CW01188652

ROLLING STONE

FOR ROLLING STONE
MANAGING EDITOR *Jason Fine*
EDITORS *Corey Seymour and Jon Dolan*
EXECUTIVE EDITORS *Nina Pearlman and Alison Weinflash*
EDITORIAL INTERNS *William Goodman and Hannah Pasternak*

DESIGN DIRECTORS *Amid Capeci and Joe Hutchinson*
CREATIVE DIRECTOR *Jodi Peckman*
ART DIRECTOR *Mark Maltais*
DESIGNER *Lou Dilorenzo*

BUSINESS AFFAIRS *Maureen Lamberti and Sandford Griffin*

PRODUCTION MANAGER *KellyAnn S. Kwiatek*
PHOTOGRAPHER *Robert Buckley*

FOR ABRAMS
EDITORS *Andrea Danese and Garrett McGrath*
DESIGNERS *Robert McKee and Darilyn Lowe Carnes*
MANAGING EDITOR *Gabriel Levinson*
PRODUCTION MANAGER *Rebecca Westall*

Library of Congress Control Number: 2017944981

ISBN: 978-1-4197-2902-7
eISBN: 978-1-68335-214-3

FRONT COVER: *Cover courtesy of Rolling Stone LLC*
PHOTOGRAPH BY *Annie Leibovitz*
BACK COVER: *Cover courtesy of Rolling Stone LLC*
PHOTOGRAPH BY *Theo Wenner*
ON THE BELLYBAND: *Front: Covers courtesy of Rolling Stone LLC. Photographs, from left to right: Albert Watson, John Zimmerman, Mark Seliger, Theo Wenner and Albert Watson. Back: Covers courtesy of Rolling Stone LLC. Photographs, clockwise from top left: Annie Leibovitz, Annie Leibovitz, Patrick Demarchelier, Annie Leibovitz, Danny Clinch, David LaChapelle, David LaChapelle, Herb Ritts, Mark Seliger and Herb Ritts.*

COPYRIGHT © 2018 ROLLING STONE LLC
ROLLING STONE COVERS © ROLLING STONE LLC
COVER © 2018 ABRAMS

Published in 2018 by Abrams, an imprint of ABRAMS. All rights reserved. No portion of this book may be reproduced, stored in a retrieval system, or transmitted in any form or by any means, mechanical, electronic, photocopying, recording, or otherwise, without written permission from the publisher.

PRINTED AND BOUND IN CHINA
10 9 8 7 6 5 4 3 2 1

Abrams books are available at special discounts when purchased in quantity for premiums and promotions as well as fundraising or educational use. Special editions can also be created to specification. For details, contact specialsales@abramsbooks.com or the address below.

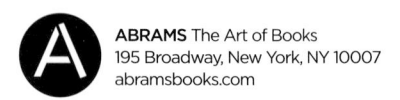

ABRAMS The Art of Books
195 Broadway, New York, NY 10007
abramsbooks.com

Rolling Stone

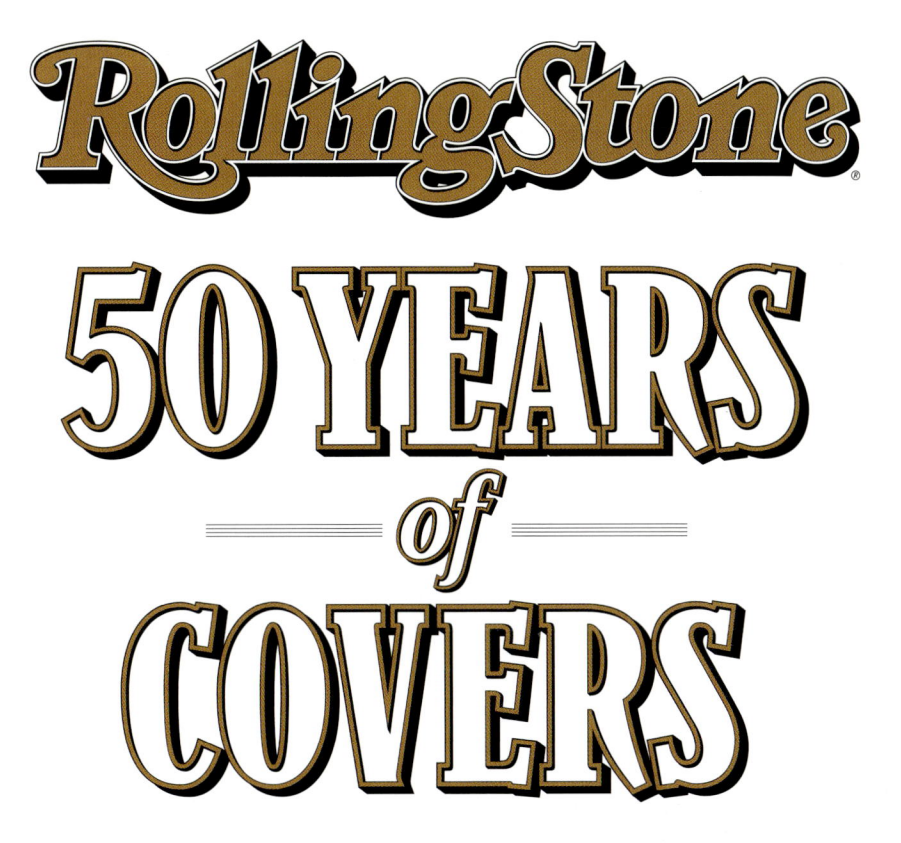

50 YEARS of COVERS

A HISTORY OF THE MOST INFLUENTIAL MAGAZINE IN POP CULTURE

INTRODUCTION BY
Jann S. Wenner

ABRAMS, NEW YORK

ROLLING STONE

NOVEMBER 9, 1967
VOL. I, NO. 1

OUR PRICE:
TWENTY-FIVE CENTS

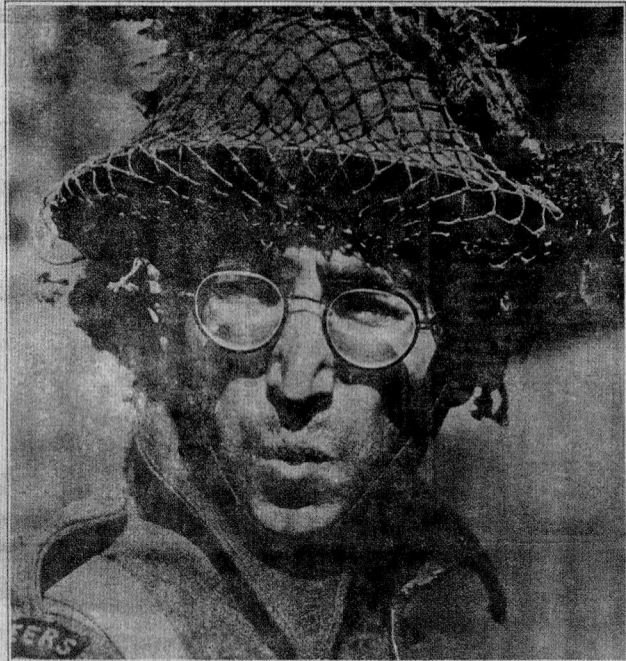

MFP

Recognize Private Gripeweed? He's actually John Lennon in Richard Lester's new film, How I Won the War. An illustrated special preview of the movie begins on page 16.

IN THIS ISSUE:

DONOVAN: An incredible Rolling Stone Interview with this manchild of magic .... Page 14

GRATEFUL DEAD: A photographic look at a rock and roll group after a dope bust .... Page 8

BYRD IS FLIPPED: Jim McGuinn kicks out David Crosby .... Page 4

RALPH GLEASON: The color bar on American television .... Page 11

Tom Rounds Quits KFRC

Tom Rounds, KFRC Program Director, has resigned. No immediate date has been set for his departure from the station. Rounds quit to assume the direction of Charlatan Productions, an L.A. based film company experimenting in the contemporary pop film.

Rounds spent seven years as Program Director of KPOI in Hawaii before coming to San Francisco in 1966. He successfully effected the tight format which made KFRC the number one station in San Francisco.

Les Turpin, former program director of KGB in San Diego will replace Tom Rounds at KFRC. Turpin has spent the last year as a consultant in the Drake-Chenault programming service.

The new appointment could mean a tightening up of programming policies. Rounds liberalization of KFRC's play-list may well become more restricted.

Airplane high, but no new LP release

Jefferson Airplane has been taking more than a month to record their new album for RCA Victor. In a recording period of five weeks only five sides have been completed. No definite release date has been set.

Their usual recording schedule in Los Angeles begins at 11:00 p.m. in the evening and extends through six or seven in the morning. When they're not in the studios, they stay at a fabulous pink mansion which rents for $5,000 a month. The Beatles stayed at the house on their last American tour.

The house has two swimming pools and a variety of recreational facilities. It's a small small little paradise in the hills above Hollywood. Maybe suntans and guitars don't make it together.

THE HIGH COST OF MUSIC AND LOVE: WHERE'S THE MONEY FROM MONTEREY?

BY MICHAEL LYDON

A weekend of "music, love, and flowers" can be done for a song (plus cost) or can be done at a cost (plus songs). The Monterey International Pop Festival, a non-profit, charity event, was, despite its own protestations, of the second sort: a damn extravagant three days.

The Festival's net profit at the end of August, the last date of accounting, was $211,451. The costs of the weekend were $290,233. Had it not been for the profit from the sale of television rights to ABC-TV of $288,843, the whole operation would have ended up a neat $77,392 in the red.

The Festival planned to have all the artists, while in Monterey, submit ideas for use of the proceeds.

In the confusion the plan miscarried and the decision on where the profits should go has still not been finally made.

So far only $50,000 has definitely been been allocated to anyone: to a unit of the New York City Youth Board which will set up classes for many ghetto children to learn music on guitars donated by Fender. Paul Simon, a Festival governor, will personally over see the program.

Plans to give more money to the Negro College Fund for college scholarships is now being discussed; another idea is a sum between ten and twenty thousand for the Monterey Symphony.

However worthy these plans, they are considerably less daring and innovative than the projects mentioned in the spring: the Diggers, pop conferences, and any project which would "tend to further national interest in and knowledge and enjoyment of popular music." The present plans suggest that the Board of Governors, unable or unwilling to make their grandiose schemes reality, fell back on traditional charity.

The Board of Governors did decide that the money would be given out in a small number of large sums. This has meant, for instance, that the John Edwards Memorial Foundation, a folk music archive at the University of California at Los Angeles, had its small request overlooked.

In ironic fact, what happened at the Festival and its financial affairs looks in many ways like the traditional Charity Ball in hippie drag.

The overhead was high and the net was low. "For every dollar spent, there was a reason," says Derek Taylor, the Festival's PR man and one of its original officers.

Yet many of the Festival's expenses, however reasonable to Taylor, seem out of keeping with its announced spirit, The Festival management, with amateurish good will, lavished generosity on their friends.

● Producer Lou Adler was able to find a spot in the show for his own property, Johnny Rivers; Paul Simon for his friend, English folk singer Beverly; John Phillips for the Group Without A Name and Scott MacKenzie. None of them had the musical status for an international pop music festival.

It is ironic that the Rivers and the rest appeared "free," but the money it cost the Festival to get them to Monterey and back, feed them, put them up (Beverly

—Continued on Page 7

4 • ROLLING STONE

RS 1 – RS 49

1967

This book, the complete collection of ROLLING STONE's covers from 1967 to the present, represents not just the evolution of a magazine but a record of our times. For almost four decades, no surer sign has heralded the arrival of a performer, artist or personality than an appearance on the cover of ROLLING STONE. Virtually every important rock musician and movie star has appeared on one of the nearly one thousand covers reproduced here, along with the politicians, comedians, cartoon characters, filmmakers, pop singers and TV actors who have helped to shape our era.

Many of them have gladly turned up time and again: Mick Jagger, who has been on the cover twenty-seven times – sometimes alone, sometimes with the band or Keith – claims the all-time record. The shrewdest among our cover subjects collaborated with us in the creation and refinement of their public images. Many of those powerful pictures have since grown to define an era. When I started ROLLING STONE in November 1967, the magazine's initial charter was to cover rock & roll music with intelligence and respect. Even then, we knew the fervor sweeping our generation encompassed more than just music. And so we gradually broadened the charter to include everything the music touched, embraced or informed: politics, movies, television, video games, the Internet, sports, crime, comic books, gurus, groupies, hippies, Jesus freaks, narcs, pimps, drugs and all the other forms of American social behavior, pathological, heroic and otherwise.

These events and personalities were captured for the cover of ROLLING STONE by some of the finest photographers of our time. A partial list would include Annie Leibovitz, Mark Seliger, Richard Avedon, Anton Corbijn, Albert Watson, Herb Ritts, David LaChapelle, Martin Schoeller, Hiro, Platon, Francesco Scavullo, Matt Mahurin and Matthew Rolston. In addition, a great roster of illustrators and cartoonists have conjured and invented for the cover: Matt Groening, Mike Judge, Garry Trudeau, Trey Parker and Matt Stone, Ralph Steadman, Maurice Sendak, Paul Davis, Milton Glaser, Robert Grossman, Gottfried Helnwein, Daniel Maffia, Andy Warhol and Anita Kunz, among others.

Many of these covers have been controversial, even shocking, so

---

RS 1 | **JOHN LENNON** | November 9th, 1967 | 'HOW I WON THE WAR' FILM STILL

[RS 1] Under the art direction of John Williams, ROLLING STONE makes its debut as an 11-by-17-inch magazine, printed on newsprint and folded in half. The cover/first page is black and white with a publicity photograph of John Lennon from the film *How I Won the War*.

1960s

here now is fair warning to those who are offended by flesh: Plenty of skin has been artfully arranged and displayed beneath our famous logo. ROLLING STONE pioneered the trend of nude "star" covers with John Lennon and Yoko Ono's full-body shots in November 1968. At the time, nudity was a political statement, health clubs were for the weird and obsessed, and I had yet to fully appreciate readers' insatiable curiosity about the naked bodies of their heroes and heroines.

John and Yoko's self-portraits were taken in their London flat for the front and back covers of their album *Two Virgins* – which their label's distributor had issued wrapped in brown paper, despite John's status as the leader of the Beatles. At the suggestion of ROLLING STONE's cofounder, writer Ralph J. Gleason, I telexed our friend Derek Taylor, the Beatles' publicist and soul mate, in London with an offer to print said pictures in our magazine. The photo wound up on the cover of our first anniversary issue (RS 22) – our first sellout issue, and the first time we went back to press. Although it may seem tame from today's perspective, the idea of someone so famous and so physically average standing stark naked for all the world to see was quite extraordinary – shocking, to be sure, but above all revolutionary and moving.

Magazine-making is a collaborative art, and over the years I have worked with the most dedicated and talented people in publishing, including editors whose duties included writing the lines of cover text that tease the newsstand browser into a purchase. "Dial Om for Murder," for an account of criminal behavior in a religious sect, "He's Hot, He's Sexy and He's Dead," for a story on Jim Morrison's posthumous

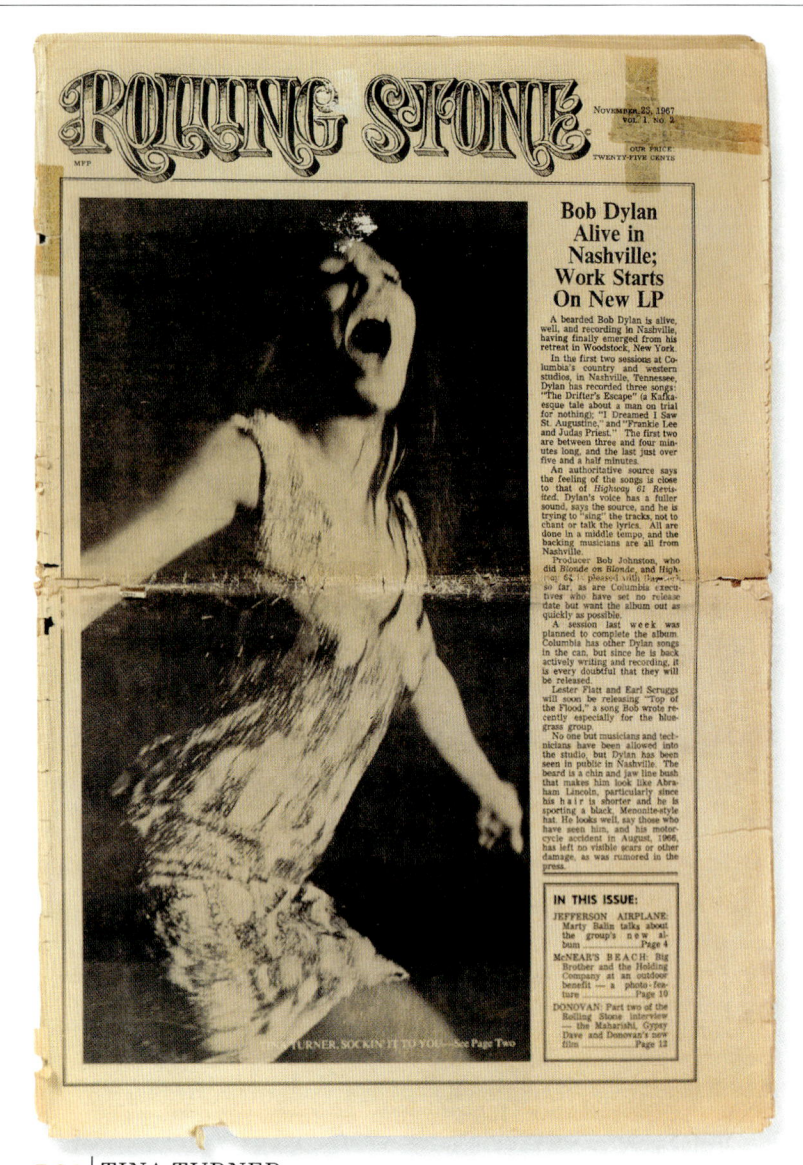

RS 2 | TINA TURNER | November 23rd, 1967 | PHOTOGRAPH BY BARON WOLMAN

"IT WAS RAUNCHY TINA, LEGS OPEN, HER RED lips, her long hair. Wild! They thought I was just another of those raunchy singers 'cause no one knew the other side. Only people very close to me knew. I've always been very spiritual but my image – in terms of my work – was very far from that."

—*Tina Turner*

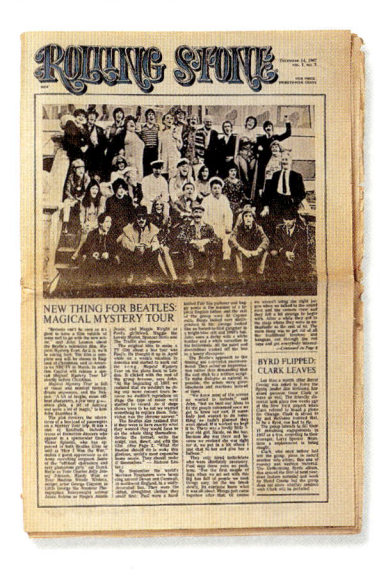

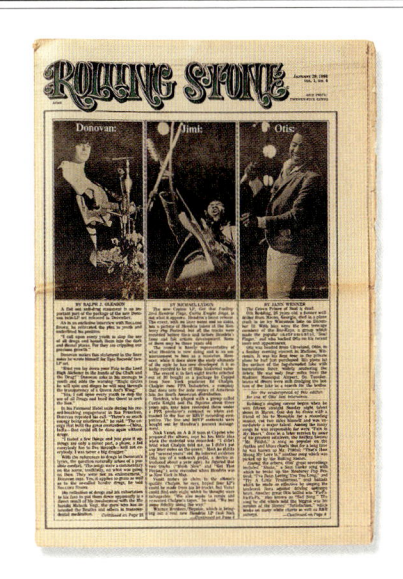

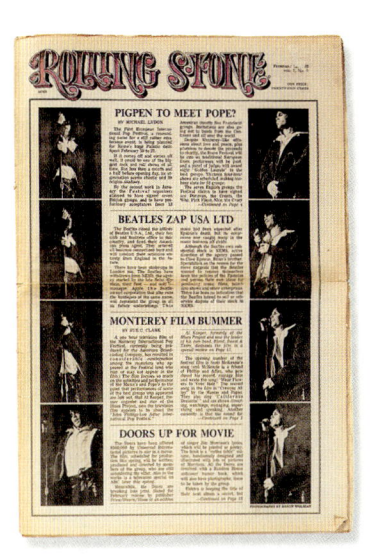

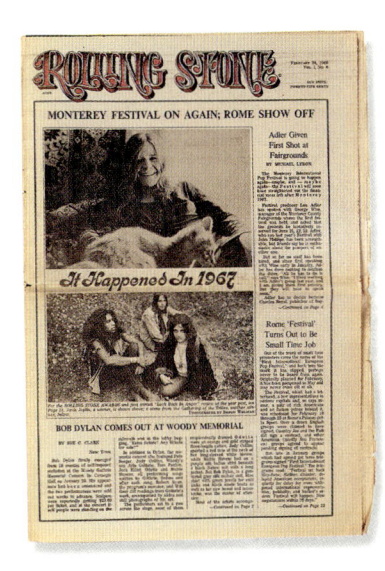

RS 3 | THE BEATLES'
'MAGICAL MYSTERY TOUR'
December 14th, 1967
PHOTOGRAPHER UNKNOWN

RS 5 | JIM MORRISON
February 10th, 1968
PHOTOGRAPHS BY BARON WOLMAN

RS 4 | DONOVAN, JIMI
HENDRIX, OTIS REDDING
January 20th, 1968
VARIOUS PHOTOGRAPHERS

RS 6 | JANIS JOPLIN,
GATHERING OF THE
TRIBES BE-IN
February 24th, 1968
PHOTOGRAPHS BY BARON WOLMAN

[RS 3] The ROLLING STONE logo gets color. Further production changes of the magazine continue to affect the cover; on RS 8, for instance, an extra quarter-fold alters the cover's size, decreasing it to 8 1/2 inches by 11 inches, and a bit more color is used.

success and "Naked Lunch Box," for Annie Leibovitz's provocative undressed shots of teen idol David Cassidy, are among my favorites.

✻ ✻ ✻ ✻ ✻

WHEN THE MAGAZINE STARTED IN 1967, I didn't understand the importance of a cover and all the things it could do. It not only defines a magazine's identity, but greatly determines sales and also confers a special status to the cover subject. There were some odd choices in the early years, but on the whole they were adventurous, and often powerful – we simply weren't driven by newsstand considerations in the first ten years.

The cover of RS 1 – November 9th, 1967 – was a wonderful, revealing accident. The photograph of John Lennon was a publicity still from a mostly forgotten film by Richard Lester called *How I Won the War*. (The ROLLING STONE logo was an unfinished draft of a design by San Francisco psychedelic-poster artist Rick Griffin, who was planning to refine it until I used his sketch in order to get it to the printer on time.) In hindsight, it was prescient of us to feature John Lennon on the first cover. That one image speaks volumes about the marriage of music and movies and politics that came to define ROLLING STONE.

In the early Sixties, there was no tradition of rock photography. In London some good photographers – David Bailey, Snowden and Sir Cecil Beaton among them – had shot the Stones, the Beatles and a few other bands. In San Francisco, New York and Los Angeles, however, that hadn't happened yet. Photographs of rock

50 YEARS OF COVERS • 7

1960s

> "I started playing the camera [shooting at concerts]. I could almost anticipate the licks. It sounds really hokey, but I got fabulous photos, one after another, because I was really in tune with what [Jimi] was doing."
>
> —*Baron Wolman*

stars were generally publicity stills or shots from the stage, with a microphone obscuring much of the performer's face. I decided we should do better than that and took on a friend and professional, Baron Wolman, as our first staff photographer. Bringing Baron into the mix, along with the feisty Jim Marshall, a San Franciscoan who had been avidly shooting the jazz and folk scene, and a few other West Coast photographers who were just beginning to do good work, distinguished us quickly. They didn't create a particular look or impose a particular style on the bands as much as produce clean, crisp photography, well-composed and artfully lit. Perhaps most valuably, they lived the life, knew the bands and understood what they wanted to say.

Our first full-time art director was Robert Kingsbury, a wood sculptor and teacher who had never worked for a publication. Bob turned out to be brilliant at sifting through all the black-and-white stills we were accumulating to find a striking image. It was still a few years before we were shooting photographs specifically for covers, and Bob did wonders with what we had on hand.

Those covers were done on the fly, and yet many of them stand up. The blue solarized cover of Eric Clapton (*RS 10*) was taken by Linda Eastman, later to become Linda McCartney – the first woman to shoot a ROLLING STONE cover. Linda went on to take many memorable early photographs, including some of Jimi Hendrix and Janis Joplin.

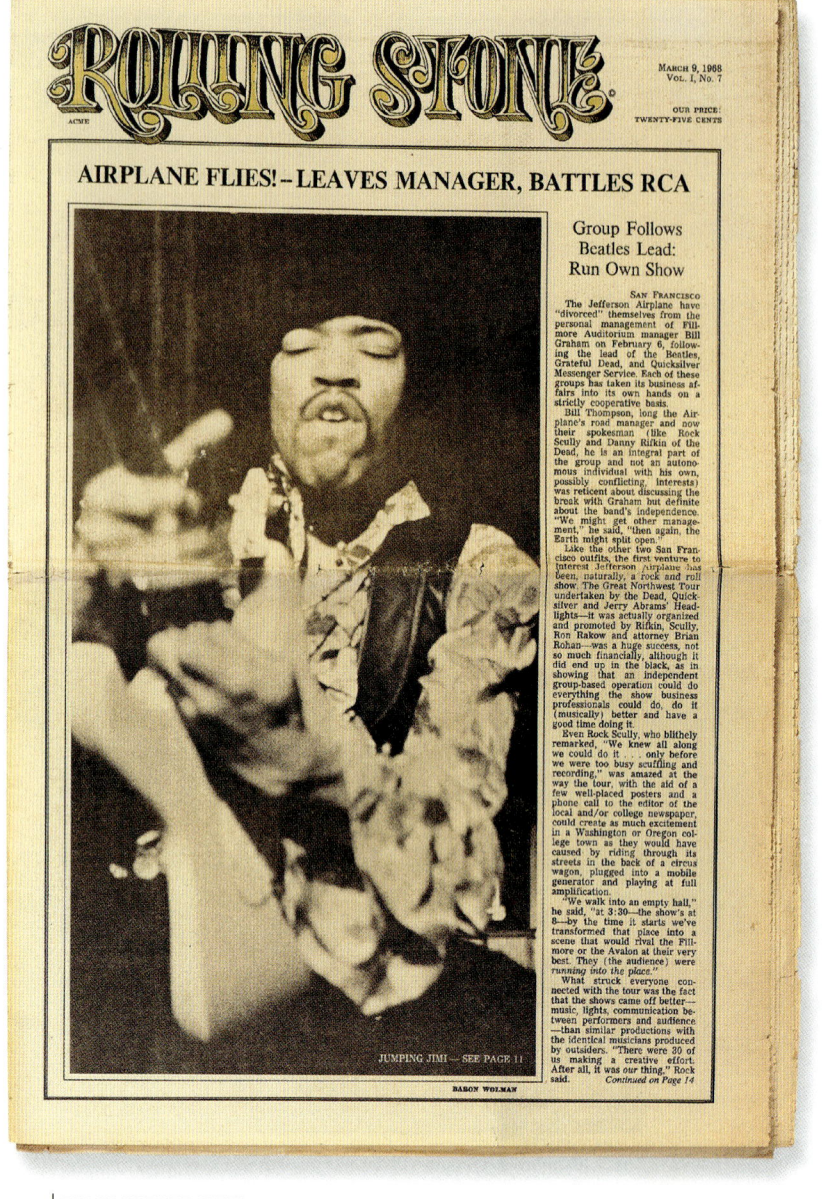

RS 7 | JIMI HENDRIX | March 9th, 1968 | PHOTOGRAPH BY BARON WOLMAN

* * * * *

ANOTHER OF OUR EARLY LESSONS in publishing was that death sells. When Janis Joplin and Jimi Hendrix died within weeks of each other, our staff placed simple, classic portraits on the cover, with type stating just the artist's name and dates of birth and death. There was nothing more to say. That began a form of tribute that we've followed ever since. When somebody in the magazine's purview dies, the cover is created with dignity and respect,

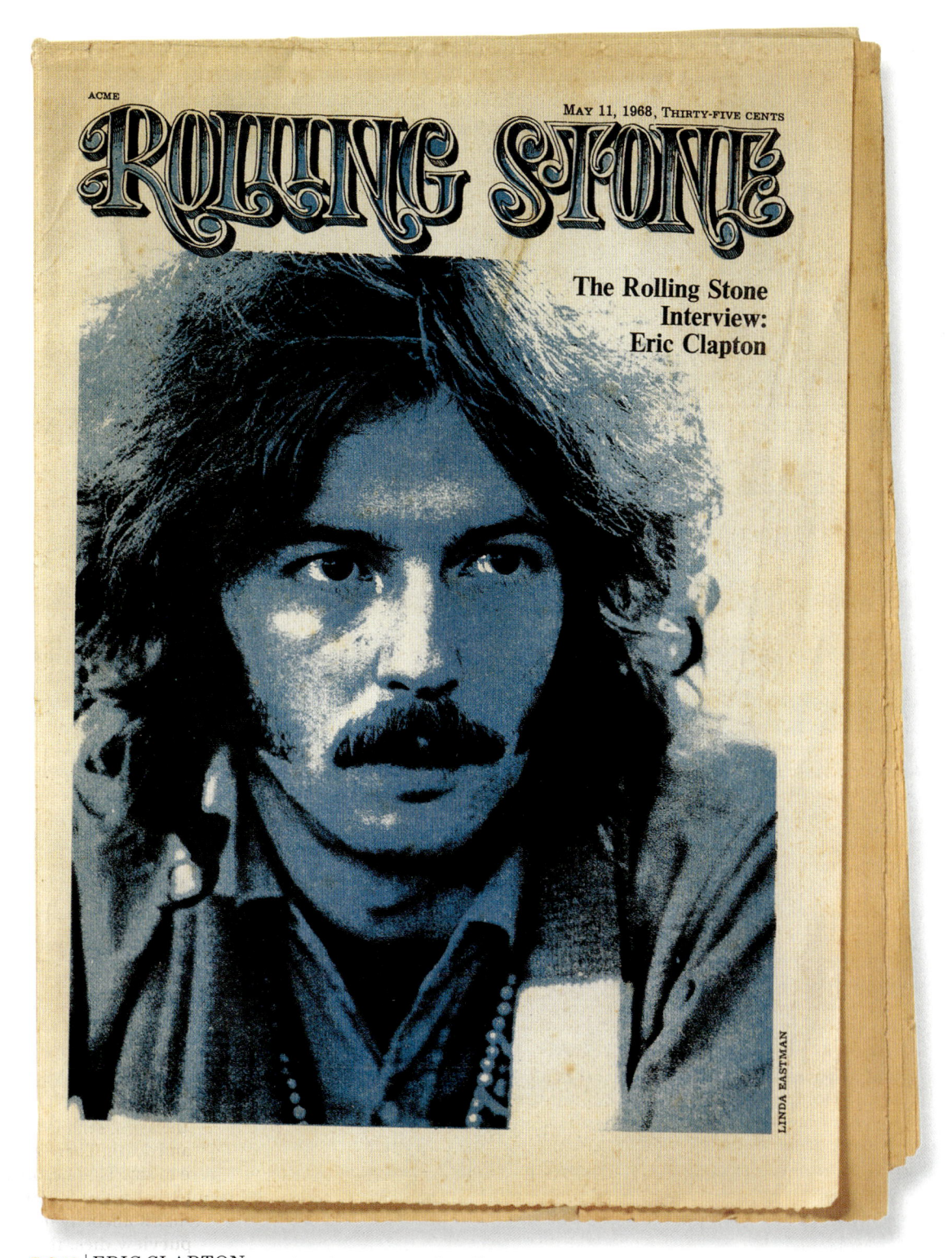

RS 10 | ERIC CLAPTON | May 11th, 1968 | Photograph by Linda Eastman

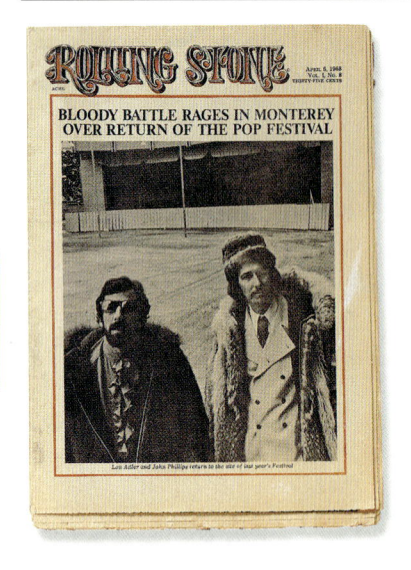

1960s

RS 8 | MONTEREY POP FESTIVAL
April 6th, 1968
PHOTOGRAPHER UNKNOWN

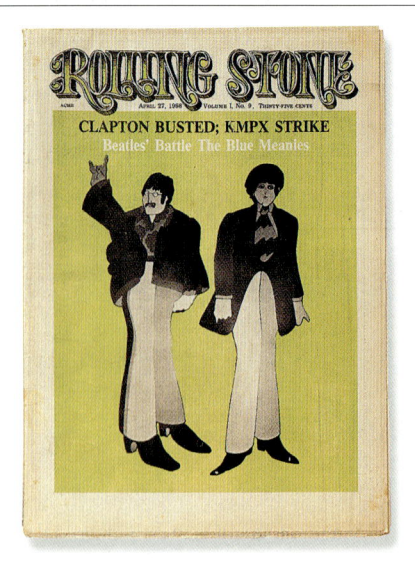

RS 9 | JOHN LENNON & PAUL McCARTNEY
April 27th, 1968
ILLUSTRATION BY HEINZ EDELMANN

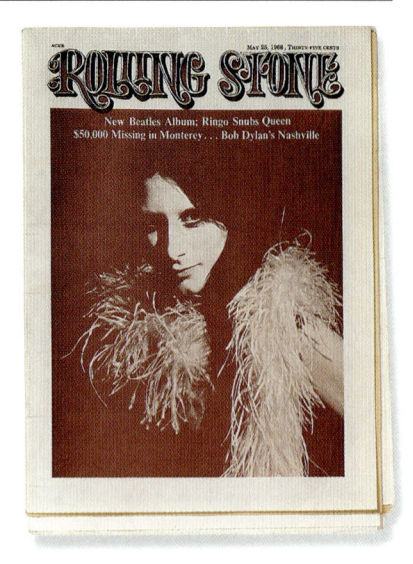

RS 11 | ROCK FASHION
May 25th, 1968
PHOTOGRAPH BY BARON WOLMAN

and the coverage inside is exhaustive, sometimes highly personal and in many cases brilliant.

In 1970, a twenty-year-old art student named Annie Leibovitz brought her portfolio to us. "She had just returned from a year in Israel," Bob Kingsbury remembers, "and I liked one of her pictures from the trip. I thought she showed a lot of potential, and she was just a kid. We hired her." While still attending the San Francisco Art Institute, Annie became the magazine's second staff photographer. Later that year, she flew with me to New York for her first major assignment, a commissioned cover portrait of John Lennon to accompany my historic interview "Lennon Remembers."

What turned out to be the cover shot was taken during a light-meter reading. John, who was "thinking nothing," as he later recalled, looked right through the lens at Annie. For her (and for the magazine), this was a defining moment, what she has called her "first encounter" with a subject. It's John's humanity that comes through in the shot. It was not the one she had wanted as our cover, but to me this photo was so simple and so stark, it was a natural choice. The directness of the eye contact, the simplicity and the truth in it all presage the best of Annie's work. I still have the framed picture near my desk. I've carried it around with me from office to office since 1971.

Annie considered herself a photojournalist at the time, working with a thirty-five-millimeter camera and, for the most part, natural lighting, which was the foundation for most of her later work. Over the next three or four years, her work began to mature, and the ROLLING STONE covers became portraits. And so for a while the covers are portrait after portrait; not all of them are Annie's, but they're all in the mold we began to establish with the John Lennon cover.

* * * * *

IN FEBRUARY 1973, WE CHANGED printers and began regularly publishing four-color covers. After years of black-and-white or two-color covers, the new format opened up endless possibilities and challenges. A few months later we went from a quarter-fold to a tabloid format, increasing the size of our covers from $8 \frac{1}{2}$ inches by 11 inches to

[RS 8] ROLLING STONE's first-ever news cover featured the Monterey Pop Festival and its organizers, producer Lou Adler and John Phillips of the Mamas and the Papas.

[RS 11] The first concept cover: "Rock Fashion." According to photographer Baron Wolman, art director John Williams didn't care for his proposed cover portraits of B.B. King and Johnny Cash, but loved a photo Wolman had taken of his wife, Julianna. Since there was a fashion story and Ms. Wolman looked very stylish, she became the cover.

10 • ROLLING STONE

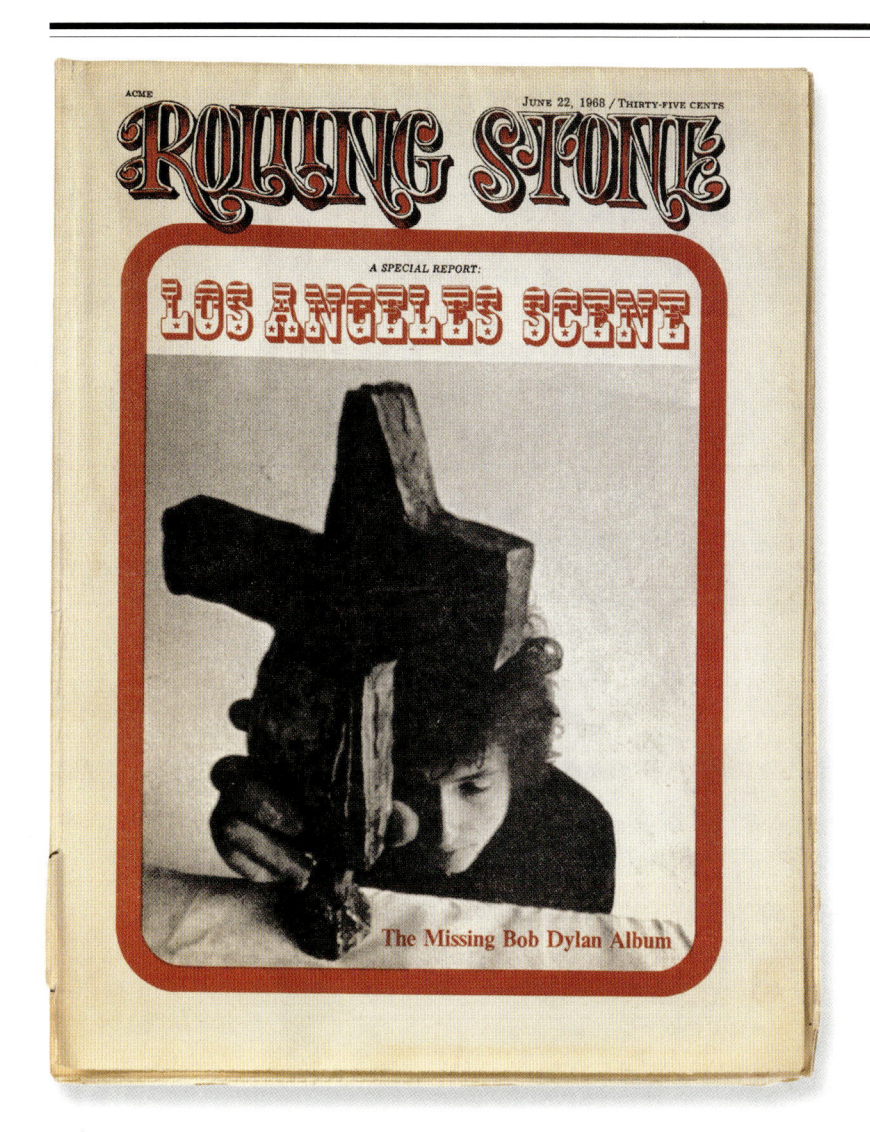

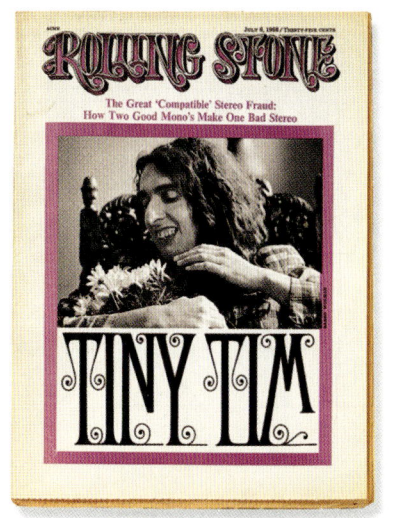

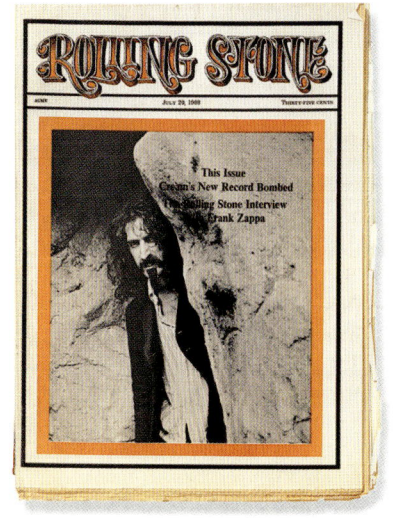

10 ½ inches by 15 inches. I brought in Michael Salisbury, the very imaginative and brash art director of the Sunday rotogravure magazine of the *Los Angeles Times*. He was our first professional art director – with a live-wire personality and his own historical references as the one-time art director of *Surfer* magazine.

Michael brought us into the world of illustration and "concept covers," and we started getting a little crazier. Michael's first cover was an illustration for an interview I'd done with Daniel Ellsberg, of "Pentagon Papers" fame (*RS 147*). Michael showed it to me at the last minute (which would become a habit of his), so there was no chance of changing it. But it was perfect: a heroic profile of Ellsberg – as if on a coin or a sculpture – accompanied by a cover line we took from the Declaration of Independence: "Let facts be submitted to a candid world." The image illustrated the point exactly.

"ROLLING STONE's identity was in not only how it read, but also how

RS 12 | BOB DYLAN
June 22nd, 1968
PHOTOGRAPHER UNKNOWN

RS 13 | TINY TIM
July 6th, 1968
PHOTOGRAPH BY BARON WOLMAN

RS 14 | FRANK ZAPPA
July 20th, 1968
PHOTOGRAPH BY BARON WOLMAN

50 YEARS OF COVERS • 11

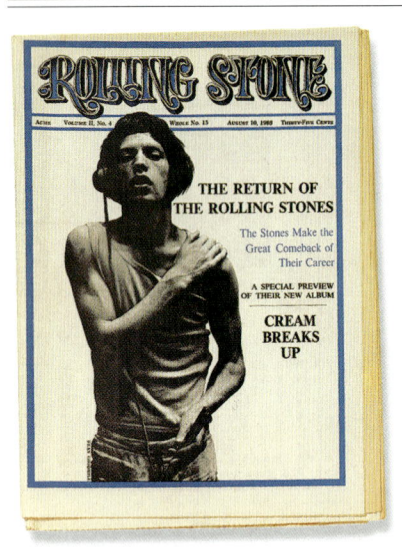

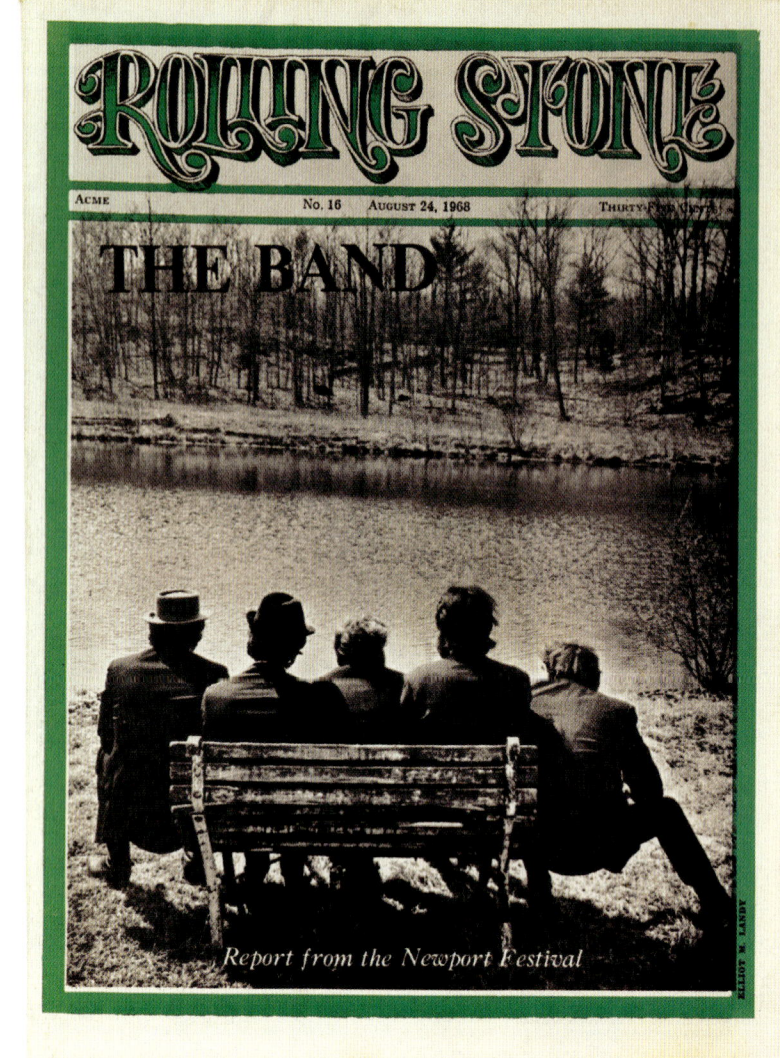

1960s

RS 15 | MICK JAGGER
August 10th, 1968
Photograph by Dean Goodhill

RS 16 | THE BAND
August 24th, 1968
Photograph by Elliott Landy

it looked," Michael says. "And that was defined by the photography. The typography and the newspaper format gave a young publication legitimacy and credibility, but the pictures added personality and depth."

Our illustrated covers were often as whimsical as they were memorable: Witness Robert Grossman's visions of a blimp-like Jerry Garcia (*RS 148*) and the members of the Who tangled in microphone cords (*RS 275*). "Artwork can be more iconic than photos," says Grossman, who calls ROLLING STONE "a friend to illustrators." Doonesbury creator Garry Trudeau has drawn four covers for the magazine so far, beginning with an image of his Uncle Duke character, whom he had based on Hunter S. Thompson (*RS 194*). "That cover was my hip moment – which meant I had to pretend it was no big deal," Trudeau says. "But of course it was. I may have hung it in my closet, but it was framed. Nicely." Sought-after illustrator Daniel Maffia took an alternate, more photorealistic approach, creating evocative watercolor images of Jackson Browne (*RS 228*) and Pete Townshend (*RS 252*). "I wasn't into music, but I respected the magazine very much," says Maffia. "It gave me a lot of creative freedom."

[RS 16] The magazine's first full-time art director, sculptor Robert Kingsbury, designs his inaugural issue.

In September 1974, Tony Lane became the magazine's third full-time art director. Tony, who came from *Holiday* and *Harper's Bazaar*, had a distinct vision and style, and he wanted badly to work with Annie. Tony proceeded to take the cover to a

12 • ROLLING STONE

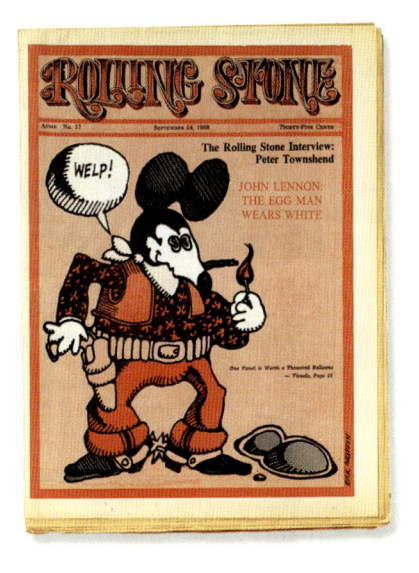

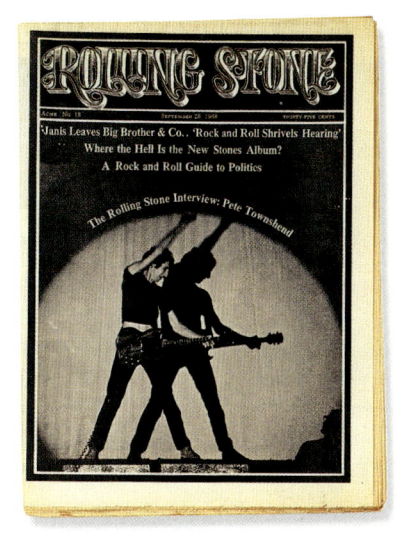

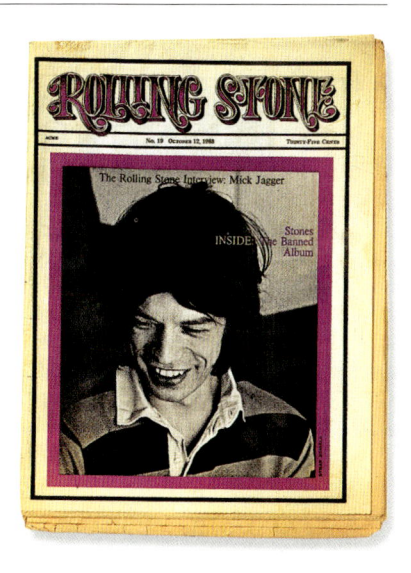

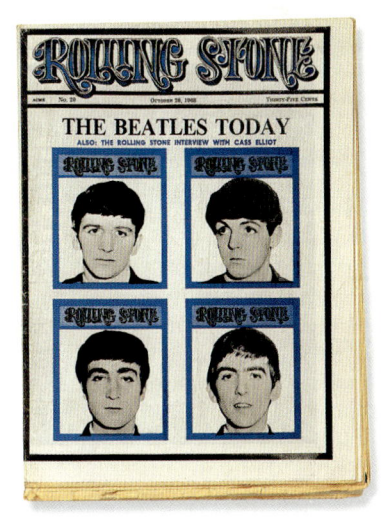

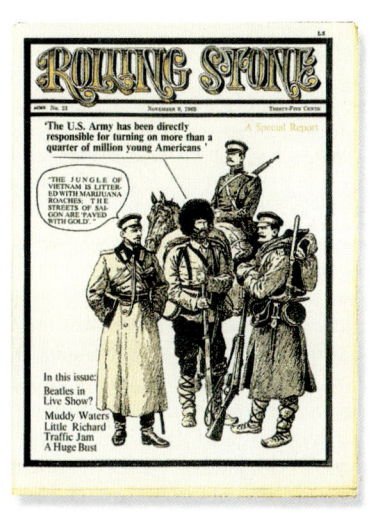

RS 17 | ZAP COMIX
September 14th, 1968
ILLUSTRATION BY RICK GRIFFIN

RS 18 | PETE TOWNSHEND
September 28th, 1968
PHOTOGRAPH BY JANN WENNER

RS 19 | MICK JAGGER
October 12th, 1968
PHOTOGRAPH BY ETHAN RUSSELL

RS 20 | THE BEATLES
October 26th, 1968
PHOTOGRAPHER UNKNOWN

RS 21 | DRUGS IN THE ARMY
November 9th, 1968
ILLUSTRATOR UNKNOWN

sparer, poster-type look. Annie was still learning, soaking up everything, honing her craft and doing a great number of covers along the way.

The next year, Annie came with me to lunch at the studio of Richard Avedon. I had begun discussions with him about photographic coverage of the 1976 presidential elections and thought it would be fun for Annie to meet Dick, and to explore new ideas and new directions for the magazine.

That day we planned the heroic black-and-white cover photograph of Mick and Keith that appeared on our July 17th, 1975, issue (*RS 191*). I was trying to get Annie to imitate Avedon's more formal style of working, and suggested she make it very simple and shoot the two Stones as partners. It worked brilliantly and is still one of my favorites.

Annie busted loose with marvelous covers: Bob Marley in the throes of ecstasy (*RS 219*), Paul Simon in his window overlooking Central Park (*RS 216*). One of the most memorable to me is the portrait of Beach Boys founder Brian Wilson, reemerged after years of exile inside his bedroom (*RS 225*). Annie shot a black-and-white pho-

1960s

to of Brian as surf patriarch in his bathrobe, holding a board. We had it hand-colored in the style of an old pastel postcard.

Another of my favorites is the Fleetwood Mac cover (RS 235). Annie posed them on an unmade bed, which brilliantly solved the perennial graphic problem of getting multiple group members in the frame in a new and interesting way. And I loved Annie's lush image of Bette Midler on a bed of roses (RS 306): What a beauty.

Annie's attitude was, "Give me a great idea – who cares where it comes from?" Our collaboration was nearly always a happy one. We

"I hadn't posed nude for pictures before. We were just being honest – that was its strength."

were working together constantly, thinking up things to do with the cover, and our work was *us*.

In 1976, ROLLING STONE published "The Family," a special issue of Avedon's portraits (RS 224), for which we won the magazine industry's highest honor, a National Magazine Award. Dick wanted to shoot the entire political and economic power structure of the United States. It was a months-long adventure, with Dick traveling around the country shooting presidents, corporate bosses, labor leaders and family matriarch Rose Kennedy: the real American establishment. It was an instant classic. I don't think any magazine had ever before done anything like it. This marked the start of Avedon's relationship with ROLLING STONE. In a few years, we had him collaborating with the likes of Prince and Eddie Murphy.

We had the access. The world inhabited by ROLLING STONE and its subjects was tighter, smaller and, for the most part, devoid of the public-relations mavens who attend to celebrities now. Those we didn't know personally, we certainly knew by reputation. And they knew us.

In 1977, we moved our entire operation from the San Francisco warehouse district to New York's Fifth Avenue. Within five days of our arrival, somebody walked into my new office and said, "Elvis is dead." We postponed the planned special issue celebrating our move and found a great picture of a smiling Elvis in his prime – an obscure old poster none of us had ever seen.

In April 1976, Roger Black, who

—Yoko Ono

was a typographer by training, took over as art director. Suddenly, type became very important. The Roman numeral *X* was Roger's idea for our Tenth Anniversary cover, which also marked the end of our funky, hand-drawn logo and the initiation of a new, bolder logo typeface. We took it from all caps to upper- and lowercase characters and eliminated the swashes and ligatures between some of the letters. (Jim Parkinson, who did the new version, became our in-house type designer.) It was the beginning of another phase, and in my Editor's Note I wrote that the new logo "symbolizes as much as anything what we are up to: respectful of our origins, considerate of new ideas and open to the times to come."

Annie's covers at this time were, as always, brilliant: The Blues Brothers painted blue (RS 285) seemed so clichéd but turned out to be timeless. Years later, when Annie's work was hung at the National Portrait Gallery in Washington, D.C., outside the columned building two large images were suspended from the arches: Gilbert Charles Stuart's George Washington and Annie's cover portrait of Patti Smith before a wall of flames (RS 270).

In 1980, Mick Jagger and I were having a late-night discussion about ROLLING STONE. Mick is a very serious reader; he understands how the magazine works. He didn't really like the new logo because, he said, we had taken out much of the character, the funkiness. So we put back the curlicue at the end of the *E*, made the loop on the bottom of the *G*, restored ligatures and swashes and brought the "roll" back in to the *R*. Thanks Mick, you were right.

We planned to unveil the "new" logo – the Jagger revision – simultaneously with another paper-quality upgrade and a different trim size. Our first issue of 1981 was to feature a new Annie photograph of John and Yoko timed with the completion of their upcoming album, *Double Fantasy*.

At this session, on December 8th, 1980, they greeted Annie like an old friend, and the pictures show three people working with commitment. From a Polaroid test shot, John and Yoko chose the image they wanted for the cover. That night John was assassinated outside his home. The haunting, spectral image of John, naked and curled around Yoko in the fetal position – along with the photos inside – were the last portraits taken of him. In the wake of his death, there was no need for a headline, and for the first time in the magazine's history, we ran a cover without one. If I had to choose, I guess this is the best cover we've ever done.

In 1983, after ten years as chief photographer and 142 covers, Annie left the magazine. Her legacy and remarkable body of work con-

ROLLING STONE

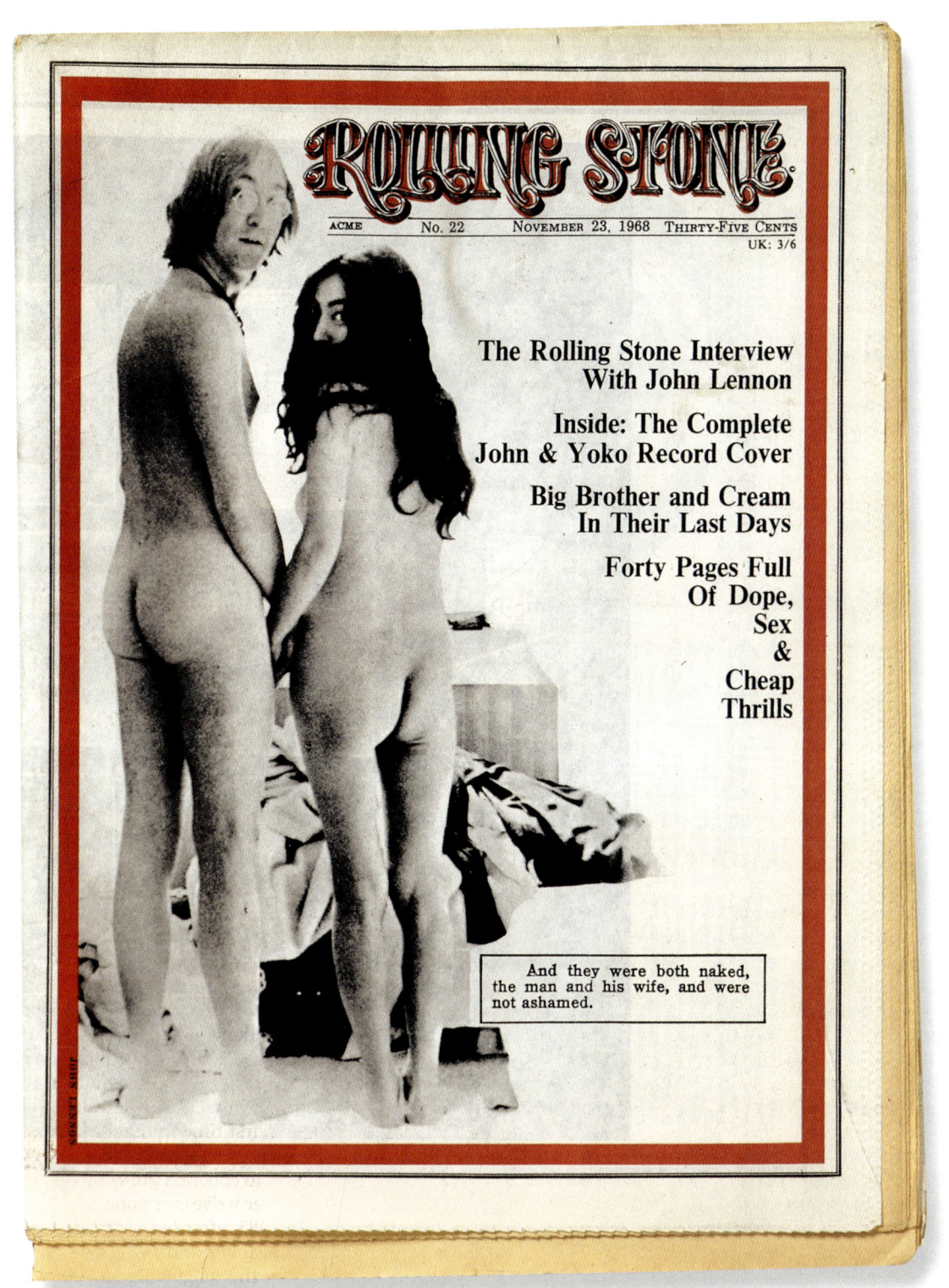

ACME · No. 22 · NOVEMBER 23, 1968 · THIRTY-FIVE CENTS
UK: 3/6

The Rolling Stone Interview With John Lennon

Inside: The Complete John & Yoko Record Cover

Big Brother and Cream In Their Last Days

Forty Pages Full Of Dope, Sex & Cheap Thrills

And they were both naked, the man and his wife, and were not ashamed.

RS 22 | JOHN LENNON & YOKO ONO | November 23rd, 1968 | Photograph by John Lennon

50 YEARS OF COVERS · 15

tinue to influence the art of photography and the lives of young photographers, and she is one of the handful of people who can be said to have been a principal in creating what ROLLING STONE became.

We could not replace Annie, so we took the opportunity to use a wide array of photographers. Avedon shot covers, as did Albert Watson, David Bailey, Hiro, Bonnie Schiffman, Steven Meisel and Matthew Rolston.

Herb Ritts, a master of celebrity portraiture, captured the look of the Eighties in his best work. For a good stretch he became our most-featured cover photographer, contributing forty-six covers over two decades. He ran his sessions like a sure-handed movie director, confident in his ability to create a hip, stylized kind of beauty. The understated sexiness of Herb's covers flows naturally from attitude, not props or tricks. He photographed Bruce Springsteen, Tom Cruise, Michael Jackson, David Bowie, Paul McCartney, Claudia Schiffer, Warren Beatty, Julia Roberts, Arnold Schwarzenegger and many more stars for us. "At the end of the day, Herb loved shooting for ROLLING STONE because he was allowed to create the images he wanted to create," says Herb's longtime executive producer, Mark McKenna. "Herb thrived on spontaneity."

Herb's shot of a topless Cindy Crawford standing on a Malibu beach at sunset (RS 672/673) proved to be one of our best-selling covers ever. He believed that everybody should look beautiful, and he could make anybody look like an idol or a god, whether that person was Cindy Crawford or a sixty-year-old Bob Dylan (RS 882). His final cover for the magazine, depicting a shirtless Justin Timberlake (RS 914), was on the newsstands

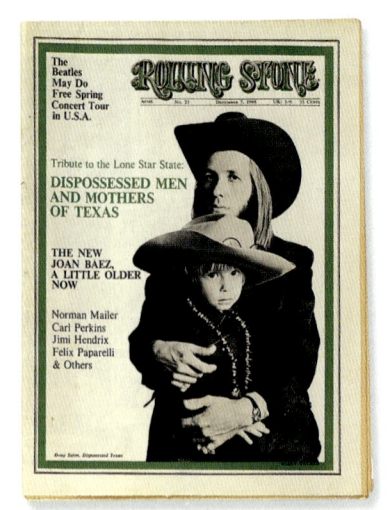

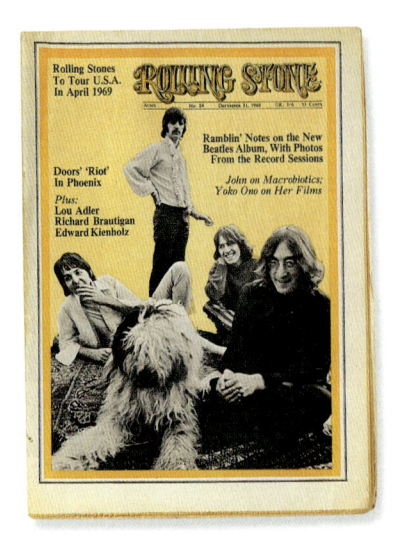

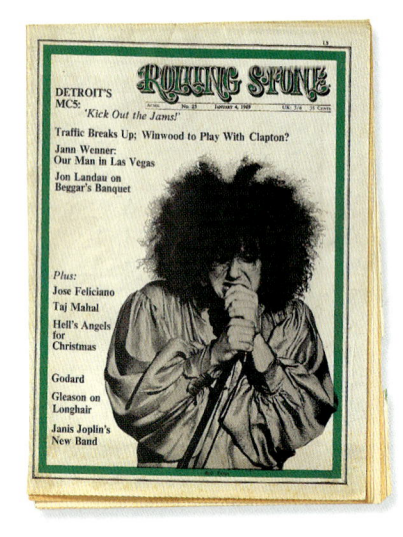

RS 23 | DOUG & SEAN SAHM
December 7th, 1968
PHOTOGRAPH BY BARON WOLMAN

RS 25 | ROB TYNER
January 4th, 1969
PHOTOGRAPHER UNKNOWN

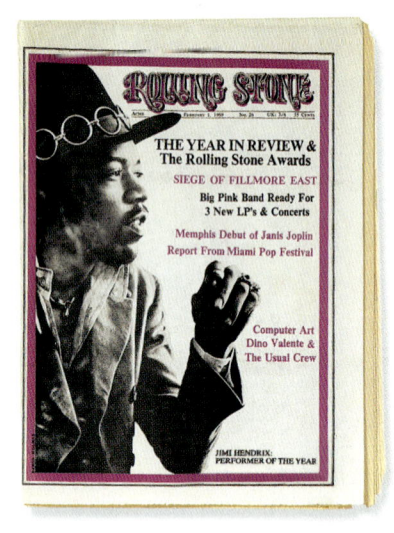

RS 24 | THE BEATLES
December 21st, 1968
PHOTOGRAPHER UNKNOWN

RS 26 | JIMI HENDRIX
February 1st, 1969
PHOTOGRAPH BY BARON WOLMAN

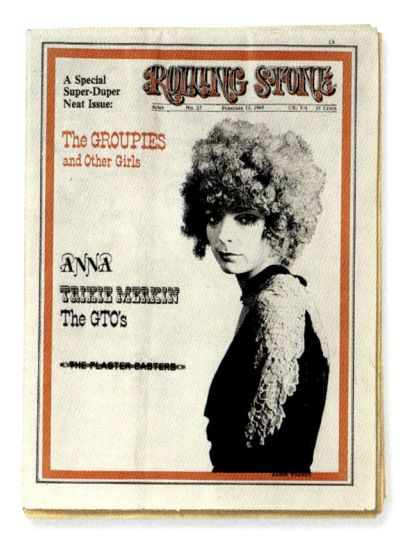

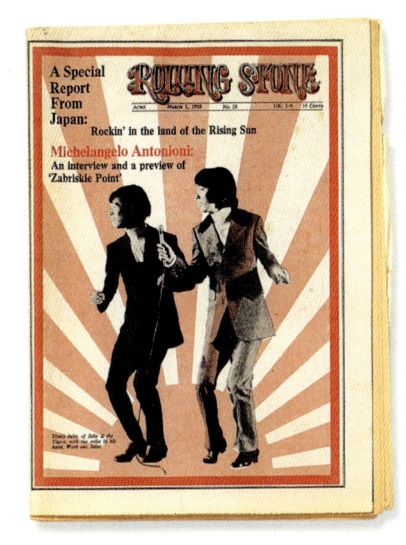

$\mathcal{RS}$ 27 | GROUPIES
February 15th, 1969
PHOTOGRAPH BY BARON WOLMAN

$\mathcal{RS}$ 28 | JAPANESE ROCK
March 1st, 1969
PHOTOGRAPH BY NAOKO LASH

just after the photographer died of pneumonia in 2002 at age fifty. It's one of our sexiest male covers ever.

* * * * *

BY 1987, I'D BECOME RESTLESS AND wanted a new art director, a fresh collaboration. Fred Woodward, whom we had been watching set fire to *Texas Monthly*, confessed to me in our initial meeting that he had dreamed of being the art director of ROLLING STONE since he was fifteen. Fred arrived at his dream job as we were counting down to a Twentieth Anniversary special issue. It was perfect timing. He and his new staff hit the bound volumes of past issues to conduct a blitzkrieg retrospective of our design history – on deadline. "I was running on pure adrenaline, and I was scared to death," Fred recalls. "I wanted to do work that measured up to that twenty-year legacy."

Fred successfully reconnected the magazine's new look to its past, producing an amazing body of work that not only kept ROLLING STONE supplied with awards for design excellence but earned him a place in the Art Director's Hall of Fame, as its youngest member ever. At one time or another, his covers violated every rule. Only someone of Fred's idiosyncratic vision could have seen the dark graphic power of the Batman cape ($\mathcal{RS}$ 634/635) or chosen to illustrate our "Portraits" issue with a simple, stunning shot of Elvis's gold lamé Nudie suit on a hanger ($\mathcal{RS}$ 643). Over fifteen years as art director, Fred's imagination wove itself into the life of ROLLING STONE.

In the Nineties, we hired Mark Seliger as our new chief photographer, the first since Annie and only the third in our history. "Shooting your first cover of ROLLING STONE is like your first romance, or the first time you got a car – except magnified ten-fold," Mark says. "It was a big world to step into, but once I gained momentum, I tried to push it in every way." Mark told me that from his teenage years, he was a student of ROLLING STONE, and it shows. There were qualities in Mark's early work – his wit, his use of space – that were as close to Annie as I had ever seen. "Mark brought back the kind of concept cover that Annie invented," says our current director of photography, Jodi Peckman. "A whole new generation started getting the excitement of these wonderfully produced photographs." On more than a hundred covers – Neil Young in a scarecrow pose ($\mathcal{RS}$ 648), the *Seinfeld* cast in black leather ($\mathcal{RS}$ 660/661), Jennifer Aniston nude at the peak of her early fame ($\mathcal{RS}$ 729) – Mark created high-gloss, vivid images that helped us capture the spirit of a new decade.

Mark took definitive shots of the Nineties' new breed of rock bands, including Pearl Jam, Red Hot Chili Peppers, Soundgarden and Smashing Pumpkins. But the most compelling among them was our first Nirvana cover ($\mathcal{RS}$ 628). Before a brief photo shoot in Melbourne, Australia, Mark gave the trio a routine warning not to wear shirts with writing on them. Kurt Cobain, who was in a foul mood and complaining of stomach pain, responded by scrawling "corporate magazines still suck" on his ragged T-shirt. "He wouldn't change the shirt, and I felt like I hadn't delivered," Mark recalls. "On the way back, I was sweating in my seat, feeling like a complete failure." I thought it was great from the moment I saw it – it was funny. In the end, it was Cobain's endorsement of the magazine, a witty acknowledgement of the power and importance of ROLLING STONE to him.

Mark's 1994 cover shot of Brad Pitt ($\mathcal{RS}$ 696) came to life after the two drove together from California

50 YEARS OF COVERS • 17

1960s

to Mexico. Pitt wanted the photos to feel real, according to Mark. "We hoped to model it after an old, traditional ROLLING STONE shoot where you're living with a person for a period of time, rather than it just being a two-hour experience in a studio," Mark says. For the record, Mark came up with the idea of pairing Jenny McCarthy with a hot dog (*RS 738/739*) and dressing Ice-T, the rapper behind "Cop Killer," in a policeman's uniform (*RS 637*). "I don't know if Ice-T thought it was funny," Mark says. "But he just loved it."

During his years on staff, Mark took some extraordinary pictures of politicians, including three Clinton covers and one of Al Gore. Political leaders are challenging to shoot – they tend to be stiff and formal – but Mark managed to transcend that. When the Gore cover (*RS 853*) came out, someone on the radio took note of the bulge in his pants, and it became one of those mindless reverberating media things for a while. Al called me up and said, "Everybody's talking about this. Is this OK? Is this a bad thing?" How could it be anything but a good thing?

The late Nineties saw a new boom in slick teen pop, and in the tradition of our shirtless David Cassidy cover almost three decades earlier, we found its provocative side. Enter David LaChapelle. In the spring of 1999, he shot a seventeen-year-old Britney Spears in her bra and polka-dot panties (*RS 810*), lying on satin sheets and clutching a purple Teletubby. When Spears's then-manager objected to the pose during the shoot, she overruled him, LaChapelle recalls: "Britney said, 'Lock the door,' and unbuttoned her shirt wide open." This was the teenage version of Madonna, and it had not been seen before.

Spears's male counterparts – 'NSync (with future solo star Justin

[**RS 30**] **This issue marked the first special issue devoted to a political topic, in this case the social movements and unrest prevalent in the late Sixties. Contributors included Black Panther Party Minister of Education George Mason Murray and Berkeley Free Speech Movement leader Michael Rossman.**

Timberlake) and Backstreet Boys – all went on to collaborate with us on sexy, occasionally subversive covers. At the peak of that period, we shot five separate covers for one issue, each with a different member of 'NSync (*RS 875*). It was a fun gimmick, and they were all delighted.

Music's divas – including Spears, Mariah Carey, Courtney Love, Christina Aguilera and, of course, Madonna – have all worked closely with us over the years, helping to create some of our most unforgettable images. Madonna's work with Herb Ritts stands apart, with a series of iconographic covers that traced the trajectory of a superstar: cheek to cheek with Rosanna Arquette for their starring roles in *Desperately Seeking Susan* (*RS 447*), a Kabuki-painted Nefertiti in three-quarter profile (*RS 508*), the reigning queen of pop frolicking in the surf (*RS 561*). "Madonna liked to play with her image," says Mark McKenna, Herb's executive producer. "And she wanted to have fun. So Herb was able to bring a crew in and really collaborate on things."

The younger divas tend to arrive with large entourages (Aguilera, for one, brought bodyguards and two dogs to a shoot), and strong ideas of what they want. But with the help of our reputation and long history, we nearly always succeed in convincing them to collaborate.

Other artists need less prodding to participate in the give and take. Mick Jagger has always been a partner in shaping his image. He knows

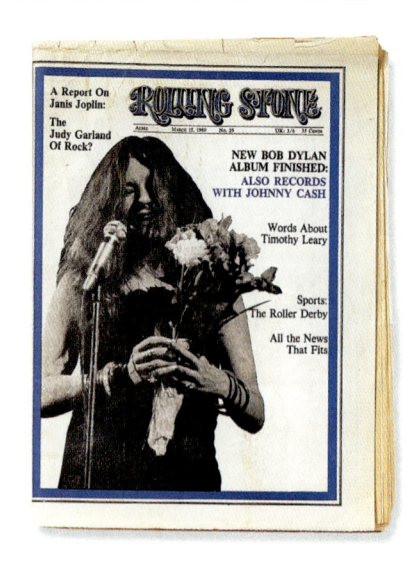

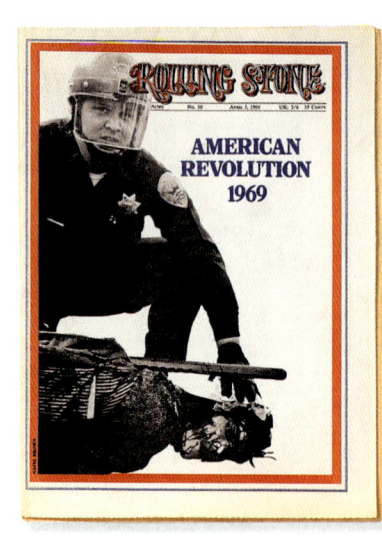

RS 29 | JANIS JOPLIN
March 15th, 1969
PHOTOGRAPHER UNKNOWN

RS 30 | AMERICAN REVOLUTION IN 1969
April 5th, 1969
PHOTOGRAPH BY NACIO BROWN

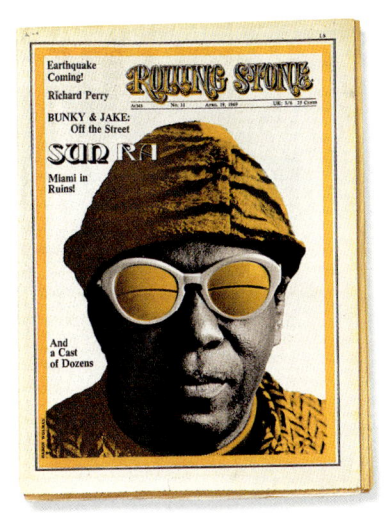

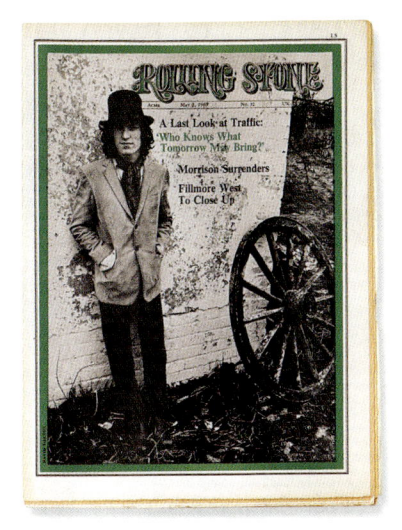

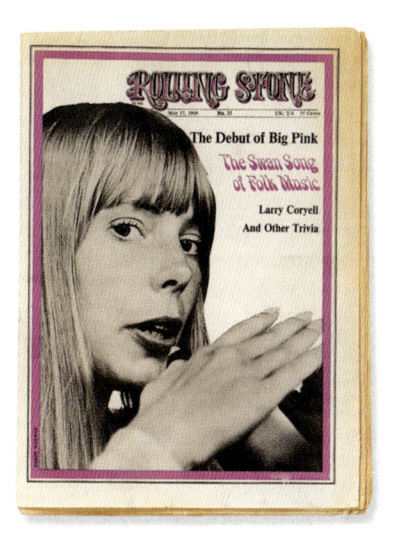

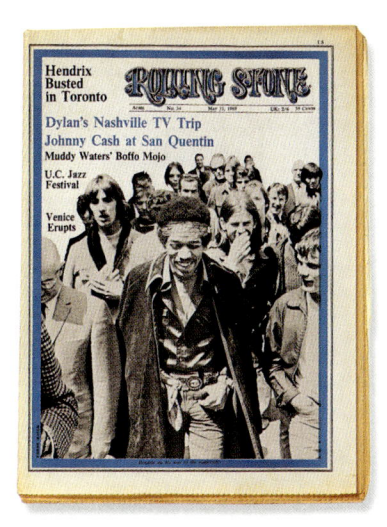

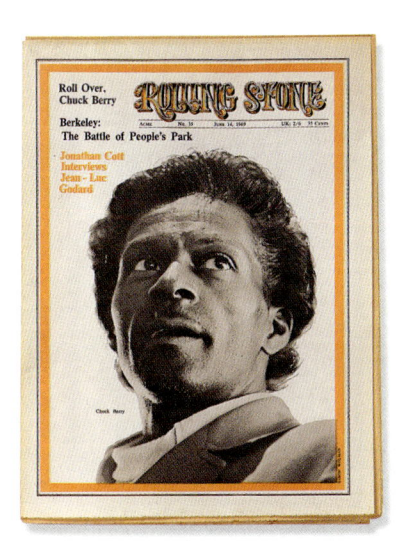

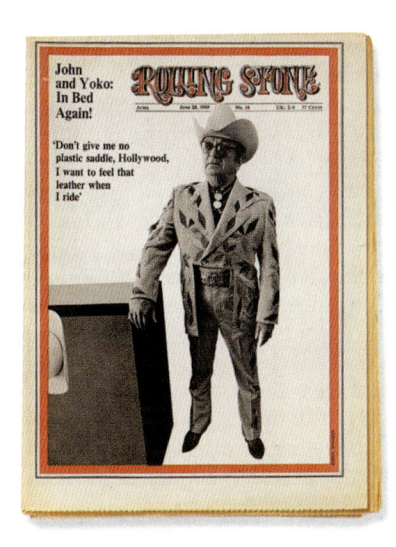

RS 31 | SUN RA
April 19th, 1969
PHOTOGRAPH BY BARON WOLMAN

RS 32 | STEVIE WINWOOD
May 3rd, 1969
PHOTOGRAPH BY DAVID DALTON

RS 33 | JONI MITCHELL
May 17th, 1969
PHOTOGRAPH BY BARON WOLMAN

RS 34 | JIMI HENDRIX
May 31st, 1969
PHOTOGRAPH BY FRANZ MAIER

RS 35 | CHUCK BERRY
June 14th, 1969
PHOTOGRAPH BY BARON WOLMAN

RS 36 | NUDIE COHN
June 28th, 1969
PHOTOGRAPH BY BARON WOLMAN

[RS 36] **This little cowboy is Nudie Cohn, the flamboyant western-wear designer responsible for the lavishly decorated outfits favored by country stars of the Fifties and Sixties. He also created Elvis Presley's famous gold lamé suit, which graces the cover of RS 643.**

50 YEARS OF COVERS • 19

1960s

what he wants to look like, but he's also fascinated by the photo-taking process, and is eager to hear our suggestions on photographers and concepts. Few artists would have posed for our cover wearing an ornate mask (*RS 689*) – and even fewer would have remained utterly recognizable.

Comic actors have been similarly eager to lend their ideas, from Steve Martin (who asked to be painted onto Franz Kline's artwork [*RS 363*]) to Jim Carrey (who gamely allowed a dog to pull off his bathing suit, recreating a Coppertone ad [*RS 712/713*]). During the Nineties, the *Seinfeld* cast posed as *Wizard of Oz* characters, while Jerry Seinfeld appeared solo as both the young and old Elvis Presley. Jerry was up for just about anything in these Mark Seliger shoots – though understandably, he did decline to wear a grotesque prosthetic tongue in imitation of Kiss' Gene Simmons.

* * * *

WHEN THE WORLD TRADE CENter fell on September 11th, 2001, we had Alicia Keys scheduled for our cover. Keys happened to be wearing a New York T-shirt in the photograph we were planning to use, so we considered going with it. Within about five minutes, it became clear that we wanted to have our say about an era-defining event. We debated various red-white-and-blue treatments, and thought about using the "11" in "9/11" to represent the towers. Then I found a flag lapel-pin in my desk drawer at home. When I brought it into the office, everyone agreed: "That's the cover."

In the early 2000s, we experimented for a while with a flashier look, and a style influenced by a new breed of British magazines. But even in that period, the covers that worked best looked like traditional ROLLING STONE, whether it was the stark, black-and-white Seliger portrait of an aged Johnny Cash we ran

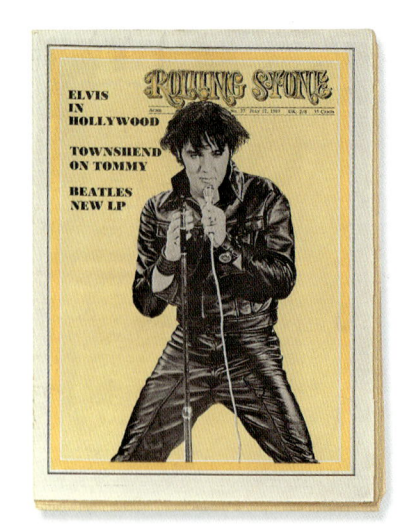

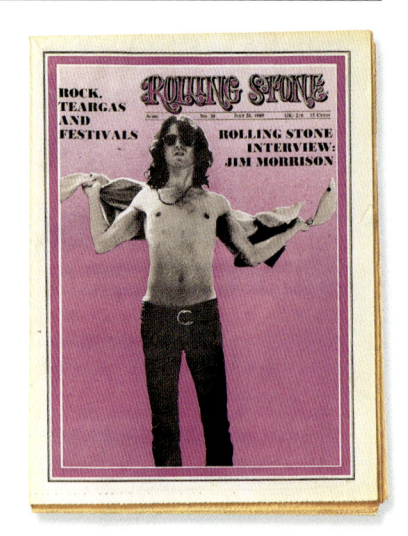

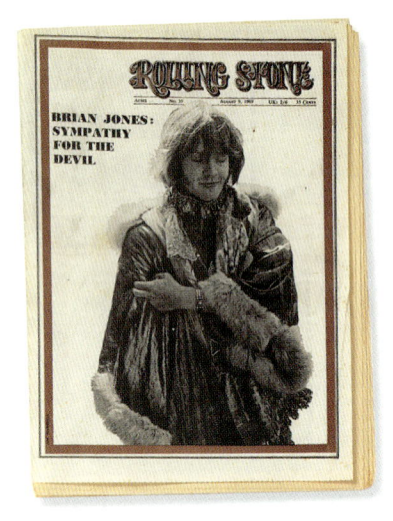

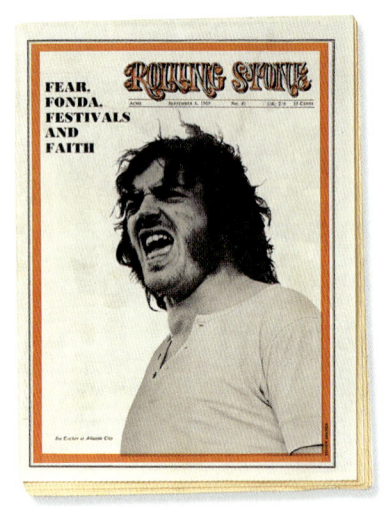

RS 37 | ELVIS PRESLEY
July 12th, 1969
PHOTOGRAPHER UNKNOWN

RS 38 | JIM MORRISON
July 26th, 1969
PHOTOGRAPHER UNKNOWN

RS 39 | BRIAN JONES
August 9th, 1969
PHOTOGRAPH BY JIM MARSHALL

RS 41 | JOE COCKER
September 6th, 1969
PHOTOGRAPH BY STEVEN SHAMES

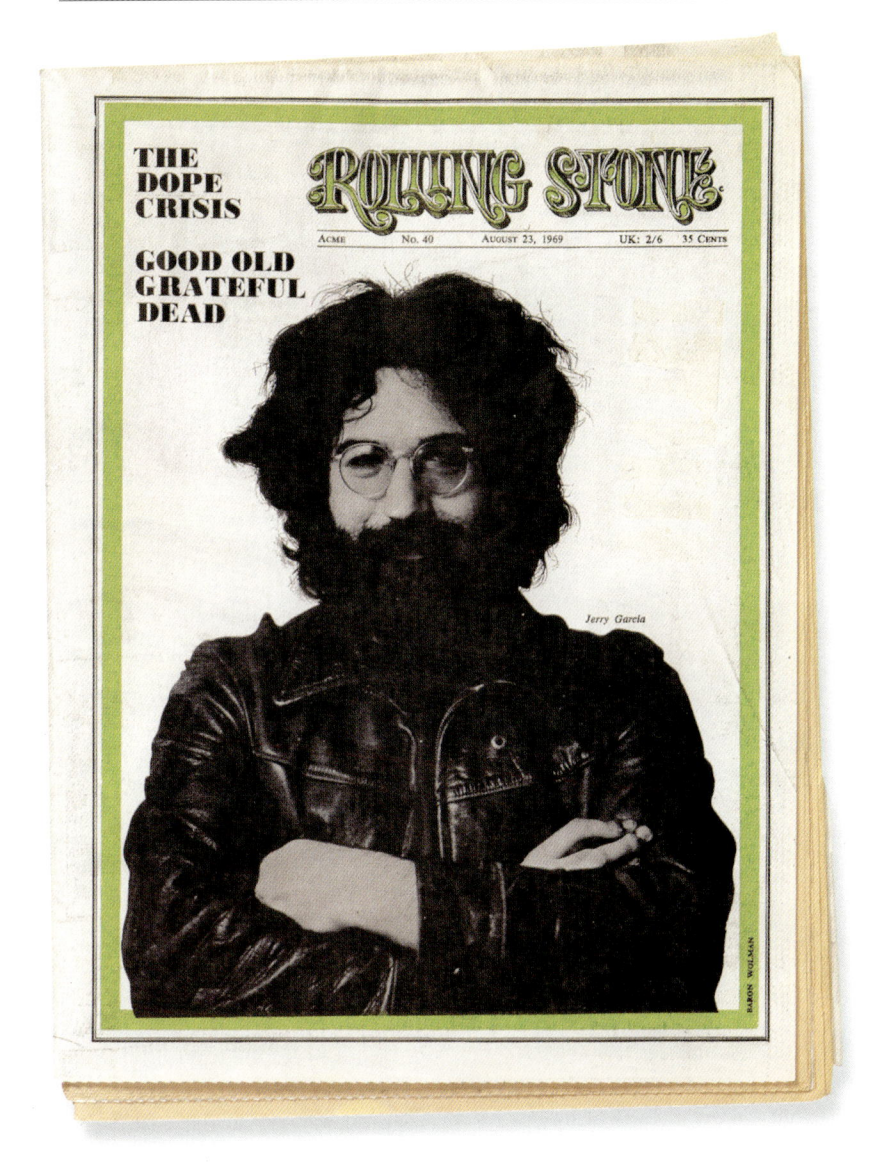

RS 40 | **JERRY GARCIA** | August 23rd, 1969 | Photograph by Baron Wolman

"HOW'D I GET TO people? They accepted me because *I was as fuckin' nuts as they were!"*
—Jim Marshall

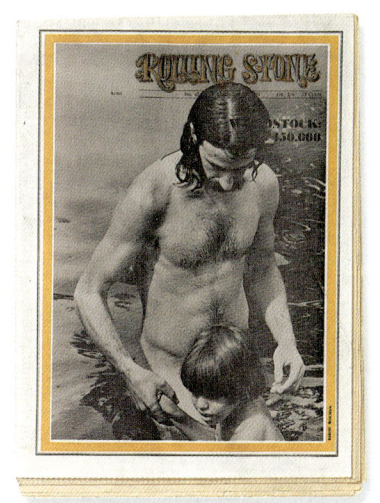

RS 42 | **WOODSTOCK**
September 20th, 1969
Photograph by Baron Wolman

upon his death (*RS 933*), or Martin Schoeller's shot of Bruce Springsteen standing in front of a vast green field (*RS 903*). "Bruce has this humongous property in New Jersey, with all these great vistas, but he limited us to a very small corner that we could photograph in," Schoeller remembers. "I finally convinced him to move fifty feet to that field. I like that shot a lot – it feels very American, somehow."

In 2004, we wanted to send a signal that we were going back to the core journalistic values of ROLLING STONE, regardless of the newsstand sales consequences. In an effort to shift the magazine to be more topical, we proceeded with a series of political covers: Garry Trudeau's rendering of the war in Iraq (*RS 954*), Michael Moore (*RS 957*), the Vote for Change tour (*RS 959*), Jon Stewart (*RS 960*), John Kerry (*RS 961*). That created new energy and purpose, almost a kind of renewal. With our current art director, the news-oriented *Newsweek* alum Amid Capeci, we entered a new period of

50 YEARS OF COVERS • 21

1960s

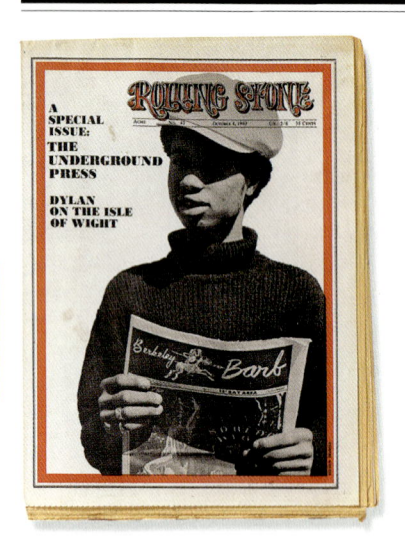

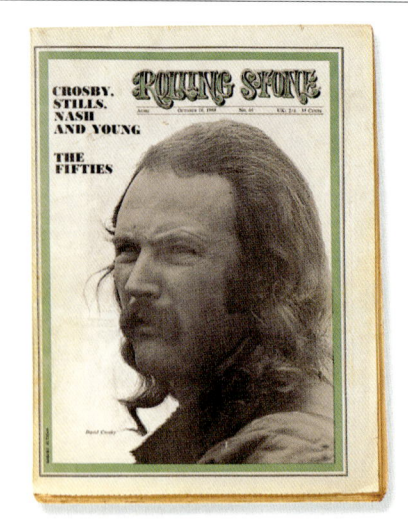

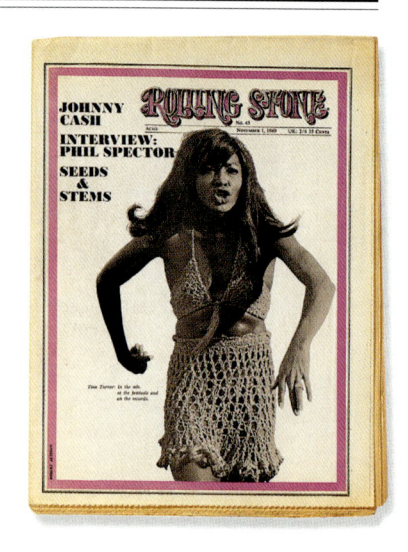

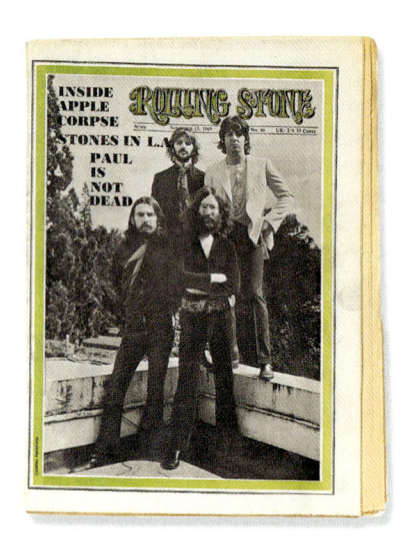

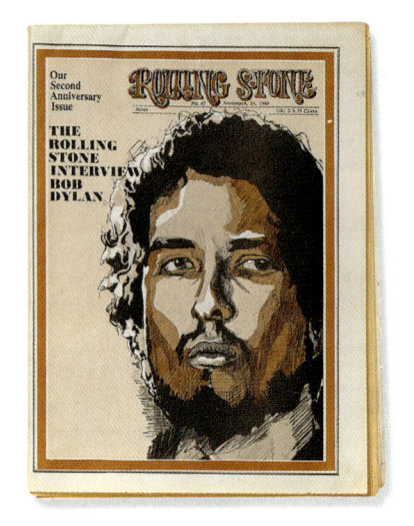

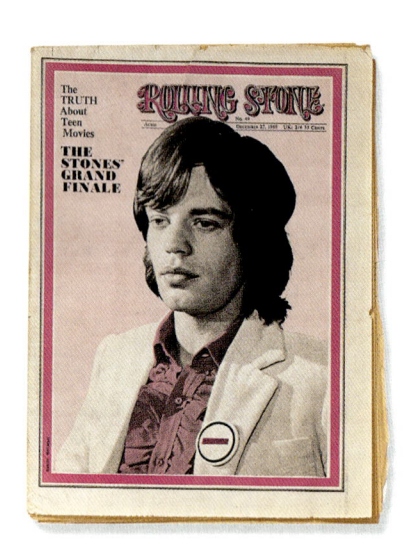

RS 43 | THE UNDERGROUND PRESS
October 4th, 1969
Photograph by Steven Shames

RS 46 | THE BEATLES
November 15th, 1969
Photographer unknown

RS 44 | DAVID CROSBY
October 18th, 1969
Photograph by Robert Altman

RS 47 | BOB DYLAN
November 29th, 1969
Illustrator unknown

RS 45 | TINA TURNER
November 1st, 1969
Photograph by Robert Altman

RS 49 | MICK JAGGER
December 27th, 1969
Photograph by Baron Wolman

RS 48 | MILES DAVIS
December 13th, 1969
PHOTOGRAPHER UNKNOWN

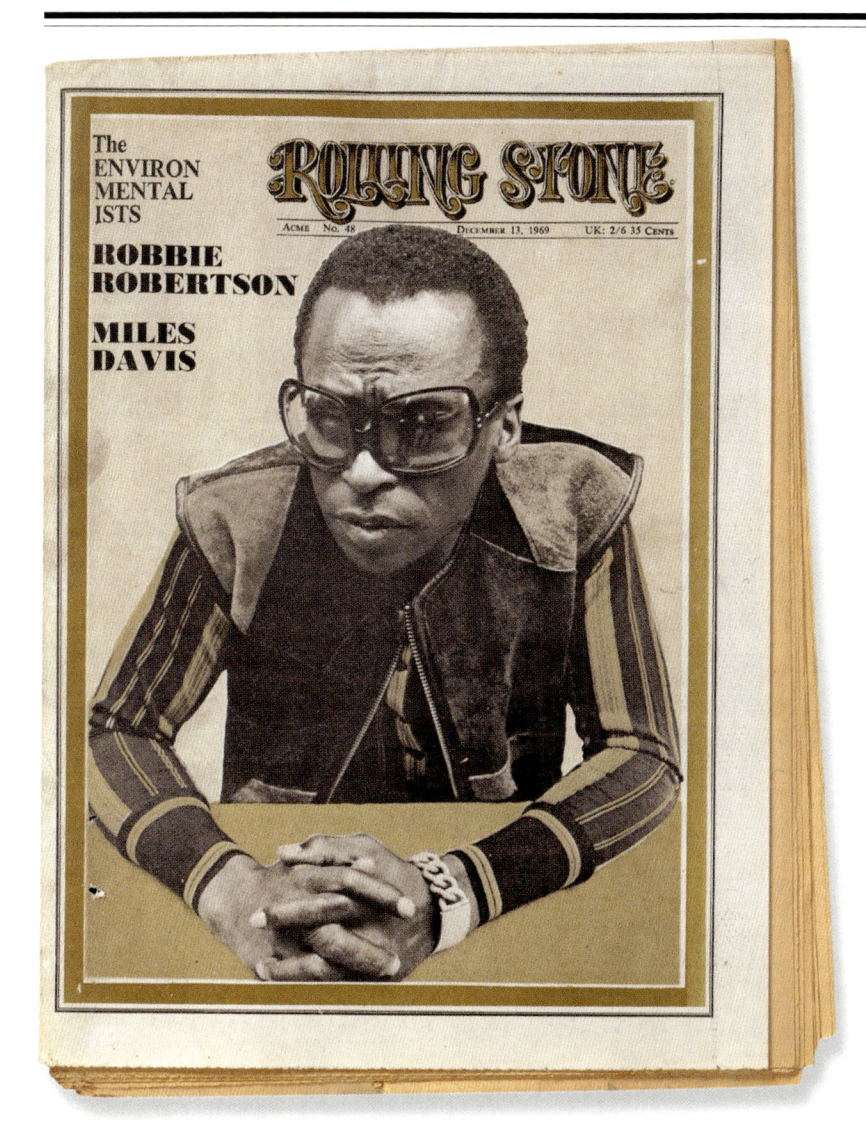

and created a 3-D cover inspired by the album art for *Sgt. Pepper's Lonely Hearts Club Band*. In 2008, the actual size of the magazine changed. But as we pass our 50th year, our mission remains the same.

We are still looking for cover subjects who are authentic and honest, iconic or hot, people who stand for something, whether it's U2's Bono or Kendrick Lamar. In the Nineties, we felt comfortable with the direction our nation was going, so we could go out and have some fun. In the Bush, Obama and Trump years, the stakes were raised, and we've had a lot of serious things to say.

Still, in the end, the cover is forever a work in progress. There are rules, but it is so alive, so vital, so in the moment. That's part of what has made the cover of ROLLING STONE so thrilling over the years: It has always been unpredictable.

* * * * *

WHAT A LONG, STRANGE TRIP IT truly has been. Our mission took us from the Haight-Ashbury to the Oval Office, bringing us face-to-face with the cultural events and influential people of our time. Our readers have come along for the journey, cheering us on with their love letters and advice. Our subjects have been the architects of their times – presidents and poets, the outsiders and insiders. In the end, this collection of covers is a sprawling archive of the five decades we've been around – and a testament to the great work of our photographers, illustrators, art directors, photo editors and the cover subjects themselves. We have devoted ourselves to our task with all the passion, energy and talent that we had to give.

classic ROLLING STONE covers. "We moved toward a stripped-down, bold, newsy design," Amid says. "And we started photographing cover subjects in a serious light."

When my friend and longtime star writer and collaborator Hunter S. Thompson died on February 20th, 2005, there was no question that he would appear on our next cover. As we prepared a memorial package that filled much of the issue, the debate was whether to picture him in his youth or as a more recognizable and iconic older man. We decided on a little-seen vintage black-and-white shot of Hunter holding a cigarette. Surrounded by wisps of smoke, Hunter looks so handsome and elegant in the image; it's from the year we met and began to work together.

As our thousandth issue approached, we searched for a cover treatment worthy of the occasion,

—*Jann S. Wenner*

ROLLING STONE

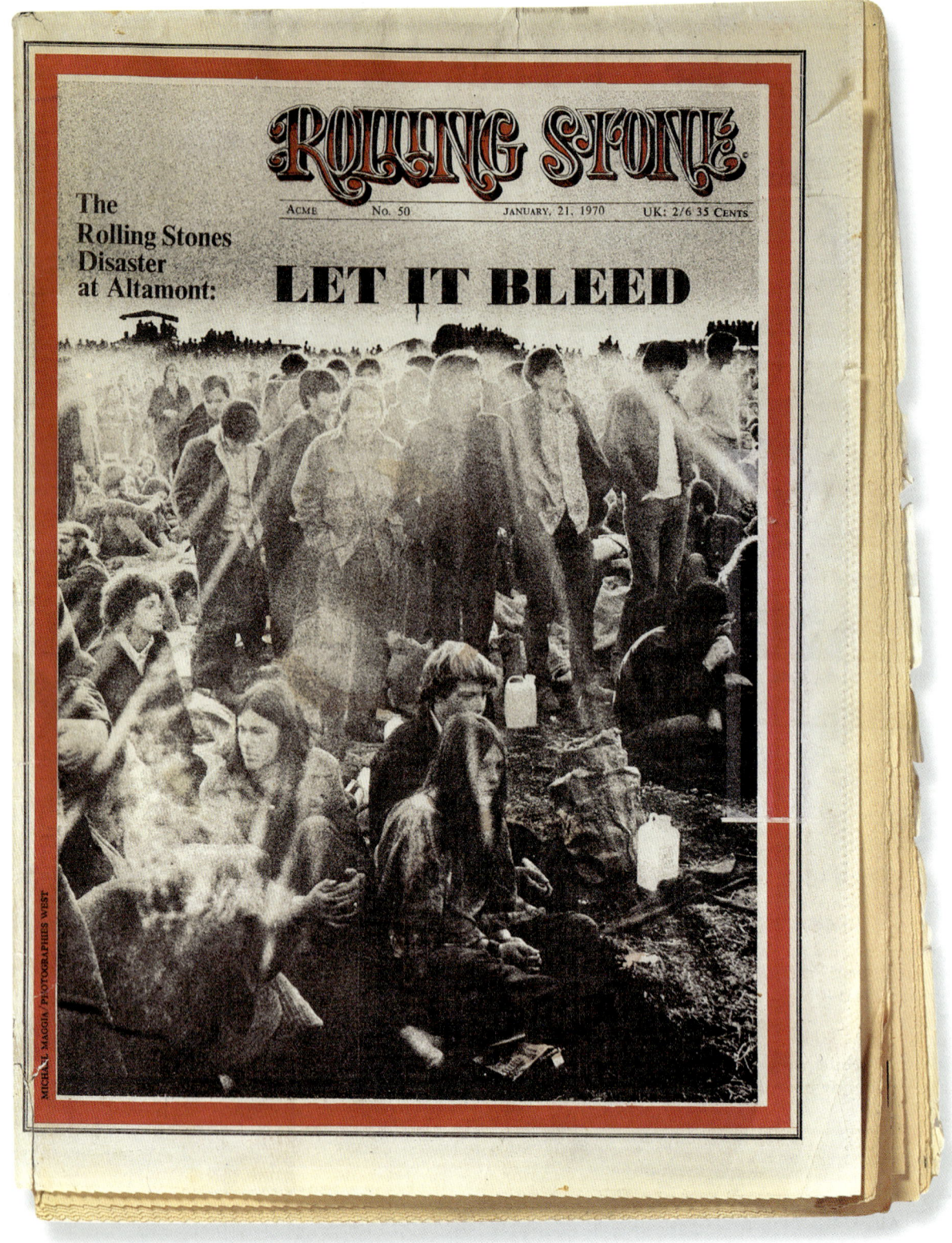

ACME · No. 50 · JANUARY, 21, 1970 · UK: 2/6 35 CENTS

The Rolling Stones Disaster at Altamont:

LET IT BLEED

RS 50 – RS 308

1970

"I didn't know his name or anything, but he

was standing alongside of me. You know, we were both watching Mick Jagger, and a Hell's Angel – the fat one; I don't know his name or anything – he reached over. He didn't like us being so close or something, you know, we were seeing Mick Jagger too well, or something. He was just being uptight. He reached over and grabbed the guy beside me by the ear and hair and yanked on it, thinking it was funny, you know, kind of laughing. And so this guy shook loose; he yanked away from him."

"Now this guy that you're talking about, is this the black guy that got killed?"

"Yeah, right. He shook loose, and the Hell's Angel hit him in the mouth and he fell back into the crowd, and he jumped offstage and jumped at him. And he tried to scramble, you know, through the crowd to run from the Hell's Angel, and four other Hell's Angels jumped on him."

Robert Hiatt, a medical resident at the Public Health Hospital in San Francisco, was the first doctor to reach eighteen-year-old Meredith Hunter after the fatal wounds. He was behind the stage and responded to Jagger's call from the stage for a doctor. When Hiatt got to the scene, people were trying to get Hunter up on the stage, apparently in the hope that the Stones would stop playing and help could get through quicker.

"I carried him myself back to the first-aid area," Hiatt said. "He was limp in my hands and unconscious. He was breathing quite shallowly, and he had a very weak pulse. It was obvious he wasn't going to make it, but if anything could be done, he would have to get to a hospital quickly.

"He had very serious wounds. He had a wound in the lower back, which could have gone into the lungs; a wound in the back near the spine, which could have severed a major vessel; and a fairly large wound in the left temple. You couldn't tell how deep the wounds were, but each was about three-fourths of an inch long, so they would have been fairly deep.

"It was just obvious he wasn't going to make it."

[EXCERPT FROM RS 50 COVER STORY REPORTED BY LESTER BANGS, RENY BROWN, JOHN BURKS, SAMMY EGAN, MICHAEL GOODWIN, GEOFFREY LINK, GREIL MARCUS, JOHN MORTHLAND, EUGENE SCHOENFELD, PATRICK THOMAS AND LANGDON WINNER]

RS 50 | ALTAMONT | January 21st, 1970 | Photograph by Michael Maggia

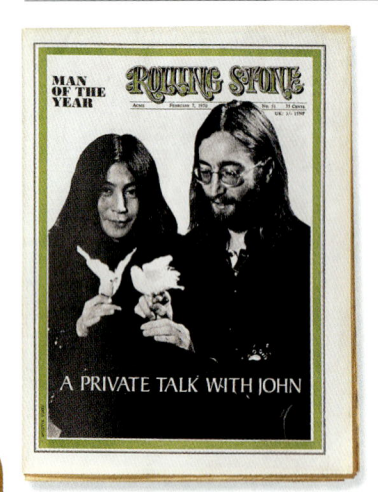

RS 51 | **JOHN LENNON & YOKO ONO**
February 7th, 1970
PHOTOGRAPH BY ANNETTE YORKE

Which of the John-and-Paul songs do you think were good?

I can't... well, you know, the early stuff like "I Wanna Hold Your Hand," "She Loves You" and stuff that was written together. I can't think of any others but things like that.

Not long ago, you told me you thought the 'Abbey Road' album was as good as 'Sgt. Pepper' and the White Album was also as good.

Yeah, yeah. I mean, I think each album since *Pepper* has been better. People just have this dream about *Pepper*. I mean, it was good for then, but it wasn't that spectacular when you look back on it. Like anything, it was great then. But I certainly prefer some of the tracks off the double album and some of the tracks off *Abbey Road* than all the tracks on *Pepper*. When you think back on *Pepper*, what do you remember? Just "A Day in the Life." You know. I go for individual songs, not for whole albums.

[EXCERPT FROM JOHN LENNON INTERVIEW BY RITCHIE YORKE]

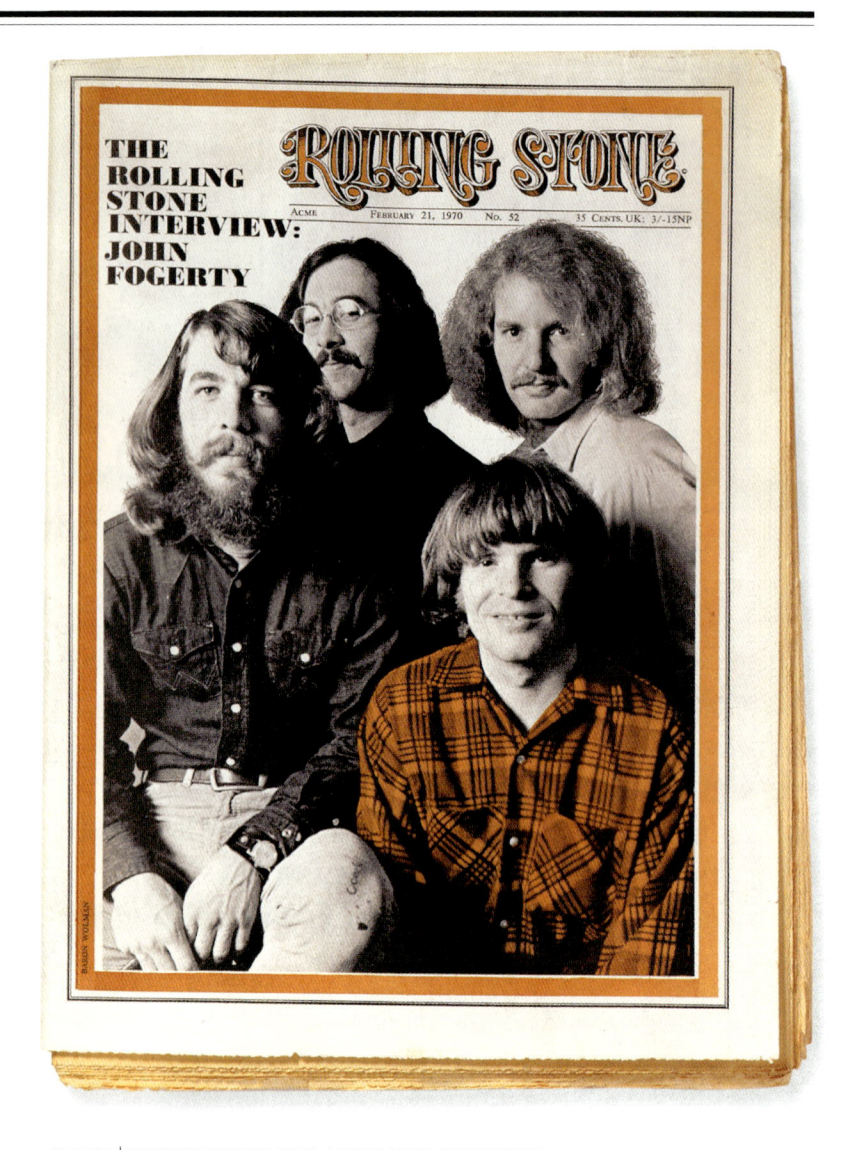

RS 52 | **CREEDENCE CLEARWATER REVIVAL**
February 21st, 1970
PHOTOGRAPH BY BARON WOLMAN

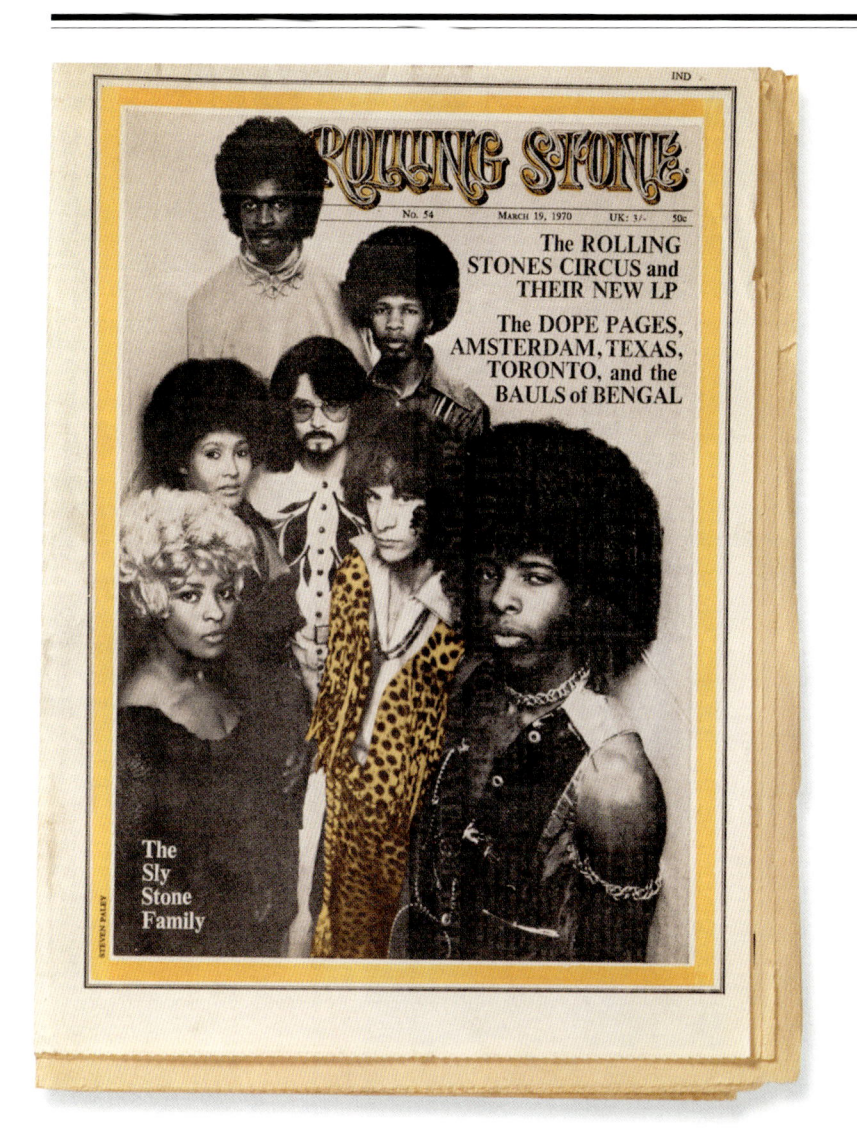

RS 54 | SLY & THE FAMILY STONE
March 19th, 1970
PHOTOGRAPH BY STEPHEN PALEY

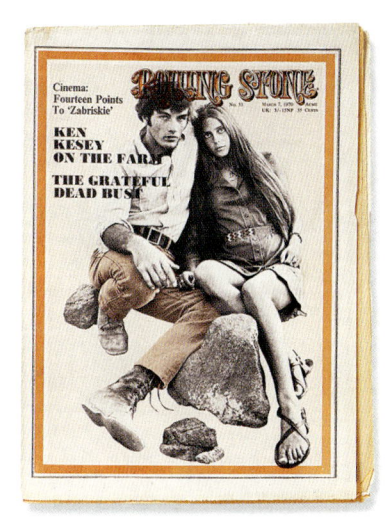

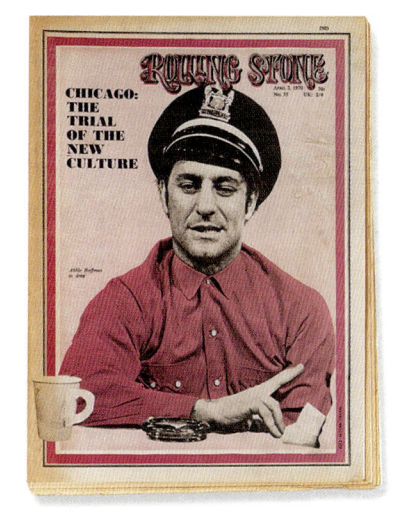

"**THE CONCEPT BEHIND** Sly and the [Family] Stone: I wanted everyone to get a chance to sweat. If there was anything to be happy about, then everybody'd be happy about it. Then, if we have a cross to bear, we bear it together." —*Sly Stone*

RS 53 | MARK FRECHETTE & DARIA HALPRIN
March 7th, 1970
'ZABRISKIE POINT' FILM STILL

RS 55 | ABBIE HOFFMAN
April 2nd, 1970
PHOTOGRAPH BY BILL MYERS

50 YEARS OF COVERS • 27

1970s

ROLLING STONE

April 30, 1970 • No. 57 • UK: 3/- • 50c

Neil Young, Pharoah Saunders & The Great Africa Dope Burn

Paul McCartney Returns!

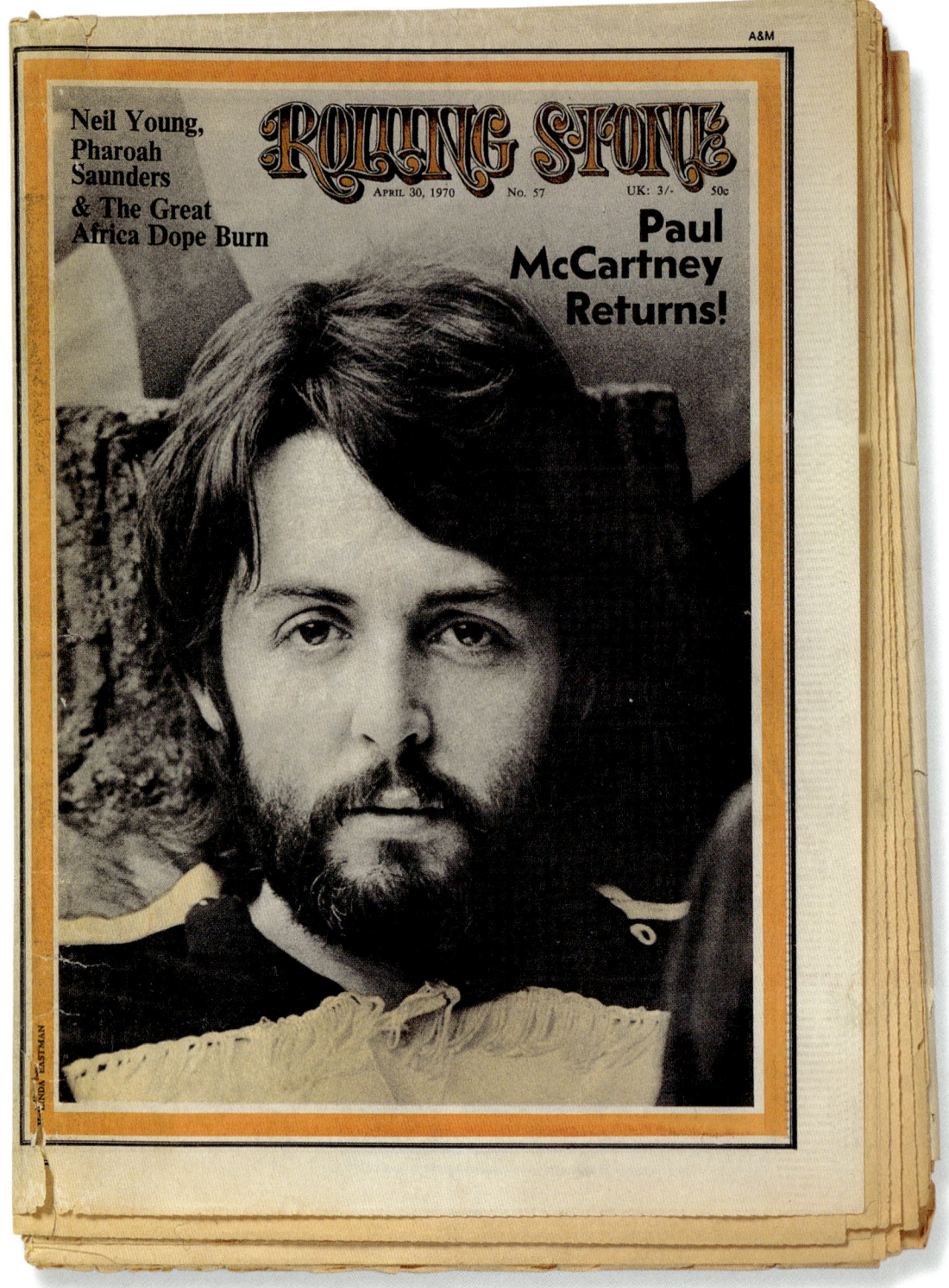

RS 57 | PAUL McCARTNEY | April 30th, 1970 | Photograph by Linda Eastman

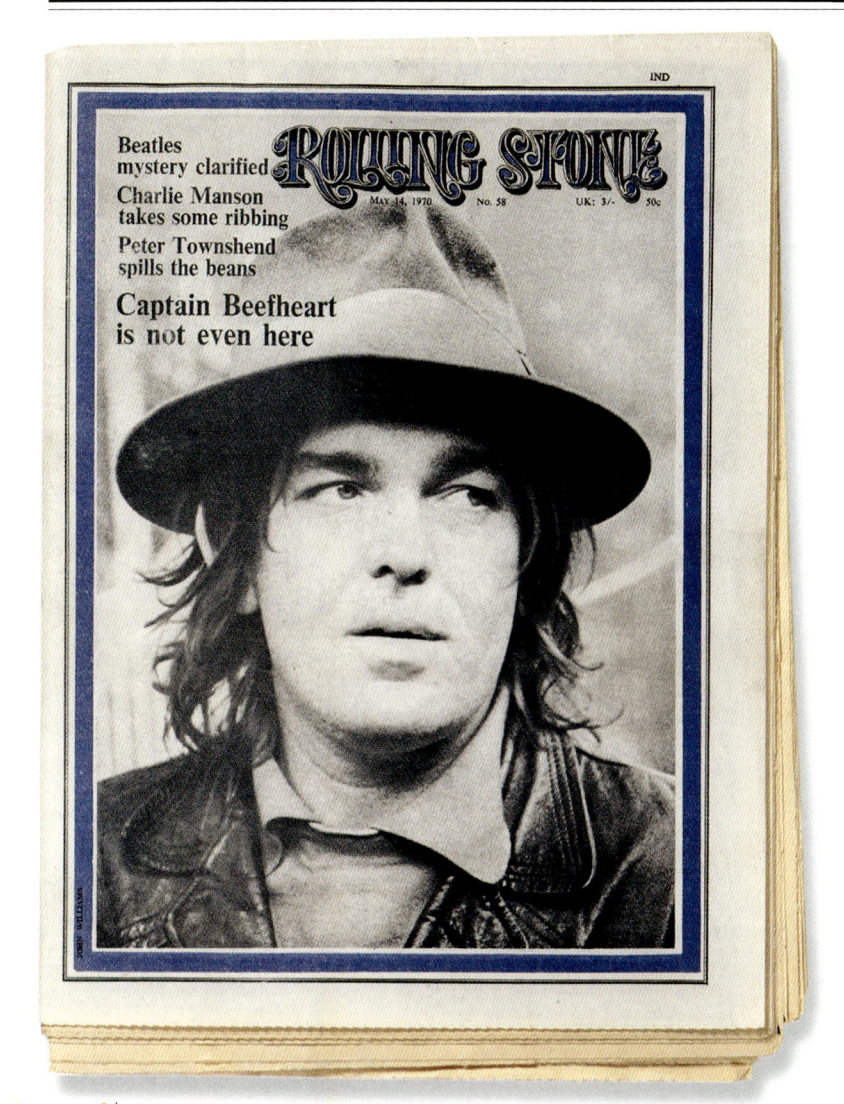

RS 58 | CAPTAIN BEEFHEART | May 14th, 1970 | Photograph by John Williams

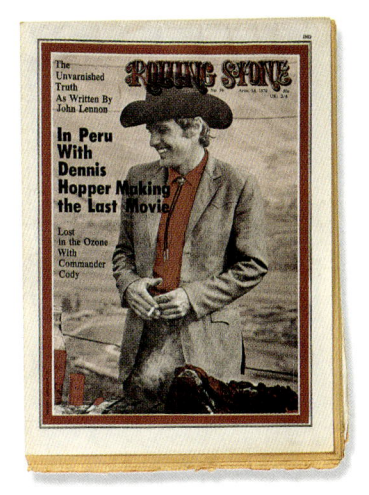

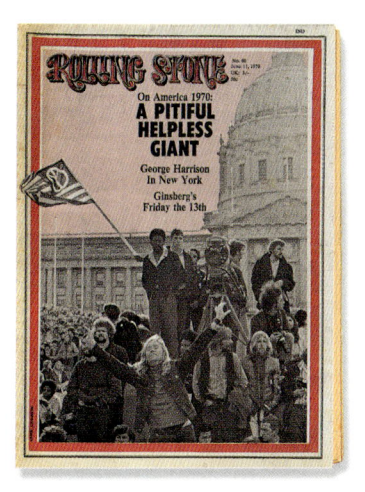

RS 56 | DENNIS HOPPER
April 16th, 1970
Photograph by Michael Anderson Jr.

RS 60 | ANTIWAR
DEMONSTRATORS
June 11th, 1970
Photograph by Annie Leibovitz

50 YEARS OF COVERS • 29

1970s

ROLLING STONE
No. 59 | May 28, 1970 | UK: 3/- | 50¢

Dylan in the Studio With George

Paul Simon, If Anybody Asks

Little Richard Child of God

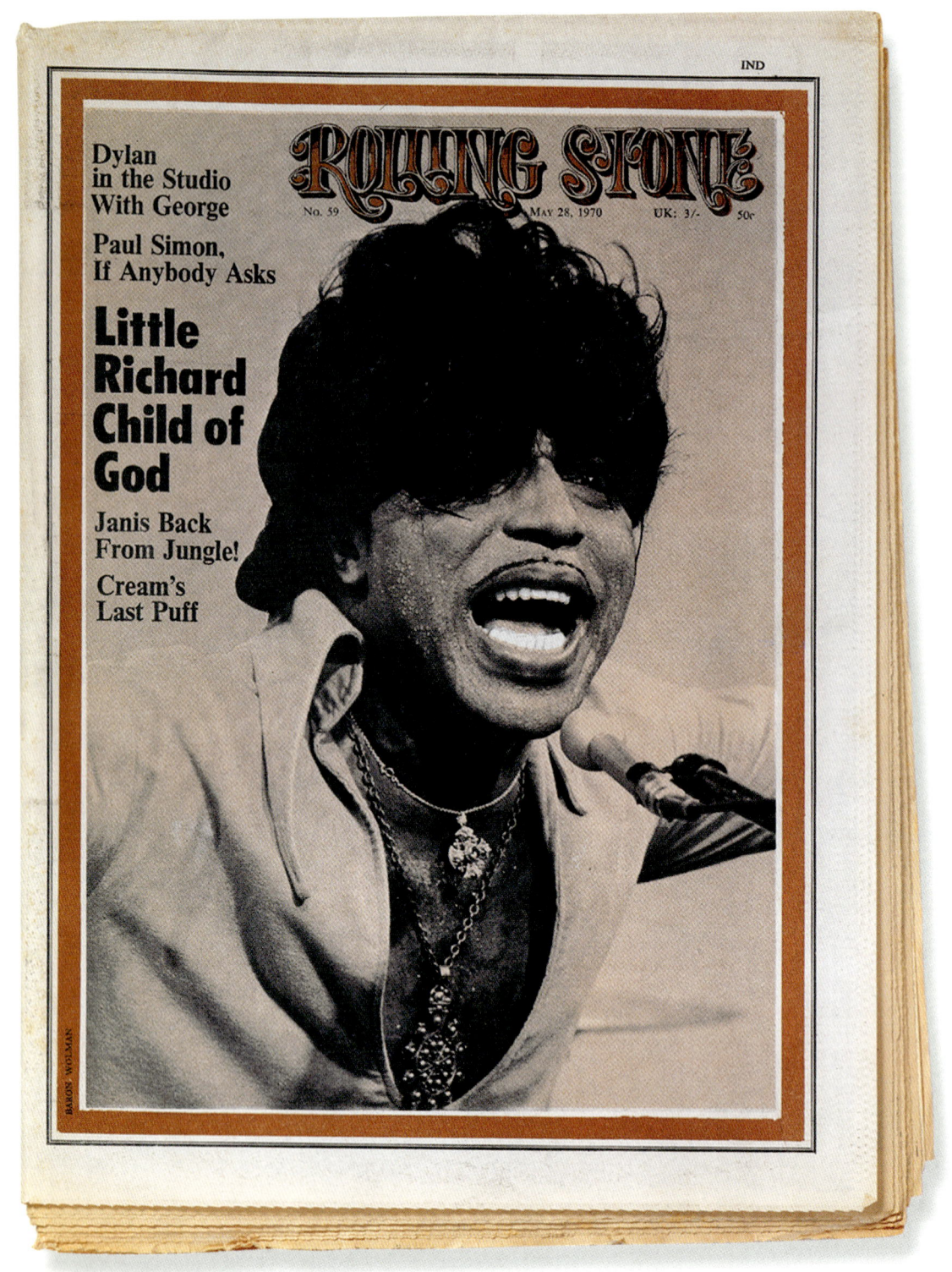

Janis Back From Jungle!

Cream's Last Puff

RS 59 | LITTLE RICHARD | May 28th, 1970 | Photograph by Baron Wolman

RS 61 | CHARLES MANSON | June 25th, 1970 | Photographer Unknown

"Jann Wenner... suggested that I and David Dalton do a story on Charles Manson. None of the editors liked the idea, including myself, but Jann figured there was a story there.

"It turned out he was amazingly perceptive. Because Manson wanted his album plugged, he granted us an exclusive prison interview. Because an assistant prosecutor thought we were a cute hippie rag with a circulation of maybe 10,000 (it was then about 250,000), he gave us a detailed on-the-record account of his case before trial, enabling us to scoop the established dailies. Because the Manson family thought of us as brothers under the ground, they let us view their mercenary attempts to cash in on their leader's story. After a few weeks, we knew we had something bigger than even Jann had anticipated.

"And certainly *longer* than Jann had anticipated – eventually the story took some 20,000 words and, more to the point, three months to write. And it was this *time* thing, I soon discovered, that tended to make Jann fret. I've always felt that anything worth doing is worth doing slowly. ('The Tortoise and the Hare' is one of my favorite stories, and someday I'm going to finish reading it.) But for some reason, Jann has never warmed to the idea. I remember the time I flew up to San Francisco to show him an outline for one section of the Manson story. I figured I would meet with him for about an hour, then fly home. But when I walked into Jann's office, he seemed disturbed and a little chagrined, like someone who'd just learned of a bad investment. He'd been talking to my previous employer. 'I understand,' he said with a weak smile, 'that at the *L.A. Times* they called you the Stonecutter.' With that, he forbade me to leave the office until the section was completely written. I stayed there a week, night and day, without a toothbrush or a change of clothing, a rather unpleasant situation for both me and anyone in the immediate vicinity.

"That should have been the tipoff right there: clearly a violation of adult labor laws. But in fact I fell into Jann's trap again a month later while working on the introduction and was imprisoned for another week without warning or underwear. The end result was a six-part epic, which I still consider the best thing written on Manson and the culture. ROLLING STONE won a National Magazine Award for it. The assistant prosecutor was removed from the case because he talked too much."

—*David Felton*

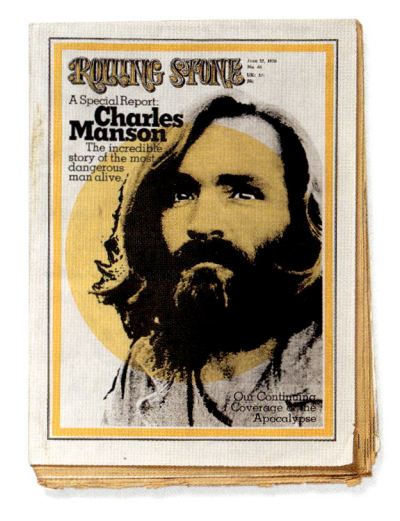

Can you explain the prophecies you found in the Beatles' double album?

[*Charlie starts drawing some lines on the back of a sheet of white paper. In the bottom area he writes the word SUB.*]

OK. Give me the names of four songs on the album.

[*We choose "Piggies," "Helter Skelter," "Blackbird," and he adds "Rocky Raccoon."*]

This bottom part is the subconscious. At the end of each song there is a little tag piece on it, a couple of notes. Or like in "Piggies" there's "oink, oink, oink." And all these sounds are repeated in "Revolution 9." Like in "Revolution 9," all these pieces are fitted together and they predict the violent overthrow of the white man. Like you'll hear "oink, oink," and then right after that, machine gun fire. AK-AK-AK-AK-AK-AK!

Do you really think the Beatles intended to mean that?

I think it's a subconscious thing. I don't know whether they did or not. But it's there. This music is bringing on the revolution, the unorganized overthrow of the Establishment. The Beatles know in the sense that the subconscious knows.

[EXCERPT FROM RS 61 COVER STORY BY DAVID FELTON AND DAVID DALTON]

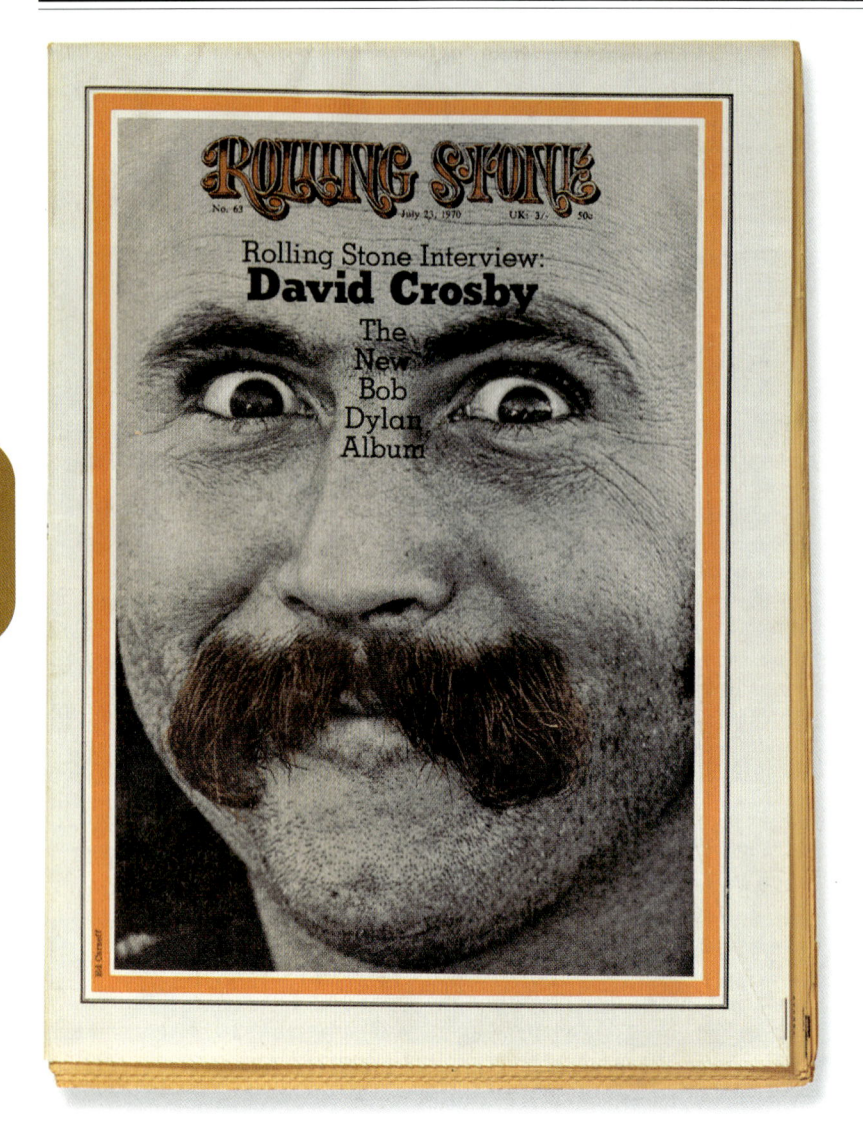

1970s

RS 63 | DAVID CROSBY
July 23rd, 1970
PHOTOGRAPH BY ED CARAEFF

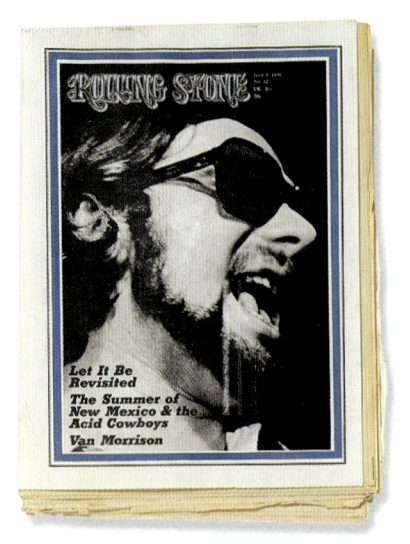

RS 62 | VAN MORRISON
July 9th, 1970
PHOTOGRAPHER UNKNOWN

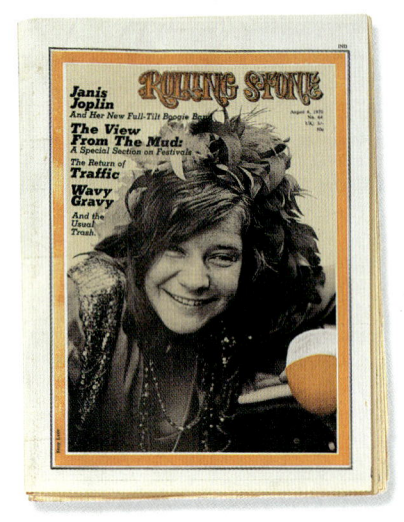

RS 64 | JANIS JOPLIN
August 6th, 1970
PHOTOGRAPH BY TONY LANE

"EVERY TIME, MAN, that I get stoned and put on a guitar and somebody points me at a microphone, I have – I can't say every time – 99 times out of a hundred – I have as good a time as most people do balling." —*David Crosby*

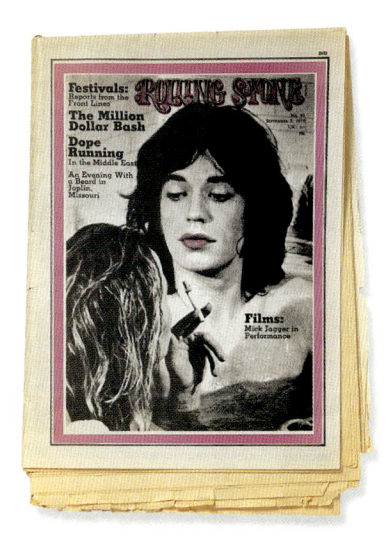

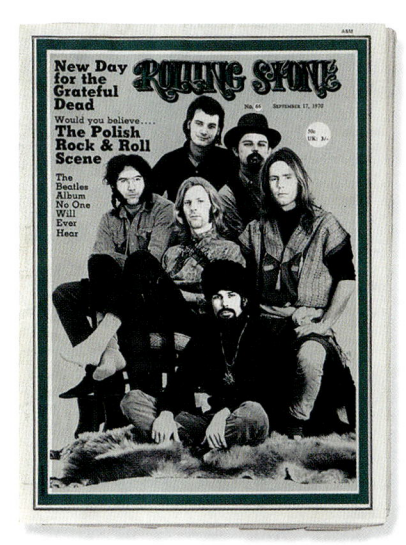

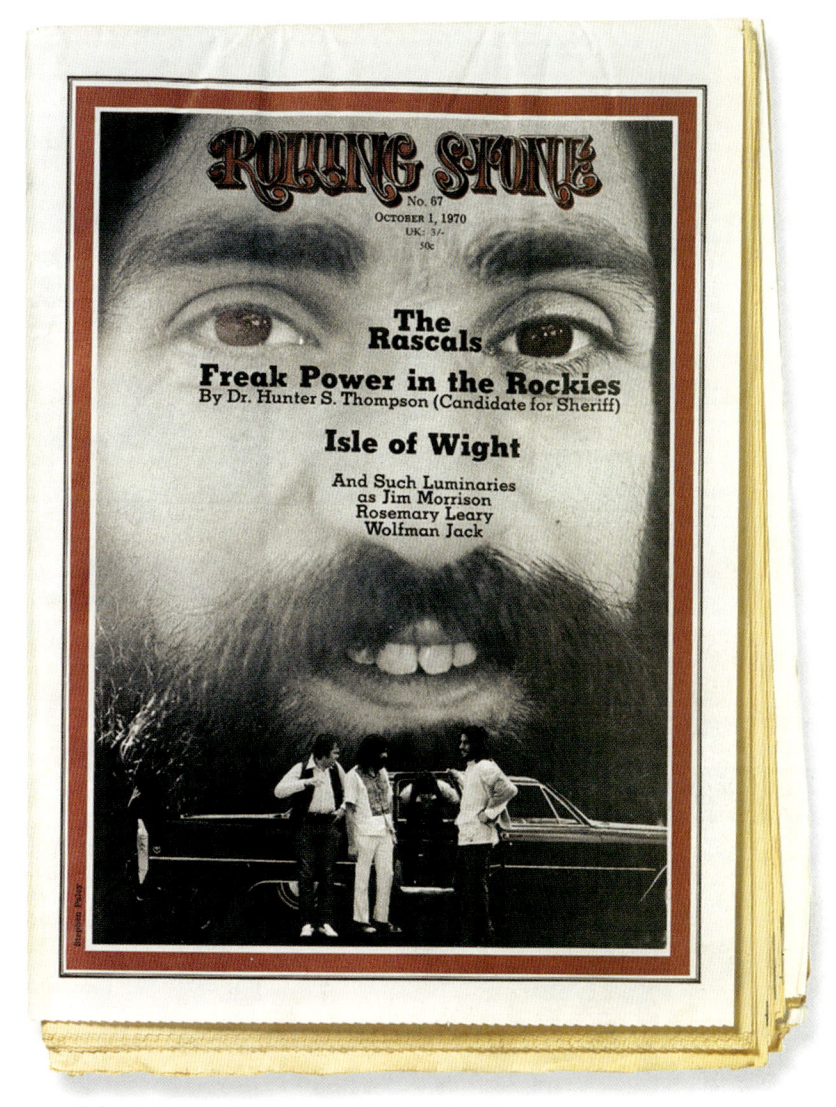

RS 65 | MICK JAGGER &
ANITA PALLENBERG
September 3rd, 1970
'Performance' film still

RS 67 | FELIX CAVALIERE & THE RASCALS
October 1st, 1970
Photograph by Stephen Paley

RS 66 | THE GRATEFUL DEAD
September 17th, 1970
Photograph by Jim Marshall

50 YEARS OF COVERS • 33

1970s

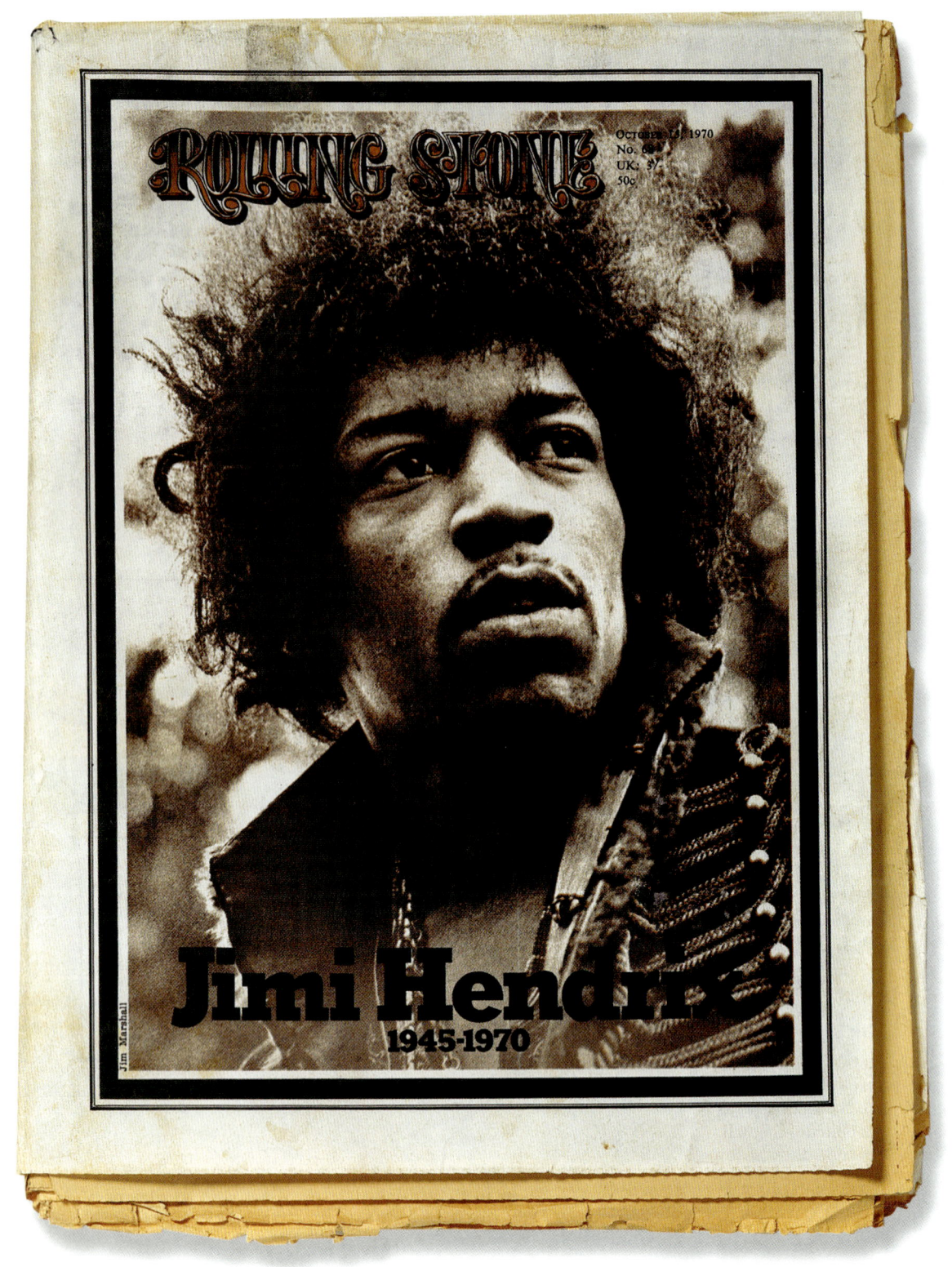

RS 68 | JIMI HENDRIX
October 15th, 1970
PHOTOGRAPH BY JIM MARSHALL

In 1967, Hendrix burst onto the rock & roll scene not initially because of his music. Sure, it was far-out, but the most significant thing was the Hendrix Presence. The sexual savage electric dandy rock & roll nigger Presence! The voodoo child run wild in electric ladyland!

Fully aware that this would be Jimi's best starting image, his first LP and singles were heavy on Presence, light on his (ultimately) strongest facet. It was through live performances and the later recordings that the rock & roll audience was to discover his greatly more astounding side: He was perhaps the master virtuoso of electric guitar. It was Jimi Hendrix, more than any other guitarist, who brought the full range of sound from all the reaches of serious electronic music – a wider palette of sound than any other performing instrumentalist in the history of music ever had at his fingertips – plus the fullest tradition of black music – from Charley Patton and Louis Armstrong all the way to John Coltrane and Sun Ra – to rock & roll. Nobody could doubt that Jimi Hendrix was a rock & roll musician, yet to jazz musicians and jazz fans, he was also a jazz performer. When Jimi Hendrix took a solo, it had everything in it.

It is only three years and three months since [the Jimi Hendrix Experience made its first American appearance at the Monterey Pop Festival]. Most master musicians are granted a good deal more time to make their statement. (Charlie Parker lived thirty-five years.) The amazing thing is how rich a musical legacy Hendrix has left in so short a time.

Certainly there is a place in the chapter on rock & roll lyrics (in the *Whole History of Rock and Roll*, to be published a few years hence, when the whole trip is dead) for Jimi. It's not just that he was adept at slinging the words together. But clearly Hendrix has got to be viewed as the father of Narcotic Fantasia imagery. This was his role as a lyricist at the start of his career. It was important to the voodoo child image that his songs came off as far out as possible, and how are you going to come off farther out than by asking your listeners to " 'Scuse me while I kiss the sky . . ."? What about "Queen Jealousy, Envy, waits behind him, her fiery green gown sneers at the grassy ground"? . . .

Hendrix told interviewers that he had been scared to sing for a long time because he thought his voice wasn't up to it. Then he heard Dylan and dug what Dylan was doing and figured, What the hell, if that cat can do that much with no more voice than *he's* got, what's holding me back? In fact, he was a great singer, as distinctive as Neil Young, and a harder wailer (swinger, mover) than either of them. It was a light but rich voice, perfectly suited to the laughter-from-the-shadows insinuations, the purrs and gurgles and the high crooning shouts that were his means to a super-expressive style. . . .

There will never be another like him.

—*John Burks*
[EXCERPT FROM JIMI HENDRIX TRIBUTE]

ROLLING STONE

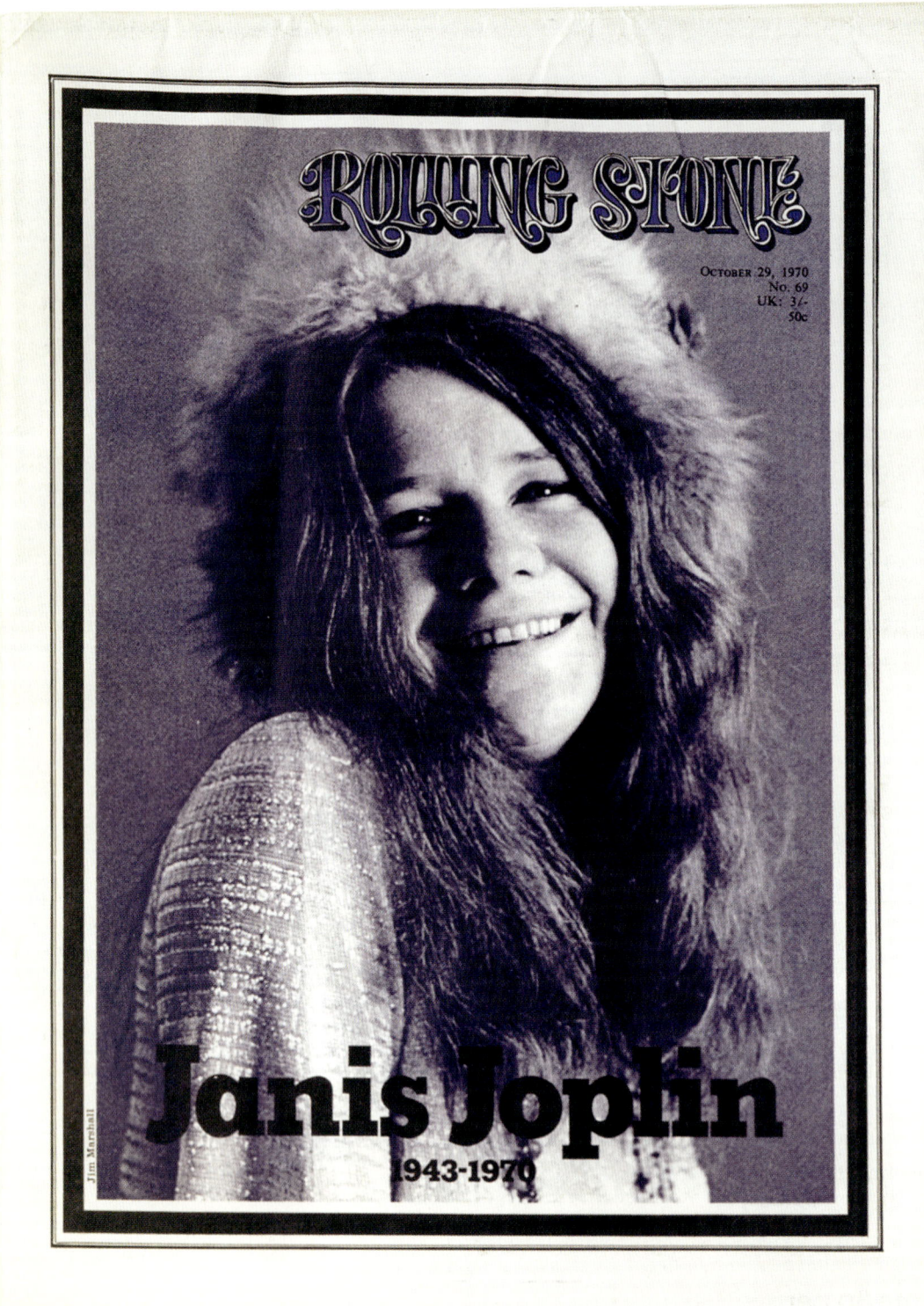

October 29, 1970
No. 69
UK: 3/-
50c

Janis Joplin
1943-1970

RS 69 | JANIS JOPLIN
October 29th, 1970
PHOTOGRAPH BY JIM MARSHALL

"*Janis was like a real person,* man. She went through all the changes we did. She went on the same trips. She was just like the rest of us – fucked up, strung out, in weird places. Back in the old days, the pre-success days, she was using all kinds of things, just like anybody, man.

"When she went out after something, she went out after it really hard, harder than most people ever think to do, ever conceive of doing.

"She was on a real hard path. She picked it, she chose it, it's okay. She was doing what she was doing as hard as she could, which is as much as any of us could do. She did what she had to do and closed her books. I don't know whether it's *the* thing to do, but it's what she had to do."
—*Jerry Garcia*

"SHE WAS IMPULSIVE, GENEROUS, SOFTHEARTED, SHY AND DETERMINED. She had style and class, and in a way, she didn't believe it. What did she want? It was all there for her but something that she knew wasn't fated to happen. Many people loved her a very great deal, like many people loved Billie Holiday, but somehow that was not enough.

"We'll never know and it doesn't matter, in a sense, because that brightly burning candle made an incredibly strong light in its brief life.

"They heard Janis Joplin 'round the world, loud and clear, and they will continue to hear her. I am only sorry for those who never had the flash of seeing her perform.

"Janis and Big Brother sang hymns at Monterey. It never seemed to me to be just music. I hope now that she's freed herself of that ball and chain, that she is at rest. She gave us a little piece of her heart and all of her soul every time she went onstage.

"Monterey, 1967. Otis, Jimi, Brian, Janis. Isn't that enough?

"Little girl blue, with the floppy hats and the brave attempt to be one of the guys. She took a little piece of all of us with her when she went. She was beautiful. That's not corny. It's true."
—*Ralph J. Gleason*

"WE USED TO GET DRUNK and play pool together. She beat me 80 percent of the time." —*Pigpen*

[EXCERPTS FROM JANIS JOPLIN TRIBUTE]

1970s

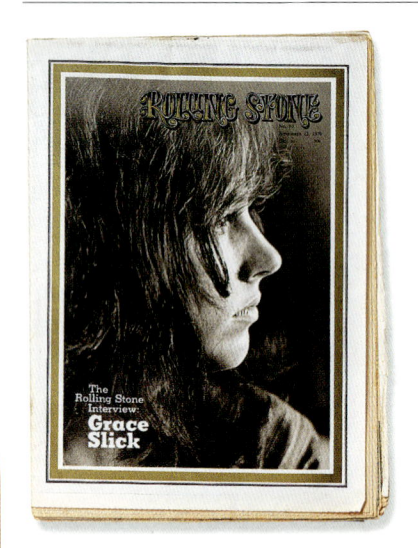

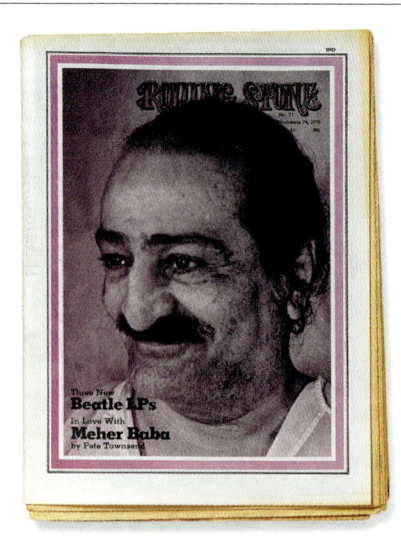

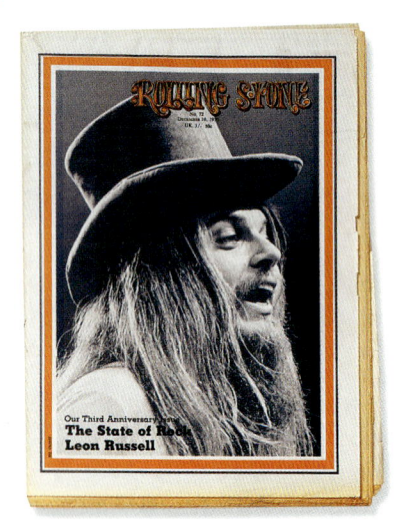

RS 70 | **GRACE SLICK**
November 12th, 1970
Photograph by Annie Leibovitz

RS 72 | **LEON RUSSELL**
December 10th, 1970
Photograph by Ed Caraeff

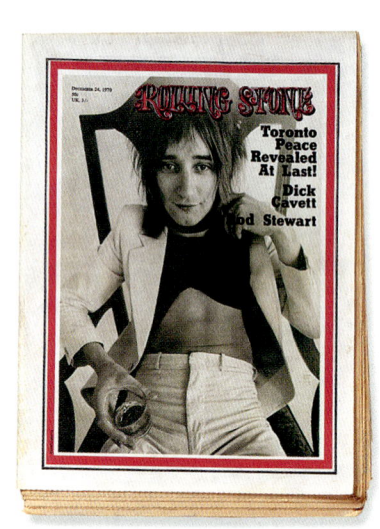

RS 71 | **MEHER BABA**
November 26th, 1970
Photographer unknown

RS 73 | **ROD STEWART**
December 24th, 1970
Photograph by Annie Leibovitz

[RS 71] Just why was Meher Baba on the cover of ROLLING STONE – and who was he, again? He was a sort of peace-extolling, mystical personal-actualization cult leader. The Who's Pete Townshend followed him (remember "Baba O'Riley" from *Who's Next*?) and wrote the accompanying cover story.

"JOHN LENNON was one of my first covers for ROLLING STONE [it was her first commissioned portrait]. At the time – I was still in school – I felt the cover shot was, like, the mediocre picture, the secondary consideration. A photograph to me was not a portrait – anyone can do that. I was addicted to hardcore journalism, newspaper stuff, capture the moment in time, Cartier-Bresson. I liked to combine the composition with the action. I carried a camera every second, and I was constantly framing life into little thirty-five-millimeter squares.

"So when I shot Lennon I was carrying three thirty-five-millimeter cameras, and on one of them I kept a 105 lens, which I used for light-meter readings. It was a long lens, I came in close on Lennon's face, and while I was taking the light-meter reading, he looked at me, and I just snapped one picture. And then I did all my other pictures. But I got back to ROLLING STONE, and Jann Wenner went through the contact sheets and immediately pulled out that picture for a cover. I said, 'Oh Jann, ughhhh!' I couldn't understand why he liked that picture. I think it took me ten, twelve years to come to an understanding of what that picture was. Maybe I was a little bit reluctant to have somebody look back at me.... And that shooting, at the very beginning of my career, set a precedent for my work with anyone of any notoriety or fame after that."

—*Annie Leibovitz*

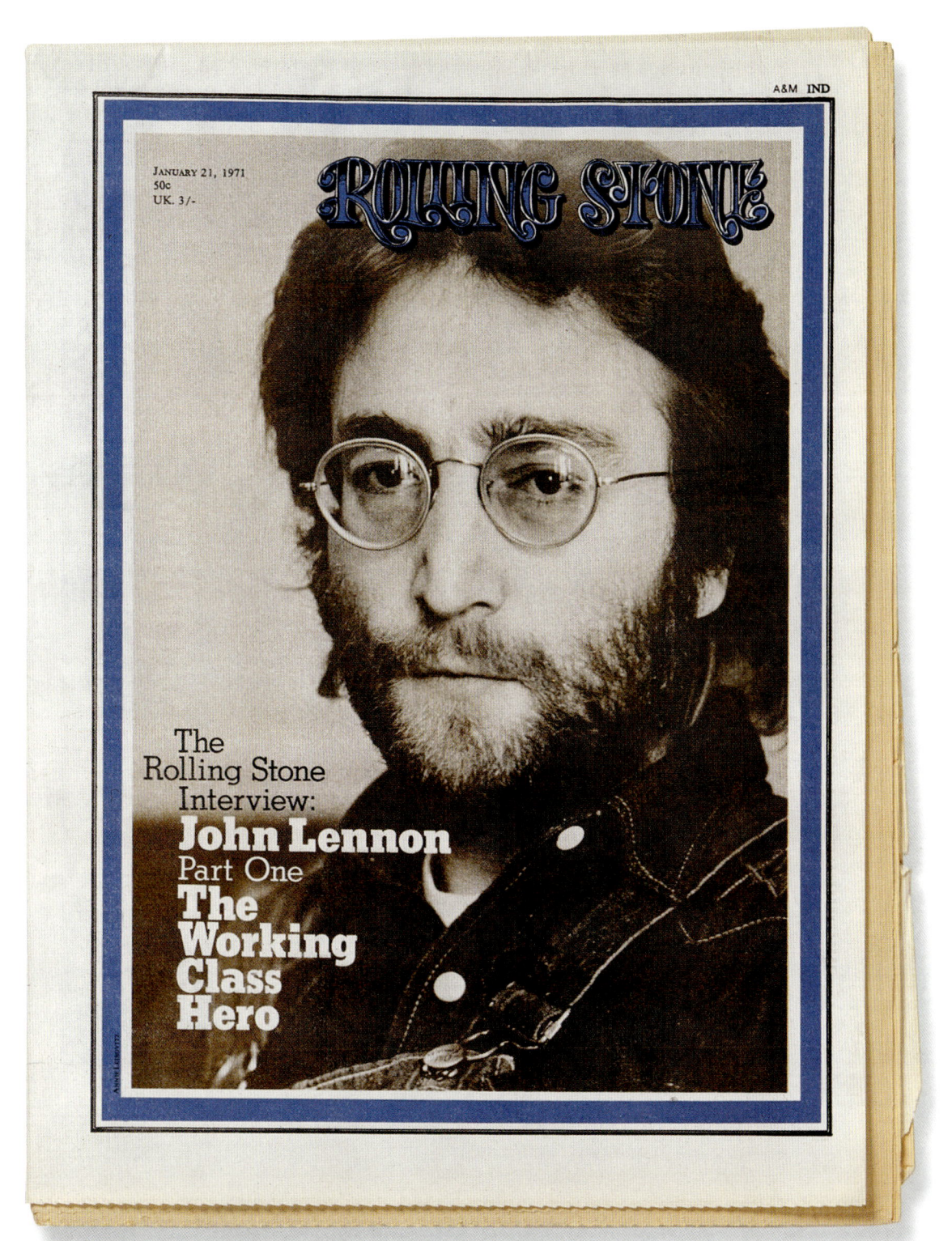

RS 74 | JOHN LENNON | January 21st, 1971 | Photograph by Annie Leibovitz

1970s

FEBRUARY 18, 1971
50c   UK. 3/-
No. 76

ROLLING STONE

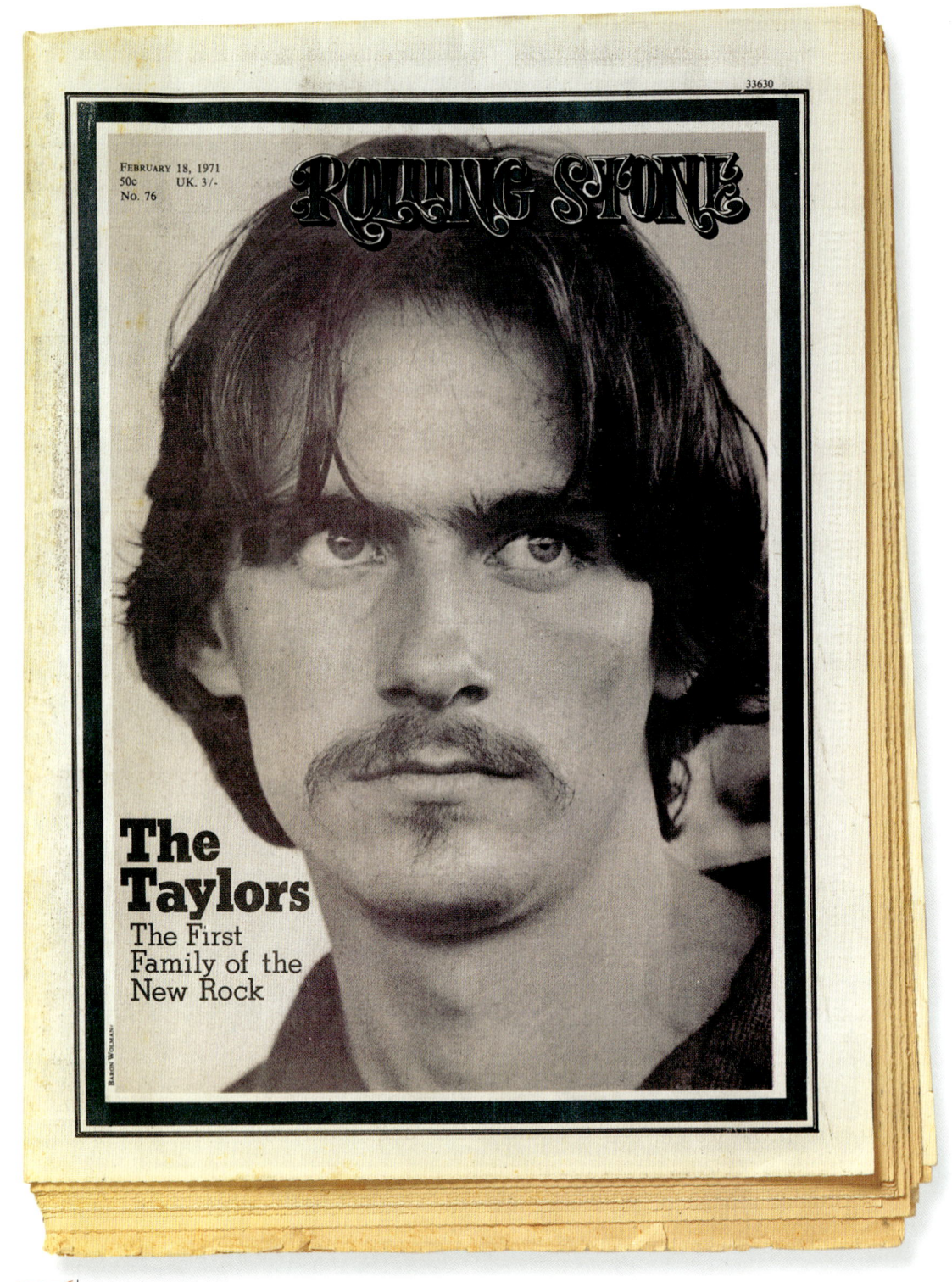

The Taylors
The First Family of the New Rock

RS 76 | JAMES TAYLOR | February 18th, 1971 | Photograph by Baron Wolman

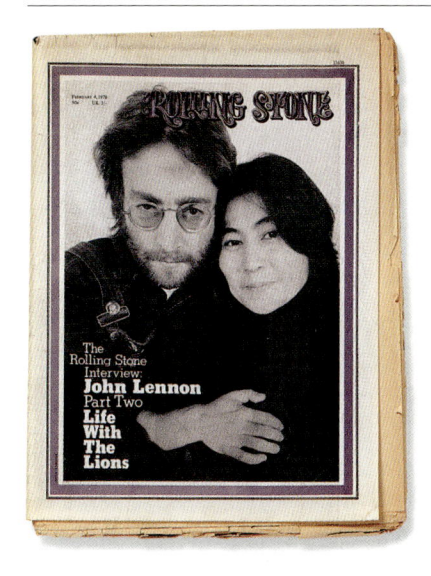

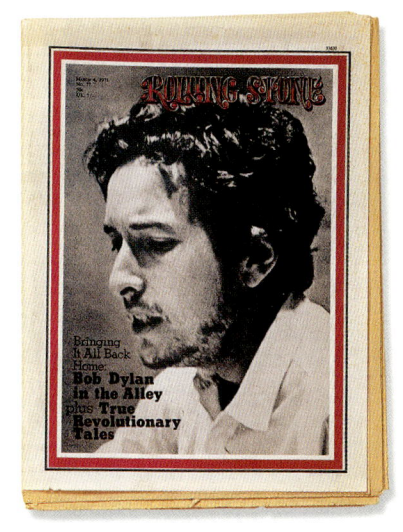

[RS 78] Muhammad Ali was the first athlete to grace the cover of ROLLING STONE. He remains the athlete with the most cover appearances, four. Brian Hamill's photo shows the then-undefeated champ as unscratched (the only scar on his face came from running his bicycle into a wall as a child).

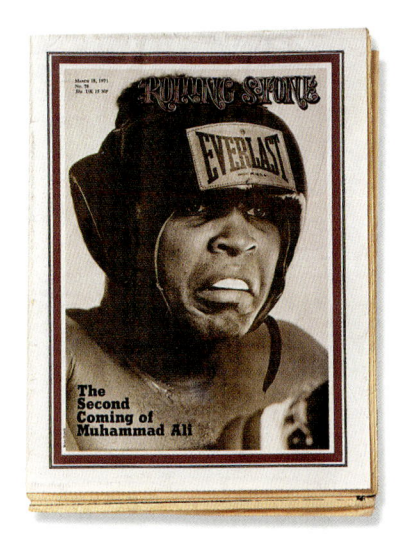

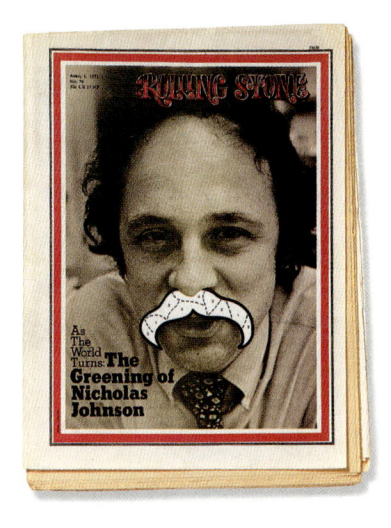

RS 75 | JOHN LENNON & YOKO ONO
February 4th, 1971
PHOTOGRAPH BY ANNIE LEIBOVITZ

RS 78 | MUHAMMAD ALI
March 18th, 1971
PHOTOGRAPH BY BRIAN HAMILL

RS 77 | BOB DYLAN
March 4th, 1971
PHOTOGRAPHER UNKNOWN

RS 79 | NICHOLAS JOHNSON
April 1st, 1971
PHOTOGRAPH BY ANNIE LEIBOVITZ

1970s

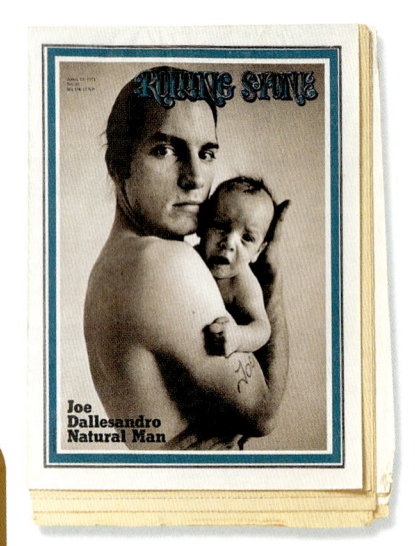

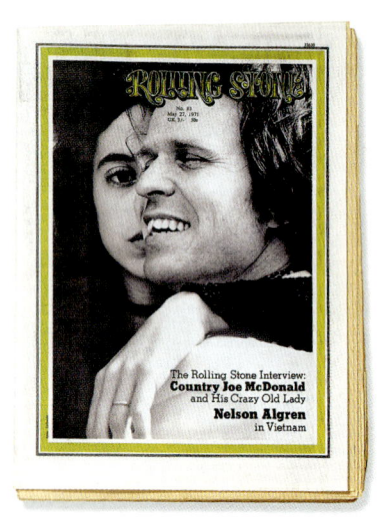

RS 80 | JOE DALLESANDRO
April 15th, 1971
Photograph by Annie Leibovitz

RS 83 | COUNTRY JOE
McDONALD & ROBIN MENKEN
May 27th, 1971
Photograph by Annie Leibovitz

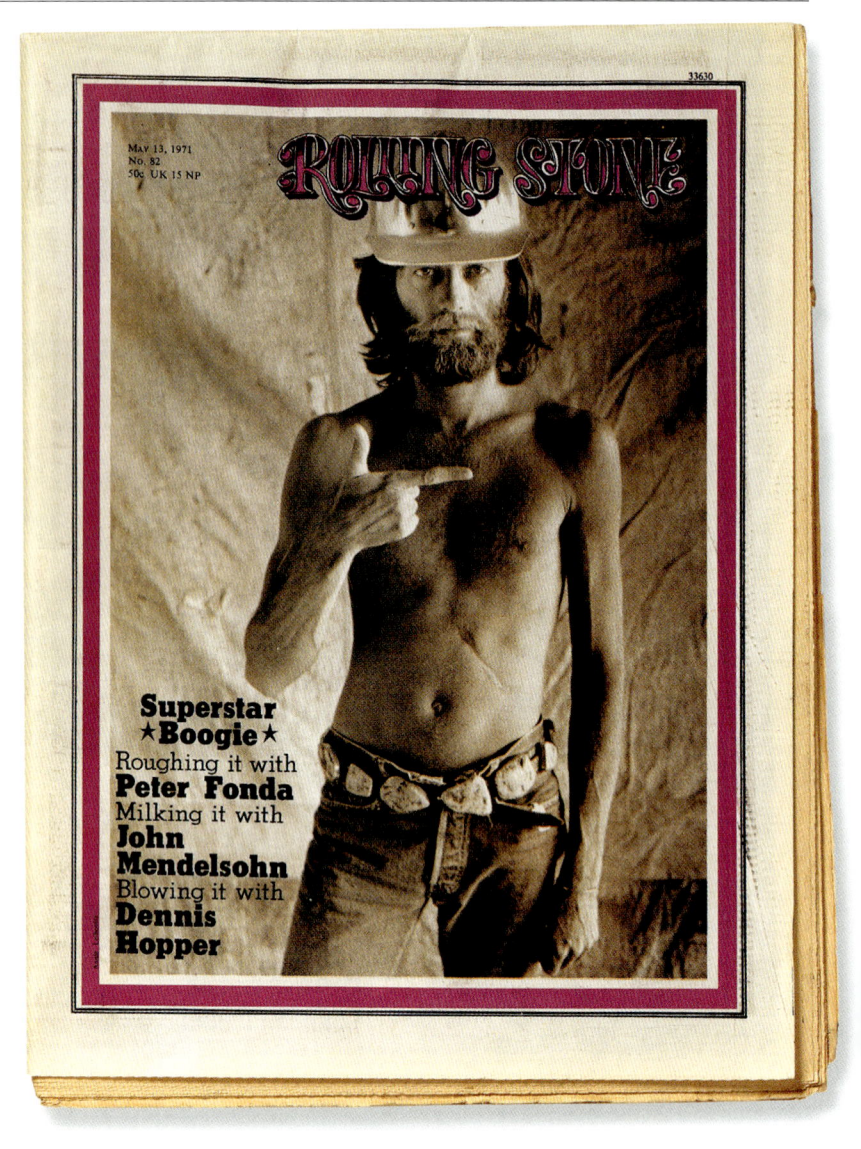

RS 82 | PETER FONDA
May 13th, 1971
Photograph by Annie Leibovitz

42 • ROLLING STONE

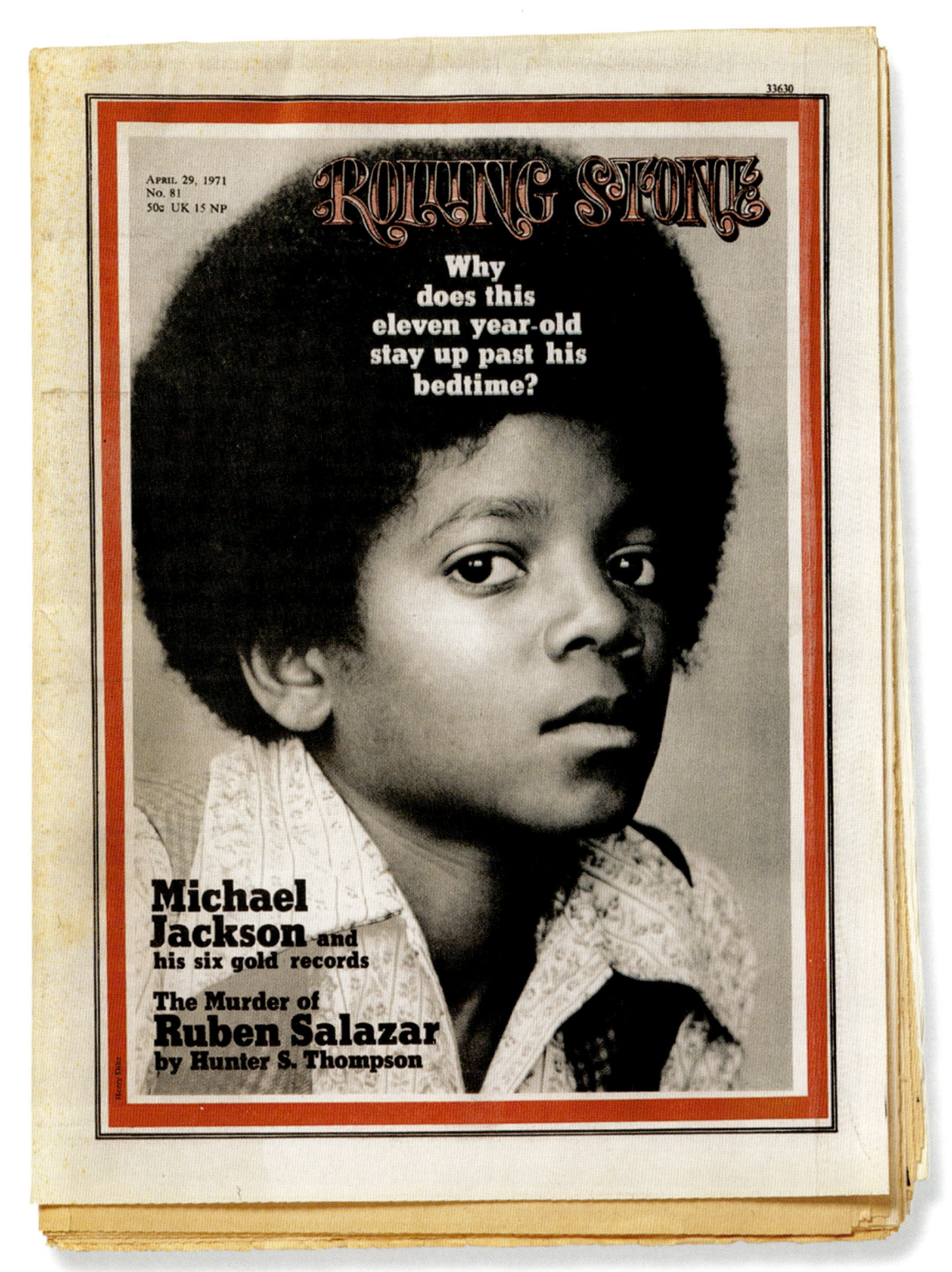

RS 81 | MICHAEL JACKSON | April 29th, 1971 | Photograph by Henry Diltz

1970s

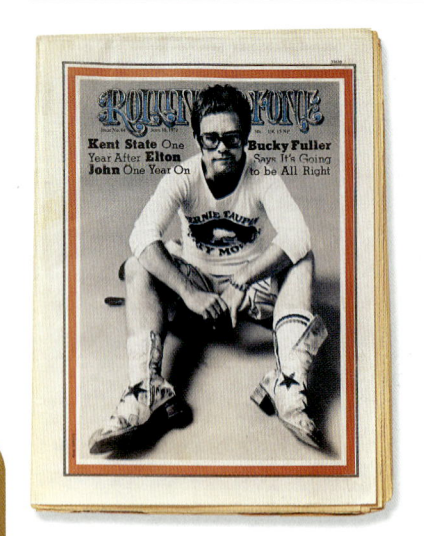

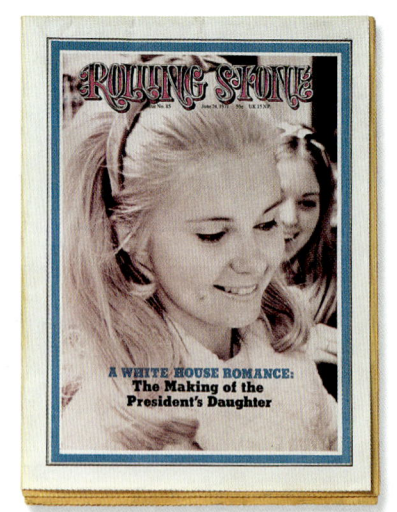

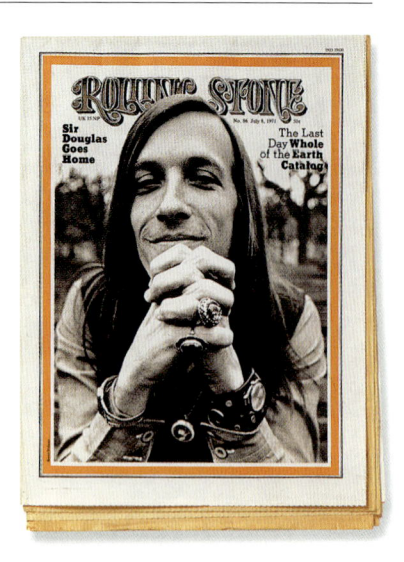

RS 84 | ELTON JOHN
June 10th, 1971
PHOTOGRAPH BY ANNIE LEIBOVITZ

RS 85 | TRICIA NIXON
June 24th, 1971
PHOTOGRAPHER UNKNOWN

RS 86 | DOUG SAHM
July 8th, 1971
PHOTOGRAPH BY BARON WOLMAN

I woke up one morning,

pretty hung over, and started poking around the apartment looking for something to read, and I found Jim's poetry manuscript. I sat down and read it and thought, Holy smoke, this is fantastic, and I was just sort of like ragingly delighted to find such a beautiful first book of poetry. When Jim came down later, I told him what I thought, and we talked about it a bit, and he was interested in what to do with it. . . . Jim was very serious about being a poet, and he didn't want to come in on top of being Jim-Morrison-the-big-rock-singer. . . .

Later, when the book had been published and the first copies arrived by mail in L.A., I found Jim in his room, crying. He was sitting there, holding the book, crying, and he said, "This is the first time I haven't been fucked." He said that a couple of times, and I guess he felt that that was the first time he'd come through as himself. . . .

I think that any two people who know each other closely probably influence each other. If I influenced him, he influenced me as well. It's hard to have a friend whose work you like where there's not some kind of mutual feedback. It's perfectly obvious in reading this book that Jim already had his own style and that he was already his own person. As to his potential for growth – well, he started out so good that I don't know how much better he could've gotten. He started off like a heavyweight.

[EXCERPT FROM TRIBUTE TO JIM MORRISON BY MICHAEL McCLURE]

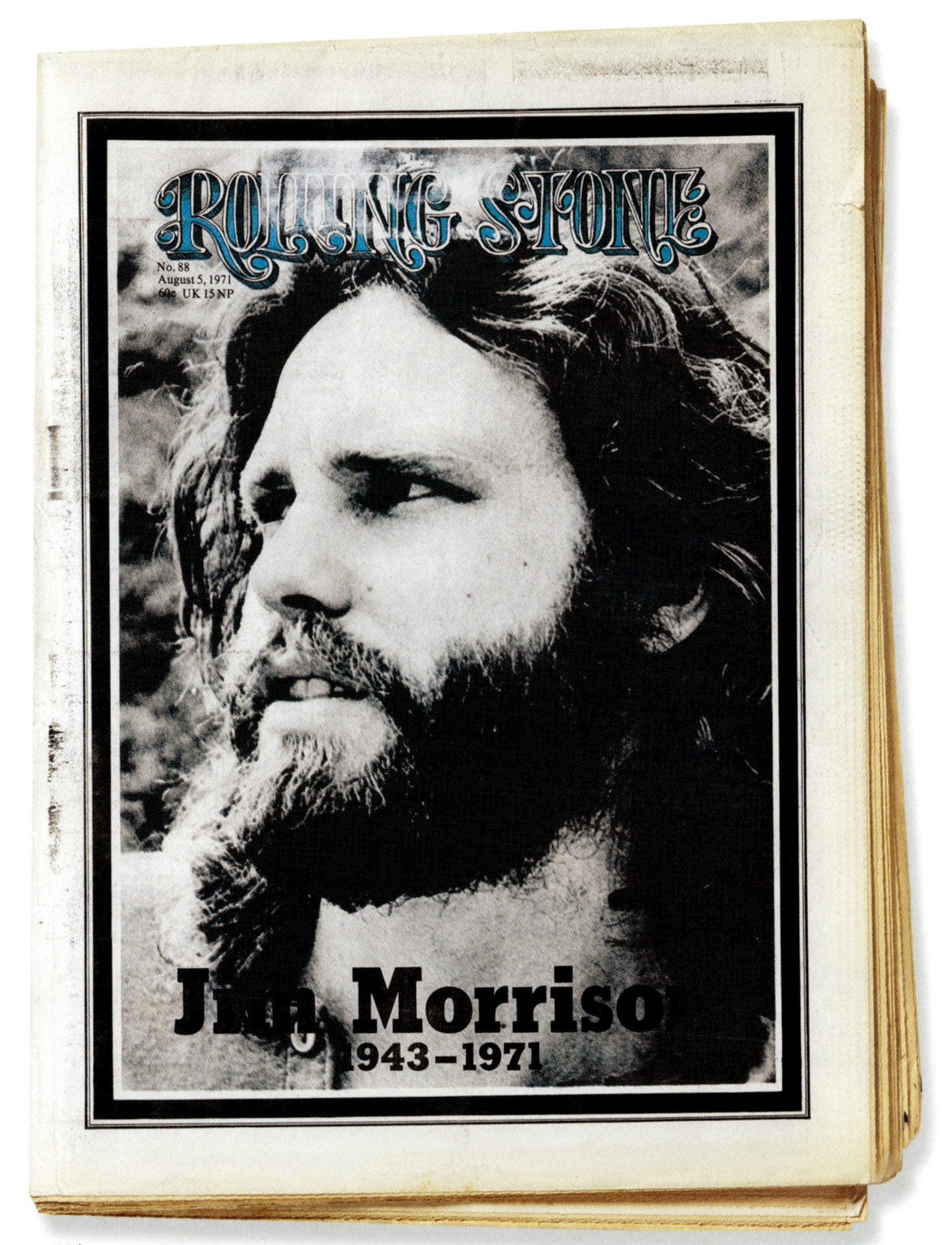

RS 88 | JIM MORRISON | August 5th, 1971 | Photographer unknown

1970s

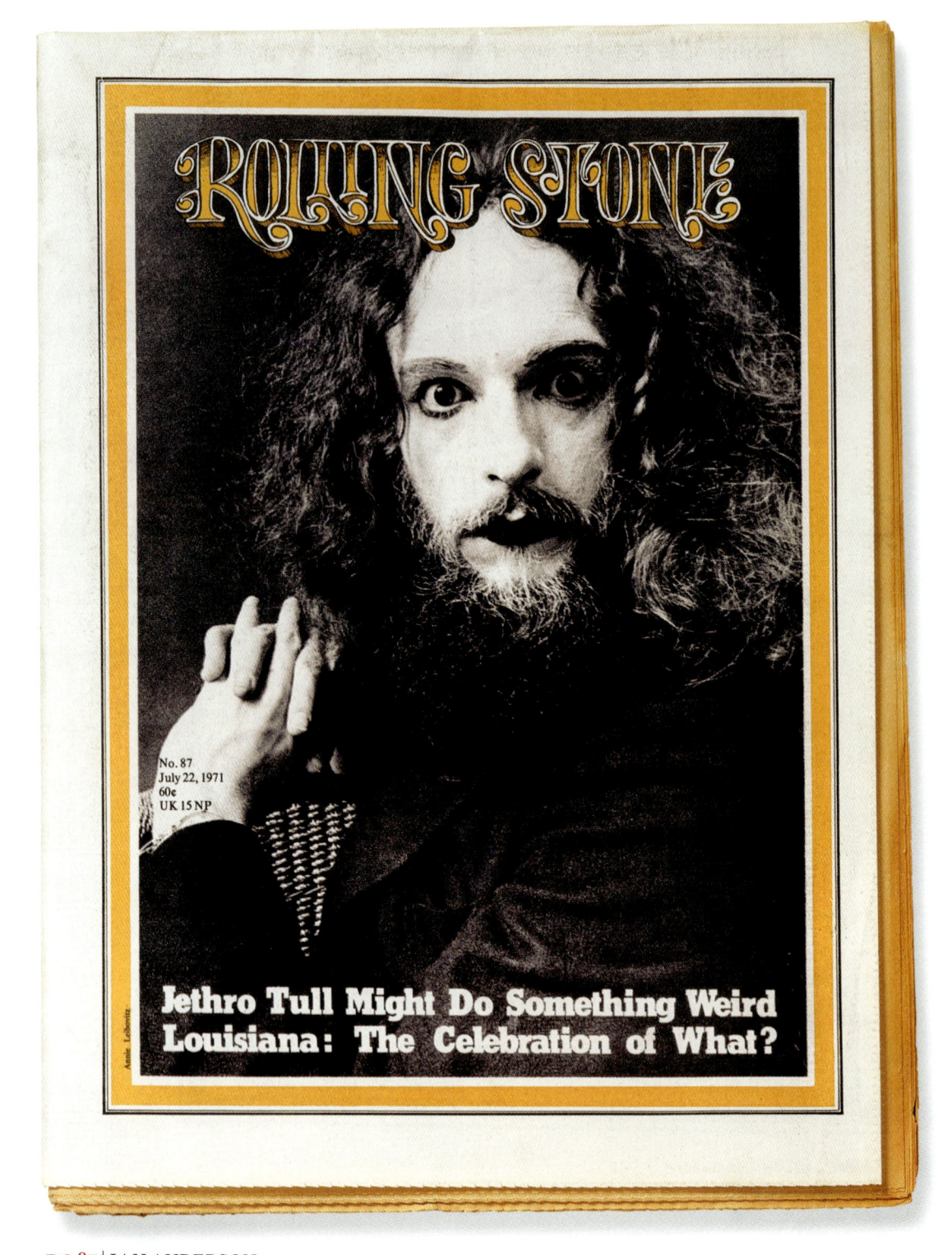

No. 87
July 22, 1971
60¢
UK 15 NP

Jethro Tull Might Do Something Weird
Louisiana: The Celebration of What?

RS 87 | IAN ANDERSON | July 22nd, 1971 | Photograph by Annie Leibovitz

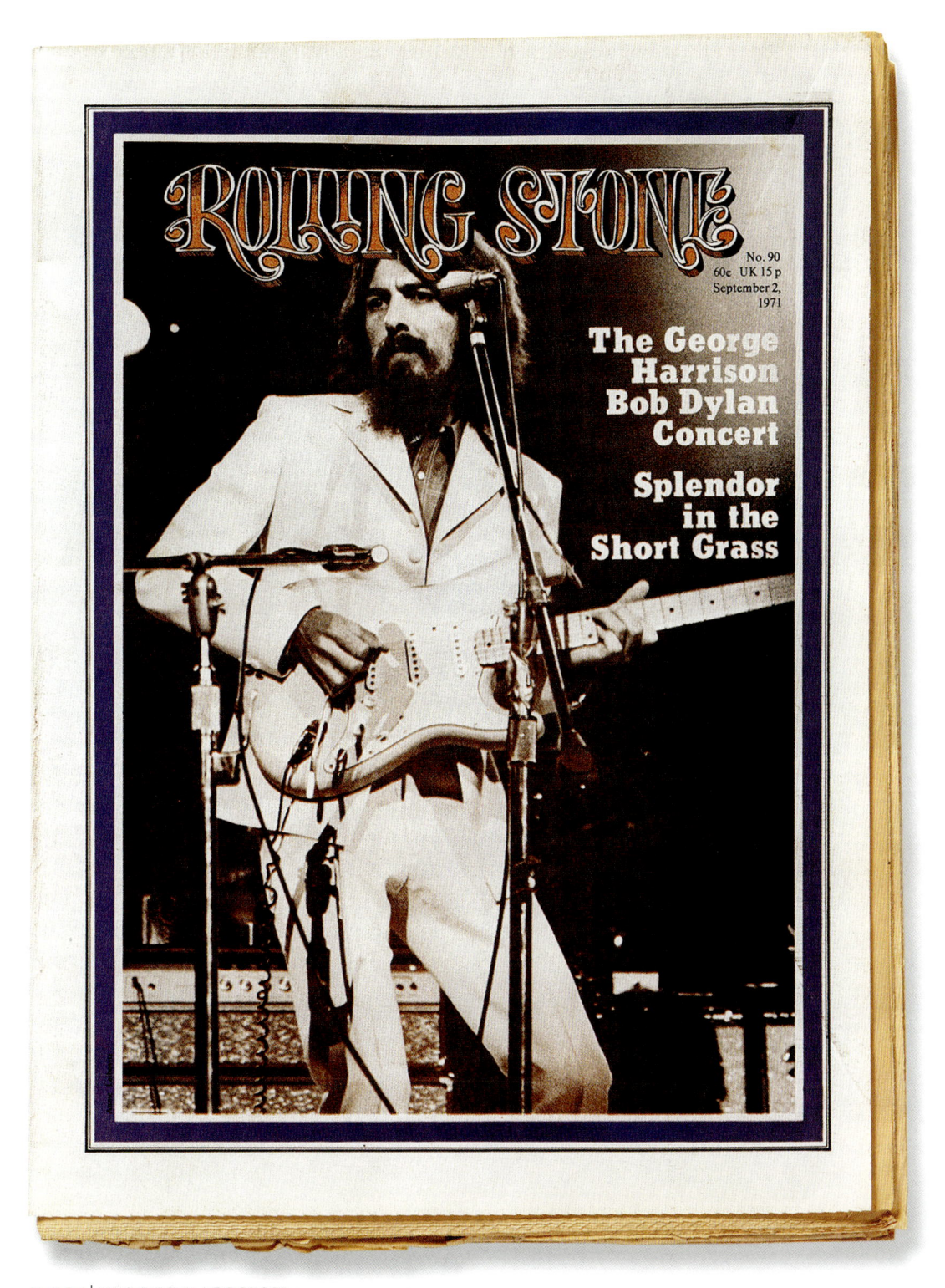

RS 90 | GEORGE HARRISON | *September 2nd, 1971* | PHOTOGRAPH BY ANNIE LEIBOVITZ

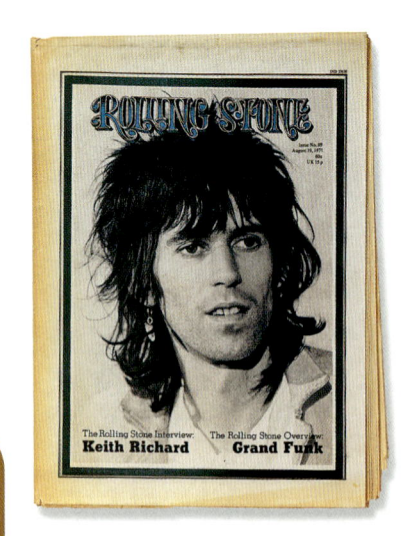

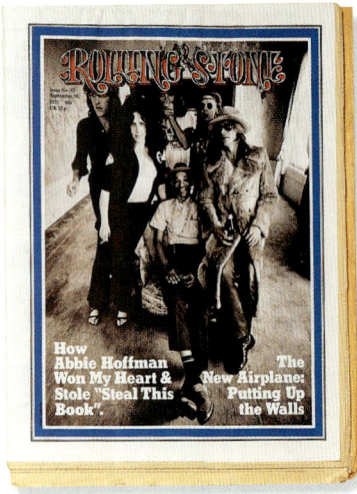

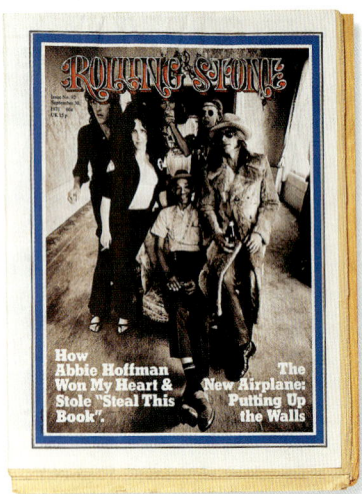

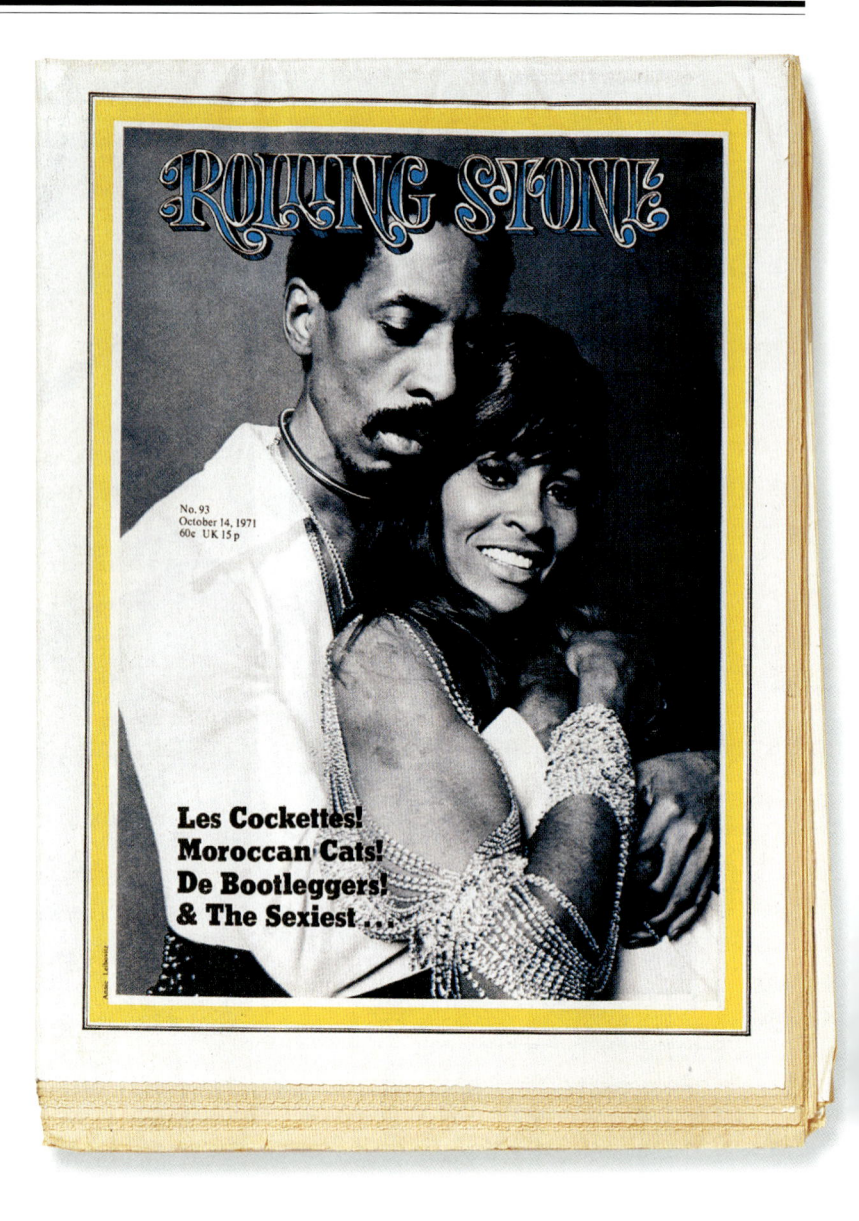

1970s

RS 89 | KEITH RICHARDS
August 19th, 1971
PHOTOGRAPH BY ROBERT ALTMAN

RS 92 | JEFFERSON AIRPLANE
September 20th, 1971
PHOTOGRAPH BY ANNIE LEIBOVITZ

RS 93 | IKE & TINA TURNER | October 14th, 1971 | PHOTOGRAPH BY ANNIE LEIBOVITZ

48 • ROLLING STONE

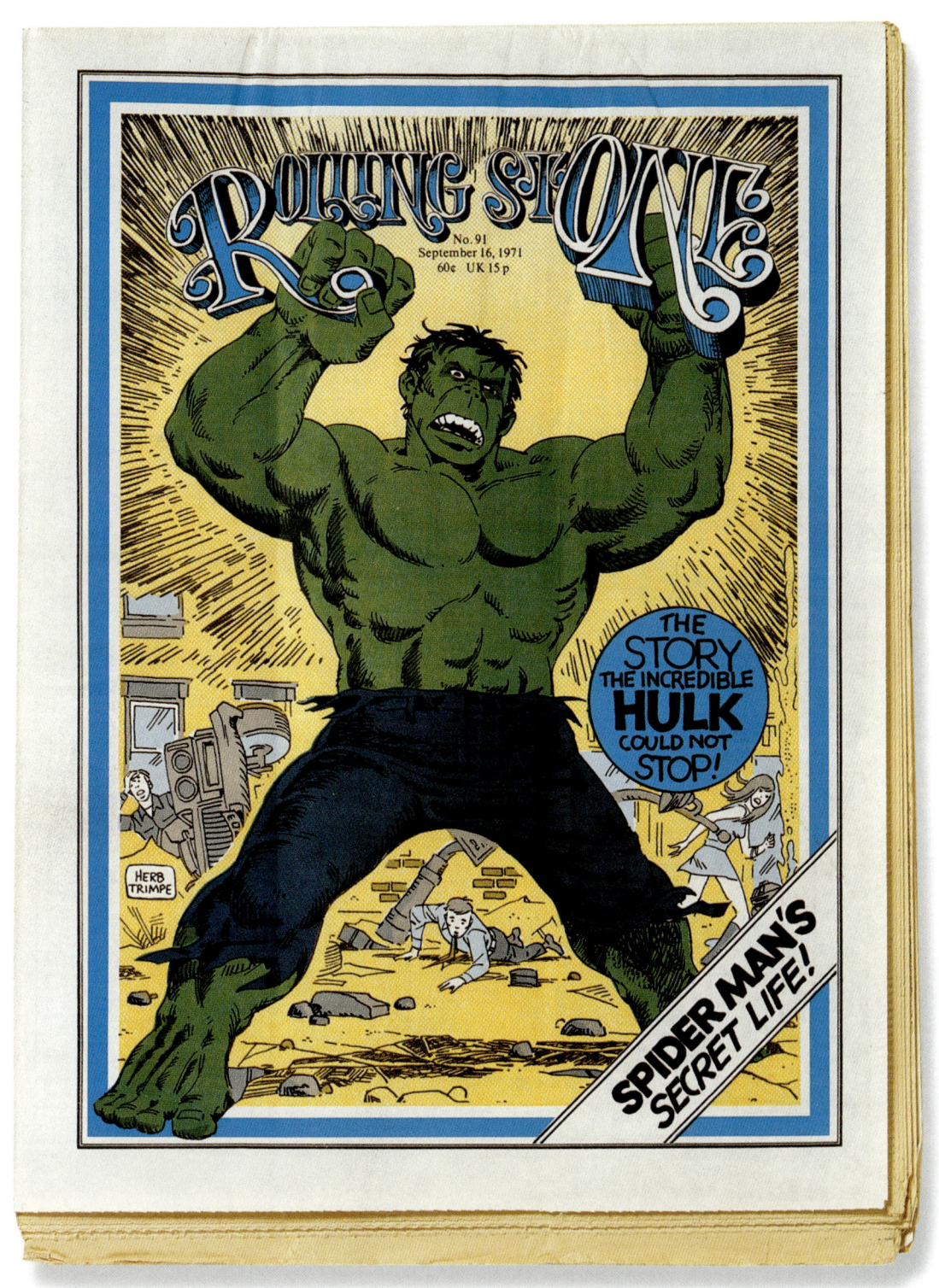

RS 91 | THE INCREDIBLE HULK | September 16th, 1971 | Illustration by Herb Trimpe

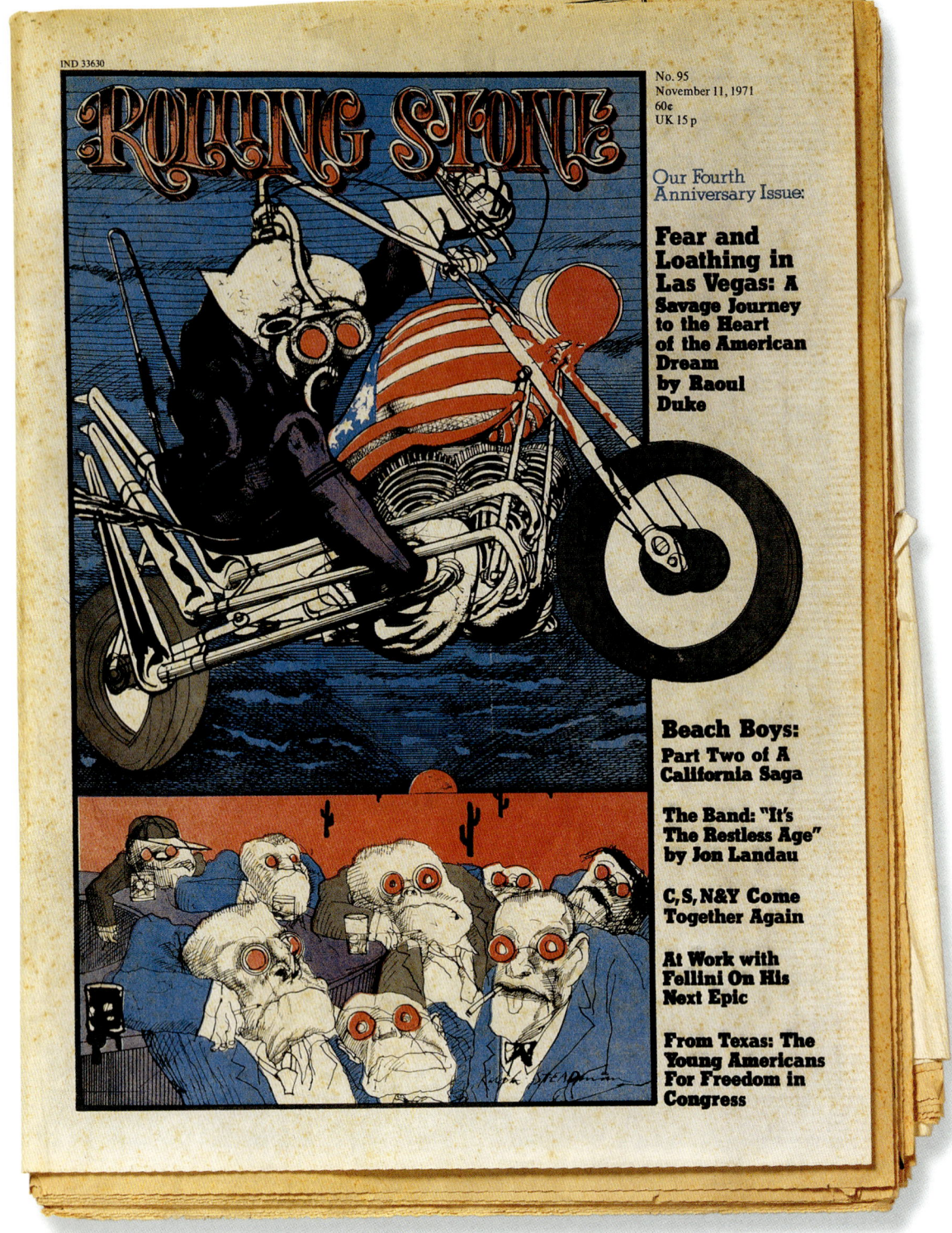

RS 95 | FEAR AND LOATHING IN LAS VEGAS | November 11th, 1971 | Illustration by Ralph Steadman

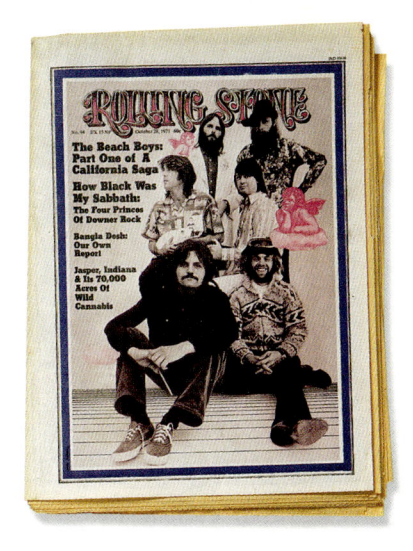

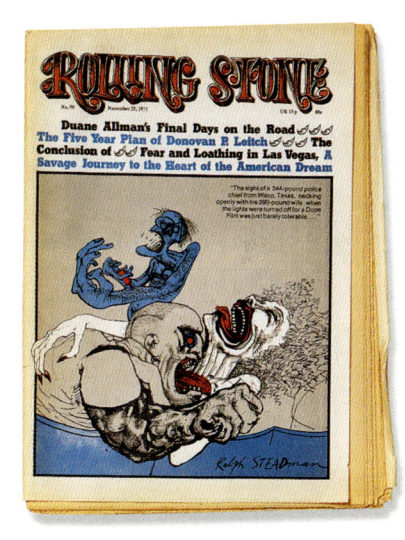

[**RS 98**] The name the Lyman family doesn't ring a bell? Its leader Mel Lyman was yet another "spiritual" leader prominent in the early Seventies. He was a sort of death-extolling quasi-mystical cult guru and author of *Mirror at the End of the Road*. He had some interesting ideas: "I am going to turn ideals to shit. I am going to shove hope up your ass." Ditto infrastructure renovations: "I am going to burn down the world, and then I am going to burn the rubble." This cover assignment, reportedly, was a day in the park for David Felton, coauthor of the six-part Charles Manson exposé.

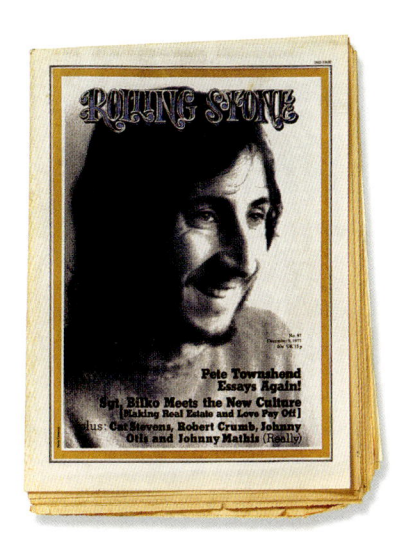

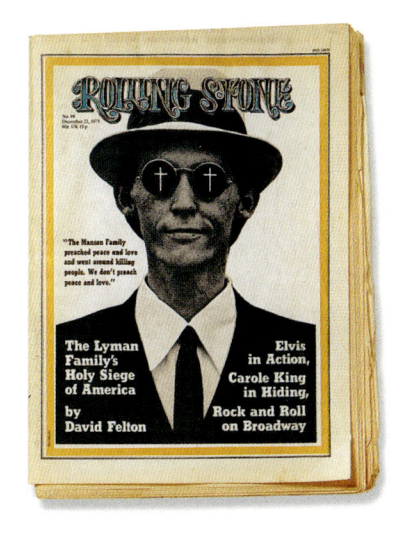

RS 94 | THE BEACH BOYS
October 28th, 1971
PHOTOGRAPH BY ANNIE LEIBOVITZ

RS 96 | FEAR AND LOATHING IN LAS VEGAS, PART TWO
November 25th, 1971
ILLUSTRATION BY RALPH STEADMAN

RS 97 | PETE TOWNSHEND
December 9th, 1971
PHOTOGRAPH BY NEVIS CAMERON

RS 98 | EVANGELIST MEL LYMAN
December 23rd, 1971
PHOTOGRAPH BY DAVID GAHR

50 YEARS OF COVERS • 51

1970s

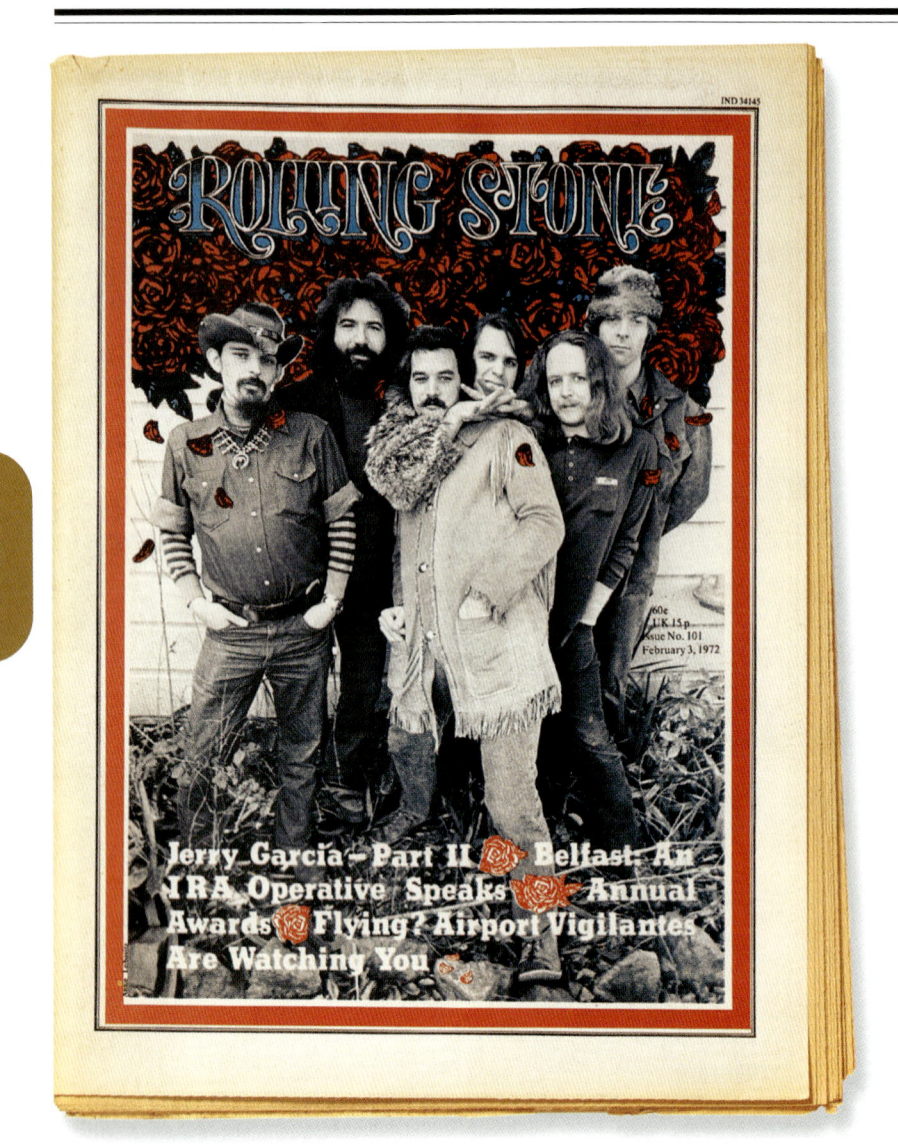

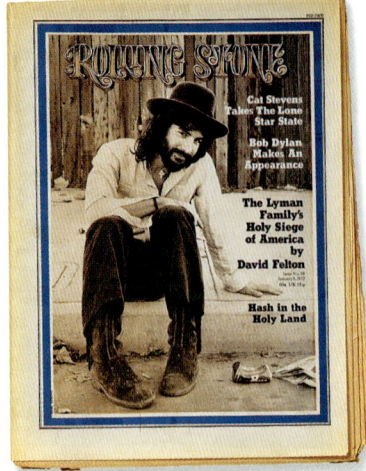

RS 101 | THE GRATEFUL DEAD | February 3rd, 1972 | Photograph by Annie Leibovitz

RS 99 | CAT STEVENS
January 6th, 1972
Photograph by Annie Leibovitz

RS 100 | JERRY GARCIA
January 20th, 1972
Photograph by Annie Leibovitz

52 • ROLLING STONE

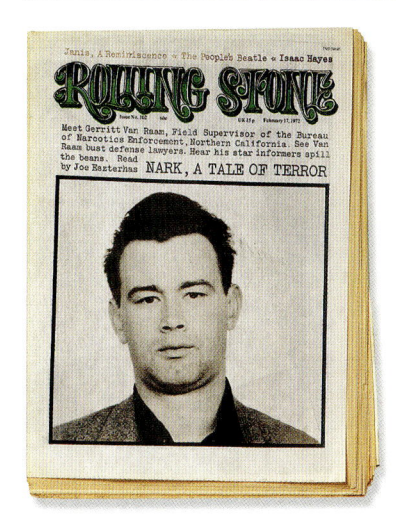

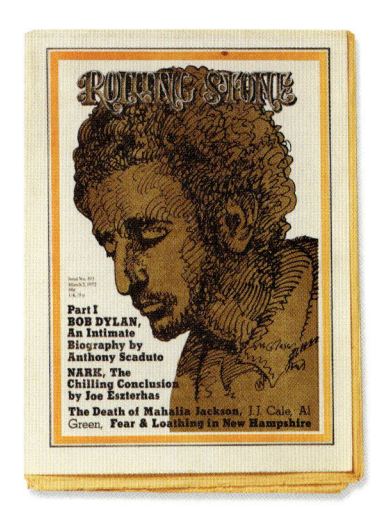

$\mathcal{RS}$ 102 | GERRITT VAN RAAM, NARCOTICS AGENT
February 17th, 1972
Photographer unknown

$\mathcal{RS}$ 103 | BOB DYLAN
March 2nd, 1972
Illustration by Milton Glaser

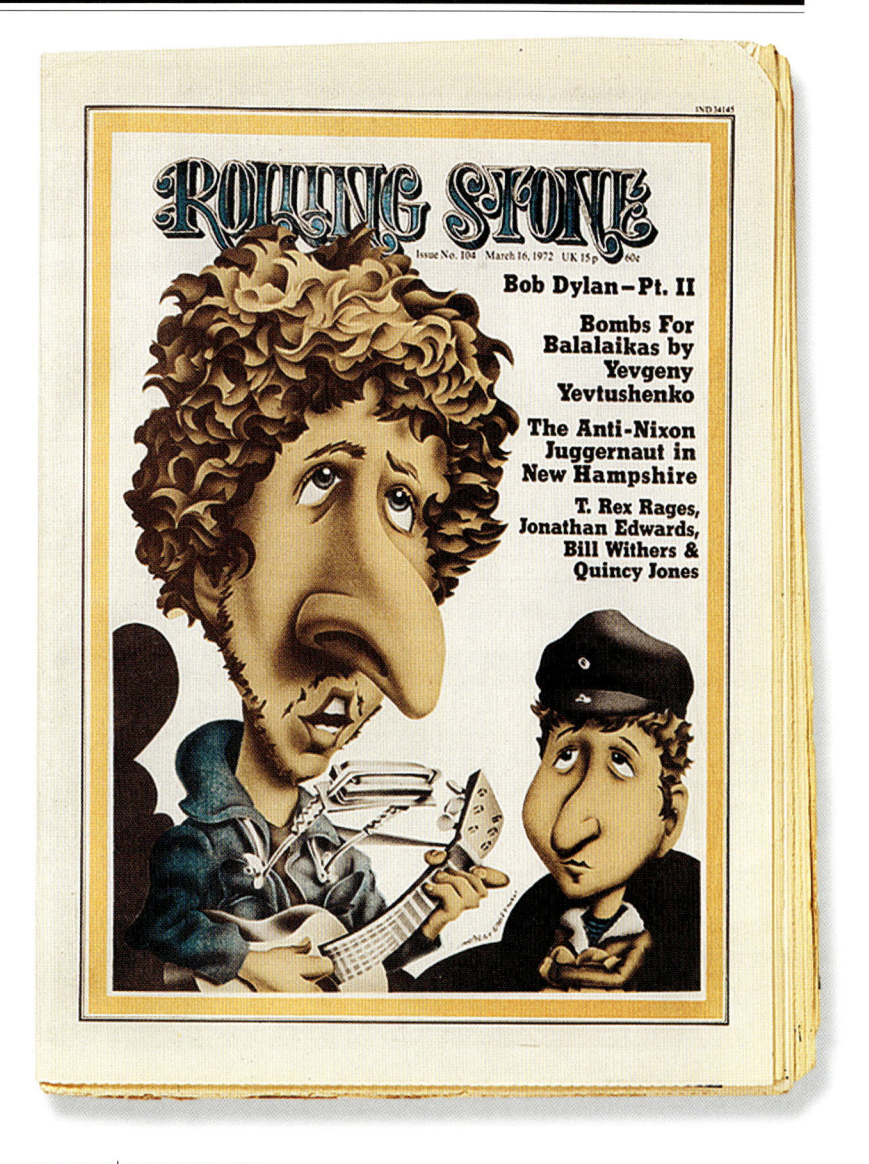

$\mathcal{RS}$ 104 | BOB DYLAN | March 16th, 1972 | Illustration by Robert Grossman

50 YEARS OF COVERS • 53

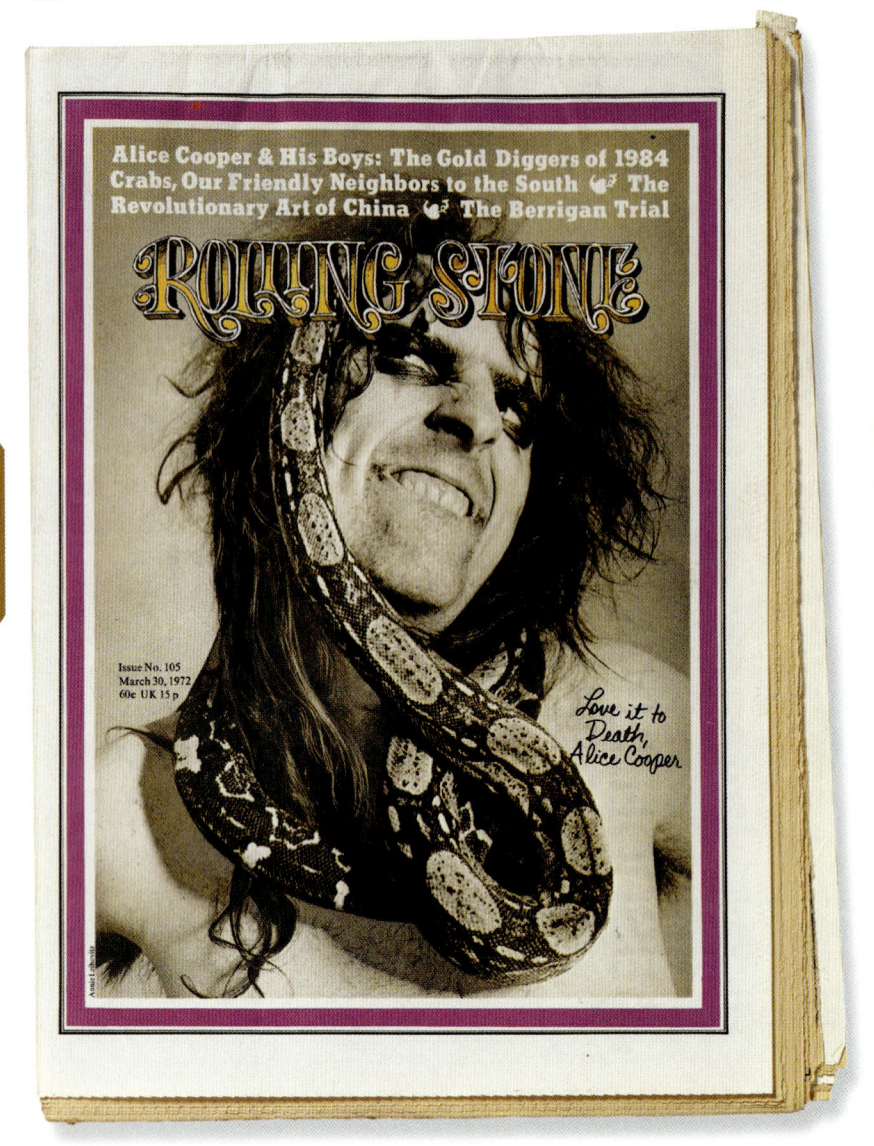

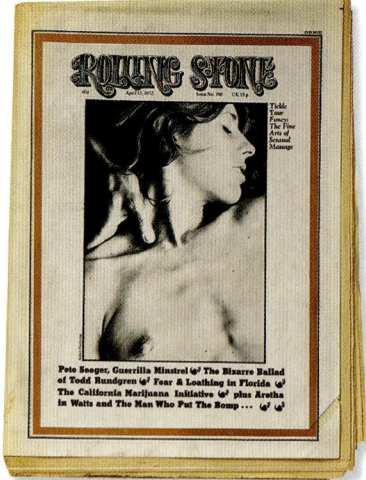

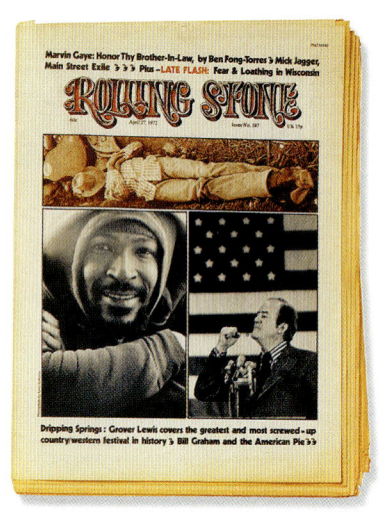

RS 105 | ALICE COOPER | March 30th, 1972 | Photograph by Annie Leibovitz

RS 106 | THE ART OF SENSUAL MASSAGE
April 13th, 1972
Photograph by Robert Foothorap

RS 107 | VARIOUS
April 27th, 1972
Photographs by Annie Leibovitz

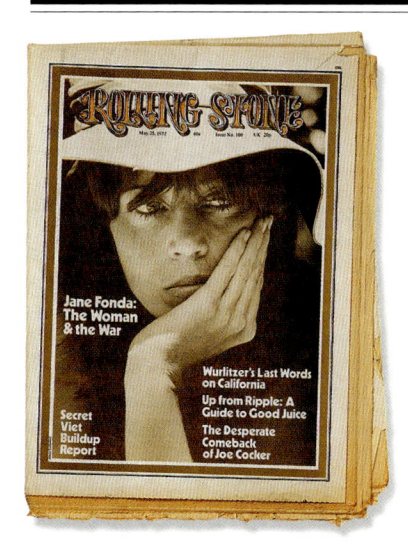

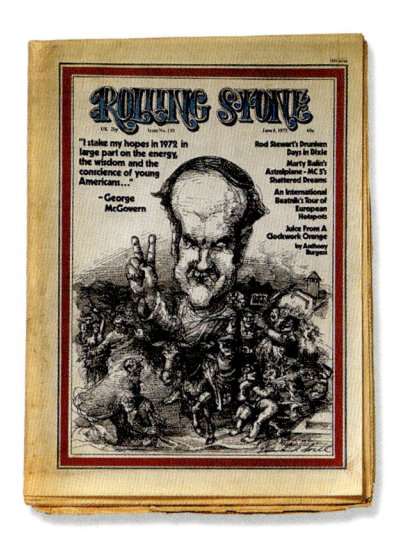

RS 109 | JANE FONDA
May 25th, 1972
Photograph by Annie Leibovitz

RS 110 | GEORGE McGOVERN
June 8th, 1972
Illustration by Edward Sorel

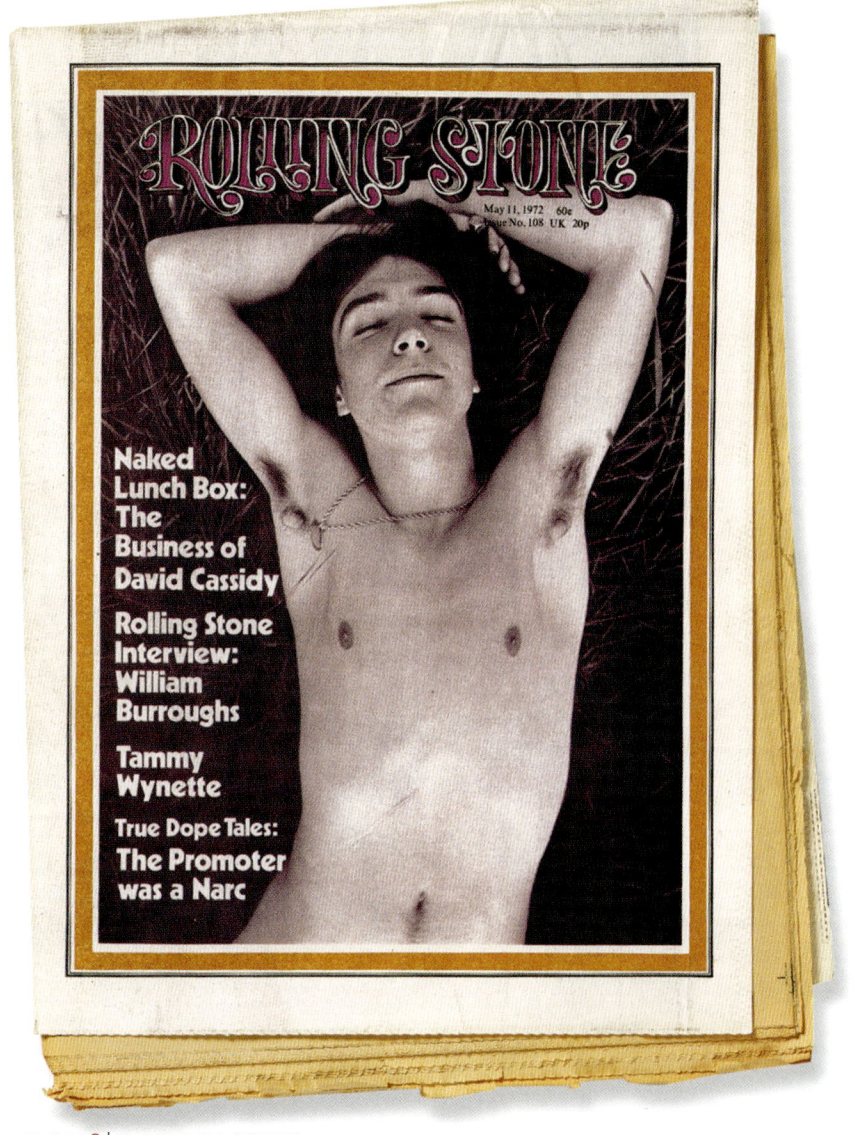

RS 108 | DAVID CASSIDY | May 11th, 1972 | Photograph by Annie Leibovitz

"IT PISSED OFF EVERYBODY that was really profiting from the business of David Cassidy. I had fan letters that came to me – and there were hundreds of thousands of them, literally – in defense of me by fans of mine, that said, 'Oh David, I know that you couldn't possibly have done this because I know that you would never have posed nude for photographs.' And the fact was, I had, had willingly done so, had thought about it. I scratched my head and thought, You know, this David Cassidy business has really gotten outta hand."

—*David Cassidy*

50 YEARS OF COVERS • 55

1970s

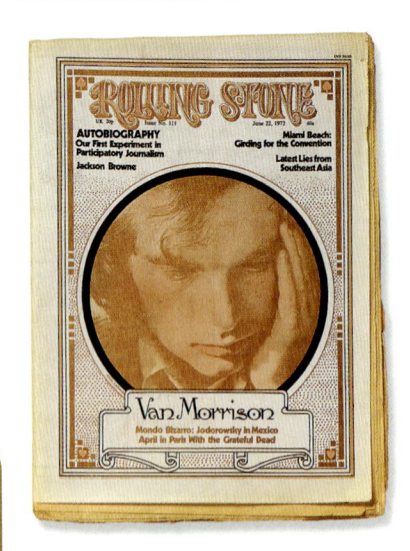

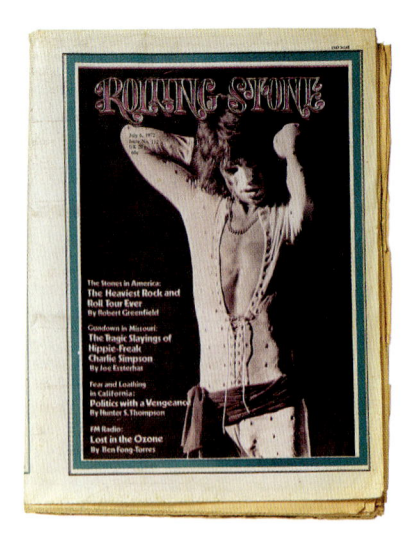

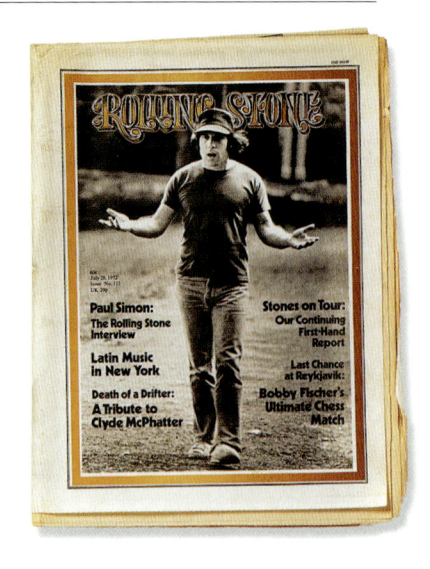

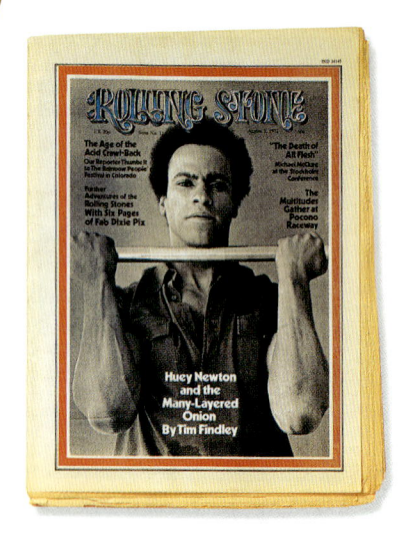

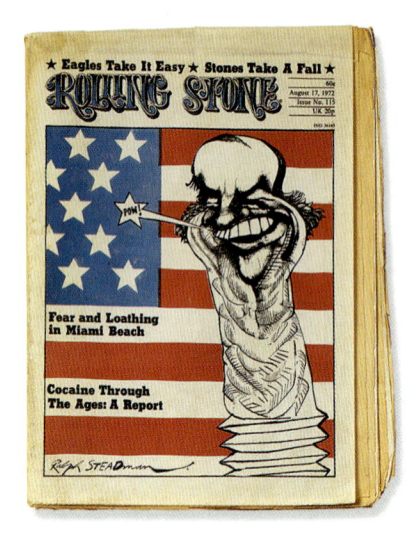

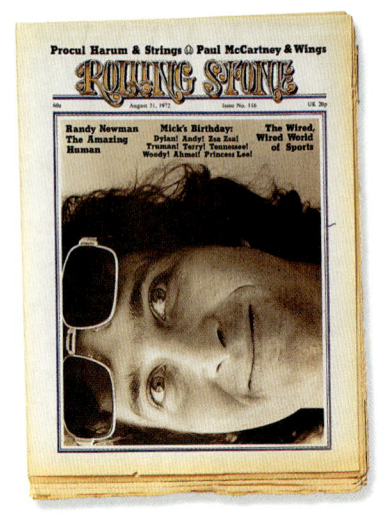

RS 111 | VAN MORRISON
June 22nd, 1972
PHOTOGRAPH BY ANNIE LEIBOVITZ

RS 112 | MICK JAGGER
July 6th, 1972
PHOTOGRAPH BY ANNIE LEIBOVITZ

RS 113 | PAUL SIMON
July 20th, 1972
PHOTOGRAPH BY PETER SIMON

RS 114 | HUEY NEWTON
August 3rd, 1972
PHOTOGRAPH BY ANNIE LEIBOVITZ

RS 115 | 1972 DEMOCRATIC CONVENTION
August 17th, 1972
ILLUSTRATION BY RALPH STEADMAN

RS 116 | RANDY NEWMAN
August 31st, 1972
PHOTOGRAPH BY ANNIE LEIBOVITZ

RS 117 | THREE DOG NIGHT
September 14th, 1972
PHOTOGRAPH BY ANNIE LEIBOVITZ

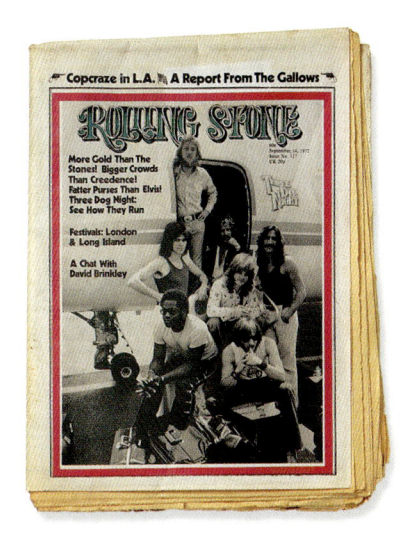

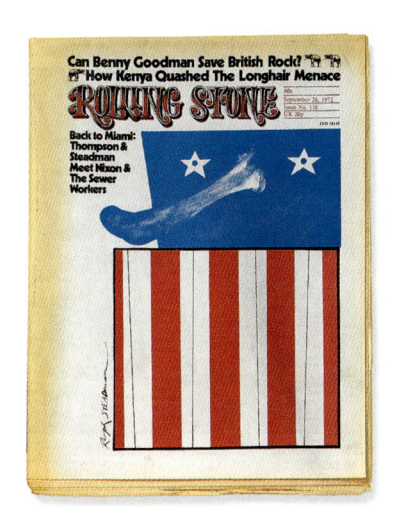

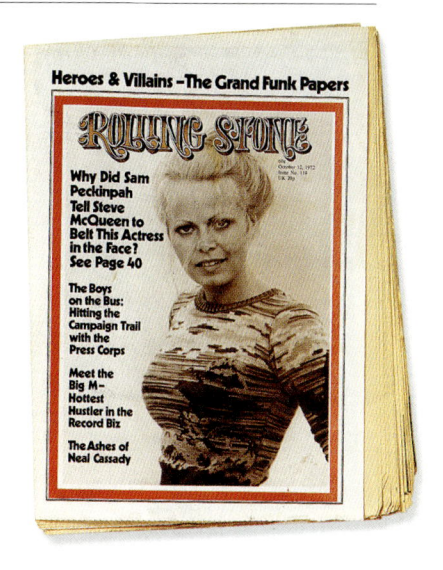

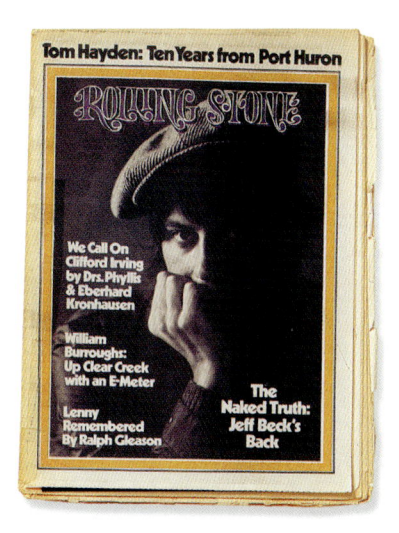

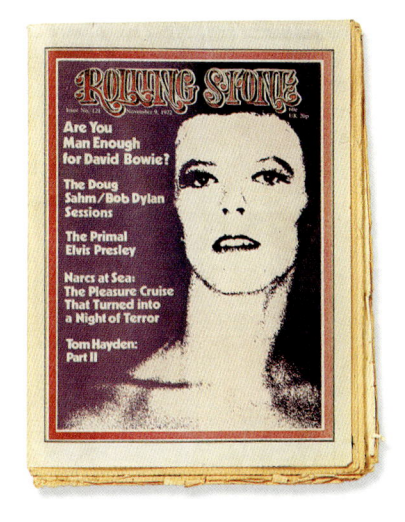

RS 120 | JEFF BECK
October 26th, 1972
PHOTOGRAPH BY HERBIE GREENE

RS 118 | 1972 REPUBLICAN CONVENTION
September 28th, 1972
ILLUSTRATION BY RALPH STEADMAN

RS 121 | DAVID BOWIE
November 9th, 1972
PHOTOGRAPH BY MICK ROCK

RS 119 | SALLY STRUTHERS
October 12th, 1972
PHOTOGRAPH BY MEL TRAXEL

RS 122 | PIMP JOE CONFORTE & HIS WORKING GIRLS
November 23rd, 1972
PHOTOGRAPH BY ANNIE LEIBOVITZ

50 YEARS OF COVERS • 57

1970s

"*I suppose* to most people I'm probably seen as an amiable idiot... a genial twit. I think I must be the victim of circumstance, really. Most of it's me own doing. I'm a victim of me own practical jokes."

—Keith Moon

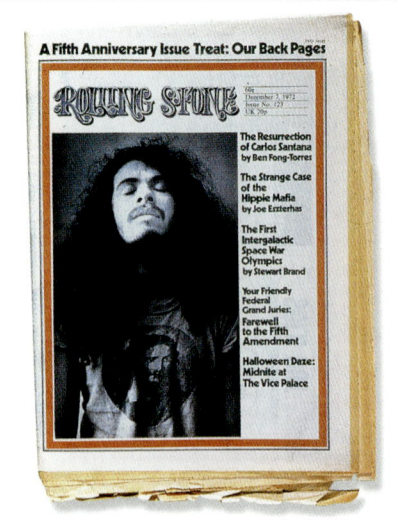

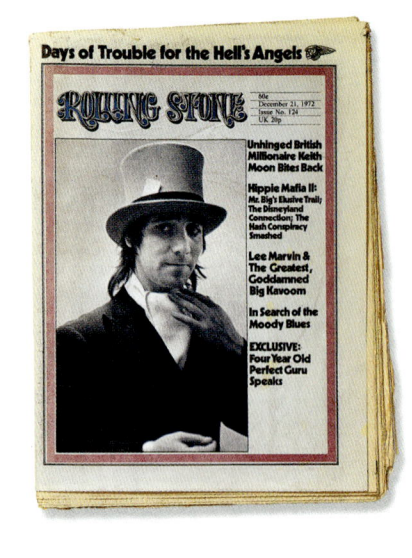

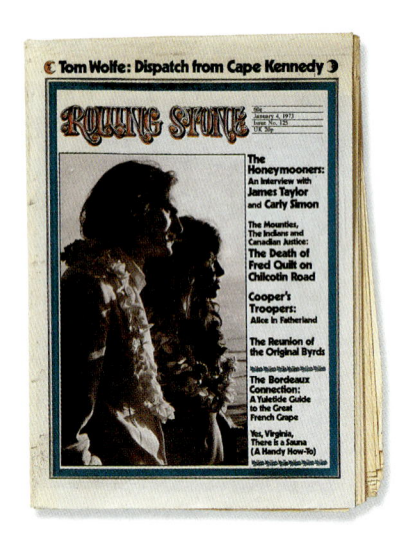

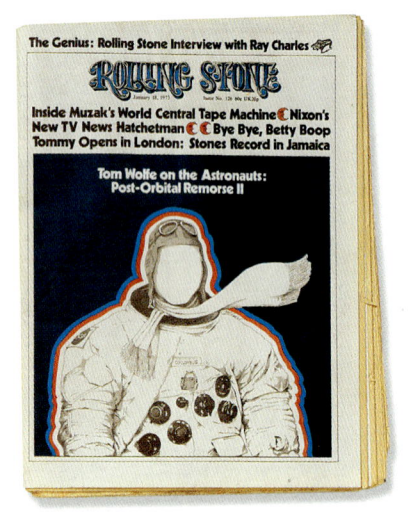

RS 123 | CARLOS SANTANA
December 7th, 1972
Photograph by Annie Leibovitz

RS 124 | KEITH MOON
December 21st, 1972
Photograph by Bob Gruen

RS 125 | JAMES TAYLOR & CARLY SIMON
January 4th, 1973
Photograph by Peter Simon

RS 126 | APOLLO ASTRONAUT
January 18th, 1973
Illustration by Dugald Stermer

You Won't Have 1972 to Kick Around Anymore (See Page 32)

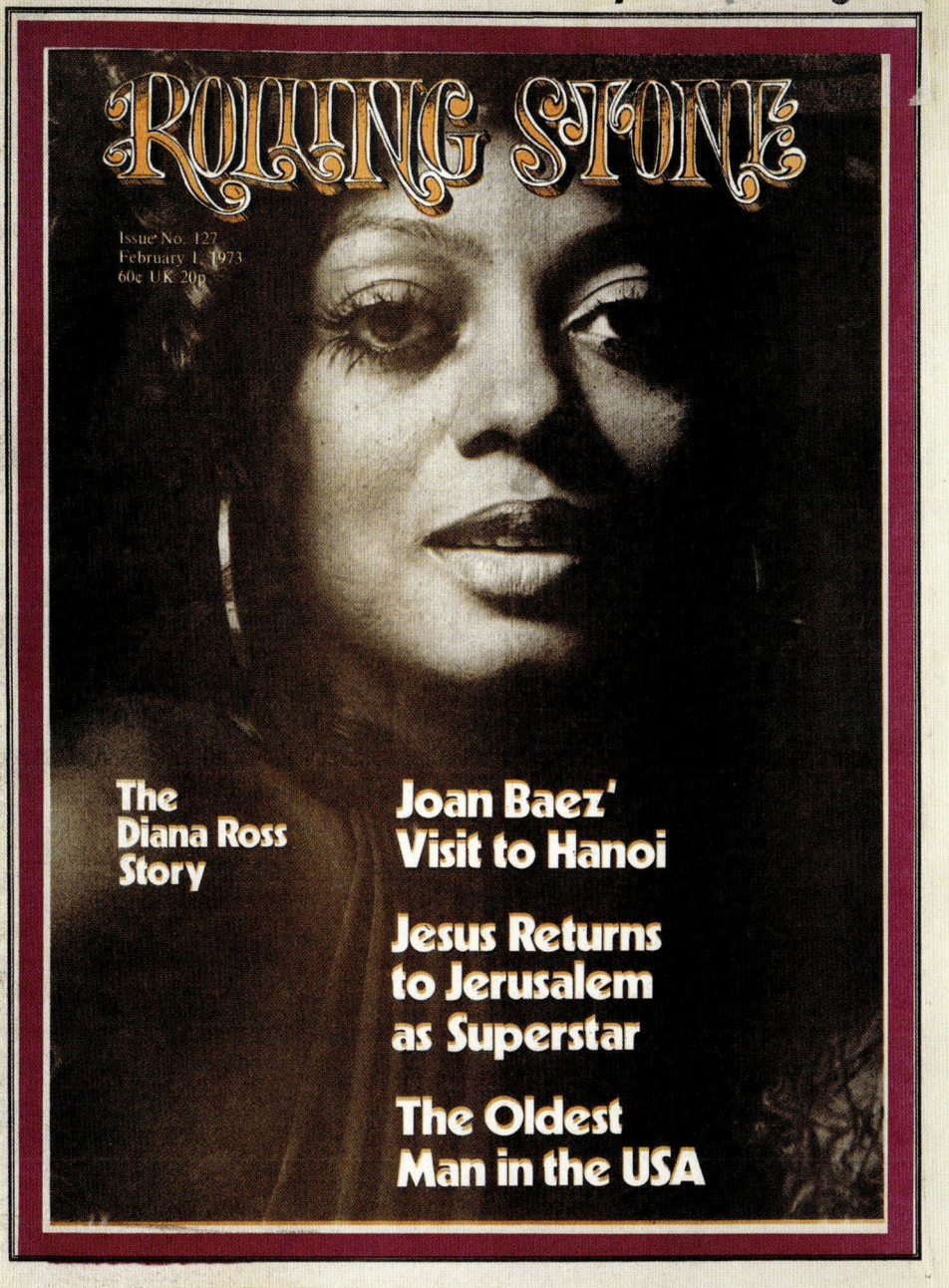

Rolling Stone

Issue No. 127
February 1, 1973
60¢ UK 20p

The Diana Ross Story

Joan Baez' Visit to Hanoi

Jesus Returns to Jerusalem as Superstar

The Oldest Man in the USA

RS 127 | DIANA ROSS | February 1st, 1973 | PHOTOGRAPH BY ANNIE LEIBOVITZ

50 YEARS OF COVERS • 59

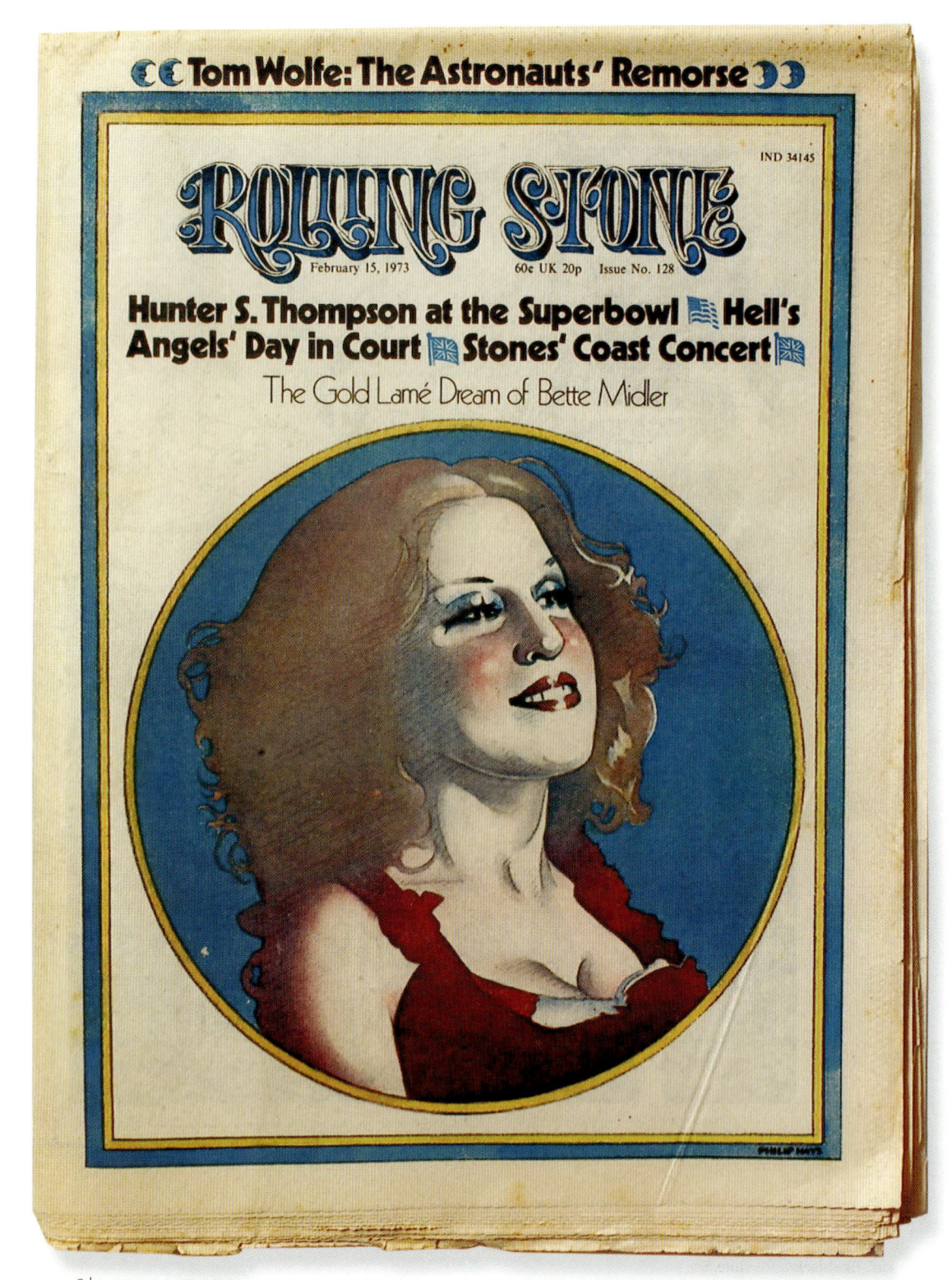

RS 128 | BETTE MIDLER | February 15th, 1973 | Illustration by Philip Hays

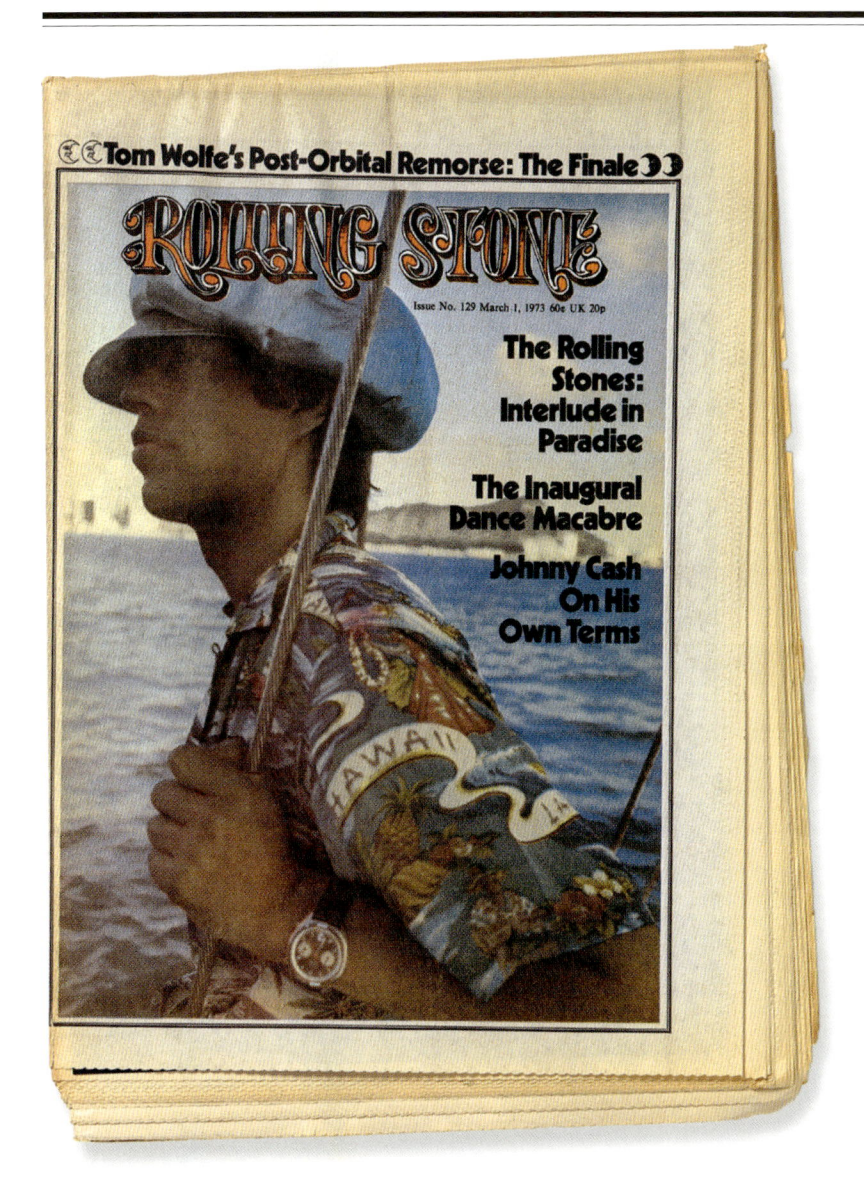

RS 129 | MICK JAGGER | March 1st, 1973 | Photograph by Annie Leibovitz

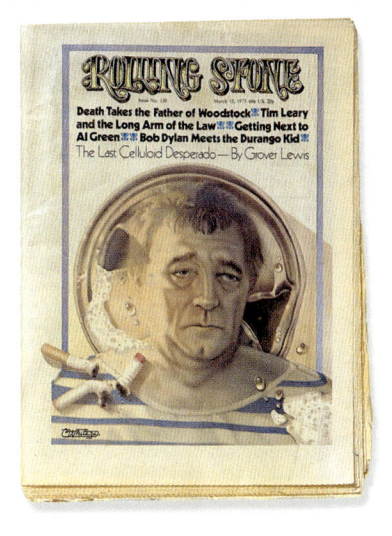

"I THINK [I REALLY STARTED TO ENJOY SHOOTING THE COVER] WHEN 'ROLLING STONE' went to color [RS 128]. I had to change to color, too, and it was very scary. I was glad I came from a school of black-and-white, because I learned to look at things in tones, highlights. Rolling Stone was printed on newsprint, rag print, and ink sinks into the magazine. So the only thing that would make it on the cover were pictures that had two or three colors, primary colors, a very posterlike effect. In a strange way, you almost had to make the color look like black-and-white. So I developed a very graphic use of form and color just to survive the printing process."
—*Annie Leibovitz*

RS 130 | ROBERT MITCHUM
March 15th, 1973
Illustration by Charles E. White III

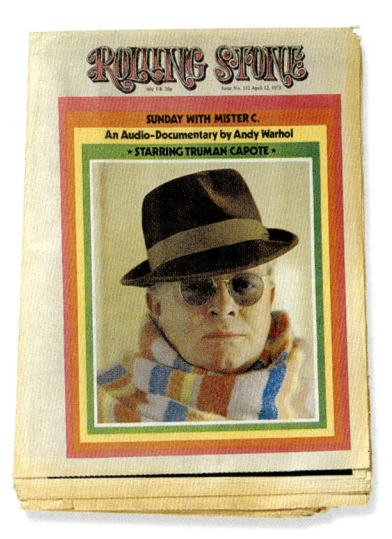

RS 132 | TRUMAN CAPOTE
April 12th, 1973
Photograph by Henry Diltz

50 YEARS OF COVERS • 61

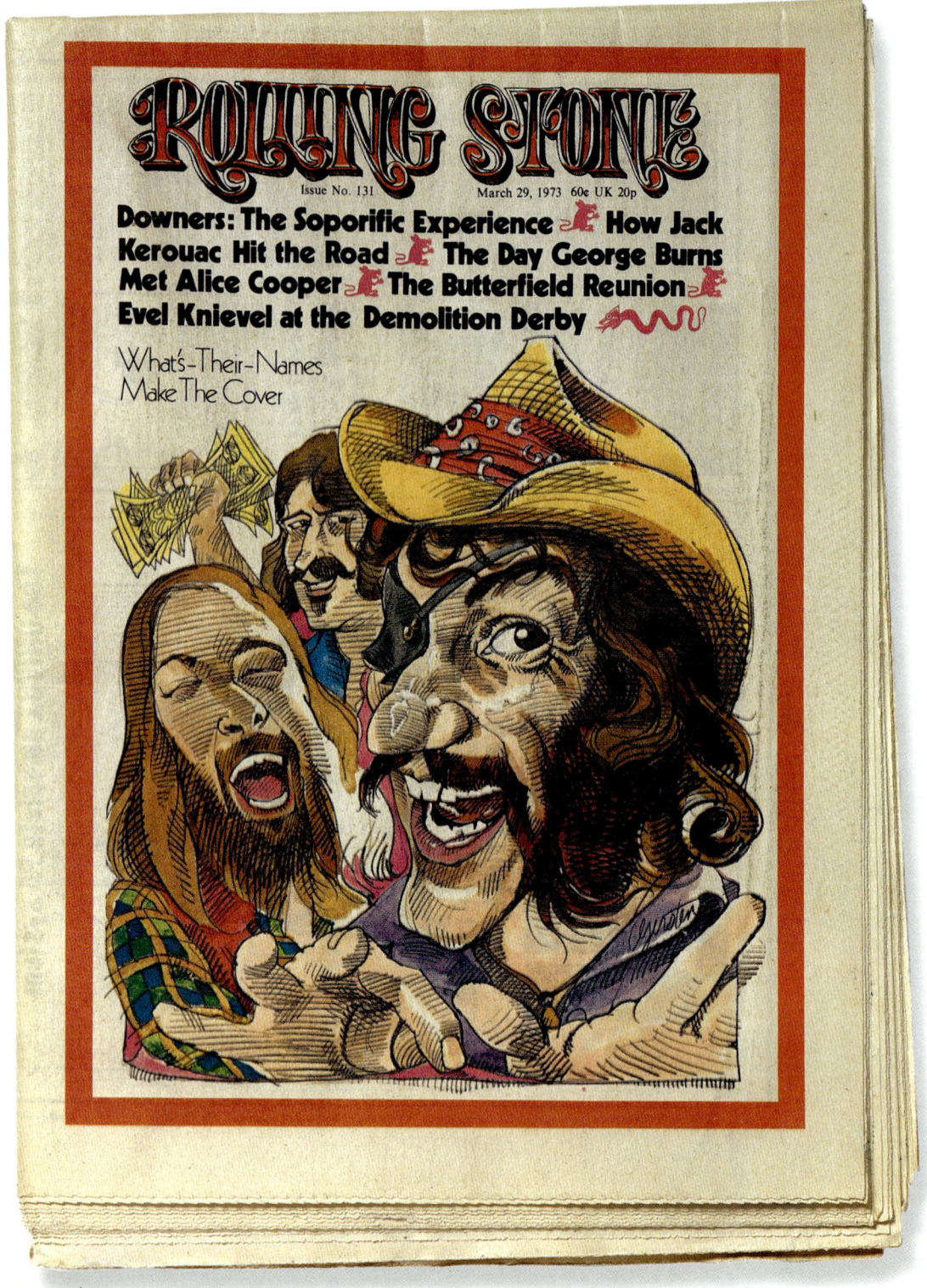

RS 131 | DR. HOOK & THE MEDICINE SHOW | March 29th, 1973 | Illustration by Gerry Gersten

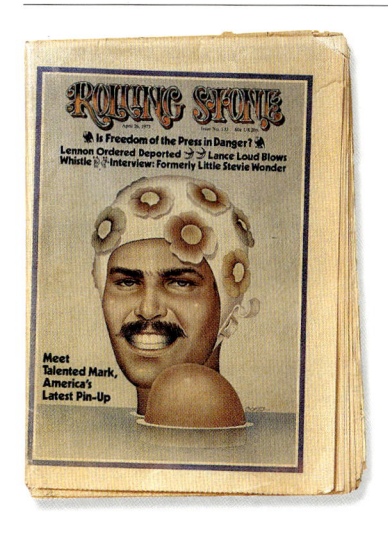

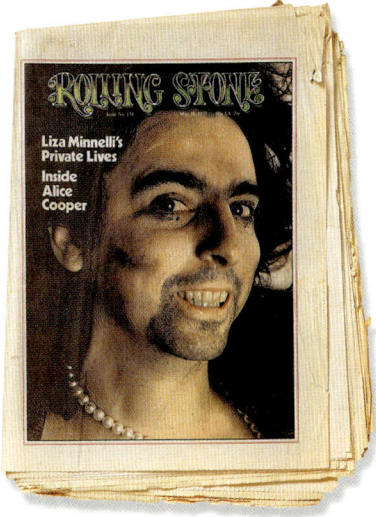

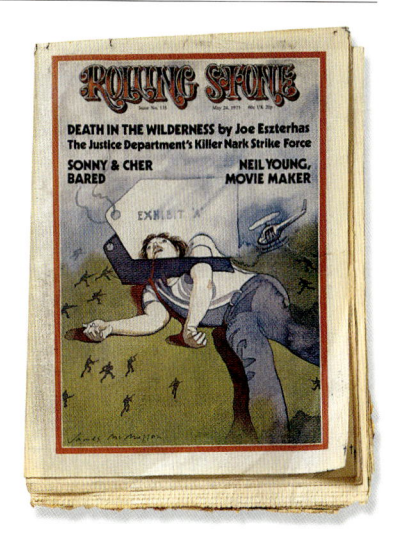

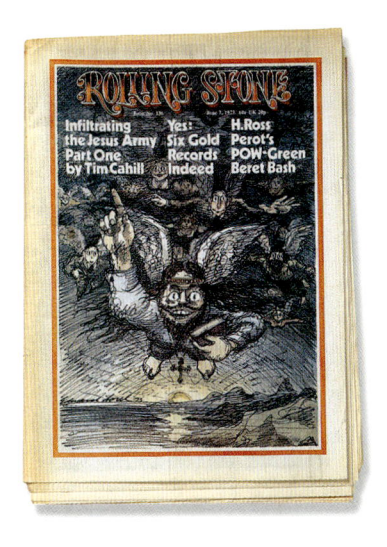

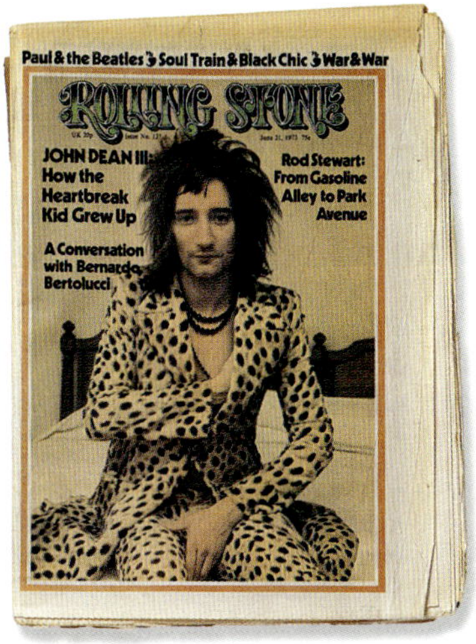

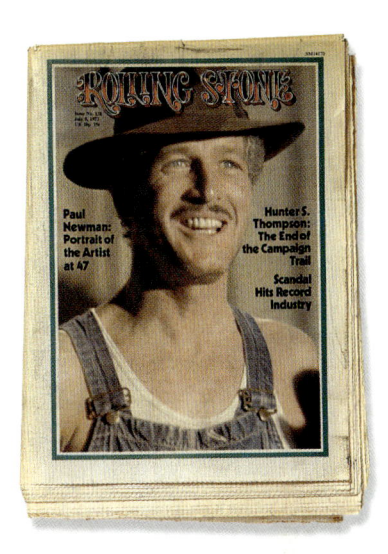

$\mathcal{RS}$ 133 | MARK SPITZ
April 26th, 1973
ILLUSTRATION BY IGNACIO GOMEZ

$\mathcal{RS}$ 134 | ALICE COOPER
May 10th, 1973
PHOTOGRAPH BY ANNIE LEIBOVITZ

$\mathcal{RS}$ 135 | CRIME VICTIM DIRK DICKENSON
May 24th, 1973
ILLUSTRATION BY JAMES MCMULLAN

$\mathcal{RS}$ 136 | JESUS FREAKS
June 7th, 1973
ILLUSTRATION BY EDWARD SOREL

$\mathcal{RS}$ 137 | ROD STEWART
June 21st, 1973
PHOTOGRAPH BY CHARLES GATEWOOD

$\mathcal{RS}$ 138 | PAUL NEWMAN
July 5th, 1973
PHOTOGRAPH BY STEPHEN SHUGRUE

[RS 131] How could ROLLING STONE not give them a cover? Dr. Hook & the Medicine Show's "The Cover of Rolling Stone" hit Number Six on the *Billboard* chart, March 17th, 1973.

50 YEARS OF COVERS • 63

1970s

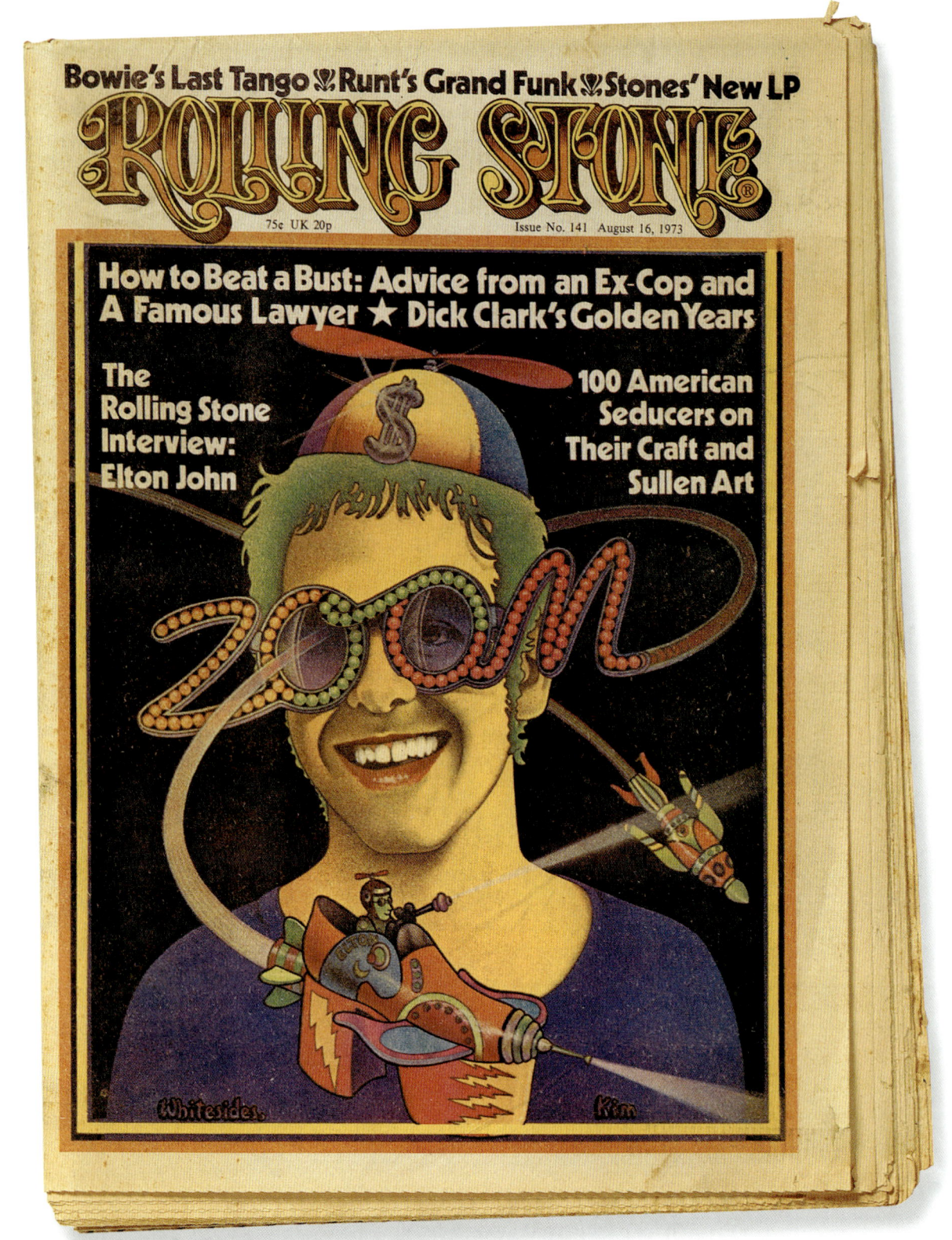

Bowie's Last Tango ❦ Runt's Grand Funk ❦ Stones' New LP

ROLLING STONE

75¢ UK 20p   Issue No. 141 August 16, 1973

How to Beat a Bust: Advice from an Ex-Cop and A Famous Lawyer ★ Dick Clark's Golden Years

The Rolling Stone Interview: Elton John

100 American Seducers on Their Craft and Sullen Art

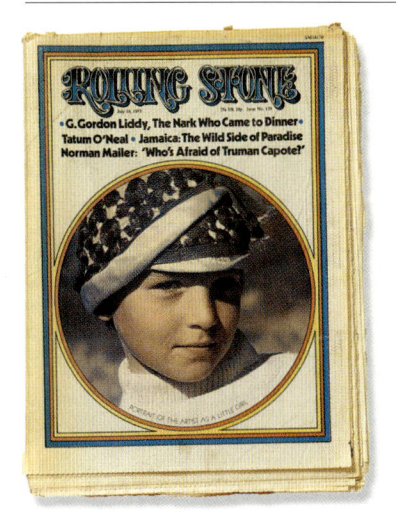

RS 141 | ELTON JOHN
August 16th, 1973
ILLUSTRATION BY KIM WHITESIDES

One report in the national press awhile back said you'd once almost gotten married to a millionairess.
ELTON: Me?
And called it off three weeks before?
ELTON: Oh, that's true. I wouldn't say she was a millionairess, that's the national press boosting their headlines – "One-Armed Man Swims Channel" or something like that, you know what I mean. It was a girl I met when I was in Sheffield one miserable Christmas doing cabaret with John Baldry. She was six foot tall and going out with a midget in Sheffield who drove around in a Mini with special pedals on. He sued to beat her up! I felt so sorry for her and she followed me up the next week to South Shields – and I fell desperately in love and said to come to London and we'll find a flat. Eventually we got a nice flat in this dismal area. It was a very stormy six months, after which I was on the verge of a nervous breakdown. I attempted suicide and various other things, during which Bernie [Taupin] and I wrote nil, absolutely nothing.
BERNIE: Don't forget the gas.
ELTON: I tried to commit suicide one day. It was a very Woody Allen–type suicide. I turned on the gas and left all the windows open.

[EXCERPT FROM ELTON JOHN INTERVIEW BY PAUL GAMBACCINI]

RS 139 | TATUM O'NEAL
July 19th, 1973
PHOTOGRAPH BY STEVE JAFFE

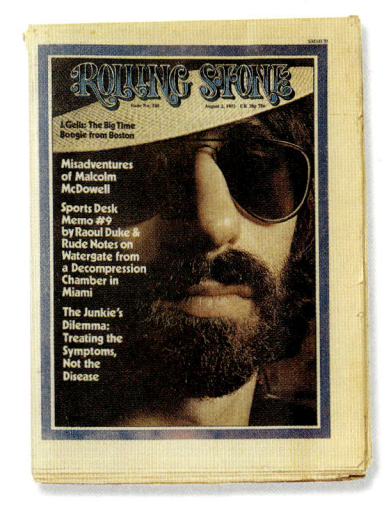

RS 140 | PETER WOLF
August 2nd, 1973
PHOTOGRAPH BY ANNIE LEIBOVITZ

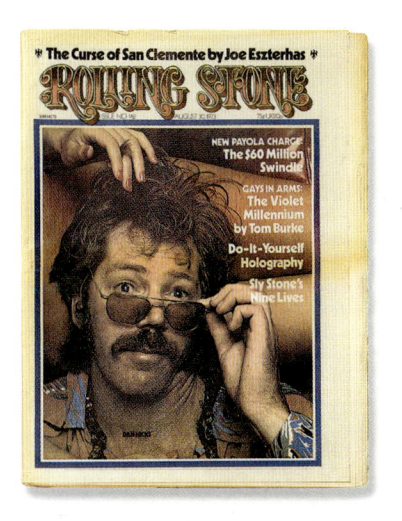

RS 142 | DAN HICKS
August 30th, 1973
PHOTOGRAPH BY ANNIE LEIBOVITZ

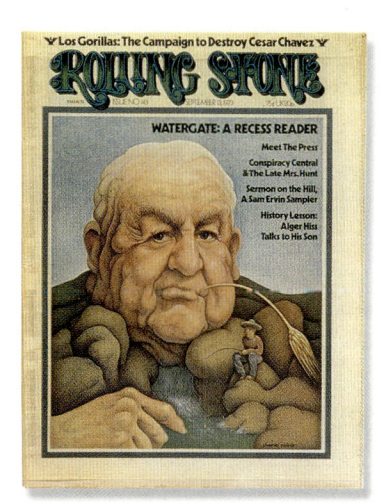

RS 143 | SENATOR SAM ERVIN
September 13th, 1973
ILLUSTRATION BY CHARLES SHIELDS

1970s

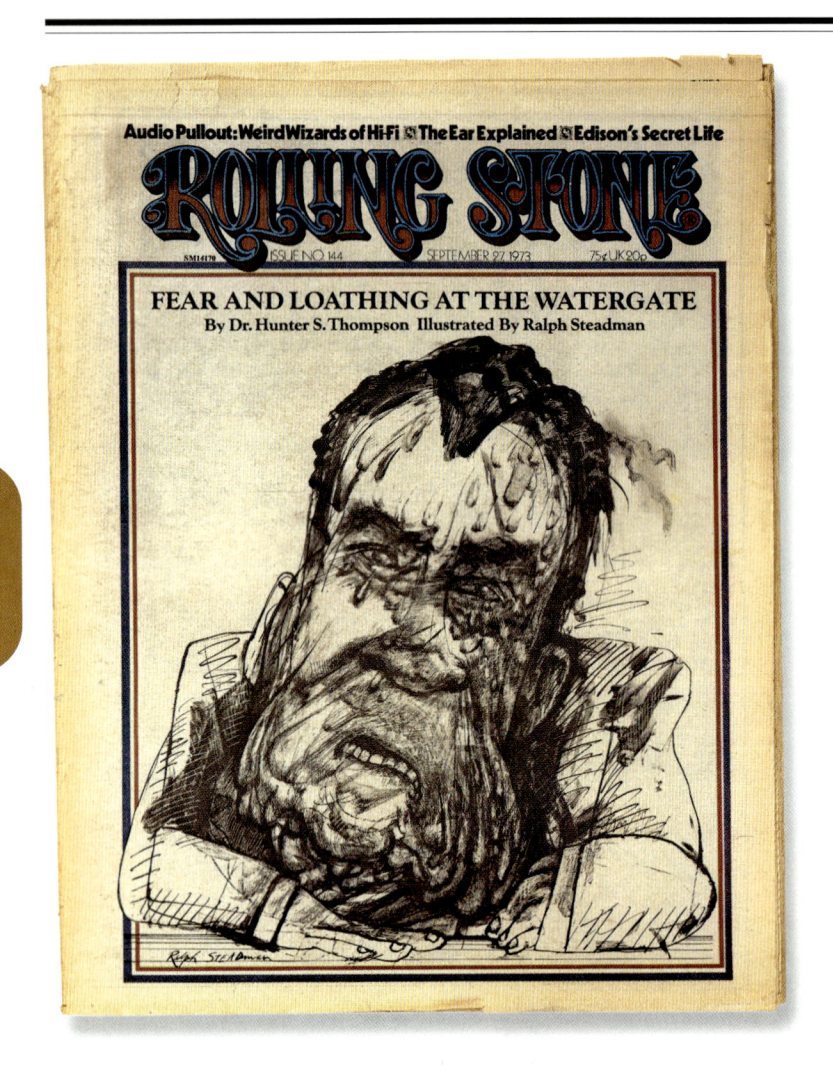

RS 144 | RICHARD NIXON
September 27th, 1973
ILLUSTRATION BY RALPH STEADMAN

RS 145 | ART GARFUNKEL
October 11th, 1973
PHOTOGRAPH BY JIM MARSHALL

RS 146 | GENE AUTRY
October 25th, 1973
ILLUSTRATION BY GARY OVERACRE

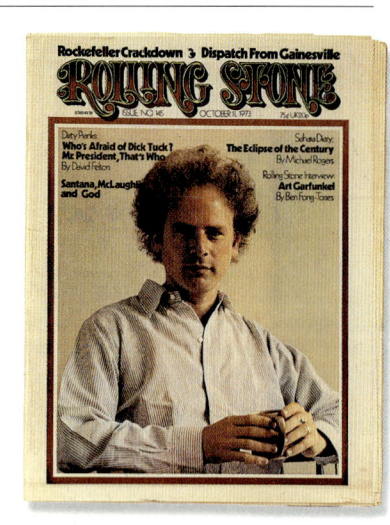

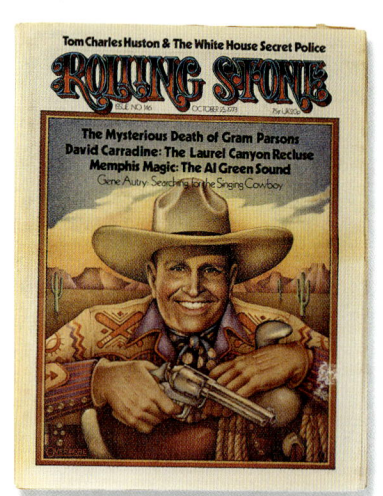

"*I wanted to* do something big and powerful because that's apparently what [Jerry] represents to the industry."

—*Robert Grossman*

66 • ROLLING STONE

RS 148 | JERRY GARCIA | November 22nd, 1973 | Illustration by Robert Grossman

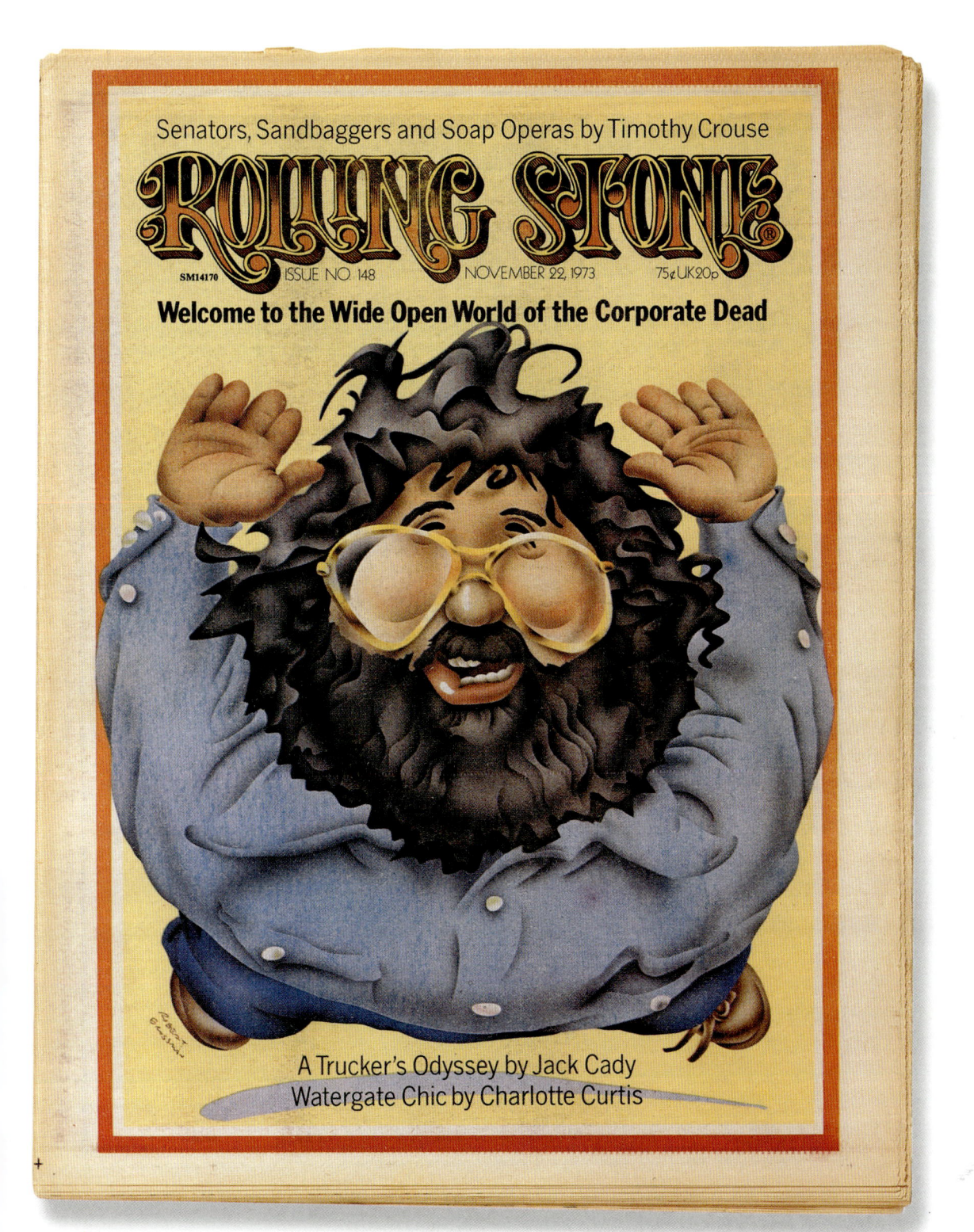

1970s

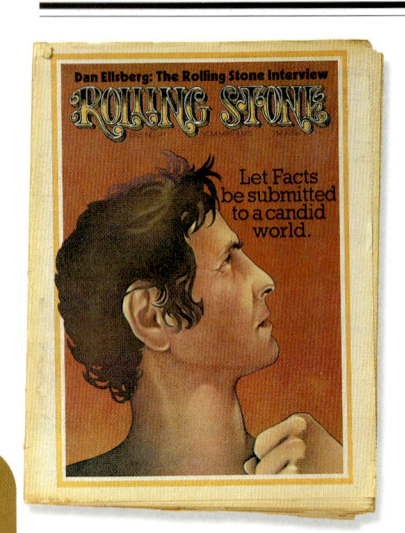

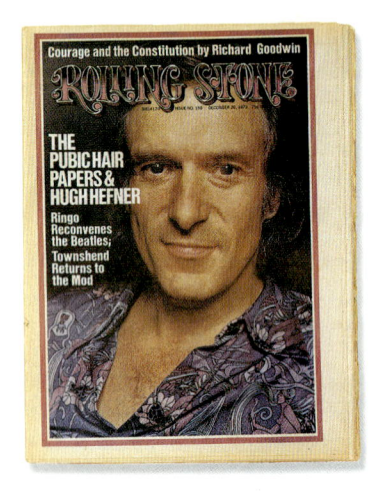

RS 147 | DANIEL ELLSBERG
November 8th, 1973
ILLUSTRATION BY DAVE WILLARDSON

RS 150 | HUGH HEFNER
December 20th, 1973
PHOTOGRAPH BY ANNIE LEIBOVITZ

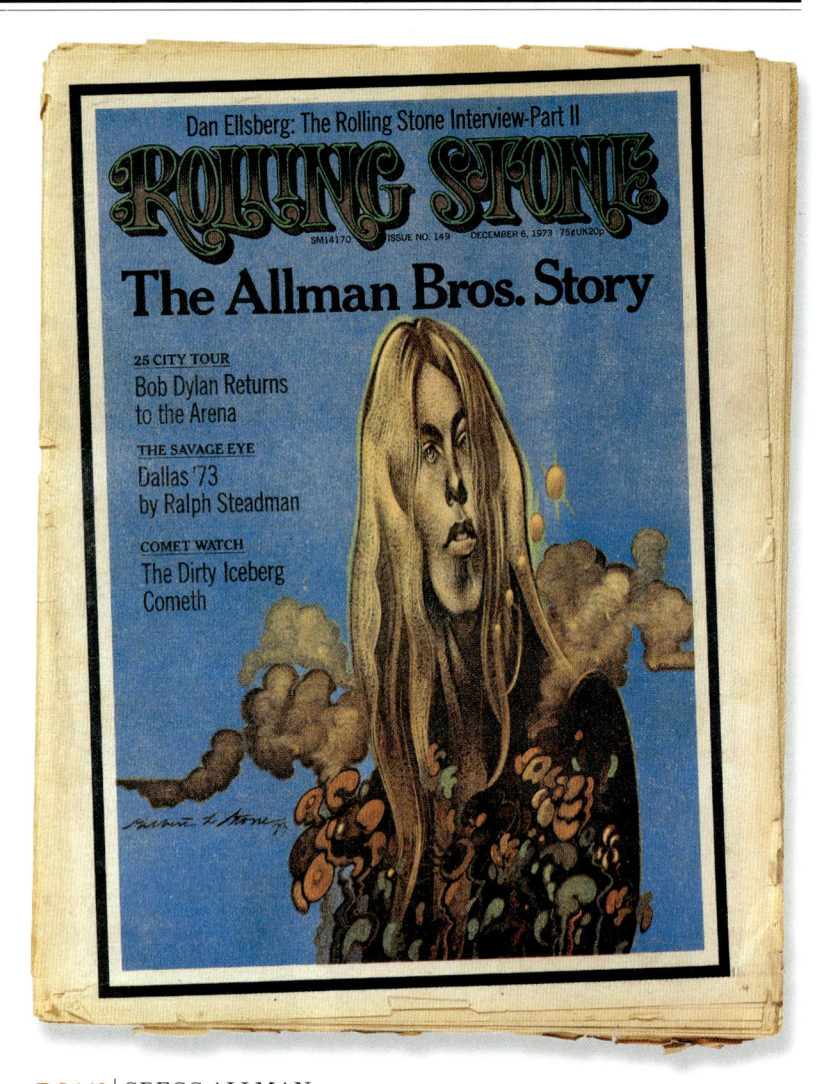

RS 149 | GREGG ALLMAN | December 6th, 1973 | ILLUSTRATION BY GILBERT STONE

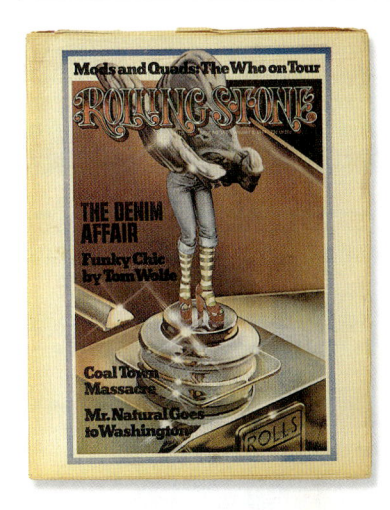

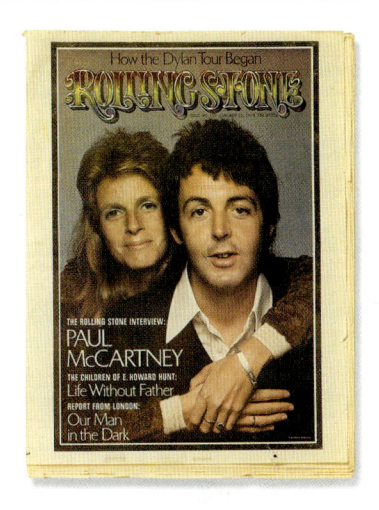

$\mathcal{RS}$ 153 | PAUL & LINDA MCCARTNEY
January 31st, 1974
PHOTOGRAPH BY FRANCESCO SCAVULLO

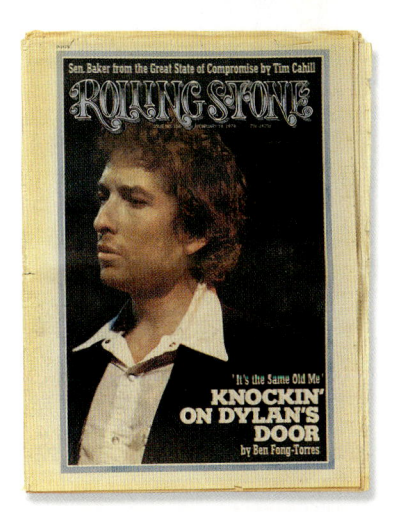

[RS 147] Michael Salisbury, a renowned Los Angeles designer, and his associate Lloyd Ziff temporarily move into Annie Leibovitz's San Francisco loft and take over ROLLING STONE's design while Robert Kingsbury is on a leave of absence for nine covers (RS 147–RS 155). They collaborate on RS 156, with Salisbury taking the helm officially for RS 157.

$\mathcal{RS}$ 151 | FUNKY CHIC
January 3rd, 1974
ILLUSTRATION BY PETER PALOMBI

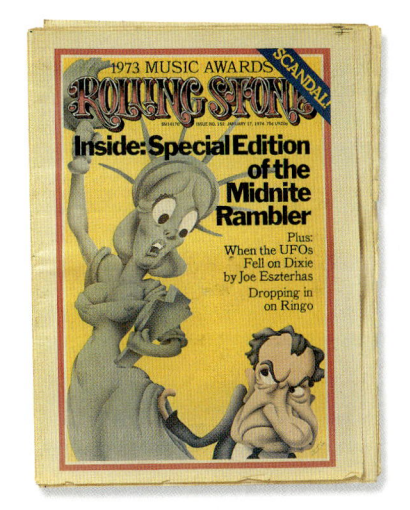

$\mathcal{RS}$ 152 | RICHARD NIXON
January 17th, 1974
ILLUSTRATION BY ROBERT GROSSMAN

$\mathcal{RS}$ 154 | BOB DYLAN
February 14th, 1974
PHOTOGRAPH BY BARRY FEINSTEIN

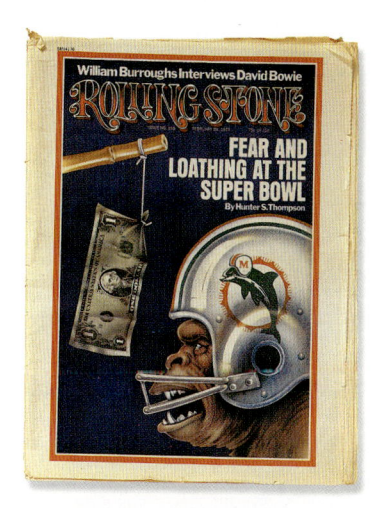

$\mathcal{RS}$ 155 | FEAR AND LOATHING AT THE SUPER BOWL
February 28th, 1974
ILLUSTRATION BY HANK WOODWARD

50 YEARS OF COVERS • 69

Dismantle the Presidency by Richard N. Goodwin

ROLLING STONE

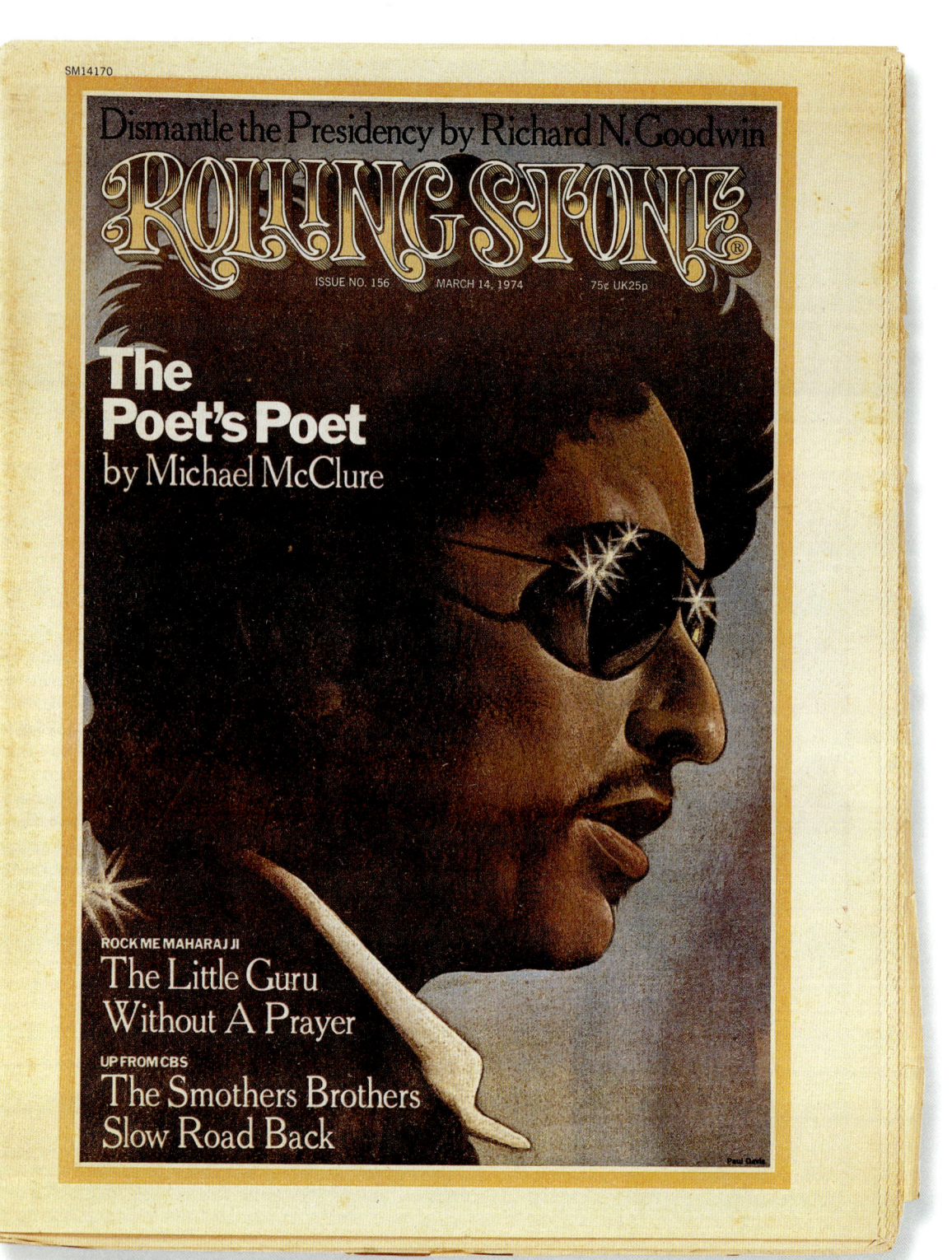

ISSUE NO. 156 — MARCH 14, 1974 — 75¢ UK25p

The Poet's Poet
by Michael McClure

ROCK ME MAHARAJ JI
The Little Guru Without A Prayer

UP FROM CBS
The Smothers Brothers Slow Road Back

RS 156 | BOB DYLAN | March 14th, 1974 | ILLUSTRATION BY PAUL DAVIS

RS 158 | MARVIN GAYE | April 11th, 1974 | Photograph by Annie Leibovitz

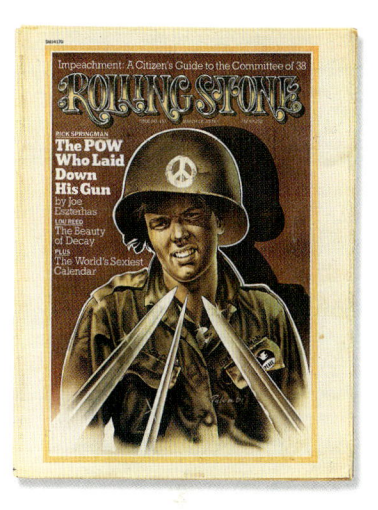

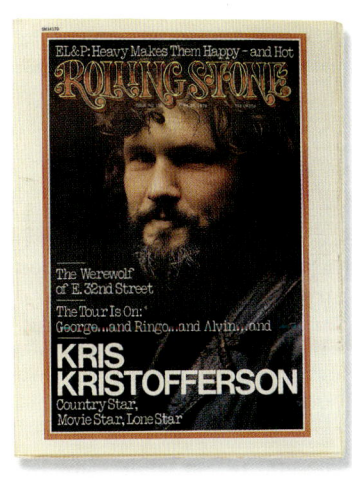

RS 157 | P.O.W. RICK SPRINGMAN
March 28th, 1974
Illustration by Peter Palombi

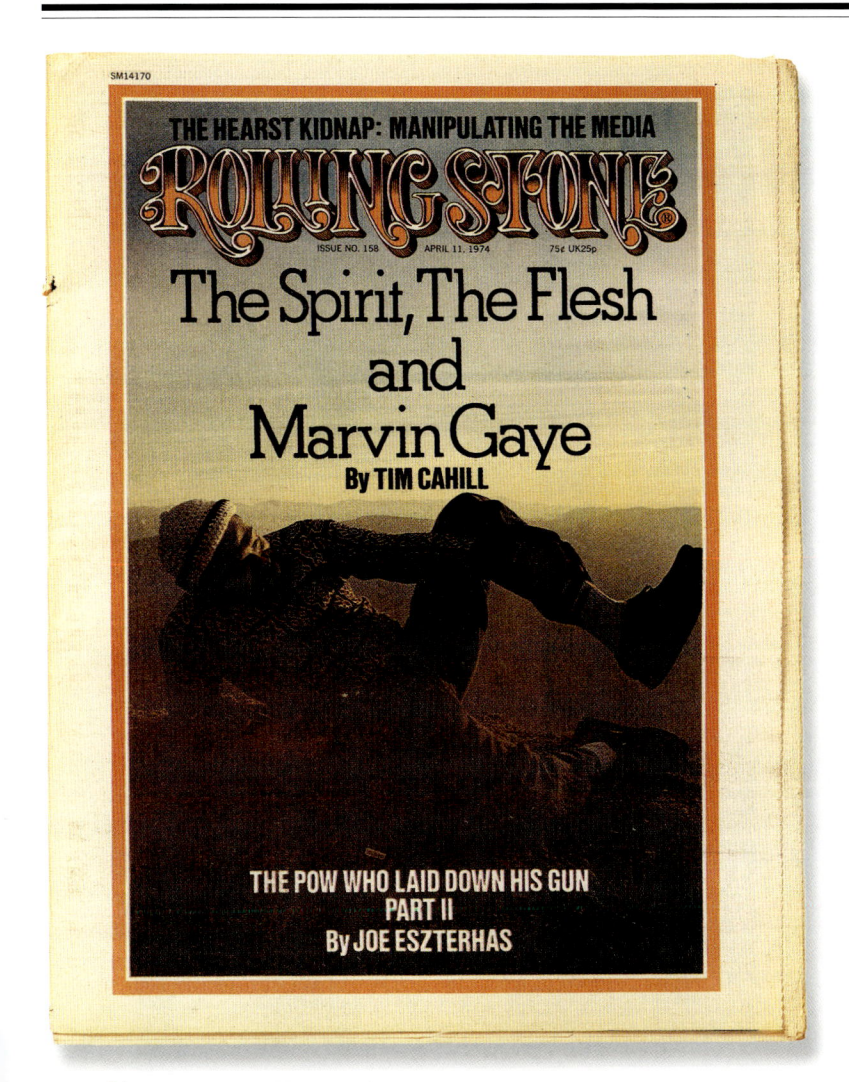

RS 159 | KRIS KRISTOFFERSON
April 25th, 1974
Photograph by Annie Leibovitz

"MARVIN LIKED THOSE SHOTS [I TOOK OF HIM IN 1971] AND AGREED TO several sessions. I had always thought there was something regal about Marvin Gaye, and I saw him with mountains in the background. When I drove up to his house outside of Los Angeles, I was amazed. There were mountains all around. Just before sunset, Marvin took the jeep out over the trails. The cover photo is one shot from that day."

—*Annie Leibovitz*

50 YEARS OF COVERS • 71

1970s

RS 161 | JACKSON & ETHAN BROWNE
May 23rd, 1974
PHOTOGRAPH BY ANNIE LEIBOVITZ

BOXES OF WIPE DIPE are in both the living room and the adjoining bedroom, where the baby's crib sits at the foot of his parents' tattered-quilt-covered bed. On one shelf, tucked back against a wall, is an unopened box of IT'S A BOY! ROI-TAN cigars. Outside, across the patio that serves as the cover of *For Everyman*, past the well and under the bambooed eaves of one walkway, a voice sings a lullaby in a foreign tongue. It is the housekeeper, a woman from San Salvador, and she is in the kitchen, cradling Ethan in her arms while his father is out shopping....

Jackson picks Ethan up and begins to pose for a photographer. He flips through the Polaroids and finds the one shot he'd like to duplicate: of him holding a broadly laughing Ethan. Back in the bedroom, he works with his free hand, slapping fingers together, and he makes gurgling noises and sings the refrain from "The Cover of ROLLING STONE." Ethan laughs, and Jackson is as unknowingly open as his baby: "I love it when he laughs," he says. "His little voice. His little throat."

[EXCERPT FROM RS 161 COVER STORY BY CAMERON CROWE]

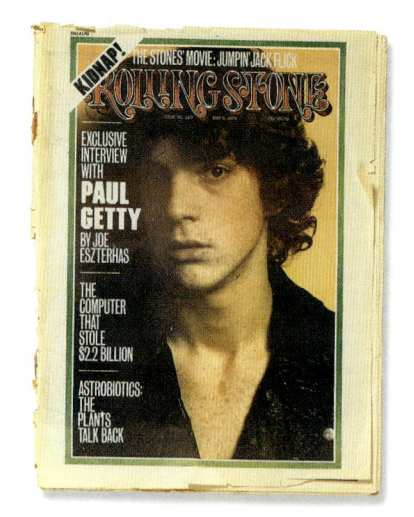

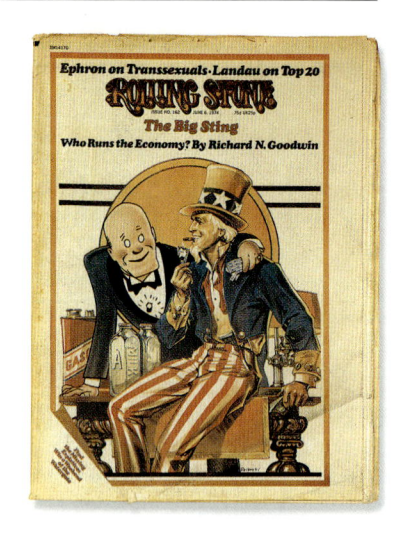

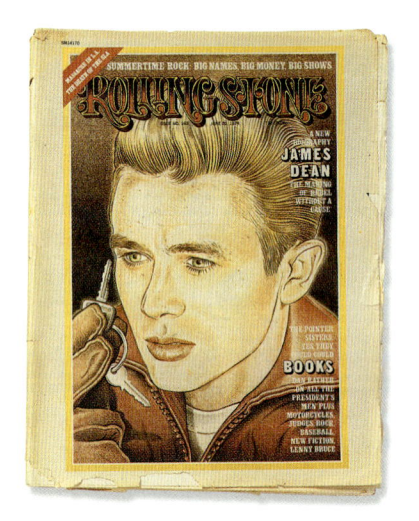

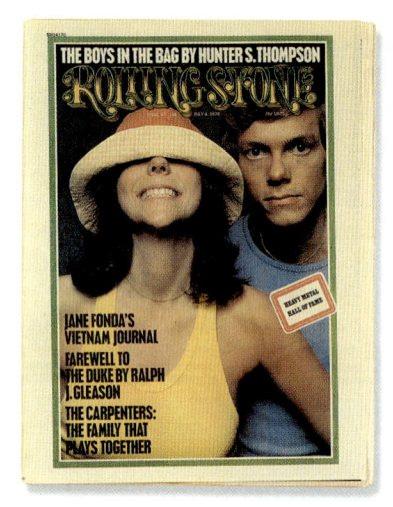

RS 160 | PAUL GETTY
May 9th, 1974
PHOTOGRAPH BY ANNIE LEIBOVITZ

RS 163 | JAMES DEAN
June 20th, 1974
ILLUSTRATION BY JOHN VAN HAMERSVELD

RS 162 | THE ECONOMY
June 6th, 1974
ILLUSTRATION BY PETER PALOMBI

RS 164 | KAREN & RICHARD CARPENTER
July 4th, 1974
PHOTOGRAPH BY ANNIE LEIBOVITZ

Rolling Stone

The Strange Behavior of the SLA

NO. 161 1974 75¢ UK25p

BOY WONDER GROWS UP
Jackson Browne

Aretha Franklin
THE MAGNIFICENT HOMEBODY

TRAVEL SPECIAL:
Get Lost

YOUTH FARE LIVES

PAUL BOWLES IN MOROCCO

ALLEN GINSBERG EVERYWHERE

THE SECRET NEGOTIATIONS TO FREE PATTY HEARST

ROLLING STONE

ISSUE NO. 165 — JULY 18, 1974 — 75c UK 25p

THE RESTORATION OF ROMAN POLANSKI
By TOM BURKE

THE FRIED ICE CREAM PAPERS
By KEN KESEY

THE ROLLING STONE INTERVIEW: ERIC CLAPTON

PHILIP HAYS

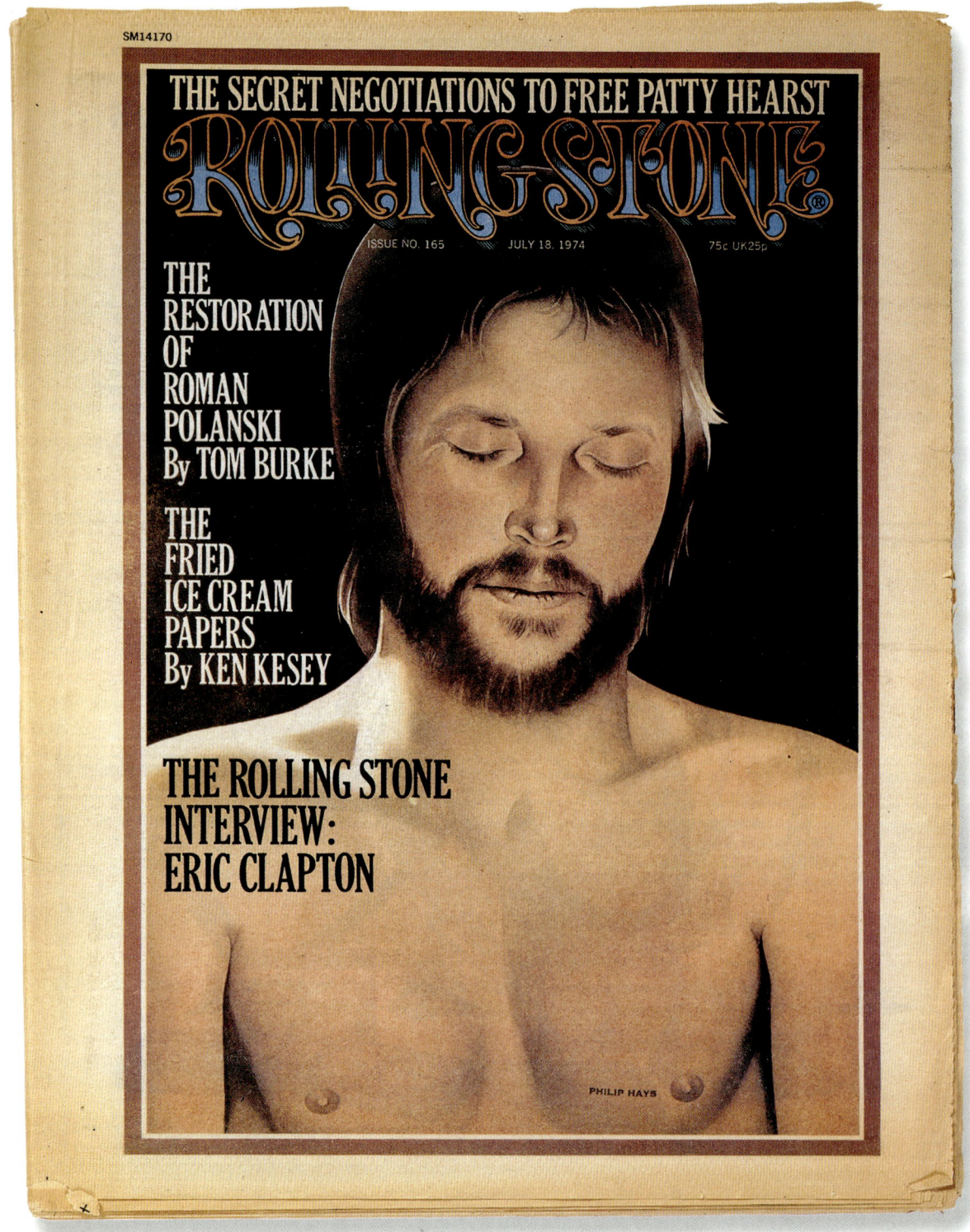

RS 165 | ERIC CLAPTON | July 18th, 1974 | Illustration by Philip Hays

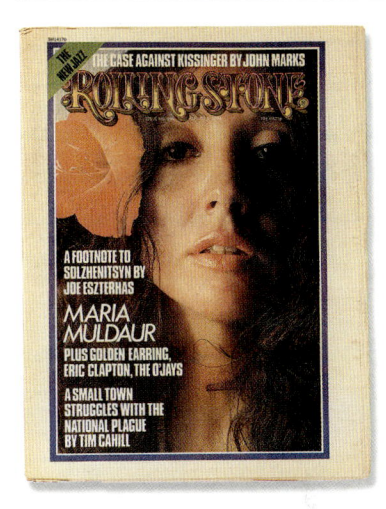

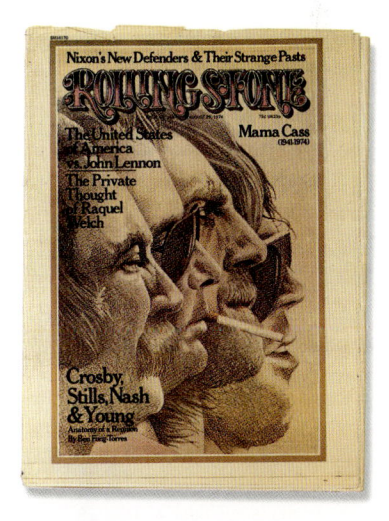

RS 166 | MARIA MULDAUR
August 1st, 1974
PHOTOGRAPH BY ANNIE LEIBOVITZ

RS 168 | CROSBY, STILLS, NASH & YOUNG
August 29th, 1974
ILLUSTRATION BY DUGALD STERMER

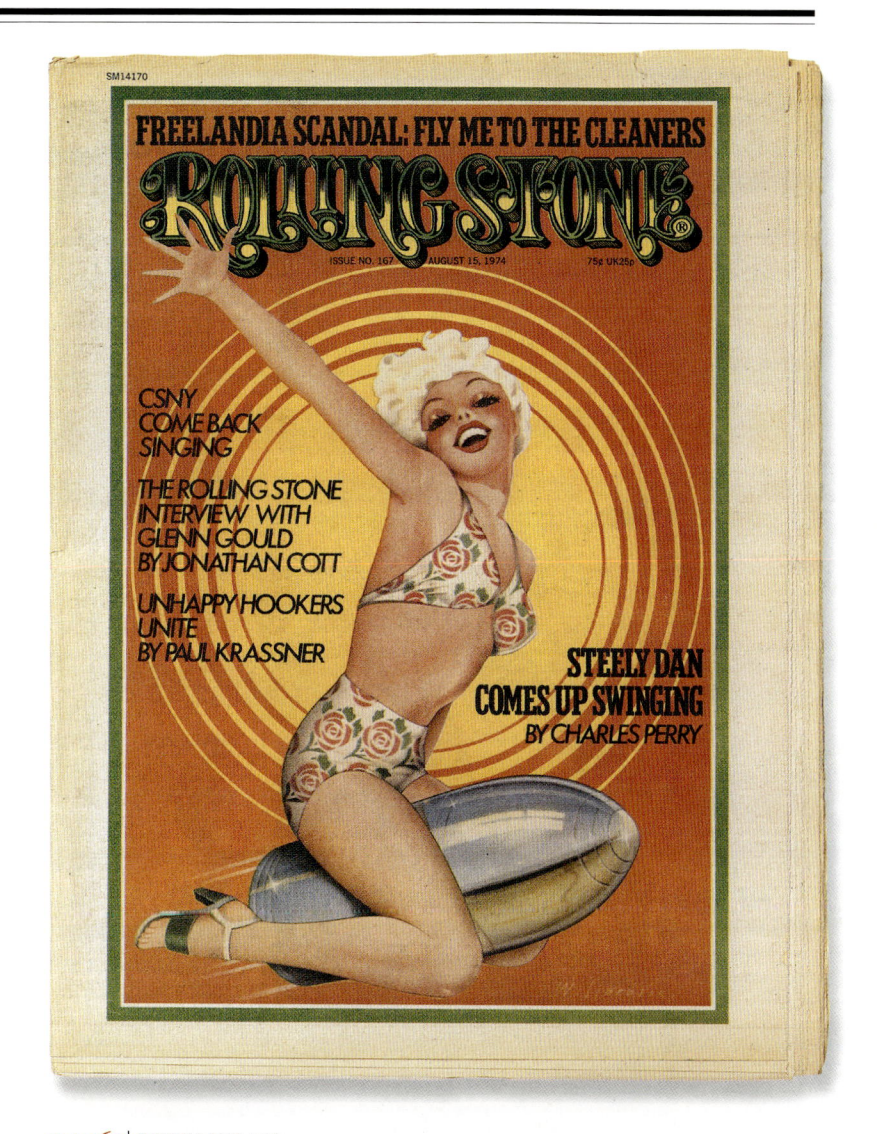

RS 167 | STEELY DAN | August 15th, 1974 | ILLUSTRATION BY DAVE WILLARDSON

[**RS 167**] Though ROLLING STONE has raised eyebrows over many of its covers, most have been more overtly controversial than the illustration for this Steely Dan story. Is the bathing-suit-clad cover girl riding a silver vibrator? Yes, the concept was this: Walter Becker and Donald Fagen named their group after a vibrator called Steely Dan in William S. Burroughs's *Naked Lunch*. Apparently, when Dave Willardson completed his airbrushed image, art director Michael Salisbury hid it from the rest of the staff until the issue was running on press – just in case there was any nay-saying.

50 YEARS OF COVERS • 75

ROLLING STONE

ISSUE NO. 169   SEPTEMBER 12, 1974   75¢ UK25p

THE QUITTER
Our Memories of a Broken Ruler

Nixon's Last Days by Annie Leibovitz

The Tragic History of Jan & Dean

1946-1974

RS 169 | **RICHARD MILHOUS NIXON** | September 12th, 1974 | Photograph by Annie Leibovitz

WHEN RICHARD NIXON RESIGNED IN 1974, Rolling Stone had been around only slightly longer than Nixon had been president. From time to time, the magazine commented on the former president and his actions. For RS 169, seven editors read over the preceding 168 issues to see what had been written about Nixon. They looked for "bright, breezy material as well as the kind of vicious, distorted, hysterical reporting that got Rolling Stone banned from the White House for all but the last months, when the pit began to open up at Nixon's feet."

Meanwhile, writer Richard Goodwin and Annie Leibovitz had been busy with, respectively, an essay on Nixon and a photo record of his last days. Goodwin had been in Washington setting up the Rolling Stone operation there. Leibovitz appeared twice on television: once in San Clemente climbing the podium of Nixon's Special Counsel James St. Clair and the other time shooting the former president's long and lachrymose walk from the Oval Office to the waiting helicopter.

DICK AND PAT THOUGHT THAT CHINA WAS A very funny place. Everywhere they went, they found things to laugh at. Dick especially liked to make jokes.

They visited a place called the Forbidden City. Their new friend Chou showed them a pretty room in an old palace. Once, Chou told them, a child emperor ruled the country in this room. His mother hid behind the screen to tell him what to do.

"It's the same today," joked Dick. "The women are always the backseat drivers!"

Then Chou showed Dick a pair of ear stoppers. Emperors used to put them in their ears. That way they could not hear when people said bad things about them.

"Give me a pair of those. Then you can only hear the questions you want to!" said clever Dick.

[RS WHITE HOUSE CORRESPONDENTS, MARCH 30TH, 1972]

We urge the Congress to vote impeachment proceedings before Nixon can escape through resignation. And, in either event, we then want a trial to determine innocence or a conviction.

And that is just the first step.

—*The Editors* [JUNE 7TH, 1973]

HE ATE A LOT OF CORNMEAL and pumped gas for his father's gas station. His father bought a Quaker meeting-house across the road and expanded the gas station into a grocery store. The boy took to studying in the bell-tower of the church/store. He was devoted to his mother. He once wrote her a letter that began: "My Dear Master" and ended "Your Good Dog, Richard." He had a habit of sitting in a big chair and staring into space . . .

He mixed with few people and hardly ever dated. When he did date, he asked the girls intimate questions: What would have happened to the world if Persia had conquered Greece? What would have happened if Plato had never lived?

—*Joe Eszterhas* [AUGUST 30TH, 1973]

Six months ago, Richard Nixon was the most powerful political leader in the history of the world, more powerful than Augustus Caesar, when he had his act rolling full bore – six months ago.

Now, with the passing of each sweaty afternoon, into what history will call "the Summer of '73," Richard Nixon is being dragged closer and closer – with all deliberate speed, as it were – to disgrace and merciless infamy. His place in history is already fixed: He will go down with Grant and Harding as one of democracy's classic mutations.

—*Hunter S. Thompson* [SEPTEMBER 27TH, 1973]

50 YEARS OF COVERS • 77

1970s

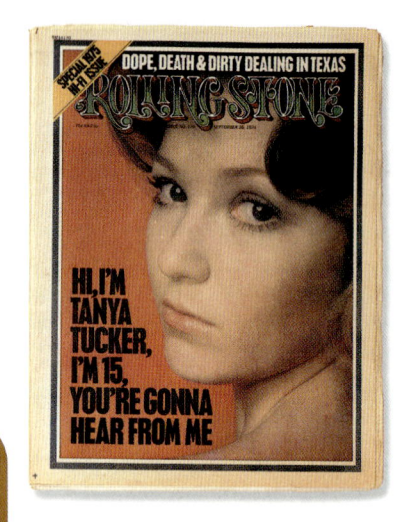

> "*I love Lily. I have this thing* about her, a little crush. She's so good I get embarrassed, I get in awe of her. I'd seen her on *Laugh-In* and shit, and something about her is very sensual. You know, when she works, I'd like to ball her in all them different characters she does sometimes. Wouldn't you? I mean, have her around the house and have her do all that – be Ernestine one minute [*he imitates Ernestine, Lily's telephone operator*]: 'Oh [*snort, snort*], just put it in the proper place. Thank you [*snort, snort*].'"
>
> —Richard Pryor

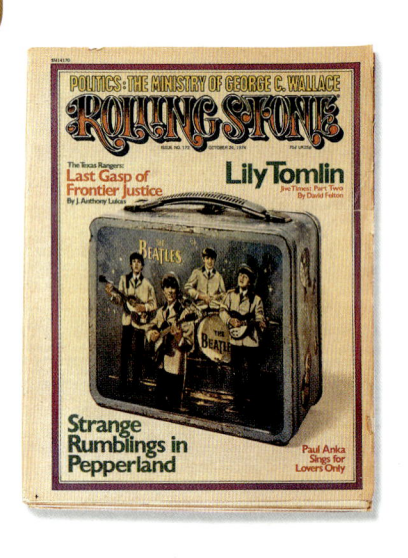

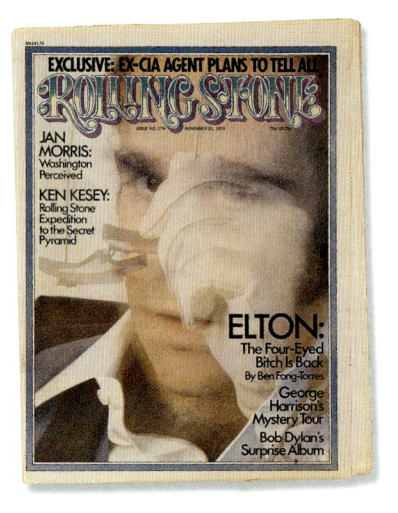

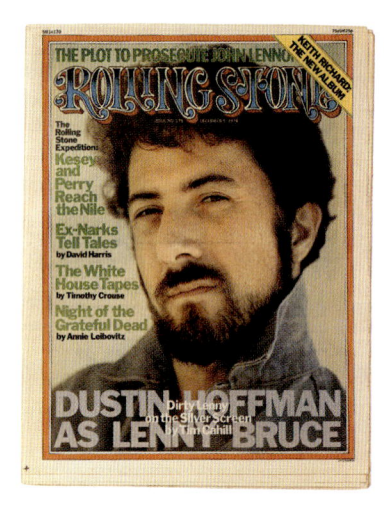

RS 170 | TANYA TUCKER
September 26th, 1974
PHOTOGRAPH BY DOUG METZLER

RS 172 | THE BEATLES
October 24th, 1974
PHOTOGRAPH BY TOM ROSE

RS 174 | ELTON JOHN
November 21st, 1974
PHOTOGRAPH BY ANNIE LEIBOVITZ

RS 175 | DUSTIN HOFFMAN
December 5th, 1974
PHOTOGRAPH BY STEVE SCHAPIRO

78 · ROLLING STONE

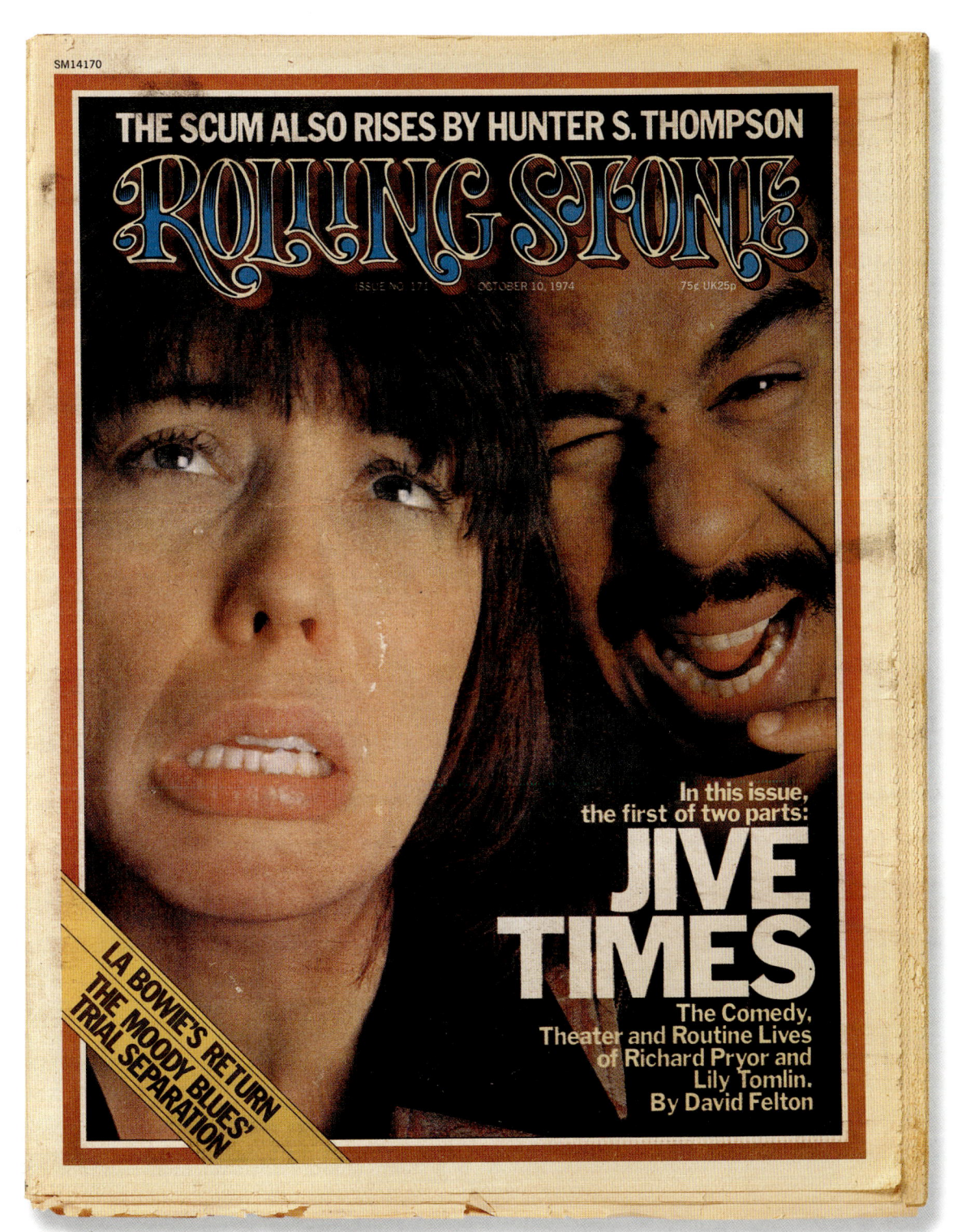

RS 171 | LILY TOMLIN & RICHARD PRYOR | October 10th, 1974 | Photograph by Annie Leibovitz

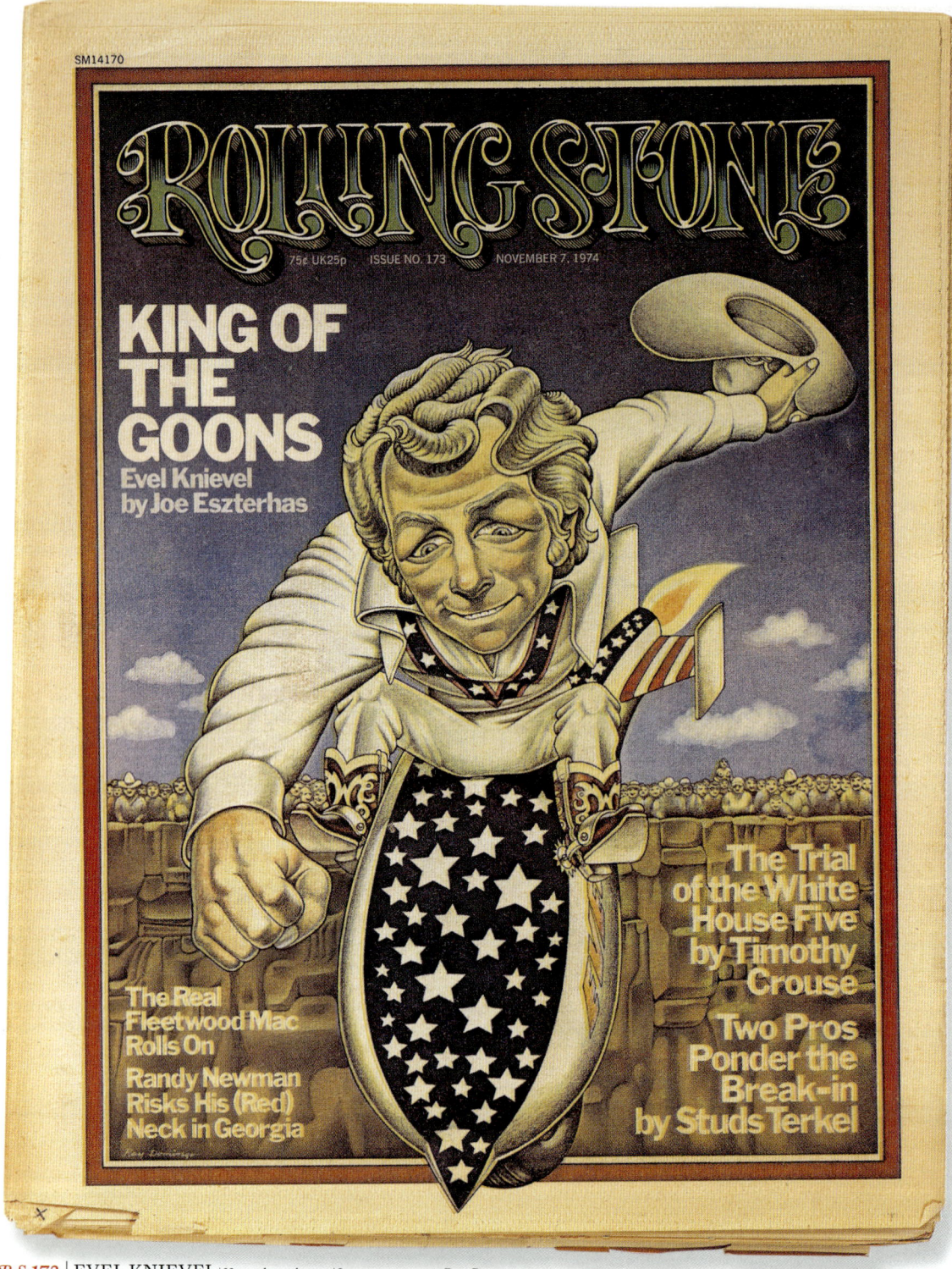

RS 173 | EVEL KNIEVEL | November 7th, 1974 | ILLUSTRATION BY RAY DOMINGO

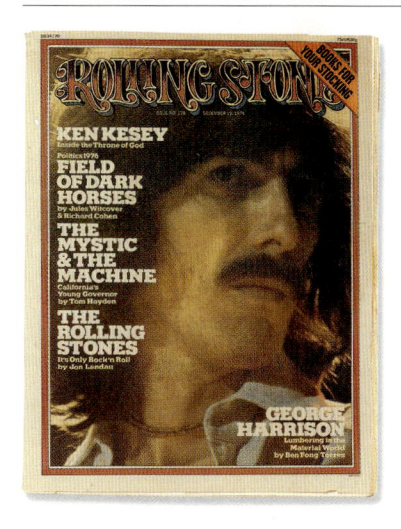

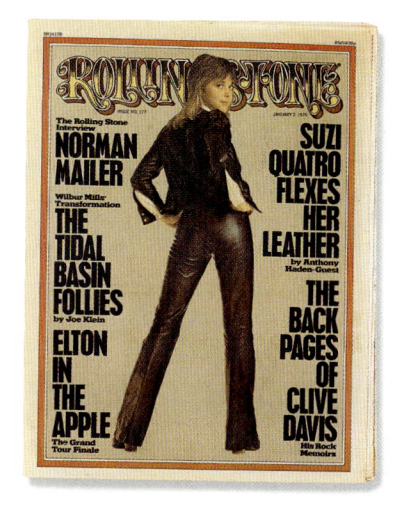

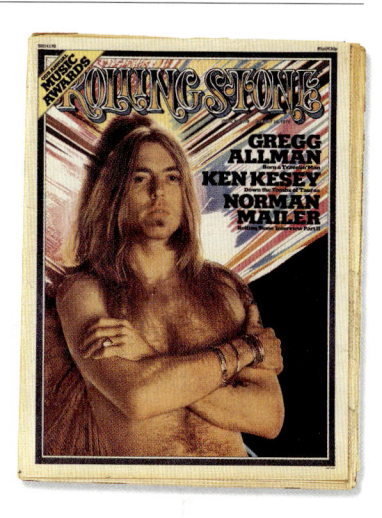

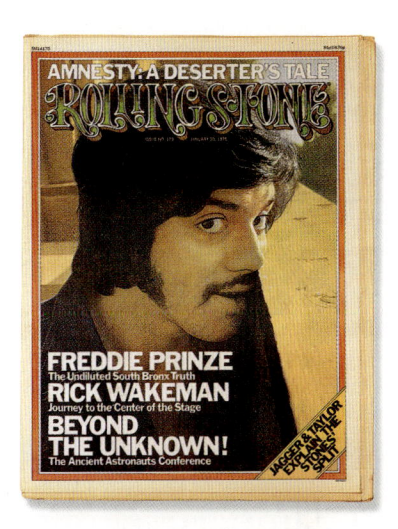

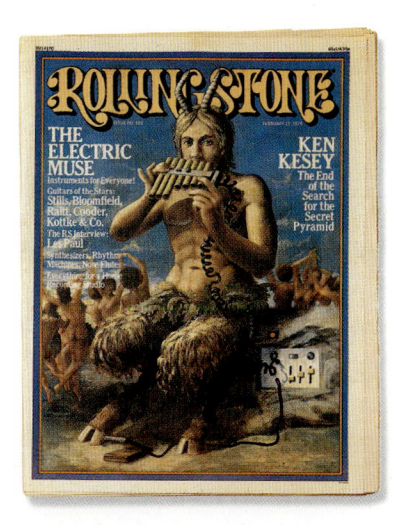

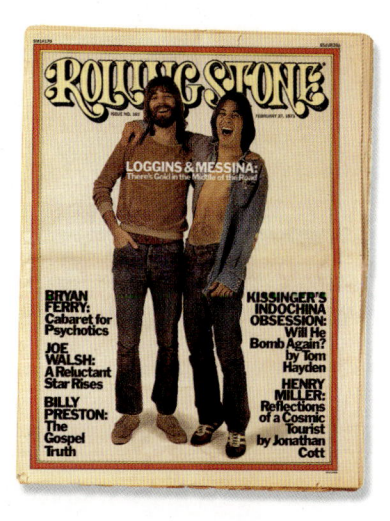

RS 176 | GEORGE HARRISON
December 19th, 1974
PHOTOGRAPH BY MARK FOCUS

RS 177 | SUZI QUATRO
January 2nd, 1975
PHOTOGRAPH BY PETER GOWLAND

RS 178 | GREGG ALLMAN
January 16th, 1975
PHOTOGRAPH BY PETE TURNER

RS 179 | FREDDIE PRINZE
January 30th, 1975
PHOTOGRAPH BY DON PETERSON

RS 180 | THE ELECTRIC MUSE
February 13th, 1975
ILLUSTRATION BY PHIL CARROLL

RS 181 | KENNY LOGGINS & JIM MESSINA
February 27th, 1975
PHOTOGRAPH BY ANNIE LEIBOVITZ

50 YEARS OF COVERS • 81

ROLLING STONE

APRIL 10th, 1975 / ISSUE NO. 184

What's Deaf, Dumb & Blind and Costs $3½ Million?

Tommy

Peter Bogdanovich and Cybill Shepherd Paint It White

Belfast, City of Sorrows by Gloria Emerson

A Big Hand for Little Feat

Rolling Stone Interview: Seymour Hersh, Toughest Reporter in America by Joe Eszterhas

The Secret Foreign Policy of Standard Oil: A Slippery Tale of Double Agents, Forgers and Arab Kings

---

RS 184 | ROGER DALTREY | April 10th, 1975 | PHOTOGRAPHER UNKNOWN

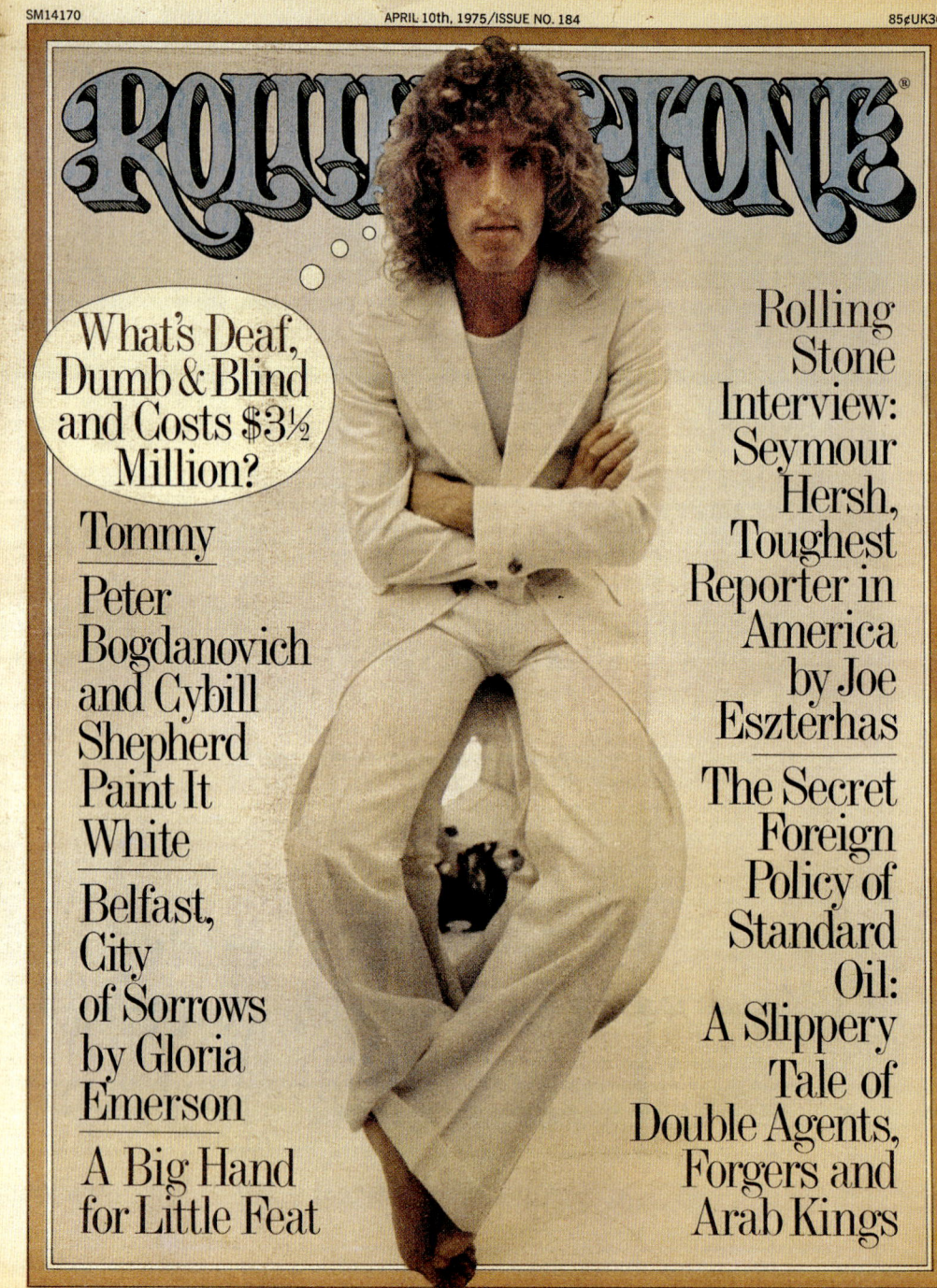

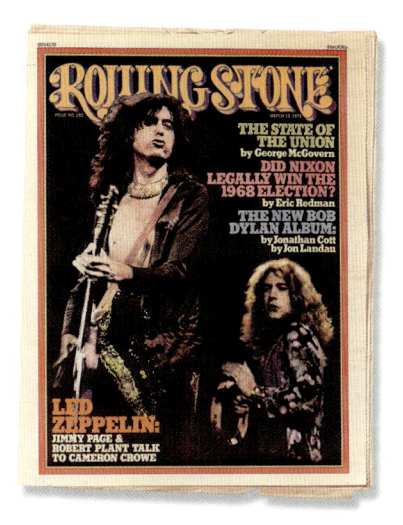

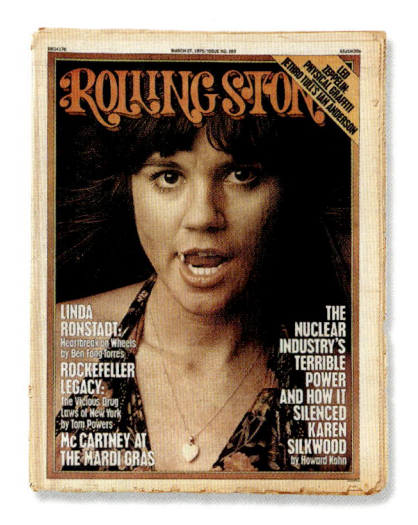

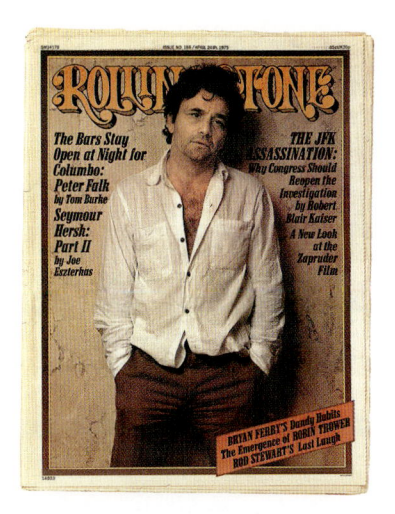

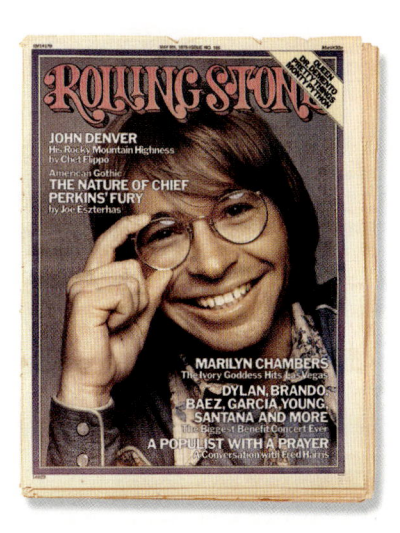

"**THE QUEST TO LAND THE MAGAZINE'S** first interview with Led Zeppelin was a rough one. The magazine had been tough on the band. Guitarist Jimmy Page vowed never to talk with them. While touring with the band for the *Los Angeles Times*, I attempted to talk them into speaking with me for ROLLING STONE, too. One by one they agreed, except for Page. I stayed on the road for three weeks, red-eyed from no sleep, until he finally relented ... out of sympathy, I think. My mother was about ready to call the police to drag me home." —*Cameron Crowe*

LINDA RONSTADT WAS ALWAYS a lover. She learned about the birds and the bees, the boys and the girls, at age seven from a cousin who was one year older. In junior high in Tucson, Arizona, she started dressing up sexy. "I was trying to be Brigitte Bardot," she said. In rebellion against the nuns at the school – St. Peter and Paul – she went "boy crazy." At Catalina High, she went out with older men, among them a steel-guitar enthusiast with whom she left town at age 18. In Los Angeles, she sought a career in music and became the object of attention – the kind that led to too many wrong relationships, too many years of hating her own records and concerts, too many sad songs to sing and, today, to a still uncertain Linda Ronstadt.

[EXCERPT FROM RS 183 COVER STORY BY BEN FONG-TORRES]

RS 182 | **JIMMY PAGE & ROBERT PLANT**
March 13th, 1975
PHOTOGRAPH BY NEAL PRESTON

RS 185 | **PETER FALK**
April 24th, 1975
PHOTOGRAPH BY ANNIE LEIBOVITZ

RS 183 | **LINDA RONSTADT**
March 27th, 1975
PHOTOGRAPH BY ANNIE LEIBOVITZ

RS 186 | **JOHN DENVER**
May 8th, 1975
PHOTOGRAPH BY FRANCESCO SCAVULLO

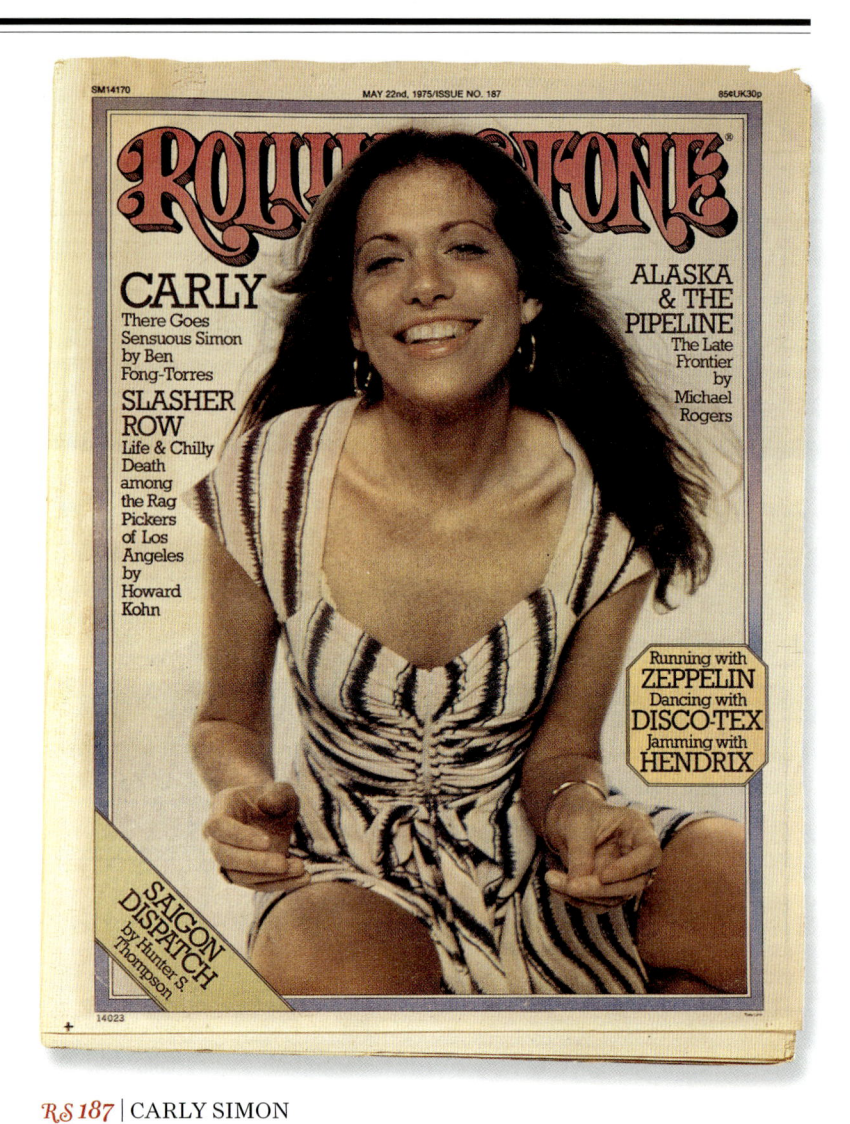

1970s

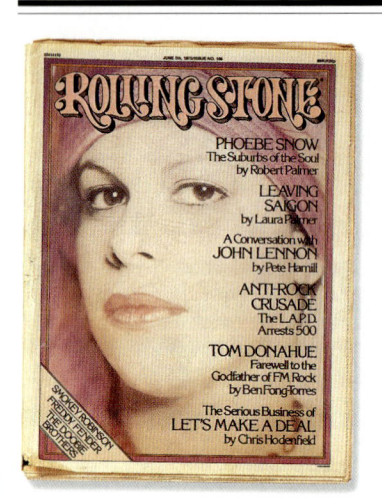

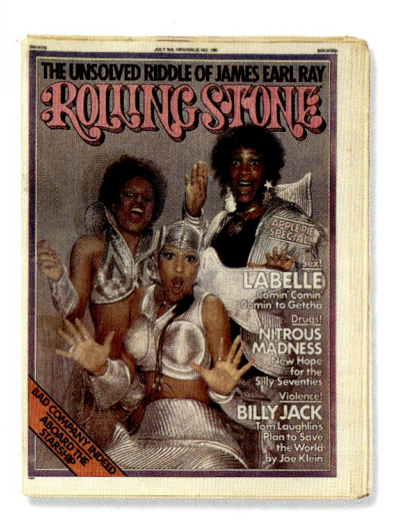

RS 188 | PHOEBE SNOW
June 5th, 1975
PHOTOGRAPH BY ANNIE LEIBOVITZ

RS 187 | CARLY SIMON
May 22nd, 1975
PHOTOGRAPH BY TONY LANE

RS 190 | LABELLE
July 3rd, 1975
PHOTOGRAPH BY HIRO

"ANNIE ALWAYS likes to get your shirt off by the end of the shoot." —*Mick Jagger*

84 • ROLLING STONE

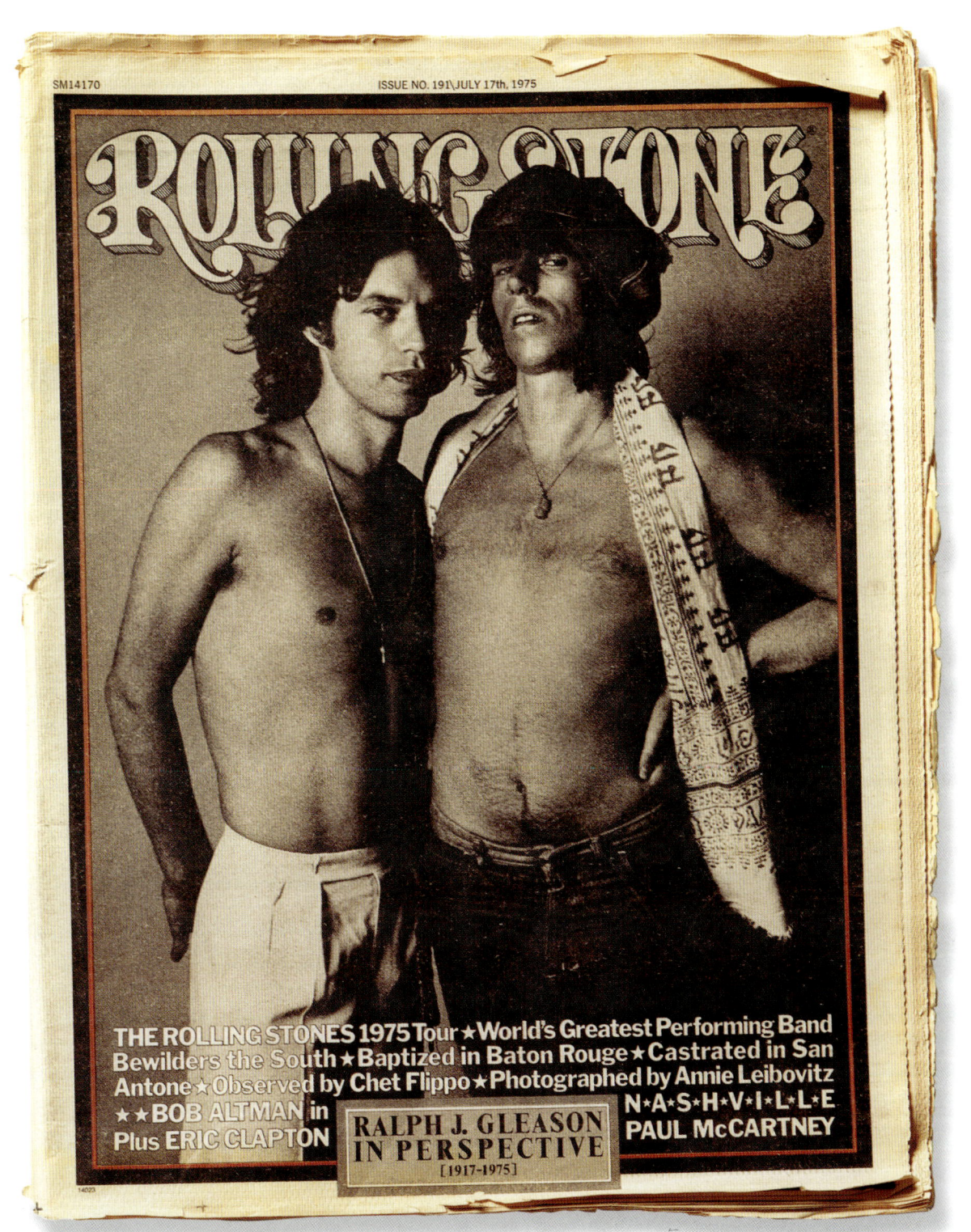

RS 191 | MICK JAGGER & KEITH RICHARDS | July 17th, 1975 | Photograph by Annie Leibovitz

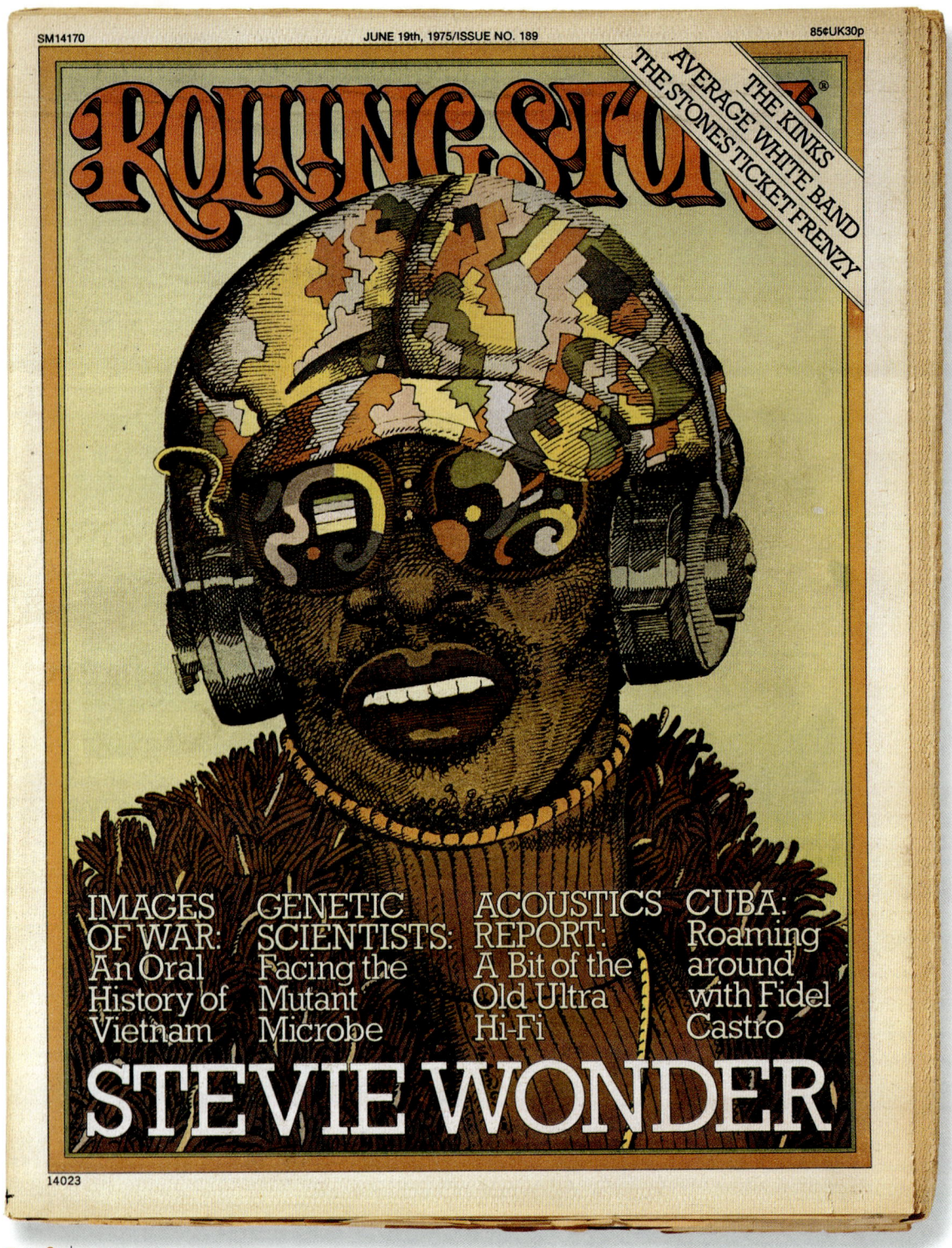

RS 189 | STEVIE WONDER | June 19th, 1975 | ILLUSTRATION BY MILTON GLASER

SM14170 AUGUST 14th, 1975 / ISSUE NO. 193 85¢ UK 30p

Rolling Stone

Americans Tortured & Lost in Mexico's Jails

NEIL YOUNG
The Rolling Stone Interview
by Cameron Crowe

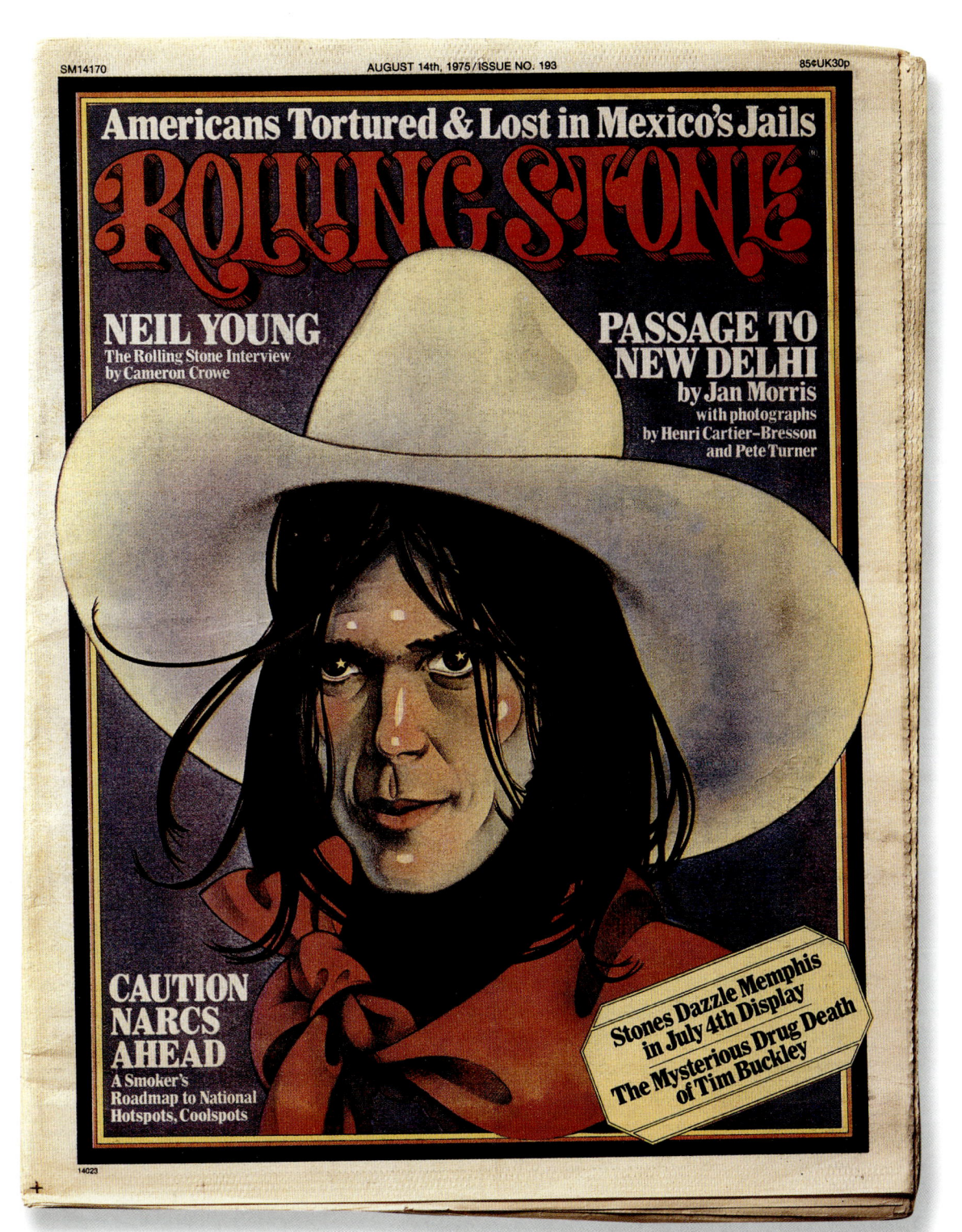

PASSAGE TO NEW DELHI
by Jan Morris
with photographs by Henri Cartier-Bresson and Pete Turner

CAUTION NARCS AHEAD
A Smoker's Roadmap to National Hotspots, Coolspots

Stones Dazzle Memphis in July 4th Display
The Mysterious Drug Death of Tim Buckley

RS 193 | NEIL YOUNG | August 14th, 1975 | ILLUSTRATION BY KIM WHITESIDES

50 YEARS OF COVERS • 87

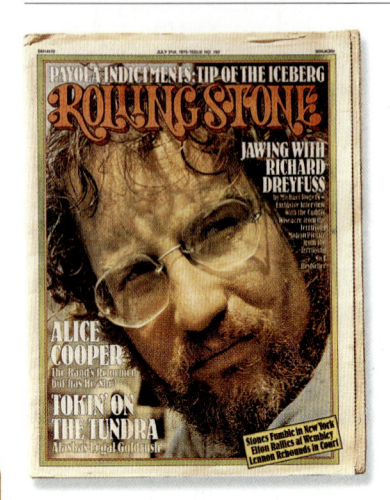

1970s

RS 192 | RICHARD DREYFUSS
July 31st, 1975
PHOTOGRAPH BY BUD LEE

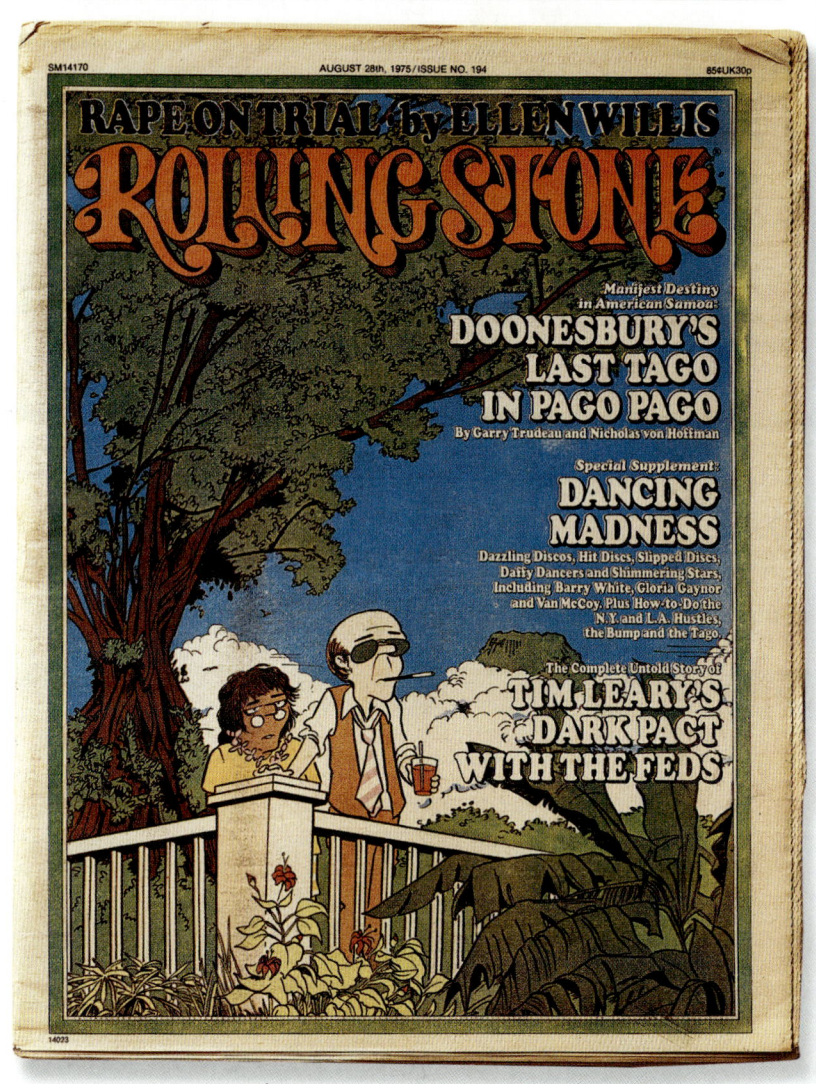

RS 194 | DOONESBURY'S UNCLE DUKE
August 28th, 1975 | ILLUSTRATION BY GARRY TRUDEAU

[RS 194] This is the first of four covers that Pulitzer Prize–winning cartoonist Garry Trudeau has illustrated for ROLLING STONE. Doonesbury's gonzoid Uncle Duke arrived on the cover after he'd been appointed governor of American Samoa. The character infuriated the real Raoul Duke, Hunter S. Thompson, on whom the character is directly based. (Thompson had once claimed that Democratic Party Chairman Larry O'Brien had offered him the governorship.) Thompson said of Trudeau, characteristically, "If I ever catch that little bastard, I'll rip his lungs out."

SM14170   SEPTEMBER 11th, 1975 / ISSUE NO. 195   85¢ UK30p

ROLLING STONE

ROLLING STONES
Jumping, Booming,
Bumping, Grinding
to a Halt.
Chronicled by
Jonathan Cott,
Dave Marsh,
Jann Wenner &
Annie Leibovitz

The Rolling Stone
Interview with
**ELDRIDGE
CLEAVER**
His Bold New Allegiance
to the Flag and to the Republic
for Which It Stands

Ganja Din:
**REGGAE'S
HAIRY EXPLOSION**
Bob Marley & the Wailers
Toots and the Maytals
Secrets of Rasta Revealed!

RS 195 | MICK JAGGER | September 11th, 1975 | Photograph by Annie Leibovitz

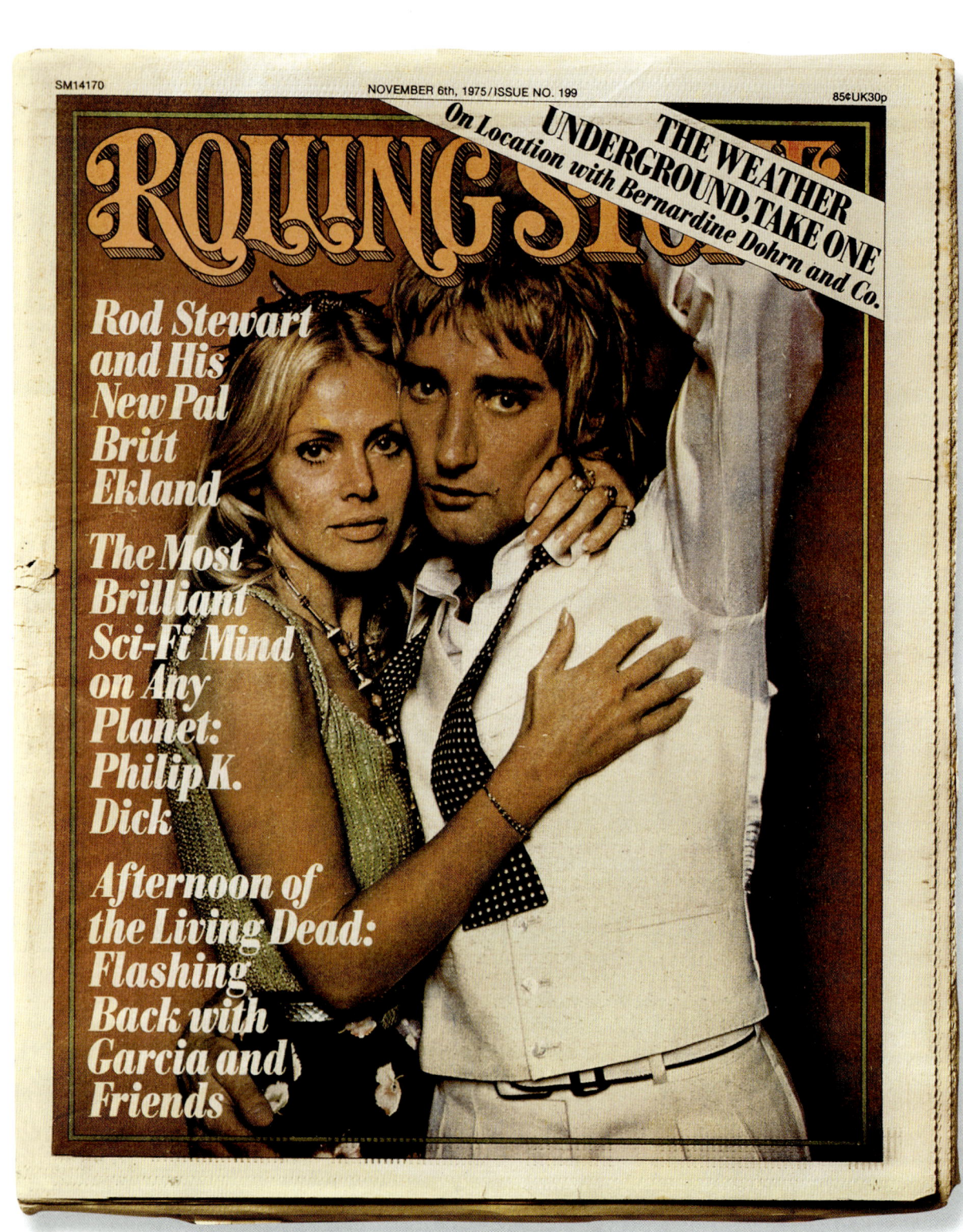

ROLLING STONE

NOVEMBER 6th, 1975 / ISSUE NO. 199

SM14170 • 85¢ UK30p

THE WEATHER UNDERGROUND, TAKE ONE On Location with Bernardine Dohrn and Co.

Rod Stewart and His New Pal Britt Ekland

The Most Brilliant Sci-Fi Mind on Any Planet: Philip K. Dick

Afternoon of the Living Dead: Flashing Back with Garcia and Friends

1970s

RS 199 | ROD STEWART & BRITT EKLAND | November 6th, 1975 | Photograph by Annie Leibovitz

90 • ROLLING STONE

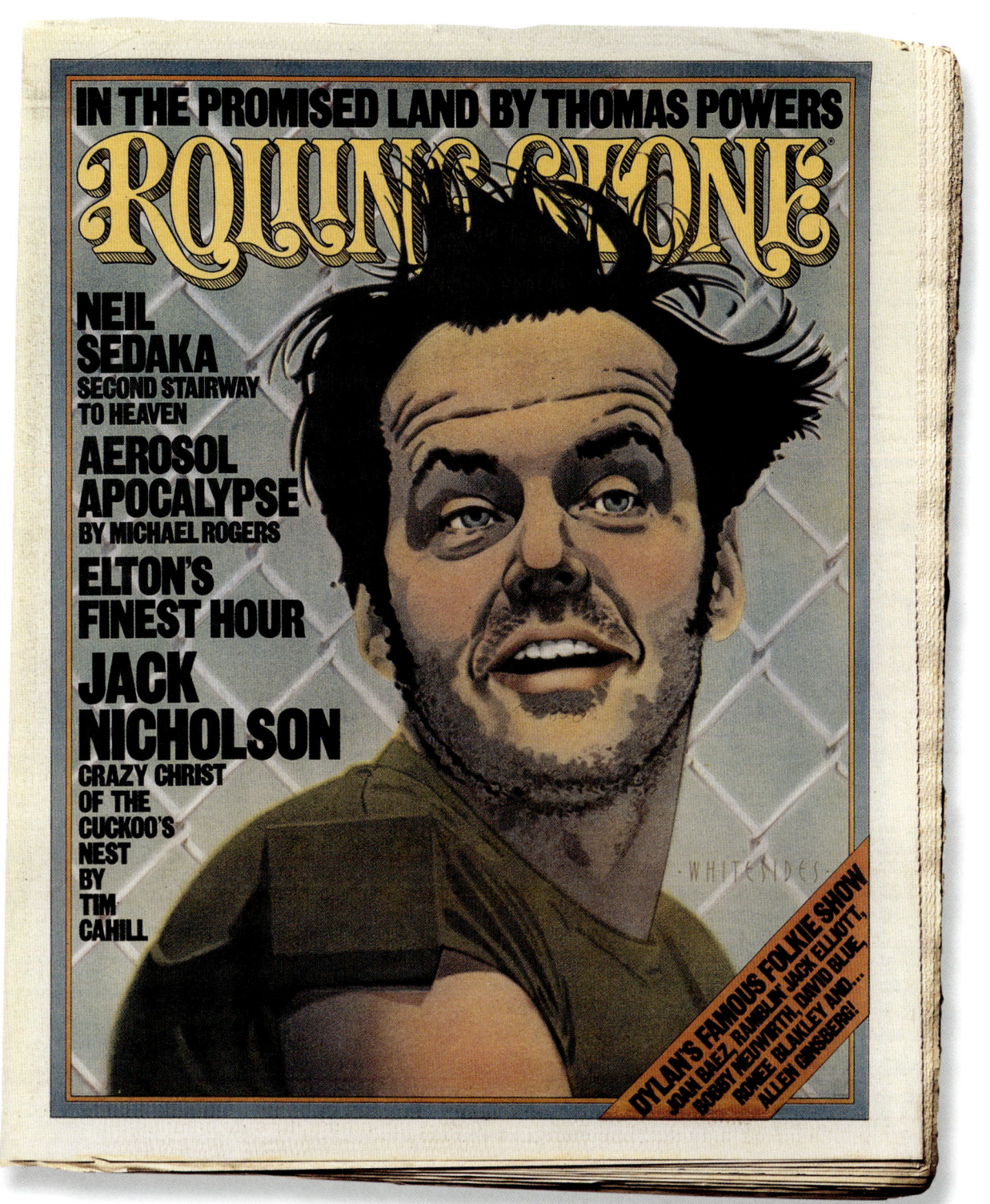

RS 201 | JACK NICHOLSON | December 4th, 1975 | ILLUSTRATION BY KIM WHITESIDES

RS 198 | PATTY HEARST
October 23rd, 1975
ILLUSTRATION BY JAMIE PUTNAM

1970s

[RS 198 AND RS 200] About this groundbreaking scoop, the editors wrote: "To obtain the interviews, Howard Kohn and David Weir had to promise they would go to jail before revealing the names of their sources (a promise they would have made in any case). They were not allowed to tape the interviews, so to keep things as accurate as possible, separate notes were taken by the two journalists and Alison Weir, an editor of *Womensports*. The material was then checked with independent outside sources. The entire process – negotiations, interviews, research and writing – took four months, during which time Kohn and Weir retraced Patty's trail across America, including a visit to the farmhouse rented by Jack and Micki Scott in Pennsylvania. Ironically, as the layouts were being readied for the printer, Patty Hearst and the Harrises were apprehended in San Francisco. But the narrative remains a scoop in itself – the first detailed account of Tania's conversion, her paranoid flights across the country, her hiding out with the Scotts. Part Two will cover her life leading up to the bust, secret meetings between her friends and her parents and how the FBI finally broke the case. You might want to send $1 (for the issue plus postage) to Inside Story, Rolling Stone, 625 Third Street, San Francisco, CA 94107, and get Part Two before the FBI."

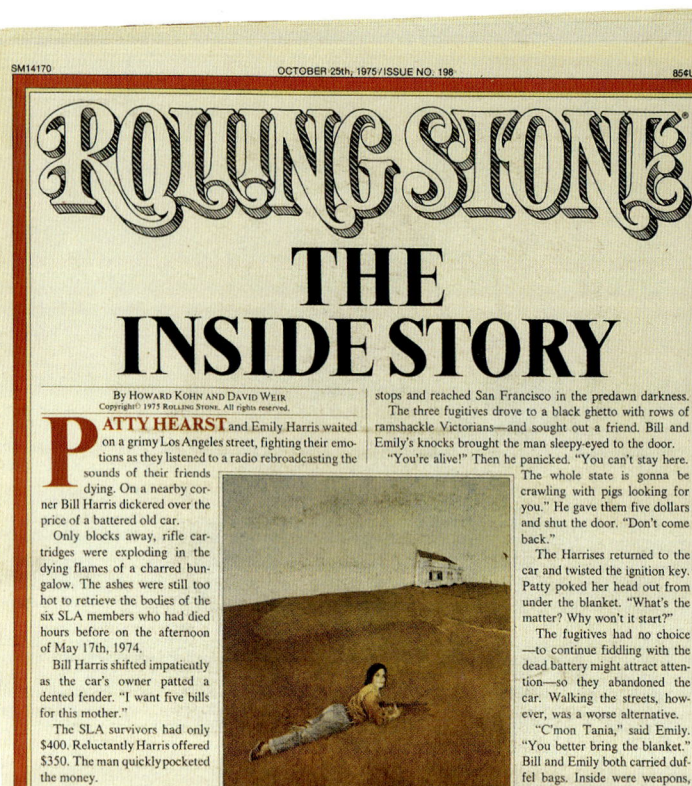

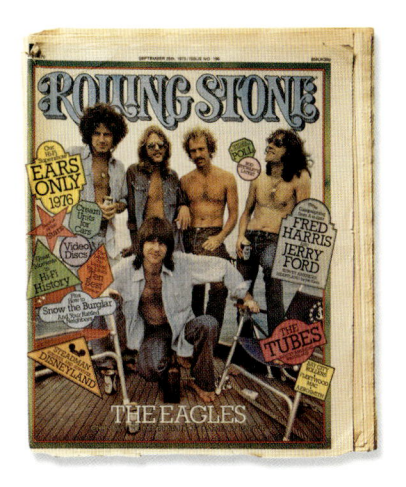

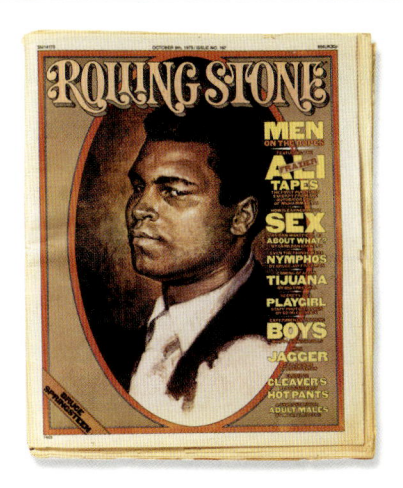

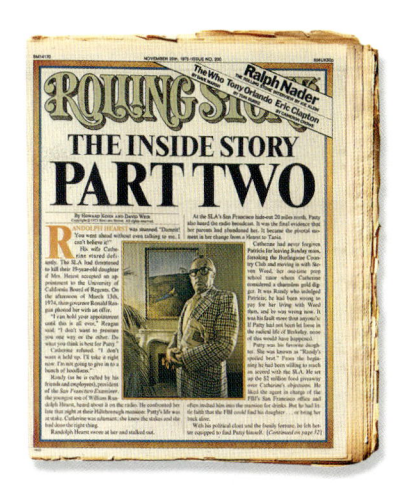

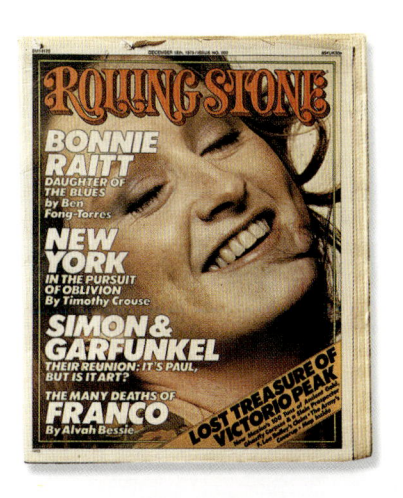

RS 196 | THE EAGLES
September 25th, 1975
PHOTOGRAPH BY NEAL PRESTON

RS 202 | BONNIE RAITT
December 18th, 1975
PHOTOGRAPH BY BILL KING

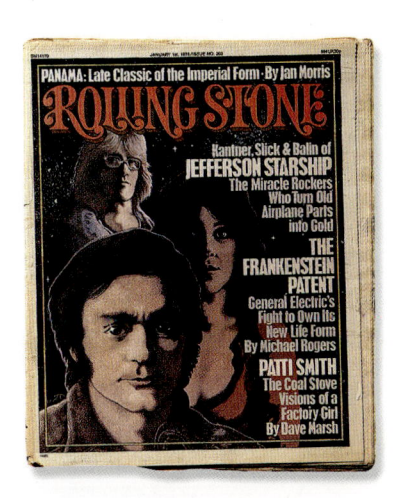

RS 197 | MUHAMMAD ALI
October 9th, 1975
ILLUSTRATION BY BRUCE WOLFE

RS 203 | JEFFERSON STARSHIP
January 1st, 1976
ILLUSTRATION BY GREG SCOTT

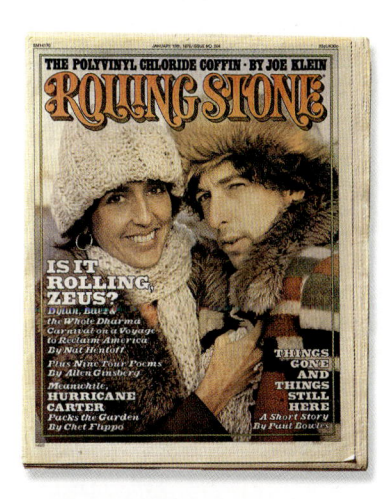

RS 200 | THE PATTY HEARST STORY, PART TWO
November 20th, 1975
PHOTOGRAPH BY TONY LANE

RS 204 | JOAN BAEZ & BOB DYLAN
January 15th, 1976
PHOTOGRAPH BY KEN REGAN

50 YEARS OF COVERS · 93

RS 206 | DAVID BOWIE | February 12th, 1976 | Photograph by Steve Schapiro

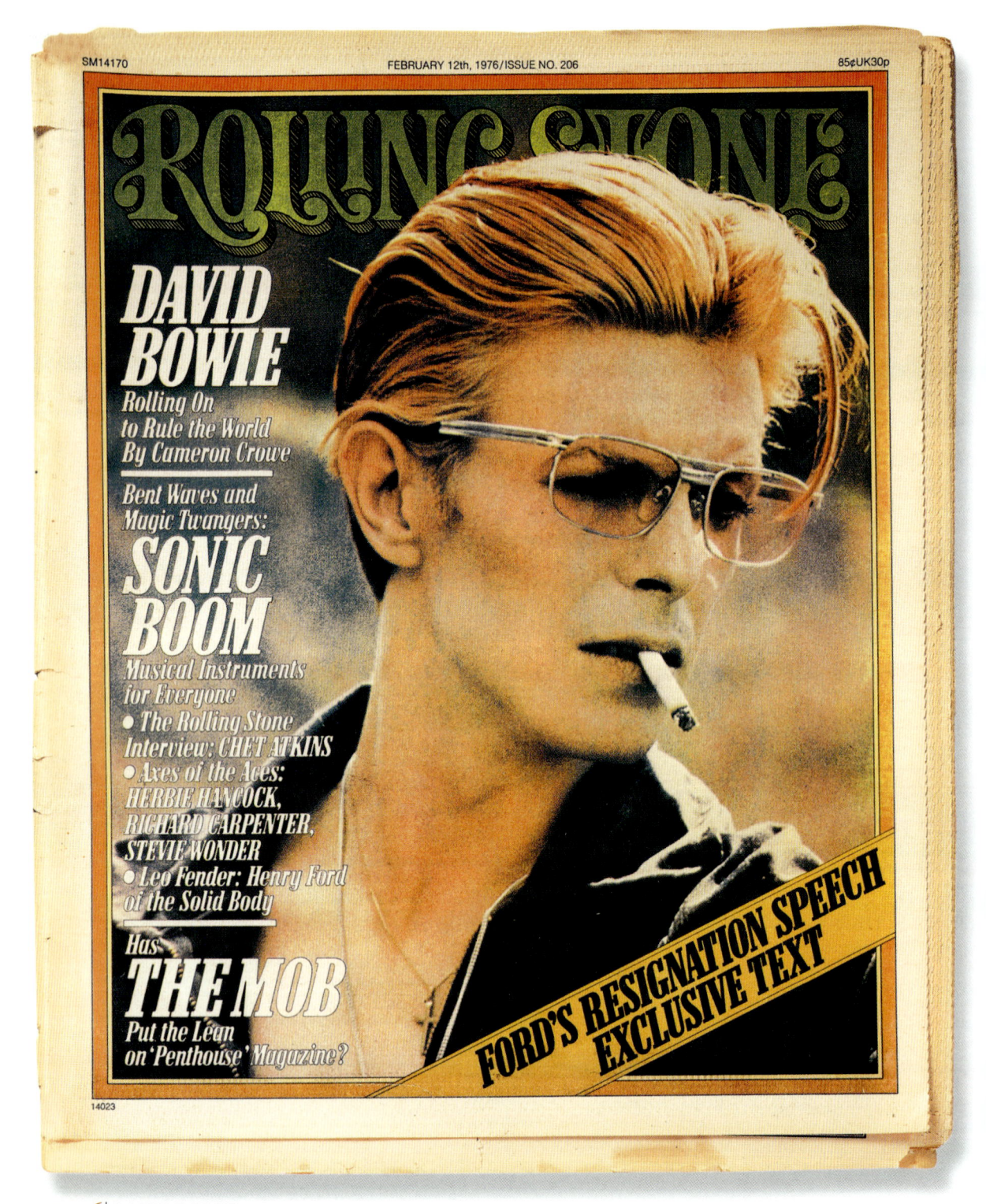

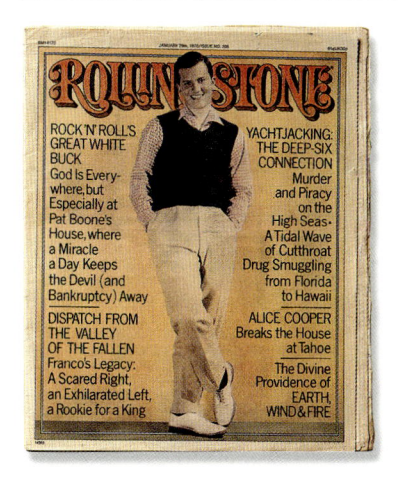

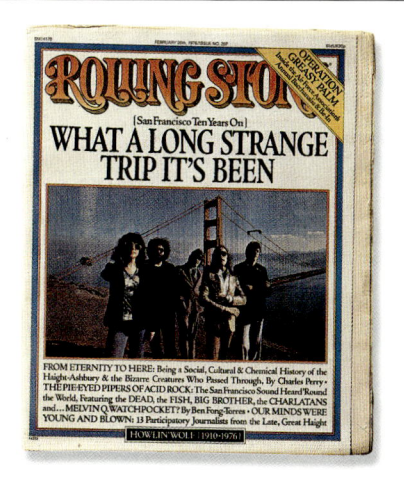

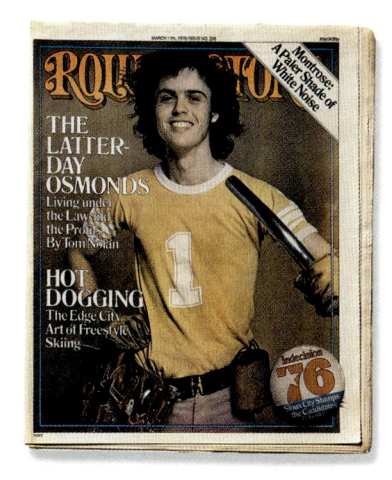

$\mathcal{RS}$ 205 | PAT BOONE
January 29th, 1976
PHOTOGRAPH BY BRUNO OF HOLLYWOOD

"THE CAMERA NEVER LIES. IN this case [RS 206], it only tells half the story. With a small target set up a few yards away, [I'd been] taking potshots with an oversized pistol. The gun was a present from one of my mid-Seventies 'friends.' I was definitely under the impression that I was merely 'passing through this world.' I didn't care where I came from and cared less where I was going; the present was futile and surreal. I ate little, but ingested a critically unfair amount of chemicals...."

—*David Bowie*

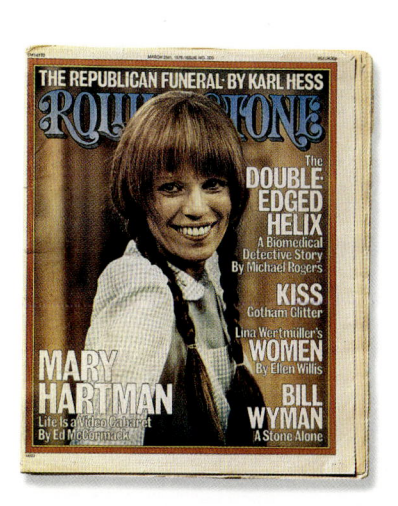

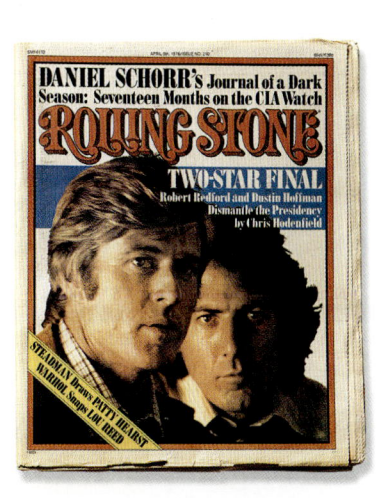

$\mathcal{RS}$ 207 | SAN FRANCISCO ROCKERS
February 26th, 1976
PHOTOGRAPH BY JIM MARSHALL

$\mathcal{RS}$ 209 | LOUISE LASSER
March 25th, 1976
PHOTOGRAPH BY BILL EPPRIDGE

$\mathcal{RS}$ 208 | DONNY OSMOND
March 11th, 1976
PHOTOGRAPH BY ANNIE LEIBOVITZ

$\mathcal{RS}$ 210 | ROBERT REDFORD & DUSTIN HOFFMAN
April 8th, 1976
PHOTOGRAPH BY STANLEY TRETICK

[RS 211] For this issue, Jann Wenner commissioned two photographs of Peter Frampton by two different photographers, was talked into using one image, then changed his mind and insisted on the other shot the day the cover was due to the printer. Different photographs appeared on early and later shipments.

It's like stepping into a scene

from *Blow-Up*. The white walls of Francesco Scavullo's Manhattan studio are covered with black-and-white portraits of blank-expressioned models. Young male assistants scurry around, each of them trying to act more hassled than the next.

In another room, looking very much out of place, twenty-five-year-old Peter Frampton waits to have his picture taken for the cover of ROLLING STONE. He squirms while a makeup man dabs colors on his cheeks and eyelids, readying him for a session with one of the world's most renowned fashion photographers. It's all happening so fast. Three months ago, Frampton was just another hardworking British rocker, crisscrossing the country with a four-album repertoire. Today, he is the brightest new star of '76.

Frampton pries himself away from the makeup man to greet his visitor. "You mean you still recognize me?" he jokes a little uneasily. "I'm in such a daze. Do you believe all that's happened? Number One? Do you believe it? What a giggle." He is quickly led before the camera and the blitz-clicking is on.

[EXCERPT FROM RS 211 COVER STORY BY CAMERON CROWE]

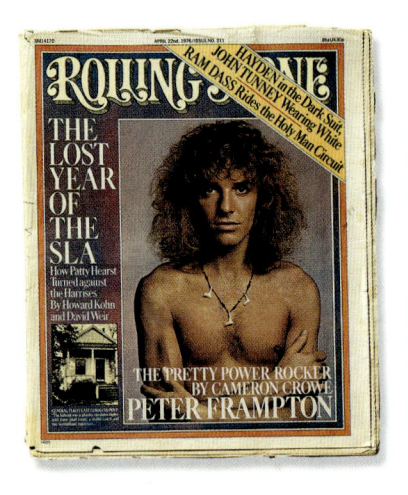

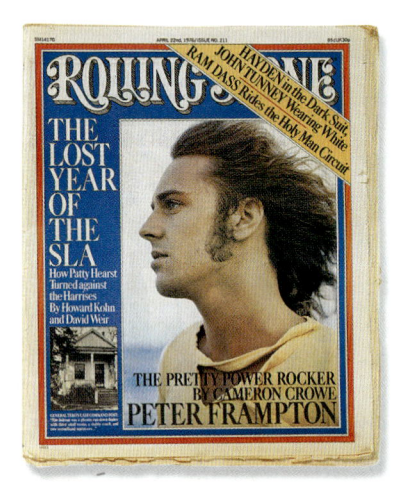

1970s

RS 211 | PETER FRAMPTON
April 22nd, 1976
PHOTOGRAPH BY FRANCESCO SCAVULLO

RS 211 | PETER FRAMPTON
April 22nd, 1976
PHOTOGRAPH BY BUD LEE

SM14170   MAY 6th, 1976/ISSUE NO. 212   85¢ UK30p

ROLLING STONE

SEVEN MASTERS OF PHOTOGRAPHY
Ansel Adams, Avedon, Cartier-Bresson, J.H. Lartigue, Helmut Newton, Ken Regan and Warhol By Annie Leibovitz

BLOODSHED IS MY BUSINESS
The Hair-Curling Exploits of John Dane, International Mercenary, Troublemaker and Gentleman

KING QUEEN
Meet Steve Ostrow, Pitchman for the Pansexual Revolution By Tom Burke

The Mission Street Mystic Returns to His Earthy Ways By Rich Wiseman

SANTANA COMES HOME

RS 212 | CARLOS SANTANA | May 6th, 1976 | Photograph by Annie Leibovitz

1970s

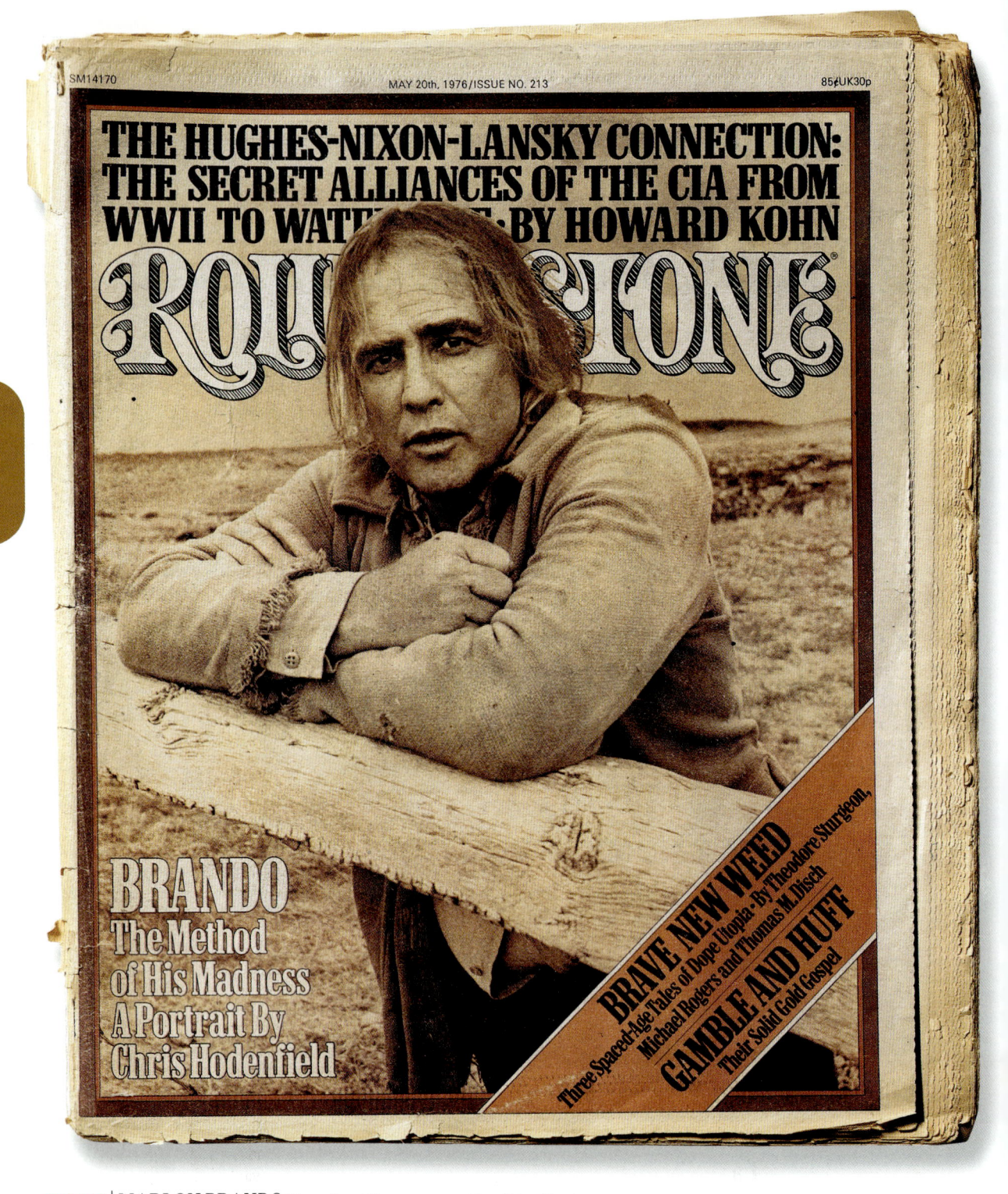

SM14170 — MAY 20th, 1976/ISSUE NO. 213 — 85¢/UK30p

THE HUGHES-NIXON-LANSKY CONNECTION: THE SECRET ALLIANCES OF THE CIA FROM WWII TO WATERGATE · BY HOWARD KOHN

ROLLING STONE

BRANDO
The Method of His Madness
A Portrait By Chris Hodenfield

BRAVE NEW WEED
Three Spaced-Age Tales of Dope Utopia · By Theodore Sturgeon, Michael Rogers and Thomas M. Disch

GAMBLE AND HUFF
Their Solid Gold Gospel

RS 213 | MARLON BRANDO | May 20th, 1976 | Photograph by Mary Ellen Mark

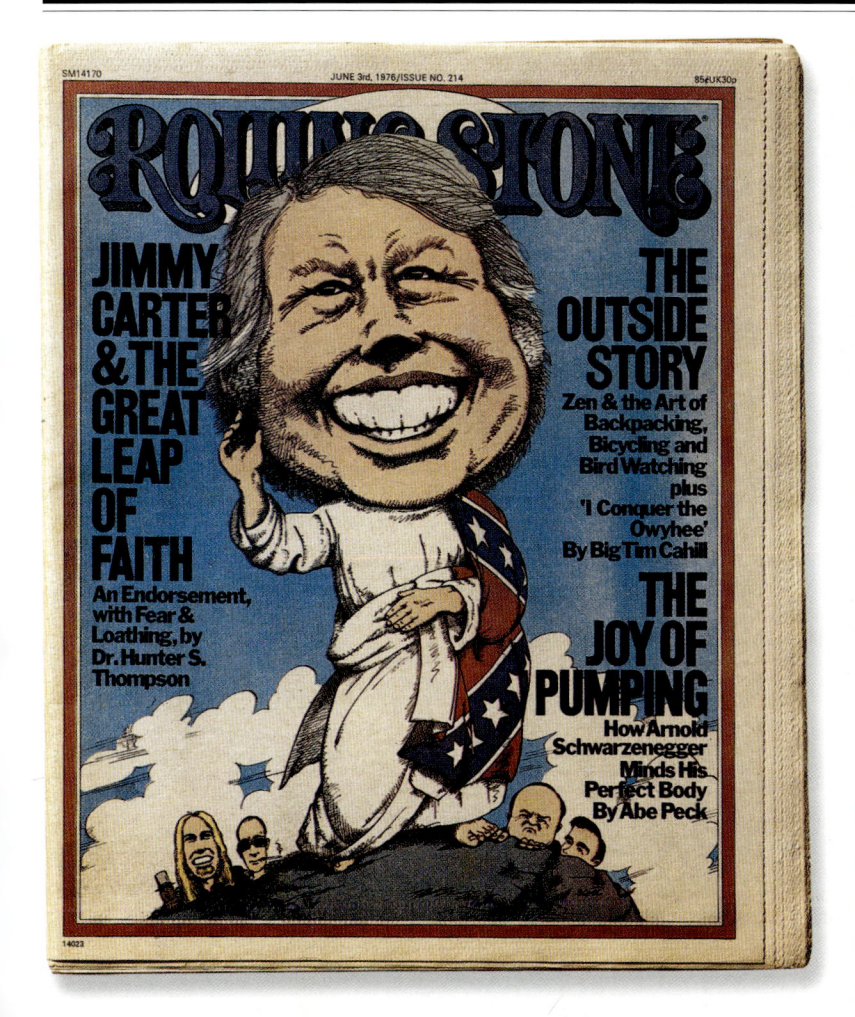

RS 214 | JIMMY CARTER | June 3rd, 1976 | ILLUSTRATION BY GREG SCOTT

"*Jimmy Carter's Law Day* speech was and still is the heaviest and most eloquent thing I have ever heard from the mouth of a politician."

—*Hunter S. Thompson*

"WHEN I FIRST HOISTED MYSELF into Marlon Brando's Dodge van, I was struggling badly with the electric shakes. It was the summer of 1975, and in the world of maximum-charisma actors, Brando was the unassailable king. Jack Nicholson had warned me that whatever I imagined Brando was going to be, in person he was going to be a *lot more*. You'd have thought I was meeting Mao Ze-dong.

"I was but a fresh-faced, longhaired punk, just twenty-five, in a psychedelic shirt out of *Arabian Nights*. I had flown to Montana on the promise of getting perhaps an hour with Brando, who was there filming *The Missouri Breaks*. The reasons for my stroke of good fortune were not entirely clear. Something I had written about director Robert Altman had appealed to one of Brando's allies. But the real reason, I expect, was that I was carrying credentials from ROLLING STONE. . . . Brando had a subscription. When Daniel Schorr wrote a big story about the CIA, for instance, Brando would call down for ten extra copies. A ROLLING STONE guy would want to know if the situation was cool. . . .

"The only other person I would meet with an equal physical force field would be Kareem Abdul-Jabbar, who is seven feet tall. As I sat with Brando for what turned out to be a week of conversation, I was hanging onto a runaway train. But I had the ROLLING STONE writer's attitude to remind me that, loud shirt and all, I was in charge."

—*Chris Hodenfield*

1970s

RS 215 | **PAUL & LINDA McCARTNEY**
June 17th, 1976
PHOTOGRAPH BY ANNIE LEIBOVITZ

No one seems perturbed that the leader of Wings is not on the loose, the way a Robert Plant or Roger Daltrey or Mick Jagger seems to be. And even if they're married, they don't display their wives up onstage with them.

I used to think of that, when we first got together, had Linda in the group. Oh, oh, we've had it with the groupies now! Everyone's gonna think we're real old squares – *blimey!* Married! God, at least we could have just lived together or something – that would have been a bit hip. Then you realize it doesn't matter. They really come for the music. At first it did seem funny to be up there with a wife instead of just friends or people associated with the game. But I think the nice thing that's happened is it seems to be part of a trend anyway, where women are getting in a bit more, families are a bit cooler than they were. Things change.

[EXCERPT FROM PAUL McCARTNEY INTERVIEW BY BEN FONG-TORRES]

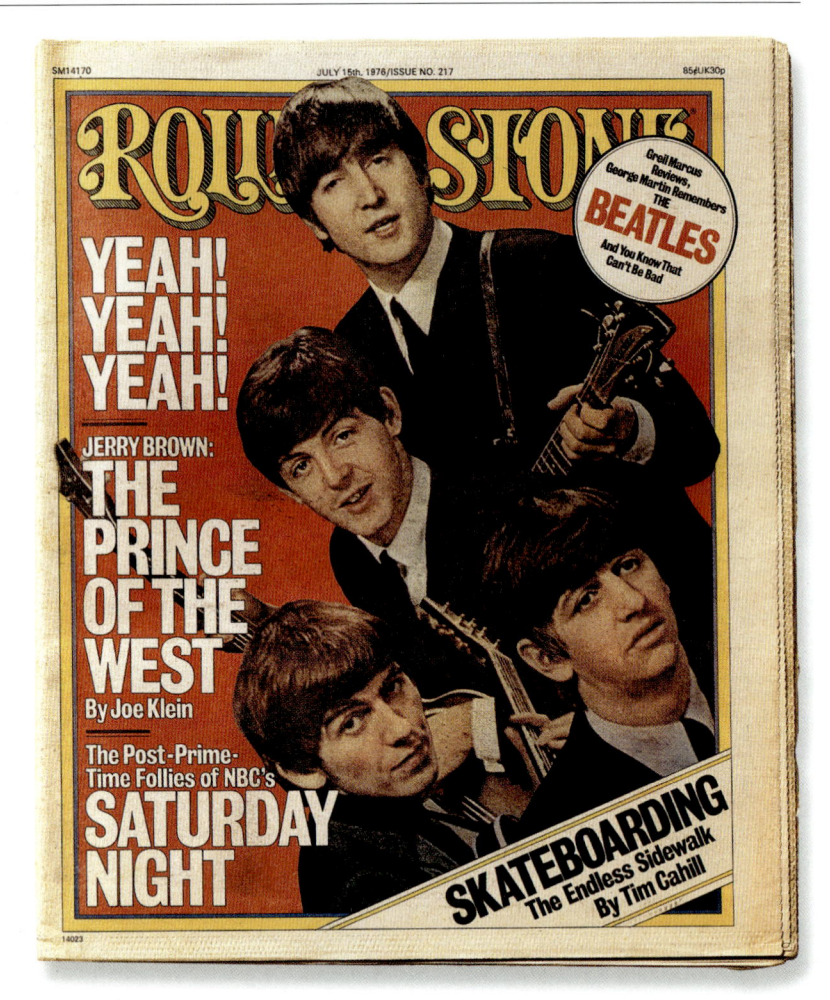

RS 217 | THE BEATLES | July 15th, 1976 | PHOTOGRAPH BY JOHN ZIMMERMAN

There's not a reason in the world to think that were John, Paul, George and Ringo to get together today they'd do more than bump into each other. Yet when geniuses collide... whoever said pop dreams were rational? Hearing what the Beatles did, one can hardly suppress the desire to turn artifact back into process.

[EXCERPT FROM RS 217 COVER STORY BY GREIL MARCUS]

ROLLING STONE

JUNE 17th, 1976/ISSUE NO. 215

YESTERDAY TODAY & PAUL

A Beatle on the Wing, a Band on the Run... but Not Quite the Act You've Known for All These Years By Ben Fong-Torres

STEVE MILLER
More Disguises from the Gangster of Love

THE ART OF UNCLOTHING THE EMPEROR
Jonathan Cott Meets ORIANA FALLACI in the Rolling Stone Interview

BUKOWSKI IN THE RAW
The Dirtiest Old Man in L.A.

1970s

"I STARTED TO follow musical examples, not sociological examples. I realized that how you dressed or how you looked or what you said wasn't as important as whether you had the musical goods.

"I could certainly see George Gershwin as somebody to measure against. Leonard Bernstein is somebody to measure against. Which is not to say that I aspire to write songs like Leonard Bernstein or George Gershwin. But there was an excellence they achieved that was right for their time. . . .

"I don't feel that it is truly significant that my record goes to Number One or that I win a Grammy. Those things are pleasant rewards. . . . But I understand there's a higher standard that can be applied to the work. And then there's a higher standard even than that. When you get to be Gershwin, that doesn't make you Bartók."

—*Paul Simon*

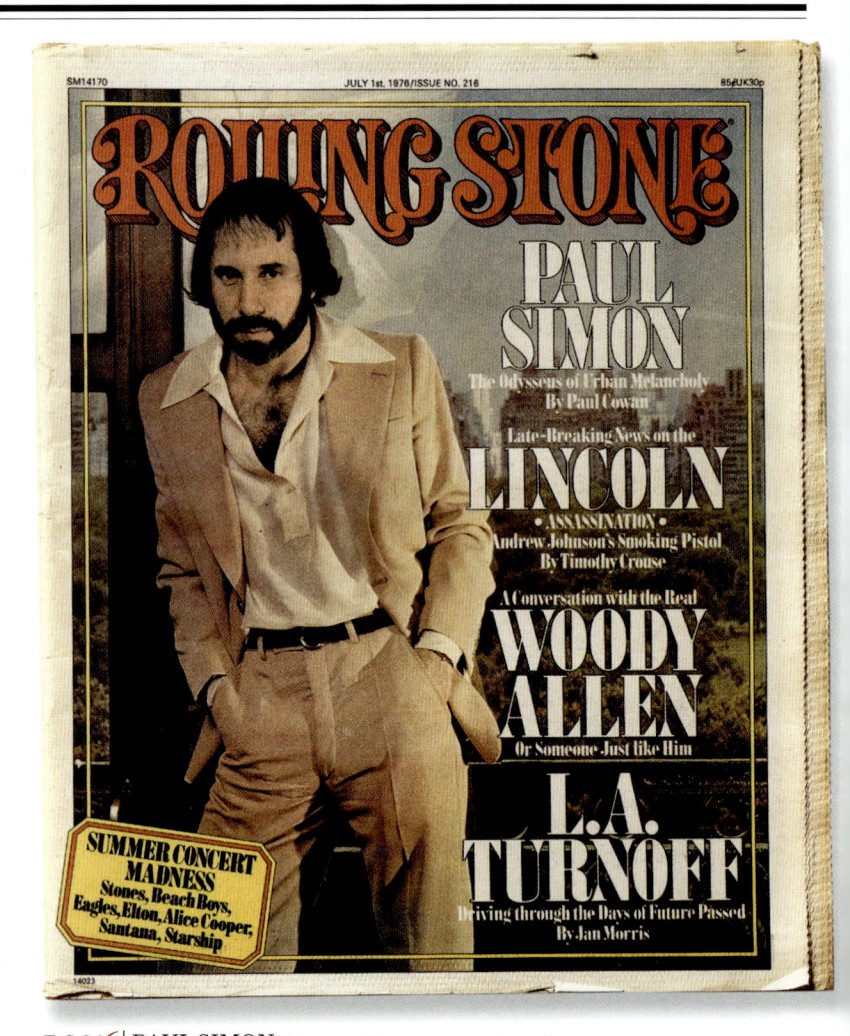

RS 216 | PAUL SIMON | July 1st, 1976 | PHOTOGRAPH BY ANNIE LEIBOVITZ

JULY 29th, 1976/ISSUE NO. 218

ROLLING STONE

WHY JACK FORD STILL LIVES WITH HIS PARENTS
A White House Portrait · By Cameron Crowe

ALFRED HITCHCOCK
Muuuurder... by the Babbling Brook
By Chris Hodenfield

LOGGINS AND MESSINA BREAK UP
A Happy Ending at the Middle of the Road

HEY, DION! MY MAN!
The Return of the Mean Street Wanderer
By Richard Price

RS 218 | JACK FORD | July 29th, 1976 | Photograph by Annie Leibovitz

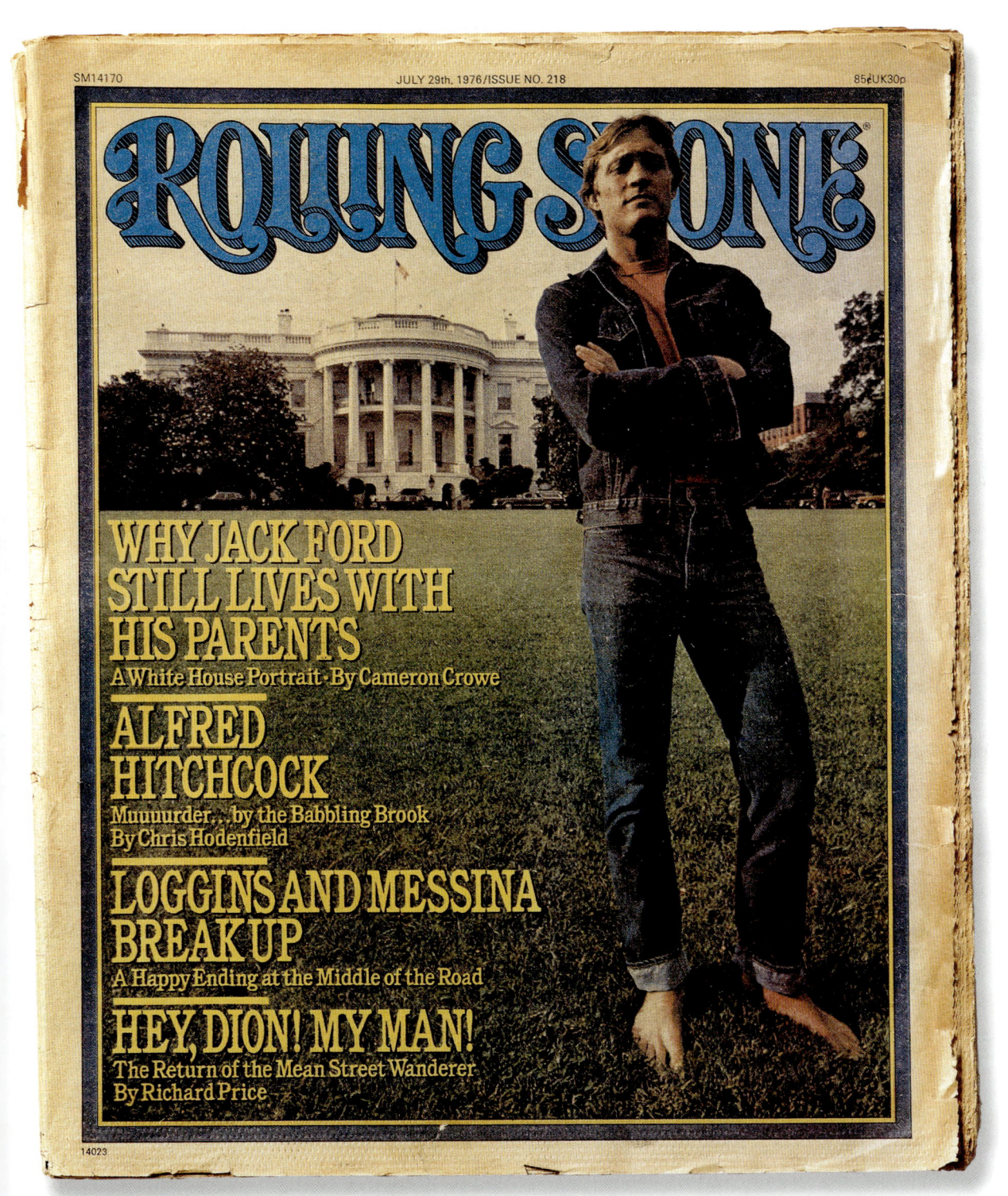

SM11417   AUGUST 12th, 1976 · ISSUE NO. 219   85¢ UK30p

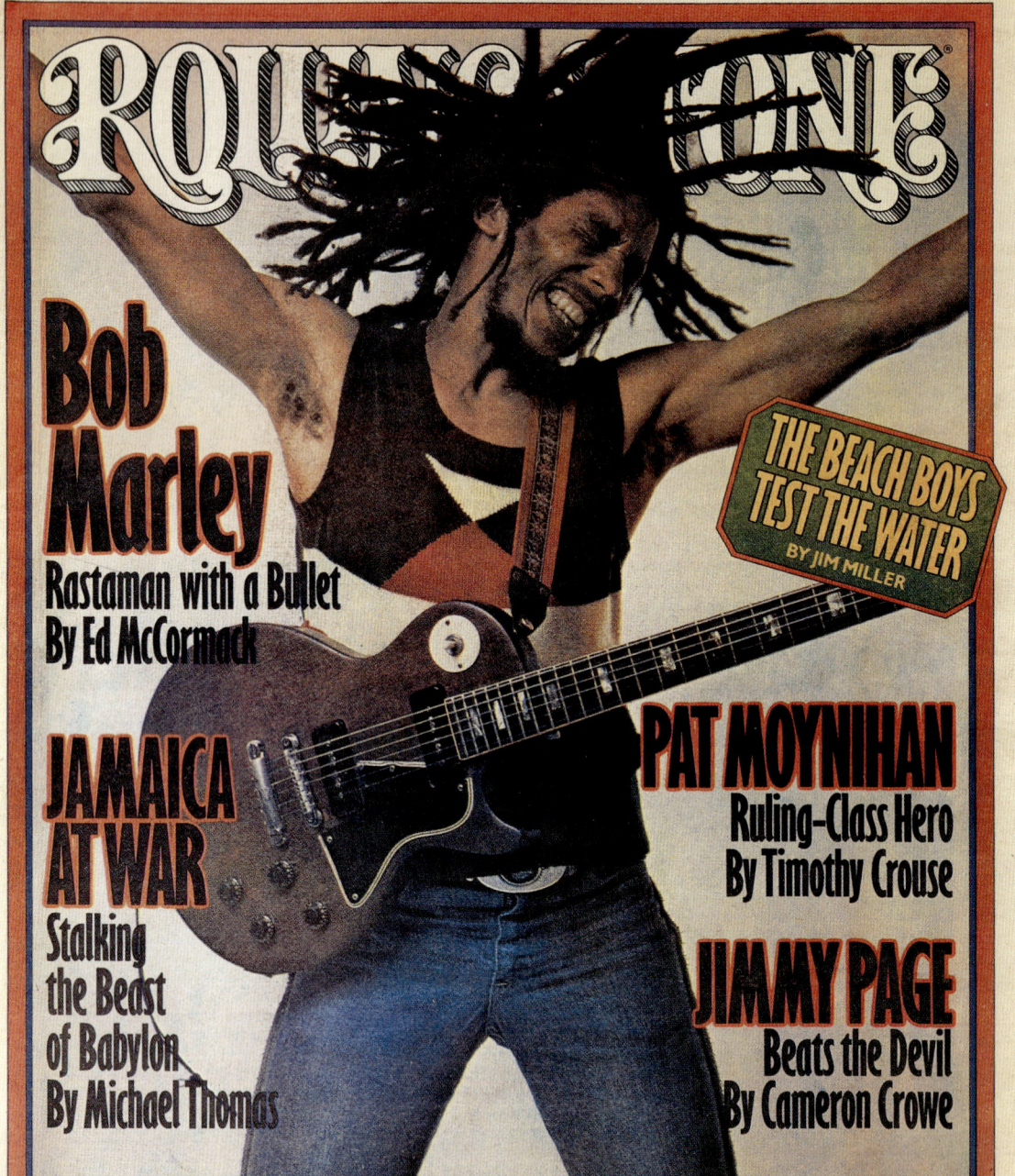

ROLLING STONE

1970s

Bob Marley
Rastaman with a Bullet
By Ed McCormack

JAMAICA AT WAR
Stalking the Beast of Babylon
By Michael Thomas

THE BEACH BOYS TEST THE WATER
By Jim Miller

PAT MOYNIHAN
Ruling-Class Hero
By Timothy Crouse

JIMMY PAGE
Beats the Devil
By Cameron Crowe

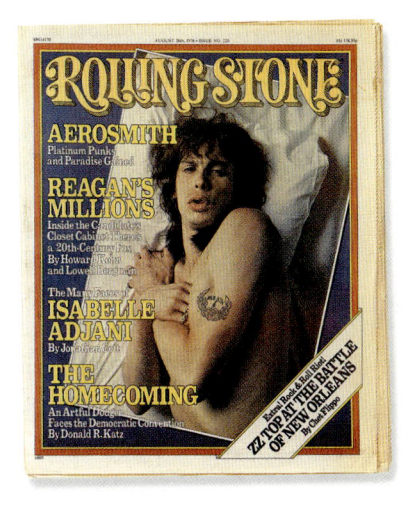

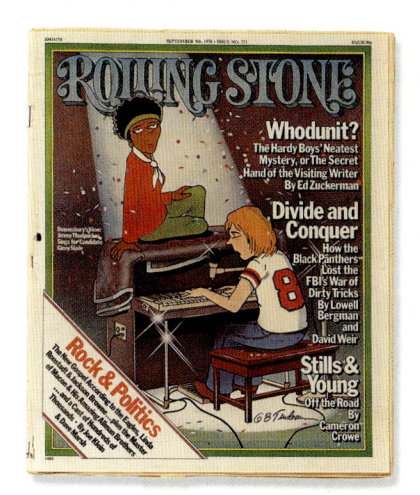

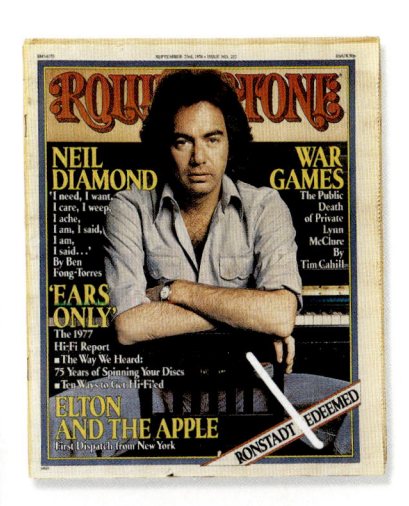

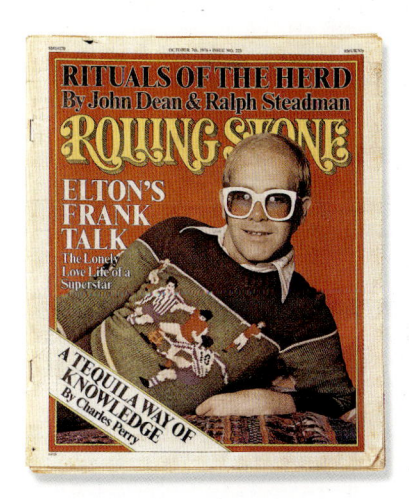

RS 219 | BOB MARLEY
August 12th, 1976
Photograph by Annie Leibovitz

"I FOUND THAT by taking the studio to the person, it looked like they posed for our cover and it built our credibility. With Bob Marley, I set up a studio in his dressing room and waited around. After two nights he started to feel sorry for me and posed for the cover shot."

—*Annie Leibovitz*

RS 220 | STEVEN TYLER
August 26th, 1976
Photograph by Annie Leibovitz

RS 222 | NEIL DIAMOND
September 23rd, 1976
Photograph by Annie Leibovitz

RS 221 | DOONESBURY'S GINNY SLADE & JIMMY THUDPUCKER
September 9th, 1976
Illustration by Garry Trudeau

RS 223 | ELTON JOHN
October 7th, 1976
Photograph by David Nutter

50 YEARS OF COVERS • 105

1970s

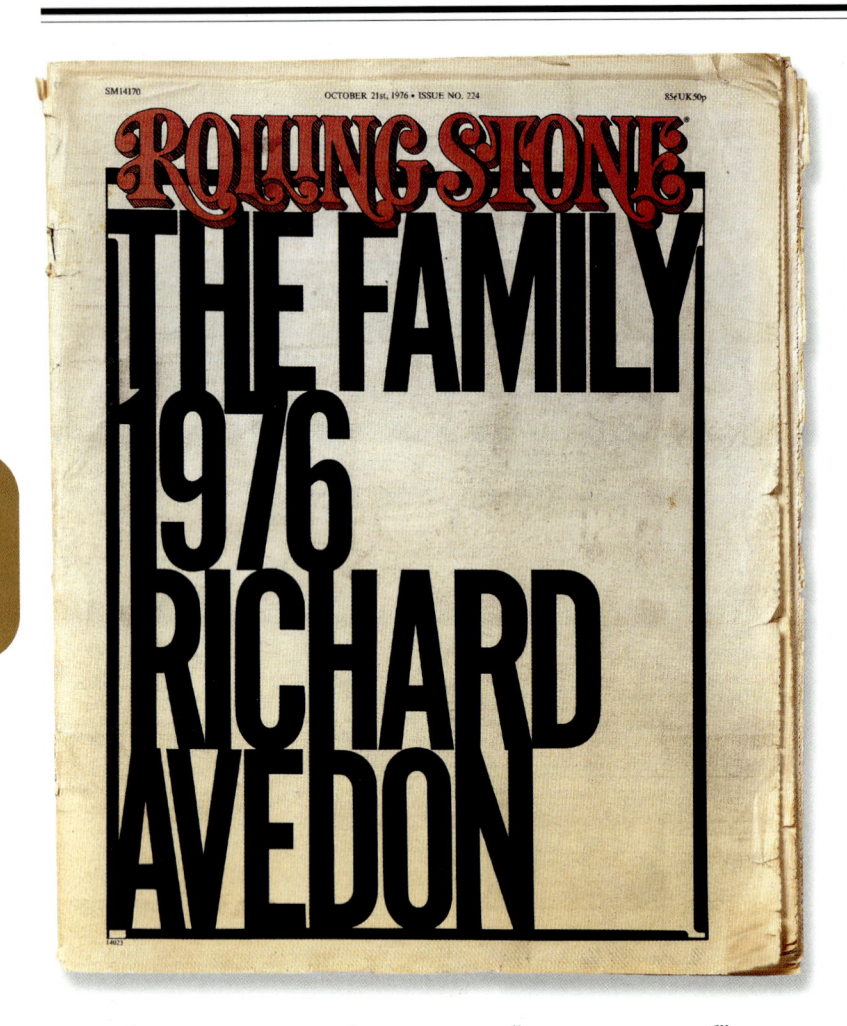

RS 224 | RICHARD AVEDON'S PORTFOLIO "THE FAMILY 1976"
October 21st, 1976 | Typography by Elizabeth Paul

Early this year
we asked Richard Avedon – one of the world's greatest photographers – to cover America's bicentennial presidential election. Our original idea was to publish a chronicle of the campaign – the candidates and the conventions – from beginning to end. Shortly after accepting our commission, Mr. Avedon called to say that there was more to the election than met the eye; that the real story was not simply the candidates, but a broad group of men and women – some of whom we had never heard of before – who constitute the political leadership of America. Thus began a special issue of ROLLING STONE, a collection of seventy-three portraits. This project was edited by Renata Adler, author of *Toward a Radical Middle* and the recently published novel *Speedboat*. Aside from the accompanying *Who's Who* biographies, there is no text; we think the portraits speak for themselves. [RS 224 EDITORS' NOTE]

RS 225 | BRIAN WILSON
November 4th, 1976
PHOTOGRAPH BY ANNIE LEIBOVITZ

> "BRIAN SEEMS to be on acid all the time.... except when he's in his room, where he's completely normal."
> —*Annie Leibovitz*

I HAVE A WRITING BLOCK RIGHT NOW. Even today I started to sit down to write a song, and there was a block there. God knows what that is. Unless it's supposed to be there. I mean, it's not something you just kick and say, "Come on, let's go, let's get a song writ." If the block is there, it's there.

I believe that writers run out of material, I really do. I believe very strongly in the fact that when the natural time is up, writers actually do run out of material. To me, it's black-and-white. When there's a song, there's a song; when there's not, there's not. Of course, you run out, maybe not indefinitely, but everybody that writes runs out of some material for a while. And it's a very frightening experience....

Another thing, too, is that I used to write on pills. I used to take uppers and write, and I used to like that effect. In fact, I'd like to take uppers now and write, because they give me, you know, a certain lift and a certain outlook. And it's not an unnatural thing. I mean, the pill might be unnatural and the energy, but the song itself doesn't turn out unnatural on the uppers. The creativity flows through. I'm thinking of asking the doctor if I can go back to those, yeah.

[EXCERPT FROM BRIAN WILSON INTERVIEW BY DAVID FELTON]

ROLLING STONE

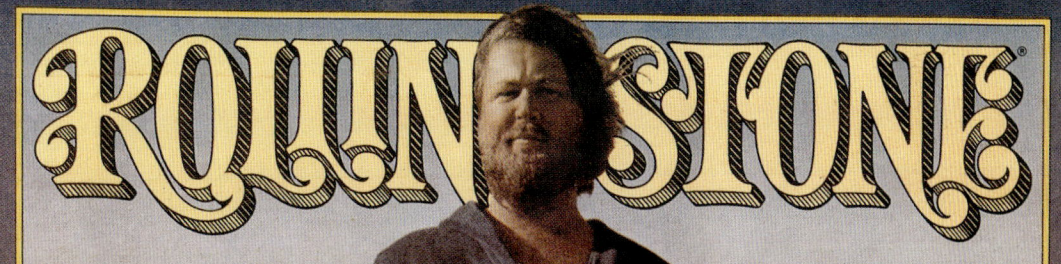

NOVEMBER 4th, 1976 • ISSUE NO. 225

THE HEALING OF BROTHER BRIAN

A Multitrack Interview with Beach Boys Brian, Dennis, Carl, Mike and Al, plus Brian's Mom, His Dad, His Wife and His Shrink
By David Felton

DRAWING FIRE: BILL MAULDIN

and His 35-Year Fight for Truth, Justice and the American Way
By Donald R. Katz

GREGG ALLMAN'S UNHAPPY CONFESSIONS

50 YEARS OF COVERS • 107

1970s

RS 227 | LINDA RONSTADT
December 2nd, 1976
Photograph by Annie Leibovitz

"**BEFORE I OPENED THE BOX,** I gave her a fifteen-minute preamble. 'Now Linda, this is a little far-out, let's try something real different. A fantasy.' I was scared stiff she would flip out. But I opened the box, and she just died. She loved it and put it on immediately. She sent her art director out to get red nail polish to match the underwear."
—*Annie Leibovitz*

RS 226 | JANIS JOPLIN | November 18th, 1976 | Photograph by David Gahr

Janis Joplin belonged to that select group of pop figures who matter as much for themselves as for their music; among American rock performers she was second only to Bob Dylan in importance as a creator/recorder/embodiment of her generation's history and mythology. She was also the only woman to achieve that kind of stature in what was basically a male club, the only Sixties culture hero to make visible and public women's experience of the quest for individual liberation, which was very different from men's. If Janis's favorite metaphors – singing as fucking (a first principle of rock & roll) and fucking as liberation (a first principle of the cultural revolution) – were equally approved by her male peers, the congruence was only on the surface. Underneath – just barely – lurked a feminist (or prefeminist) paradox.

[EXCERPT FROM RS 226 COVER STORY BY ELLEN WILLIS]

SM14170 DECEMBER 2nd, 1976 • ISSUE NO. 227 85¢ UK 50p

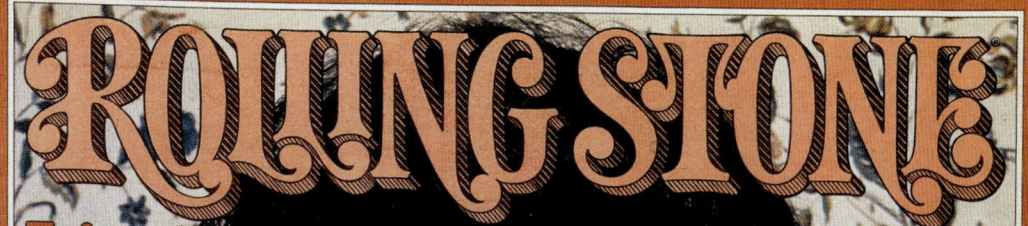

ROLLING STONE

Linda Ronstadt
The Million-Dollar Woman

THE RAPE OF Jimi Hendrix
A Scandal of Lawsuits and Laundered Money

THE NATURAL ACTS OF WINTER
Outside!
Adventure by Tim Cahill, Fiction by Michael Rogers, plus Hardware-Software and the Armchair Rambler

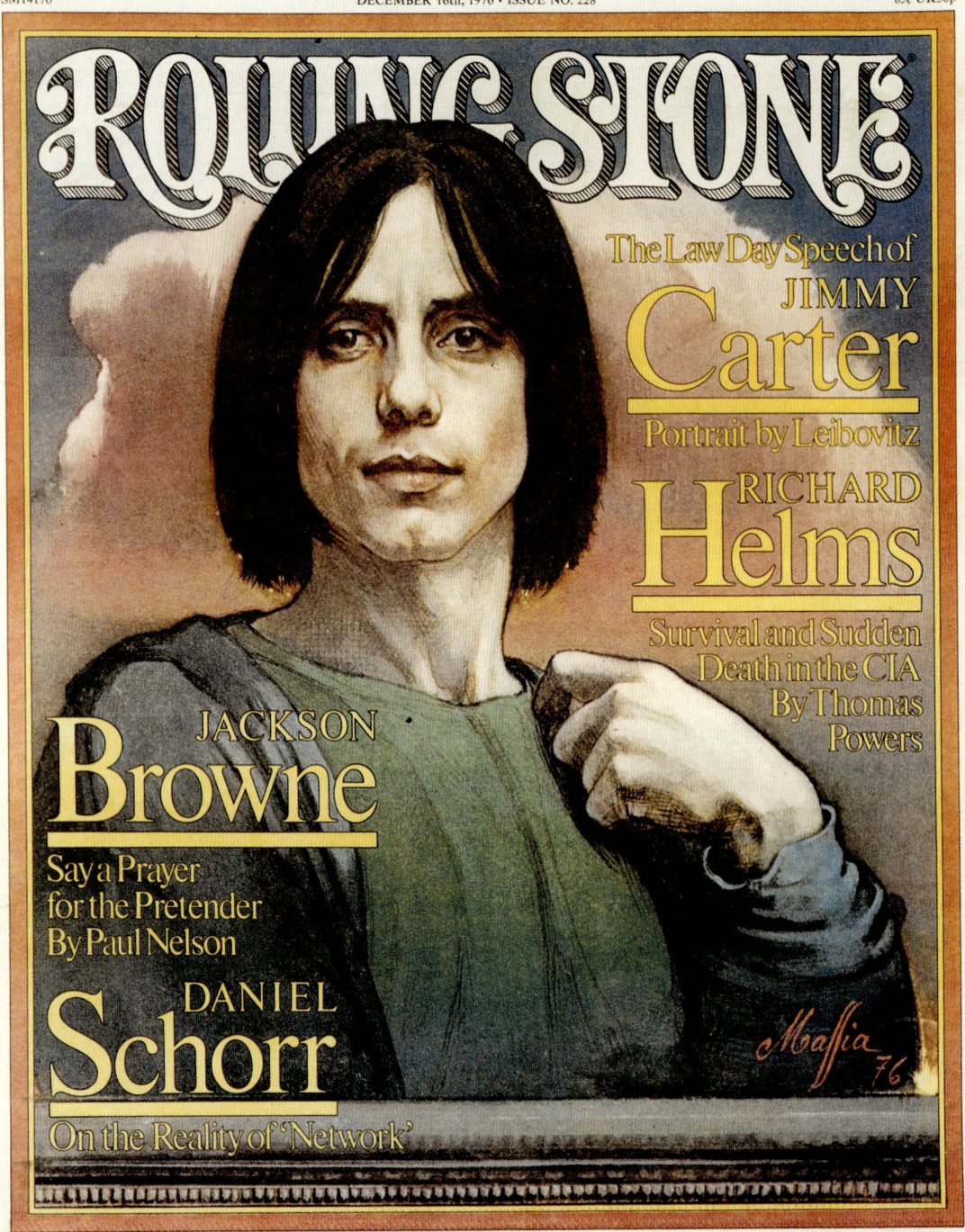

RS 228 | JACKSON BROWNE | December 16th, 1976 | Illustration by Daniel Maffia

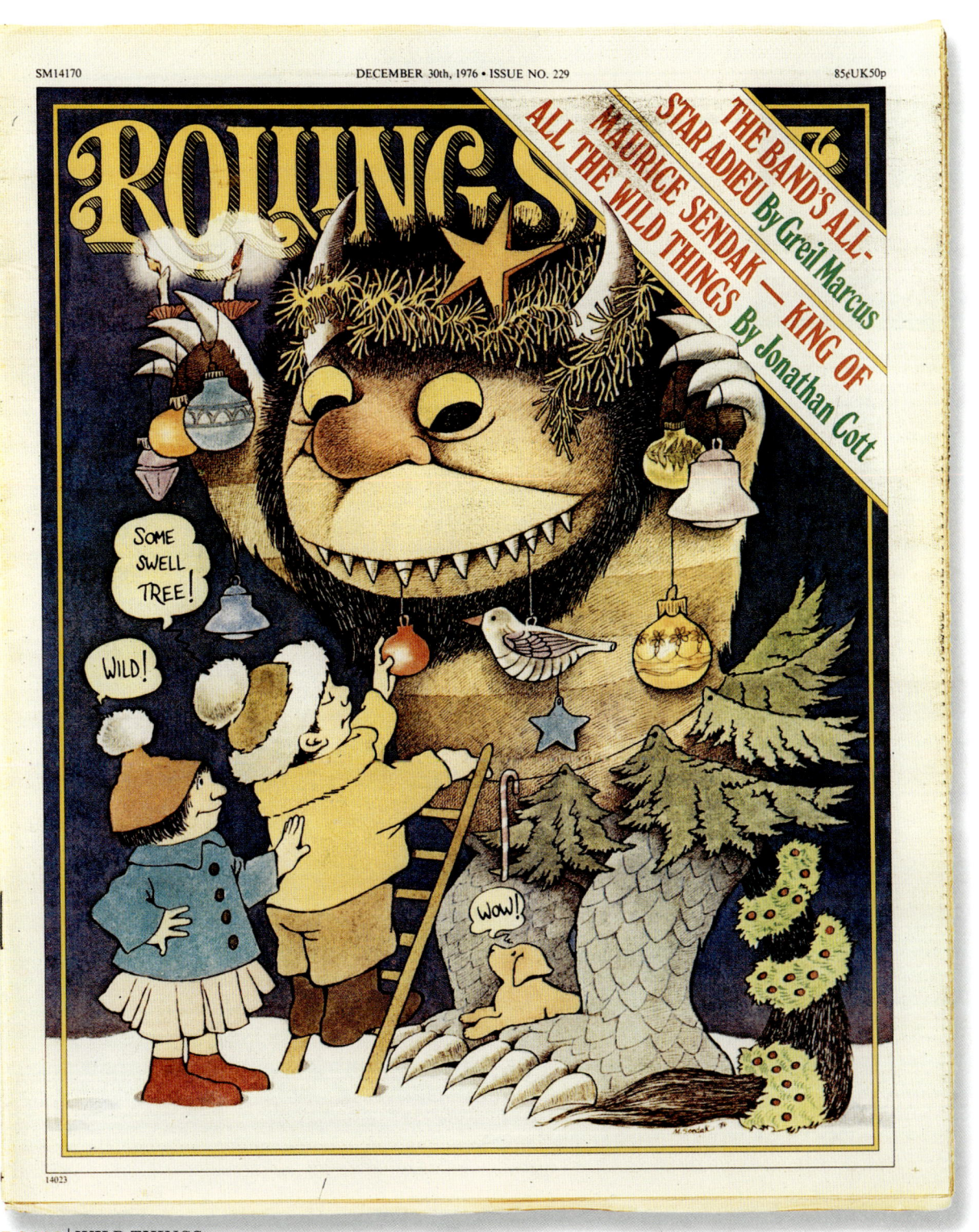

RS 229 | WILD THINGS | December 30th, 1976 | Illustration by Maurice Sendak

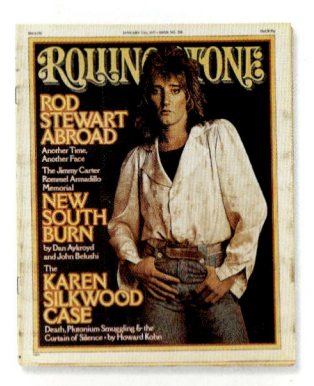

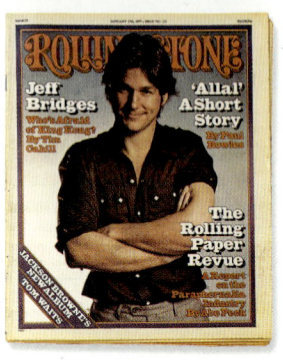

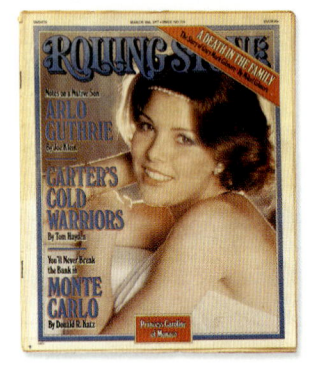

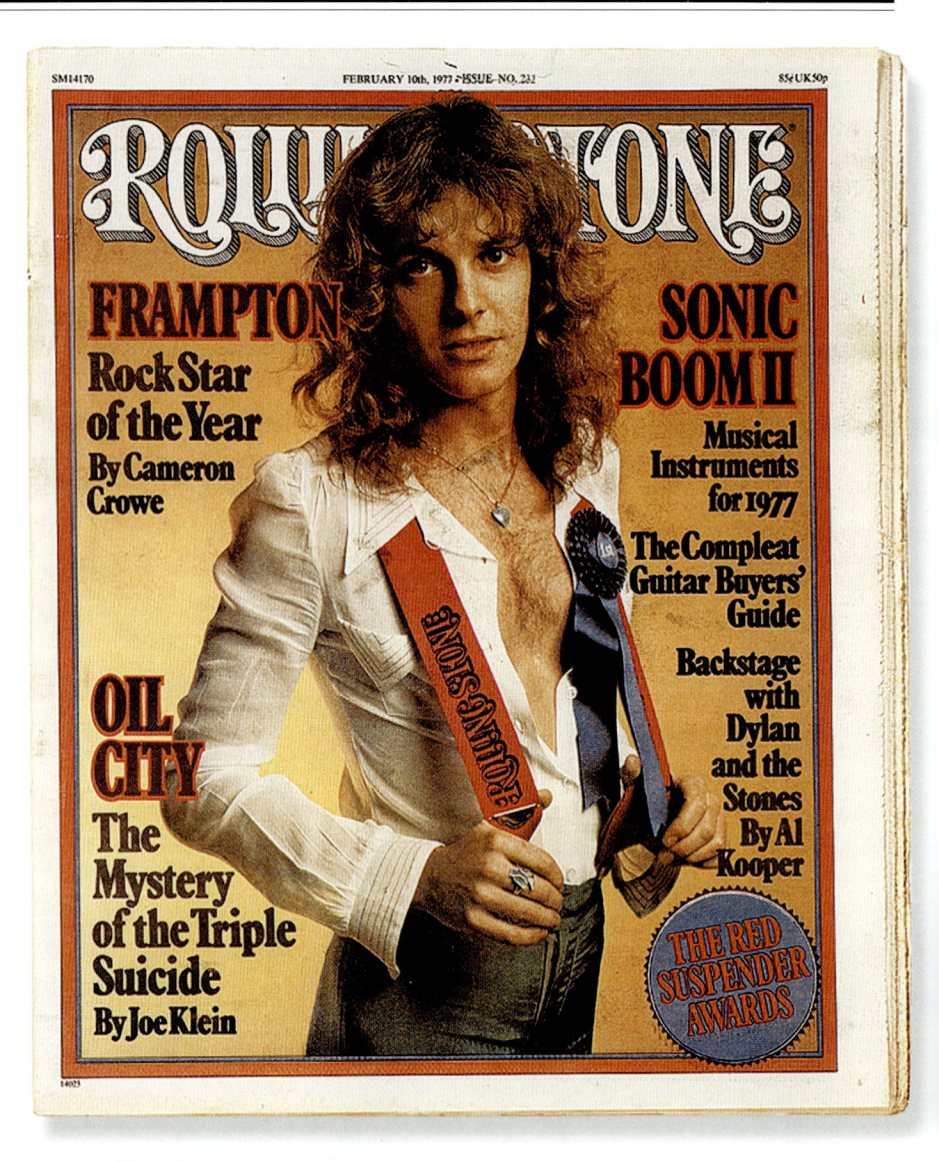

1970s

$\mathcal{RS}$ 230 | ROD STEWART
January 13th, 1977
PHOTOGRAPH BY DAVID MONTGOMERY

$\mathcal{RS}$ 232 | PETER FRAMPTON
February 10th, 1977
PHOTOGRAPH BY ANNIE LEIBOVITZ

$\mathcal{RS}$ 231 | JEFF BRIDGES
January 27th, 1977
PHOTOGRAPH BY ANNIE LEIBOVITZ

$\mathcal{RS}$ 234 | PRINCESS CAROLINE
March 10th, 1977
PHOTOGRAPH BY NORMAN PARKINSON

112 • ROLLING STONE

ROLLING STONE

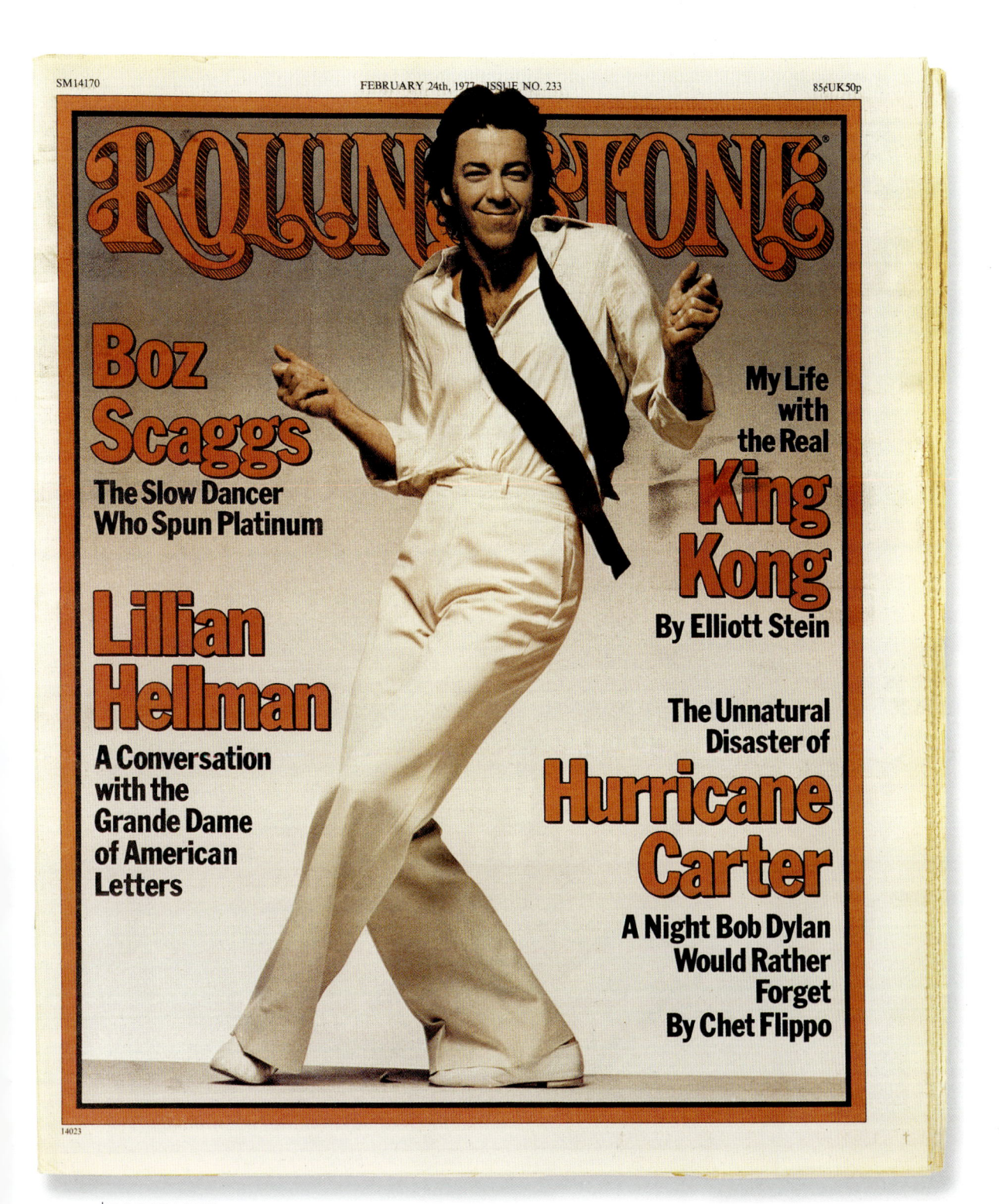

FEBRUARY 24th, 1977 · ISSUE NO. 233

Boz Scaggs
The Slow Dancer Who Spun Platinum

Lillian Hellman
A Conversation with the Grande Dame of American Letters

My Life with the Real King Kong
By Elliott Stein

The Unnatural Disaster of Hurricane Carter
A Night Bob Dylan Would Rather Forget
By Chet Flippo

RS 233 | BOZ SCAGGS | February 24th, 1977 | Photograph by Annie Leibovitz

50 YEARS OF COVERS • 113

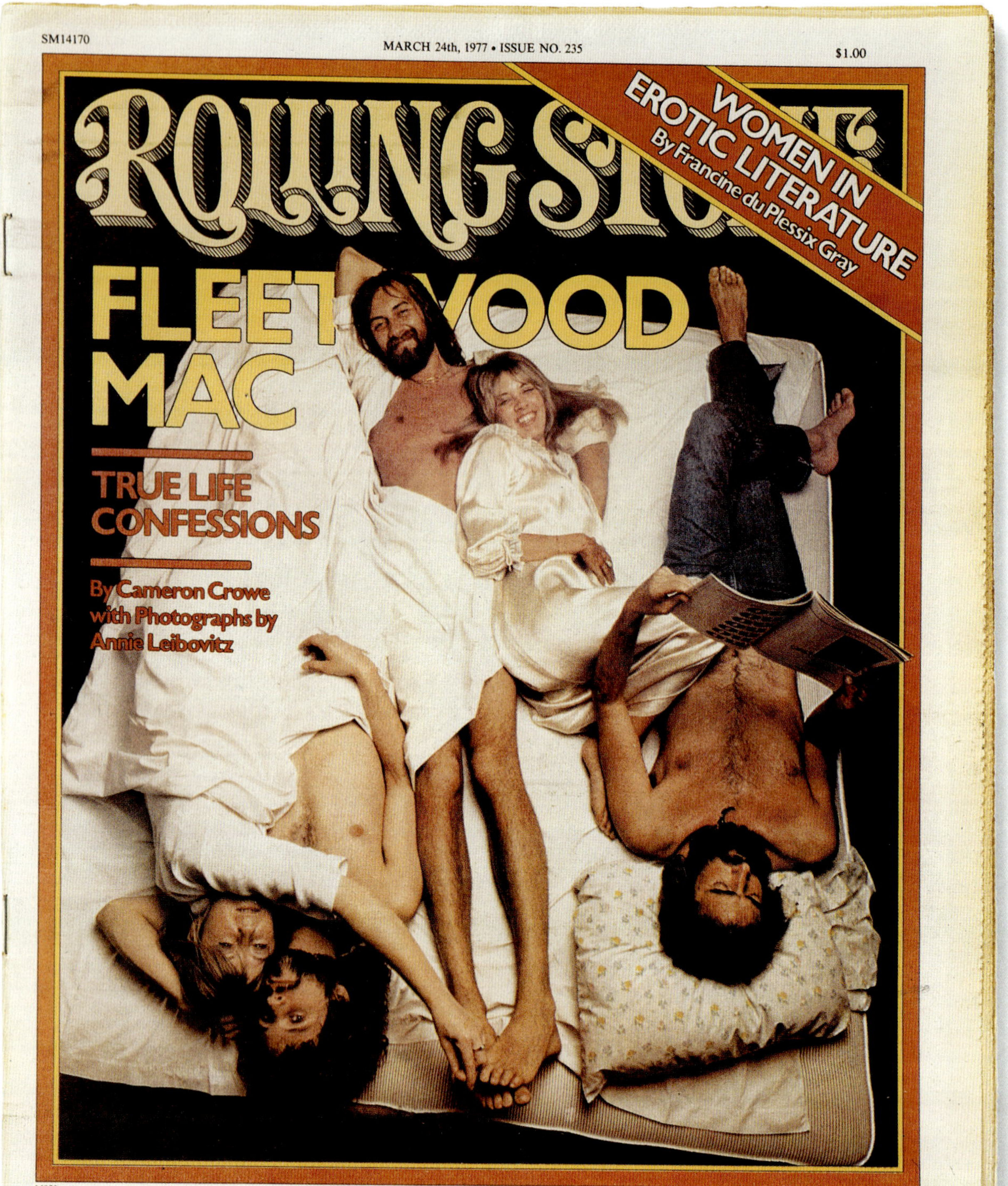

SM14170   MARCH 24th, 1977 • ISSUE NO. 235 $1.00

ROLLING STONE

WOMEN IN EROTIC LITERATURE
By Francine du Plessix Gray

FLEETWOOD MAC
TRUE LIFE CONFESSIONS

By Cameron Crowe
with Photographs by
Annie Leibovitz

1970s

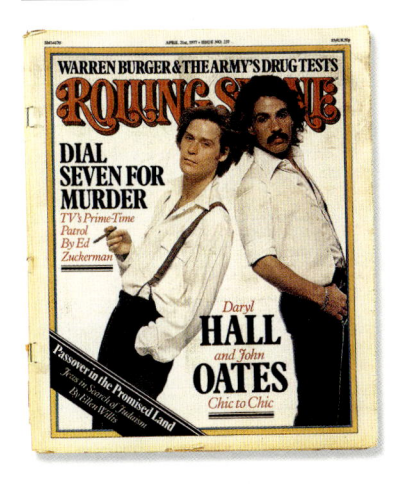

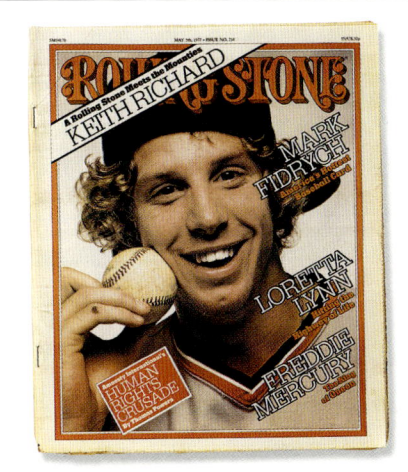

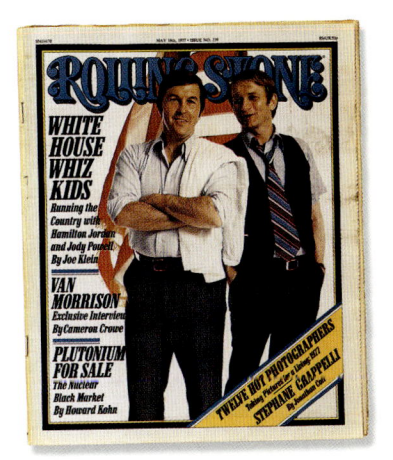

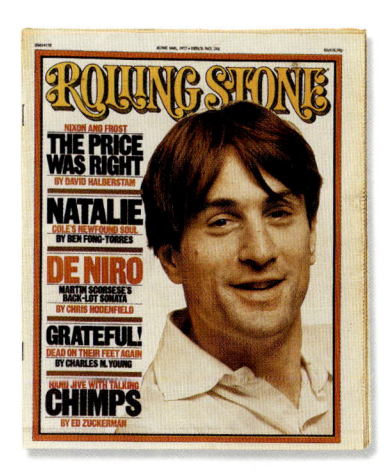

RS 235 | FLEETWOOD MAC
March 24th, 1977
Photograph by Annie Leibovitz

"[FLEETWOOD MAC] was sort of a soap opera – who was with whom, someone had just split up with another one. It was as if each one of them was sort of jumping from bed to bed. It seems like they'd all passed through each other's lives yet were still a *band*."

—*Annie Leibovitz*

RS 237 | DARYL HALL & JOHN OATES
April 21st, 1977
Photograph by Annie Leibovitz

RS 239 | HAMILTON JORDAN & JODY POWELL
May 19th, 1977
Photograph by Annie Leibovitz

RS 238 | MARK FIDRYCH
May 5th, 1977
Photograph by Annie Leibovitz

RS 241 | ROBERT DE NIRO
June 16th, 1977
Photograph by Leonard De Raemy

[RS 238] Mark Fidrych, 1976's Rookie of the Year, is the only baseball player to appear on the cover of Rolling Stone. The six-foot-three Detroit Tigers all-star pitcher – nicknamed "the Bird" for his resemblance to Big Bird from *Sesame Street* – failed to live up to this early promise.

50 YEARS OF COVERS • 115

RS 236 | LILY TOMLIN | April 7th, 1977 | Photograph by Annie Leibovitz

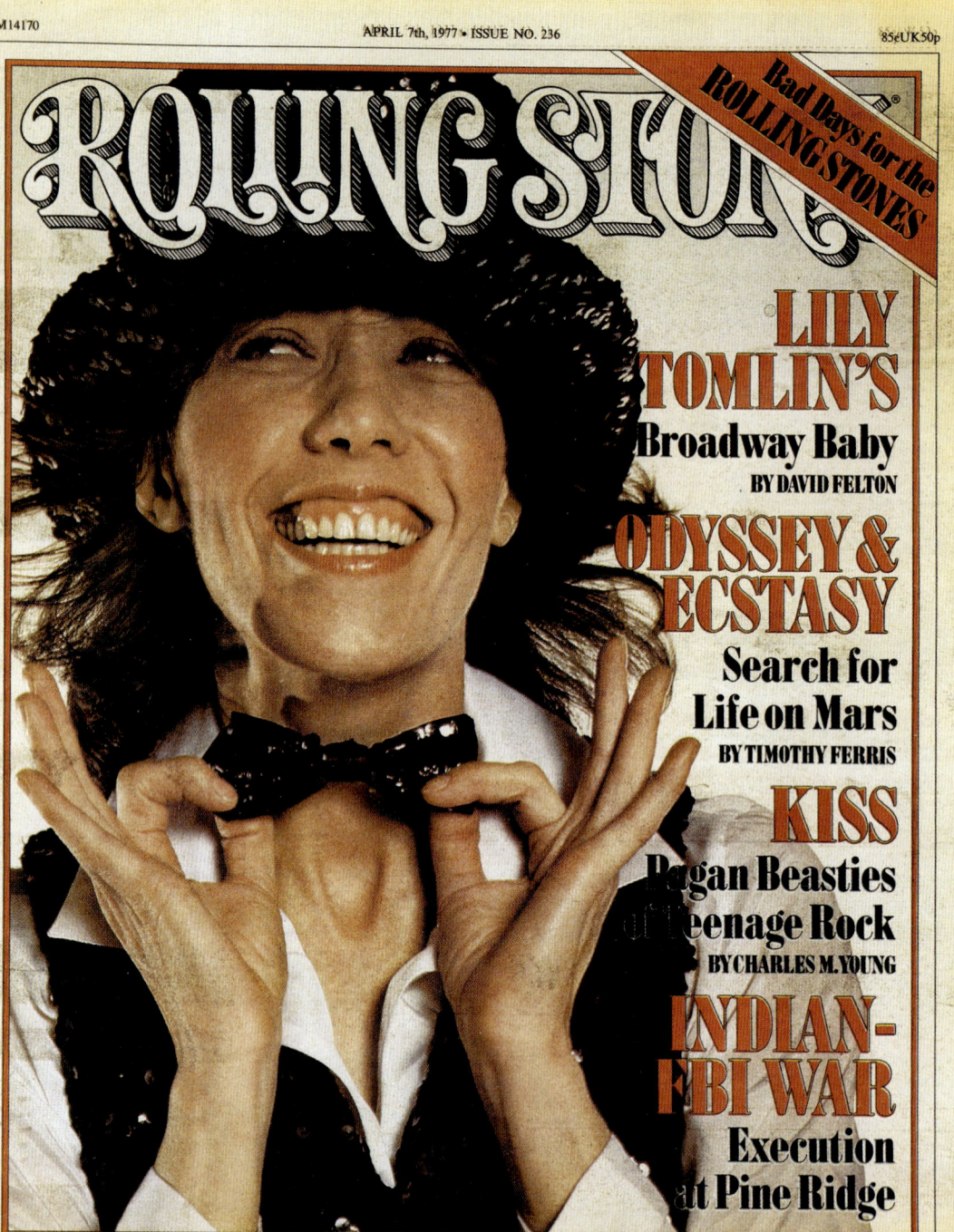

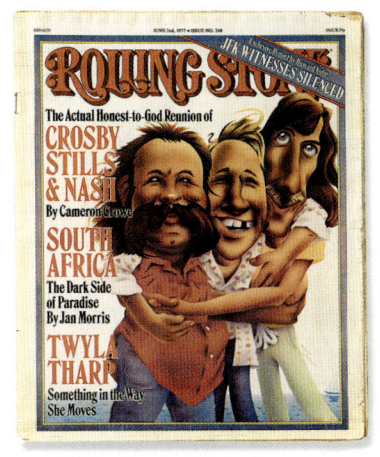

RS 240 | CROSBY, STILLS & NASH
June 2nd, 1977
ILLUSTRATION BY ROBERT GROSSMAN

So Crosby, Stills and Nash –

CSN – are back together. It's 1977, eight years since their first and only album became a rallying point for a budding Woodstock generation. But now Richard Nixon is out of office, the war is over, marijuana is slowly being "decriminalized," and a Democrat is in the White House. Rock music is bigger business than ever, and artists like Peter Frampton and Fleetwood Mac easily outsell the entire CSN catalogue (with or without Neil Young) with a single album.

And yet Young is back with his band, Crazy Horse, and CSN are back in the studio. Another turn around the wheel . . .

There was a time in late 1970, with *Déjà Vu* at its peak, when CSNY were just about the American Beatles. The four of them had clear and separate, slightly adversary identities: Crosby, the former Byrd, the political voice, the California dreamer; Nash, the Briton, the former Hollie, the spiritually hungry searcher; Stills, the guitar hero from Buffalo Springfield; and Young, the brooding dark horse from Canada. They were, at once, steeped in mystique and still the guys next door. . . .

In 1970, after less than two years, CSNY shattered into four directions several months after recording the single "Ohio," backed, ironically, with "Find the Cost of Freedom." . . . But every year or so there was a tease. At least three times they announced attempts to record another CSNY studio album, but each one collapsed in bitterness. In their place, bands like the Eagles, whose members once idolized them, emerged.

And then, two months ago, I got a phone call and invitation from Crosby: "We're doin' it, man. It's CSN, just us this time, and it's coming out. C'mon down and have a listen." A plane flight later, I learned that he was right. For the first time since those nights in 1969, Crosby, Stills and Nash are in harmony. Only one question: Does anybody out there still care?

[EXCERPT FROM RS 240 COVER STORY BY CAMERON CROWE]

1970s

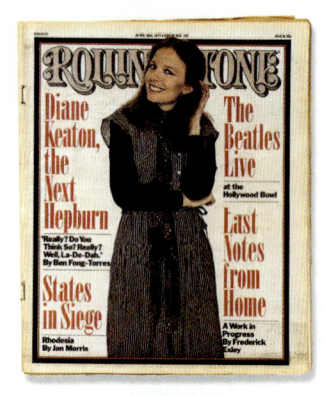

RS 242 | **DIANE KEATON**
June 30th, 1977
Photograph by Hiro

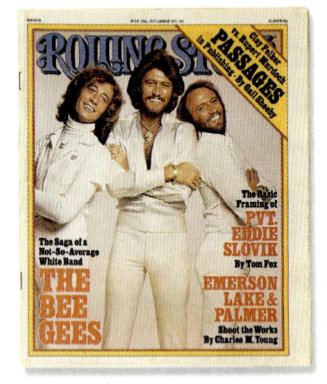

RS 243 | **THE BEE GEES**
July 14th, 1977
Photograph by Francesco Scavullo

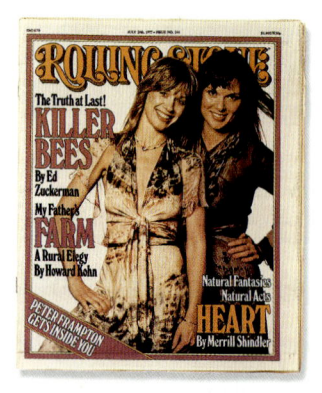

RS 244 | **ANN & NANCY WILSON**
July 28th, 1977
Photograph by Eric Meola

RS 245 | **DIANA ROSS** | August 11th, 1977 | Photograph by Annie Leibovitz

"*I remember* at one point glancing in the mirror and once again saying to myself, Will I have to sit in front of this mirror and spend hours putting on makeup for the rest of my life? This is what I have been doing since I was a child, putting this stuff on my face, then going onstage for two or two and a half hours, maybe three at the most and then having to undergo the misery of taking it all off again. It's not any fun, but there's no getting around it. The lights do strange things to the skin, and heavy stage makeup is necessary. So when I'm not working, I try not to wear much makeup. Particularly in the daytime. . . .

"Back to the face in the mirror. Who is this looking back at me? A woman who with each stroke of the eyeliner, with each brush of the rouge, is transforming into a stage personality. I breathe deeply, searching for relief from the reality in front of me. My mind wanders to distant places, anywhere but here, away from the pressure. When I travel, I love to be invited to use someone's private plane, because that way I can look funky. But that isn't always possible. Sometimes I have to walk through public airports where people see me, and there is this expectation that I look a certain way. I have to be Diana Ross, the performer, the star, not Diana, the human being, the weary traveler. This makes me smile as I write. It is yet another situation where my seemingly glamorous life is really quite difficult."

—*Diana Ross*

AUGUST 11th, 1977 • ISSUE NO. 245

ROLLING STONE

DIANA
(Ross)
Reflections
By O'Connell
Driscoll

A Question of Style
DIANA
(Vreeland)
By Lally Weymouth

CSN AND YOUNG

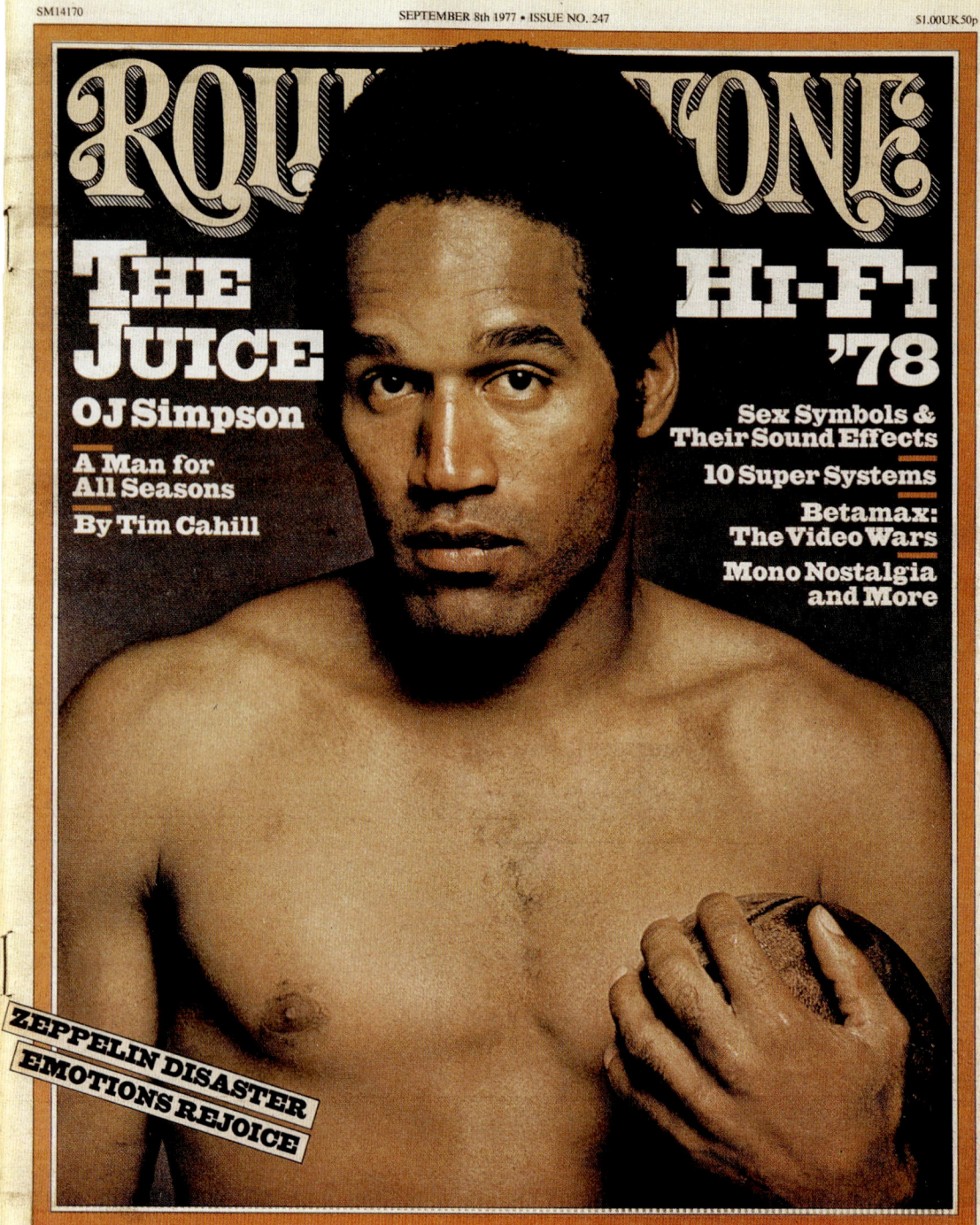

ROLLING STONE

SEPTEMBER 8th 1977 • ISSUE NO. 247

THE JUICE
OJ Simpson
A Man for All Seasons
By Tim Cahill

HI-FI '78
Sex Symbols & Their Sound Effects
10 Super Systems
Betamax: The Video Wars
Mono Nostalgia and More

**ZEPPELIN DISASTER
EMOTIONS REJOICE**

1970s

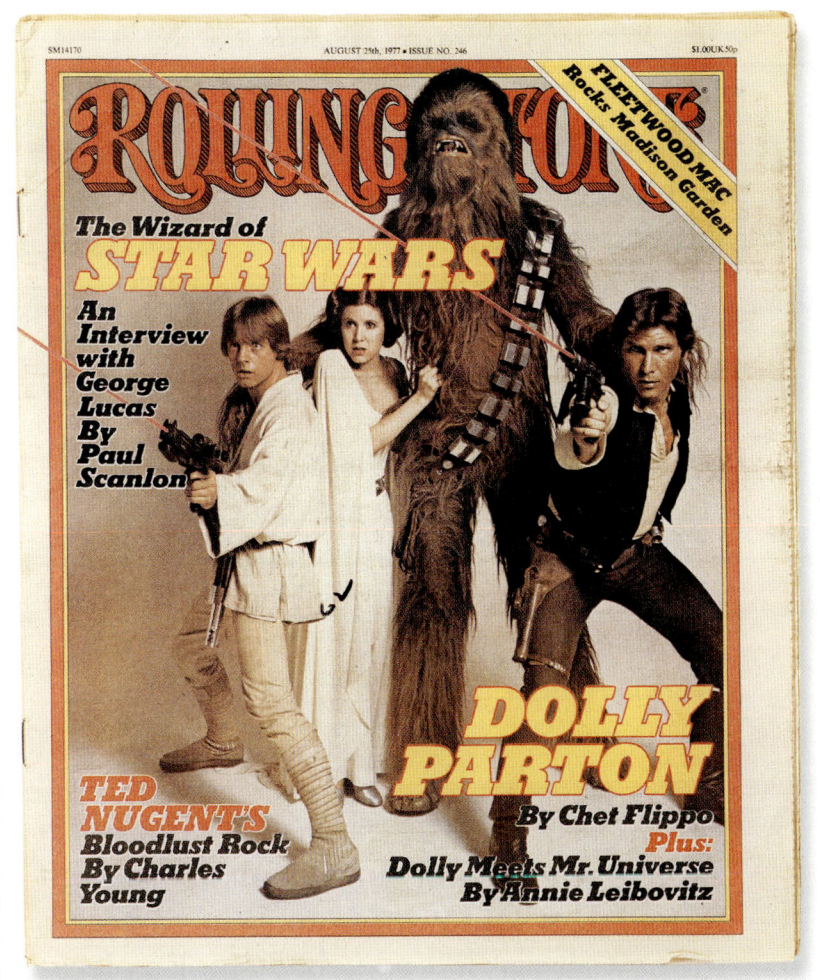

RS 246 | CAST OF 'STAR WARS' | August 25th, 1977 | Photograph by Terry O'Neill

RS 247 | O.J. SIMPSON
September 8th, 1977
Photograph by Annie Leibovitz

[RS 247] The first football player to grace the cover of ROLLING STONE, O.J. Simpson was dabbling in film and becoming known as the TV spokesman for Hertz; his future notoriety was nearly two decades away.

"'Star Wars' is about 25 percent of what I wanted it to be. It's really down there quite a bit. It's still a good movie, but it fell so short of what I wanted it to be. And everyone said, 'Well, Jesus, George, you wanted the moon for Chrissake.' I think the sequels will be much, much better."

—George Lucas

RS 248 | ELVIS PRESLEY | September 22nd, 1977 | PHOTOGRAPHER UNKNOWN

ELVIS PRESLEY was generally considered an overweight Las Vegas nightclub throwback by many rock fans when he died on August 16th, 1977. On the other hand, Jann Wenner, convinced that the man still mattered, decided to scrap an issue ready for the printer and create a brand-new one in honor of the King. His decision was the right one: The issue sold more copies than any other in the history of ROLLING STONE.

1970s

"**THE FIRST TIME I EVER HEARD HIS** music, back in '54 or '55, I was in a car and heard the announcer say, 'Here's a guy who, when he appears onstage in the South, the girls scream and rush the stage.' Then he played 'That's All Right, Mama.' I thought his name was about the weirdest I'd ever heard. I thought for sure he was a black guy.

"Later on I grew my hair like him, imitated his stage act – once I went all over New York looking for a lavender shirt like the one he wore on one of his albums. I did stop liking his music pretty early, though. I felt wonderful when he sang 'Bridge Over Troubled Water,' even though it was a touch on the dramatic side – but so was the song." —*Paul Simon*

"**I LAST SAW HIM LAST DECEMBER IN** Las Vegas. Had a *fantastic* visit, almost two hours, from the time he came off to the time he went back on. We talked about the early days and the recent days. We talked about the people we admired – each other – and people who tried to really perform, from the heart, with soul, as opposed to trying to make commercial records.

"I hope people remember the impact – it's not only historical fact, but it's lingering fact." —*Roy Orbison*

Elvis was the king of rock

& roll because he was the embodiment of its sins and virtues: grand and vulgar, rude and eloquent, powerful and frustrated, absurdly simple and awesomely complex. He was the King, I mean, in our hearts, which is the place where the music really comes to life. And just as rock & roll will stand as long as our hearts beat, he will always be our King: forever, irreplaceable, corrupt and incorruptible, beautiful and horrible, imprisoned and liberated. And finally, rockin' and free, free at last.

—*Dave Marsh*
[EXCERPT FROM ELVIS PRESLEY TRIBUTE]

"**I COULD NOT IMAGINE THAT GUY DYING.** He was so incredibly important to me, to go on and do what I want to do. When I heard the news it was like somebody took a piece out of me. . . . To me, he was as big as the whole country itself, as big as the whole dream. He just embodied the essence of it and he was in mortal combat with the thing. It was horrible and, at the same time, it was fantastic. Nothing will ever take the place of that guy. Like I used to say when I introduced one of his songs: 'There have been a lotta tough guys. There have been pretenders. There have been contenders. But there is only one King.' " —*Bruce Springsteen*

ROLLING STONE

SEPTEMBER 22ND 1977 • ISSUE NO 248

ELVIS PRESLEY
1935-1977

ROLLING STONE

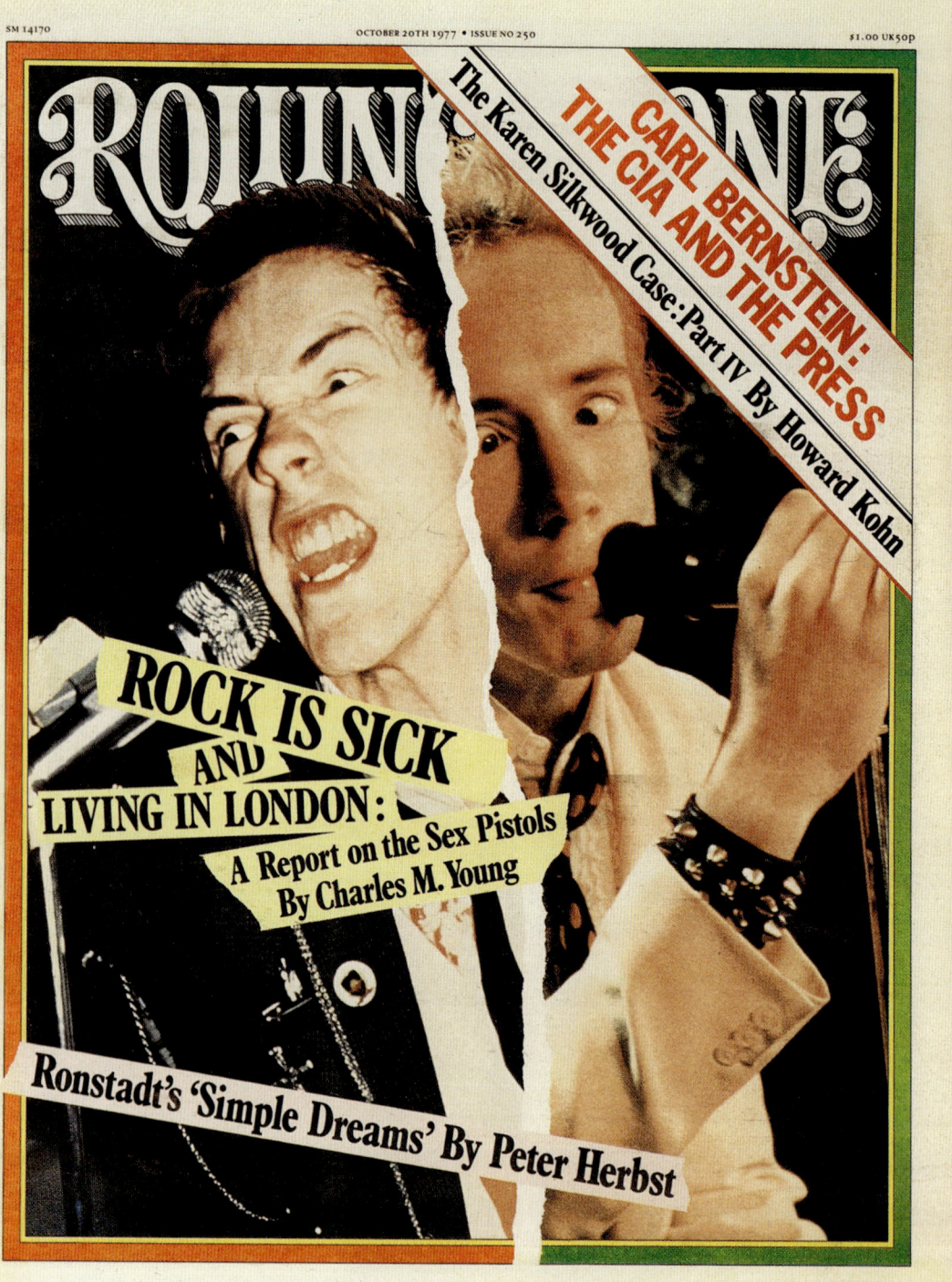

OCTOBER 20TH 1977 • ISSUE NO 250

CARL BERNSTEIN: THE CIA AND THE PRESS
The Karen Silkwood Case: Part IV By Howard Kohn

ROCK IS SICK AND LIVING IN LONDON:
A Report on the Sex Pistols By Charles M. Young

Ronstadt's 'Simple Dreams' By Peter Herbst

RS 250 | JOHNNY ROTTEN | October 20th, 1977 | Photographs by Bob Gruen, Dennis Morris

A little before midnight, my taxi arrives at a club called the Vortex. Half a block away ten or twelve teenage boys dressed like horror-movie morticians jump up and down and hit each other. Their hair is short, either greased back or combed to stick straight out with a pomade of Vaseline and talcum powder. Periodically, one chases another out of the pack, grabs the other's arm and twists it until he screams with pain. Then they rush back laughing and leap about some more. Sitting oblivious against a building, a man dressed in a burlap bag nods gently as a large puddle of urine forms between his legs.

Shouting epithets at themselves in a thick proletarian accent, the boys finally bob down the street as another cab pulls up to the entrance. A man with curly, moderately long red hair, a pale face and an apelike black sweater gets out. It is Malcolm McLaren, manager of the Sex Pistols, the world's most notorious punk band, who I have flown from New York to meet and see perform. McLaren has been avoiding me for two days. I introduce myself and suggest we get together soon. He changes the subject by introducing me to Russ Meyer, the soft-core porn king of *Supervixens* and *Beyond the Valley of the Dolls* fame, who is directing the Sex Pistols' movie. "You're a journalist?" asks Meyer. "Do you know Roger Ebert? He won the Pulitzer Prize for film criticism, and he's writing the movie with me. You should talk to him. He's really into tits."

McLaren seizes the opportunity to disappear into the Vortex and is lost to me for the rest of the evening. The dense crowd inside consists of a few curiosity seekers and four hundred to five hundred cadaverous teenagers dressed in black or gray. Often their hair is dyed shades of industrial pink, green and yellow. Several blacks, also drably dressed and with rainbow stripes dyed into their short Afros, speckle the audience. The music over the loudspeakers is about two-thirds shrieking New Wave singles and one-third reggae tunes, which the kids respond to with almost as much enthusiasm as the punk rock. The dancing is frantic as a band called the Slits sets up. The style is called pogo dancing – jumping up and down and flailing one's arms around. It is as far as one can get from the Hustle, and it is the only way one can dance if one is wearing bondage pants tied together at the knees. Most are pogoing alone. Those with partners (usually of the same sex) grasp each other at the neck or shoulders and act like they are strangling each other. Every four or five minutes, someone gets an elbow in the nose and the ensuing punch-out lasts about thirty seconds amid a swirling mass of tripping bodies.

[EXCERPT FROM RS 250 COVER STORY BY CHARLES M. YOUNG]

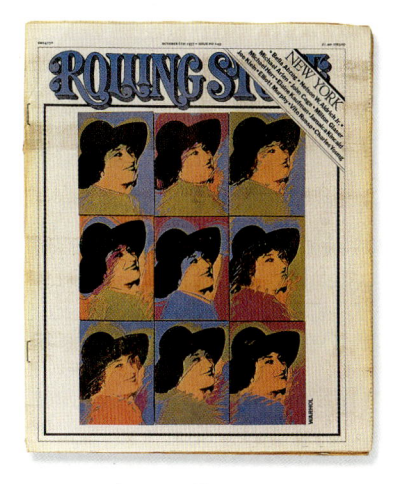

RS 249 | BELLA ABZUG
October 6th, 1977
ILLUSTRATION BY ANDY WARHOL

[RS 249] To celebrate the magazine's relocation to New York City from San Francisco, ROLLING STONE devoted the entire feature well to New York and commissioned Andy Warhol to create a cover portrait of mayoral primary candidate Bella Abzug, who contributed her own personal guide to the city (she lost the election, by the way, to Ed Koch). Wrote the editors: "A Columbia University sociologist recently published a study which suggests that people who live in big cities appear to be mentally healthier than those who live in small towns and rural areas. At a time when mere residence in New York was thought to be hazardous to the central nervous system, this study was particularly heartening to us, poised as we were for a great leap across the country to our new offices in midtown Manhattan – after all, ROLLING STONE has been coming to you from various funky offices in San Francisco for nearly ten years.... It occurred to us that an issue devoted to New York would helps us come to grips with what some call the center of the universe and others call the pits, and at the same time announce that we were here."

1970s

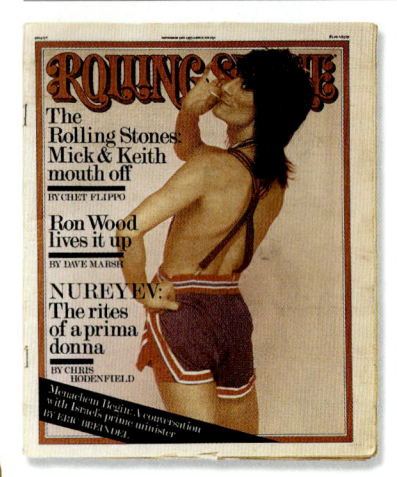

RS 251 | RON WOOD
November 3rd, 1977
Photograph by Annie Leibovitz

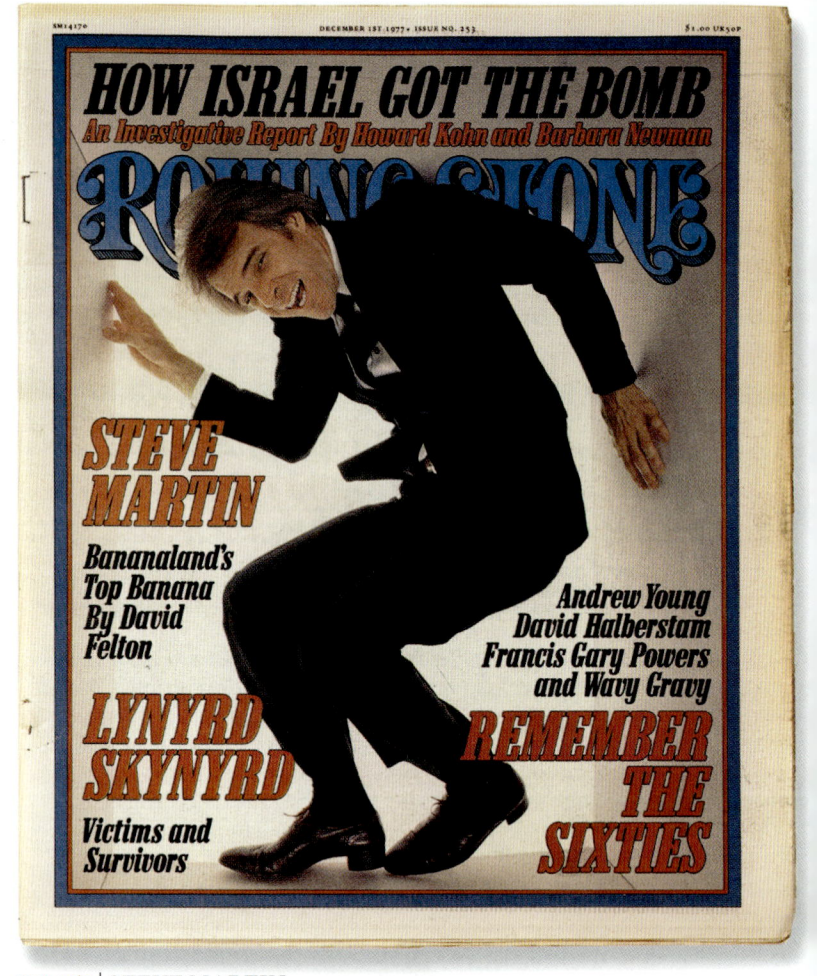

RS 253 | STEVE MARTIN | December 1st, 1977 | Photograph by Annie Leibovitz

"I remember Martin Mull
sent me a note, and he said, 'Congratulations on being on the cover of Rolling Stone. Too bad you weren't on when it really meant something.'"

—Steve Martin

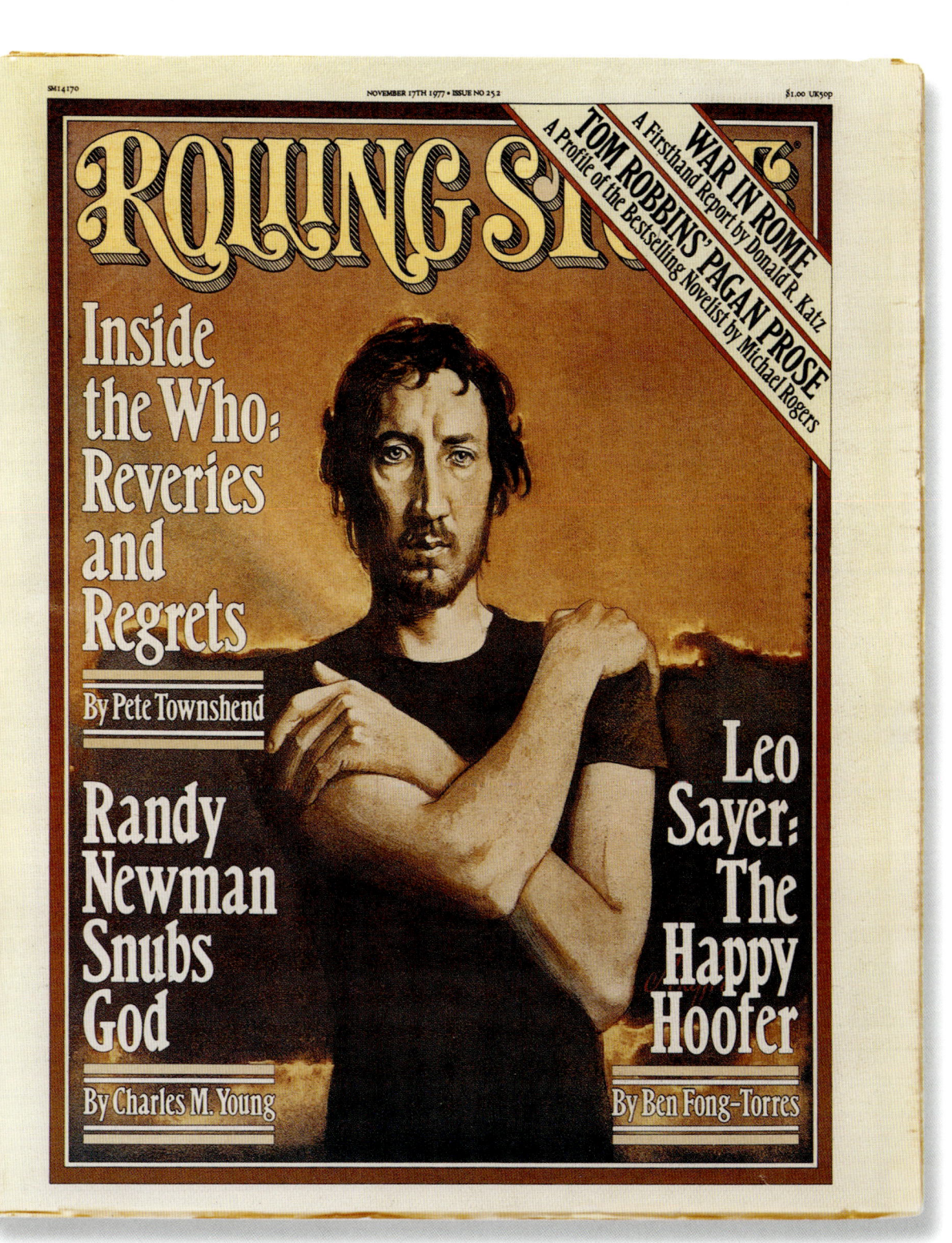

RS 252 | PETE TOWNSHEND | November 17th, 1977 | Illustration by Daniel Maffia

SM14170: ISSUE NUMBER 254 — THE TENTH ANNIVERSARY ISSUE — DECEMBER 15, 1977: $1.50 UK75P

Rolling Stone

DR. HUNTER S. THOMPSON
Fear & Loathing: The Banshee Screams for the Buffalo

ANNIE LEIBOVITZ
A special fifty-page color collection of Greatest Hits · Plus A Decade in the Life

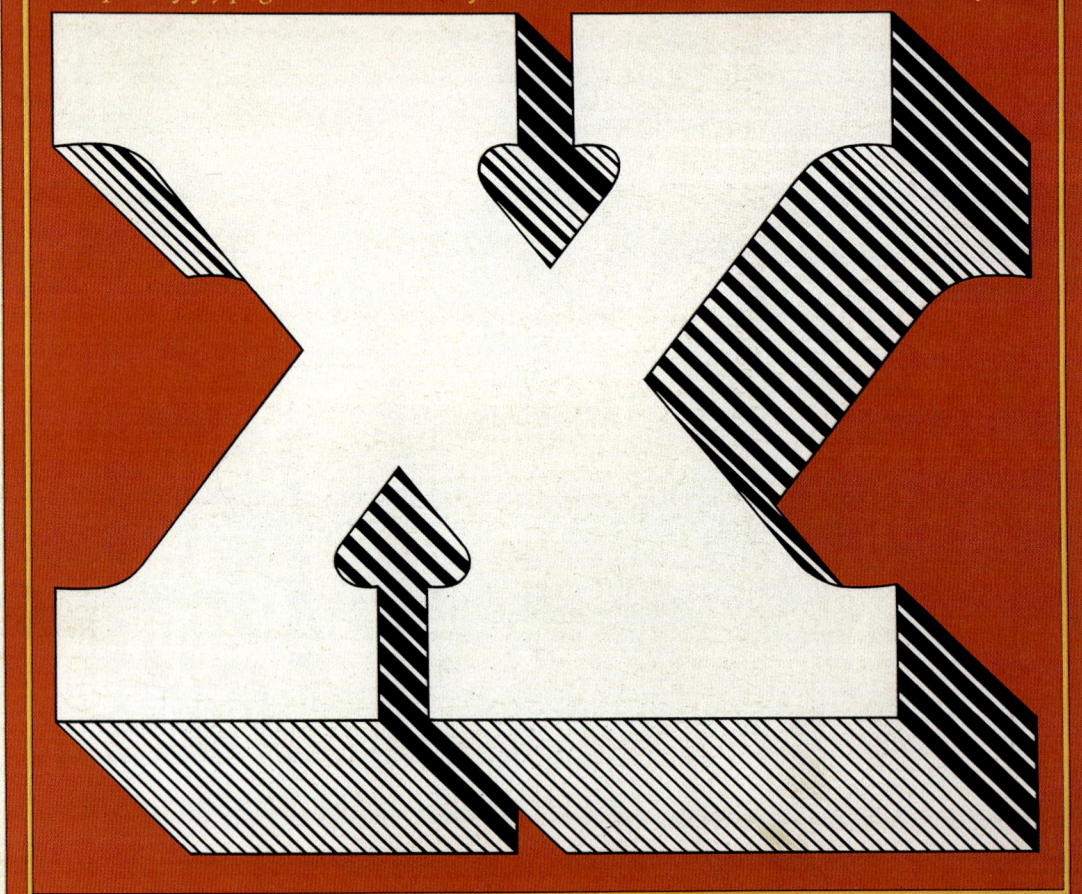

1970s

RS 254 | TENTH ANNIVERSARY | December 15th, 1977 | Typography by Jim Parkinson

Change – the ability to see it and live with it – explains much of what ROLLING STONE is about. In this issue we have yet another change: a new logo. It symbolizes as much as anything what we are up to: respectful of our origins, considerate of new ideas and open to the times to come.

—*Jann S. Wenner*

"'ROLLING STONE' HAS – FROM THE FIRST – covered events and personalities that are not always a purist's idea of rock & roll. What the purists forget is that 'rock & roll' means much more than just the music. Anyone who ever took those words to heart knows that; knows that there are books and movies and people and events and attitudes that matter more to a rock & roll way of life than do many records that are labeled rock & roll. Jack Kerouac was rock & roll; Bobby Rydell was not. Tom Robbins is rock & roll; Andy Gibb is not. *Star Wars* is rock & roll; *A Star Is Born* is not. . . .

"At this very minute, I can hear two other typewriters rattling away: Carl Bernstein is in the next office writing about the CIA, and next door to him John Swenson is hammering out a story on a near breakup of the Beach Boys. Both stories mean a great deal here, and that kind of mixture of subjects under the umbrella of rock & roll is exactly what ROLLING STONE is about."

—*Chet Flippo*
ASSOCIATE EDITOR

The Tenth Anniversary issue introduces a new logo, drawn by Jim Parkinson. It's based on "Roman and Italic typefaces that revolutionized printing in the Fifteenth Century," according to the editors. The issue's contents include a fifty-page portfolio of Annie Leibovitz's photography from 1970, when she first shot for the magazine, to 1977. Designer Bea Feitler, previously art director of *Harper's Bazaar* and *Ms.*, came aboard to work with art director Roger Black on putting together the photo section. Also featured were musings by the magazine's then so-called lifers: Hunter S. Thompson, Dave Marsh, Jon Landau, David Felton, Jonathan Cott and Chet Flippo.

"'ROLLING STONE' IS MORE than grinding out a magazine every two weeks, converting whole forests to self-serving pulp, exposing innocent lives, laughing at cripples and stomping on budding careers just to make a fast buck. It's people. Presently 101 people work full-time for the magazine, and all of them, practically without exception, are young, gifted, industrious, well groomed and ruggedly individualistic. Also completely nuts. Believe me, I know what I'm talking about; I've worked here for eight years. They are all nuts – maybe not dangerously nuts or dysfunctionally nuts or down-and-out, desperate-and-broken nuts, but they are definitely, certifiably and incorrigibly gonzo cuckoo bananas."

—*David Felton*
ASSOCIATE EDITOR

1970s

Rock & roll isn't rock & roll anymore.
You're right, there's no more rock & roll. It's an imitation, we can forget about that. Rock & roll has turned itself inside out. I never did do rock & roll, I'm just doing the same old thing I've always done.
You've never sung a rock & roll song?
No, I never have, only in spirit.
You can't really dance to one of your songs.
I couldn't.
Imagine dancing to "Rainy Day Woman #12 & 35." It's kind of alienating. Everyone thought it was about being stoned, but I always thought it was about being alone.
So did I. You could write about that for years.... Rock & roll ended with Phil Spector. The Beatles weren't rock & roll either. Nor the Rolling Stones. Rock & roll ended with Little Anthony and the Imperials. Pure rock & roll.
With "Goin' Out of My Head"?
The one before that. Rock & roll ended in 1959.

[EXCERPT FROM BOB DYLAN INTERVIEW BY JONATHAN COTT]

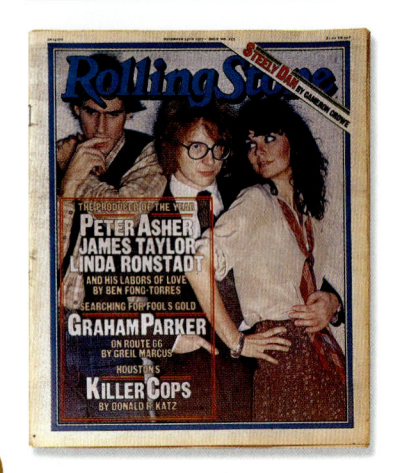

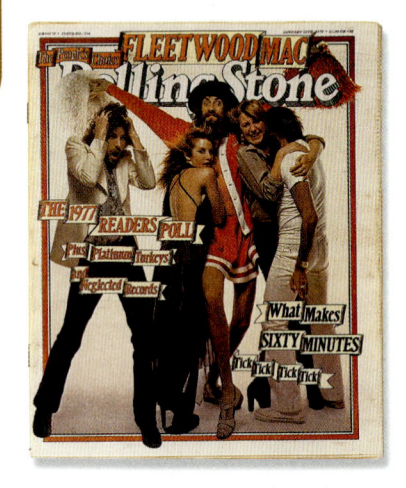

RS 255 | JAMES TAYLOR, PETER ASHER & LINDA RONSTADT
December 29th, 1977
Photograph by Annie Leibovitz

RS 256 | FLEETWOOD MAC
January 12th, 1978
Photograph by Annie Leibovitz

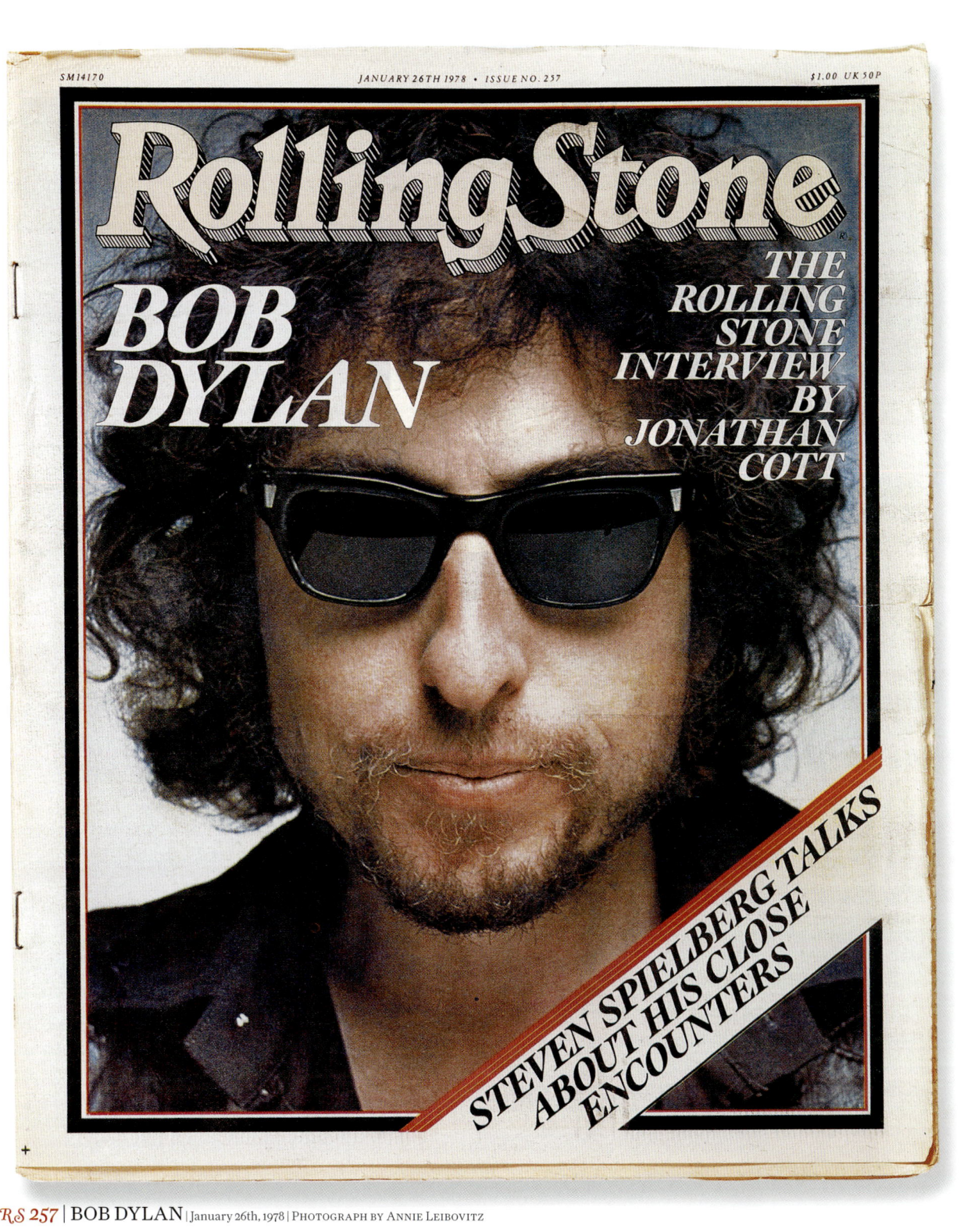

RS 257 | BOB DYLAN | January 26th, 1978 | Photograph by Annie Leibovitz

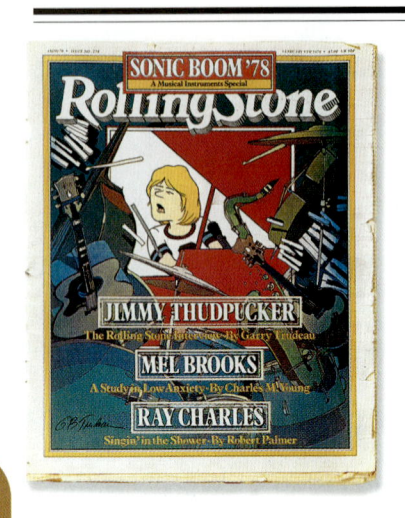

1970s

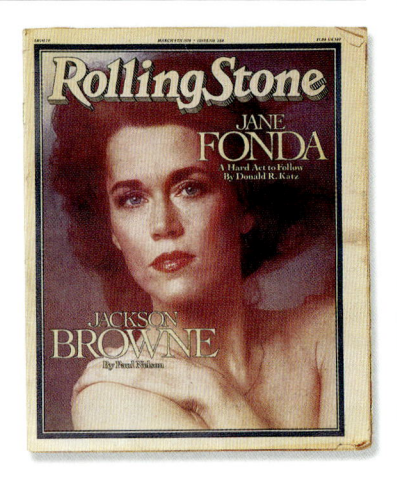

RS 260 | JANE FONDA
March 9th, 1978
PHOTOGRAPH BY ANNIE LEIBOVITZ

"WHEN I WAS TWELVE I WAS on the cover, and it was the first time I'd been on the cover, and I was thrilled. I felt so cool and so hip."
—*Brooke Shields*

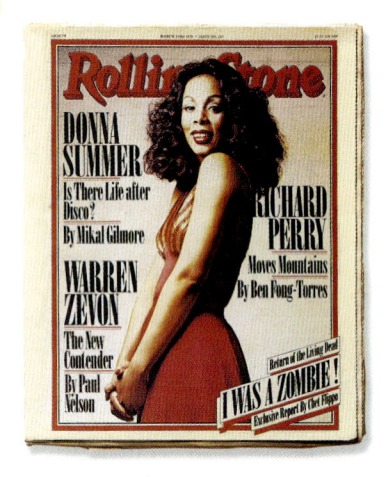

RS 258 | DOONESBURY'S JIMMY THUDPUCKER
February 9th, 1978
ILLUSTRATION BY GARRY TRUDEAU

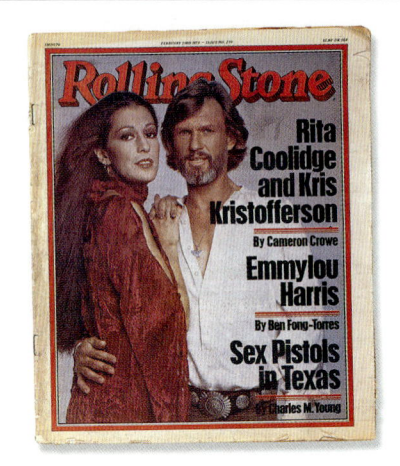

RS 259 | RITA COOLIDGE & KRIS KRISTOFFERSON
February 23rd, 1978
PHOTOGRAPH BY FRANCESCO SCAVULLO

RS 261 | DONNA SUMMER
March 23rd, 1978
PHOTOGRAPH BY BRIAN LEATART

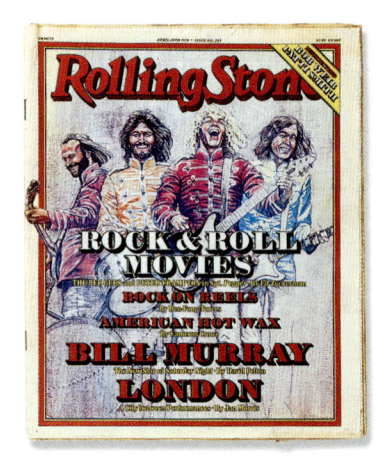

RS 263 | THE BEE GEES & PETER FRAMPTON
April 19th, 1978
ILLUSTRATION BY BRUCE WOLFE

SM14170   APRIL 6TH 1978 • ISSUE NO. 262 $1.00 UK 60P

Rolling Stone

Pretty Baby's Pretty Baby
Brooke Shields
By The Children's Express

Louis Malle
Her Director • By Jonathan Cott

Rod Stewart
Under Siege • By Paul Nelson

Lou Reed's
Street Hassle

PARLIAMENT'S FUNK APOCALYPSE
By Charles M. Young

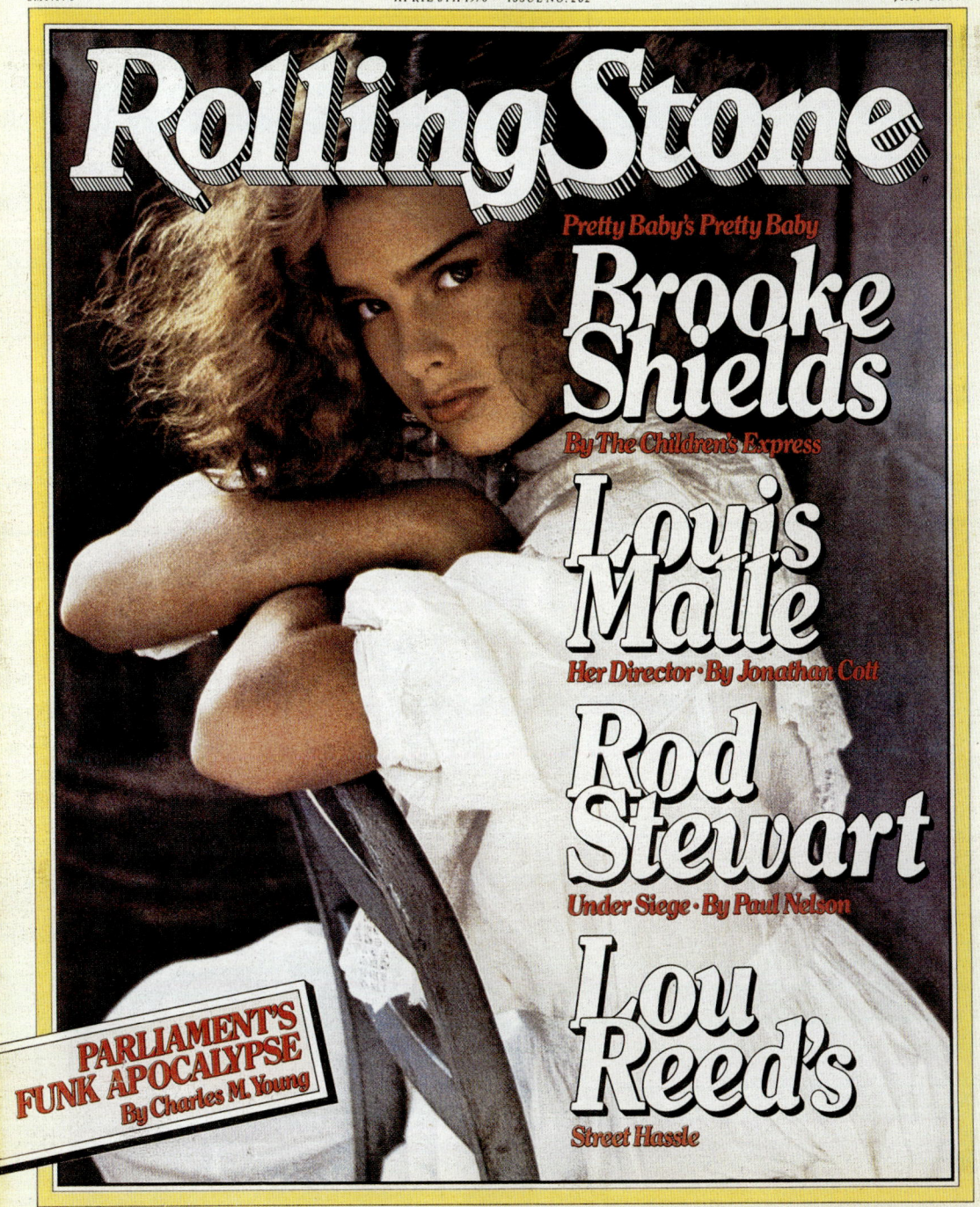

RS 262 | BROOKE SHIELDS | April 6th, 1978 | Photograph by Maureen Lambray

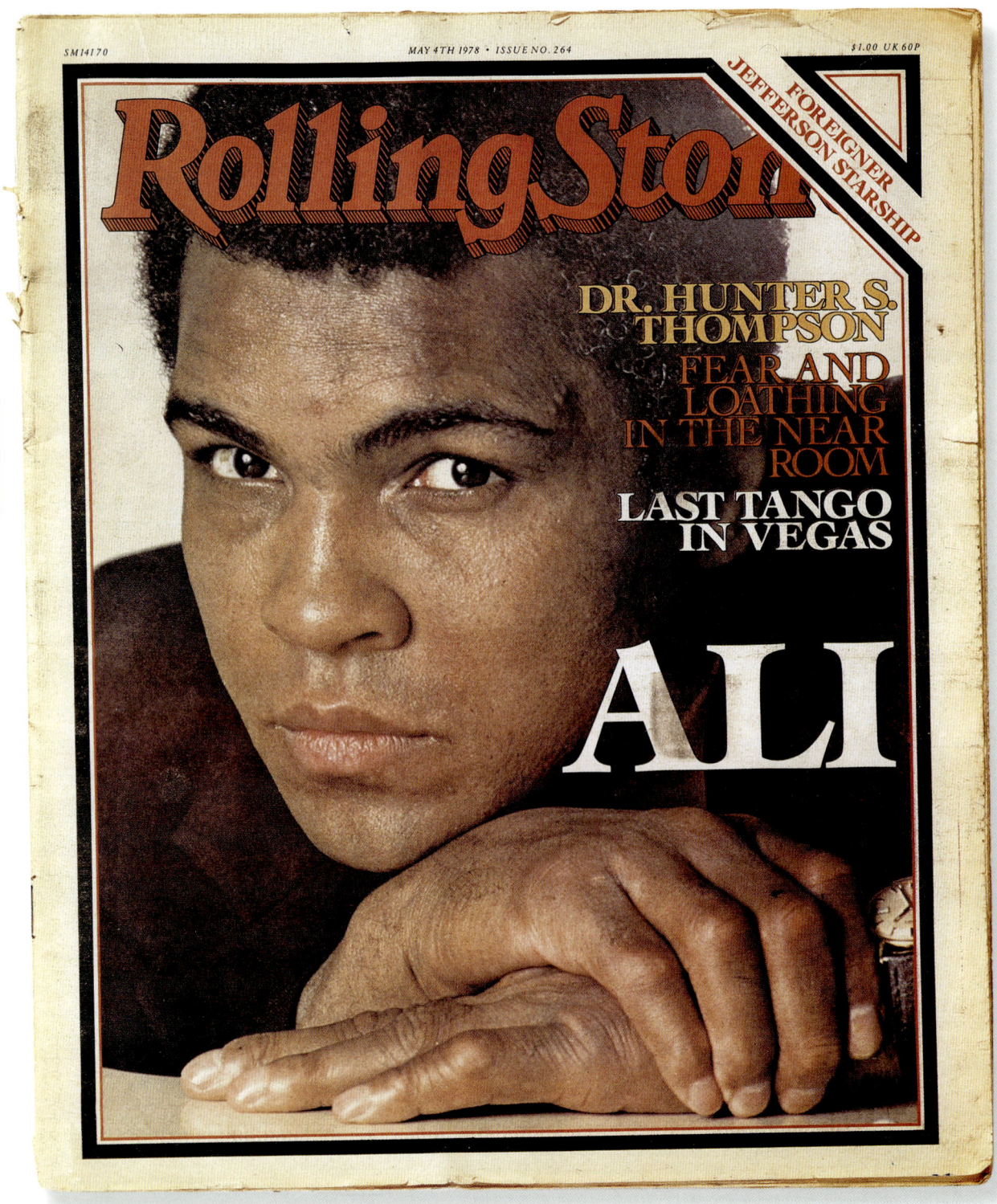

RS *264* | MUHAMMAD ALI | May 4th, 1978 | Photograph by Annie Leibovitz

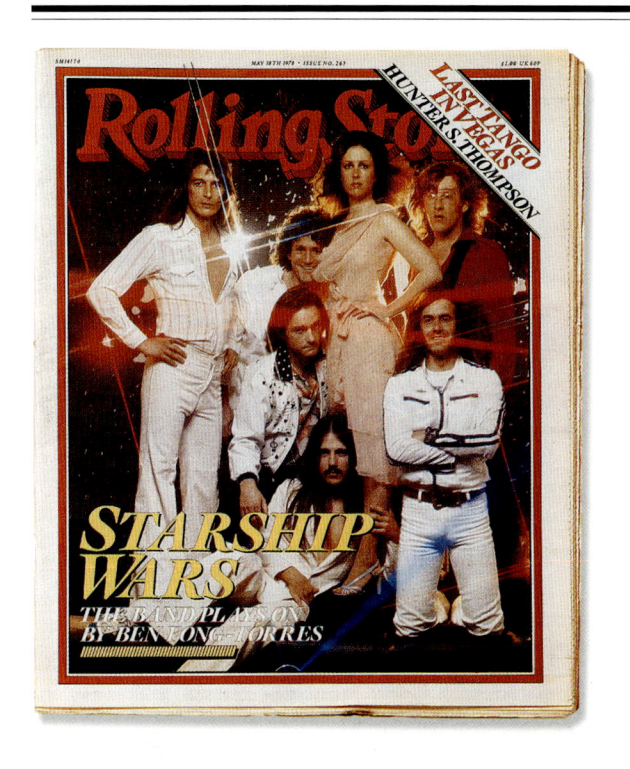

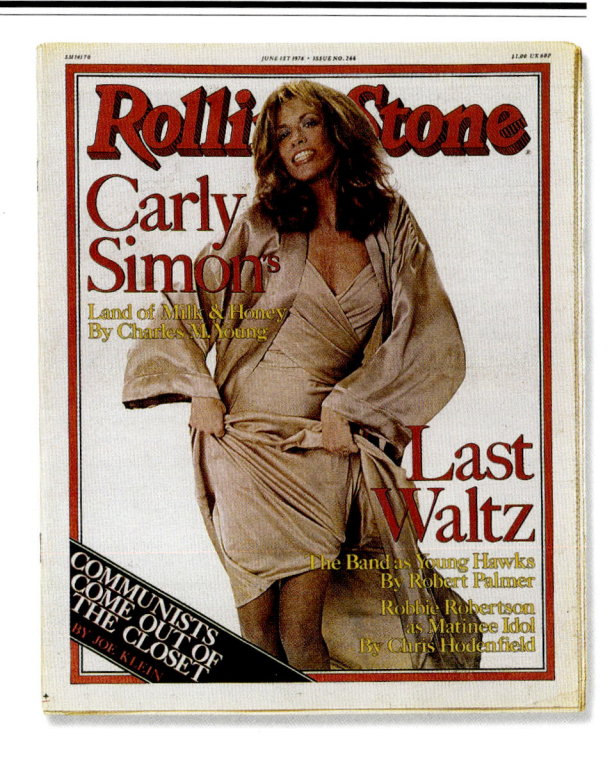

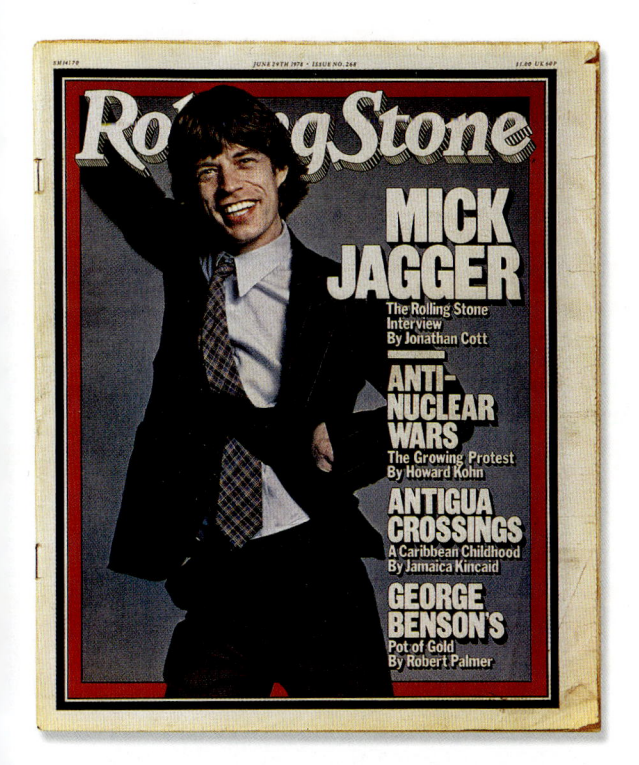

RS 265 | **JEFFERSON STARSHIP**
May 18th, 1978 | Photograph by Annie Leibovitz

RS 266 | **CARLY SIMON**
June 1st, 1978 | Photograph by Hiro

RS 268 | **MICK JAGGER**
June 29th, 1978 | Photograph by Annie Leibovitz

50 YEARS OF COVERS • 135

RS 267 | JOHN TRAVOLTA | June 15th, 1978 | Photograph by Annie Leibovitz

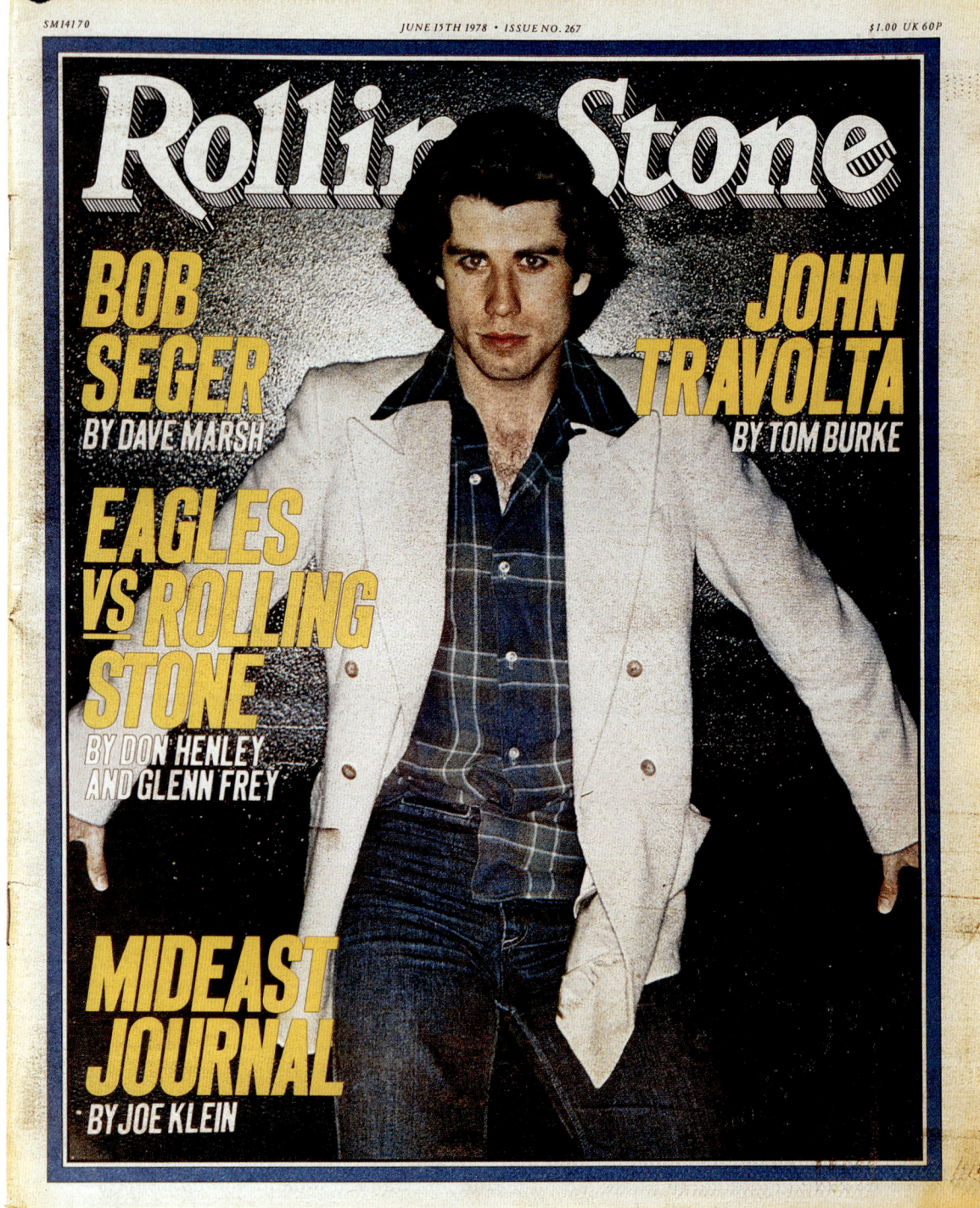

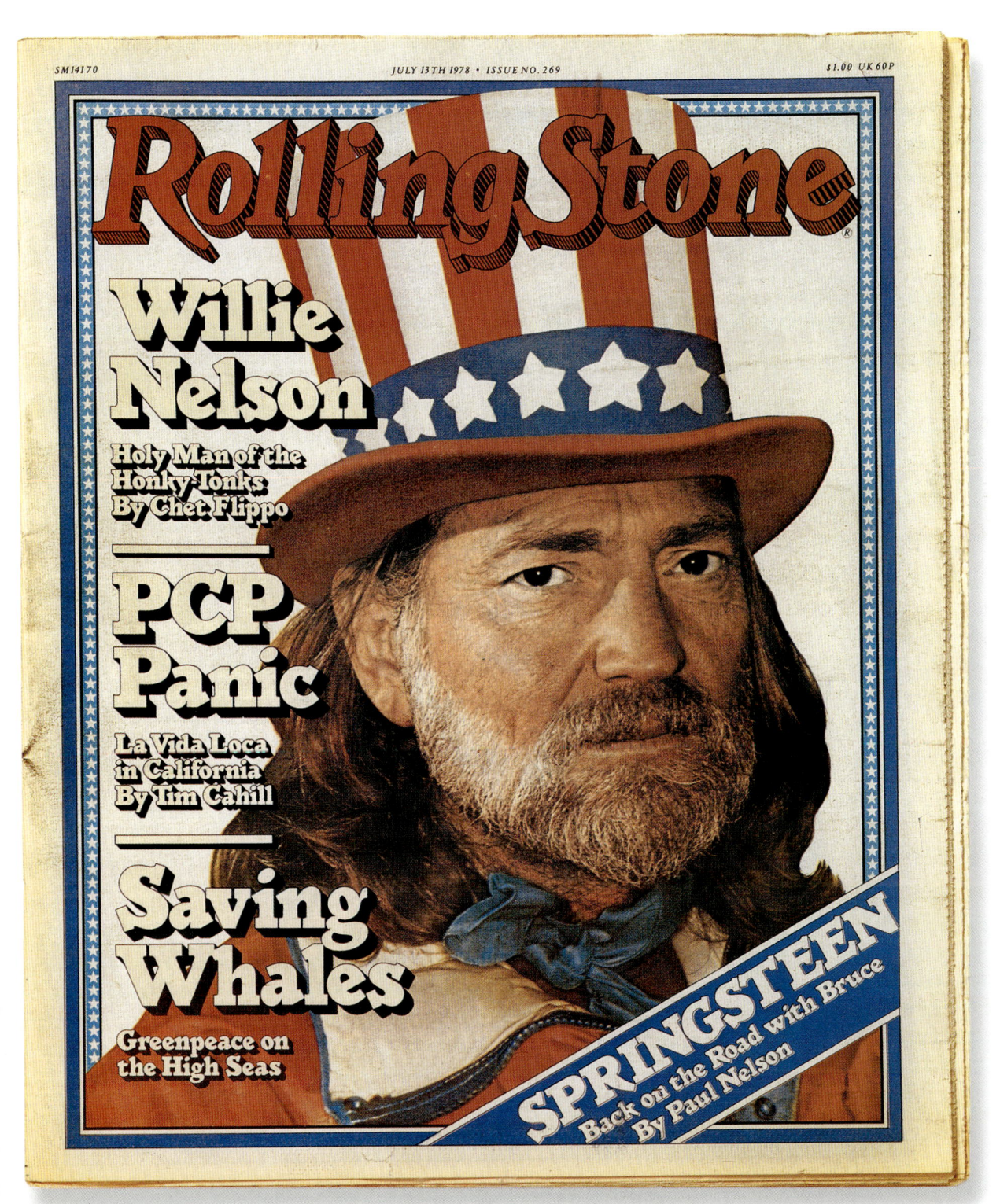

RS 269 | WILLIE NELSON | July 13th, 1978 | Photograph by Beverly Parker, Painted by Jack Doonan

Rolling Stone

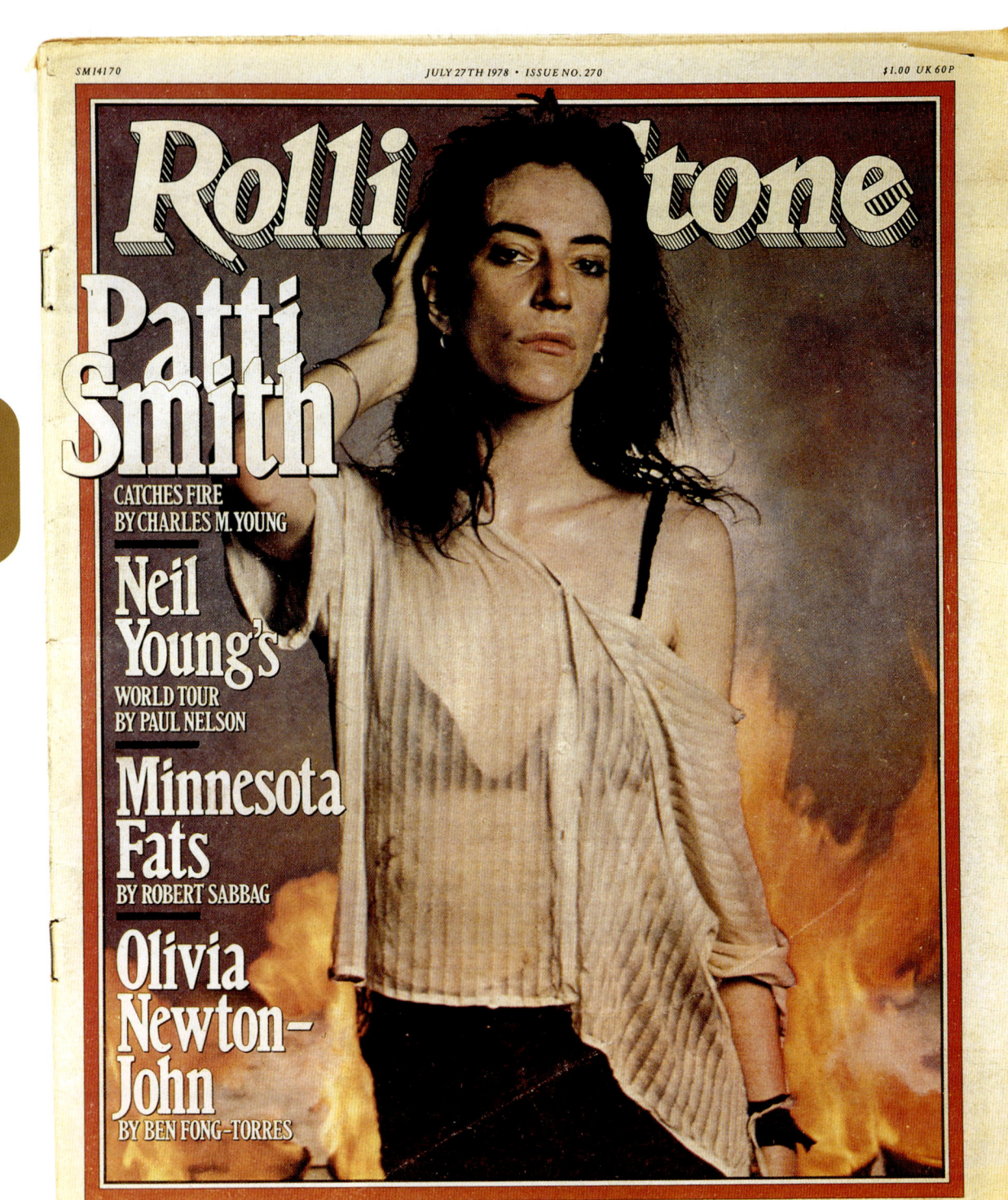

JULY 27TH 1978 • ISSUE NO. 270

1970s

Patti Smith
CATCHES FIRE
BY CHARLES M. YOUNG

Neil Young's
WORLD TOUR
BY PAUL NELSON

Minnesota Fats
BY ROBERT SABBAG

Olivia Newton-John
BY BEN FONG-TORRES

RS 270 | PATTI SMITH | July 27th, 1978 | Photograph by Annie Leibovitz

"People say to me, 'Do you think you sold out?' To me, they should be saying, 'Oh wow, you're on AM radio.' Kids come up to me on the street and say, 'Patti, we're on ABC.' Because they fought with me, they know that the past four years it's been a tough struggle. They can see I was the black sheep. I'll probably always be a black sheep, maybe a richer one instead of a poorer one, but they see someone who felt alienated, who didn't belong anywhere. I stuck it out, you know, I stuck it out. And I'm determined to make us kids, us fuckups, us ones who could never get a degree in college, whatever, have a family, or do regular stuff, social stuff, prove that there's a place for us. So I think it's great that I have a hit single ['Because the Night']. To me, the place for us would be right out on the front line."

[EXCERPT FROM RS 270 COVER STORY BY CHARLES M. YOUNG]

"**[THE PATTI SMITH SHOT IS] REALLY A GOOD** story on how a lot of planning can be worthless sometimes. I had an assistant come out from California – I was just starting to work with assistants then – and I said to him, 'Listen, I want this huge wall of flame behind Patti Smith, I don't care how you do it.' He said, 'I have it all figured out.' His idea was like this kerosene-soaked net behind her. Needless to say, it lasted about five seconds, because as soon as it burned out, it fell down to the floor. So then we lit big barrels of kerosene and practically burned down the place. I think Patti did get a burn on the back of her *tutu*. The whole backside of her was red.

"It's really a lot of fun taking pictures with me. And then I slap them in the mud! And then I hang them from the ceiling! And they say, 'I heard you were hard, Leibovitz. I heard it wasn't easy.'"

—*Annie Leibovitz*

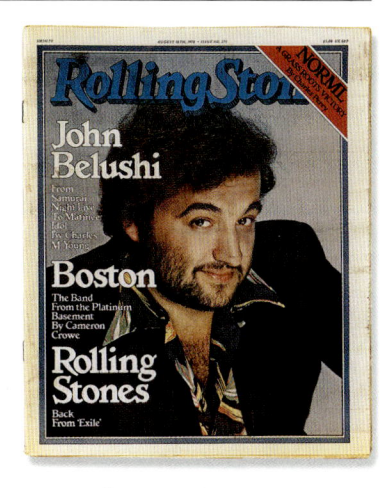

RS 271 | JOHN BELUSHI
August 10th, 1978
Photograph by Hiro

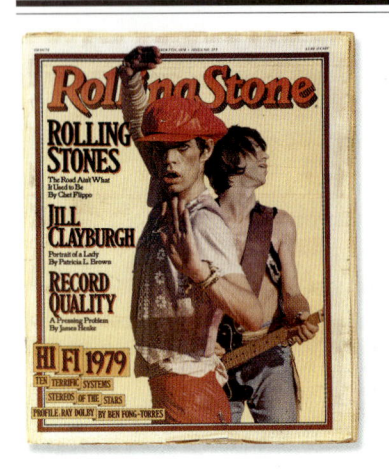

> "**With all this attention, you** become a child. It's awful to be at the center of attention. You can't talk about anything apart from your own experience, your own dopey life. I'd rather do something that can get me out of the center of attention. It's very dangerous. But there's no way, really, to avoid that."
>
> — *Mick Jagger*

RS 273 | MICK JAGGER & KEITH RICHARDS
September 7th, 1978
PHOTOGRAPH BY LYNN GOLDSMITH

WALKING THROUGH THE LOBBY OF THE MARQUIS LAST NIGHT, JUST after 2 a.m., I ran into Bruce, who asked if I wanted to walk over to Ben Frank's for something to eat. On the way I mentioned that there must be a lot of people in line at the Roxy just up the street. Bruce gave me a look. "I don't like people waiting up all night for me," he said.

Bruce ate another prodigious meal: four eggs, toast, a grilled-cheese sandwich, large glasses of orange juice and milk. And the talk ranged widely: surfing (Bruce had lived with some of the Jersey breed for a while in the late Sixties, and he's a little frustrated with trying to give a glimmer of its complexity to a landlocked ho-dad like me), the new album and its live recording ("I don't think I'll ever go back to the overdub method," he said, mentioning that almost all of the LP was done completely live in the studio, and that "Streets of Fire" and "Something in the Night" were first takes). But mostly we talked, or rather, Bruce talked and I listened.

Springsteen can be spellbinding, partly because he is so completely ingenuous, partly because of the intensity and sincerity with which he has thought out his role as a rock star. He delivers these ideas with an air of conviction, but not a proselytizing one; some of his ideas are radical enough for Patti Smith or the punks, yet lack their sanctimonious rhetoric.

I asked him why the band plays so long – their shows are rarely less than three hours – and he said: "It's hard to explain. 'Cause every time I read stuff that I say, like in the papers, I always think I come off sounding like some kind of crazed fanatic. When I read it, it sounds like that, but it's the way I am about it. It's like you have to go the whole way because . . . that's what keeps everything *real*. It all ties in with the records and the values, the morality of the records. There's a certain morality of the show, and it's very strict." Such comments can seem not only fanatical but also self-serving. The great advantage of the sanctimony and rhetoric that infests the punks is that such flaws humanize them. Lacking such egregious characteristics, Bruce Springsteen seems too good to be true when reduced to cold type. Nice guys finish last, we are told, and here's one at the top. So what's the catch? I just don't know.

[EXCERPT FROM RS 272 COVER STORY BY DAVE MARSH]

RollingStone

AUGUST 24TH, 1978 • ISSUE NO. 272

BRUCE
SPRINGSTEEN BY DAVE MARSH

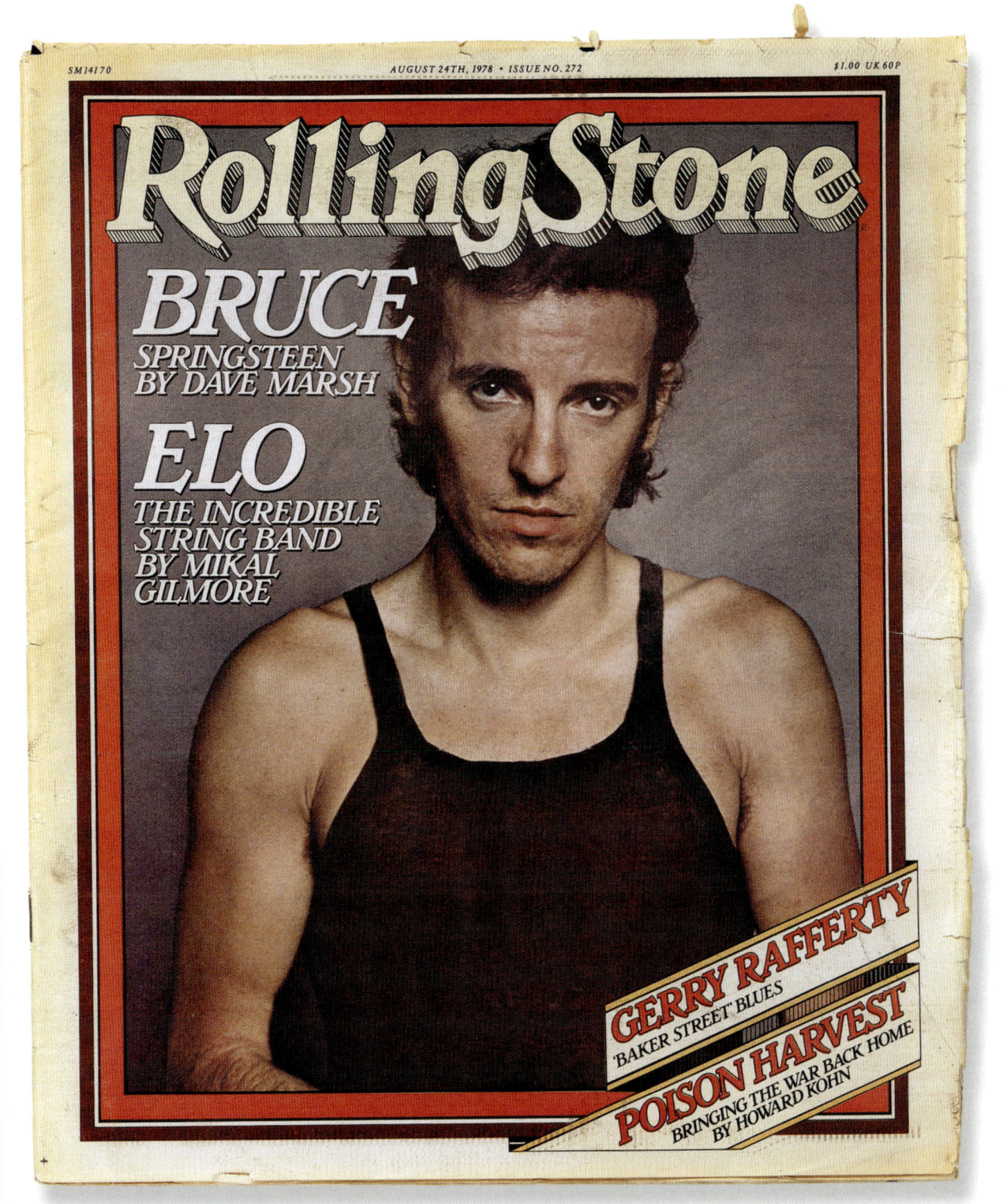

ELO
THE INCREDIBLE STRING BAND BY MIKAL GILMORE

GERRY RAFFERTY
'BAKER STREET' BLUES

POISON HARVEST
BRINGING THE WAR BACK HOME BY HOWARD KOHN

RS 272 | BRUCE SPRINGSTEEN | August 24th, 1978 | Photograph by Lynn Goldsmith

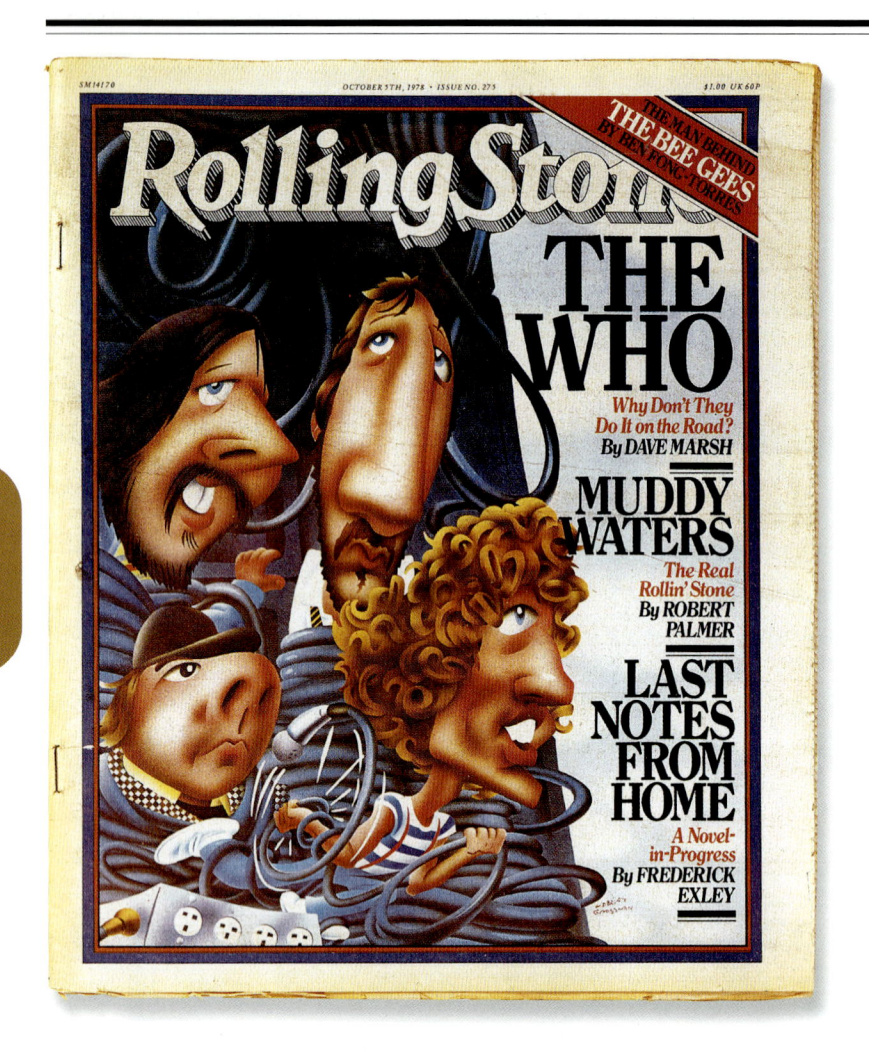

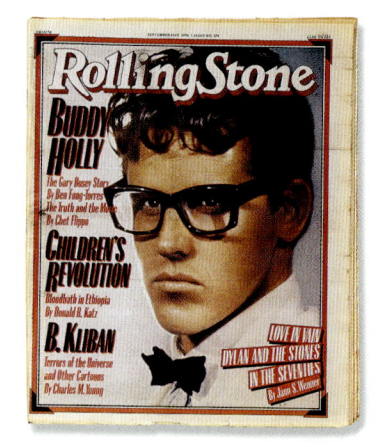

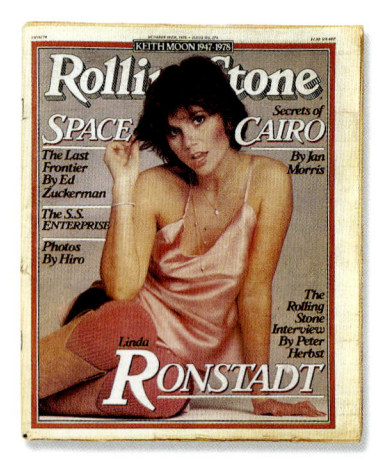

𝓡𝓢 275 | THE WHO | October 5th, 1978 | ILLUSTRATION BY ROBERT GROSSMAN

𝓡𝓢 274 | GARY BUSEY
AS BUDDY HOLLY
September 21st, 1978
PHOTOGRAPH BY GEMMA LAMANA

𝓡𝓢 276 | LINDA RONSTADT
October 19th, 1978
PHOTOGRAPH BY FRANCESCO SCAVULLO

𝓡𝓢 277 | GILDA RADNER
November 2nd, 1978
Photograph by Francesco Scavullo

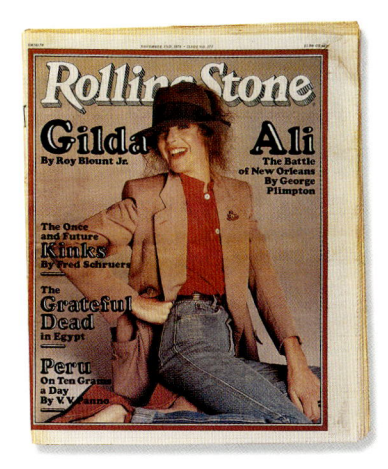

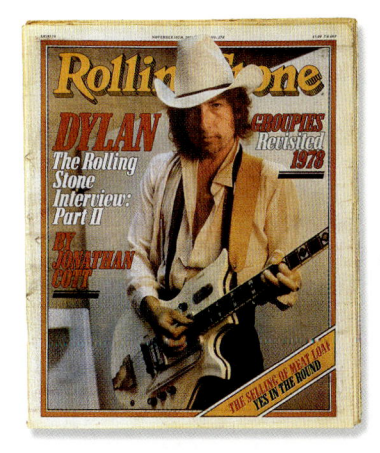

𝓡𝓢 278 | BOB DYLAN
November 16th, 1978
Photograph by Morgan Renard

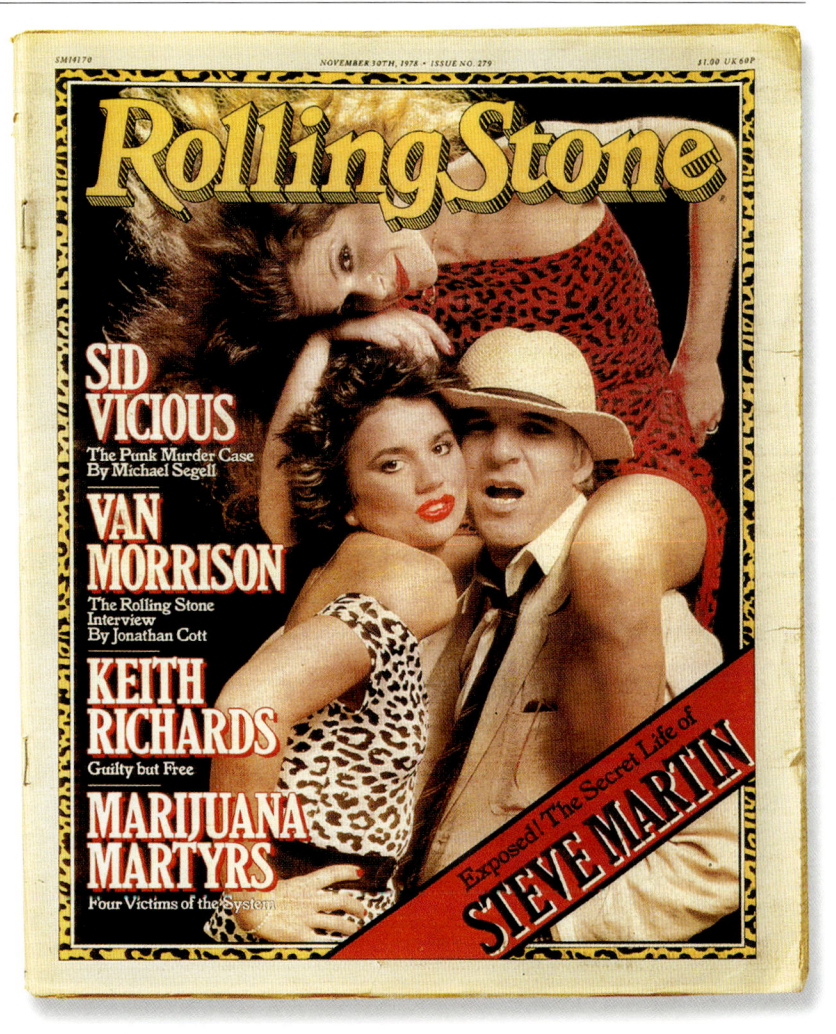

𝓡𝓢 279 | LINDA RONSTADT, GILDA RADNER & STEVE MARTIN
November 30th, 1978 | Photograph by Annie Leibovitz

[RS 278] Bob Dylan had apparently run out of patience with photo shoots by the time he appeared on the magazine's cover for the tenth time. For this cover, he refused to let Rolling Stone's photographer snap the portrait. Instead, he had his friend Morgan Renard take his picture in the backstage men's room at Madison Square Garden. (Note the urinal in the background.) This cover would be the last one designed by Roger Black; Mary Shanahan, Rolling Stone's first and only female art director, would begin her term the following issue.

50 YEARS OF COVERS · 143

1970s

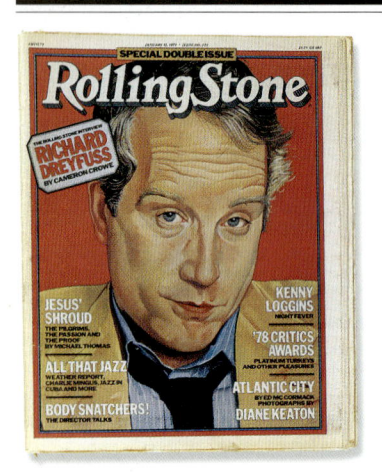

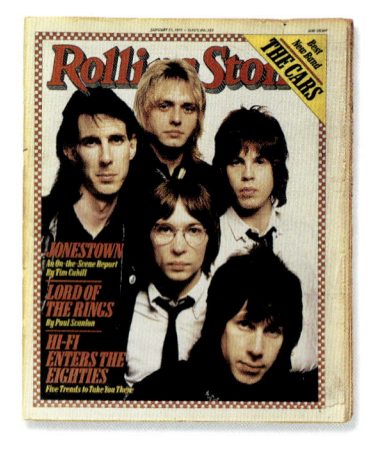

RS 281/282 | RICHARD DREYFUSS
December 28th, 1978 – January 11th, 1979
ILLUSTRATION BY JULIAN ALLEN

RS 283 | THE CARS
January 25th, 1979
PHOTOGRAPH BY JIM HOUGHTON

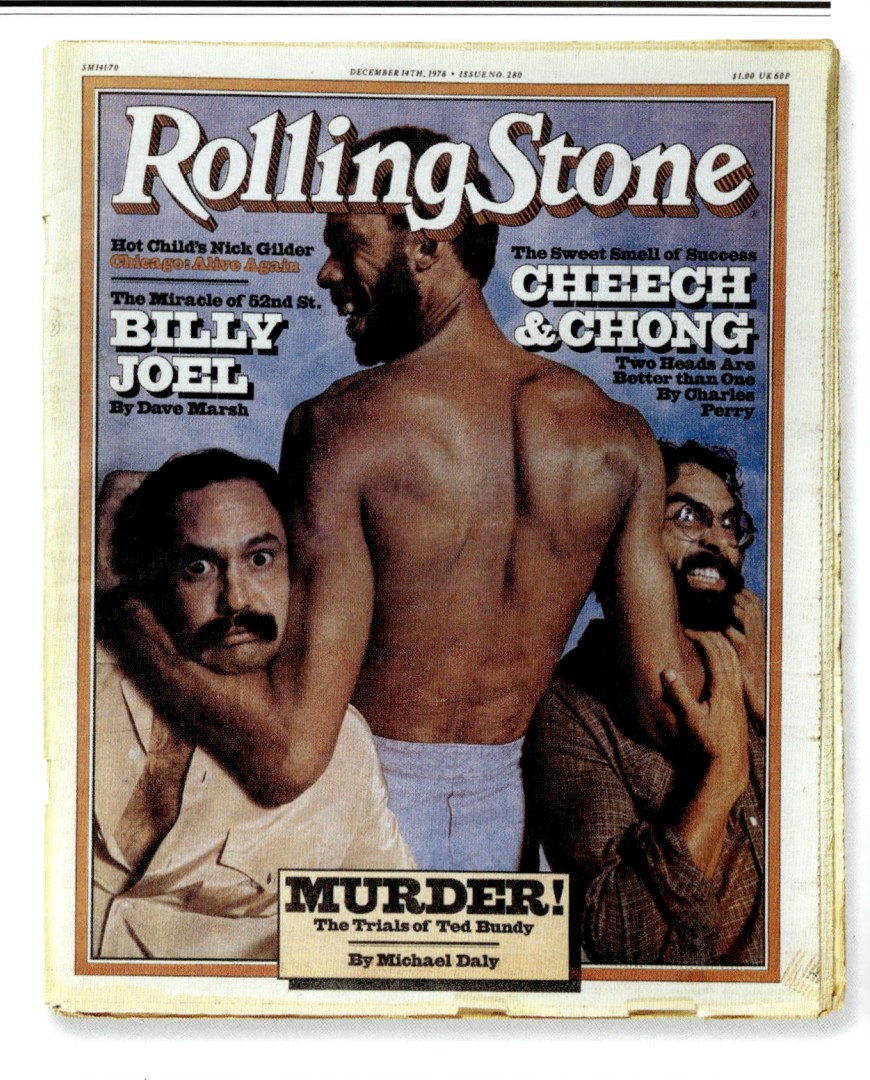

RS 280 | CHEECH & CHONG WITH KAREEM ABDUL-JABBAR
December 14th, 1978 | PHOTOGRAPH BY DAVID ALEXANDER

"THERE'S A CULTURE THAT A LOT OF PEOPLE ARE TRYING TO BURY, like they tried to bury rock & roll after a couple of years and said, 'Rock's dead.' They want to say, 'This is the Seventies, that stuff's dead.' But we will keep it alive for the rest of our lives. We are so much a part of the culture we make fun of, whatever comes down we will still be a part of it."
—*Tommy Chong*

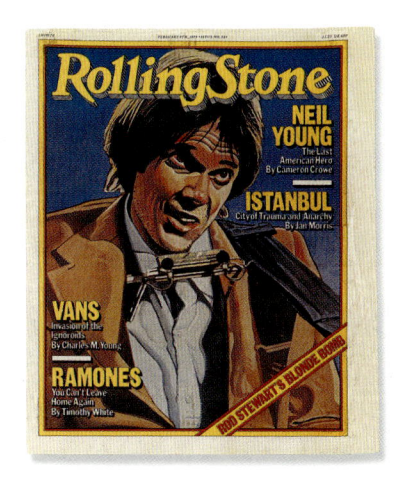

RS 284 | NEIL YOUNG
February 8th, 1979
ILLUSTRATION BY JULIAN ALLEN

My parents occupied the bedroom above mine while I was growing up. Luckily they were heavy sleepers, and loud music late at night didn't seem to bother them – unless it was the high-pitched guitar or vocal work of Neil Young. On such occasions, my mother would trudge downstairs, rap at the door and stand there with a look that suggested the wrath of every deprived sleeper over the ages.

There was a time, sure, when I tried to explain to them what it was to be a Neil Young fan. "How important is an in-tune vocal?" "But it's *great* when he hits the same note thirty-eight times in 'Down by the River.'" Here was an *artist,* as opposed to an entertainer.

In 1972, my parents would hear "Heart of Gold" played in the supermarket, find it tuneful and begin to see things differently. When Neil Young announced he would be playing San Diego, our hometown, on a rare concert tour, it became a family outing.

Neil Young appeared right on time, nervously walking out in front of the screaming crowd, one arm upraised. He looked skittish and tired as he picked up a guitar and began to sing an acoustic song, called "Sugar Mountain." The audience rushed the stage, shouted for the electric songs and Young called his band out onstage. But instead of standards like "Down by the River," they played a set of reckless new music, causing no small tension in the arena. Then, during the final song of the evening, the pressure seemed to cause Neil Young to crack. He began to shout, "Wake up, San Diego. Get up, San Diego." The houselights were turned on and the hall was filled with an eerie silence. We didn't talk about Neil Young for the next few years.

Recently, I found myself back in the same old room late one night, typing this article and listening to Neil Young records, when a familiar knock came at the door. "Well," said my mother with a note of sentimentality. "A *survivor.*"

[EXCERPT FROM RS 284 COVER STORY BY CAMERON CROWE]

FEBRUARY 22ND, 1979 • ISSUE NO. 285

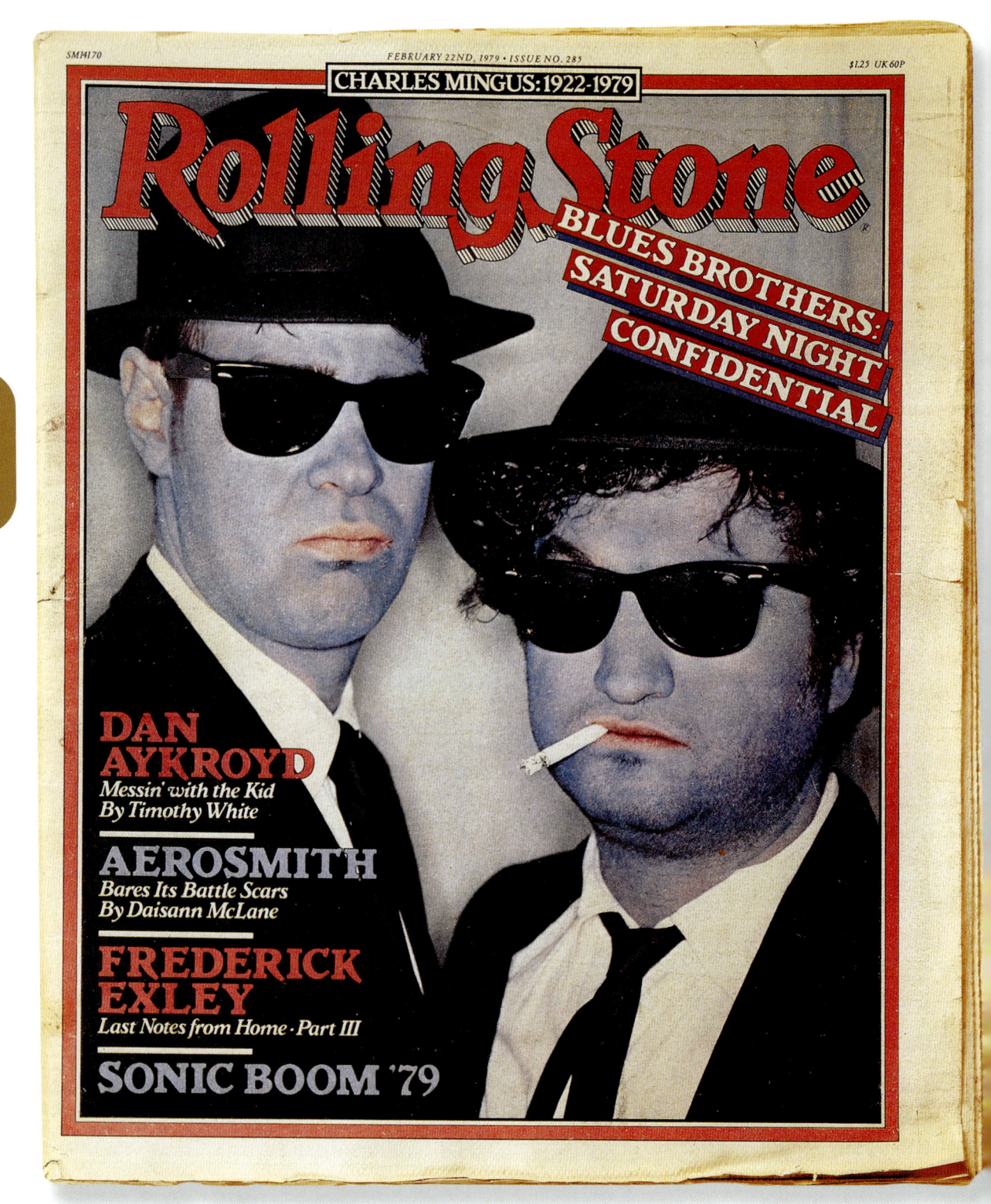

CHARLES MINGUS: 1922-1979

Rolling Stone

BLUES BROTHERS: SATURDAY NIGHT CONFIDENTIAL

1970s

DAN AYKROYD
Messin' with the Kid
By Timothy White

AEROSMITH
Bares Its Battle Scars
By Daisann McLane

FREDERICK EXLEY
Last Notes from Home · Part III

SONIC BOOM '79

RS 285 | THE BLUES BROTHERS, DAN AYKROYD
& JOHN BELUSHI | February 22nd, 1979 | PHOTOGRAPH BY ANNIE LEIBOVITZ

"BY THE WAY, HOW DID YOU ASSEMBLE THE ORIGINAL BAND?"
"It was agony," says Jake, burying his face in his hands. "Elwood and I were a duo and when word got out we were forming a group, I got phone calls immediately, calls from heavy stars, saying, 'I wanna be in your band!' And it was a question of whether to assemble one or just get a band that was already established – some guys together for ten years so we could put 'em up there and let 'em just groove. I was thinking about getting Delbert McClinton's band, and Roomful of Blues, too. When we first resurfaced, Elwood and I did a gig at the Lone Star Café in New York in June [of 1978] with Roomful of Blues."

"But finally we just decided, 'Fuck the cost and the damage it will do to the feelings of people who aren't asked, and let's go for the best band we can get, *piece by piece.*' We got Bones Malone first and he recommended Cropper and Dunn. We really didn't know who they were," Jake snorts. "Then when he [Malone] said, 'You know, from "Knock on Wood" and "Soul Man," ' we said, 'Would *they* do it?!'

"I called them up, acting real arrogant," Jake recounts, "saying, '*Wellllll*, all right Cropper, you're in the group but you're a rhythm guitar player – ya got that?' and he went [*meekly*], 'I like playing rhythm guitar; I don't like all that lead stuff.' So I said [*sarcastically*], 'Oh, you're hard to work with, aren't ya?'

"Then I called Dunn up and said, 'I never met you but I'd like you to be in a group – but I understand you don't get along with Cropper.' He said, '*Aw no*, we get along all right!' I was just giving them all kinda shit, bustin' their balls," Jake guffaws, slapping Elwood on the back.

"But they both said yes, and, uh, incidentally . . . they didn't know who *we* were either."

[EXCERPT FROM RS 285 COVER STORY BY TIMOTHY WHITE]

"THE IDEA OF PAINTING THE BLUES BROTHERS BLUE IS TOO STUPID. IT'S JUST TOO stupid. But it's something I've learned to trust: The stupider the idea is, the better it looks. Painting the Blues Brothers blue is as stupid as the Blues Brothers being the Blues Brothers. They were taking themselves so seriously about being musicians, they were forgetting that they were actors and comedians. I mean, Belushi was saying, 'Did you hear Aykroyd on the harp? Better than Paul Butterfield!' And I said, 'Whoa . . . time to remember who you are.' That's when my job gets a little dangerous. Belushi didn't talk to me for six months. But Aykroyd always knew it was good. I knew it was good, too. It was a healthy thing to do, it was funny."

—*Annie Leibovitz*

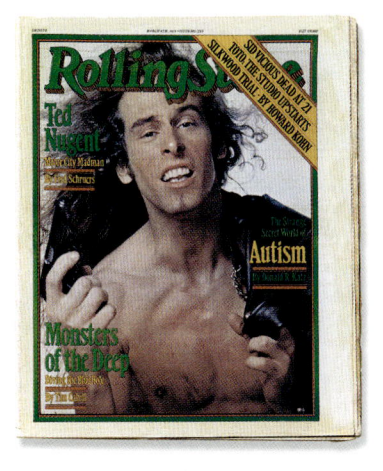

RS 286 | TED NUGENT
March 8th, 1979
PHOTOGRAPH BY BILL KING

SM14170　　　　　　　MARCH 22ND, 1979 • ISSUE NO. 287　　　　　　　$1.00 UK 60P

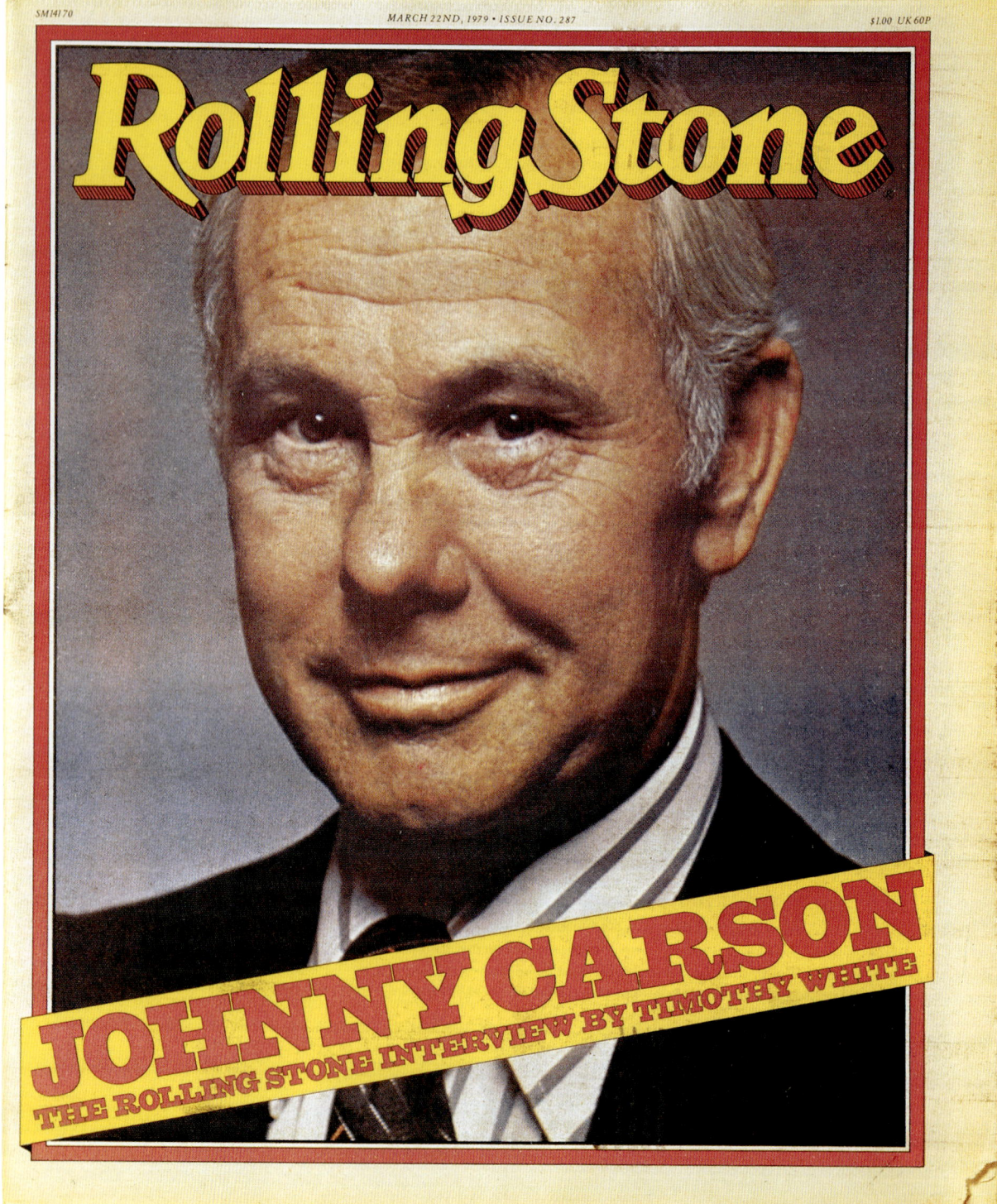

Rolling Stone

1970s

JOHNNY CARSON
THE ROLLING STONE INTERVIEW BY TIMOTHY WHITE

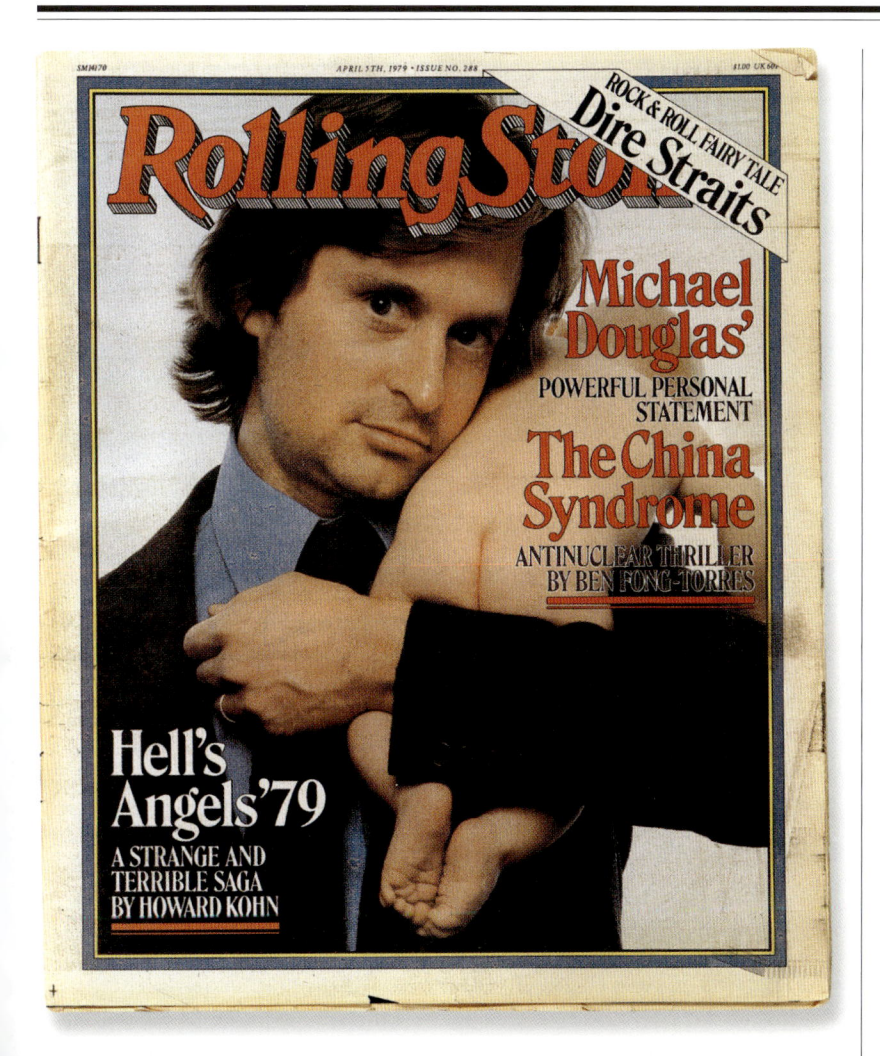

RS 288 | MICHAEL
& CAMERON DOUGLAS
April 5th, 1979
PHOTOGRAPH BY ANNIE LEIBOVITZ

RS 287 | JOHNNY CARSON
March 22nd, 1979
PHOTOGRAPH BY ANNIE LEIBOVITZ

I've wondered if there was a certain moment of self-esteem and self-worth upon which you built every other experience.

There comes a time or a moment when you know in which direction you're going to go, but you don't know why exactly. I think that probably happened to me in grade school, where I could get attention by being different, by getting up in front of an audience and calling attention to myself. And I said, "Hey, I like that feeling." When I was a kid, I was shy, and to get that reaction is a strange feeling. It is a high that I don't think you can get from drugs or from anything else. It's a great feeling, and that's why many performers have very big highs and very big lows. I know I do.

So you had shyness to conquer?

[*Sheepishly*] Yeah, oh, yeah. I still feel uncomfortable in large groups of people. Not audiences, mind you. I can go out in front of 20,000 people because I'm in charge. Most entertainers feel that way. I think people who are creative, in the arts, also seem to have larger appetites for life than most people, to excess usually. Whether it be drinking, sex, anything, the appetites seem larger. Because I guess you are always trying to prove yourself. You're only as good as your last performance.

All things considered, are you happy with the way everything has turned out?

Yes, but it depends. Do you have a capacity for happiness? A lot of people don't have a capacity. I don't know how big my capacity is. It's not as big as a lot of people's, but I'm getting better at it all the time.

[EXCERPT FROM JOHNNY CARSON INTERVIEW BY TIMOTHY WHITE]

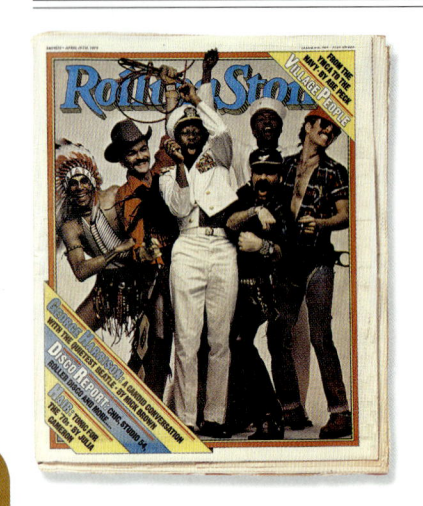

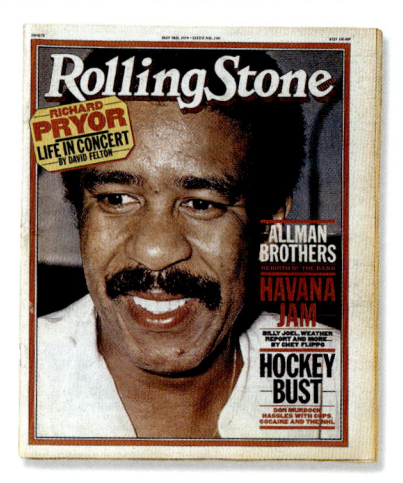

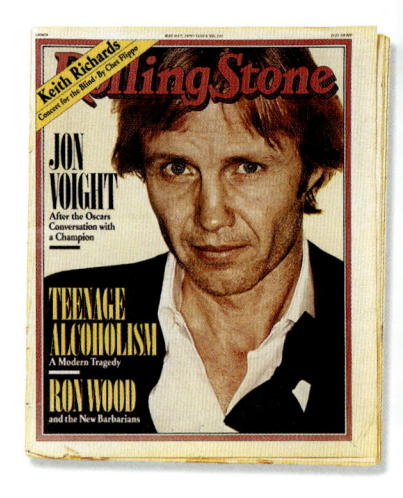

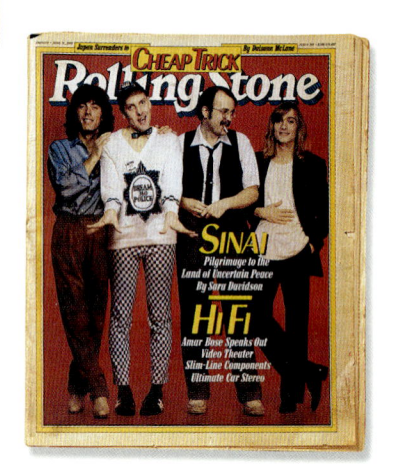

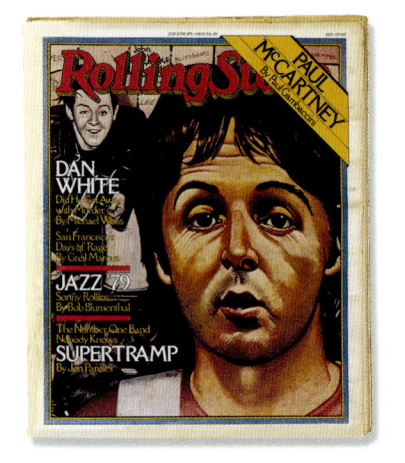

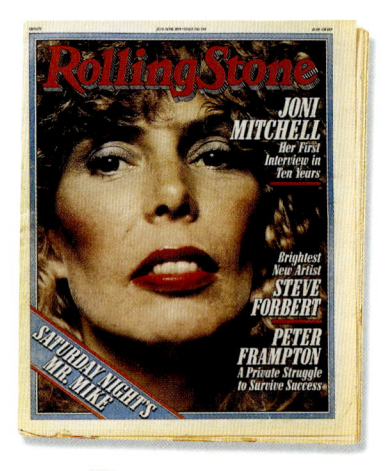

1970s

RS 289 | THE VILLAGE PEOPLE
April 19th, 1979
PHOTOGRAPH BY BILL KING

RS 290 | RICHARD PRYOR
May 3rd, 1979
PHOTOGRAPH BY DAVID ALEXANDER

RS 292 | JON VOIGHT
May 31st, 1979
PHOTOGRAPH BY ANNIE LEIBOVITZ

RS 293 | CHEAP TRICK
June 14th, 1979
PHOTOGRAPH BY ANNIE LEIBOVITZ

RS 295 | PAUL McCARTNEY
July 12th, 1979
ILLUSTRATION BY JULIAN ALLEN

RS 296 | JONI MITCHELL
July 26th, 1979
PHOTOGRAPH BY NORMAN SEEFF

150 • ROLLING STONE

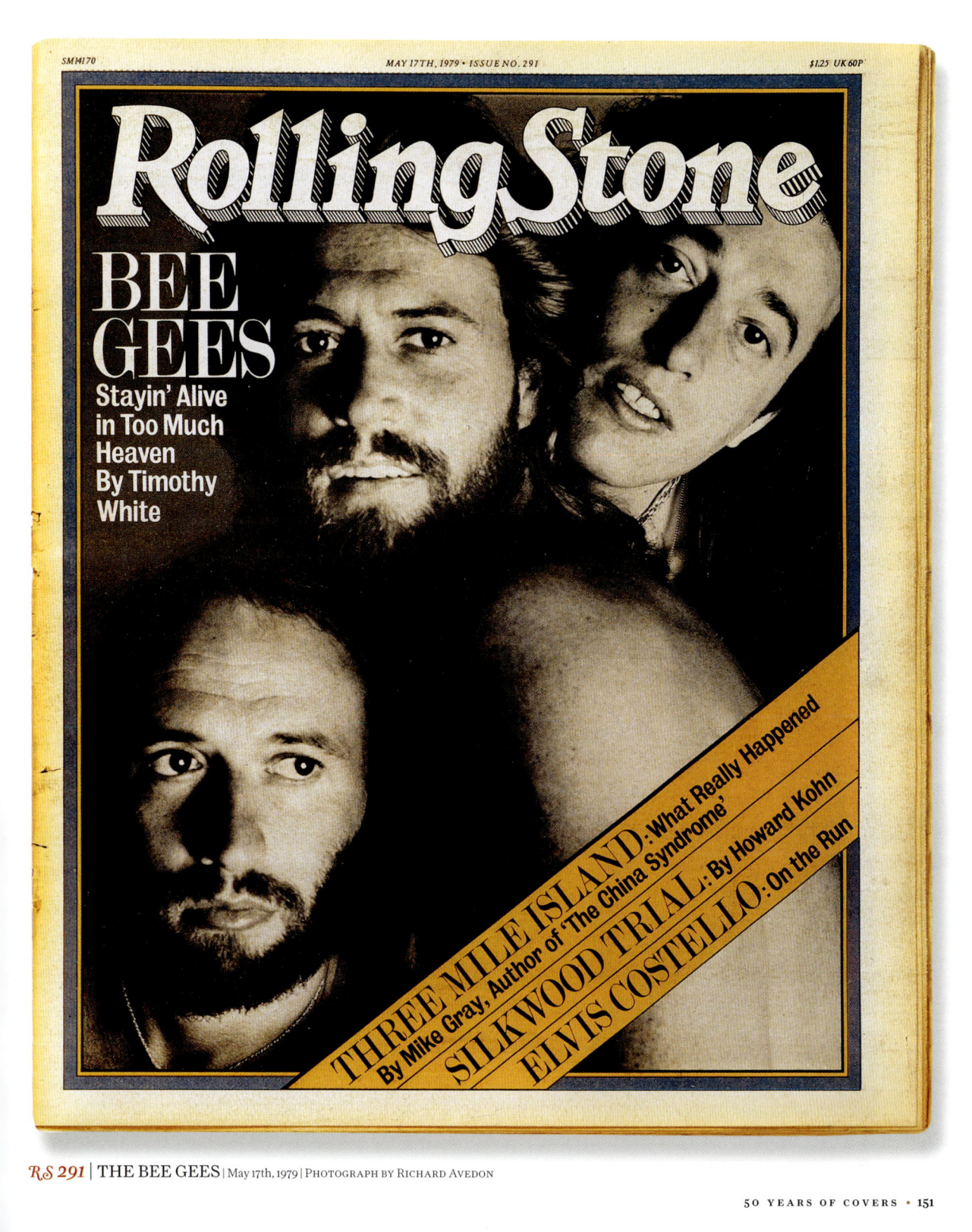

RS 291 | THE BEE GEES | May 17th, 1979 | Photograph by Richard Avedon

50 YEARS OF COVERS • 151

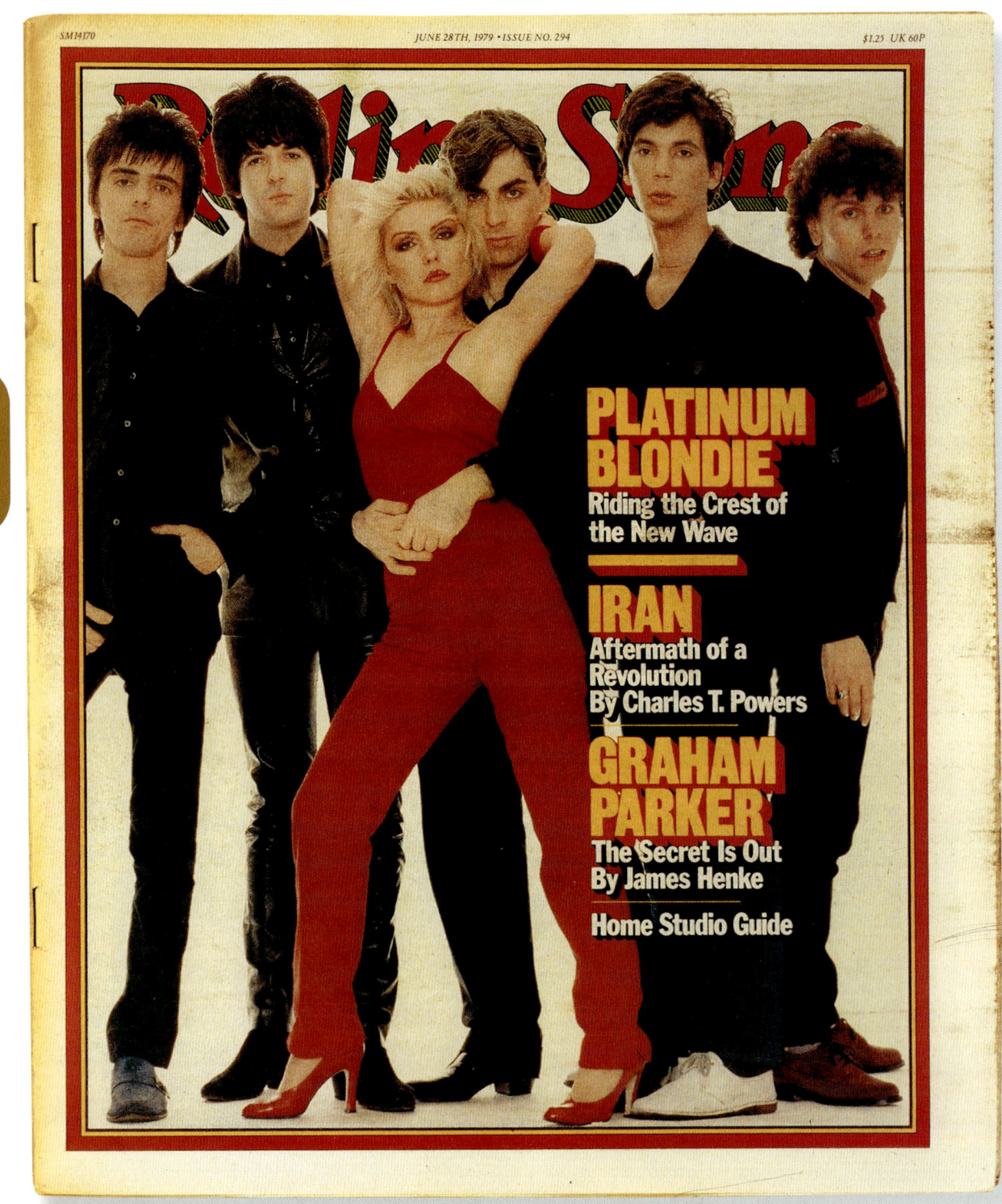

RS 294 | BLONDIE | June 28th, 1979 | Photograph by Annie Leibovitz

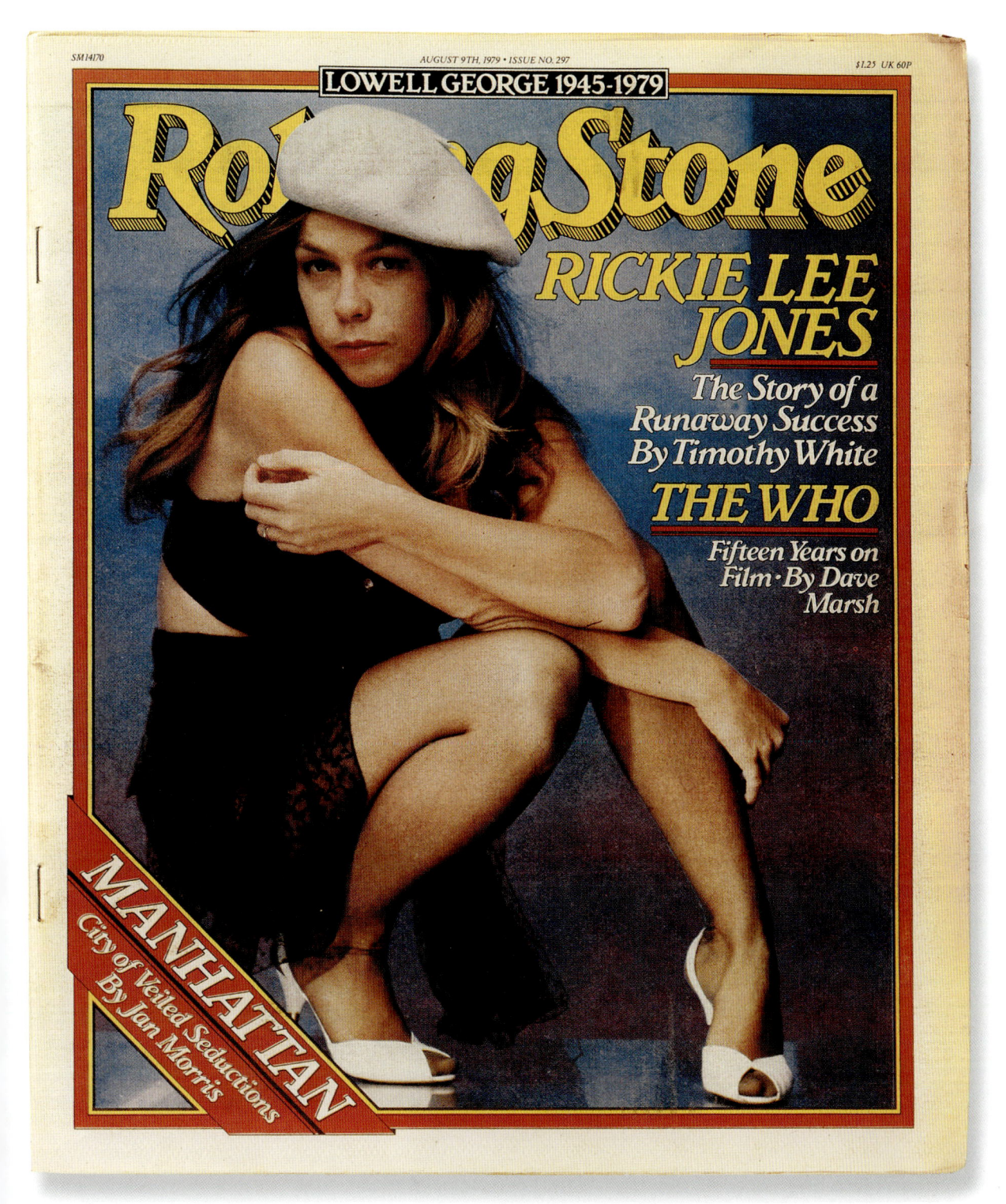

RS 297 | RICKIE LEE JONES | August 9th, 1979 | Photograph by Annie Leibovitz

50 YEARS OF COVERS • 153

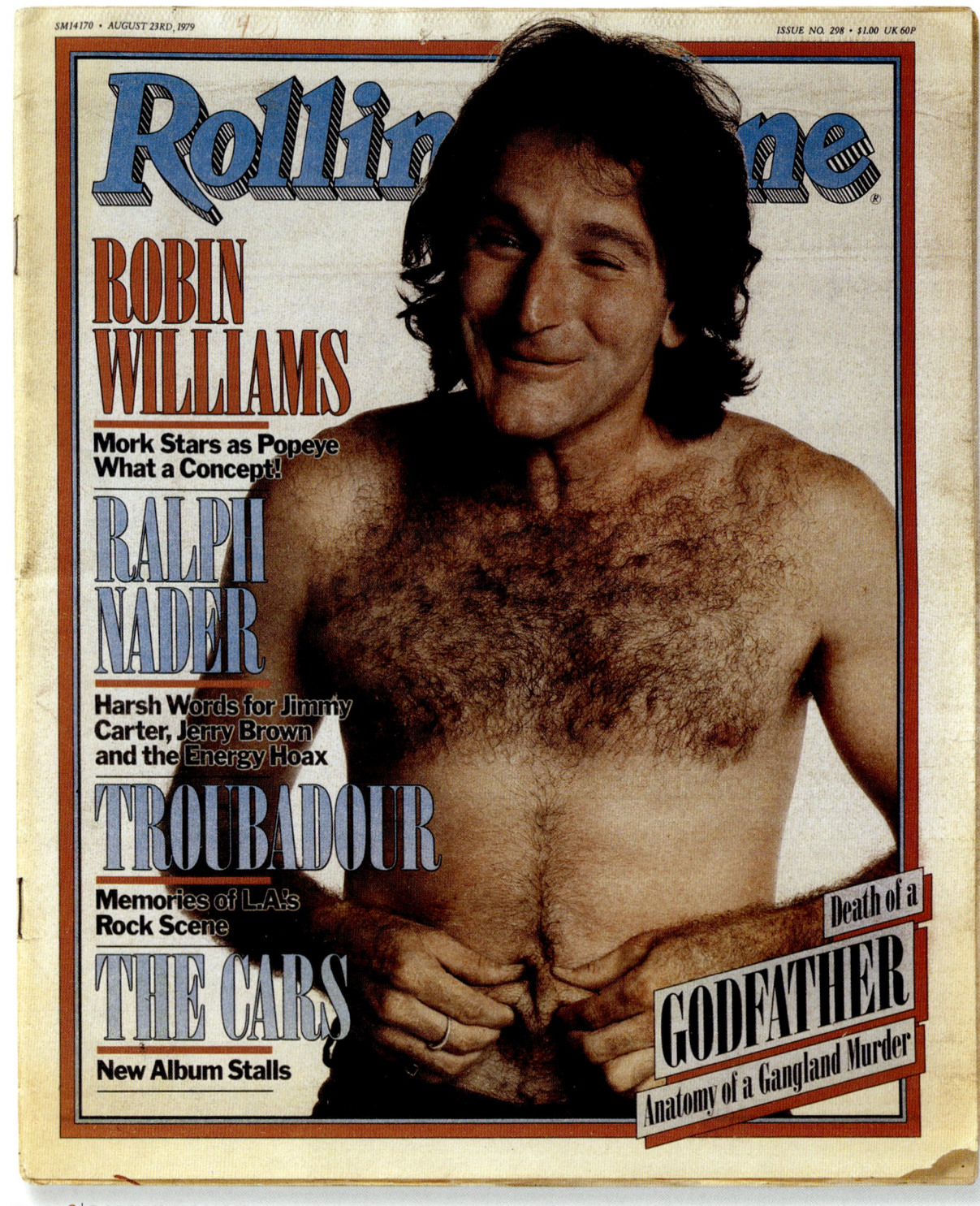

RS 298 | ROBIN WILLIAMS | August 23rd, 1979 | Photograph by Richard Avedon

SM14170 • SEPTEMBER 6TH, 1979 $1.25 UK 60P

Rolling Stone

MARIJUANA Stalking Hawaii's Number One Cash Crop

JAMES TAYLOR

The Rolling Stone Interview
By Peter Herbst

REGGIE JACKSON CLOSE UP

Baseball's Most Volatile Player
By Roy Blount Jr.

RS 299 | JAMES TAYLOR | September 6th, 1979 | Photograph by Annie Leibovitz

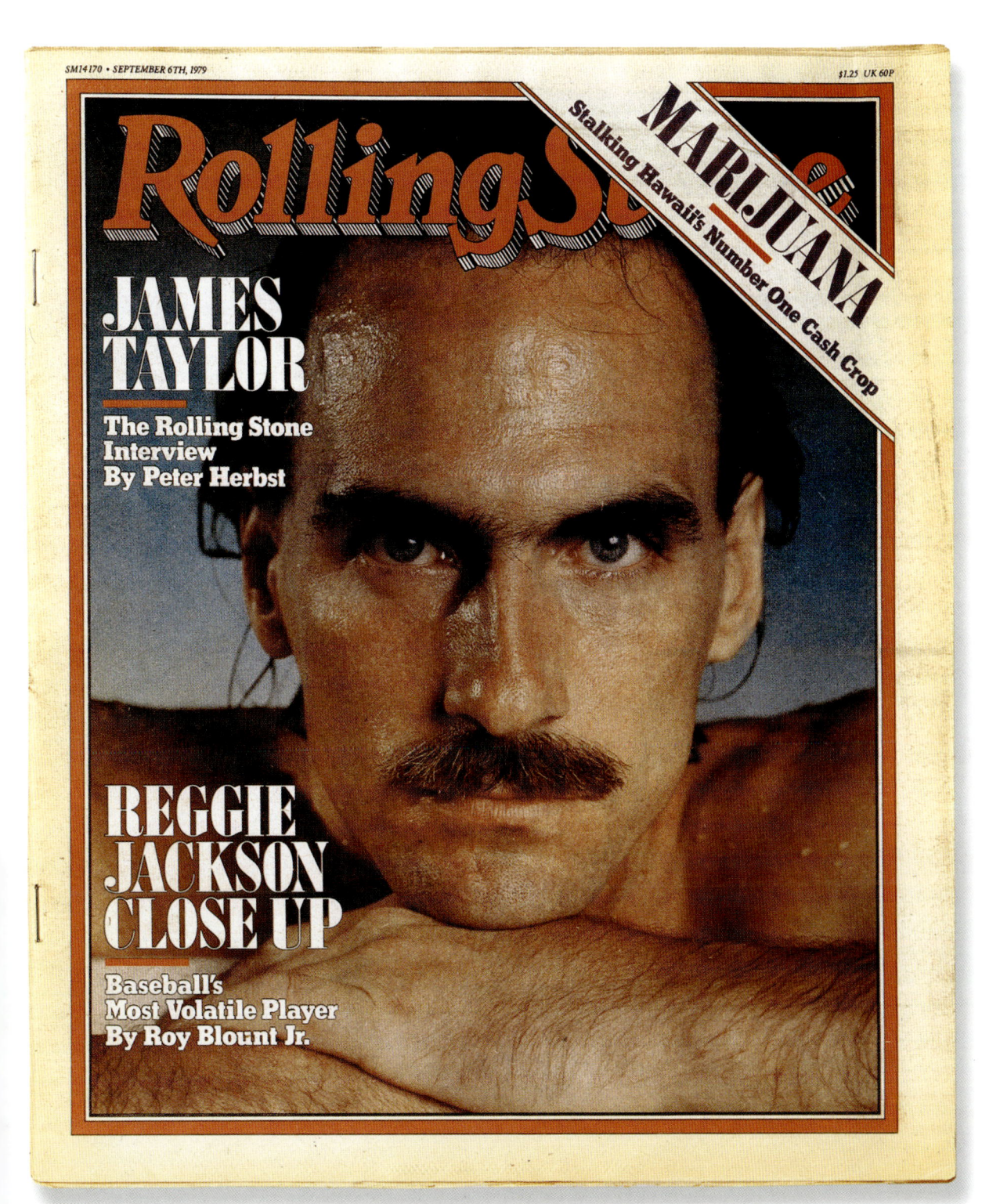

1970s

[RS 305] What's wrong with this picture? Look closely at the Eagles' lower extremities. Norman Seeff shot the band against a dark backdrop, so when ROLLING STONE decided to run the picture using an orange background on the cover, one of the magazine's crack photo strippers had to cut around the band's silhouette. In doing so, he left guitarist Don Felder (second from left) legless. Though sources deny there was any connection with the goof, the Eagles disbanded (for the first time) shortly thereafter. (Conspiracy theorists take note: In an infamous softball game prior to this cover, the Eagles beat ROLLING STONE staffers 15–8.)

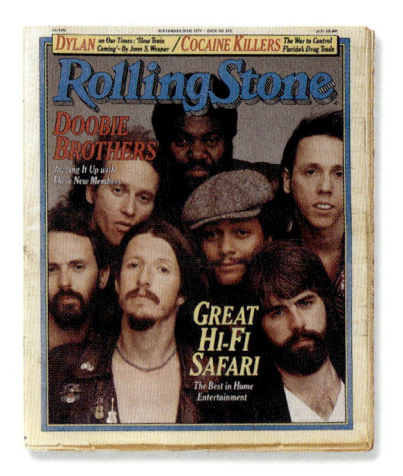

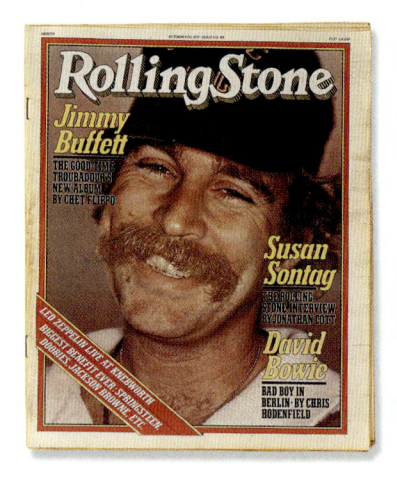

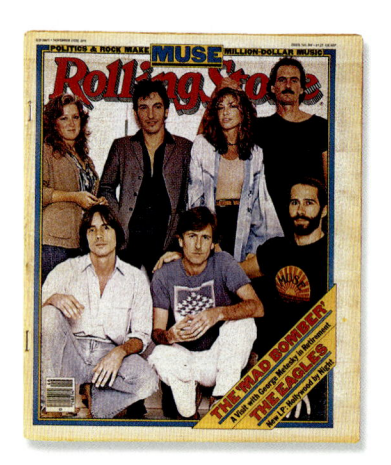

RS 300 | THE DOOBIE BROTHERS
September 20th, 1979
PHOTOGRAPH BY ANNIE LEIBOVITZ

RS 304 | MUSICIANS UNITED FOR SAFE ENERGY
November 15th, 1979
PHOTOGRAPH BY ANNIE LEIBOVITZ

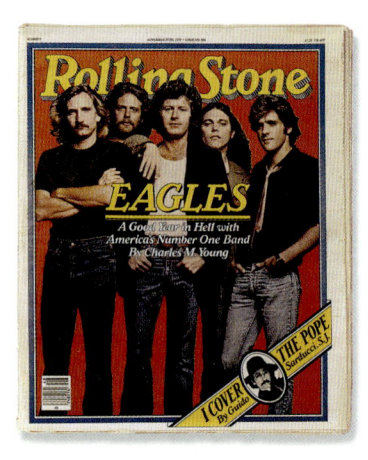

RS 301 | JIMMY BUFFETT
October 4th, 1979
PHOTOGRAPH BY ANNIE LEIBOVITZ

RS 305 | THE EAGLES
November 29th, 1979
PHOTOGRAPH BY NORMAN SEEFF

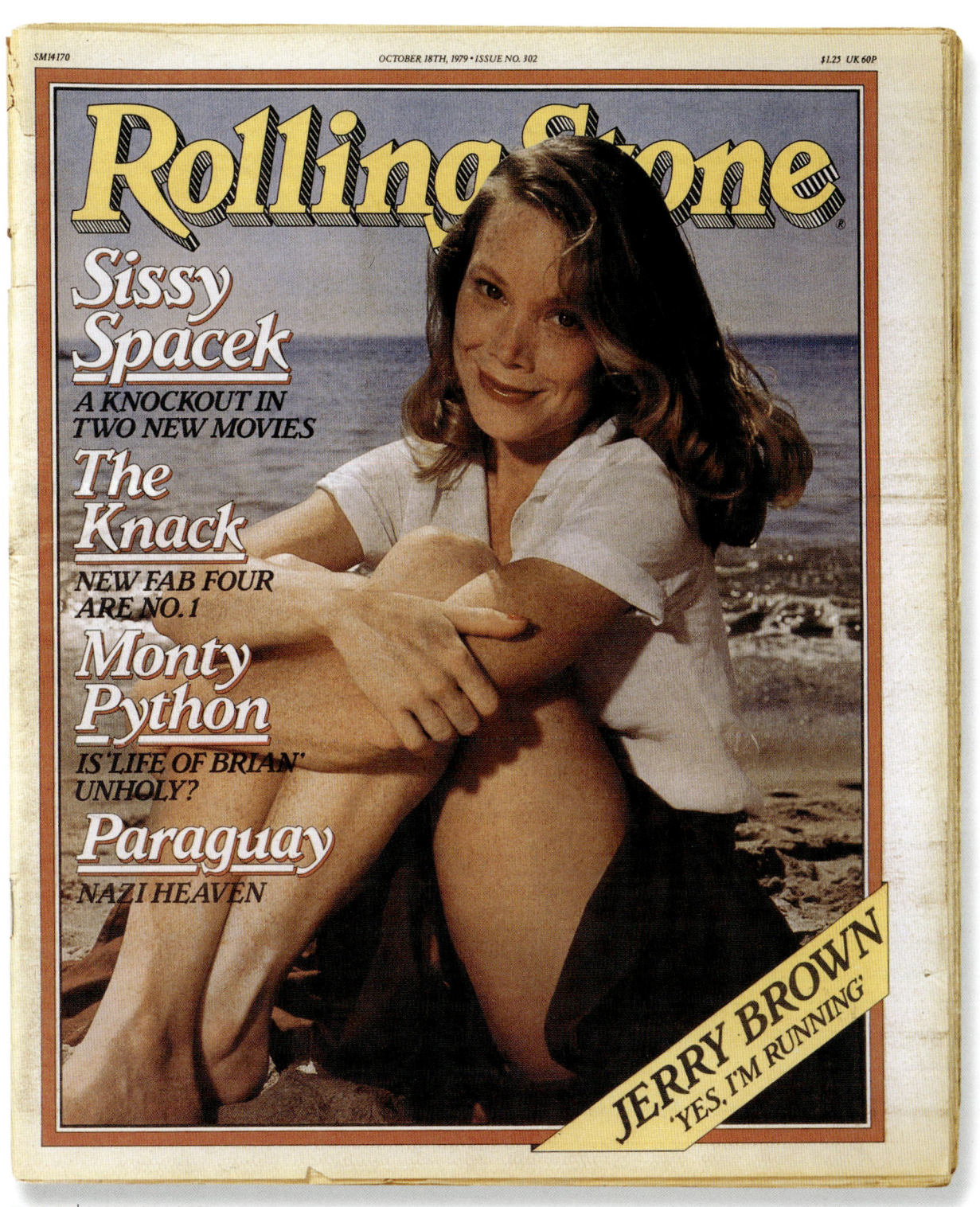

RS 302 | SISSY SPACEK | October 18th, 1979 | Photograph by Annie Leibovitz

50 YEARS OF COVERS • 157

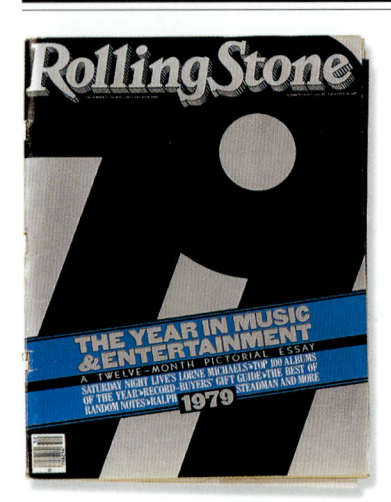

1970s

RS 307/308 | **1979 YEAR IN REVIEW**
December 27th, 1979 – January 10th, 1980
TYPOGRAPHER UNKNOWN

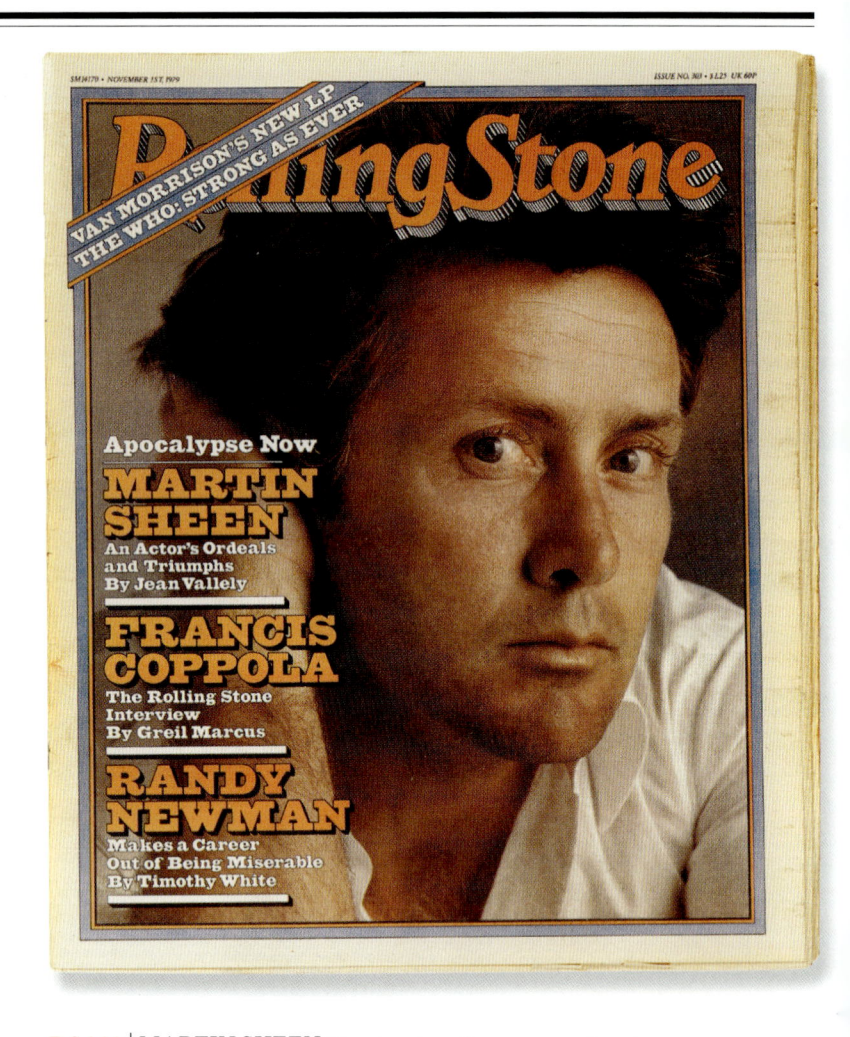

RS 303 | MARTIN SHEEN | November 1st, 1979 | PHOTOGRAPH BY ANNIE LEIBOVITZ

"*I remember some poor guy* was sitting there with bleeding hands from removing all the thorns on the roses. But it was a fabulously pleasant experience when [Annie] laid me down in all those flowers."

—*Bette Midler*

158 • ROLLING STONE

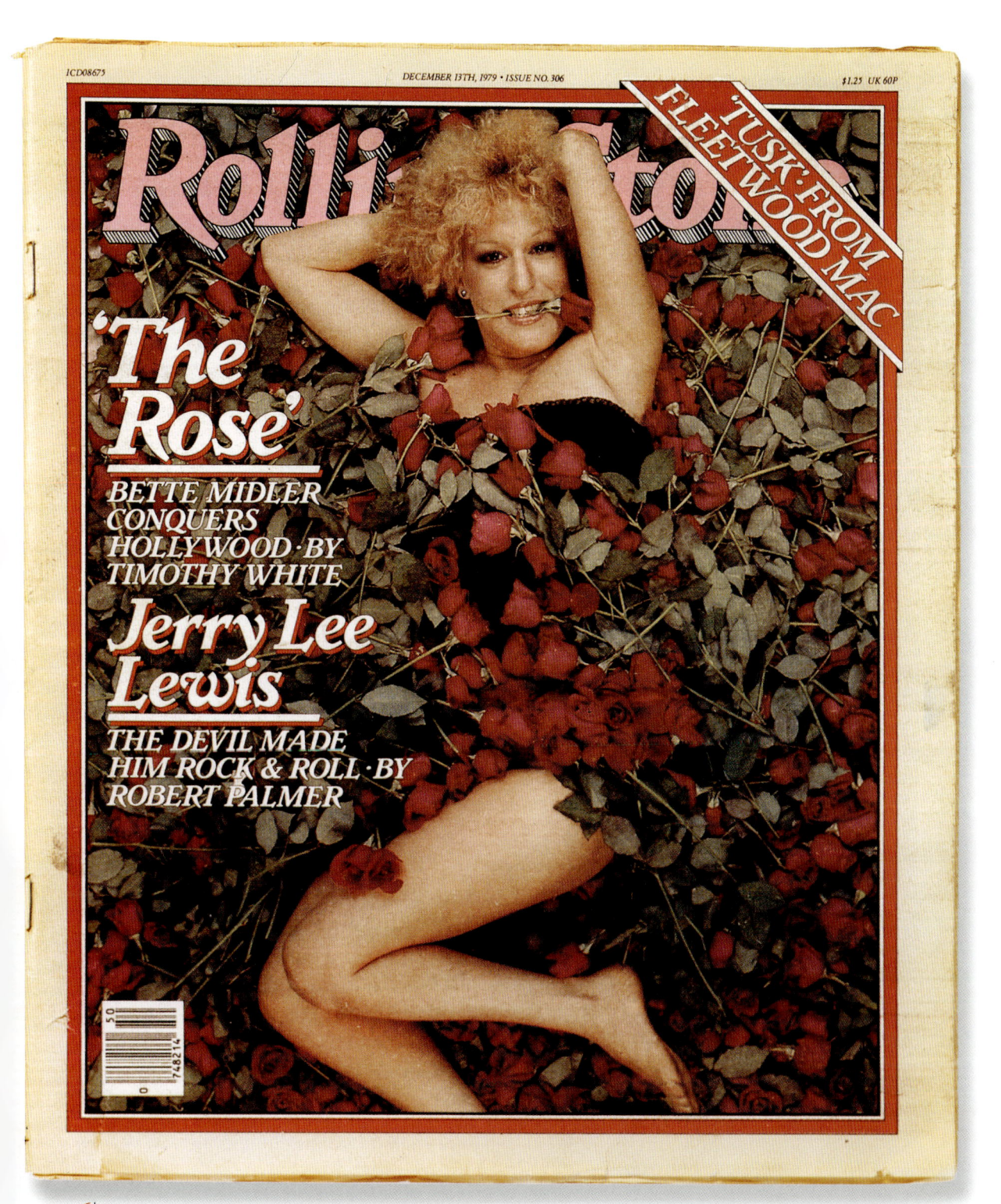

RS 306 | BETTE MIDLER | December 13th, 1979 | Photograph by Annie Leibovitz

50 YEARS OF COVERS • 159

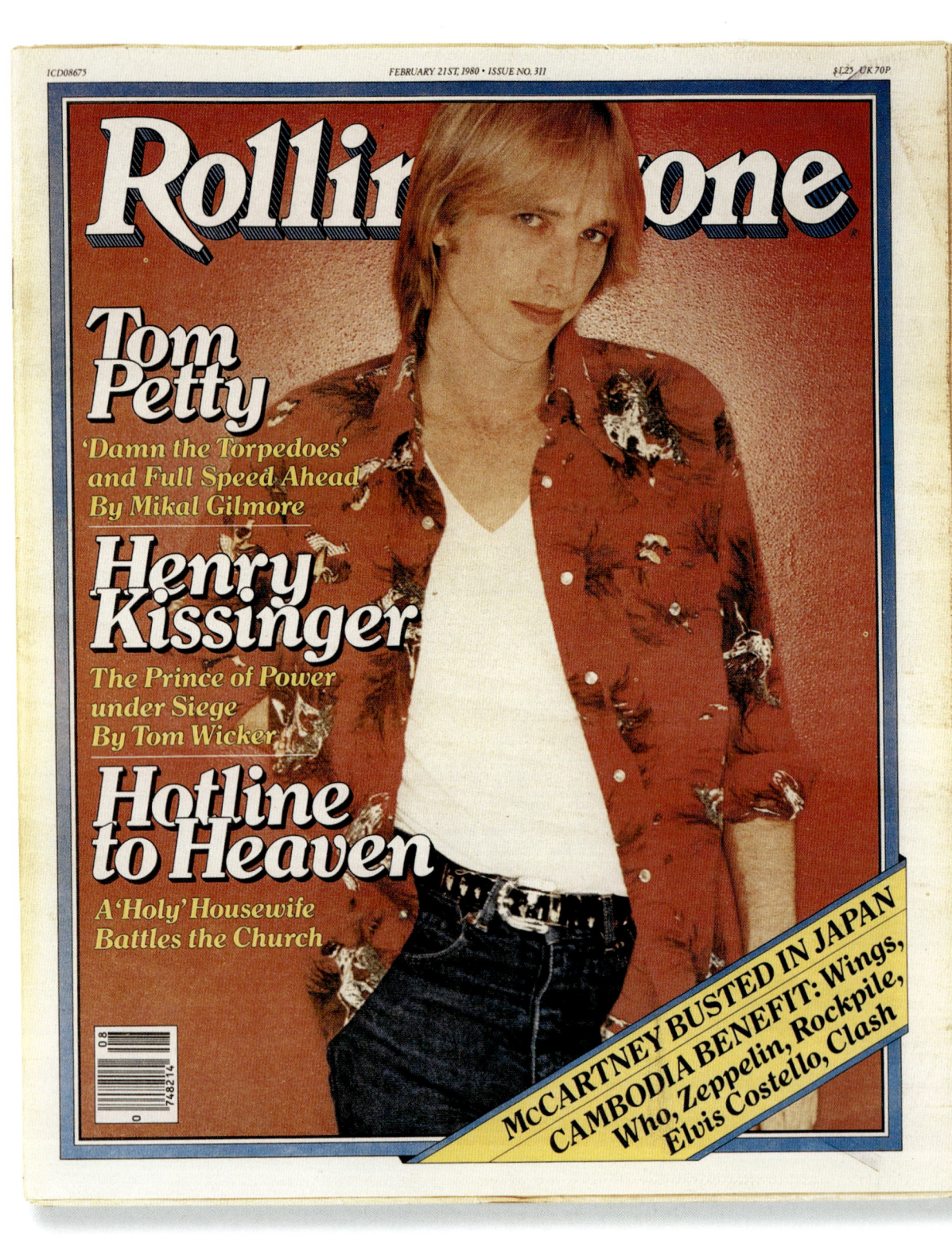

Rolling Stone

FEBRUARY 21ST, 1980 • ISSUE NO. 311

Tom Petty
'Damn the Torpedoes' and Full Speed Ahead
By Mikal Gilmore

Henry Kissinger
The Prince of Power under Siege
By Tom Wicker

Hotline to Heaven
A 'Holy' Housewife Battles the Church

McCARTNEY BUSTED IN JAPAN
CAMBODIA BENEFIT: Wings, Who, Zeppelin, Rockpile, Elvis Costello, Clash

1980s

RS 309 – RS 568

1980

Leafy ashes of vinyl, the byproduct of a Christmas rock & roll record-burning party, are still blowing around a frigid St. Paul parking lot when Petty and the Heartbreakers' tour bus pulls into town the next afternoon. These guys still remember the South Bible Belt bonfires that followed John Lennon's declaration in 1966 that the Beatles were "more popular than Jesus Christ." Maybe for that reason their show that evening seems to try to boast its own kind of hellfire.

"I called my mama on the phone today," Petty tells the audience in his introduction to Solomon Burke's "Cry to Me" (the song Petty performs on the *No Nukes* album). "I said, 'Mamma, I'm in St. Paul.' '*St. Paul?*' she said. 'I hear it gets pretty cold there.'"

Petty pauses and flashes the crowd a knowing grin. "'Yeah, mamma, but last night it got pretty hot.'" The audience lavishes him with a volley of cheers and a houseful of flickering Bic lights.

Tom Petty and the Heartbreakers' shows vary little from one to the next, but they do get more assaultive, like a blaring replication of *Torpedoes*' steam. And the older material benefits from that verve. In "American Girl," Mike Campbell and Benmont Tench embellish Petty's rock-constant rhythm guitar with fierce melodic undercuts, while Stan Lynch and Ron Blair direct the gun-burst tempo changes. In that majestic moment, the Heartbreakers fulfill a lot of promises that Roger McGuinn and company long ago forgot.

Petty, though, is the fulcrum. Yet it's something more than his mannered cockiness and stealthy catwalk that move me tonight. For one thing, it's the way he sings the pained pronouncement at the opening of "Even the Losers" – "I showed you the stars you could never see/Baby, it couldn't have been that easy to forget about me" – in a voice that sounds like it lost more than it could afford, and will probably lose it all again.

It occurs to me, standing at the back of the hall, that most people I know who have ever found meaning in rock & roll have done so because they saw something heroic or romantic or intellectual or transcendent about the idiom. Petty's music offers a curious kind of transcendence, one that reminds me of something crime novelist James M. Cain once wrote about his own books: "I . . . write of the wish that comes true, for some reason a terrifying concept, at least to my imagination. [The reader realizes] that the characters cannot have this particular wish and survive."

[EXCERPT FROM RS 311 COVER STORY BY MIKAL GILMORE]

RS 311 | TOM PETTY | February 21st, 1980 | PHOTOGRAPH BY ANNIE LEIBOVITZ

1980s

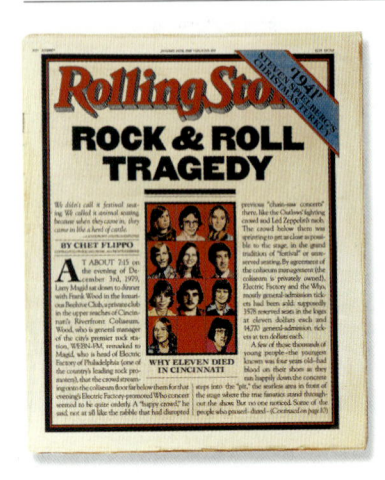

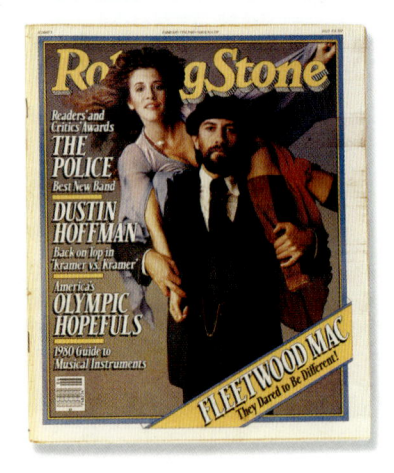

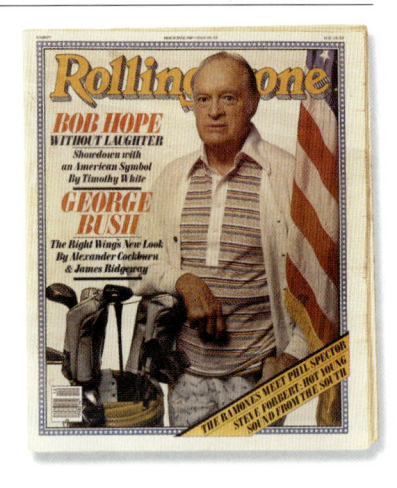

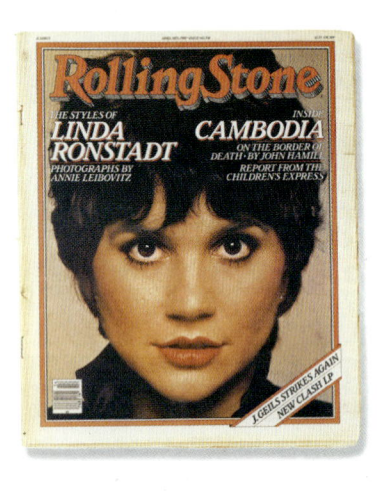

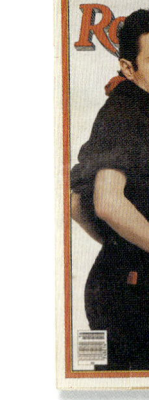

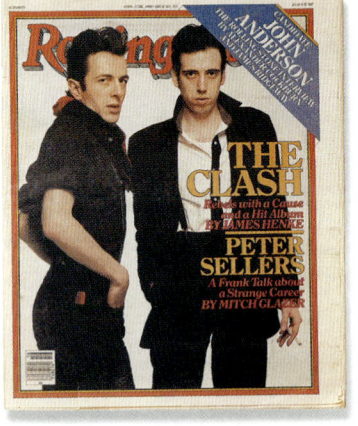

RS 309 | THE WHO
CONCERT TRAGEDY
January 24th, 1980
PHOTOGRAPHERS UNKNOWN

RS 314 | LINDA RONSTADT
April 3rd, 1980
PHOTOGRAPH BY ANNIE LEIBOVITZ

RS 310 | STEVIE NICKS
& MICK FLEETWOOD
February 7th, 1980
PHOTOGRAPH BY RICHARD AVEDON

RS 315 | JOE STRUMMER
& MICK JONES
April 17th, 1980
PHOTOGRAPH BY ANNIE LEIBOVITZ

RS 313 | BOB HOPE
March 20th, 1980
PHOTOGRAPH BY RICHARD AVEDON

RS 316 | BOB SEGER
May 1st, 1980
PHOTOGRAPH BY ANNIE LEIBOVITZ

"THIS IS AN IMPORTANT FACT: PEOPLE PREFER TO DANCE THAN to fight wars. In these days, when everybody's fighting, mostly for stupid reasons, people forget that. If there's anything we can do, it's to get them dancing again."
—*Mick Jones*

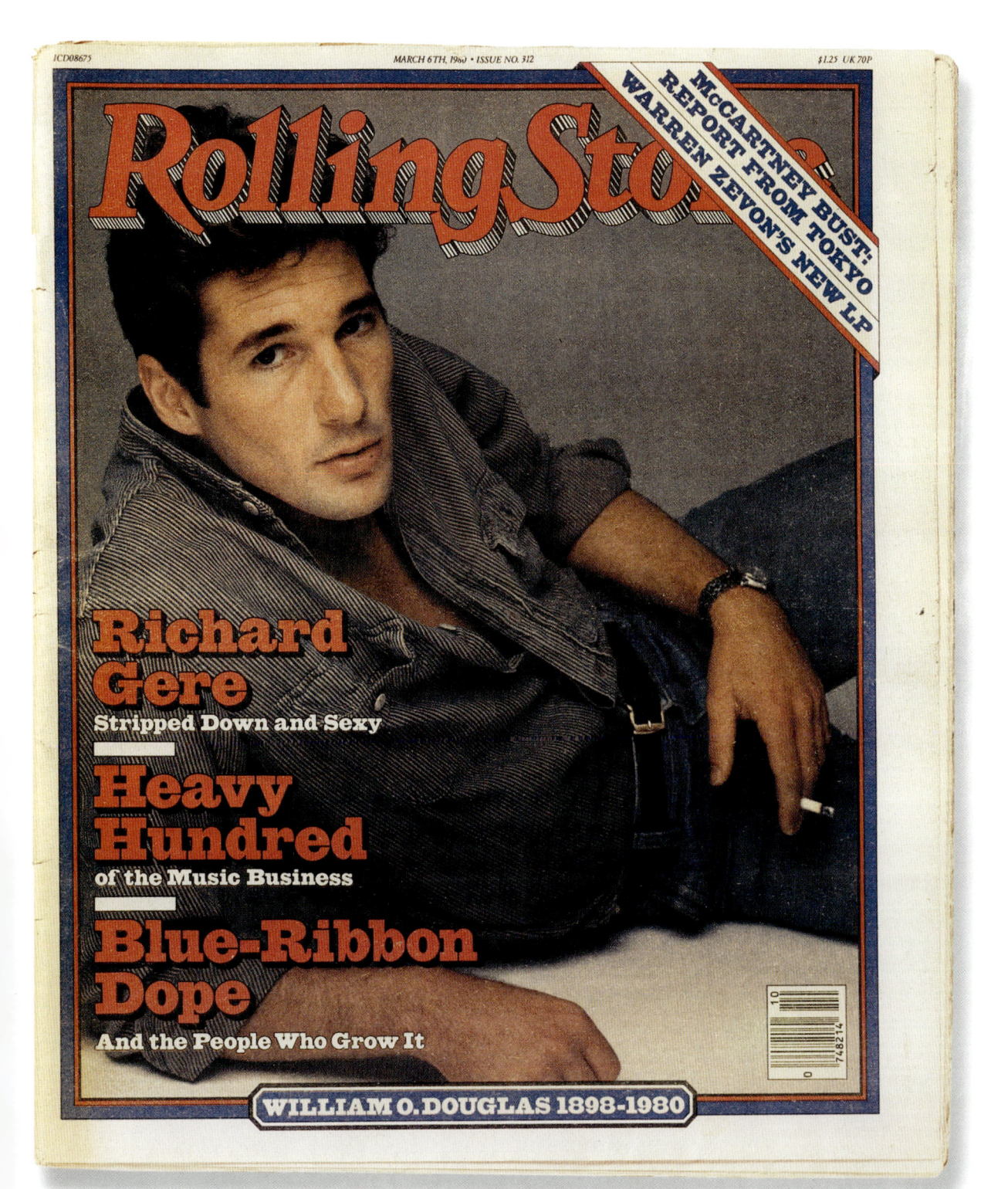

RS 312 | RICHARD GERE | March 6th, 1980 | Photograph by Terry O'Neill

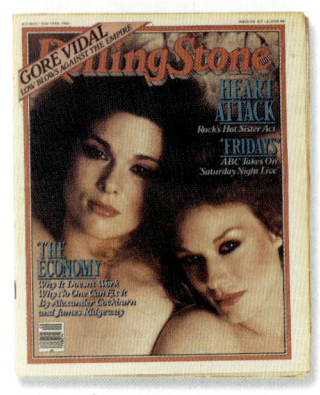

RS 317 | ANN & NANCY WILSON
May 15th, 1980
PHOTOGRAPH BY ANNIE LEIBOVITZ

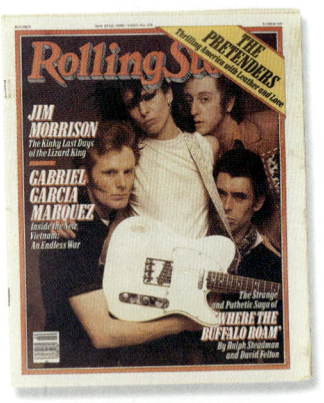

RS 318 | THE PRETENDERS
May 29th, 1980
PHOTOGRAPH BY ANNIE LEIBOVITZ

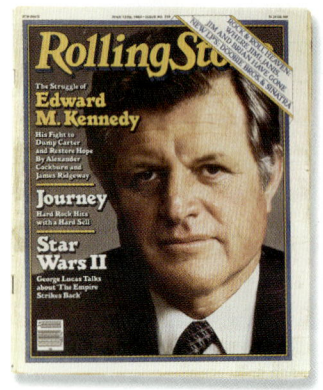

RS 319 | EDWARD KENNEDY
June 12th, 1980
PHOTOGRAPH BY ANNIE LEIBOVITZ

RS 320 | PETE TOWNSHEND | June 26th, 1980 | PHOTOGRAPH BY ANNIE LEIBOVITZ

"*In Britain,* at the moment, we've got 2-Tone, we've still got punk, we've got Mod bands, we've got heavy-metal bands, we've got established supergroups, we've got all kinds of *different* families of music – *each* of which takes an enormous amount of adjustment. They're intense, and very socially . . . jagged. They don't fit neatly into existing society: They challenge it. . . .

"When you listen to the Sex Pistols, to 'Anarchy in the U.K.' and 'Bodies' and tracks like that, what immediately strikes you is that *this is actually happening.* This is a bloke, with a brain on his shoulders, who is actually saying something he *sincerely* believes is happening in the world, saying it with real venom and real passion. It touches you, and it scares you – it makes you feel uncomfortable. It's like somebody saying, 'The Germans are coming! And there's no way we're gonna stop 'em!' . . .

"You read the fucking words, they scare the shit out of you. The Pretenders – Chrissie Hynde's got a sweet voice, but she writes in double-speak: She's talking about getting laid by Hell's Angels on her latest record! And *raped.* The words are full of the most *brutal,* head-on feminism that has ever come out of any band, anywhere. . . ."

[EXCERPT FROM PETE TOWNSHEND INTERVIEW BY GREIL MARCUS]

Rolling Stone

ICD 08675 · JUNE 26TH, 1980 · ISSUE NO. 320 — $1.25 UK 70P

PETE TOWNSHEND
THE ROLLING STONE INTERVIEW

PAUL McCARTNEY
TALKS ABOUT JAIL IN JAPAN AND HIS ONE-MAN BAND

SUGAR RAY LEONARD
BOXING'S KNOCKOUT SENSATION

HI-FI 1980
STEREOS OF THE STARS: BOB SEGER, TED NUGENT, NICOLETTE LARSON & MORE

ROBBIE ROBERTSON
TAKES A CHANCE ON 'CARNY'

1980s

ICD 08675 — JULY 10TH, 1980 • ISSUE NO. 321 — $1.25 UK 70P

Rolling Stone

JOHN TRAVOLTA
The Pain and Passion
of a Private Life
By Timothy White

**NICARAGUA
ONE YEAR
AFTER**
The Revolution That
Actually Might Work

**LOS ANGELES
RENAISSANCE**
Local Bands
Thrive in Clubs

How to Choose
an Acoustic Guitar

The Pros Pick
the Best Keyboards

RS 321 | JOHN TRAVOLTA | July 10th, 1980 | Photograph by Annie Leibovitz

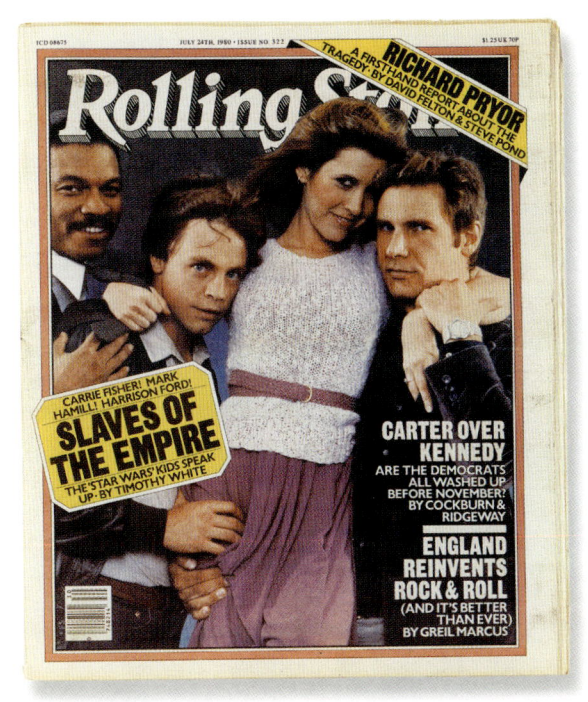

RS 322 | CAST OF 'THE EMPIRE STRIKES BACK'
July 24th, 1980
PHOTOGRAPH BY ANNIE LEIBOVITZ

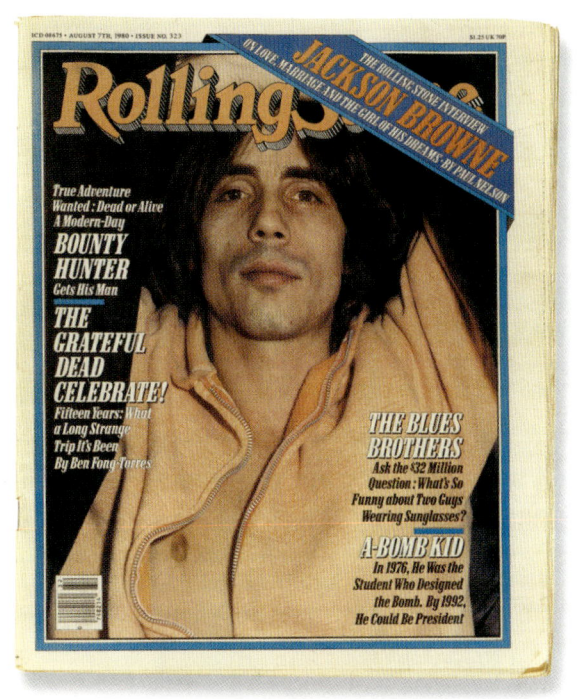

RS 323 | JACKSON BROWNE
August 7th, 1980
PHOTOGRAPH BY ANNIE LEIBOVITZ

Truly, there is a different John Travolta

making movies these days than the one who soared in *Saturday Night Fever*. He has developed the instincts to exploit the charisma that moved *New Yorker* film critic Pauline Kael to dub him "an original presence." Professionally, he has become as insulated as a working actor can possibly be. As for the mystery surrounding his personal life, it can be no accident that after years of extraordinary press coverage, we've learned precious little about who he is.

And so, when Travolta, 26, ambles in for an informal lunch, it isn't surprising that he exudes no particular panache beyond a boyish likability. He arrives alone, as he will for subsequent meetings. He shakes my hand, plops into a chair opposite mine and puzzles over the menu, trying to decide whether he should eat something nourishing or go straight for brownie cake topped with whipped cream. (He eventually opts for the latter.)

[EXCERPT FROM RS 321 COVER STORY BY TIMOTHY WHITE]

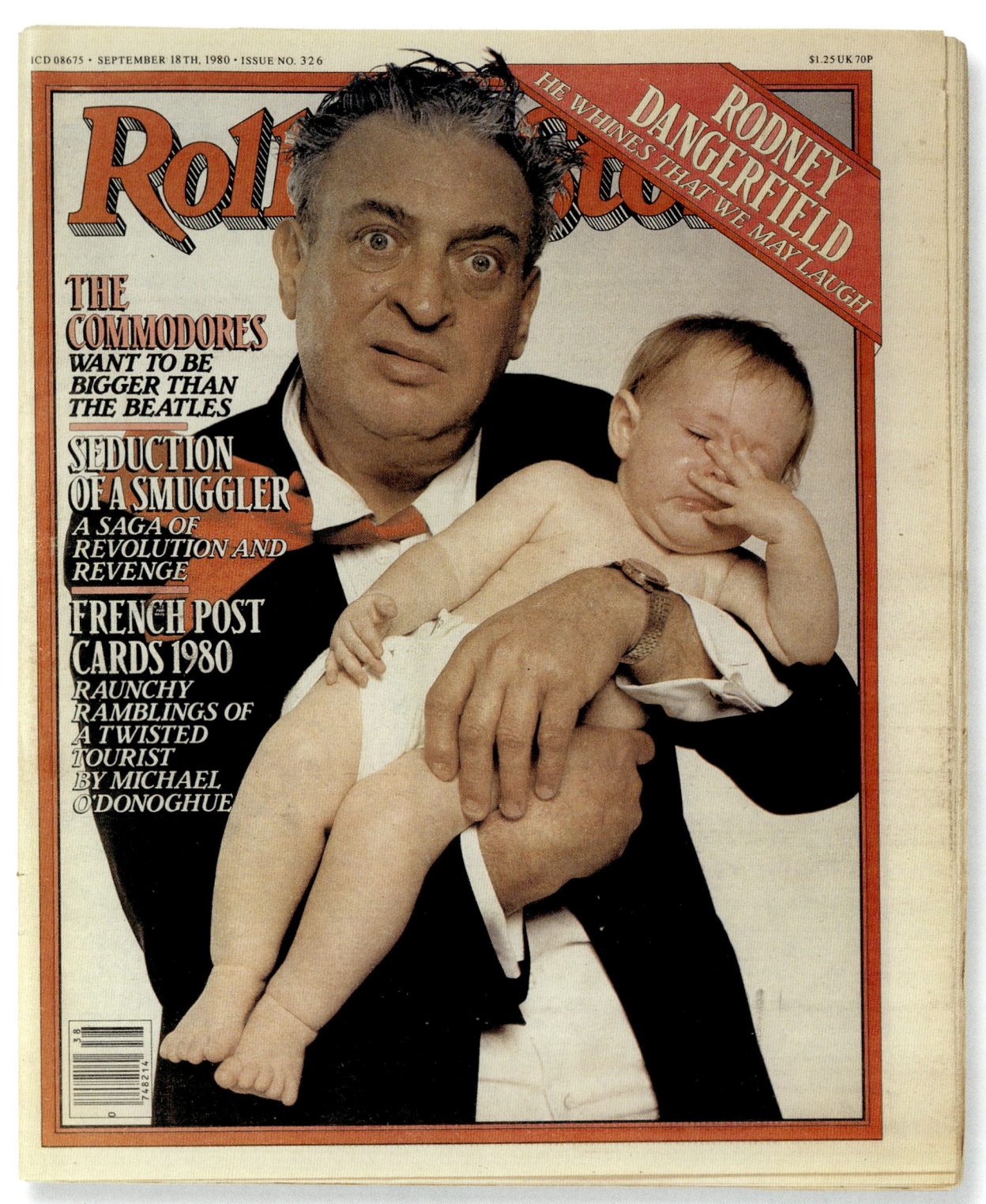

RS 326 | **RODNEY DANGERFIELD** | September 18th, 1980 | Photograph by Annie Leibovitz

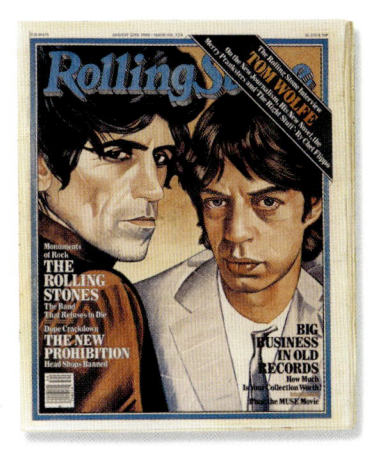

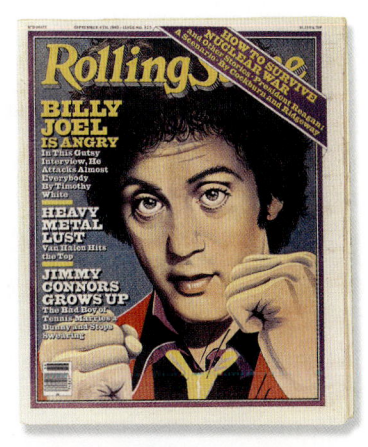

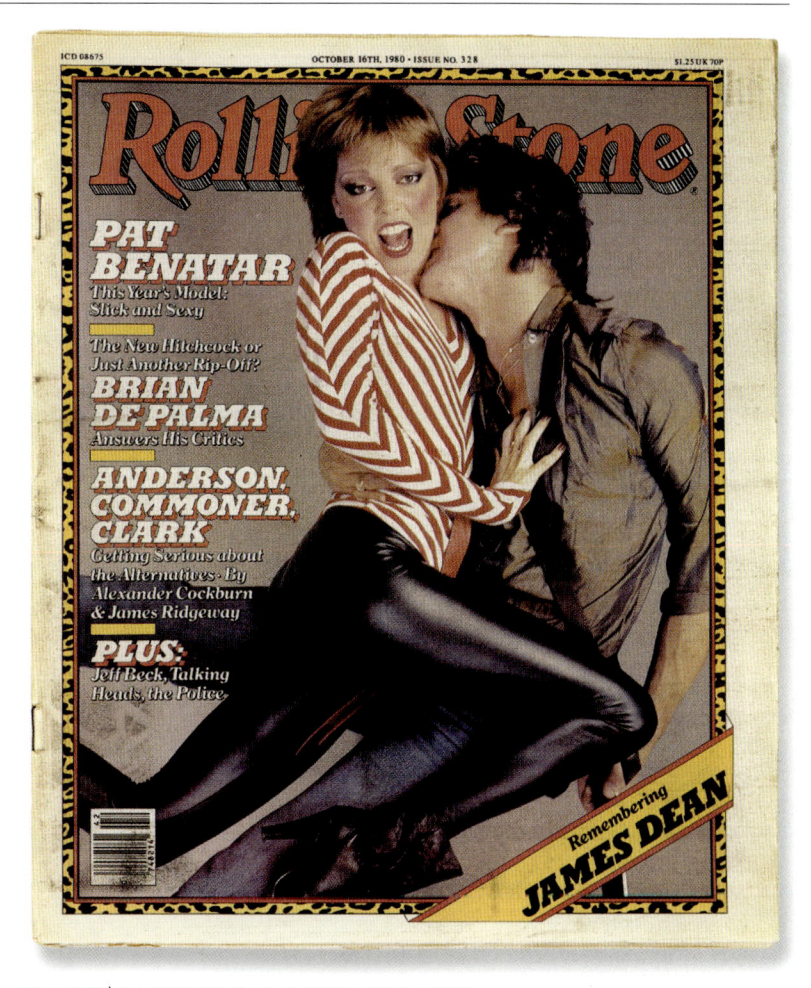

$\mathcal{RS}$ 324 | KEITH RICHARDS
& MICK JAGGER
August 21st, 1980
ILLUSTRATION BY JULIAN ALLEN

$\mathcal{RS}$ 325 | BILLY JOEL
September 4th, 1980
ILLUSTRATION BY KIM WHITESIDES

$\mathcal{RS}$ 328 | PAT BENATAR & NEIL GERALDO
October 16th, 1980
PHOTOGRAPH BY ANNIE LEIBOVITZ

"THE SHIT THE RECORD COMPANY puts out is embarrassing. I came back from the last tour and found out they'd made a cardboard cutout of me in my little tights. What has that got to do with anything? They also took out an ad in *Billboard* and airbrushed part of my top off. They knew I'd never pose like that, so they took the cover of the new record, moved the bottom line up a bit and airbrushed it to look like I'm naked. If that is gonna sell records, then it's a real sorry thing.

"The strange thing is, the bigger you get, the less control you really have. So when something gets really screwed up, you have to pull out the big guns and say, 'Look, cut it out or I won't sing.' I'm not ready to be Farrah Fawcett."

—*Pat Benatar*

1980s

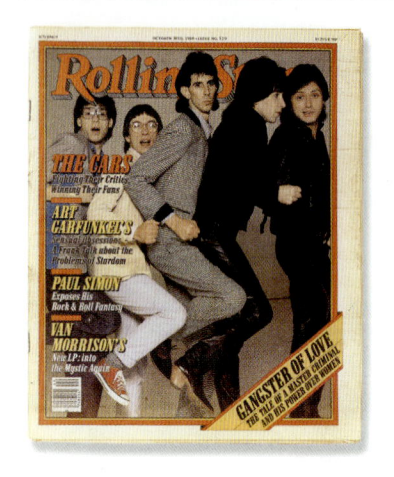

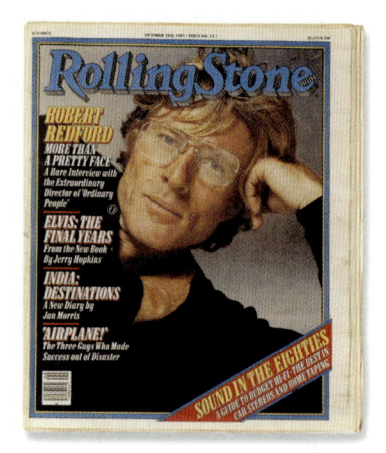

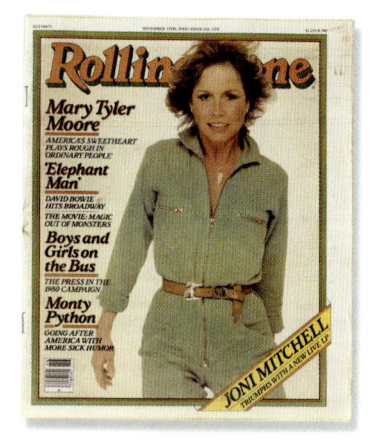

RS 329 | THE CARS
October 30th, 1980
PHOTOGRAPH BY ANNIE LEIBOVITZ

"IT'S FUNNY, BUT WHEN I wasn't a so-called star, I still used to get recognized a lot, although for other reasons. I've felt rather like an outcast for most of my life, and I became comfortable with it at a young age. But it's not easy sometimes telling yourself that there's hope for your future, there's a reason to go on." Ocasek sits quietly for several seconds, staring down at his long, bony hands. "I used to think about how it would be turned around someday."

And now that things have turned around?

He shrugs casually. "That's the joke of the thing: you *can't* be loved by everybody. I know that, and I've really come to accept it. That denial of love, in fact, eases my mind."

[EXCERPT FROM RS 329 COVER STORY BY MIKAL GILMORE]

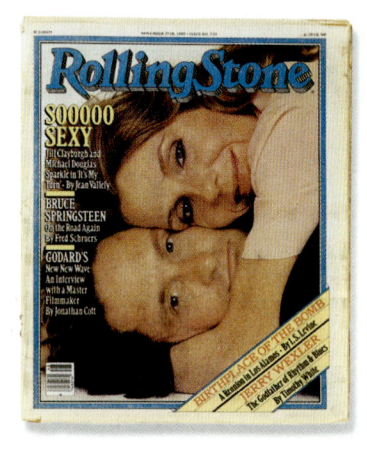

RS 327 | ROBERT REDFORD
October 2nd, 1980
PHOTOGRAPH BY ANNIE LEIBOVITZ

RS 331 | JILL CLAYBURGH & MICHAEL DOUGLAS
November 27th, 1980
PHOTOGRAPH BY ANNIE LEIBOVITZ

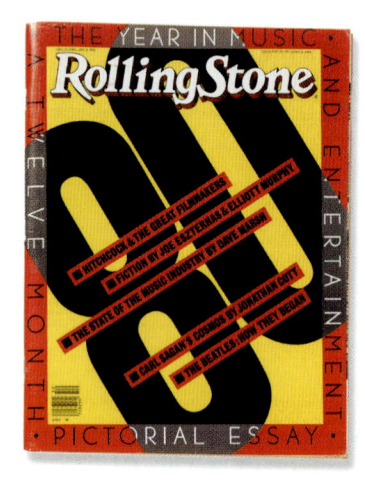

RS 330 | MARY TYLER MOORE
November 13th, 1980
PHOTOGRAPH BY ANNIE LEIBOVITZ

RS 333/334 | 1980 YEARBOOK
December 25th, 1980 – January 8th, 1981
TYPOGRAPHER UNKNOWN

Rolling Stone

DECEMBER 11TH, 1980 · ISSUE NO. 332

ICD 08675 $1.50 UK 70P

THE UNSINKABLE DOLLY PARTON
Bursts into the Movies
By Chet Flippo

B-52'S
What Makes This Tacky Little Dance Band Tick?

PEKING GIRL
A Tender Encounter with a Victim of the Gang of Four

KENNY STABLER
Peter Gent Sacks Houston's Elusive Quarterback

THE HITMAKERS
A REPORT ON THE MOST SENSITIVE SECRET IN THE RECORD BUSINESS

RS 332 | DOLLY PARTON | December 11th, 1980 | Photograph by Richard Avedon

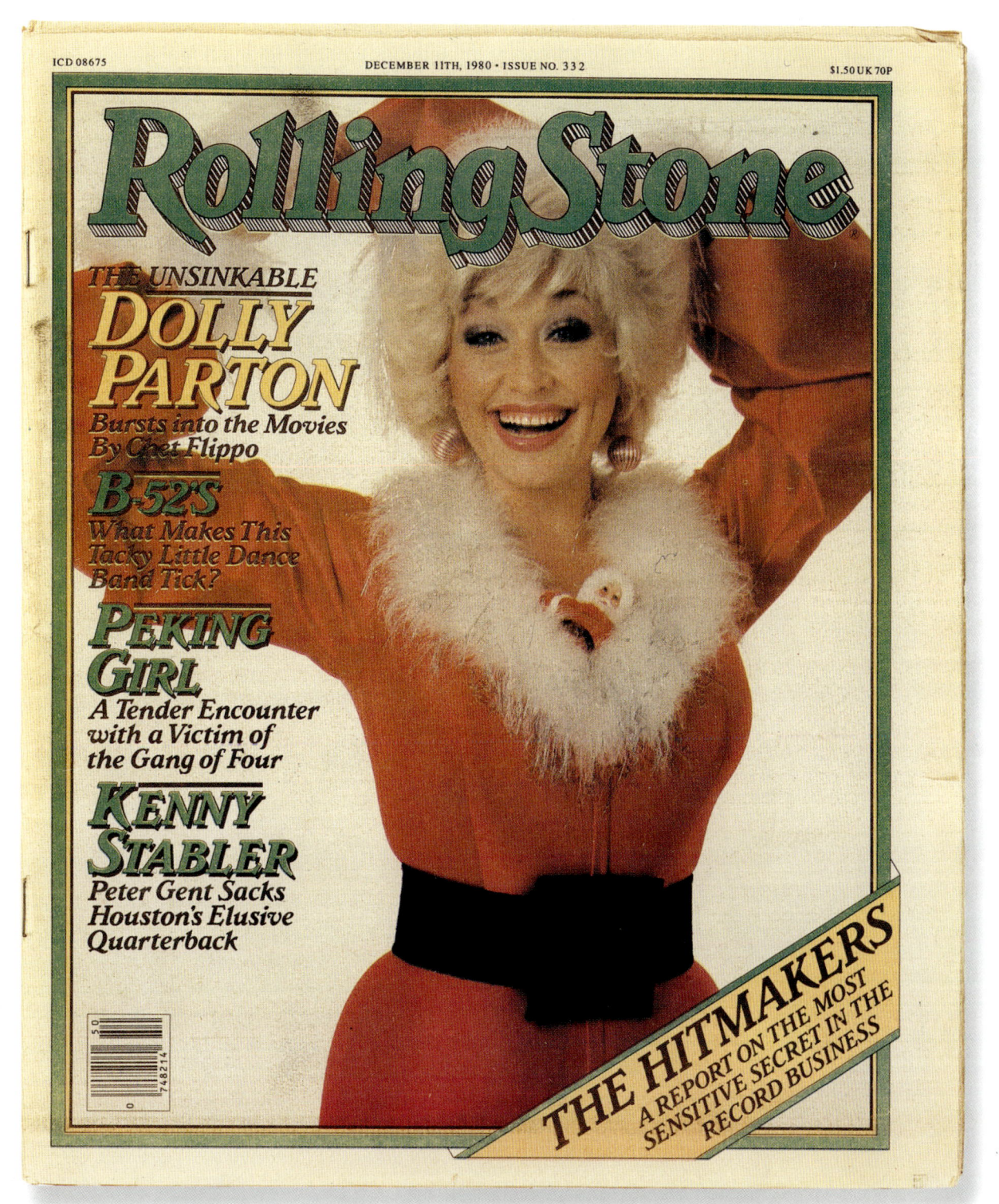

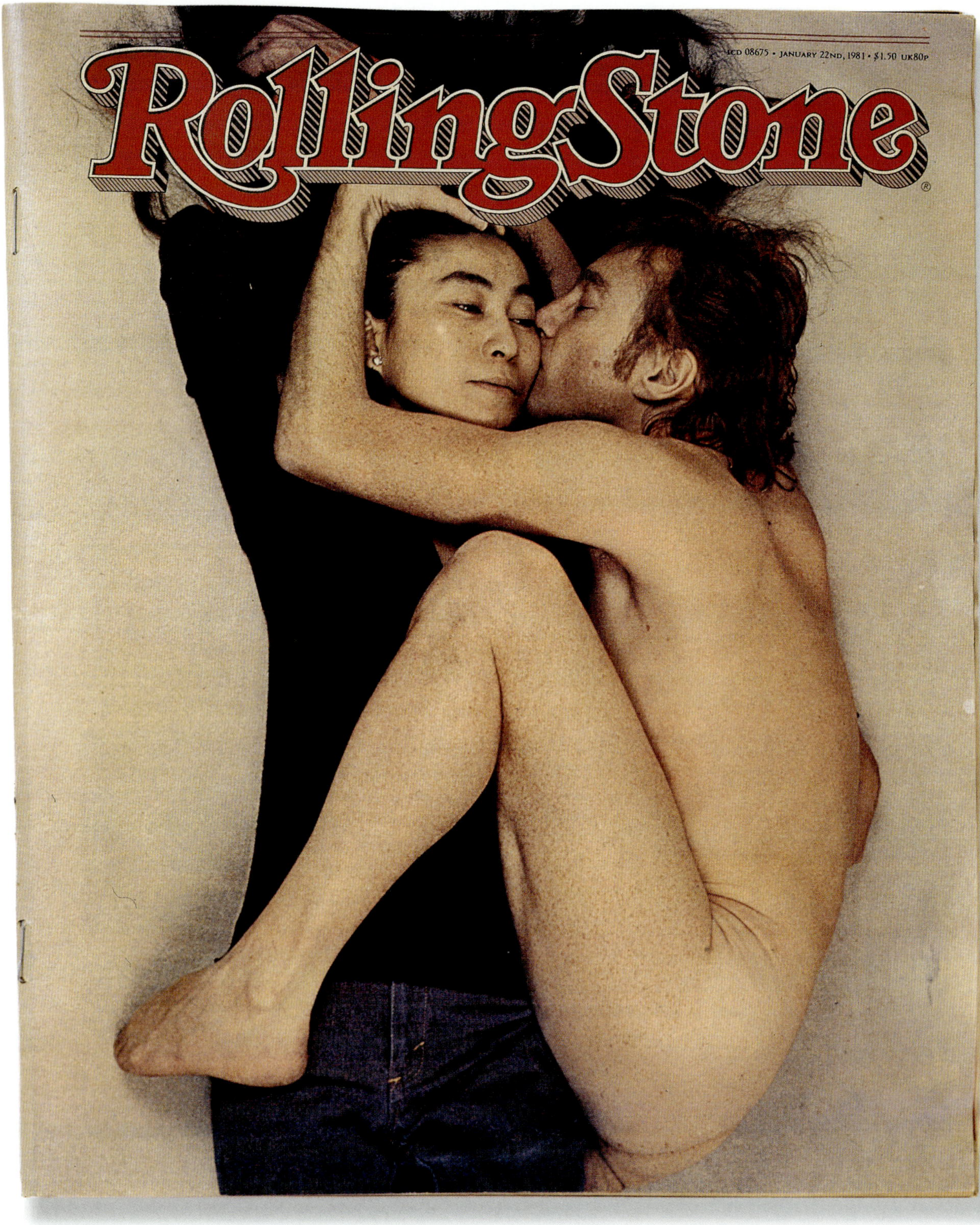
Rolling Stone
LCD 08675 • JANUARY 22ND, 1981 • $1.50 UK80P

RS 335 | JOHN LENNON & YOKO ONO | January 22nd, 1981 | Photograph by Annie Leibovitz

"*Man shot,* One West Seventy-second" was the call on the police radio just before eleven p.m. Officers Jim Moran and Bill Gamble were in the third blue-and-white that screamed to a halt outside the Dakota apartment building. The man who had been shot couldn't wait for an ambulance. They stretched him out on the backseat of their car and raced to Roosevelt Hospital, at the corner of Fifty-ninth Street and Ninth Avenue. They lifted the bloody body onto a gurney and wheeled it into the emergency room. There was nothing the doctors could do. They pronounced John Lennon dead at 11:07 p.m. . . .

Within minutes, the small, brick-walled ambulance courtyard outside the emergency room was filled with at least 200 people who were staring dumbly at the closed double doors. Some of the cabdrivers, who were depositing reporters at the rate of two or three a minute, joined the throng. One of them volunteered loudly that he had it from a good source that John Lennon had been dead on arrival. One young woman stood alone in the middle of Ninth Avenue and wept.

—*Chet Flippo* [EXCERPT FROM RS 335]

"I REMEMBER ARRIVING AT THE apartment that morning, December 8th, and John taking me aside and saying, 'Listen, I know they want to run me by myself on the cover, but I really want Yoko to be on the cover with me. It's really important.' They had just finished their *Double Fantasy* album, and I remember seeing the cover and being very *moved* by it, so of course when they lay down together, and John was nude curled up against her clothed, it was much more poignant. He looked much more vulnerable. I remember peeling the Polaroid and him looking at it and saying, 'This is it. This is our relationship.'

Several hours later John was murdered. I went to the Roosevelt Hospital waiting for an announcement. Early in the morning, the doctor came out – I remember that I was completely numb – I stood on a chair and I photographed the doctor giving the death announcement. I came in [to ROLLING STONE] the following day, and they were mocking up covers with John's portrait [close-ups of his face] and I said, 'Jann, I promised John that the cover would be him and Yoko.' And Jann backed me up. I said it was the last promise." —*Annie Leibovitz*

"We have lost a genius of the spirit."

—*Norman Mailer*

MORE THAN ANY OTHER ROCK MUSICIAN (with the possible exception of Bob Dylan), John Lennon personalized the political and politicized the personal, often making the two stances interchangeable but sometimes ripping out the seams altogether. Whereas Dylan expressed his personal and political iconoclasm mainly by expanding and exploding the narrative line, Lennon assaulted pop music from a dozen different directions. He not only attacked the war – any war – but questioned and confronted the very methods and structures he'd utilized in his attack, thereby pushing rock & roll up against the wall to test limits and demand answers. John Lennon believed passionately that popular music could and should do more than merely entertain. He changed the face of rock & roll forever. —*Stephen Holden* [EXCERPT FROM RS 335]

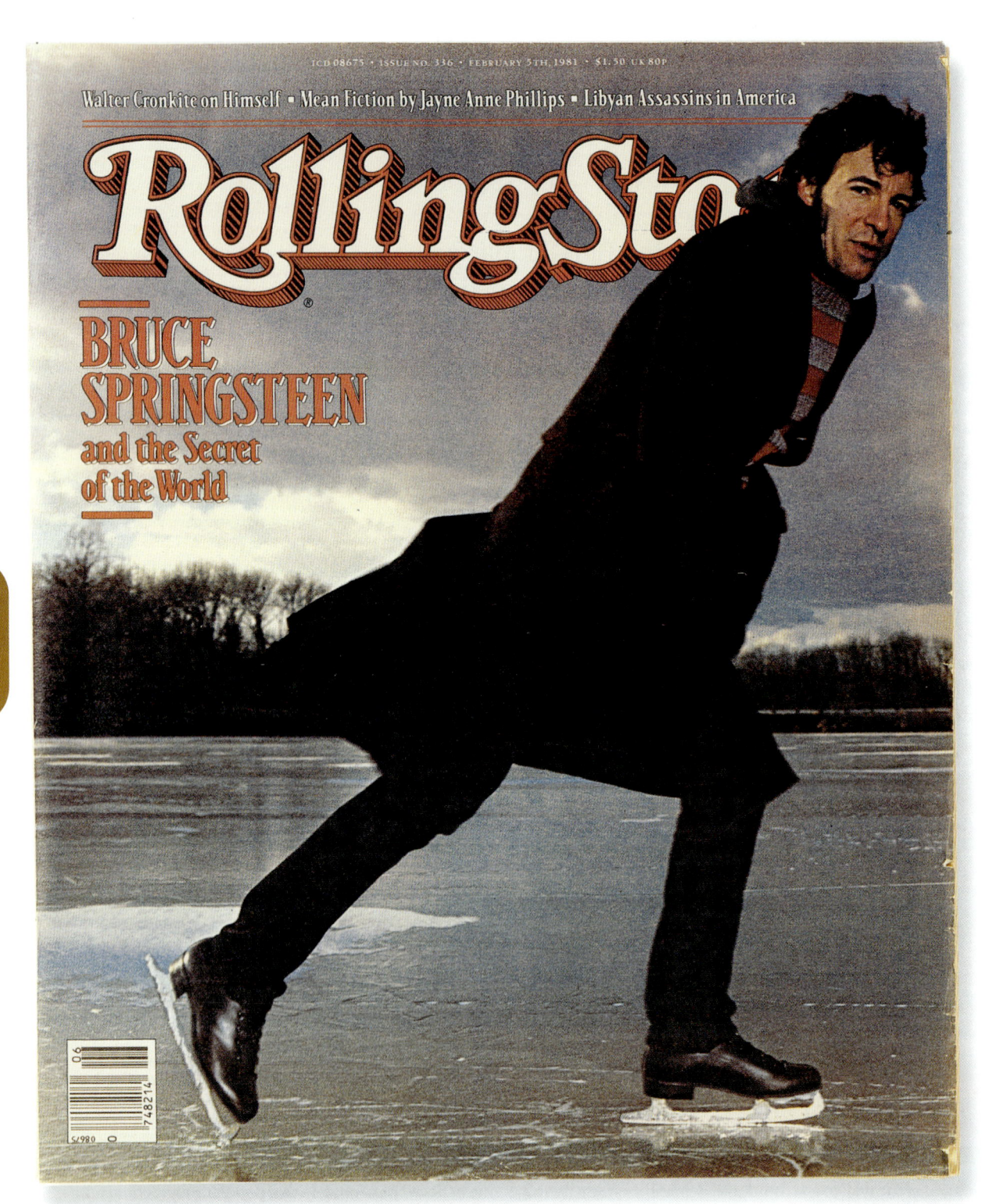

RS 336 | **BRUCE SPRINGSTEEN** | February 5th, 1981 | Photograph by Annie Leibovitz

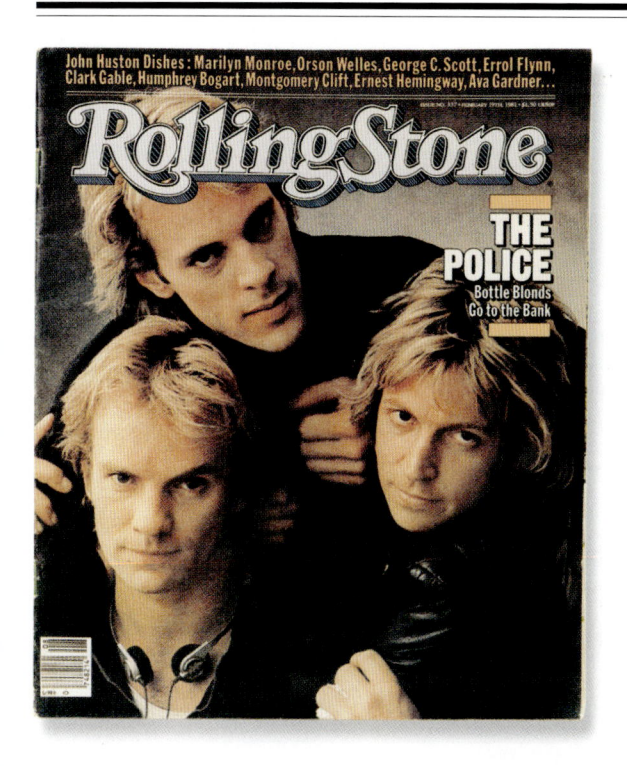

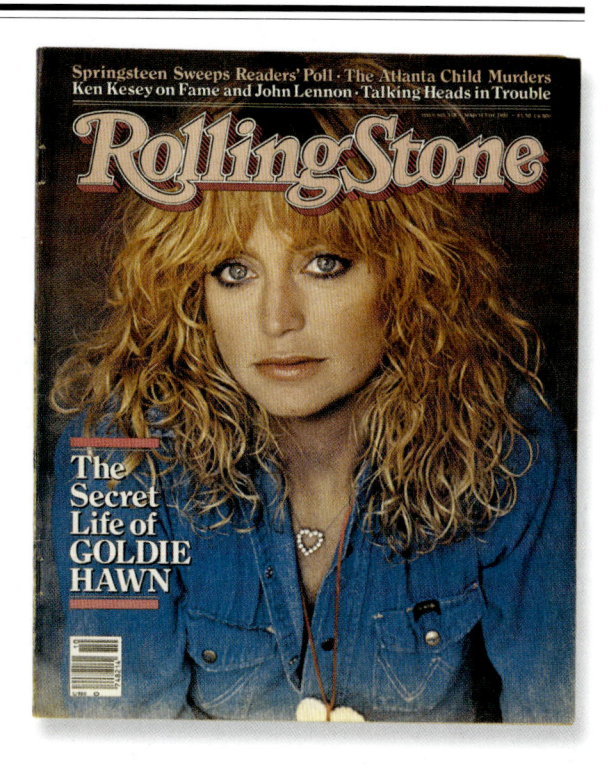

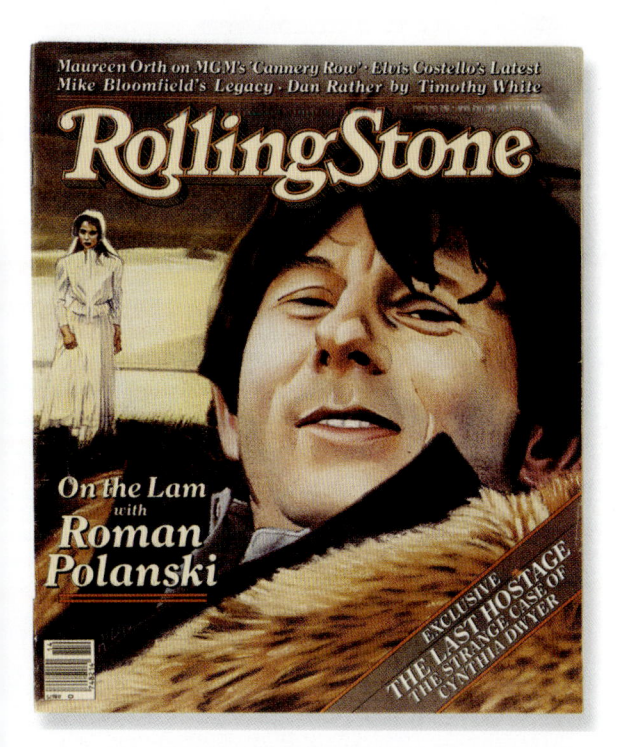

RS 337 | THE POLICE
February 19th, 1981
Photograph by Klaus Lucka

RS 338 | GOLDIE HAWN
March 5th, 1981
Photograph by Denis Piel

RS 340 | ROMAN POLANSKI
April 2nd, 1981
Illustration by Julian Allen

[*RS 336*] In discussing Rolling Stone with Jann Wenner, Mick Jagger implies that the logo lost its character when it lost its balls. Hence the introduction of a redesigned logo by typographer Jim Parkinson combining elements of the previous logos. In addition, glossy paper and trimmed pages replace rough-edged newsprint, and the cover's dimensions decrease to 10 by 12 inches, the size it has remained ever since.

50 YEARS OF COVERS • 175

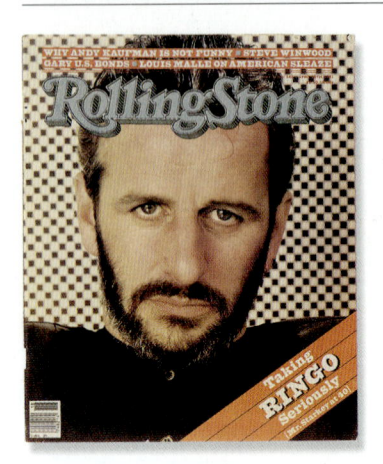

RS 342 | RINGO STARR
April 30th, 1981
PHOTOGRAPH BY MICHAEL CHILDERS

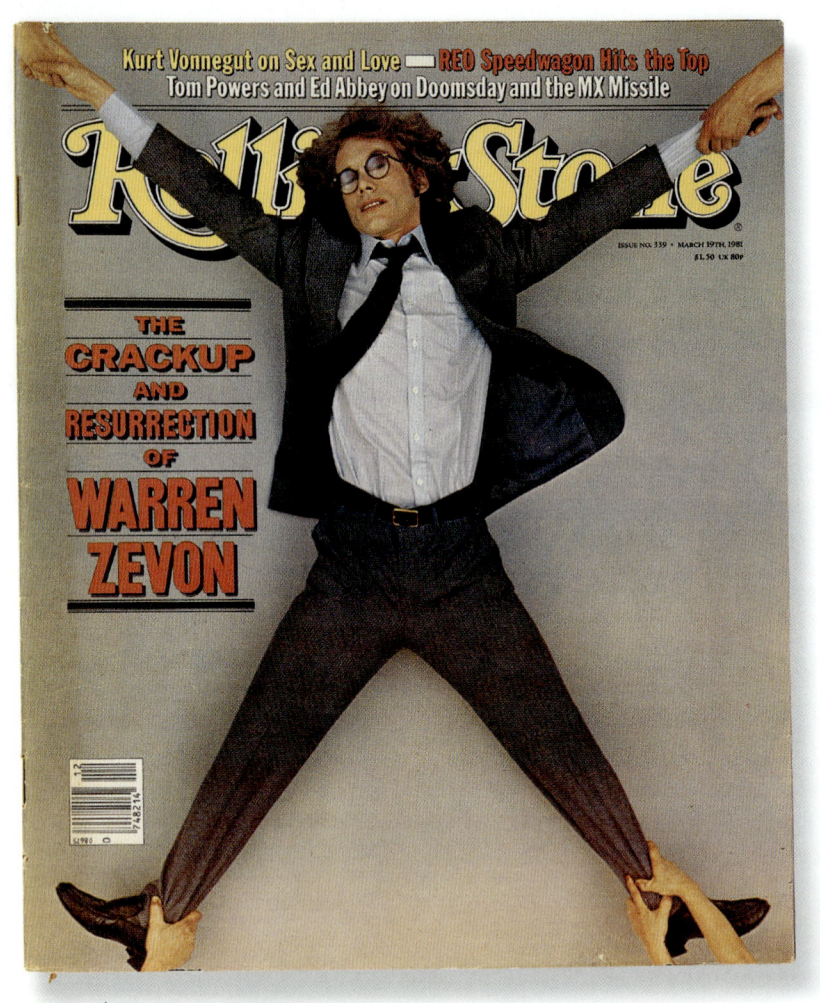

1980s

RS 339 | WARREN ZEVON | March 19th, 1981 | PHOTOGRAPH BY ANNIE LEIBOVITZ

[RS 341] Albert Watson traveled to Jack Nicholson's house in Aspen, Colorado, for this cover shot. When snow started falling hard, the actor asked Watson to leave him alone outdoors for fifteen minutes. Nicholson, by the way, had just completed work on *The Shining*, in which his character freezes to death. Perhaps still in character, Nicholson waited until he had slightly more than a dusting before getting his photo taken.

RS 341 | JACK NICHOLSON | April 16th, 1981 | Photograph by Albert Watson

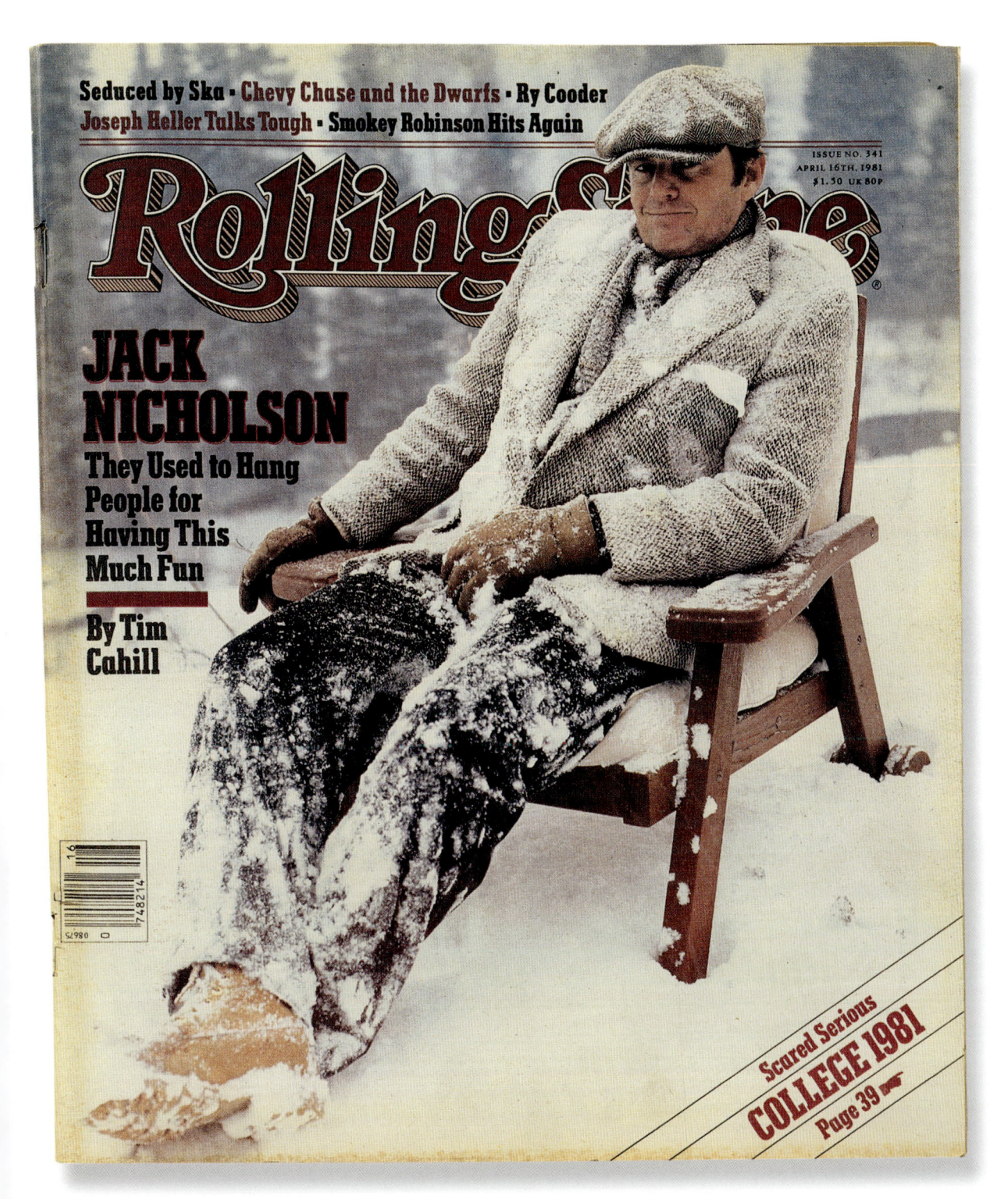

50 YEARS OF COVERS • 177

JAMES CAAN ▪ SLAM DANCING IN L.A. ▪ THE WHO

Rolling Stone

ISSUE NO. 343 • MAY 14TH, 1981
$1.50 UK 80P

INSIDE THE GUN LOBBY

THE NATIONAL RIFLE ASSOCIATION
BY HOWARD KOHN

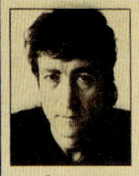

After each assassination, from John Kennedy to John Lennon, there has been a public outcry for gun control. And each time, new membership cards have come firing in to the National Rifle Association. Since 1960, membership has jumped from 250,000 to 1.8 million. It appears that the gun-control issue is the best thing that's ever happened to the NRA. I suggested this to their chief lobbyist, Neal Knox. "No question about it."
[CONTINUED ON PAGE 19]

1980s

RS 343 | GUN CONTROL & JOHN LENNON | May 14th, 1981 | Photograph by Annie Leibovitz

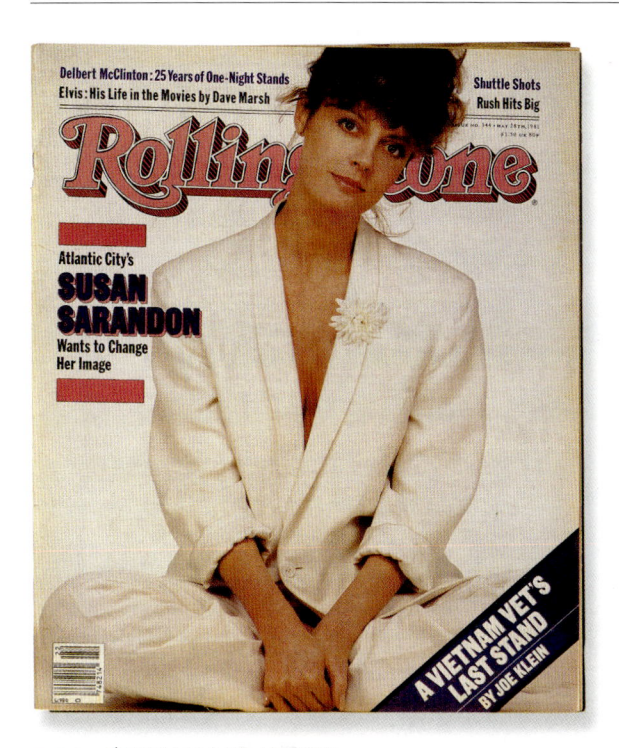

RS 344 | SUSAN SARANDON
May 28th, 1981
PHOTOGRAPH BY ALBERT WATSON

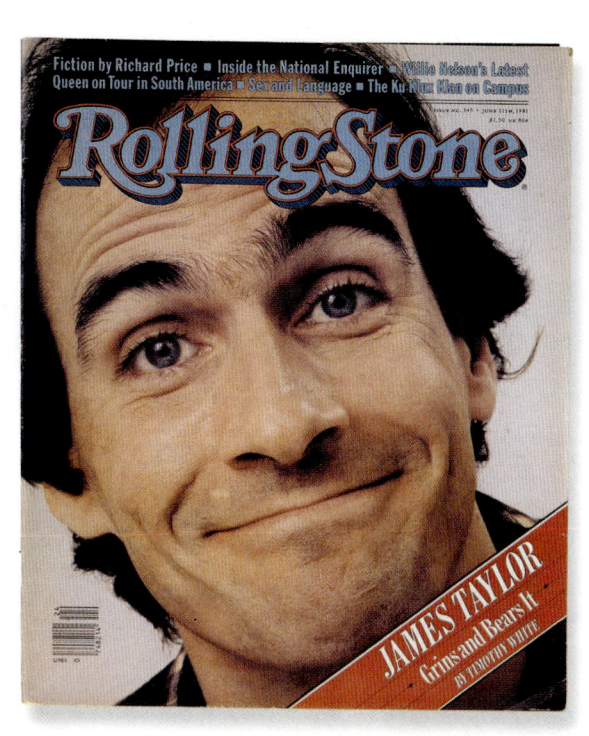

RS 345 | JAMES TAYLOR
June 11th, 1981
PHOTOGRAPH BY AARON RAPOPORT

MIDNIGHT, SATURDAY NIGHT. After I came clean with the cop and told him I was a reporter working on a story, he volunteered to put me in touch with a black-market gun dealer. The meeting place was the gunrunner's car in a motel parking lot. He patted me down for a hidden mike and then we drove around aimlessly, until he was satisfied there was no tail. He spoke with a Brooklyn accent, but his guns were from Florida – RG guns, the brand John Hinckley used.

The triggers and barrels and cylinders are imported from Germany and assembled in Miami, where labor is cheap. The RG Industries factory is a small whitewashed structure that looks as if it has been thrown up, ready to be abandoned at a moment's notice. Approximately 350,000 guns are assembled there each year.

"I don't buy right out of the factory. I buy wholesale," the gunrunner said. He showed me a large metal-frame suitcase. Zip-lock plastic bags were arranged by size among three dividers, and inside each bag was an RG Special. He conducts his business from motel rooms. Three or four times a week he changes locations in the suburbs around Washington. You have to find him. A lot of people do. "You betcha," he said. "Some of my best customers are cabbies."

What if Congress were to pass a federal law like the one in D.C.? "Suits me. Business would go sky-high. I'd have to open franchises." How big is the black market today? A grin. No answer. Is the mob involved? "Not with me, no way. But you go ahead and get gun control passed and the mob's gonna be all over this business like flies over candy." He says he's a pessimist. Guns are part of America. Shut down RG Industries, lock up the gunrunners, legislate and confiscate all you want, and there will still be guns. Zip guns made from car aerials. Starter pistols with the barrels hollowed out and the gas ports covered with Silly Putty and needles for ammo. Shotguns fashioned from pipes, rubber bands, blocks of wood, firing nails. On the black market, the quality of merchandise varies, but prices tend to level out. The RG guns are bottom-of-the-line – Saturday-night specials. But you can buy a Smith & Wesson as well. Statistically, in gun crimes, quality merchandise is used as often as junk. As the National Rifle Association will tell you, all guns are equal before the Constitution.

[EXCERPT FROM RS 343 COVER STORY BY HOWARD KOHN]

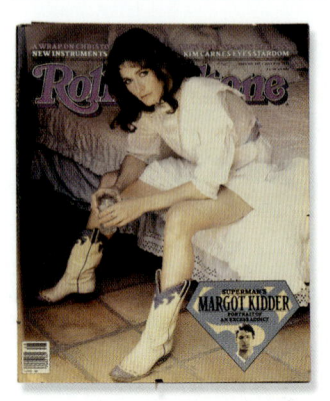

1980s

RS 347 | MARGOT KIDDER
July 9th, 1981
PHOTOGRAPH BY DENIS PIEL

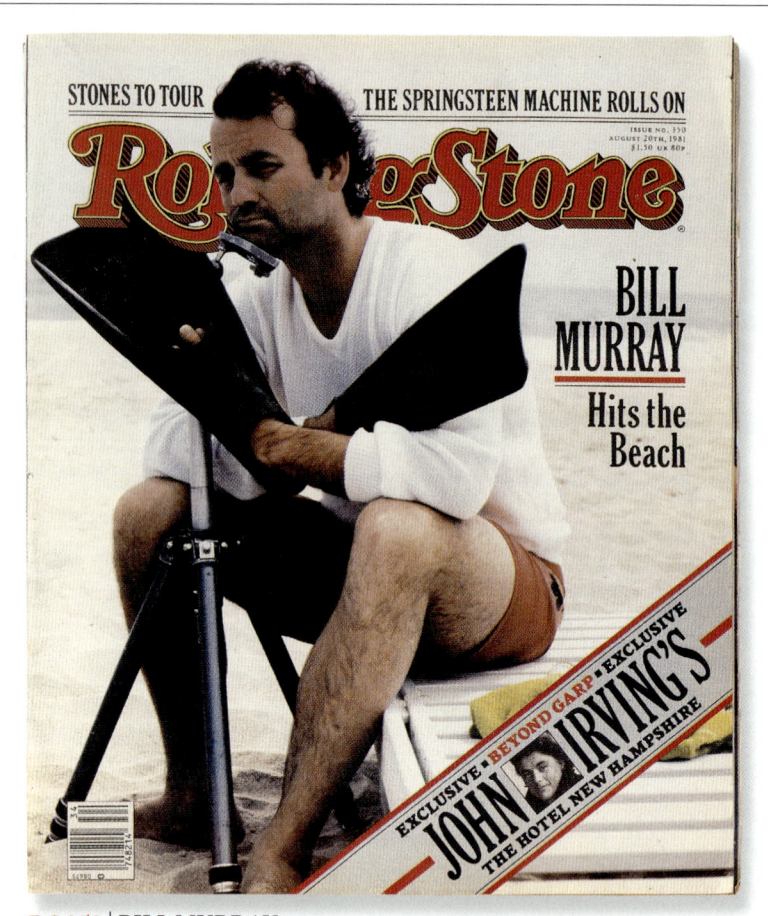

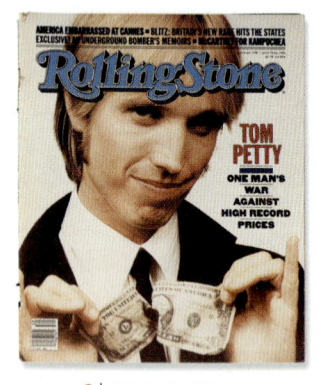

RS 348 | TOM PETTY
July 23rd, 1981
PHOTOGRAPH BY AARON RAPOPORT

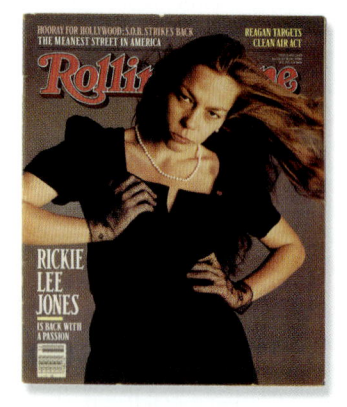

RS 350 | BILL MURRAY | August 20th, 1981 | PHOTOGRAPH BY ANDREA BLANCH

RS 349 | RICKIE LEE JONES
August 6th, 1981
PHOTOGRAPH BY ANNIE LEIBOVITZ

"I WAS FIGHTING THE RECORD INDUSTRY TO KEEP PRICES DOWN TO $8.98. So ROLLING STONE wanted me in a suit and tie to reflect some kind of corporate angle. It really looked silly to me – like my head had been cut off and pasted onto another body. I was not really all that comfortable with it. But Mick Jagger told me not long afterwards that that cover had helped them. The Stones really wanted to keep the price down on their upcoming record, and they were at a meeting about it, and someone brought that cover in, and it helped to resolve the whole argument. It really did hold prices down for quite a while after that. I was sort of proud of that – it's a case of using your position to speak to the masses and send your opinion out."

—*Tom Petty*

The Irish at War by Warren Hinckle
Bob Marley [1945-1981] ■ **Summer Hi-fi, Video Guide**

ISSUE NO. 346 • JUNE 25TH, 1981
$1.50 UK 80P

RollingStone

RAIDERS *of the* **LOST ARK**

George Lucas and Steven Spielberg **TEAM UP TO TOP STAR WARS**

Harrison Ford as Indiana Jones

RS 346 | HARRISON FORD | June 25th, 1981 | Photograph by Bill King

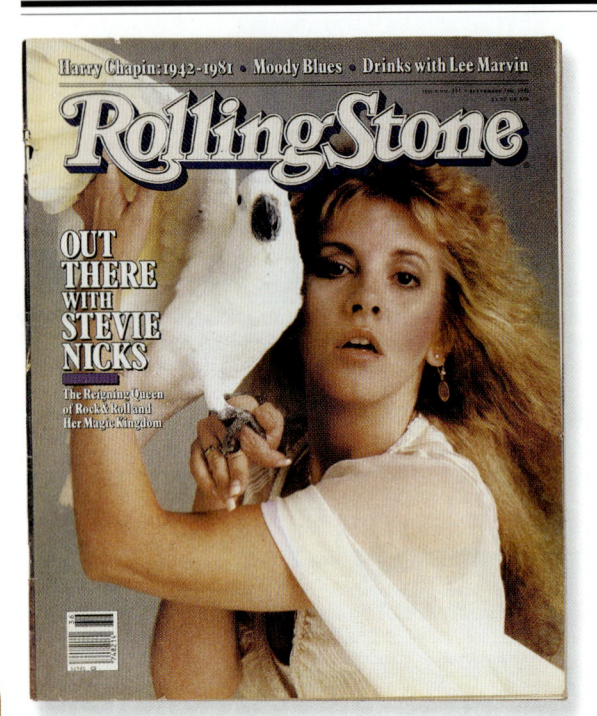

RS 351 | STEVIE NICKS
September 3rd, 1981
PHOTOGRAPH BY ANNIE LEIBOVITZ

RS 352 | JIM MORRISON
September 17th, 1981
PHOTOGRAPH BY GLORIA STAVERS

THE MOST FAMOUS (or infamous) cover line ROLLING STONE ever ran accompanied a 1968 photograph of Jim Morrison taken by his lover/confidante, longtime *16* magazine editor Gloria Stavers. During her stint (from 1957 to 1975) at the preeminent teen 'zine, Stavers – who would die two years after this issue, in 1983, of lung cancer – practically invented provocative cover lines. She was also an early champion of ROLLING STONE, writing a feature in *16* about the new rock rag not long after it began publication and later giving Jann Wenner advice about rock photography.

As for ROLLING STONE's cover line, a handful of staffers have taken credit for writing it, and, simply put, it works. As the cover story detailed, a full ten years after Morrison's death, Doors records were selling better than ever, hordes of kids were making the pilgrimage to his grave in Paris's Père-Lachaise cemetery and the lead singer's poetry was being revered.

The State of the Democrats by Joe Klein ■ **Smart Audio 1981**
Was Elvis Cheated? ■ **Wheelsucking in Boulder, Colorado**

RollingStone

SEPTEMBER 17TH, 1981
ISSUE NO. 352
$1.50 UK 80p

Jim Morrison

He's hot, he's sexy and he's dead

Santana Surfaces • A Special Report: College Life 1981

ISSUE NO. 353 • OCTOBER 1ST, 1981
$1.50 UK 80p

Rolling Stone

Yoko

An Intimate Conversation

Photographs by Annie Leibovitz

By Barbara Graustark

1980s

RS 353 | YOKO ONO | October 1st, 1981 | Photograph by Annie Leibovitz

184 • ROLLING STONE

"[WHEN THIS PHOTO was taken] I was walking in a daze. But I think it helped that it was Annie [who took the picture] rather than a stranger."

—*Yoko Ono*

I THINK JOHN'S DEATH MADE SEAN and me very strong. A lot of people are saying that because of what happened, he's going to grow up to be a neurotic kid, and I worried about that. But looking at Sean, I see only strength in him. And somehow I think that Sean is going to be all right. Not just all right, but beautiful.

"It's like this event – isn't that a terrible way of putting it? – affected us all in different ways, but we are all stronger and more aware for it, and probably for the better.

"I can't think it was all for the worse.

"When John and I were saying 'The world is one, one world,' it's almost like fate told us, 'Okay, prove it. Prove it with your life.' And that's what John did. At the time of his death, the world definitely became one. And though we might forget it, we're never going to lose that sense. It's in us, and it always will be. Somehow we're gonna be different. And the sense of oneness that we preached, well, John actually had to show it physically, and somehow he did it. That was his fate. And I keep thinking of it.

"It's like preaching is not enough. Let the whole world feel it. Let it happen."

[EXCERPT FROM YOKO ONO INTERVIEW BY BARBARA GRAUSTARK]

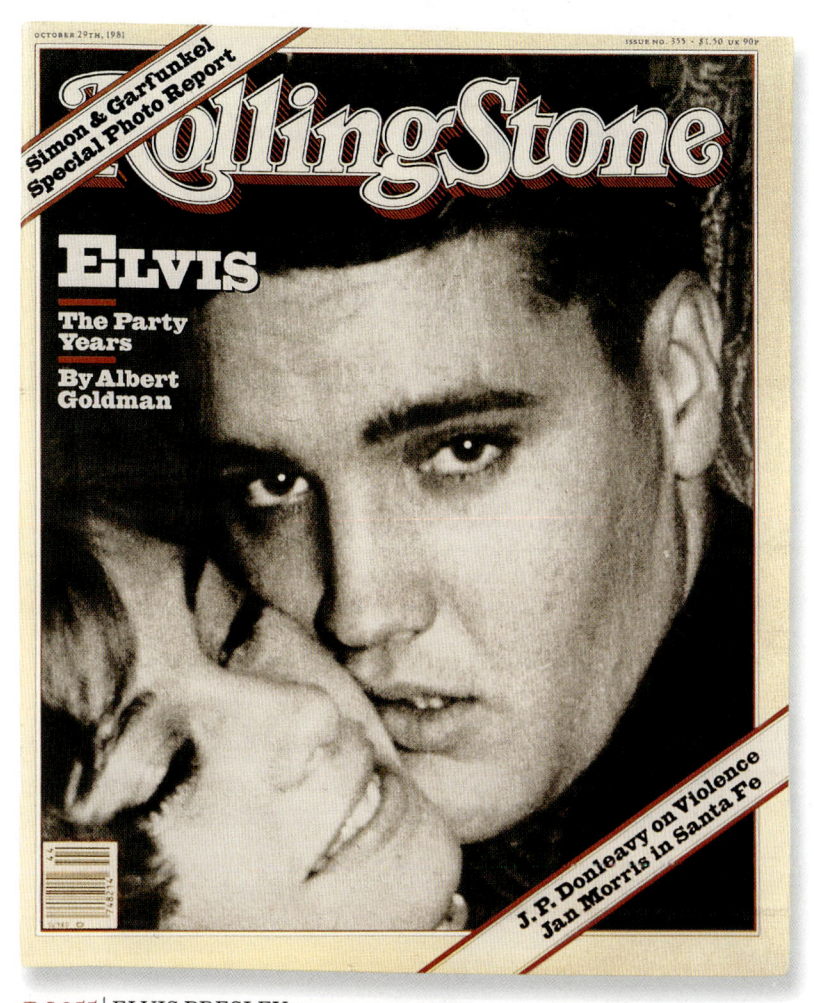

RS 355 | ELVIS PRESLEY | October 29th, 1981 | PHOTOGRAPH BY RUDOLF PAULINI

Foreigner Gets Good, Stones Get Great, Simon & Garfunkel Get Back

ISSUE NO. 354 • OCTOBER 15TH, 1981
$1.50 UK 80p

Rolling Stone

MERYL STREEP

1980s

RS 354 | MERYL STREEP | October 15th, 1981 | Photograph by Annie Leibovitz

"**PUT YOURSELF IN THIS POSITION.** You're passing the newsstand at Fifty-seventh Street and Sixth Avenue, and there's your face on the cover of a magazine. And one week later, you're on the subway, and there's that cover, with your face, on the floor. Somebody's probably pissed on it."

—*Meryl Streep*

"*I was scheduled to shoot* [Meryl Streep] for the cover of ROLLING STONE, *The French Lieutenant's Woman* was coming out, and that week [Francesco] Scavullo had shot her for the cover of *Time*, I think. And she'd had such a miserable time at that shooting – she was becoming this very big star, they wanted her to look like a big star, and she couldn't deal with it – that she canceled my shooting. So I called up her agent and screamed for forty-five minutes, and finally the agent said, 'She won't go anywhere with you. She'll come to your studio and give you between nine-thirty and twelve in the morning, and that's it.'

"I was shooting [John] Belushi at the time, I had all these clown books around the studio, and I was even thinking of a whiteface for Belushi. Actually, I bought the clown books originally for James Taylor, who had hepatitis and didn't want to be on the cover of ROLLING STONE because his face was all yellow.

"So she came to the studio and she told me about the *Time* shooting, and she said how she didn't want to be anybody, she was nobody, all she was was an actress. So I said, 'Well, be no one, be a mime. Let's try the whiteface.' And she really loved it. That's when she started to pull her cheeks out like this – she did that herself. It's just great when that stuff starts to happen."

—*Annie Leibovitz*

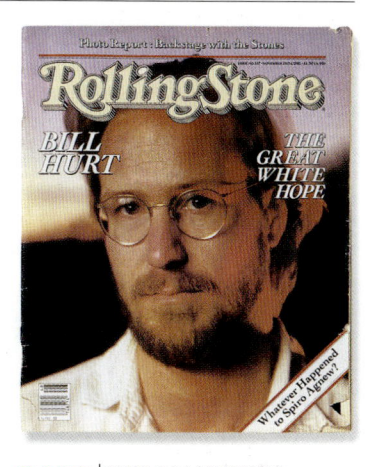

RS 357 | WILLIAM HURT
November 26th, 1981
PHOTOGRAPH BY ANNIE LEIBOVITZ

Back to the Barricades : inside the Environmental Movement

Rolling Stone

ISSUE NO. 356 · NOVEMBER 12TH, 1981 · $1.50 UK 90P

1980s

KEITH RICHARDS
No Regrets
The Rolling Stone Interview
By Kurt Loder

RS 356 | KEITH RICHARDS | November 12th, 1981 | Photograph by Annie Leibovitz

Stones Tour from the Front Row • Jamie Lee Curtis

ISSUE NO. 358 · DECEMBER 10TH, 1981 · $1.50 UK 90P

RollingStone

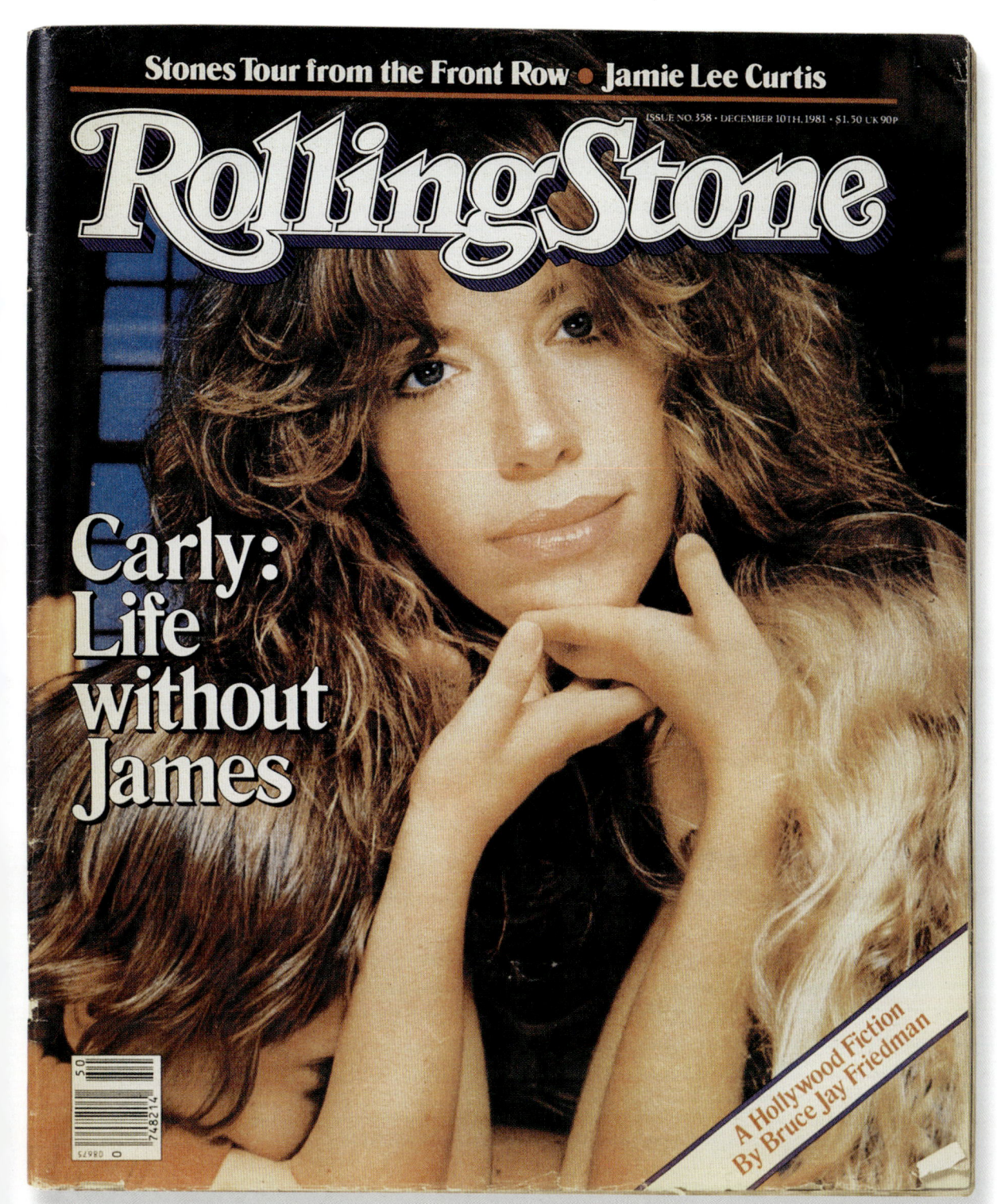

Carly: Life without James

A Hollywood Fiction By Bruce Jay Friedman

RS 358 | CARLY SIMON | December 10th, 1981 | PHOTOGRAPH BY JIM VARRIALE

RS 361 | JOHN BELUSHI | January 21st, 1982 | Photograph by Annie Leibovitz

SCTV's Best Joke • The Paranoid Millionaires Convention

Rolling Stone

ISSUE NO. 362 • FEBRUARY 4TH, 1982 • $1.50 UK 90P

Timothy Hutton Is Too Good To Be True

Ali's Last Stand By Harold Conrad

RS 362 | TIMOTHY HUTTON | February 4th, 1982 | Photograph by Annie Leibovitz

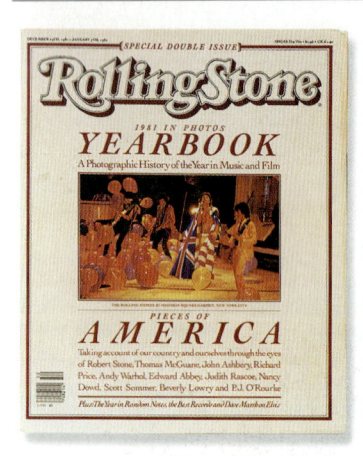

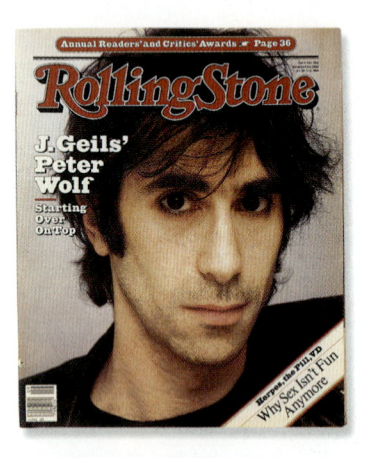

1980s

"**Steve Martin,** actually, he says to me, 'Annie, I've pushed myself in my movies and in my career; everything's gone further except for the photographs of myself.' And he was really interested in trying to take a new picture. He had just bought that Franz Kline, it was the kind of thing only museums can afford, and it seemed so strange to have it in his home. And he was just in love with it. He said, 'I see myself in that picture.'

"When I went out there I wanted to do him in tails, but then I realized he was already beyond the tails. This was a way of throwing away the tails so he could move forward – he could have been stuck in that *Pennies From Heaven* genre for some time. Originally we were going to paint him black, put him in the painting, but then I came up with the idea of painting the tux like the painting."

—*Annie Leibovitz*

RS 359/360 | THE ROLLING STONES
December 24th, 1981 – January 7th, 1982
Photograph by Lynn Goldsmith

RS 364 | PETER WOLF
March 4th, 1982
Photograph by Annie Leibovitz

Rolling Stone

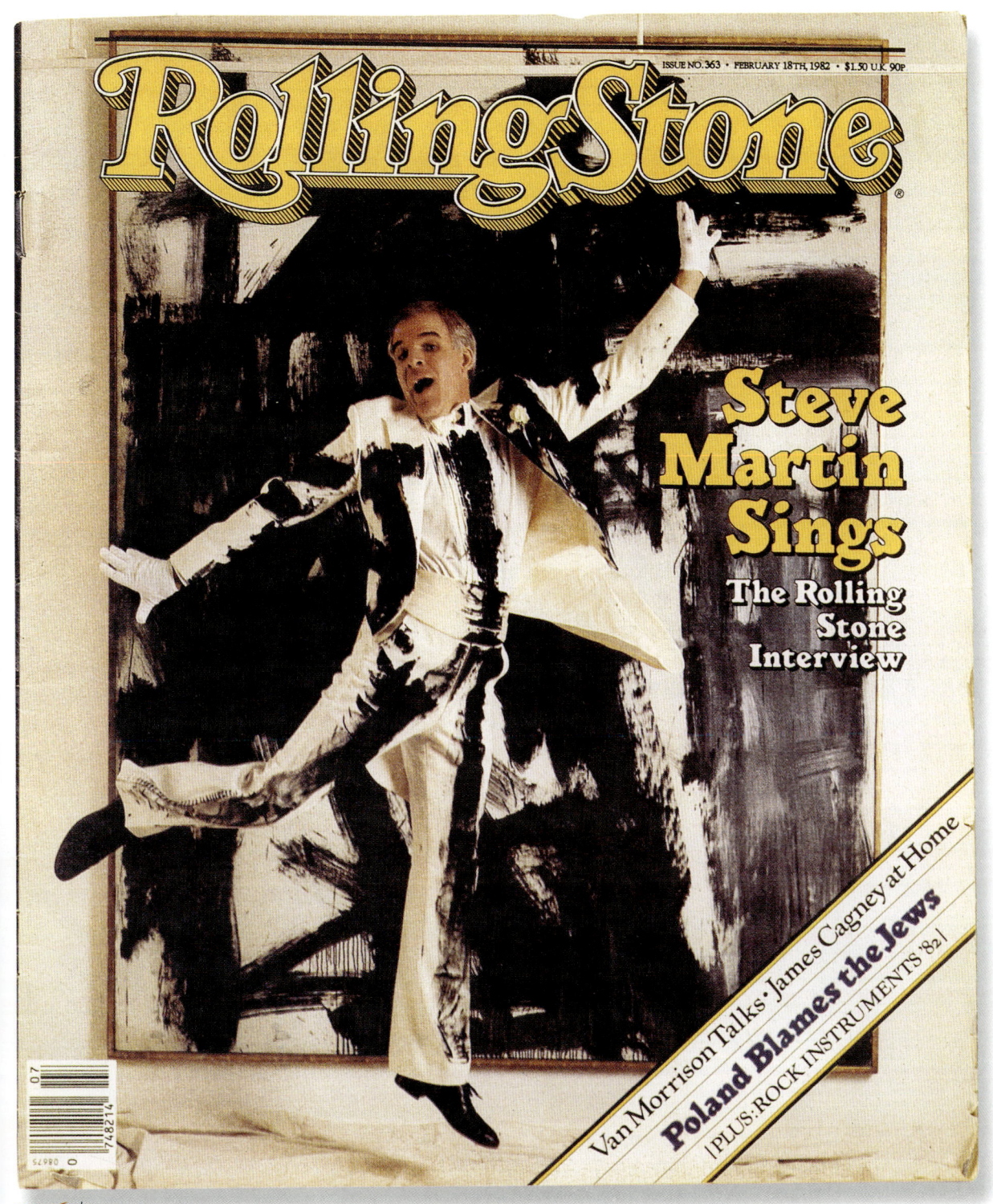

ISSUE NO. 363 • FEBRUARY 18TH, 1982 • $1.50 U.K. 90P

Steve Martin Sings
The Rolling Stone Interview

Van Morrison Talks • James Cagney at Home
Poland Blames the Jews
[PLUS: ROCK INSTRUMENTS '82]

RS 363 | STEVE MARTIN | February 18th, 1982 | Photograph by Annie Leibovitz

COLLEGE PAPERS 1982

ISSUE NO. 367 • APRIL 15TH, 1982 • $1.50 U.K. 90P

RollingStone

1980s

Mariel Hemingway

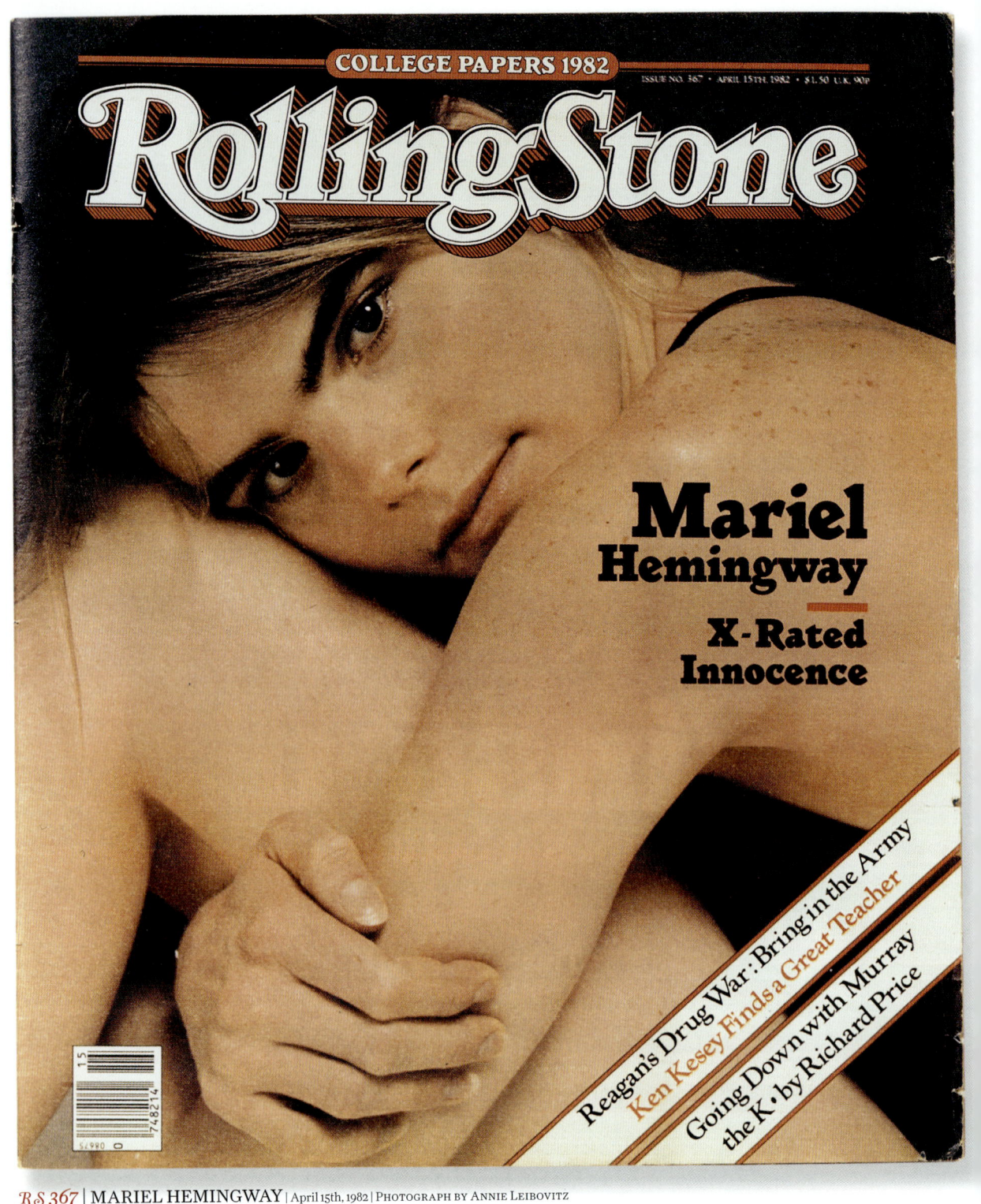

X-Rated Innocence

Reagan's Drug War: Bring in the Army
Ken Kesey Finds a Great Teacher
Going Down with Murray the K • by Richard Price

RS 367 | MARIEL HEMINGWAY | April 15th, 1982 | Photograph by Annie Leibovitz

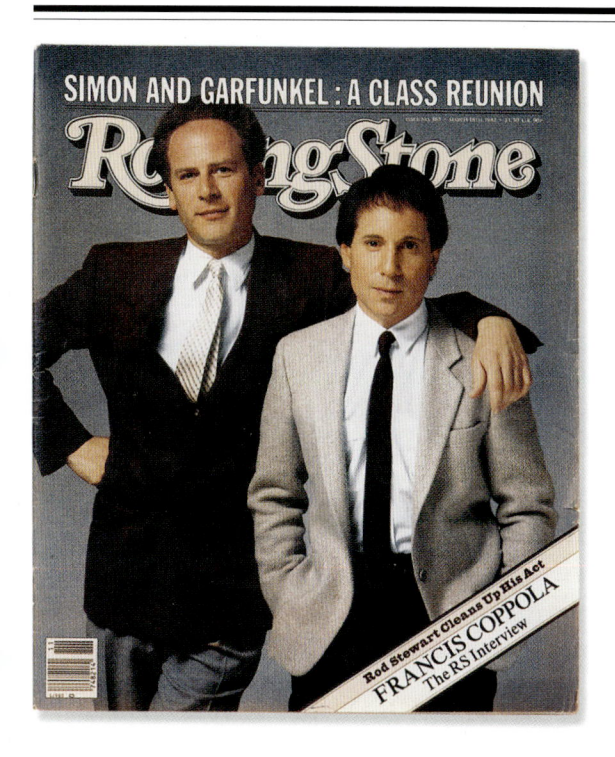

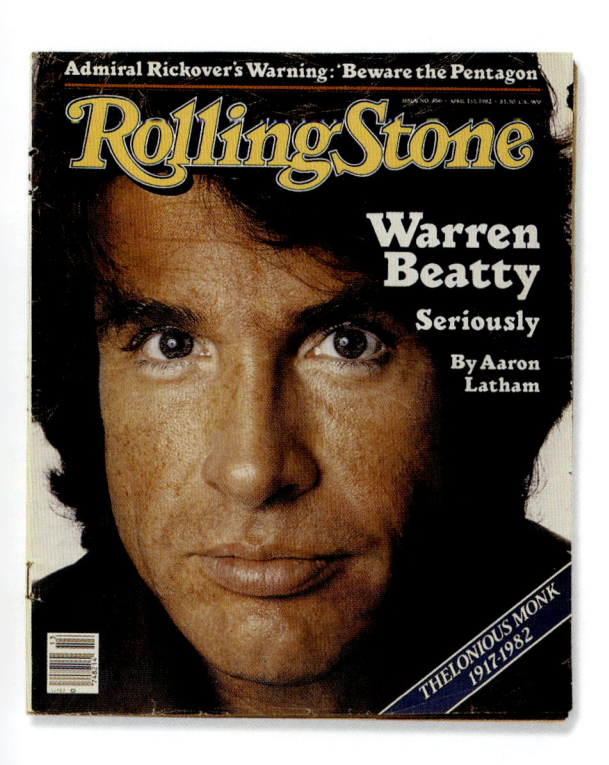

RS 365 | ART GARFUNKEL & PAUL SIMON
March 18th, 1982
PHOTOGRAPH BY ANNIE LEIBOVITZ

RS 366 | WARREN BEATTY
April 1st, 1982
PHOTOGRAPH BY JACK MITCHELL

IT MAY BE AN IDEA WHOSE TIME HAS COME – AGAIN.
Two men, one guitar, a body of beautifully crafted songs. Sounds retrograde, you say? Well, until six months ago, Paul Simon and Art Garfunkel probably would have agreed. But then, last September 19th, Simon and Garfunkel played a free concert in New York's Central Park. It was their first full performance together in eleven years, and nearly half a million people flocked to see it. In the aftermath of that unexpectedly successful event, as they worked on a live album and video, Simon and Garfunkel talked seriously about getting back together again. Now, they're considering a tour of Europe in May, and possibly some U.S. dates this summer. And if things go well, there may even be a new Simon and Garfunkel studio album.

If things go well. In all their years as a singing team, these two boyhood buddies somehow never learned how to talk to each other. Personal tics caused tension, and quibbles accumulated into quarrels. Nothing major, but unpleasant memories lingered. In fact, the Central Park show almost didn't come off.

"The weeks before the concert were so tense that there were times I really regretted having agreed to do it," said Simon, sitting in the palatial study of his apartment, which overlooks Central Park. "It was very rushed. Artie had to learn a lot of material very quickly. Basically, the show combined old Simon and Garfunkel arrangements with expanded orchestrations of arrangements I used on my *One-Trick Pony* tour. We didn't have time to make new arrangements."

It didn't matter – the concert was a spontaneous smash. And in the postconcert projects that followed – polishing the tapes for the recently released live double album, *The Concert in Central Park*; editing videotapes for a February 21st airing on Home Box Office; and planning a videocassette for commercial release – Simon and Garfunkel discovered that they could work together again. Better yet, they *wanted* to work together again. With their music as the focus, the old disputes fell away. As Garfunkel said, "We had a rapprochement."

[EXCERPT FROM RS 365 COVER STORY BY STEPHEN HOLDEN]

50 YEARS OF COVERS • 195

RS 368 | JOHN BELUSHI | April 29th, 1982 | Photograph by Annie Leibovitz

1980s

"*Even though he* was a bit of a monster, he was *our* monster, as well as a damned good person you could count on for help in the dark times. There was a ten-day period one recent summer when I sought refuge with him. We fooled around in his speedboat, dug clams and steamed them, and he lifted me out of the pit with his considerable powers as a host. The most drugs we did was a little pot, and he seemed as peaceful as I'd ever seen him.

"The last time he visited me, he caught my neighbor a bit offguard by 'borrowing' his truck for a spell. But, hell, he brought it back in pretty good condition. As far as I'm concerned, John is welcome at my house anytime, dead or alive. For me, John's epitaph is: THIS MAN WAS THE REAL THING. HE NEVER NEEDED PROPS."

—*Hunter S. Thompson*

"'NATIONAL LAMPOON'S ANIMAL HOUSE' was a lowball project in Hollywood when Sean Daniels asked me to develop it. I read the script and loved it, but the studio said no movie unless I got this guy named Belushi to play Bluto Blutarski. I flew to New York and arranged a meeting with John at the Drake Hotel. He came up to my room, ordered ten shrimp cocktails, twenty beers and ten Perriers. I told him that Bluto would be on screen less time than any of the other characters and that he'd have the least dialogue. In the end, the film was to be designed for Bluto's entrances and exits.

"John threw out ideas. I said no to all of them, thinking at the moment that I was losing my star and my movie.

"'No?' he said.

"'No,' I said.

"'Good,' he said. 'I was just testing you. I'll do the film.' He got up and left, and then, of course, all the food and drink arrived."

—*John Landis*

"I NOT ONLY WORKED with John on the *Blues Brothers* film, I also worked with him on *Saturday Night Live*. He was the kind of guy who would volunteer to sit with me and help me prepare my lines, since I obviously could not rely on cue cards. He was a sweet, thoughtful man who did everything he could think of to make me feel comfortable.

"John was a loyal fan of rhythm & blues, and the Blues Brothers movie got a hell of a lot of people back into R&B. They especially helped people like Aretha Franklin and me reach the young kids who might not have even known we existed. As far as commercial interest in R&B is concerned, John helped get the ball rolling again. Man, we owe him."

—*Ray Charles*

"WHEN I WAS ON THE ROAD with John in *Lemmings*, we used to room together occasionally. I had a habit of putting my girlfriend's picture up on my bureau. John walked in one night, looked at the photo and said, 'Oh, you've got one of her too, eh? I've got the version with the donkey in the picture.'"

—*Chevy Chase*

"A FEW WEEKS BEFORE HE DIED, JOHN grabbed me at a party in New York, threw me into the bathroom, barricaded the door and said, 'Listen, I want you to tell George Lucas that Danny and I want to be space monsters in the next *Star Wars* sequel! We're not leaving this bathroom till you agree.' I agreed. They would have been ideal as funky space monsters. I liked those little unexpected get-togethers with John. He once sat with me for three hours in a Beverly Hills beauty salon while I had my hair done, and he was like the world's largest puppy, charming the whole place."

—*Carrie Fisher*

ISSUE NO. 368 · APRIL 29TH, 1982

$1.50 U.K. 90P

RollingStone

John Belushi

By Dan Aykroyd, Jim Belushi, Mitchell Glazer, Brian Doyle-Murray, Michael O'Donoghue, Jack Nicholson, Hunter S. Thompson, Laraine Newman, Don Novello and friends...

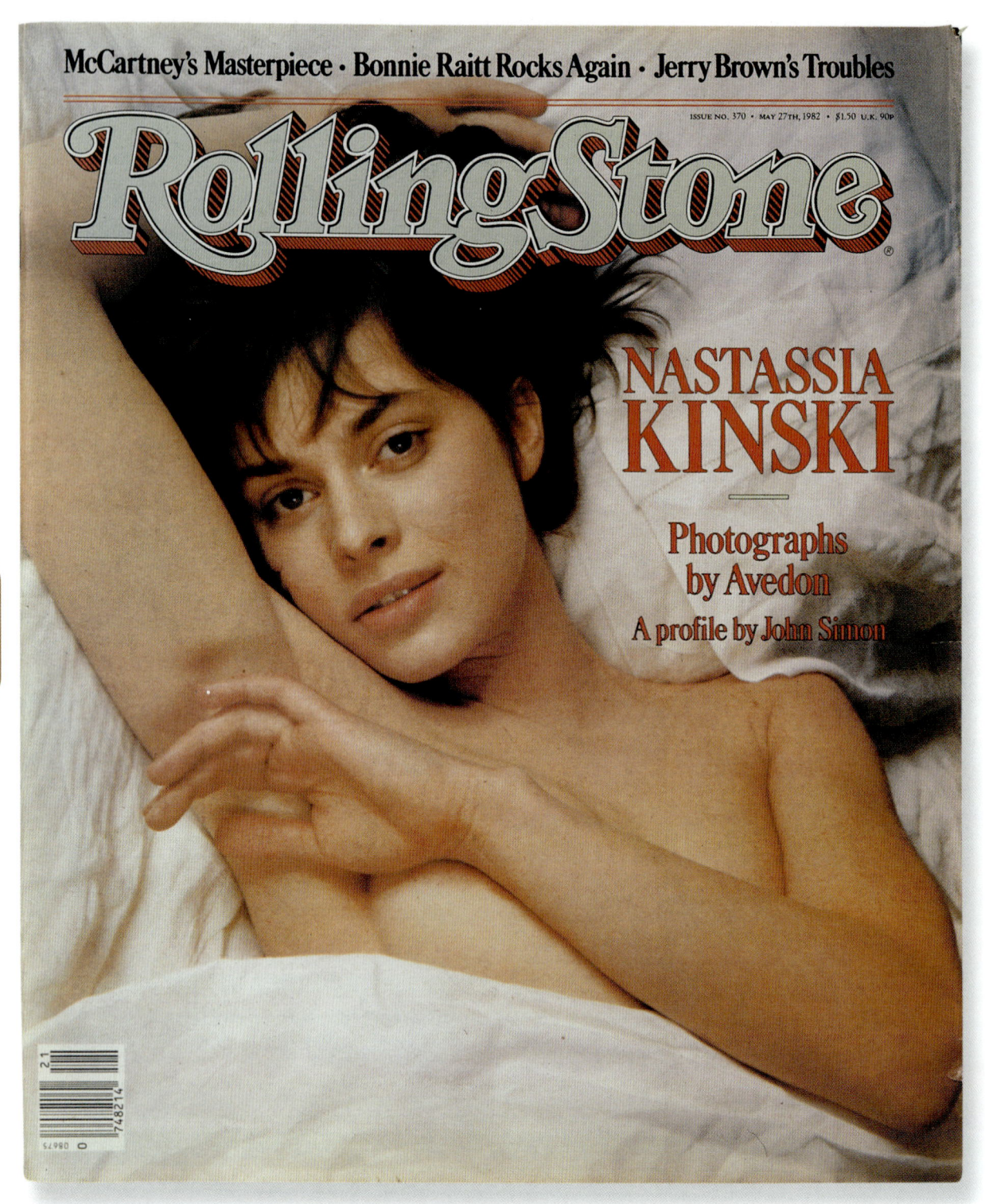

RS 370 | NASTASSIA KINSKI | May 27th, 1982 | Photograph by Richard Avedon

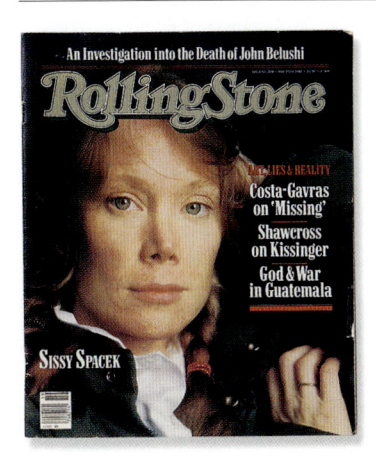

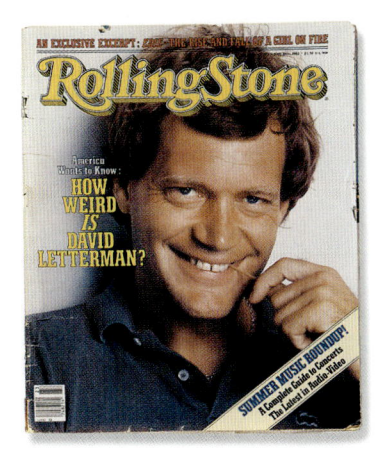

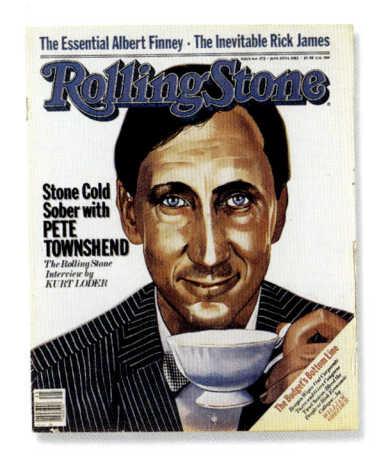

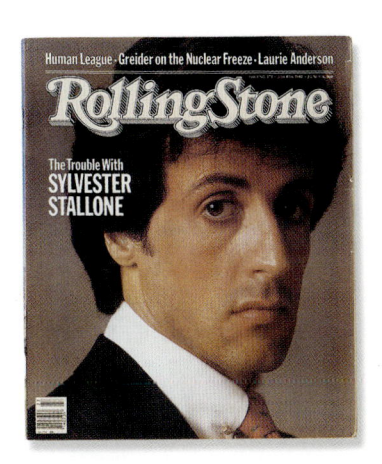

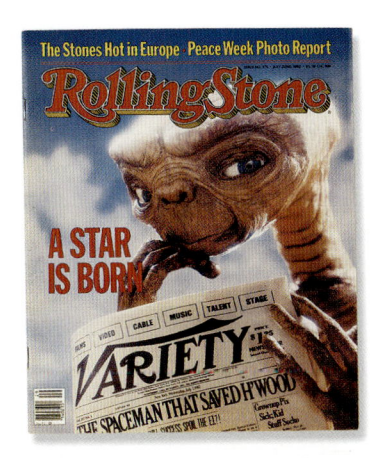

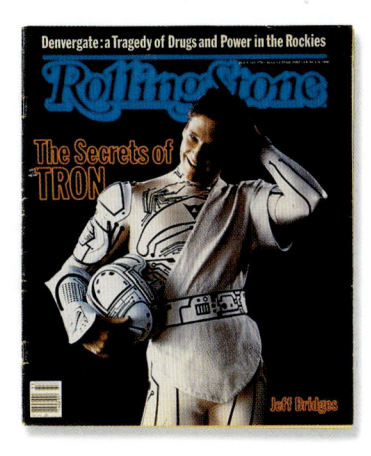

RS 369 | SISSY SPACEK
May 13th, 1982
PHOTOGRAPH BY ANNIE LEIBOVITZ

RS 373 | SYLVESTER STALLONE
July 8th, 1982
PHOTOGRAPH BY ANNIE LEIBOVITZ

RS 371 | DAVID LETTERMAN
June 10th, 1982
PHOTOGRAPH BY HERB RITTS

RS 374 | E.T.
July 22nd, 1982
PHOTOGRAPH BY AARON RAPOPORT

RS 372 | PETE TOWNSHEND
June 24th, 1982
ILLUSTRATION BY JULIAN ALLEN

RS 376 | JEFF BRIDGES
August 19th, 1982
PHOTOGRAPH BY ANNIE LEIBOVITZ

[RS 373] Jann Wenner hires art director Derek Ungless, whose background was in European magazine design, to give ROLLING STONE a cleaner, more spare look.

50 YEARS OF COVERS • 199

The Journey of John W. Hinckley, Jr. • Shark Attacks

Rolling Stone

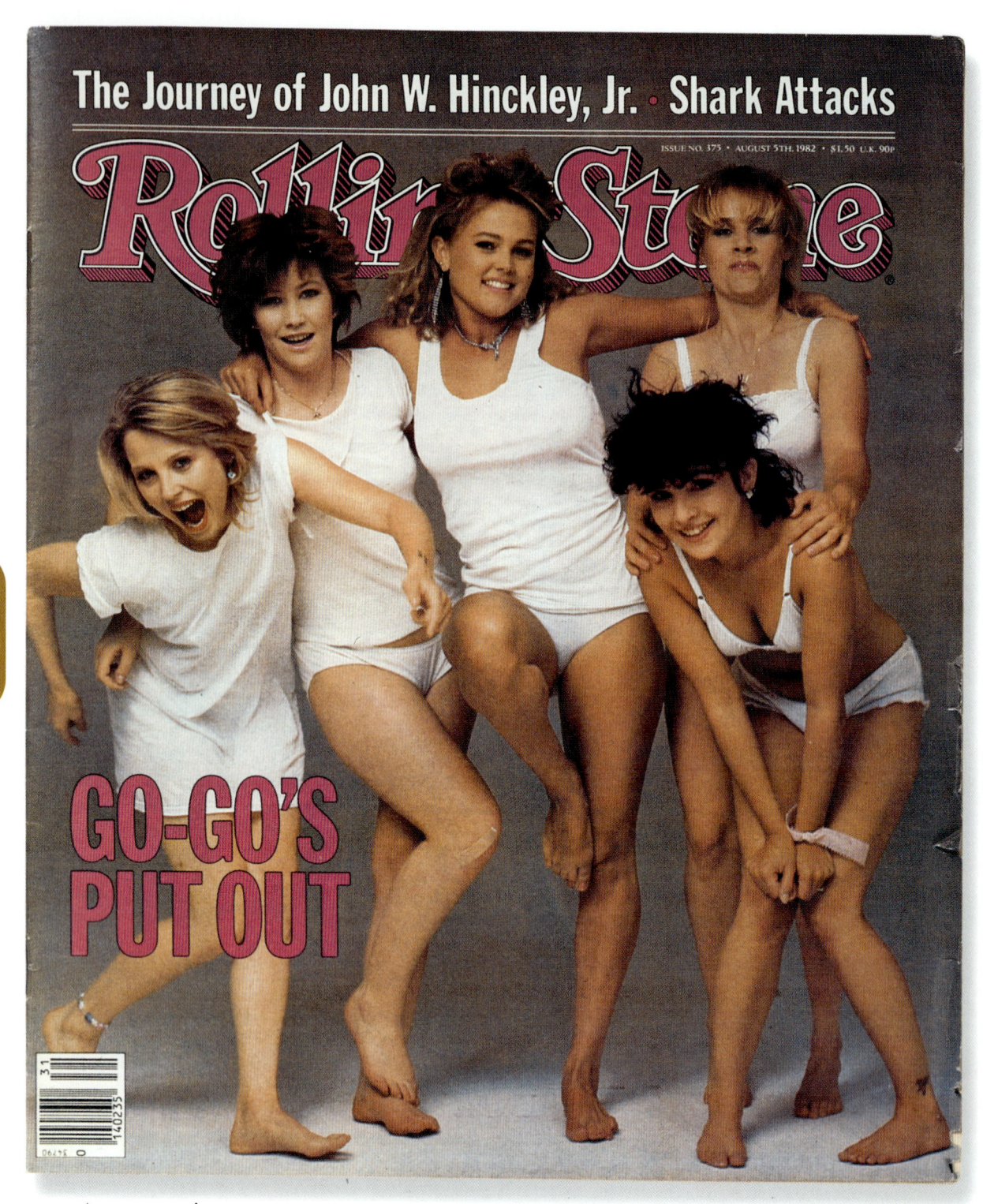

ISSUE NO. 375 • AUGUST 5TH, 1982 • $1.50 U.K. 90P

1980s

GO-GO'S PUT OUT

RS 375 | THE GO-GO'S | August 5th, 1982 | Photograph by Annie Leibovitz

End of an Era: Why the Sixties Generation Has Quit Smoking Pot

ISSUE NO. 377 · SEPTEMBER 2ND, 1982 · $1.50 U.K. 90P

RollingStone

ELVIS COSTELLO REPENTS

The Rolling Stone Interview by Greil Marcus

RS 377 | ELVIS COSTELLO | September 2nd, 1982 | Photograph by Annie Leibovitz

1980s

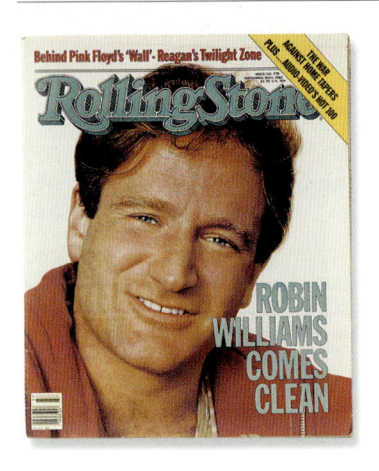

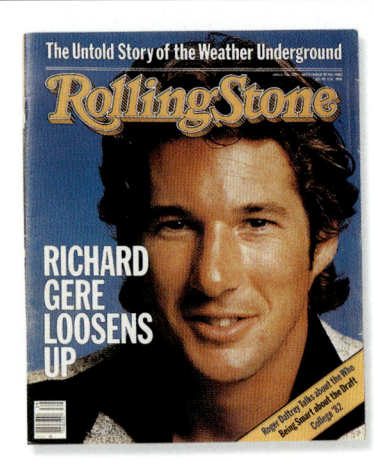

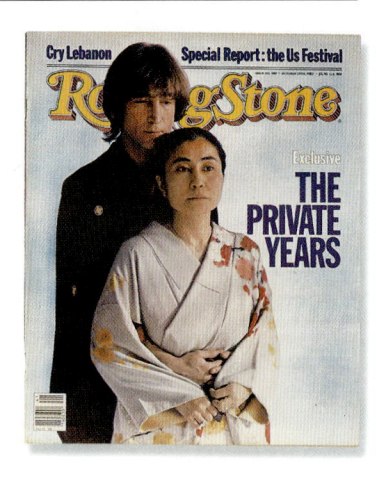

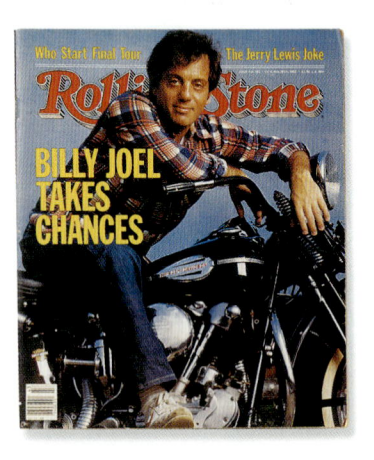

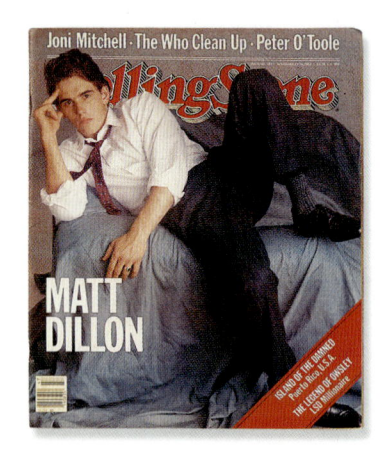

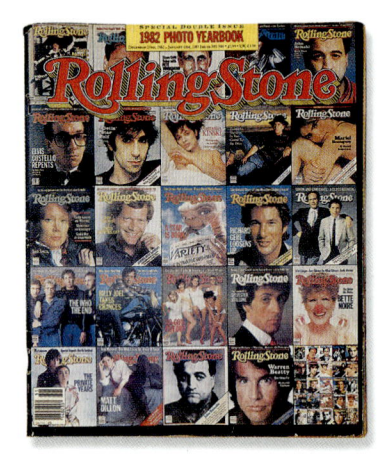

RS 378 | ROBIN WILLIAMS
September 16th, 1982
PHOTOGRAPH BY BONNIE SCHIFFMAN

RS 381 | BILLY JOEL
October 28th, 1982
PHOTOGRAPH BY ANNIE LEIBOVITZ

RS 379 | RICHARD GERE
September 30th, 1982
PHOTOGRAPH BY HERB RITTS

RS 383 | MATT DILLON
November 25th, 1982
PHOTOGRAPH BY ANNIE LEIBOVITZ

RS 380 | JOHN LENNON
& YOKO ONO
October 14th, 1982
PHOTOGRAPH BY ALLAN TANNENBAUM

RS 385/386 | 1982 YEARBOOK
December 23rd, 1982 – January 6th, 1983
VARIOUS PHOTOGRAPHERS

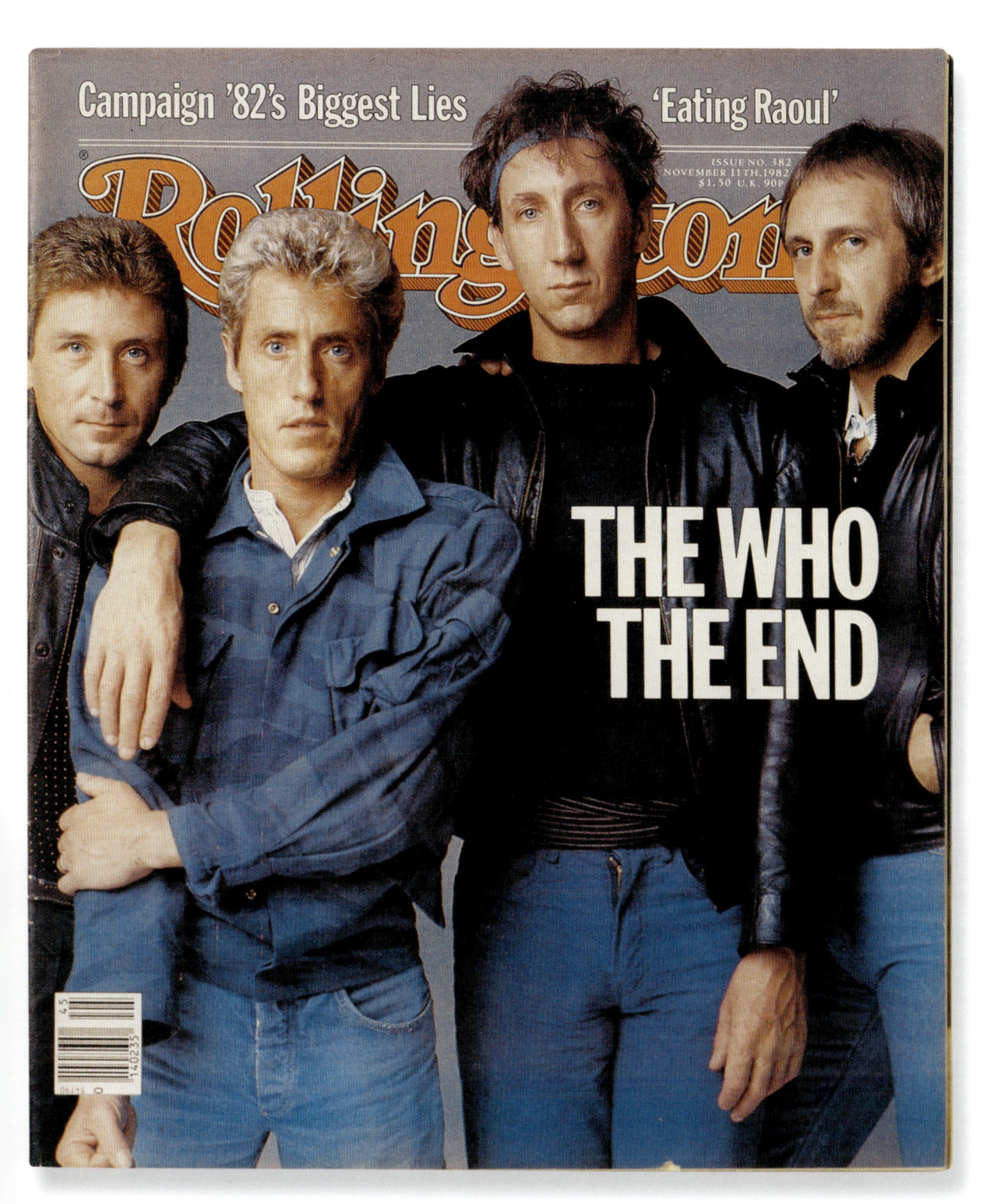

RS 382 | THE WHO | November 11th, 1982 | Photograph by Annie Leibovitz

John Cougar • Gary Gilmore by Mikal Gilmore • Radio Racism

ISSUE NO. 384 • DECEMBER 9TH, 1982 • $1.50 U.K. 90P

RollingStone

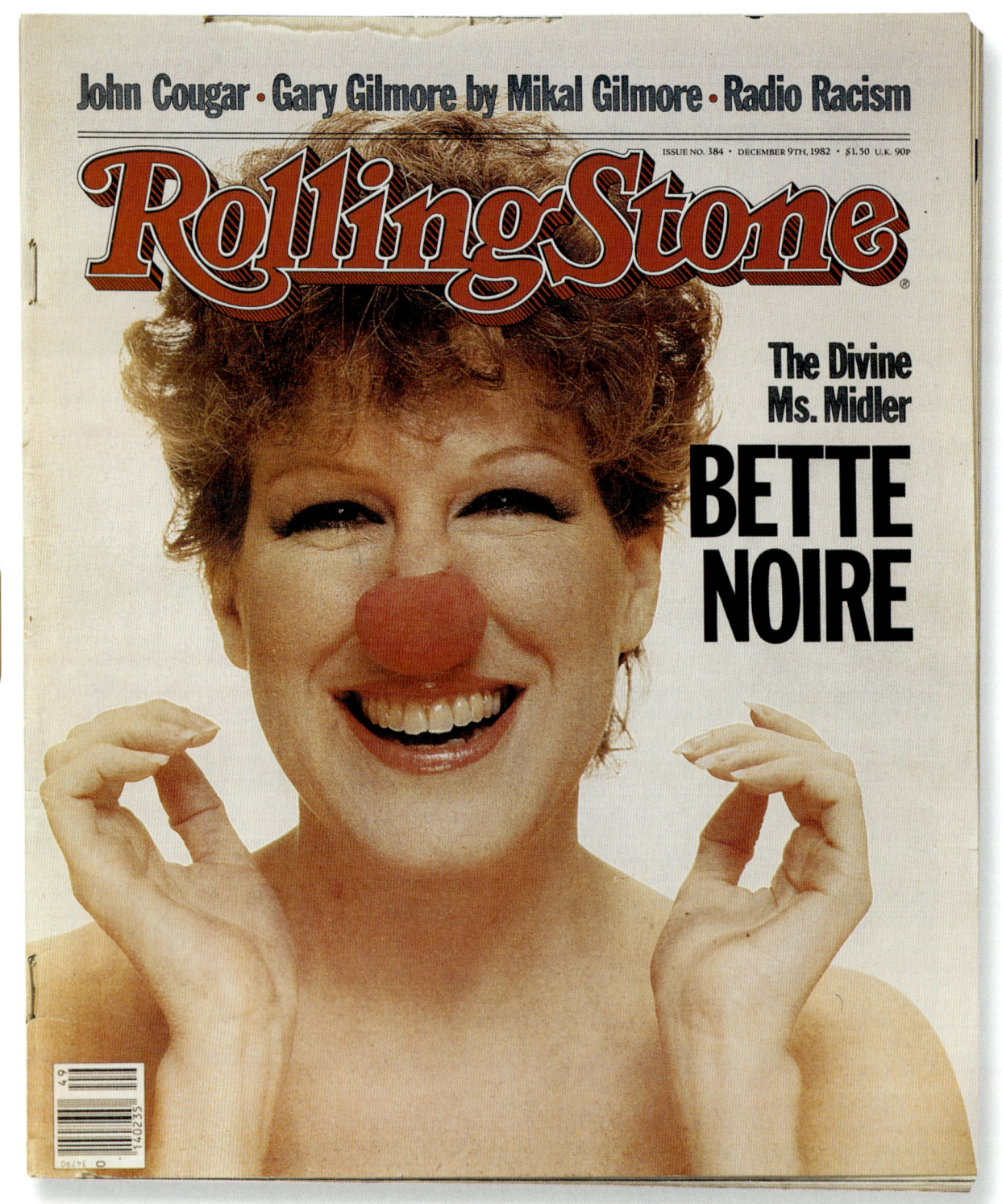

1980s

The Divine Ms. Midler

BETTE NOIRE

RS 384 | BETTE MIDLER | December 9th, 1982 | Photograph by Greg Gorman

America's New Plague: Contagious Sexual Cancer • Bob Seger

RollingStone

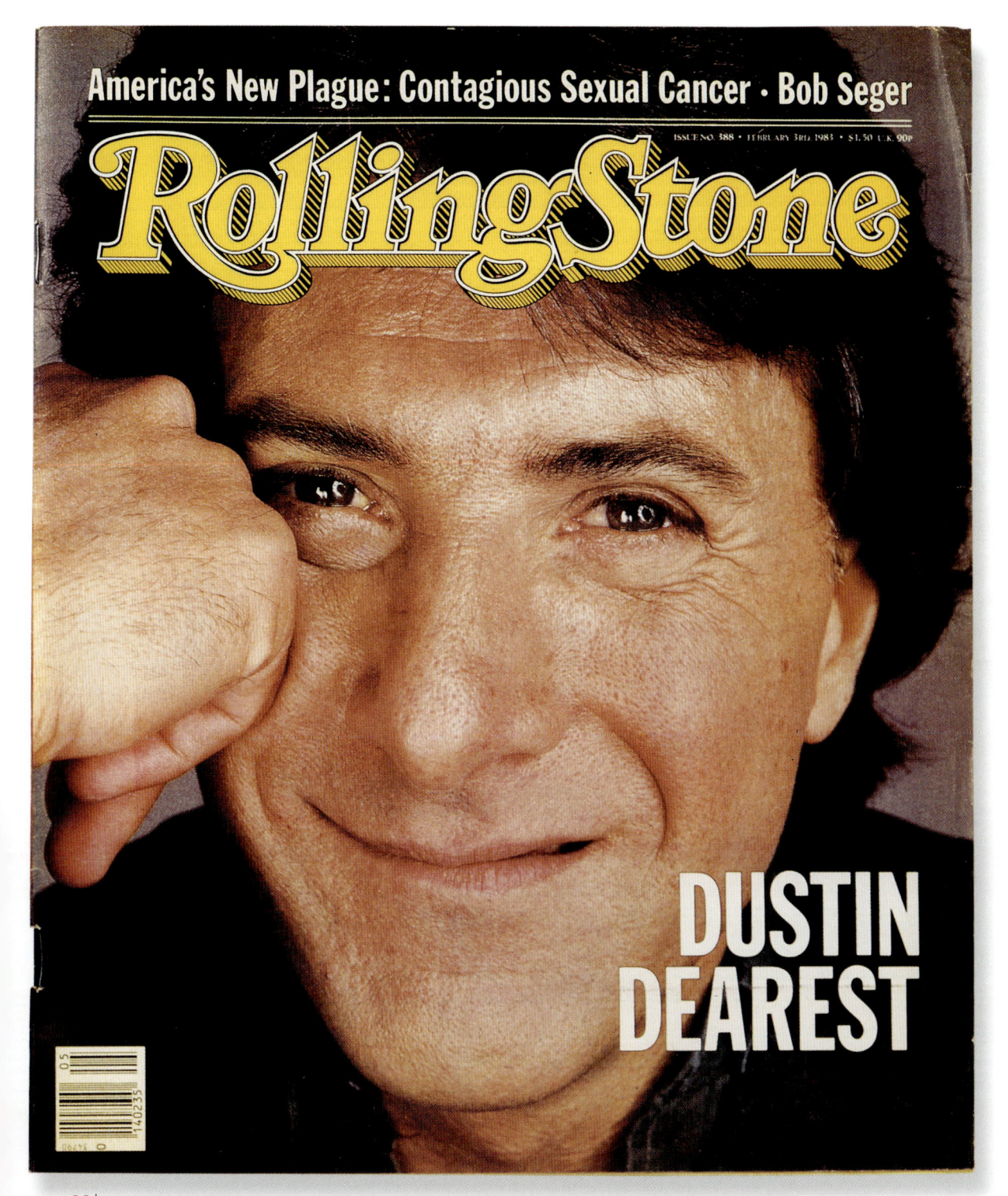

ISSUE NO. 388 • FEBRUARY 3RD 1983 • $1.50 U.K. 90P

DUSTIN DEAREST

RS 388 | DUSTIN HOFFMAN | February 3rd, 1983 | Photograph by Richard Avedon

Rolling Stone

Greider on Kennedy · Dire Straits · Hot Computers

ISSUE NO. 387 · JANUARY 20TH, 1983 · $1.50 U.K. 90P

PAUL NEWMAN
The Real Thing

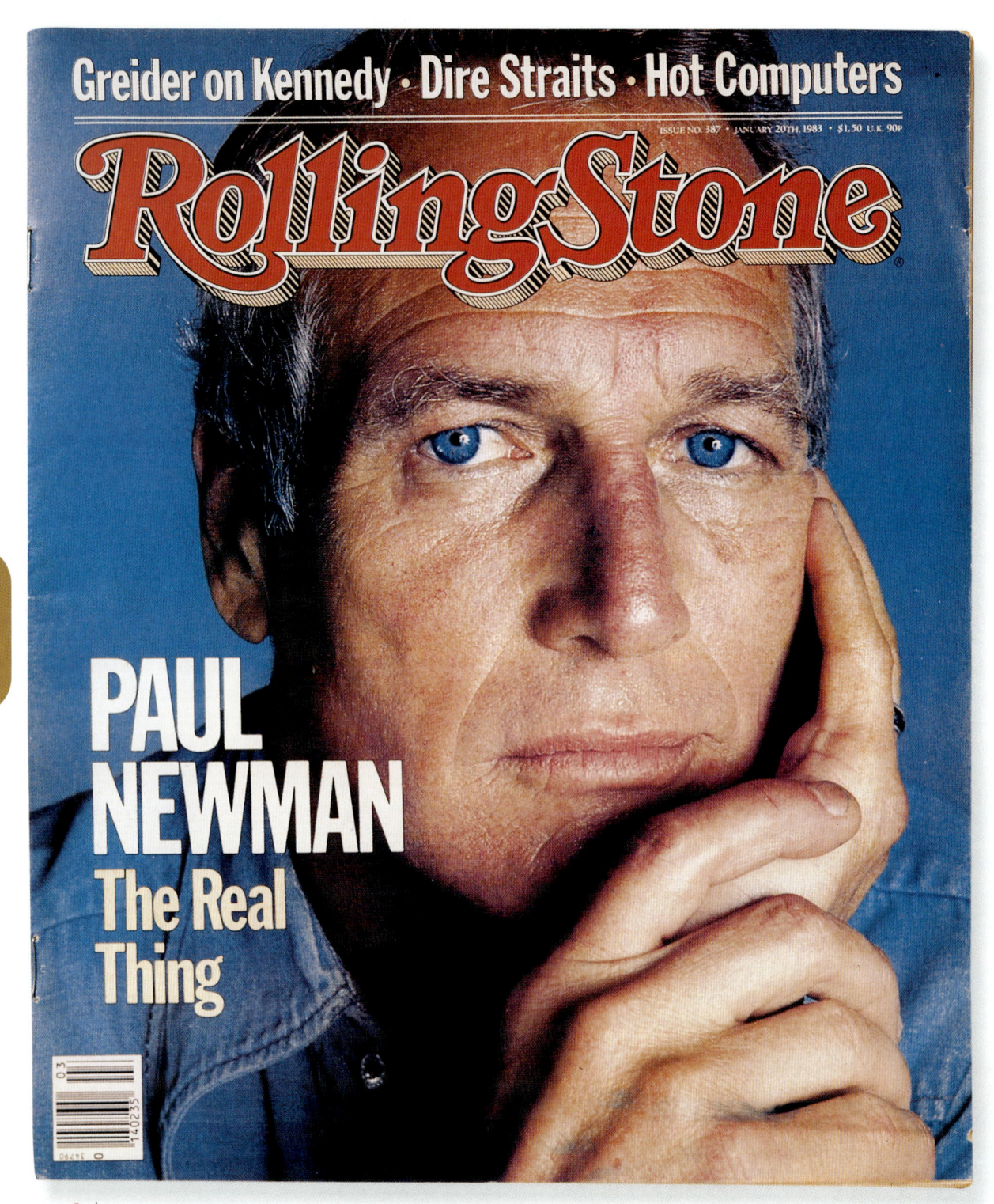

1980s

RS 387 | PAUL NEWMAN | January 20th, 1983 | Photograph by Jim Varriale

California's Handgun Vote • Ray Mancini: a Death in the Ring

Rolling Stone

ISSUE NO. 389
FEBRUARY 17TH, 1983
$1.50 U.K. £1

MICHAEL JACKSON
Life as a Man

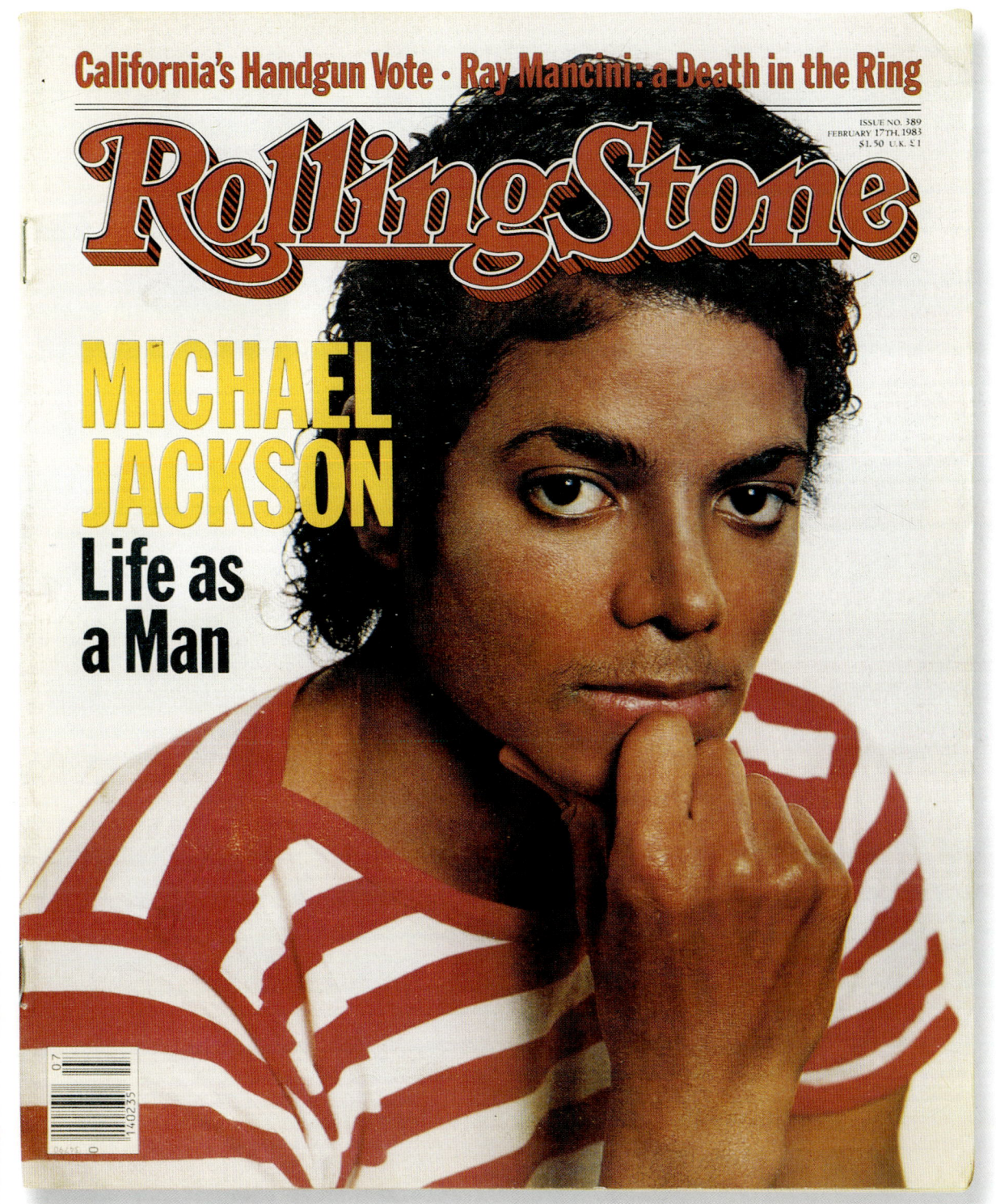

RS 389 | MICHAEL JACKSON | February 17th, 1983 | Photograph by Bonnie Schiffman

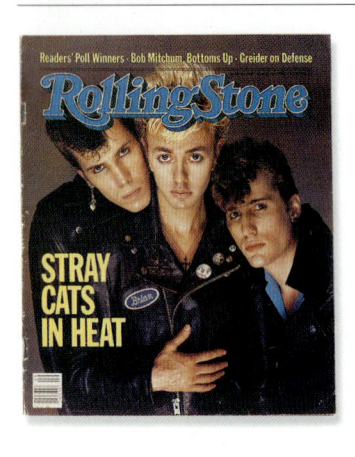

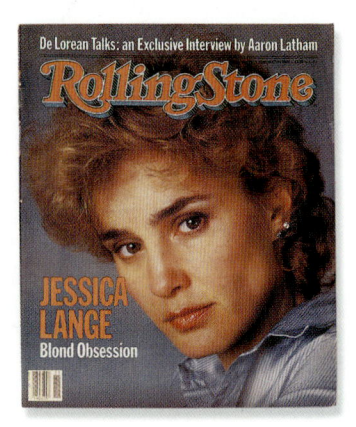

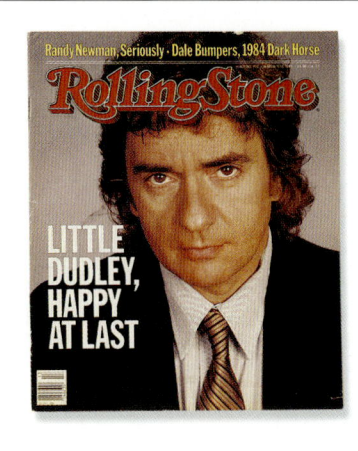

1980s

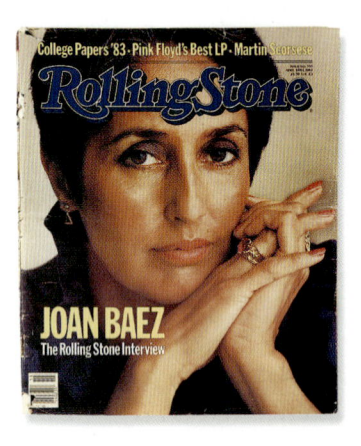

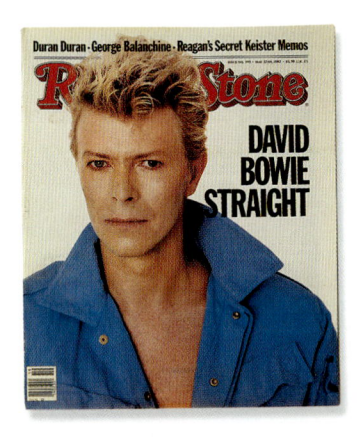

RS 390 | THE STRAY CATS
March 3rd, 1983
PHOTOGRAPH BY RICHARD AVEDON

RS 391 | JESSICA LANGE
March 17th, 1983
PHOTOGRAPH BY JIM VARRIALE

RS 392 | DUDLEY MOORE
March 31st, 1983
PHOTOGRAPH BY BONNIE SCHIFFMAN

RS 393 | JOAN BAEZ
April 14th, 1983
PHOTOGRAPH BY DAVID MONTGOMERY

RS 395 | DAVID BOWIE
May 12th, 1983
PHOTOGRAPH BY DAVID BAILEY

"THE BEST THING IS TO HAVE absolutely no idea what you're doing. I much prefer the planned accident to the 'Well, if you turn your head this way, deah, your cheekbone stands out' approach. I've got to have a photograph that's sort of extraordinary looking rather than beautiful."
—*David Bowie*

Rolling Stone

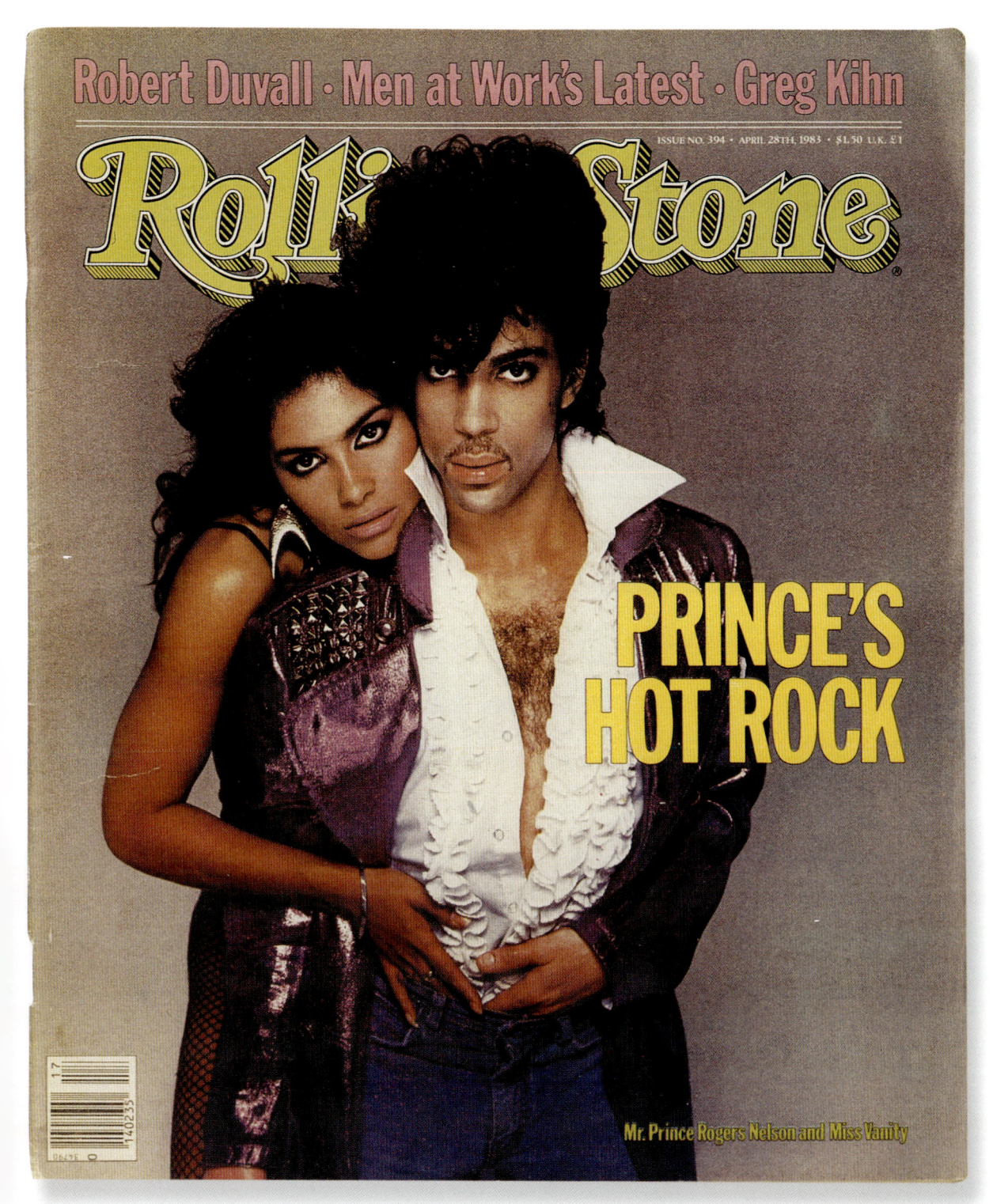

Robert Duvall · Men at Work's Latest · Greg Kihn

ISSUE NO. 394 · APRIL 28TH, 1983 · $1.50 U.K. £1

PRINCE'S HOT ROCK

Mr. Prince Rogers Nelson and Miss Vanity

RS 394 | PRINCE & VANITY | April 28th, 1983 | Photography by Richard Avedon

1980s

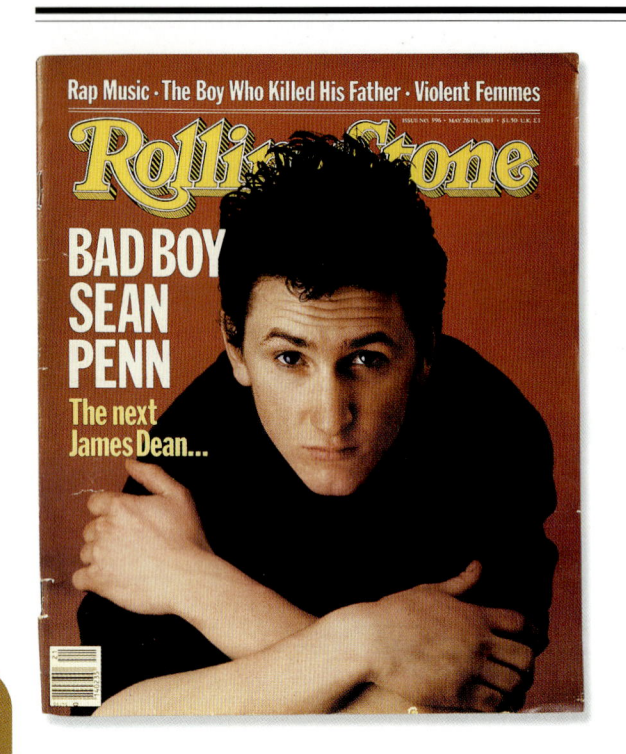

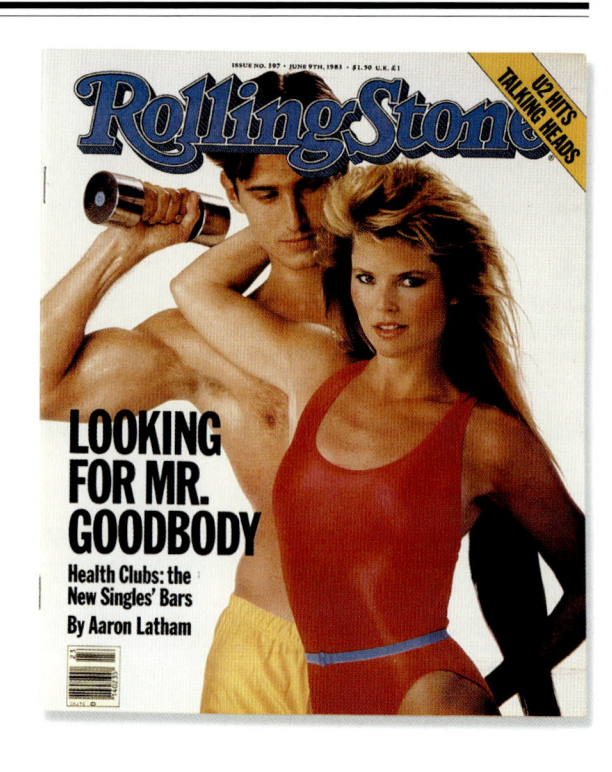

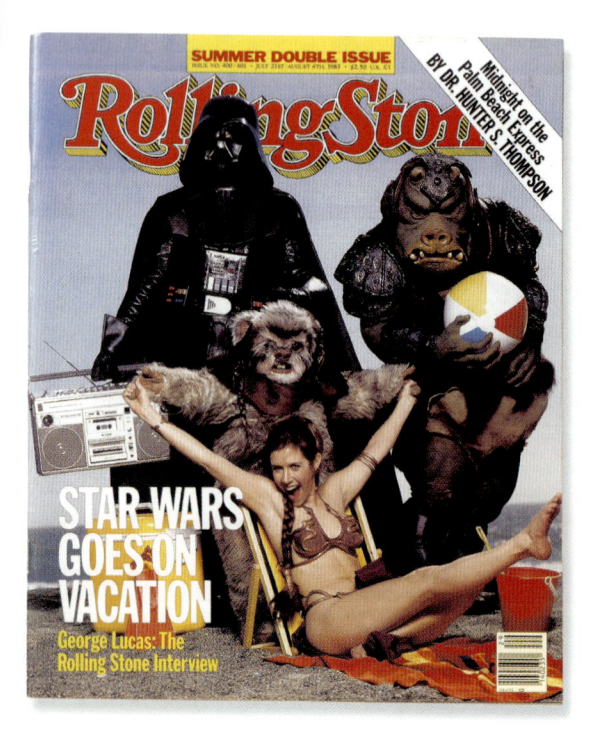

RS 396 | SEAN PENN
May 26th, 1983
PHOTOGRAPH BY MARY ELLEN MARK

RS 397 | CHRISTIE BRINKLEY
& MICHAEL IVES
June 9th, 1983
PHOTOGRAPH BY E.J. CAMP

RS 400/401 | CAST OF 'RETURN
OF THE JEDI'
July 21st – August 4th, 1983
PHOTOGRAPH BY AARON RAPOPORT

210 • ROLLING STONE

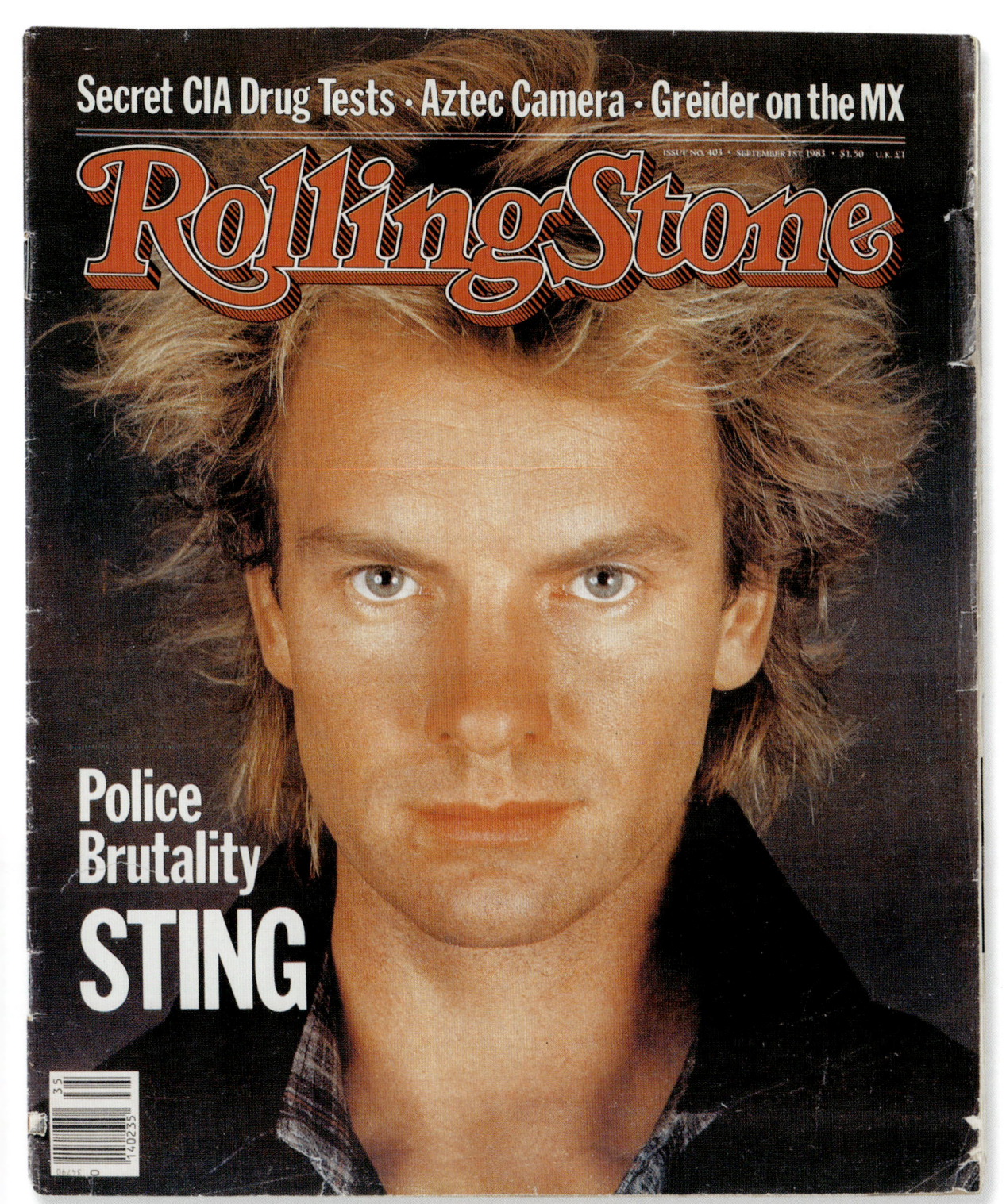

Secret CIA Drug Tests · Aztec Camera · Greider on the MX

RollingStone

ISSUE NO. 403 · SEPTEMBER 1ST 1983 · $1.50 · U.K. £1

Police Brutality
STING

RS 403 | STING | September 1st, 1983 | Photograph by Lynn Goldsmith

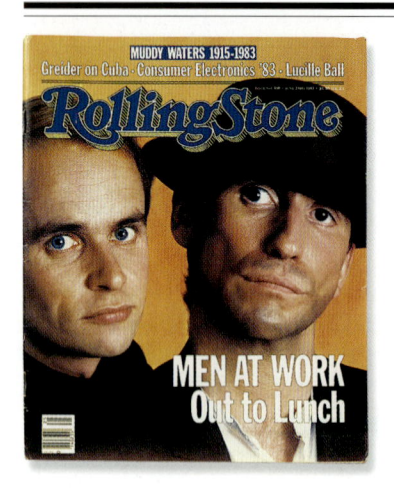

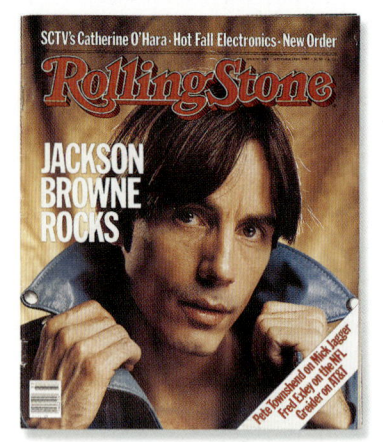

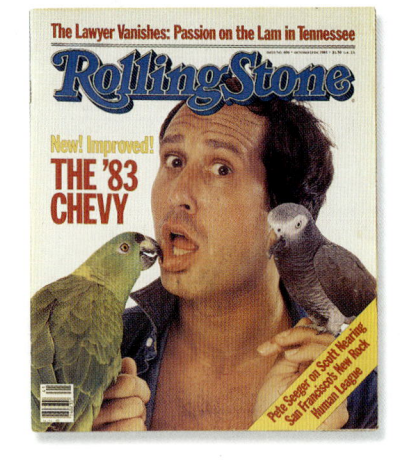

RS 398 | MEN AT WORK
June 23rd, 1983
PHOTOGRAPH BY AARON RAPOPORT

RS 404 | JACKSON BROWNE
September 15th, 1983
PHOTOGRAPH BY AARON RAPOPORT

RS 406 | CHEVY CHASE
October 13th, 1983
PHOTOGRAPH BY BONNIE SCHIFFMAN

1980s

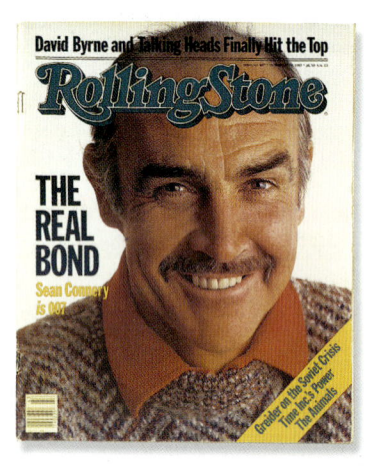

RS 407 | SEAN CONNERY
October 27th, 1983
PHOTOGRAPH BY DAVID MONTGOMERY

RS 405 | ANNIE LENNOX
September 29th, 1983
PHOTOGRAPH BY E.J. CAMP

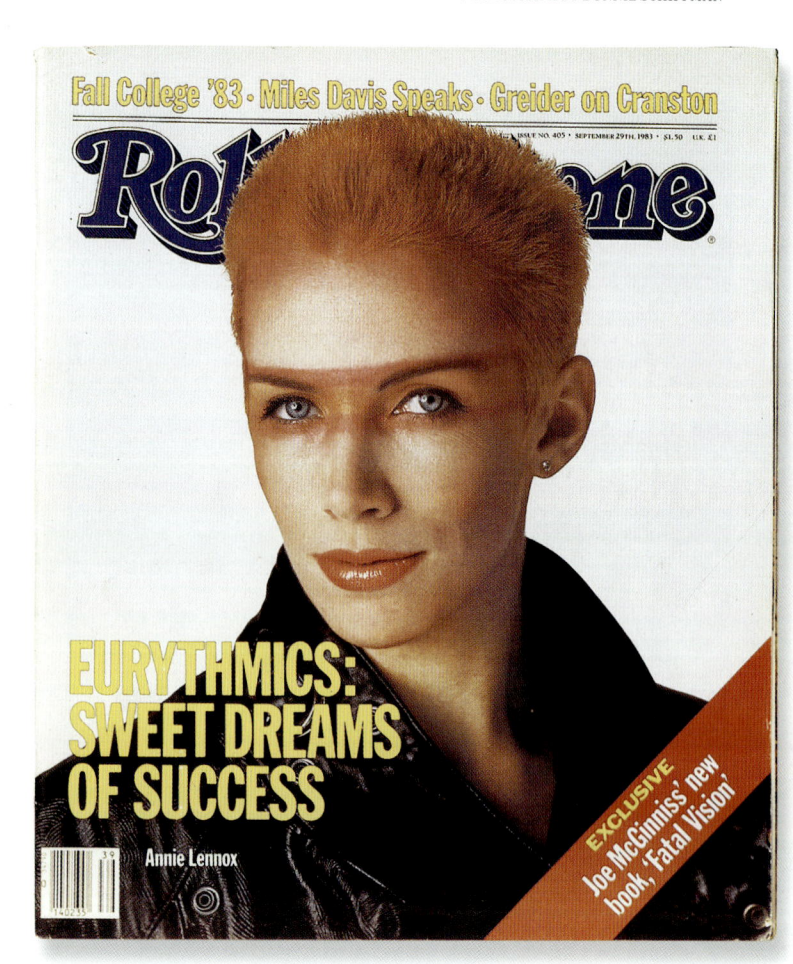

Stevie Nicks • The Young, the Rich & Heroin • Def Leppard

RollingStone

ISSUE NO. 399 • JULY 7TH, 1983 • $1.50 U.K. £1

EDDIE MURPHY
Goes for the Gold

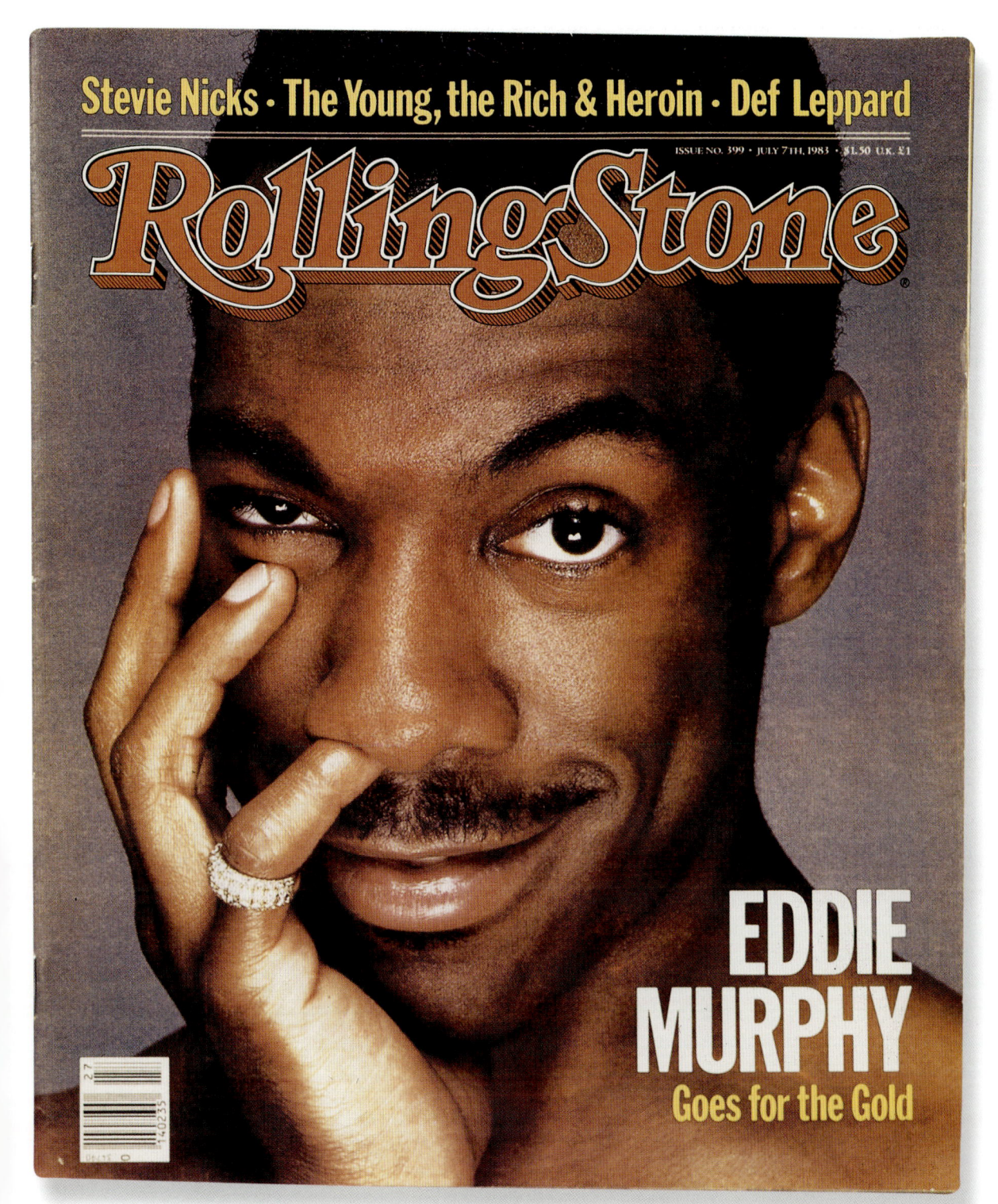

RS 399 | EDDIE MURPHY | July 7th, 1983 | Photograph by Richard Avedon

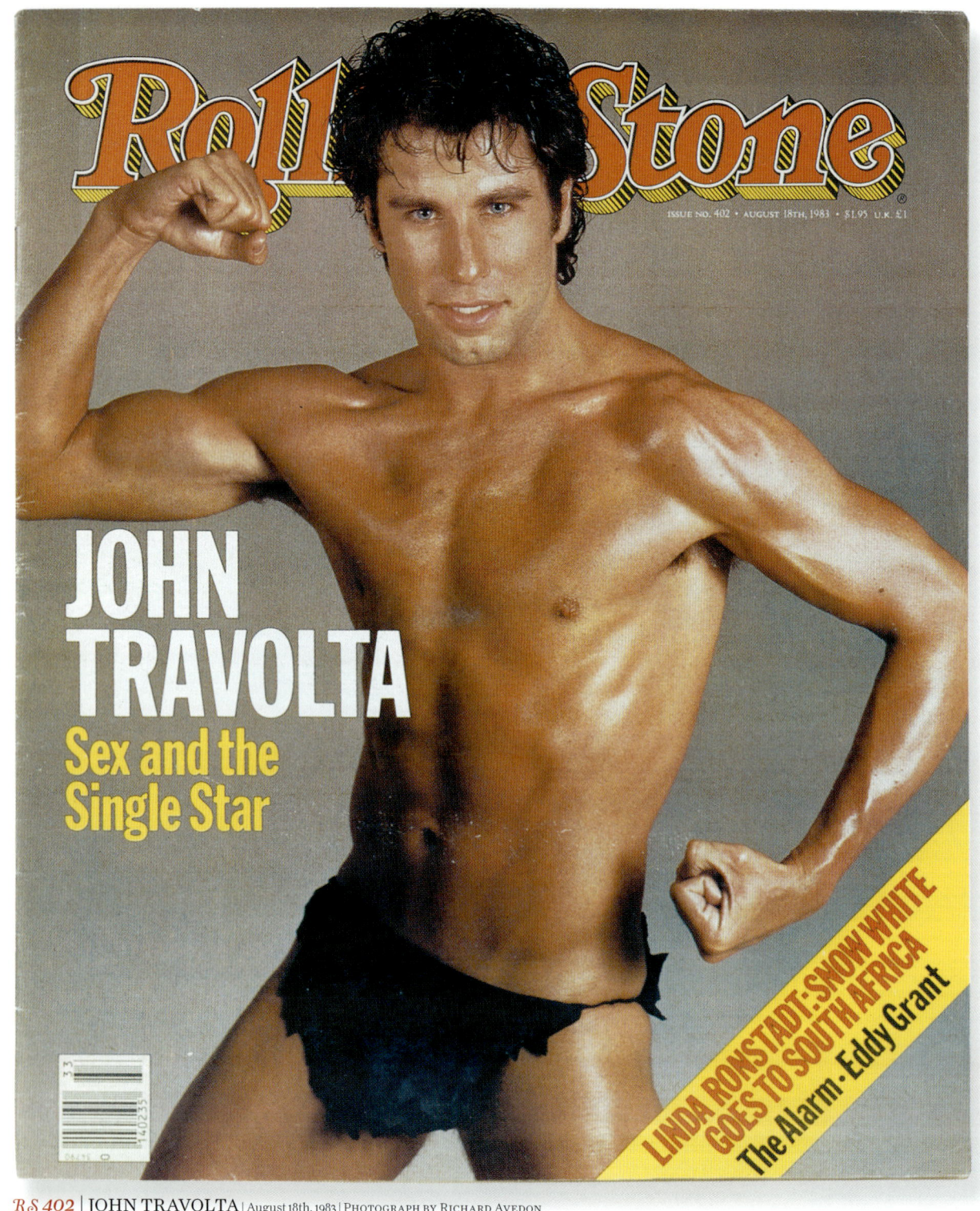

RS 402 | JOHN TRAVOLTA | August 18th, 1983 | Photograph by Richard Avedon

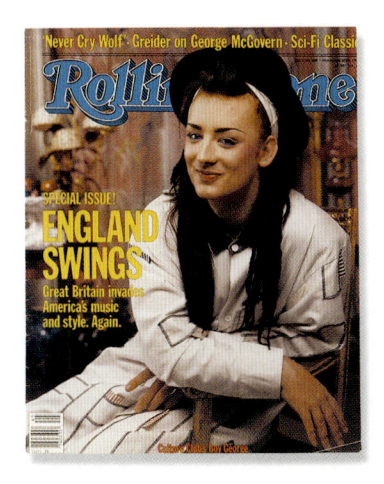

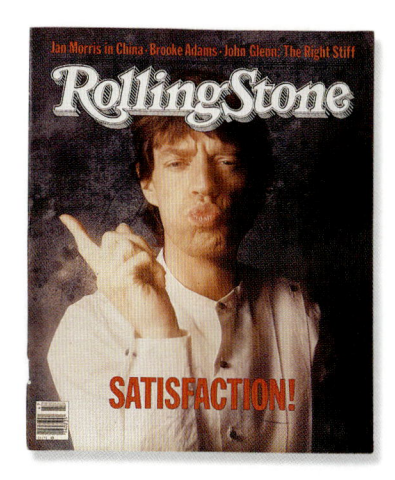

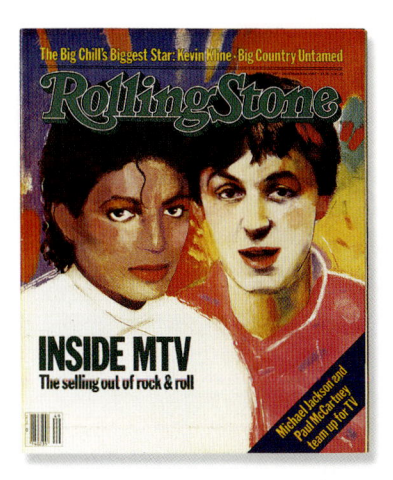

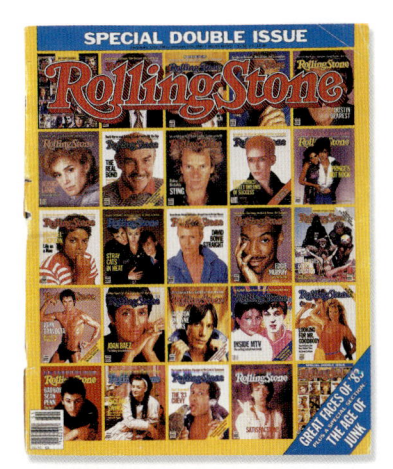

MTV IS PERFECT for a generation never weaned from television, because its videos contain few lines between fantasy and reality. Sexual fantasies blend with toothless gossip about a rock community that really does not exist, having dissipated maybe a decade ago. It doesn't matter. There are no dissenting opinions or alternative views telecast on MTV. Profit-making television creates an unreal environment to get people into what is called a "consumer mode"; MTV, as its executives boast, is pure environment. It is a way of thought, a way of life. It is the ultimate junk-culture triumph. It is a sophisticated attempt to touch the post-Woodstock population's lurking G spot, which is unattainable to those advertisers sponsoring *We Got It Made*.

It is easy to get lost in the fun-house environment of MTV, to spend idle hours in a dull stereo stupor, watching video clips and Martha Quinn, without glimpsing what is behind the visions with which MTV so relentlessly provides us. Behind the fun-house mirror is another story, one that makes the musical energy and optimism of the Sixties seem a thousand light-years ago. After watching hours and days of MTV, it's tough to avoid the conclusion that rock & roll has been replaced by commercials.

[EXCERPT FROM RS 410 COVER STORY BY STEVEN LEVY]

RS 408 | BOY GEORGE
November 10th, 1983
PHOTOGRAPH BY DAVID MONTGOMERY

RS 409 | MICK JAGGER
November 24th, 1983
PHOTOGRAPH BY WILLIAM COUPON

RS 410 | MICHAEL JACKSON & PAUL McCARTNEY
December 8th, 1983
ILLUSTRATION BY VIVIENNE FLESHER

RS 411/412 | 1983 YEARBOOK
December 22nd, 1983 – January 5th, 1984
VARIOUS PHOTOGRAPHERS

50 YEARS OF COVERS • 215

1980s

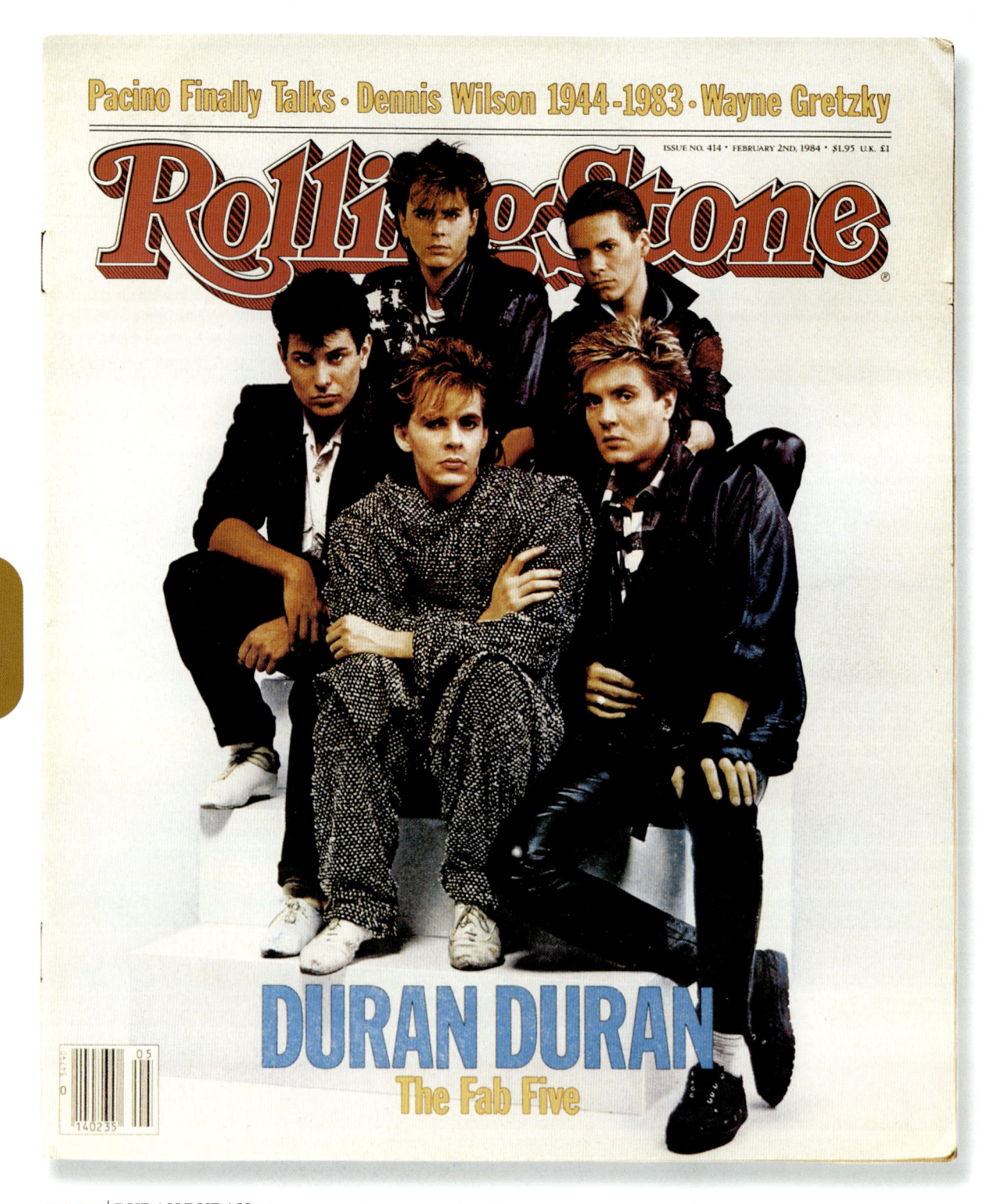

Pacino Finally Talks · Dennis Wilson 1944-1983 · Wayne Gretzky

Rolling Stone

ISSUE NO. 414 · FEBRUARY 2ND, 1984 · $1.95 U.K. £1

DURAN DURAN
The Fab Five

RS 414 | DURAN DURAN | February 2nd, 1984 | Photograph by David Montgomery

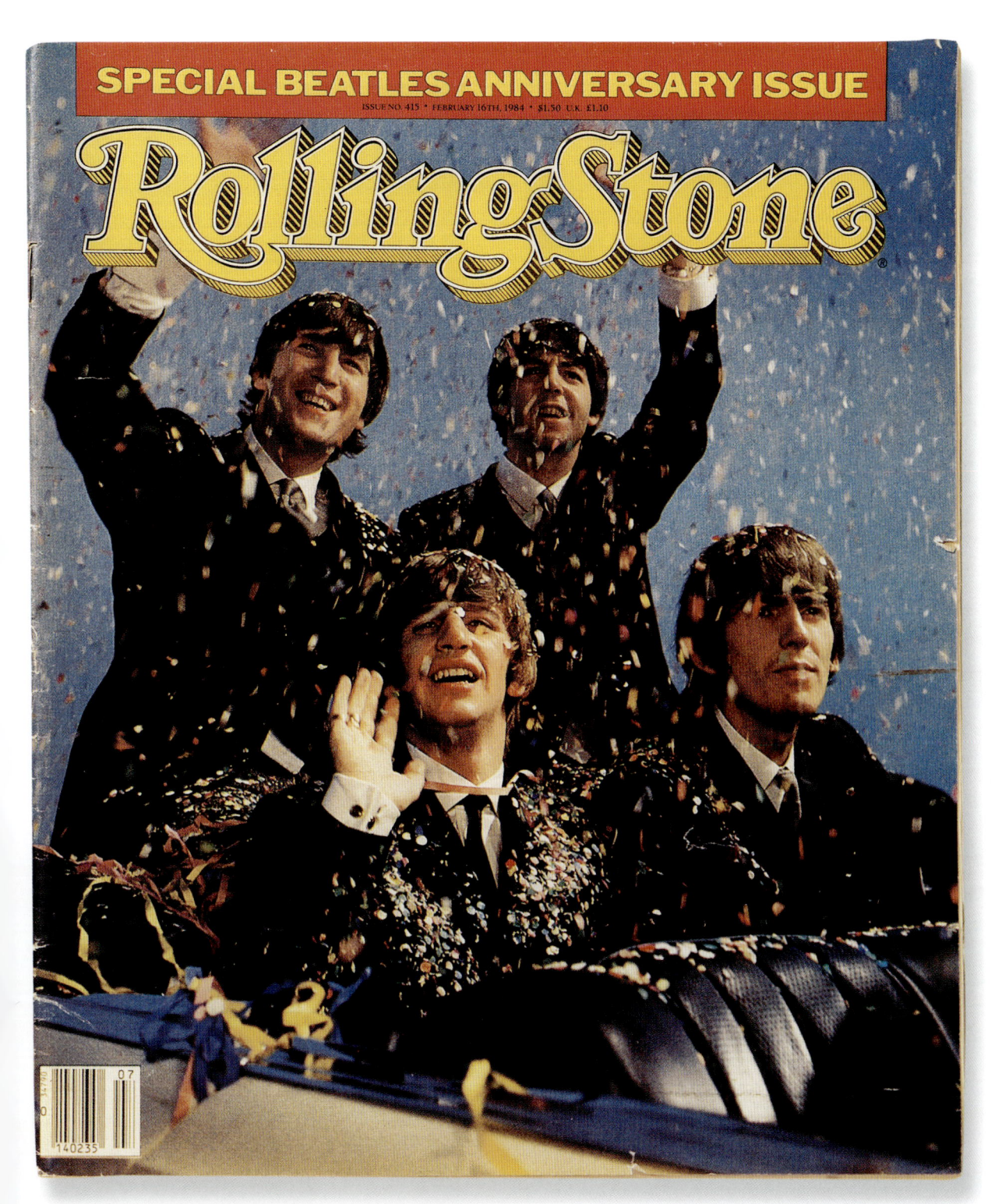

RS 415 | THE BEATLES | February 16th, 1984 | Photograph by John Launois

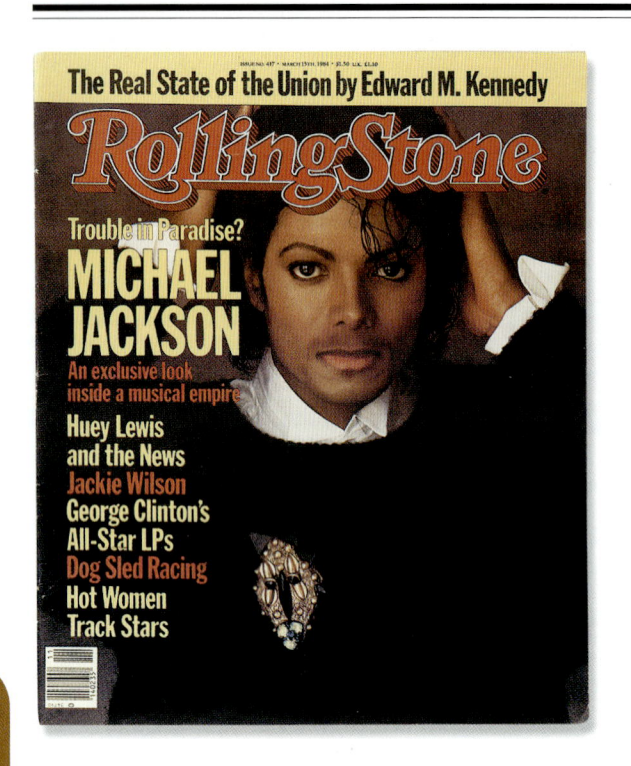

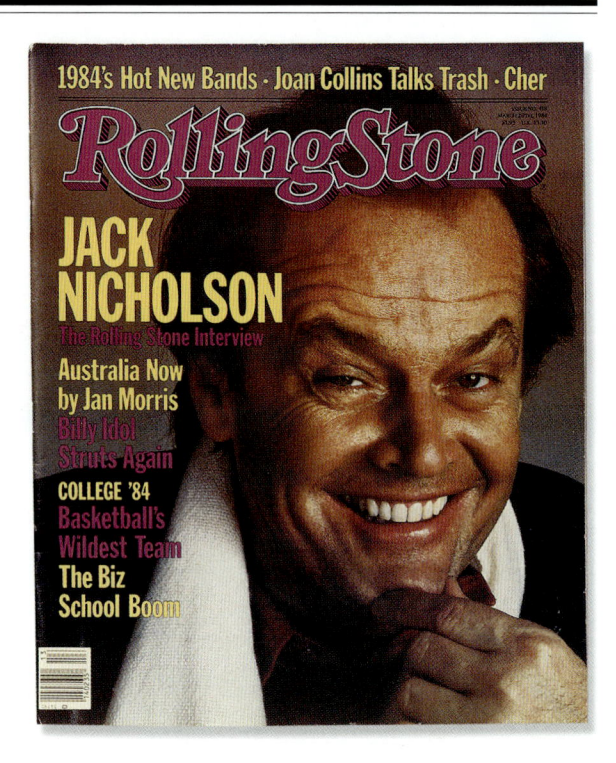

1980s

RS 417 | MICHAEL JACKSON
March 15th, 1984 | Photograph by Matthew Rolston

RS 418 | JACK NICHOLSON
March 29th, 1984 | Photograph by Richard Avedon

RS 419 | EDDIE MURPHY
April 12th, 1984 | Photograph by Richard Avedon

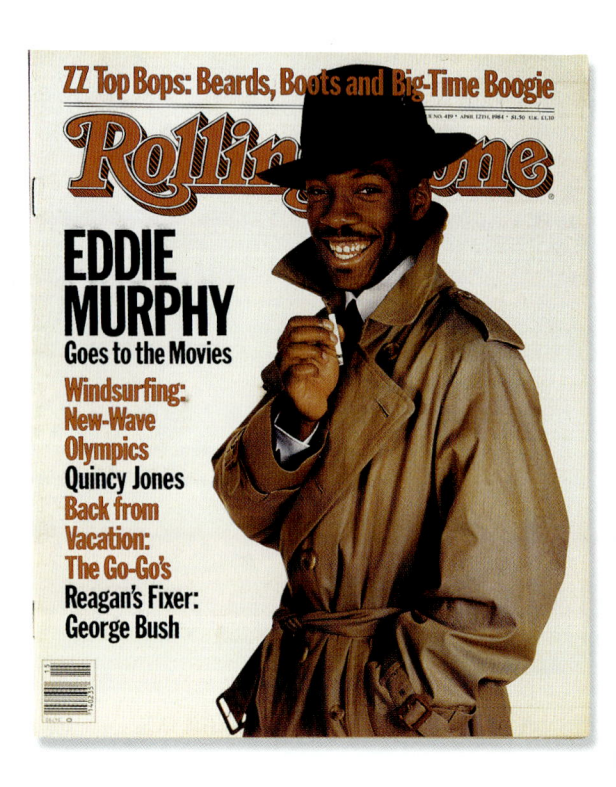

"HERE'S WHAT I LEARNED FROM MICHAEL Jackson. Michael will always ask everybody questions, questions that sound very naive. It was his form of research. And he was as curious about why this wardrobe person was using a certain kind of Scotch tape on the hem of the trouser to whatever light or lens or where I put the camera. It was like, 'Why does the snow fall, Daddy?' And that was a very intelligent thing to do. I started doing it, too, on commercials."

—*Matthew Rolston*

218 • ROLLING STONE

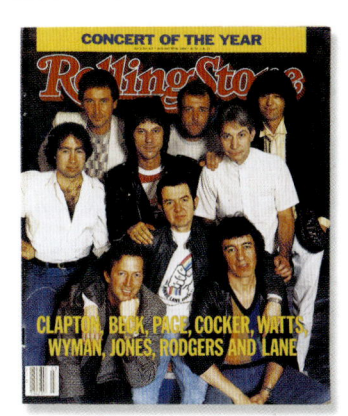

RS 413 | ARMS CONCERT PARTICIPANTS
January 19th, 1984
Photograph by Bonnie Schiffman

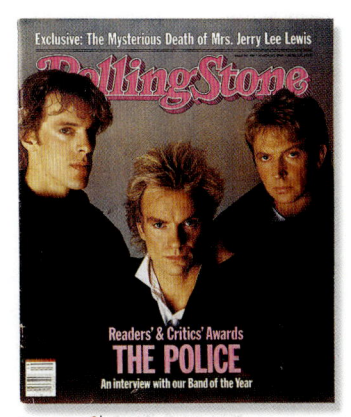

RS 416 | THE POLICE
March 1st, 1984
Photograph by David Bailey

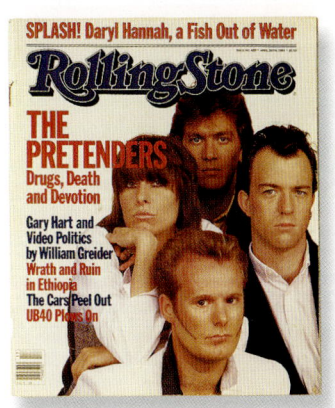

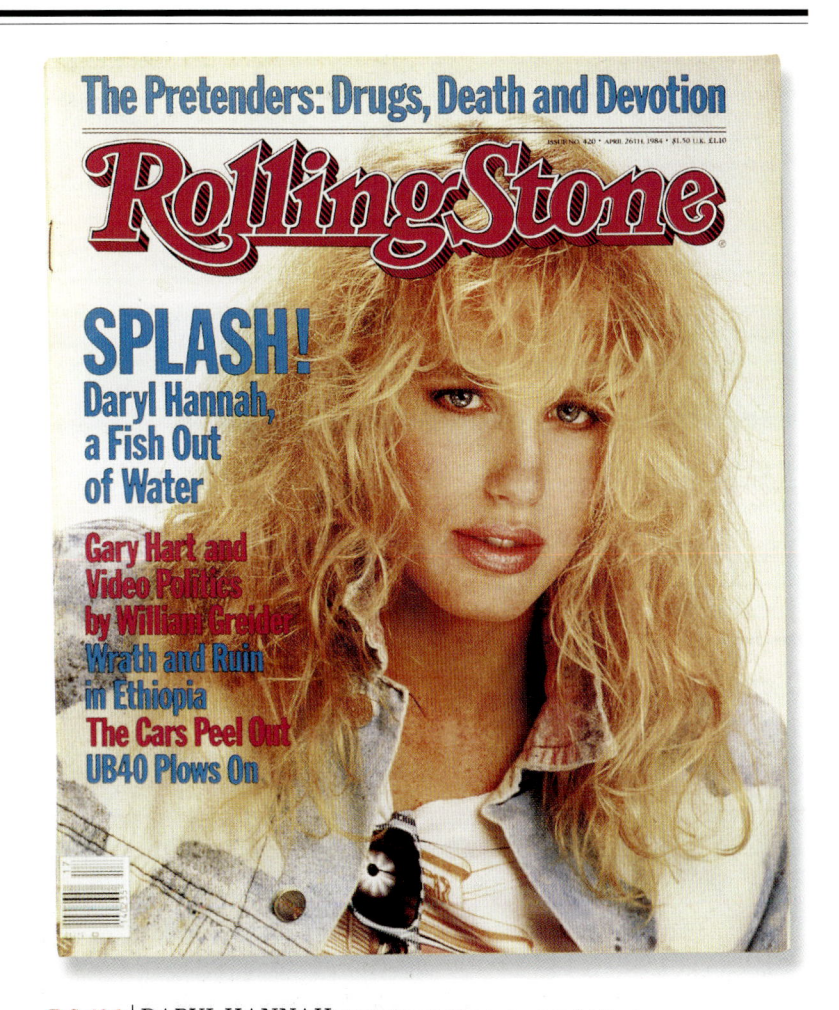

RS 420 | DARYL HANNAH | April 26th, 1984 | Photograph by E.J. Camp

RS 420 | THE PRETENDERS
April 26th, 1984
Photograph by Aaron Rapoport

[**RS 420**] In response to an angry reader's complaint at putting Daryl Hannah on the cover while granting the Pretenders nothing more than a cover line, one ROLLING STONE editor had this to say: "In a marketing test for issue 420, the Pretenders did appear on the cover of newsstand copies distributed on the West Coast. Our advice to disgruntled Pretenders fans in other regions of the country echoes that of a great newspaperman: Go West."

RollingStone

ISSUE NO. 421 • MAY 10TH, 1984 • $1.50 U.K. £1.10

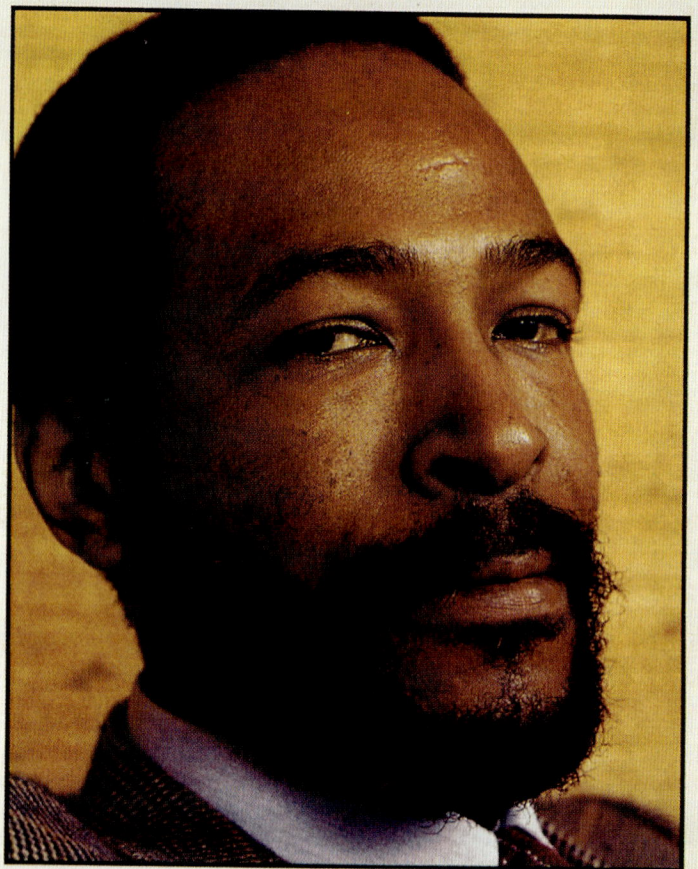

1980s

THE DEATH OF MARVIN GAYE
The Nightmare of the Final Days
The Genius of a Troubled Soul
A Look Back at Motown's Sexiest Singer

He was, above all, a preacher.
He came to preach to his people, to all people. He did so once, calling his sermon *What's Going On*. I believe he was called to preach again, to write and sing songs about the Jesus he loved so sincerely. But now we'll never know. A great artist – of the magnitude of Michelangelo and the sweetness of Mozart – is dead, and all we can do is praise the power that brought him forth.

His Oedipal struggle, his battles with the elements are finally laid to rest. He has written his own Greek tragedy – the story of a boy who became a man who became a god, only to be devoured, like Dionysus, by some demonic, self-destructive bent. The dark cloud that had long hung over his head has exploded. In his softly sloped eyes, in his exquisitely high-pitched speaking voice, even in his lighthearted, quick-witted banter, one heard the troubled vibe, the aching blue note. Marvin Gaye sang with a tear in his voice. He had the blues. His depressions were as deep as the Grand Canyon, his heartaches painful and prolonged. His romantic aura brings to mind Keats, a poet "half in love with easeful Death."

Like Mahalia Jackson's, his cry soars far beyond this world, reaching its crescendo in the arms of God. It is there where Marvin Gaye rests, peaceful at last. Whenever the voice of an angel is set free, there is cause for celebration. With Marvin, there is much to celebrate. He left behind a golden legacy. The gift of his genius and the truth of his preaching are now matters of historical record. He has not died, nor will he ever die. The message of his music is rooted in love, and love lives forever.

[EXCERPT FROM MARVIN GAYE TRIBUTE BY DAVID RITZ]

RS 421 | MARVIN GAYE
May 10th, 1984
PHOTOGRAPH BY NEAL PRESTON

Rolling Stone

ISSUE NO. 422 · MAY 24TH, 1984 · $1.50 U.K. £1.10

A SURPRISE HIT
Making
Romancing

CYNDI LAUPER
Laughs Last

Why Jesse Jackson Should Remember George Wallace
By William Greider

THE MARINES IN NICARAGUA
The War of 1927

1980s

RS 422 | CYNDI LAUPER | May 24th, 1984 | Photograph by Richard Avedon

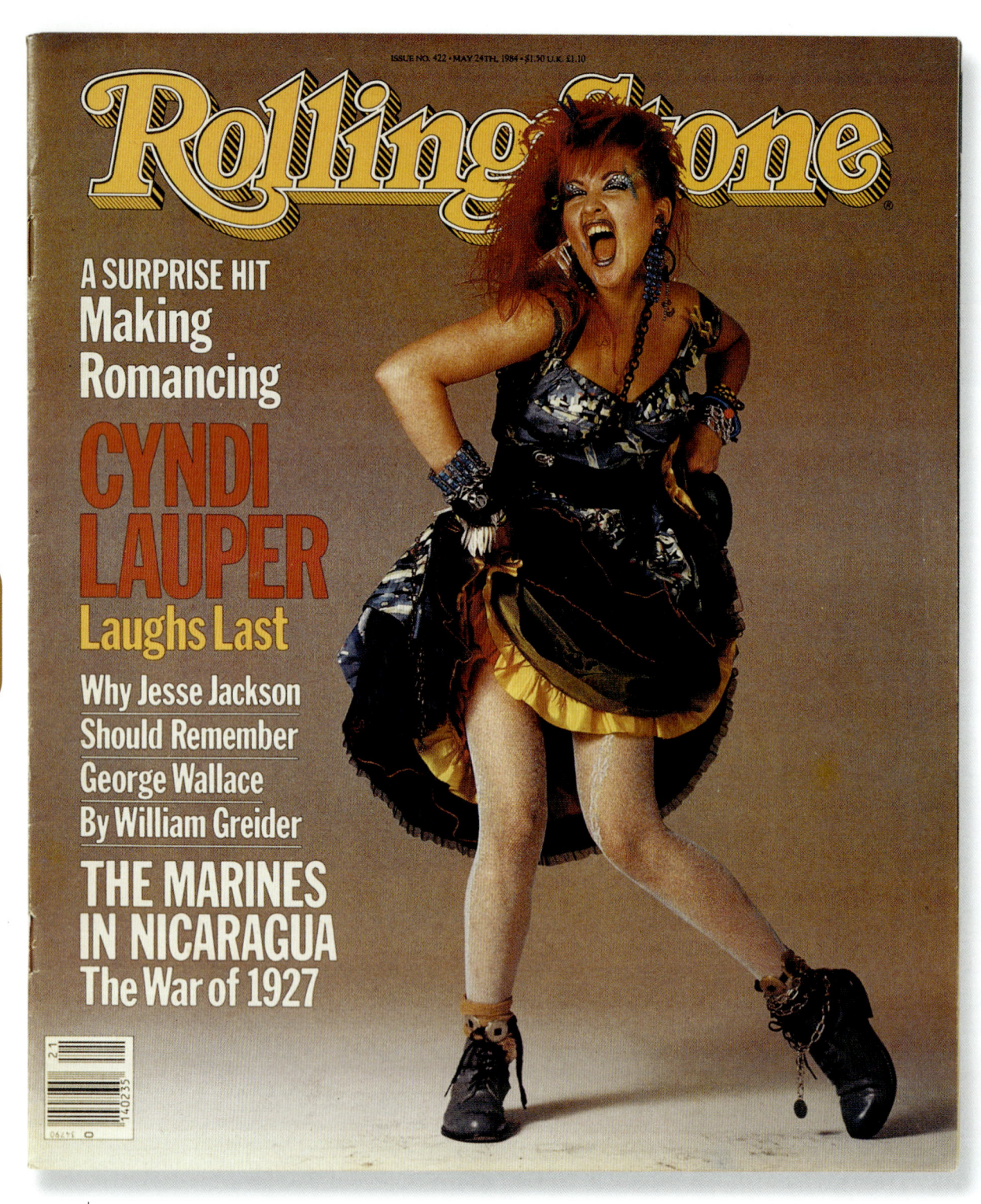

VAN HALEN: Thud Rock's Two-Headed Monster

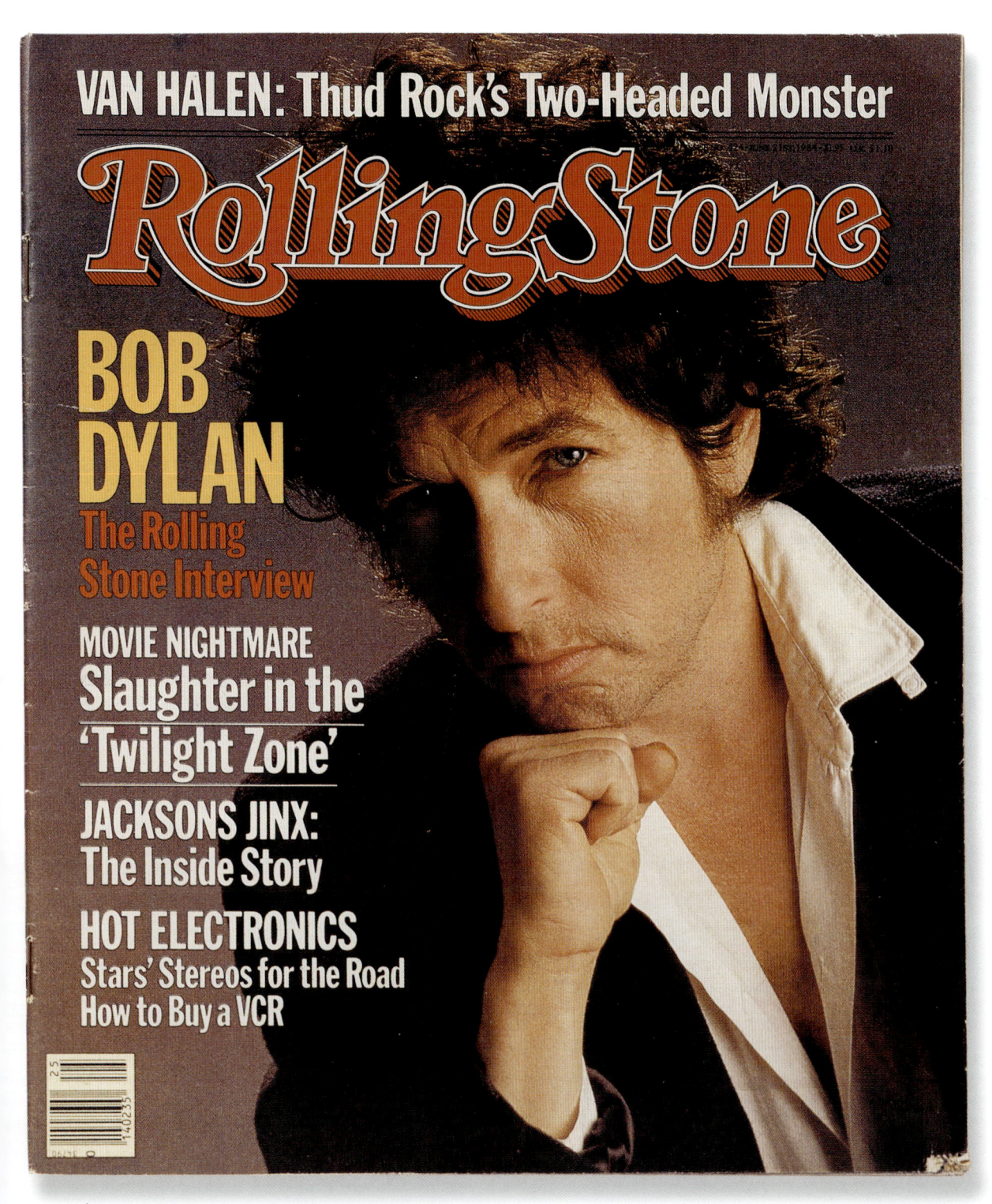

Rolling Stone

BOB DYLAN
The Rolling Stone Interview

MOVIE NIGHTMARE
Slaughter in the 'Twilight Zone'

JACKSONS JINX:
The Inside Story

HOT ELECTRONICS
Stars' Stereos for the Road
How to Buy a VCR

RS 424 | BOB DYLAN | June 21st, 1984 | Photograph by Ken Regan

Rolling Stone

ISSUE NO. 423 · JUNE 7TH, 1984 · $1.50 U.K. £1.16

CULTURE CLUB'S
BOY GEORGE
The Rolling Stone Interview

The Last Days of Dennis Wilson

HOW TO GET OFF COCAINE

Jacksons Tour in Chaos

1980s

RS 423 | CULTURE CLUB | June 7th, 1984 | Photograph by Richard Avedon

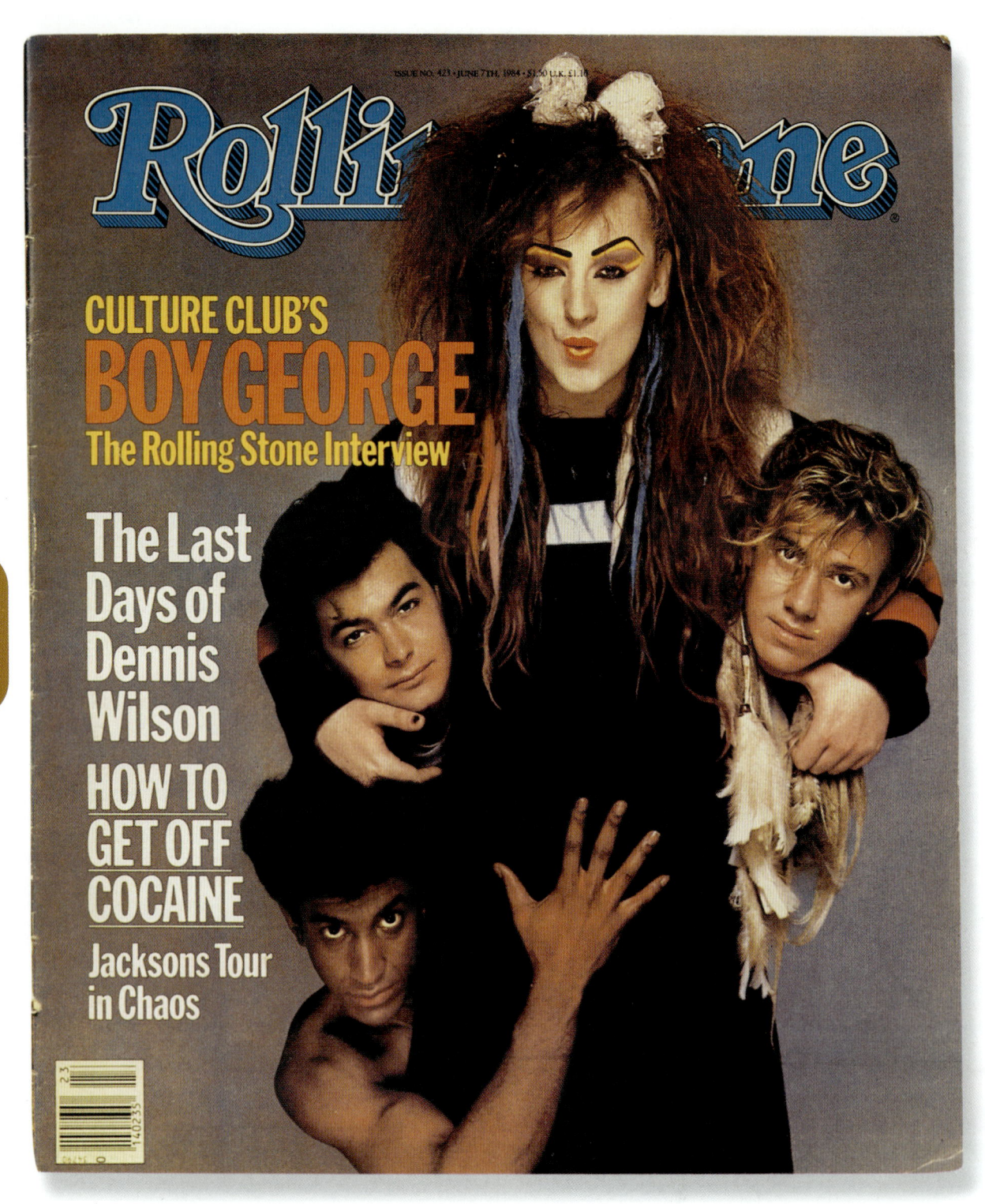

ISSUE NO. 429 · AUGUST 30TH, 1984 · $1.50 U.K. £1.20

RollingStone

PRINCE SCORES
A Hit Album
A Hot Movie

WILLIAM GREIDER
The Democratic Convention

TOM WOLFE
'The Bonfire of the Vanities'

RS 429 | PRINCE | August 30th, 1984 | Photograph by Richard Avedon

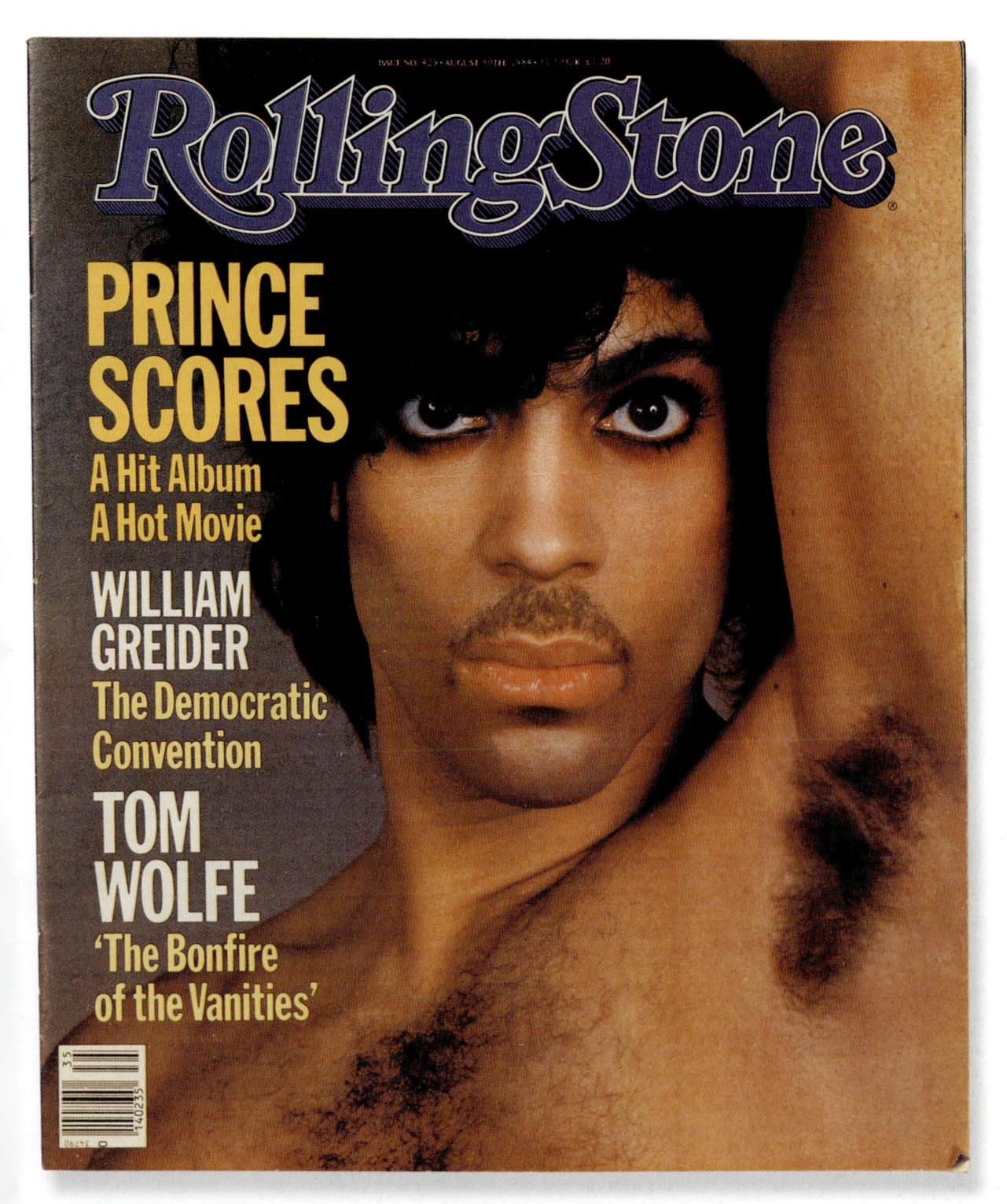

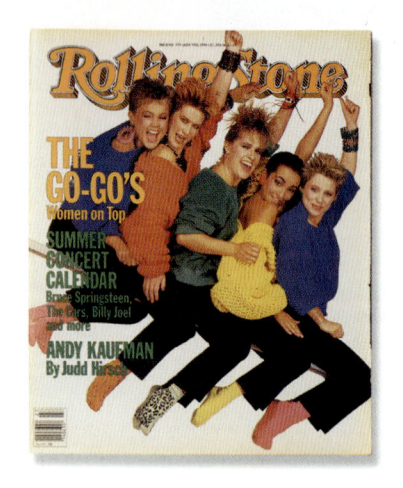

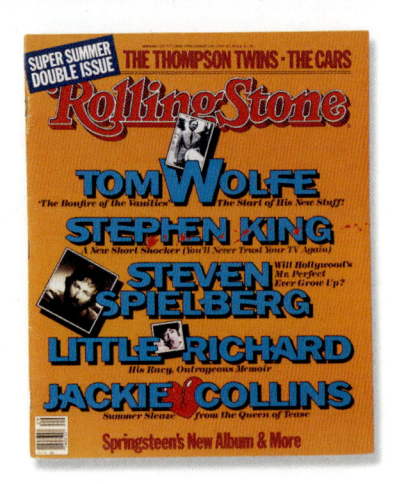

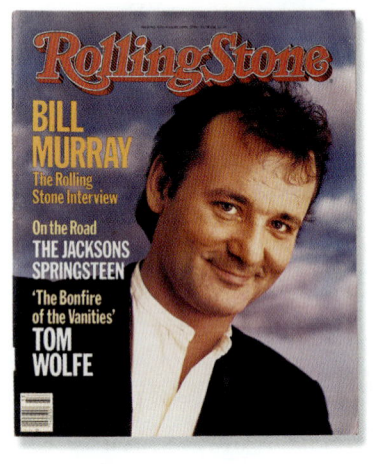

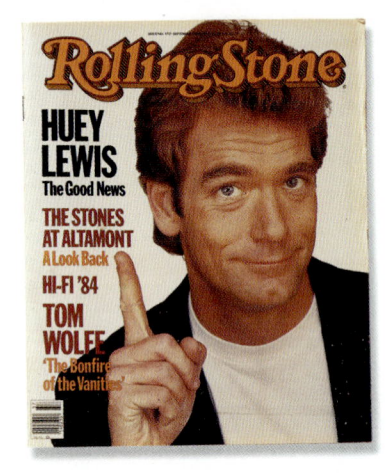

$\mathcal{RS}$ 432 | TINA TURNER
October 11th, 1984
PHOTOGRAPH BY STEVEN MEISEL

Today, Tina looks better than ever, sings better than ever, and says she's now happier than ever, too. She has a new boyfriend – a younger man she'd rather not name – and is now attempting to find the "balance of equality between men and women." She sees herself performing until she's fifty, perhaps, and says she'd then like to become a teacher, a propagator of her beloved Buddhist beliefs. Apparently, it's preordained.

"I'm gonna focus on this," she says. "I think that's gonna be my message, that's why I'm here. And I think that's why I'm gonna be as powerful as I am. Because in order to get people to listen to you, you've got to be some kind of landmark, some kind of foundation. You don't listen to people that don't mean anything to you. You have to have something there to make people believe you. And so I think that's what's going on now. I'm getting their attention now, and then when I'm ready, they'll listen. And they'll hear."

[EXCERPT FROM RS 432 COVER STORY BY KURT LODER]

$\mathcal{RS}$ 425 | THE GO-GO'S
July 5th, 1984
PHOTOGRAPH BY ALBERT WATSON

$\mathcal{RS}$ 428 | BILL MURRAY
August 16th, 1984
PHOTOGRAPH BY BARBARA WALZ

$\mathcal{RS}$ 426/427 | TOM WOLFE, STEVEN SPIELBERG, LITTLE RICHARD
July 19th – August 2nd, 1984
VARIOUS PHOTOGRAPHERS

$\mathcal{RS}$ 430 | HUEY LEWIS
September 13th, 1984
PHOTOGRAPH BY AARON RAPOPORT

1980s

226 • ROLLING STONE

Rolling Stone

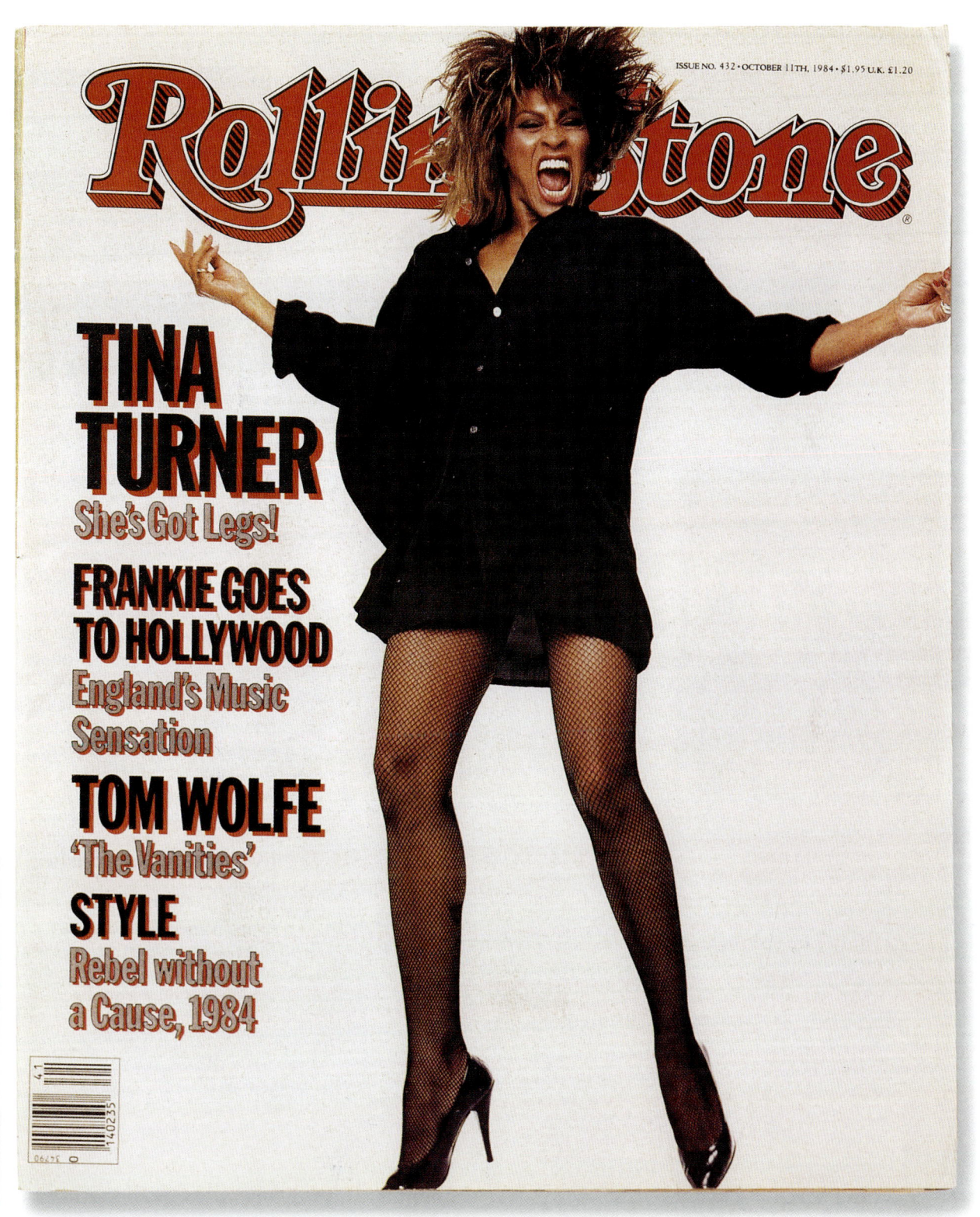

ISSUE NO. 432 • OCTOBER 11TH, 1984 • $1.95 U.K. £1.20

TINA TURNER
She's Got Legs!

FRANKIE GOES TO HOLLYWOOD
England's Music Sensation

TOM WOLFE
'The Vanities'

STYLE
Rebel without a Cause, 1984

1980s

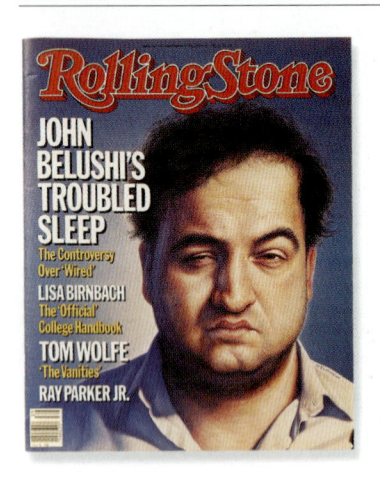

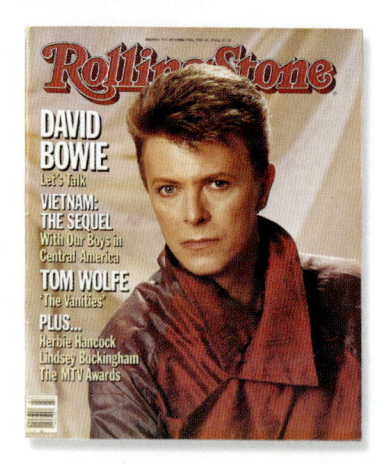

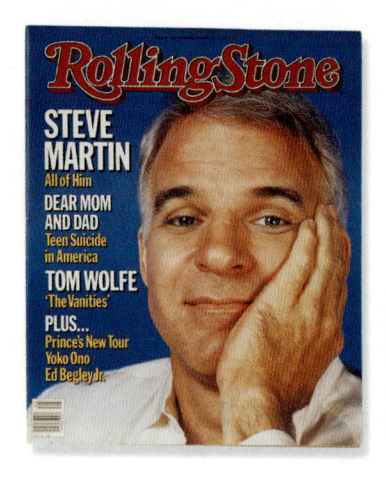

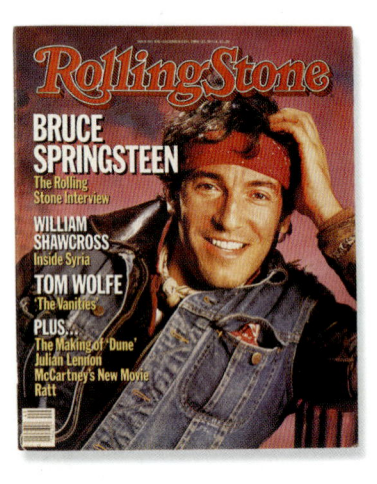

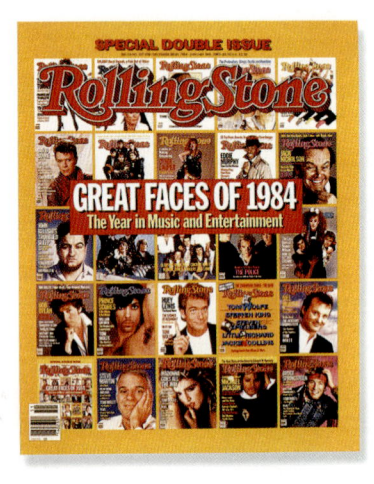

RS 431 | JOHN BELUSHI
September 27th, 1984
ILLUSTRATION BY GOTTFRIED HELNWEIN

RS 436 | BRUCE SPRINGSTEEN
December 6th, 1984
PHOTOGRAPH BY AARON RAPOPORT

RS 433 | DAVID BOWIE
October 25th, 1984
PHOTOGRAPH BY GREG GORMAN

RS 437/438 | GREAT FACES OF 1984
December 20th, 1984 – January 3rd, 1985
VARIOUS PHOTOGRAPHERS

RS 434 | STEVE MARTIN
November 8th, 1984
PHOTOGRAPH BY BONNIE SCHIFFMAN

IT'S LIKELY THAT HER VIDEOS were the breakthrough, as Madonna perfectly merged her dance training with her knowledge of the randier things in life. How did she manage to put across such seething sexuality where so many others have tried and failed? "I think that has to do with them not being in touch with that aspect of their personality," according to Madonna. "They say, 'Well, I have to do a video now, and a pop star has to come on sexually, so how do I do that?' instead of being in touch with that part of their self to begin with. I've been in touch with that aspect of my personality since I was five."

[EXCERPT FROM RS 435 COVER STORY BY CHRISTOPHER CONNELLY]

ISSUE NO. 435 • NOVEMBER 22TH, 1984 • $1.50 U.K. £1.20

RollingStone

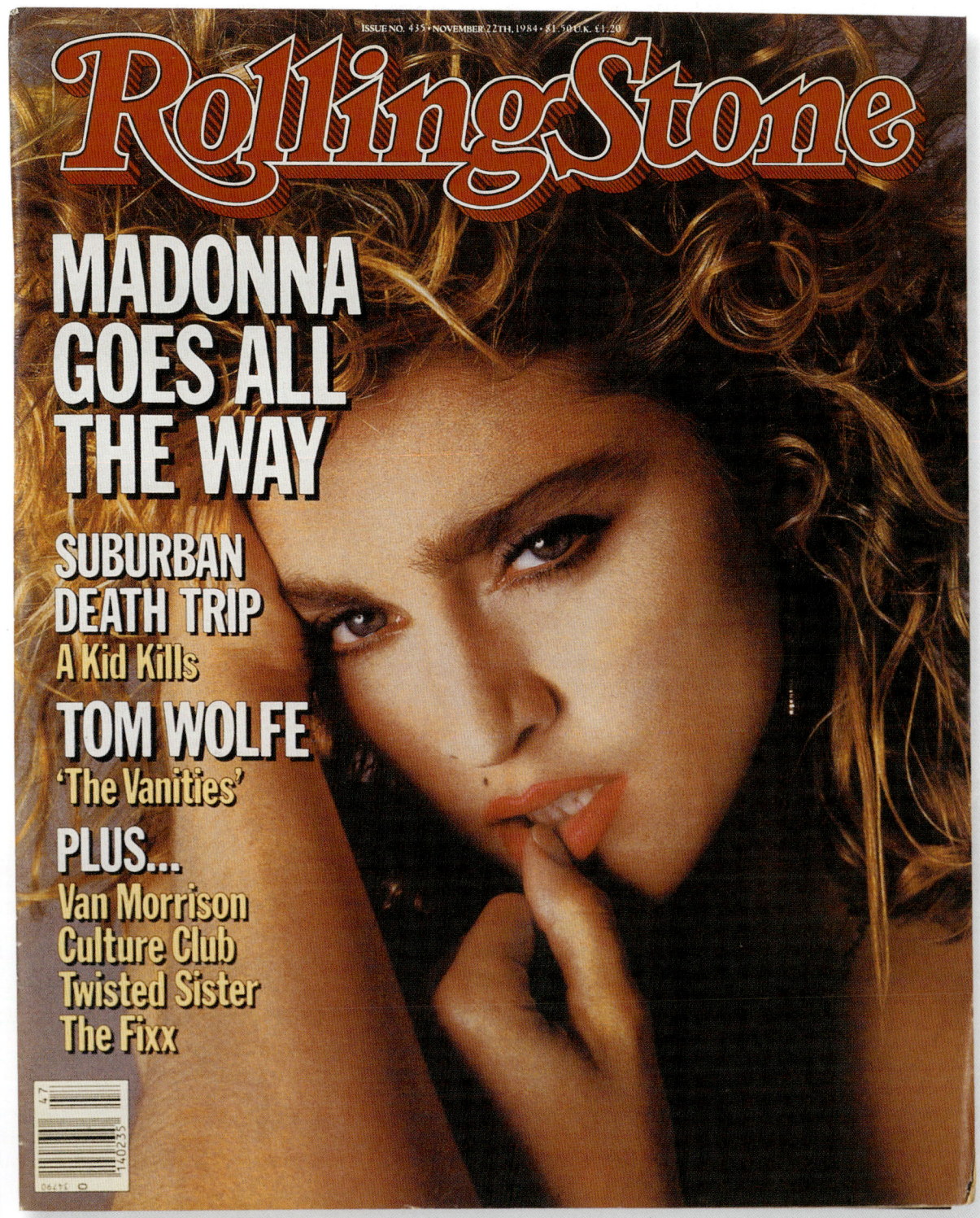

MADONNA GOES ALL THE WAY

SUBURBAN DEATH TRIP
A Kid Kills

TOM WOLFE
'The Vanities'

PLUS...
Van Morrison
Culture Club
Twisted Sister
The Fixx

RS 435 | MADONNA | November 22nd, 1984 | Photograph by Steven Meisel

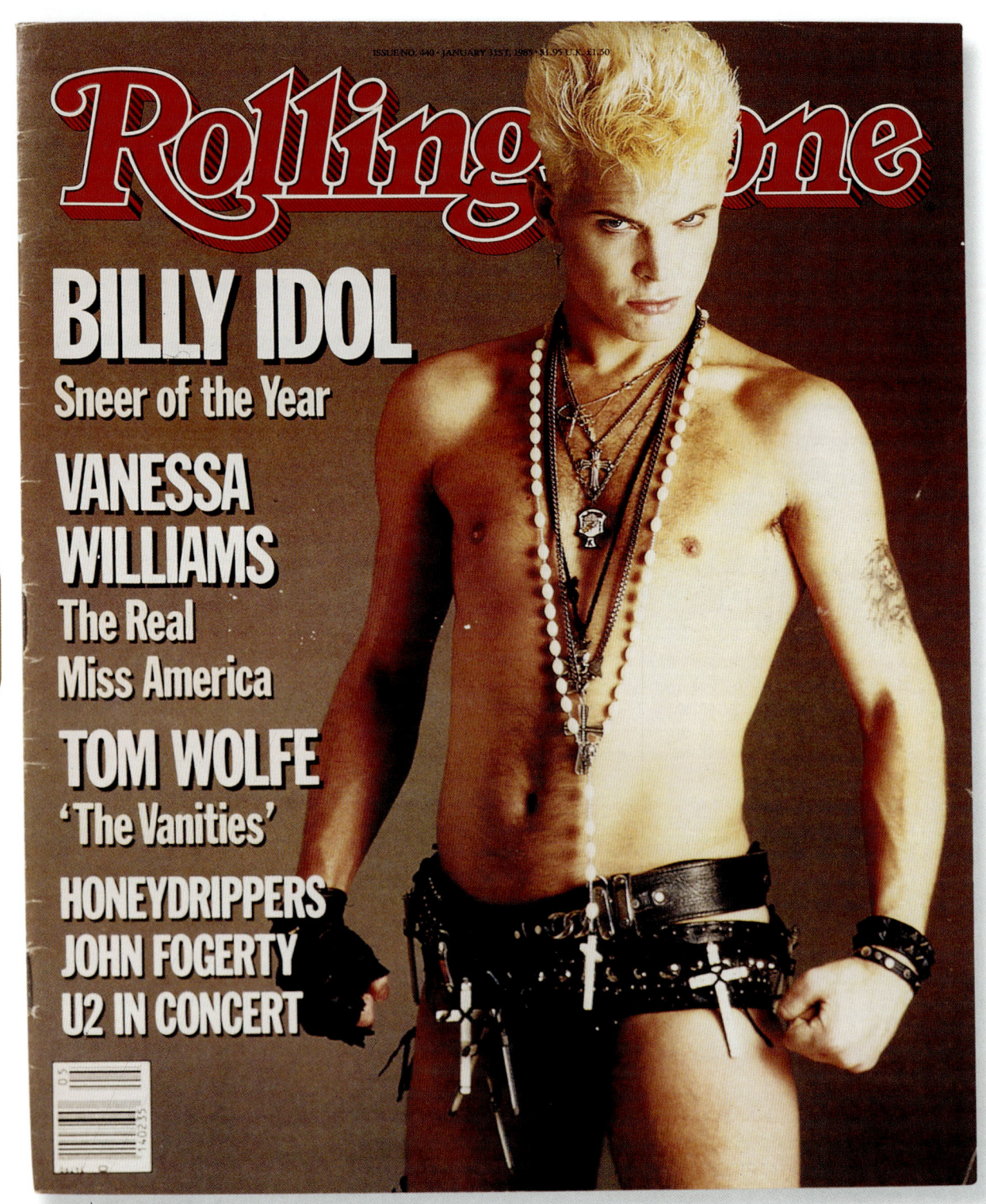

RS 440 | BILLY IDOL | January 31st, 1985 | Photograph by E.J. Camp

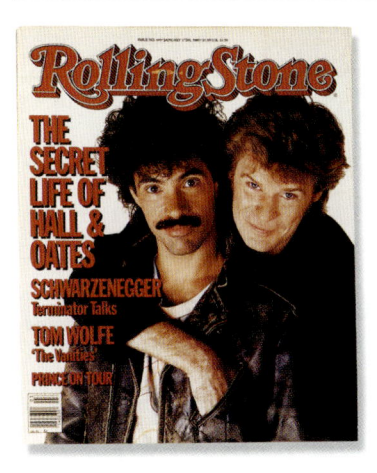

RS 439 | DARYL HALL
& JOHN OATES
January 17th, 1985
PHOTOGRAPH BY BERT STERN

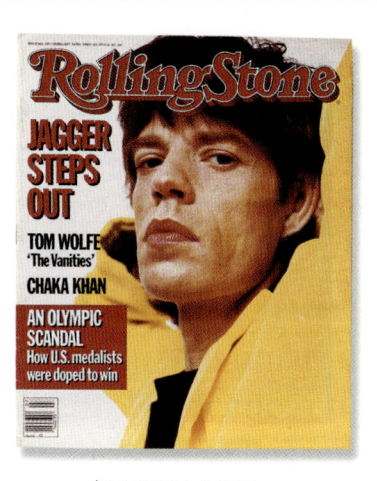

RS 441 | MICK JAGGER
February 14th, 1985
PHOTOGRAPH BY STEVEN MEISEL

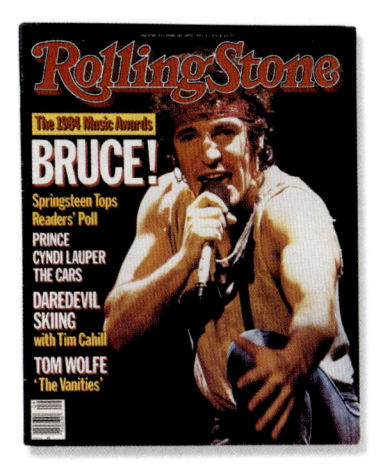

RS 442 | BRUCE SPRINGSTEEN
February 28th, 1985
PHOTOGRAPH BY NEAL PRESTON

HERE'S THE CHECK.

"I'll let you pay," says Billy, "but it better be a good article, you cunt."

"Right," I say.

"Otherwise, stick it up your ass. Don't tell me you'll pay for it."

"Okay," I say, laughing.

We are in a back booth at Emilio's in New York City's Greenwich Village. We are on a date set up by ROLLING STONE. Billy Idol has had two bottles of wine. It is one in the morning.

"Anyway, ROLLING STONE sucks," says Billy, affably. "If ROLLING STONE was clever, they would have bought their own TV channel. And put me on it. I *know* they're rich enough."

He's in a high mood.

"That's why, 'Don't fuck with me, motherfuckers!' " He bangs on the table. " 'Cause I'm going to be rich enough soon, I'll be at your economic level, and then fuck *you*, ROLLING STONE."

"Right," I say, paralyzed with delight.

"I want to be on the *back* of that motherfucker!" says Billy. "Don't put me on the front!" He pushes his dark glasses up on his nose. "I think it sucks being on the front of ROLLING STONE!" He bends toward the tape recorder. "I love you *all*, you motherfuckers. But you should have fucking had a bit more respect when I came up in 1977, '78 to see you in your Fifth Avenue offices! But I don't care. Now maybe you understand that I *am* worth being on the front cover of your magazine, for the *right* reasons, motherfuckers! Don't put me on if you don't like me! Fucking *don't* put me on it!"

"Well, you're probably going to be on it," I say.

He drops his lower lip and looks for the cigarettes.

"Well, I better be real on there," he says, slapping his coat for the lighter. "We don't want no Cyndi Lauper this year."

"You'll be real," I say.

"I didn't like the picture they put of me in the year-end issue."

He lights up.

"You didn't?"

"No, I thought it sucked." He takes the cigarette out of his mouth and leans toward the recorder again. "You put the wrong picture in, and you know you did . . . ooooaaaah [*chuckling*] I know. I know. Don't fuck with me. All right. Let's go."

[EXCERPT FROM RS 440 COVER STORY BY E. JEAN CARROLL]

In America, their names are not household words, and their faces are unfamiliar even to some of their fans. They have yet to notch a Top Ten album or single. Only now are they beginning to tour arena-sized venues. But for a growing number of rock & roll fans, U2 – vocalist Paul "Bono" Hewson, twenty-four; guitarist Dave "the Edge" Evans, twenty-two; bassist Adam Clayton, twenty-four; and drummer Larry Mullen Jr., twenty-two – has become the band that matters most, maybe even the only band that matters. It's no coincidence that U2 sells more T-shirts and merchandise than groups that sell twice as many records, or that four of U2's five albums are currently on *Billboard*'s Top 200. The group has become one of the handful of artists in rock & roll history (the Who, the Grateful Dead, Bruce Springsteen) that people are eager to identify themselves with. And they've done it not just with their music but with a larger message as well – by singing "Pride (In the Name of Love)" while most other groups sing about pride in the act of love.

The band's appeal doesn't seem to be sexual; no member of U2 appears to have seen the inside of a health club or a New Wave haberdashery, and only Mullen could pass for a Cute Guy. U2's strength, it seems, goes deeper. Like most rock & roll bands, U2 articulates, at top volume, the alienation that young people can feel from their country, their hometown, their family, their sexuality. Like some of the best rock & roll bands, U2 also shows how that alienation might be overcome. But unlike anyone else in rock & roll, U2 also addresses the most ignored – and most volatile – area of inquiry: alienation from religion.

"Sadomasochism is not taboo in rock & roll," notes Bono. "Spirituality is." Indeed, when religion in America seems sadly synonymous with the electronic evangelism of Jimmy Swaggart and Jerry Falwell, U2 dares to proclaim its belief in Christianity – at top volume – while grappling with the ramifications of its faith. Each member is careful to avoid discussing the specifics of his beliefs (the perfectly amiable Mullen, in fact, customarily declines to give interviews), and the band's musical message is hardly a proselytizing one. But even to raise the issue, to suggest that a person who loves rock & roll can unashamedly find peace with God as well, is a powerful statement. This is a band that onstage and offstage seems guided by a philosophy not included in such yuppie maxims as "feeling good" and "go for it": not how might we live our lives (what we can get away with) but how ought we to live our lives.

Lofty goals, but while the promise of U2's records has always been great, it is a promise that remains largely unfulfilled. In the past year and a half, U2 has found itself faced with several critical decisions: artistic, financial, personal, even patriotic. Each choice represented a test of whether the band could continue to articulate its message and fulfill its promise without drowning in contradictions. And while the outcome isn't settled yet, U2 seems to have come through its crises in good shape – due in large part, perhaps, to the band members' willingness to acknowledge their own weaknesses.

"It interests me that I'm portrayed as some sort of strong man," says Bono with genuine perplexity. "I don't see myself in that way. I know my weaknesses. When I see the albums, I don't see them as anthemic. I think that's what's uplifting, that's what connects with people. I think people relate to U2 because they've seen us fall on our face so many times."

[EXCERPT FROM RS 443 COVER STORY BY CHRISTOPHER CONNELLY]

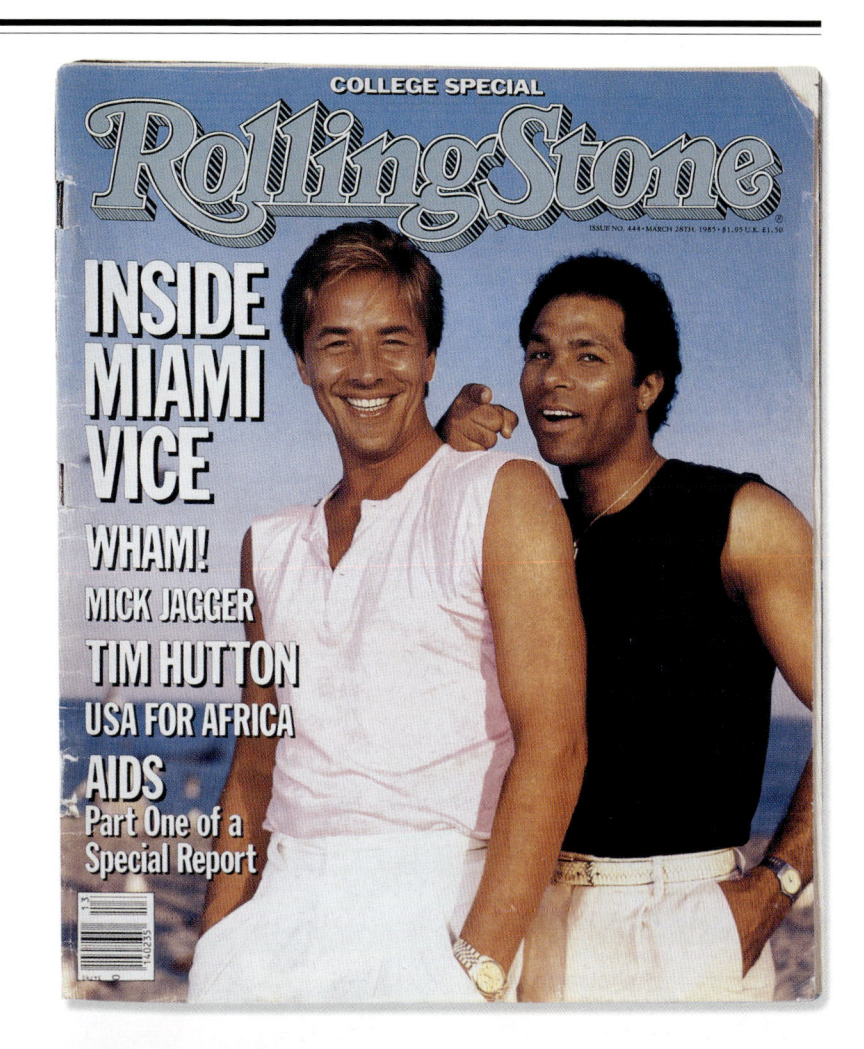

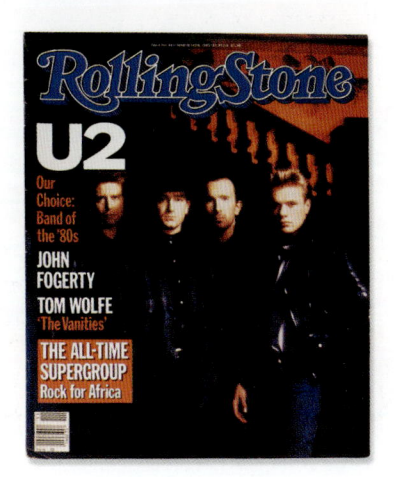

RS 444 | DON JOHNSON & PHILLIP MICHAEL THOMAS
March 28th, 1985
PHOTOGRAPH BY DEBORAH FEINGOLD

RS 443 | U2
March 14th, 1985
PHOTOGRAPH BY REBECCA BLAKE

ISSUE NO. 445 • APRIL 11TH, 1985 $1.95 U.K. £1.50

RollingStone

Van Halen's DAVID LEE ROTH

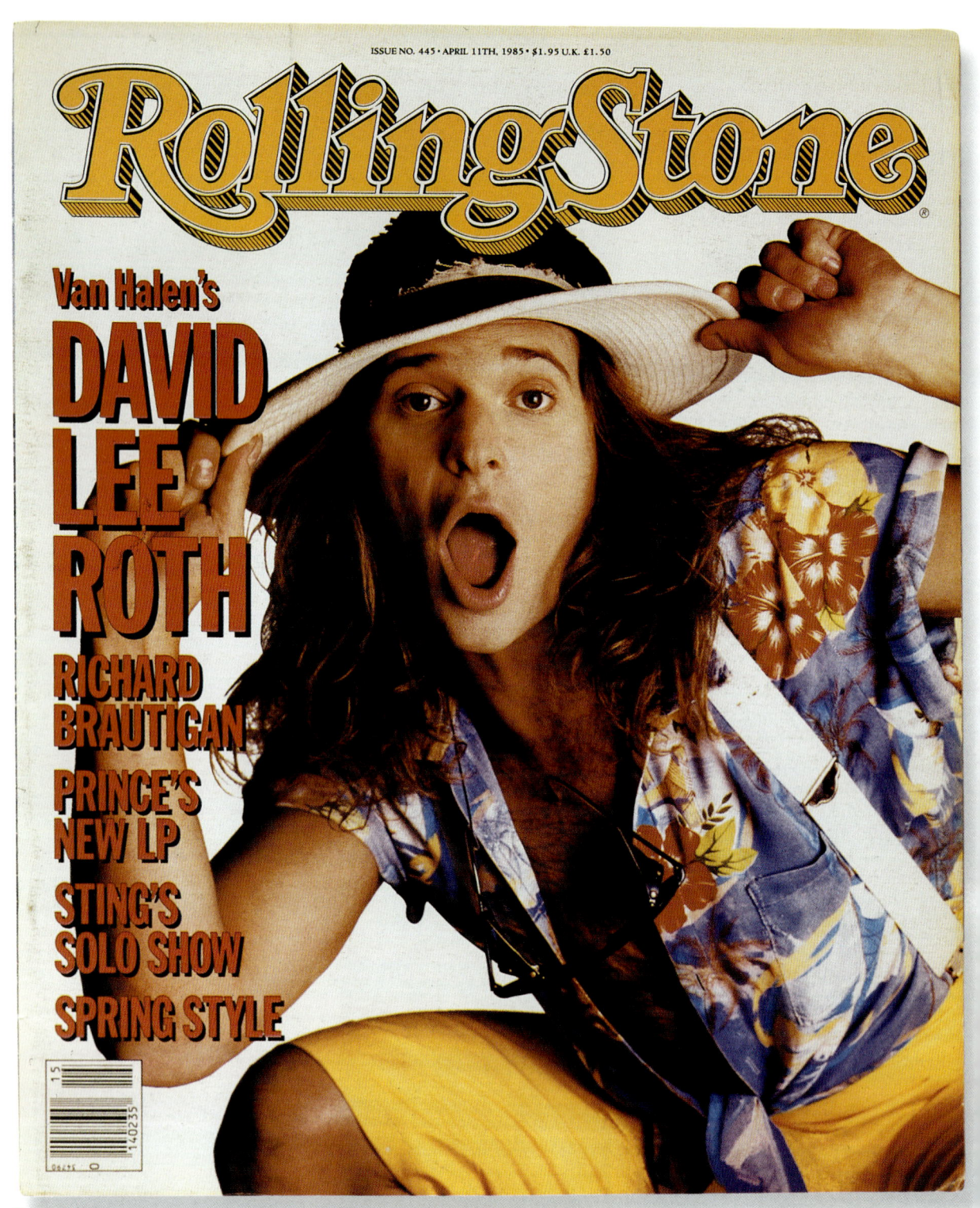

RICHARD BRAUTIGAN

PRINCE'S NEW LP

STING'S SOLO SHOW

SPRING STYLE

1980s

RS 445 | DAVID LEE ROTH | April 11th, 1985 | Photograph by Bradford Branson

ISSUE NO. 447 • MAY 9TH, 1985 • U.K. £1.50 • $1.95

RollingStone

MADONNA AND ROSANNA
Their New Movie's Hot

HUNTER S. THOMPSON
The Fall of Saigon

MARTIN SHORT

TOM WOLFE

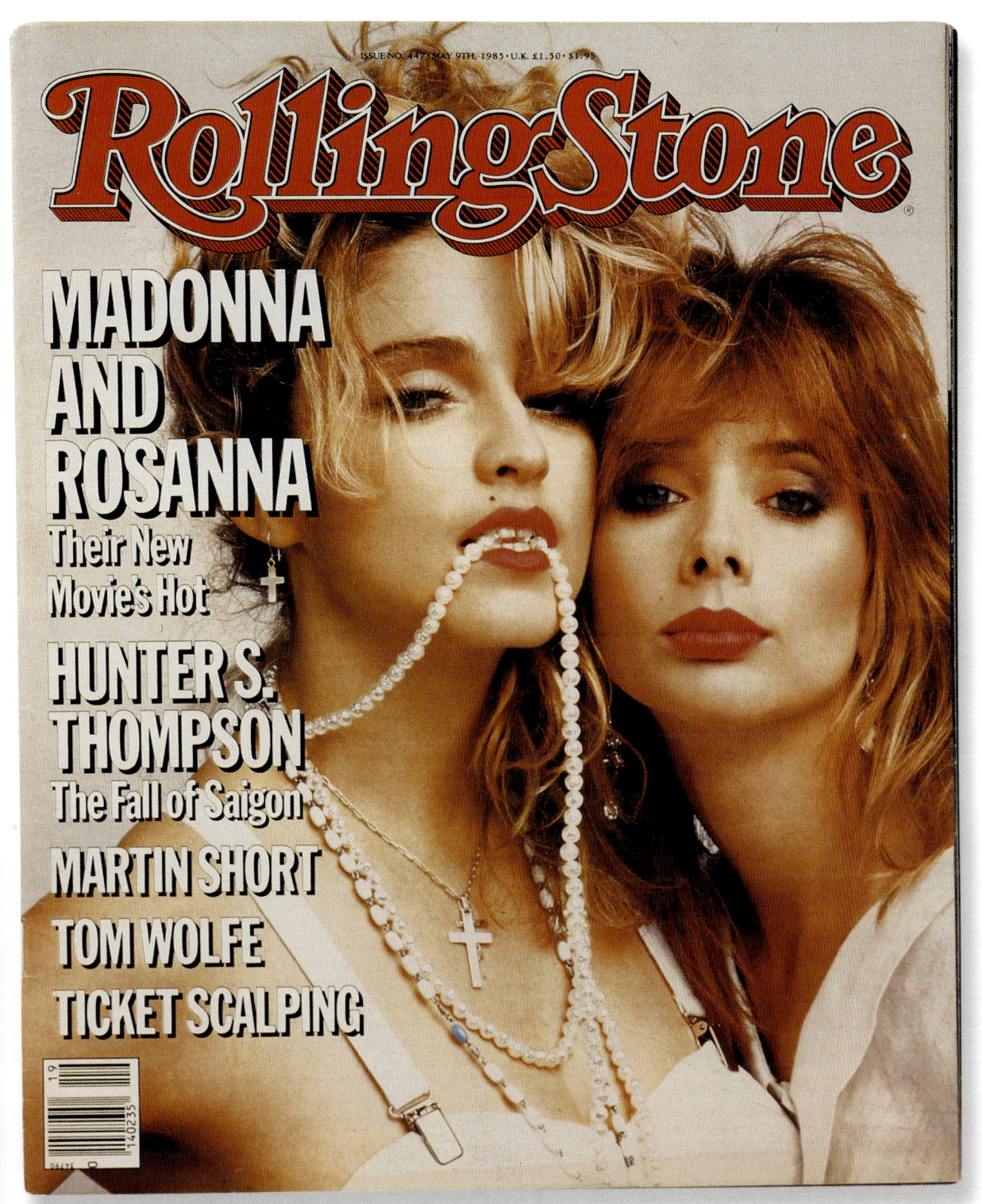

TICKET SCALPING

RS 447 | MADONNA & ROSANNA ARQUETTE | May 9th, 1985 | Photograph by Herb Ritts

ISSUE NO. 446 • APRIL 25TH, 1985 • U.K. £1.50 • $1.95

Rolling Stone

RICHARD GERE: ACTOR

AIDS
Special Report

DON HENLEY

England's Songbirds:
SADE
ALISON MOYET

TOM WOLFE

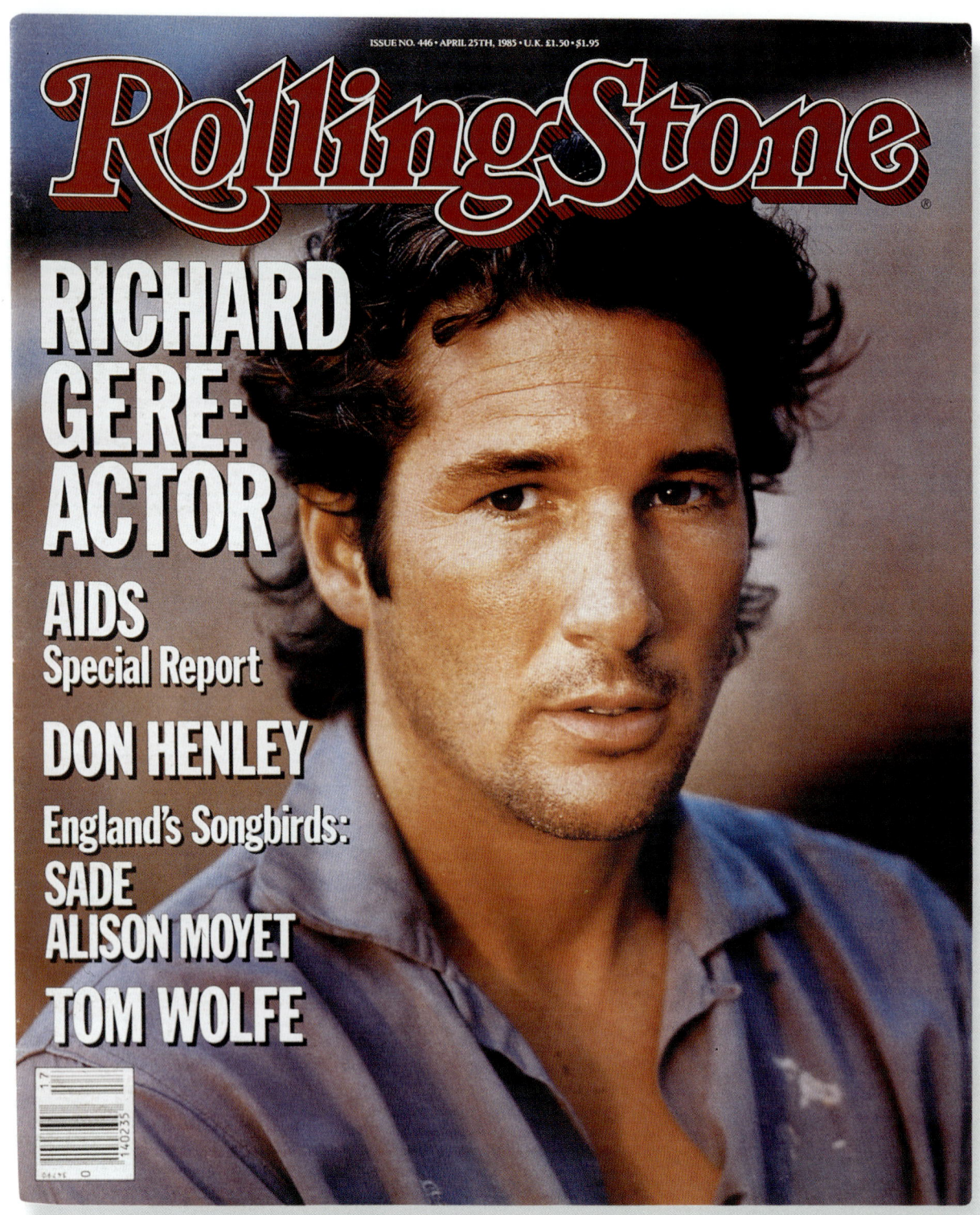

1980s

RS 446 | RICHARD GERE | April 25th, 1985 | Photograph by Herb Ritts

ISSUE NO. 448 • MAY 23RD, 1985 • U.K. £1.50 • $1.95

RollingStone

PHIL COLLINS BEATS THE ODDS

L.A. Clubs: THE ZERO GENERATION

SADE

TOM PETTY

POWER STATION

TOM WOLFE

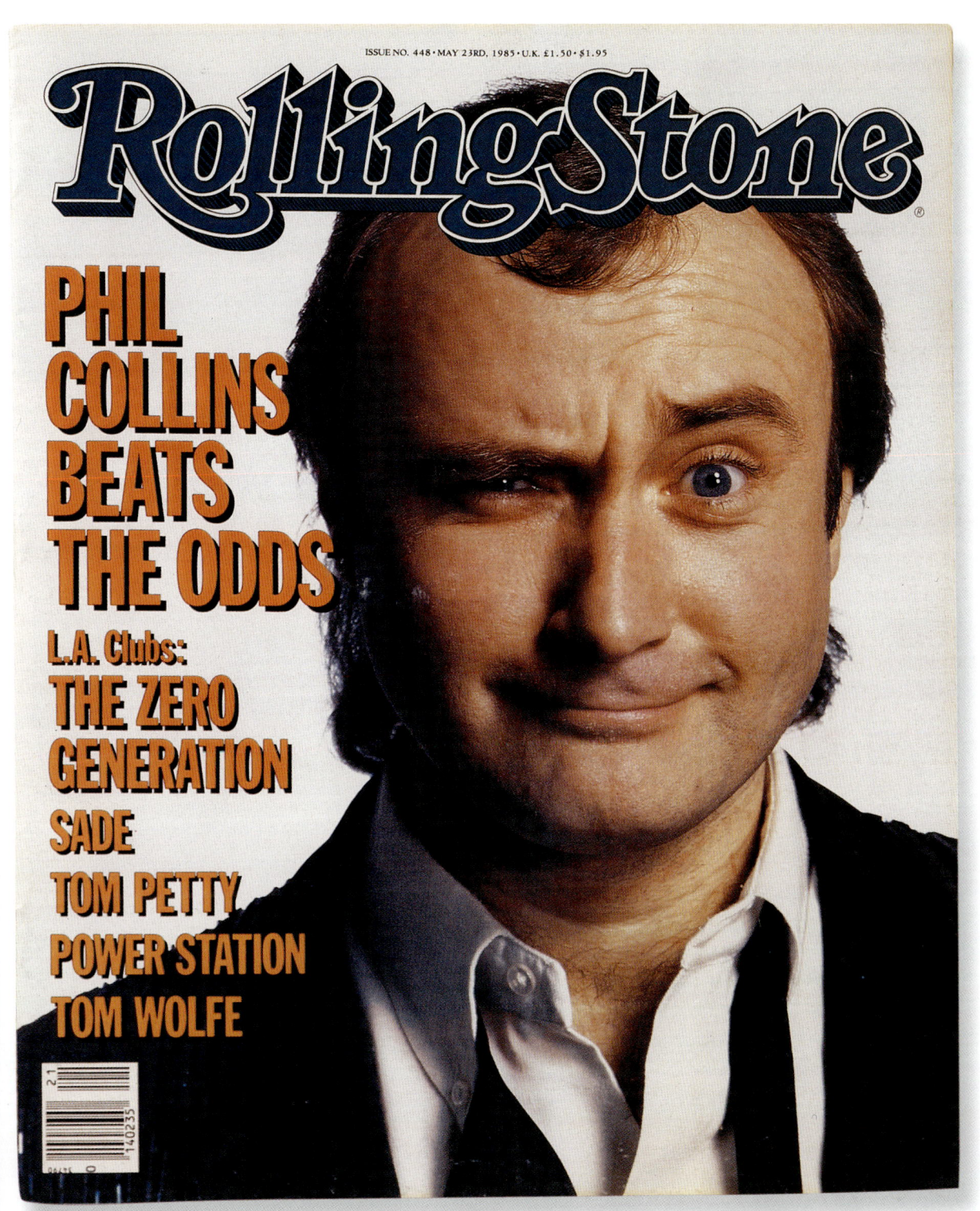

RS 448 | PHIL COLLINS | May 23rd, 1985 | Photograph by Aaron Rapoport

1980s

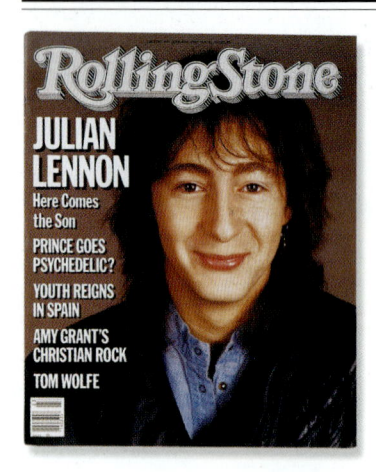

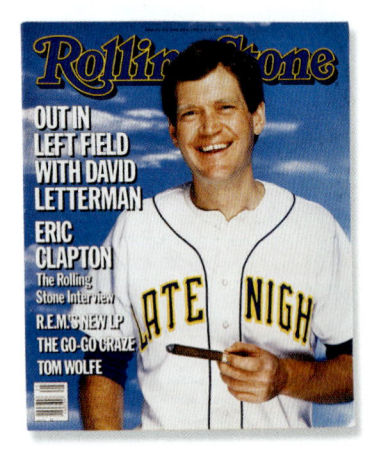

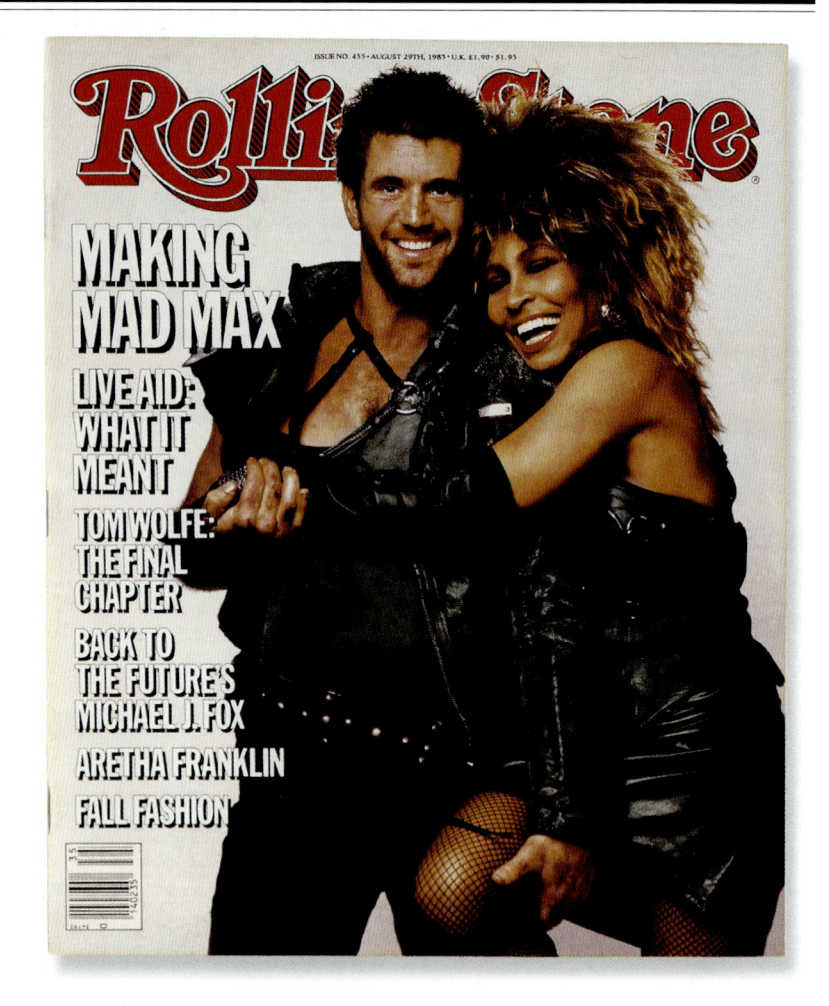

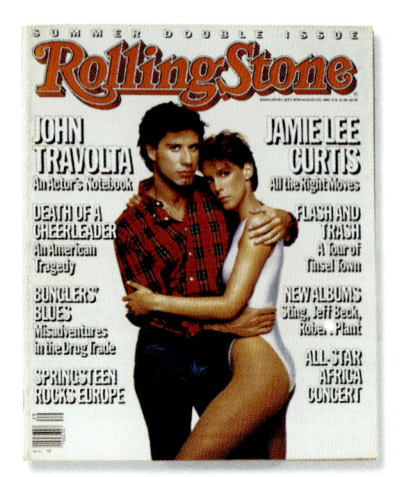

RS 449 | JULIAN LENNON
June 6th, 1985
PHOTOGRAPH BY RICHARD AVEDON

RS 450 | DAVID LETTERMAN
June 20th, 1985
PHOTOGRAPH BY DEBORAH FEINGOLD

RS 452/453 | JOHN TRAVOLTA
& JAMIE LEE CURTIS
July 18th – August 1st, 1985
PHOTOGRAPH BY PATRICK DEMARCHELIER

RS 455 | MEL GIBSON
& TINA TURNER
August 29th, 1985
PHOTOGRAPH BY HERB RITTS

ISSUE NO. 451 • JULY 4TH, 1985 • U.K. £1.50 • $1.95

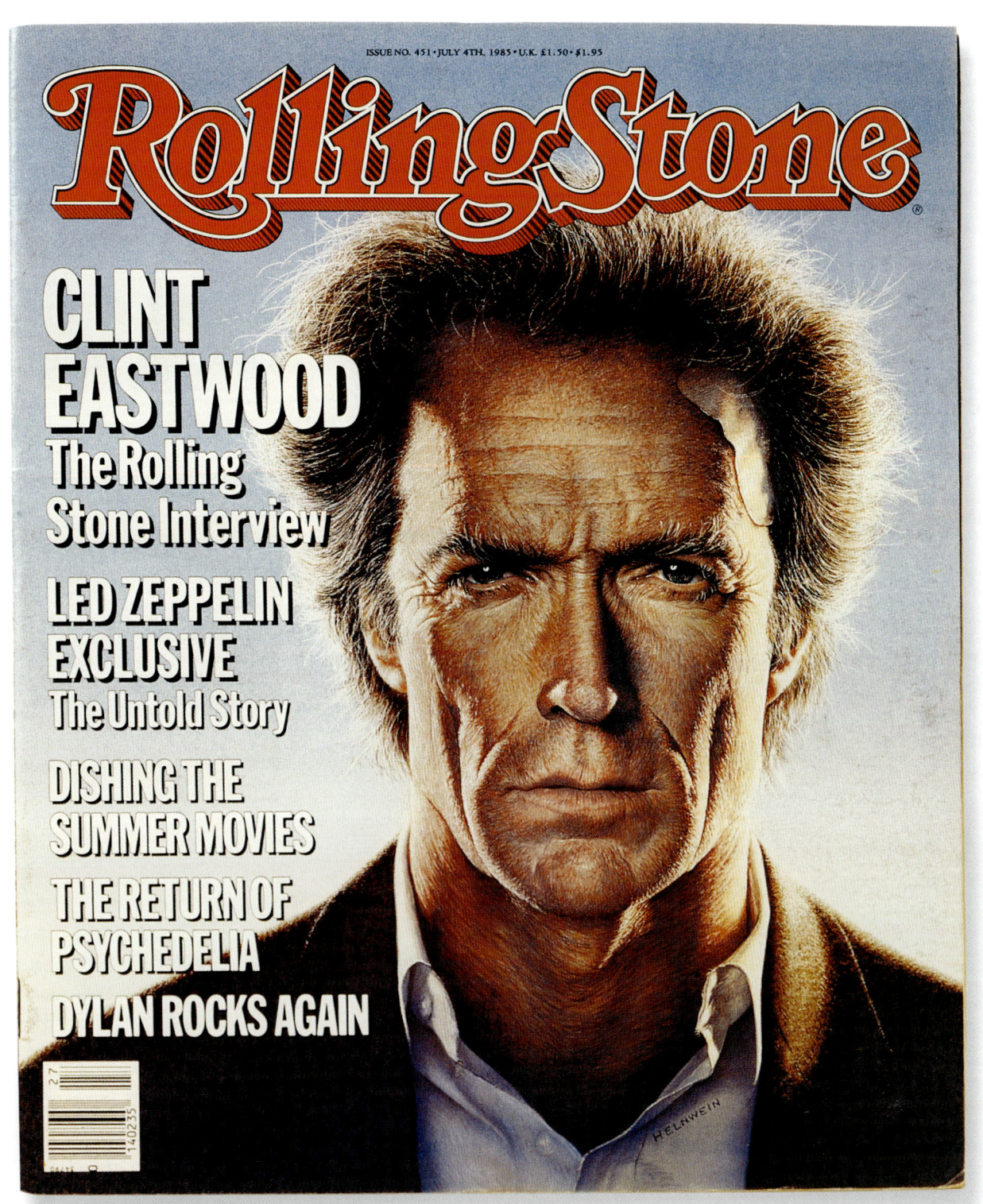

RollingStone

CLINT EASTWOOD
The Rolling Stone Interview

LED ZEPPELIN EXCLUSIVE
The Untold Story

DISHING THE SUMMER MOVIES

THE RETURN OF PSYCHEDELIA

DYLAN ROCKS AGAIN

RS 451 | CLINT EASTWOOD | July 4th, 1985 | Illustration by Gottfried Helnwein

1980s

RS 454 | LIVE AID PARTICIPANTS
August 15th, 1985
VARIOUS PHOTOGRAPHERS

RS 458 | BRUCE SPRINGSTEEN
October 10th, 1985
PHOTOGRAPH BY NEAL PRESTON

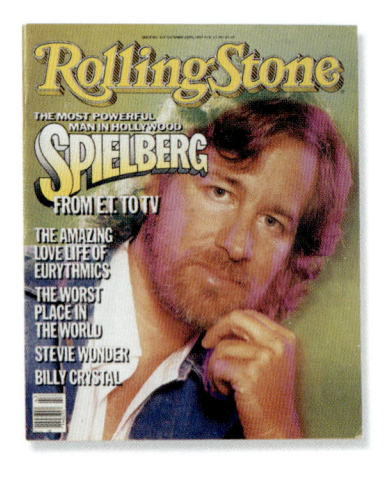

RS 456 | PRINCE
September 12th, 1985
"RASPBERRY BERET" VIDEO STILL

RS 459 | STEVEN SPIELBERG
October 24th, 1985
PHOTOGRAPH BY MOSHE BRAKHA

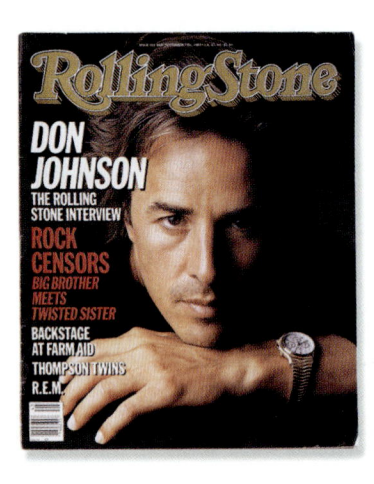

RS 457 | STING
September 26th, 1985
PHOTOGRAPH BY ERIC BOMAN

RS 460 | DON JOHNSON
November 7th, 1985
PHOTOGRAPH BY HERB RITTS

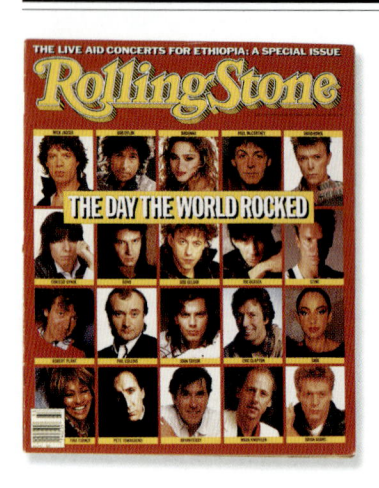

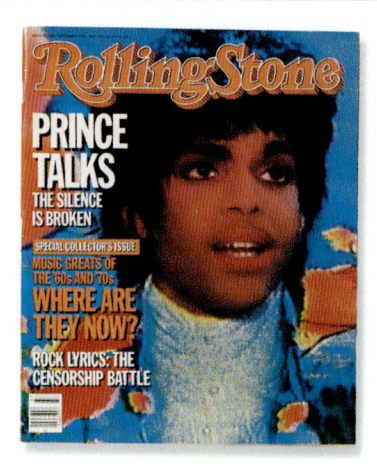

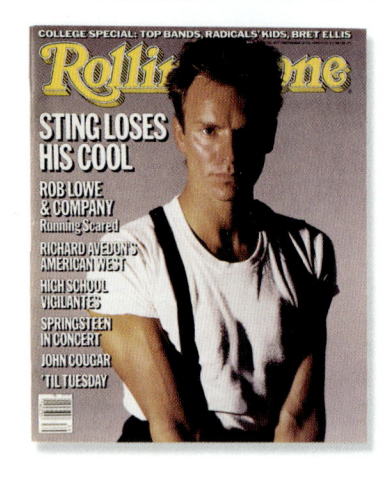

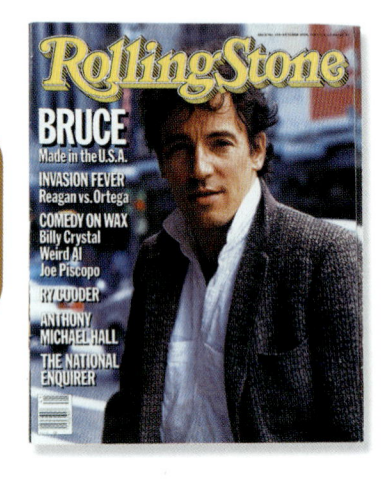

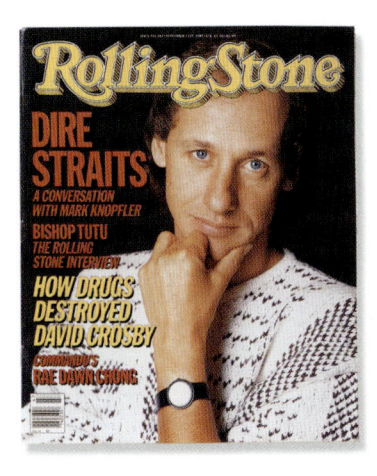

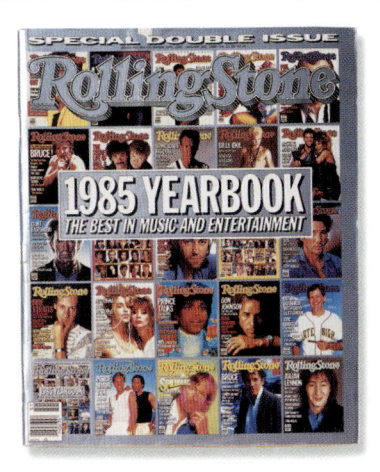

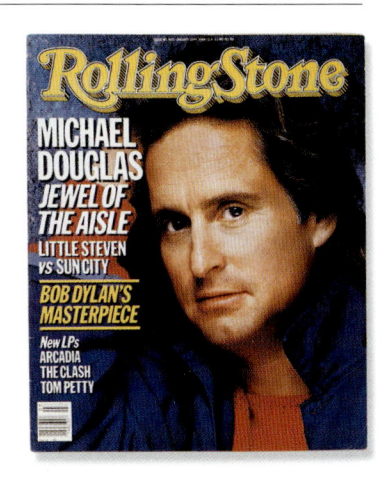

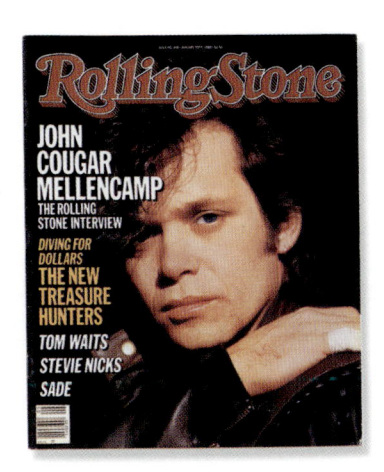

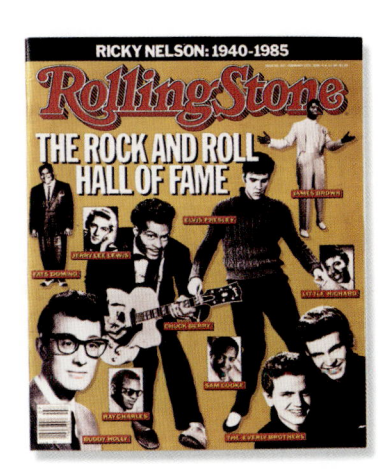

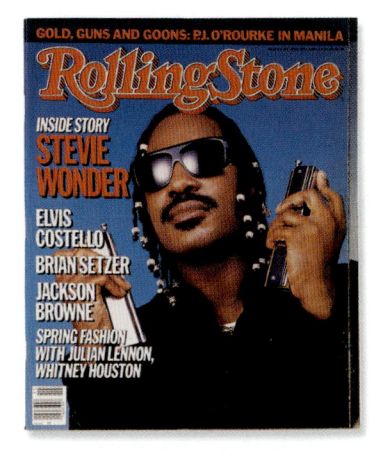

RS 461 | MARK KNOPFLER
November 21st, 1985
PHOTOGRAPH BY DEBORAH FEINGOLD

RS 463/464 | 1985 YEARBOOK
December 19th, 1985 – January 2nd, 1986
VARIOUS PHOTOGRAPHERS

RS 465 | MICHAEL DOUGLAS
January 16th, 1986
PHOTOGRAPH BY E.J. CAMP

RS 466 | JOHN COUGAR MELLENCAMP
January 30th, 1986
PHOTOGRAPH BY HERB RITTS

RS 467 | ROCK AND ROLL HALL OF FAME INDUCTEES
February 13th, 1986
VARIOUS PHOTOGRAPHERS

RS 471 | STEVIE WONDER
April 10th, 1986
PHOTOGRAPH BY MARK HANAUER

50 YEARS OF COVERS • 241

1980s

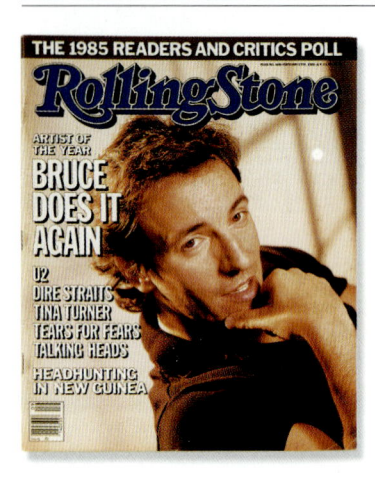

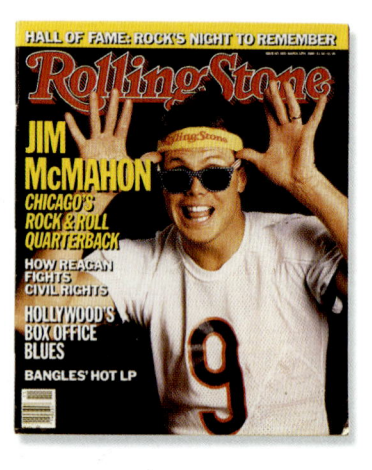

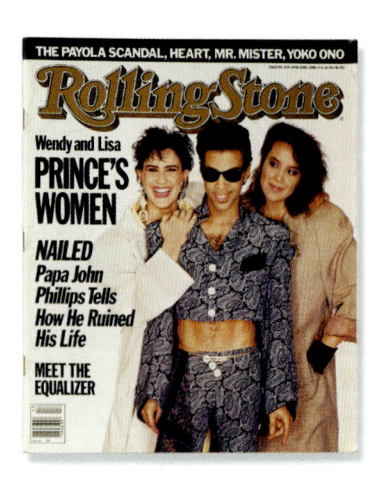

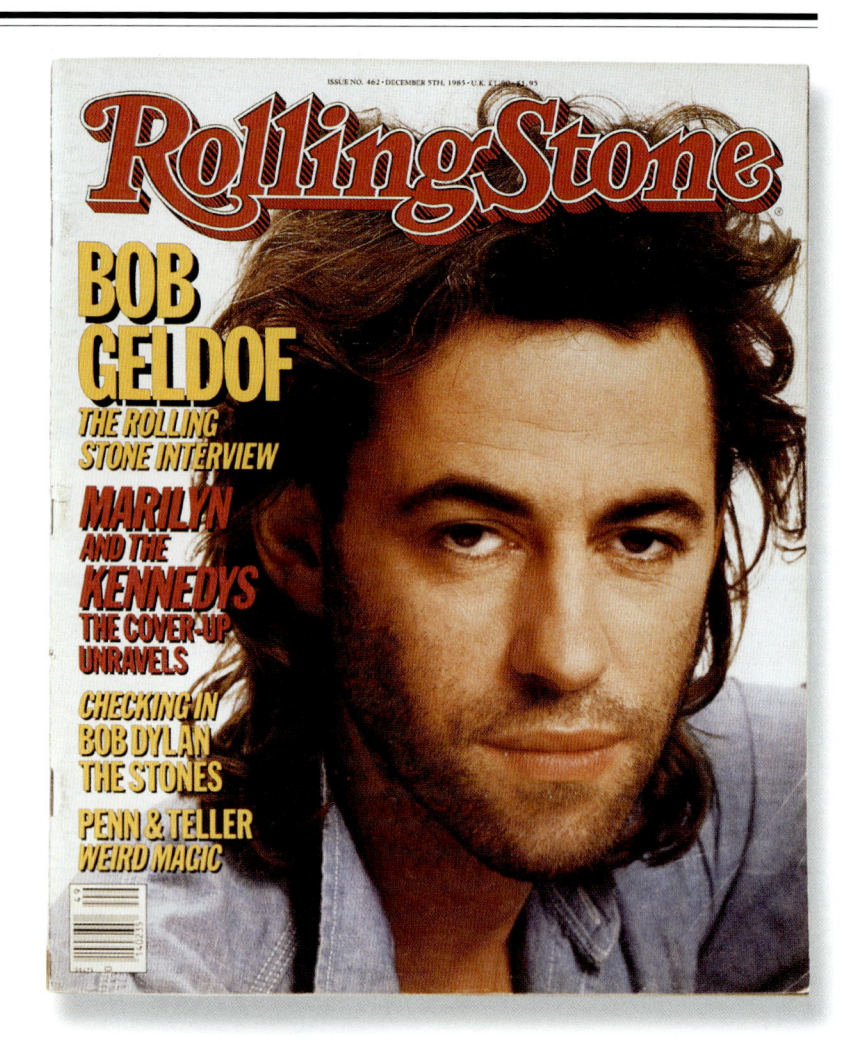

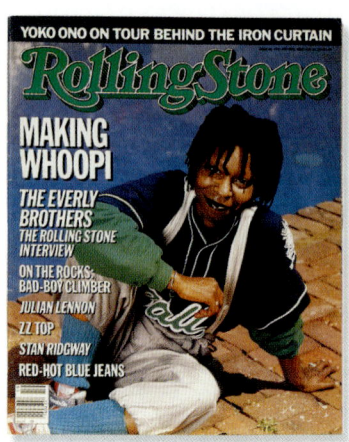

RS 462 | BOB GELDOF
December 5th, 1985
PHOTOGRAPH BY DAVIES & STARR

RS 468 | BRUCE SPRINGSTEEN
February 27th, 1986
PHOTOGRAPH BY AARON RAPOPORT

RS 469 | JIM McMAHON
March 13th, 1986
PHOTOGRAPH BY KEN REGAN

RS 472 | PRINCE WITH WENDY & LISA
April 24th, 1986
PHOTOGRAPH BY JEFF KATZ

RS 473 | WHOOPI GOLDBERG
May 8th, 1986
PHOTOGRAPH BY BONNIE SCHIFFMAN

242 • ROLLING STONE

THE BANGLES, AL GREEN, ELVIS COSTELLO, JOE JACKSON

ISSUE NO. 470 • MARCH 27TH, 1986 • U.K. £1.90 • $1.95

RollingStone

EXCLUSIVE

MEET BRUCE WILLIS

BAD COPS

ON CAMPUS
IS BIZ SCHOOL WORTH IT?
RATING THE COLLEGE PRESS
RIGHT vs LEFT AT DARTMOUTH

RS 470 | BRUCE WILLIS | March 27th, 1986 | Photograph by Bonnie Schiffman

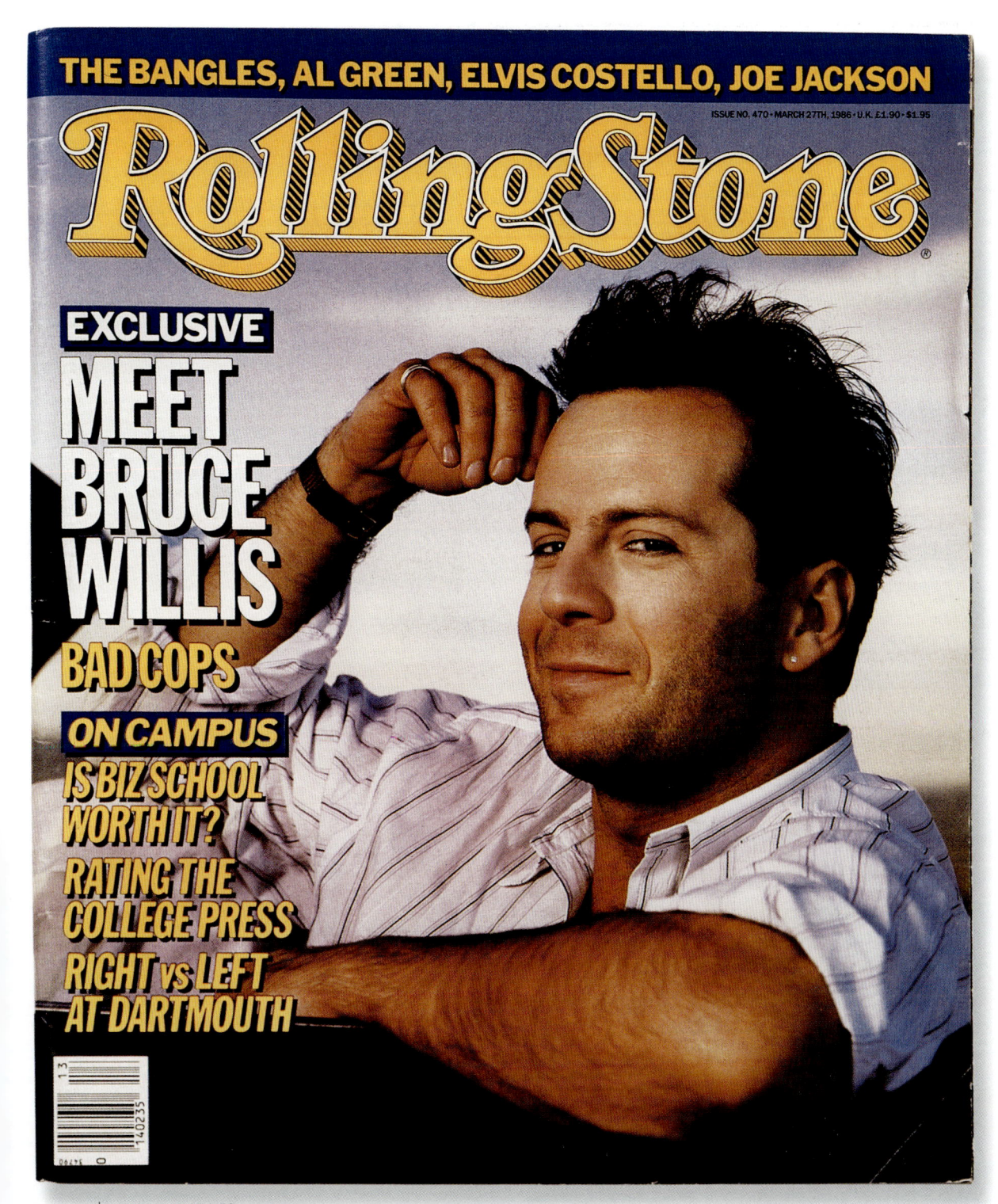

1980s

Rolling Stone

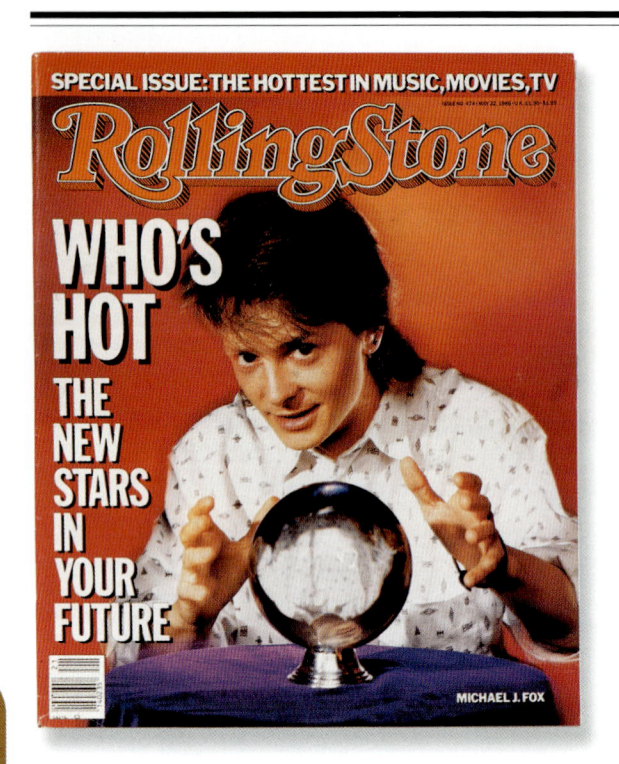

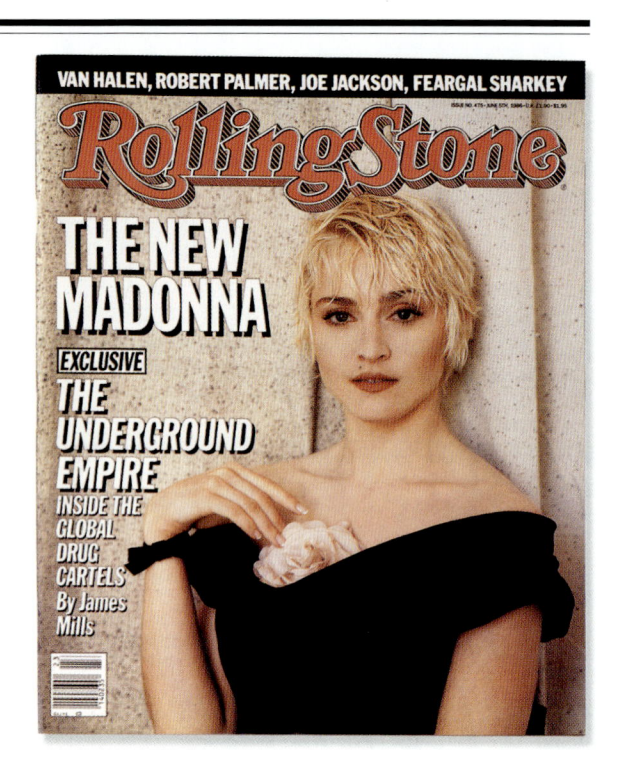

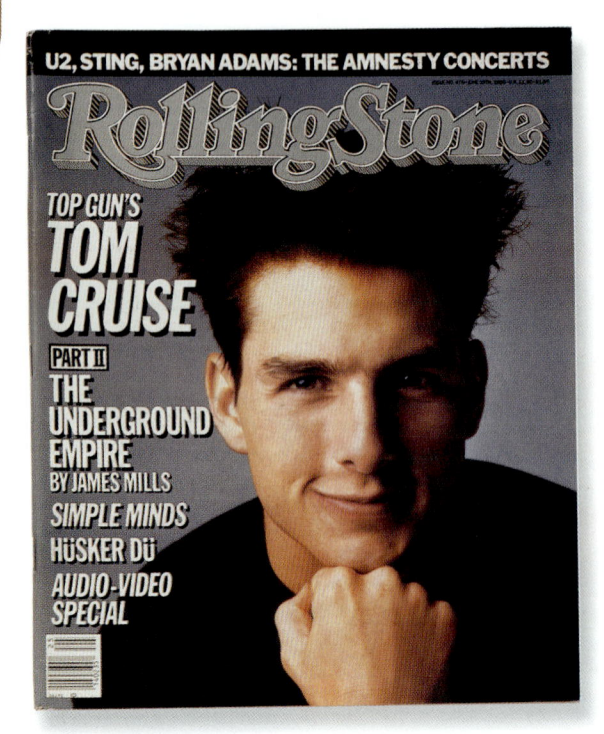

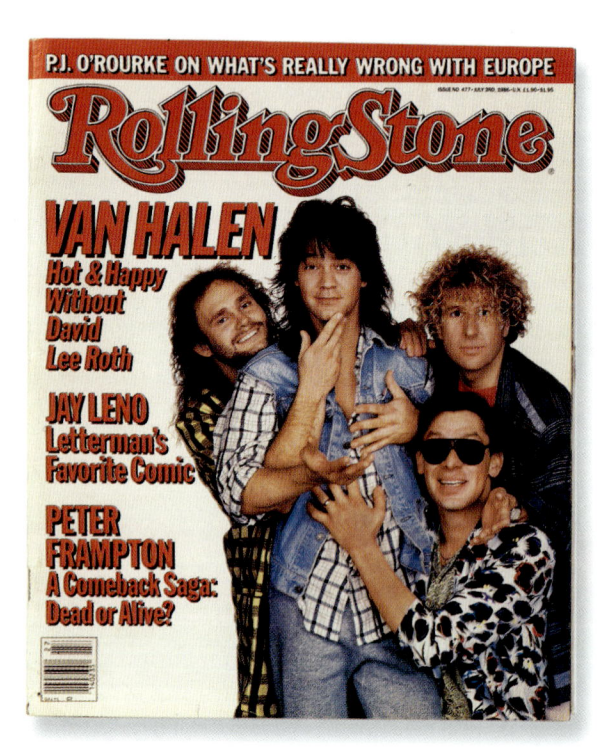

SPECIAL ISSUE: THE HOTTEST IN MUSIC, MOVIES, TV

WHO'S HOT
THE NEW STARS IN YOUR FUTURE

MICHAEL J. FOX

Rolling Stone

VAN HALEN, ROBERT PALMER, JOE JACKSON, FEARGAL SHARKEY

THE NEW MADONNA

EXCLUSIVE
THE UNDERGROUND EMPIRE
INSIDE THE GLOBAL DRUG CARTELS
By James Mills

Rolling Stone

U2, STING, BRYAN ADAMS: THE AMNESTY CONCERTS

TOP GUN'S TOM CRUISE

PART II
THE UNDERGROUND EMPIRE
BY JAMES MILLS
SIMPLE MINDS
HÜSKER DÜ
AUDIO-VIDEO SPECIAL

Rolling Stone

P.J. O'ROURKE ON WHAT'S REALLY WRONG WITH EUROPE

VAN HALEN
Hot & Happy Without David Lee Roth

JAY LENO
Letterman's Favorite Comic

PETER FRAMPTON
A Comeback Saga: Dead or Alive?

244 • ROLLING STONE

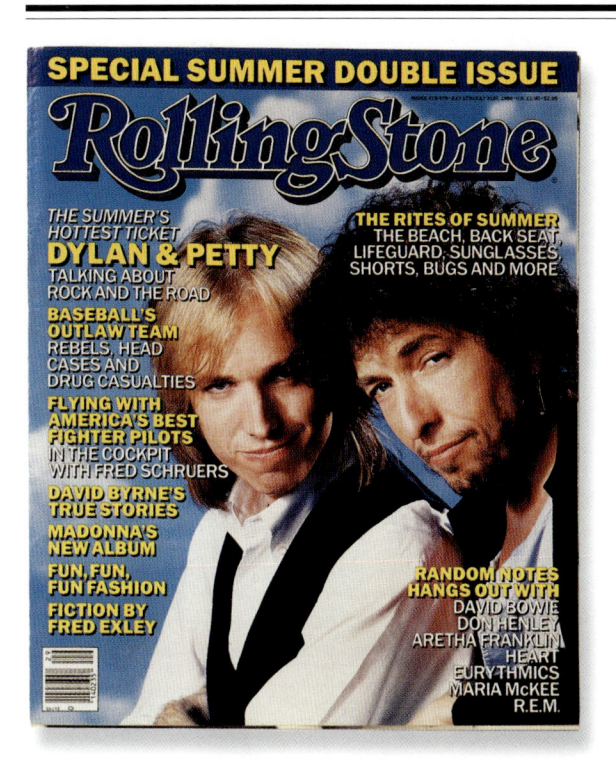

RS 474 | MICHAEL J. FOX
May 22nd, 1986
PHOTOGRAPH BY CHRIS CALLIS

RS 475 | MADONNA
June 5th, 1986
PHOTOGRAPH BY MATTHEW ROLSTON

RS 476 | TOM CRUISE
June 19th, 1986
PHOTOGRAPH BY HERB RITTS

RS 477 | VAN HALEN
July 3rd, 1986
PHOTOGRAPH BY DEBORAH FEINGOLD

RS 478/479 | TOM PETTY & BOB DYLAN
July 17th – July 31st, 1986
PHOTOGRAPH BY AARON RAPOPORT

RS 480 | JACK NICHOLSON
August 14th, 1986
PHOTOGRAPH BY HERB RITTS

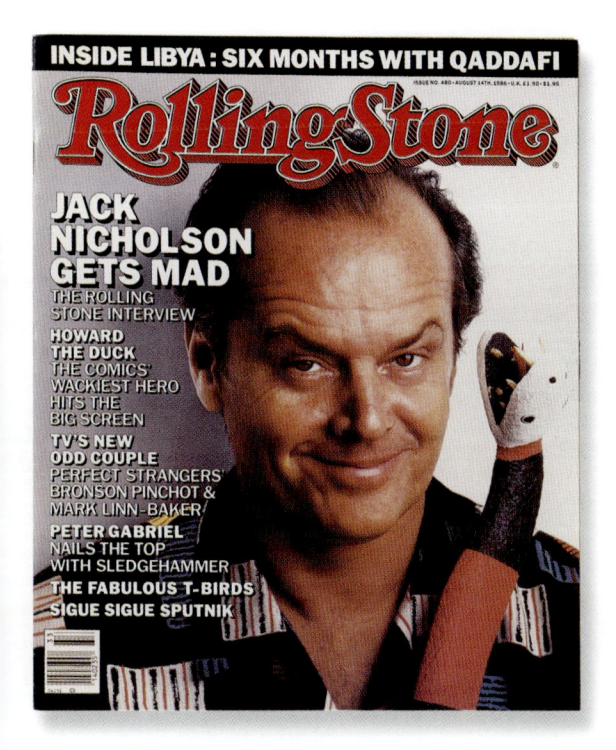

[**RS 478/479**] Though Bob Dylan has been one of ROLLING STONE's most frequent cover subjects (twenty-four times), he's also been one of the most elusive. On one occasion, he refused to allow RS's photographer to shoot him; instead, he enlisted a buddy, Morgan Renard, to photograph him in the backstage men's room at Madison Square Garden (RS 278). For this cover, Dylan only showed up at the last minute for the shoot with Tom Petty. The session started without him, and the next thing Petty knew, "Bob arrived, came straight across the room and just stepped into the frame with me. I don't think he really said anything to anyone. After they'd shot two pictures, Bob leaned over to me and said, 'I gotta go,' and then left. I remember trying to get it across to Aaron [Rapoport] that he was actually gone." ROLLING STONE wasn't happy with the two shots, so after a rehearsal one night, Petty recalls, "We went back and did the shot they actually used. That time we were both there."

50 YEARS OF COVERS • 245

BELINDA CARLISLE, R.E.M., VAN MORRISON, TOM WAITS

Rolling Stone

ISSUE NO. 481
AUGUST 28TH, 1986
U.K. £1.90 • $1.95

BOY GEORGE'S TRAGIC FALL

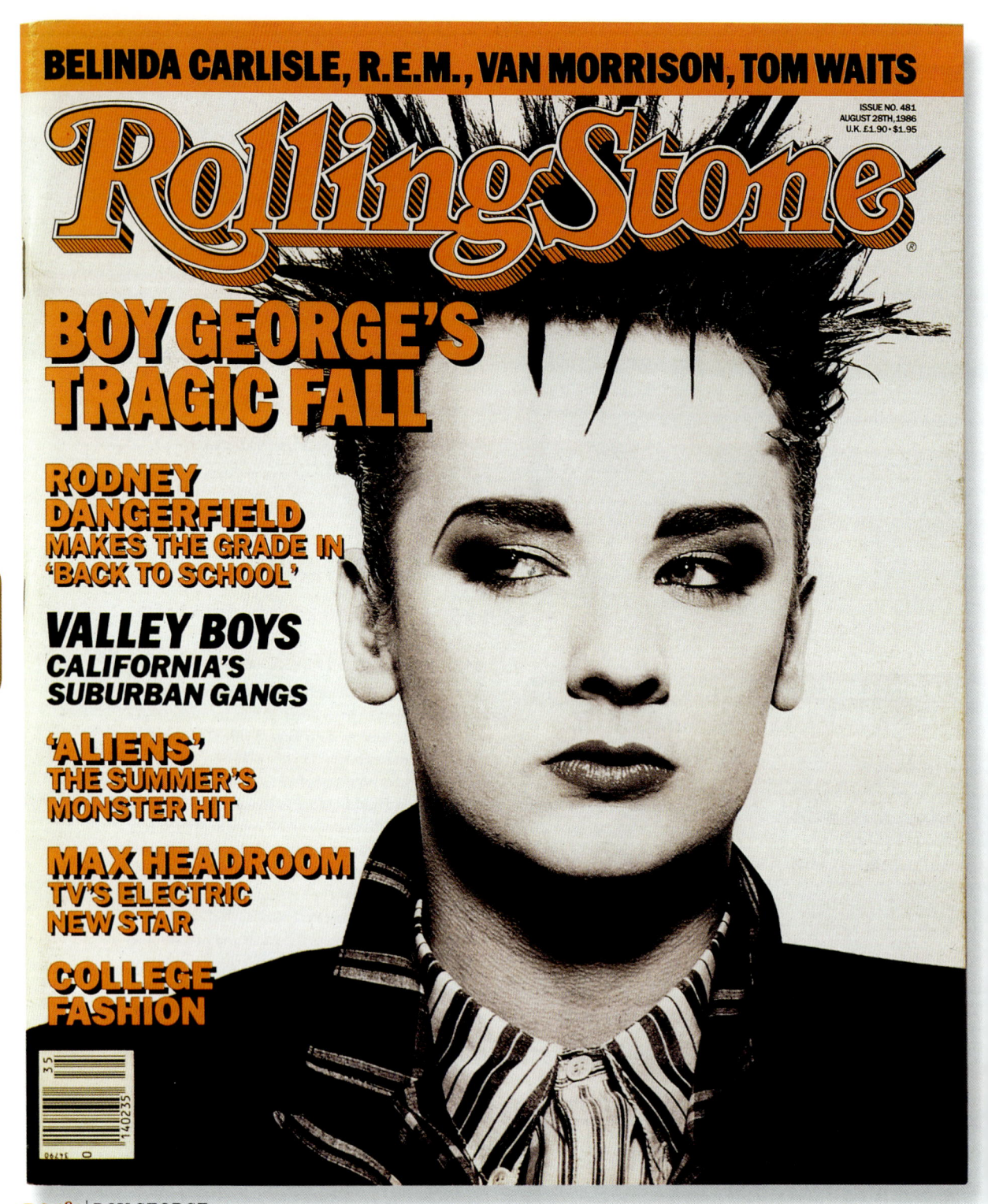

RODNEY DANGERFIELD MAKES THE GRADE IN 'BACK TO SCHOOL'

VALLEY BOYS CALIFORNIA'S SUBURBAN GANGS

'ALIENS' THE SUMMER'S MONSTER HIT

MAX HEADROOM TV'S ELECTRIC NEW STAR

COLLEGE FASHION

1980s

RS 481 | BOY GEORGE | August 28th, 1986 | PHOTOGRAPH BY Norman Watson

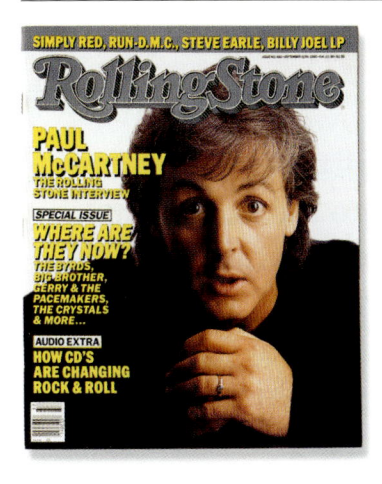

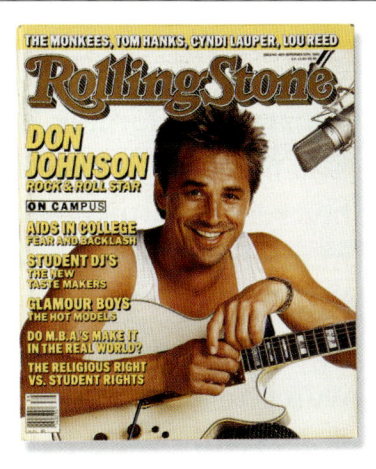

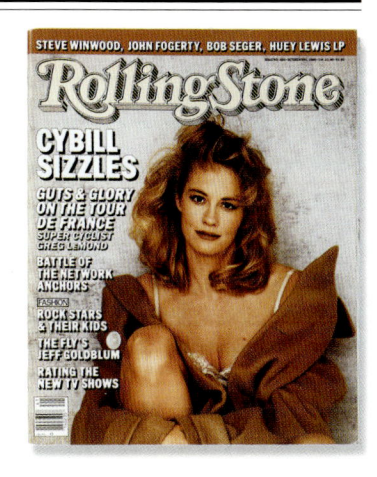

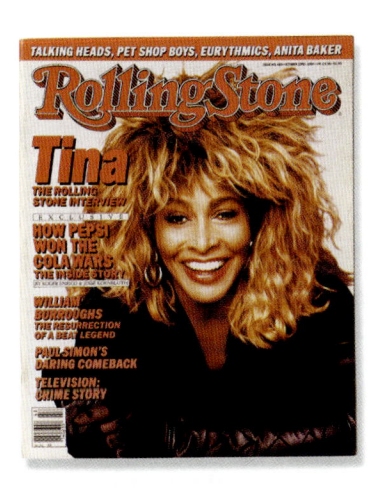

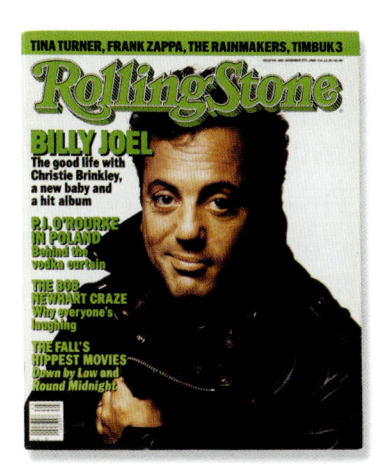

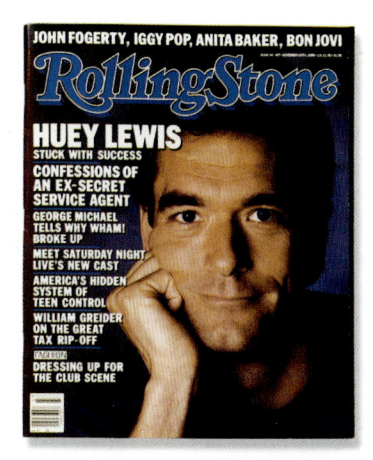

RS 482 | PAUL MCCARTNEY
September 11th, 1986
PHOTOGRAPH BY HARRY DEZITTER

RS 483 | DON JOHNSON
September 25th, 1986
PHOTOGRAPH BY E.J. CAMP

RS 484 | CYBILL SHEPHERD
October 9th, 1986
PHOTOGRAPH BY MATTHEW ROLSTON

RS 485 | TINA TURNER
October 23rd, 1986
PHOTOGRAPH BY MATTHEW ROLSTON

RS 486 | BILLY JOEL
November 6th, 1986
PHOTOGRAPH BY ALBERT WATSON

RS 487 | HUEY LEWIS
November 20th, 1986
PHOTOGRAPH BY TIM BOOLE

Run (Joe Simmons), D.M.C.

(Darryl McDaniels, also known as D) and Jam Master Jay (Jason Mizell) – the trio that has recently injected rap into the American mainstream with its double-platinum album *Raising Hell* – are blasting Michael Jackson and other glitzy pop stars. Run says, "Michael wants us to make a record with him, and we don't really want to make a record with Michael. We really dig Barry White."

"Michael's not really us," says Jay.

"He doesn't fit the program," says Darryl.

Run-D.M.C. is now at a crossroads. Having broken through to white radio with "Walk This Way," its collaboration with the hard-rock group Aerosmith, Run-D.M.C. must decide how to be pop and streetwise at the same time. Run-D.M.C. also faces another crisis. As its fame has increased, the trio has consistently been associated with violence. A riot between two youth gangs at the Long Beach Arena last August left forty-two people injured. It was the fifth time this past summer that a Run-D.M.C. concert led to mass arrests or serious injuries. While promoters have canceled Run-D.M.C. shows or added to the hysteria with talk of hiring extra security guards for concerts, more dispassionate observers have suggested that the group is getting a bum rap.

Yet the image has stuck. To much of white America, rap means mayhem and bloodletting.

[EXCERPT FROM RS 488 COVER STORY BY ED KIERSH]

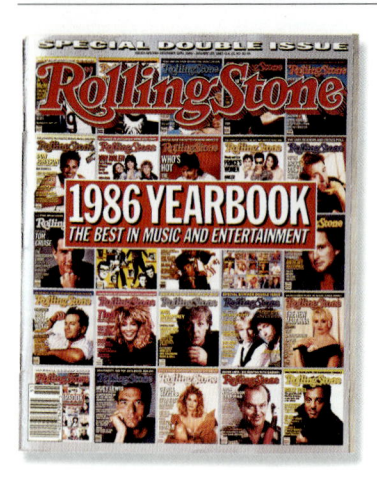

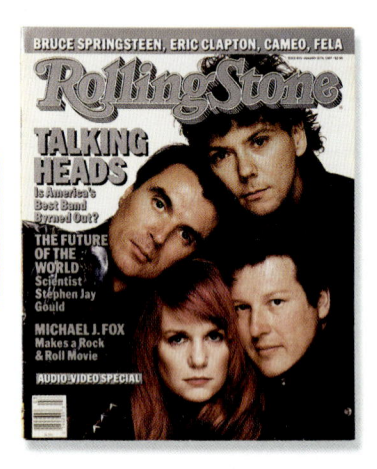

RS 489/490 | 1986 YEARBOOK
December 18th, 1986 – January 7th, 1987
VARIOUS PHOTOGRAPHERS

RS 491 | TALKING HEADS
January 15th, 1987
PHOTOGRAPH BY RICHARD CORMAN

CHUCK BERRY, BILLY IDOL, HOWARD JONES, UB40

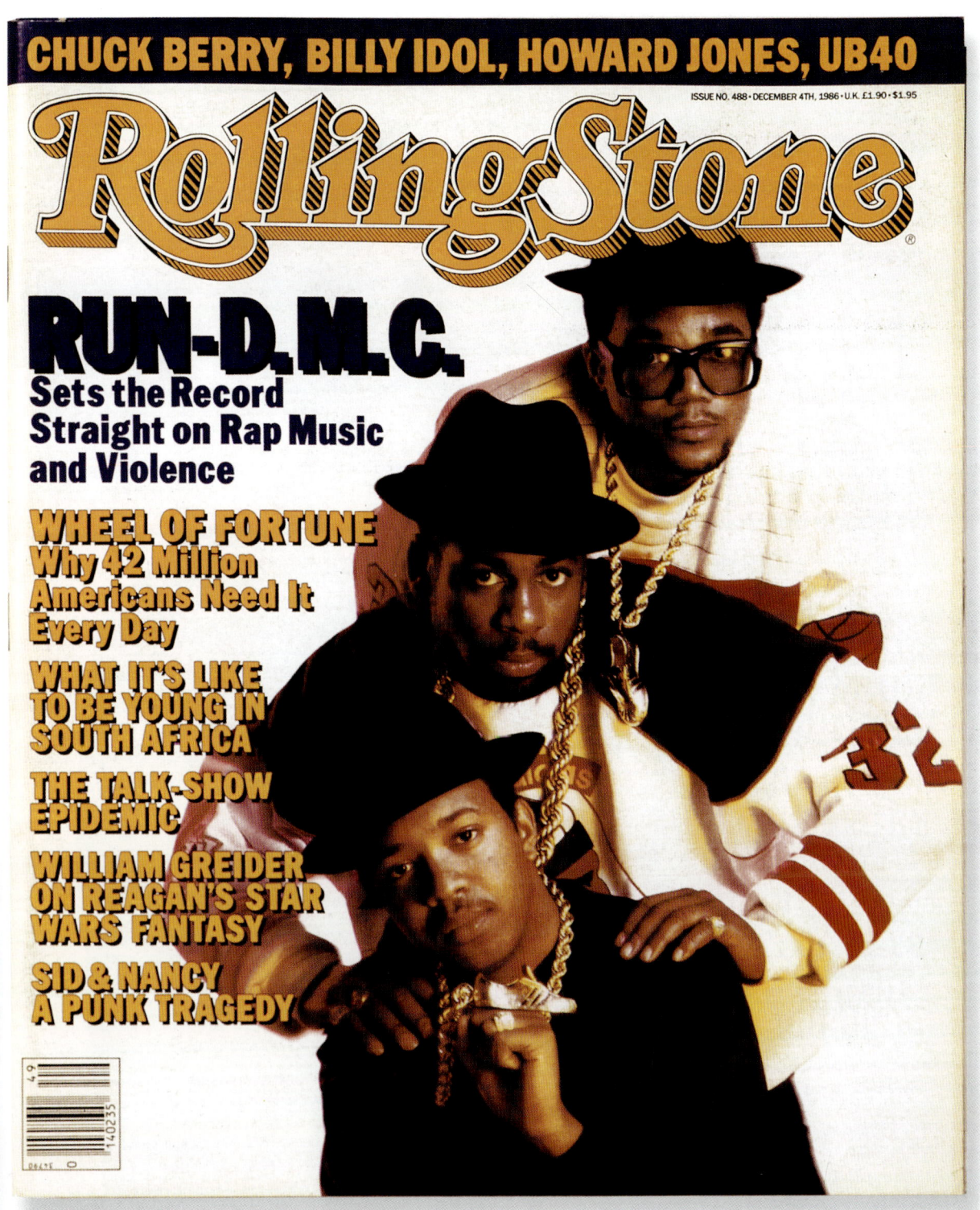

ISSUE NO. 488 · DECEMBER 4TH, 1986 · U.K. £1.90 · $1.95

RollingStone

RUN-D.M.C.
Sets the Record Straight on Rap Music and Violence

WHEEL OF FORTUNE
Why 42 Million Americans Need It Every Day

WHAT IT'S LIKE TO BE YOUNG IN SOUTH AFRICA

THE TALK-SHOW EPIDEMIC

WILLIAM GREIDER ON REAGAN'S STAR WARS FANTASY

SID & NANCY A PUNK TRAGEDY

RS 488 | RUN-D.M.C. | December 4th, 1986 | Photograph by Moshe Brakha

BRUCE HORNSBY, CYNDI LAUPER, BEASTIE BOYS

Rolling Stone

ISSUE 493 · FEBRUARY 12TH, 1987
U.K. £1.90 · $1.95

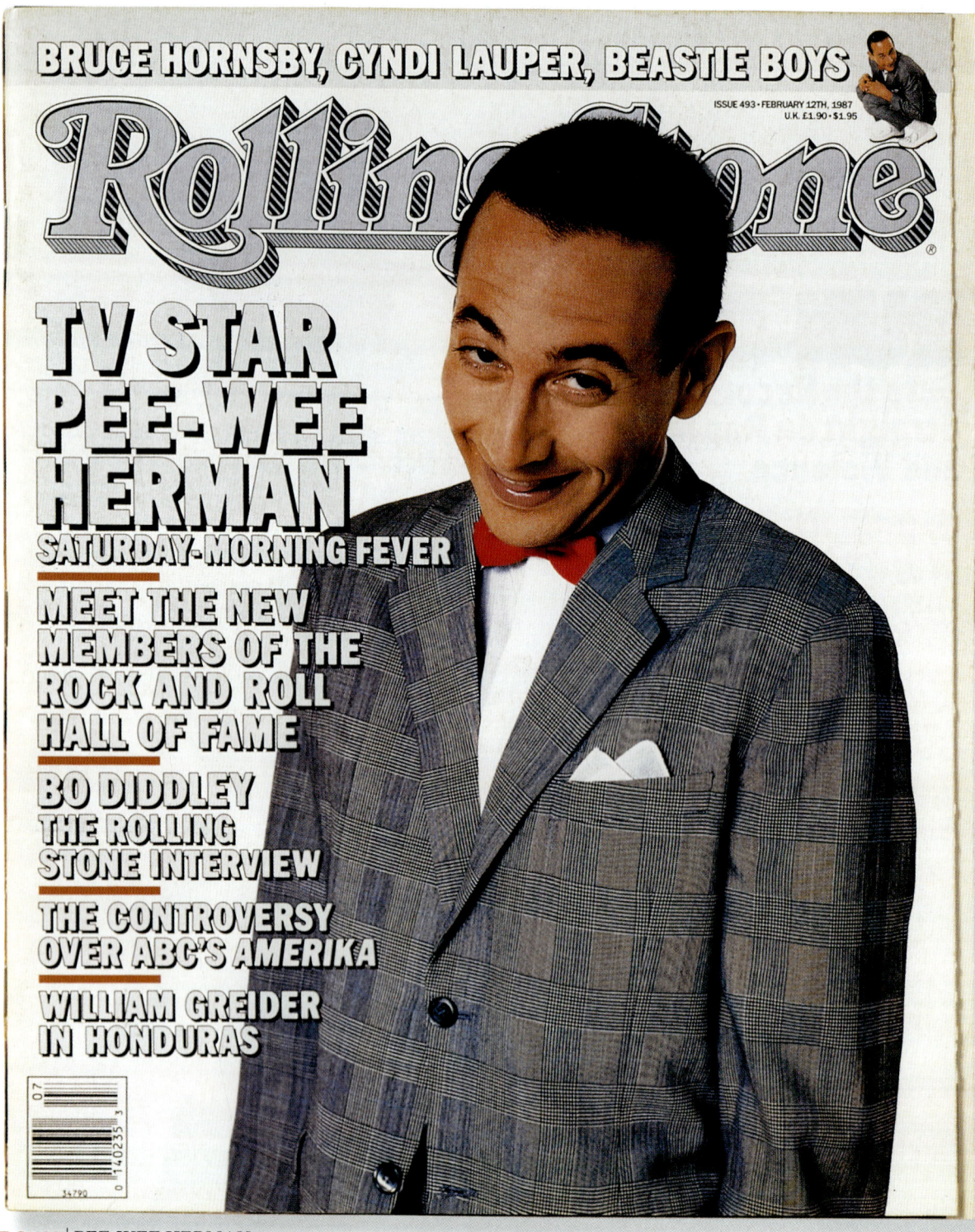

1980s

TV STAR PEE-WEE HERMAN
SATURDAY-MORNING FEVER

MEET THE NEW MEMBERS OF THE ROCK AND ROLL HALL OF FAME

BO DIDDLEY THE ROLLING STONE INTERVIEW

THE CONTROVERSY OVER ABC'S AMERIKA

WILLIAM GREIDER IN HONDURAS

RS 493 | PEE-WEE HERMAN | February 12th, 1987 | Photograph by Janette Beckman

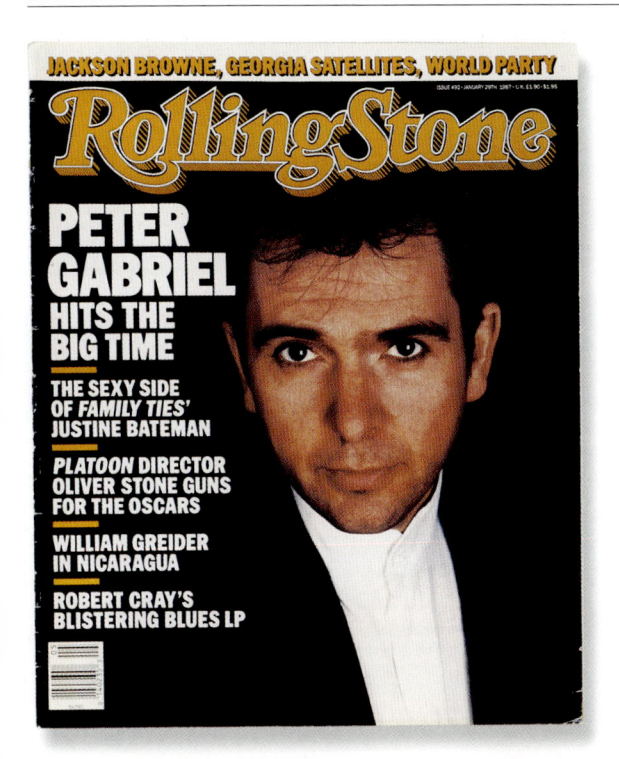

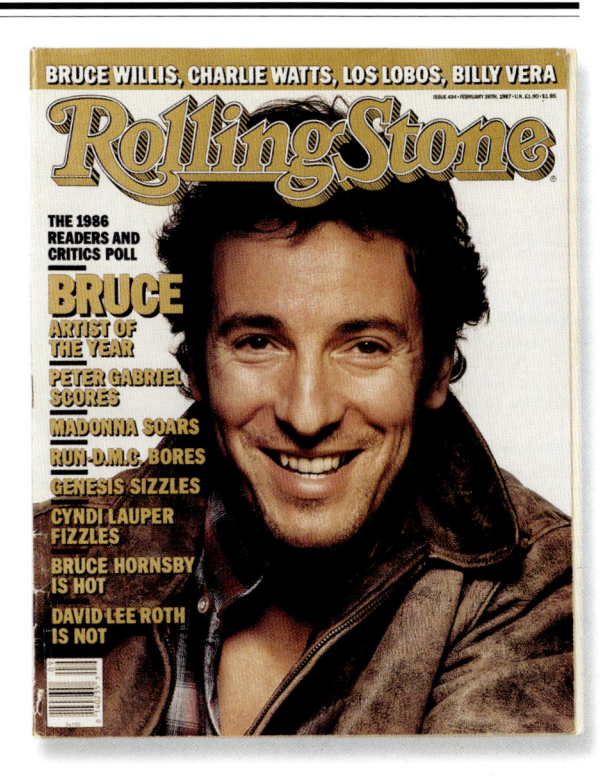

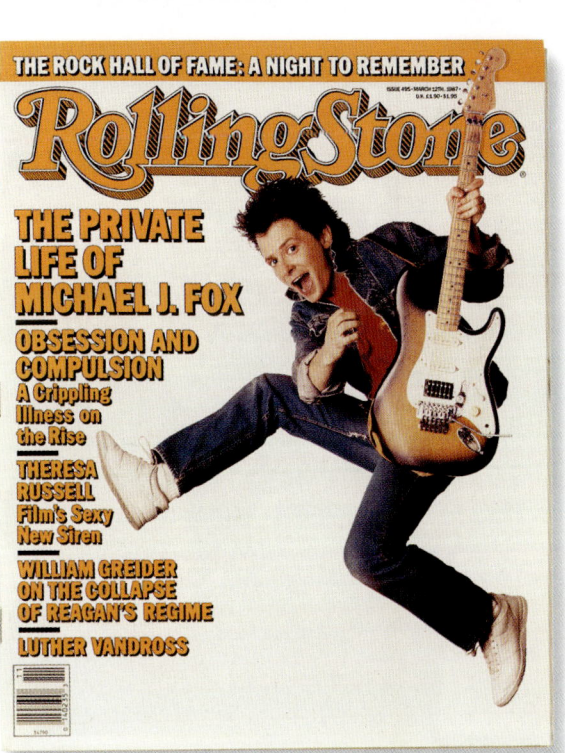

RS 492 | PETER GABRIEL
January 29th, 1987
PHOTOGRAPH BY ROBERT MAPPLETHORPE

RS 494 | BRUCE SPRINGSTEEN
February 26th, 1987
PHOTOGRAPH BY ALBERT WATSON

RS 495 | MICHAEL J. FOX
March 12th, 1987
PHOTOGRAPH BY DEBORAH FEINGOLD

50 YEARS OF COVERS • 251

1980s

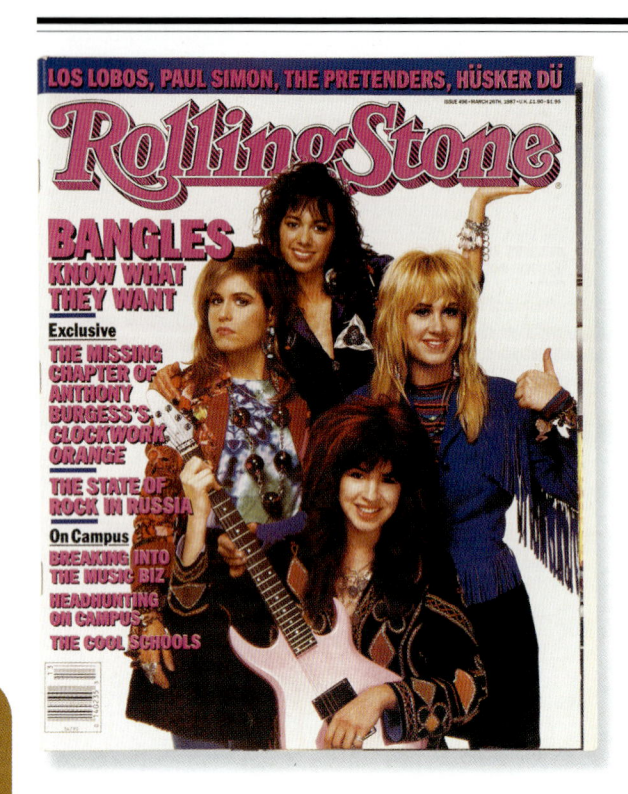

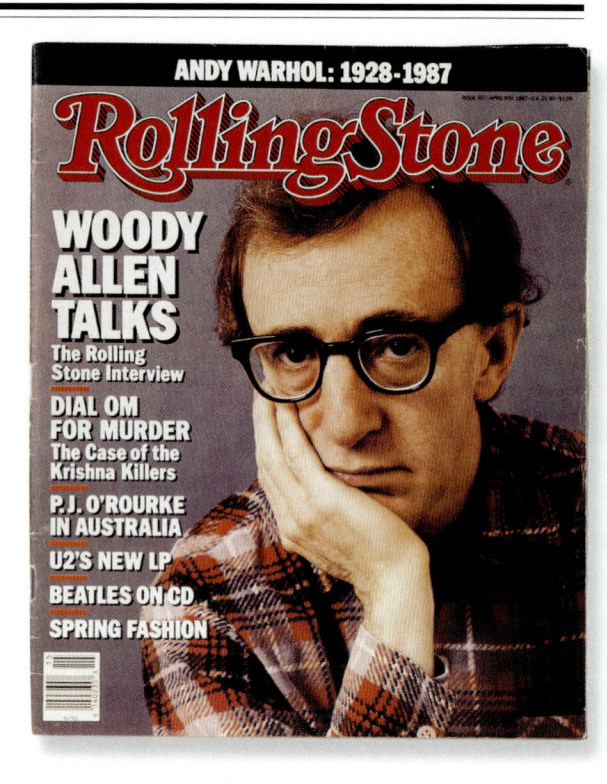

RS 496 | THE BANGLES
March 26th, 1987
PHOTOGRAPH BY BONNIE SCHIFFMAN

RS 497 | WOODY ALLEN
April 9th, 1987
PHOTOGRAPH BY BRIAN HAMILL

RS 499 | U2
May 7th, 1987
PHOTOGRAPH BY ANTON CORBIJN

[RS 498] For its twentieth anniversary, ROLLING STONE produced three special issues: this one on style, one on the best live performances ever (RS 501) and one on the best albums recorded since the magazine's inception (RS 507). Ranking among the greatest live performances were Cream at London's Royal Albert Hall on November 26th, 1968 and Bruce Springsteen at New York's Bottom Line from August 13th to 17th, 1975. The top three albums were the Beatles' *Sgt. Pepper's Lonely Hearts Club Band*, the Sex Pistols' *Never Mind the Bollocks, Here's the Sex Pistols* and the Rolling Stones' *Exile on Main Street.*

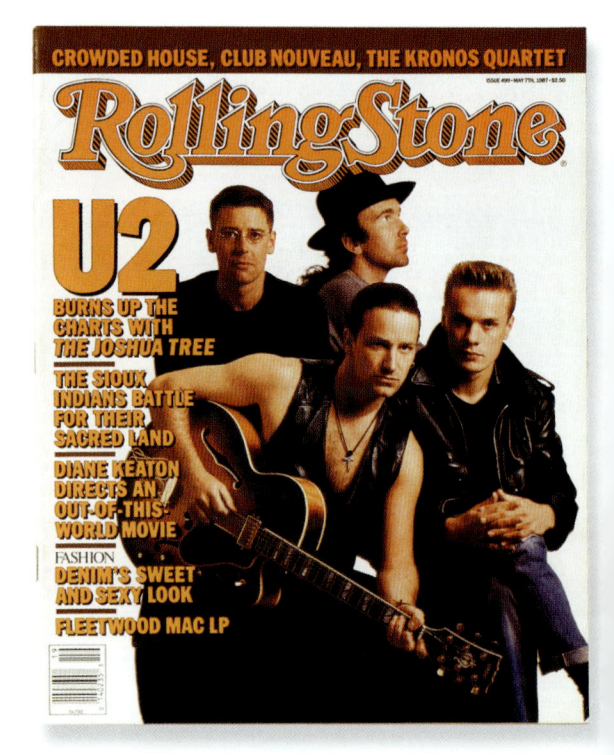

Rolling Stone

1967 1987 · A TWENTIETH-ANNIVERSARY SPECIAL ISSUE

ISSUE 498 · APRIL 23RD, 1987 · U.K. £1.90 · $1.95

STYLE

David Bowie

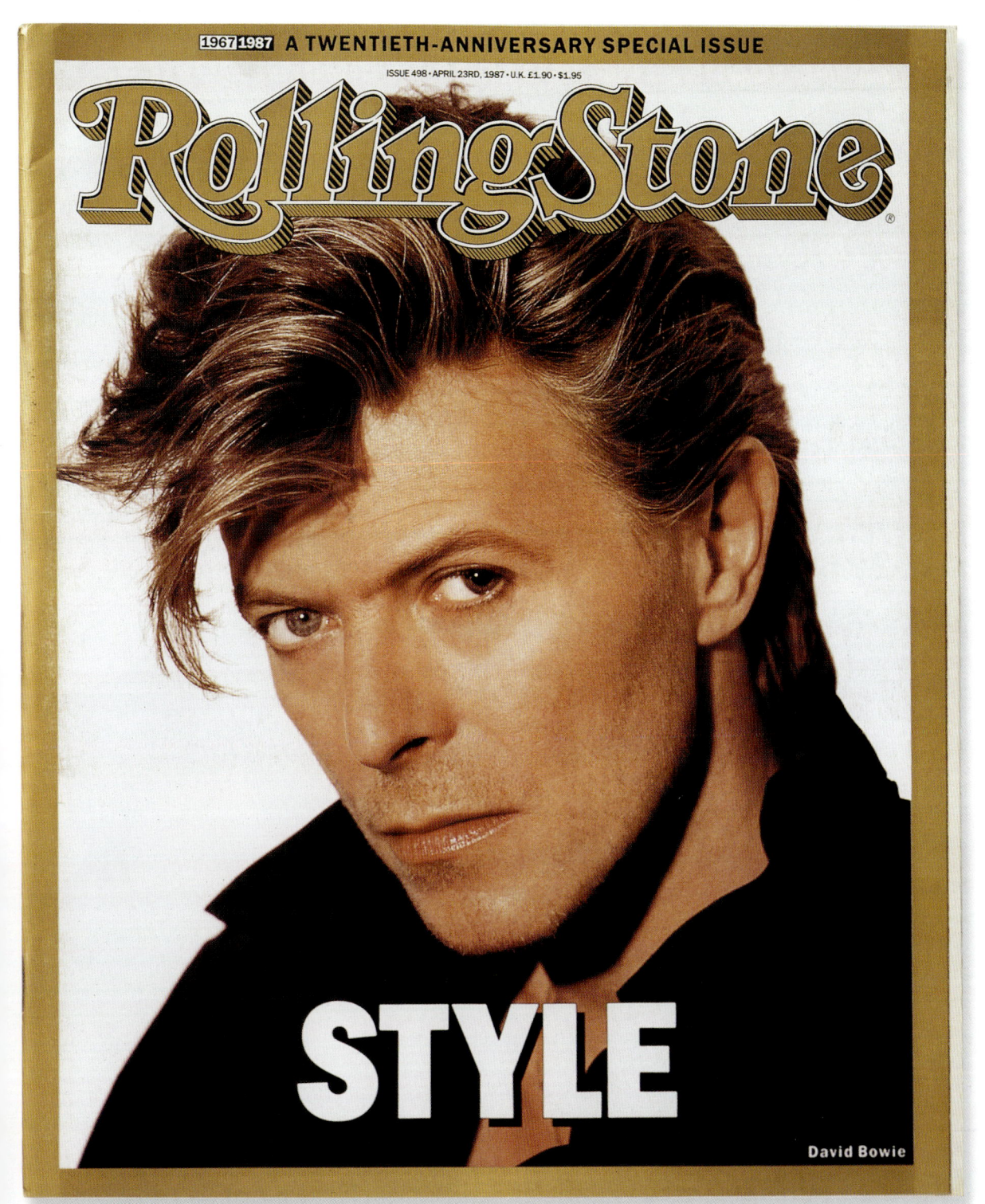

RS 498 | TWENTIETH ANNIVERSARY: STYLE – DAVID BOWIE | April 23rd, 1987 | Photograph by Herb Ritts

SPECIAL ISSUE: THE HOTTEST IN MUSIC, MOVIES, TV

ISSUE 500 • MAY 21ST, 1987 • $2.50

Rolling Stone

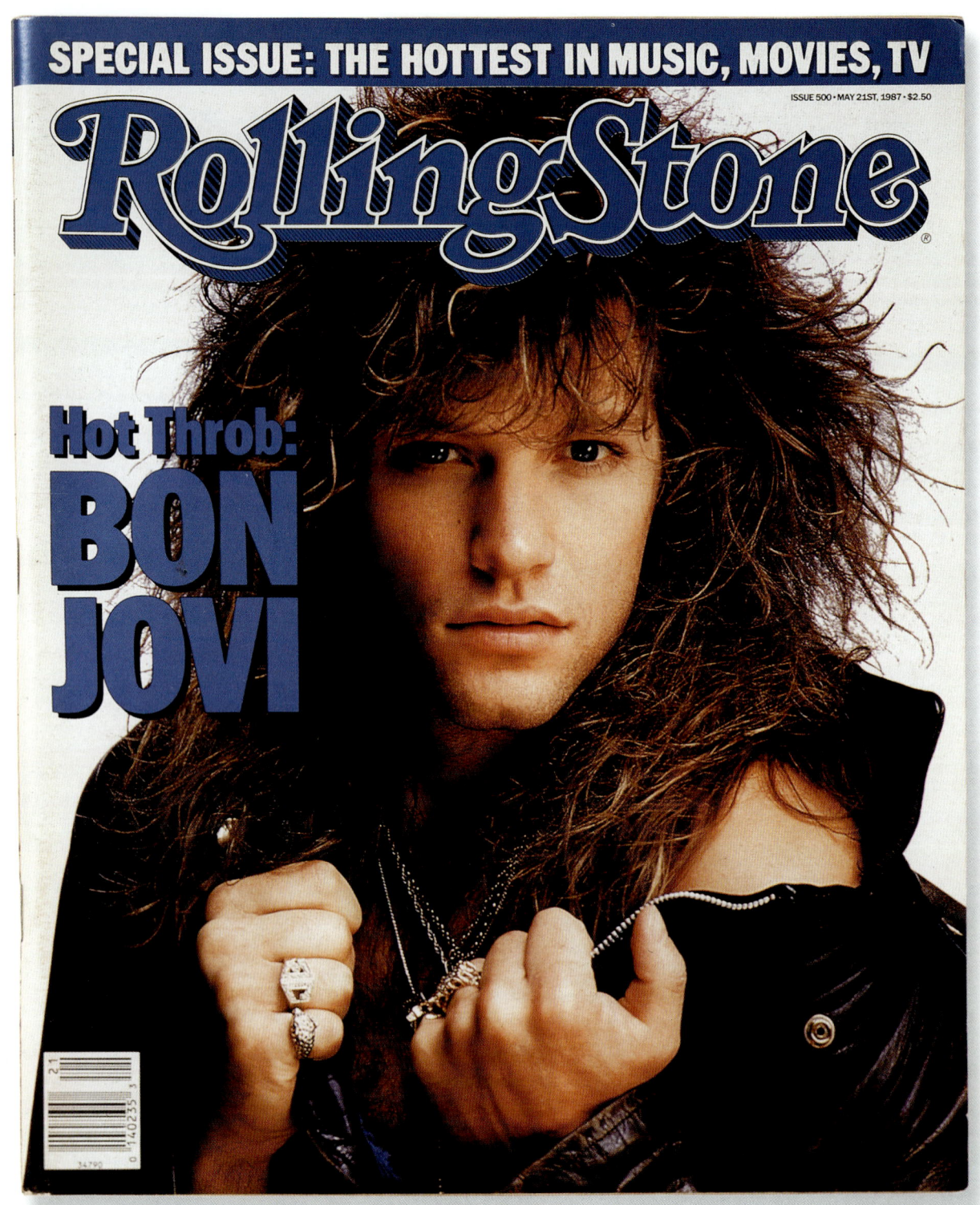

1980s

Hot Throb: BON JOVI

RS 500 | JON BON JOVI | May 21st, 1987 | Photograph by E.J. Camp

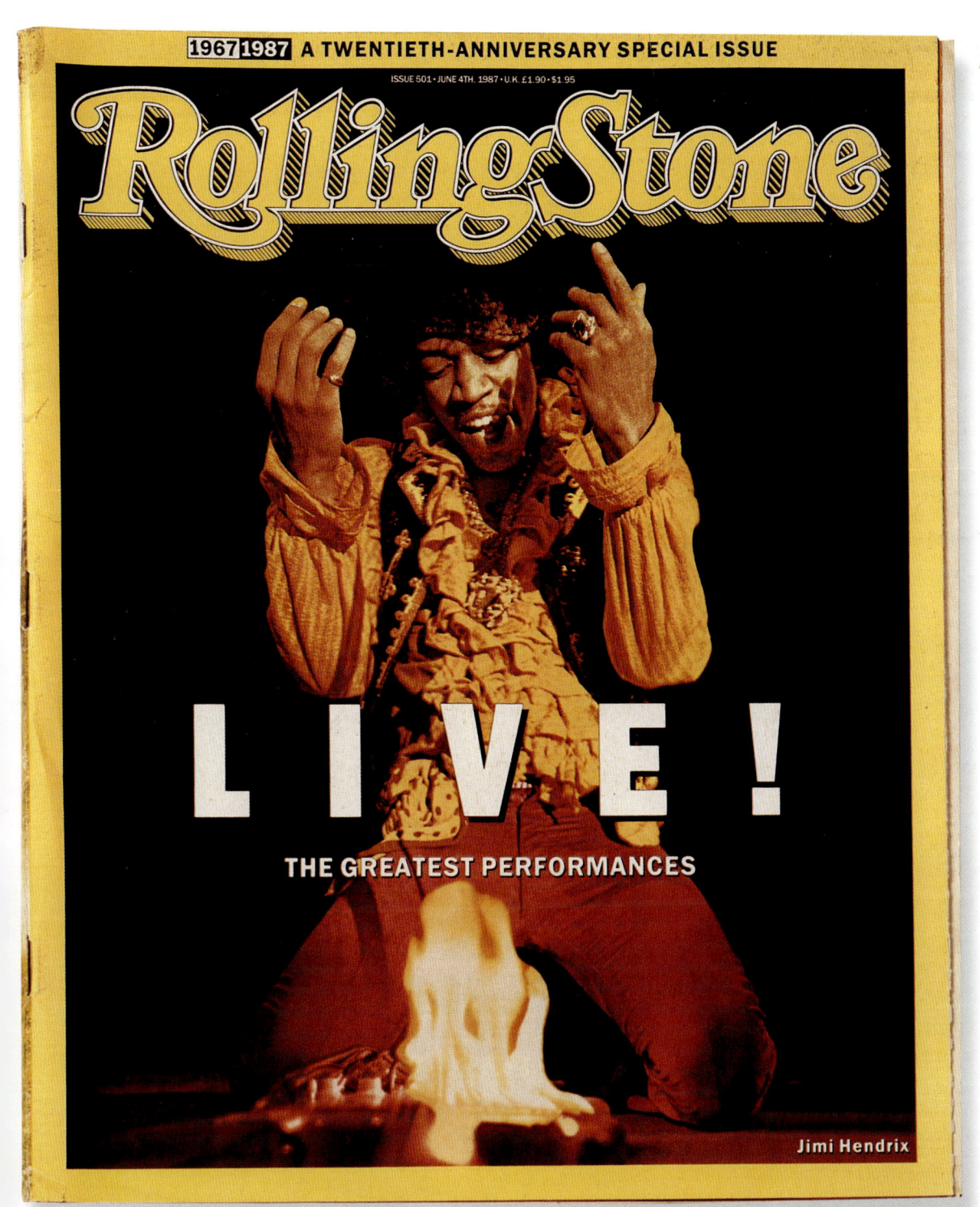

RS 501 | TWENTIETH ANNIVERSARY: THE GREATEST PERFORMANCES – JIMI HENDRIX
June 4th, 1987 | Photograph by Ed Caraeff

EDDIE MURPHY, PRINCE, THE JUDDS, THE NEVILLE BROTHERS

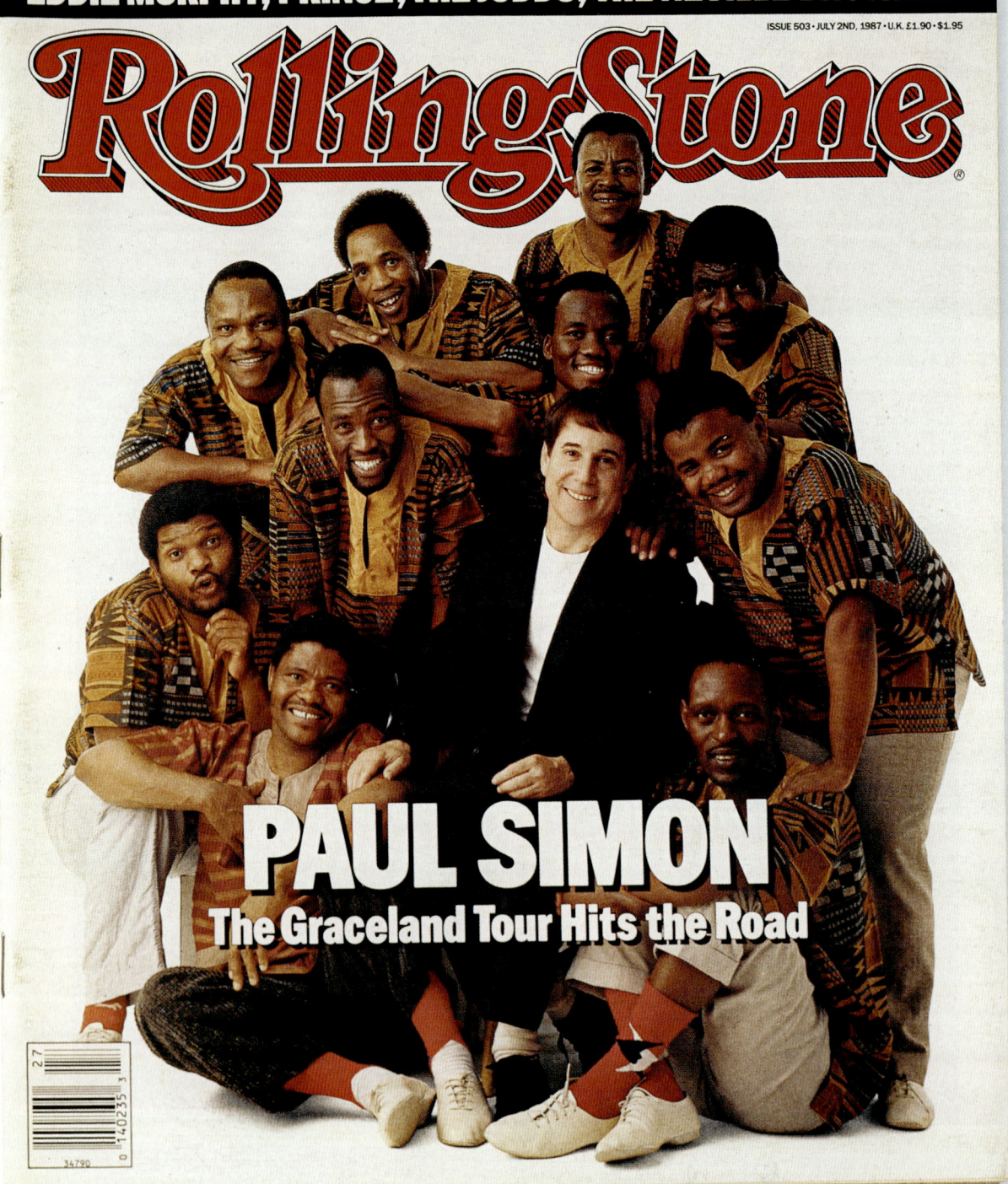

ISSUE 503 • JULY 2ND, 1987 • U.K. £1.90 • $1.95

Rolling Stone

PAUL SIMON
The Graceland Tour Hits the Road

RS 503 | PAUL SIMON & LADYSMITH BLACK MAMBAZO | July 2nd, 1987 | Photograph by Mark Seliger

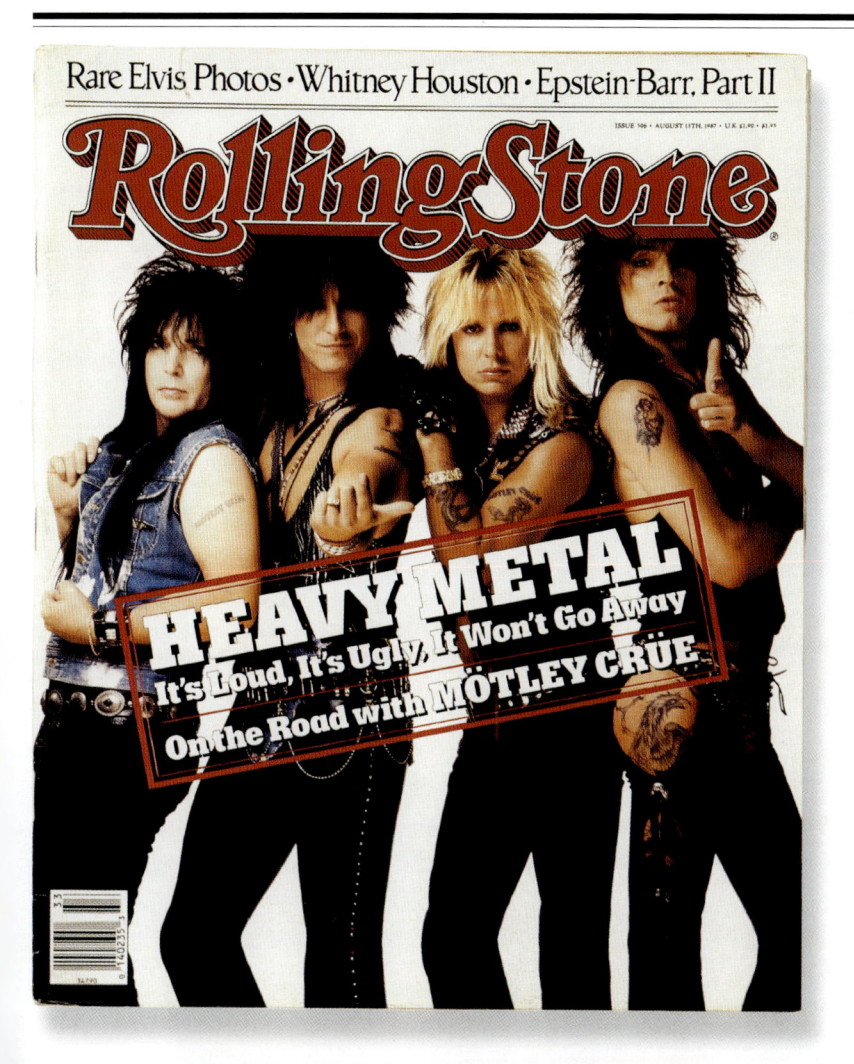

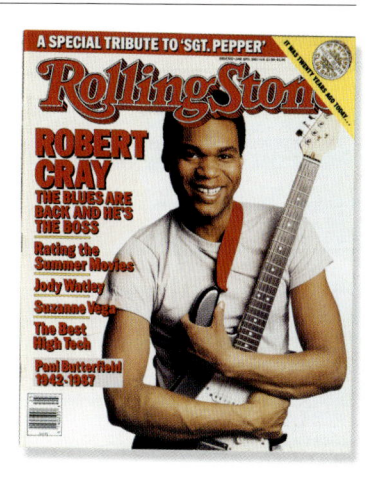

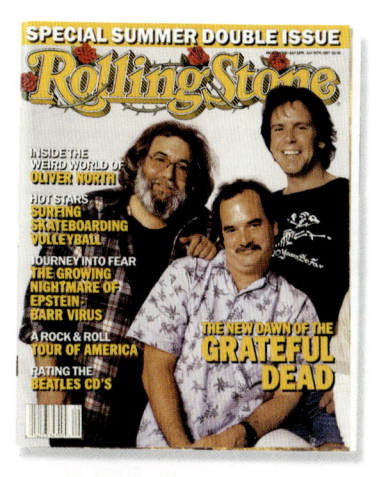

RS 506 | MÖTLEY CRÜE | August 13th, 1987 | Photograph by E.J. Camp

RS 502 | ROBERT CRAY
June 18th, 1987
Photograph by Deborah Feingold

RS 504/505 | THE GRATEFUL DEAD
July 16th – July 30th, 1987
Photograph by Michael O'Neill

"*I remember very well they* told me that they couldn't put five guys on the cover [RS 500]. That was exactly how they sold it to us: 'You can't put five guys on the cover.' And then we saw Paul Simon and twelve guys on the cover [RS 503]. And we went, 'uh-huh!'"
—*Jon Bon Jovi*

50 YEARS OF COVERS • 257

1980s

1967-1987 A TWENTIETH·ANNIVERSARY SPECIAL ISSUE

Rolling Stone

ISSUE 507 · AUGUST 27TH, 1987 · U.K. £1.90 · $1.95

THE 100 BEST ALBUMS OF THE LAST TWENTY YEARS

RS 507 | THE 100 BEST ALBUMS OF THE LAST TWENTY YEARS | August 27th, 1987 | Photograph by Constance Hansen

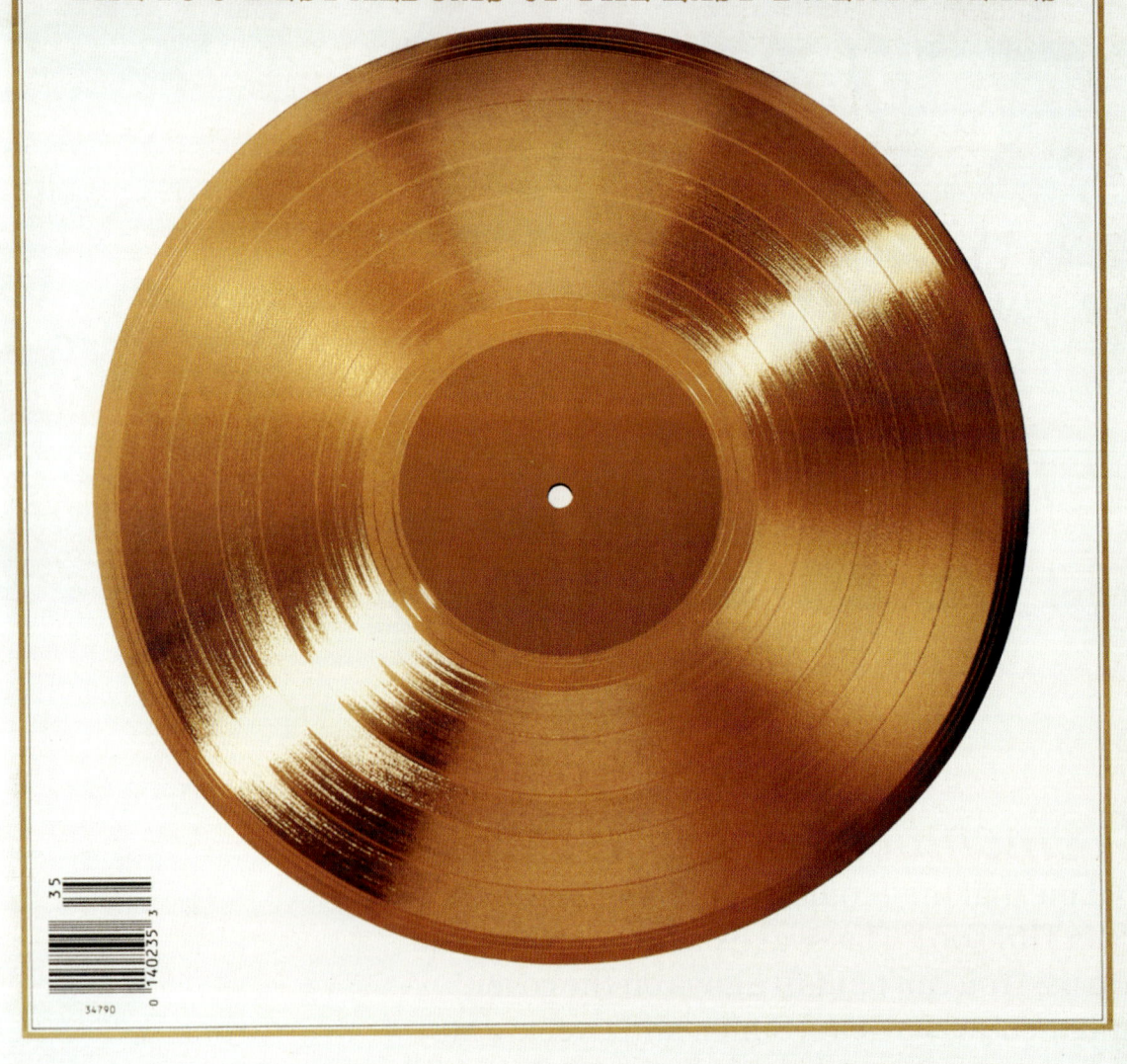

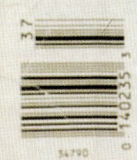

RS 508 | MADONNA | September 10th, 1987 | Photograph by Herb Ritts

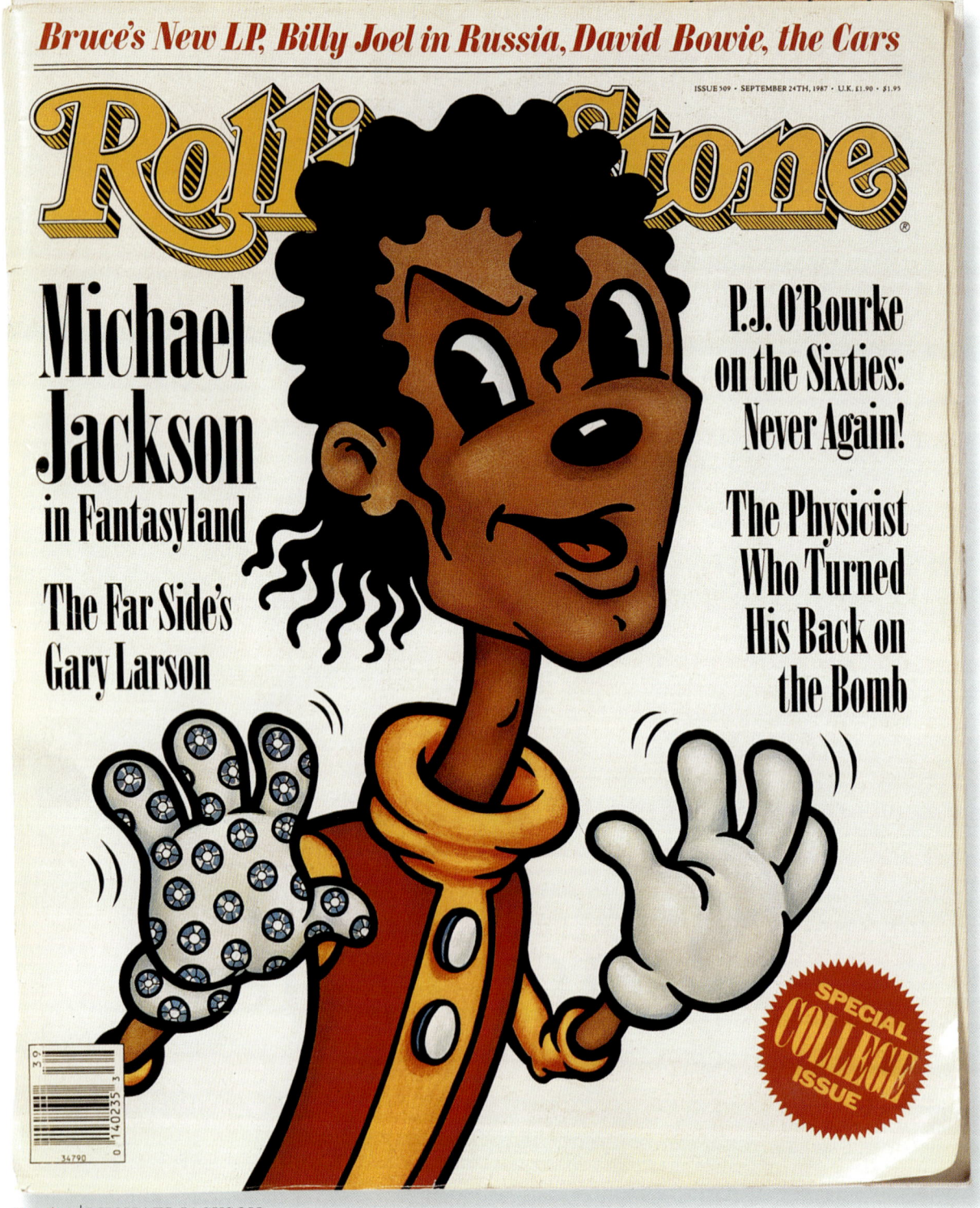

Bruce's New LP, Billy Joel in Russia, David Bowie, the Cars

Rolling Stone

ISSUE 509 · SEPTEMBER 24TH, 1987 · U.K. £1.90 · $1.95

Michael Jackson in Fantasyland

The Far Side's Gary Larson

P.J. O'Rourke on the Sixties: Never Again!

The Physicist Who Turned His Back on the Bomb

1980s

SPECIAL COLLEGE ISSUE

RS 509 | MICHAEL JACKSON | September 24th, 1987 | ILLUSTRATION BY ANITA KUNZ

260 • ROLLING STONE

When Michael Jackson kicks off his first solo tour in Tokyo this month, he will be sharing his two-bedroom suite with one of his closest friends. Michael's friend is a three-year-old named Bubbles.

Bubbles is a chimpanzee.

Bubbles is just one of the many real-life characters who populate the elaborate fantasy world that the superstar has constructed around himself. Playing and chatting with Bubbles or Louie the Llama or Crusher, his new 300-pound python, Michael can effortlessly become one of those Disney characters he so loves.

Bubbles goes everywhere with Michael. They are a classic TV-style duo, like Timmy and Lassie or Wilbur and Mister Ed. Bubbles was in the recording studio with Michael for much of the two years it took to make *Bad*, the follow-up to *Thriller*. Bubbles accompanied Michael to New York for Martin Scorsese's filming of the "Bad" video. Bubbles is a star of the new line of stuffed animals known as Michael's Pets, which will also be the basis for a children's cartoon series. Bubbles even has a crib in Michael's bedroom. And when Michael threw an elaborate dinner party at his Encino, California, mansion on a warm July night to begin the promotion of *Bad*, it was Bubbles, not the pop star, who worked the room, truly the life of the party.

[EXCERPT FROM RS 509 COVER STORY BY MICHAEL GOLDBERG AND DAVID HANDELMAN]

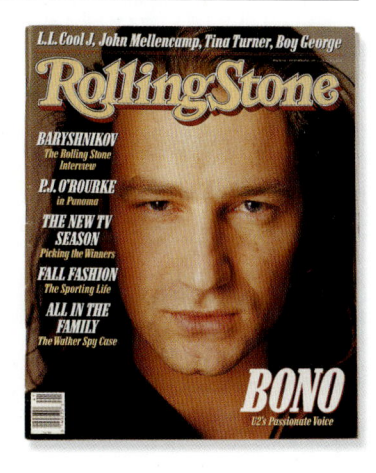

RS 510 | BONO
October 8th, 1987
PHOTOGRAPH BY MATTHEW ROLSTON

DYLAN IN ISRAEL, R.E.M.'S NEW ALBUM, PINK FLOYD, ROGER WATERS

Rolling Stone

ISSUE 511 · OCTOBER 22ND, 1987 · U.K. £1.90 · $1.95

1980s

The Return of George Harrison

The Phony Freedom Fighters
How Reagan Duped Congress on Aid to the Contras

The Man Who Turns On America
NBC's Brandon Tartikoff

How Good Is Michael Jackson's 'Bad'?

RS 511 | GEORGE HARRISON | October 22nd, 1987 | Photograph by William Coupon

A LETTER FROM THE EDITOR

'Rolling Stone' turns twenty

years old with this issue. What was started with $7,000 in a loft above a printer in San Francisco is now one of America's leading publications, with offices in six cities and a paid circulation of more than one million.

That ROLLING STONE survived and prospered is due in part to the talent and devotion of the people who have worked on it; to the vitality and growth of the music and culture from which it came and which it covers; and to its own deeply held beliefs and values. This twentieth anniversary is, in a sense, an affirmation of what ROLLING STONE writes about and what it stands for.

We read and hear a lot about the Sixties these days. We are told that they were the most exciting of times, years of great passion and commitment. We are also told that those passions and ideals were full of sound and fury, signifying nothing, that no beliefs or tangible benefits came from that period, and that everyone grew up to be a stockbroker. A lot of people would like to have us believe that what we stood for and what we believed in was childish, shallow and powerless stuff.

In our series of twentieth-anniversary issues, we have attempted to assess those times. In this final anniversary issue we have asked people whose work has stood out and whose voices have often been heard in the pages of ROLLING STONE to talk about their experiences during the past two decades, their understanding of what has survived and what they see ahead.

ROLLING STONE, at age twenty, holds these things dear: high standards in its own craft – writing, reporting, photography, editing, design, publishing; rock & roll music and the popular arts it touches; a commitment to stimulating and nourishing musicians and artists; and having a voice of reason that will be heard in the politics and policies of this country.

We will continue to try our best. We ain't perfect. But we're good, and we're getting better.

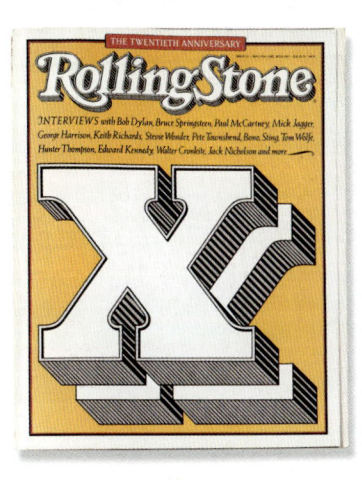

—*Jann S. Wenner*
[OCTOBER 1987]

RS 512 | TWENTIETH ANNIVERSARY
November 5th – December 10th, 1987
TYPOGRAPHY BY JIM PARKINSON

Three decades on, ROLLING STONE's twentieth-anniversary issue still stands as one of its best-selling issues. It is also the only all-type cover to make it in the magazine's top bestsellers. It was the seventh issue designed by art director Fred Woodward.

♦ P.J. O'Rourke in Korea; The New Masters of Horror Fiction ♦
The Rock & Roll Hall of Fame; On Location: The U2 Movie

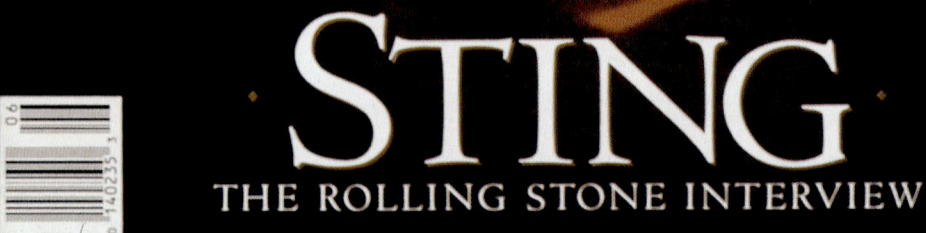

Rolling Stone

STING
THE ROLLING STONE INTERVIEW

RS 519 | STING | February 11th, 1988 | Photograph by Matt Mahurin

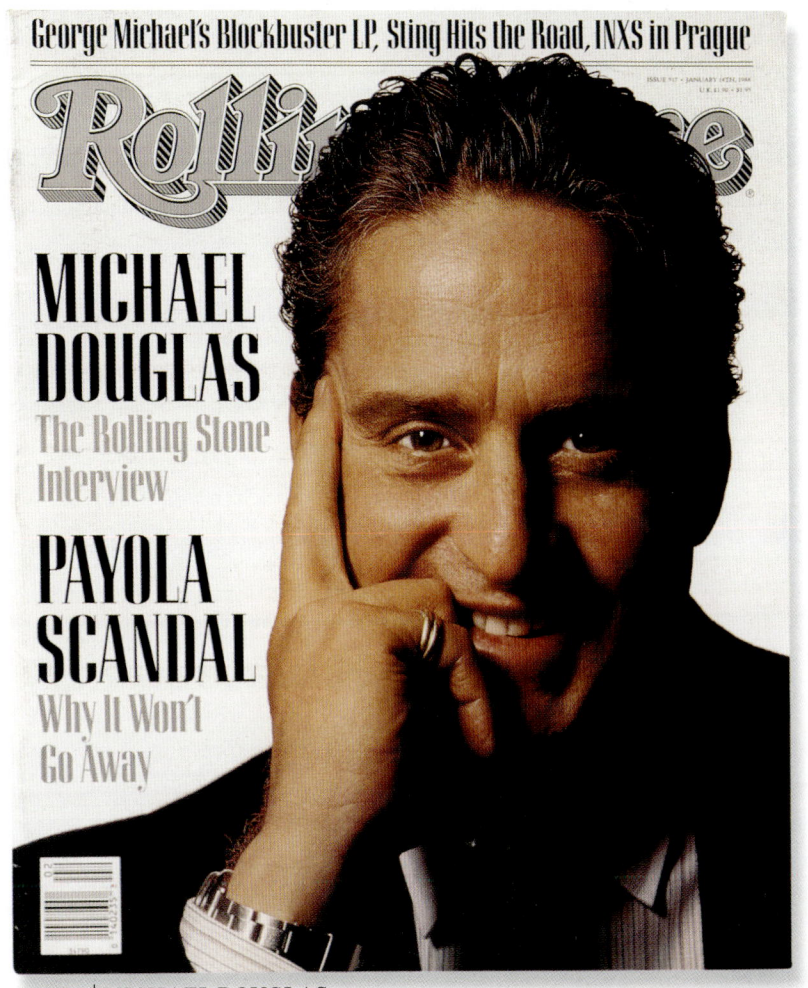

RS 517 | MICHAEL DOUGLAS | January 14th, 1988 | Photograph by Albert Watson

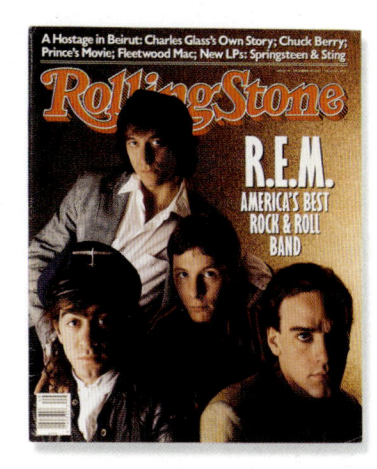

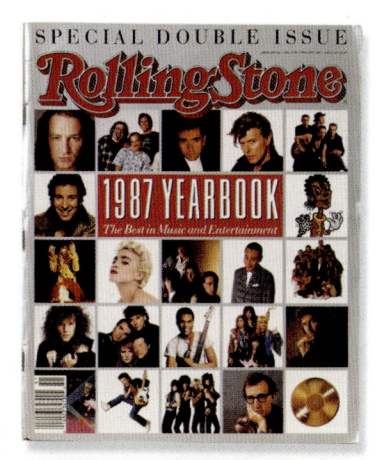

RS 513 | PINK FLOYD
November 19th, 1987
Illustration by Melissa Grimes

RS 514 | R.E.M.
December 3rd, 1987
Photograph by Brian Smale

RS 515/516 | 1987 YEARBOOK
December 17th – December 31st, 1987
Various photographers

RS 521 | U2
March 10th, 1988
Photograph by Matthew Rolston

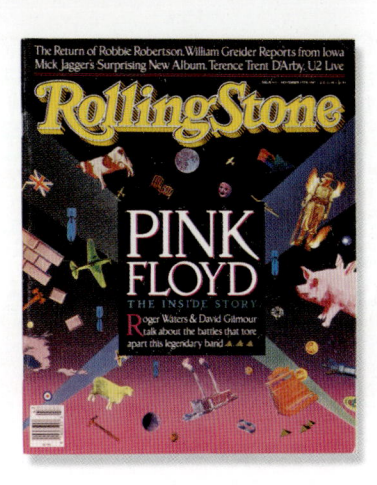

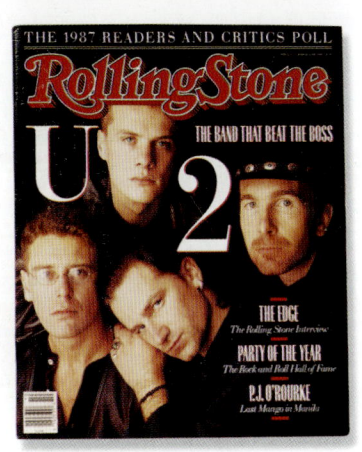

50 YEARS OF COVERS • 265

ISSUE 518 · JANUARY 28TH, 1988 · U.K. £1.90 · $2.50

Rolling Stone

1980s

GEORGE MICHAEL
Life After Wham!: No More Kid Stuff

GORBY DOES WASHINGTON
William Greider & P.J. O'Rourke at the Summit

BROADCAST NEWS
Behind the Scenes

RS 518 | GEORGE MICHAEL | January 28th, 1988 | Photograph by Matthew Rolston

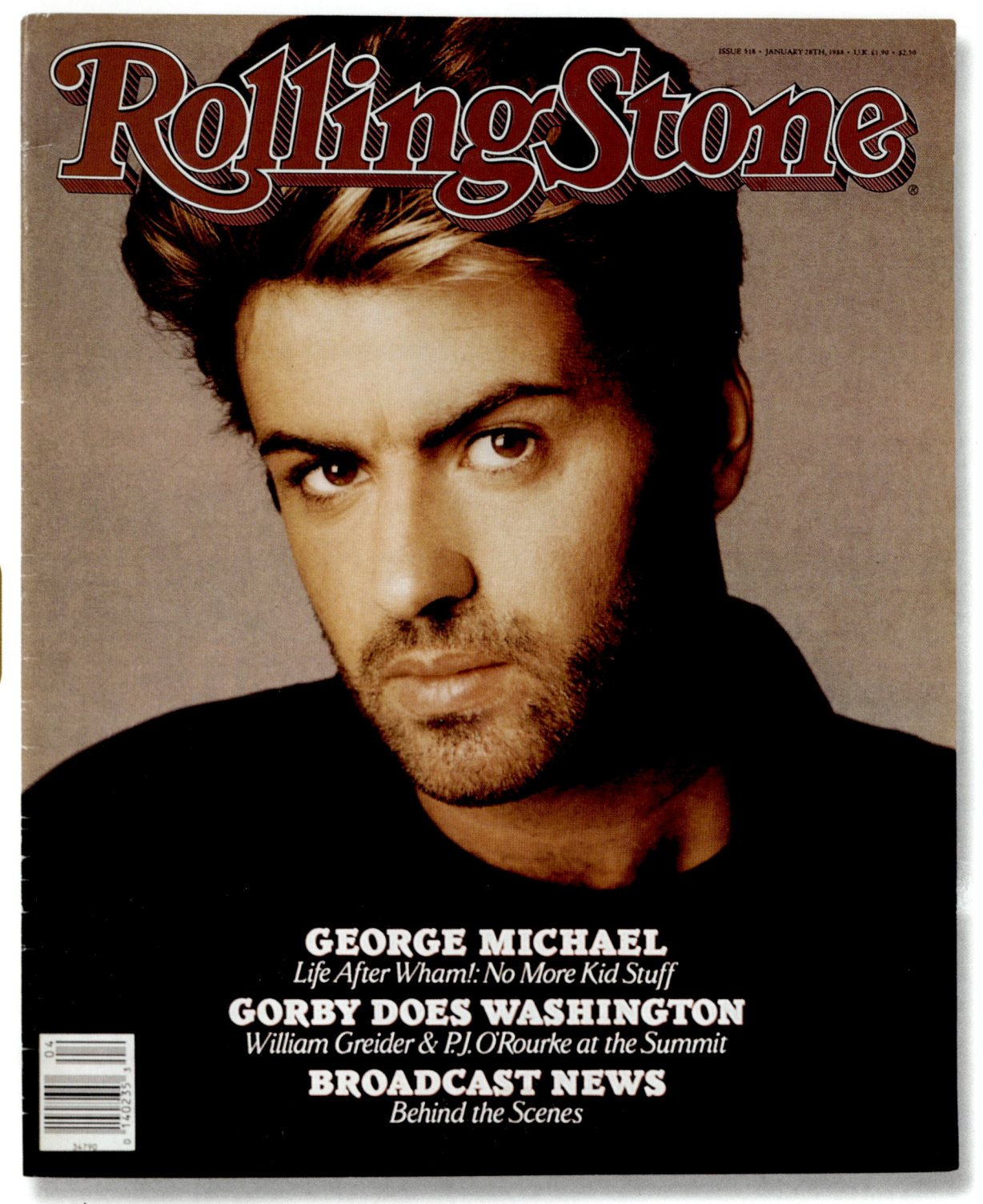

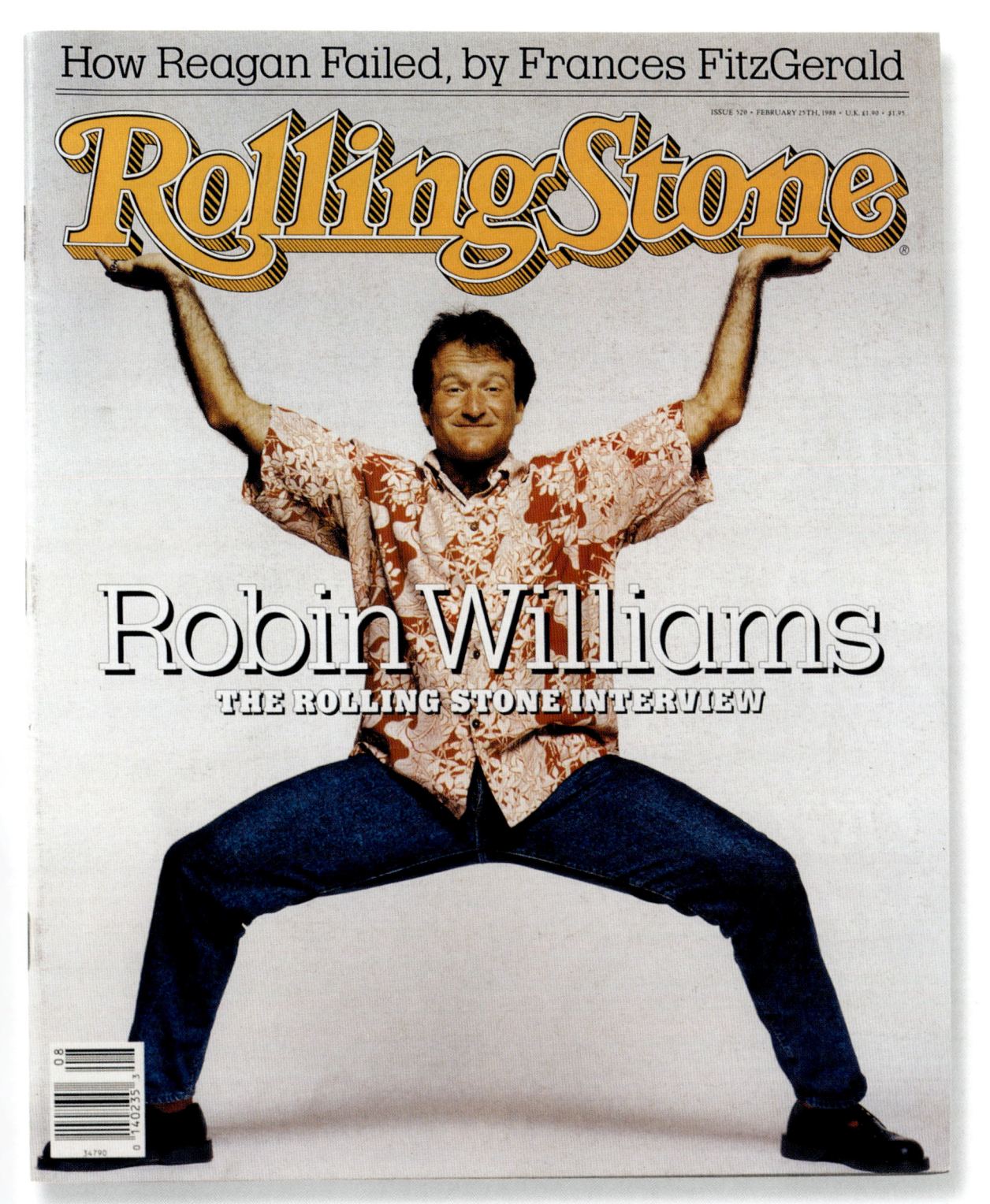

How Reagan Failed, by Frances FitzGerald

ISSUE 520 • FEBRUARY 25TH, 1988 • U.K. £1.90 • $1.95

Rolling Stone

Robin Williams
THE ROLLING STONE INTERVIEW

RS 520 | ROBIN WILLIAMS | February 25th, 1988 | Photograph by Bonnie Schiffman

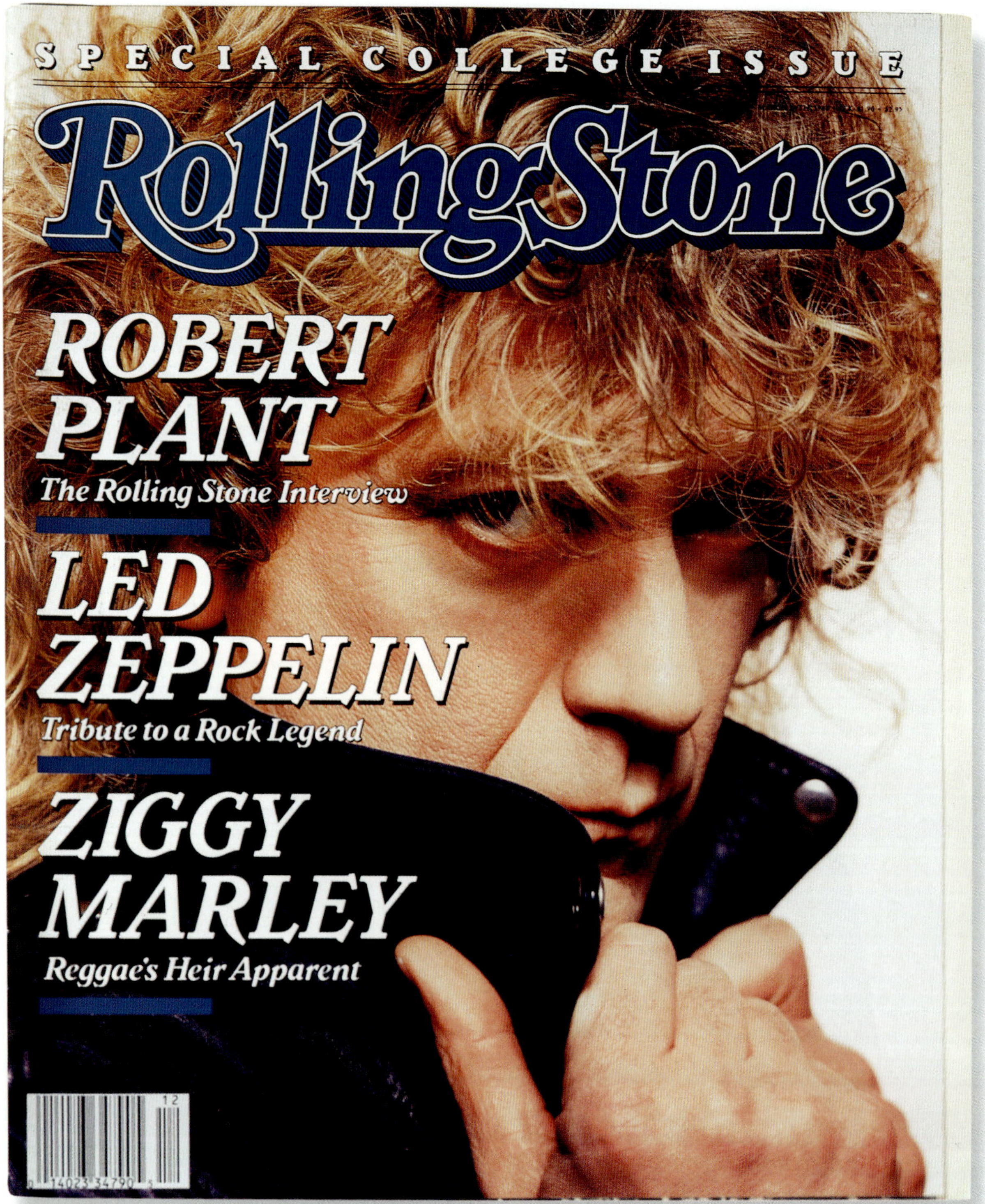

SPECIAL COLLEGE ISSUE

Rolling Stone

ROBERT PLANT
The Rolling Stone Interview

LED ZEPPELIN
Tribute to a Rock Legend

ZIGGY MARLEY
Reggae's Heir Apparent

1980s

RS 522 | ROBERT PLANT | March 24th, 1988 | Photograph by David Montgomery

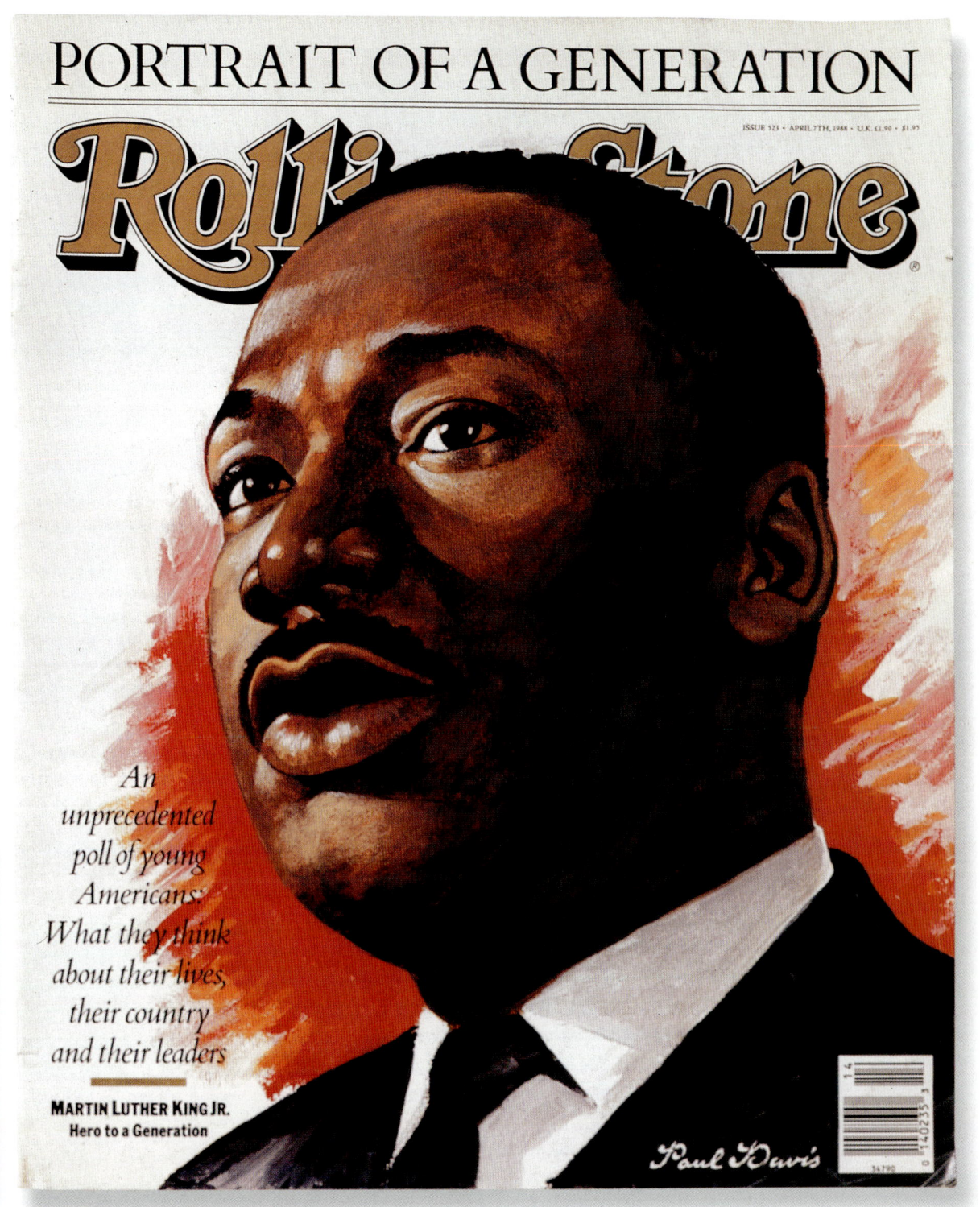

RS 523 | **MARTIN LUTHER KING JR.** | April 7th, 1988 | Illustration by Paul Davis

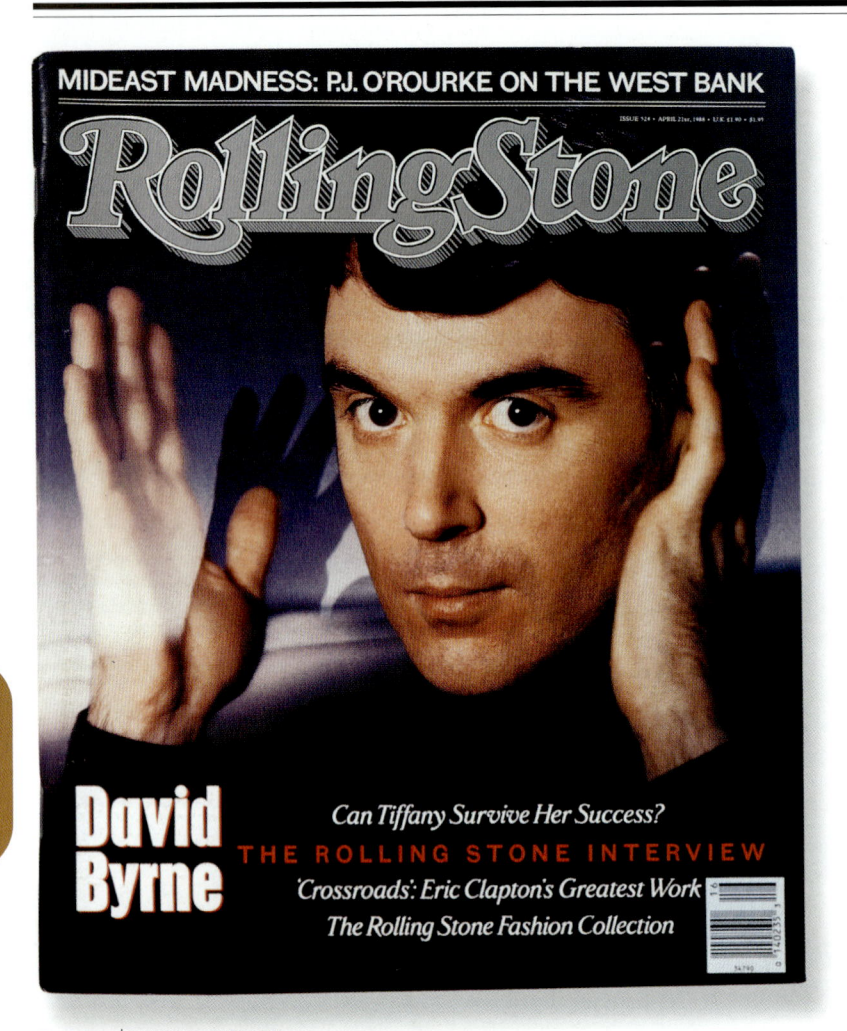

1980s

RS 524 | **DAVID BYRNE** | April 21st, 1988 | Photograph by Hiro

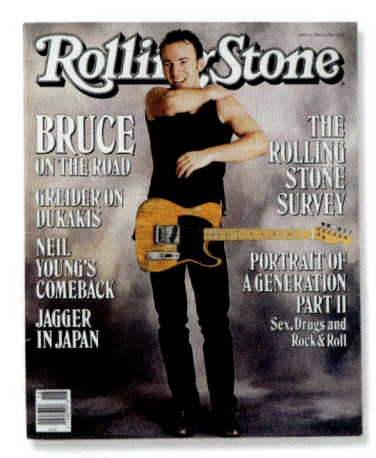

RS 525 | **BRUCE SPRINGSTEEN**
May 5th, 1988
Photograph by Neal Preston

[*RS 526*] At twenty, Lisa Bonet was looking for a new image. She'd just completed a stint on the wholesome *Cosby Show* and was pregnant with her first child by then-husband Lenny Kravitz. At the photo session, her publicist insisted that there be no nude shots. But once Matthew Rolston started shooting, her clothes started dropping faster than the camera could click. Later, when Bonet learned that Rolling Stone didn't choose the totally nude shot for the cover (it appeared inside), she came to the magazine's offices to lobby – unsuccessfully – for it. The white blouse obviously did not hurt sales.

Rock & roll is an obsessive state. You dared to enter into that obsessive state. What kind of insights have you gotten from it?

Rock music makes the obsessive okay and turns it into a creative act. Rock deflects that energy and channels it into something creative. Which is odd, because at a certain point you realize that it's not enough to just be obsessive in front of an audience. There's also craft to it. You have to achieve a balance between obsession and craftsmanship. Otherwise, you're just screaming in somebody's ear.

What do you think is going to happen to rock in the 1990s?

Rock's probably going to go two ways. There will be music from many cultures that crosses the generations, that speaks to the greater humanity that we are. That's one kind of thing. And I think we and other musicians are searching for a way to do that. We're certainly not alone. And I think, at the same time, there will always be younger musicians who have a more frantic set of hormones rushing through the body.

[EXCERPT FROM DAVID BYRNE INTERVIEW BY ROBERT FARRIS THOMPSON]

Rolling Stone

ISSUE 526 · MAY 19TH, 1988 · U.K. £1.90 · $1.95

The
HOT
Issue

Starring
Lisa Bonet

1988's Hottest People, Places & Things

RS 526 | LISA BONET | May 19th, 1988 | Photograph by Matthew Rolston

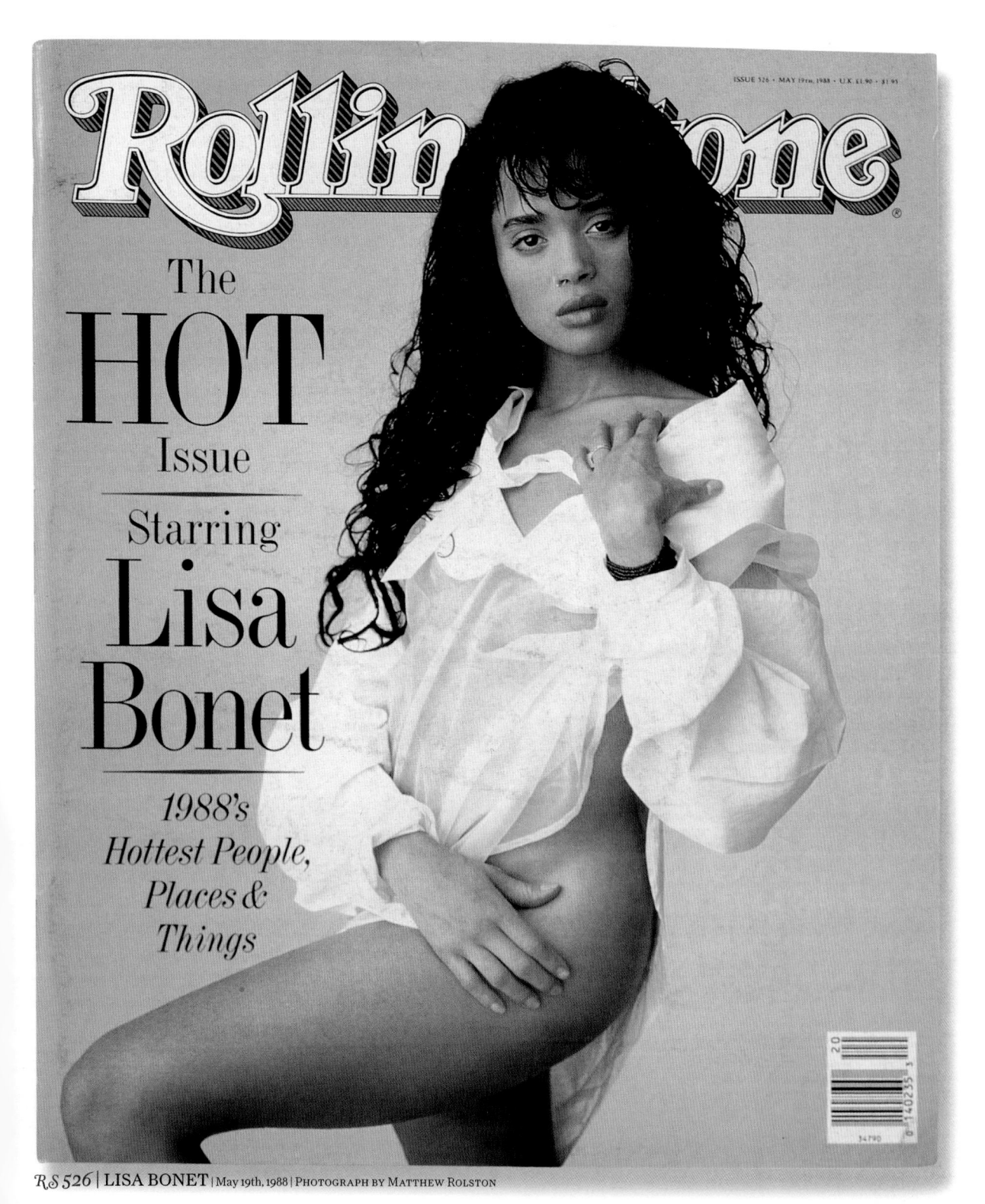

50 YEARS OF COVERS · 271

'ST. ELSEWHERE' CHECKS OUT; BEETLEJUICE: ULTIMATE DEAD HEAD

Rolling Stone

ISSUE 527 • JUNE 2nd, 1988 • $2.50

The Rolling Stone Interview

NEIL YOUNG

Talks About His New Album and the CSNY Reunion

DEATH OF A HIGH-SCHOOL NARC

1980s

RS 527 | NEIL YOUNG | June 2nd, 1988 | Photograph by William Coupon

PRINCE IN PARIS, PATTI SMITH'S NEW ALBUM, FALL TV

ISSUE 533 · AUGUST 25TH, 1988 · $2.50

Rolling Stone

ERIC CLAPTON
The Rolling Stone Interview

ROBERT DE NIRO
A Rare Talk with the Star of 'Midnight Run'

WHERE ARE THEY NOW?
Cat Stevens, the Box Tops, Billy J. Kramer and more

FALL FASHION
The Rolling Stone Collection

RS 533 | ERIC CLAPTON | August 25th, 1988 | Photograph by David Bailey

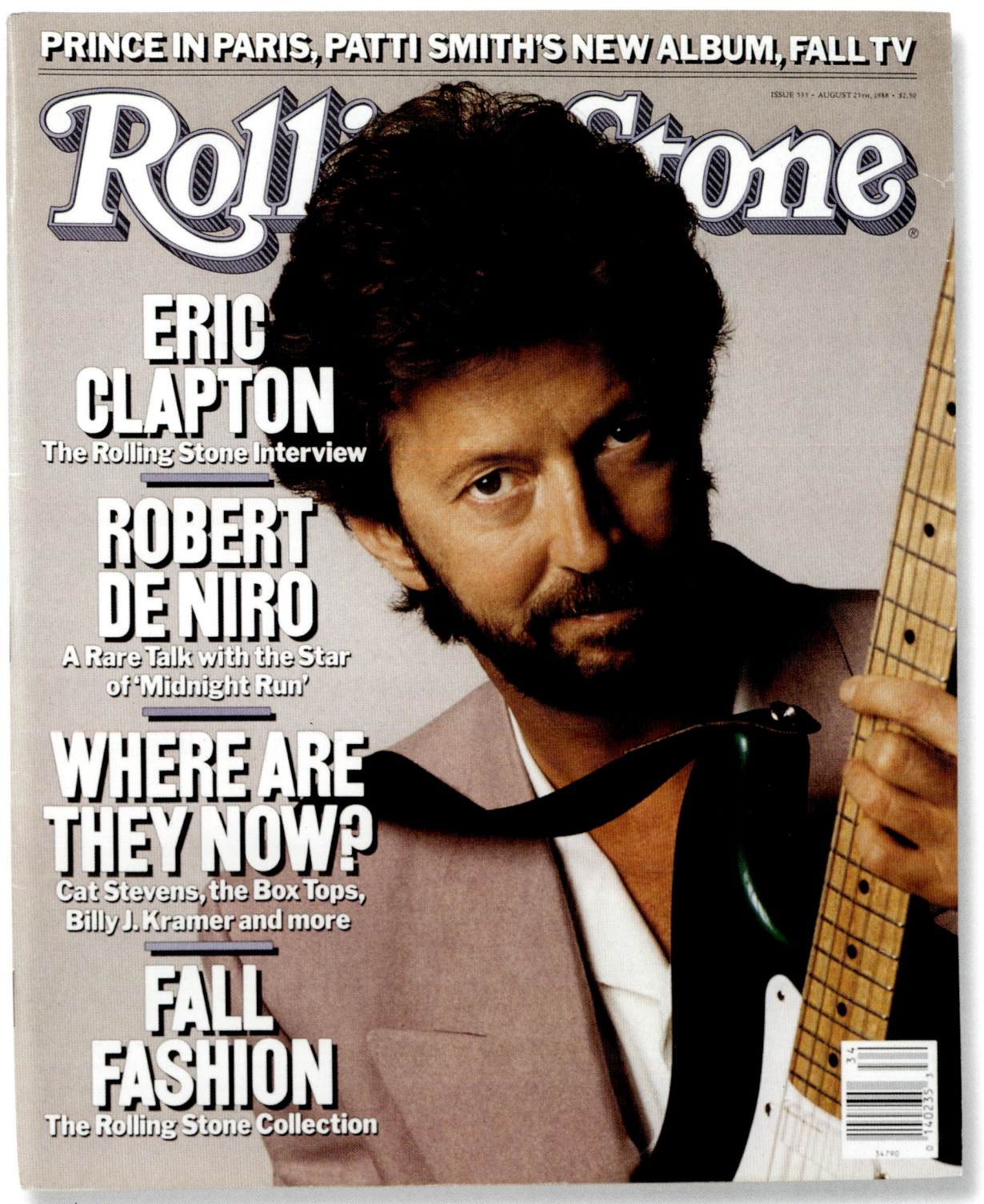

50 YEARS OF COVERS • 273

1980s

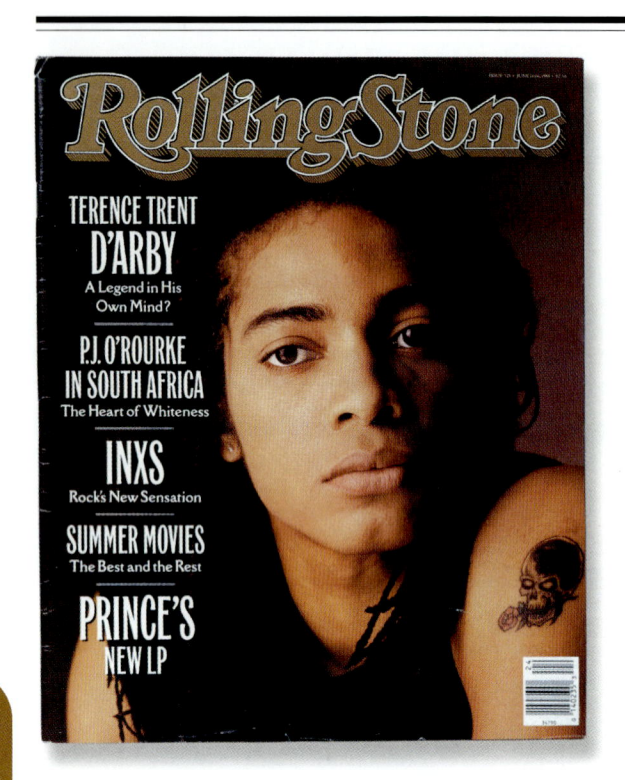

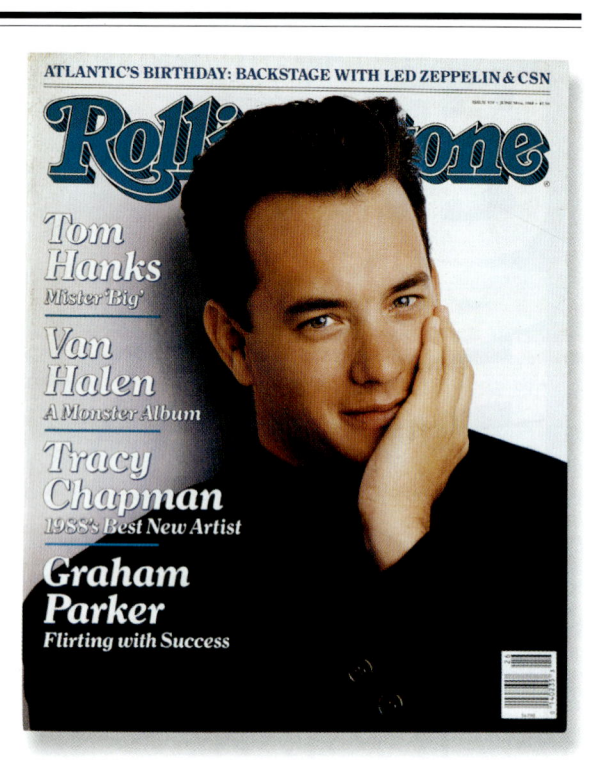

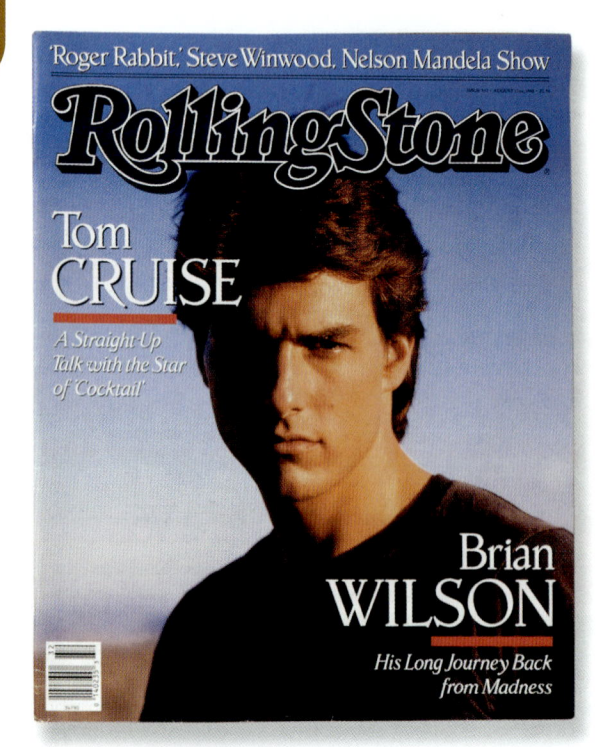

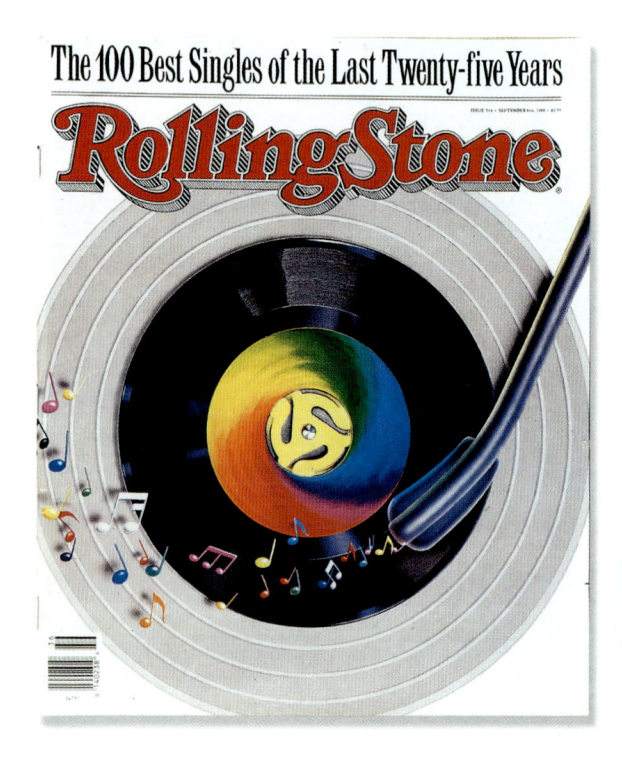

274 • ROLLING STONE

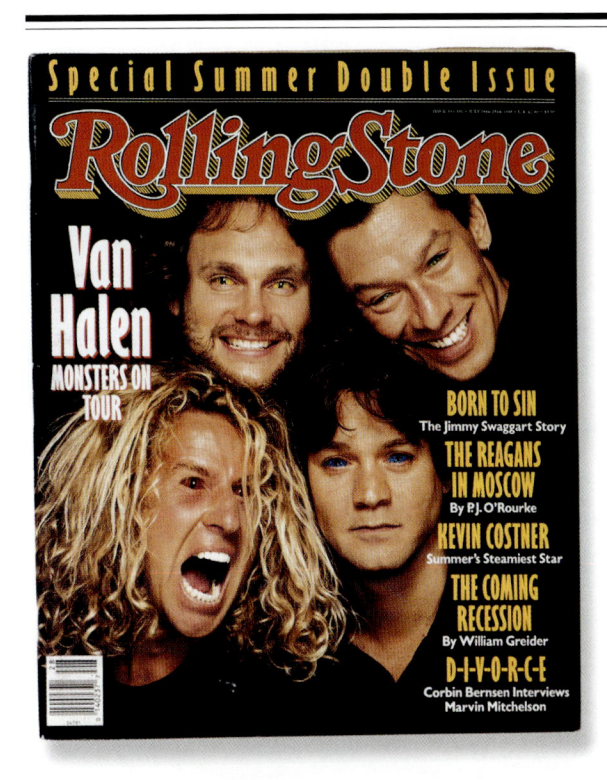

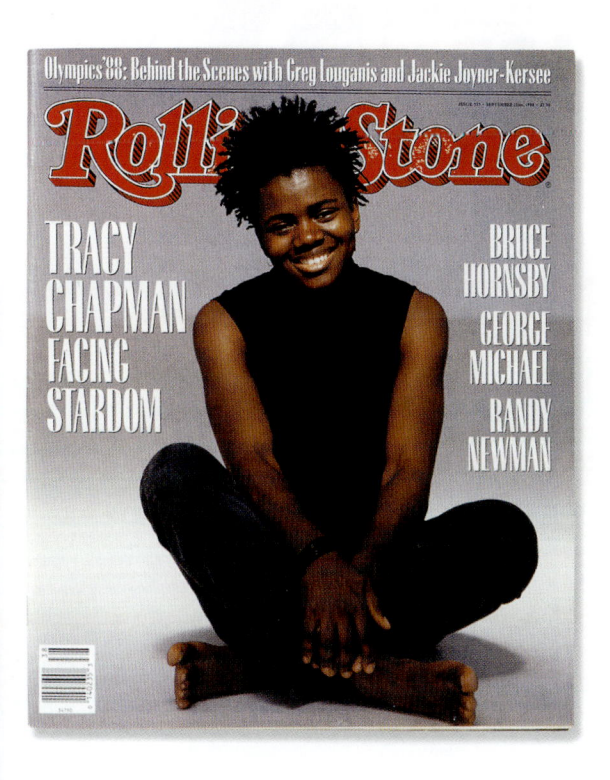

RS 528 | TERENCE TRENT D'ARBY
June 16th, 1988
Photograph by Matthew Rolston

RS 529 | TOM HANKS
June 30th, 1988
Photograph by Herb Ritts

RS 530/531 | VAN HALEN
July 14th – July 28th, 1988
Photograph by Timothy White

RS 532 | TOM CRUISE
August 11th, 1988
Photograph by Herb Ritts

RS 534 | THE 100 BEST SINGLES OF THE LAST TWENTY-FIVE YEARS
September 8th, 1988
Illustration by Steve Pietzsch

RS 535 | TRACY CHAPMAN
September 22nd, 1988
Photograph by Herb Ritts

50 YEARS OF COVERS • 275

RS 538 | JOHNNY CARSON & DAVID LETTERMAN | November 3rd, 1988 | Photograph by Bonnie Schiffman

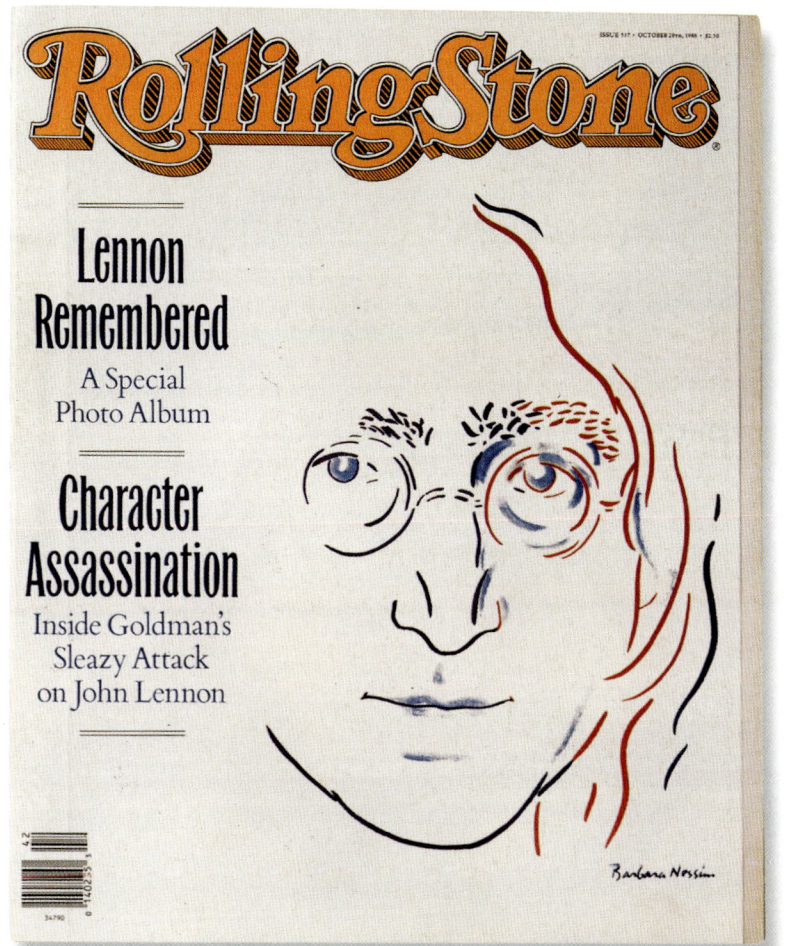

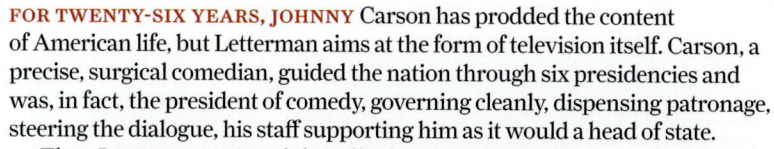

RS 537 | JOHN LENNON | October 20th, 1988 | ILLUSTRATION BY BARBARA NESSIM

FOR TWENTY-SIX YEARS, JOHNNY Carson has prodded the content of American life, but Letterman aims at the form of television itself. Carson, a precise, surgical comedian, guided the nation through six presidencies and was, in fact, the president of comedy, governing cleanly, dispensing patronage, steering the dialogue, his staff supporting him as it would a head of state.

Then Letterman entered the talk-show mainstream by reinventing the genre called found comedy, which casts a cold video eye on the conventions of the landscape – dumb ads, bad TV, stores that advertise things they don't have. It was the high point of consumer comedy: Letterman got on the telephone and sent out cameras to try and gauge the disparity between what television had told us and what really existed. For six years and eight months, he has been shooting arrows at television, at the culture, and they never seem to fall back to earth, like the pencils that still hang from the acoustically dotted ceiling of his office. "I mean," he often says on the show, "what's the *deal* here?"

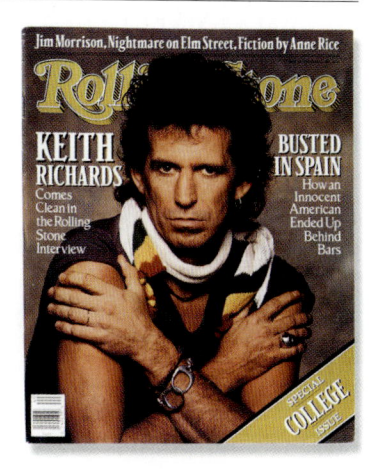

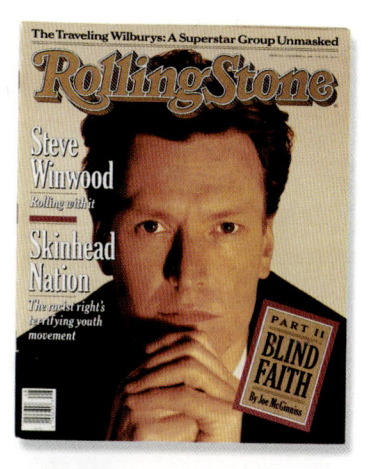

[EXCERPT FROM RS 538 COVER STORY BY PETER W. KAPLAN]

RS 536 | KEITH RICHARDS
October 6th, 1988
PHOTOGRAPH BY ALBERT WATSON

RS 540 | STEVE WINWOOD
December 1st, 1988
PHOTOGRAPH BY HERB RITTS

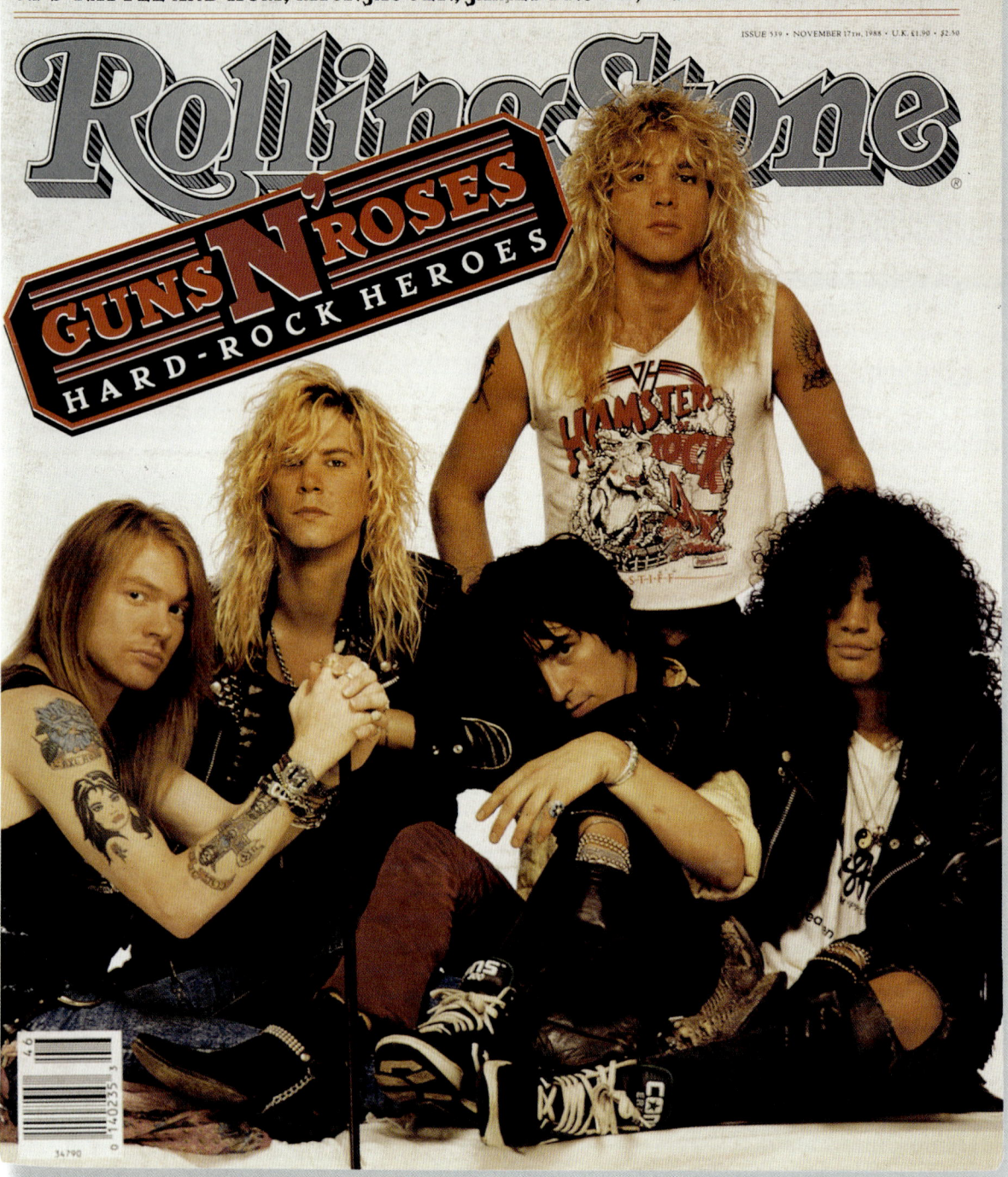

RS 539 | GUNS N' ROSES | November 17th, 1988 | Photograph by Timothy White

SPECIAL COLLEGE ISSUE

ISSUE 548 · MARCH 23RD, 1989 · U.K. £1.90 · $2.95

RollingStone

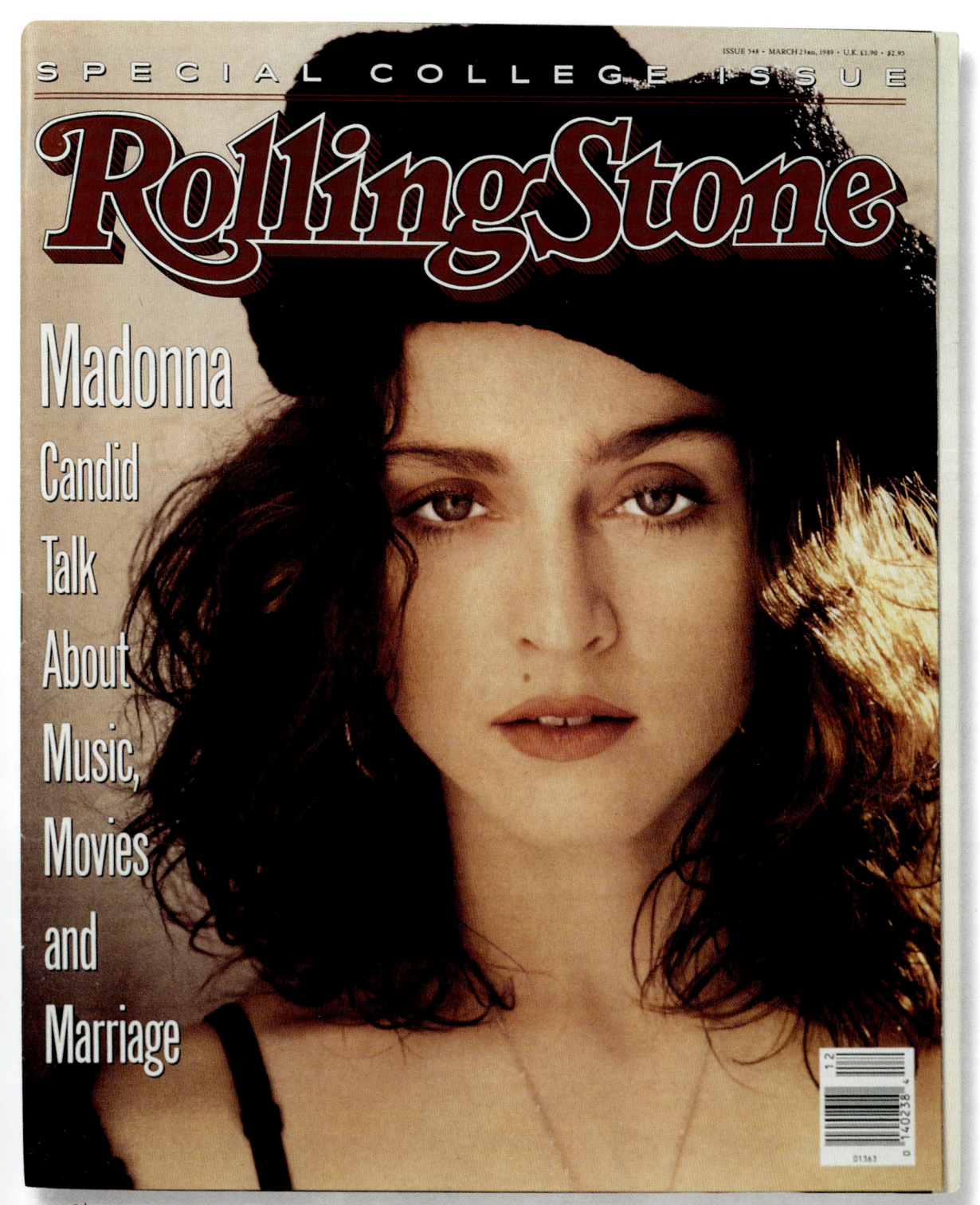

Madonna Candid Talk About Music, Movies and Marriage

RS 548 | MADONNA | March 23rd, 1989 | Photograph by Herb Ritts

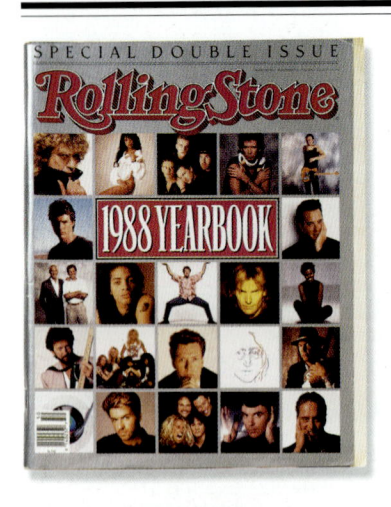

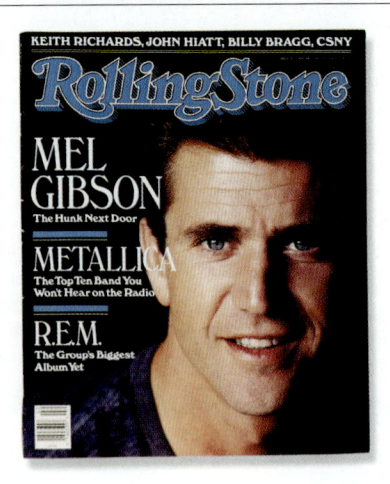

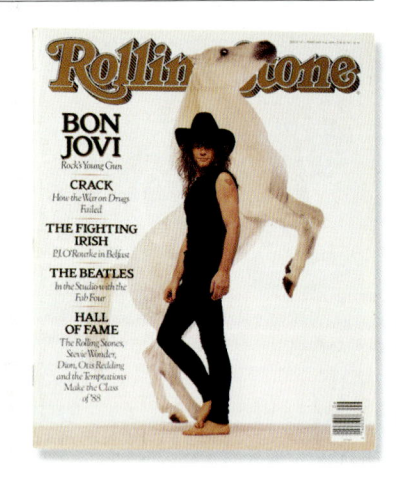

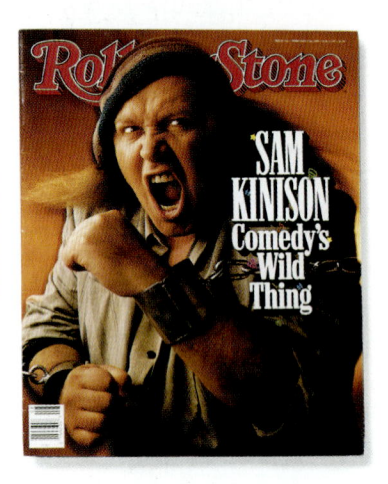

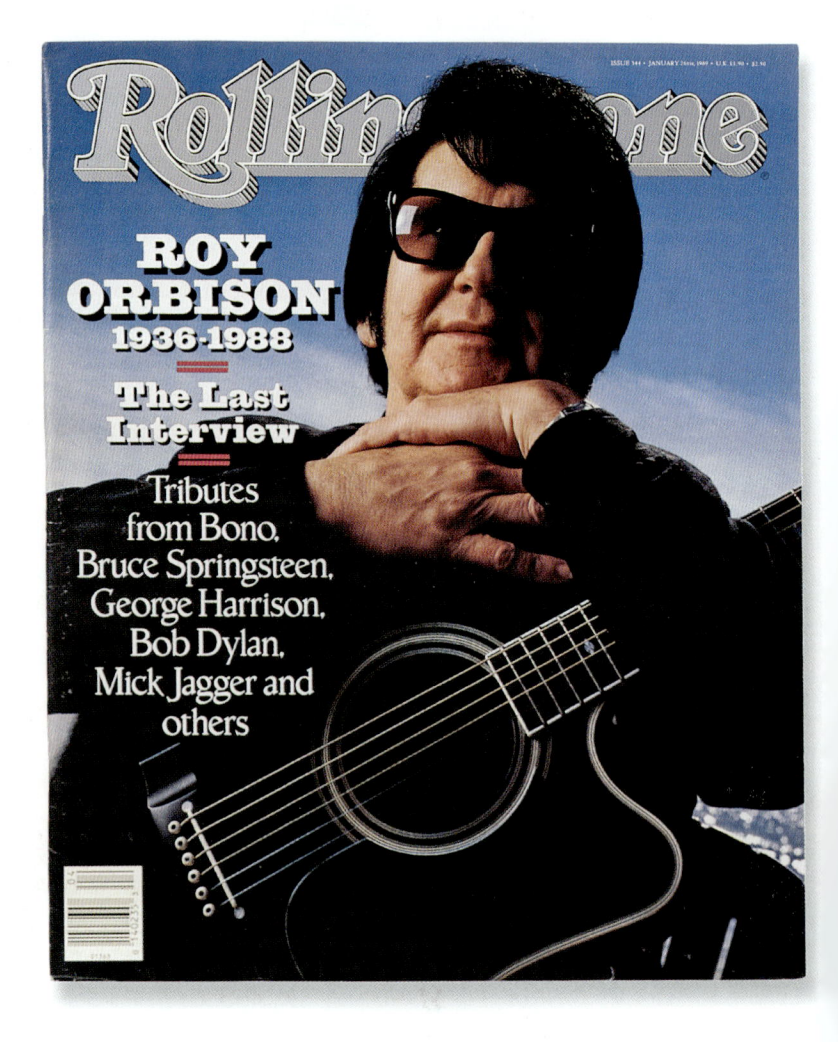

1980s

RS 541/542 | 1988 YEARBOOK
December 15th – December 29th, 1988
VARIOUS PHOTOGRAPHERS

RS 543 | MEL GIBSON
January 12th, 1989
PHOTOGRAPH BY HERB RITTS

RS 545 | JON BON JOVI
February 9th, 1989
PHOTOGRAPH BY TIMOTHY WHITE

RS 544 | ROY ORBISON
January 26th, 1989
PHOTOGRAPH BY ANN SUMMA

RS 546 | SAM KINISON
February 23rd, 1989
PHOTOGRAPH BY MARK SELIGER

280 • ROLLING STONE

1988 READERS AND CRITICS POLL

Rolling Stone

U2
BAND OF THE YEAR

BONO
VOICE OF THE YEAR

LOYALTIES
THE NEW BOOK
BY CARL BERNSTEIN

P.J.
O'ROURKE ON GEORGE
BUSH

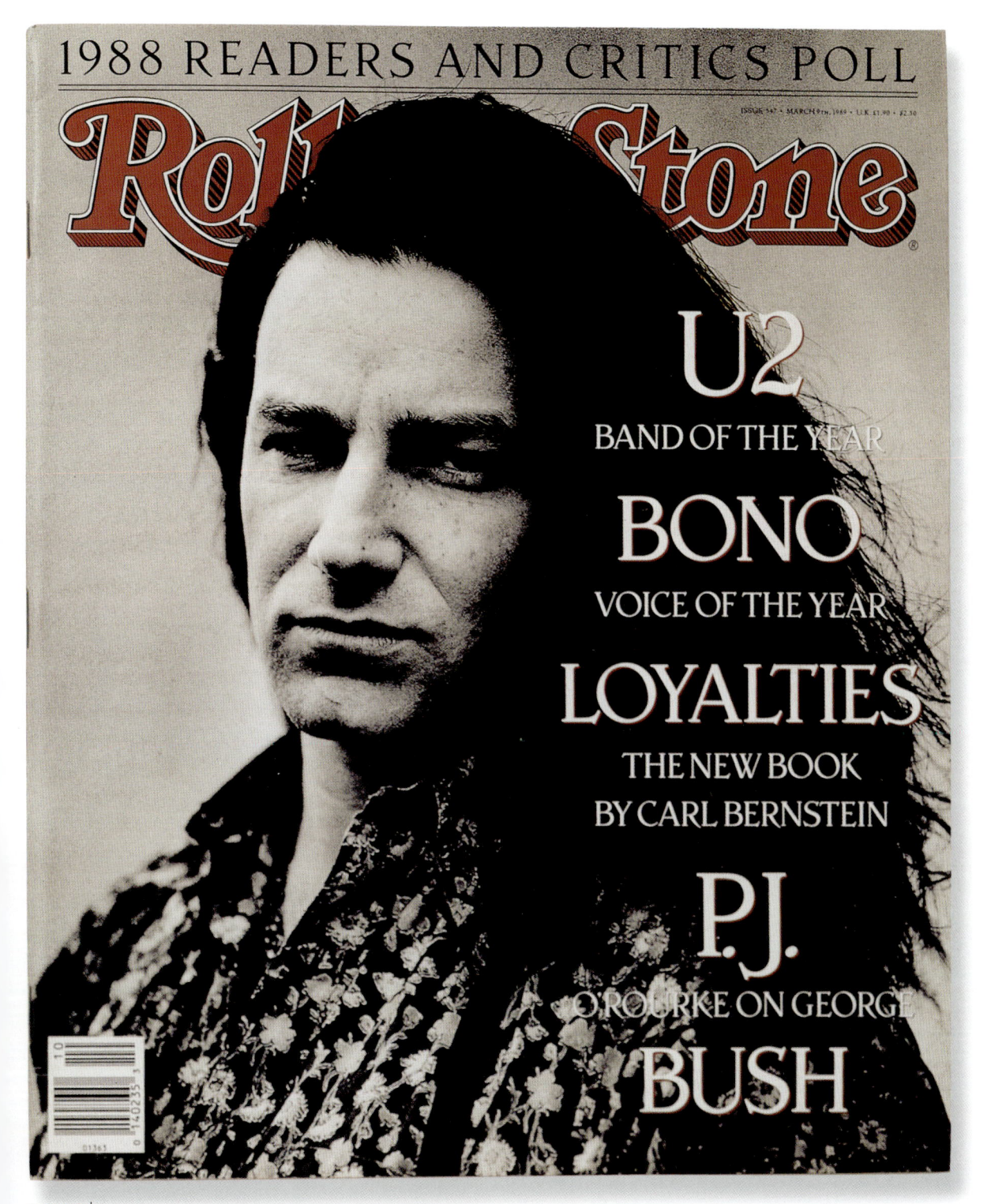

RS 547 | BONO | March 9th, 1989 | Photograph by Anton Corbijn

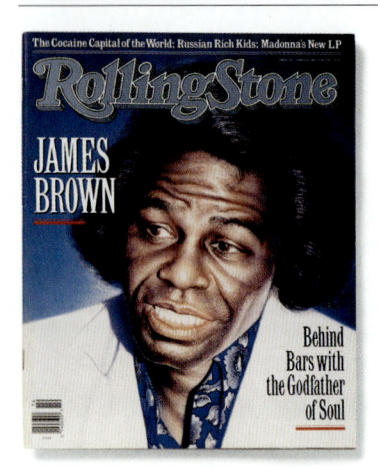

RS 549 | JAMES BROWN
April 16th, 1989
ILLUSTRATION BY GOTTFRIED HELNWEIN

1980s

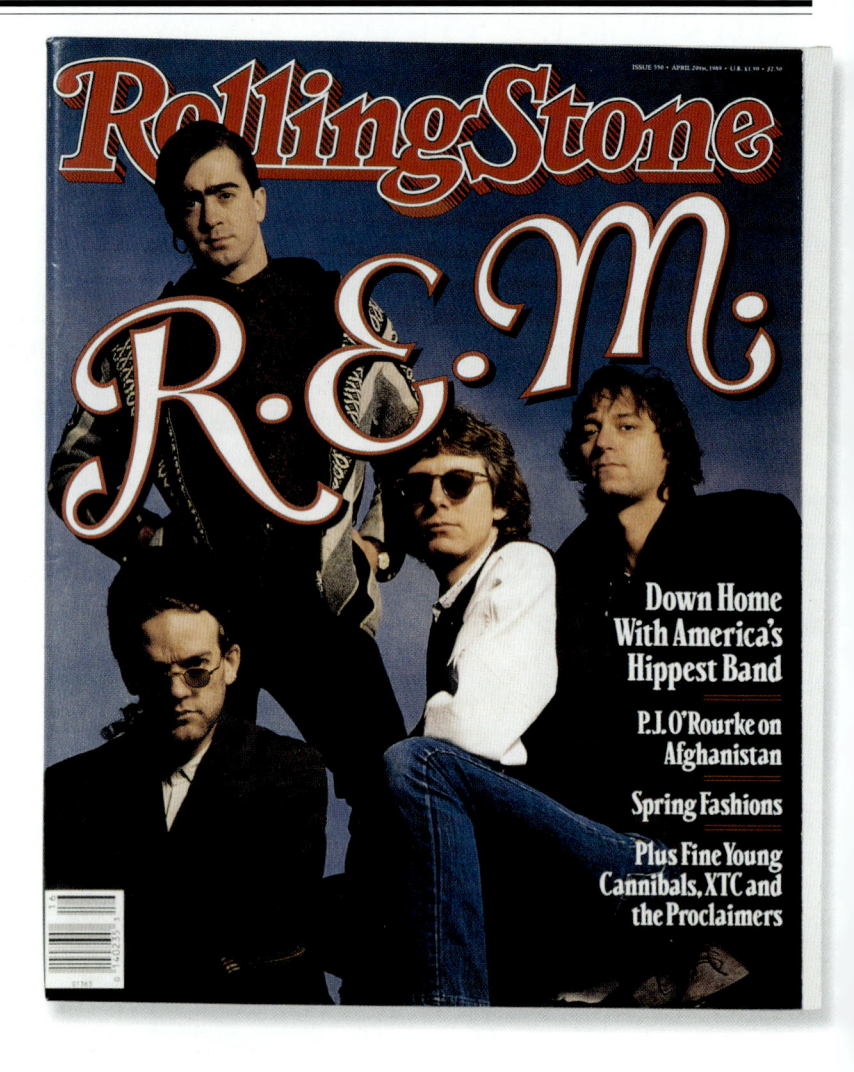

RS 550 | R.E.M.
April 20th, 1989
PHOTOGRAPH BY TIMOTHY WHITE

RS 551 | LOU REED | May 4th, 1989 | Photograph by Mark Seliger

RS 552 | UMA THURMAN | May 18th, 1989 | Photograph by Matthew Rolston

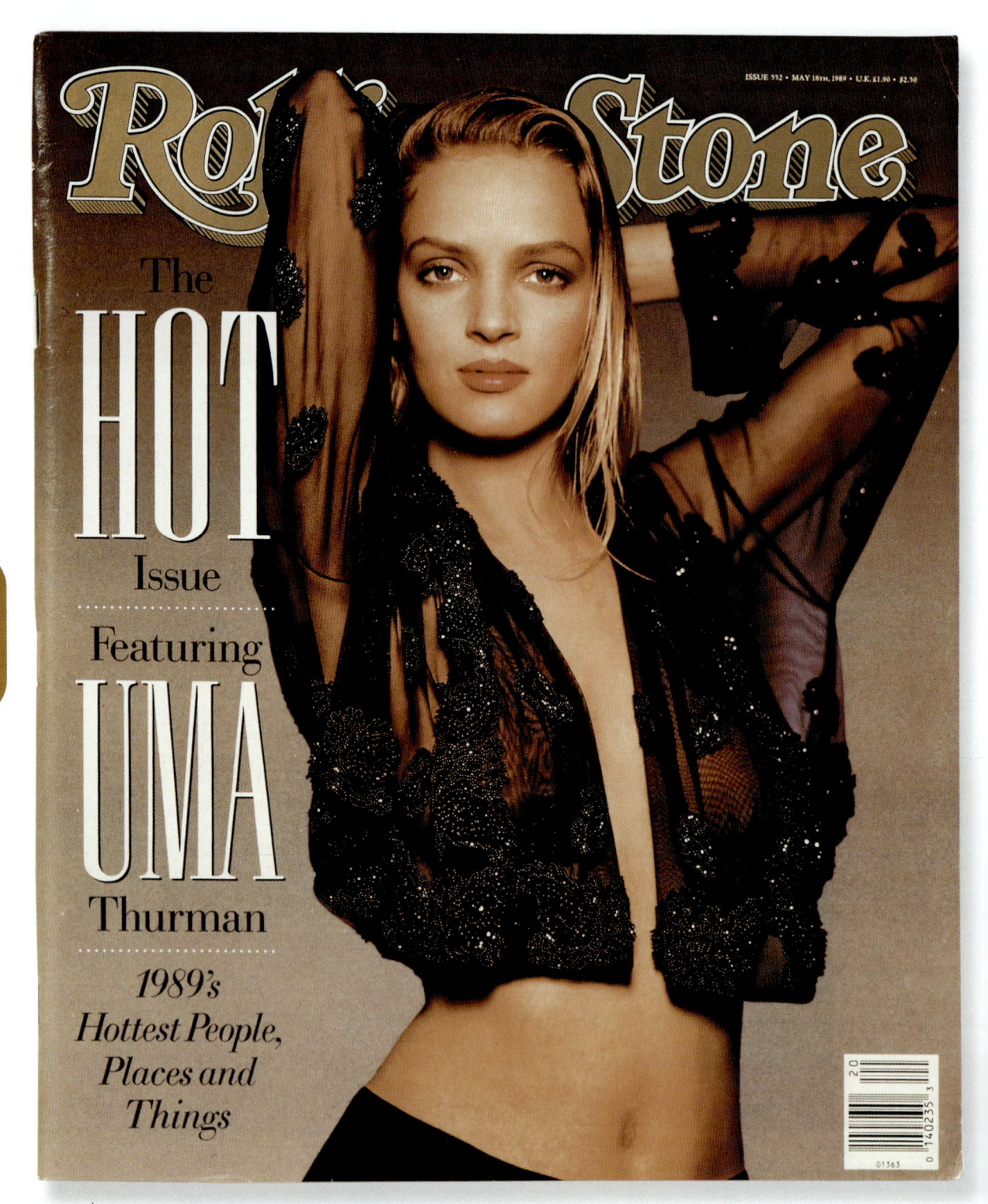

# Rolling Stone

ISSUE 556/557 · JULY 13TH-27TH, 1989 · UK £1.90 · $3.50

SPECIAL DOUBLE ISSUE

ROCK & ROLL SUMMER *A Coast-to-Coast Guide to Hot Fun in the Sun With Bryan Adams, Cowboy Junkies, Sammy Hagar, Bo Deans, Lisa Lisa and Others* **THE WHO** *Back Together on the Road* **THE BEATLES** *Rare Photos From Their 1964 Tour* **GILDA RADNER** *An Intimate Tribute* **GREAT BALLS OF FIRE** *Behind the Scenes in Memphis With Dennis Quaid and Jerry Lee Lewis* **PEACE** *A Special Report by Lawrence Wright* **SPIKE LEE** *His Controversial New Movie* **THE CULT** *British Rockers Conquer America*

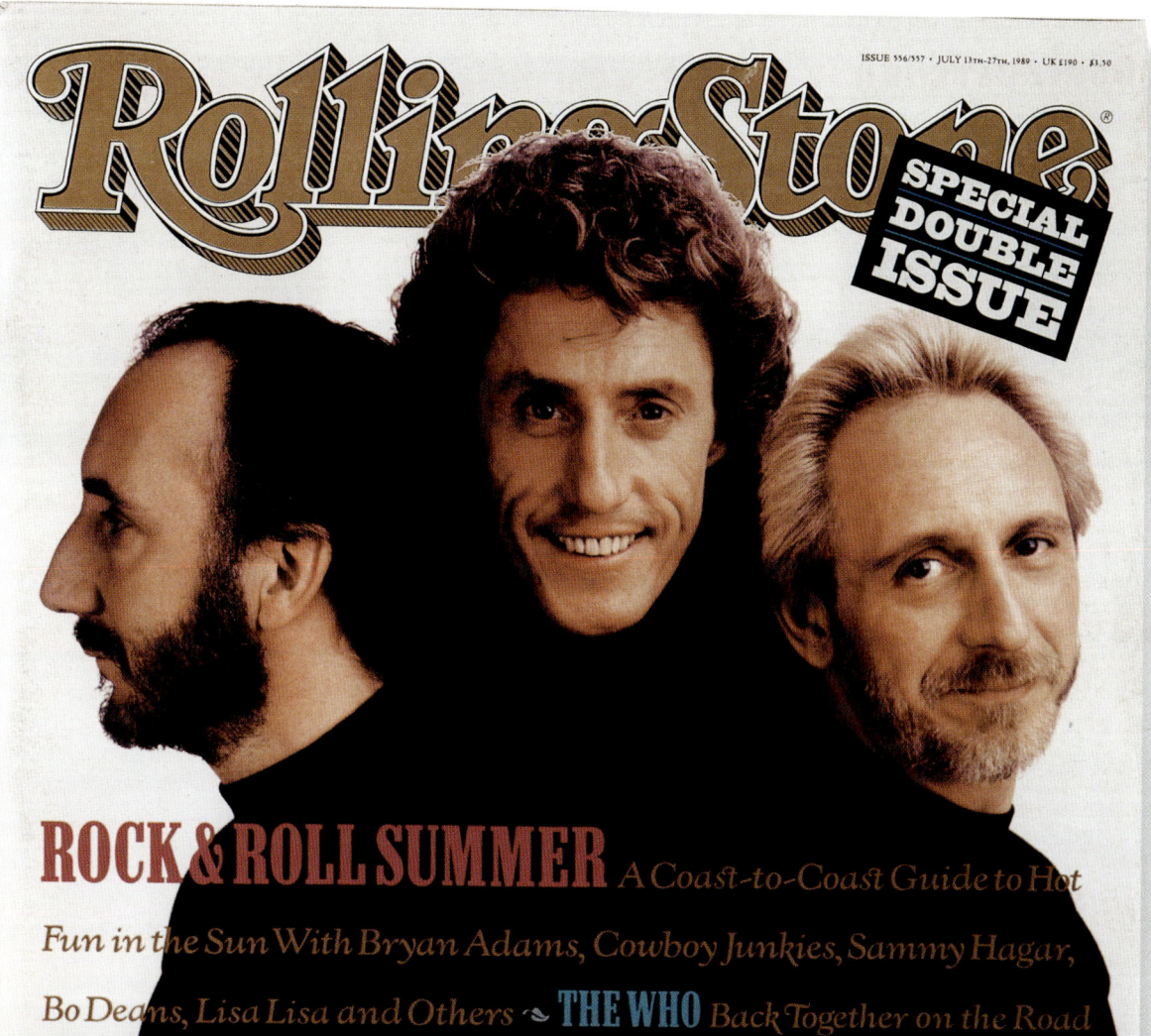

RS 556/557 | THE WHO | July 13th – July 27th, 1989 | Photograph by Davies & Starr

50 YEARS OF COVERS · 285

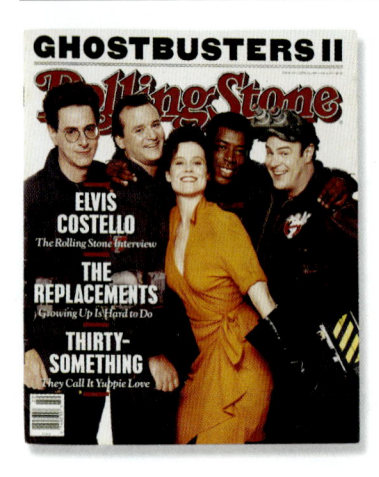

1980s

RS 553 | CAST OF 'GHOSTBUSTERS II'
June 1st, 1989
PHOTOGRAPH BY TIMOTHY WHITE

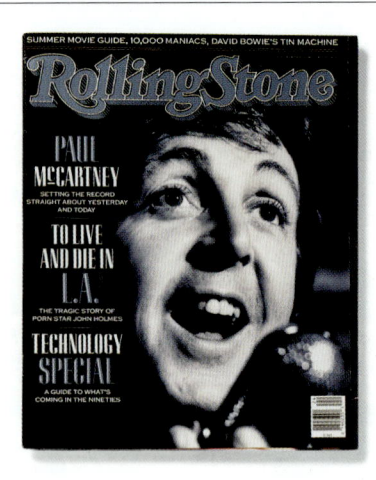

RS 554 | PAUL McCARTNEY
June 15th, 1989
PHOTOGRAPH BY HERB RITTS

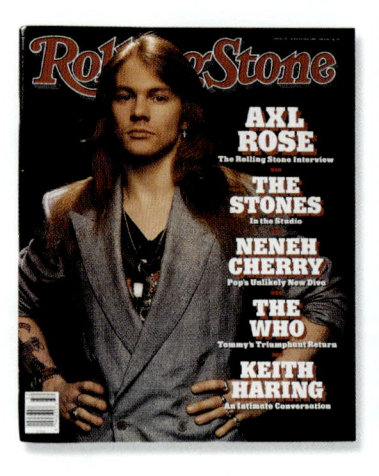

RS 558 | AXL ROSE
August 10th, 1989
PHOTOGRAPH BY ROBERT JOHN

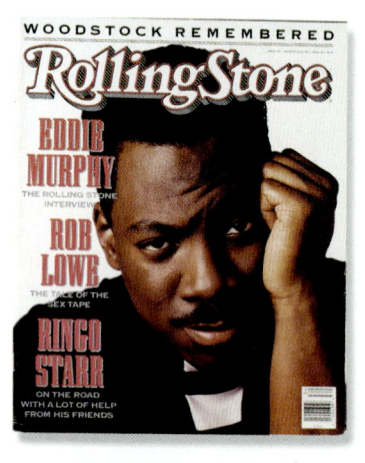

RS 559 | EDDIE MURPHY
August 24th, 1989
PHOTOGRAPH BY BONNIE SCHIFFMAN

HIS FRIENDS CALL HIM MONEY. He looks like money, like $40 million, if perchance one speculates. He looks crisp, controlled. He is twenty-eight yet not terribly youthful; he fancies himself much older, more world-weary. He stares straight ahead and seems to notice no one, but he sees all and hears even more. Unless he's erupting into his deft repertoire of character voices, his presence is shy, inscrutable. Usually he is sullen, almost somber – but this creates a quiet aura of power.

You've probably heard this before, but you don't smile much for someone with such a famous smile.

People come up to me and ask me to smile all the time. The thing I hear most is "Yo, smile! Why aren't you smiling? *Smile*. Smile for me!" And it gets irritating. Sometimes in restaurants, I'll see people across the room pressing their fingers into the corners of their mouths, showing me how to smile. I kid you not. When I'm driving down the street, people pull up to me and ask why I'm not smiling. Never mind that if I was driving around with a big smile, then people would think I was a lunatic.

Maybe you're just shy.

That, and I've got a mouth full of fillings. I'm a sugar freak – that's my one indulgence, so I get a lot of cavities, and I have to go to the dentist more often than most.

So the million-dollar smile is fake?

The million-dollar smile is hollow, actually. At any moment, the teeth could all fall out. It's the sad truth: The million-dollar smile is rotten. So I'll fucking smile when I want!

[EXCERPT FROM EDDIE MURPHY INTERVIEW BY BILL ZEHME]

286 • ROLLING STONE

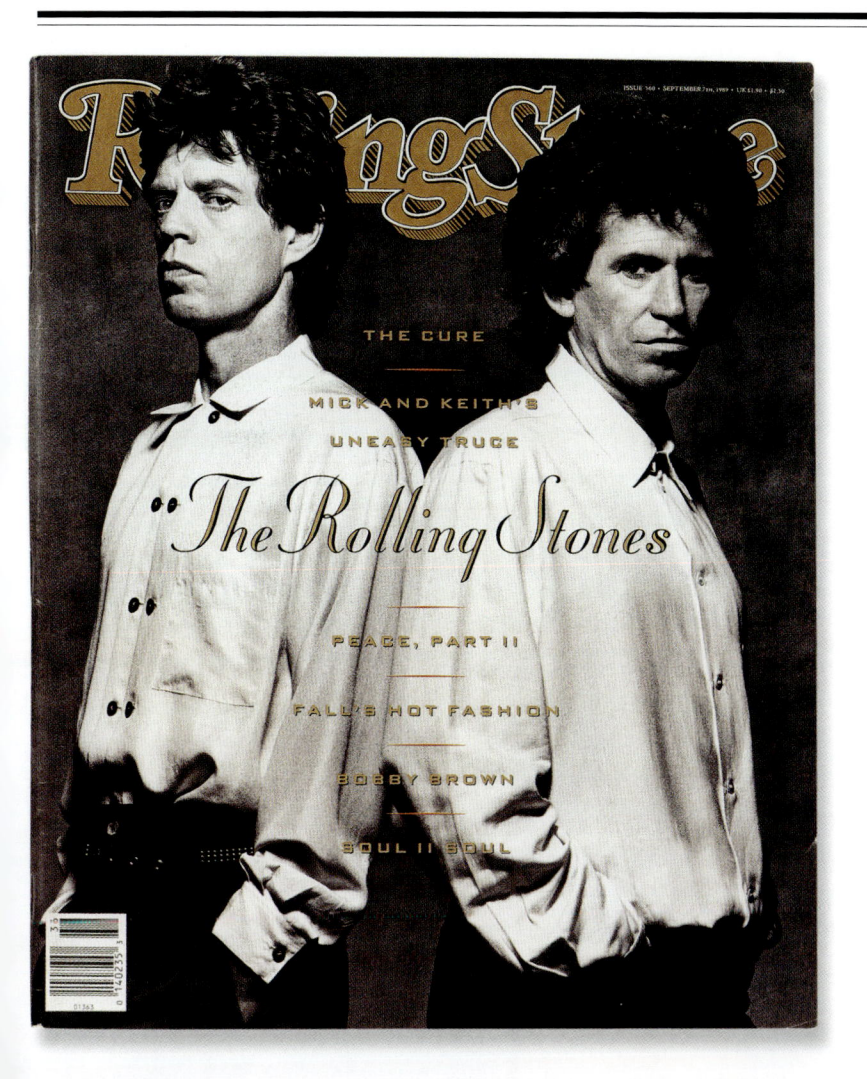

RS 560 | MICK JAGGER & KEITH RICHARDS
September 7th, 1989
PHOTOGRAPH BY ALBERT WATSON

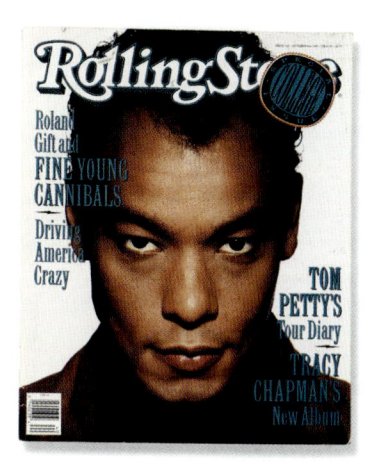

RS 562 | ROLAND GIFT
October 5th, 1989
PHOTOGRAPH BY ANDREW MACPHERSON

50 YEARS OF COVERS • 287

Rock & Roll Photo Album

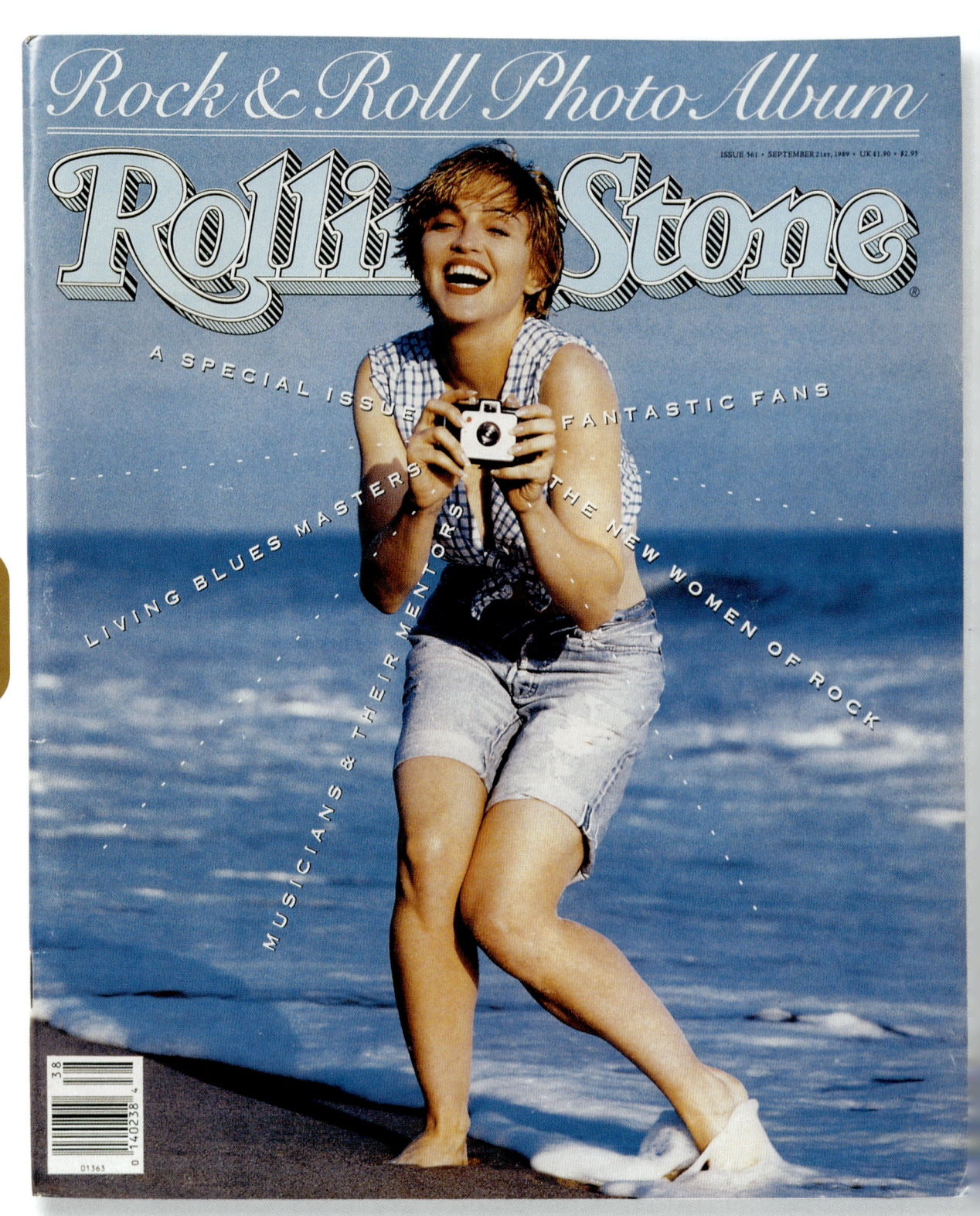

Rolling Stone

ISSUE 561 • SEPTEMBER 21st, 1989 • UK £1.90 • $2.95

A SPECIAL ISSUE

FANTASTIC FANS

LIVING BLUES MASTERS

THE NEW WOMEN OF ROCK

MUSICIANS & THEIR MENTORS

1980s

RS 561 | MADONNA
September 21st, 1989
PHOTOGRAPH BY HERB RITTS

AS ROCK STARS COME TO EXERCISE increasing control over their images, photographers face the challenge of finding ways to exercise their own powerful art, finding ways to say something unique and penetrating about people who are often extremely wary – or manipulatively savvy – about how they are represented. Photographers must also search for surprising aspects of the world of music to bring to light.

In this Rock & Roll Photo Album, ROLLING STONE's photographers do both with wit and flair. Herb Ritts captures a frolicsome Madonna turning the tables on her fans – and doctoring still another spin of the carefully crafted image that has helped make her one of the most recognizable stars in the world.

[EXCERPT FROM RS 561 ESSAY BY ANTHONY DeCURTIS]

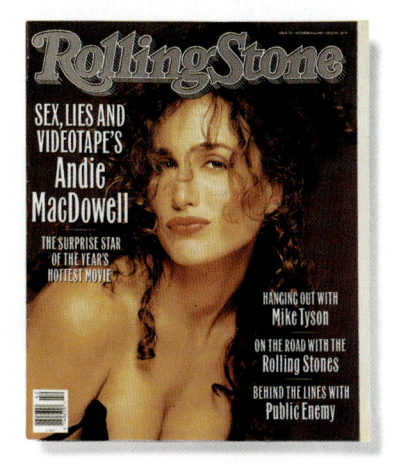

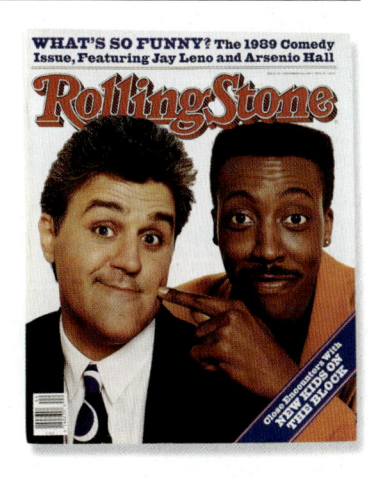

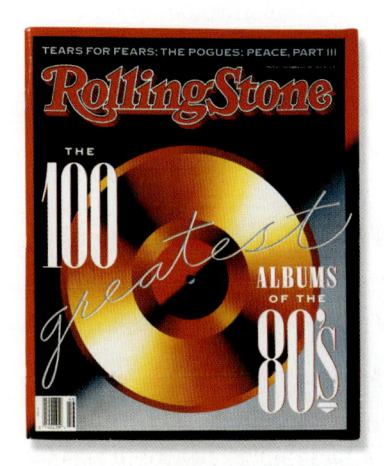

RS 563 | ANDIE MacDOWELL
October 19th, 1989
PHOTOGRAPH BY MATTHEW ROLSTON

RS 565 | THE 100 GREATEST ALBUMS OF THE EIGHTIES
November 16th, 1989
ILLUSTRATION BY TERRY ALLEN

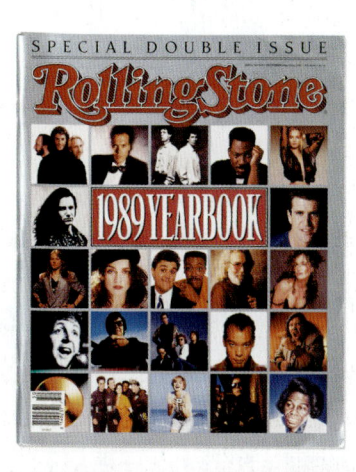

RS 564 | JAY LENO & ARSENIO HALL
November 2nd, 1989
PHOTOGRAPH BY BONNIE SCHIFFMAN

RS 567/568 | 1989 YEARBOOK
December 14th – December 28th, 1989
VARIOUS PHOTOGRAPHERS

JOHN MELLENCAMP'S BROKEN HEARTLAND

ISSUE 555 • JUNE 29TH, 1989 • U.K. £1.90 • $2.50

Rolling Stone

BAT-MAN

Can Michael Keaton Fill the Cape?

1980s

RS 555 | MICHAEL KEATON | June 29th, 1989 | Photograph by Bonnie Schiffman

ISSUE 566 • NOVEMBER 30TH, 1989 • UK £2.00 • $2.50

RollingStone

P.J. O'Rourke Tackles the Drug Problem

The Rolling Stone Interview

JERRY GARCIA

Paula Abdul, Terence Trent D'Arby, Milli Vanilli, Jeff Beck and Stevie Ray Vaughan

RS 566 | JERRY GARCIA | November 30th, 1989 | Photograph by William Coupon

50 YEARS OF COVERS • 291

RollingStone

ISSUE 572 • FEBRUARY 22ND, 1990 • $2.50 • UK £2.00

1990s

Janet Jackson
MICHAEL'S LITTLE SISTER GROWS UP

RS 569 – RS 831
1990

Even by California's peerless standard, the day is exquisite: sunny, impossibly clear, surprisingly warm for late November. Janet Jackson sits on a bench in a narrow park overlooking the ocean and the beach in Pacific Palisades, on the edge of Los Angeles. She's out of the quasi-military regalia that constitutes what by now might be thought of as the Janet Jackson uniform and looking almost preppy in bluejeans, white sneakers with black stripes, a white Raiders cap, a ski sweater and a shirt with pictures of cartoon characters on it. Bugs Bunny and Woody Woodpecker peer over the collar of the sweater. Her large silver earrings, with African designs, catch the glint of the sun as she speaks.

Pedestrians stroll by, joggers jog, the occasional person or couple saunters along the shore. The appearance of a dog within fifty yards in any direction triggers heart-rending paroxysms of longing in Puffy, the charmingly good-natured – and evidently quite lonely – mixed-breed bitch Jackson brought along to the interview. Fondness for pets is, of course, a Jackson family trait, and Janet had phoned my hotel that morning to ask if it would be all right if one of her dogs came along with her.

Puffy's function today is to help Jackson contend with her reluctance to deal with the press. She has not done any major interviews since her 1986 album *Control* – with its quintuple-platinum sales and string of hit singles – established her, at the age of twenty, as one of the most popular recording artists in the world. A preliminary meeting in Paris on the set of the video shoot for "Come Back to Me," a luxurious ballad from Jackson's latest album, *Janet Jackson's Rhythm Nation 1814*, had taken place a month earlier at Jackson's request.

Like virtually everyone else in the public eye, Jackson doesn't feel she's been treated particularly well by the press, and she's sensitive about the media's portrayal of her brother Michael, to whom she is still extremely close. Also, after working so hard to break away from her family and build an independent identity, Janet isn't especially inclined to enter situations over which she doesn't have ultimate control. When she was first approached about doing this story, she requested the right to approve it before it was published – a request that was denied. Finally, you don't grow up in the preeminent entertainment family in America without learning that maintaining an air of mystery about yourself is an acutely effective marketing technique.

[EXCERPT FROM RS 572 COVER STORY BY ANTHONY DECURTIS]

RS 572 | JANET JACKSON | February 22nd, 1990 | PHOTOGRAPH BY MATTHEW ROLSTON

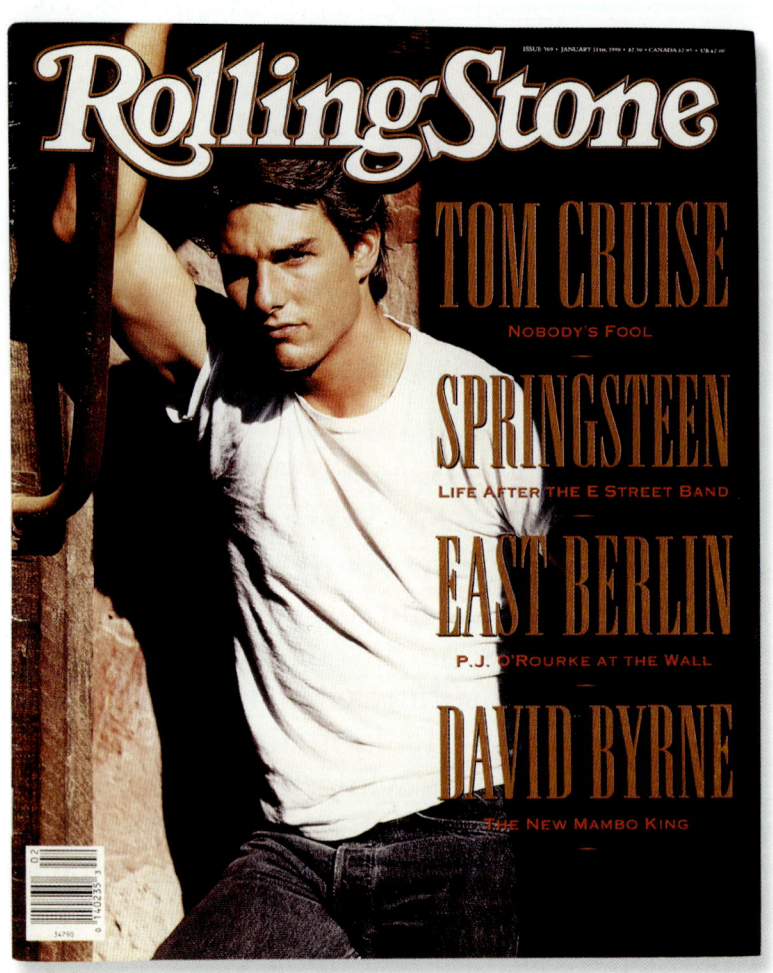

RS 569 | TOM CRUISE | January 11th, 1990 | Photograph by Herb Ritts

RS 570 | BILLY JOEL
January 25th, 1990
Photograph by Timothy White

"THE CRITICS DON'T SEE ME AS this authentic rock & roller. I'm not an authentic rock & roller. I never pretended to be one. I never hid my influences. The thing that pissed me off is when people compared me to Elton John when I was copying McCartney, you know? My God, I was straightforward about this stuff. I remember one guy said I was 'the Irving Berlin of narcissistic alienation.' I kinda like that – the Irving Berlin part anyway. Listen, I wrote some reviews when I was young for small rock magazines. But then I trashed this album by Al Cooper, and I realized that if I were him, I'd want to wring my neck. I didn't have the stomach for it. Now I say, 'You think I stink. I think your opinion stinks.' Have I read bad reviews onstage? Of course. Would I do it again? No. Nowadays it just bugs me when they say something about my wife or my kid.

"Listen, I might be an antique, just like the Stones, but antiques are of value. Antiques hold their value. We even get more valuable with age. And people want collectibles. Also, maybe people are finally getting tired of paying hard-earned money to see nothing up there. Maybe folks are tired of video stars who can't deliver live. They want substance, too."

—*Billy Joel*

ISSUE 570 · JANUARY 25TH, 1990 · $2.50 · UK £2.00

Rolling Stone

billy joel

*On Fire Again:
The Rolling Stone
Interview*

*Guitar Heroes:
Jeff Beck
and Stevie Ray
Vaughan*

ROLLING STONE

ISSUE 571
FEBRUARY 8TH, 1990
$2.50 • UK £2.00

HALL OF FAME
The Who, the Kinks and the Class of '89

THE ICE AGE
A New Drug Epidemic Threatens America

PAUL McCARTNEY
A Backstage Look at His U.S. Tour

1990s

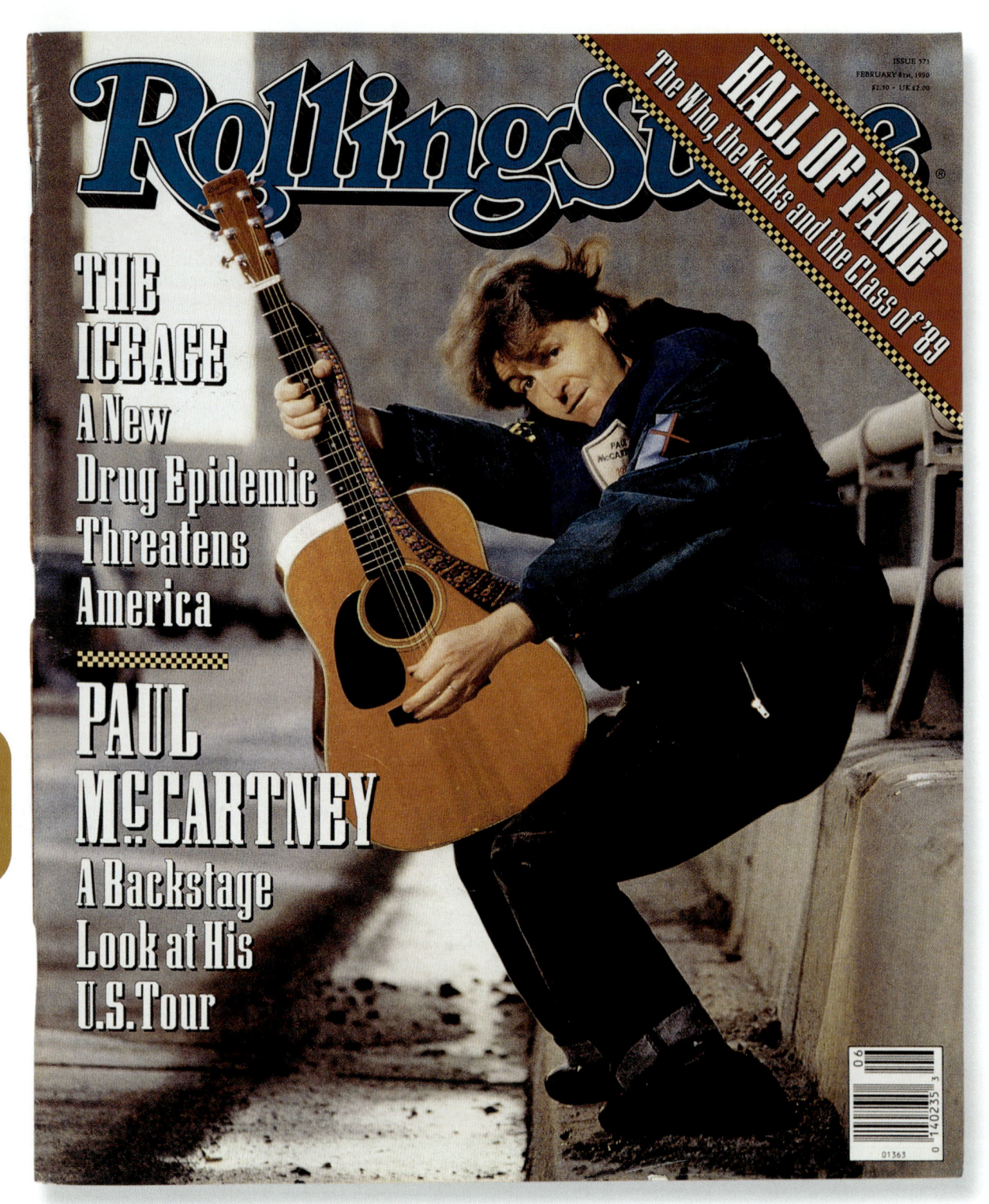

RS 571 | PAUL McCARTNEY | February 8th, 1990 | Photograph by Timothy White

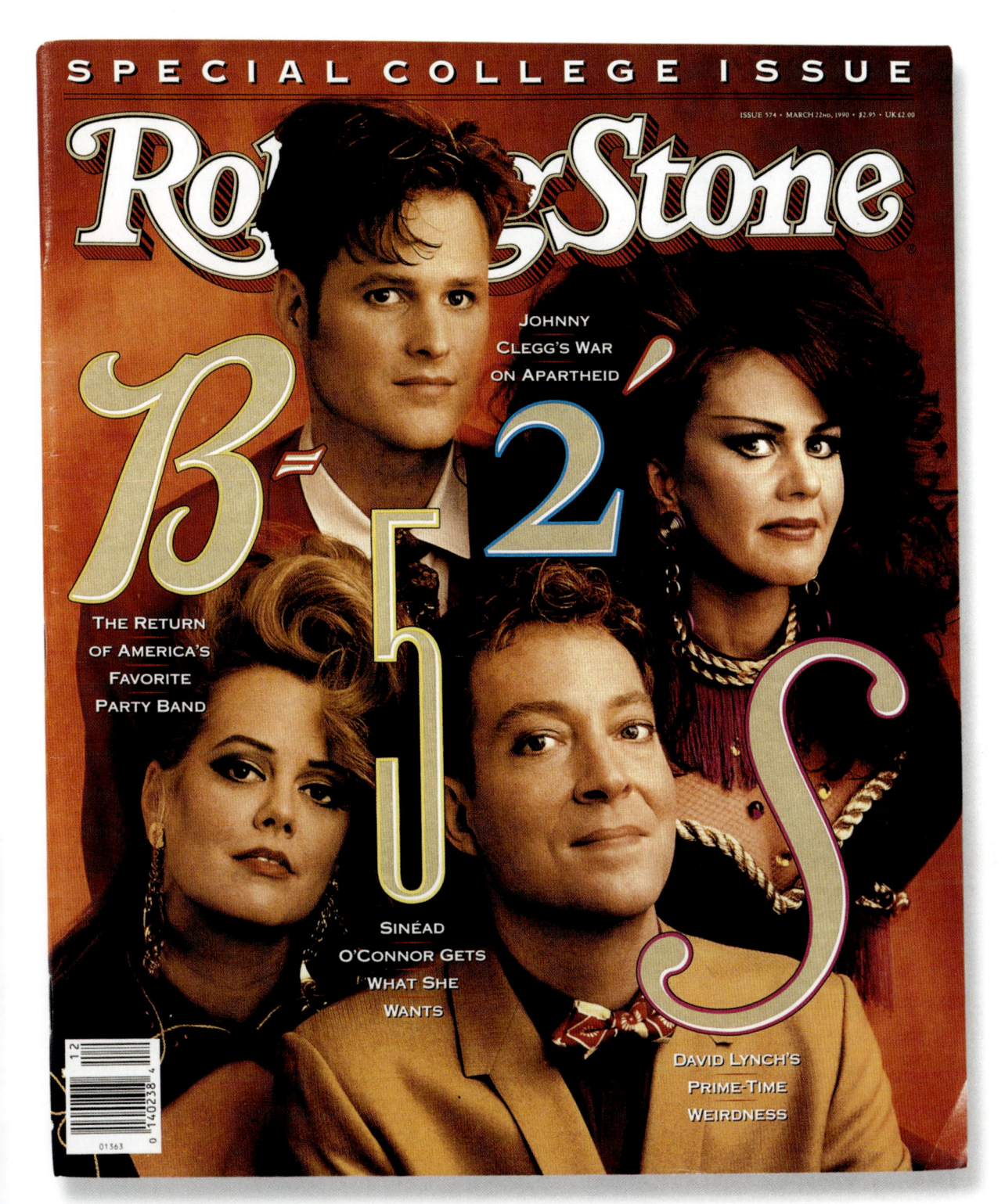

RS 574 | THE B-52'S | March 22nd, 1990 | Photograph by Mark Seliger

50 YEARS OF COVERS • 297

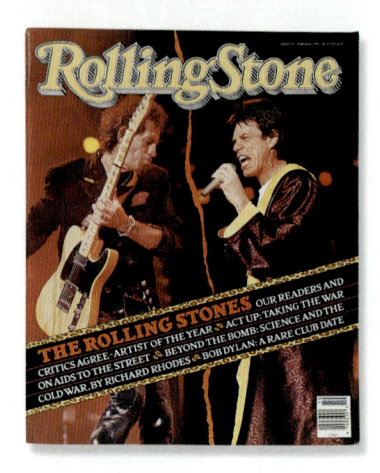

RS 573 | **KEITH RICHARDS & MICK JAGGER**
March 8th, 1990
PHOTOGRAPH BY NEAL PRESTON

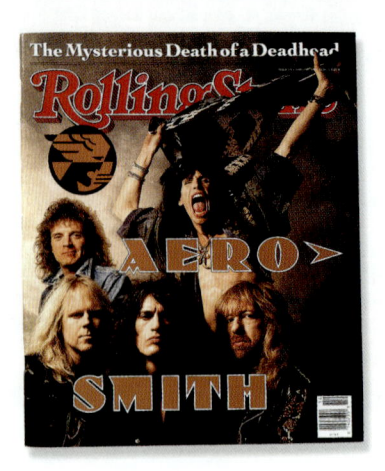

RS 575 | **AEROSMITH**
April 5th, 1990
PHOTOGRAPH BY MARK SELIGER

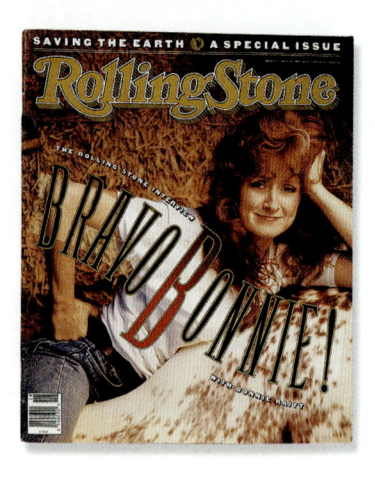

RS 577 | **BONNIE RAITT**
May 3rd, 1990
PHOTOGRAPH BY E.J. CAMP

1990s

For some of us, it began late at night: huddled under bedroom covers with our ears glued to a radio pulling in black voices charged with intense emotion and propelled by a wildly kinetic rhythm through the after-midnight static. Growing up in the white-bread America of the Fifties, we had never heard anything like it, but we reacted, and were converted. We were believers before we knew what it was that had so spectacularly ripped the dull, familiar fabric of our lives. We asked our friends, maybe an older brother or sister. We found out they called it rock & roll. It was so much more vital and alive than any music we had ever heard before. Rock & roll was much more than new music for us. It was an obsession, and a way of life.

For some of us, it began a little later, with our first glimpse of Elvis on the family television set. But for those of us growing up in the Fifties, it didn't seem to matter how or where we first heard the music. Our reactions were remarkably uniform. Here was a sonic cataclysm come bursting (apparently) out of nowhere, with the power to change our lives forever. Because it was obviously, inarguably *our* music. If we had any initial doubt about that, our parents' horrified – or at best dismissive – reactions banished those doubts. Growing up in a world we were only beginning to understand, we had finally found something for us.

[EXCERPT FROM ESSAY ON THE FIFTIES BY ROBERT PALMER]

RS 576 | THE FIFTIES | April 19th, 1990 | Illustration by Terry Allen & Dennis Ortiz-Lopez

1990s

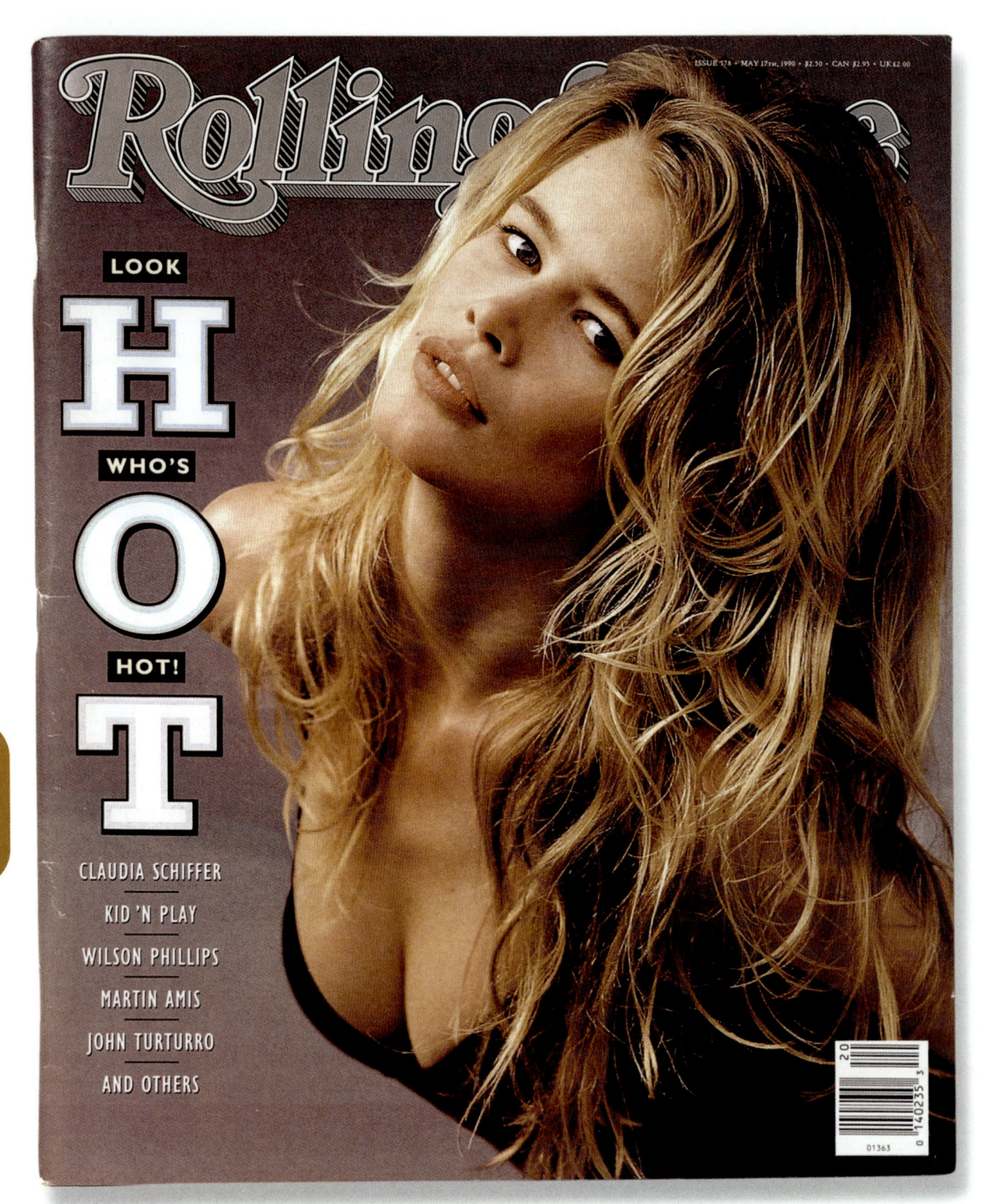

RS 578 | CLAUDIA SCHIFFER | May 17th, 1990 | Photograph by Herb Ritts

300 • ROLLING STONE

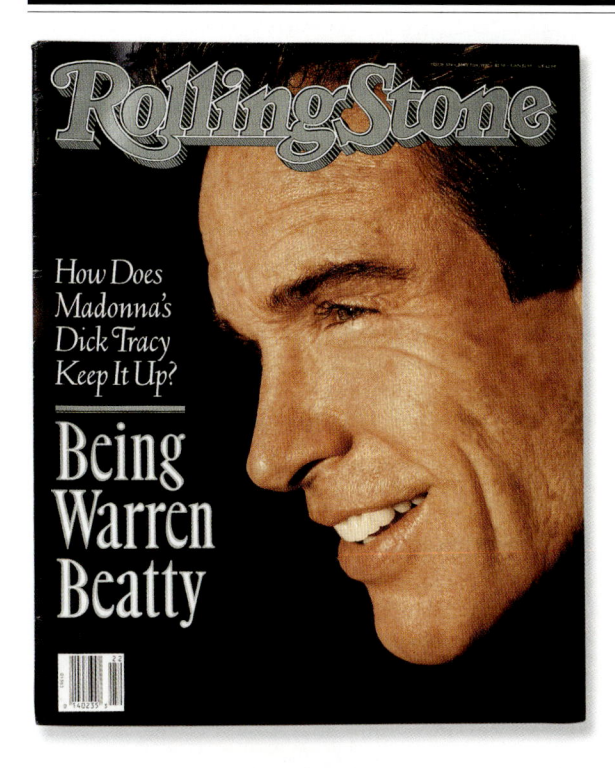

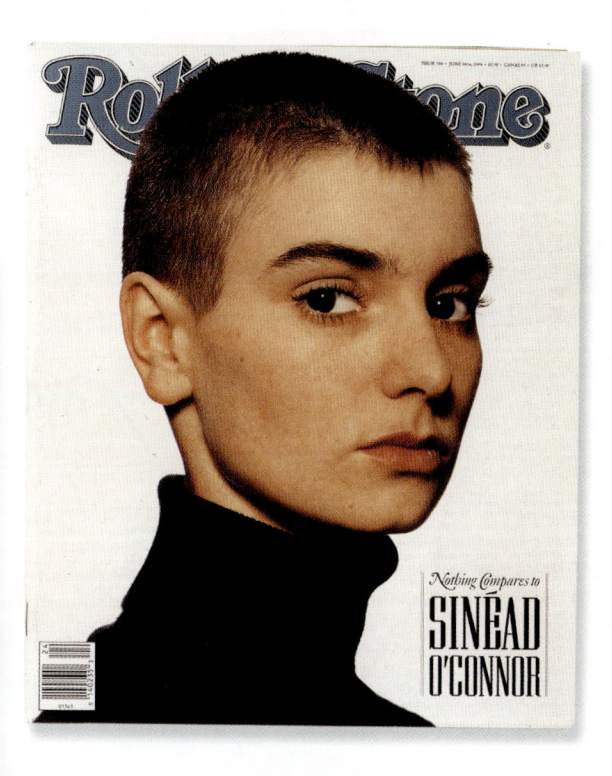

RS 579 | WARREN BEATTY
May 31st, 1990
Photograph by Herb Ritts

RS 580 | SINÉAD O'CONNOR
June 14th, 1990
Photograph by Andrew MacPherson

HE IS A GHOST. HE IS HUMAN ECTOPLASM. HE IS HERE, and then he is gone, and then you aren't sure he was ever here to begin with. He has had sex with everyone, or at least tried. He has had sex with someone you know or someone who knows someone you know or someone you wish you knew, or at least tried. He is famous for sex, he is famous for having sex with the famous, he is famous. He makes mostly good films when he makes films, which is mostly not often. He has had sex with most of his leading ladies. He befriends all women and many politicians and whispers advice to them on the telephone in the dead of night. Or else he does not speak at all to anyone ever, except to those who know him best, if anyone can really know him. He is an adamant enigma, elusive for the sake of elusiveness, which makes him desirable, although for what, no one completely understands. He is much smarter than you think but perhaps not as smart as he thinks, if only because he thinks too much about being smart. He admits to none of this. He admits to nothing much. He denies little. And so his legend grows.

He has talked. And talked. For days, I have listened to him talk. I have listened to him listen to himself talk. I have probed and pelted and listened some more. For days. He speaks slowly, fearfully, cautiously, editing every syllable, slicing off personal color and spontaneous wit, steering away from opinion, introspection, humanness. He is mostly evasive. His pauses are elephantine. Broadway musicals could be mounted during his pauses. He works at this. Ultimately, he renders himself blank. In *Dick Tracy*, he battles a mysterious foe called the Blank. In life, he is the Blank doing battle with himself. It is a fascinating showdown, exhilarating to behold.

To interview Warren Beatty is to want to kill him.

[EXCERPT FROM WARREN BEATTY INTERVIEW BY BILL ZEHME]

ISSUE 581 · JUNE 28TH, 1990 · $2.50 · CAN $2.95 · UK £2.00

RollingSto

THE TRIAL OF ·HUNTER· THOMPSON

EXCLUSIVE!

At Home With

BART SIMPSON

Underachiever or Just a Kid?

MIDNIGHT OIL
Turns to Gold

P.J. O'ROURKE'S
Earth Day

World Party
Soul II Soul
New Girl Groups

MATT GROENING

1990s

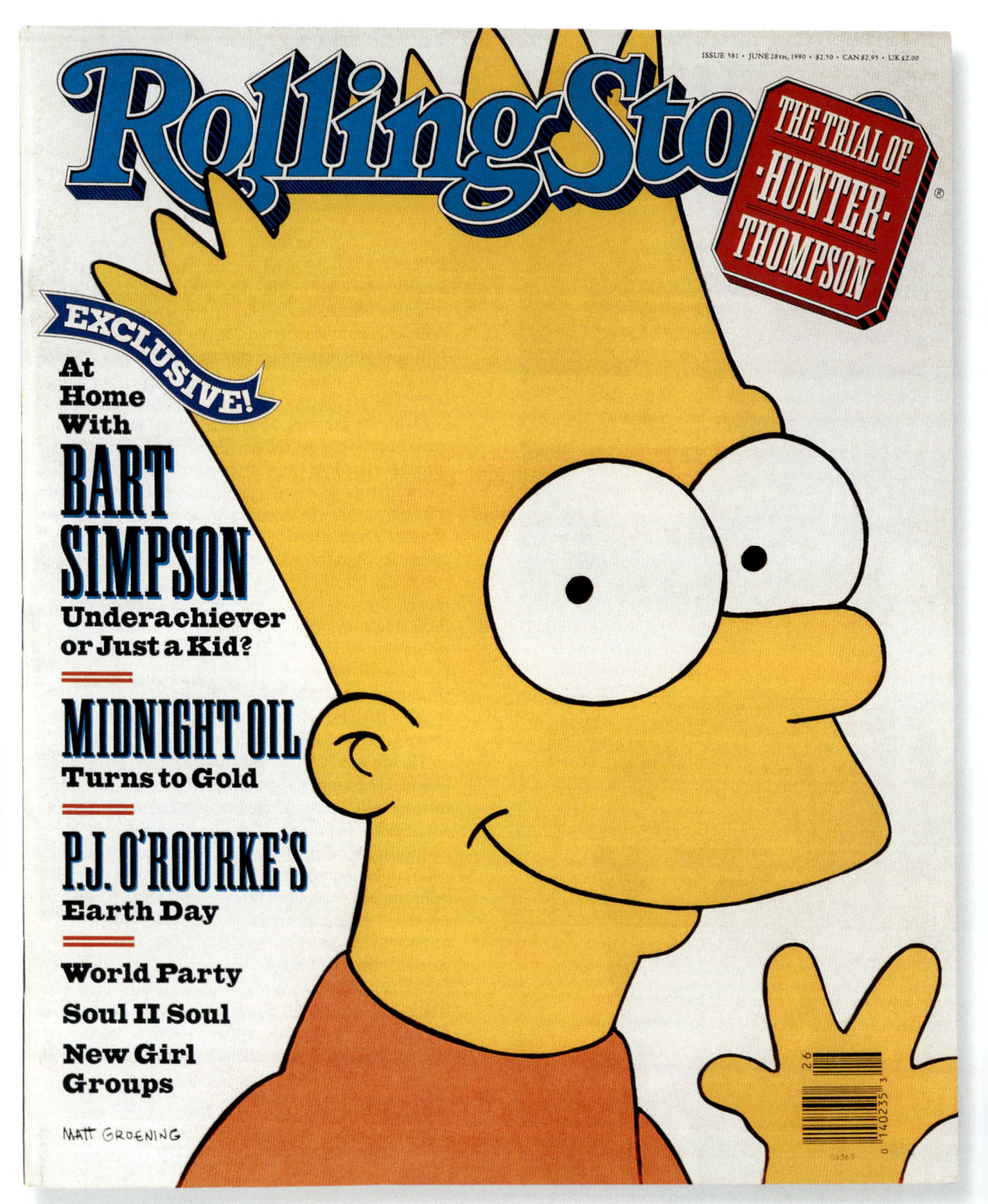

RS 581 | BART SIMPSON | June 28th, 1990 | ILLUSTRATION BY MATT GROENING

SPECIAL DOUBLE ISSUE

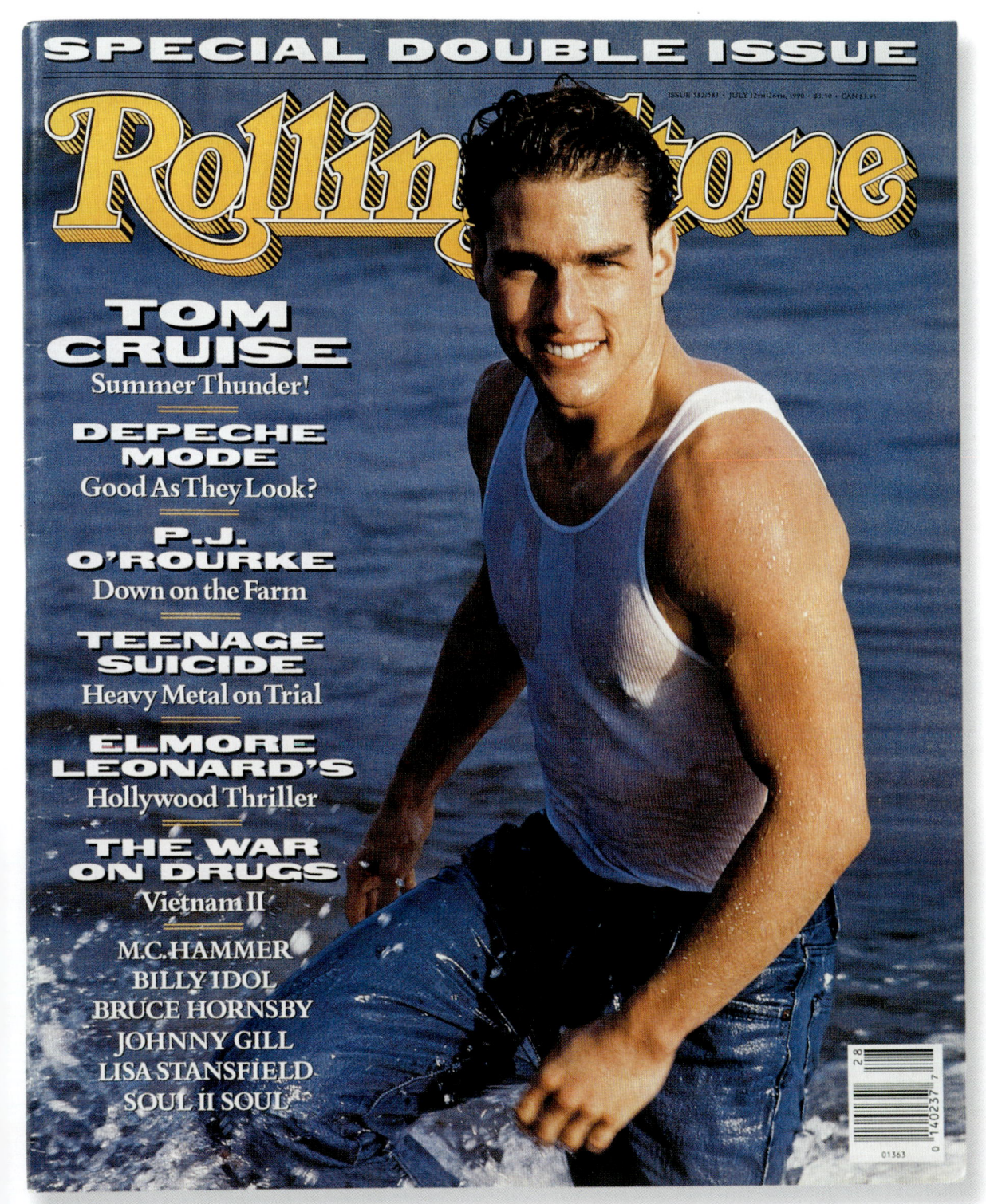

Rolling Stone

TOM CRUISE
Summer Thunder!

DEPECHE MODE
Good As They Look?

P.J. O'ROURKE
Down on the Farm

TEENAGE SUICIDE
Heavy Metal on Trial

ELMORE LEONARD'S
Hollywood Thriller

THE WAR ON DRUGS
Vietnam II

M.C. HAMMER
BILLY IDOL
BRUCE HORNSBY
JOHNNY GILL
LISA STANSFIELD
SOUL II SOUL

RS 582/583 | TOM CRUISE | July 12th – July 26th, 1990 | PHOTOGRAPH BY HERB RITTS

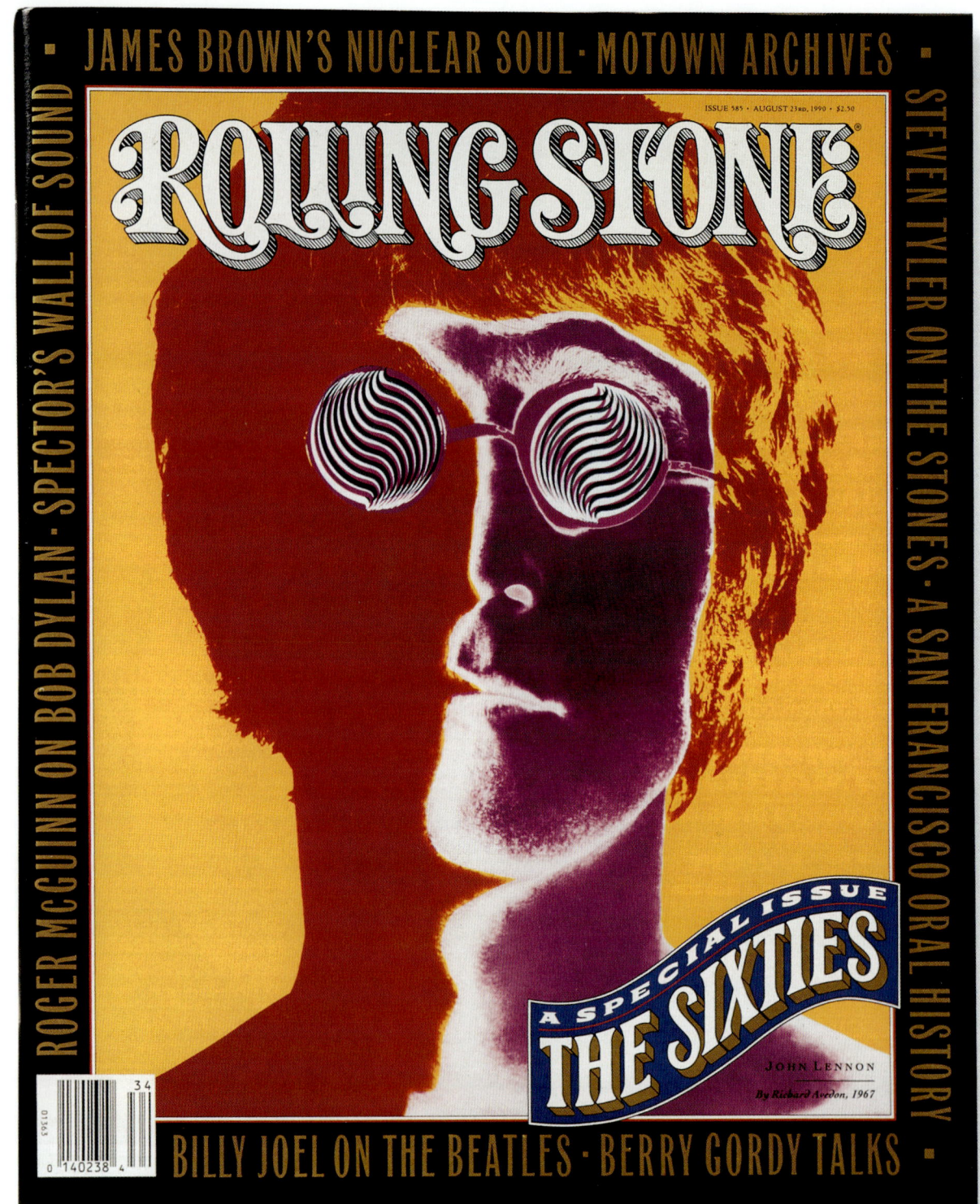

RS 585 | THE SIXTIES – JOHN LENNON | August 23rd, 1990 | Photograph by Richard Avedon

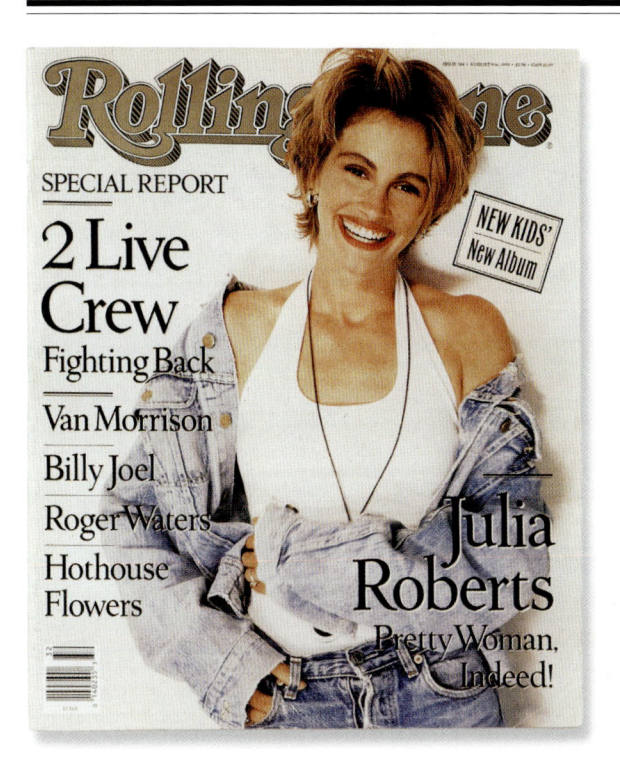

RS 584 | JULIA ROBERTS
August 9th, 1990
PHOTOGRAPH BY HERB RITTS

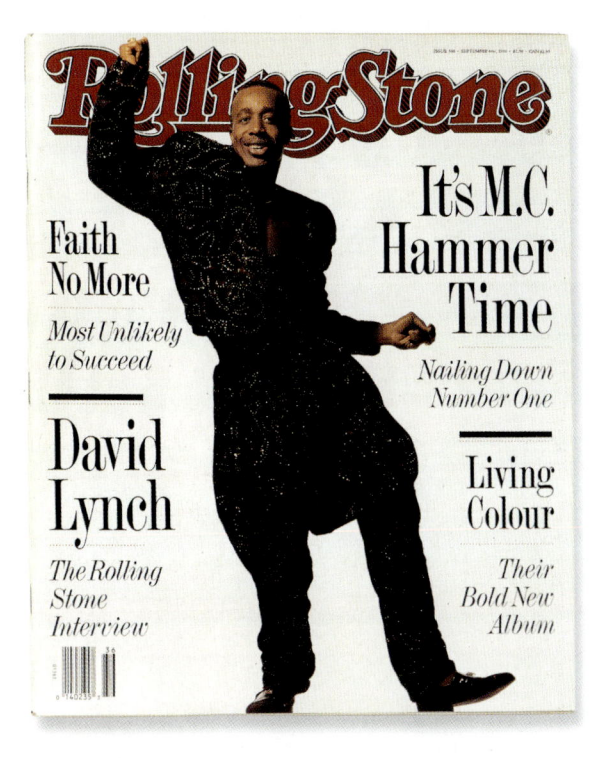

RS 586 | M.C. HAMMER
September 6th, 1990
PHOTOGRAPH BY FRANK W. OCKENFELS 3

FOR A LONG AND UNFORGETTABLE SEASON, ROCK was a voice of unity and liberty. In the 1950s, rock & roll meant disruption: It was the clamor of young people, kicking hard against the Eisenhower era's ethos of vapid repression. By the onset of the 1960s, that spirit had been largely tamed or simply impeded by numerous misfortunes, including the film and army careers of Elvis Presley, the death of Buddy Holly, the blacklisting of Jerry Lee Lewis and Chuck Berry and the persecution of DJ Alan Freed, who had been stigmatized by payola charges by Tin Pan Alley interests and politicians angered with his championing of R&B and rock & roll. In 1960, the music of Frankie Avalon, Paul Anka, Connie Francis and Mitch Miller (an avowed enemy of rock & roll) ruled the airwaves and the record charts, giving some observers the notion that decency and order had returned to the popular mainstream. But within a few years, rock would regain its disruptive power with a joyful vengeance until, by the decade's end, it would be seen as a genuine force of cultural and political consequence. For a long and unforgettable season, it was a truism – or threat, depending on your point of view – that rock & roll could (and should) make a difference: that it was eloquent and inspiring and principled enough to change the world – maybe even to save it.

[EXCERPT FROM THE SIXTIES ESSAY BY MIKAL GILMORE]

1990s

RS 587 | THE SEVENTIES – JIMMY PAGE & ROBERT PLANT | September 20th, 1990 | Photograph by Bob Gruen

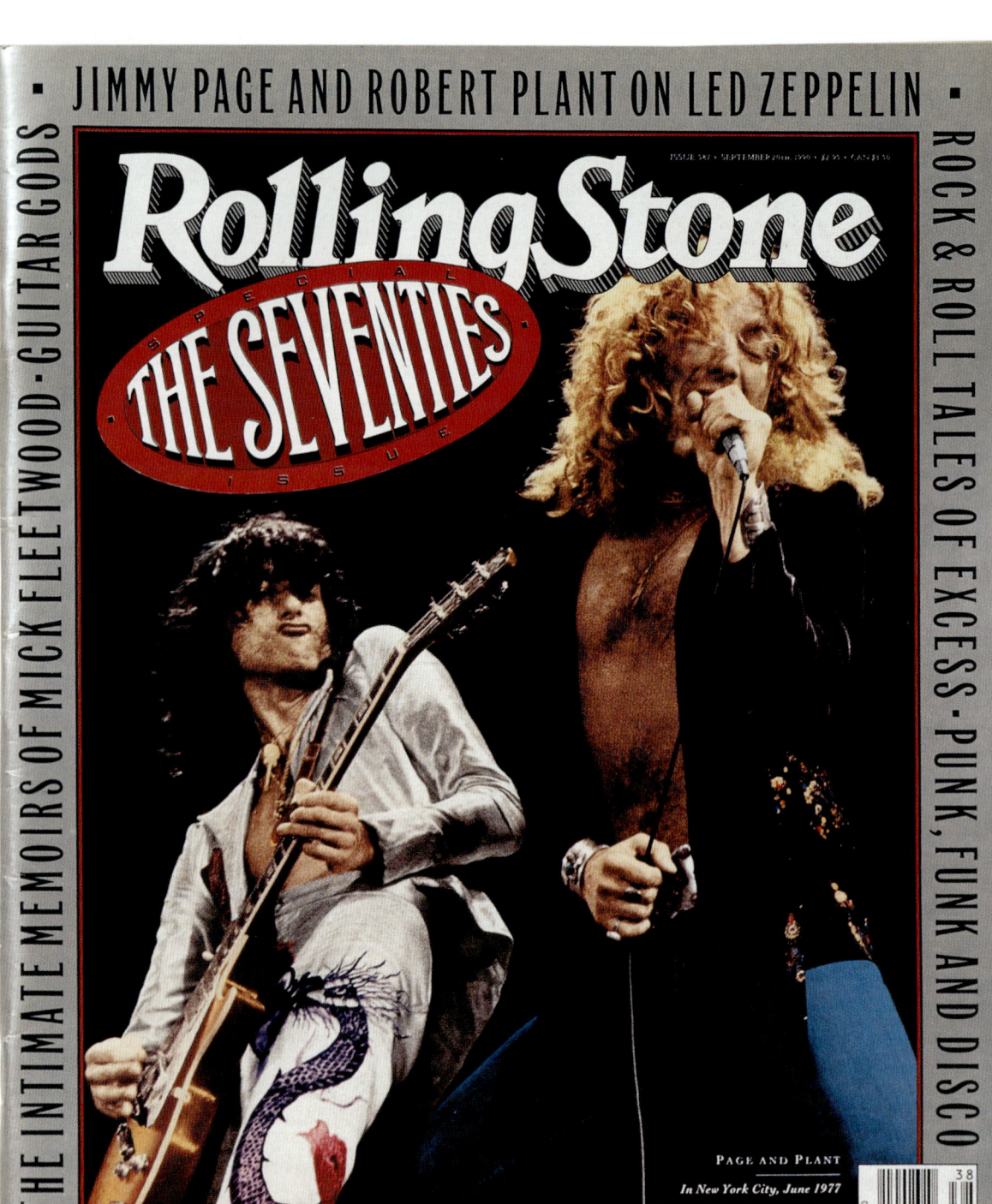

1954 · STEVIE RAY VAUGHAN · 1990

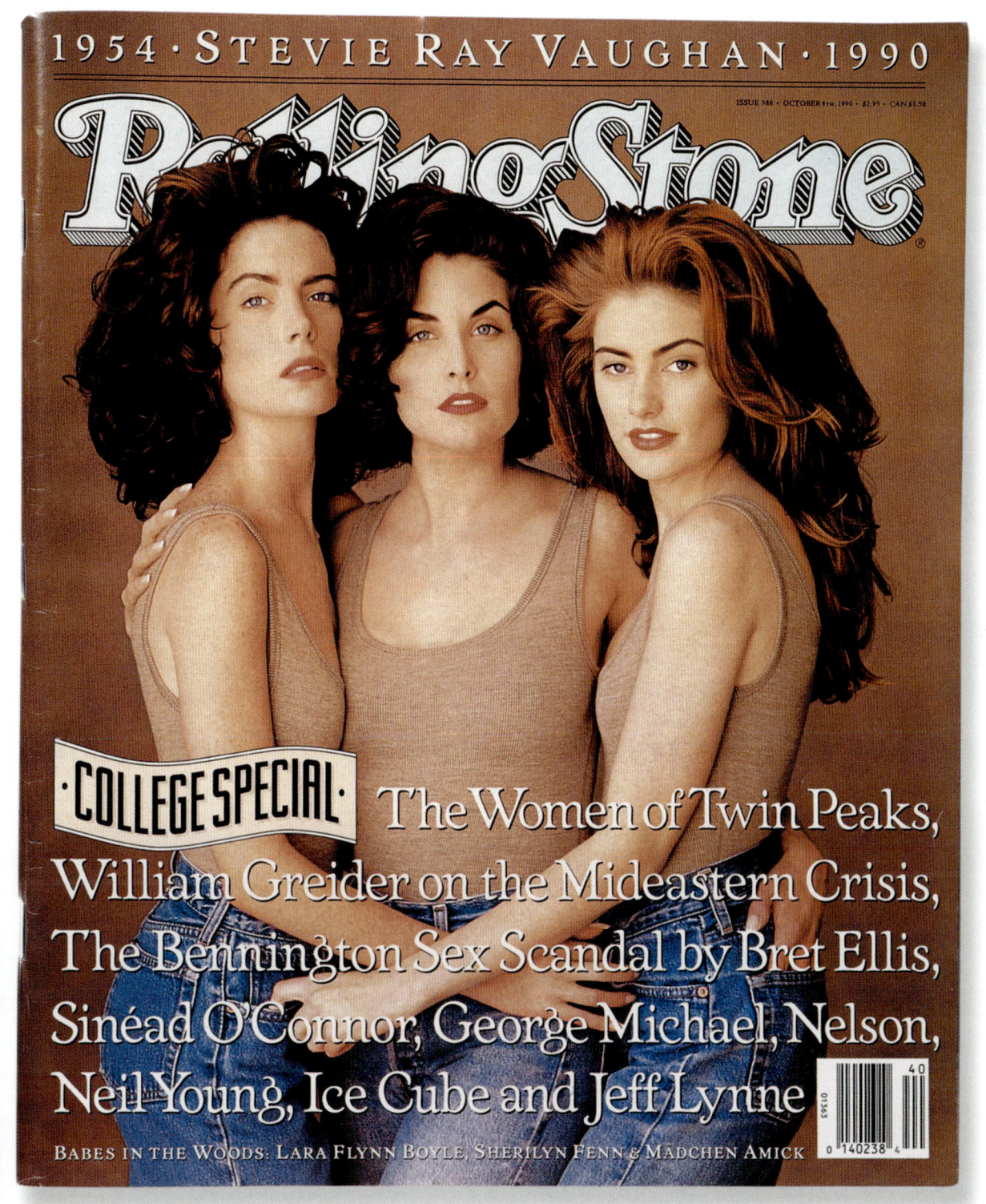

Rolling Stone

ISSUE 588 · OCTOBER 4TH, 1990 · $2.95 · CAN $3.50

· COLLEGE SPECIAL ·

The Women of Twin Peaks, William Greider on the Mideastern Crisis, The Bennington Sex Scandal by Bret Ellis, Sinéad O'Connor, George Michael, Nelson, Neil Young, Ice Cube and Jeff Lynne

BABES IN THE WOODS: LARA FLYNN BOYLE, SHERILYN FENN & MÄDCHEN AMICK

RS 588 | THE WOMEN OF 'TWIN PEAKS' | October 4th, 1990 | Photograph by Matthew Rolston

ISSUE 589 • OCTOBER 18th, 1990 • $2.50 • CAN $2.95

Rolling Stone

1990s

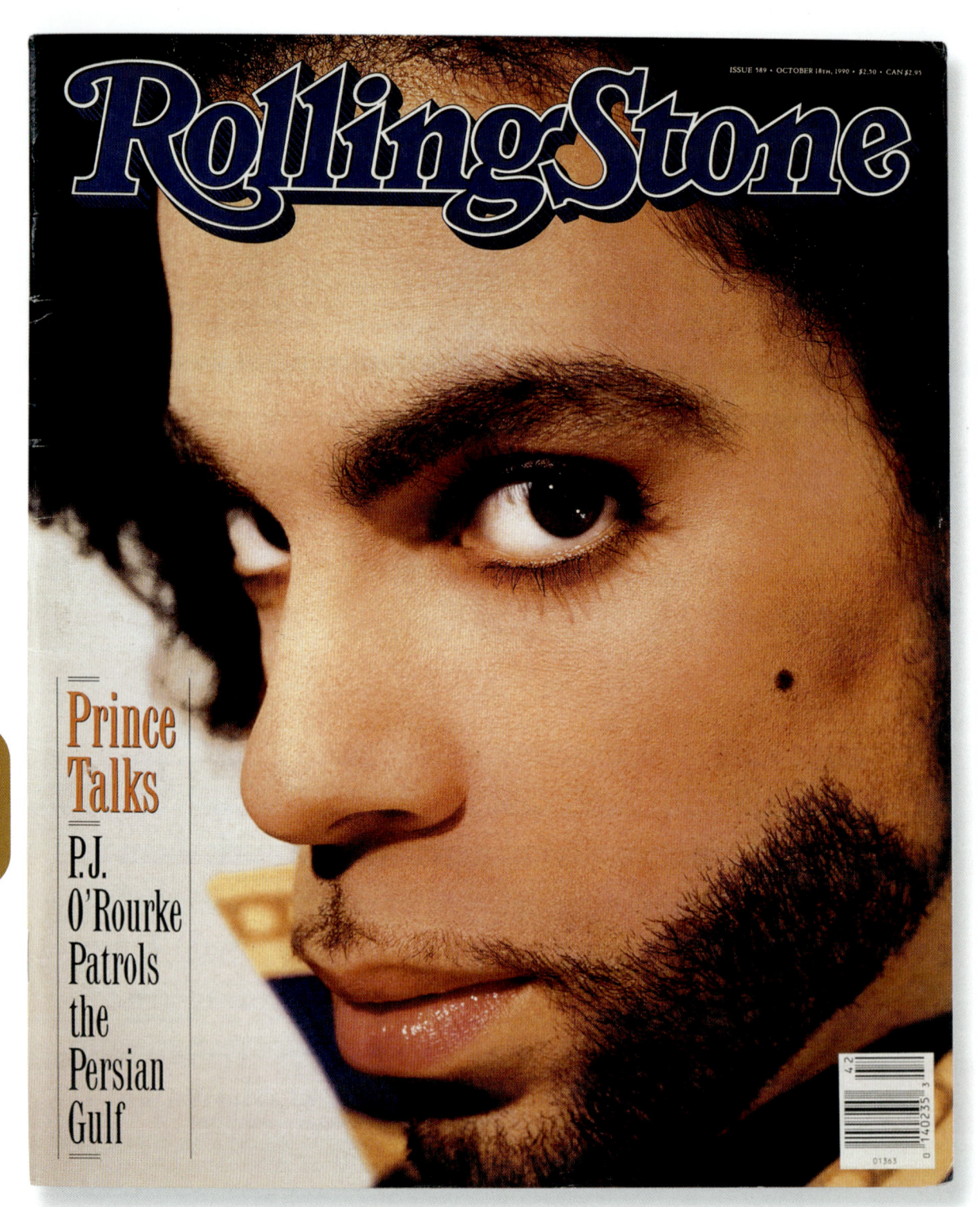

Prince Talks

P.J. O'Rourke Patrols the Persian Gulf

RS 589 | PRINCE | October 18th, 1990 | Photograph by Jeff Katz

308 • ROLLING STONE

VICTORY AND VENGEANCE, BY DR. HUNTER S. THOMPSON

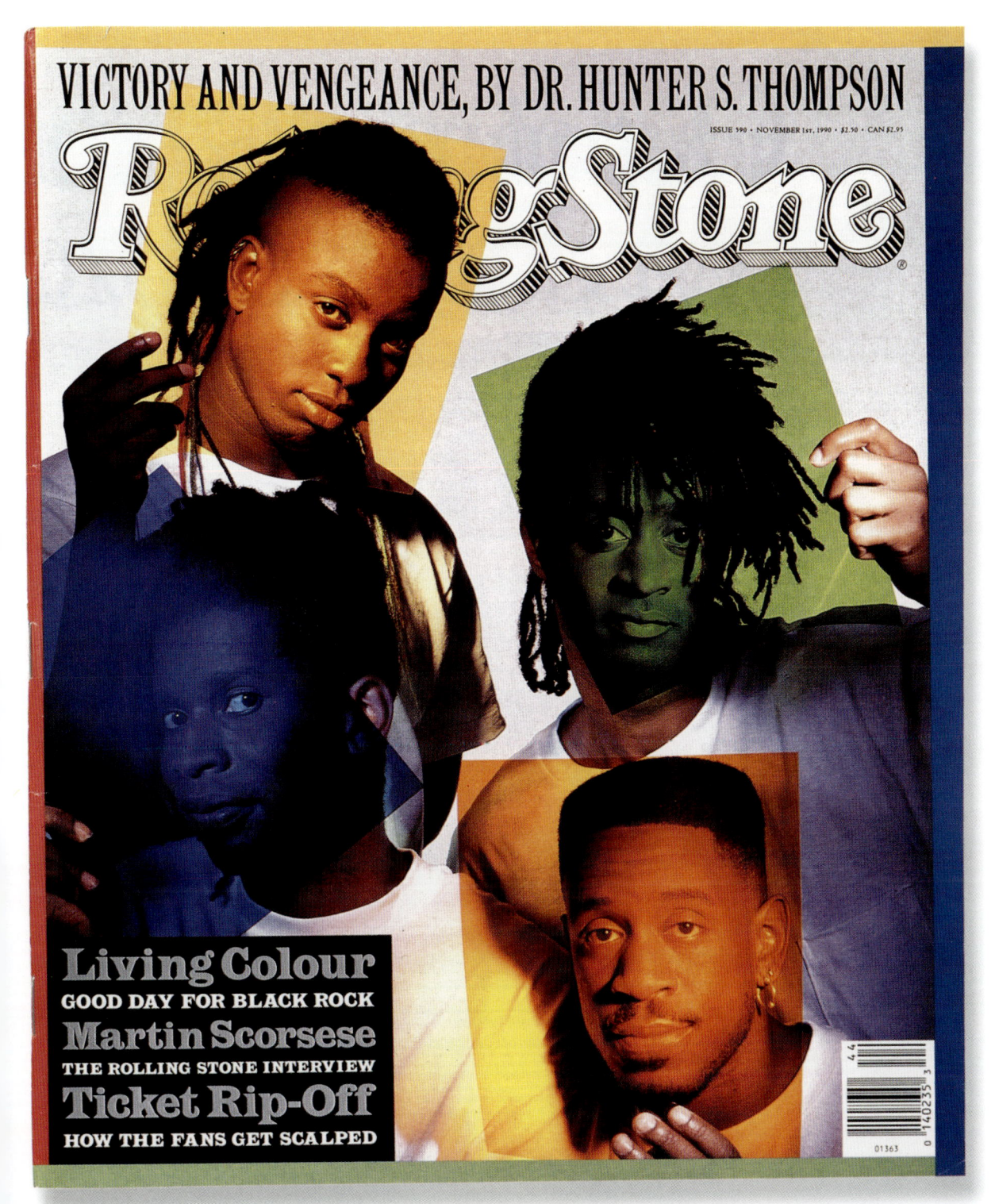

RollingStone

ISSUE 590 • NOVEMBER 1st, 1990 • $2.50 • CAN $2.95

Living Colour
GOOD DAY FOR BLACK ROCK

Martin Scorsese
THE ROLLING STONE INTERVIEW

Ticket Rip-Off
HOW THE FANS GET SCALPED

RS 590 | LIVING COLOUR | November 1st, 1990 | Photograph by Mark Seliger

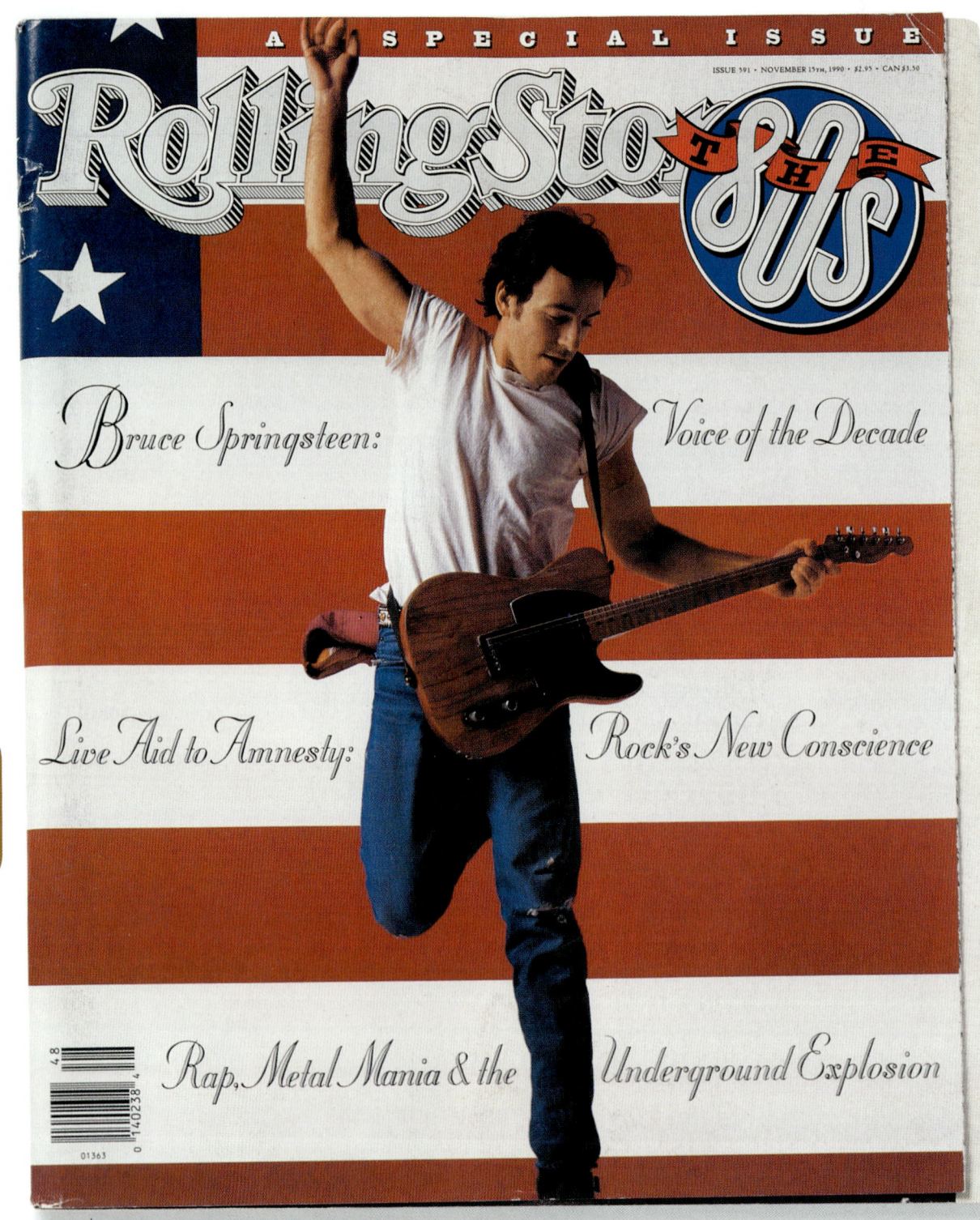

RS 591 | THE EIGHTIES – BRUCE SPRINGSTEEN | November 15th, 1990 | Photograph by Annie Leibovitz

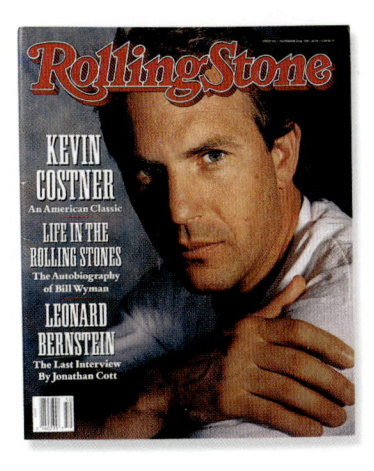

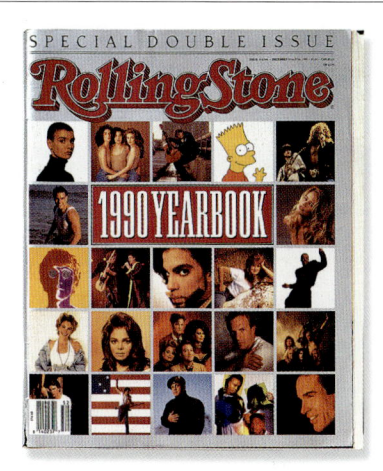

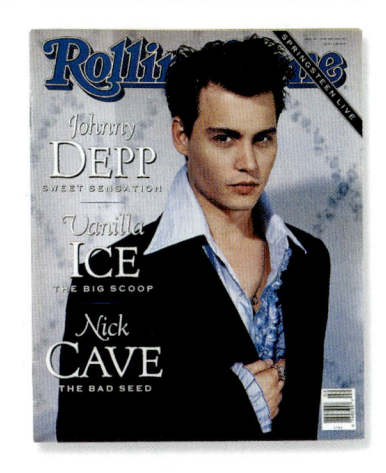

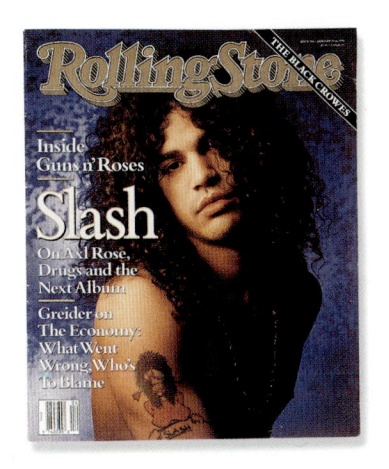

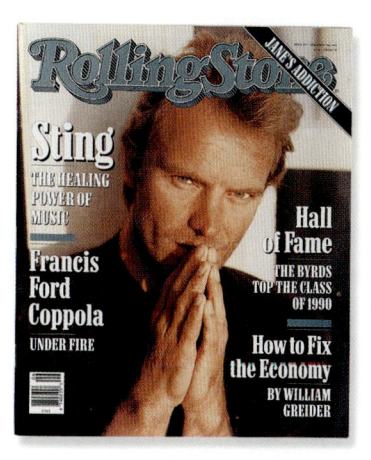

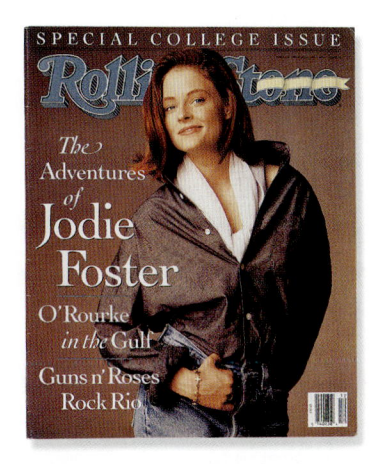

RS 592 | KEVIN COSTNER
November 29th, 1990
PHOTOGRAPH BY GWENDOLEN CATES

RS 593/594 | 1990 YEARBOOK
December 13th – 27th, 1990
VARIOUS PHOTOGRAPHERS

RS 595 | JOHNNY DEPP
January 10th, 1991
PHOTOGRAPH BY HERB RITTS

RS 596 | SLASH
January 24th, 1991
PHOTOGRAPH BY MARK SELIGER

RS 597 | STING
February 7th, 1991
PHOTOGRAPH BY HERB RITTS

RS 600 | JODIE FOSTER
March 21st, 1991
PHOTOGRAPH BY MATTHEW ROLSTON

50 YEARS OF COVERS • 311

Rolling Stone

ROBIN WILLIAMS
Fears of a CLOWN

ROGER McGUINN

STING

King's X

ISSUE 598 · FEBRUARY 21st, 1991 · $2.50 · CAN $2.95

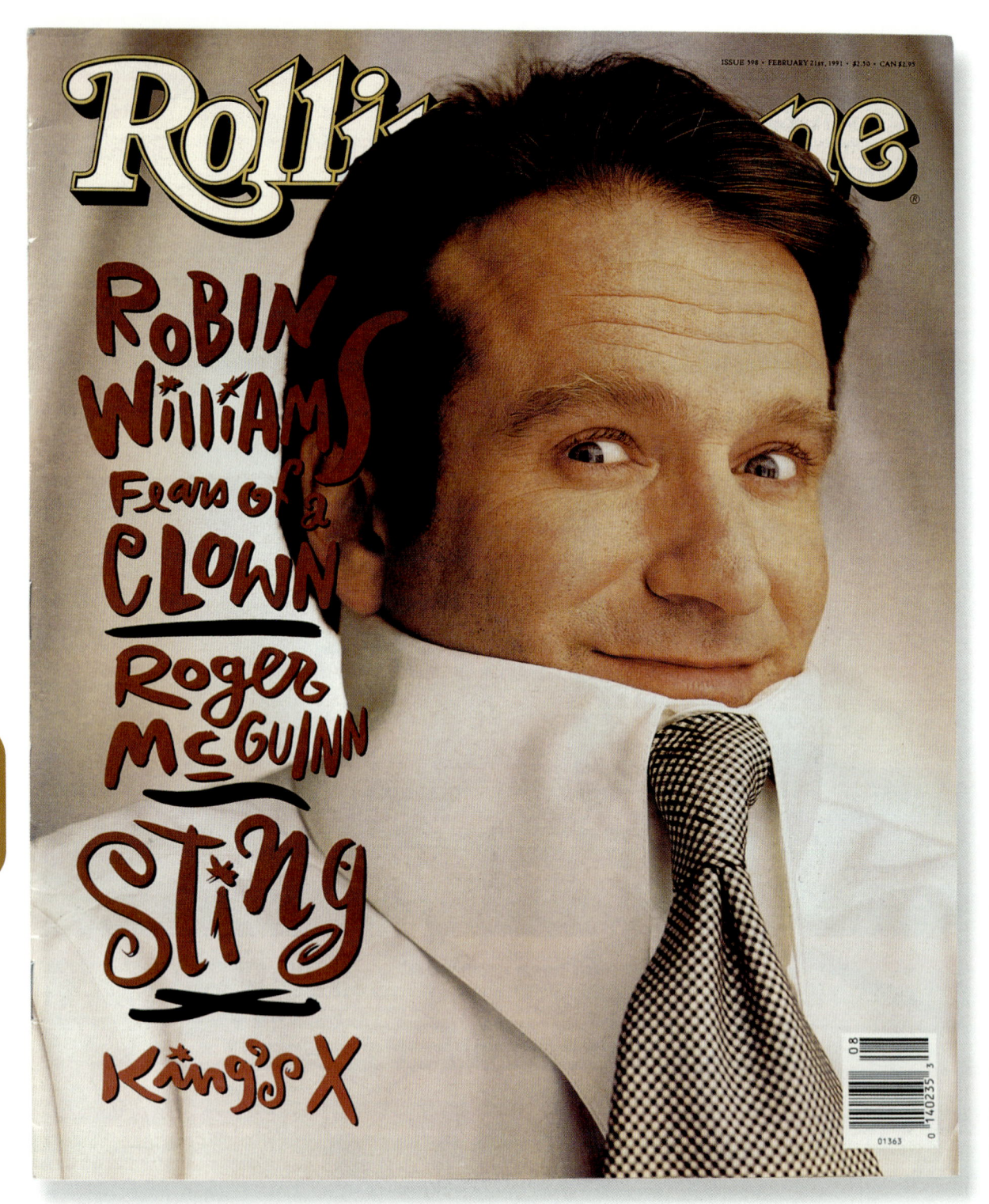

RS 598 | ROBIN WILLIAMS | February 21st, 1991 | Photograph by Mark Seliger

READERS SOUND OFF: ANNUAL MUSIC AWARDS

RollingStone

ISSUE 599 • MARCH 7TH, 1991 • $2.50 • CAN $2.95

O'ROURKE IN THE GULF

Artist
of the Year
Sinéad
O'CONNOR

The
Rolling Stone
Interview

RS 599 | SINÉAD O'CONNOR | March 7th, 1991 | Photograph by Herb Ritts

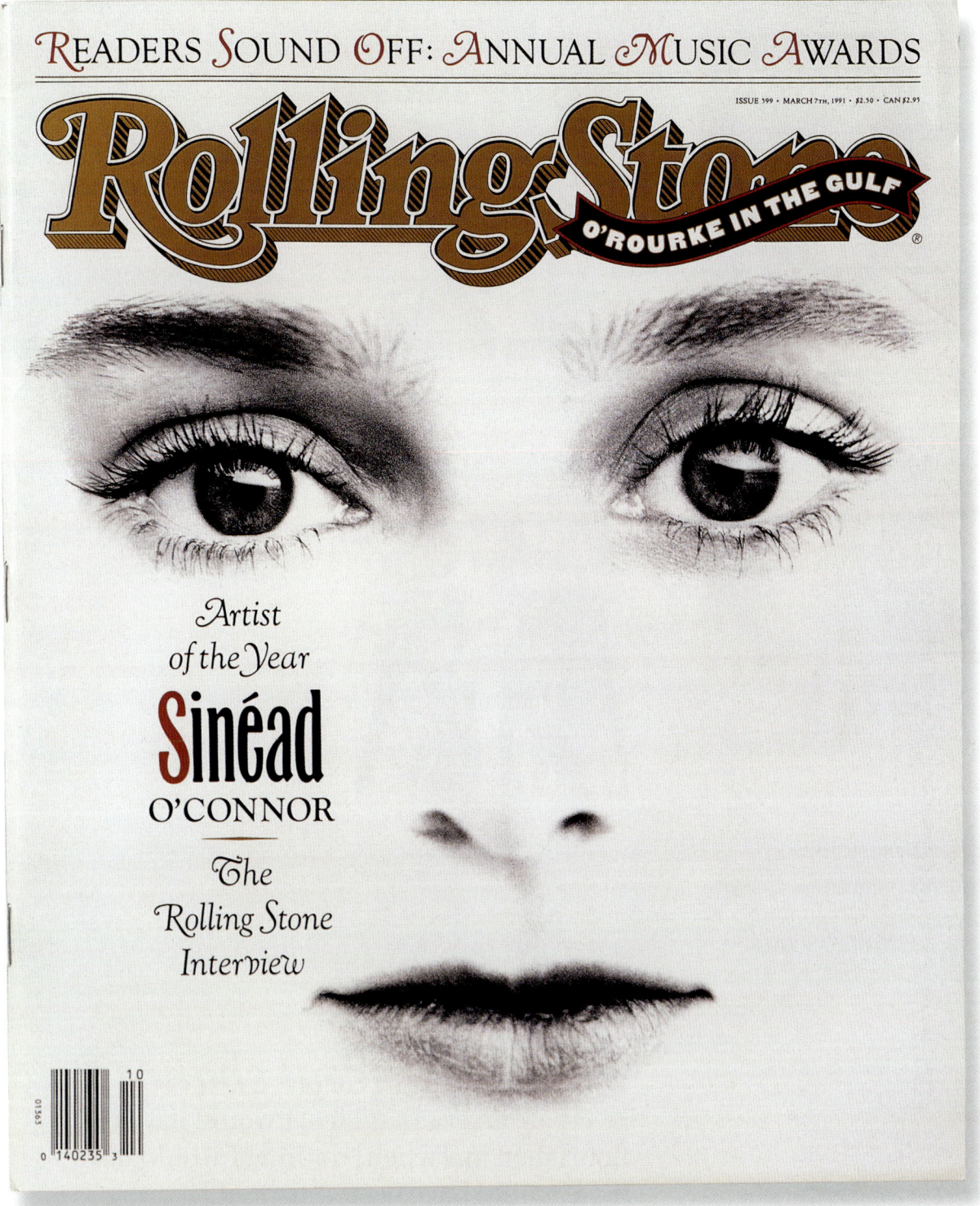

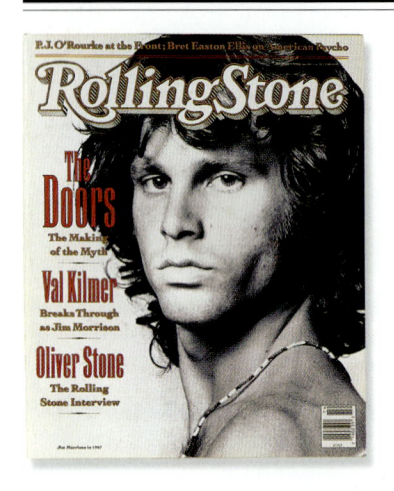

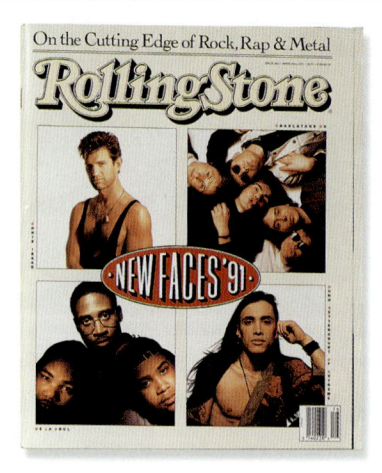

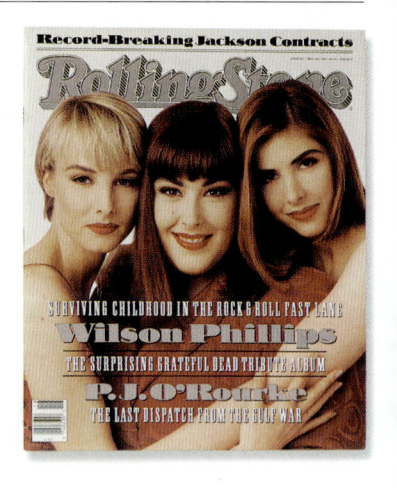

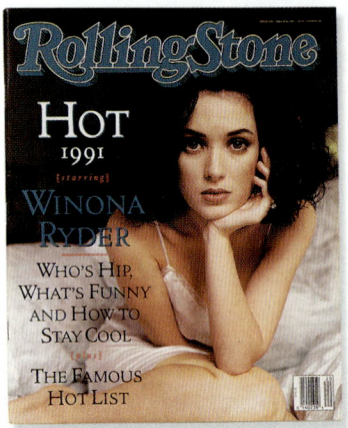

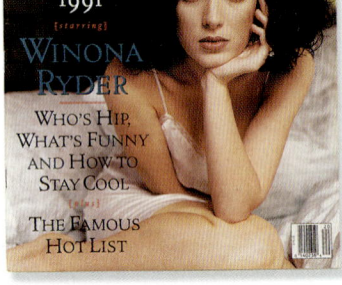

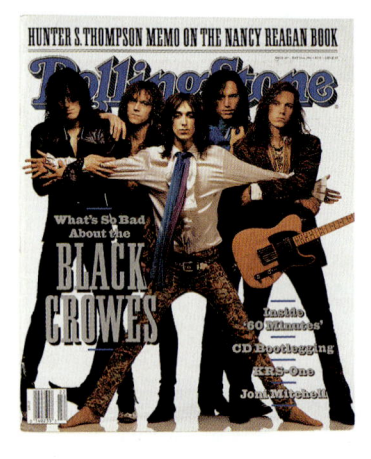

1990s

RS 601 | JIM MORRISON
April 4th, 1991
Photograph by Joel Brodsky

RS 602 | NEW FACES 1991
April 18th, 1991
Various photographers

RS 603 | WILSON PHILLIPS
May 2nd, 1991
Photograph by Andrew Eccles

RS 604 | WINONA RYDER
May 16th, 1991
Photograph by Herb Ritts

RS 605 | THE BLACK CROWES
May 30th, 1991
Photograph by Mark Seliger

"This was a great chance to re-create an era that I feel I would have really flourished in, [when] nothing I would have done would have been censored."

—*Madonna*

314 • ROLLING STONE

Madonna BIG-TIME GIRL TALK
The ROLLING STONE INTERVIEW *by* **CARRIE FISHER**

ISSUE 606 • JUNE 13TH, 1991 • $2.50 • CAN $2.95

RollingStone

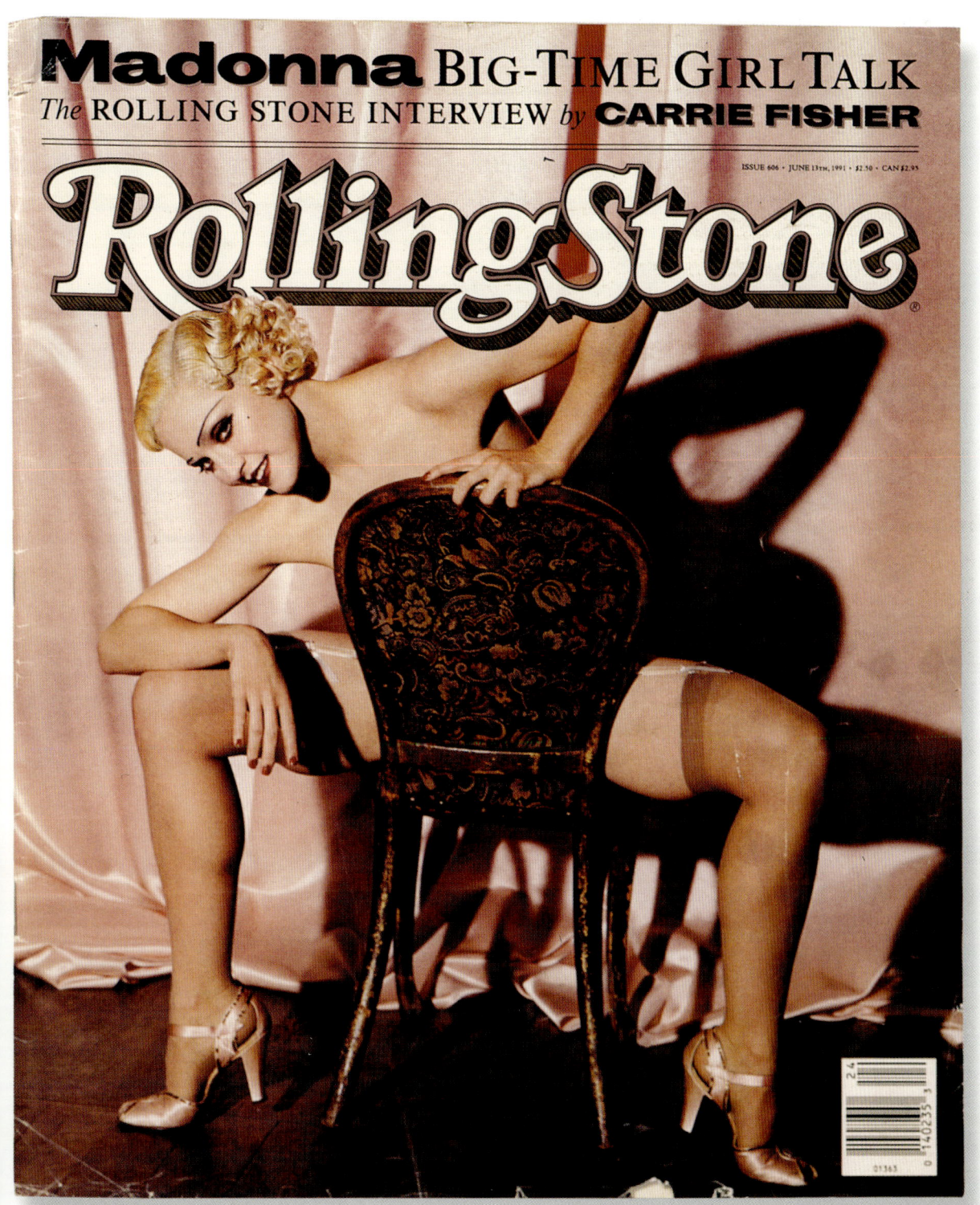

RS 606 | MADONNA | June 13th, 1991 | Photograph by Steven Meisel

50 YEARS OF COVERS • 315

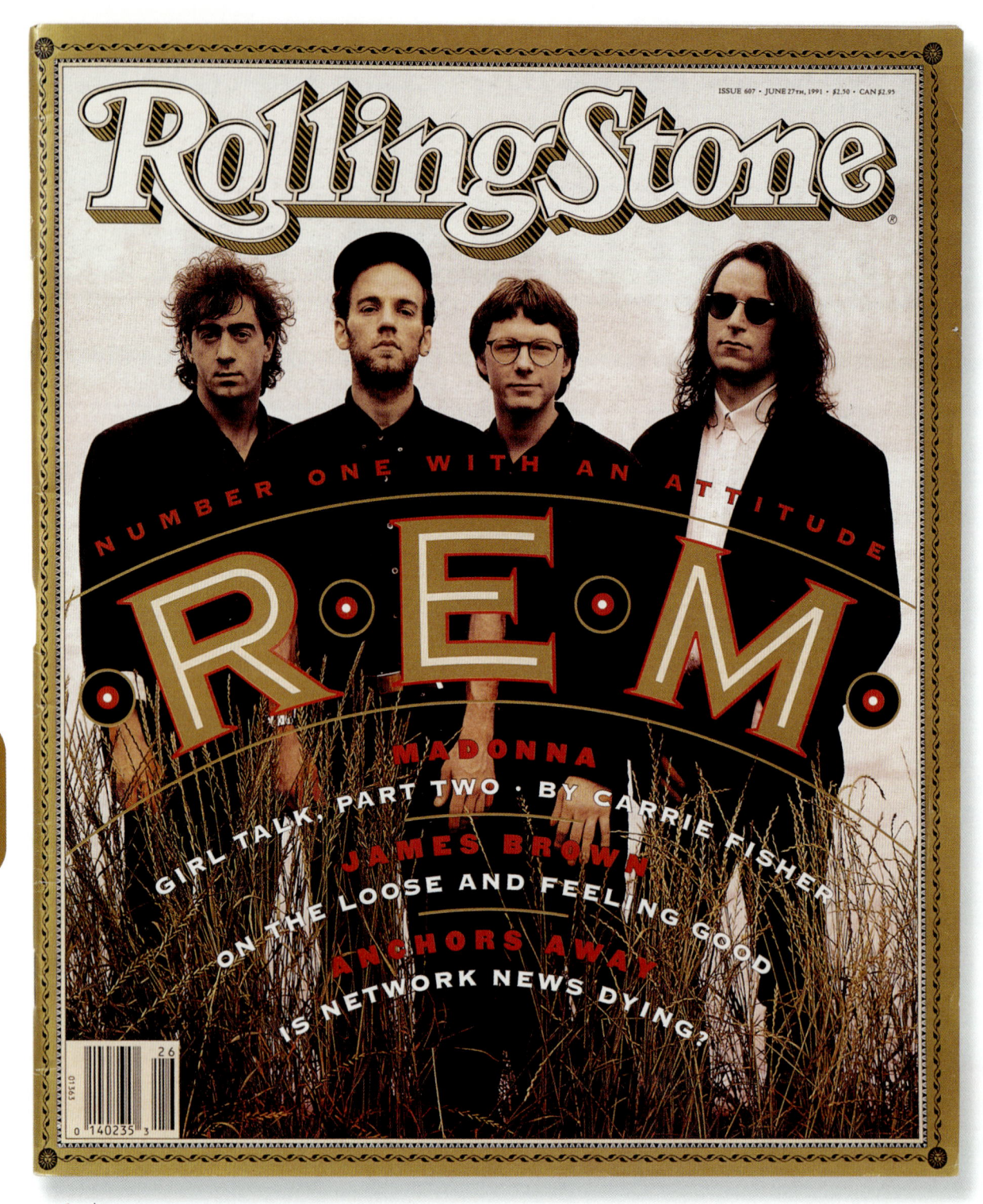

RS 607 | R.E.M. | June 27th, 1991 | Photograph by Frank W. Ockenfels 3

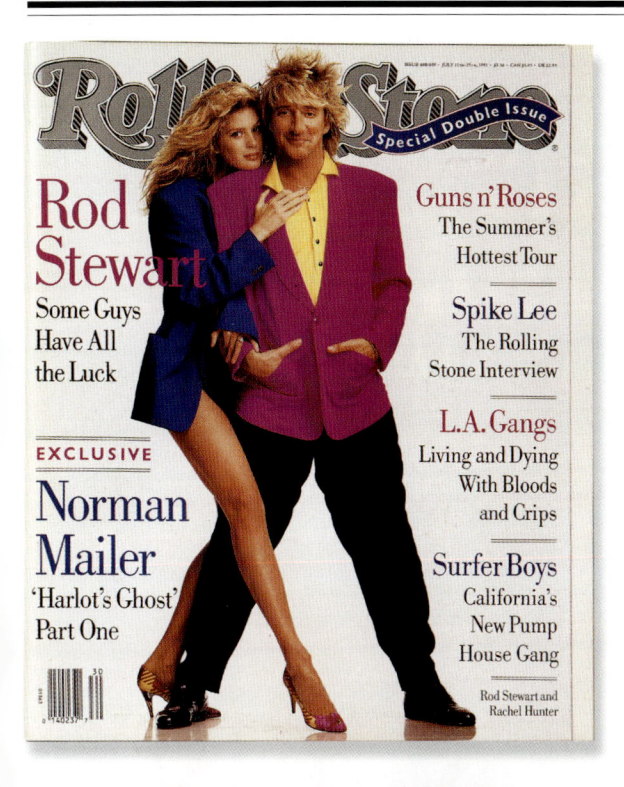

RS 608/609 | ROD STEWART
& RACHEL HUNTER
July 11th – July 25th, 1991
Photograph by Andrew Eccles

RS 610 | TOM PETTY
August 8th, 1991
Photograph by Mark Seliger

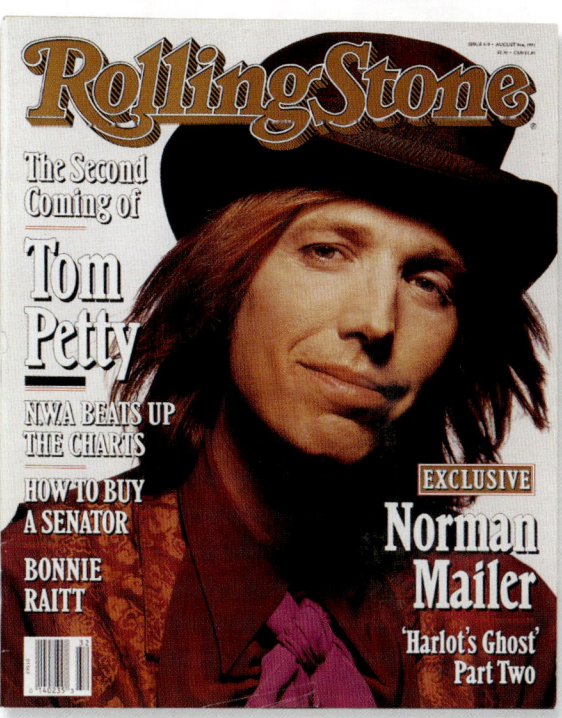

"THIS IS A DAY LIKE I THOUGHT being a pop star would be like when I was a kid. You get in the limo, you go across town to do a photo session, you buy a shirt and then wear it right away and get photographed for the cover of Rolling Stone. You get in another limo with a couple of journalists who hang on your every word, and then go speak to Southeast Asia." —*Peter Buck*

ROLLING STONE

ISSUE 611 • AUGUST 22ND, 1991 • $2.50 • CAN $2.95

GUNS N' ROSES
What Happened in St. Louis?

EXCLUSIVE NORMAN MAILER
'Harlot's Ghost' Part Three

THE BIG SHOT

Schwarzenegger

METALLICA
L.L. COOL J
SKID ROW

1990s

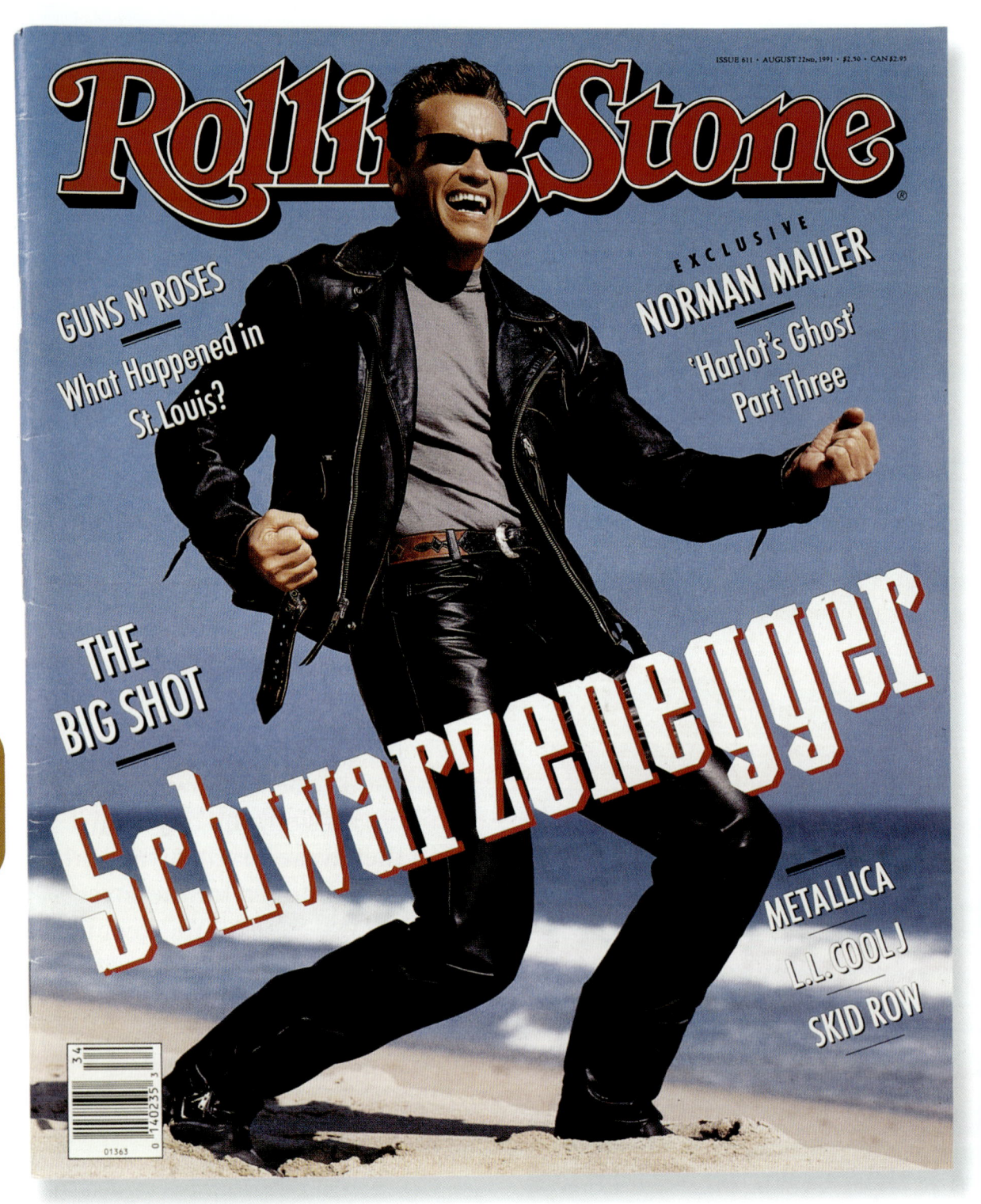

RS 611 | ARNOLD SCHWARZENEGGER | August 22nd, 1991 | Photograph by Herb Ritts

MEN ARE IN CRISIS, whereas he is not. He does not know the meaning of "crisis." Or perhaps he does, but he pretends otherwise. He is Austrian, after all, and some things do not translate easily between cultures. (Lederhosen, for instance.) Throughout the world he is called Arnold, but that is because there are too many letters in Schwarzenegger. By now everyone has come to know that the literal meaning of Schwarzenegger is "black plowman," and like many black plowmen before him, Arnold knows exactly what it feels like when a horse falls on top of him. There is much pain, yes, but pain means little to Arnold, especially when there are stuntmen available. Anyway, Arnold is never in crisis. For this reason, it is imperative that Arnold be Arnold so that others may learn. And, from what society tells us, there has never been a more crucial epoch in history for Arnold to be alive, which is, at the very least, pretty convenient.

[EXCERPT FROM RS 611 COVER STORY BY BILL ZEHME]

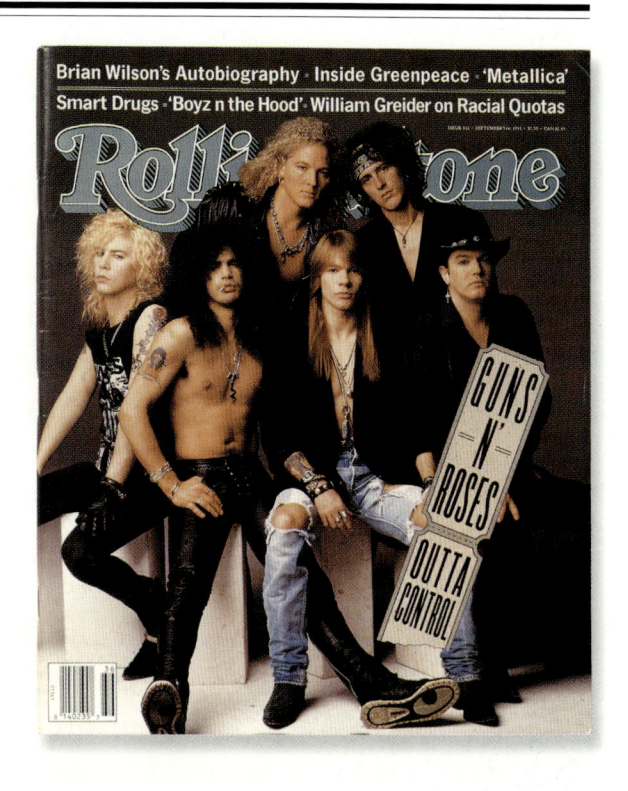

RS 612 | GUNS N' ROSES
September 5th, 1991
PHOTOGRAPH BY HERB RITTS

"PEOPLE WANT SOMETHING, AND THEY WANT IT AS soon as they can get it. Needy people. And I'm the same way, but I want it to be right – I don't want it to be half-assed. Since we put out *Appetite for Destruction*, I've watched a lot of bands put out two to four albums, and who cares? They went out, they did a big tour, they were big rock stars for that period of time. That's what everybody's used to now – the record companies push that. But I want no part of that."

—*Axl Rose*

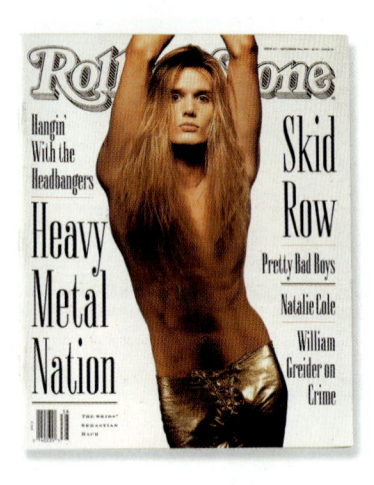

RS 613 | SEBASTIAN BACH
September 19th, 1991
Photograph by Mark Seliger

1990s

"I just got arrested," Paul said over the telephone to his sister, Abby. "I'm gonna disappear now."

A reluctant fugitive since the fateful night of July 26th, Paul Reubens has kept in touch with only three friends. He won't tell them where he is. In his house in the Hollywood Hills, an answering machine takes calls from well-wishers. Paul's secretary calls back to say thanks.

The day after he was arrested for indecent exposure in a Florida pornographic theater, the bright red door of *Pee-wee's Playhouse* – a Saturday-morning kids' show that even parents loved – was boarded up. Unsold Pee-wee Herman dolls became orphans. Disney-MGM Studios dropped him from its two-minute tour video. Executives at Disney, CBS and Toys 'R' Us had acted swiftly to protect the interests of American children.

Bad boy, Pee-wee. Rest in peace, Pee-wee Herman. *Nyah, nyah, nyah, nyah, nyah.* An adult playing a child, he needed to be punished like a child for acting like an adult. Paul's own lawyer provided an epitaph: "His career is over." It was as if redheaded Randy, the Playhouse bully, had poisoned the gestalt: no more gentle dinosaurs or anthropomorphic furniture, no more secret word.

[EXCERPT FROM RS 614 COVER STORY BY PETER WILKINSON]

Rolling Stone

ISSUE 614 · OCTOBER 3RD, 1991 · $2.95 · CAN $3.50

WHO Killed Pee wee Herman?

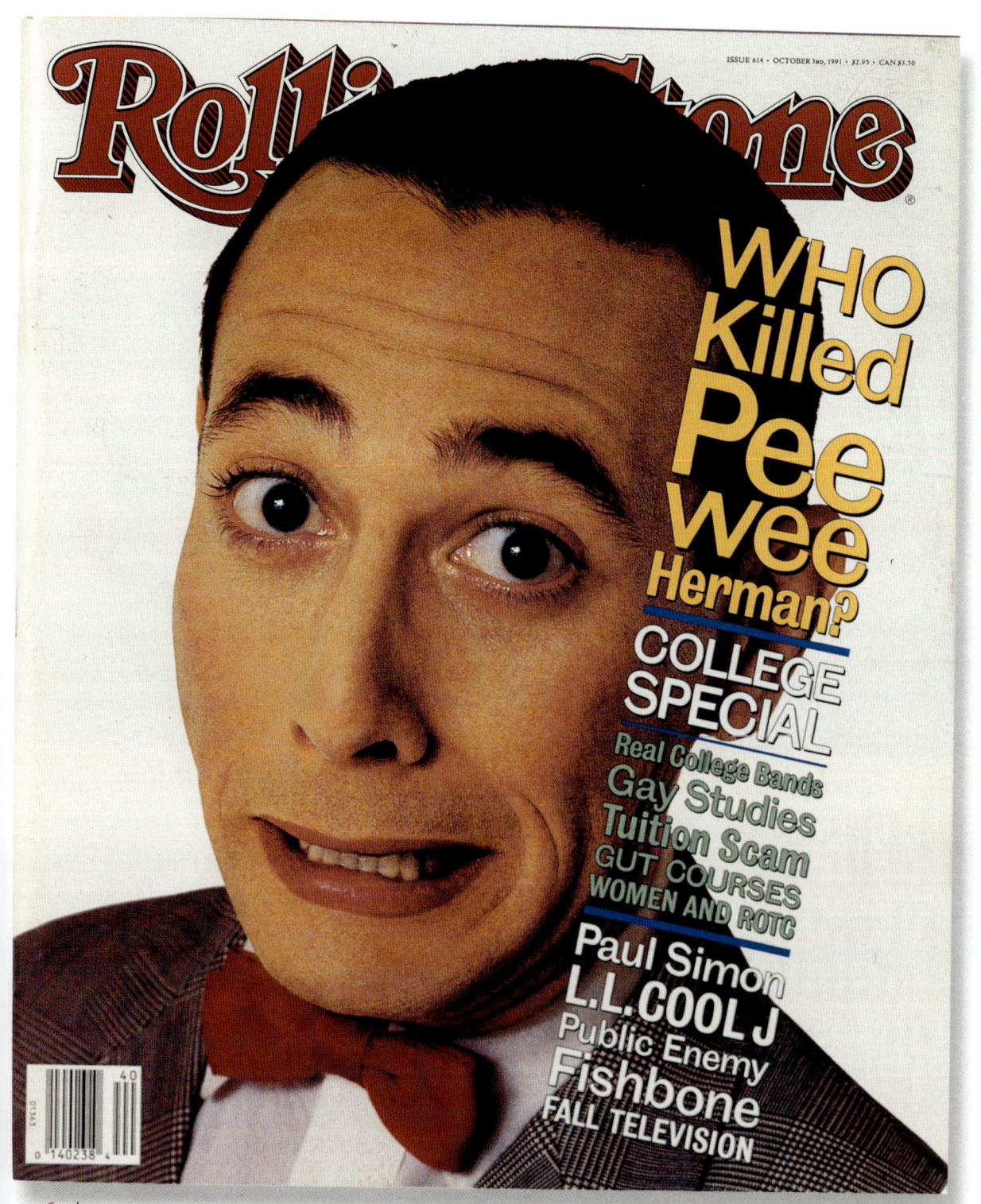

COLLEGE SPECIAL

Real College Bands
Gay Studies
Tuition Scam
GUT COURSES
WOMEN AND ROTC

Paul Simon
L.L. COOL J
Public Enemy
Fishbone
FALL TELEVISION

RS 614 | PEE-WEE HERMAN | October 3rd, 1991 | Photograph by Janette Beckman

ROLLING STONE

ISSUE 615 • OCTOBER 17TH, 1991 • $2.50 • CAN $2.95

Guns n' Roses' New LPs

Three Days at the Moscow Barricades

The Rolling Stone Interview

Eric Clapton's Blues

1990s

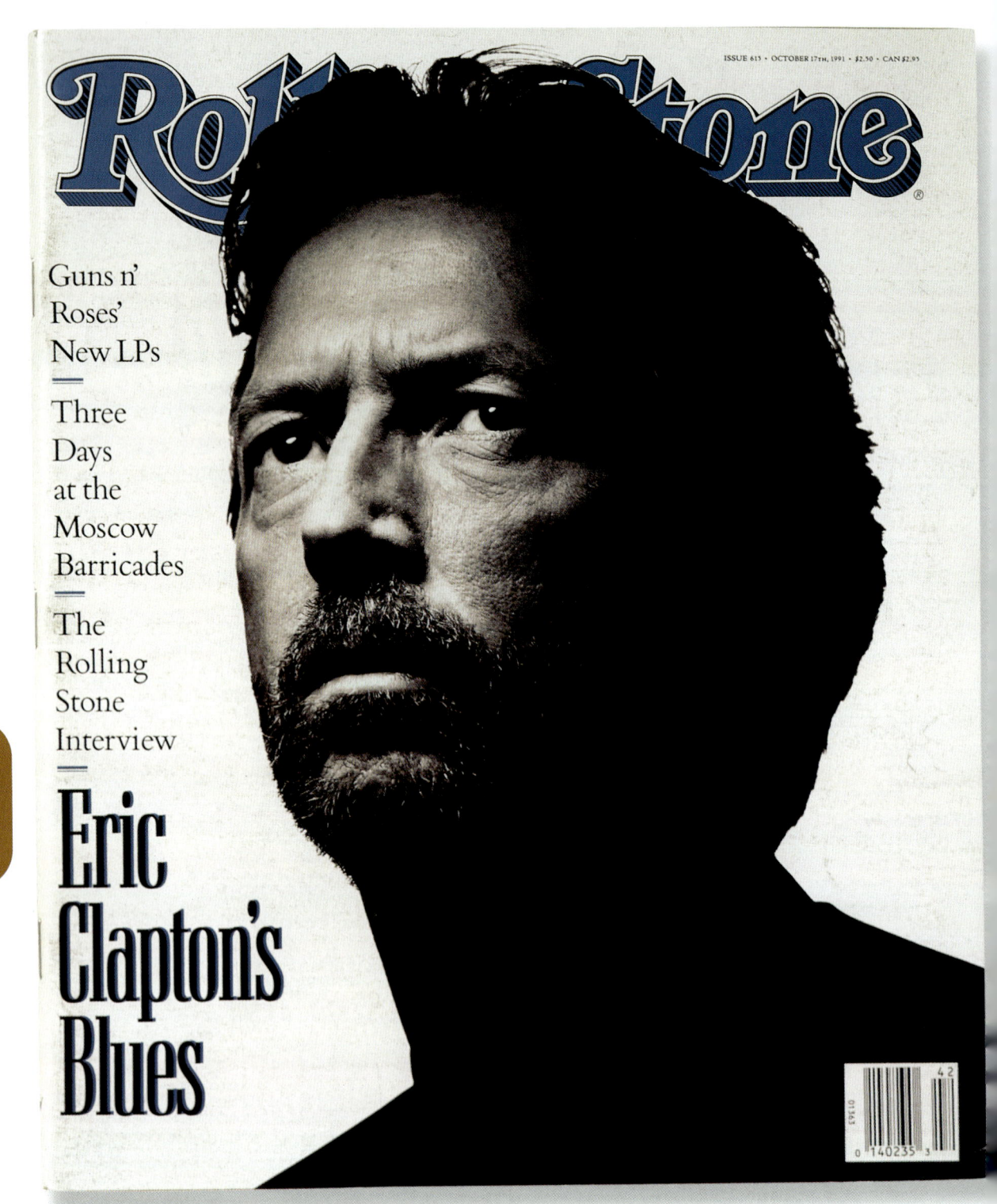

RS 615 | ERIC CLAPTON | October 17th, 1991 | Photograph by Albert Watson

ISSUE 616 • OCTOBER 31st, 1991 • $2.50 • CAN $2.95

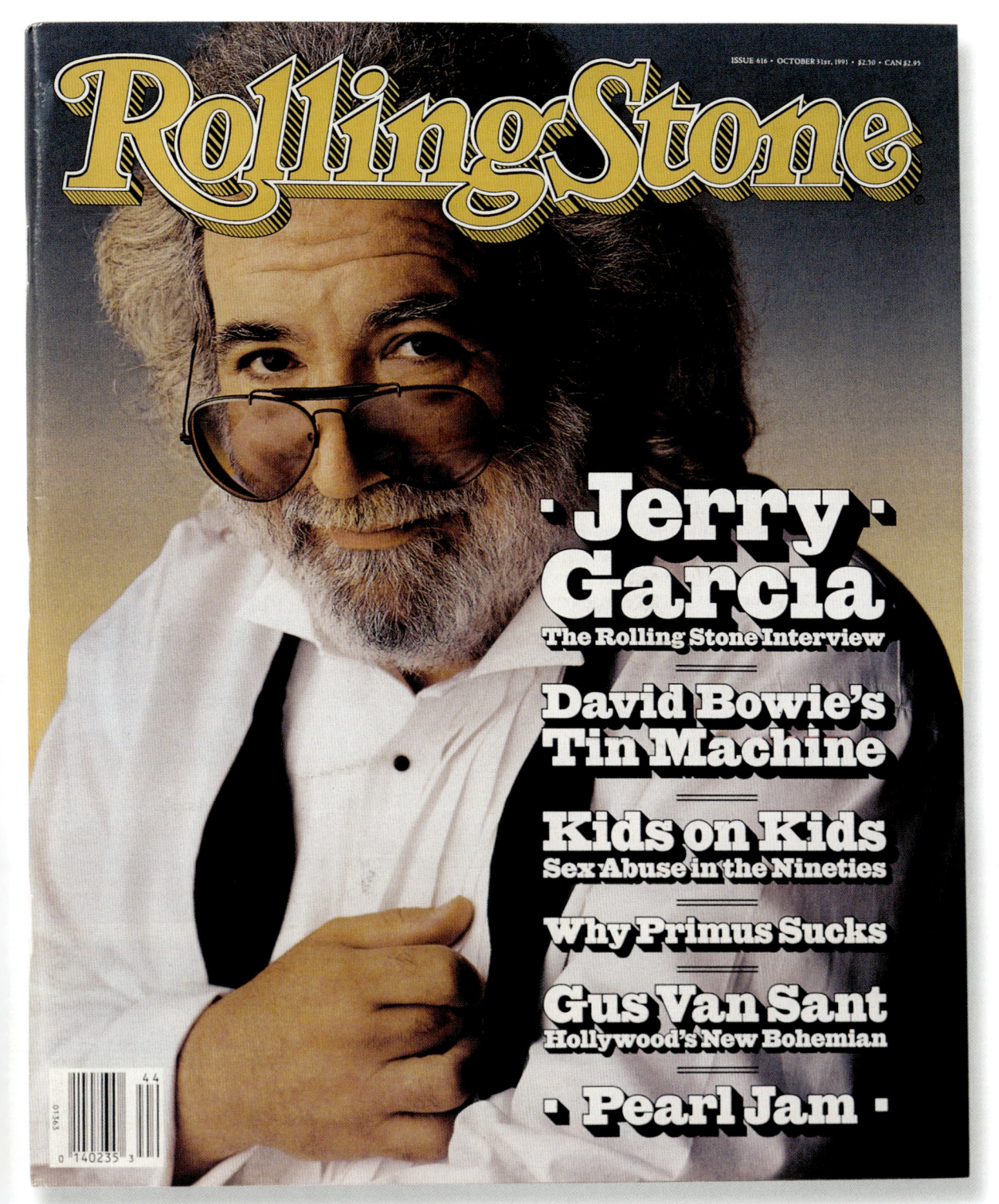

RollingStone

Jerry Garcia
The Rolling Stone Interview

David Bowie's Tin Machine

Kids on Kids
Sex Abuse in the Nineties

Why Primus Sucks

Gus Van Sant
Hollywood's New Bohemian

Pearl Jam

RS 616 | JERRY GARCIA | October 31st, 1991 | Photograph by Mark Seliger

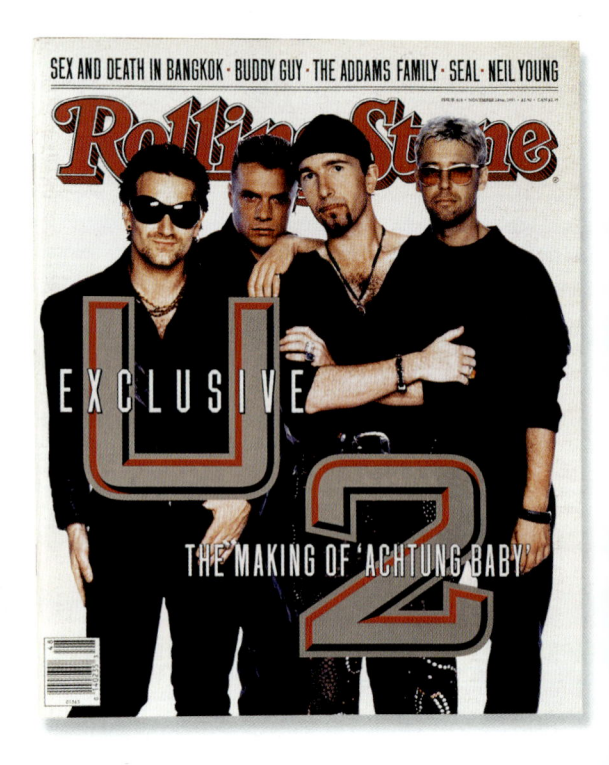

RS 617 | METALLICA
November 14th, 1991
PHOTOGRAPH BY MARK SELIGER

RS 618 | U2
November 28th, 1991
PHOTOGRAPH BY ANTON CORBIJN

HERE I AM, WRITING ABOUT THIS RECORD WITH which I had a tangential involvement, still hopefully warm from the experience. U2 had asked Dan [Lanois] and myself to produce this album with them, but I'd already made plans for much of the period. The role I thus ended up with was luxurious: I came in now and again for a week at a time, listened to what had been going on and made comments and suggestions. I can think of worse jobs than hearing something you like and then telling the people who made it why they ought to like it, too …

Working on a U2 record is a long and demanding process. The pattern seems to go like this: A couple of weeks of recording throws up dozens of promising beginnings. A big list goes up on the blackboard, songs with strange names that no one can remember ("Is that the one with the slidy bass or the sheet-of-ice guitar?"). These are wheeled out, looked at, replayed, worked on, sung to, put away, bootlegged and wheeled out again, until they start to either consolidate into something or fall away into oblivion. The list on the blackboard begins to thin down, although Bono, the Mother Teresa of abandoned songs, compassionately continues arguing the case for every single idea that has ever experienced even the most transitory existence.

[EXCERPT FROM RS 618 COVER STORY BY BRIAN ENO]

> "This must have been taken after one of Anton's jokes. It's not easy looking that serious."
> —The Edge

1990s

ISSUE 621 · JANUARY 9TH, 1992 · $2.50 · CAN $2.95

ROLLING STONE

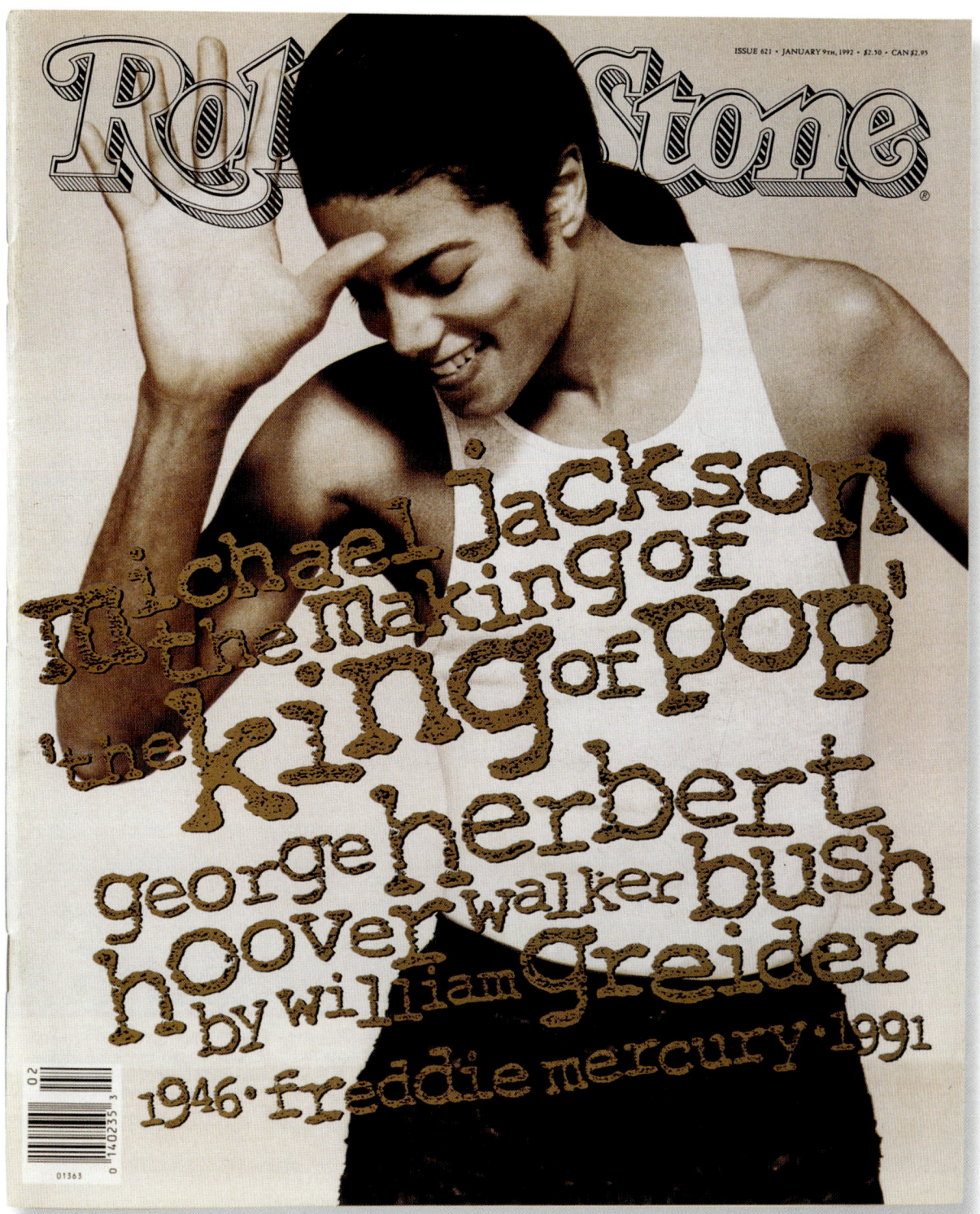

**Michael Jackson
the making of
"the king of pop"**

**george herbert
hoover walker bush
by william greider**

1946 · freddie mercury · 1991

RS 621 | MICHAEL JACKSON | January 9th, 1992 | Photograph by Herb Ritts

HUNTER S. THOMPSON
Fear and Loathing in Elko

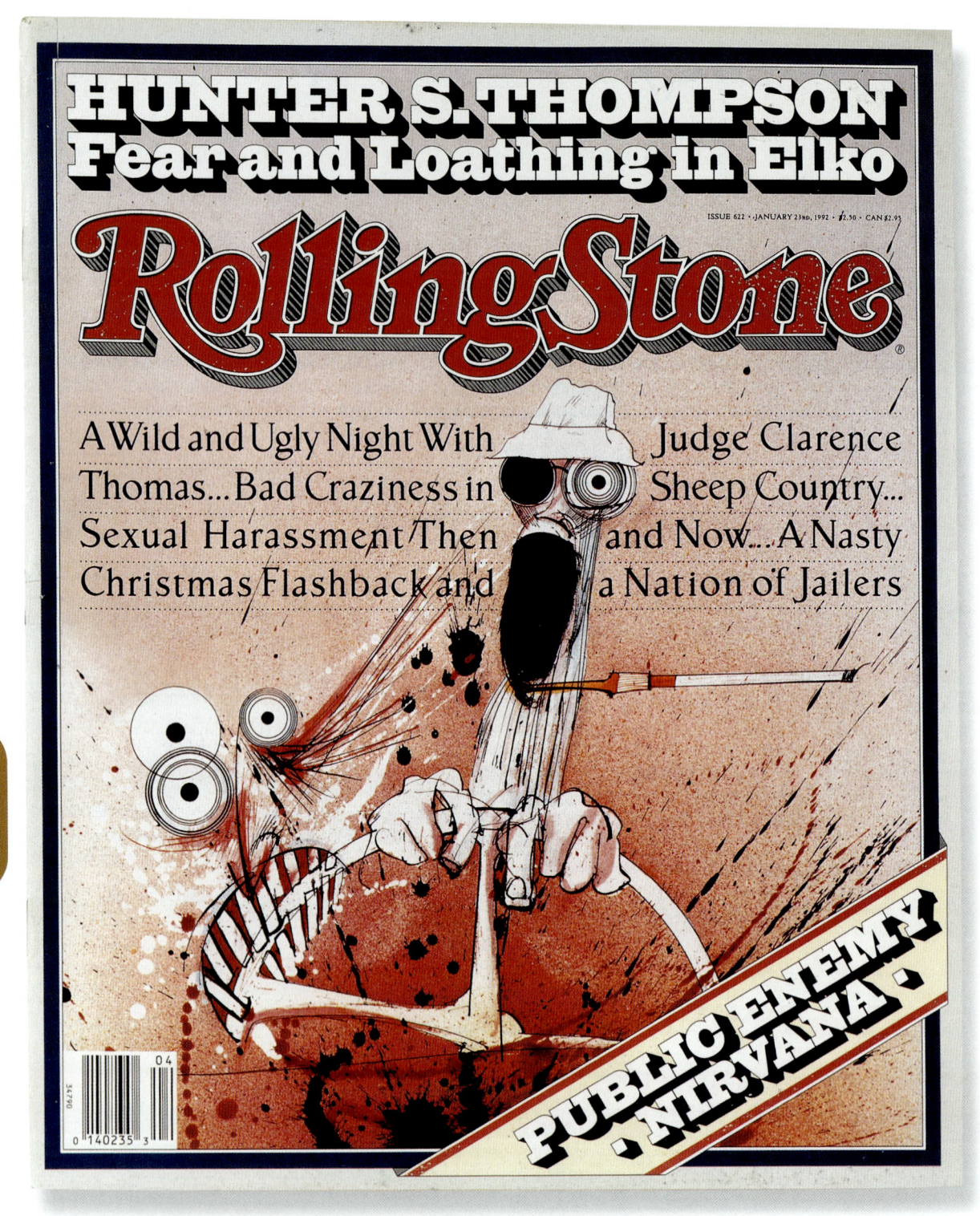

Rolling Stone

ISSUE 622 • JANUARY 23RD, 1992 • $2.50 • CAN $2.95

A Wild and Ugly Night With Thomas...Bad Craziness in Sexual Harassment Then Christmas Flashback and

Judge Clarence Sheep Country... and Now...A Nasty a Nation of Jailers

PUBLIC ENEMY · NIRVANA

RS 622 | HUNTER S. THOMPSON | January 23rd, 1992 | Illustration by Ralph Steadman

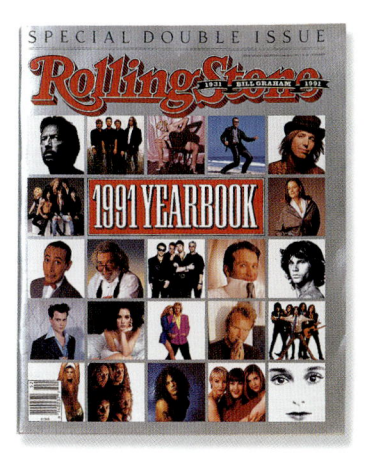

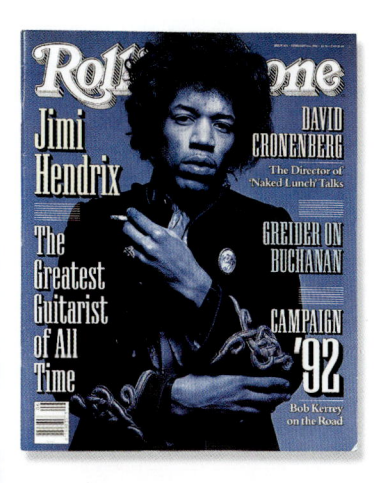

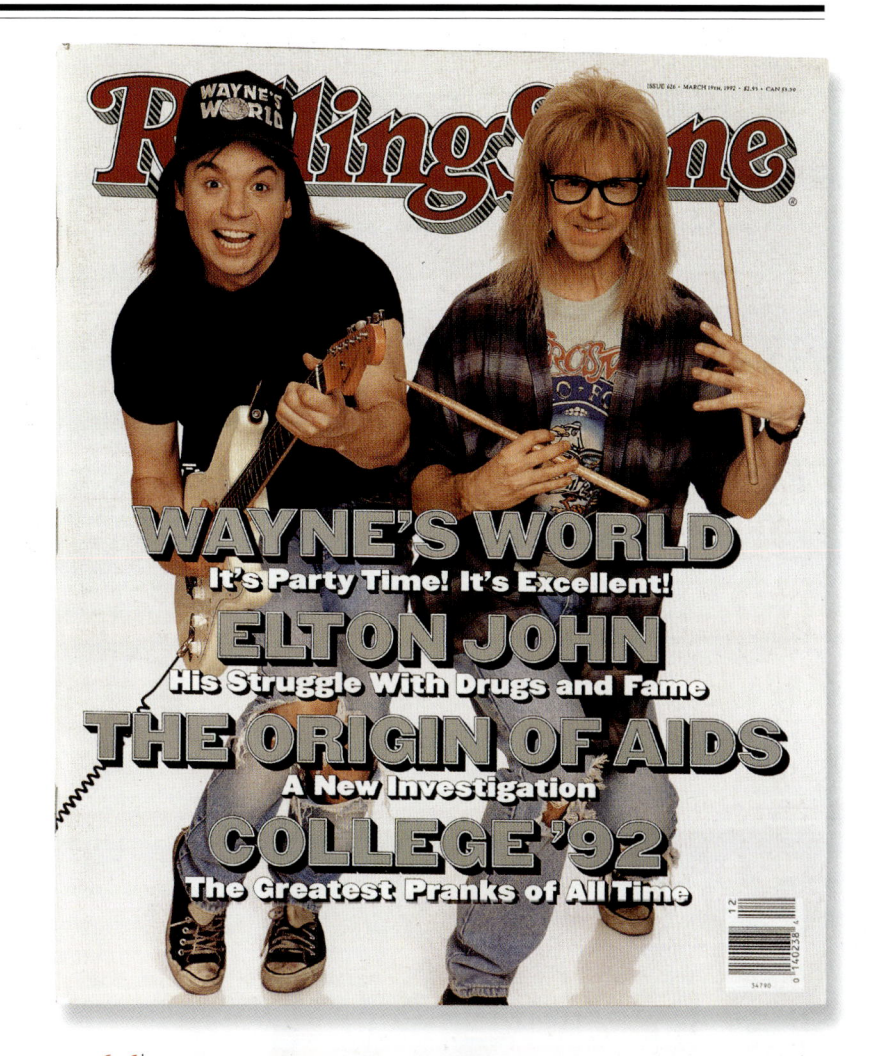

RS 619/620 | 1991 YEARBOOK
December 12th – December 26th, 1991
VARIOUS PHOTOGRAPHERS

RS 623 | JIMI HENDRIX
February 6th, 1992
PHOTOGRAPH BY GERED MANKOWITZ

RS 626 | MIKE MYERS & DANA CARVEY
March 19th, 1992
PHOTOGRAPH BY BONNIE SCHIFFMAN

50 YEARS OF COVERS • 327

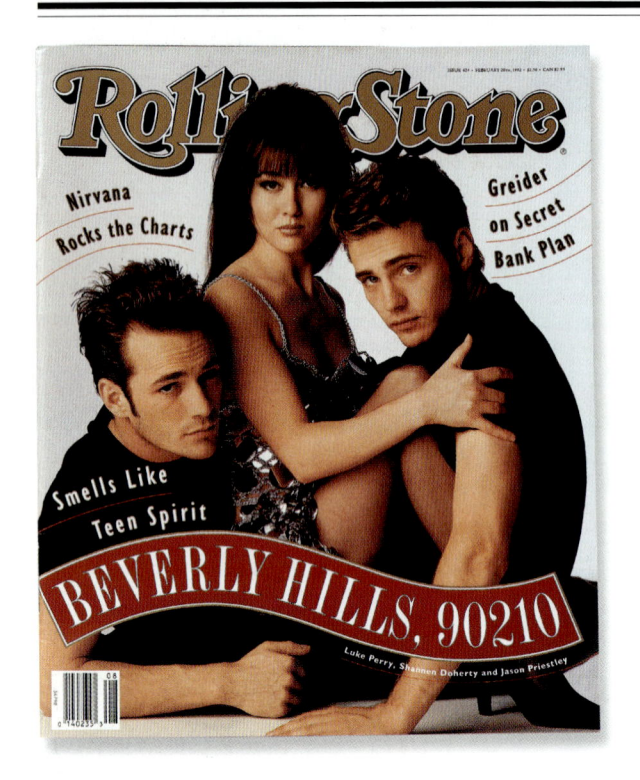

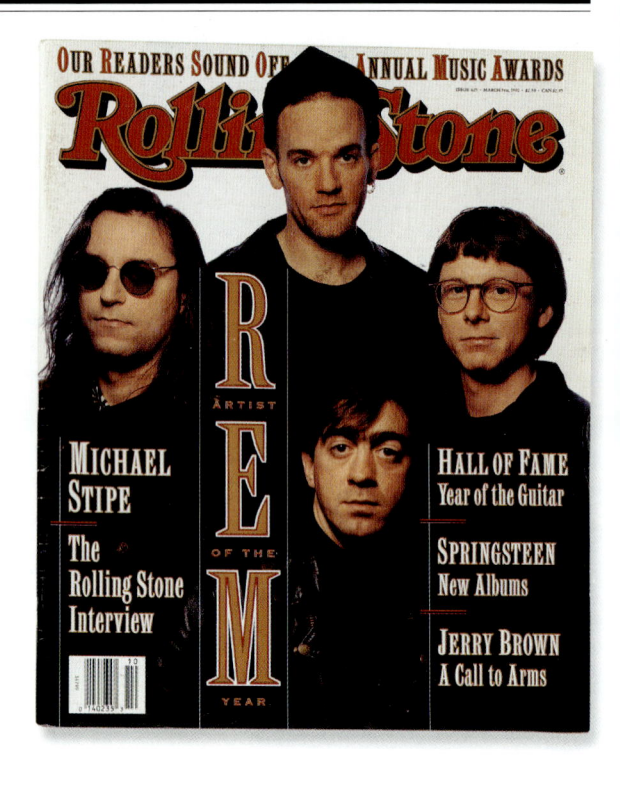

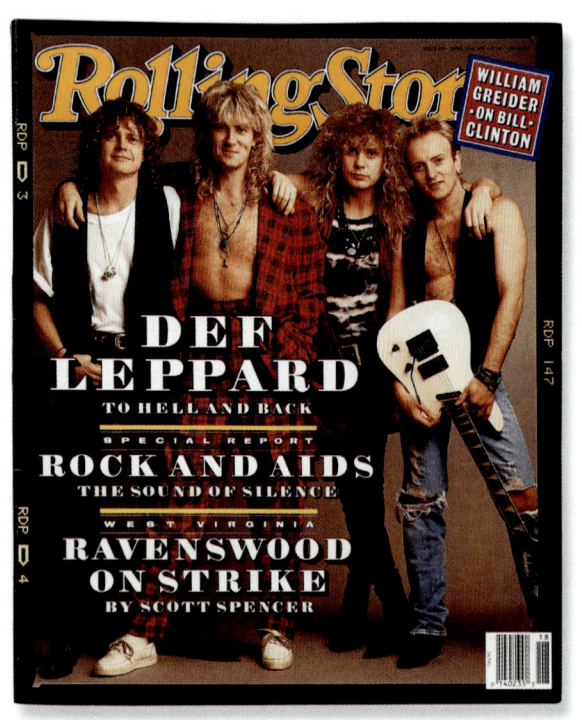

RS 624 | CAST OF 'BEVERLY HILLS, 90210'
February 20th, 1992
PHOTOGRAPH BY ANDREW ECCLES

RS 625 | R.E.M.
March 5th, 1992
PHOTOGRAPH BY ALBERT WATSON

RS 629 | DEF LEPPARD
April 30th, 1992
PHOTOGRAPH BY MARK SELIGER

"I'M DOWN ON MY ELBOW, AND SHE'S SITTING ON my kidneys, and Jason has his leg back up around her, holding her up. It looks like a wonderfully choreographed thing, but we're all in intense physical pain. I remember Jason would peek his head around her hairdo, and I'd look around the other side of her hairdo, and he'd go, 'ROLLING STONE,' and I'd go, *I know!*"

—Luke Perry

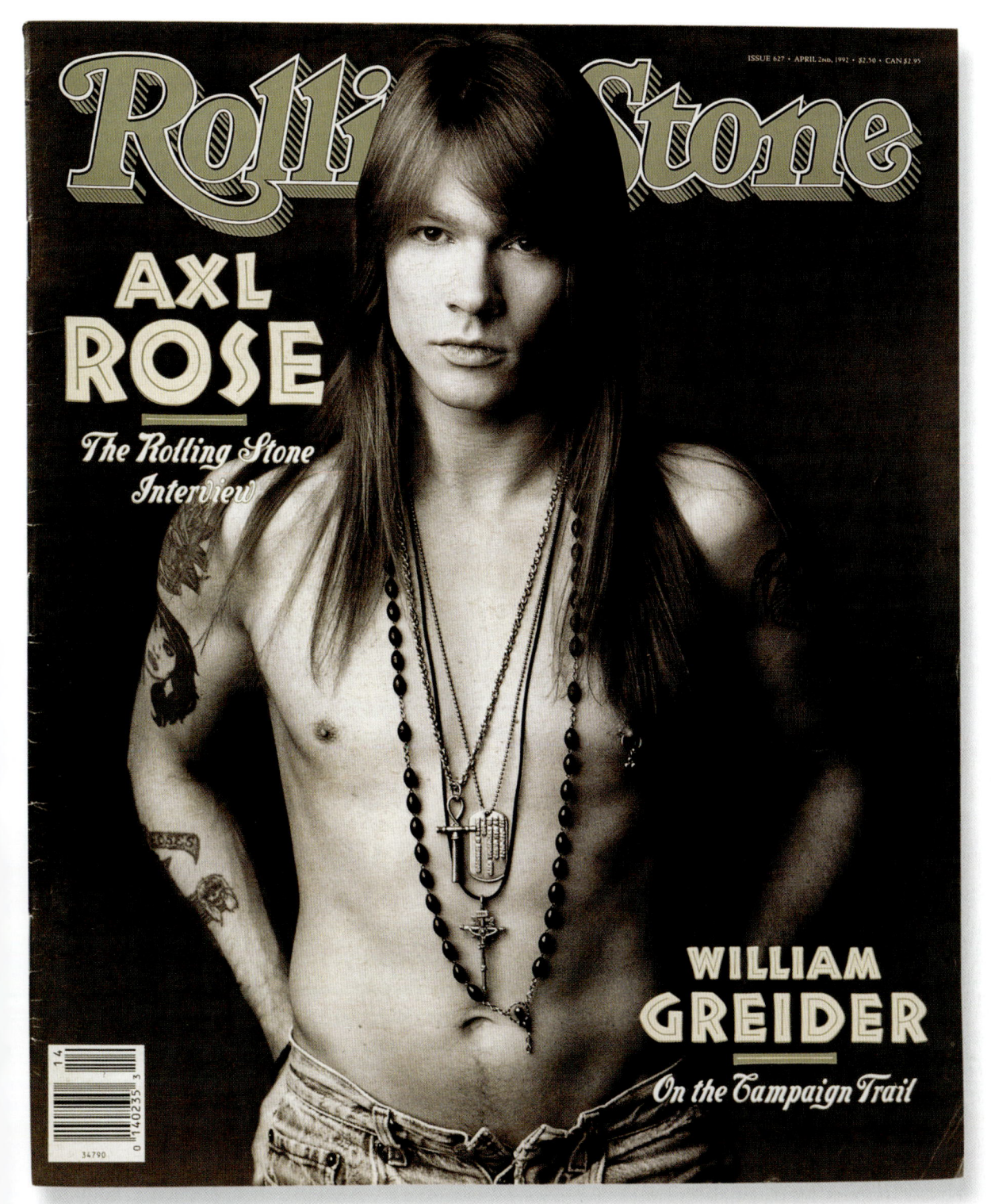

RS 627 | AXL ROSE | April 2nd, 1992 | Photograph by Herb Ritts

U2 LIVE; SPRINGSTEEN PREVIEW

Rolling Stone

ISSUE 628 • APRIL 16TH, 1992 • $2.95 • CAN $3.50

NEW FACES OF ROCK · 1·9·9·2 ·

NIRVANA

Inside the Heart and Mind of KURT COBAIN

SEATTLE SCENE
The New Liverpool

CITIZEN GE
By William Greider

1990s

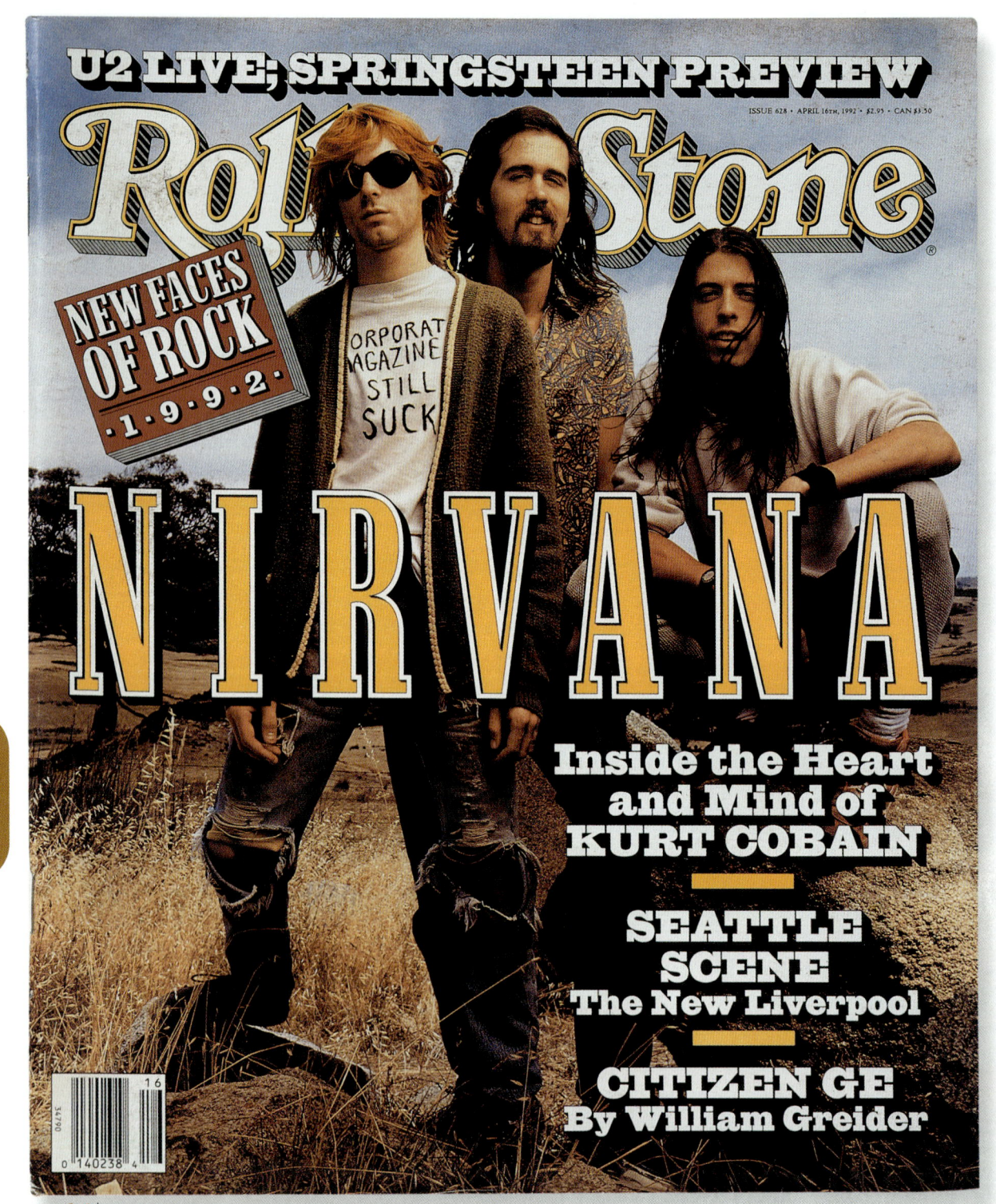

RS 628 | NIRVANA | April 16th, 1992 | Photograph by Mark Seliger

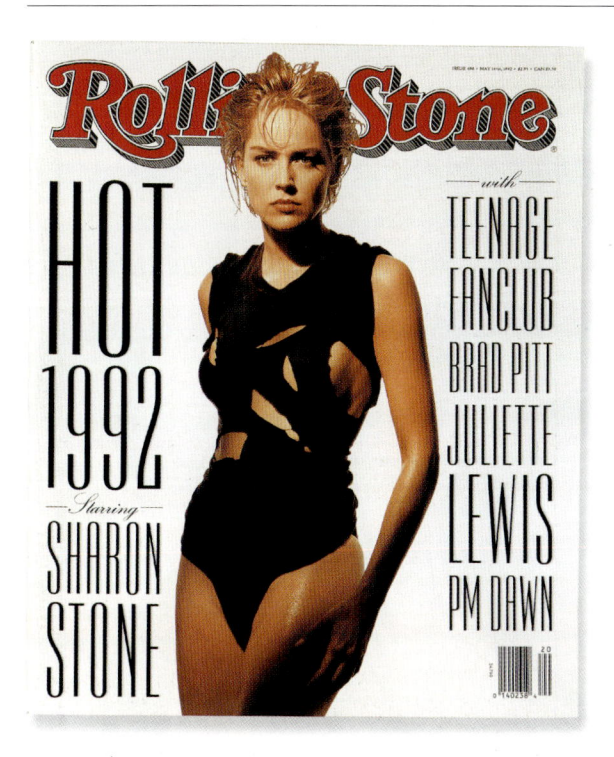

RS 630 | SHARON STONE
May 14th, 1992 | Photograph by Albert Watson

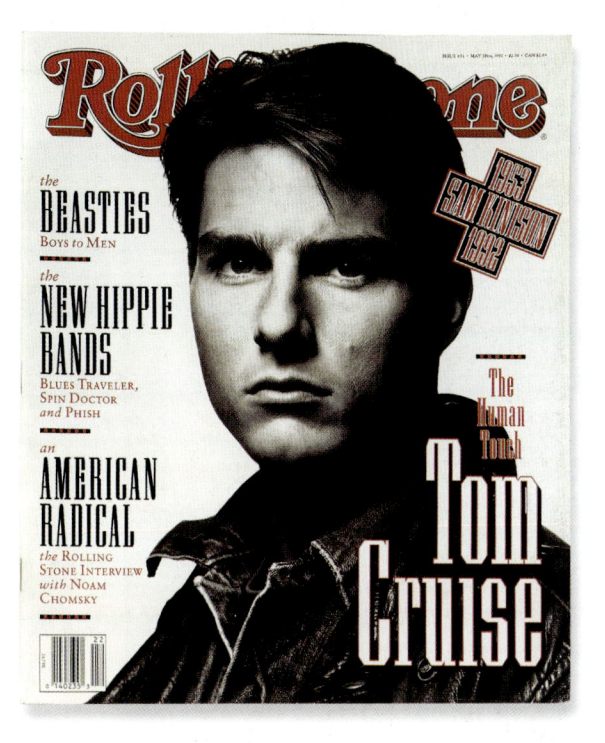

RS 631 | TOM CRUISE
May 28th, 1992 | Photograph by Albert Watson

[NIRVANA'S] 'NEVERMIND' EMBODIES A CULTURAL moment; "Smells Like Teen Spirit" is an anthem for (or is it against) the "Why Ask Why?" generation. Just don't call [Kurt] Cobain a spokesman for a generation. "I'm a spokesman for *myself*," he says. "It just so happens that there's a bunch of people that are concerned with what I have to say. I find that frightening at times because I'm just as confused as most people. I don't have the answers for anything. I don't want to be a fucking spokesperson."

"That ambiguity or confusion, that's the whole thing," says *Nevermind* producer Butch Vig. "What the kids are attracted to in the music is that he's *not* necessarily a spokesman for a generation, but all that's in the music – the passion and [the fact that] he doesn't necessarily know what he wants but he's pissed. It's all these things working at different levels at once. I don't exactly know what 'Teen Spirit' means, but you know it means *something* and it's intense as hell."

[EXCERPT FROM RS 628 COVER STORY BY MICHAEL AZERRAD]

"*I said,* 'I think that's a great shirt, I think that's great. That's a great shirt! – but let's shoot a couple, with and without it.' [Kurt Cobain] said, 'No, I'm not going to take my shirt off.'"

—*Mark Seliger*

50 YEARS OF COVERS • 331

[RS 632] To celebrate its twenty-fifth anniversary, ROLLING STONE published three special issues, beginning with this one, "The Great Stories," followed by "The Interviews" in October and "The Photographs" in November.

A LETTER FROM THE EDITOR

We see this issue as a kind of impressionistic history of the past quarter century. We started by choosing thirty of our best stories, then asked the writers to speak about themselves, about the reporting of their story and about the context of the work – i.e., what it's like to work at ROLLING STONE.

The paths that led editors and writers to ROLLING STONE are a part of [the] story. Joe Eszterhas was thought to be a narc by the mailroom guys when he first came to buy back issues (and went on to write major exposés of narcs in ROLLING STONE). Hunter S. Thompson's first assignment was to write about his nearly successful attempt to be elected sheriff in Aspen, Colorado. After that came "Fear and Loathing in Las Vegas," then the 1972 presidential campaign, and on, and on.

Within a few years we had assembled a legendary writing and reporting staff. In addition to Thompson and Eszterhas, there were Tim Cahill, Jonathan Cott, Tim Crouse, David Felton, Ben Fong-Torres, Howard Kohn, Michael Rogers, to name a few.

ROLLING STONE reporting and writing in the Eighties and the beginning of the Nineties has also leaned heavily on the talents of P.J. O'Rourke and William Greider. For P.J., the pen is the sword, and he has used it to drive liars, cheats, thieves and scoundrels out into the open. Bill Greider has been articulating his own and ROLLING STONE's political conscience with eloquence since he joined us from the *Washington Post* more than a decade ago. His essay concludes this issue and recalls our sometimes lonely political mission through the Reagan-Bush years.

I am immensely proud of all the talent that has worked at ROLLING STONE over the years – in Lawrence Wright's words, "literary hellcats who brushed aside journalistic conventions and social taboos to get at new ways of telling the truth." Larry, who joined us in 1985, goes on to write in his piece here: "One accepts a ROLLING STONE assignment knowing that not only must it be the final word on a subject, it must be freshly seen and powerfully told."

—*Jann S. Wenner*

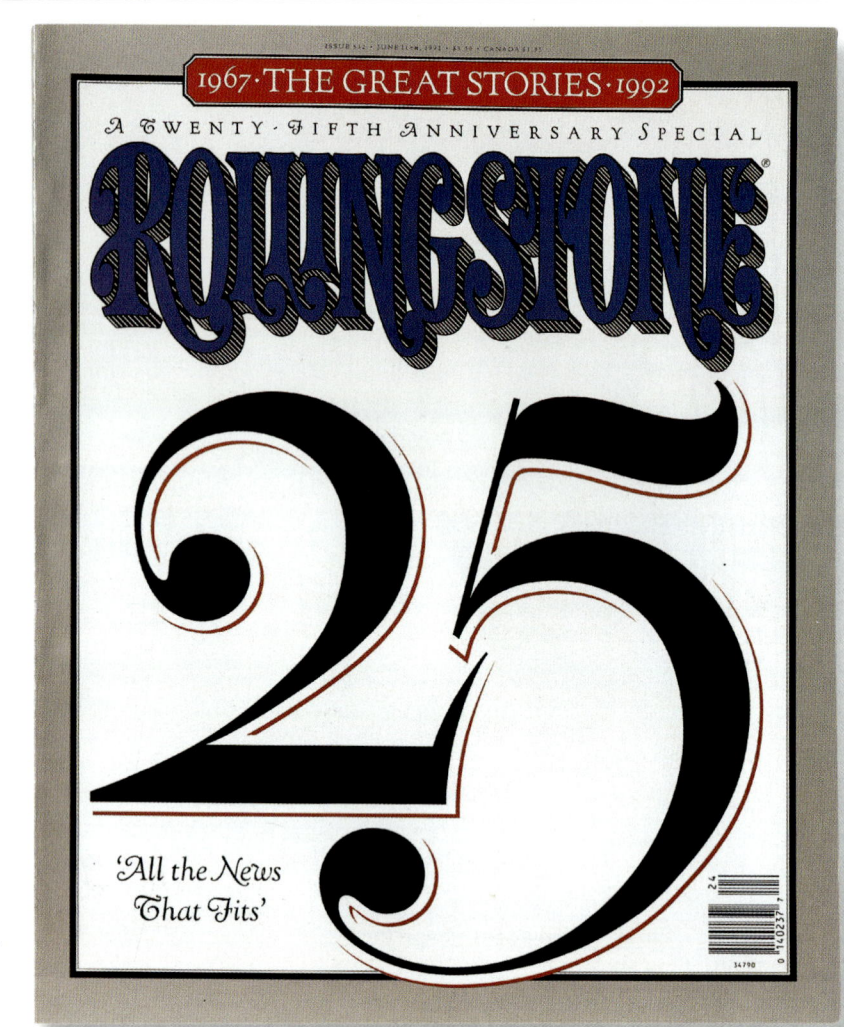

RS 632 | TWENTY-FIFTH ANNIVERSARY: THE GREAT STORIES
June 11th, 1992 | TYPOGRAPHY BY DENNIS ORTIZ-LOPEZ

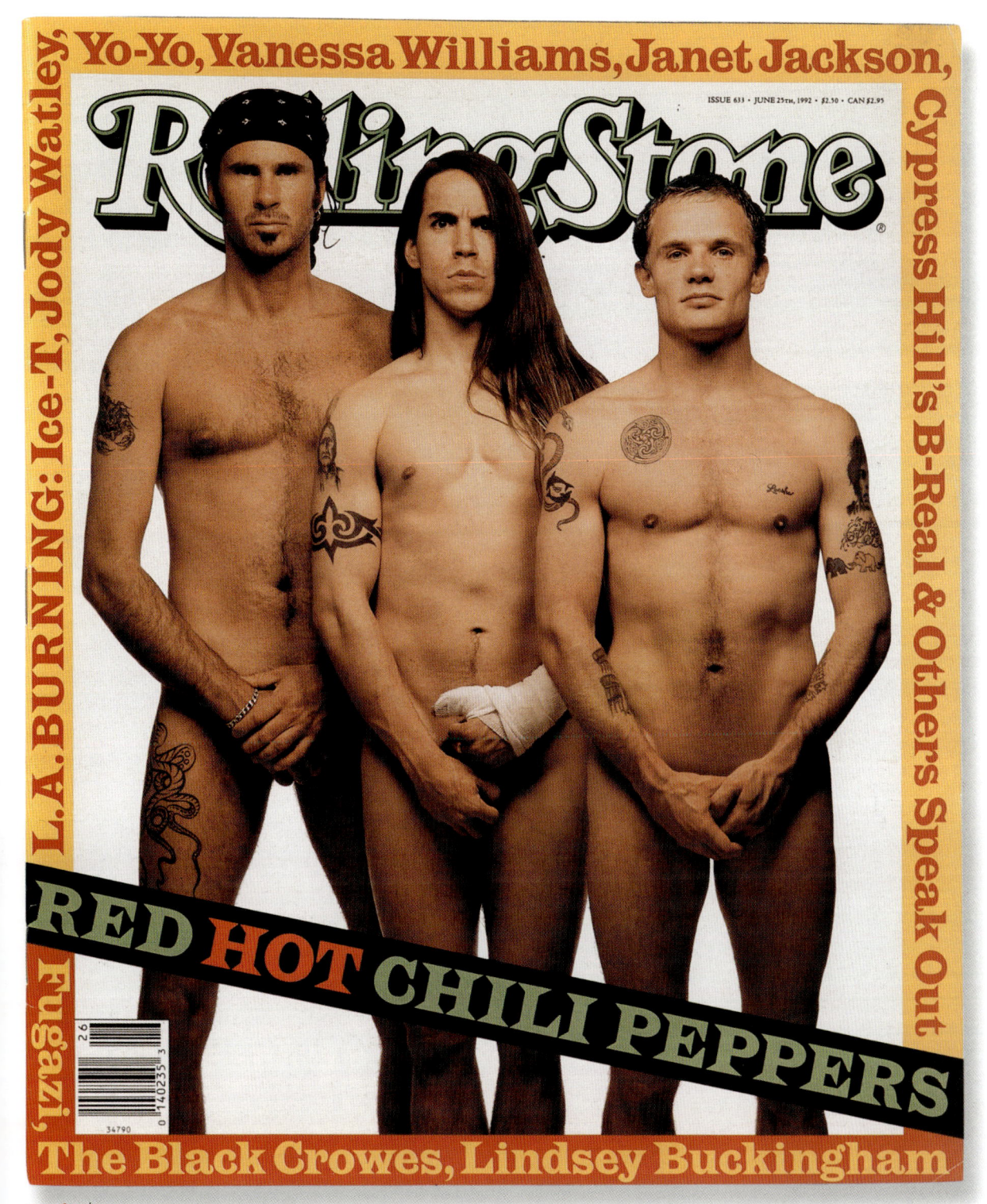

RS 633 | RED HOT CHILI PEPPERS | June 25th, 1992 | Photograph by Mark Seliger

50 YEARS OF COVERS · 333

SPECIAL DOUBLE ISSUE

Rolling Stone

P.J. O'ROURKE: ON THE ROAD IN VIETNAM

SOUNDGARDEN: ROCK'S HEAVY ALTERNATIVE

INSIDE BATMAN

THE ROLLING STONE INTERVIEW WITH DIRECTOR TIM BURTON BY DAVID BRESKIN

BEN & JERRY: THE CARING CAPITALISTS

PAULY SHORE: TOTALLY HIP COMEDY

GEARHEADS: THE BIRTH OF MOUNTAIN BIKING

RINGO STARR, SOCIAL DISTORTION, HAMMER & LINDSEY BUCKINGHAM

1990s

RS 634/635 | BATMAN'S SUIT | July 9th – July 23rd, 1992 | Photograph by Herb Ritts

GREIDER ON ROSS PEROT · JIMMY BUFFETT

RollingStone

Bruce
The Rolling Stone Interview

RS 636 | BRUCE SPRINGSTEEN | August 6th, 1992 | Photograph by Herb Ritts

ISSUE 617 · AUGUST 20TH, 1992 · $2.50 · CAN $2.95

Rolling Stone

SEARCHING FOR THE NEW NIRVANA

Ice-T Talks Back
(You Got a Problem With That?)

Greenmail in Rio: P.J. O'Rourke at the Earth Summit

1990s

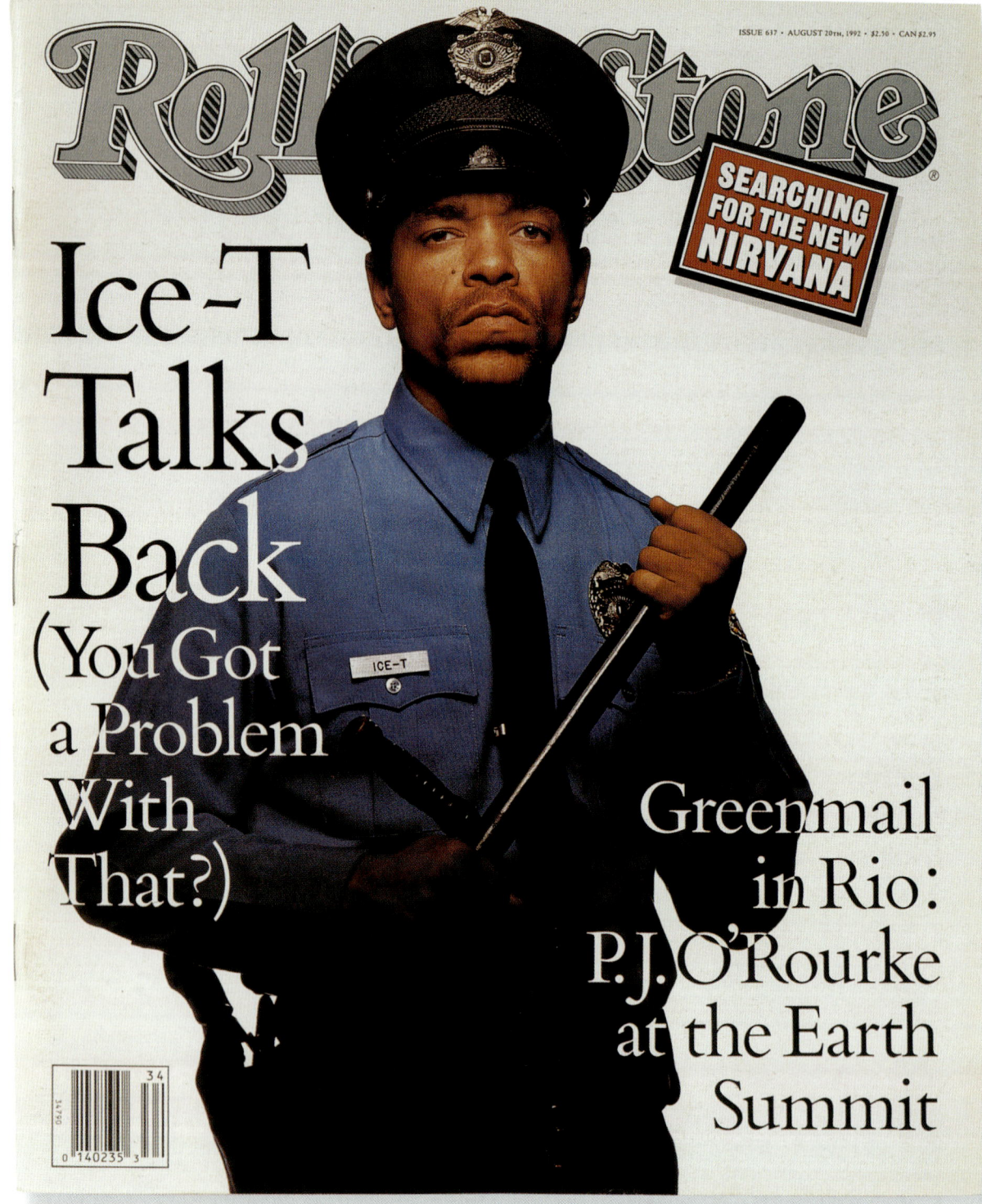

RS 637 | ICE-T | August 20th, 1992 | Photograph by Mark Seliger

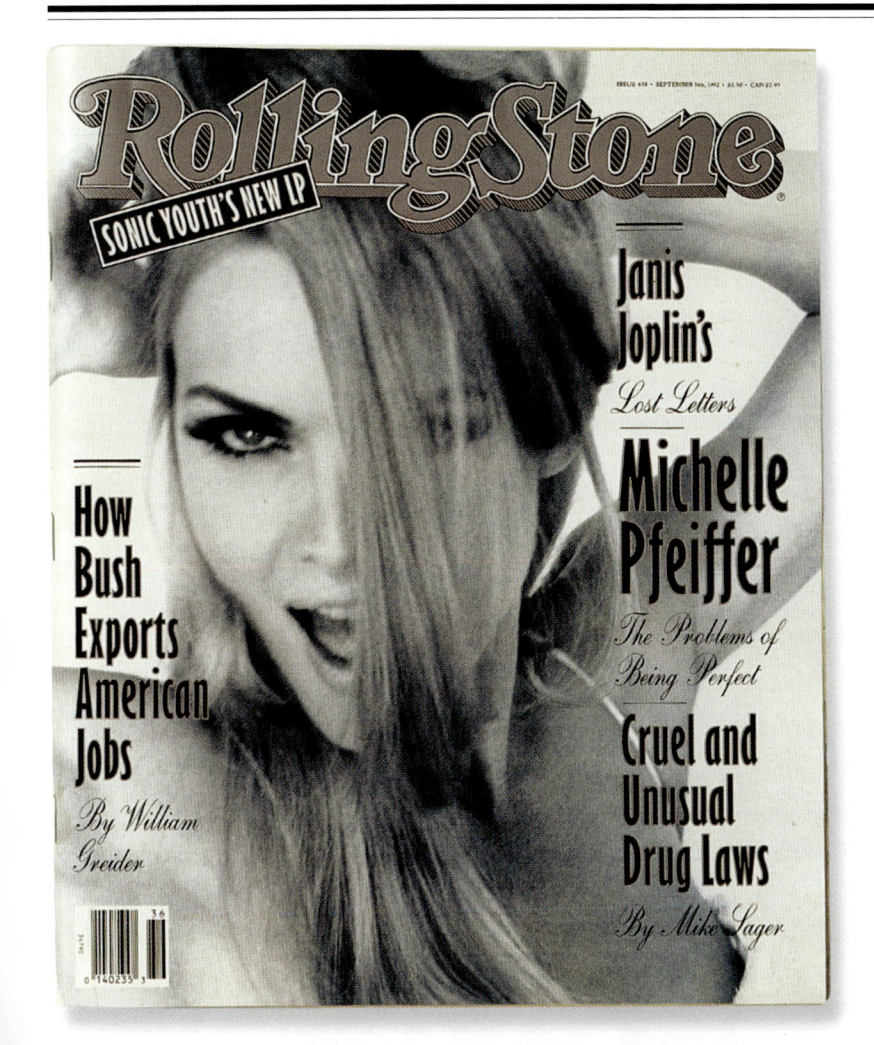

"I had to do a lot of apologizing to my hard-core fans [for wearing a policeman's uniform]. That was sacrilegious in the ghetto. 'Why did you have to be a cop? Why you got to give credit to the Man?' I had to tell them the laws of Hollywood: The only way you can run around with a gun is to be a cop."

—Ice-T

RS 638 | MICHELLE PFEIFFER
September 3rd, 1992 | Photograph by Herb Ritts

COLLEGE SPECIAL

Rolling Stone

ISSUE 639 • SEPTEMBER 17TH, 1992 • $2.95 • CAN $3.50

LOLLAPALOOZA
On the Road With
The Chili Peppers,
Pearl Jam and
Soundgarden

CLINT EASTWOOD
He Shoots, He Scores

THE ROLLING STONE INTERVIEW

BILL CLINTON

By William Greider,
P.J. O'Rourke and
Hunter S. Thompson

**DEEE-LITE
MICHAEL JACKSON
BOBBY BROWN**

1990s

RS 639 | BILL CLINTON | September 17th, 1992 | Photograph by Mark Seliger

So what did we learn here?

Bill Clinton's favorite Beatle is Paul McCartney. He voted for the skinny Elvis stamp (which doesn't show much self-knowledge). Also, he bites his nails – though they're bitten in a tidy, thoughtful manner, not gnawed to the raw quick the way crazy people do it. I'm sure this is all valuable information. I mean, *eeeeeyew, Paul?* Especially at a moment in history when America cries out for a president whose favorite Beatle is Ringo.

—P.J. O'Rourke

MEMO FROM THE NATIONAL AFFAIRS DESK

DATE: August 4th, '92
FROM: Dr. Hunter S. Thompson
SUBJECT: THE THREE STOOGES GO TO LITTLE ROCK

I have just returned, as you know, from a top-secret Issues Conference in Little Rock with our high-riding Candidate, Bill Clinton – who is also the five-term Governor of Arkansas and the only living depositor in the Grameen Bank of Bangladesh who wears a ROLLING STONE T-shirt when he jogs past the hedges at sundown. Ah, yes – the hedges. How little is know of them, eh? And I suspect, in fact, that the truth will never be known.... I wanted to check them out, but it didn't work. My rented Chrysler convertible turned into a kind of Trojan Horse in reverse – and frankly, I was deeply afraid to stay for even one night in Little Rock, by myself, for fear of being tracked and seized and perhaps even jailed and humiliated, on instructions from some nameless Clinton factotum.

MAYBE WEIRD POLITICS RUNS IN TWENTY-YEAR CYCLES. The last time I became ensnared in Dr. Hunter S. Thompson's delusional reality was on the campaign trail in 1972, when Richard Nixon was trashing George McGovern and the Constitution. The Doctor's apocalyptic rumblings turned out to be the only accurate account of that doomed presidential election. This time around, the year had already turned strange by the time I found myself in the back room of a Little Rock, Arkansas, restaurant, sitting around a checker-clothed table with ROLLING STONE's political team.... HST appeared to believe that this meeting constituted a high-level political parley in which we would deliver the "ROLLING STONE vote" to Bill Clinton. P.J. O'Rourke, meanwhile, determined to play the right-wing hit man, had loaded up with hard facts from the *Statistical Abstract* to zing Clinton and unmask his mush-headed liberalism. Jann Wenner, our always wise and generous leader, seemed blissfully oblivious to the potential for humiliation.

—*William Greider*
[EXCERPTS FROM RS 639 COVER STORY]

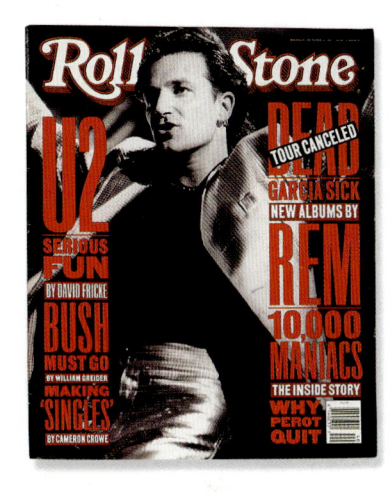

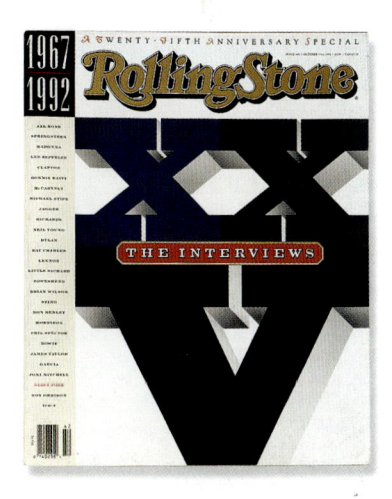

RS 640 | BONO
October 1st, 1992
Photograph by Neal Preston

RS 641 | TWENTY-FIFTH ANNIVERSARY: THE INTERVIEWS
October 15th, 1992

RS 642 | SINÉAD O'CONNOR | October 29th, 1992 | Photograph by Albert Watson

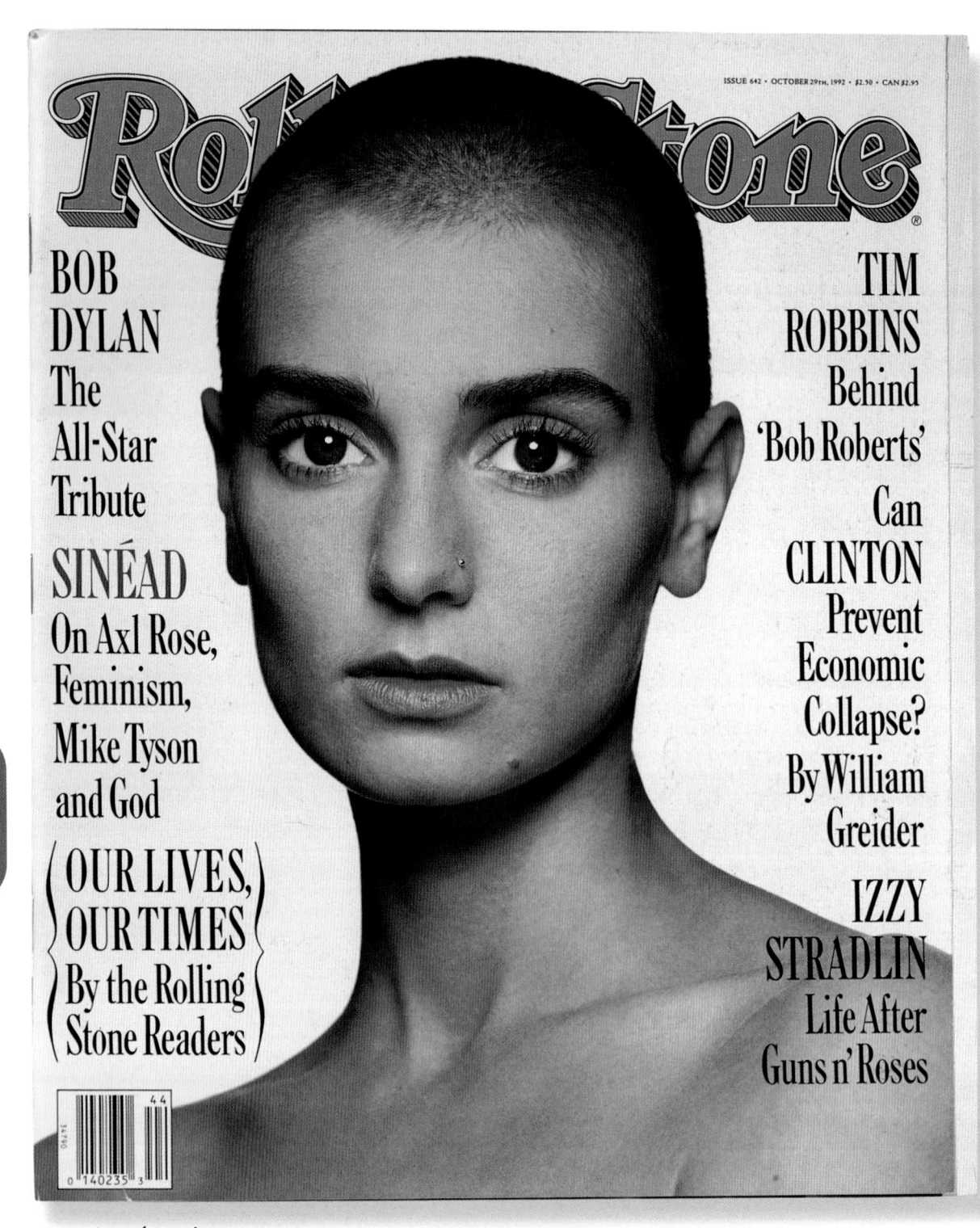

A TWENTY-FIFTH ANNIVERSARY SPECIAL

Rolling Stone

ISSUE 643 · NOVEMBER 12TH, 1992 · $3.50 CAN $1.95

The
FAMILY
of
ROCK
1992

Portraits

The
HISTORY of
ROCK & ROLL
PHOTOGRAPHY
By
GERRI HIRSHEY

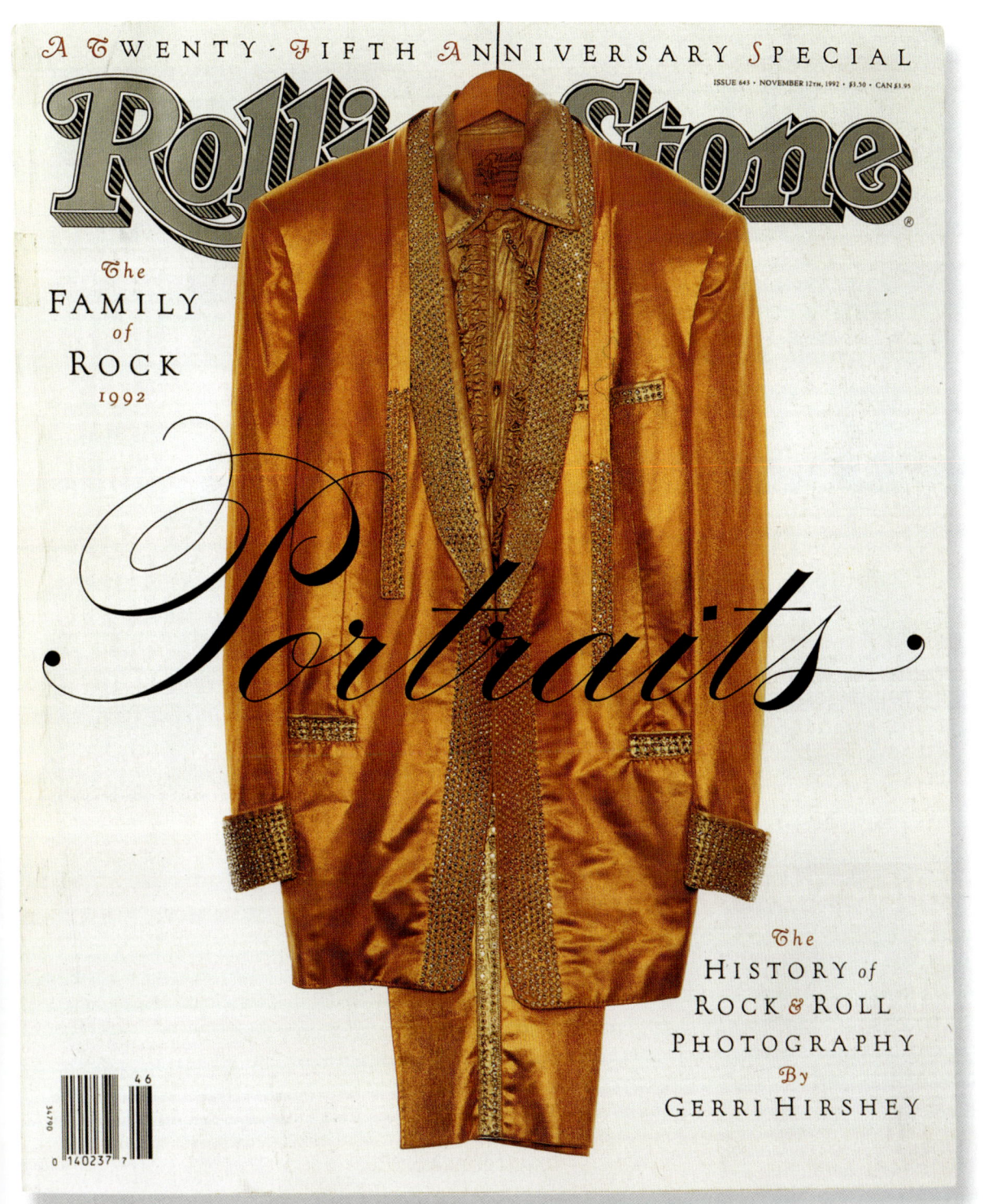

RS 643 | TWENTY-FIFTH ANNIVERSARY: THE PORTRAITS; ELVIS'S GOLD LAMÉ NUDIE SUIT
November 12th, 1992 | Photograph by Albert Watson

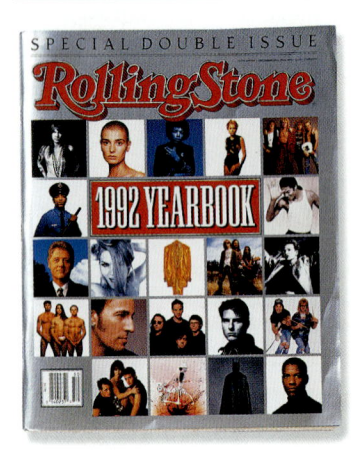

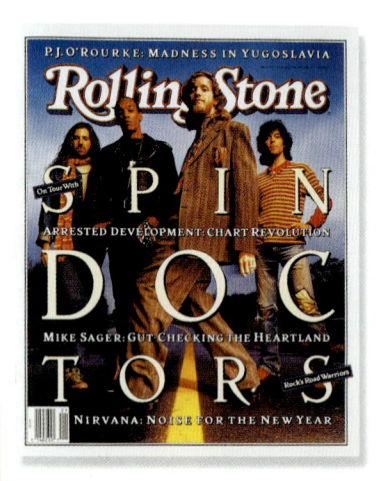

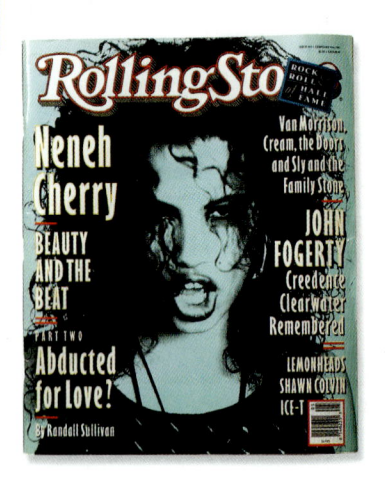

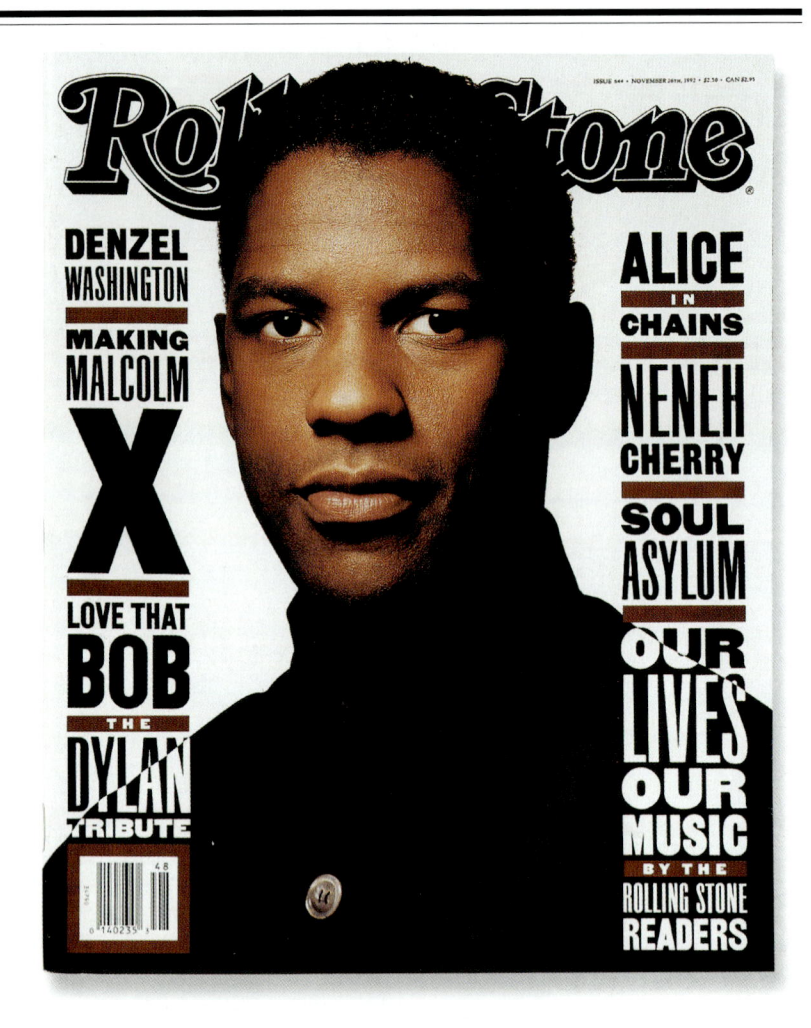

1990s

RS 644 | **DENZEL WASHINGTON**
November 26th, 1992
PHOTOGRAPH BY ALBERT WATSON

RS 645/646 | **1992 YEARBOOK**
December 10th – 24th, 1992
VARIOUS PHOTOGRAPHERS

RS 647 | **SPIN DOCTORS**
January 7th, 1993
PHOTOGRAPH BY MARK SELIGER

RS 649 | **NENEH CHERRY**
February 4th, 1993
PHOTOGRAPH BY ELLEN VON UNWERTH

"IF YOU'RE CHARGED UP AND HAVE ALL this experience, what else is there? When you're young, you don't have any experience – you're charged up, but you're out of control. And if you're old and you're not charged up, then all you have is memories. But if you're charged and stimulated by what's going on around you and you also have experience, you know what to appreciate and what to pass by. And then you're really cruising."

—*Neil Young*

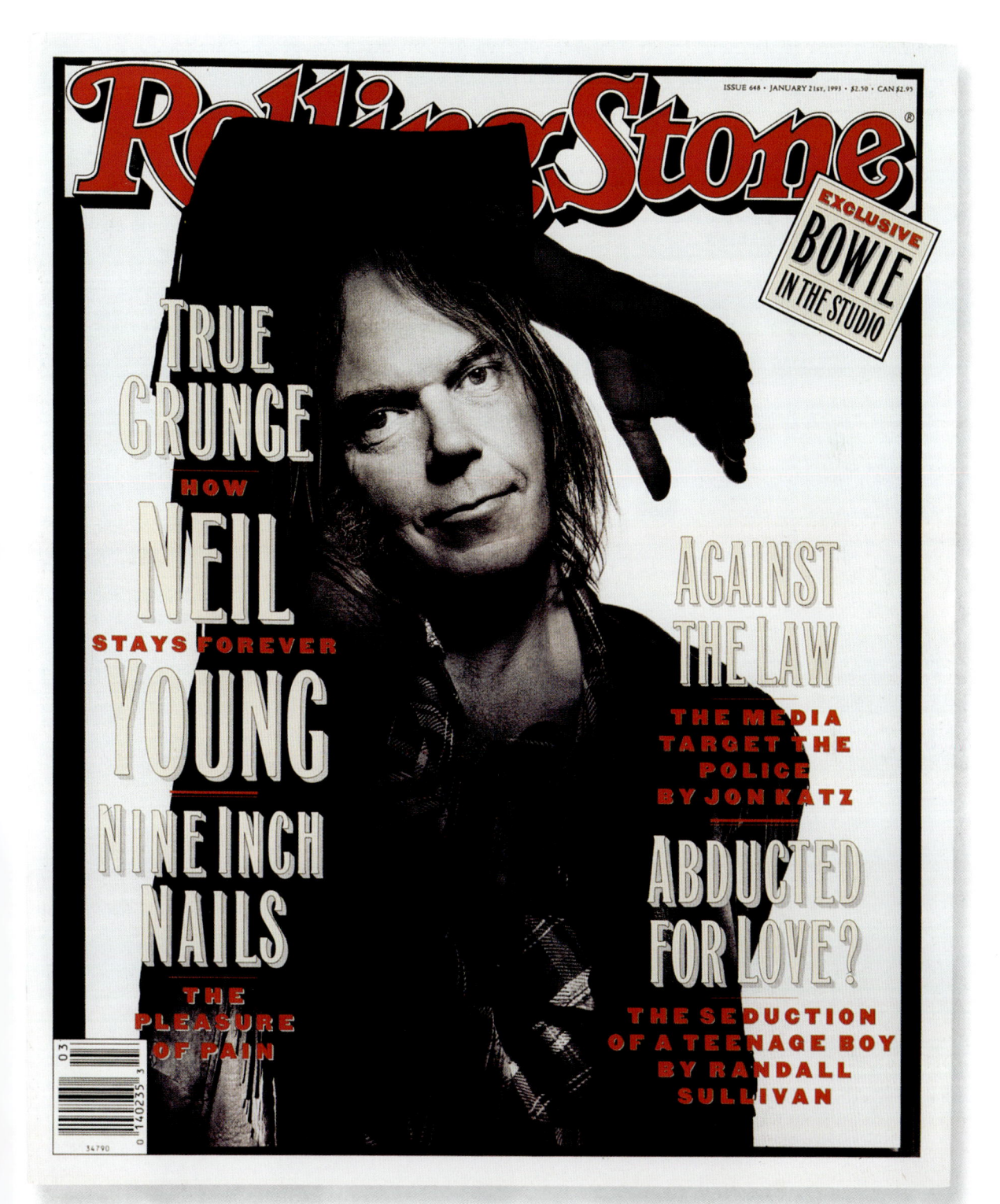

RS 648 | NEIL YOUNG | January 21st, 1993 | Photograph by Mark Seliger

Rolling Stone

SCREAMING TREES · VAN HALEN · HENRY ROLLINS

ISSUE 650 · FEBRUARY 18TH, 1993 · $2.50 · CAN $2.95

Heeeeeeeeerrre's Dave!

1990s

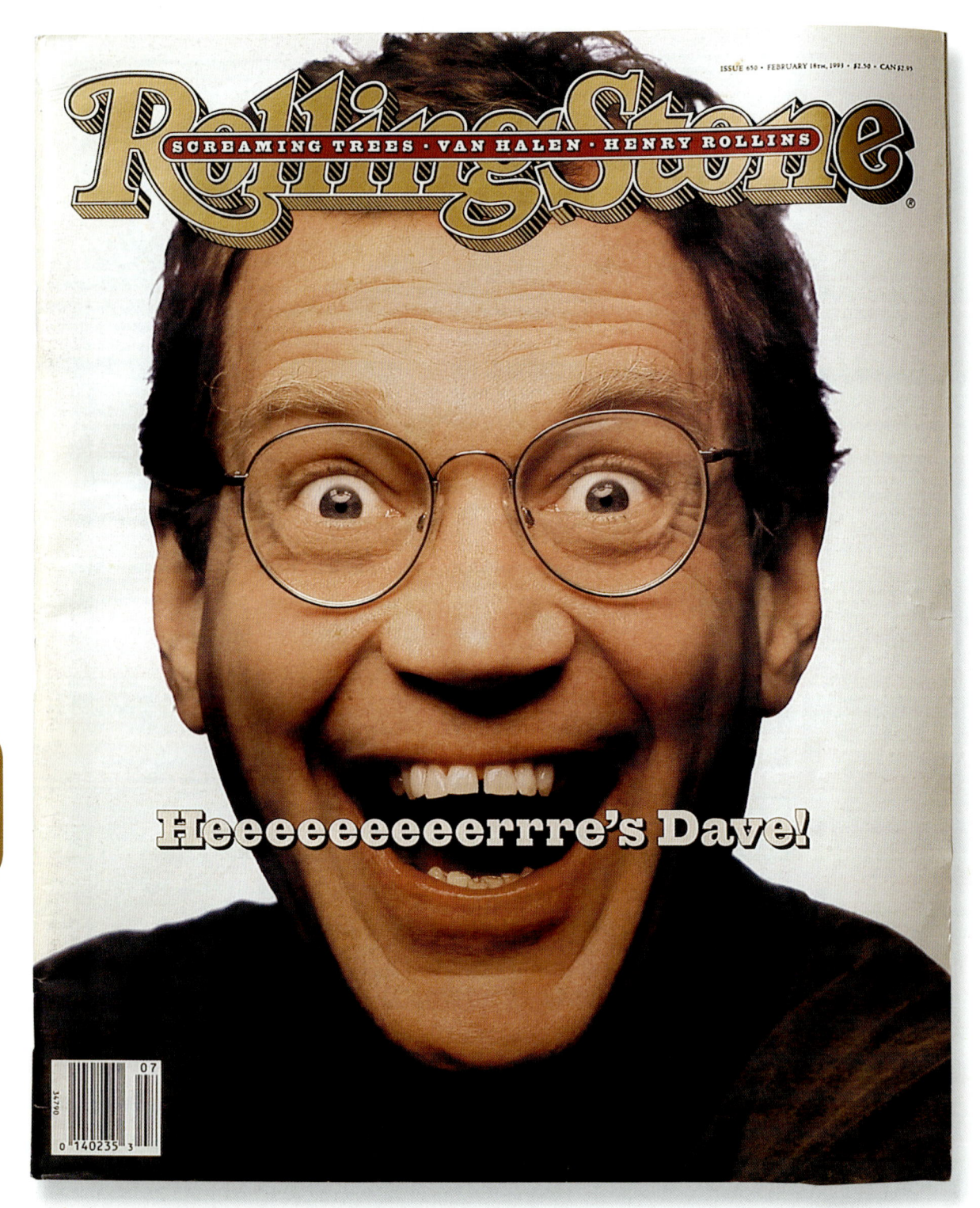

RS 650 | DAVID LETTERMAN | February 18th, 1993 | Photograph by Mark Seliger

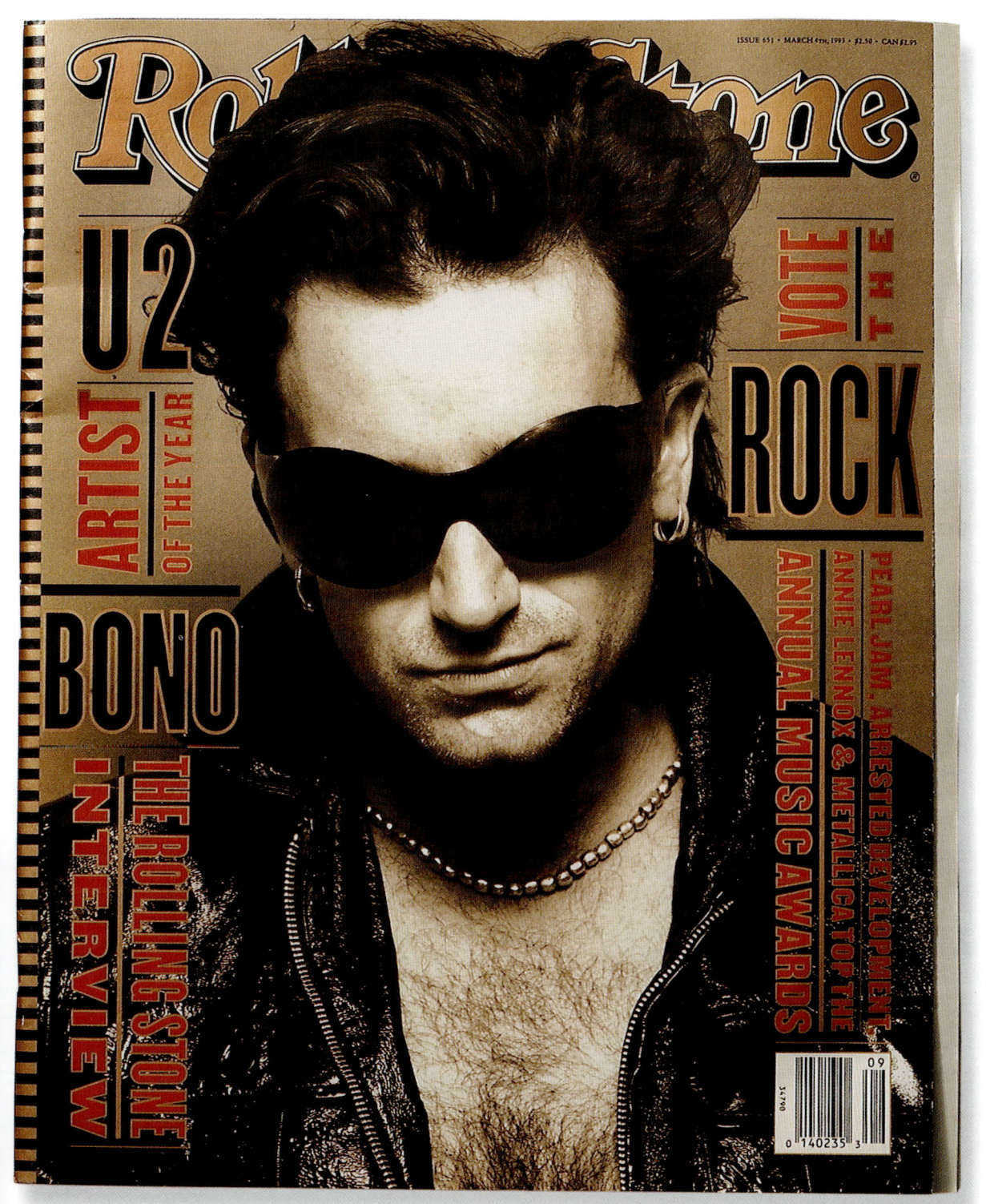

RS 651 | BONO | March 4th, 1993 | Photograph by Andrew MacPherson

Rolling Stone

ISSUE 654 · APRIL 15TH, 1993 · $2.50 · CAN $2.95

SPECIAL REPORT

CONCERT SECURITY
How Safe Are You?

ELECTRONIC BULLETIN BOARDS
The People's News

JAMES HETFIELD
OF METALLICA
The Leader of the Real Free World Speaks

EXCERPT
T. CORAGHESSAN BOYLE'S
New Novel

1990s

RS 654 | JAMES HETFIELD | April 15th, 1993 | Photograph by Mark Seliger

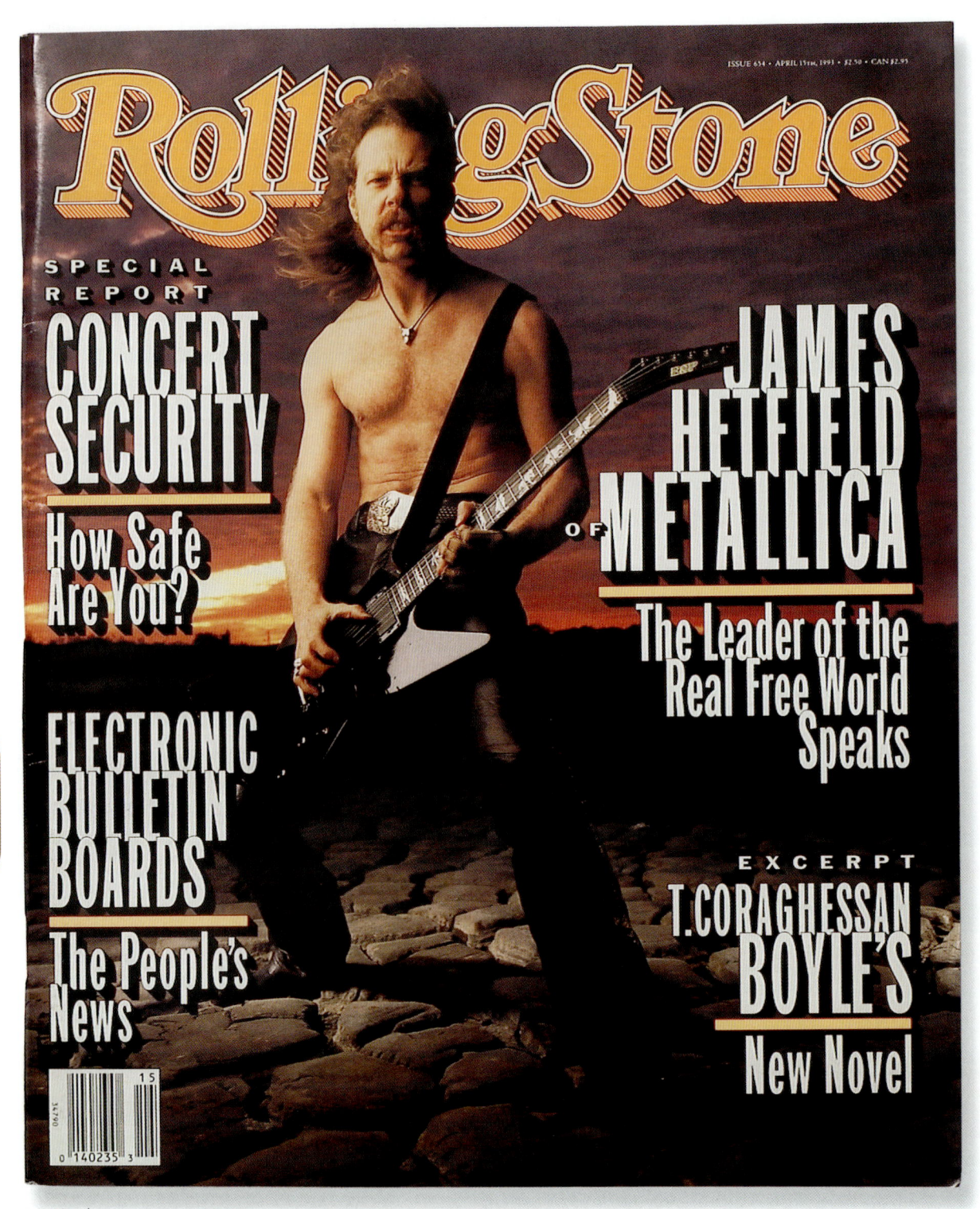

RollingStone

ISSUE 656 • MAY 13th, 1993
$2.95 • CAN $3.50

dana carvey quits

life after SNL

BY BILL ZEHME

perry farrell's bad HABITS

marisa tomei
american music club
james carville

THE **famous hot list**

shaquille o'neal
john woo
seinfeld's kramer
belly
fly girls

RS 656 | DANA CARVEY | May 13th, 1993 | Photograph by Mark Seliger

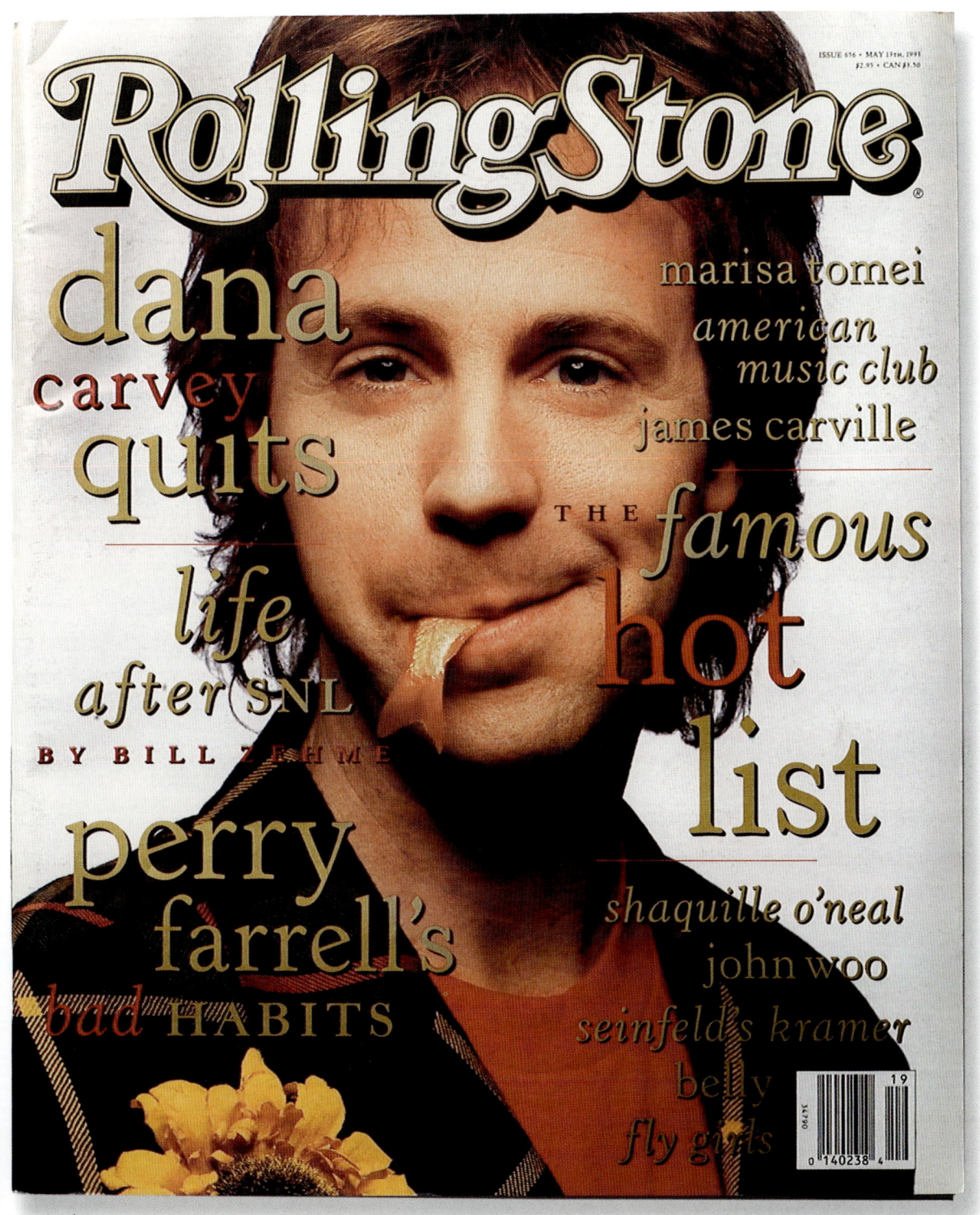

50 YEARS OF COVERS • 347

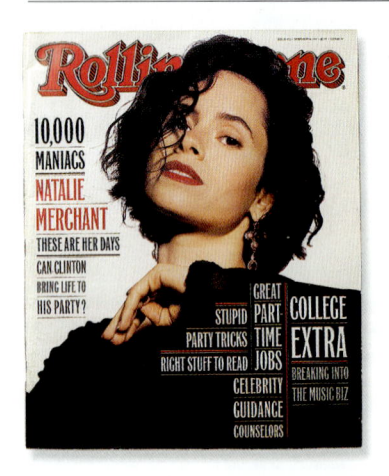

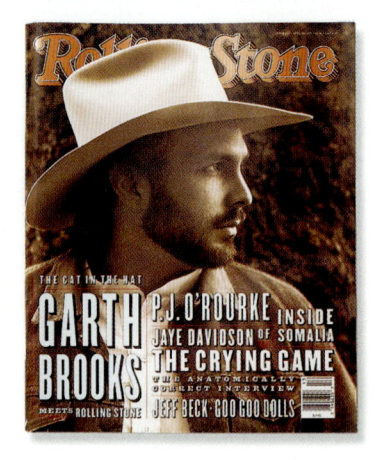

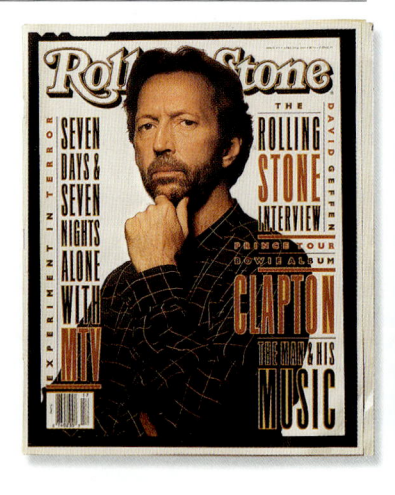

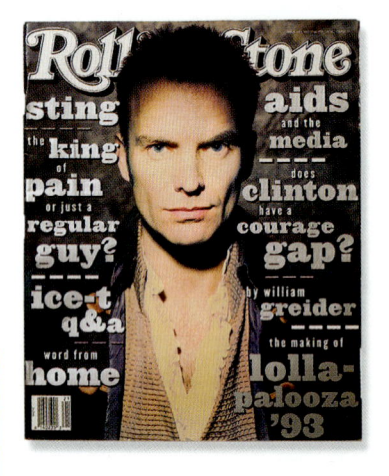

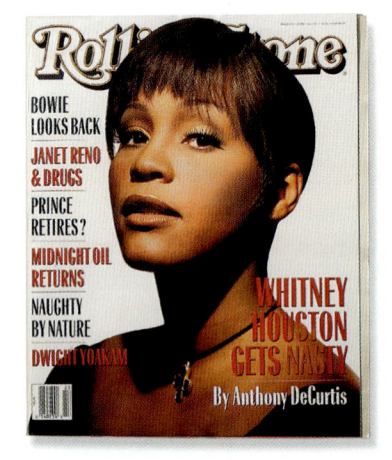

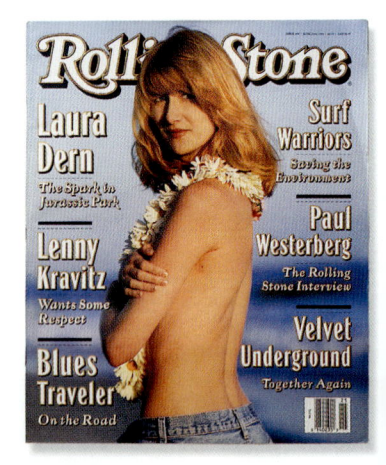

1990s

RS 652 | NATALIE MERCHANT
March 18th, 1993
PHOTOGRAPH BY JEFFREY THURNHER

RS 653 | GARTH BROOKS
April 1st, 1993
PHOTOGRAPH BY KURT MARKUS

RS 655 | ERIC CLAPTON
April 29th, 1993
PHOTOGRAPH BY ALBERT WATSON

RS 657 | STING
May 27th, 1993
PHOTOGRAPH BY ANDREW MACPHERSON

RS 658 | WHITNEY HOUSTON
June 10th, 1993
PHOTOGRAPH BY ALBERT WATSON

RS 659 | LAURA DERN
June 24th, 1993
PHOTOGRAPH BY KURT MARKUS

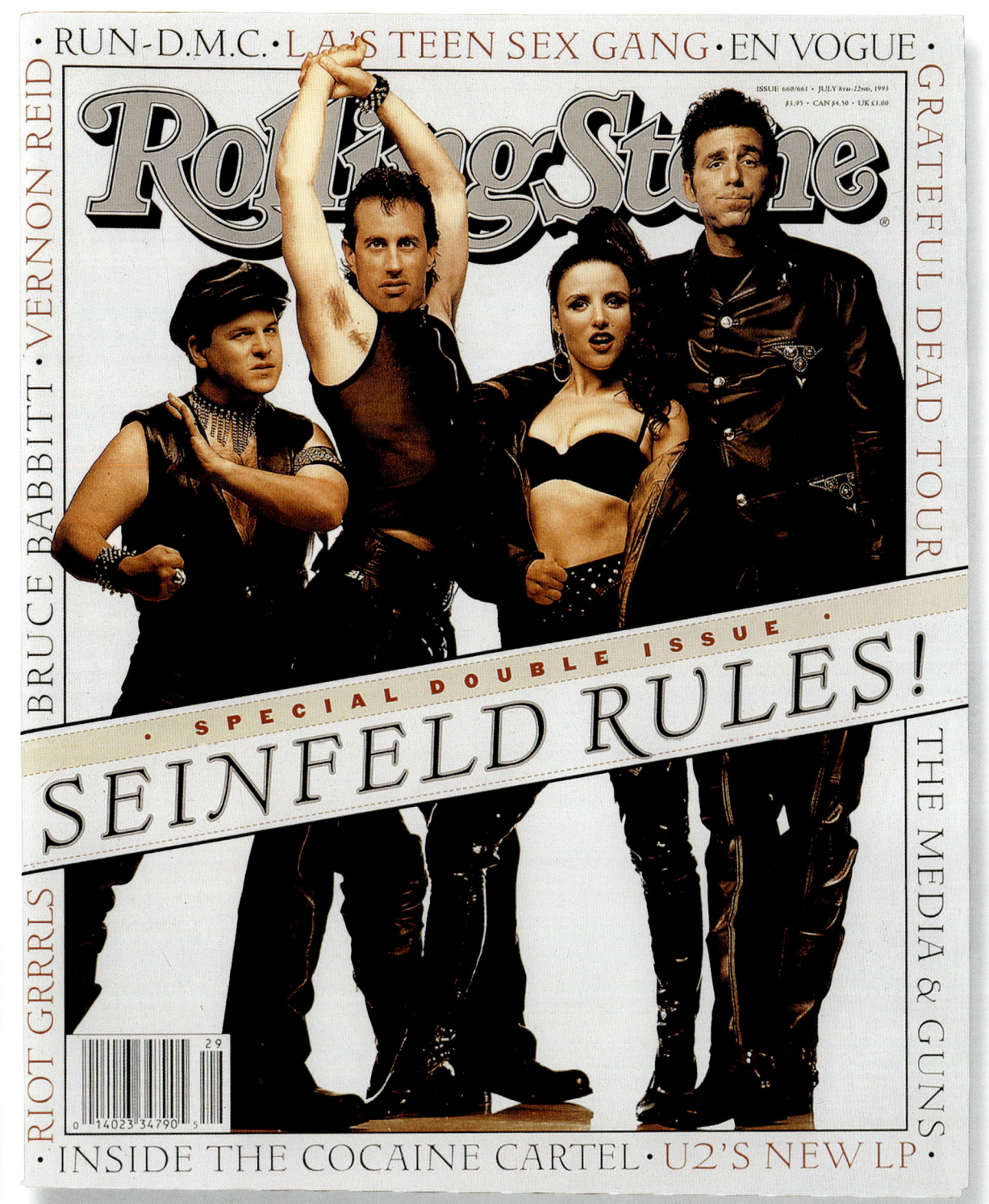

RS 660/661 | CAST OF 'SEINFELD' | July 8th – July 22nd, 1993 | Photograph by Mark Seliger

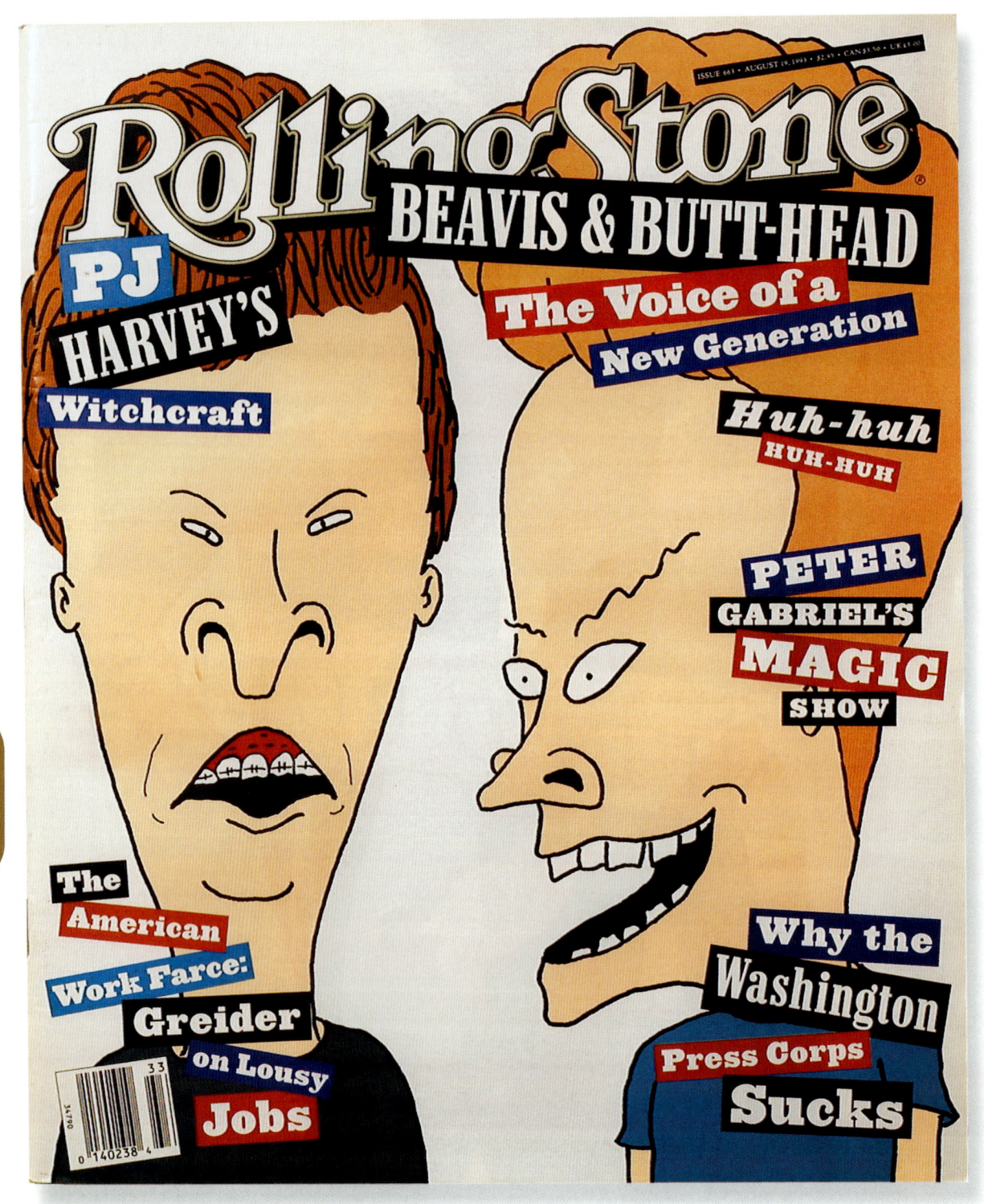

RS 663 | BEAVIS & BUTT-HEAD | August 19th, 1993 | ILLUSTRATION BY MIKE JUDGE

Rolling Stone

ISSUE 665 · SEPTEMBER 16, 1993

THE ROLLING STONE INTERVIEW

WOODY ALLEN
'no apologies'

JANET JACKSON
the joy of sex

STONE TEMPLE PILOTS

NIRVANA

SNOW

RED HOT CHILI PEPPERS

RADIOHEAD

BJÖRK

BUFFALO TOM

RS 665 | JANET JACKSON | September 16th, 1993 | Photograph by Patrick Demarchelier

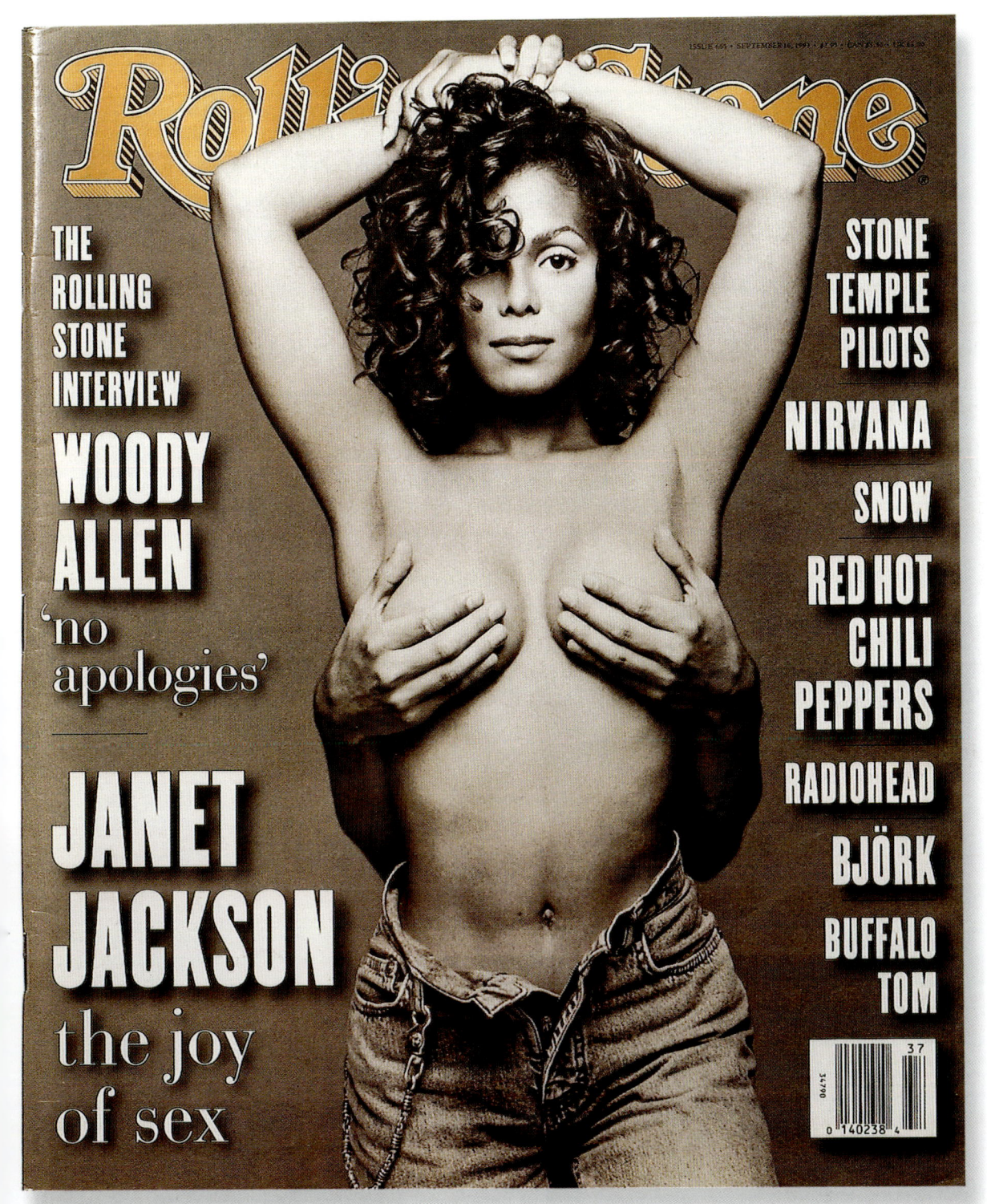

50 YEARS OF COVERS · 351

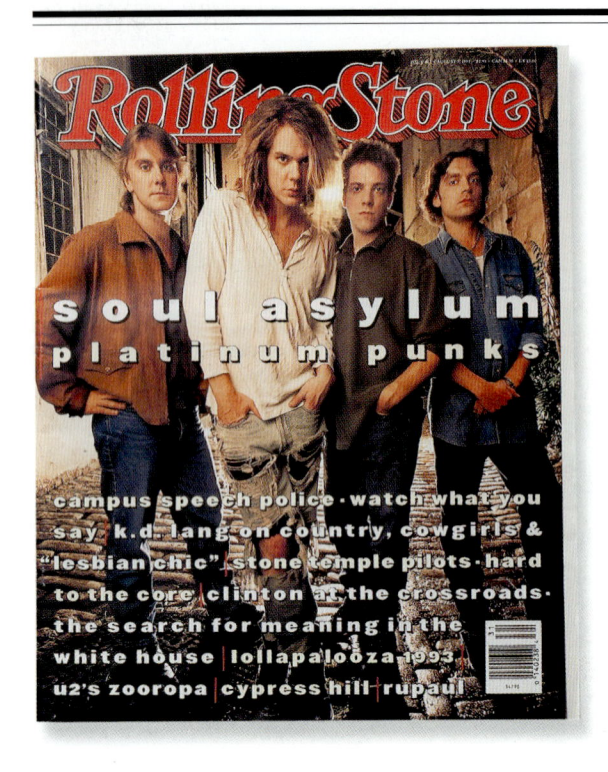

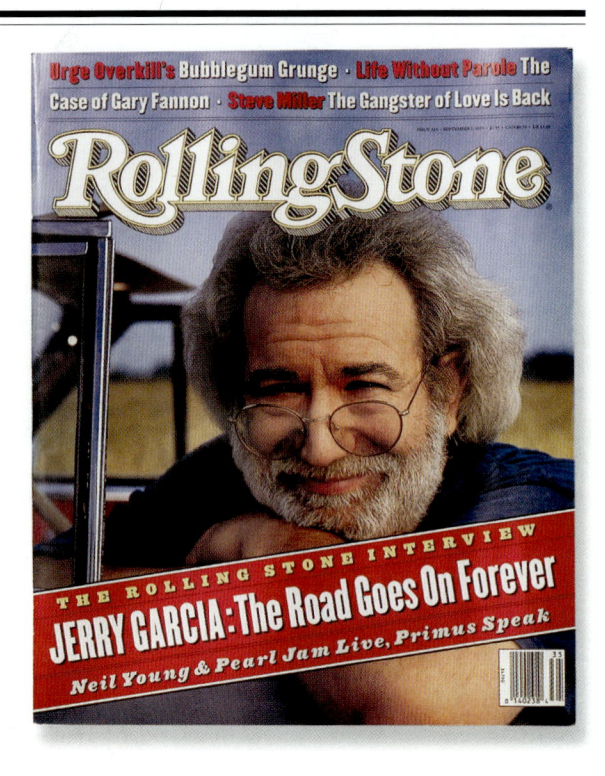

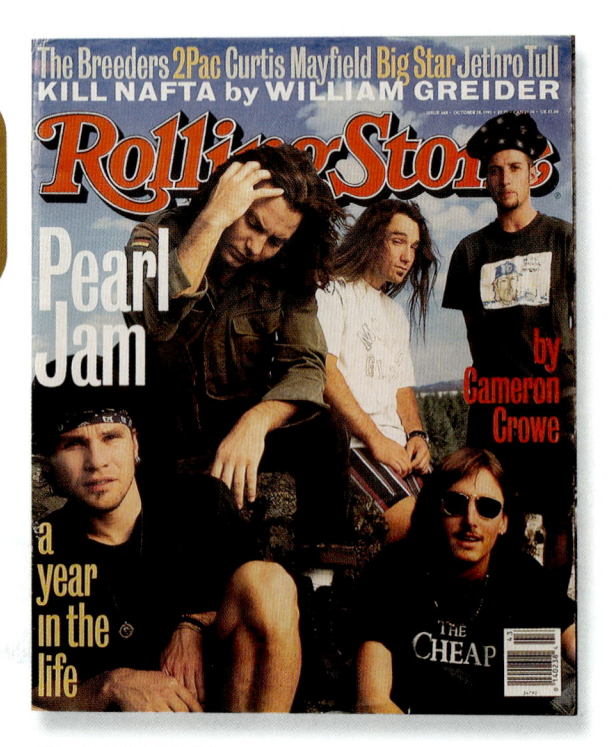

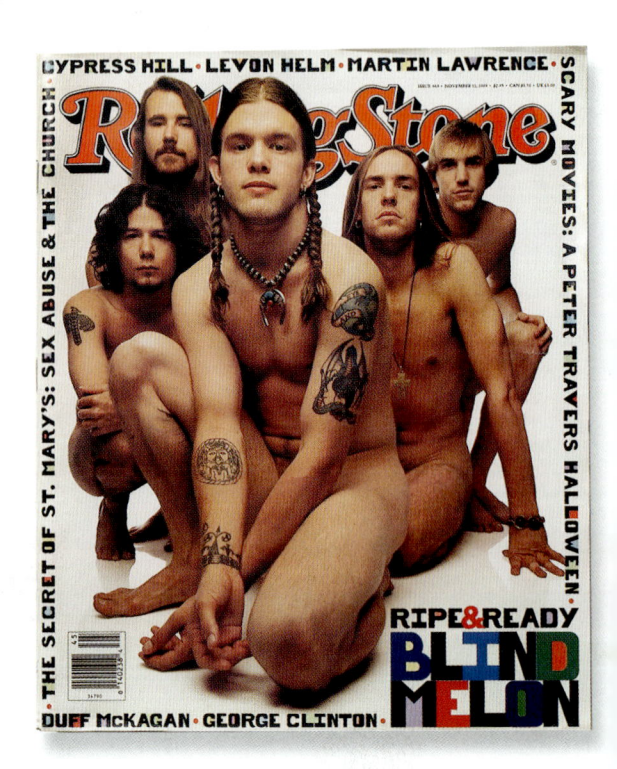

1990s

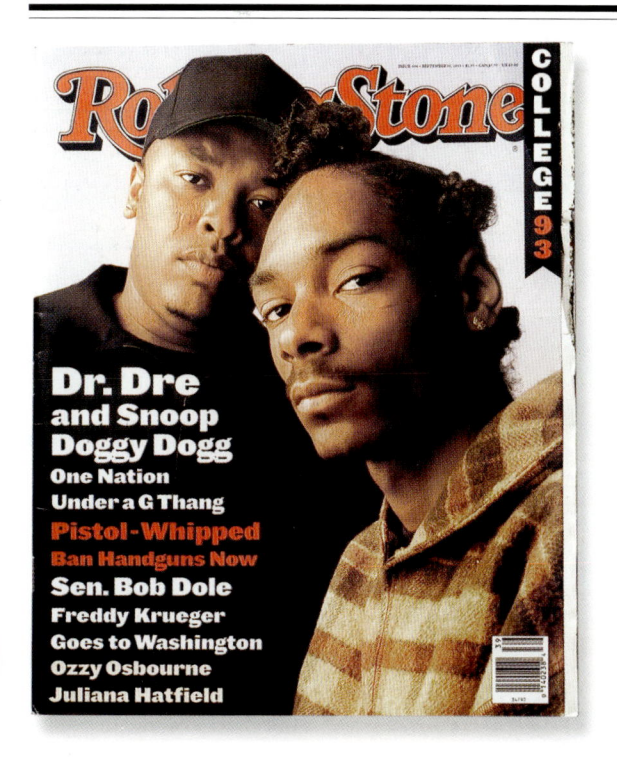

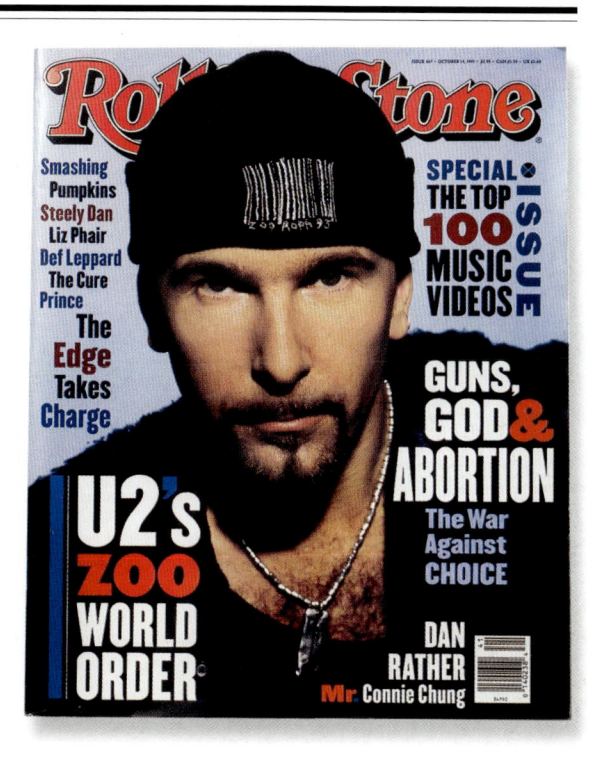

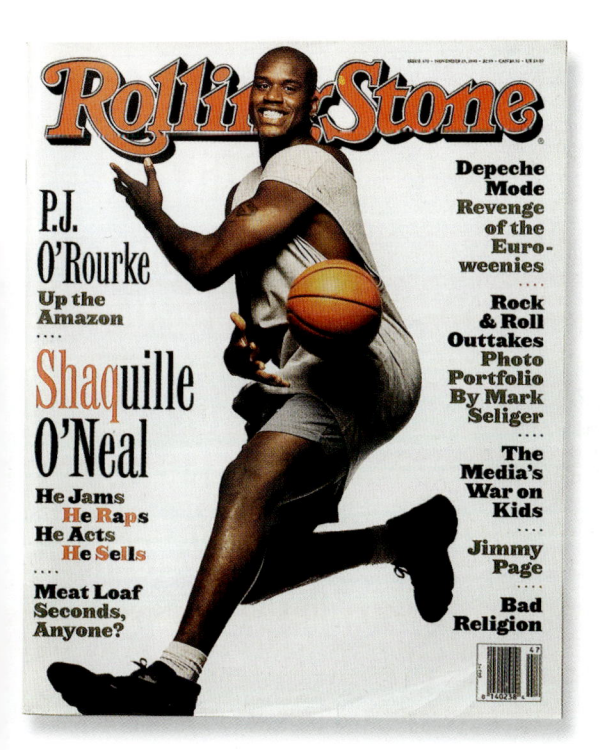

RS 662 | SOUL ASYLUM
August 5th, 1993
Photograph by Mark Seliger

RS 664 | JERRY GARCIA
September 2nd, 1993
Photograph by Mark Seliger

RS 666 | DR. DRE & SNOOP DOGGY DOG
September 30th, 1993
Photograph by Mark Seliger

RS 667 | THE EDGE
October 14th, 1993
Photograph by Andrew MacPherson

RS 668 | PEARL JAM
October 28th, 1993
Photograph by Mark Seliger

RS 669 | BLIND MELON
November 11th, 1993
Photograph by Mark Seliger

RS 670 | SHAQUILLE O'NEAL
November 25th, 1993
Photograph by Mark Seliger

PEARL JAM LIVE | WHITE ZOMBIE | GUNS N' ROSES | INXS

Rolling Stone

Life in the Fast Lane

President CLINTON

The Rolling Stone Interview

NRA ON THE RUN
The New Politics of Gun Control

ADOLESCENCE IN AMERICA

The Years of Living Dangerously

1990s

RS 671 | BILL CLINTON | December 9th, 1993 | Photograph by Mark Seliger

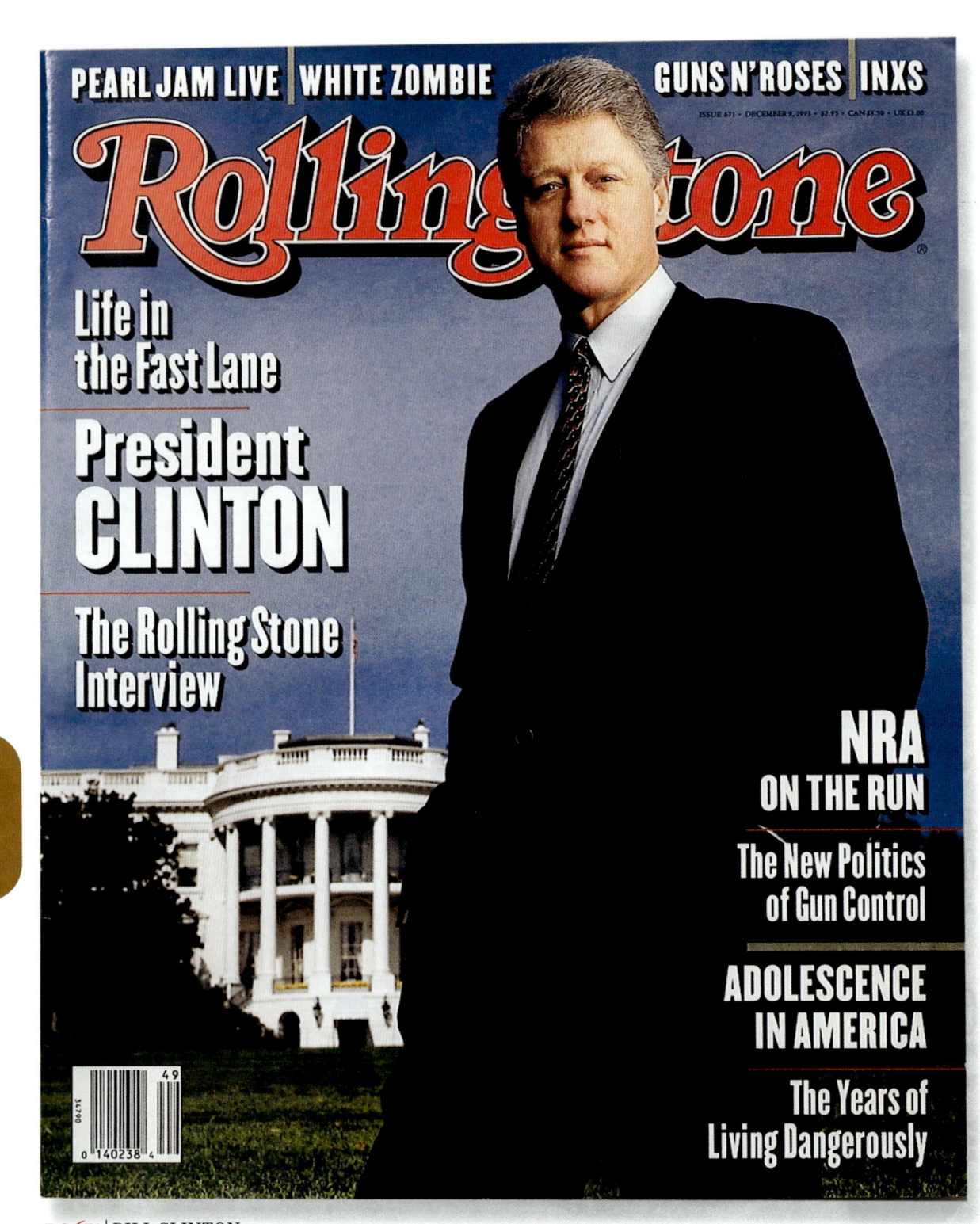

SPECIAL DOUBLE ISSUE

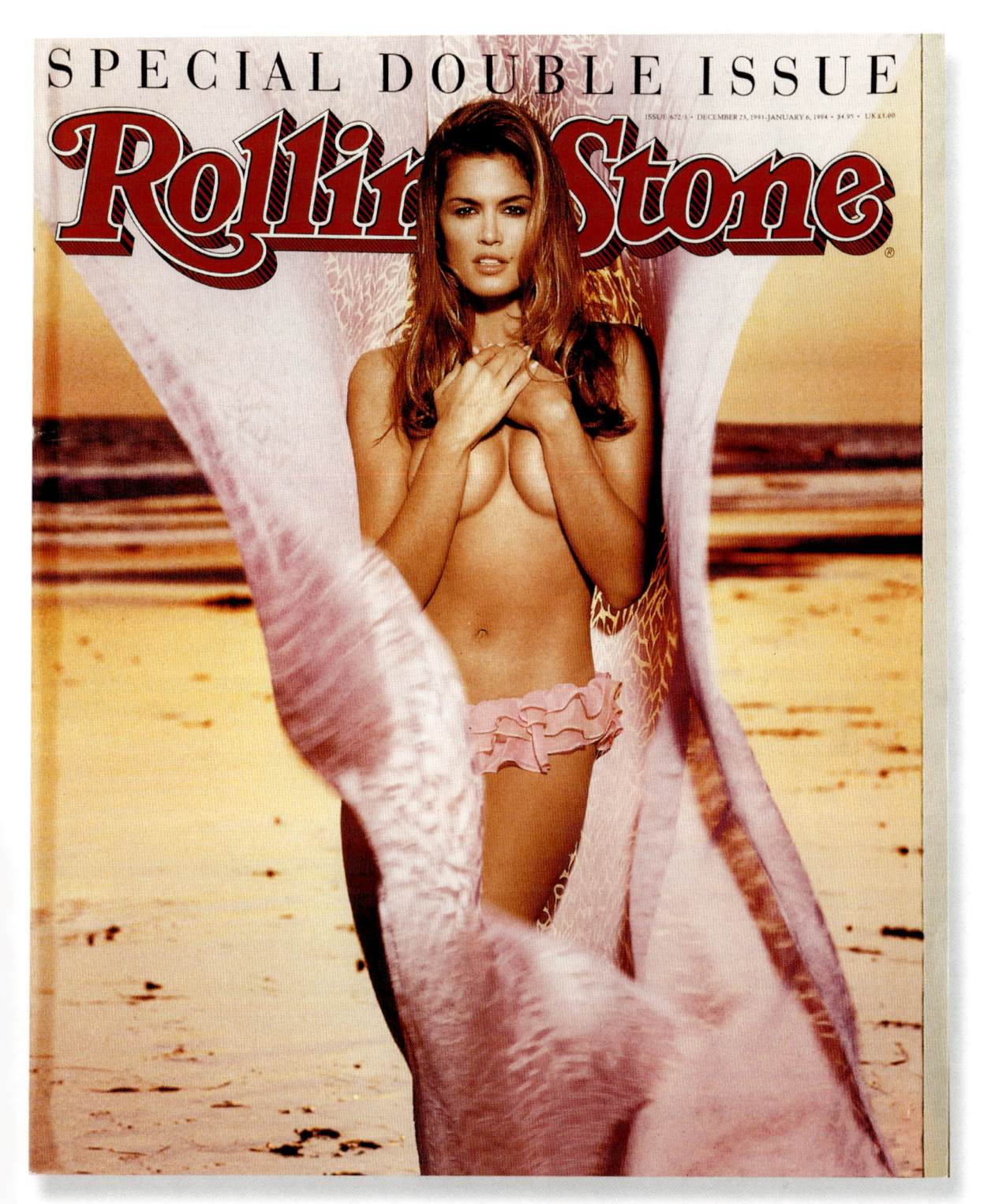

Rolling Stone

ISSUE 672/3 · DECEMBER 23, 1993-JANUARY 6, 1994 · $4.95 · UK £3.00

RS 672/673 | CINDY CRAWFORD | December 23rd, 1993 – January 6th, 1994 | Photograph by Herb Ritts

50 YEARS OF COVERS • 355

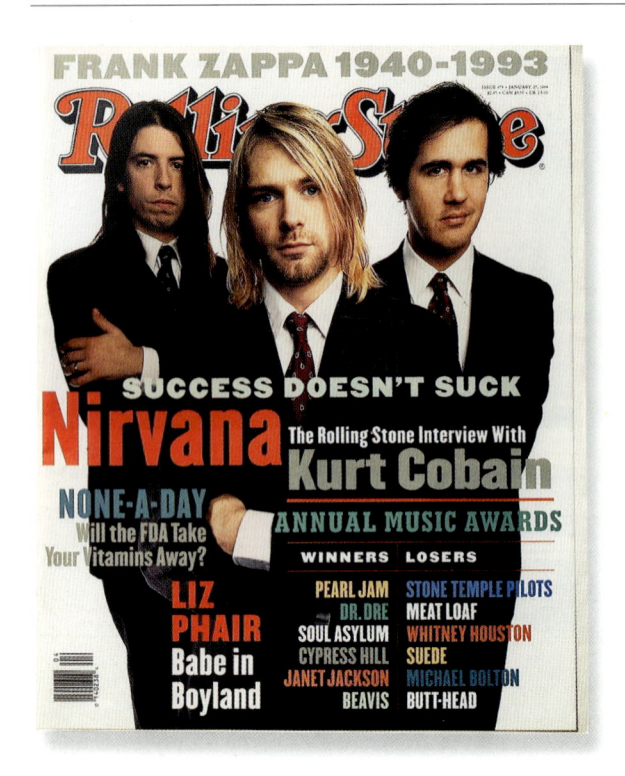

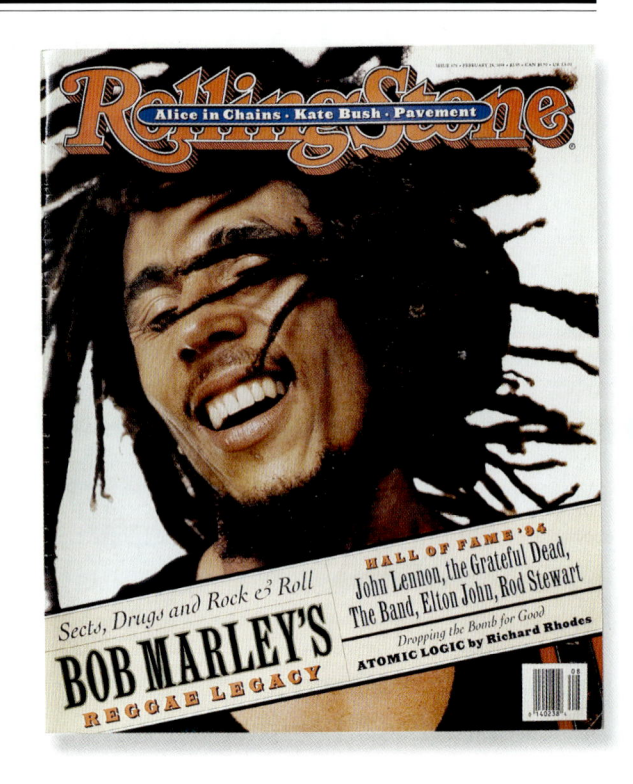

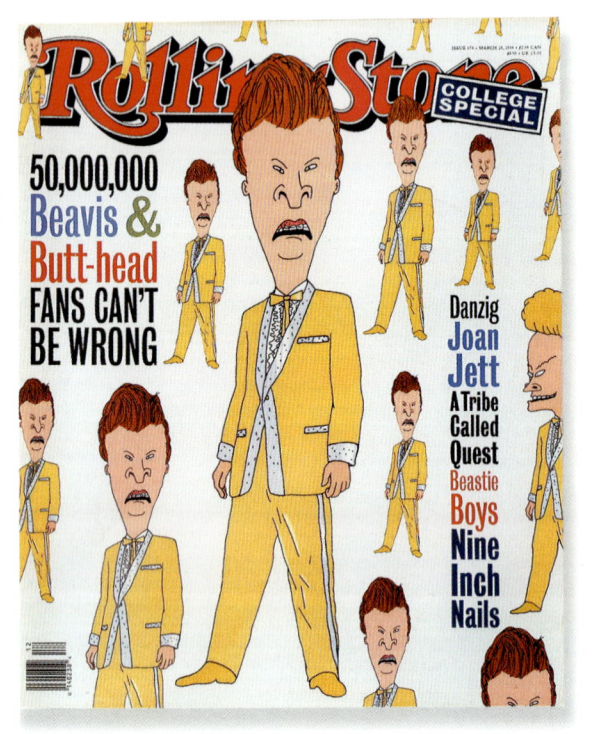

RS 674 | NIRVANA
January 27th, 1994
PHOTOGRAPH BY MARK SELIGER

RS 676 | BOB MARLEY
February 24th, 1993
PHOTOGRAPH BY ANNIE LEIBOVITZ

RS 678 | BEAVIS & BUTT-HEAD
March 24th, 1994
ILLUSTRATION BY MIKE JUDGE

1990s

356 • ROLLING STONE

Rolling Stone

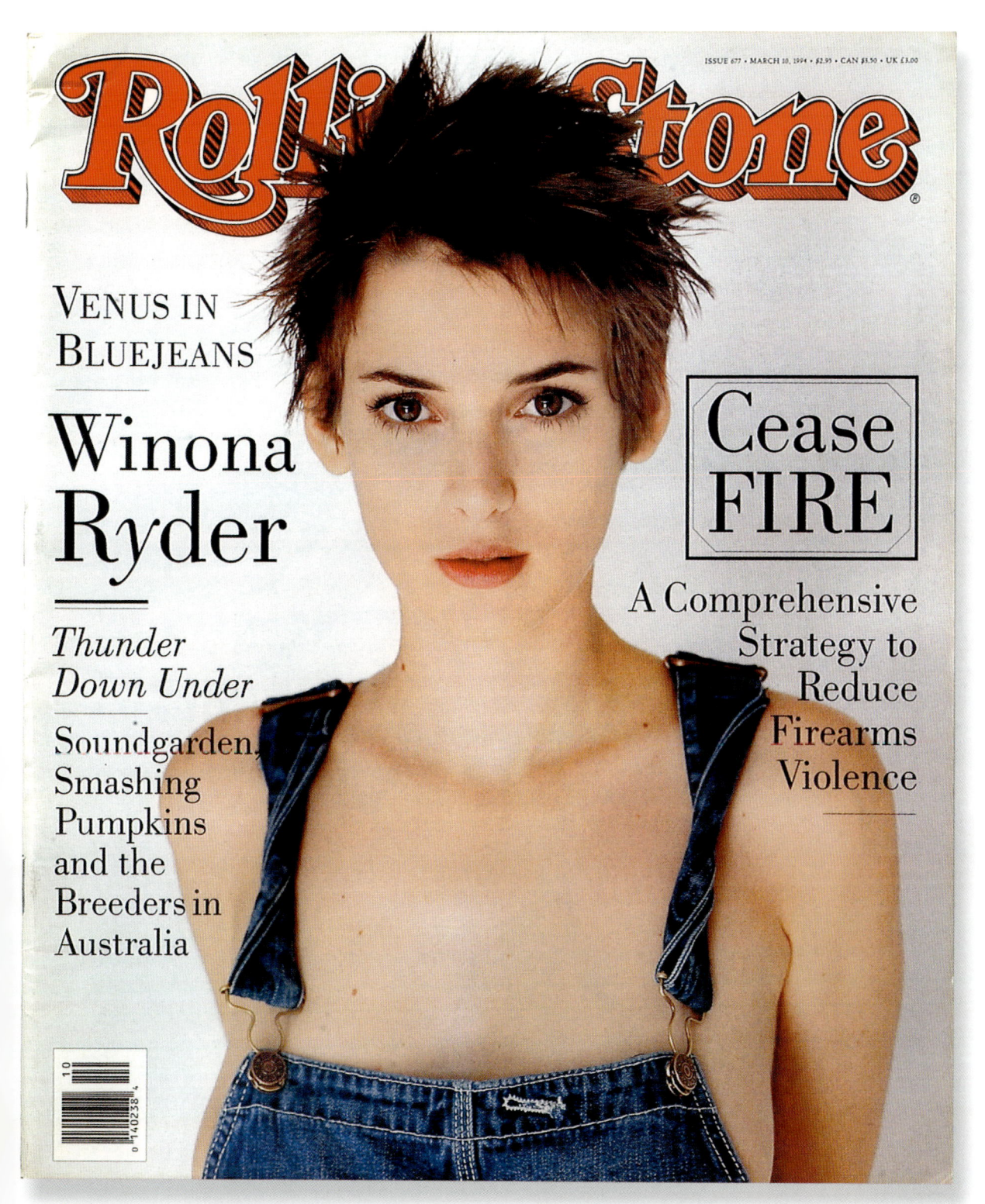

ISSUE 677 · MARCH 10, 1994 · $2.95 · CAN $3.50 · UK £3.00

VENUS IN
BLUEJEANS

Winona Ryder

Thunder Down Under

Soundgarden, Smashing Pumpkins and the Breeders in Australia

Cease FIRE

A Comprehensive Strategy to Reduce Firearms Violence

RS 677 | WINONA RYDER | March 10th, 1994 | Photograph by Herb Ritts

Rolling Stone

ISSUE 675 · FEBRUARY 10, 1994 · $2.95 · CAN $3.50 · UK £3.00

REVENGE OF THE NERD

HOWARD STERN

THE ROLLING STONE INTERVIEW

PAUL McCARTNEY

STONE TEMPLE PILOTS

THE LEMONHEADS

SEX, DRUGS & EVAN DANDO

ZZ TOP

BUZZCOCKS

1990s

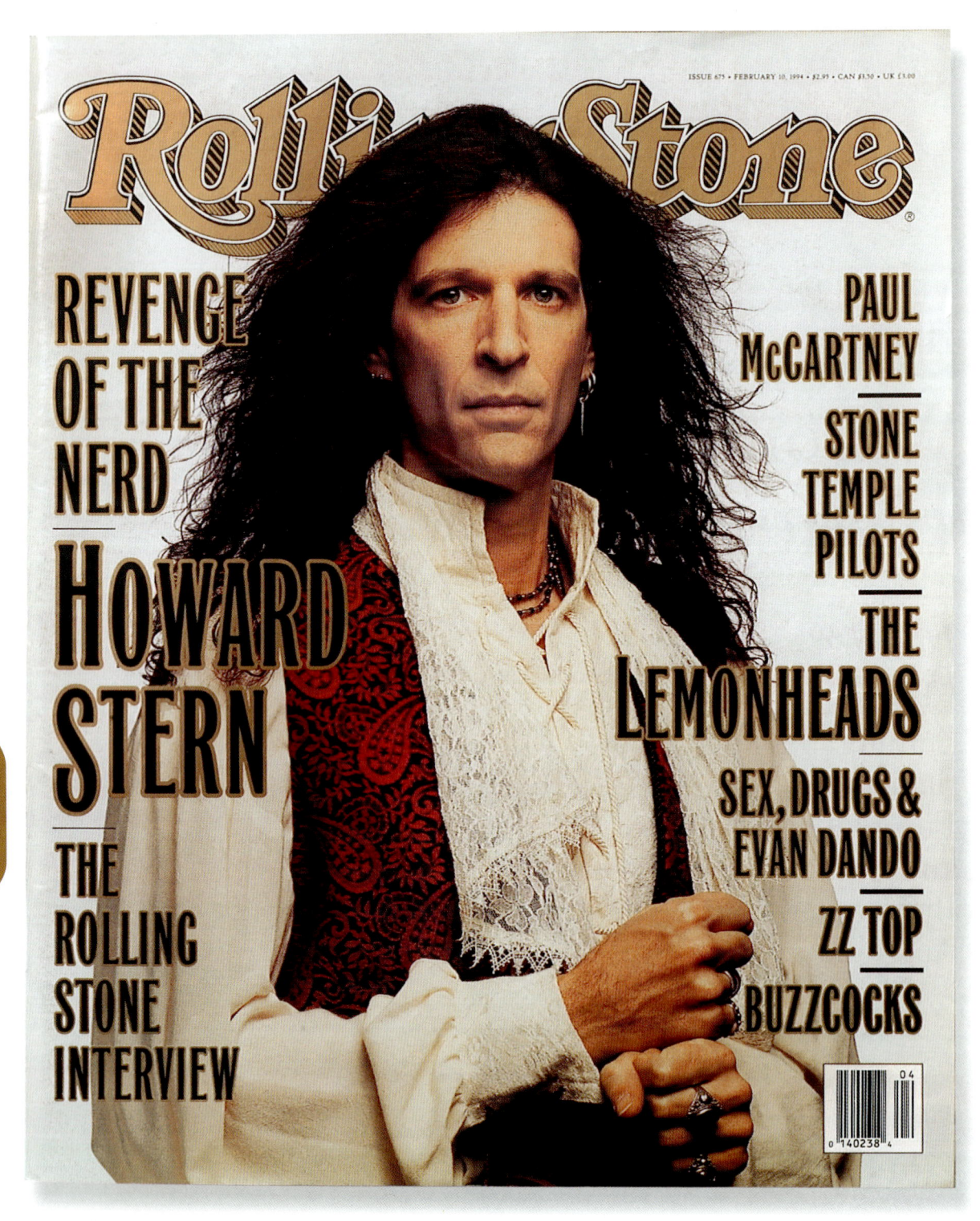

RS 675 | HOWARD STERN | February 10th, 1994 | Photograph by Mark Seliger

ISSUE 679 · APRIL 7, 1994 · $2.95 CAN $3.50 UK £3.00

Rolling Stone

RED HOT CHILI PEPPERS' ANTHONY KIEDIS

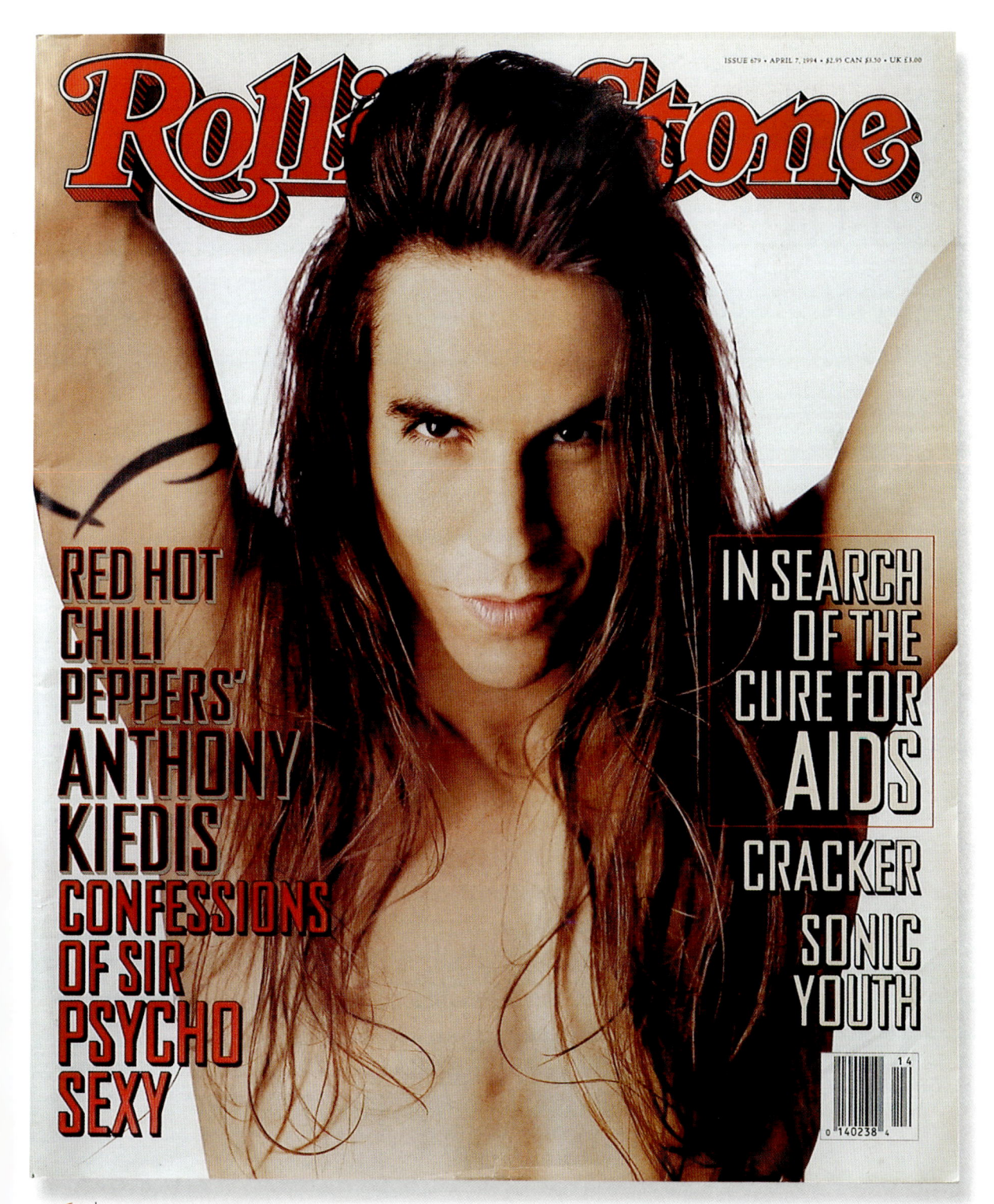

CONFESSIONS OF SIR PSYCHO SEXY

IN SEARCH OF THE CURE FOR AIDS

CRACKER

SONIC YOUTH

RS 679 | ANTHONY KIEDIS | April 7th, 1994 | PHOTOGRAPH BY MATTHEW ROLSTON

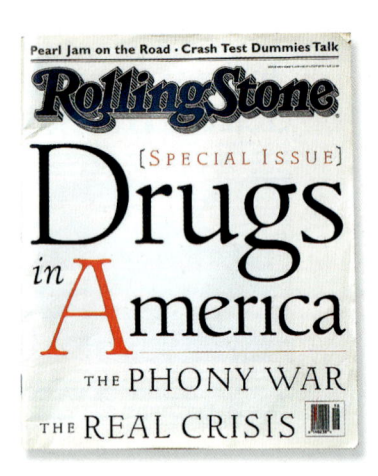

RS 681 | DRUGS IN AMERICA
May 5th, 1994

The war on drugs is over.

After eight decades of interdiction, prohibition and punishment, the results are in: There are now more than 330,000 Americans behind bars for violating the drug laws. We are spending over $20 billion per year on criminal-justice approaches, but illegal drugs are available in greater supply and purity than ever before. Cynical phrases such as *zero tolerance* and *drug-free society* substitute for thoughtful policies and realistic objectives. It's time for a change. . . .

One often forgotten lesson of Prohibition is that it was followed not by a uniform national policy but by "local option." When, in 1933, the 21st Amendment to the Constitution repealed Prohibition, the states went their own ways: Some opted for state monopolies, others for licensing schemes, and some chose to remain dry. Some legalized all alcoholic beverages, others just beer and wine. Some imposed high taxes, others low taxes.

We need local solutions to local problems. What the federal government needs to do is repeal many of the laws and regulations that stifle local initiatives and block any movement away from the war on drugs. Let towns, cities, counties and states experiment with new approaches. It's the only way to find out what really works.

[EXCERPT FROM "TOWARD A SANE NATIONAL DRUG POLICY," RS 681, BY JANN S. WENNER AND ETHAN NADELMAN]

RollingStone

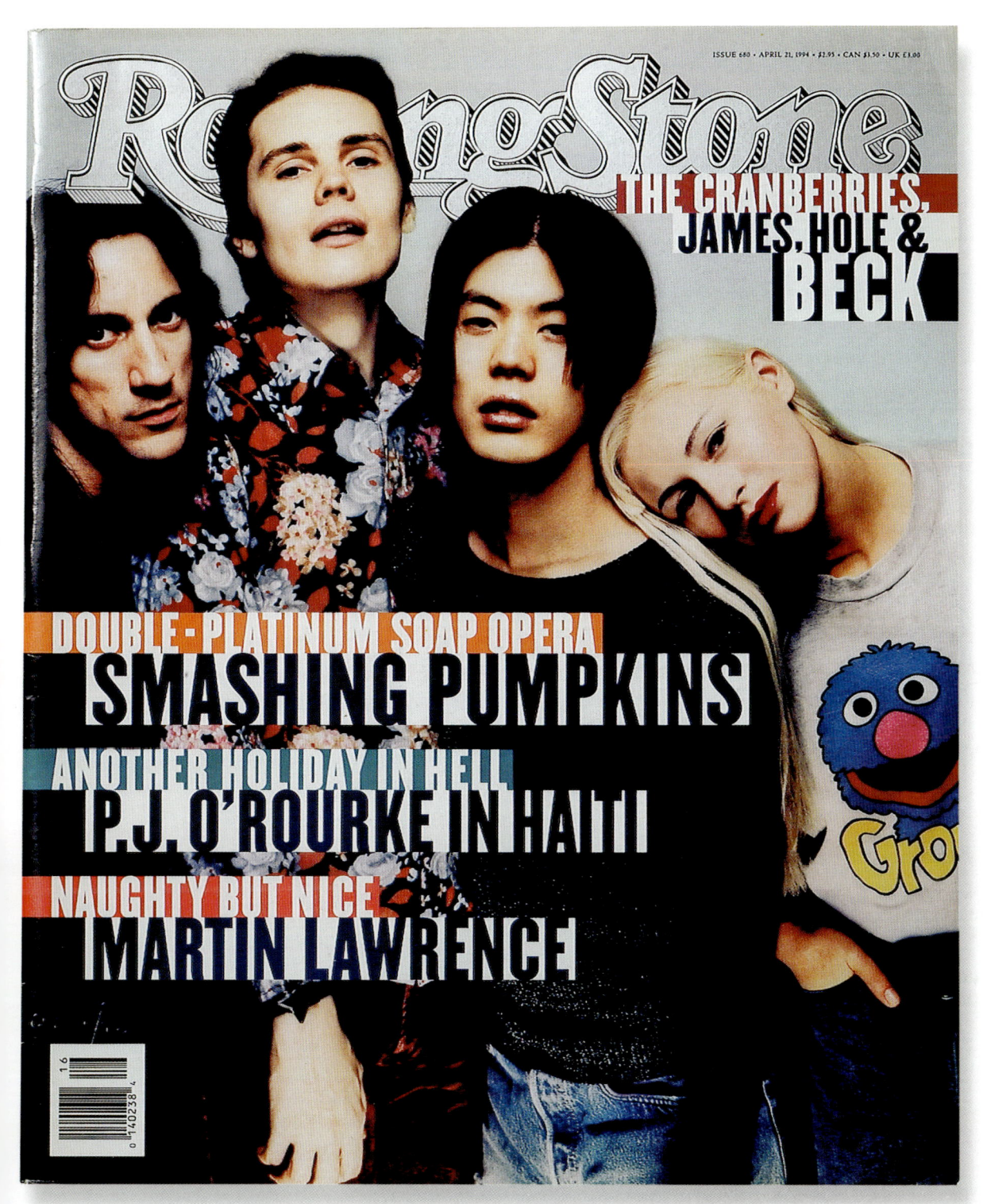

ISSUE 680 · APRIL 21, 1994 · $2.95 CAN $3.50 UK £3.00

THE CRANBERRIES, JAMES, HOLE & BECK

DOUBLE-PLATINUM SOAP OPERA
SMASHING PUMPKINS

ANOTHER HOLIDAY IN HELL
P.J. O'ROURKE IN HAITI

NAUGHTY BUT NICE
MARTIN LAWRENCE

RS 680 | SMASHING PUMPKINS | April 21st, 1994 | Photograph by Glen Luchford

the hot issue

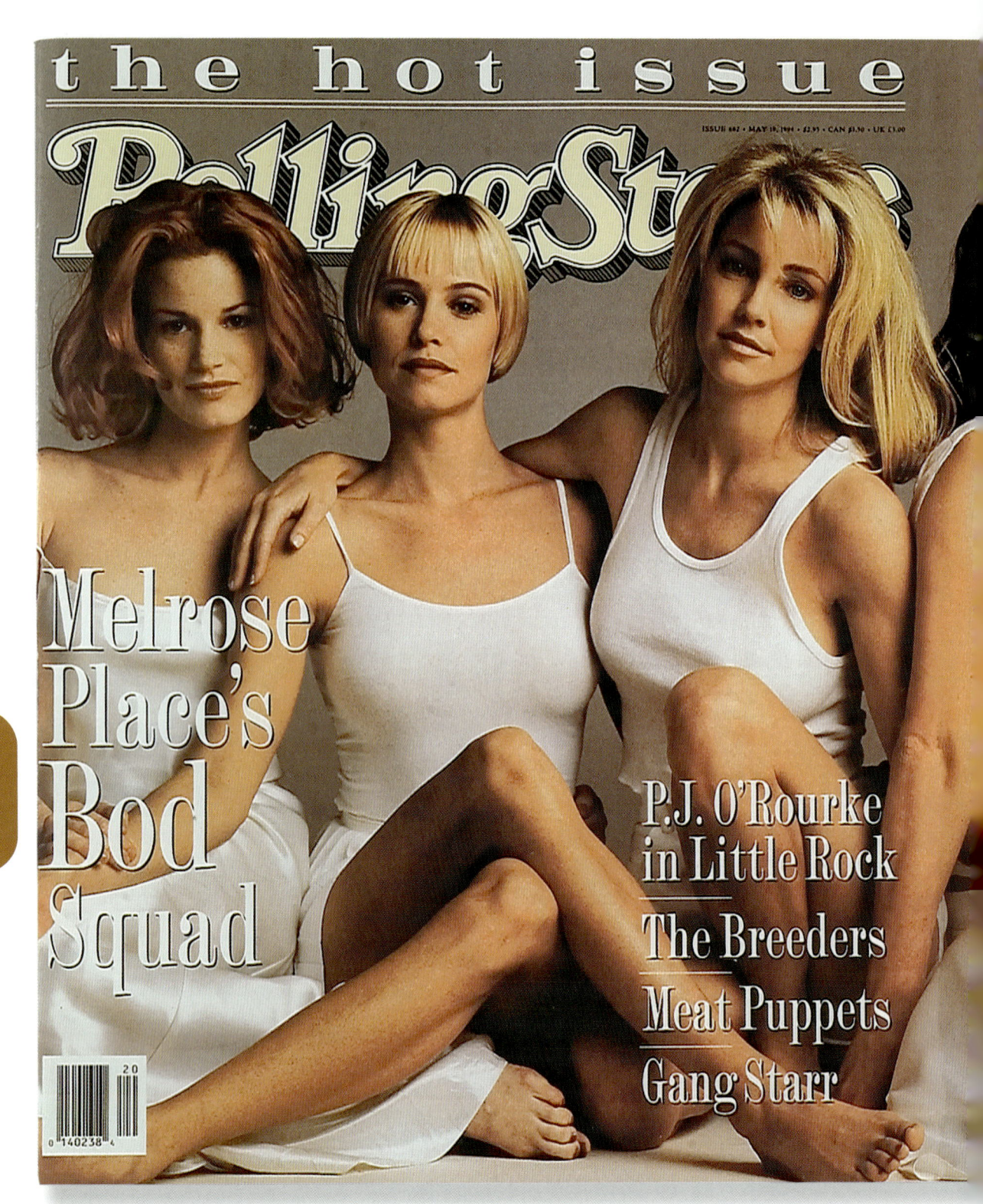

RollingStone

ISSUE 682 • MAY 19, 1994 • $2.95 • CAN $3.50 • UK £3.00

1990s

Melrose Place's Bod Squad

P.J. O'Rourke in Little Rock

The Breeders

Meat Puppets

Gang Starr

The Famous Hot List

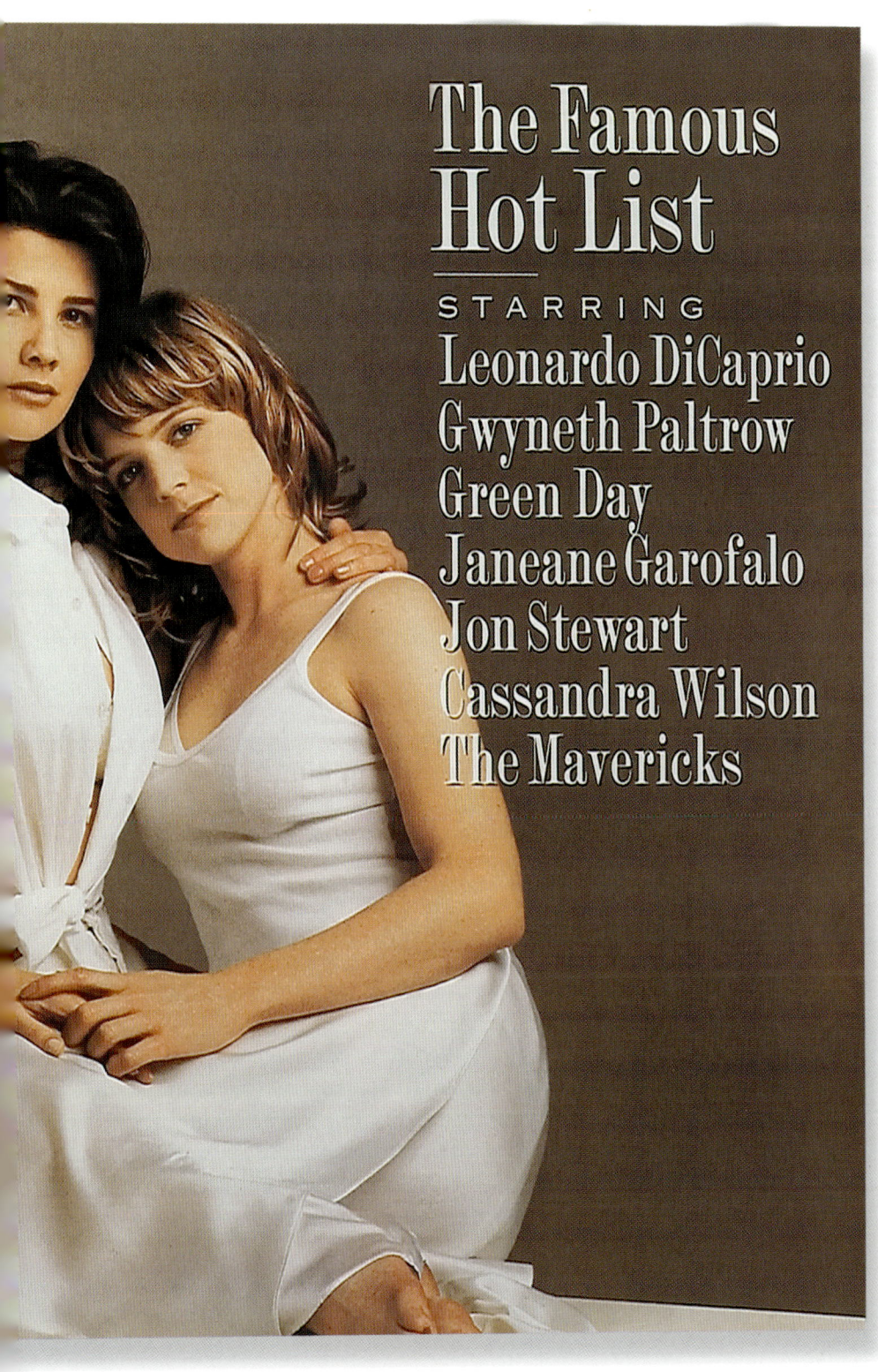

STARRING
Leonardo DiCaprio
Gwyneth Paltrow
Green Day
Janeane Garofalo
Jon Stewart
Cassandra Wilson
The Mavericks

RS 682
THE WOMEN OF 'MELROSE PLACE'
May 19th, 1994
Photograph by Mark Seliger

RS 683 | **KURT COBAIN** | June 2nd, 1994 | Photograph by Mark Seliger

"***I haven't felt*** the excitement of listening to as well as creating music, along with really writing for too many years now. I feel guilty beyond words about these things. For example, when we're backstage and the lights go out and the manic roar of the crowd begins, it doesn't affect me the way in which it did for Freddie Mercury, who seemed to love and relish in the love and admiration from the crowd which is something I totally admire and envy. The fact is, I can't fool you, any one of you. It simply isn't fair to you or to me. The worst crime I can think of would be to rip people off by faking it and pretending as if I'm having 100 percent fun."

—*Kurt Cobain's suicide note*

PEOPLE LOOKED TO KURT COBAIN because his songs captured what they felt before they knew they felt it. Even his struggles – with fame, with drugs, with his identity – caught the generational drama of our time. Seeing himself since his boyhood as an outcast, he was stunned – and confused, and frightened, and repulsed, and, truth be told, not entirely disappointed (no one forms a band to remain anonymous) – to find himself a star. If Cobain seemed more willing to play the fool than the hero and took drugs more for relief than pleasure, that was fine with his contemporaries. For people who came of age amid the designer-drug indulgence and the image-driven celebrity of the Eighties, anyone who could make an easy peace with success was fatally suspect. Whatever importance Cobain assumed as a symbol, however, one thing is certain: He and his band Nirvana announced the end of one rock & roll era and the start of another. In essence, Nirvana transformed the Eighties into the Nineties. —*Anthony DeCurtis*

SOME KIDS DON'T MAKE IT OUT OF HIGH SCHOOL ALIVE. They give up before they even try. Others stick around, wounded, just to see what happens. Introverted and depressed, Cobain maybe was born with a morbid disposition. Maybe he had a chemical imbalance that made him too sensitive to live in the world, so that even true love, a beautiful daughter, a brilliant band, detox, family life and his wholesome Northwestern community rootedness couldn't fill the hole in his soul. At twenty-seven, Cobain was tired of being alive. —*Donna Gaines*

ON APRIL 8TH, SHORTLY BEFORE 9 a.m., Kurt Cobain's body was found in a greenhouse above the garage of his Seattle home. Across his chest lay the twenty-gauge shotgun with which the twenty-seven-year-old singer, guitarist and songwriter ended his life. Cobain had been missing for six days.

An electrician installing a security system in the house discovered Cobain dead. Though the police, a private investigation firm and friends were on the trail, his body had been lying there for two and a half days, according to a medical examiner's report. A high concentration of heroin and traces of Valium were found in Cobain's bloodstream. He was identifiable only by his fingerprints. —*Neil Strauss*

LAST SPRING, KURT COBAIN sat at his kitchen table at 3 a.m., chain-smoking and toying with one of the medical mannequins he collected. "It's hard to believe that a person can put something as poisonous as alcohol or drugs in their system and the mechanics can take it – for a while," he said to me, absently removing and inserting the doll's lungs, liver, heart.

Kurt was slight, painfully thin; he'd wear several layers of clothes under his usual cardigan and ripped jeans just to appear a little more substantial. He knew well just how much abuse, self-inflicted and otherwise, that fragile frame could withstand.

—*Michael Azerrad*

[EXCERPTS FROM RS 683]

1990s

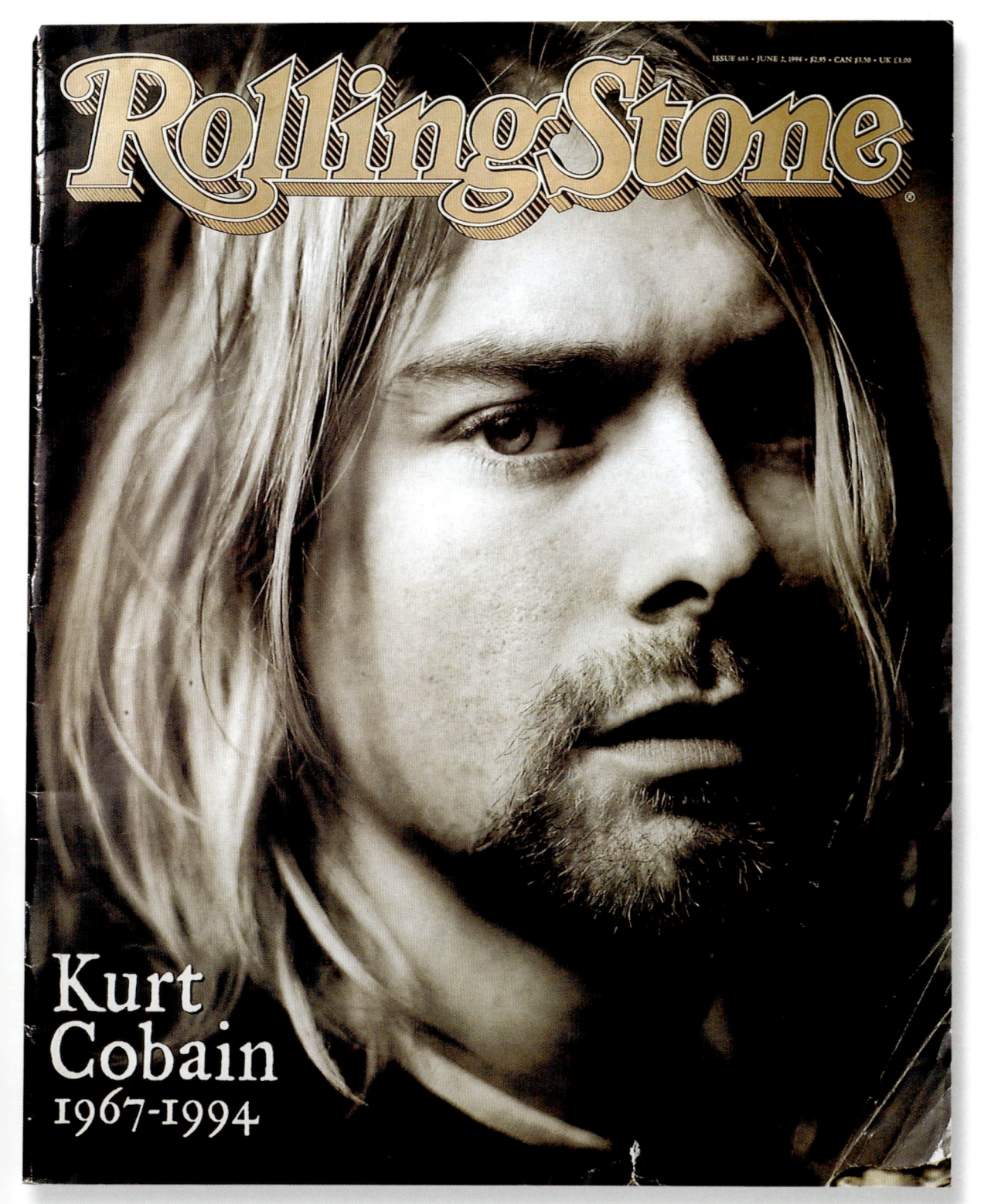

Rolling Stone

ISSUE 683 · JUNE 2, 1994 · $2.95 · CAN $3.50 · UK £1.00

Kurt Cobain
1967-1994

50 YEARS OF COVERS · 365

1990s

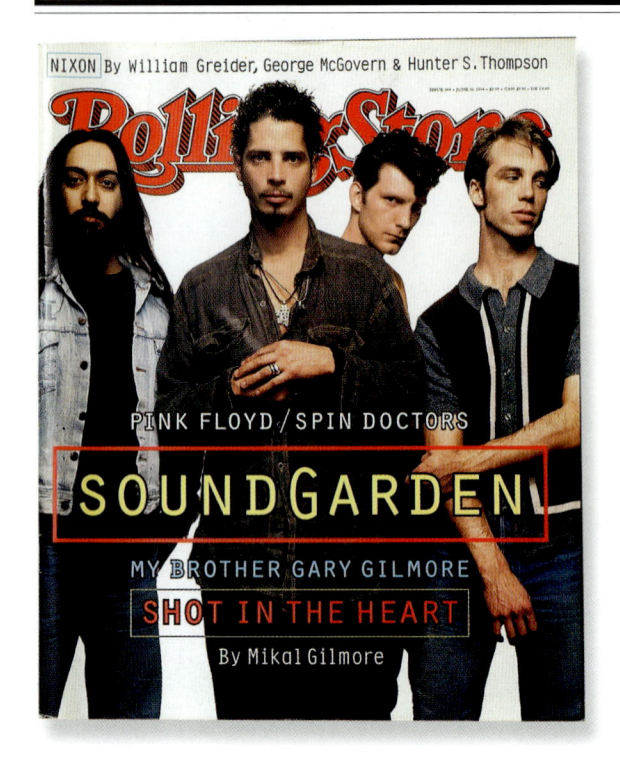

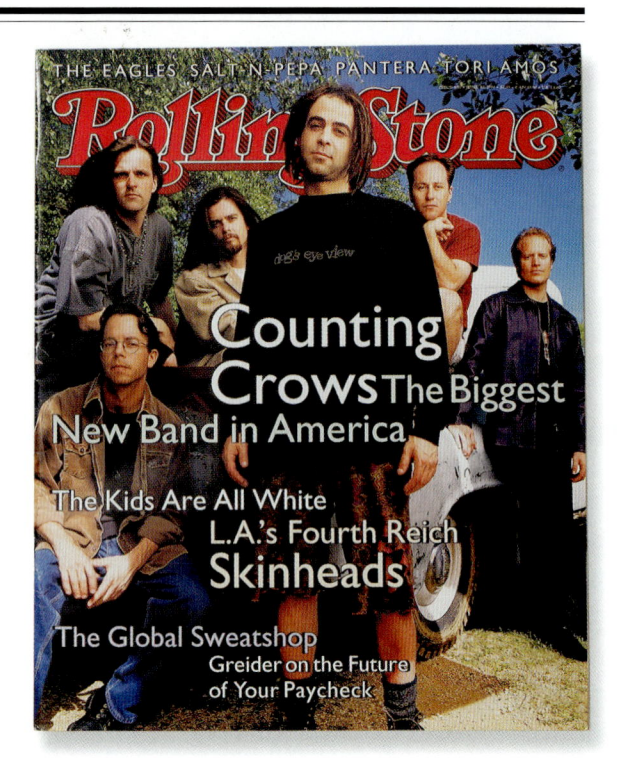

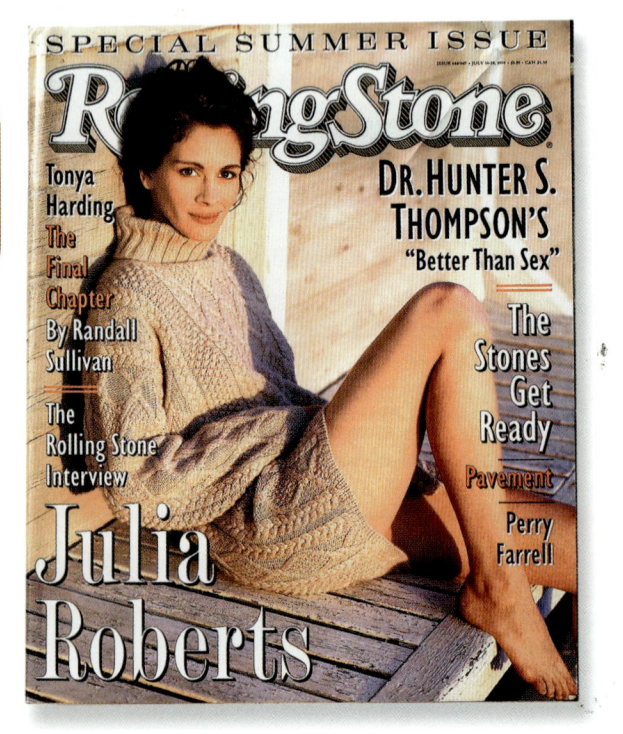

RS 684 | SOUNDGARDEN
June 16th, 1994
Photograph by Mark Seliger

RS 685 | COUNTING CROWS
June 30th, 1994
Photograph by Mark Seliger

RS 686/687 | JULIA ROBERTS
July 14th – July 28th, 1994
Photograph by Herb Ritts

"IT'S JUST SUCH A COOL CHEMISTRY BETWEEN THE three of us [Beastie Boys]. I don't even completely understand how it all interconnects. It's just that the three of us together is much stronger than any one of us working individually. We've been together for so long and care about each other so much, it's really like brothers."

—*Adam Yauch*

366 • ROLLING STONE

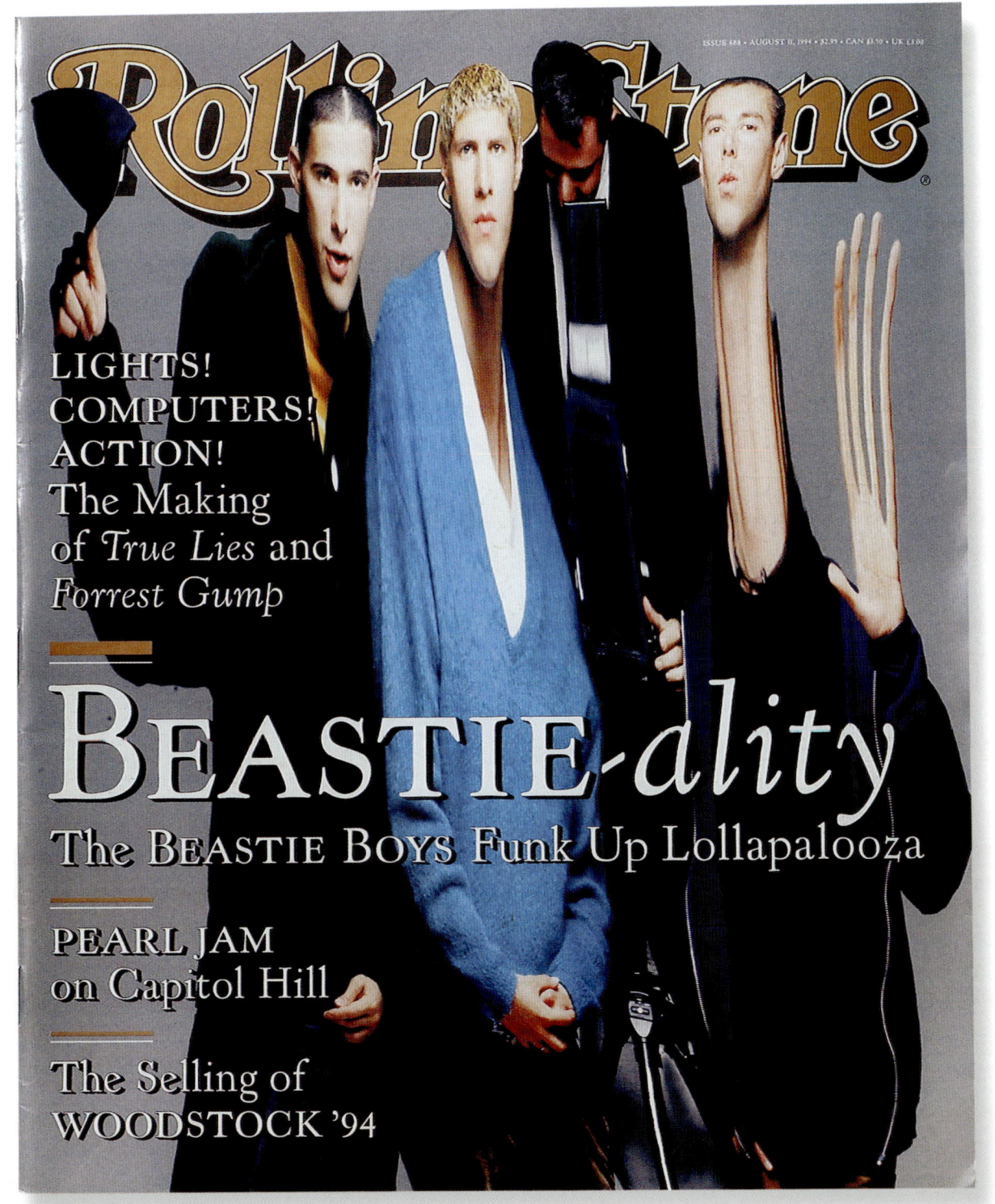

Rolling Stone

ISSUE 688 · AUGUST 11, 1994 · $2.95 · CAN $3.50 · UK £1.80

LIGHTS! COMPUTERS! ACTION! The Making of *True Lies* and *Forrest Gump*

BEASTIE-ality
The Beastie Boys Funk Up Lollapalooza

PEARL JAM on Capitol Hill

The Selling of WOODSTOCK '94

RS 688 | BEASTIE BOYS | August 11th, 1994 | Photograph by Matthew Rolston

50 YEARS OF COVERS · 367

RS 689
THE ROLLING STONES
August 25th, 1994
PHOTOGRAPH BY ANTON CORBIJN

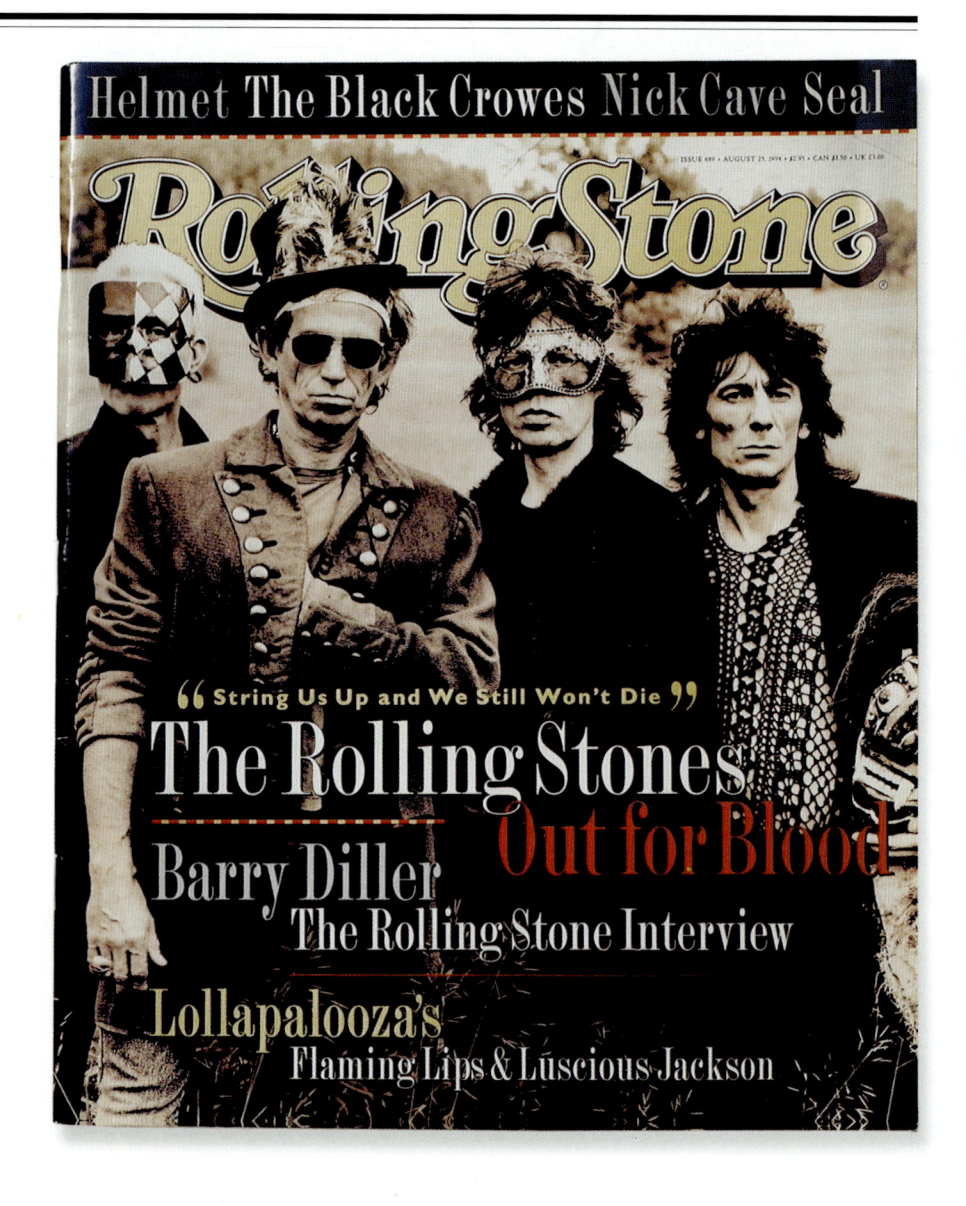

1990s

"THIS COVER WORKED OUT quite madly. The Rolling Stones don't enjoy photo sessions as a band. Because with the band, you have to get everyone in the mood, and I've found that's very difficult. People get bored. You have a good half-hour and someone else is having a bad one. So you get very, very few pictures."

—*Mick Jagger*

ROLLING Stone

NINE INCH NAILS' KILLER INSTINCT

INSIDE TRENT REZNOR'S DARK WORLD OF SEX, PAIN AND ROCK & ROLL

JOHN MELLENCAMP STRIPS DOWN

JOHN DEAN REVIEWS HALDEMAN'S DIARIES

GARRY SHANDLING

SOUNDGARDEN

FREEDY JOHNSTON

AFGHAN WHIGS

RS 690 | TRENT REZNOR | September 8th, 1994 | Photograph by Matt Mahurin

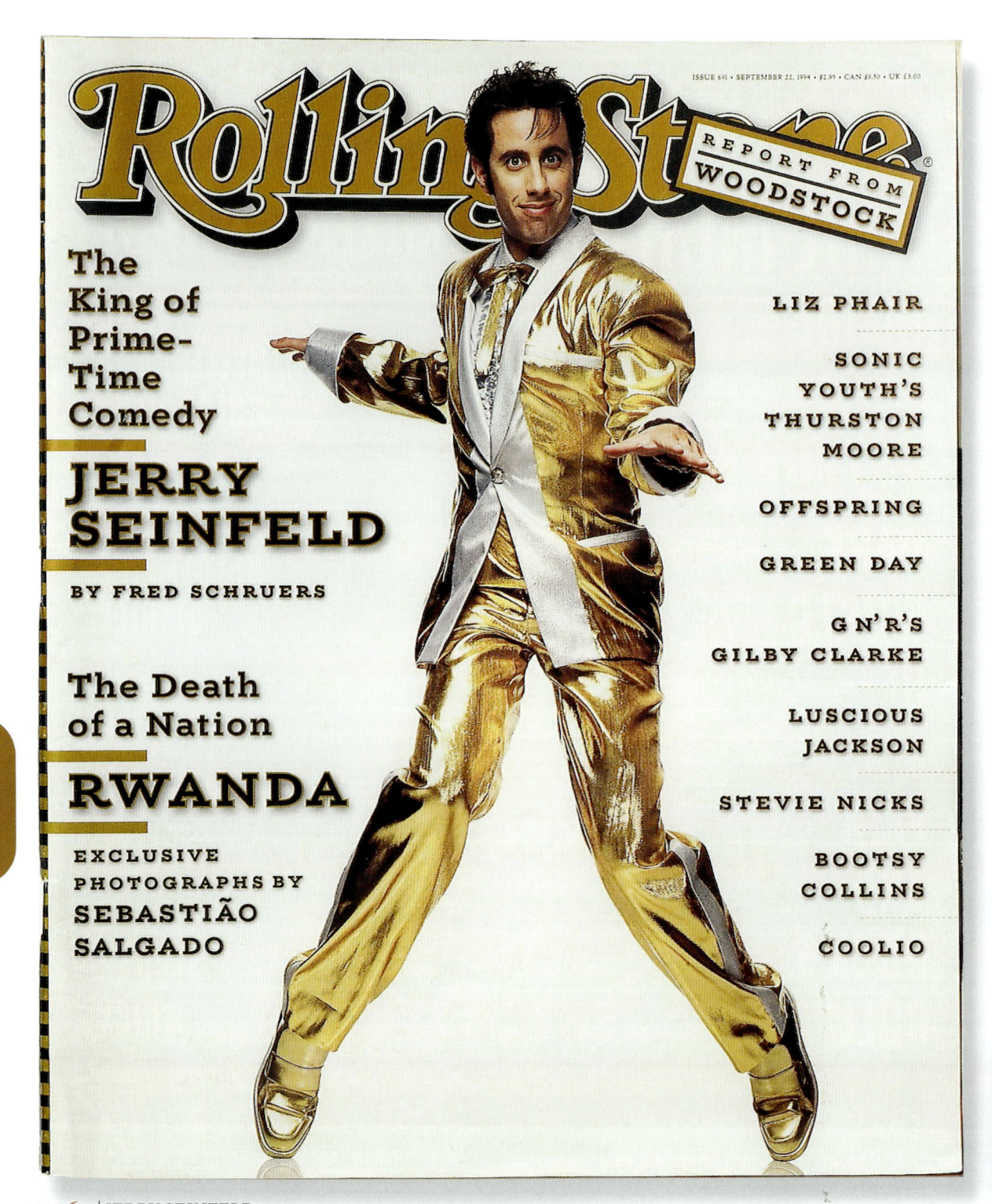

Rolling Stone

ISSUE 691 · SEPTEMBER 22, 1994 · $2.99 CAN $3.50 UK £3.00

REPORT FROM WOODSTOCK

The King of Prime-Time Comedy
JERRY SEINFELD
BY FRED SCHRUERS

The Death of a Nation
RWANDA
EXCLUSIVE PHOTOGRAPHS BY SEBASTIÃO SALGADO

LIZ PHAIR

SONIC YOUTH'S THURSTON MOORE

OFFSPRING

GREEN DAY

GN'R'S GILBY CLARKE

LUSCIOUS JACKSON

STEVIE NICKS

BOOTSY COLLINS

COOLIO

1990s

RS 691 | JERRY SEINFELD | September 22nd, 1994 | PHOTOGRAPHS BY MARK SELIGER

370 · ROLLING STONE

Rolling Stone

ISSUE 691 · SEPTEMBER 22, 1994 · $2.95 · CAN $3.50 · UK £1.00

REPORT FROM WOODSTOCK

JERRY SEINFELD
The King of Prime-Time Comedy
BY FRED SCHRUERS

The Death of a Nation
RWANDA
EXCLUSIVE PHOTOGRAPHS BY SEBASTIÃO SALGADO

- GREEN DAY
- OFFSPRING
- SONIC YOUTH'S THURSTON MOORE
- LIZ PHAIR
- BOOTSY COLLINS
- GN'R'S GILBY CLARKE
- STEVIE NICKS
- LUSCIOUS JACKSON
- COOLIO

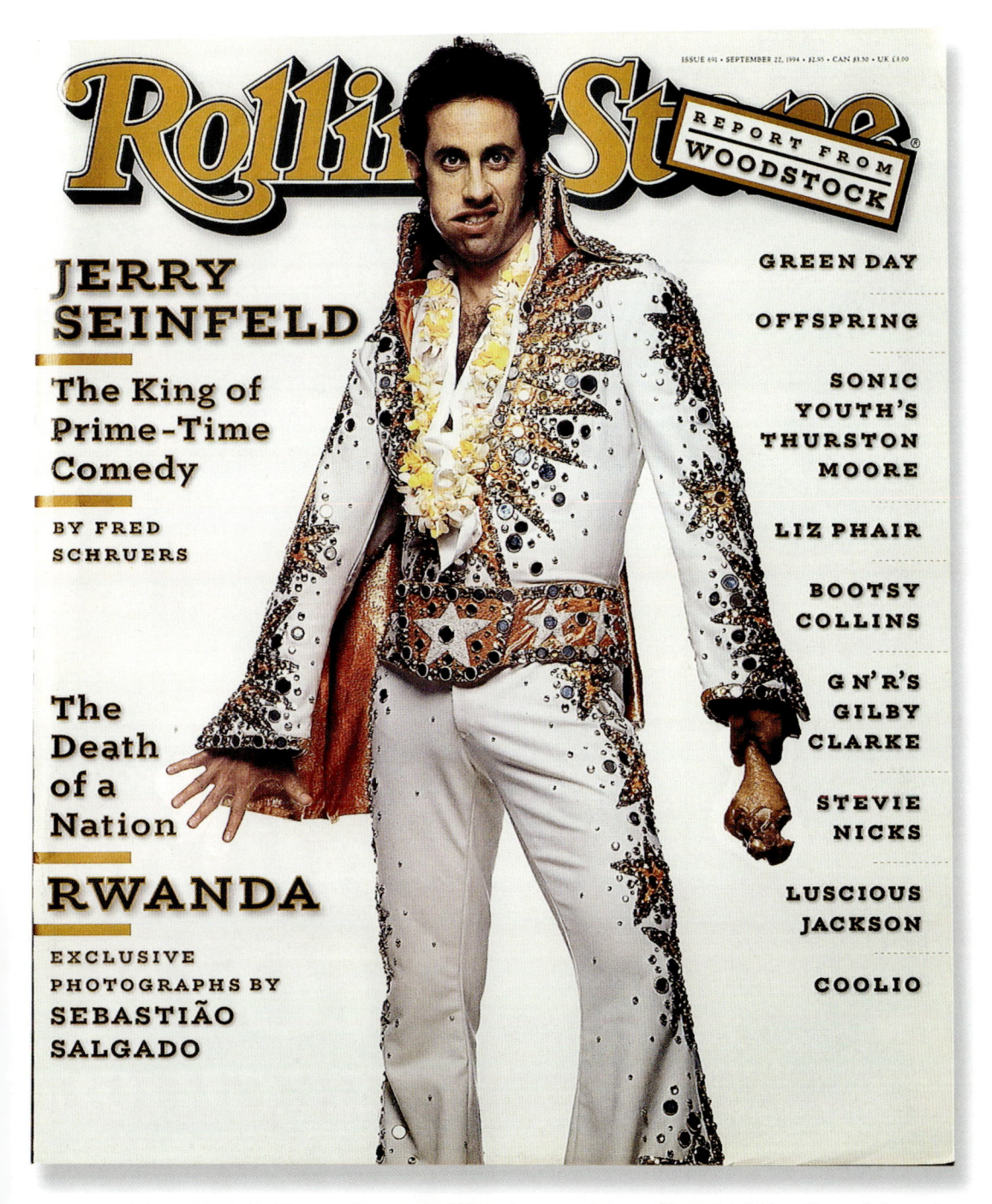

[**RS 691**] The Editor's Note tells this story: "So we're looking at these two pictures of Jerry Seinfeld, and in one he's wearing a gold lamé suit, and in the other he's got on this scary white jumpsuit, and we're saying to ourselves, 'Which do you think the readers will like – Jerry as the young Elvis or Jerry as the old Elvis?' Then we say to ourselves, 'Hey, ROLLING STONE is a democratic kind of place – let the readers decide.' So we put both pictures on the cover and sent it out random-like. But it's all the same magazine inside – take our word for it."

1990s

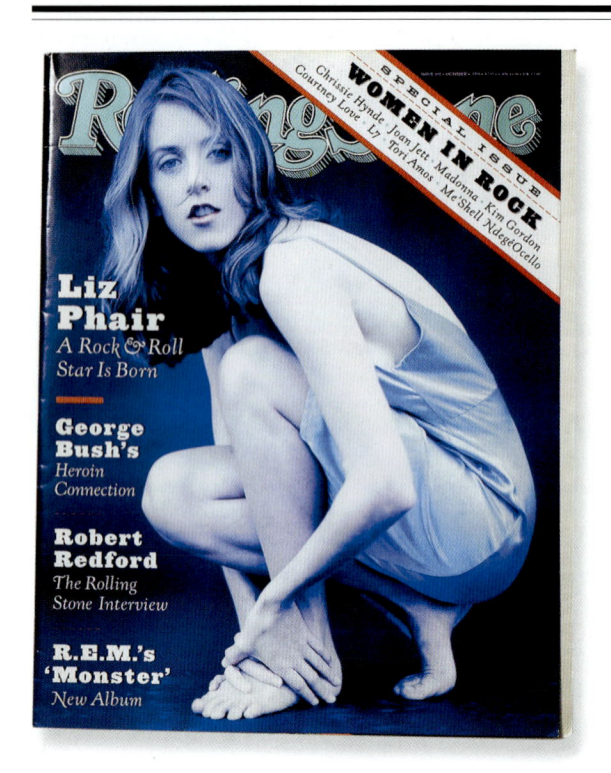

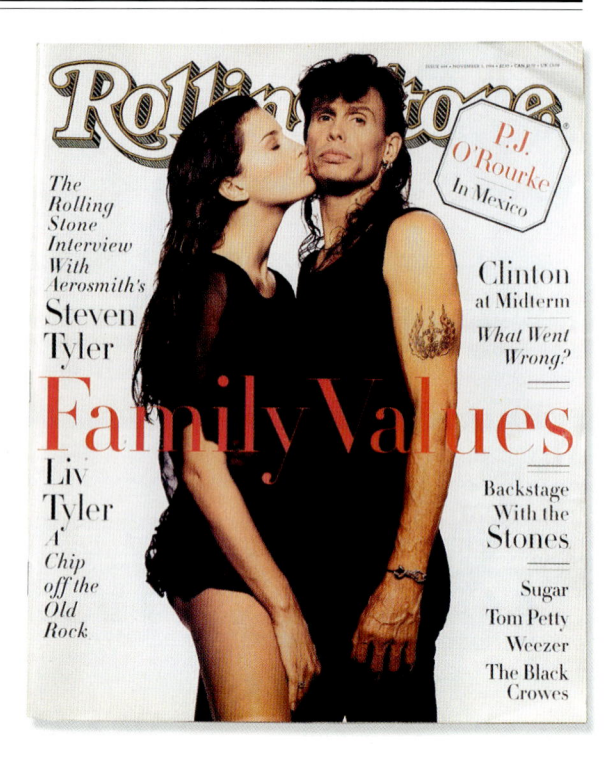

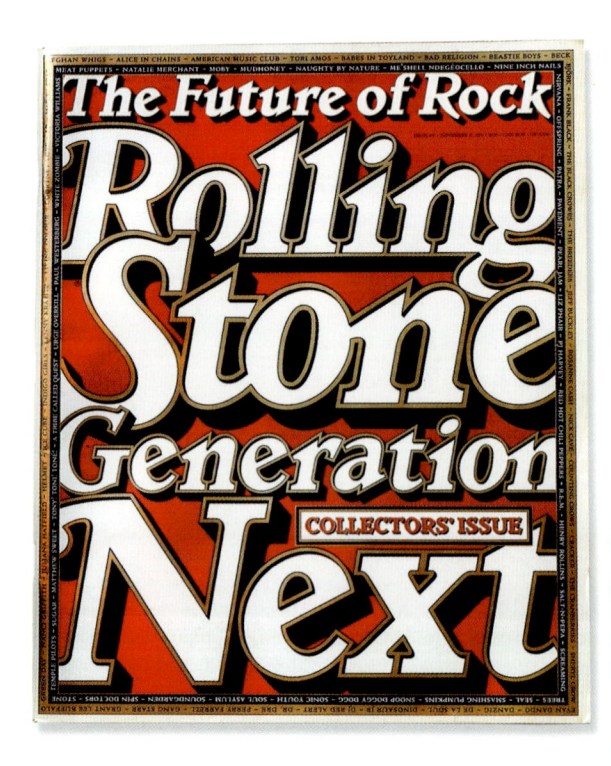

RS 692 | LIZ PHAIR
October 6th, 1994
PHOTOGRAPH BY FRANK W. OCKENFELS 3

RS 694 | LIV & STEVEN TYLER
November 3rd, 1994
PHOTOGRAPH BY ALBERT WATSON

RS 695 | GENERATION NEXT
November 17th, 1994
TYPOGRAPHY BY ERIC SIRY

"BEING ON THE COVER OF ROLLING STONE? You know, the old kiss of death. It's like *whoops*, wait a minute. It's great, no it isn't. *It is*, no it isn't."
—Steven Tyler

372 • ROLLING STONE

ERIC CLAPTON   MAZZY STAR   JEFF BUCKLEY

Rolling Stone
College Special

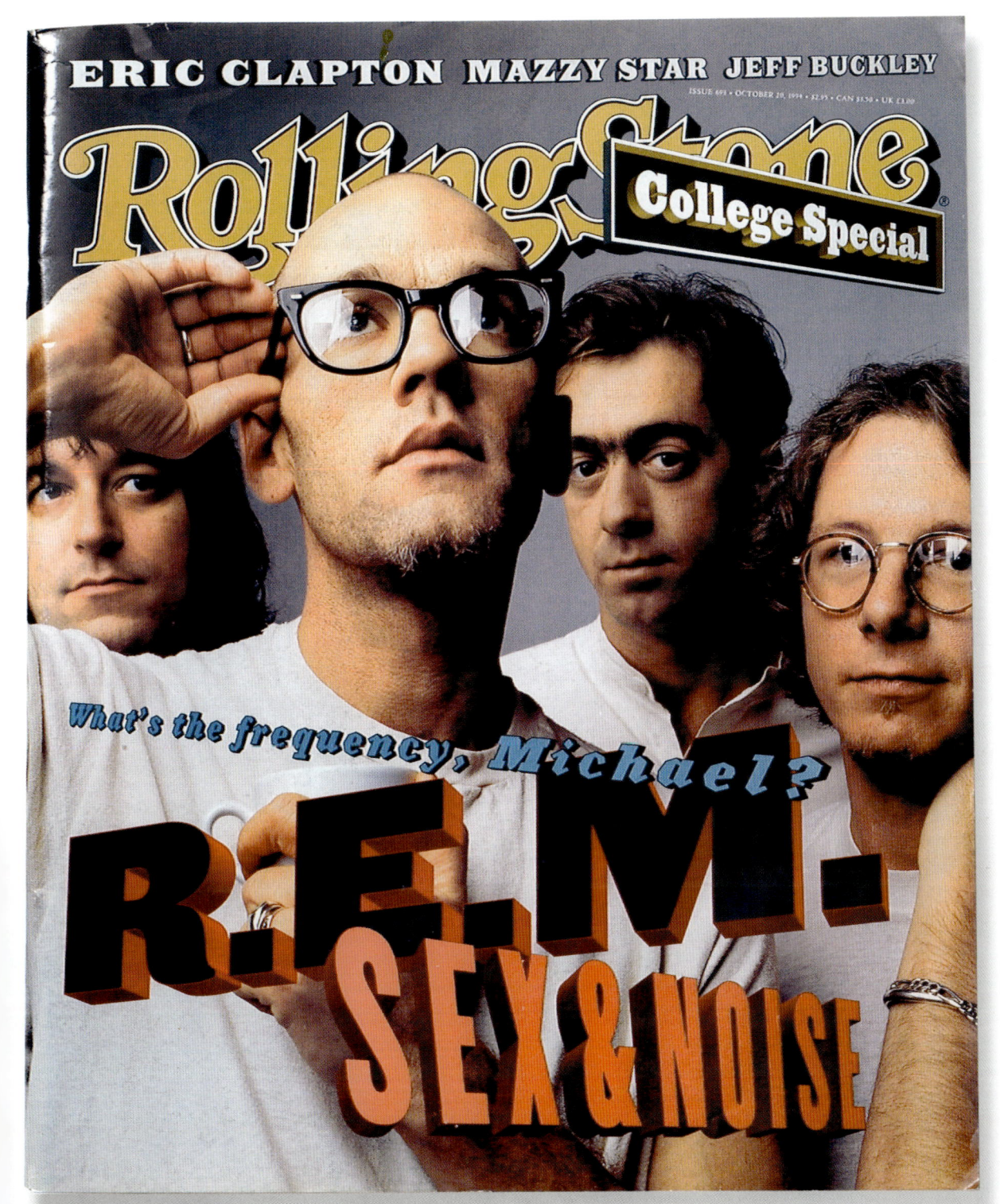

What's the frequency, Michael?

R.E.M.
SEX & NOISE

RS 693 | R.E.M. | October 20th, 1994 | Photograph by Mark Seliger

Rolling Stone

SPECIAL CYBER NATION

ROLLING STONE'S INTERVIEW WITH THE VAMPIRE

Brad Pitt Bites

NIRVANA
[UNPLUGGED]

JIMMY PAGE
and
ROBERT PLANT
[UNLEDDED]

LIVE

BABYFACE

GRANT LEE BUFFALO

1990s

RS 696 | BRAD PITT | December 1st, 1994 | Photograph by Mark Seliger

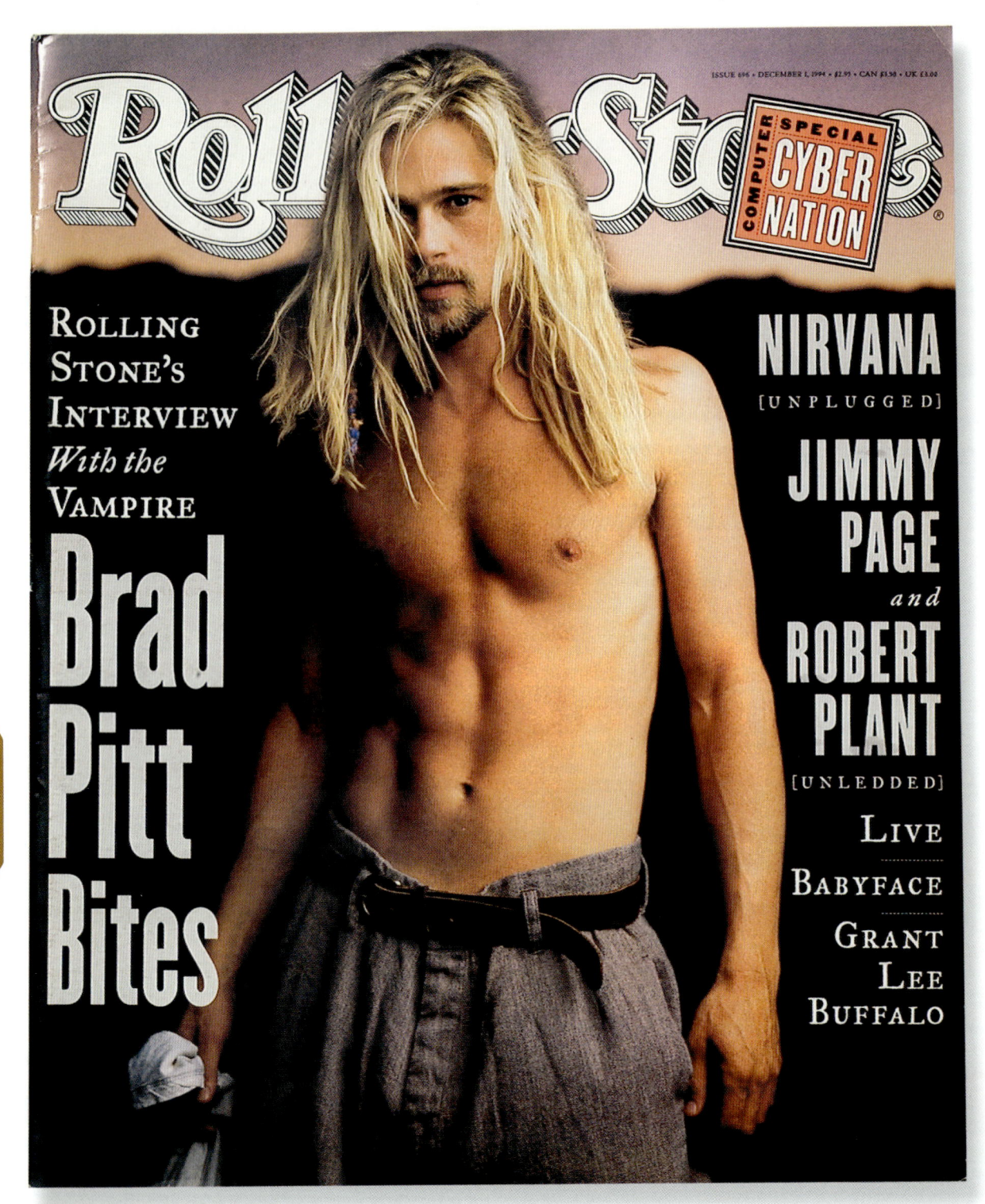

SHERYL CROW | **PEARL JAM** | **THE JAYHAWKS** | **BOB DYLAN** | **OASIS**

Rolling Stone

ISSUE 697 • DECEMBER 15, 1994 • $2.95 CAN $3.50 UK £3.00

EXCLUSIVE

Courtney Love
Talks About Music, Madness and the Last Days of Kurt Cobain

By David Fricke

The O.J. Simpson Story

By Randall Sullivan

FEAR AND LOATHING IN HORSE COUNTRY

Hunter S. Thompson
Polo Is My Life

RS 697 | COURTNEY LOVE | December 15th, 1994 | PHOTOGRAPH BY MARK SELIGER

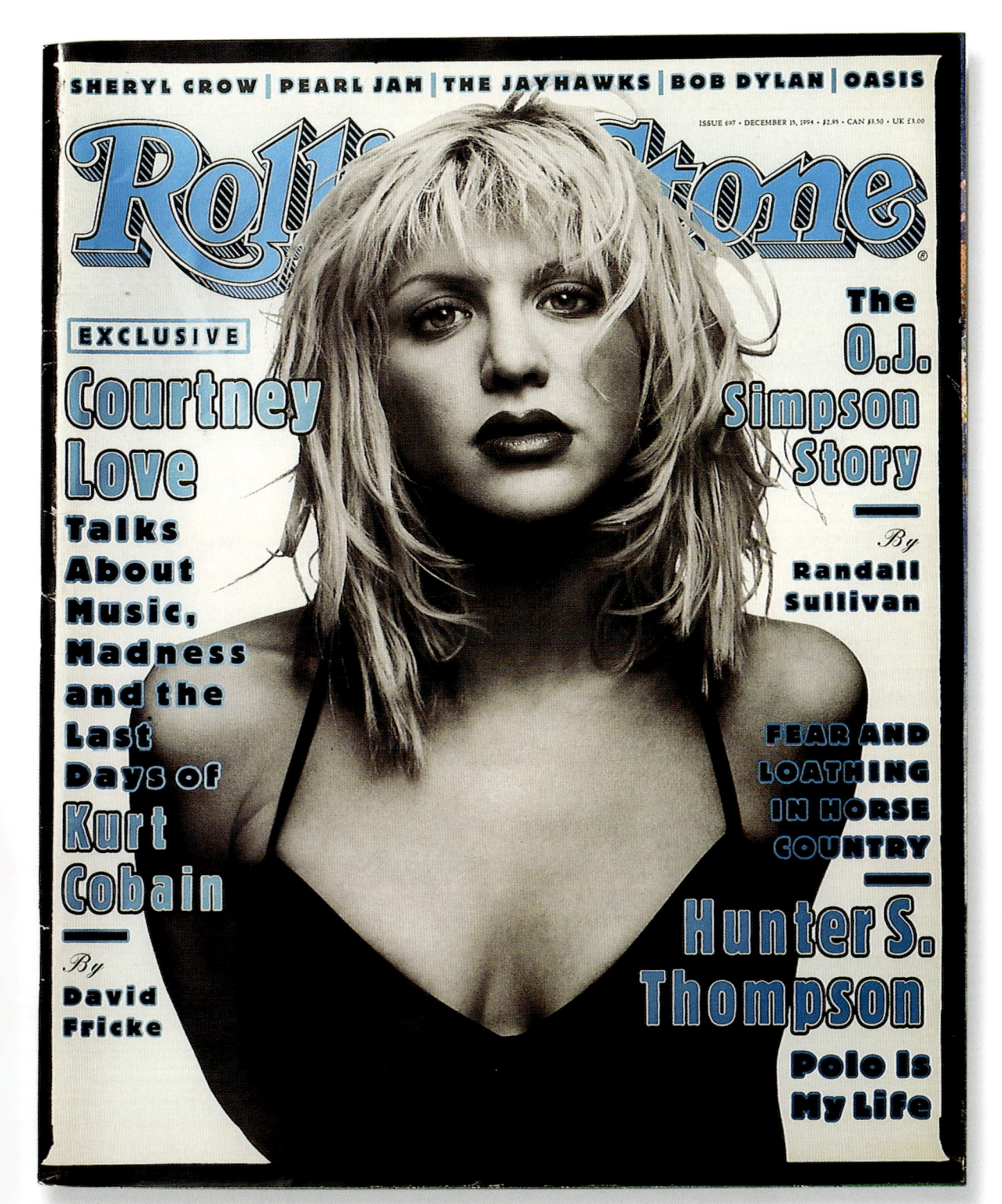

RS 698/699 | DAVID LETTERMAN
December 28th, 1994 – January 12th, 1995
PHOTOGRAPH BY FRANK W. OCKENFELS 3

RS 700 | GREEN DAY
January 26th, 1995
PHOTOGRAPH BY DAN WINTERS

[RS 701] The striking nude portrait of Demi Moore is one of only four covers to go to press without any cover lines. It is also the only textless cover that's not a tribute issue; the other three were published after John Lennon's death (RS 335) and following the passing of John's fellow Beatle George Harrison (RS 887) and Prince (RS 1261).

1990s

NOT LONG AFTER GREEN DAY PLAYED WOODSTOCK '94 – a performance that scored the band mass adulation – singer Billie Joe Armstrong received a letter from his mother.

"It was a hate letter," says Armstrong.

It seems Mrs. Armstrong ordered the concert on pay-per-view and had settled in to watch the event with a friend. That's when the melee occurred. Onstage, the Green Day set culminated in a titanic mud fight; Armstrong yanked down his pants; and bassist Mike Dirnt had his front teeth smashed when he was tackled by a security guard who thought he was a fan storming the stage. Finally a mud-covered Armstrong asked the fans to shout, "Shut the fuck up," and the band exited.

"She said that I was disrespectful and indecent," says Armstrong, "and that if my father was alive, he would be ashamed of me. She couldn't believe that I pulled my pants down and got in a fight onstage.

"Everything's fine now, but her letter was just unreal. She was not happy with my performance at all. She even talked shit about my wife, Adrienne, and said how she's supposed to be my loving wife, but she's never even come over and visited."

He pauses.

"It was pretty brutal."

[EXCERPT FROM RS 700 COVER STORY BY CHRIS MUNDY]

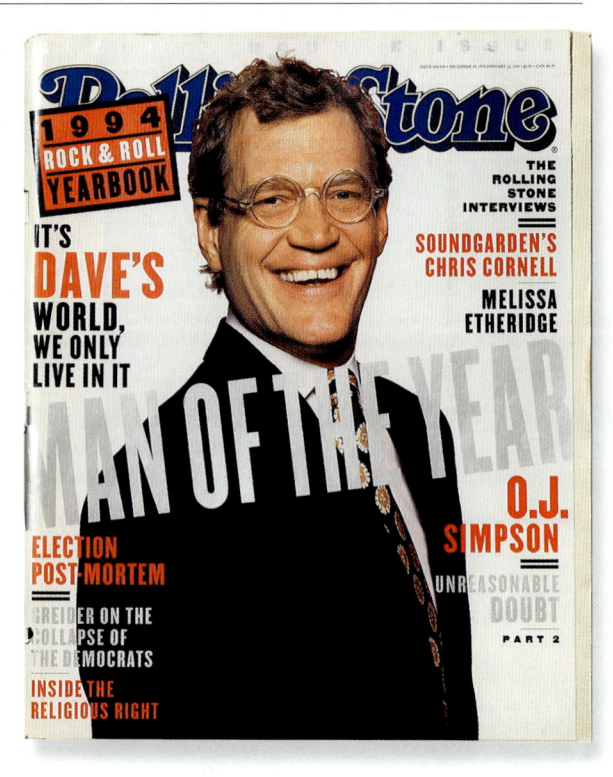

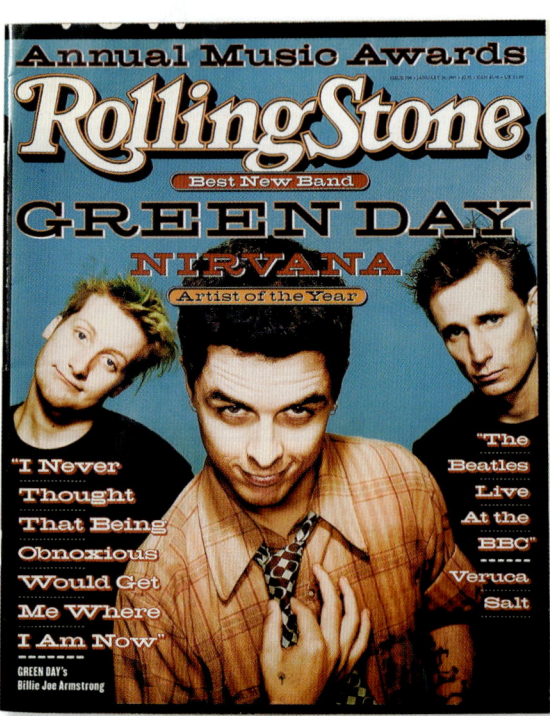

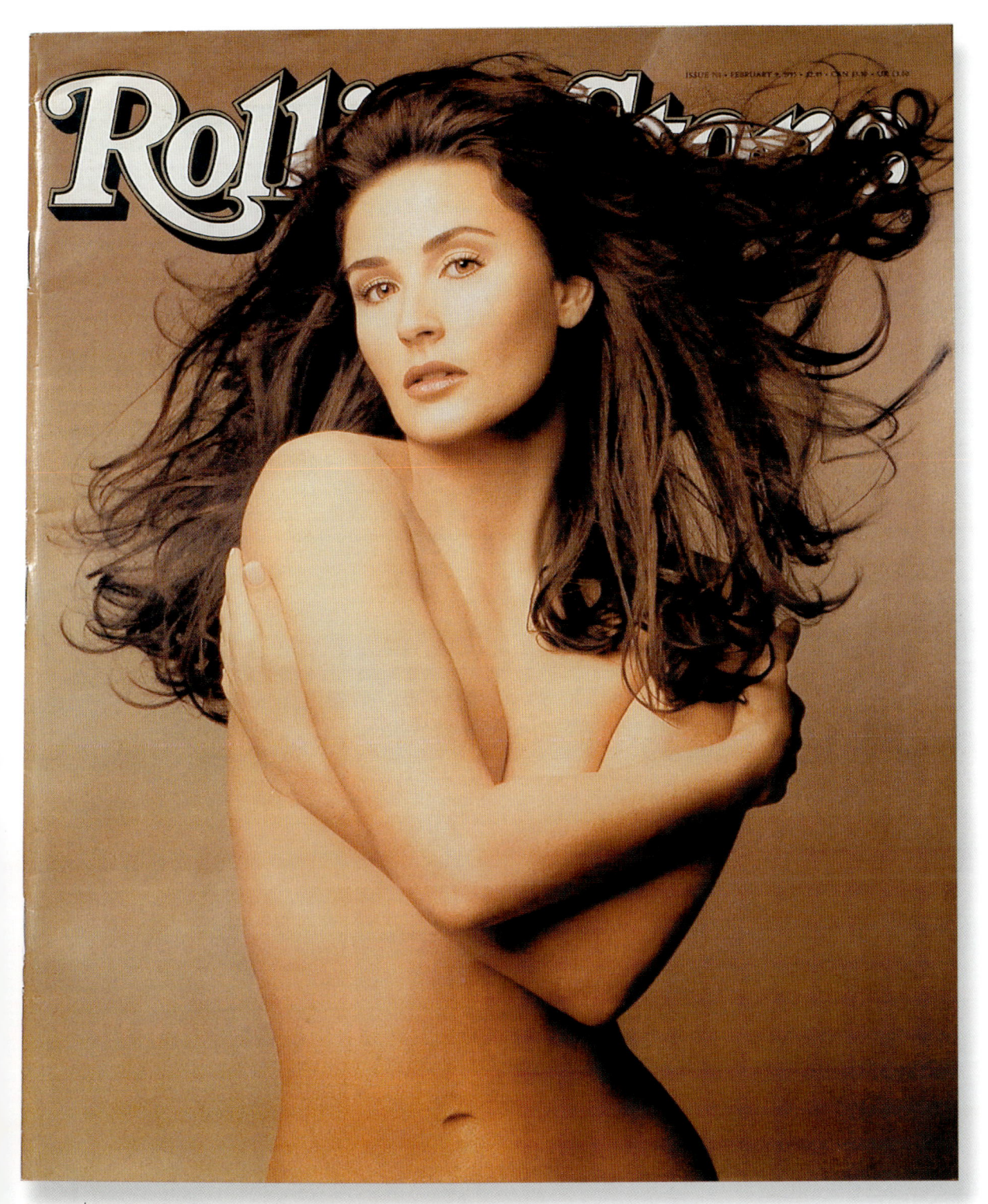

RS 701 | DEMI MOORE | February 9th, 1995 | Photograph by Matthew Rolston

HALL OF FAME SPECIAL

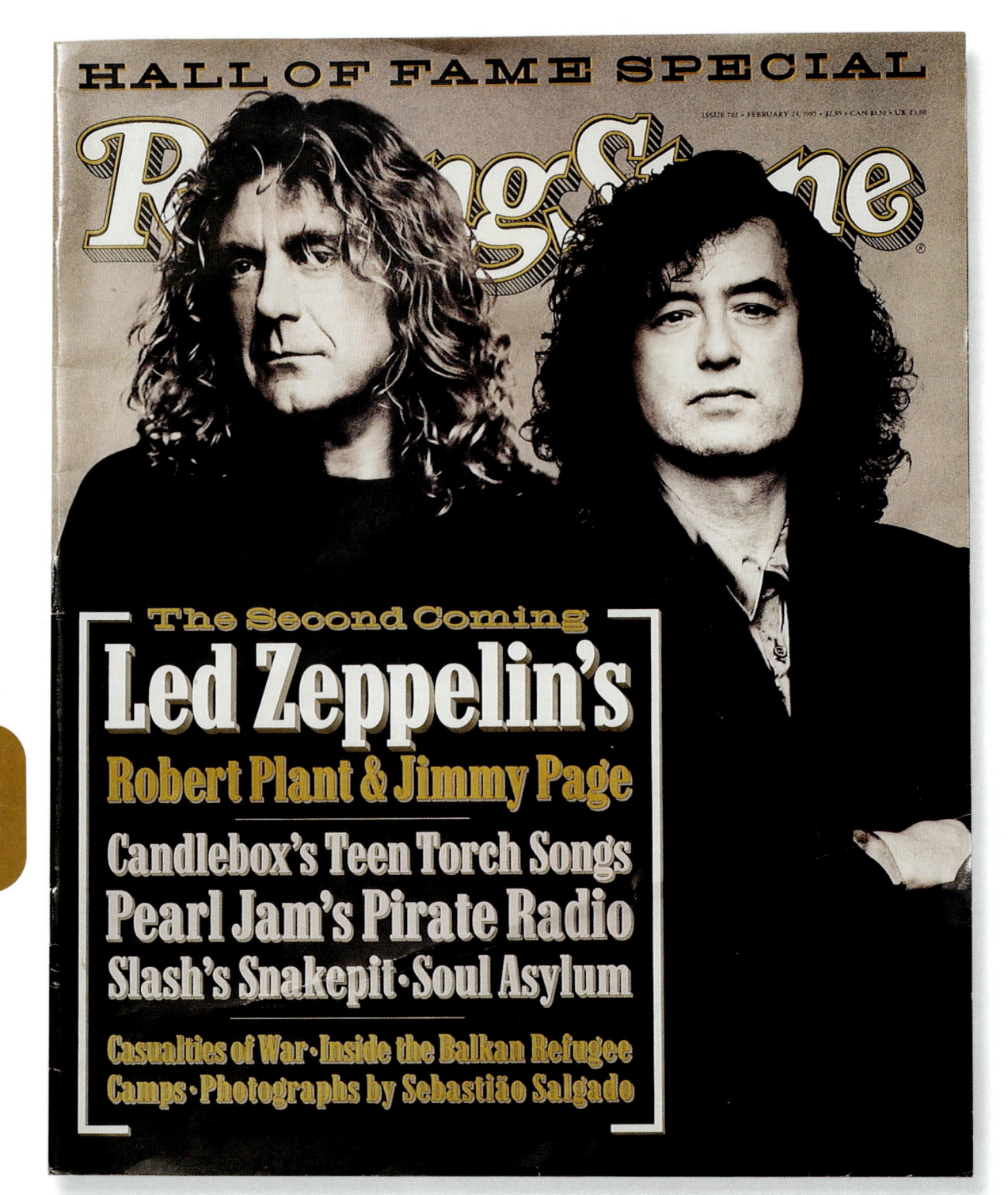

Rolling Stone

ISSUE 702 • FEBRUARY 23, 1995

The Second Coming
Led Zeppelin's
Robert Plant & Jimmy Page

Candlebox's Teen Torch Songs
Pearl Jam's Pirate Radio
Slash's Snakepit • Soul Asylum

Casualties of War • Inside the Balkan Refugee Camps • Photographs by Sebastião Salgado

1990s

RS 702 | ROBERT PLANT & JIMMY PAGE | February 23rd, 1995 | Photograph by Anton Corbijn

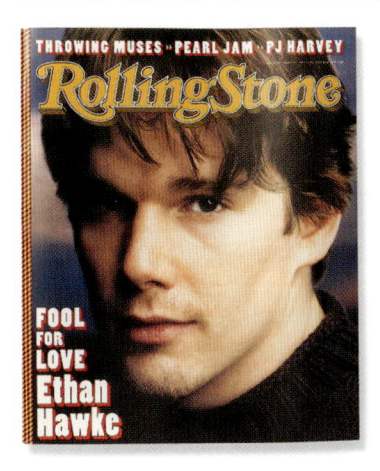

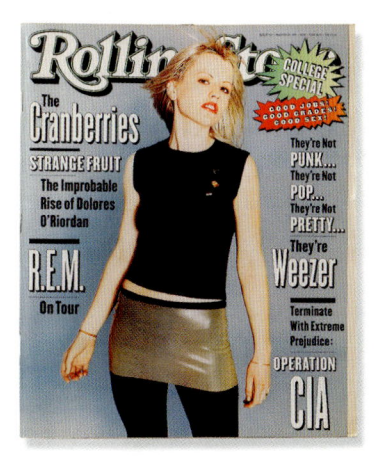

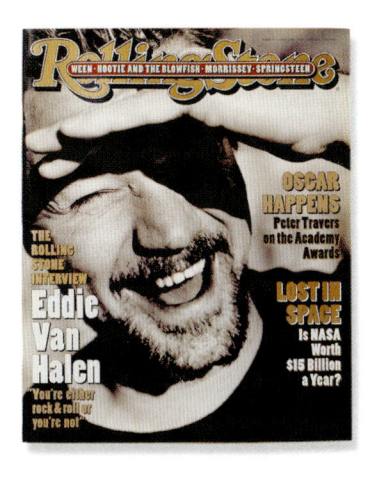

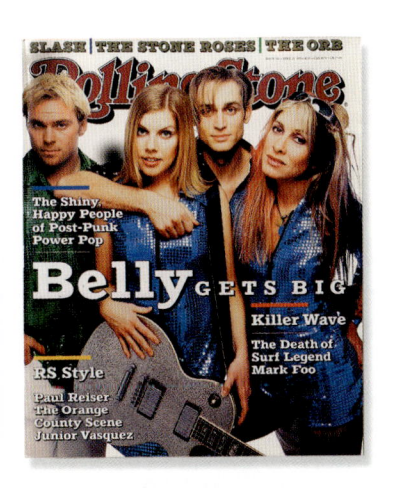

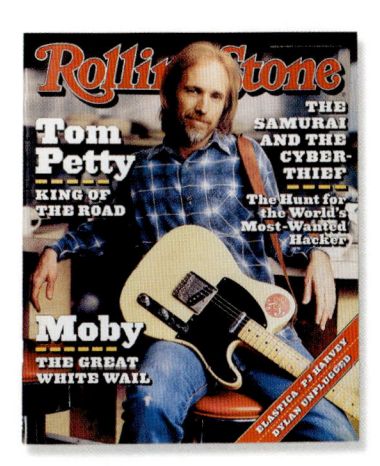

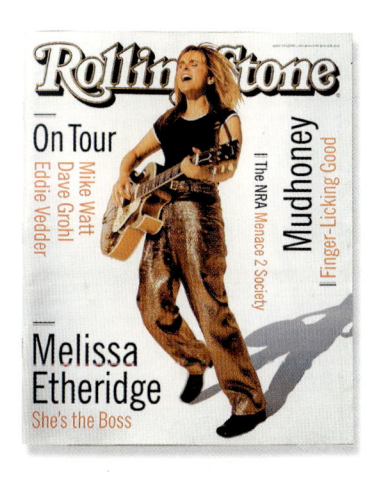

RS 703 | ETHAN HAWKE
March 9th, 1995
Photograph by Mark Seliger

RS 704 | DOLORES O'RIORDAN
March 23rd, 1995
Photograph by Corrine Day

RS 705 | EDDIE VAN HALEN
April 6th, 1995
Photograph by Mark Seliger

RS 706 | BELLY
April 20th, 1995
Photograph by Mark Seliger

RS 707 | TOM PETTY
May 4th, 1995
Photograph by Mark Seliger

RS 709 | MELISSA ETHERIDGE
June 1st, 1995
Photograph by Peggy Sirota

"There's no point in trying to pretend that you're immortal and that you've returned once again to do that ultimate version of 'Stairway to Heaven.'"
—*Robert Plant*

1990s

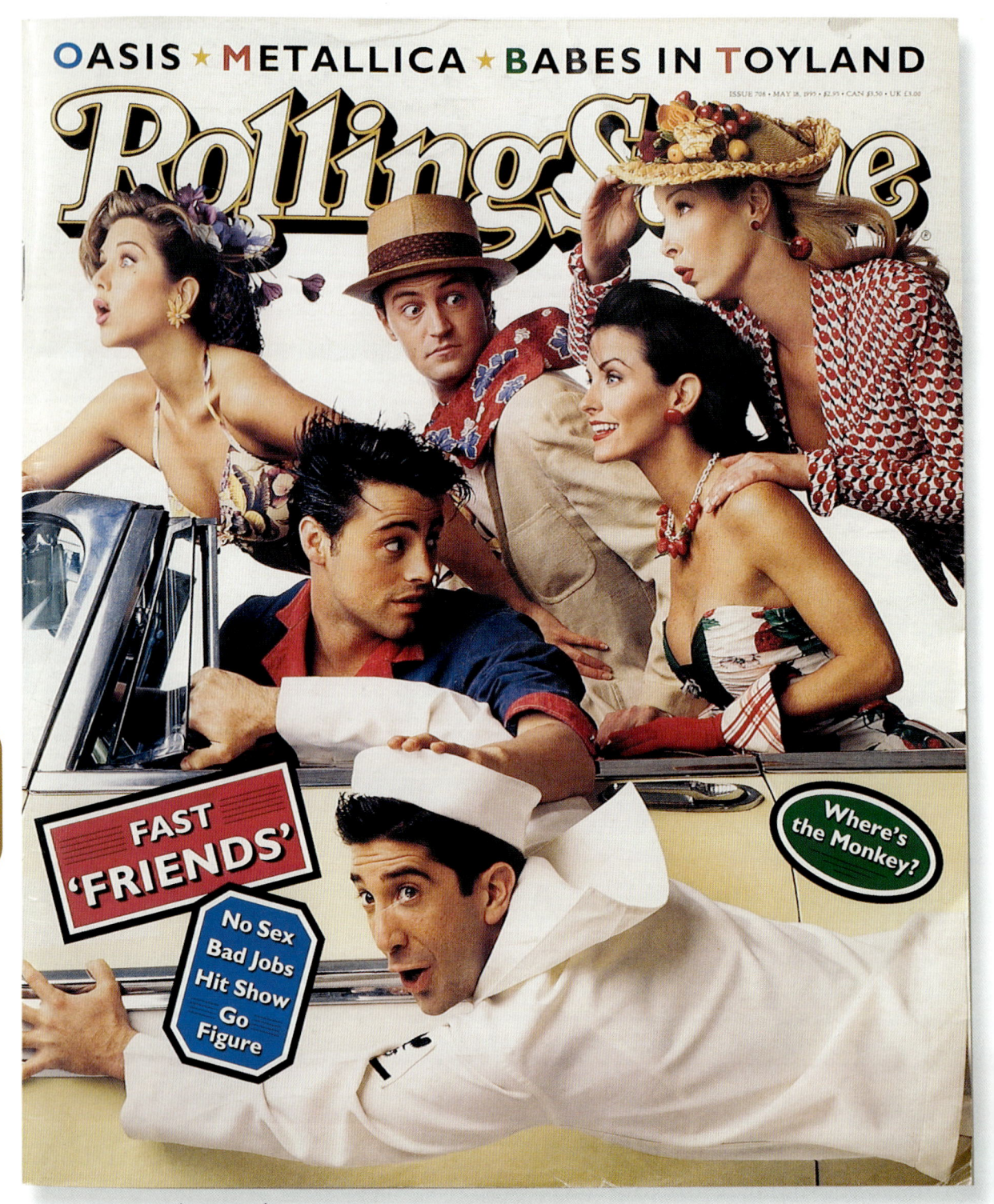

RS 708 | CAST OF 'FRIENDS' | May 18th, 1995 | Photograph by Mark Seliger

Rolling Stone
· ROCK & ROLL SUMMER ·

Wild Thing
Drew Barrymore

Hootie and the Blowfish
Nice Guys Finish First

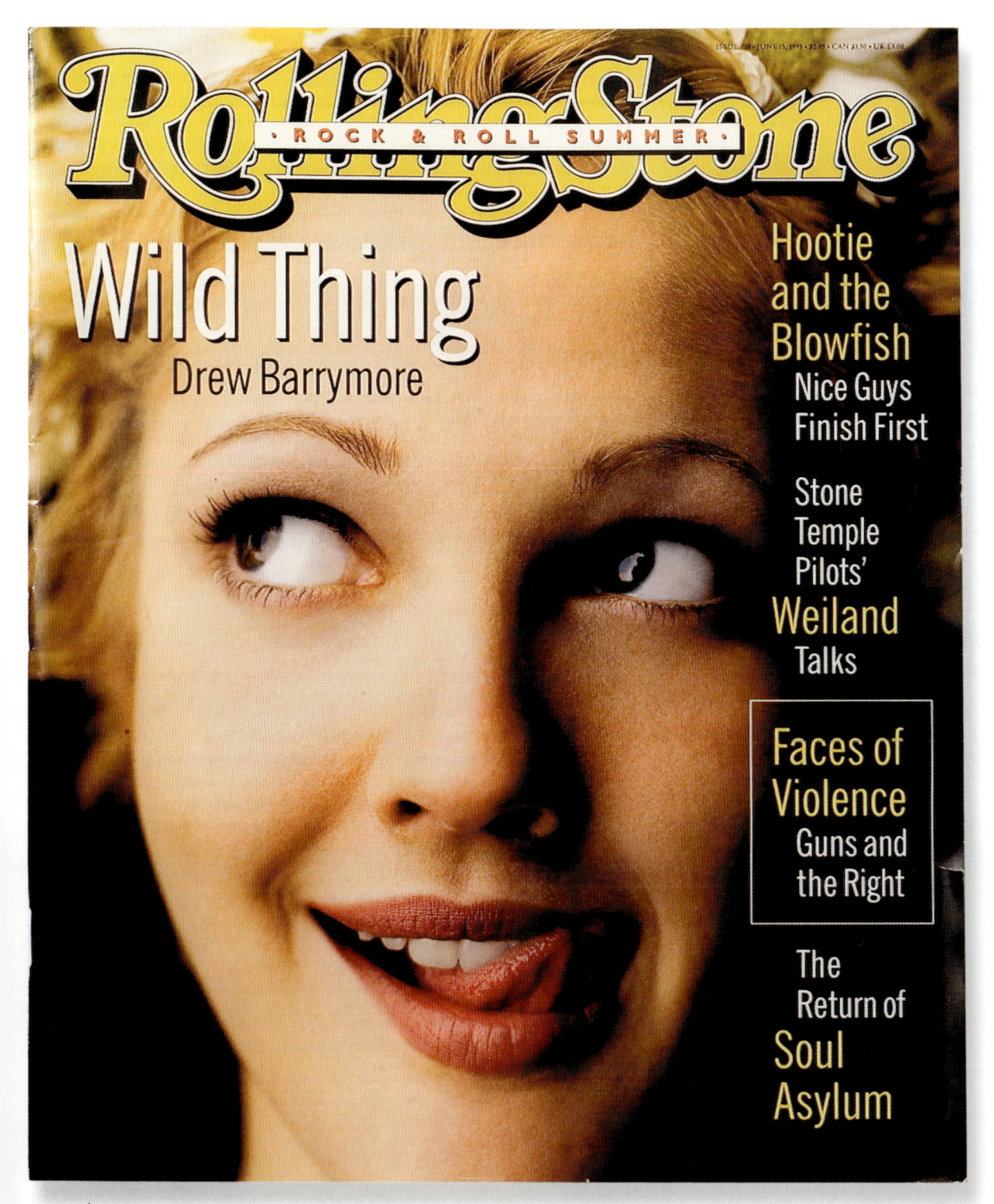

Stone Temple Pilots' Weiland Talks

Faces of Violence
Guns and the Right

The Return of **Soul Asylum**

RS 710 | DREW BARRYMORE | June 15th, 1995 | Photograph by Mark Seliger

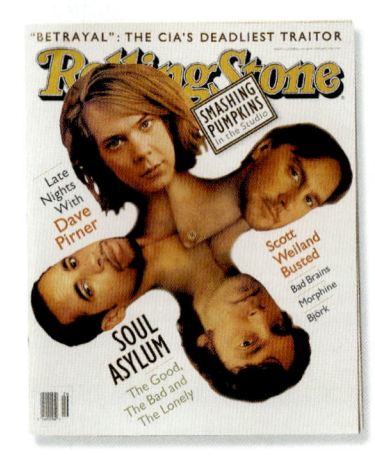

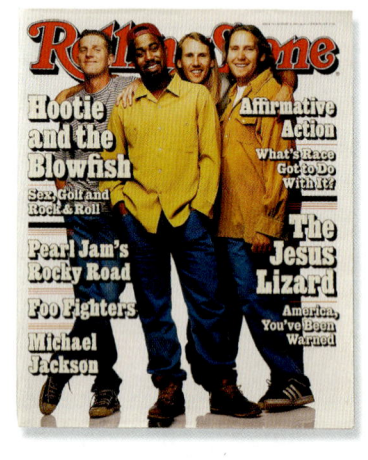

PICTURE, IF YOU WILL, A HOTEL LOUNGE. [Soul Asylum singer Dave] Pirner sits on a sofa, engaged in what seems to be a heated conversation with a reporter. Drummer Sterling Campbell sits on a chair to their right, leaning in closely.

PIRNER: But look, Socrates was fucking Greek, man. I mean, what influence has that culture had on us as a people now? Those wrapped-up leaves with rice in them . . .

[*Soul Asylum's publicist arrives.*]

PIRNER: I mean, that shit doesn't taste that good, but it tastes pretty good. And you kind of sit there, and you eat it, and you go, "All right, these motherfuckers, they ate this shit, and they made a bunch of motherfuckers drag fucking rocks up a hill to build some big old colossal thing. And they tried to create this whole society." And what was the food left over from that? These fucking grape leaves wrapped around rice.

PUBLICIST: I have a recommendation to make as a publicist. You guys could stay up all night talking, but the on-the-record portion of the interview should be over at this point.

CAMPBELL: No, no, no, no.

PIRNER: I think I can be held accountable for anything that I should say. I'll tell you what I want to know, though. What's ROLLING STONE's angle here? Do they think we're rock stars and suck or what? What do they want to know about us, just between me and you?

PUBLICIST [*coughs*]: What would be the most natural, obvious question to answer that? The new record? Coming off the tremendous success of Grave Dancers Union?

PIRNER: I mean, what the fuck could possibly be interesting about us?

[*The publicist is silent.*]

PIRNER: Exactly. That's the right answer.

PUBLICIST [*flustered*]: Is the tape recorder running? Could you turn it off?

[EXCERPT FROM RS 711 COVER STORY BY NEIL STRAUSS]

RS 711 | SOUL ASYLUM
June 29th, 1995
PHOTOGRAPH BY MATT MAHURIN

RS 714 | HOOTIE AND THE BLOWFISH
August 10th, 1995
PHOTOGRAPH BY MARK SELIGER

[**RS 712/713**] Finding a dog that could pull the skivvies off of Jim Carrey was no simple task. A casting call went out across the land and canines galore showed up. The only one with the necessary skills was a crafty fellow named Poundcake. Unfortunately, he was white – and for the setup to mirror the classic Coppertone ad, the assertive doggie had to be black. After weeks of intensive training, Poundcake consented to having his snowy coat dyed black (reportedly with shoe polish). Poundcake, now ebony, had risen to the occasion when Mr. Carrey's handlers called to say he couldn't make the shoot that day. Unfortunately, rescheduling took a month, and poor Poundcake had to go through boot camp once again – not to mention having his roots touched up. A trouper to the end, Poundcake came through, putting that Coppertone mutt to shame with his briefs-snatching antics.

SUMMER DOUBLE ISSUE

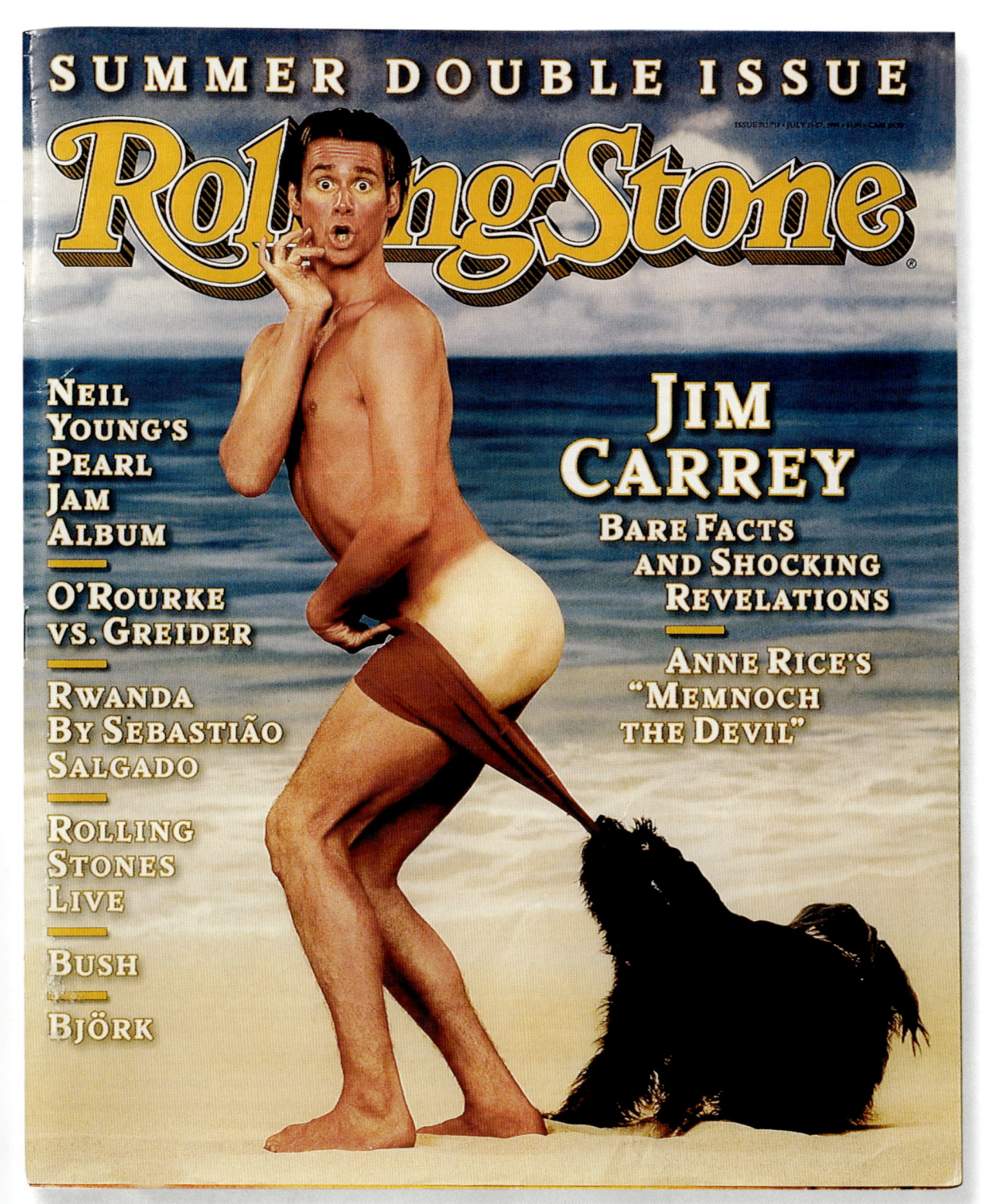

Rolling Stone

NEIL YOUNG'S PEARL JAM ALBUM

O'ROURKE vs. GREIDER

RWANDA BY SEBASTIÃO SALGADO

ROLLING STONES LIVE

BUSH

BJÖRK

JIM CARREY

BARE FACTS AND SHOCKING REVELATIONS

ANNE RICE'S "MEMNOCH THE DEVIL"

RS 712/713 | JIM CARREY | July 13th – July 27th, 1995 | Photograph by Herb Ritts

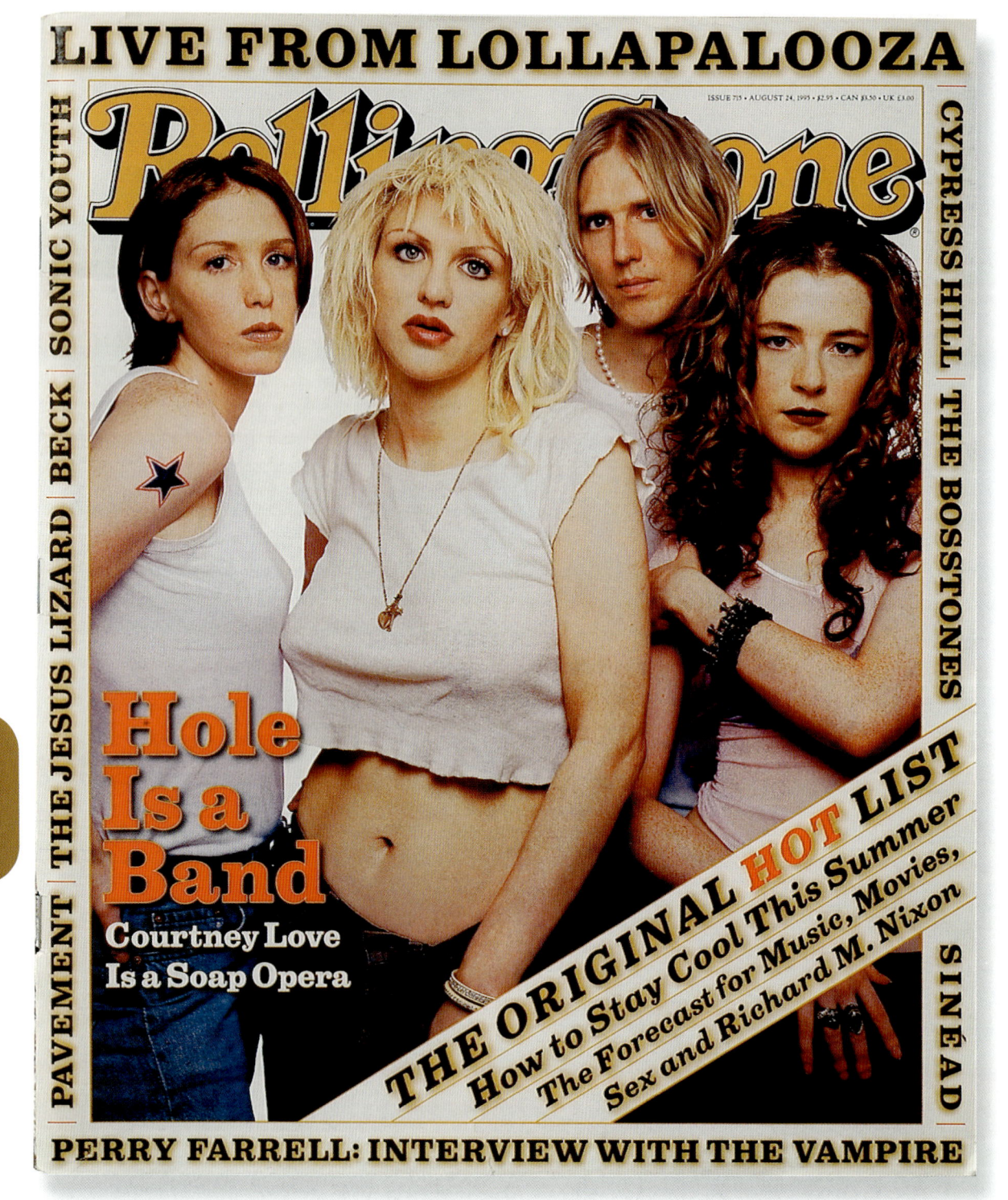

RS 715 | HOLE | August 24th, 1995 | Photograph by Mark Seliger

Rolling Stone

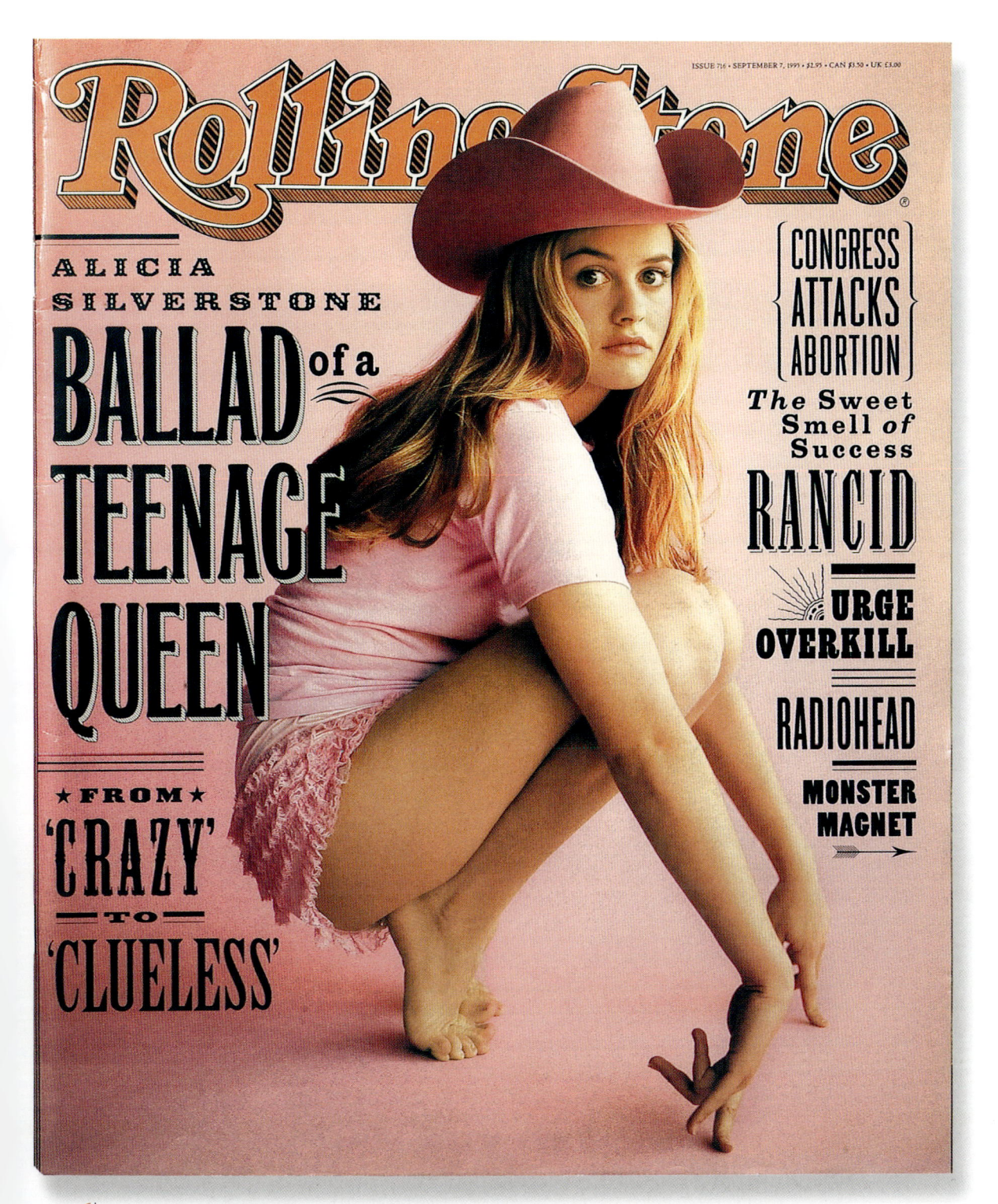

ISSUE 716 · SEPTEMBER 7, 1995 · $2.95 | CAN $3.50 | UK £3.00

ALICIA SILVERSTONE

BALLAD of a TEENAGE QUEEN

FROM ★ 'CRAZY' TO 'CLUELESS'

CONGRESS ATTACKS ABORTION

The Sweet Smell of Success
RANCID

URGE OVERKILL

RADIOHEAD

MONSTER MAGNET

RS 716 | ALICIA SILVERSTONE | September 7th, 1995 | Photograph by Peggy Sirota

50 YEARS OF COVERS • 385

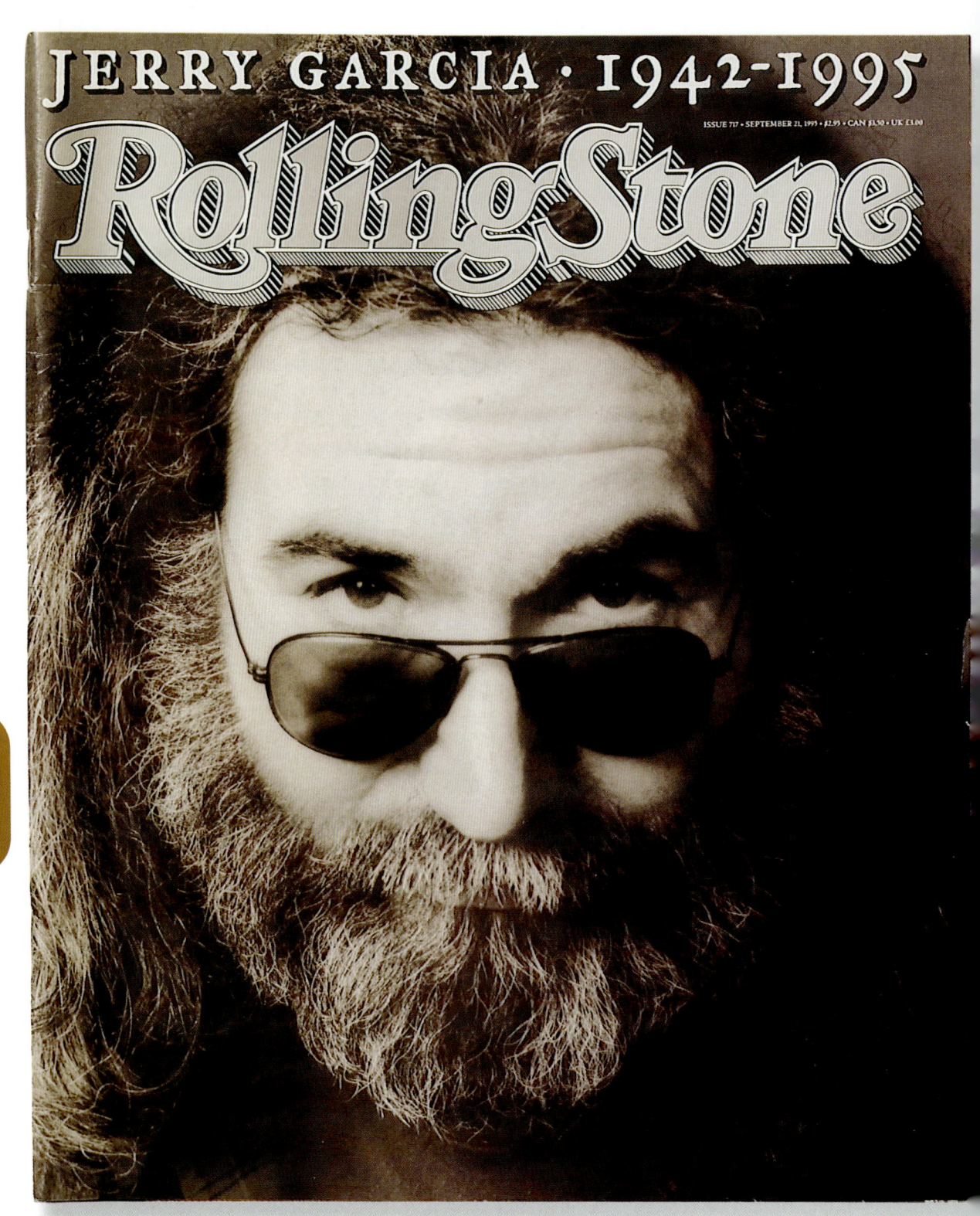

JERRY GARCIA · 1942-1995

Rolling Stone

ISSUE 717 · SEPTEMBER 21, 1995 · $2.95 · CAN $3.50 · UK £1.00

1990s

RS 717 | JERRY GARCIA | September 21st, 1995 | PHOTOGRAPH BY Herbie Greene

On August 9th, 1995, Jerry

Garcia died in his sleep at Serenity Knolls drug treatment center, in the Marin County community of Forest Knolls, north of San Francisco. He was fifty-three. . . . The memorial service transformed into a festive, open-air Grateful Dead theme park. . . . As the waft of marijuana and incense intensified, fans gathered at the alter and danced. . . .

— *Alec Foege*

HE WAS THE UNLIKELIEST OF POP STARS AND THE MOST RETICENT OF cultural icons.

Onstage he wore plain clothes – usually a sacklike T-shirt and loose jeans to fit his heavy frame – and he rarely spoke to the audience that watched his every move. Even his guitar lines – complex, lovely and rhapsodic, but never flashy – as well as his strained, weatherworn vocal style had a subdued, colloquial quality about them. Offstage he kept to family and friends, and when he sat to talk with interviewers about his remarkable music, he often did so in sly-witted, self-deprecating ways. "I feel like I'm sort of stumbling along," he said once, "and a lot of people are watching me or stumbling along with me or allowing me to stumble for them." It was as if Jerry Garcia – who, as the lead guitarist and singer of the Grateful Dead, lived at the center of one of popular culture's most extraordinary epic adventures – was bemused by the circumstances of his own renown.

— *Mikal Gilmore*

In rock & roll,

there is Grateful Dead music – and then there is everything else. No other band has been so pure in its outlaw idealism, so resolute in its pursuit of transcendence onstage and on record, and so astonishingly casual about both the hazards and rewards of its chosen, and at times truly lunatic, course. . . .

— *David Fricke*

FOR OUR VERY FIRST ISSUE – published in November 1967 – we lucked, journalistically speaking, into a story for the ages: the Grateful Dead getting busted at their Haight-Ashbury digs. The police had had it up to their badges with freaks flaunting various laws. Inviting local media along for the roust, they barged into the house at 710 Ashbury Street, where most of the Dead and their old ladies lived, and arrested two band members and nine associates and friends on dope charges (Jerry Garcia wasn't one of them; he was out at the time).

Baron Wolman, ROLLING STONE's first photographer, snapped shots of Bob Weir walking down the front steps, cuffed to Phil Lesh's girlfriend, and Ron "Pigpen" McKernan and Phil Lesh outside their bail bondsman's office across from the Hall of Justice. The next day, after a festive press conference at the house, Wolman shot photographs of a band of unrepentant freaks – now joined by Garcia, posing in front of 710, with Pigpen brandishing a rifle. The photos took up most of a two-page spread.

The lead, by an uncredited Jann S. Wenner, was textbook hook-'em news writing: " 'That's what ya get for dealing the killer weed,' laughed state narcotics agent Gerritt Van Ramm at the eleven members of the Grateful Dead household he and his agents had rounded up into the Dead's kitchen."

The band and the magazine always had a special relationship, despite the occasional negative album review or report on an unpleasant incident or ROLLING STONE's move to New York in 1977. Our common roots transcended trivia; our love of great music kept us bonded.

— *Ben Fong-Torres*

[EXCERPTS FROM RS 717]

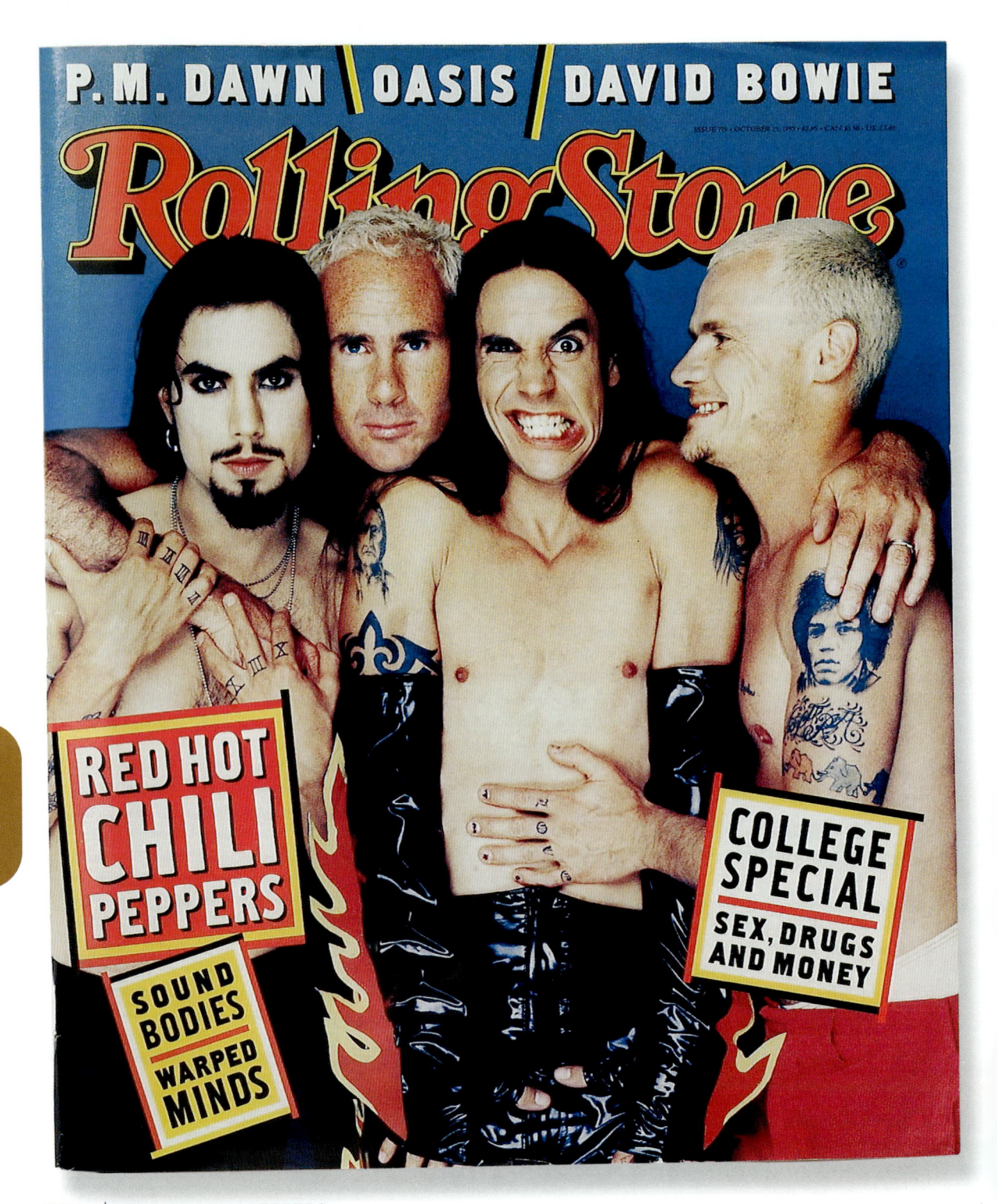

RS 719 | RED HOT CHILI PEPPERS | October 19th, 1995 | Photograph by Anton Corbijn

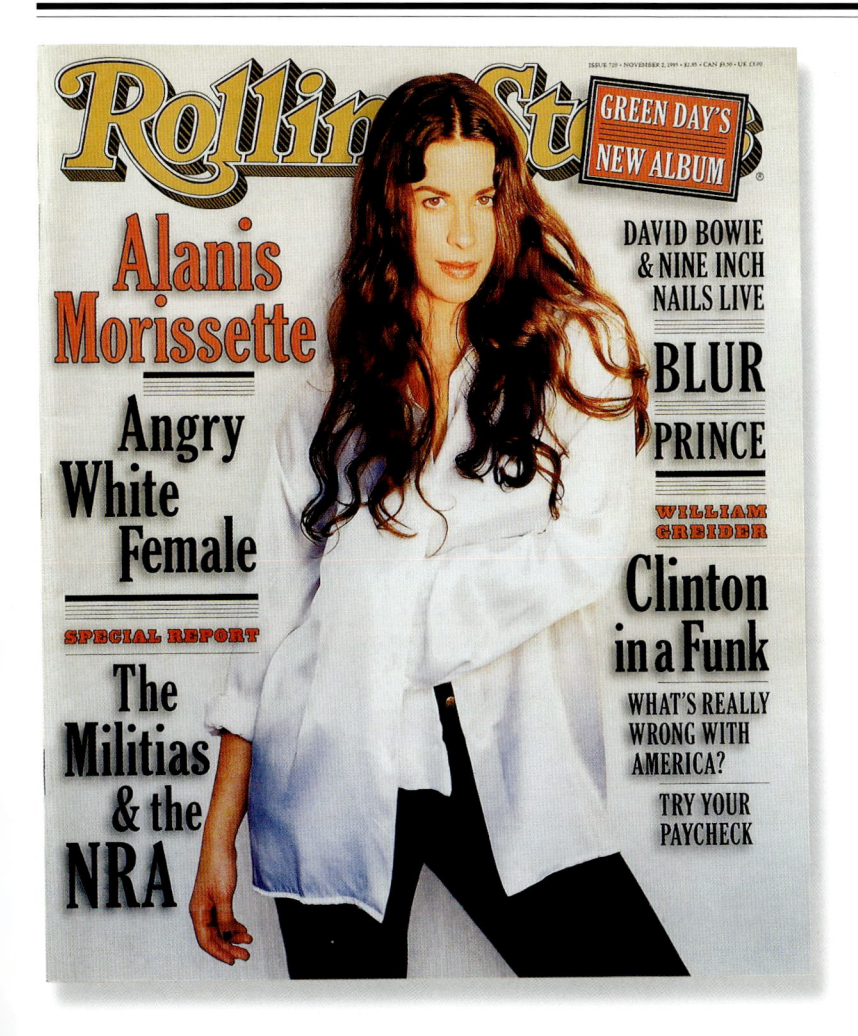

RS 720 | ALANIS MORISSETTE
November 2nd, 1995
PHOTOGRAPH BY FRANK W. OCKENFELS 3

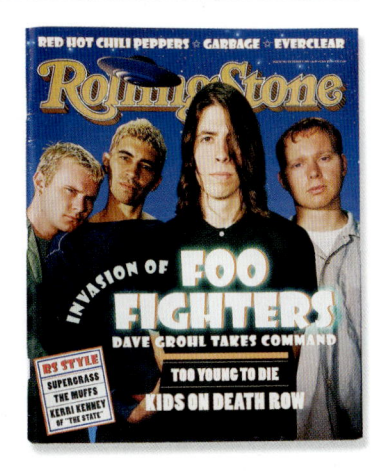

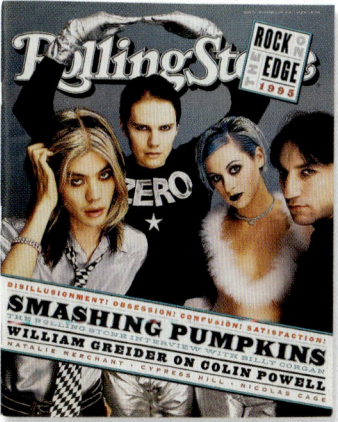

RS 718 | FOO FIGHTERS
October 5th, 1995
PHOTOGRAPH BY DAN WINTERS

RS 721 | SMASHING PUMPKINS
November 16th, 1995
PHOTOGRAPH BY MARK SELIGER

"*I learned a lot of lessons* from Nirvana. We don't want to spend too much time whoring ourselves around because not only does it make everyone sick of you, eventually you get sick of yourself."

—*Dave Grohl*

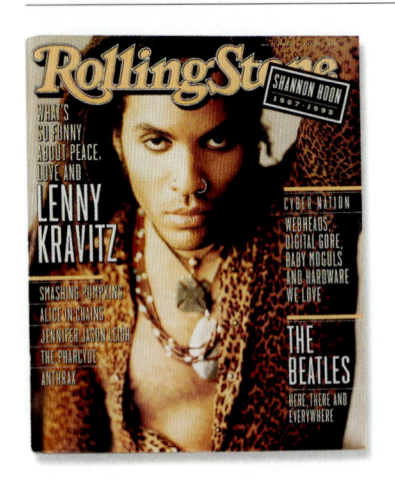

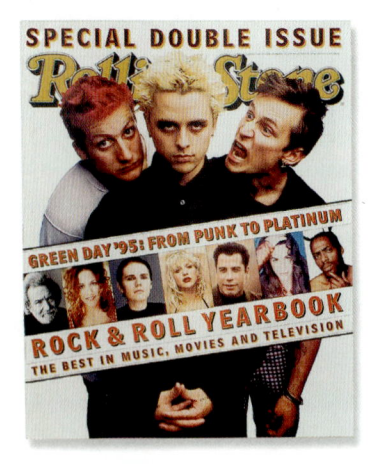

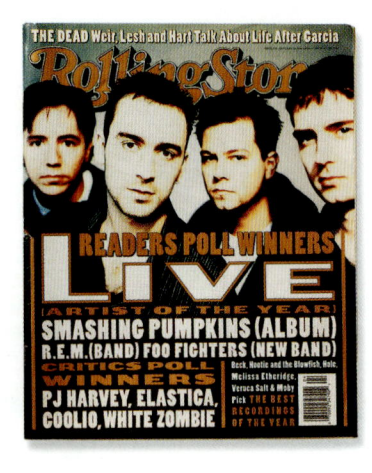

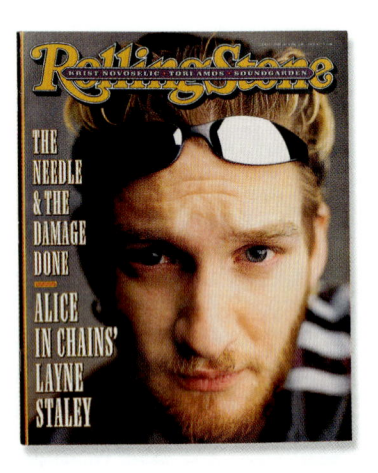

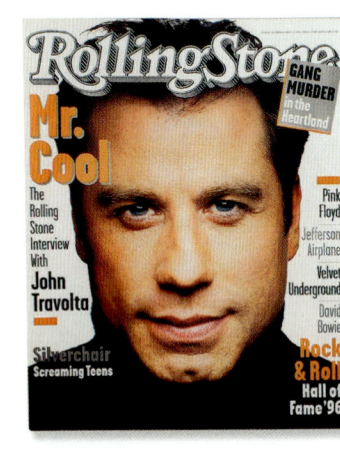

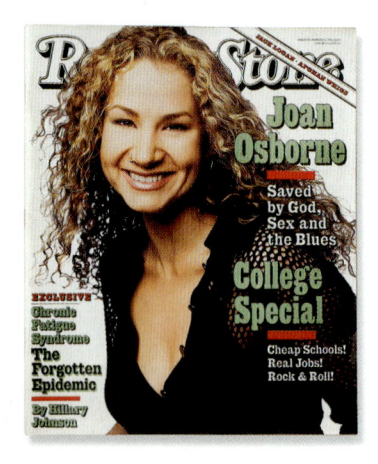

RS 722 | LENNY KRAVITZ
November 30th, 1995
PHOTOGRAPH BY MATTHEW ROLSTON

RS 727 | LAYNE STALEY
February 8th, 1996
PHOTOGRAPH BY MARK SELIGER

RS 724/725 | GREEN DAY, VARIOUS
December 28th, 1995 – January 11th, 1996
PHOTOGRAPHS BY MARK SELIGER, VARIOUS

RS 728 | JOHN TRAVOLTA
February 22nd, 1996
PHOTOGRAPH BY MARK SELIGER

RS 726 | LIVE
January 25th, 1996
PHOTOGRAPH BY JULIAN BROAD

RS 730 | JOAN OSBORNE
March 21st, 1996
PHOTOGRAPH BY MARK SELIGER

Rolling Stone

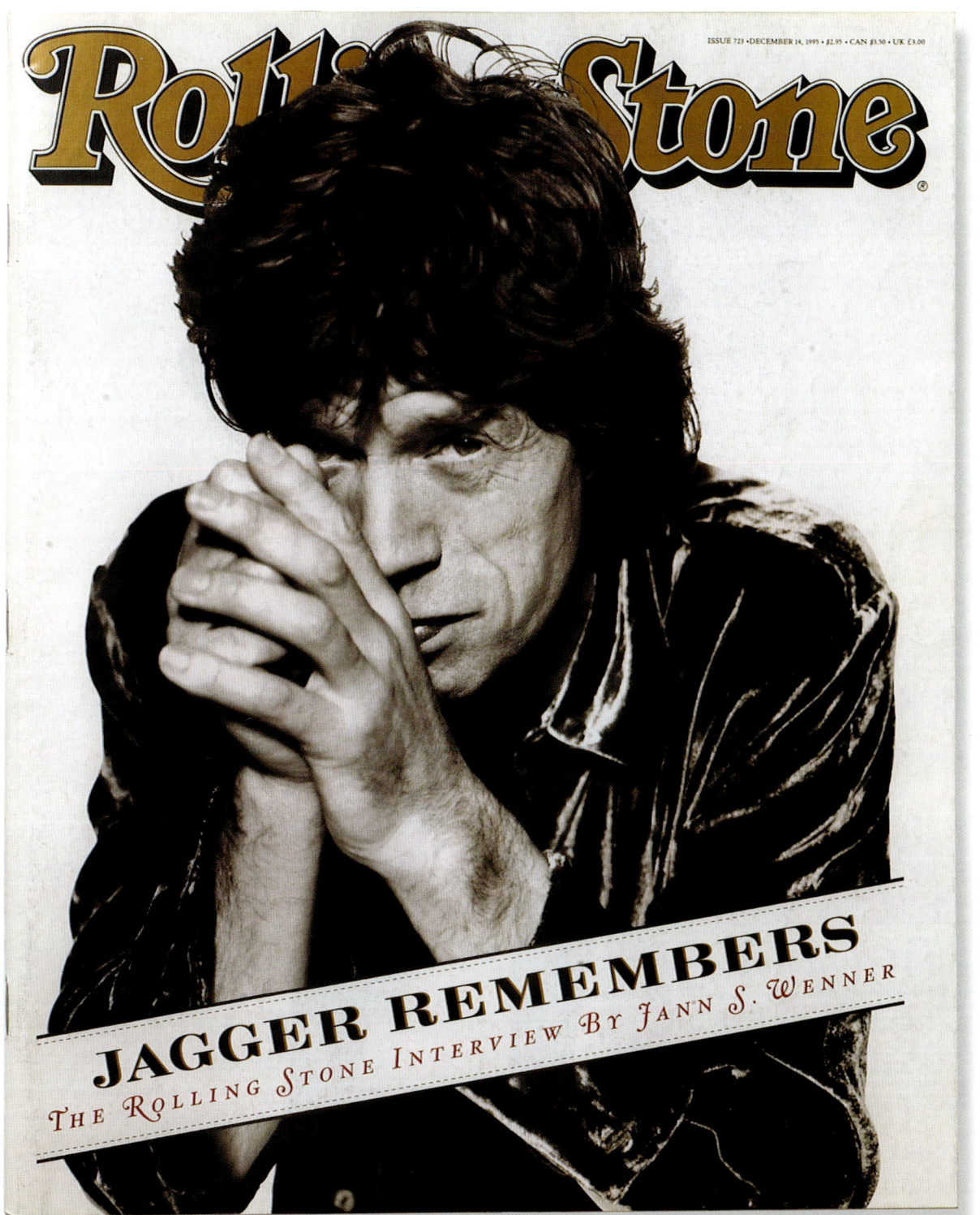

ISSUE 723 · DECEMBER 14, 1995 · $2.95 · CAN $3.50 · UK £3.00

JAGGER REMEMBERS
The Rolling Stone Interview By Jann S. Wenner

RS 723 | MICK JAGGER | December 14th, 1995 | Photograph by Peter Lindbergh

PRESIDENTS OF THE UNITED STATES | **YOKO ONO**

RollingStone

ISSUE 729 · MARCH 7, 1996

How Smashing Pumpkins Beat the Ticket Scalpers

Playing Politics With God
The Republicans and the Religious Right

1990s

Jennifer Aniston

The Girl Friend

RS 729 | JENNIFER ANISTON | March 7th, 1996 | Photograph by Mark Seliger

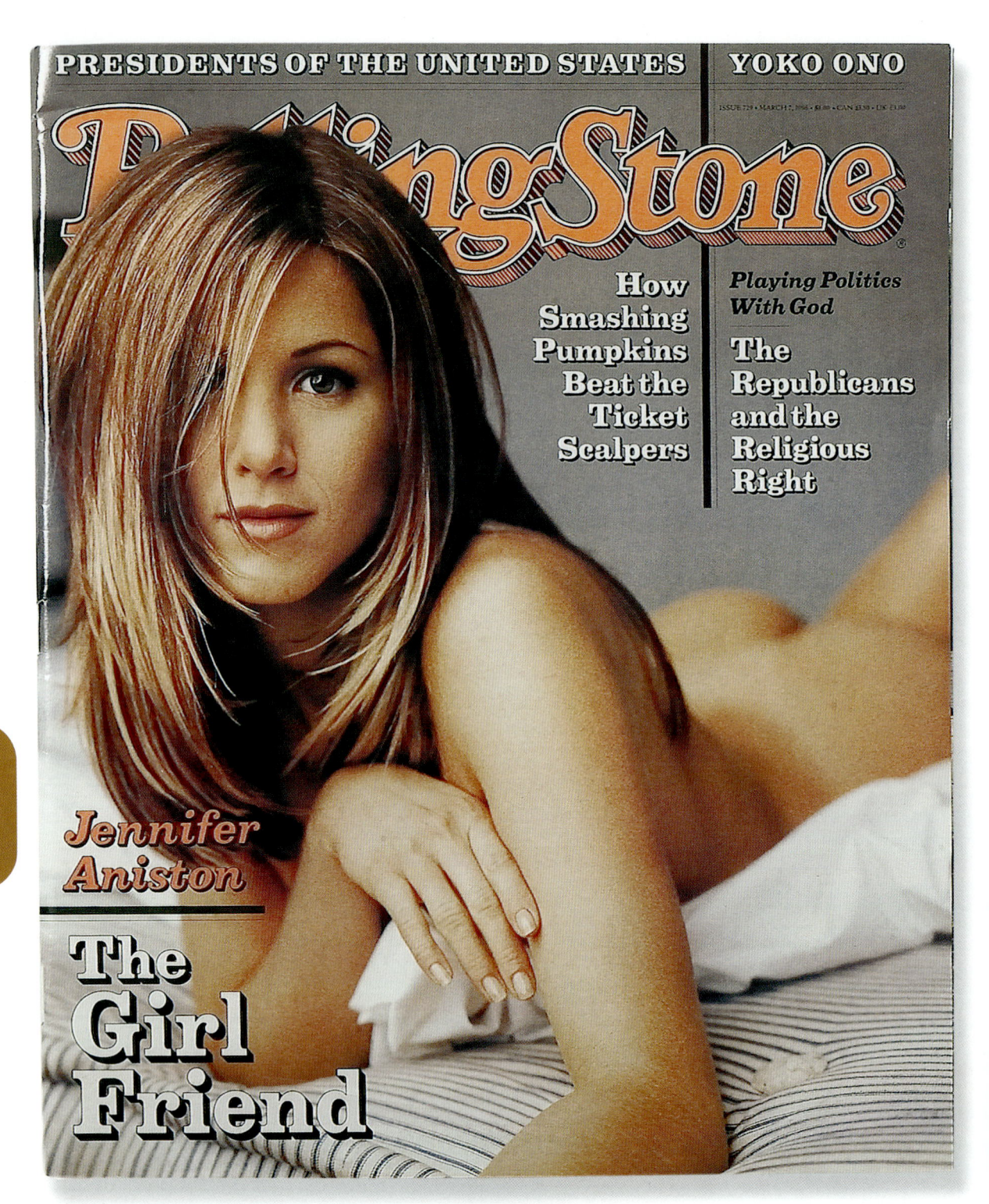

Rolling Stone

SPECIAL REPORT: THE FALL OF APPLE *By Jeff Goodell*

ISSUE 731 · APRIL 4, 1996 · $3.00 · CAN $3.50 · UK £3.00

COOL JERK

Is *Sean Penn* the greatest actor of his generation or a menace to society?

The DOGG WALKS
Snoop Doggy Dogg Beats Murder Rap

Beatles Unplugged

SEVEN MARY THREE

2PAC

STEREOLAB

PULP

RS 731 | SEAN PENN | April 4th, 1996 | PHOTOGRAPH BY MARK SELIGER

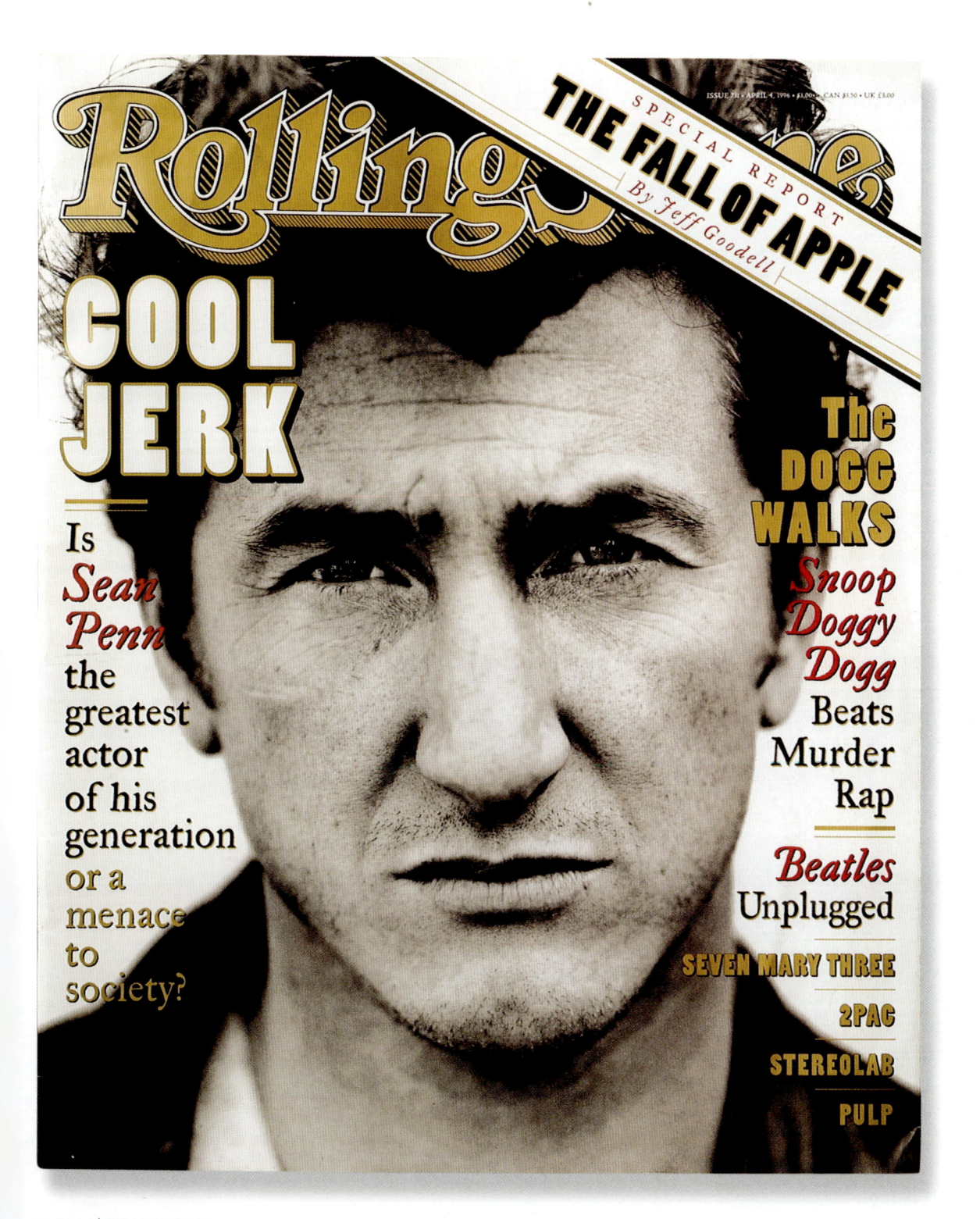

CRACKER | PULP | STEVE EARLE | RAGE AGAINST THE MACHINE

RollingStone

ISSUE 732 · APRIL 18, 1996 · $3.00 | CAN $3.50 | UK £3.00

Three million albums, five hit singles...

Bush

Why won't anyone take Gavin Rossdale seriously?

P.J. O'Rourke on Pat Buchanan

PART TWO
The Fall of
APPLE
By Jeff Goodell

ROLLING STONE
ONE HOT MINUTE
SPRING STYLE

1990s

RS 732 | GAVIN ROSSDALE | April 18th, 1996 | Photograph by MARK SELIGER

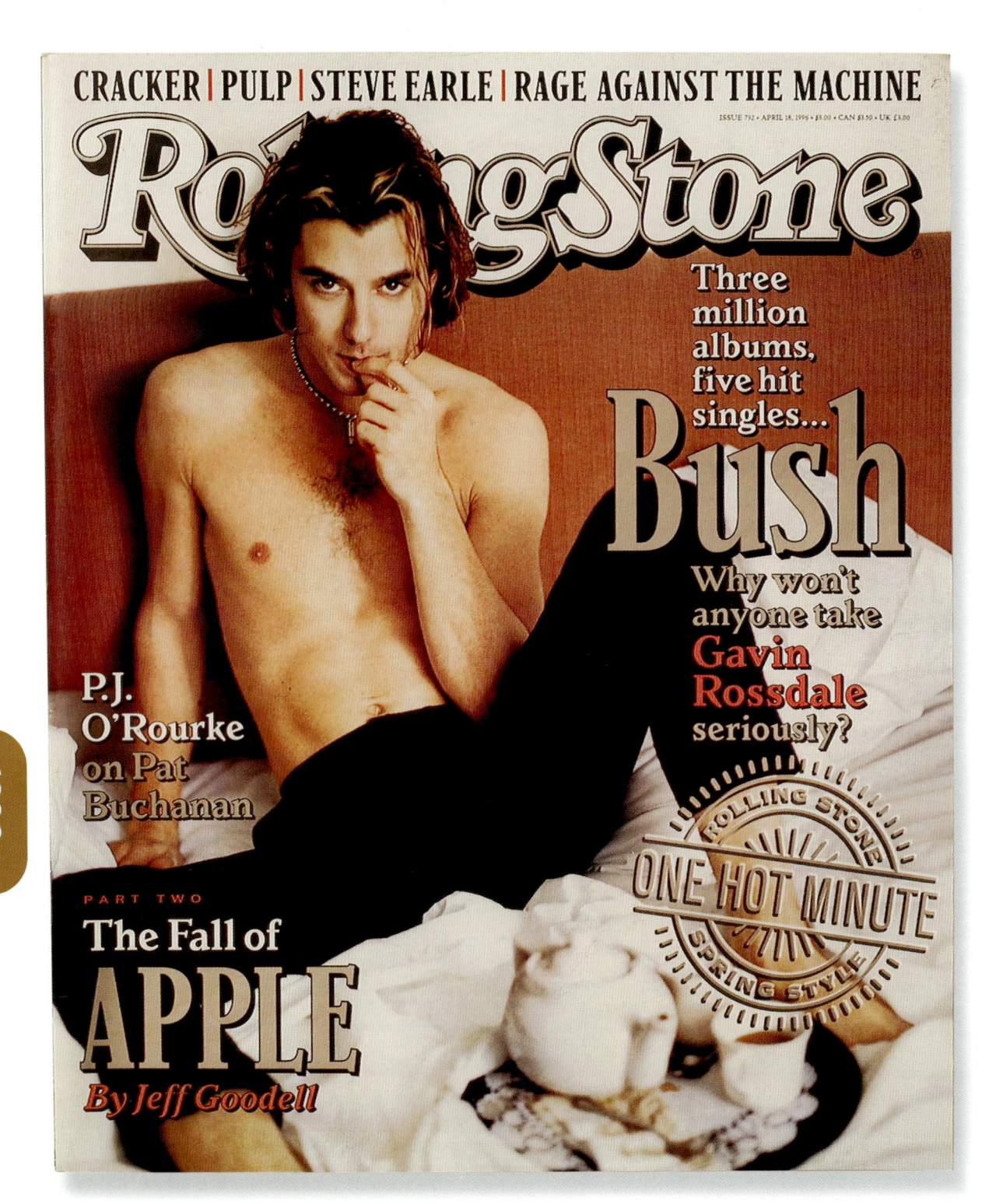

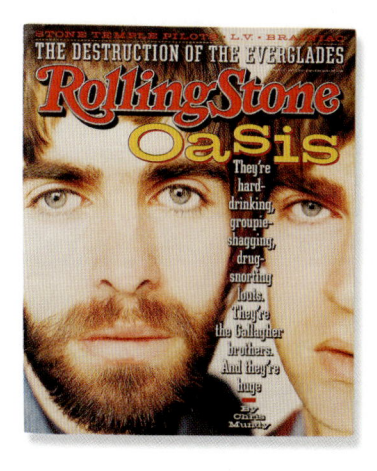

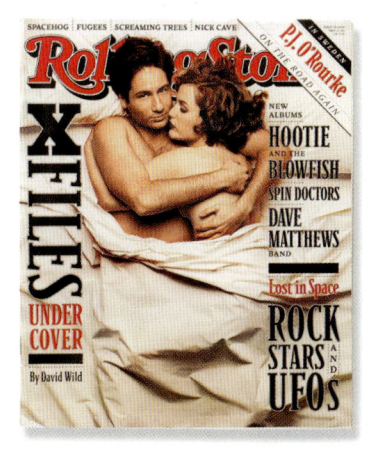

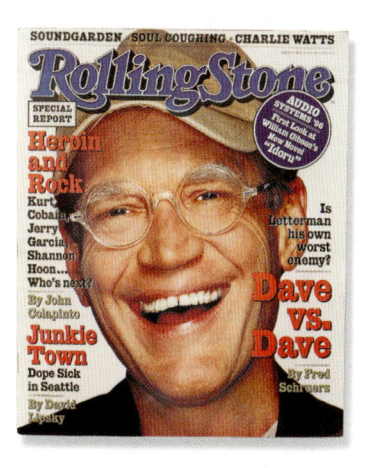

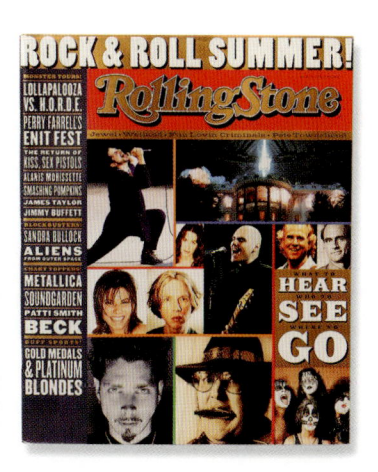

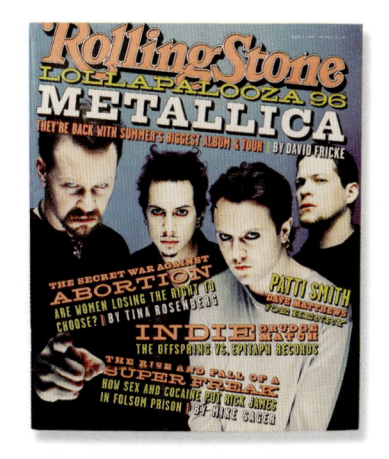

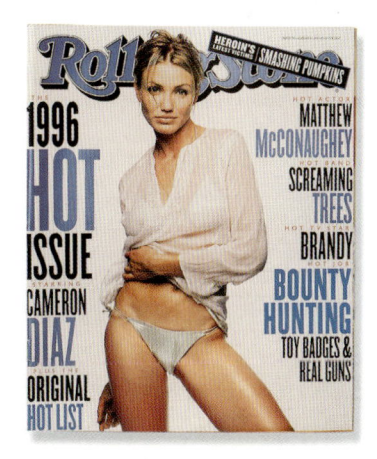

RS 733 | LIAM
& NOEL GALLAGHER
May 2nd, 1996
PHOTOGRAPH BY NATHANIEL GOLDBERG

RS 734 | DAVID DUCHOVNY
& GILLIAN ANDERSON
May 16th, 1996
PHOTOGRAPH BY MONTALBETTI/CAMPBELL

RS 735 | DAVID LETTERMAN
May 30th, 1996
PHOTOGRAPH BY ALBERT WATSON

RS 736 | ROCK & ROLL SUMMER
June 13th, 1996
VARIOUS PHOTOGRAPHERS

RS 737 | METALLICA
June 27th, 1996
PHOTOGRAPH BY ANTON CORBIJN

RS 741 | CAMERON DIAZ
August 22nd, 1996
PHOTOGRAPH BY MARK SELIGER

50 YEARS OF COVERS • 395

Rolling Stone

THE LAST DAYS OF TIM LEARY » BY MIKAL GILMORE

SUMMER DOUBLE ISSUE

ISSUE 738/739 · JULY 11-25, 1996 · $3.50 · CAN $3.95 · UK £3.00

P.J. O'ROURKE In Cuba

THE ROLLING STONE INTERVIEW
PATTI SMITH
By David Fricke

SAFETY LAST
DEATH IN THE MOSH PIT

THE GIRL WITH THE MOST MUSTARD
MTV'S JENNY McCARTHY
By Jancee Dunn

JIM CARREY
BECK
METALLICA
SCREAMING
TREES
EVERYTHING
BUT THE
GIRL

1990s

RS 738/739 | JENNY McCARTHY | July 11th – July 25th, 1996 | Photograph by Mark Seliger

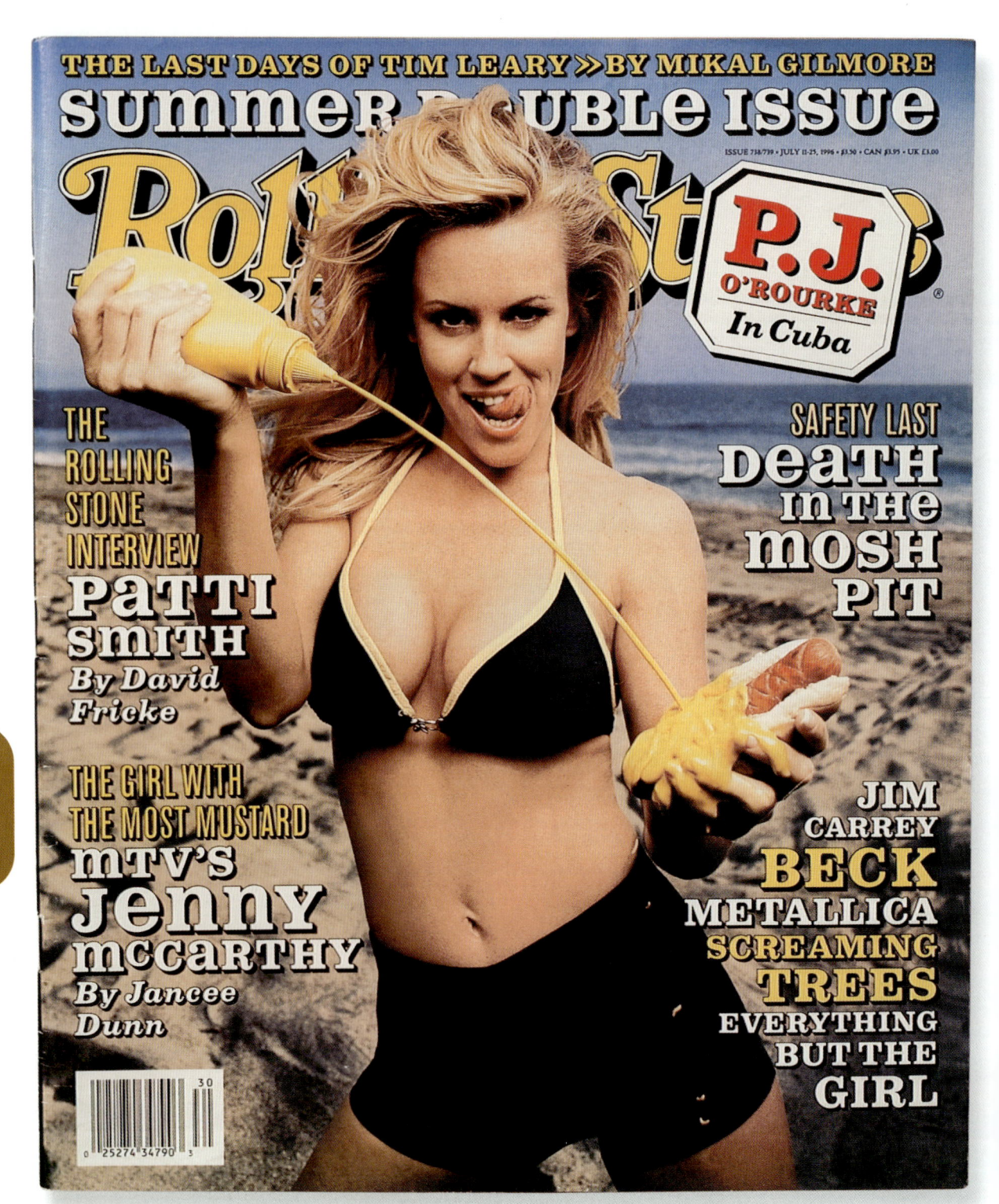

396 • ROLLING STONE

ELLA FITZGERALD 1917-1996 · BY MIKAL GILMORE

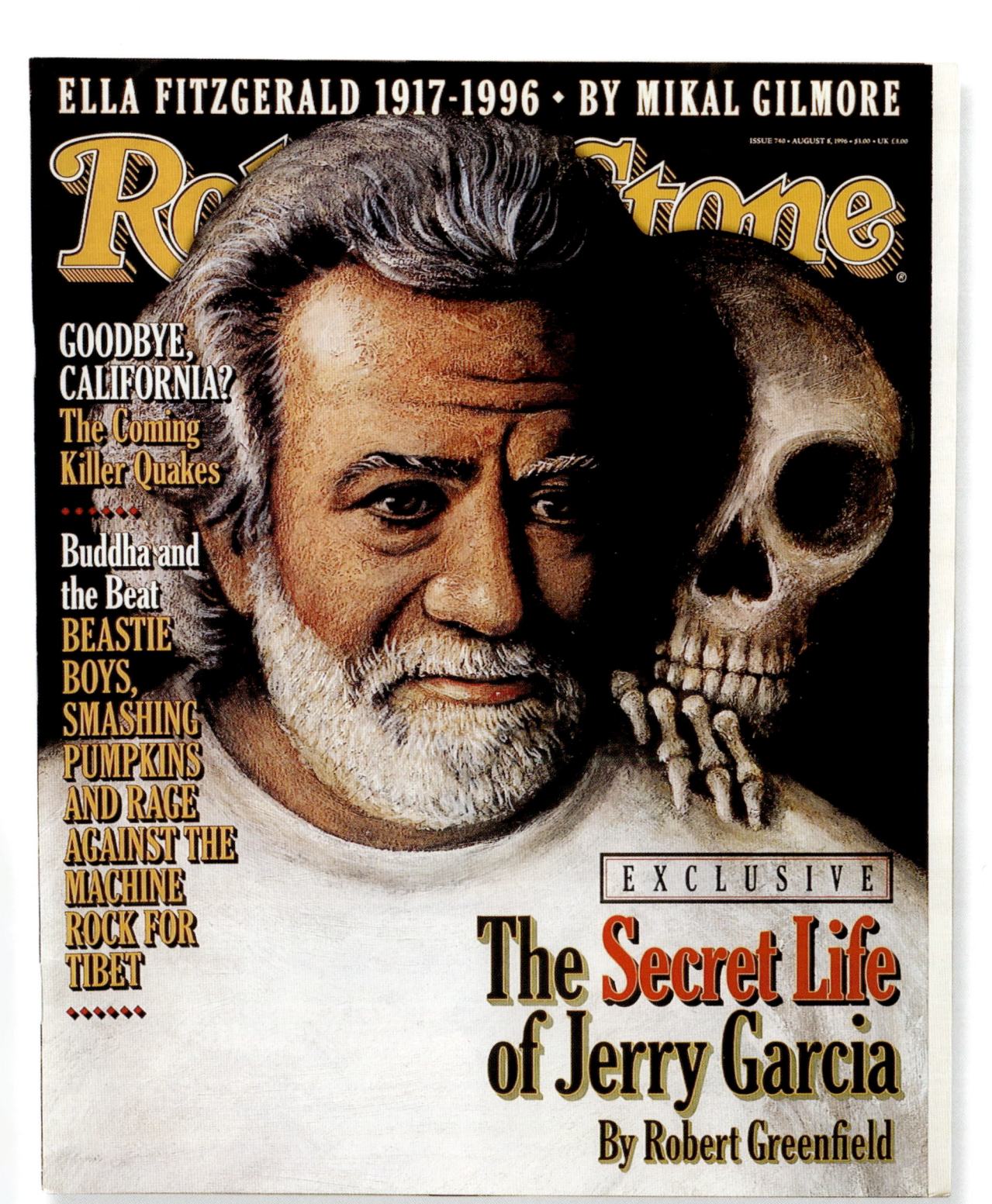

Rolling Stone

ISSUE 740 · AUGUST 8, 1996 · $3.00 · UK £1.00

GOODBYE, CALIFORNIA?
The Coming Killer Quakes

Buddha and the Beat
BEASTIE BOYS, SMASHING PUMPKINS AND RAGE AGAINST THE MACHINE ROCK FOR TIBET

EXCLUSIVE

The Secret Life of Jerry Garcia
By Robert Greenfield

RS 740 | JERRY GARCIA | August 8th, 1996 | Illustration by Paul Davis

PEARL JAM | SEX PISTOLS | 311 | CRANBERRIES | CHER | TRACY CHAPMAN

Rolling Stone

ISSUE 743 · SEPTEMBER 19, 1996 · $3.00 · UK £3.00

The Big Red One

Conan O'Brien's Three-Year Overnight Success

BY CHRIS MUNDY

R.E.M.'s Excellent 'Adventures'

P.J. O'Rourke Invades Russia

JOHN MELLENCAMP
CARDIGANS
PRODIGY
CHEAP TRICK
DUST BROTHERS

EXCLUSIVE

Billy Corgan Talks

About Heroin, Death and the Future of Smashing Pumpkins

1990s

RS 743 | CONAN O'BRIEN | September 19th, 1996 | Photograph by Mark Seliger

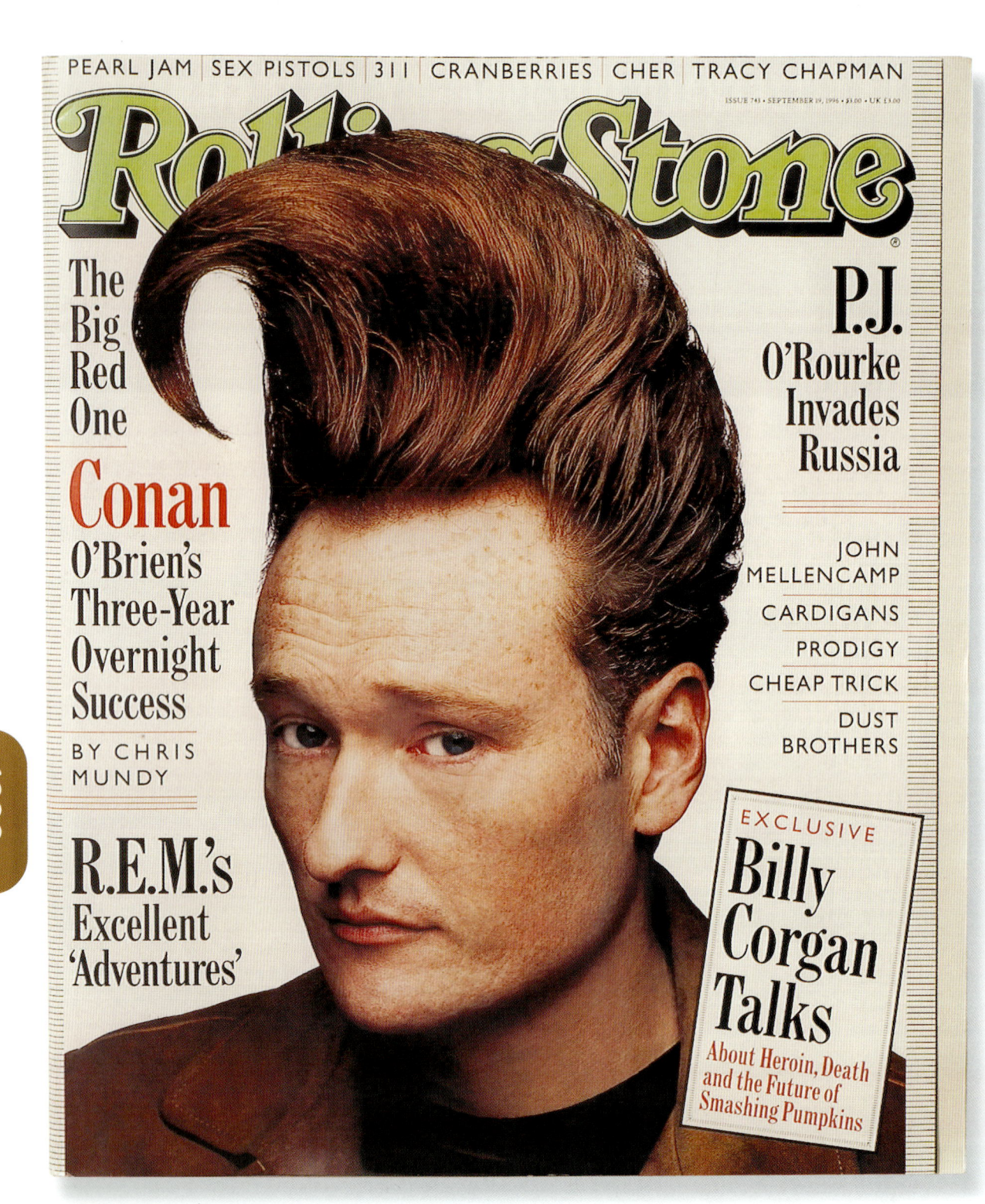

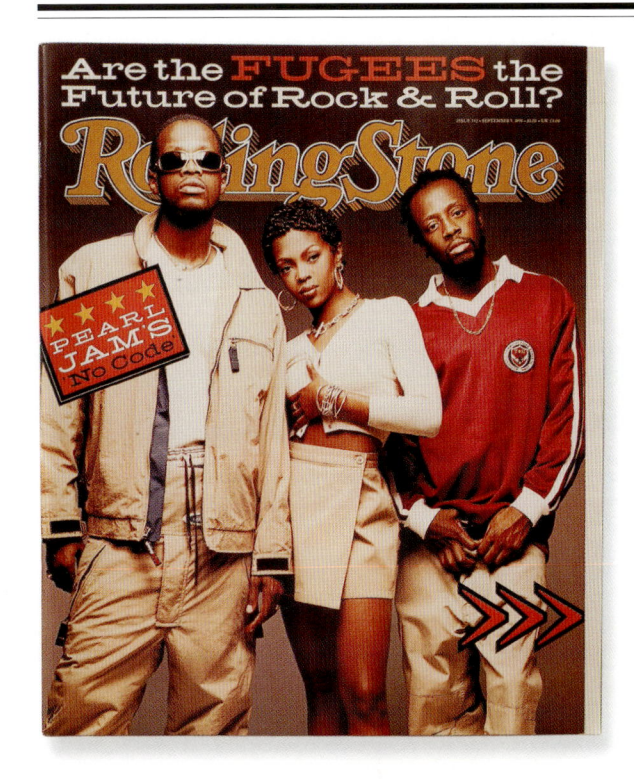

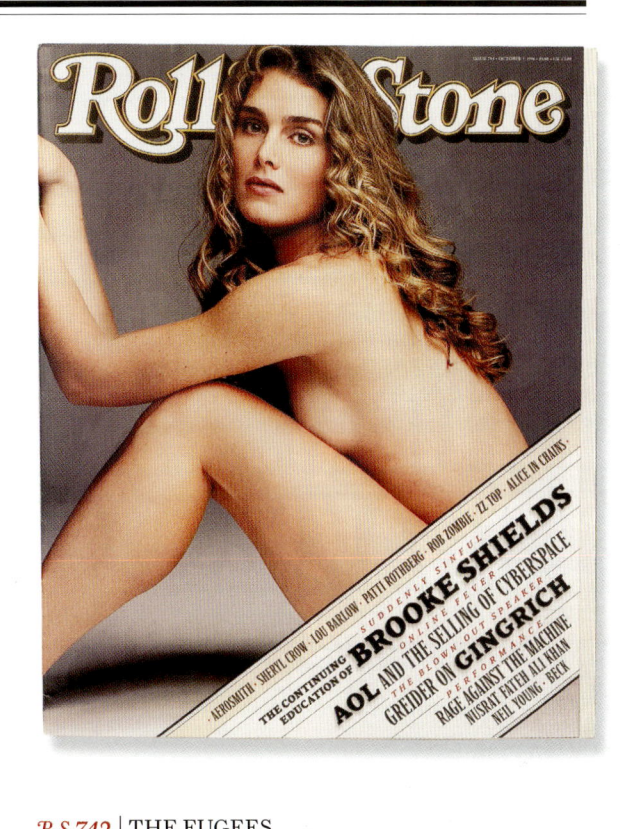

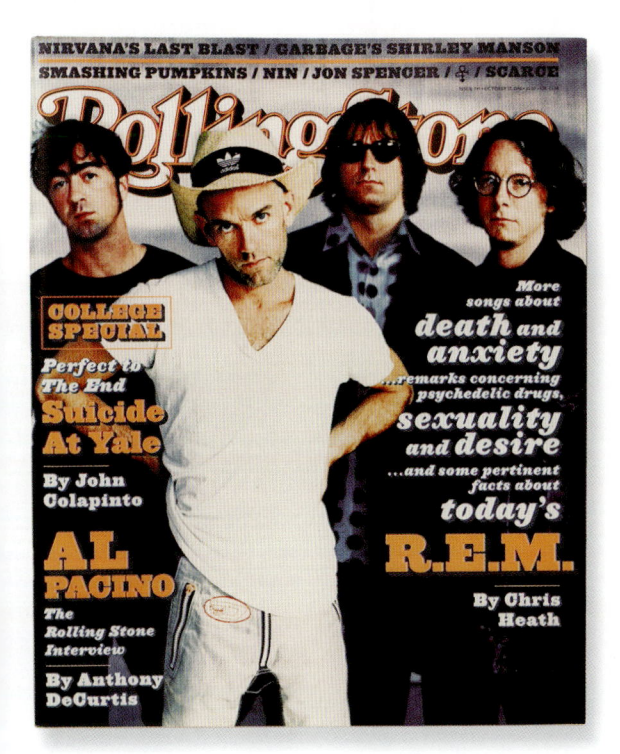

RS 742 | THE FUGEES
September 5th, 1996 | PHOTOGRAPH BY MATTHEW ROLSTON

RS 744 | BROOKE SHIELDS
October 3rd, 1996 | PHOTOGRAPH BY MARK SELIGER

RS 745 | R.E.M.
October 17th, 1996 | PHOTOGRAPH BY ANTON CORBIJN

YOU CAN CALL IT FATE OR YOU CAN CALL IT BREAKING AND entering. The differences are marginal. The time was the late Eighties, a simpler period. Back then, while David Letterman was quietly building an empire in the hours past midnight, a young Harvard grad named Conan O'Brien was making his way as a writer for the recently resuscitated *Saturday Night Live*. Every now and then, to get a break from the all-night writing binges, O'Brien would sneak downstairs, pick the lock to Studio 6A and attempt to write comedy while sitting at Letterman's desk.

"It wasn't like, 'Someday I will sit here,'" says O'Brien. "It was more like, 'This is where he sits? Cool.'" He laughs – you know the sound: high-pitched, slightly braying. "Really, the point of the story is that NBC has terrible security, and I'm sure now every night there will be a different weird person sitting at my desk."

[EXCERPT FROM RS 743 COVER STORY BY CHRIS MUNDY]

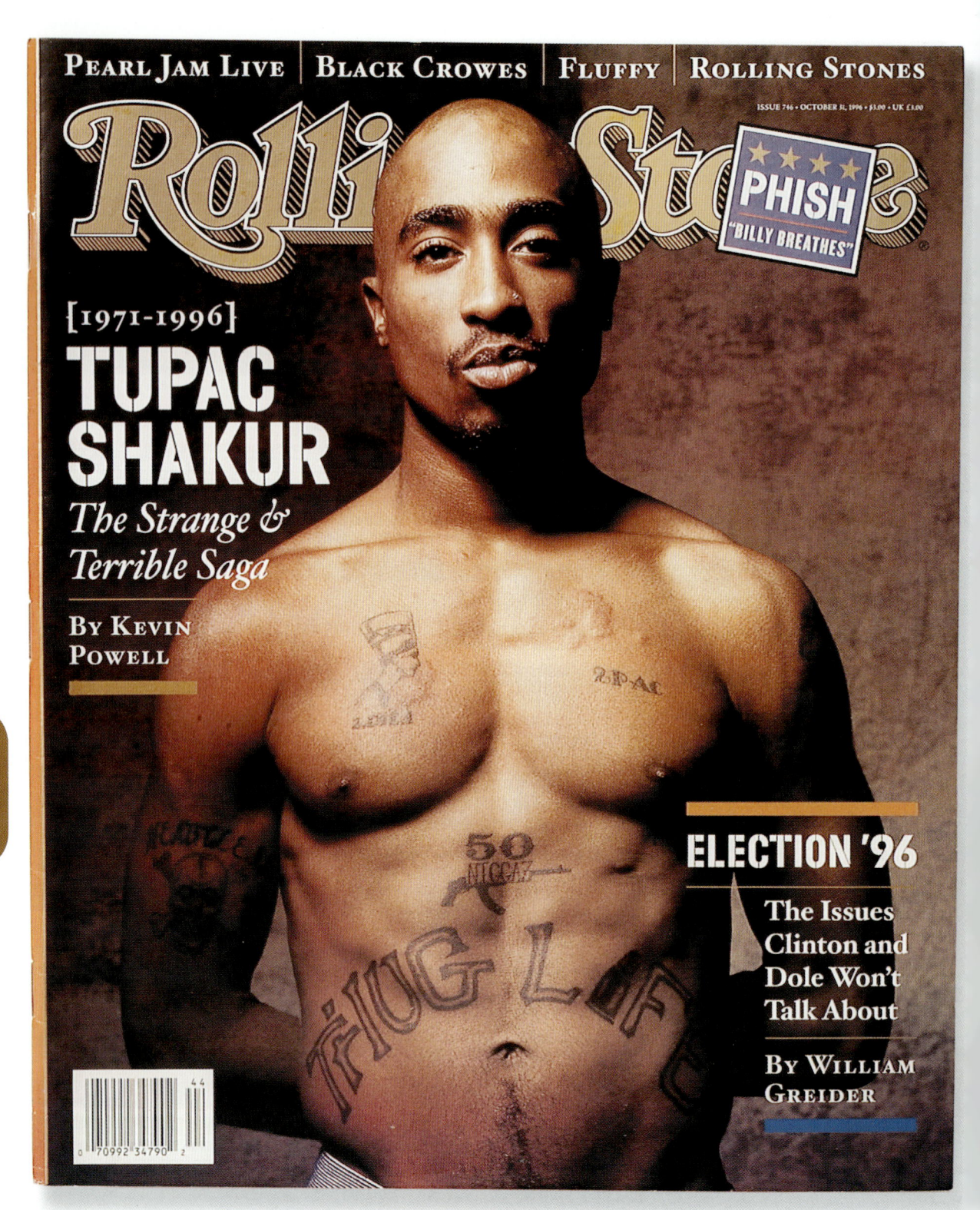

PEARL JAM LIVE | BLACK CROWES | FLUFFY | ROLLING STONES

ISSUE 746 · OCTOBER 31, 1996 · $3.00 · UK £3.00

Rolling Stone

PHISH "BILLY BREATHES"

[1971–1996]

TUPAC SHAKUR

The Strange & Terrible Saga

BY KEVIN POWELL

ELECTION '96

The Issues Clinton and Dole Won't Talk About

BY WILLIAM GREIDER

At 4:03 p.m. on September 13th, Tupac Amaru Shakur, rapper and actor, died at the University of Nevada Medical Center in the Wild West gambling town of Las Vegas, the result of gunshot wounds he had received six days earlier in a drive-by shooting near the glittery, hotel-studded strip. Shakur, a.k.a. 2Pac, was twenty-five. The rapper is survived by his mother, Afeni Shakur, his father, Billy Garland, and a half sister, Sekyiwa.

RS 746 | TUPAC SHAKUR
October 31st, 1996
PHOTOGRAPH BY DANNY CLINCH

I DON'T KNOW WHETHER TO MOURN TUPAC SHAKUR OR to rail against all the terrible forces – including the artist's own self-destructive temperament – that have resulted in such a wasteful, unjustifiable end. I do know this, though: Whatever its causes, the murder of Shakur, at age twenty-five, has robbed us of one of the most talented and compelling voices of recent years. He embodied just as much for his audience as Kurt Cobain did for his. That is, Tupac Shakur spoke to, and for, many who had grown up within hard realities – realities that mainstream culture and media are loath to understand or respect. His death has left his fans feeling a doubly sharp pain: the loss of a much-esteemed signifier and the loss of a future volume of work that, no doubt, would have proved both brilliant and provocative.

So: A man sings about death and killing, and then the man is killed. There is a great temptation for many to view one event as the result of the other. And in Tupac Shakur's case, there are some grounds for this assessment: He did more than sing about violence; he also participated in a fair amount of it. As Shakur himself once said, in words that *Time* magazine appropriated for its headline covering his murder: WHAT GOES 'ROUND COMES 'ROUND. Still, I think it would be a great disservice to dismiss Shakur's work and life with any quick and glib headline summations. It's like burying the man without hearing him.

—*Mikal Gilmore*
[EXCERPT FROM RS 746 ESSAY]

1990s

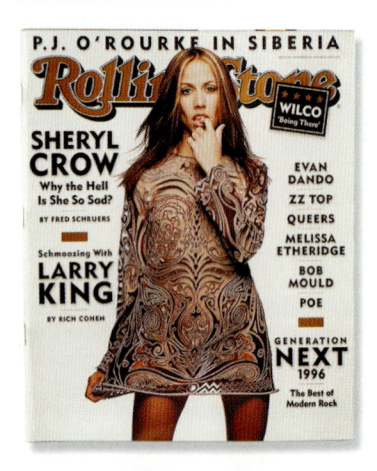

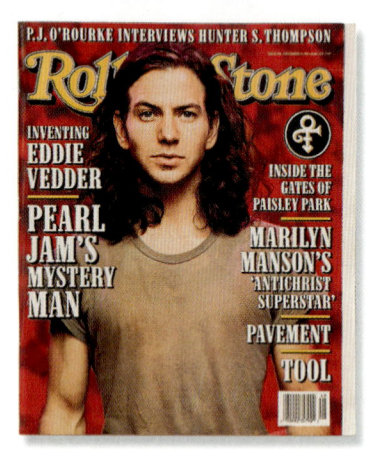

RS 747 | SHERYL CROW
November 14th, 1996
PHOTOGRAPH BY MARK SELIGER

RS 748 | EDDIE VEDDER
November 28th, 1996
PHOTOGRAPH BY ROSS HALFIN

This is a journey into the mind of Dennis Rodman. Think twice before volunteering to go further. Sometimes it will be funny, but sometimes it will be scary. Sometimes the paranoia and craziness will seep out of the page to get you. Sometimes you won't quite understand what Dennis Rodman is saying. Sometimes you will and wish you didn't. There will be casualties. Logic, love, basketball, fashion . . . these will all take a battering. You will not be lied to, but sometimes the truth will seem elusive. This trip will take in an array of guests, and not all of them will be pleased to find themselves in Rodman-land. It will be fun, in a way, but the kind of fun that gets all mixed up with trouble and sadness and never quite untangles itself. In the end, life won't seem simpler, and the world won't seem a safer place.

Don't forget: We are just tourists here. We will be going home. But Dennis Rodman can't leave. This is where he lives. . . .

Dennis Rodman lies back on the bus bed, the evening sunlight shining off his nose rings. "I totally feel like a rock star more than a basketball player. I totally think: Have I got to go and play basketball now?"

[EXCERPT FROM RS 749 COVER STORY BY CHRIS HEATH]

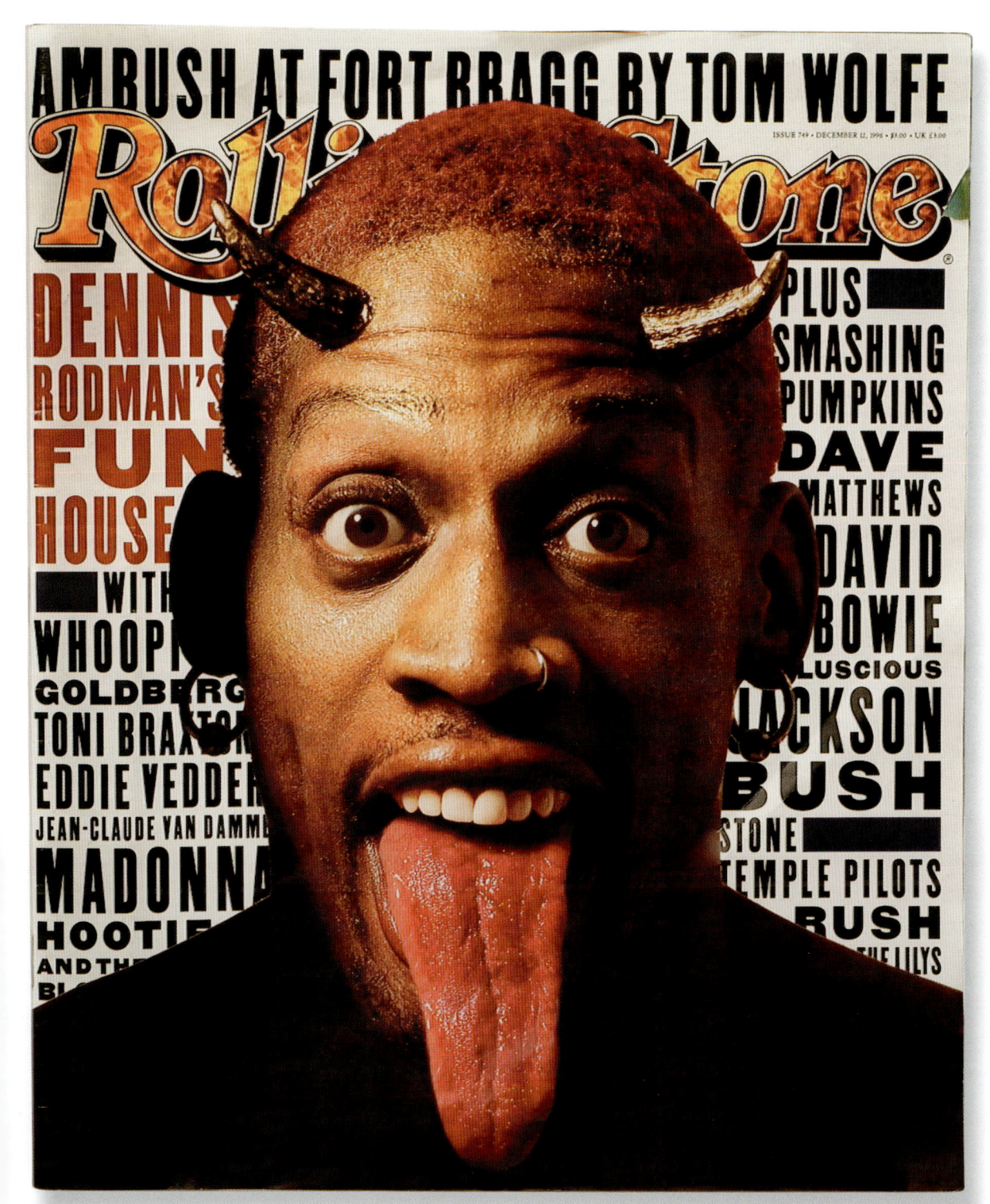

RS 749 | DENNIS RODMAN | December 12th, 1996 | Photograph by Albert Watson

50 YEARS OF COVERS • 403

RS 752 | MARILYN MANSON
January 23rd, 1997
Photograph by Matt Mahurin

Be careful when you gossip:

A little rumor can go a long way. Especially when the subject is Marilyn Manson.

"For a solid year, there was a rumor that I was going to commit suicide on Halloween," says Manson. He is sitting in a hot tub (yes, a hot tub!) in his hometown of Fort Lauderdale, Florida. "I started to think, 'Maybe I have to kill myself, maybe that's what I was supposed to do.' Then, when we were performing on Halloween, there was a bomb threat. I guess someone thought they would take care of the situation for me.

It was one of those moments where chaos had control." He pauses, raises his tattoo-covered arm from the water and stares nervously through a pair of black wraparound sunglasses at the spa door. It opens a crack, then closes. No one enters. "Sometimes I wonder if I'm a character being written, or if I'm writing myself," Manson continues. "It's confusing."

Never has there been a rock star quite as complex as Marilyn Manson, frontman of the band of the same name. In the current landscape of reluctant rock stars, Manson is a complete anomaly: He craves spectacle, success and attention. And when it comes to the traditional rock-star lifestyle, he can outdo most of his contemporaries. Manson and his similarly pseudonymed band mates – bassist Twiggy Ramirez, drummer Ginger Fish, keyboardist Madonna Wayne Gacy and guitarist Zim Zum – have shat in Evan Dando's bathtub and, just last night, they coaxed Billy Corgan into snorting sea monkeys. When it comes to getting serious about his work, Manson is among the most eloquent and artful musicians. And among the most misunderstood. The rumor-hungry fans who see him as a living demon who's removed his own ribs and testicles know just as little about Manson as the detractors who dismiss him as a Halloween-costumed shock rocker riding on Trent Reznor's coattails.

[EXCERPT FROM RS 752 COVER STORY BY NEIL STRAUSS]

1990s

ANNUAL MUSIC AWARDS ISSUE

ISSUE 752 · JANUARY 23, 1997 · $3.00 · UK £3.00

RollingStone

BEST NEW ARTIST
Marilyn Manson's Beautiful Nightmare
BY NEIL STRAUSS

ALBUM OF THE YEAR
Beck's "Odelay"

ARTIST OF THE YEAR
Smashing Pumpkins

THE HOMECOMING QUEEN MURDER
BY PETER WILKINSON

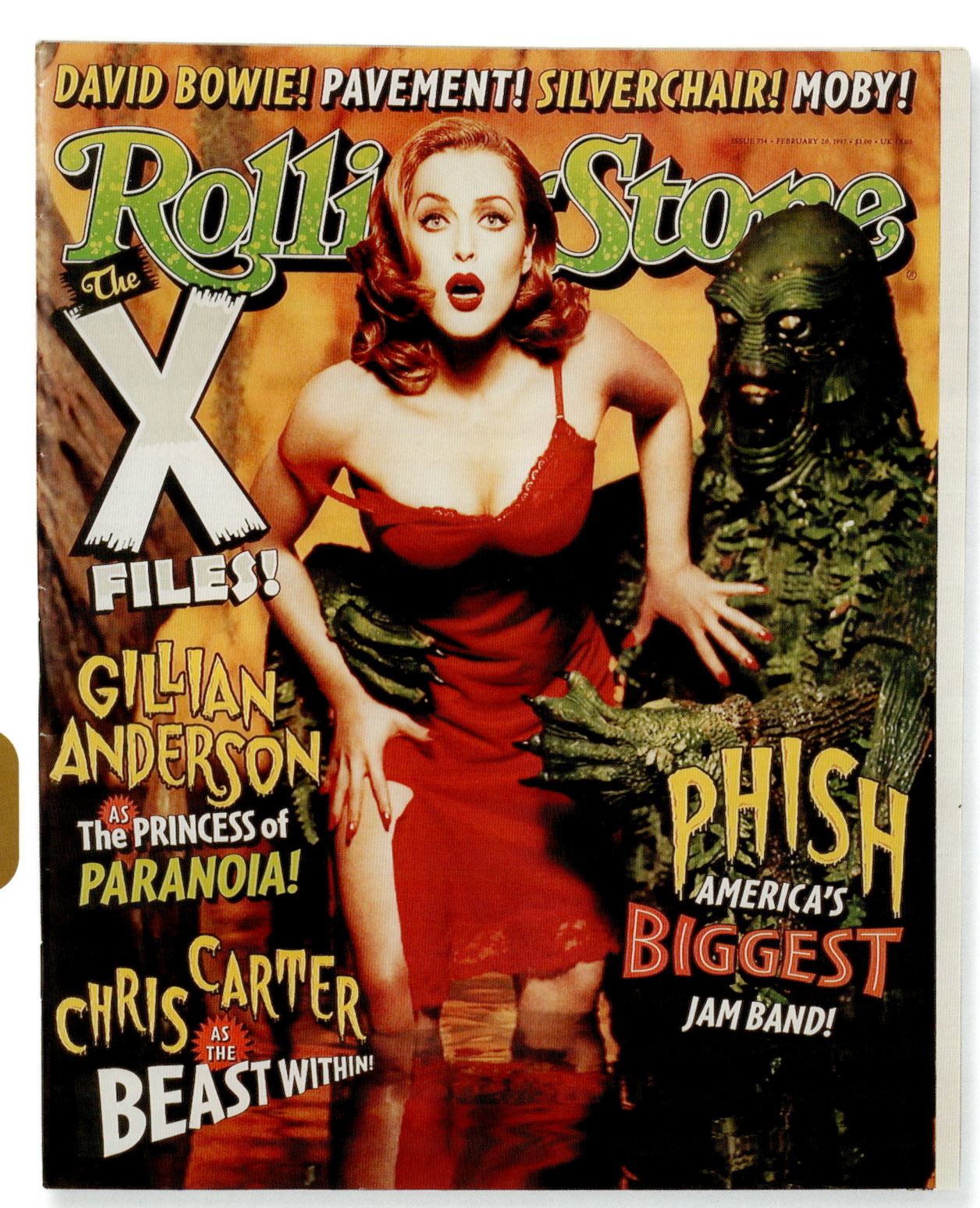

RS 754 | GILLIAN ANDERSON | February 20th, 1997 | Photograph by Matthew Rolston

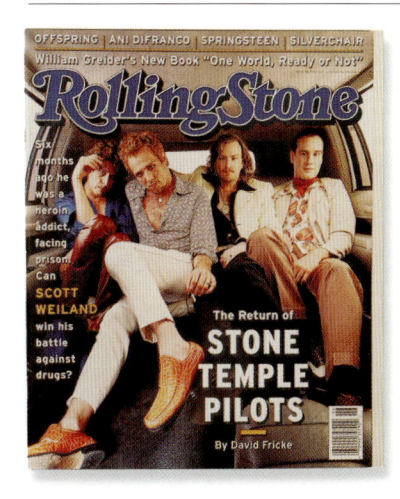

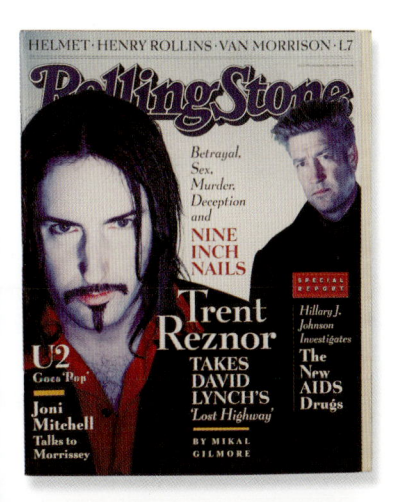

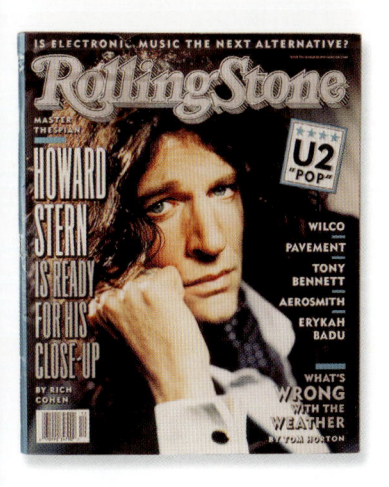

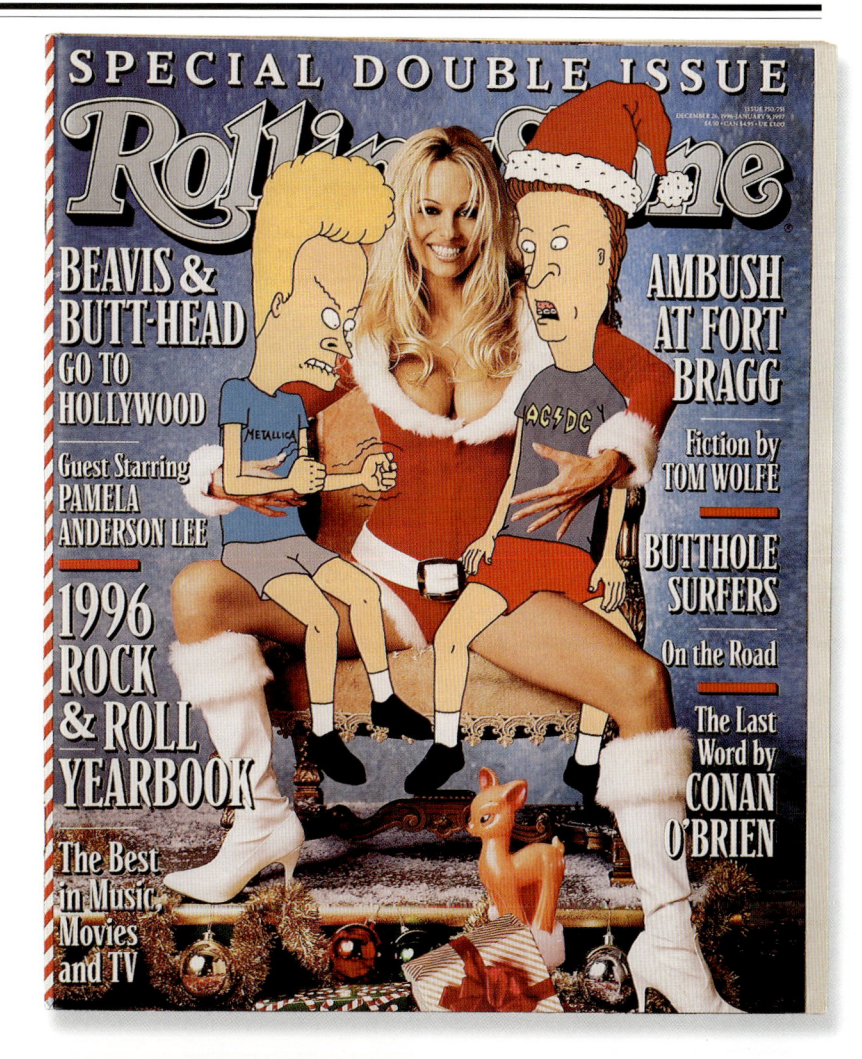

RS 750/751 | BEAVIS & BUTT-HEAD
WITH PAMELA ANDERSON LEE
December 26th, 1996 – January 9th, 1997
Photograph by Mark Seliger, Illustration by Mike Judge

RS 753 | STONE TEMPLE PILOTS
February 6th, 1997
Photograph by Mark Seliger

RS 755 | TRENT REZNOR & DAVID LYNCH
March 6th, 1997
Photograph by Dan Winters

RS 756 | HOWARD STERN
March 20th, 1997
Photograph by Mark Seliger

50 YEARS OF COVERS • 407

RS 762 | JAKOB DYLAN
June 12th, 1997
PHOTOGRAPH BY MARK SELIGER

MUCH OF TONIGHT'S AUDIENCE has no idea who Jakob's father is; everyone I've talked to couldn't care less: *Bob Dylan's just a guy in my social studies book.*

"*Jaaaaaaykob!*"

So handsome, with those sharp Armani shoulders, the startling, Samoyed-blue eyes, that cool, funky hat destined to become a video talisman . . .

"*Jaaaaaykob! Tell it!*"

What the recordmen don't know, the little girls understand. Jakob Dylan is a young man of certain passion, singing his own words with a shy, fitful intensity that seems, sometimes, to take him out and above this big, hot room. It's not the raspy, unremarkable voice so much as the delivery that draws them, some strain of the ageless troubadour DNA that goosed vestal virgins in the shadows of Stonehenge.

[EXCERPT FROM RS 762 COVER STORY BY GERRI HIRSHEY]

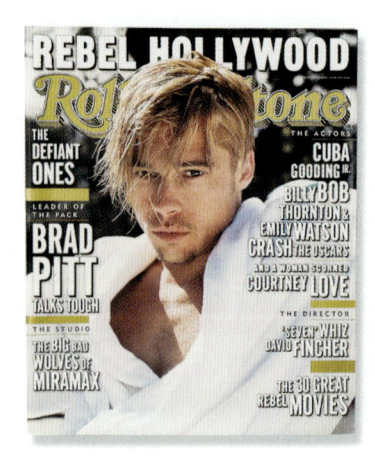

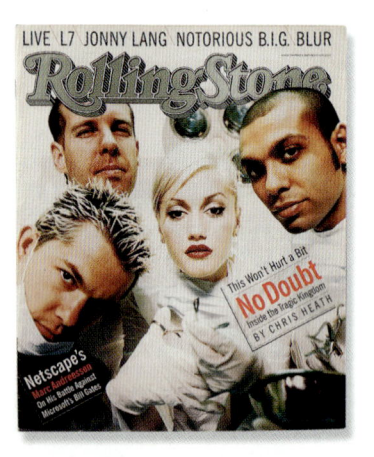

1990s

RS 757 | BRAD PITT
April 3rd, 1997
PHOTOGRAPH BY MARK SELIGER

RS 759 | NO DOUBT
May 1st, 1997
PHOTOGRAPH BY NORBERT SCHOERNER

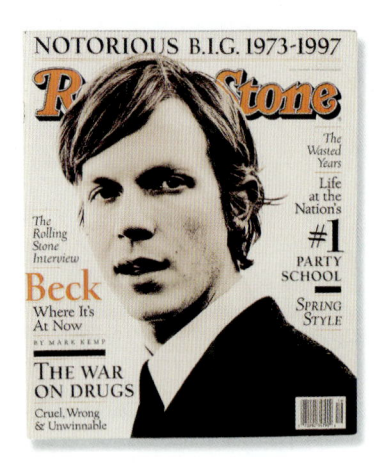

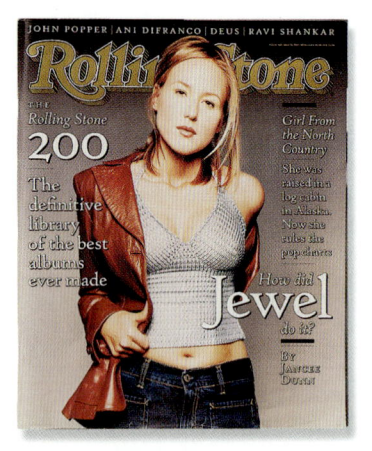

RS 758 | BECK
April 17th, 1997
PHOTOGRAPH BY ANTON CORBIJN

RS 760 | JEWEL
May 15th, 1997
PHOTOGRAPH BY MATTHEW ROLSTON

408 • ROLLING STONE

Rolling Stone

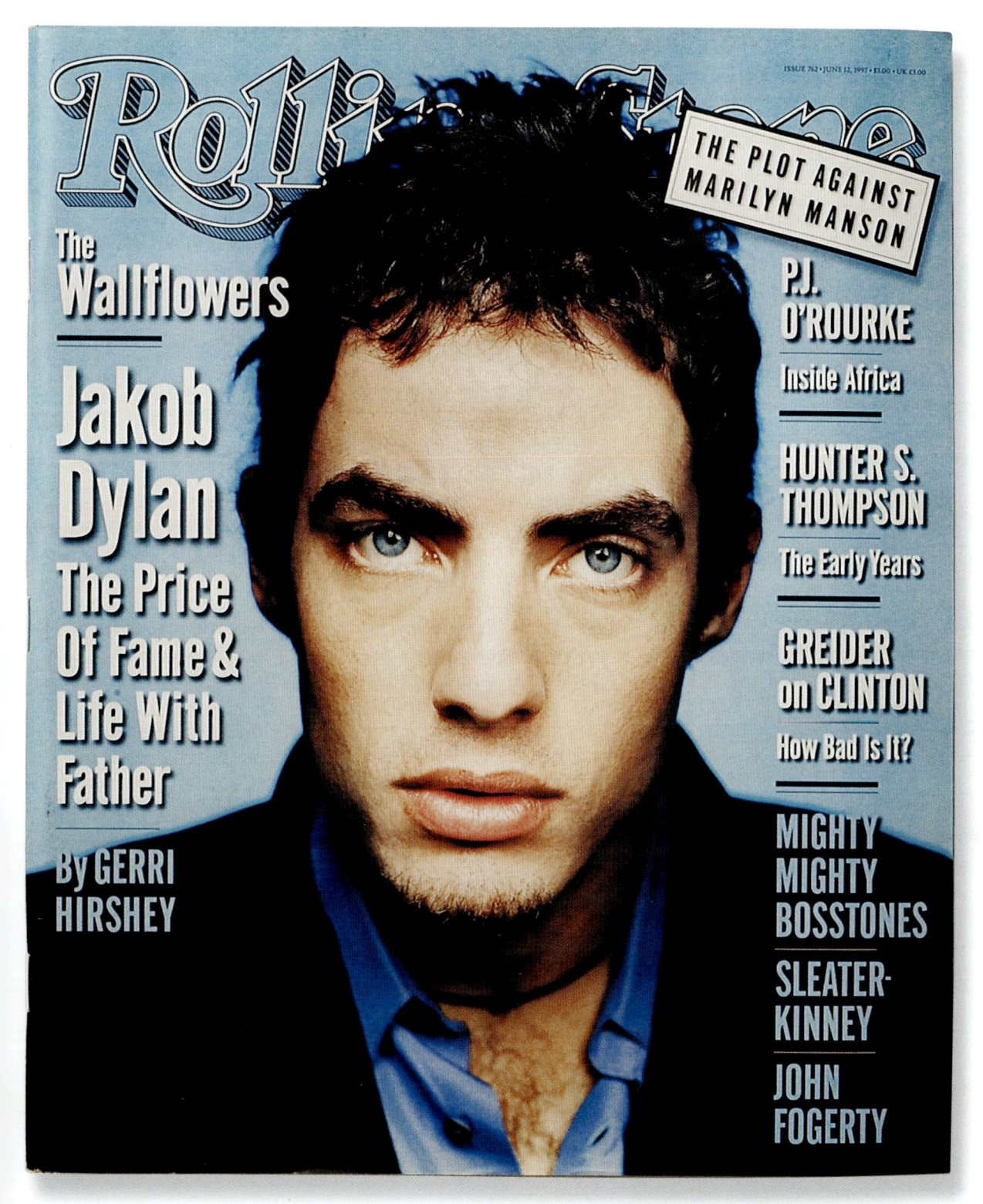

ISSUE 762 · JUNE 12, 1997 · $3.00 · UK £3.00

THE PLOT AGAINST MARILYN MANSON

The Wallflowers

Jakob Dylan
The Price Of Fame & Life With Father

BY GERRI HIRSHEY

P.J. O'ROURKE
Inside Africa

HUNTER S. THOMPSON
The Early Years

GREIDER on CLINTON
How Bad Is It?

MIGHTY MIGHTY BOSSTONES

SLEATER-KINNEY

JOHN FOGERTY

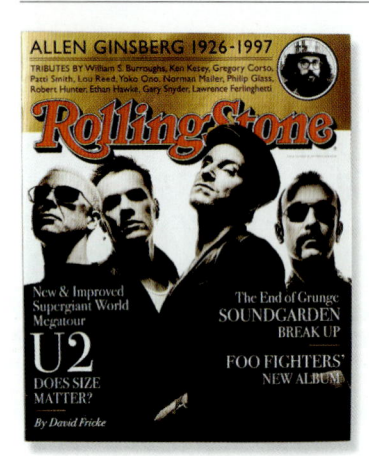

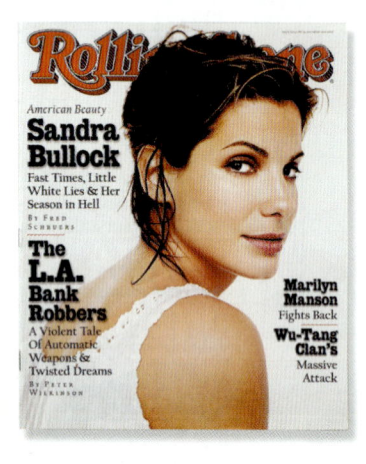

RS 764/765 | SPICE GIRLS | July 10th – July 24th, 1997 | Photograph by Mark Seliger

HERE, BEFORE THINGS GET TOO SILLY AND AGITATED, is a cut out'n'keep guide to the five Spice Girls. This is what you will need to know:

Geri Haliwell is twenty-four. She is known as Ginger Spice. . . . When Geri was young, she once poohed in the bath with her brother and sister. She is the most talkative Spice Girl and the one who is generally first to shout "girl power," the key concept in Spice Girl philosophy.

Melanie Brown (Mel B) is twenty-two. She is known as Scary Spice. . . . When she was young, Mel B used to have a boogie collection behind her bunk bed. Now she has a pierced tongue.

Emma Bunton is twenty-one. She is known as Baby Spice. She has blond hair, which she often wears in bunches. . . . When she was young, she was a child model. She recently announced, as a joke, "I don't want to be a cutie – I want to be a hot, sexy bitch," but she's now rather perturbed that the statement has been taken seriously.

Victoria Aadams is twenty-two. She is known as Posh Spice. . . . When she was young, Victoria used to beg her father not to take her to school in the Rolls-Royce. She was teased for that and for her nose. She likes to dress in Prada and Gucci and hates the way she looks when she smiles.

Melanie Chisholm is twenty-three. She is known as Sporty Spice. . . . When she was young, Melanie used to eat cat food. She wears lots of Adidas sportswear. A tattoo on her upper right arm is of two Japanese symbols: woman and strength. Girl power, in other words.

These names – Ginger, Scary, Baby, Posh, Sporty – have been a successful part of the Spice Girls package: a perfect simultaneous pop expression of heterogeneity (they're each their own person) and homogeneity (they're all disciples in the Church of Spice).

[EXCERPT FROM RS 764/765 COVER STORY BY CHRIS HEATH]

RS 761 | U2
May 29th, 1997
Photograph by Albert Watson

RS 763 | SANDRA BULLOCK
June 26th, 1997
Photograph by Brigitte Lacombe

SUMMER DOUBLE ISSUE

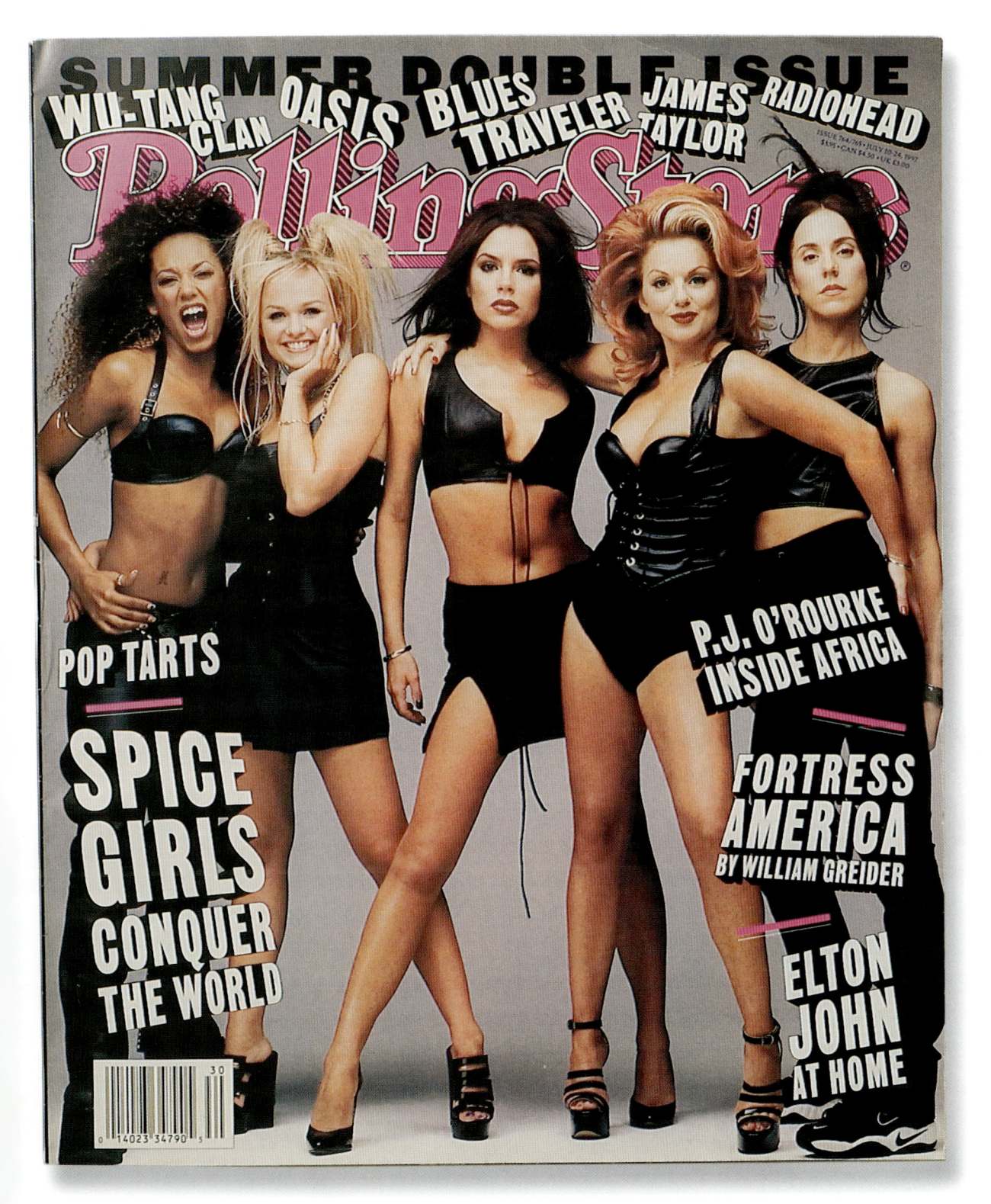

WU-TANG CLAN · **OASIS** · **BLUES TRAVELER** · **JAMES TAYLOR** · **RADIOHEAD**

Rolling Stone

POP TARTS

SPICE GIRLS CONQUER THE WORLD

P.J. O'ROURKE INSIDE AFRICA

FORTRESS AMERICA BY WILLIAM GREIDER

ELTON JOHN AT HOME

Rolling Stone

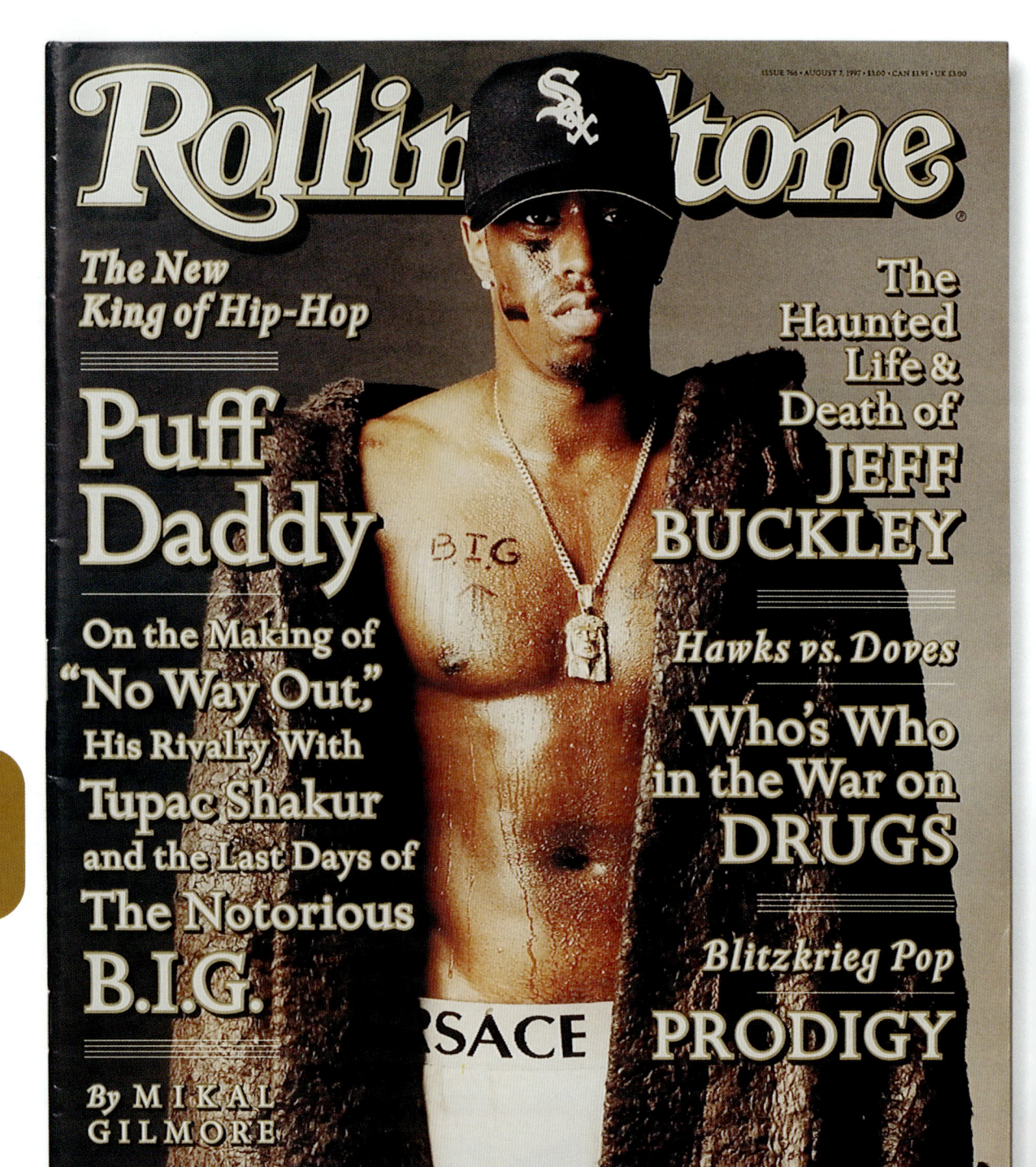

ISSUE 766 · AUGUST 7, 1997 · $3.00 · CAN $3.95 · UK £3.00

The New King of Hip-Hop

Puff Daddy

On the Making of "No Way Out," His Rivalry With Tupac Shakur and the Last Days of The Notorious B.I.G.

By MIKAL GILMORE

The Haunted Life & Death of JEFF BUCKLEY

Hawks vs. Doves

Who's Who in the War on DRUGS

Blitzkrieg Pop
PRODIGY

1990s

RS 766 | PUFF DADDY | August 7th, 1997 | Photograph by MATTHEW ROLSTON

412 · ROLLING STONE

Rolling Stone

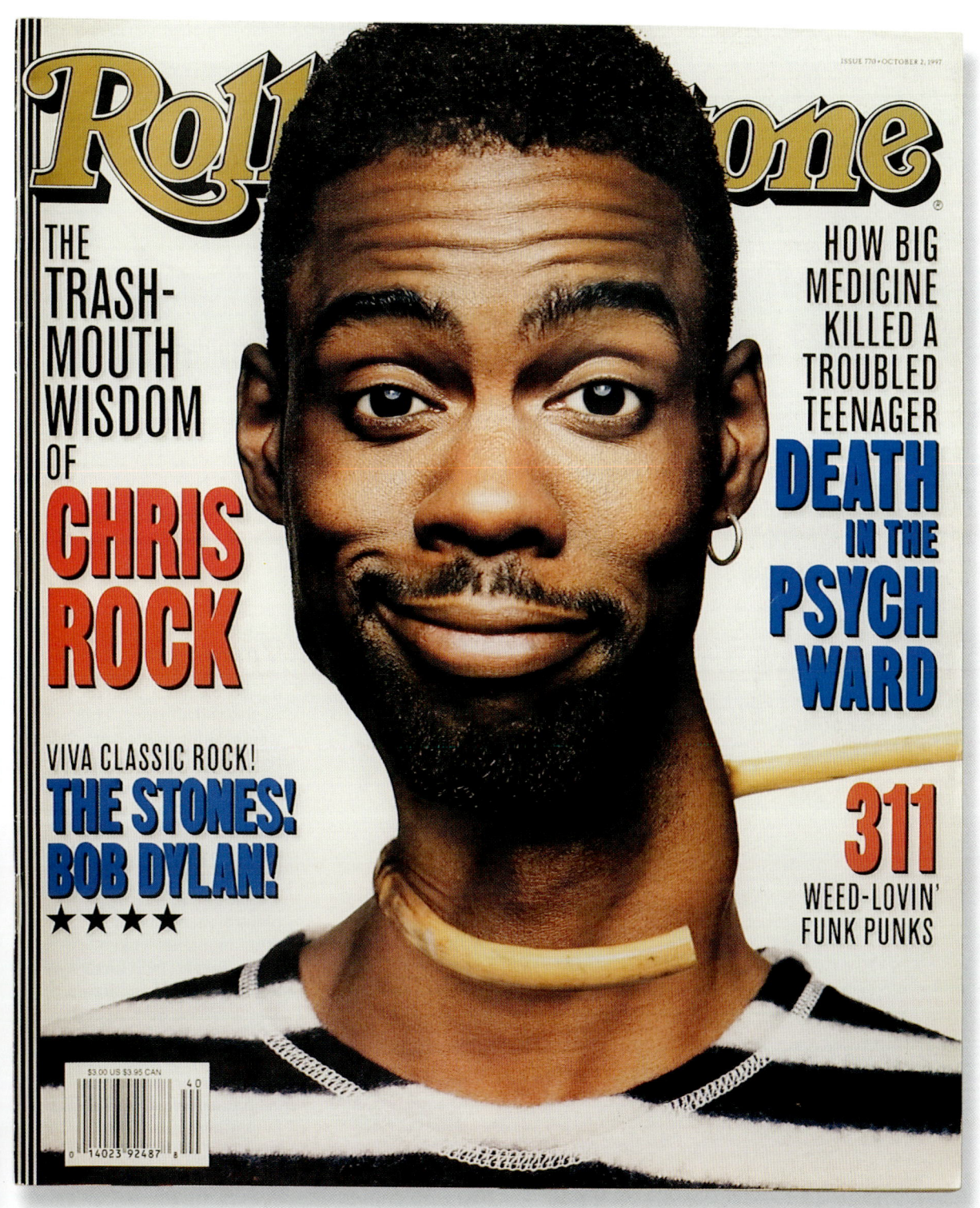

ISSUE 770 • OCTOBER 2, 1997

THE TRASH-MOUTH WISDOM OF **CHRIS ROCK**

VIVA CLASSIC ROCK!
**THE STONES!
BOB DYLAN!**
★★★★

HOW BIG MEDICINE KILLED A TROUBLED TEENAGER
DEATH IN THE PSYCH WARD

311 WEED-LOVIN' FUNK PUNKS

RS 770 | CHRIS ROCK | *October 2nd, 1997* | Photograph by Mark Seliger

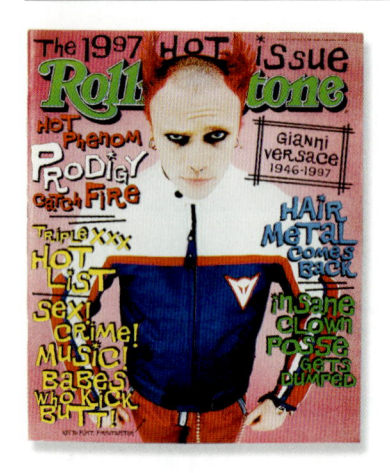

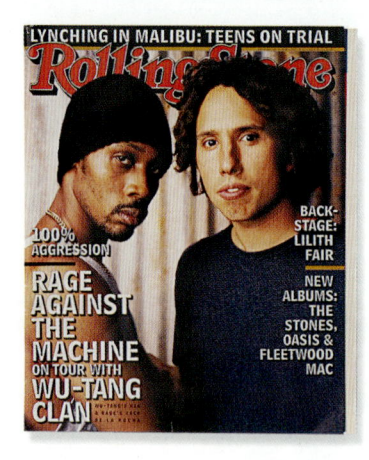

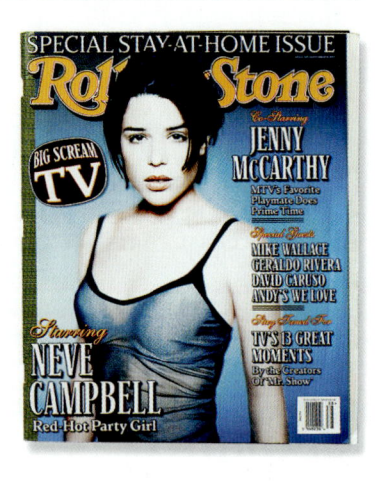

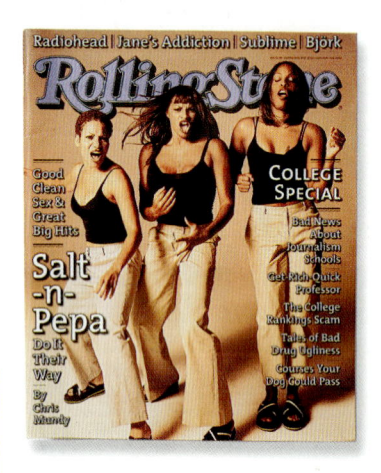

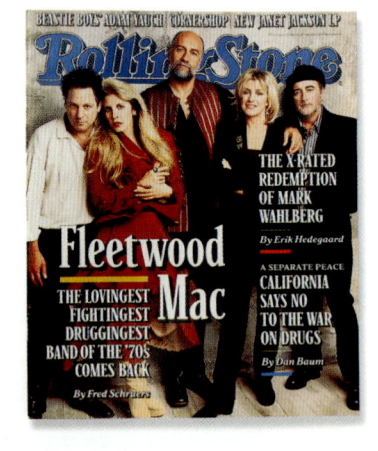

1990s

RS 767 | THE PRODIGY'S
KEITH FLINT
August 21st, 1997
PHOTOGRAPH BY PETER ROBATHAN

RS 771 | SALT-N-PEPA
October 16th, 1997
PHOTOGRAPH BY PEGGY SIROTA

RS 768 | RZA &
ZACH DE LA ROCHA
September 4th, 1997
PHOTOGRAPH BY MARK SELIGER

RS 772 | FLEETWOOD MAC
October 30th, 1997
PHOTOGRAPH BY MARK SELIGER

RS 769 | NEVE CAMPBELL
September 18th, 1997
PHOTOGRAPH BY MATTHEW ROLSTON

Women

have been at the heart of rock & roll all along. They were wailing loudest at rock's beginning – in its blues and gospel prehistory. At times, they've sung stalwart background or had their sounds and looks arranged by the whims and marketing plans of men. And at other moments – like now – they've held forth in the boldest of spotlights. They've been worshipped and objectified, overdubbed and underpaid. Like their male counterparts, they can be deeply passionate or chillingly calculated. But they have never – ever – been quiet.

[EXCERPT FROM RS 773 COVER STORY BY GERRI HIRSHEY]

414 • ROLLING STONE

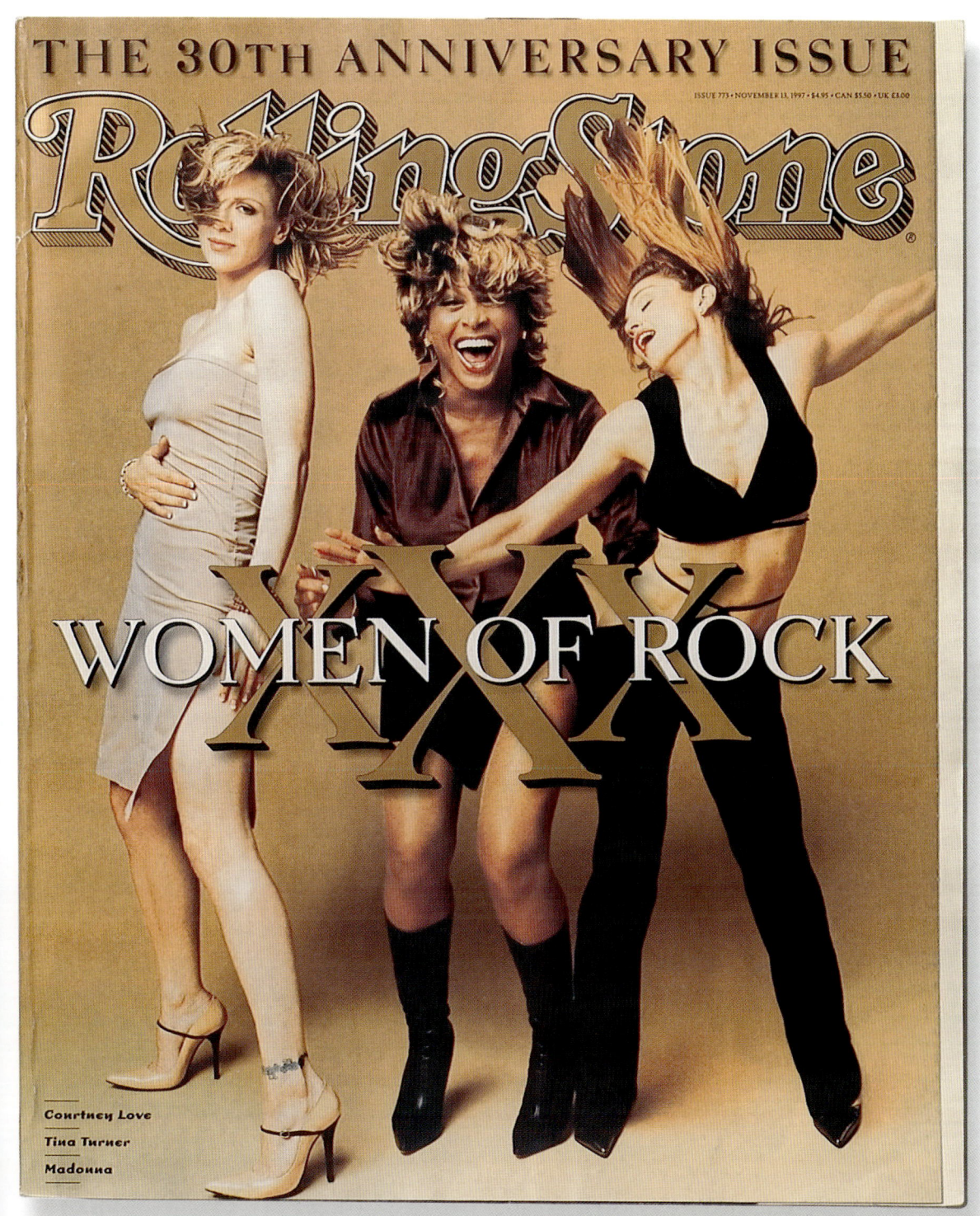

RS 773 | THIRTIETH ANNIVERSARY WITH WOMEN OF ROCK: COURTNEY LOVE, TINA TURNER & MADONNA | November 13th, 1997 | Photograph by Peggy Sirota

THE CASE OF JOHN/JOAN BY JOHN COLAPINTO

ISSUE 775 · DECEMBER 11, 1997 · $3.00 · CAN $3.95 · UK £3.00

RollingStone

R.E.M. WHAT'S NEXT?

NOTES FROM THE BABYLON BAR

THE STONES ON TOUR

THE VERVE

1990s

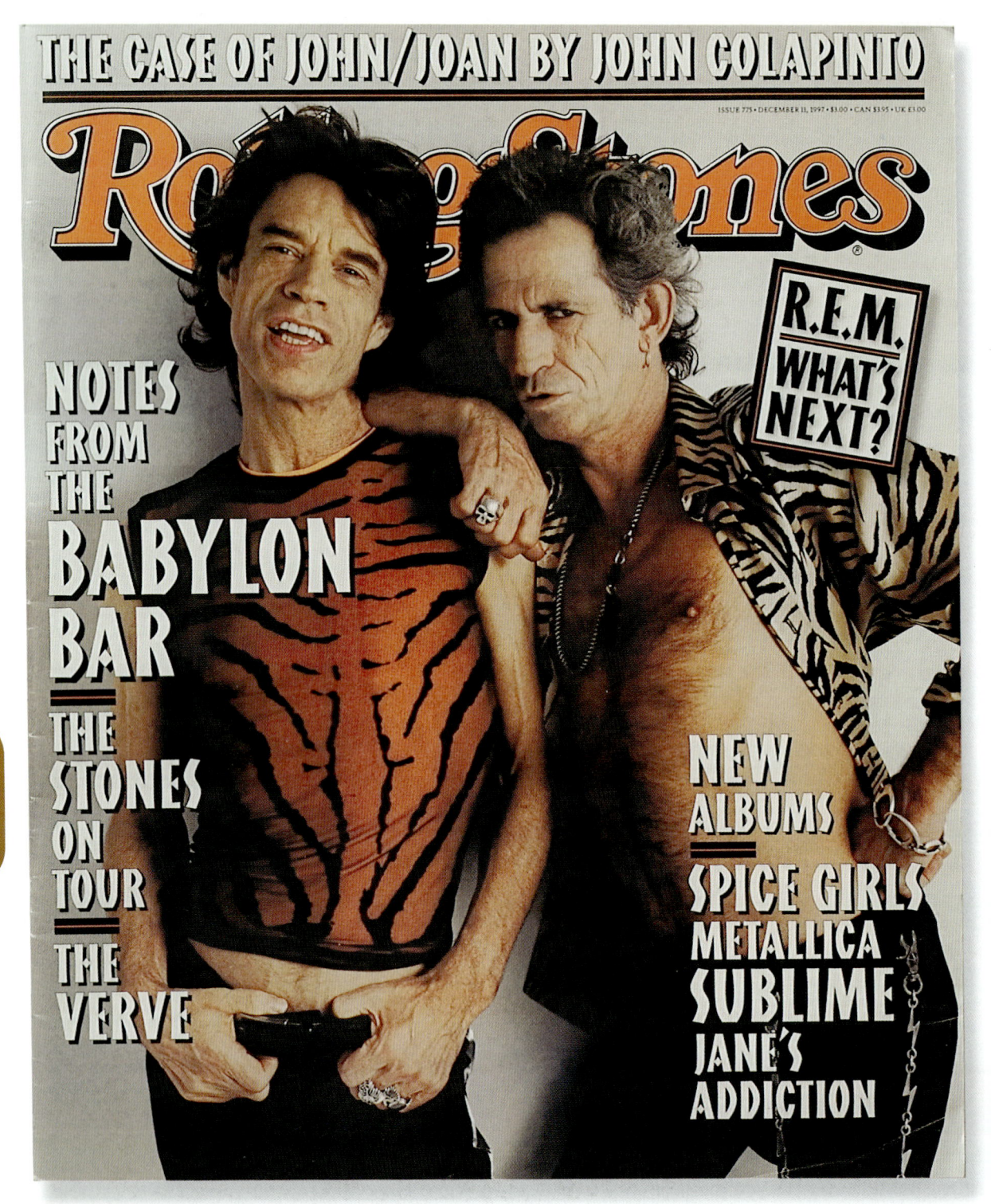

NEW ALBUMS

SPICE GIRLS
METALLICA
SUBLIME
JANE'S ADDICTION

RS 775 | MICK JAGGER & KEITH RICHARDS | December 11th, 1997 | Photograph by Mark Seliger

416 • ROLLING STONE

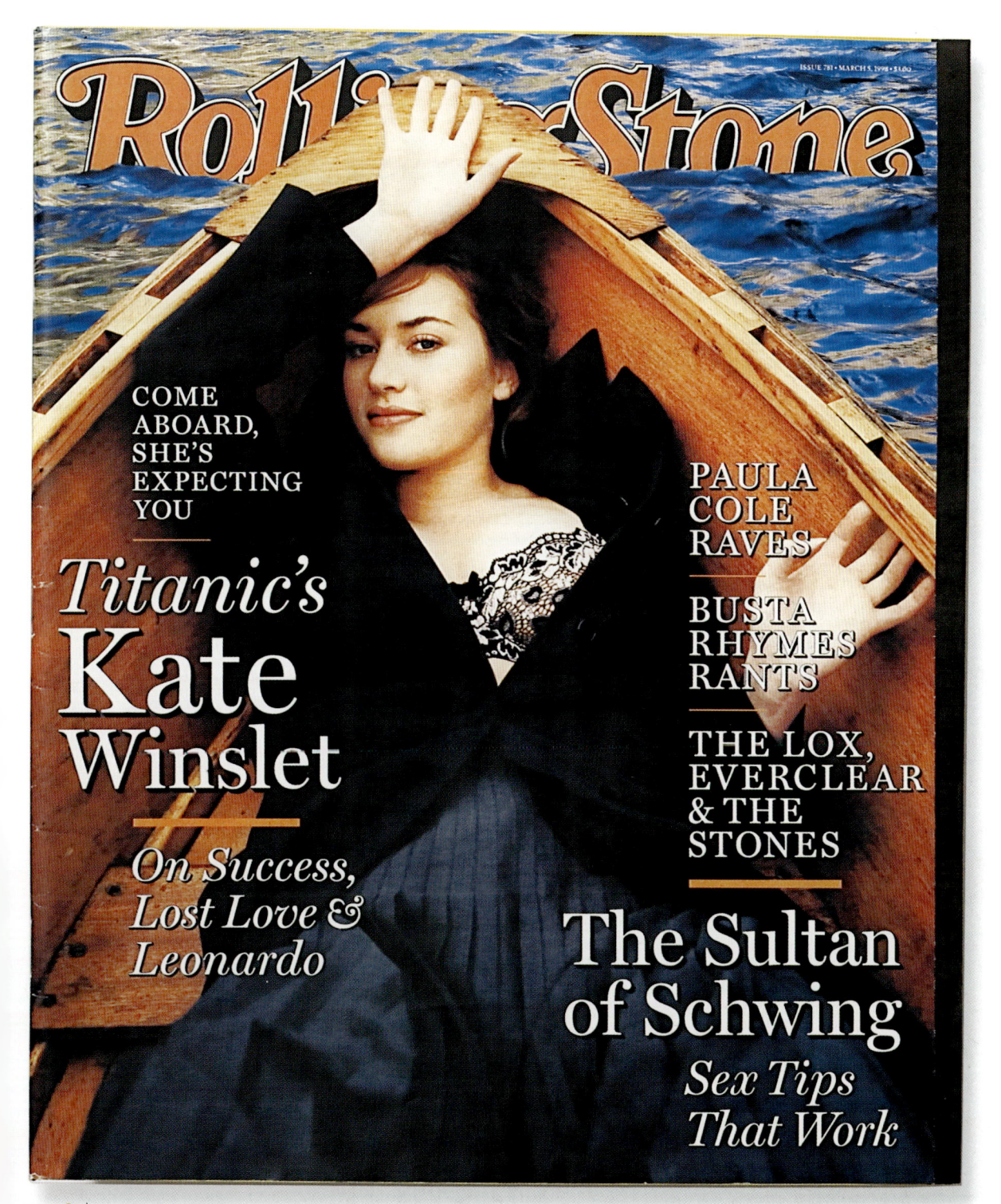

RS 781 | KATE WINSLET | March 5th, 1998 | Photograph by Peggy Sirota

RS 774 | **CAST OF 'SATURDAY NIGHT LIVE'**
November 27th, 1997
PHOTOGRAPH BY MARK SELIGER

RS 776/777 | **TORI SPELLING**
December 5th, 1997 – January 8th, 1998
PHOTOGRAPH BY MARK SELIGER

RS 778 | **FIONA APPLE**
January 22nd, 1998
PHOTOGRAPH BY MARK SELIGER

RS 779 | **MARIAH CAREY**
February 5th, 1998
PHOTOGRAPH BY ALBERT WATSON

RS 780 | **CAST OF 'SOUTH PARK'**
February 19th, 1998
ILLUSTRATION BY TREY PARKER AND MATT STONE

RS 782 | **JACK NICHOLSON**
March 19th, 1998
PHOTOGRAPH BY ALBERT WATSON

1990s

SOUTH PARK IS A POISONED PLACE IN THE HEART, a taste-free zone where kids say the darnedest, most fucked-up things. If *Seinfeld* made television history by positing that adults are petty, nasty, self-serving beasts, *South Park* has, during its nine-episode history, suggested that such lousy behavior doesn't begin at the age of eighteen.

By facing the ugly truth that our inner children are baby-faced sadists with big eyes, the show has broken our sweetest taboo and revealed childhood as a dangerous and obscene place. As the warning before the show explains, "The following program contains coarse language, and, due to its content, it should not be viewed by anyone."

"That's how we pitched the show when we went around town," says Parker. "There's this whole thing out there about how kids are so innocent and pure. That's bullshit, man. Kids are malicious little fuckers. They totally jump on any bandwagon and rip on the weak guy at any chance. They say whatever bad word they can think of. They are total fucking bastards, but for some reason everyone has kids and forgets about what they were like when they were kids."

[EXCERPT FROM RS 780 COVER STORY BY DAVID WILD]

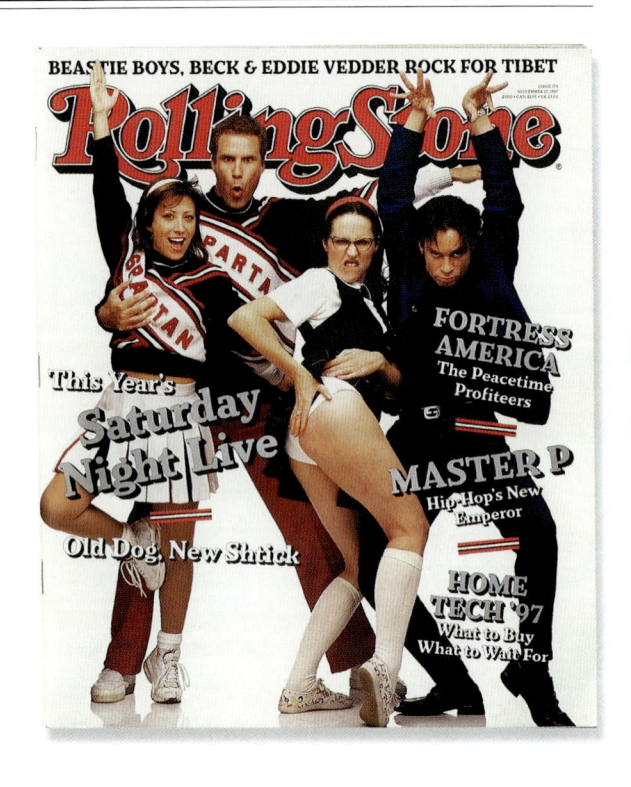

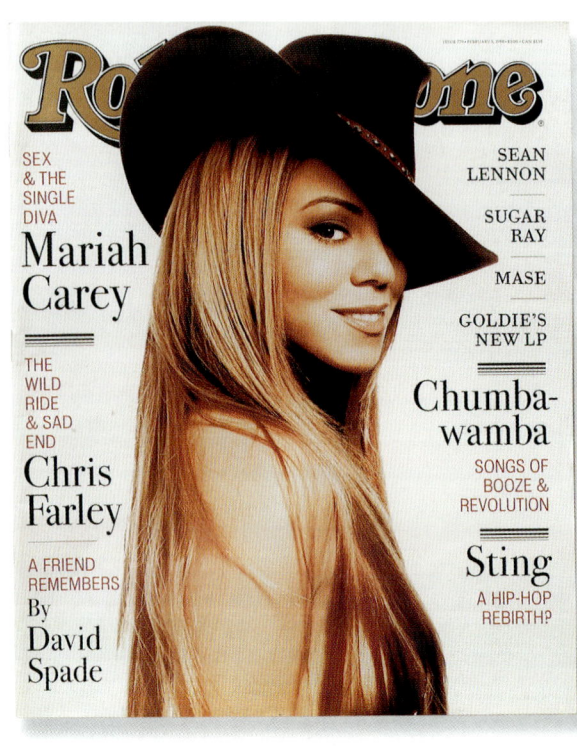

418 • ROLLING STONE

50 YEARS OF COVERS • 419

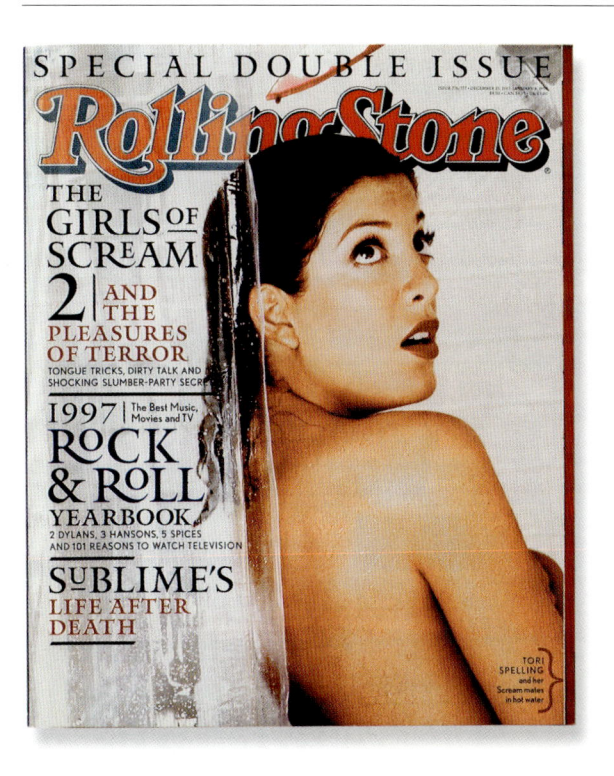

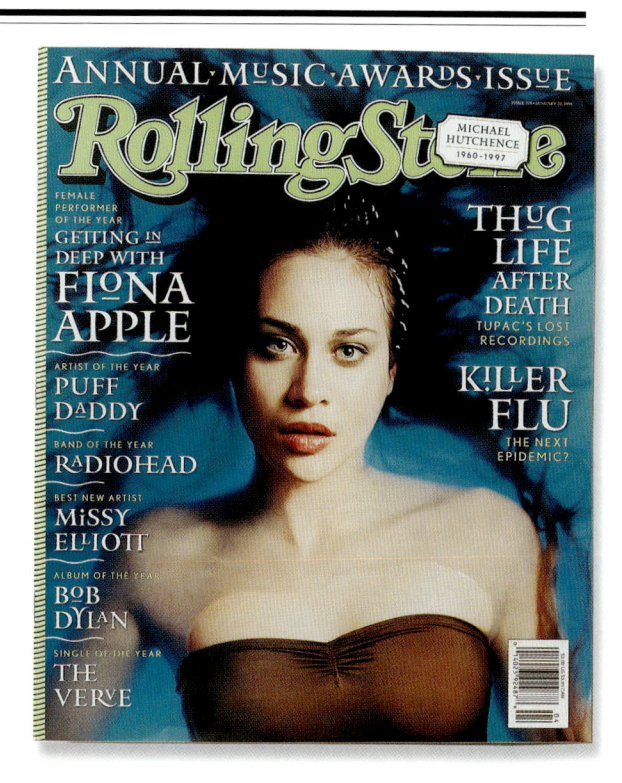

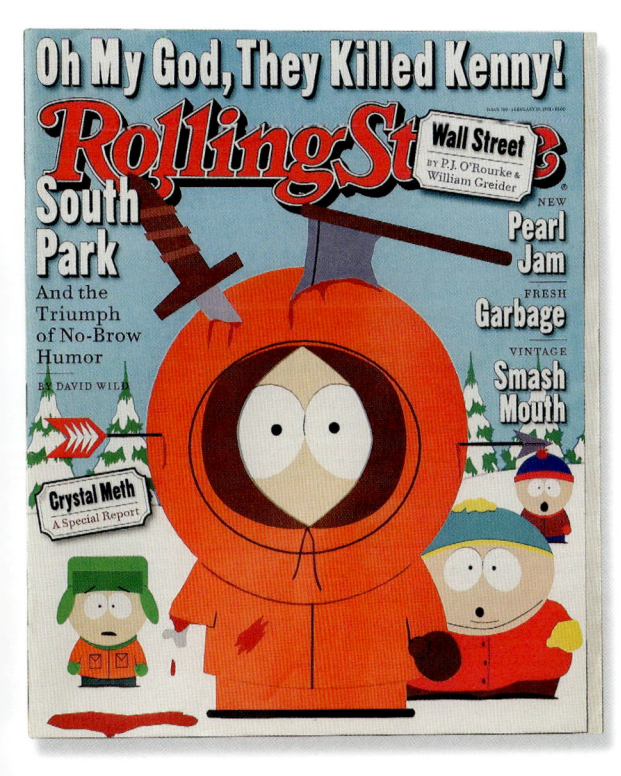

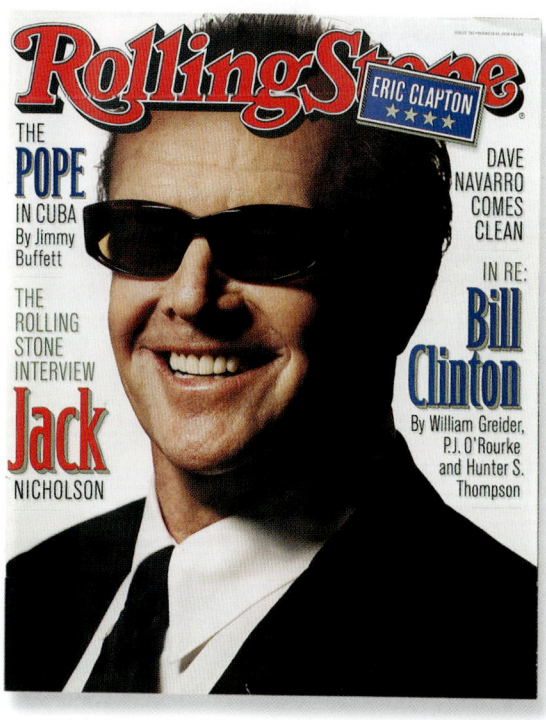

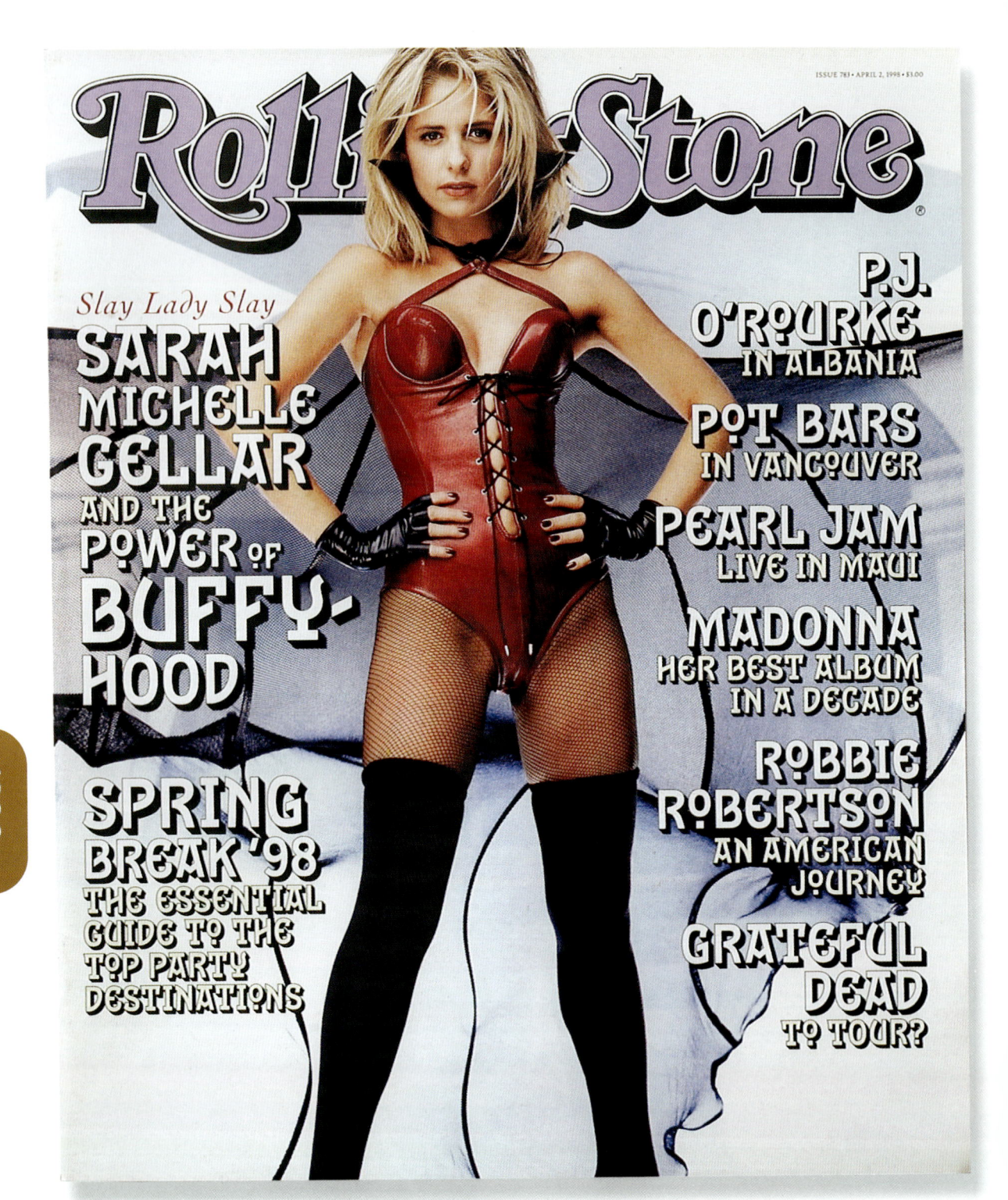

1990s

RS 783 | SARAH MICHELLE GELLAR | April 2nd, 1998 | Photograph by Mark Seliger

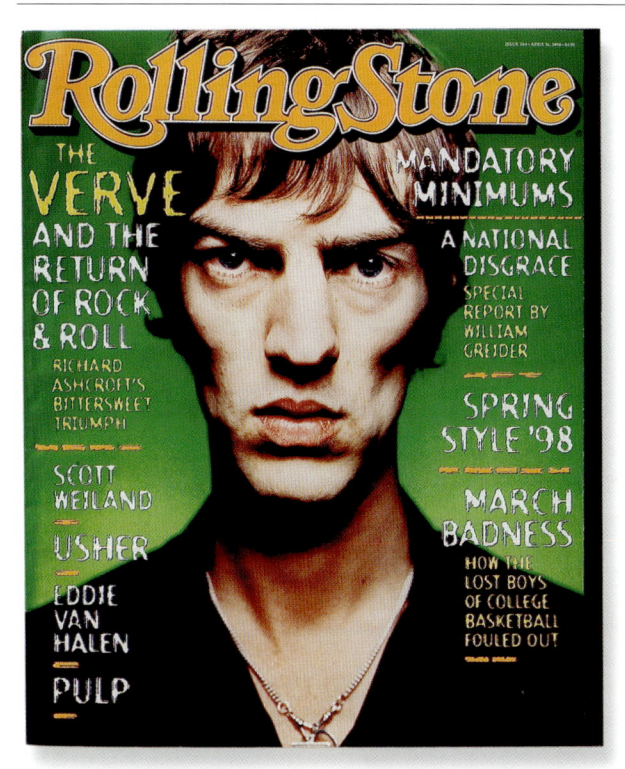

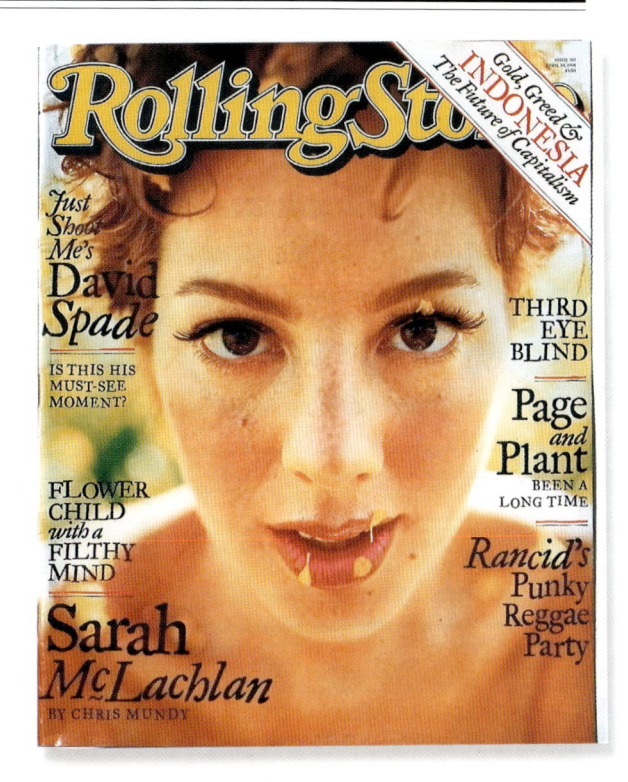

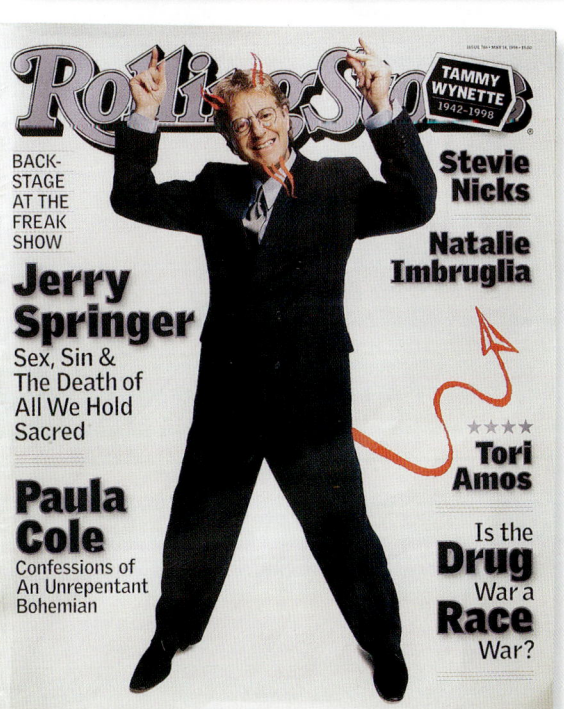

RS 784 | RICHARD ASHCROFT
April 16th, 1998
Photograph by Mark Seliger

RS 785 | SARAH McLACHLAN
April 30th, 1998
Photograph by Peggy Sirota

RS 786 | JERRY SPRINGER
May 14th, 1998
Photograph by Mark Seliger

HER LOOK IS DESIGNER FLOWER CHILD –
Stevie Nicks with an eye on fashion runways – but in person, Sarah McLachlan doesn't play the part. Perhaps it is because she doesn't bother to hide her business savvy. Or because her favorite pastime is burping louder than anyone else in the room. Whatever the reasons, the Sarah McLachlan who stands before you is not the one you recognize from the wispy photographs. For instance, she does not say, "I'm very lucky," but rather, "Don't think I don't count the horseshoes on my ass daily." Demure she is not.

[EXCERPT FROM RS 785 COVER STORY BY CHRIS MUNDY]

50 YEARS OF COVERS • 421

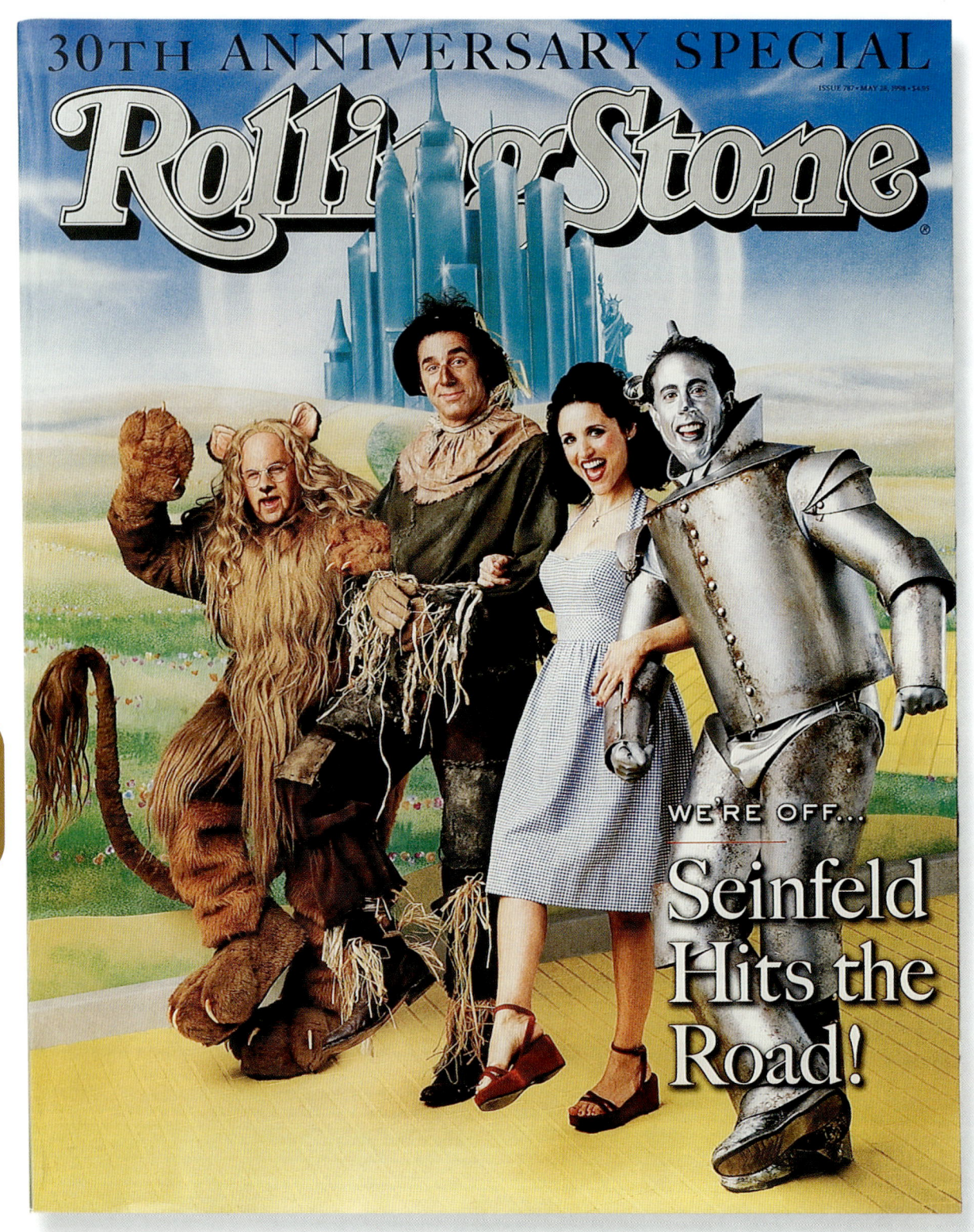

30TH ANNIVERSARY SPECIAL
Rolling Stone

1990s

WE'RE OFF...
Seinfeld Hits the Road!

422 • ROLLING STONE

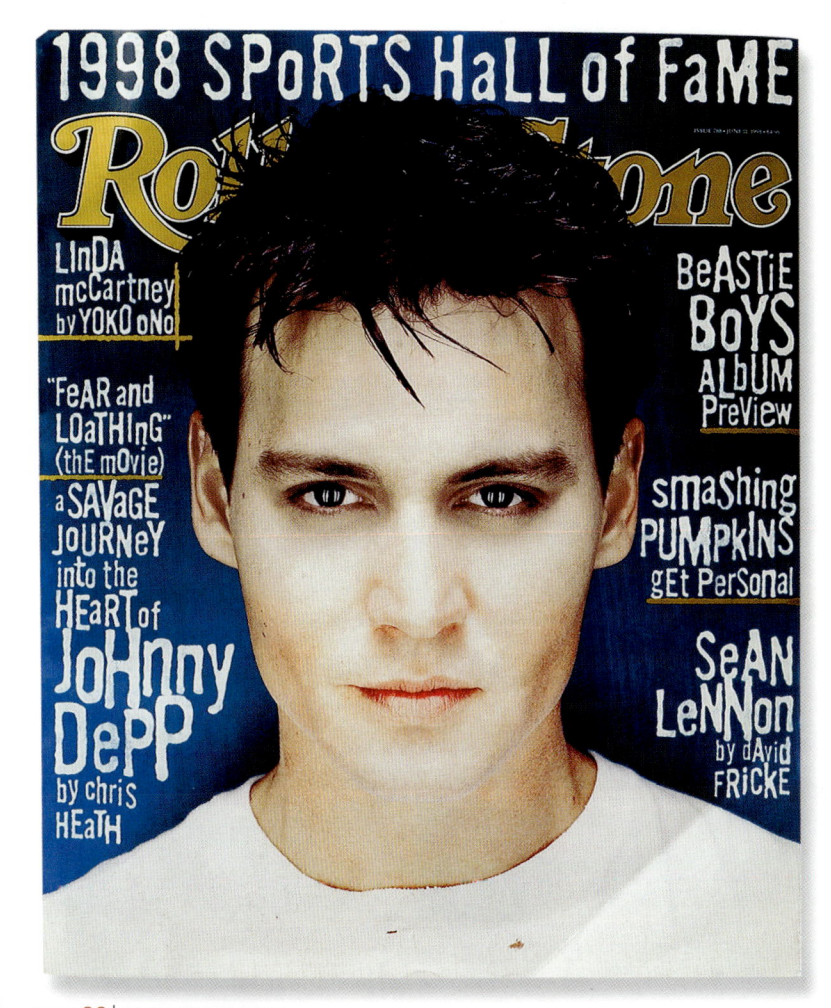

RS 788 | JOHNNY DEPP | June 11th, 1998 | Photograph by Dan Winters

[RS 788] Johnny Depp has been favored with seven covers; this is his second. This appearance was timed to his portrayal of Hunter S. Thompson's alter ego, Raoul Duke, in the film adaptation of what Thompson called "the Vegas book": *Fear and Loathing in Las Vegas.*

RS 787 | THIRTIETH ANNIVERSARY SPECIAL: CAST OF 'SEINFELD'
May 28th, 1998
Photograph by Mark Seliger

IT'S OVER. WHEN THE LIGHTS come up at the end, the cast takes its curtain call. The four of them hug each other, tightly, two by two, with moist eyes. Seinfeld takes the microphone. "Ladies and gentlemen . . ." he begins and the way he does so, it is as though he is going to say more, and as if only emotion or a desire for once not to find the funny way through to his destination stops him; anyway, the statement ends almost immediately, "that is a wrap."

The cast mingles round, hugging and tearing up, and the audience joins them on the floor. Champagne and sushi circulate. Seinfeld himself slips away backstage through his alter ego's bathroom, and stands in the craft-service area with his sister and her family. "I'm very happy," he tells them. "The past months . . . the guy in the circus with the steel balls . . ." He mimes a circular juggling motion to explain what he means. "Well, I better go and wash away my makeup."

[EXCERPT FROM RS 787 COVER STORY BY CHRIS HEATH]

"*Kramer has* no brain, George has no courage, Jerry has no heart, and Elaine has no friends."
—*Jason Alexander*

50 YEARS OF COVERS • 423

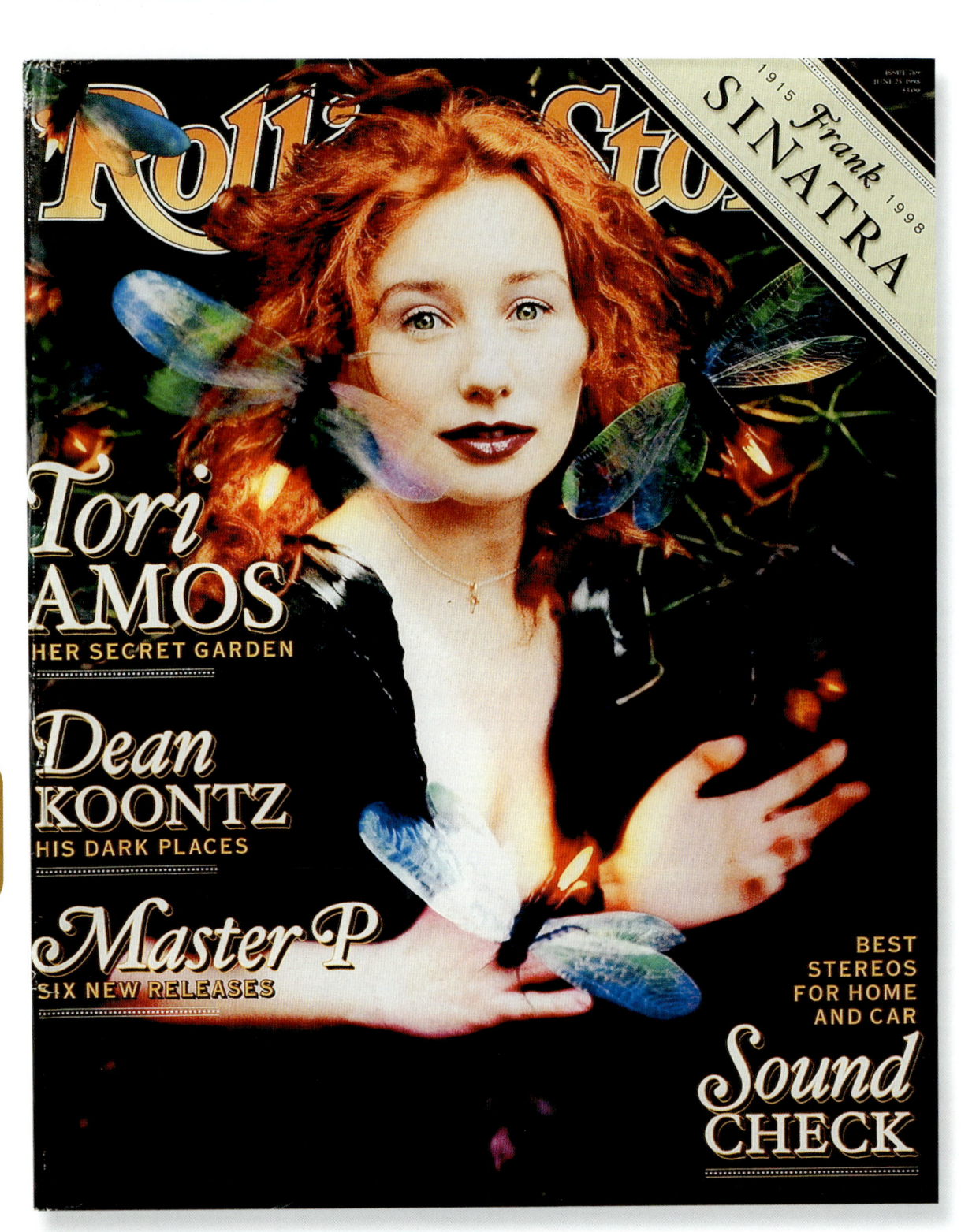

RS 789 | TORI AMOS | June 25th, 1998 | Photograph by David LaChapelle

SPECIAL DOUBLE ISSUE

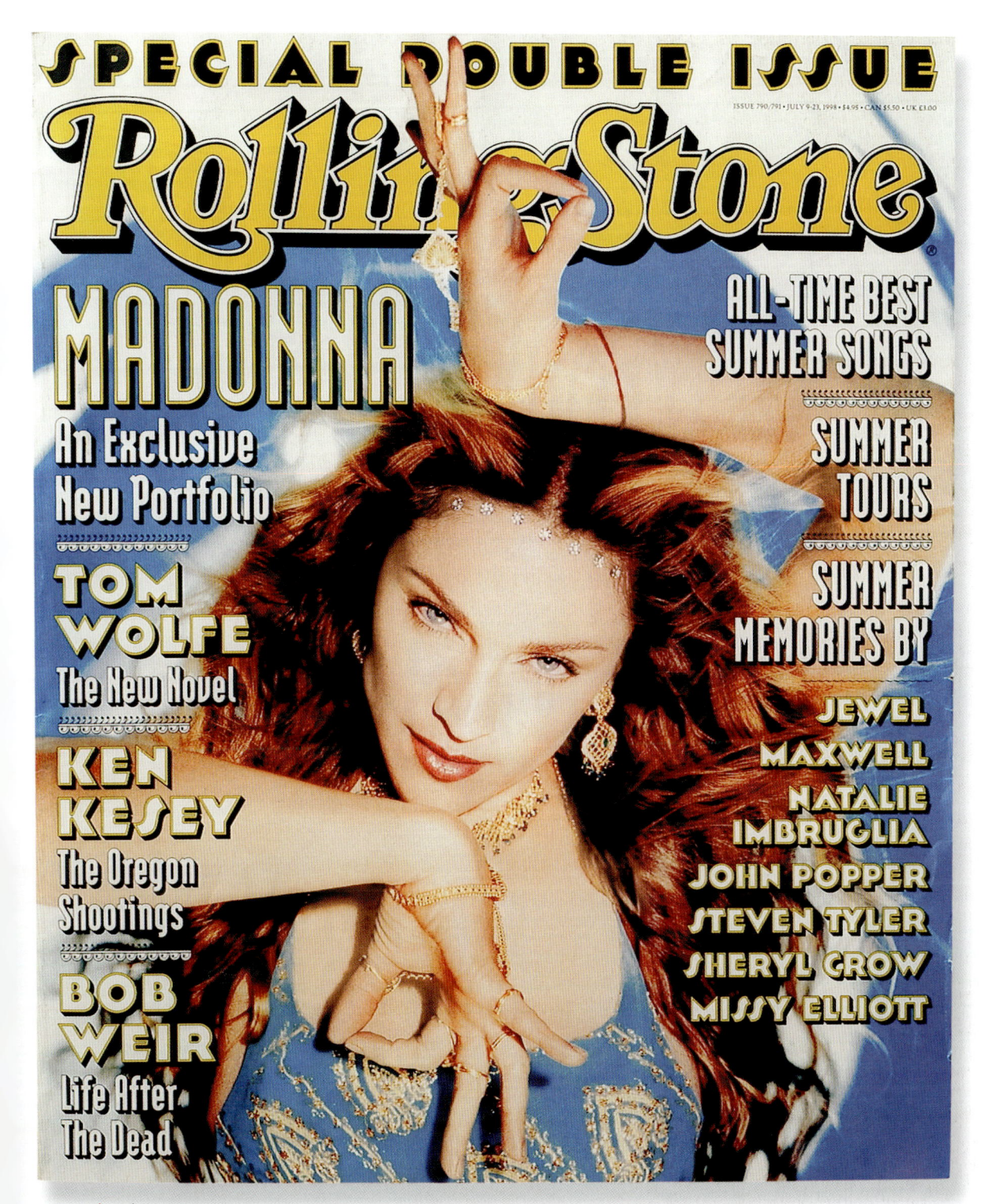

ISSUE 790/791 • JULY 9-23, 1998 • $4.95 CAN $5.50 UK £3.00

Rolling Stone

MADONNA
An Exclusive New Portfolio

TOM WOLFE
The New Novel

KEN KESEY
The Oregon Shootings

BOB WEIR
Life After The Dead

ALL-TIME BEST SUMMER SONGS

SUMMER TOURS

SUMMER MEMORIES BY

JEWEL
MAXWELL
NATALIE IMBRUGLIA
JOHN POPPER
STEVEN TYLER
SHERYL CROW
MISSY ELLIOTT

RS 790/791 | MADONNA | July 9th – July 23, 1998 | PHOTOGRAPH BY DAVID LACHAPELLE

MAXWELL • THE ARTIST • SHERYL CROW

Rolling Stone

TO BE YOUNG AND GAY
A Special Report

BEASTIE BOYS
Back in the Game

LUCINDA WILLIAMS
The Making of a Masterpiece

1990s

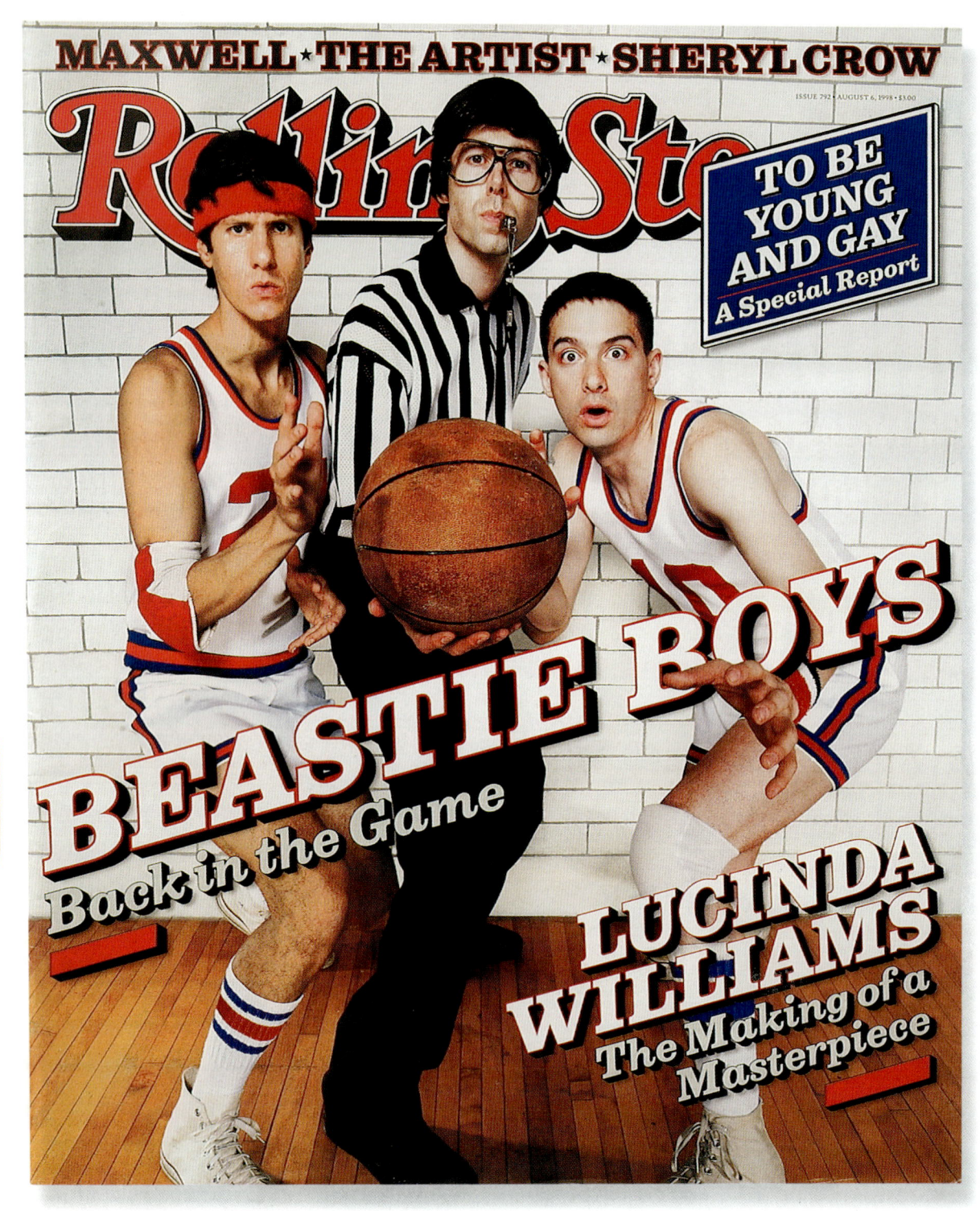

RS 792 | BEASTIE BOYS | August 6th, 1998 | Photograph by Mark Seliger

Rolling Stone

ISSUE 793 • AUGUST 20, 1998 • $3.00

Life After
Death Row

SNOOP
DOGGY
DOGG
IS BACK!

SWING
REVIVAL

Is It Jumpin'
Or Just Jive?

Blood, Dust
And Tears

INSIDE
MEXICO'S
SECRET
WAR

*The
Original*
**HOT
List**

STARRING
This Year's Model,
Laetitia
Casta

RS 793 | LAETITIA CASTA | August 20th, 1998 | PHOTOGRAPH BY HERB RITTS

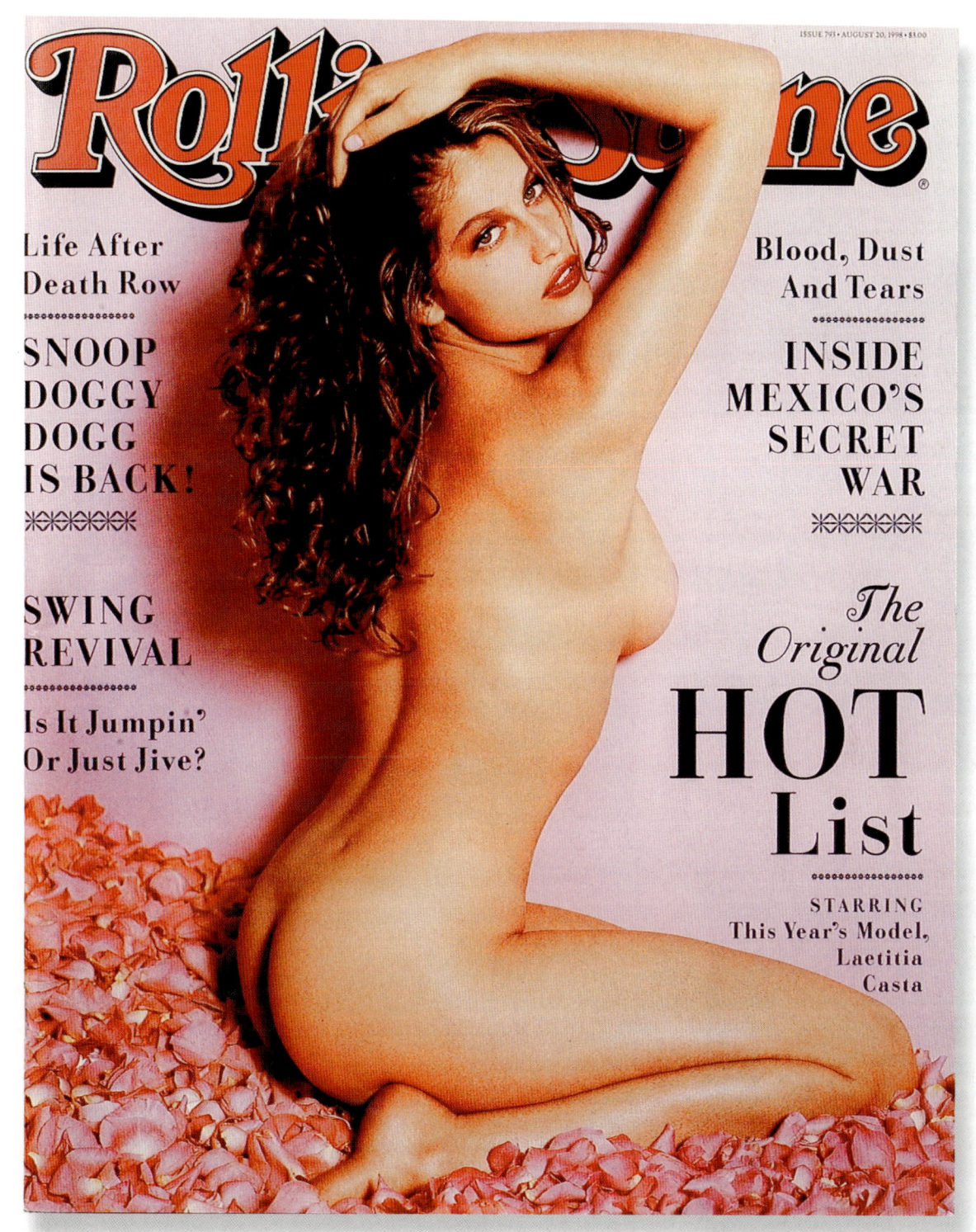

50 YEARS OF COVERS • 427

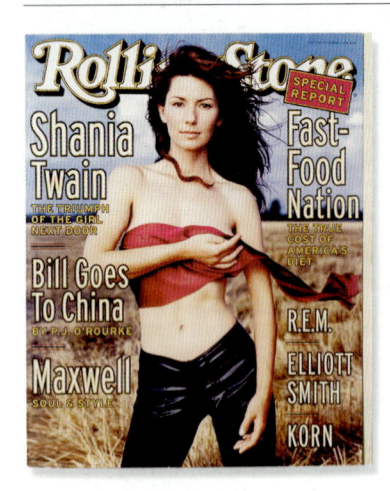

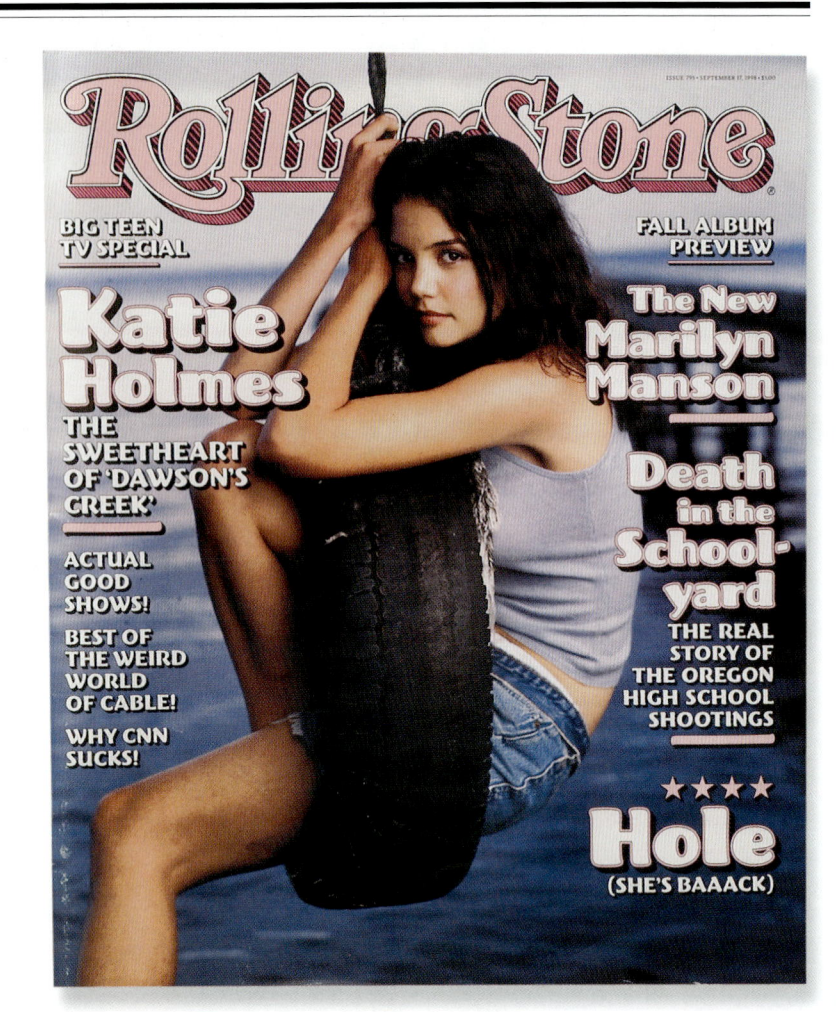

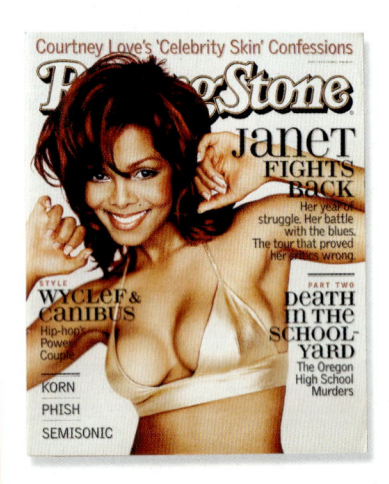

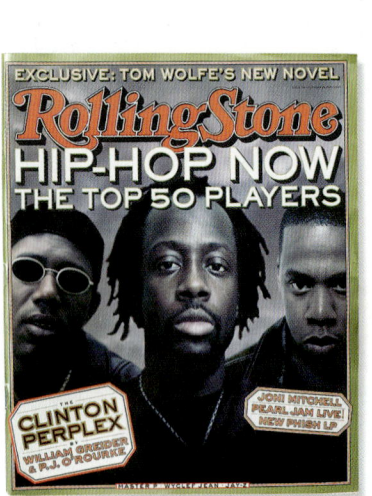

1990s

RS 795 | KATIE HOLMES
September 17th, 1998
PHOTOGRAPH BY MARK SELIGER

RS 794 | SHANIA TWAIN
September 3rd, 1998
PHOTOGRAPH BY MARK SELIGER

RS 796 | JANET JACKSON
October 1st, 1998
PHOTOGRAPH BY MARK SELIGER

RS 798 | MASTER P, WYCLEF JEAN & JAY-Z
October 29th, 1998
PHOTOGRAPH BY MATT MAHURIN

428 • ROLLING STONE

GOO GOO DOLLS • WU-TANG CLAN • SHERYL CROW

Rolling Stone

ISSUE 797 • OCTOBER 15, 1998 • $3.00

EXCLUSIVE
Sneak Preview

Tom Wolfe's New Novel

A Journey to the Heart of **Marilyn Manson**

LOVE, DRUGS AND REDEMPTION IN THE HOLLYWOOD HILLS

College Special

Inside the Cybersex Trial

Dangerous Profs

Wooing the Geeks

Sex on Campus

The Half-Price Diploma

RS 797 | MARILYN MANSON | October 15th, 1998 | Photograph by Mark Seliger

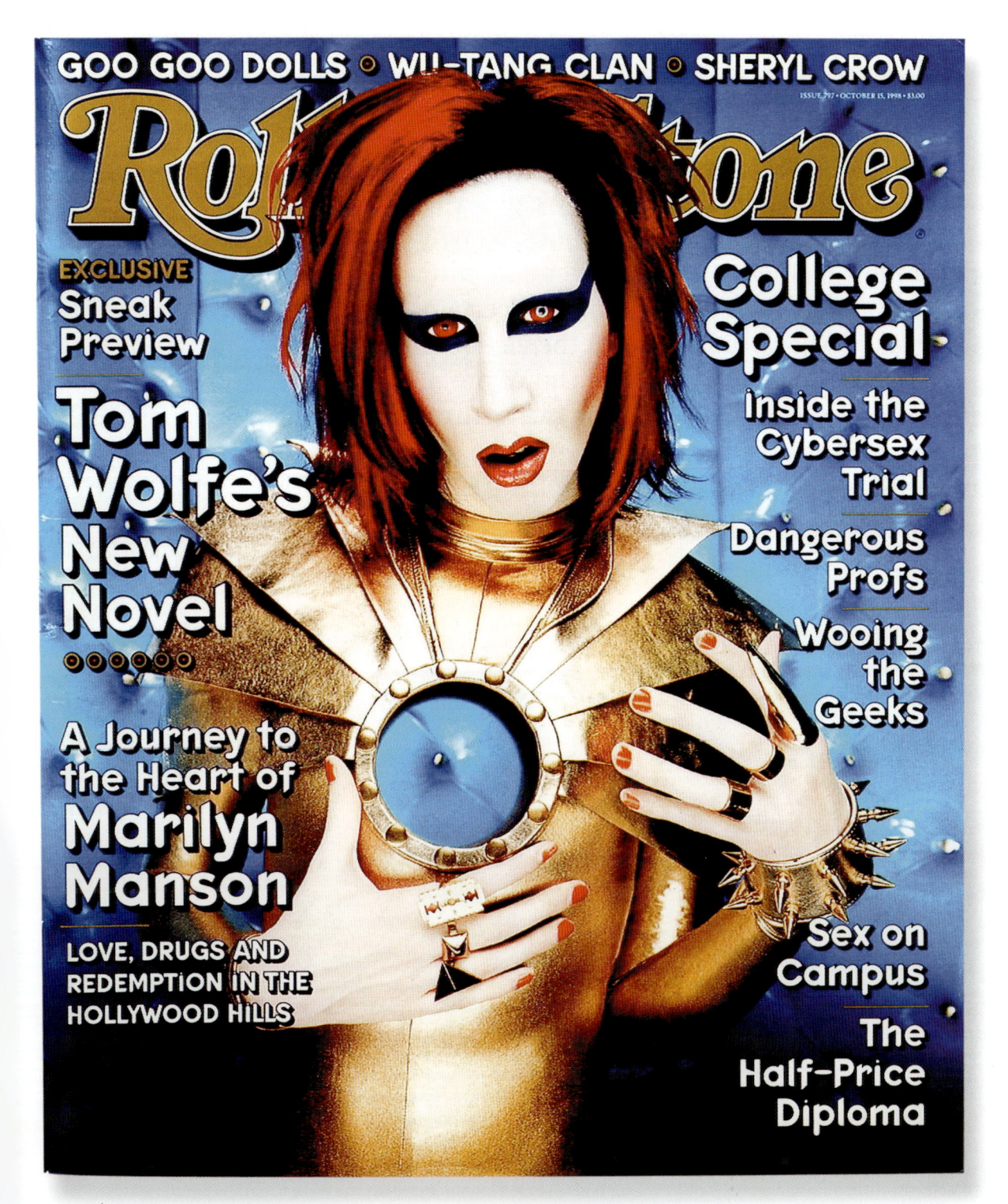

50 YEARS OF COVERS • 429

RS 799 | BILL CLINTON | November 12th, 1998 | Photograph by Mark Seliger

The current situation gives off whiffs of high school ("But why? We never went all the way") rather than high crimes. So why not settle for a high school conduct-committee solution? Suspend the president for a certain interval – 90 days, 120 days – let the vice president and his wife take over the White House, and then, after validation by the three-preacher Penitence Panel already chosen, let the president return and serve out his term.

—Tom Wolfe
[EXCERPT FROM RS 799]

"I GUESS YOU COULD SAY KEN Starr is acting responsibly – if Clinton had, in fact, killed Monica Lewinsky after blowing a load on her dress. Clinton engaged in reckless adolescent behavior, but it's not for me to forgive him. It's none of my business. I mean, if he had done it on my dress, yeah, then I think we'd have an issue here; but as far as I know, he didn't ruin any of my clothes.

In the end, something really terrible is going to happen. Truly catastrophic, like some guy is going to get anthrax in a bottle and put it in our soft drinks or something. We will look back on these days with the kind of nostalgia that people have when they talk about nickel movies. We'll look back and go, 'Oh, remember the days when all we worried about was the president blowing his load on someone's dress?'"

—Jon Stewart

"IT'S GOOD THAT AMERICA HAS someone else to scrutinize, take apart, invade. I think he's done a good job for the country, and I think there's no reason why he shouldn't be getting laid just like a rock star would. Do they have backstage passes for the Oval Office? Did Monica Lewinsky have to sleep her way to the president? Go through the tour manager first? I don't think he deserves to be impeached; but if he does get impeached, he always has a job with me. He can be my tour manager, test-drive the girls for me."

—Marilyn Manson

"WHEN I LOOK AT THE CRUCIFIXION of Clinton, I look at the crucifixion of my generation. They are finally nailing us for introducing new ideas about sexual mores, sexual freedom, personal freedom: 'OK, you wanted sexual freedom, we're gonna give it to you – to the point where it is going to saturate and sicken the whole planet.'"

—Patti Smith

"*To the rest of* the world, America looks like a teenager in a masturbatory frenzy of voyeurism and *Schadenfreude*: ratings vs. decency, a Salem witch hunt for evidence vs. the human right to some kind of privacy, even in the wrong.

Stop it – America is better than this." —Bono

"THIS IS A SLOW POLITICAL COUP D'ETAT. It is pretty obvious that we've got our tit in the wringer and we don't really know how to get out of it. I'm a big Clinton supporter. I think he understands the mechanics of the job better than anyone who has ever held the position, and that's really what I want. The degree to which he is able to wear his heart on his sleeve, for a man who has lived his life in the executive branch of the government, is somehow more impressive to me than the negative side of all this. I think the video deposition and his day in Ireland were the two times I was most moved for him. If you've ever had to settle a lawsuit in which you were not in the wrong, you understand what this feels like."

—Jack Nicholson

1990s

SEX, POWER & THE PRESIDENCY

Rolling Stone

**BEN STILLER
'N SYNC · R.E.M.
PETER WOLF**

The Clinton Conversation

EDDIE VEDDER,
TOM WOLFE,
JACK NICHOLSON,
PATTI SMITH,
MARILYN MANSON,
ROBERT REDFORD,
LOU REED, ICE CUBE,
WILLIE NELSON,
LUCINDA WILLIAMS,
SEAN LENNON,
MICHAEL DOUGLAS,
BILL MAHER,
SHIRLEY MANSON,
JON STEWART,
SUSAN SARANDON,
JIMMY BUFFETT

Speak Out

THE STINK AT THE
OTHER END OF
PENNSYLVANIA
AVENUE

Newt Gingrich
BY WILLIAM GREIDER

THE HOT-AIR
BUFFOON

Bill Bennett
BY DAVID BROCK

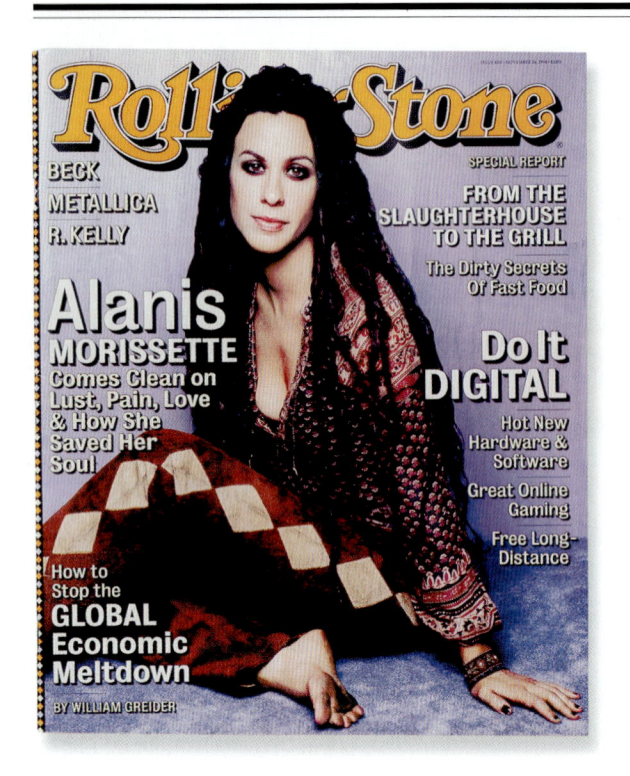

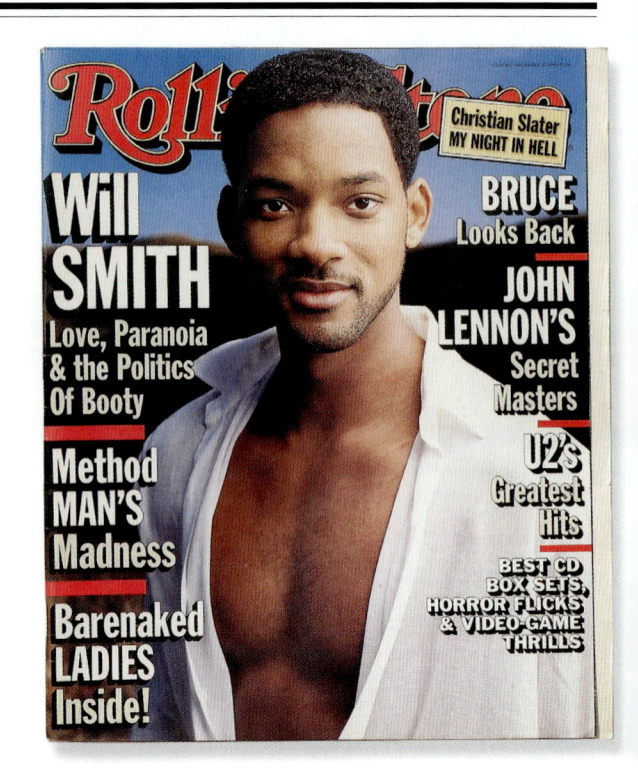

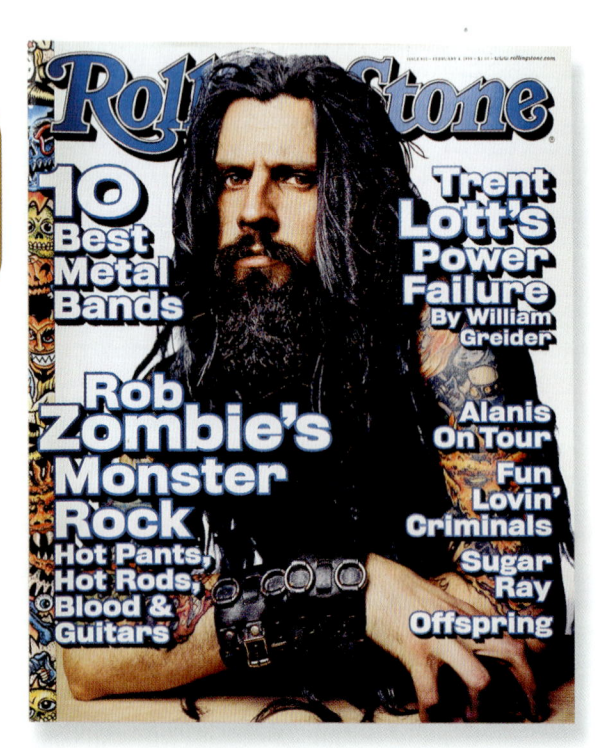

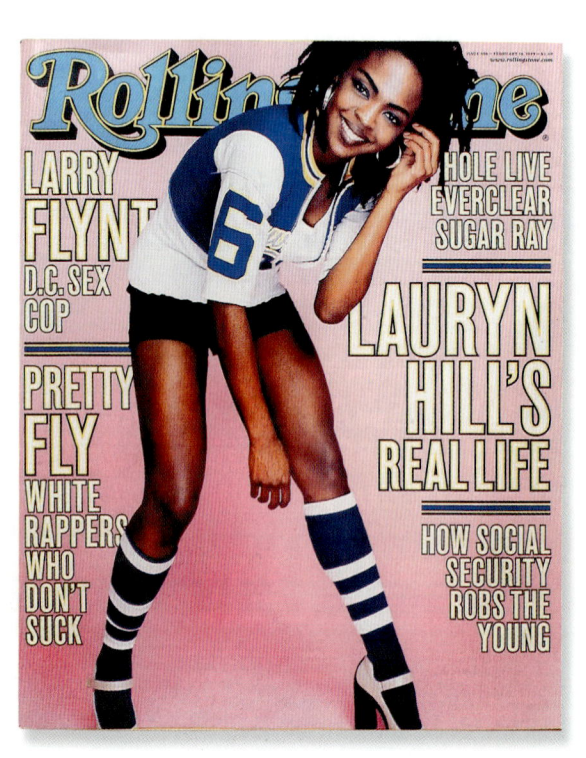

1990s

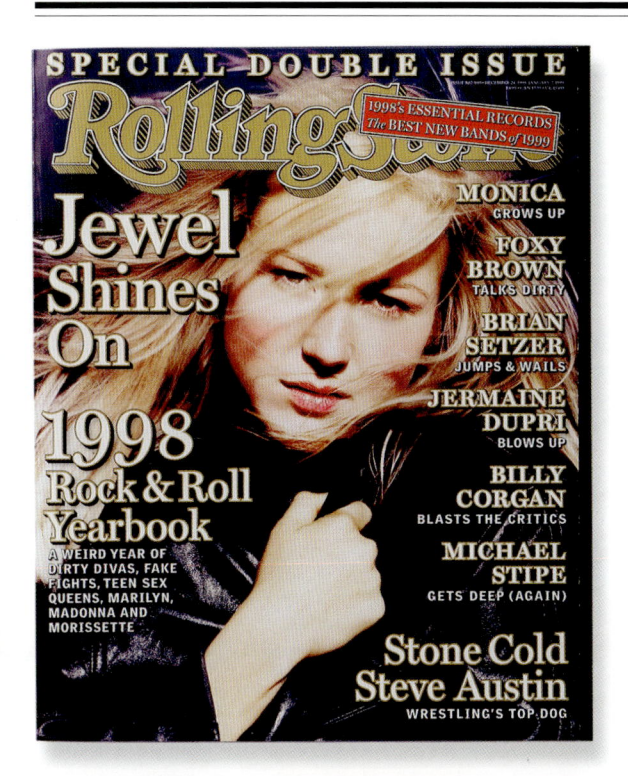

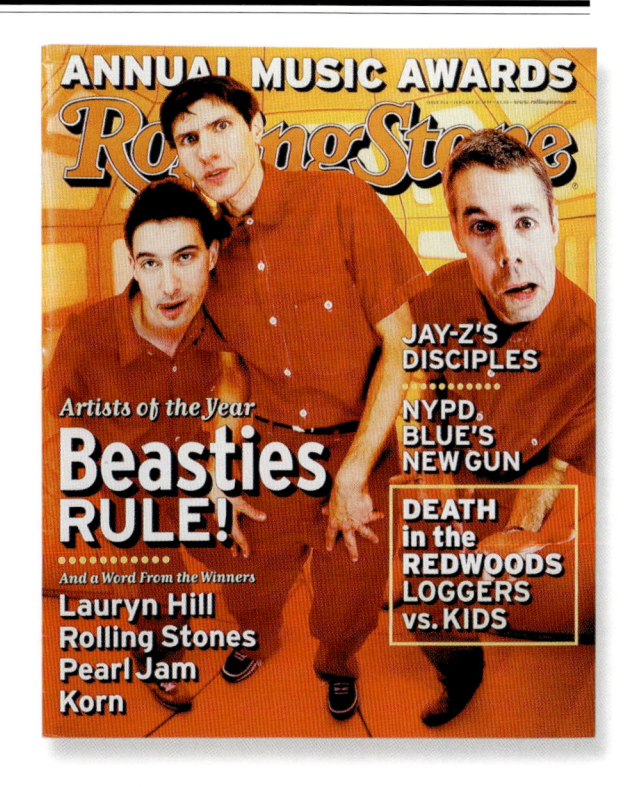

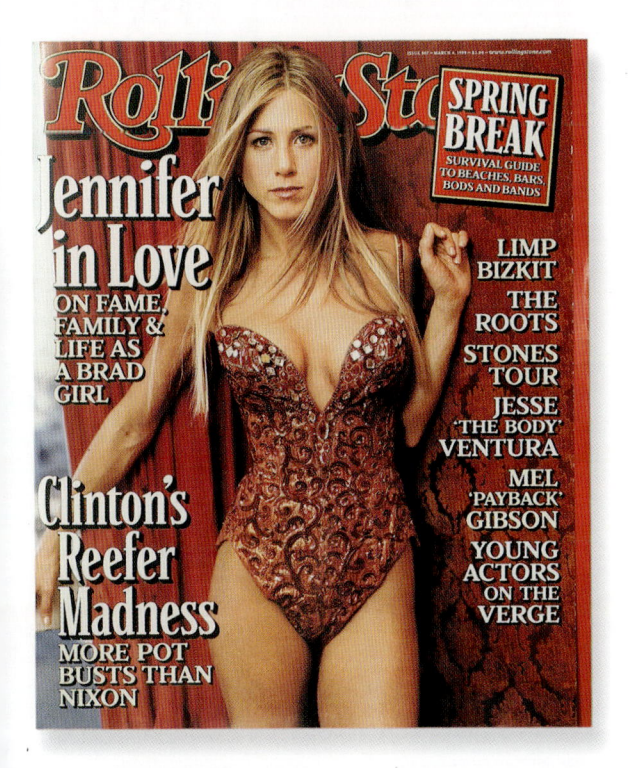

RS 800 | ALANIS MORISSETTE
November 26th, 1998
PHOTOGRAPH BY HERB RITTS

RS 801 | WILL SMITH
December 10th, 1998
PHOTOGRAPH BY MARK SELIGER

RS 802/803 | JEWEL
December 24th, 1998 – January 7th, 1999
PHOTOGRAPH BY DAVID LACHAPELLE

RS 804 | BEASTIE BOYS
January 21st, 1999
PHOTOGRAPH BY MARK SELIGER

RS 805 | ROB ZOMBIE
February 4th, 1999
PHOTOGRAPH BY MARK SELIGER

RS 806 | LAURYN HILL
February 18th, 1999
PHOTOGRAPH BY MARK SELIGER

RS 807 | JENNIFER ANISTON
March 4th, 1999
PHOTOGRAPH BY MARK SELIGER

RS 810 | BRITNEY SPEARS
April 15th, 1999
PHOTOGRAPH BY DAVID LACHAPELLE

"I SAID TO [BRITNEY], 'YOU DON'T want to be buttoned-up, like Debbie Gibson. Let's push it further and do this whole Lolita thing.' She got it. She knew it would get people talking and excited."
—*David LaChapelle*

"*Holy roller* religious people made such a big deal about that photo, and I didn't really get it. That's the way I've always been, and I thought that photo was a good representation of who I really am."
—*Britney Spears*

1990s

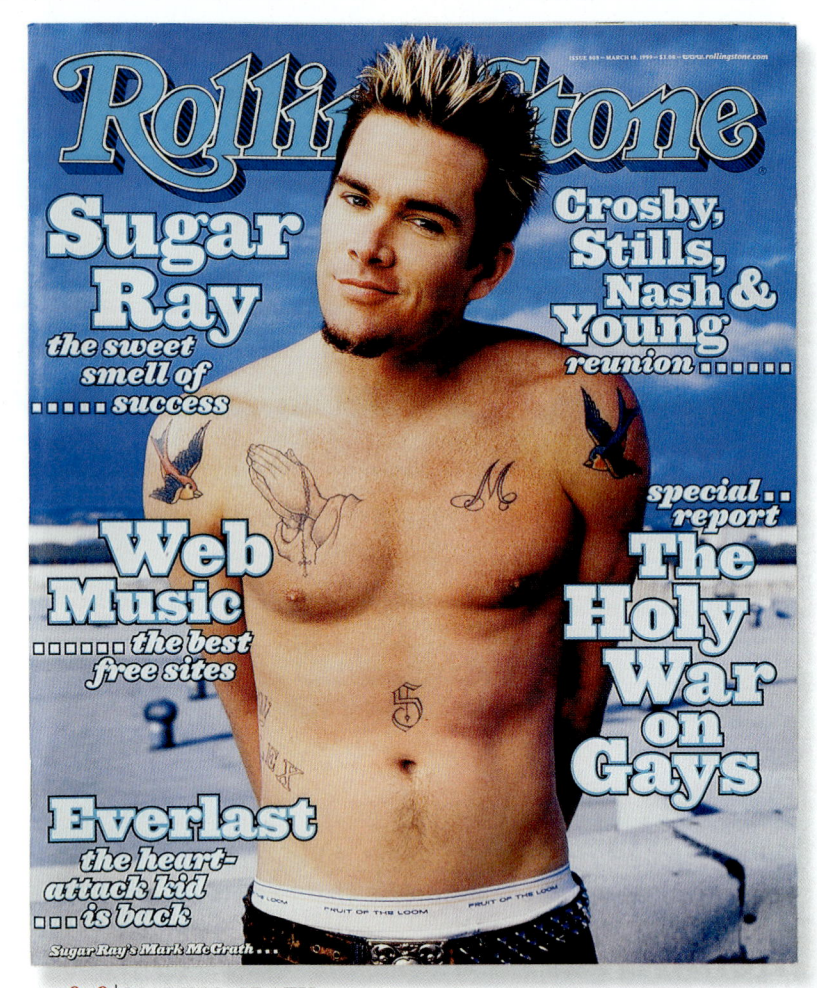

RS 808 | MARK MCGRATH | March 18th, 1999 | PHOTOGRAPH BY MARK SELIGER

434 • ROLLING STONE

Rolling Stone

ISSUE 810 · APRIL 15, 1999 · $3.00 · www.rollingstone.com

HOLE & MANSON TOUR MADNESS

Britney Spears
Inside the Heart, Mind & Bedroom Of a Teen Dream

Bill Maher
What He Won't Say on TV

Norm Macdonald
Ready or Not For Prime Time?

Lost Tribes Of the Amazon
By Sebastião Salgado

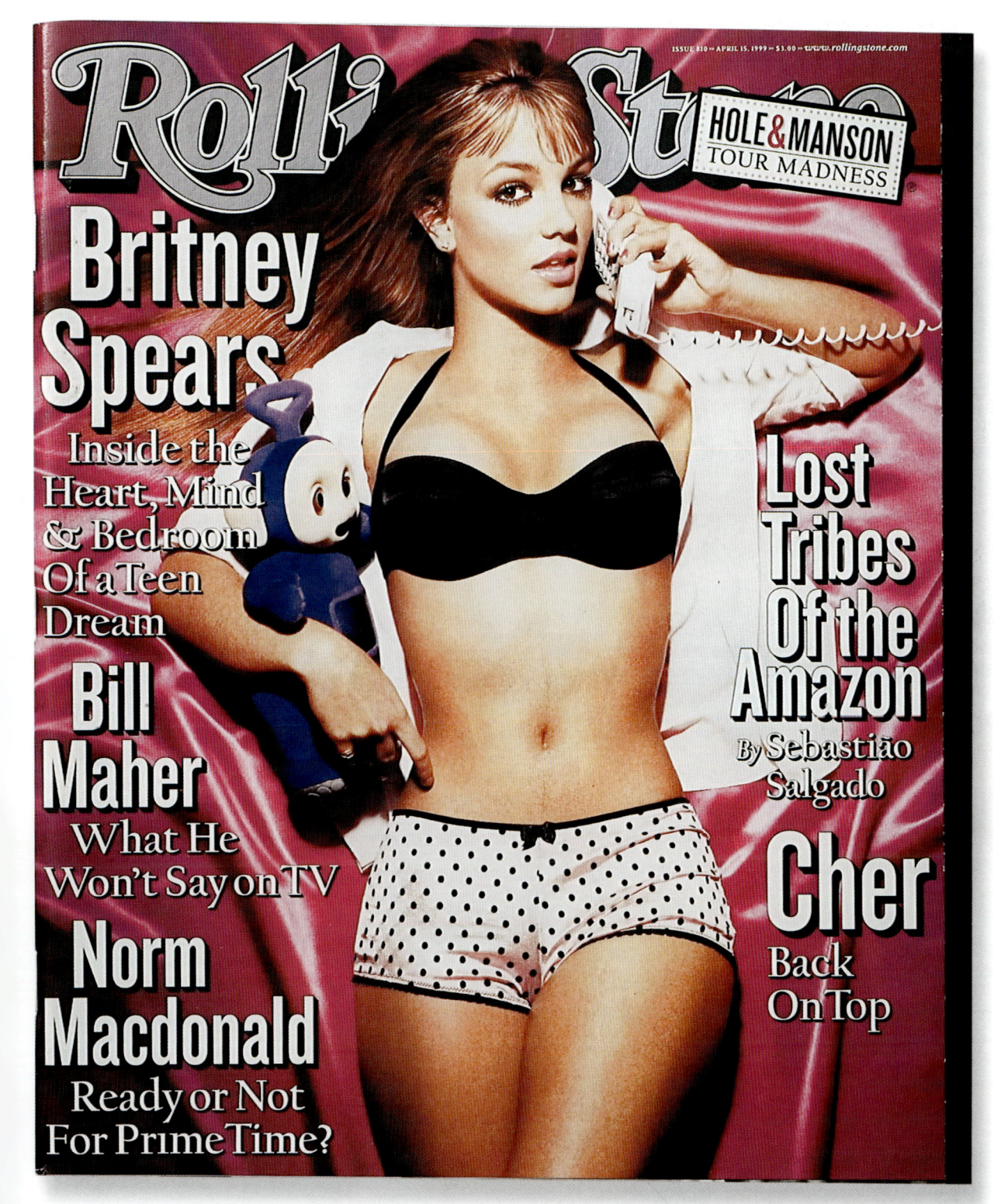

Cher
Back On Top

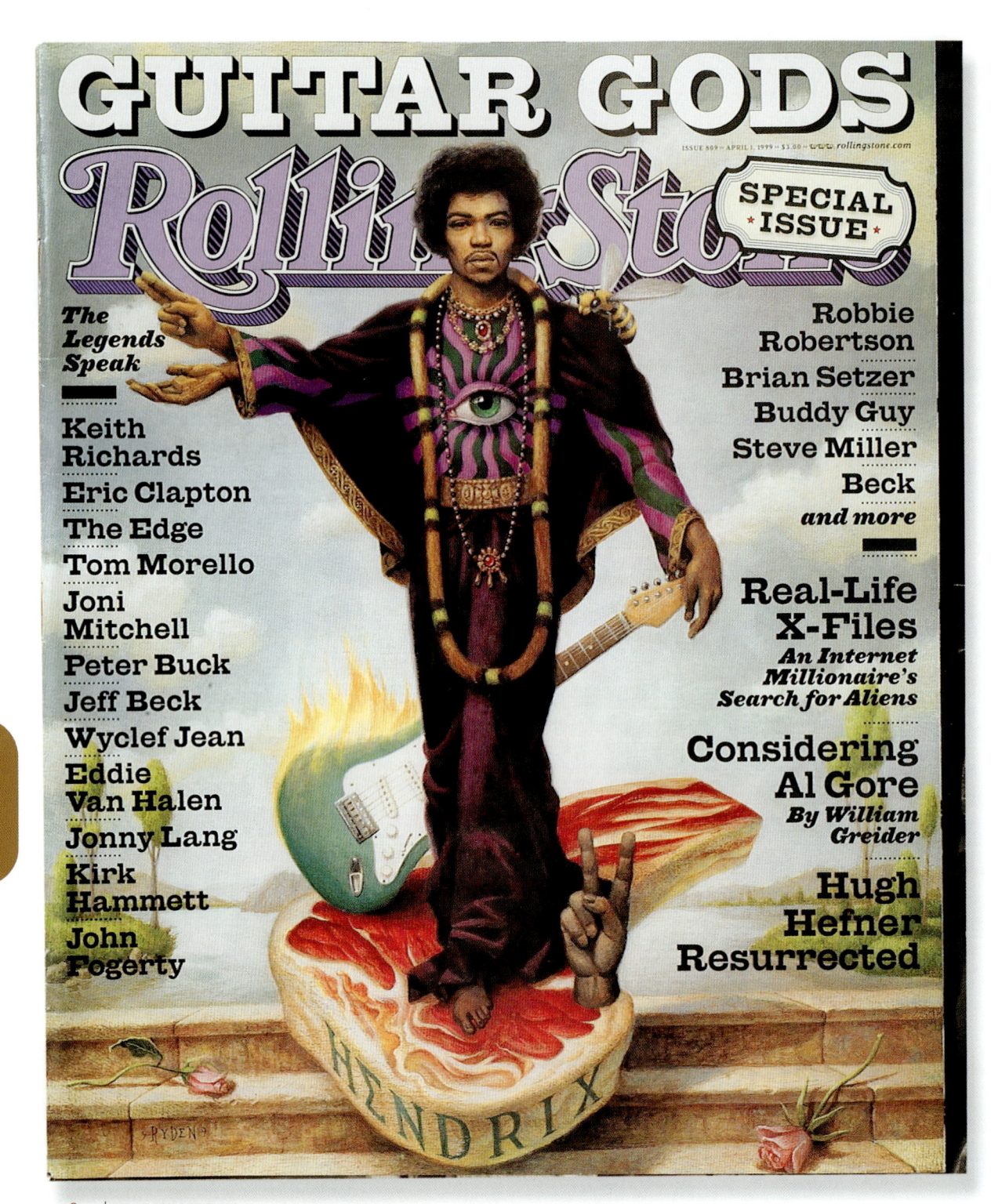

RS 809 | JIMI HENDRIX | April 1st, 1999 | ILLUSTRATION BY MARK RYDEN

The ESSENTIAL RECORDINGS of the '90s

Rolling Stone

ISSUE 812 · MAY 13, 1999 · $3.00 · www.rollingstone.com

SPECIAL ISSUE

Terror & Comedy
MTV's Tom Green

Orgy

Neil Young

Tori Amos

Jennifer Lopez

Ben Folds Five

KURT COBAIN
Artist of the Decade

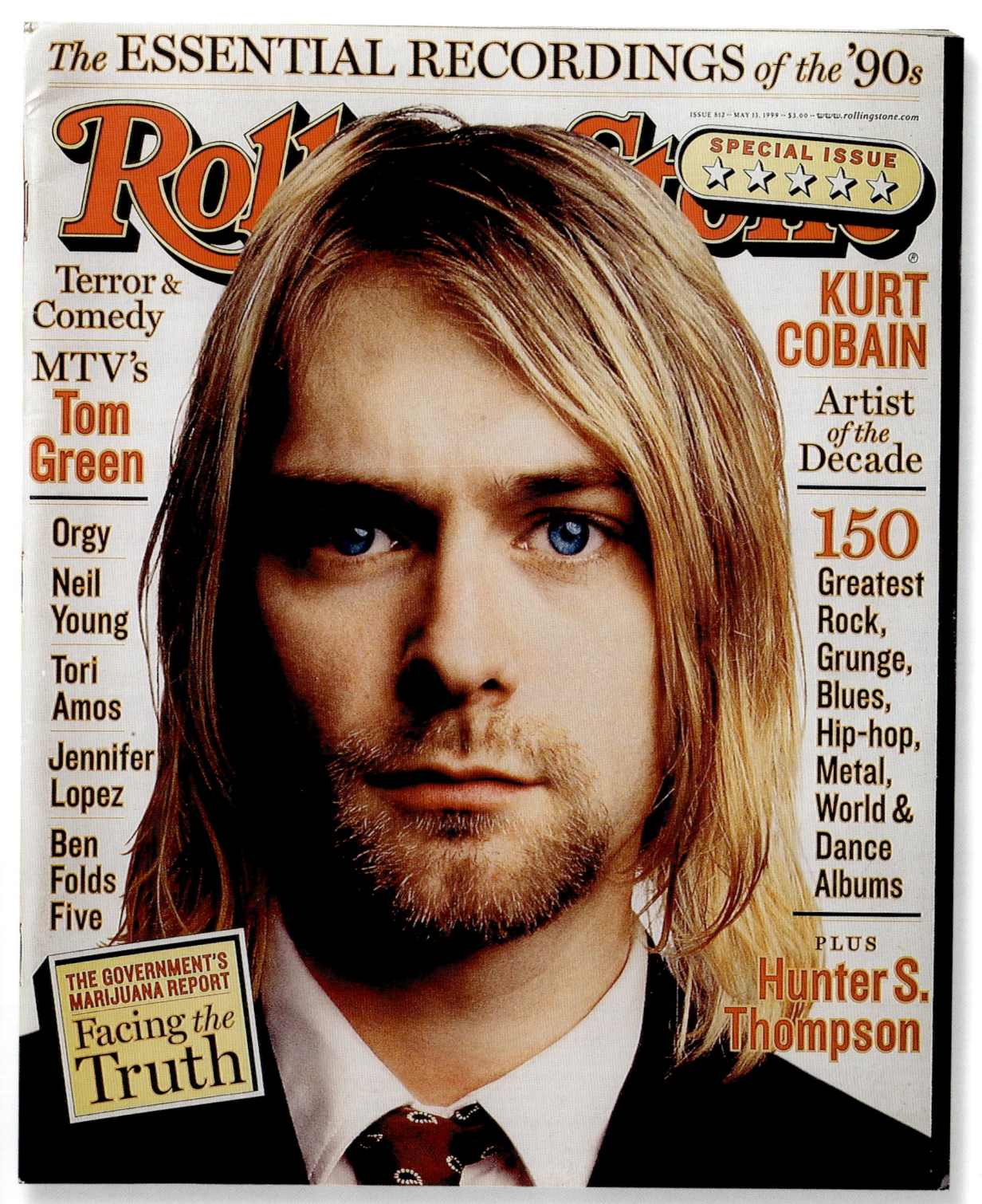

150 Greatest Rock, Grunge, Blues, Hip-hop, Metal, World & Dance Albums

PLUS Hunter S. Thompson

THE GOVERNMENT'S MARIJUANA REPORT
Facing the Truth

RS 812 | KURT COBAIN | May 13th, 1999 | Photograph by Mark Seliger

ROLLING STONE

ISSUE 811 · APRIL 29, 1999 · $3.00 · www.rollingstone.com

WOODSTOCK '99
Alanis, Aerosmith, Jewel, Korn & Rage

"Hi. My name is Slim Shady."

LOW-DOWN AND DIRTY WHITE-BOY RAP

EMINEM'S TWISTED LIFE STORY

Bad Blood
MANSON & HOLE TOUR DOA

Bono, Billy, Bruce & Eric
HALL OF FAME'S HISTORIC NIGHT

Exclusive Preview
CHILI PEPPERS' RED-HOT COMEBACK

Inside the World of
INTERNET DRIFTERS

1990s

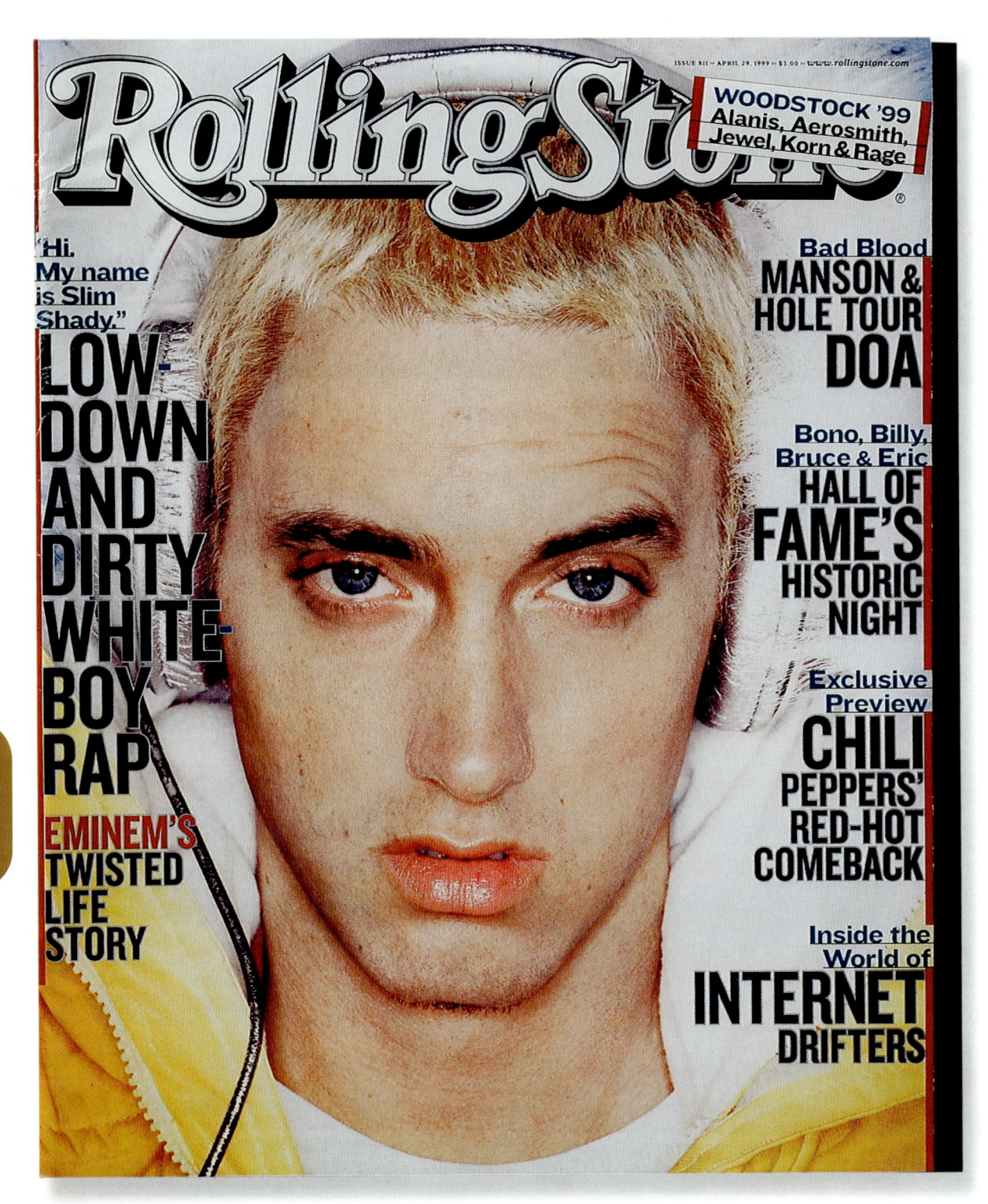

RS 811 | EMINEM | April 29th, 1999 | Photograph by David LaChapelle

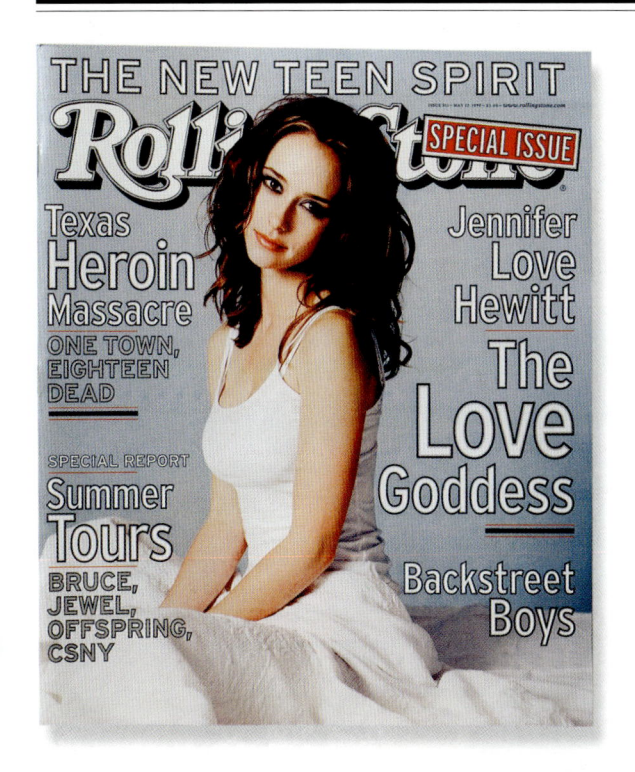

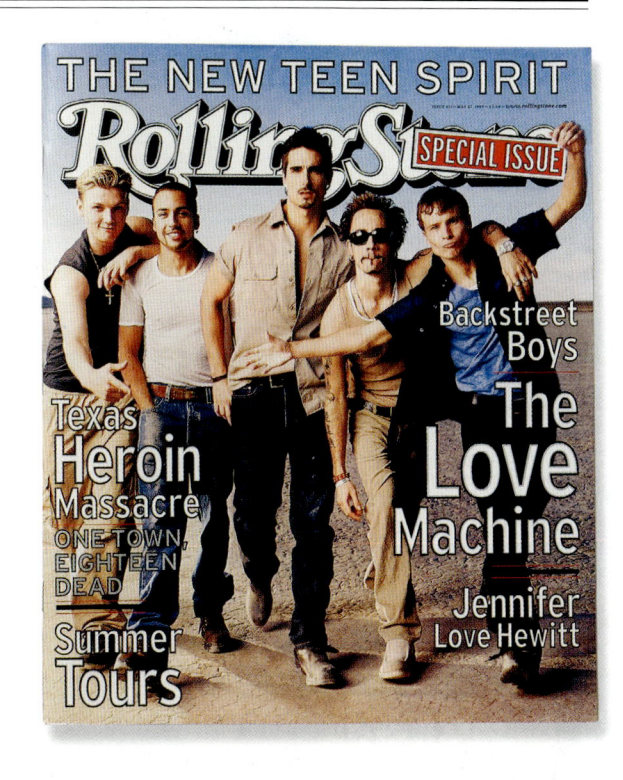

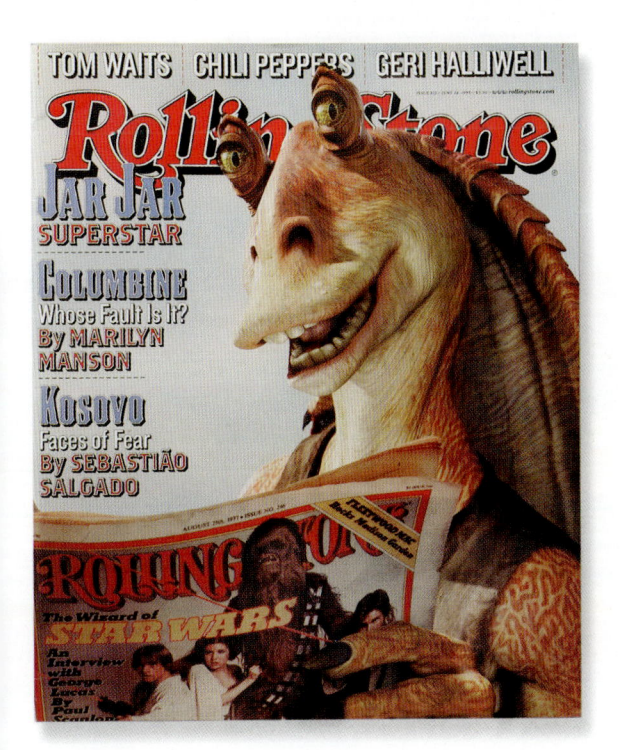

RS 813 | JENNIFER LOVE HEWITT
May 27th, 1999
PHOTOGRAPH BY STEWART SHINING

RS 813 | BACKSTREET BOYS
May 27th, 1999
PHOTOGRAPH BY MARK SELIGER

RS 815 | JAR JAR BINKS
June 24th, 1999
IMAGE CREATED BY INDUSTRIAL LIGHT & MAGIC

[RS 813] To celebrate the rise of teen culture (and to take advantage of rising teen purchasing power), ROLLING STONE published two covers for this special issue on the New Teen Spirit, putting the *Party of Five* princess on one and the reigning boy-band sensation on the other. The issue featured twenty-five stars – including Alanis Morissette, Snoop Dogg, Marilyn Manson, Lenny Kravitz and Joe Perry – reminiscing about their awkward high school years.

50 YEARS OF COVERS · 439

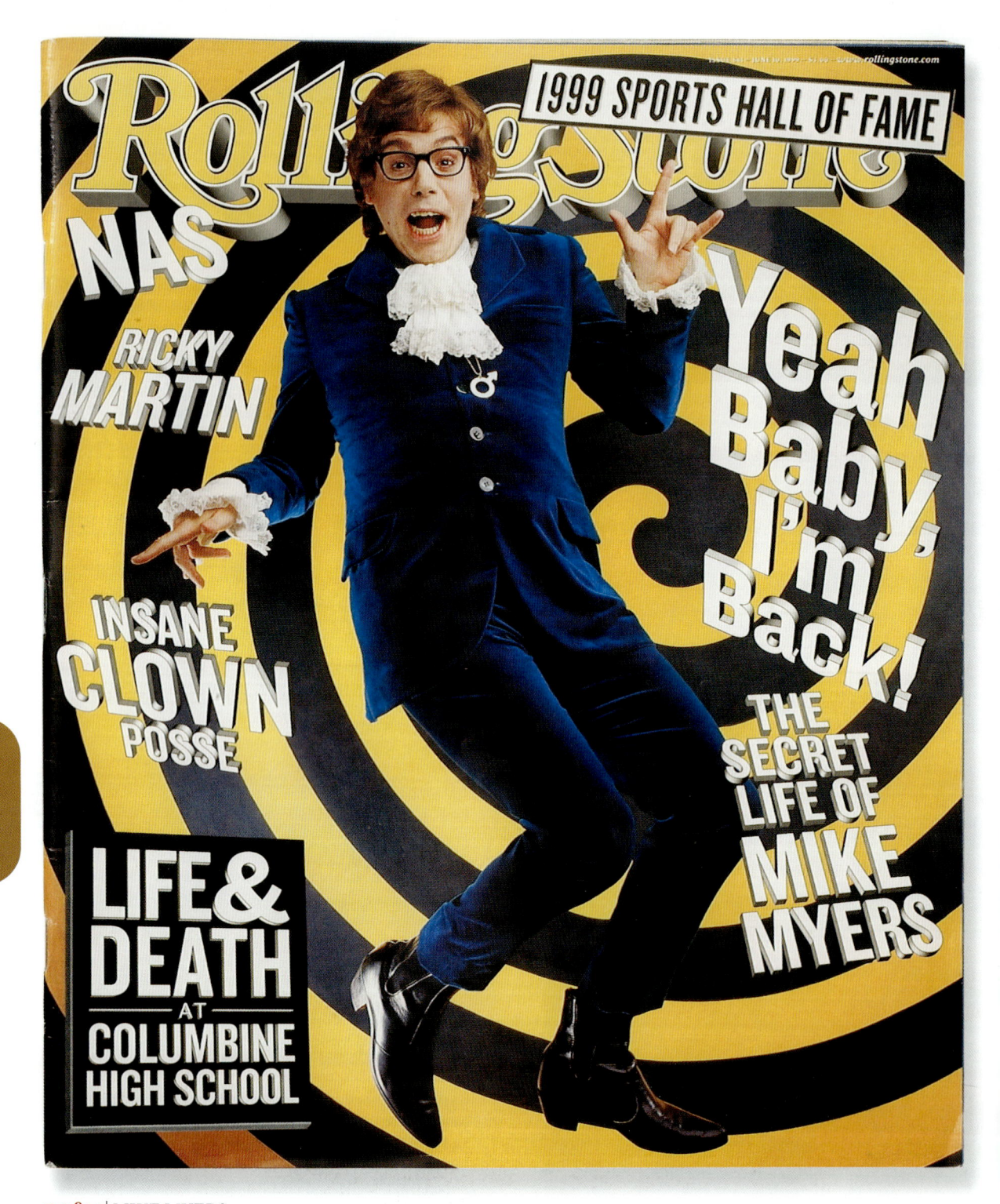

RS 814 | MIKE MYERS | June 10th, 1999 | Photograph by Mark Seliger

[MIKE] MYERS is a strange man to spend time with. He tells you a lot without showing any willingness to open himself up. Though his conversation is littered with jokes, he almost seems slightly put-off if you particularly laugh at them. He has the demeanor of a man who comes from a sweeter and kinder world than the one most of us live in and who in private tries to re-create that around him. One evening, a little frustrated, he launches into the following speed rap: "The root gratitude of it is that I love doing this stuff. It's very cool that I get to do what I do. You know, I swear on my father's grave, I could give a shit about the money. It doesn't mean anything to me. I could happily live in a socialist utopia of 'To each according to his needs and from each according to his abilities' and just have me and [my wife] Robin and an apartment that works."

[EXCERPT FROM RS 814 COVER STORY BY CHRIS HEATH]

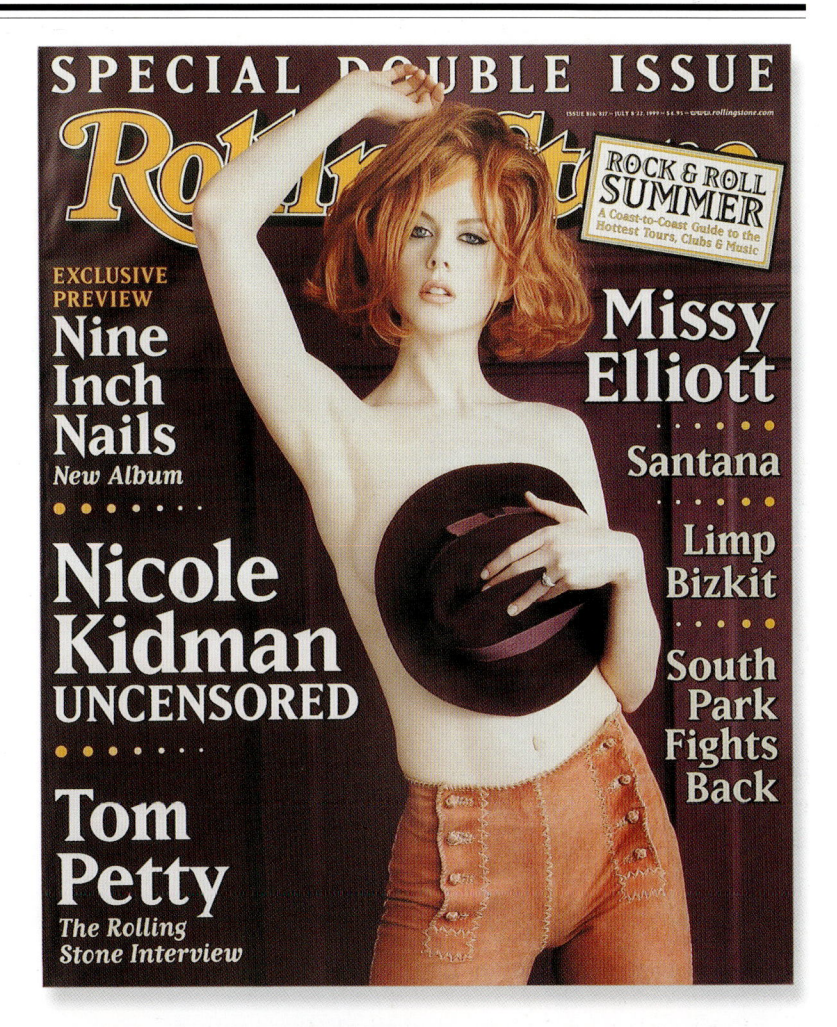

RS 816/817 | NICOLE KIDMAN | July 8th – July 22nd, 1999 | Photograph by Herb Ritts

50 YEARS OF COVERS • 441

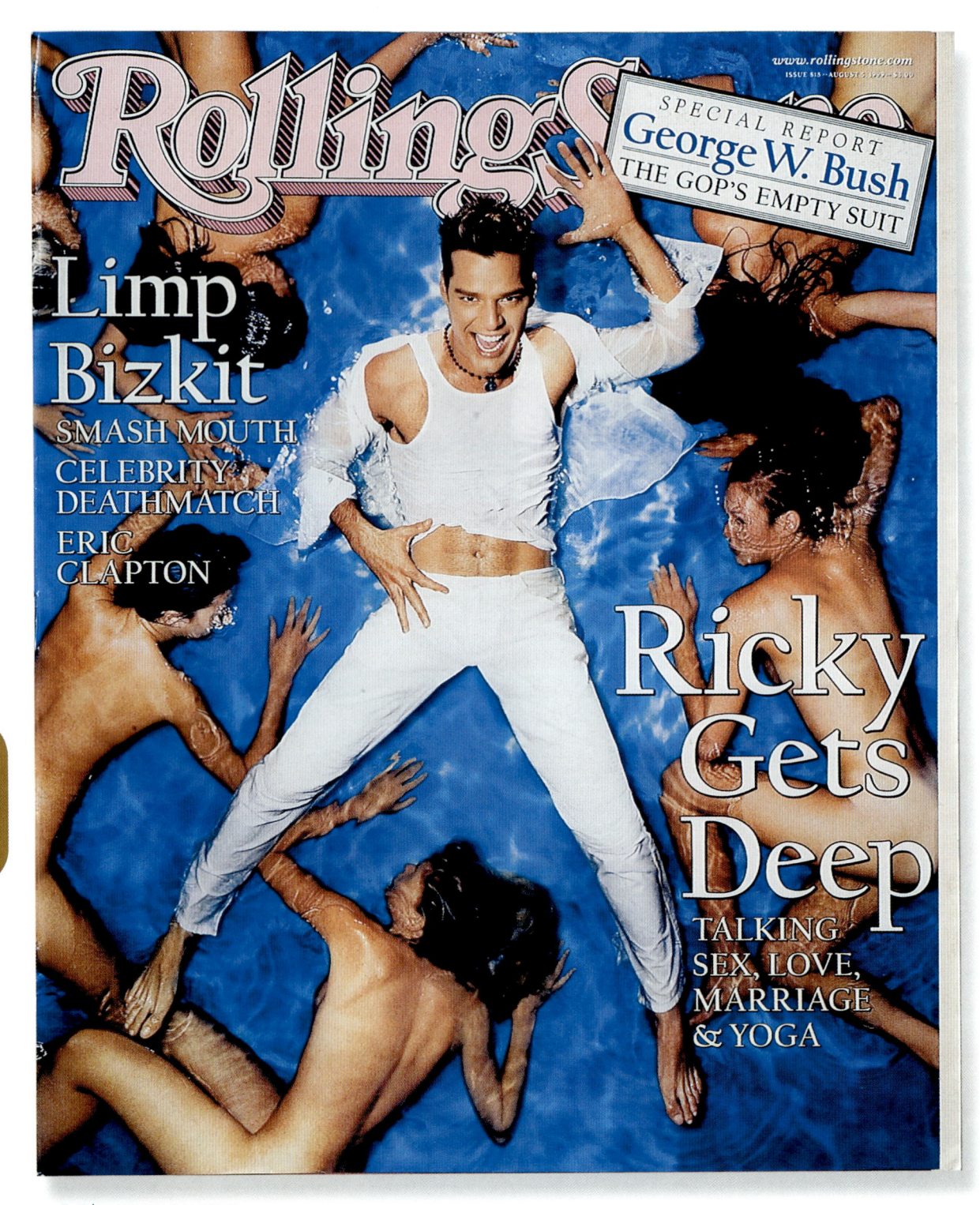

RS 818 | RICKY MARTIN | August 5th, 1999 | Photograph by David LaChapelle

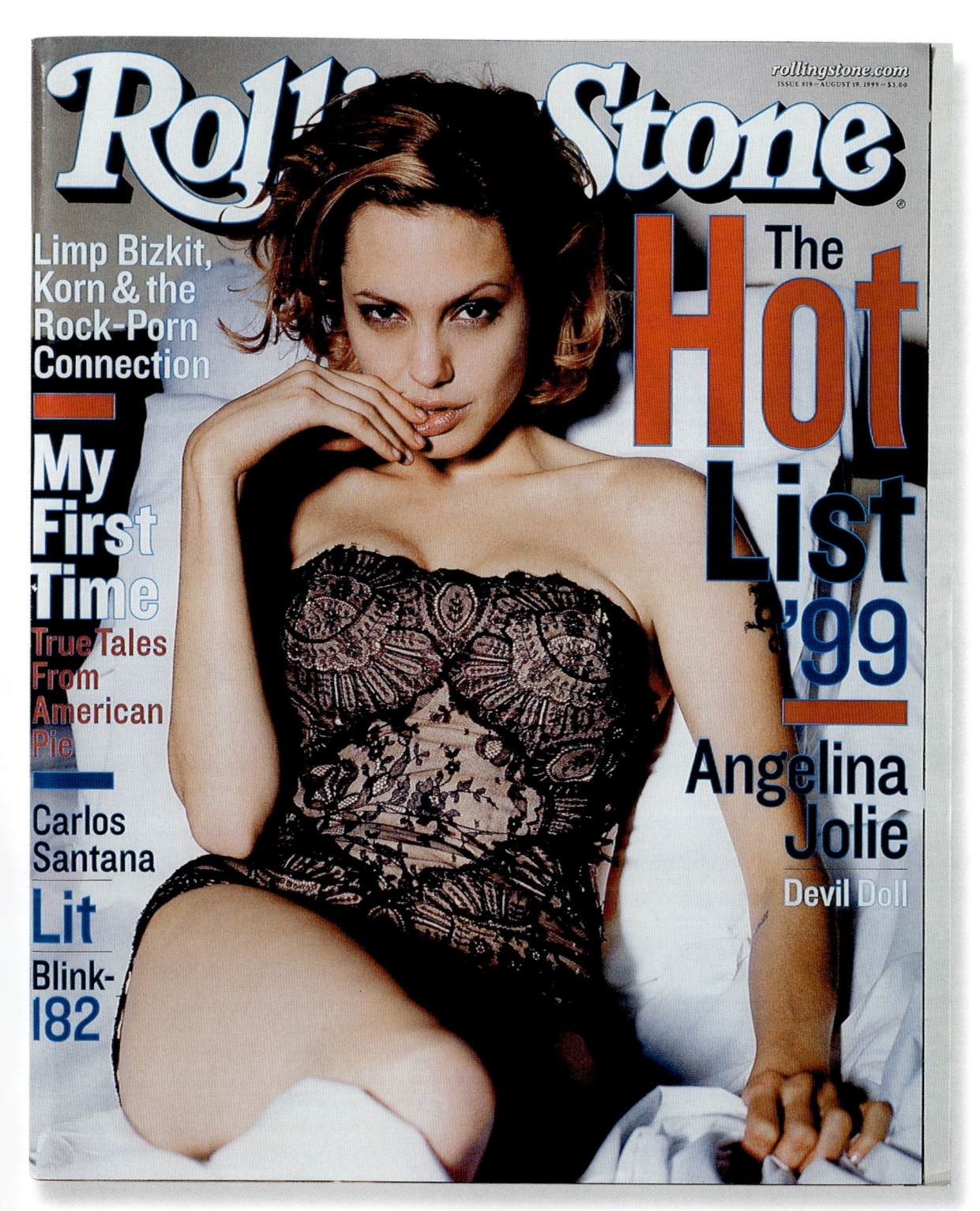

RS 819 | ANGELINA JOLIE | August 19th, 1999 | Photograph by Mark Seliger

1990s

"**Brad says,** 'I've got a real weird idea. For this movie I'm doing [*Fight Club*], I'm going to have to be pretty big. I'm going to have chipped teeth and a nice shaved head. And I thought about you shooting me in dresses – what do you think of that?' And I say, 'That sounds pretty funny.' And he says, 'But we're not talking about me in drag; we're talking about me coming from another planet.'"

—*Mark Seliger*

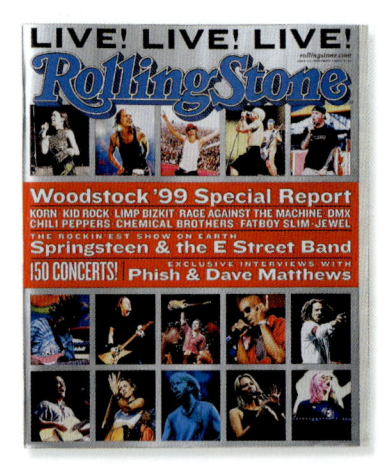

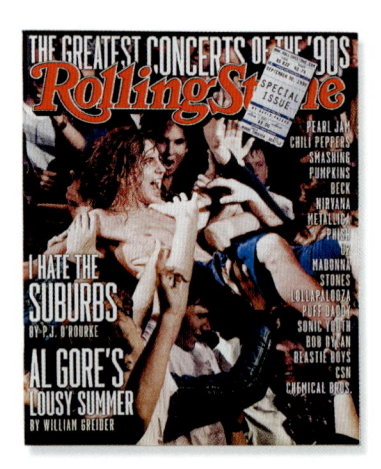

RS 820 | SUMMER CONCERTS 1999
September 2nd, 1999
Various photographers

RS 822 | THE GREATEST CONCERTS OF THE NINETIES – EDDIE VEDDER
September 30th, 1999
Photograph by Lance Mercer

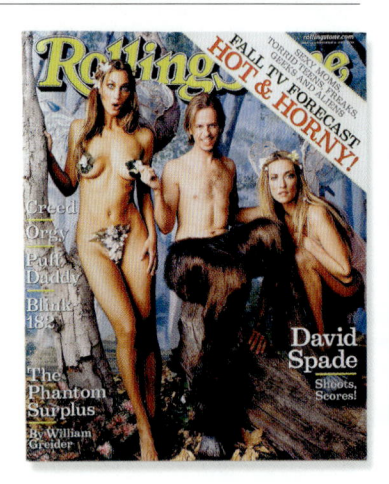

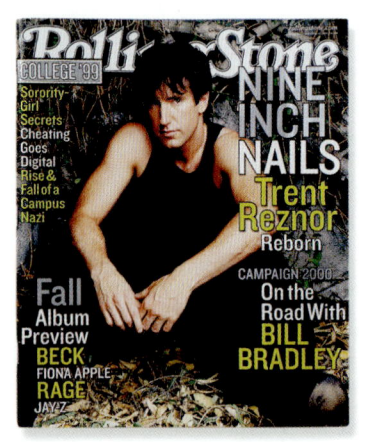

RS 821 | DAVID SPADE
September 16th, 1999
Photograph by Mark Seliger

RS 823 | TRENT REZNOR
October 14th, 1999
Photograph by Mark Seliger

Rolling Stone

rollingstone.com
ISSUE 824 · OCTOBER 28, 1999 · $3.50

Christina Aguilera

Tales of Teen Fame

❋ ❋ ❋

CAMPAIGN 2000

John McCain

❋ ❋ ❋

Being Brad
By Chris Heath

❋ ❋ ❋

Dixie Chicks

Live

Creed

Eve

RS 824 | BRAD PITT | October 28th, 1999 | Photograph by Mark Seliger

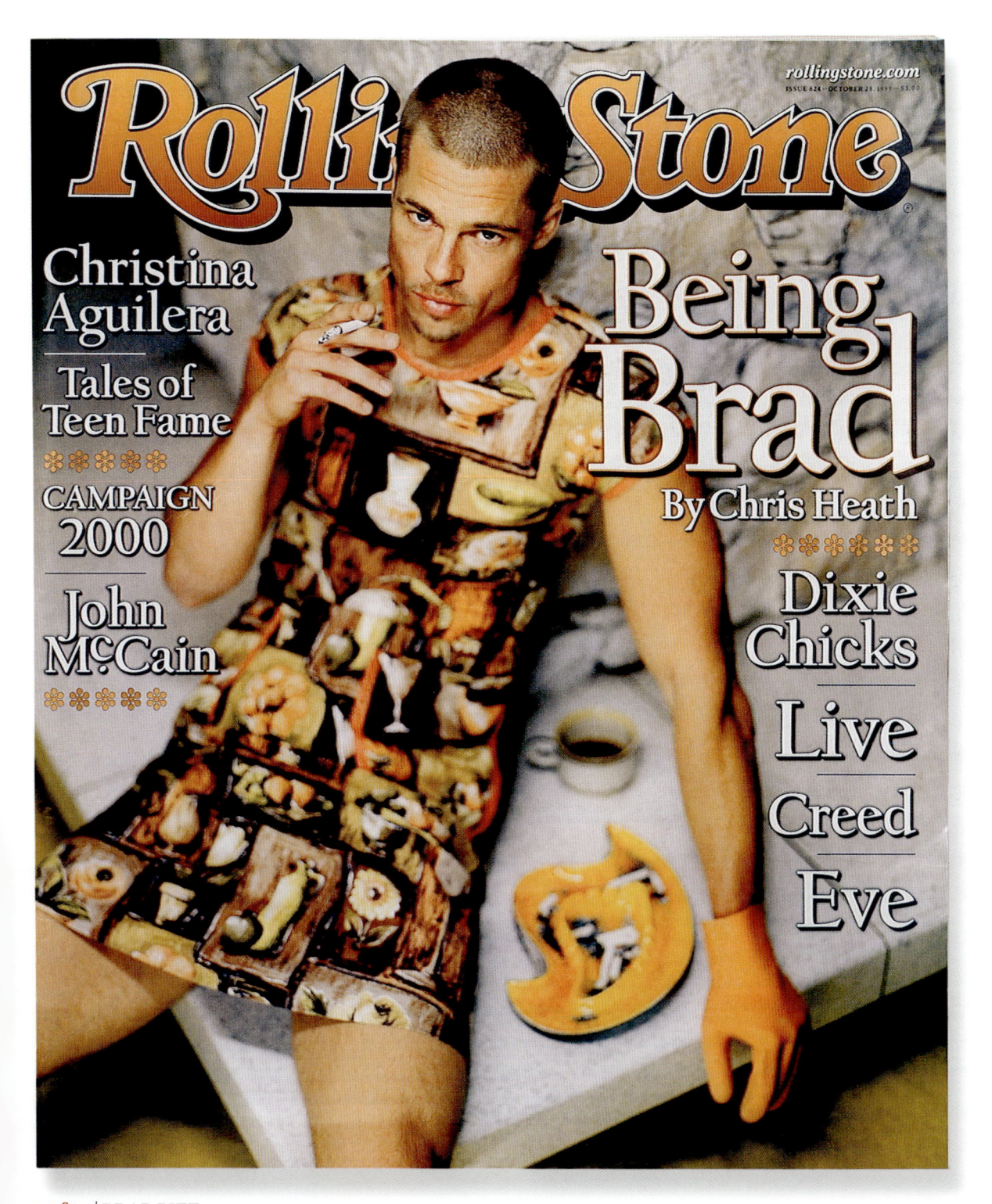

1990s

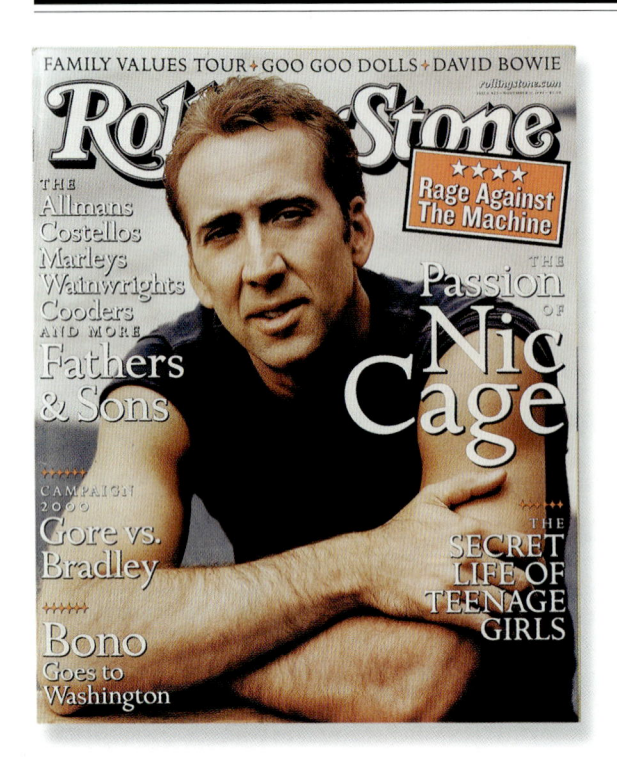

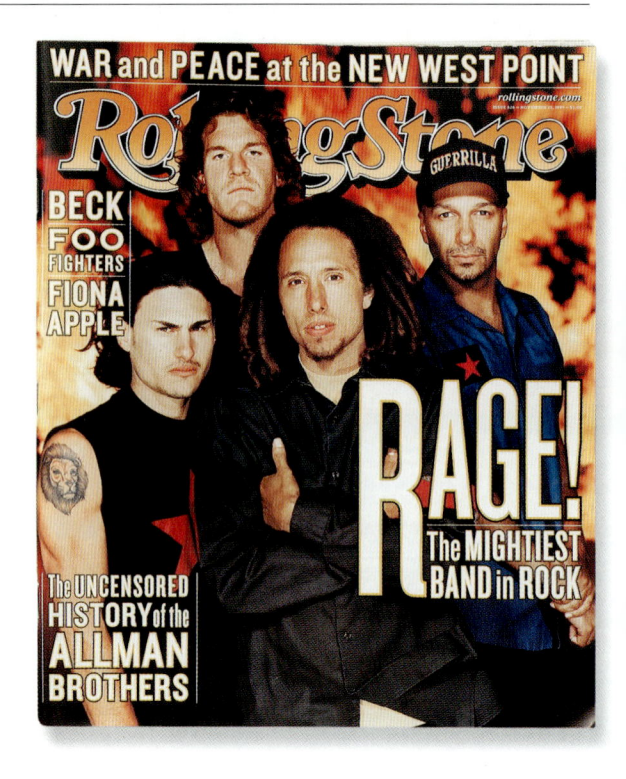

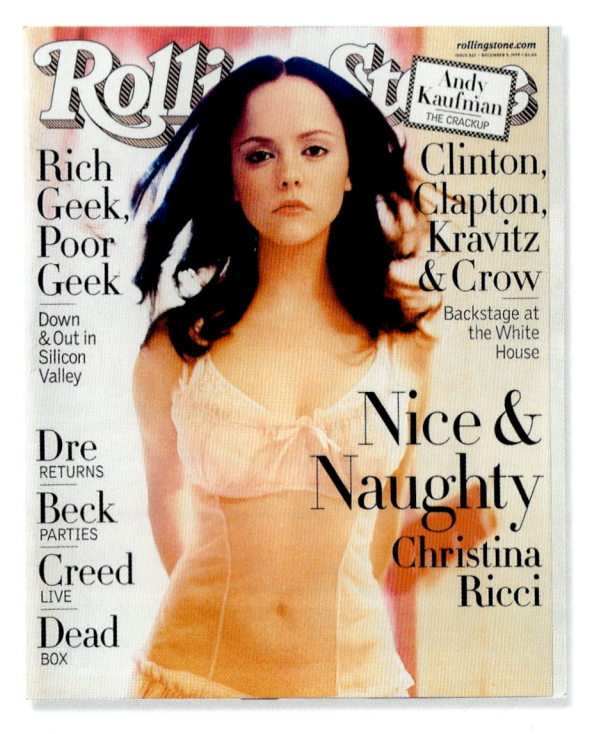

RS 825 | NICOLAS CAGE
November 11th, 1999
PHOTOGRAPH BY PETER LINDBERGH

RS 826 | RAGE AGAINST THE MACHINE
November 25th, 1999
PHOTOGRAPH BY MARTIN SCHOELLER

RS 827 | CHRISTINA RICCI
December 9th, 1999
PHOTOGRAPH BY PEGGY SIROTA

[RS 828/829] "You are about to take an insider's tour of the history of rock & roll, ROLLING STONE and three decades of photojournalism, all at once," wrote the editors by way of introducing this special issue. The issue not only showcased photographs by all of the magazine's greatest contributors – Baron Wolman, Herb Ritts, Annie Leibovitz, Anton Corbijn, Mark Seliger, David LaChapelle, and others – but also told the fabled stories behind those fantastic shots.

446 • ROLLING STONE

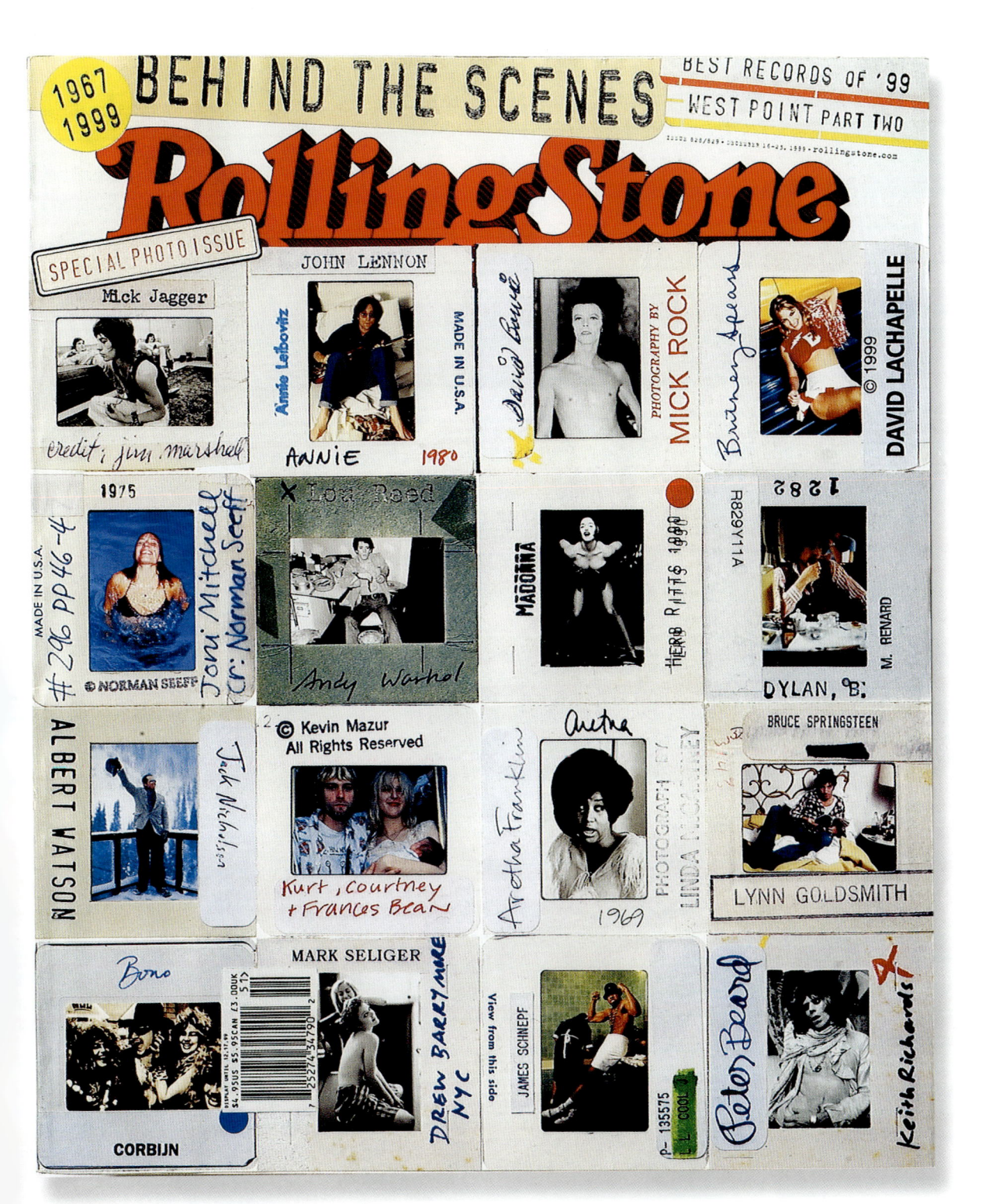

RS 828/829 | BEHIND THE SCENES: 1967–1999 | December 16th – December 23rd, 1999 | VARIOUS PHOTOGRAPHERS

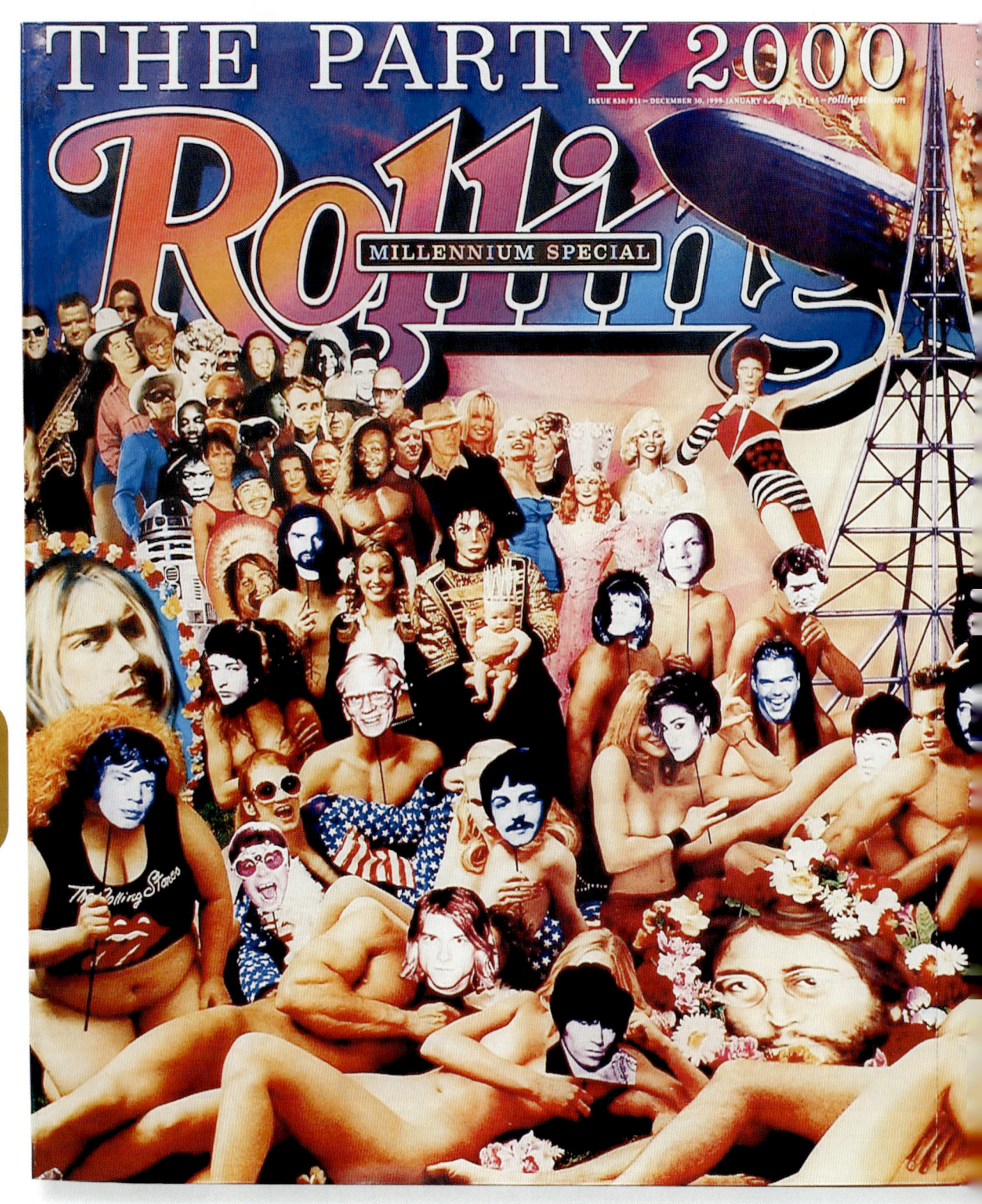

1990s

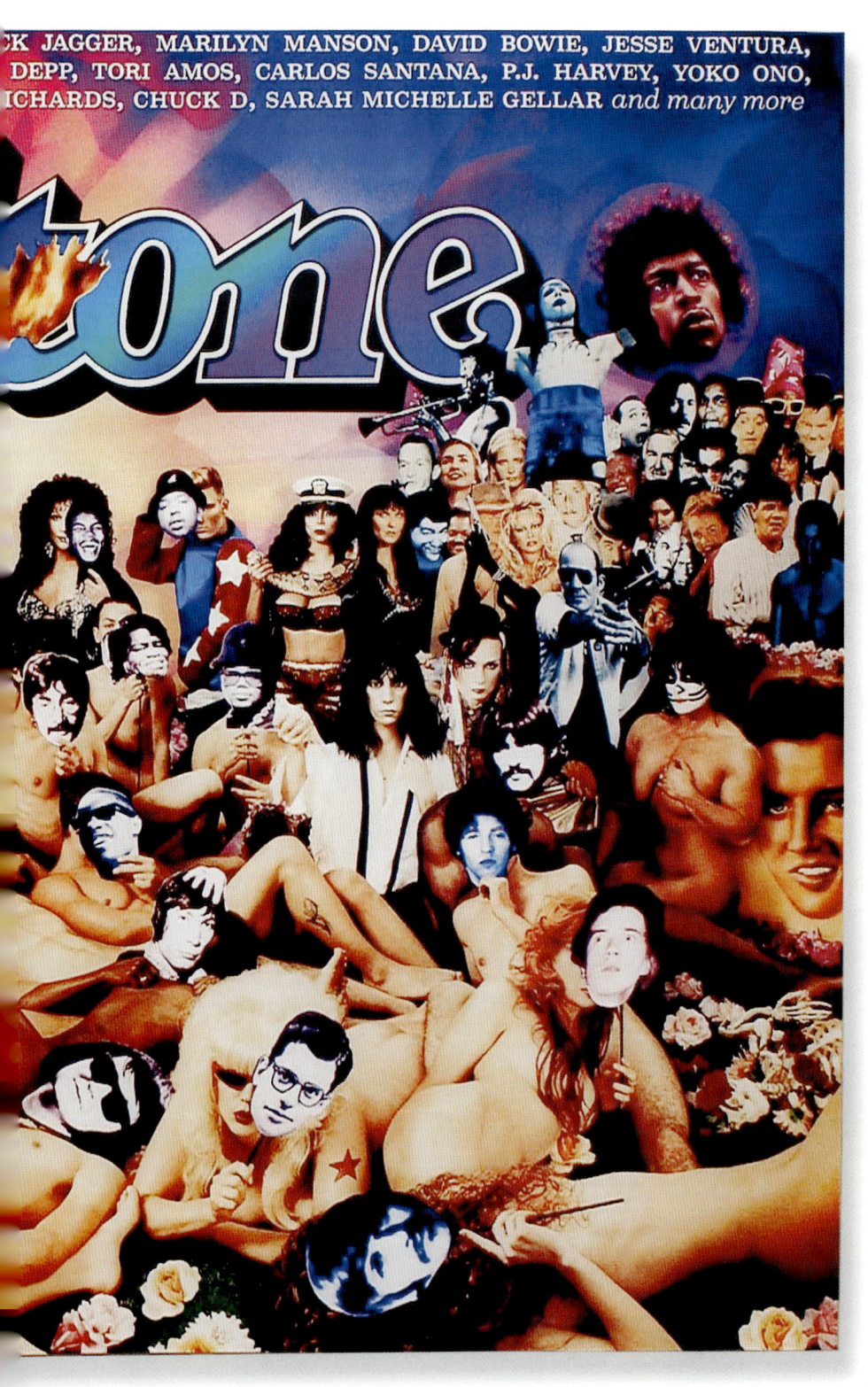

K JAGGER, MARILYN MANSON, DAVID BOWIE, JESSE VENTURA,
DEPP, TORI AMOS, CARLOS SANTANA, P.J. HARVEY, YOKO ONO,
ICHARDS, CHUCK D, SARAH MICHELLE GELLAR and many more

RS 830/831
THE PARTY 2000
December 30th, 1999 –
January 6th, 2000
PHOTOGRAPH BY
DAVID LaCHAPELLE

"**I JUST WANTED TO** throw a party. I wanted to capture that kind of anarchy and chaos and all that communal sexuality. That's why La Toya Jackson and Vanilla Ice are there – whenever you throw a party, there are strangers who show up uninvited and push their way to the front, with no rhyme or reason. And that's what rock history is like."
—*David LaChapelle*

EXCLUSIVE **MELISSA'S SECRET**

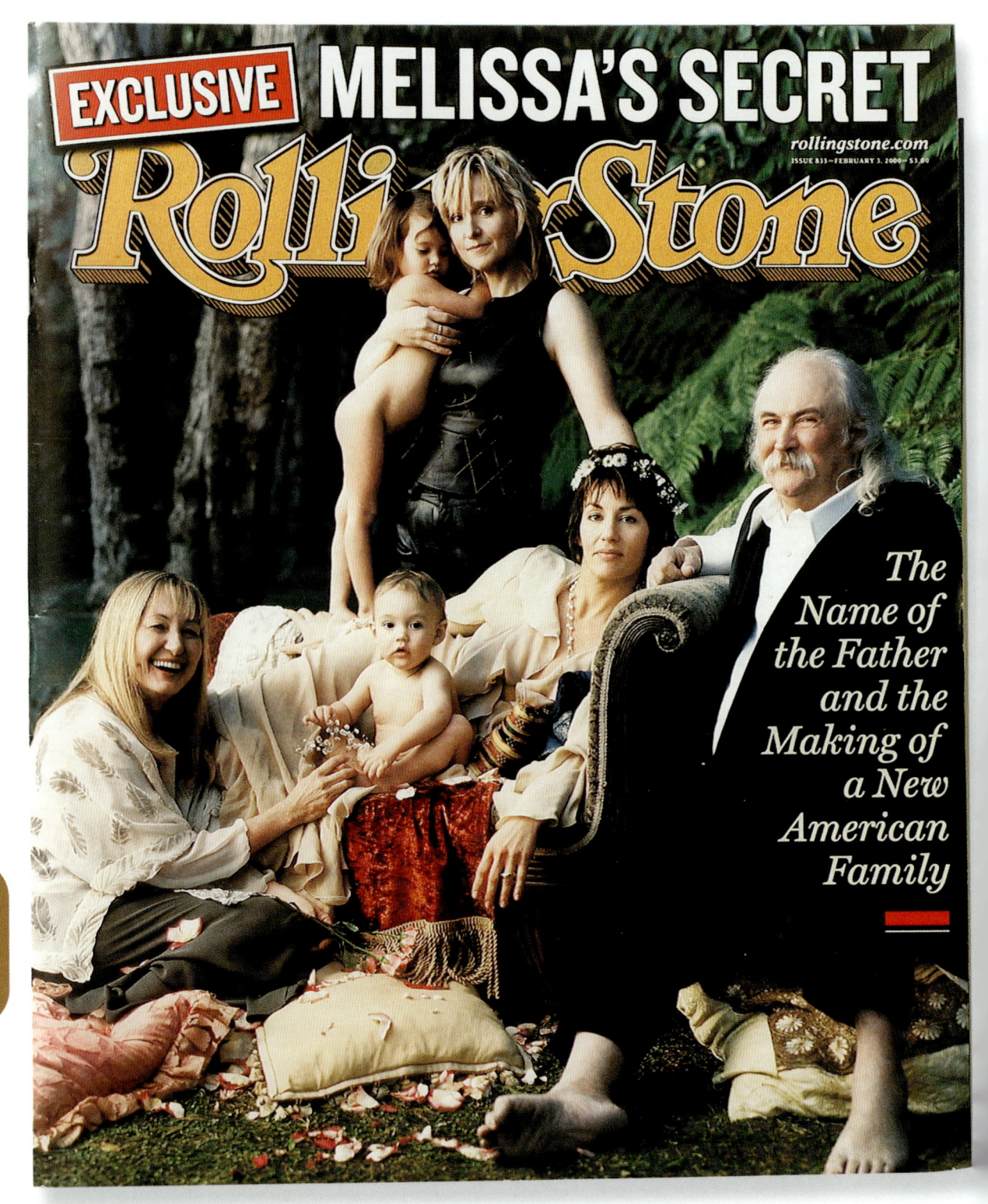

Rolling Stone

rollingstone.com
ISSUE 833 · FEBRUARY 3, 2000 · $3.50

The Name of the Father and the Making of a New American Family

2000s

450 • ROLLING STONE

RS 832 – RS 1000

2000

It was beginning to get ridiculous: the speculation... the rumors... the jokes. For three long years, Melissa Etheridge and her partner, filmmaker Julie Cypher, were asked the same question over and over: Who is the biological father of your two children? Once it was a tad amusing to the couple. Then, with the release of Etheridge's album *Breakdown*, her first in more than three years, the badgering intensified.

"We just got so tired of this secret," says Etheridge, who didn't even tell the rest of her family the father's name until the couple's first child, Bailey, was a year old. "It wears you out. And keeping this big secret goes against how we are choosing to live our lives: very openly." There was also the consideration that Bailey, now three, will attend school soon: "I didn't want my kids to ever be in a position where someone could come up to them and know something they don't."

Thus, after much discussion, the two have decided to reveal the identity of their two children's biological father. It is a man whose name, it is safe to say, has never come up on a short list of candidates. As you can see, it is – of all people – David Crosby, founding member of the Byrds and Crosby, Stills and Nash, a rock & roll bad boy with a four-decade-long career, a wife of twelve years and a thirty-five-year-old son.

A few questions:
What do the kids call you?
"I am Mama, Julie is Mamo," says Etheridge.
Not to put too fine a point on it, but how did the fertilization occur?
"It was artificial insemination, done privately," says Cypher.

It was decided that she should carry the babies because of Etheridge's work. "I was more the homebody, so to speak," Cypher says. "And I'm a health nut, a fanatic, so I was really good at making babies."
Some more questions:
Does Crosby share parental duties?
"It's not a parental thing for David," says Etheridge. "David and Jan totally understood that we are the parents."
"So we see them every once in a while," says Cypher.
Why break the news here?
Etheridge and Cypher decided to come to ROLLING STONE with their story after the two ran into editor and publisher Jann S. Wenner at VH1's Concert of the Century last October in Washington, D.C. "Julie was on a mission to tell everybody," says Etheridge. "She told Jann, and I made some sort of joke. I said, 'Oh, yeah, let it be known in ROLLING STONE.' And I remember leaving there going, 'Huh. Well, that's an idea. It's musical, which is really cool, it's funky, and we could tell the story the way we wanted to, before the world – well, I don't know about the world but whoever is interested in it – picked up on it and did what they were going to do."

[EXCERPT FROM RS 833 COVER STORY BY JANCEE DUNN]

RS 833 | MELISSA ETHERIDGE & DAVID CROSBY WITH FAMILIES | February 3rd, 2000 | PHOTOGRAPH BY MARK SELIGER

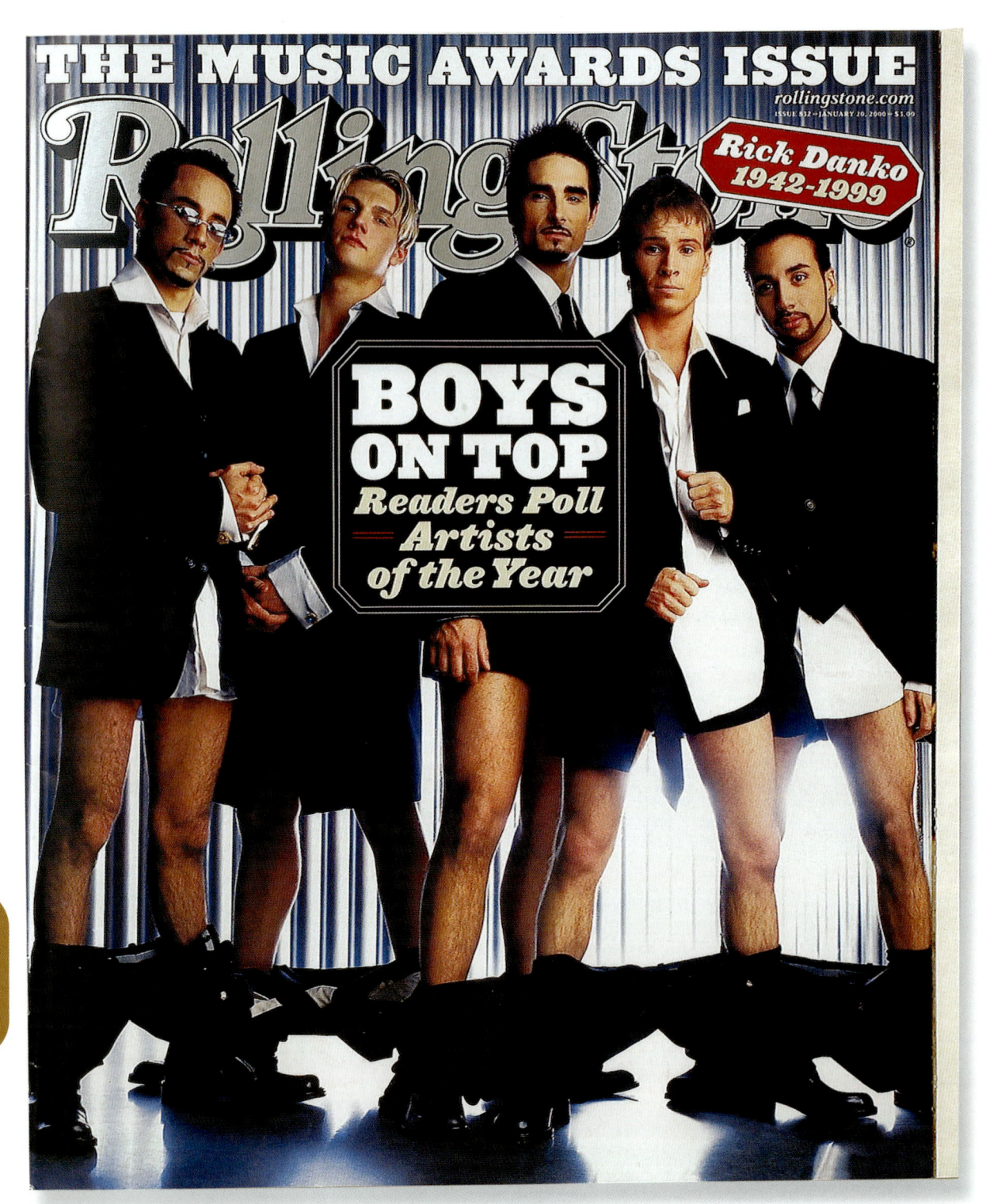

RS 832 | BACKSTREET BOYS | January 20th, 2000 | Photograph by Mark Seliger

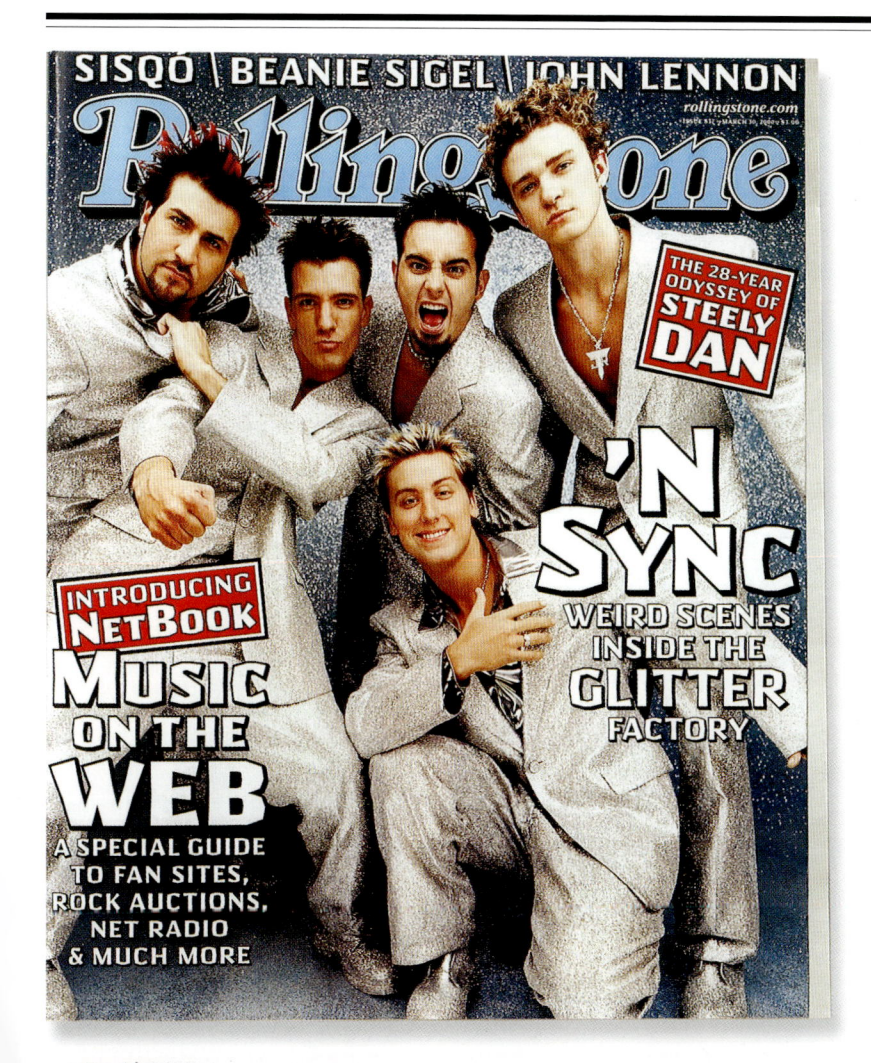

RS 837 | 'NSYNC
March 30th, 2000
Photograph by Stewart Shining

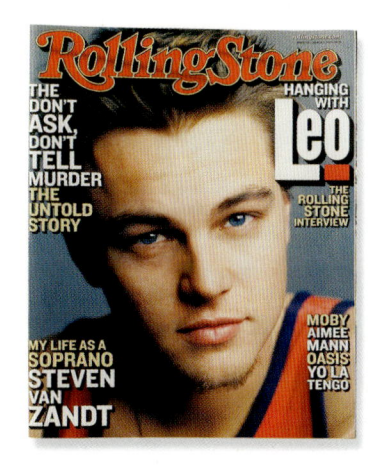

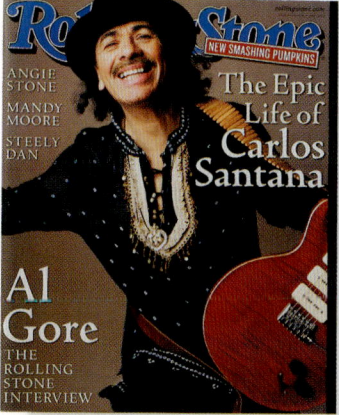

RS 835 | LEONARDO DiCAPRIO
March 2nd, 2000
Photograph by Mark Seliger

RS 836 | CARLOS SANTANA
March 16th, 2000
Photograph by Mark Seliger

"There are restrictions to [shooting] the covers. There is definitely a format that you need to follow. First, acquiesce to the idea that someone is going to put something on it. You can't be a page pig and decide that your photo is going to be the only thing on there."

—*Mark Seliger*

50 YEARS OF COVERS • 453

RS 838 | DMX
April 13th, 2000
PHOTOGRAPH BY ALBERT WATSON

RS 842 | TOM GREEN
June 8th, 2000
PHOTOGRAPH BY MARK SELIGER

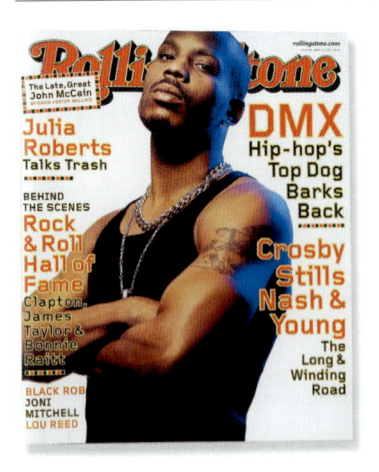

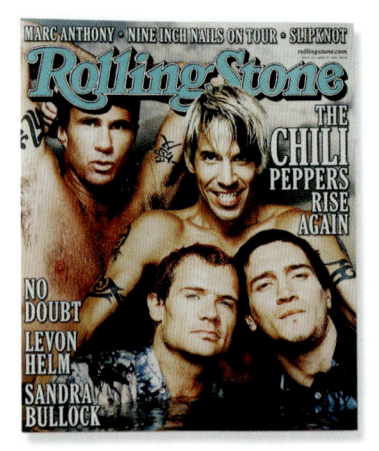

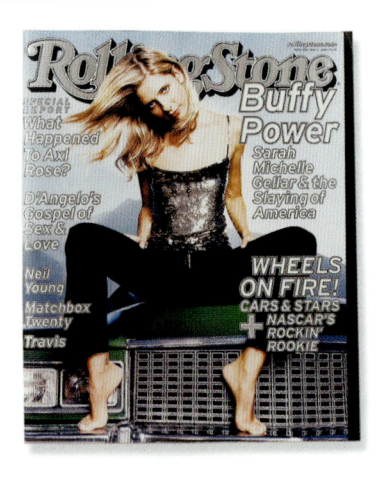

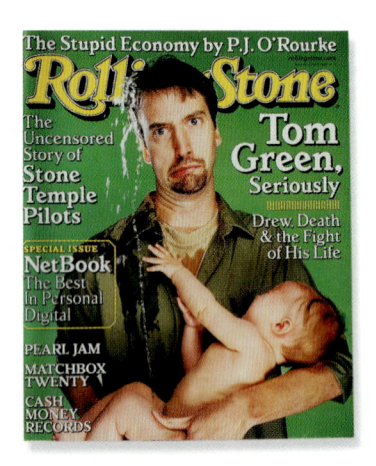

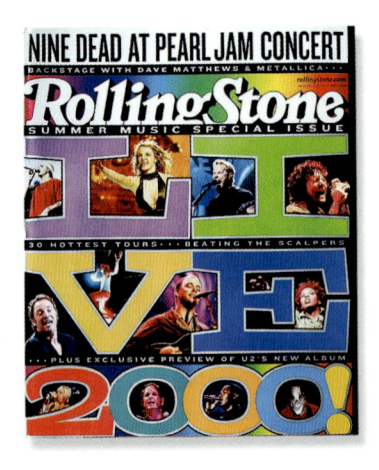

RS 839 | RED HOT CHILI PEPPERS
April 27th, 2000
PHOTOGRAPH BY MARTIN SCHOELLER

RS 847 | LIVE 2000
August 17th, 2000
VARIOUS PHOTOGRAPHERS

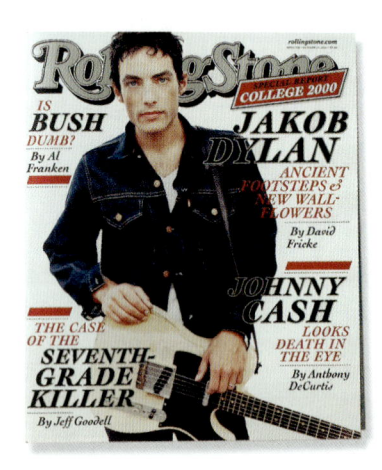

RS 840 | SARAH MICHELLE GELLAR
May 11th, 2000
PHOTOGRAPH BY STEWART SHINING

RS 852 | JAKOB DYLAN
October 26th, 2000
PHOTOGRAPH BY MARK SELIGER

RS 843 | KID ROCK | June 22nd, 2000 | Photograph by Mark Seliger

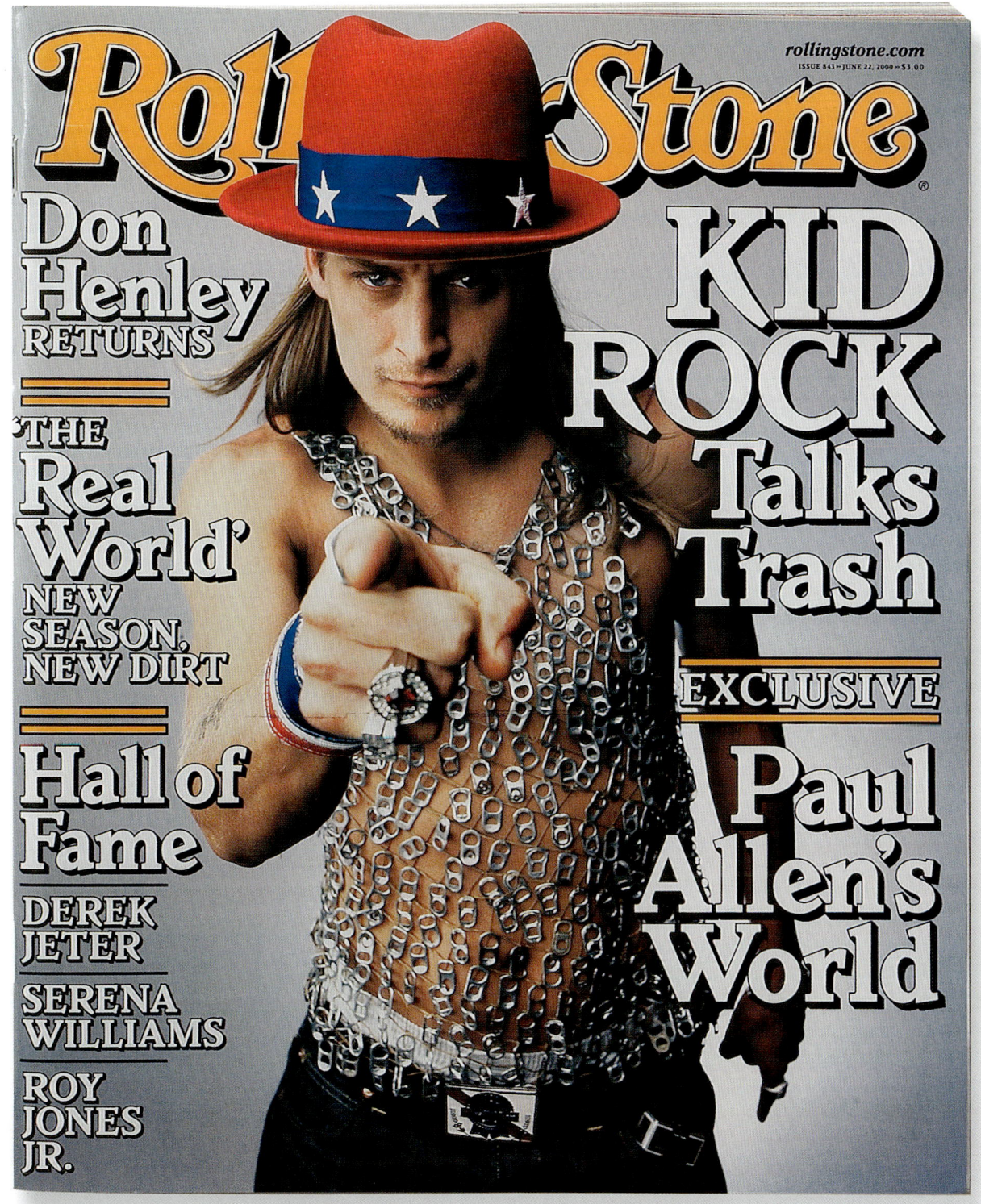

50 YEARS OF COVERS • 455

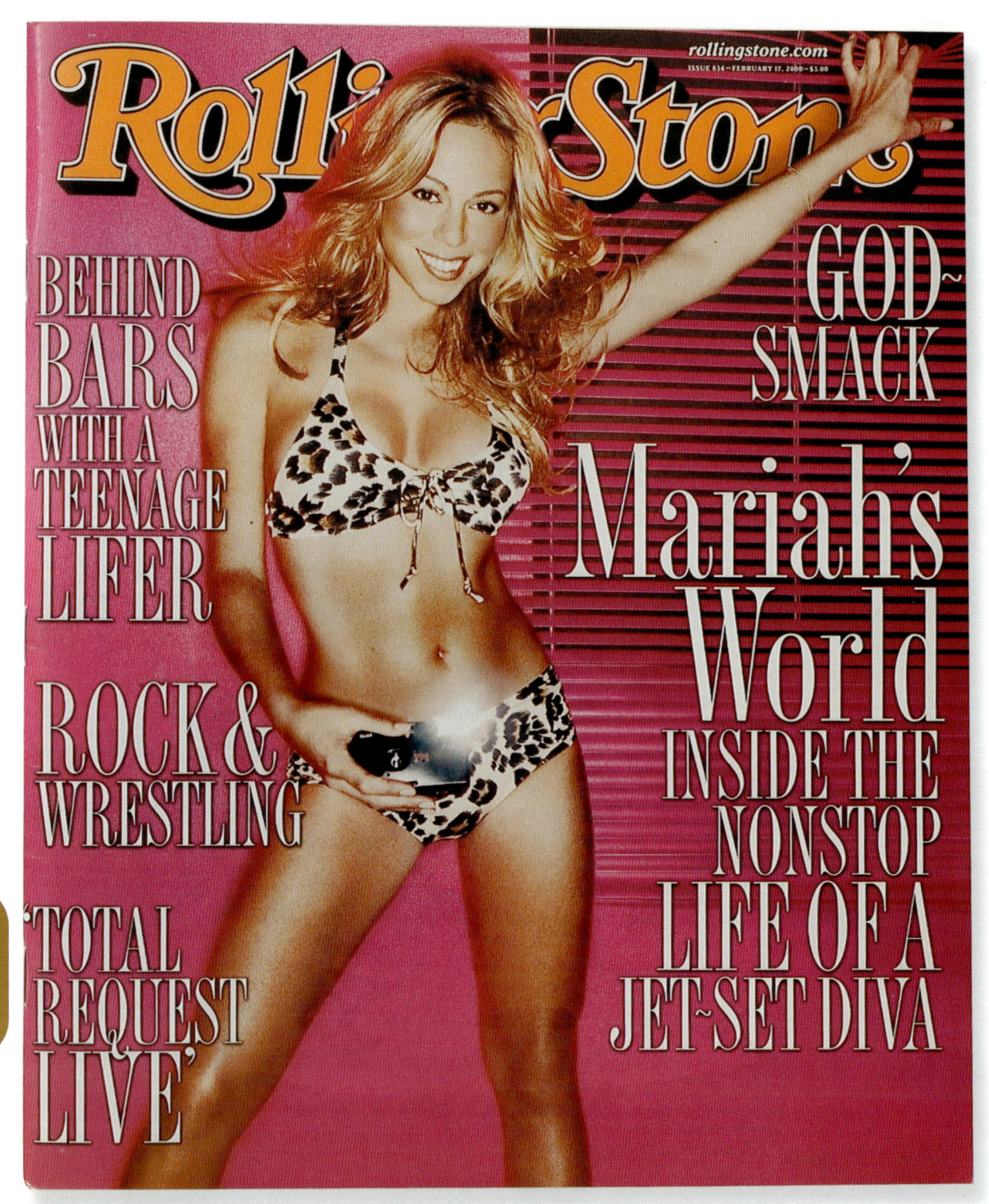

RS 834 | MARIAH CAREY | February 17th, 2000 | Photograph by David LaChapelle

Rolling Stone

rollingstone.com
ISSUE 841 · MAY 25, 2000 · $3.00

BRITNEY WANTS YOU!

THE STATE OF GAY POLITICS

HANSON

BLINK-182

KITTIE

MONEY, GREED & MYSTERY: WHO WROTE 'THE LION SLEEPS TONIGHT'?

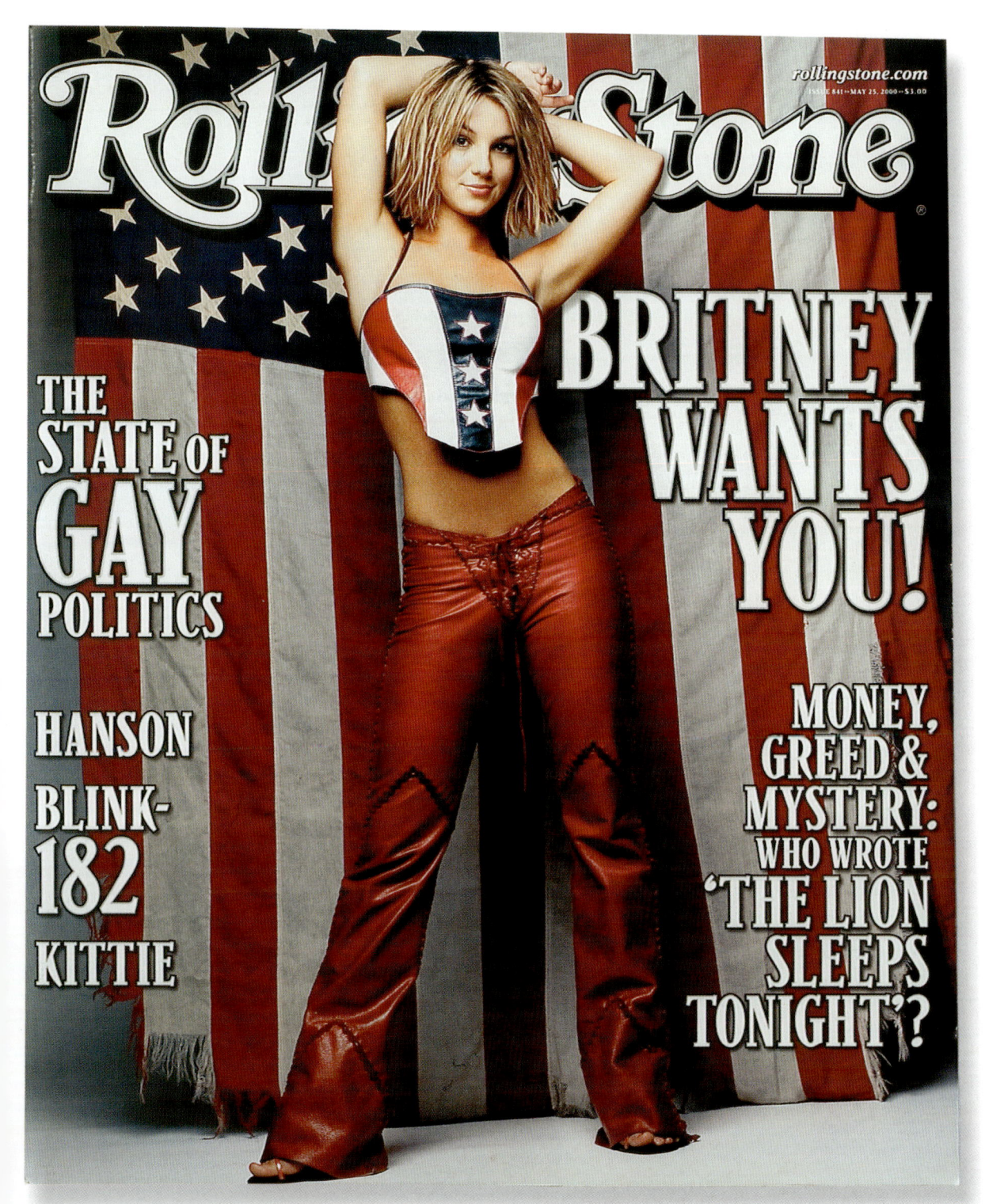

RS 841 | BRITNEY SPEARS | May 25th, 2000 | Photograph by Mark Seliger

50 YEARS OF COVERS • 457

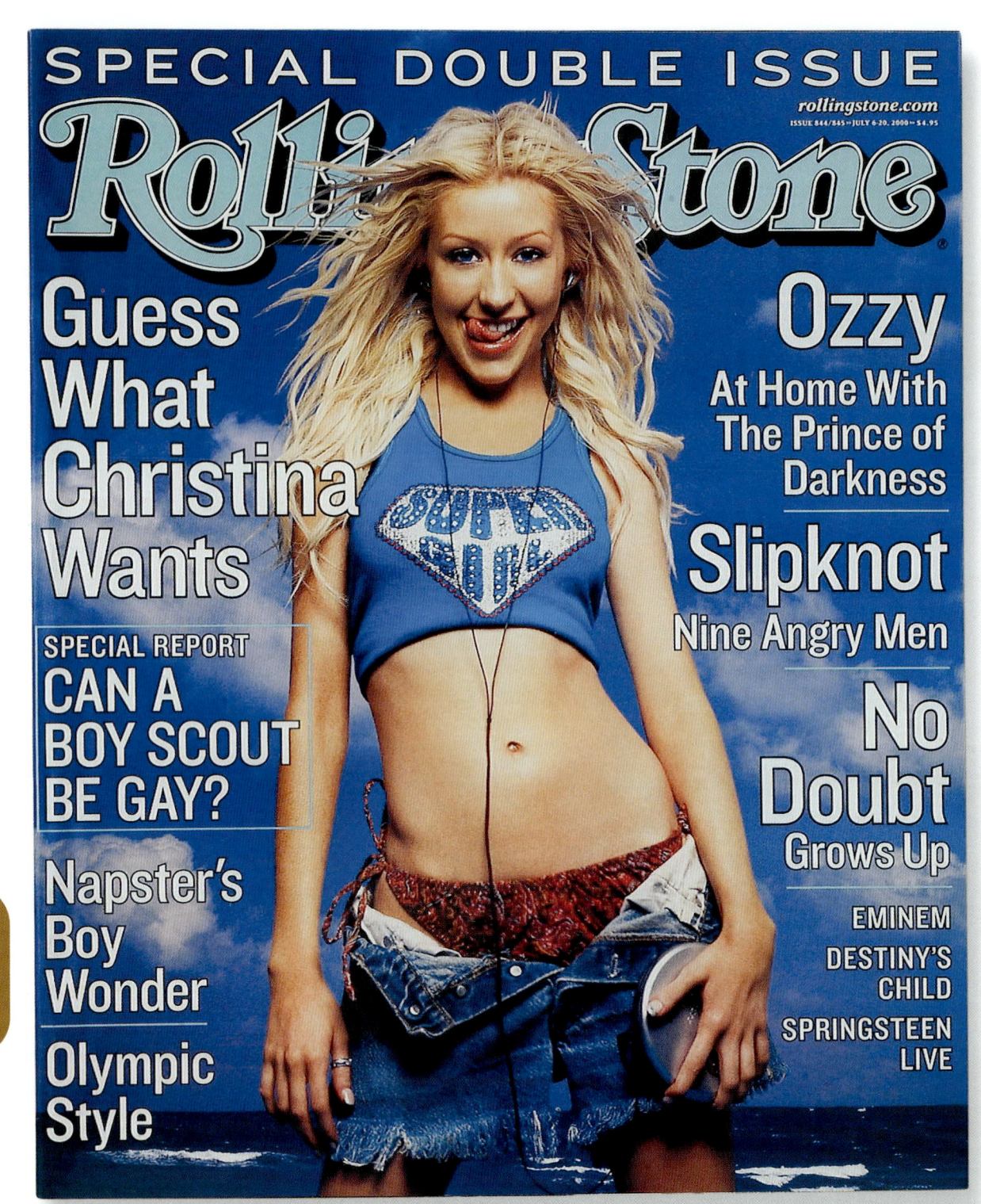

SPECIAL DOUBLE ISSUE

Rolling Stone

rollingstone.com
ISSUE 844/845 • JULY 6-20, 2000 • $4.95

Guess What Christina Wants

SPECIAL REPORT
CAN A BOY SCOUT BE GAY?

Napster's Boy Wonder

Olympic Style

Ozzy
At Home With The Prince of Darkness

Slipknot
Nine Angry Men

No Doubt
Grows Up

EMINEM
DESTINY'S CHILD
SPRINGSTEEN LIVE

2000s

RS 844/845 | CHRISTINA AGUILERA | July 6th – July 20th, 2000 | Photograph by Mark Seliger

Rolling Stone

rollingstone.com
ISSUE 850 · SEPTEMBER 28, 2000 · $3.00

INTO THE MYSTIC WITH DEEPAK CHOPRA

HOW TO TELL BUSH FROM GORE
By P.J. O'Rourke

AL GREEN
INCUBUS
DISTURBED
WALLFLOWERS

Madonna
CAN'T STOP *the* MUSIC

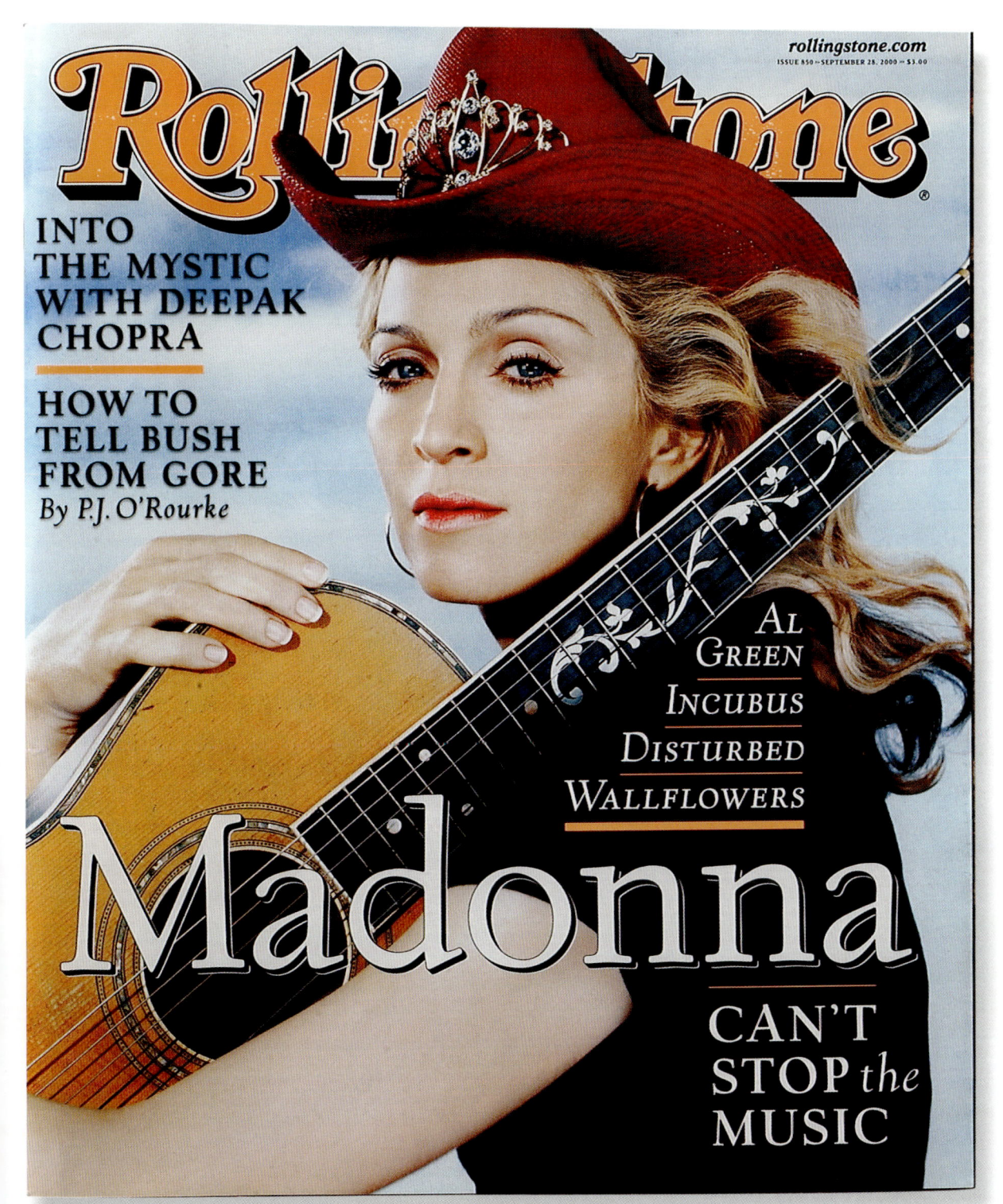

RS 850 | MADONNA | September 28th, 2000 | Photograph by Jean-Baptiste Mondino

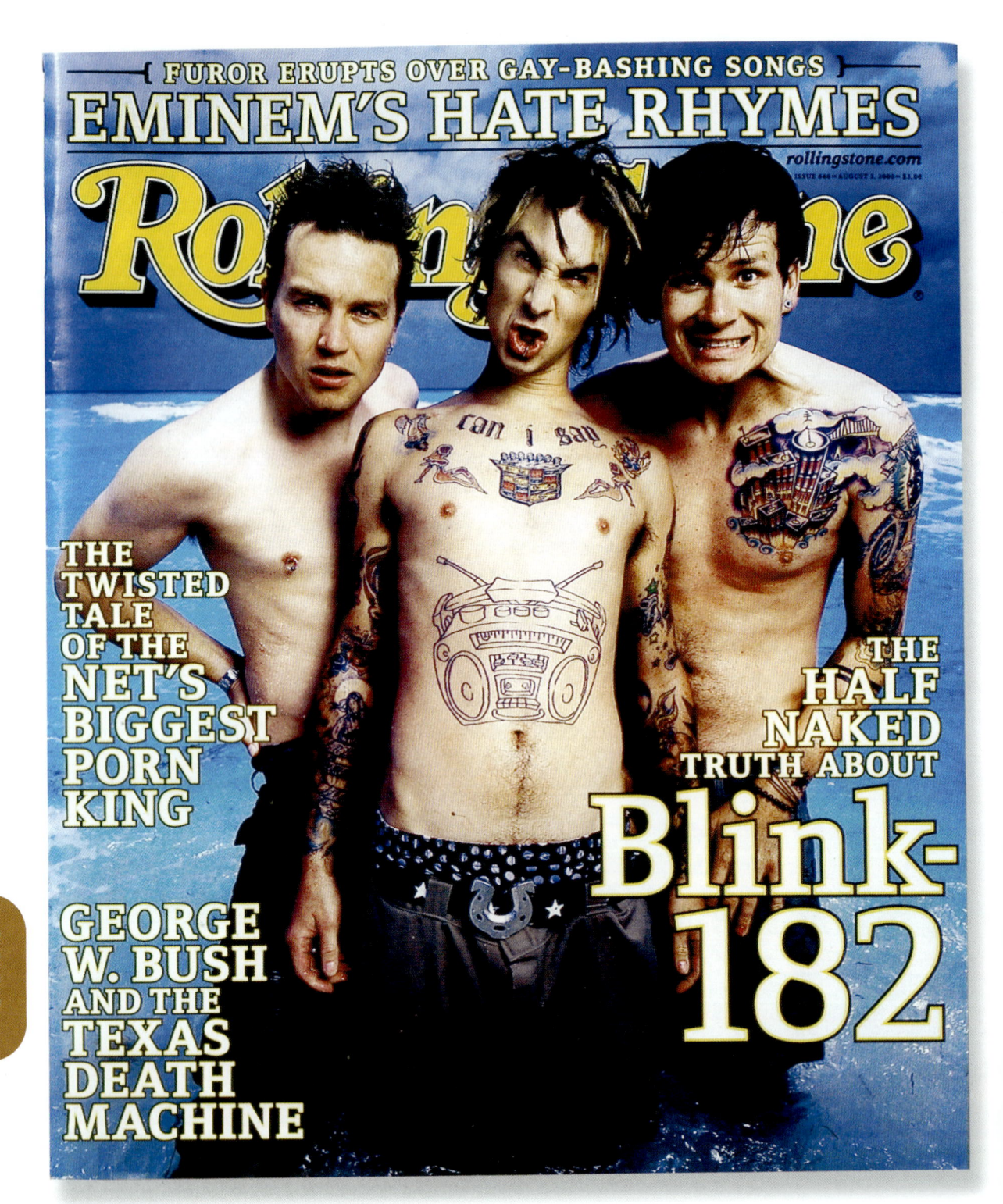

RS 846 | BLINK-182 | August 3rd, 2000 | Photograph by Mark Seliger

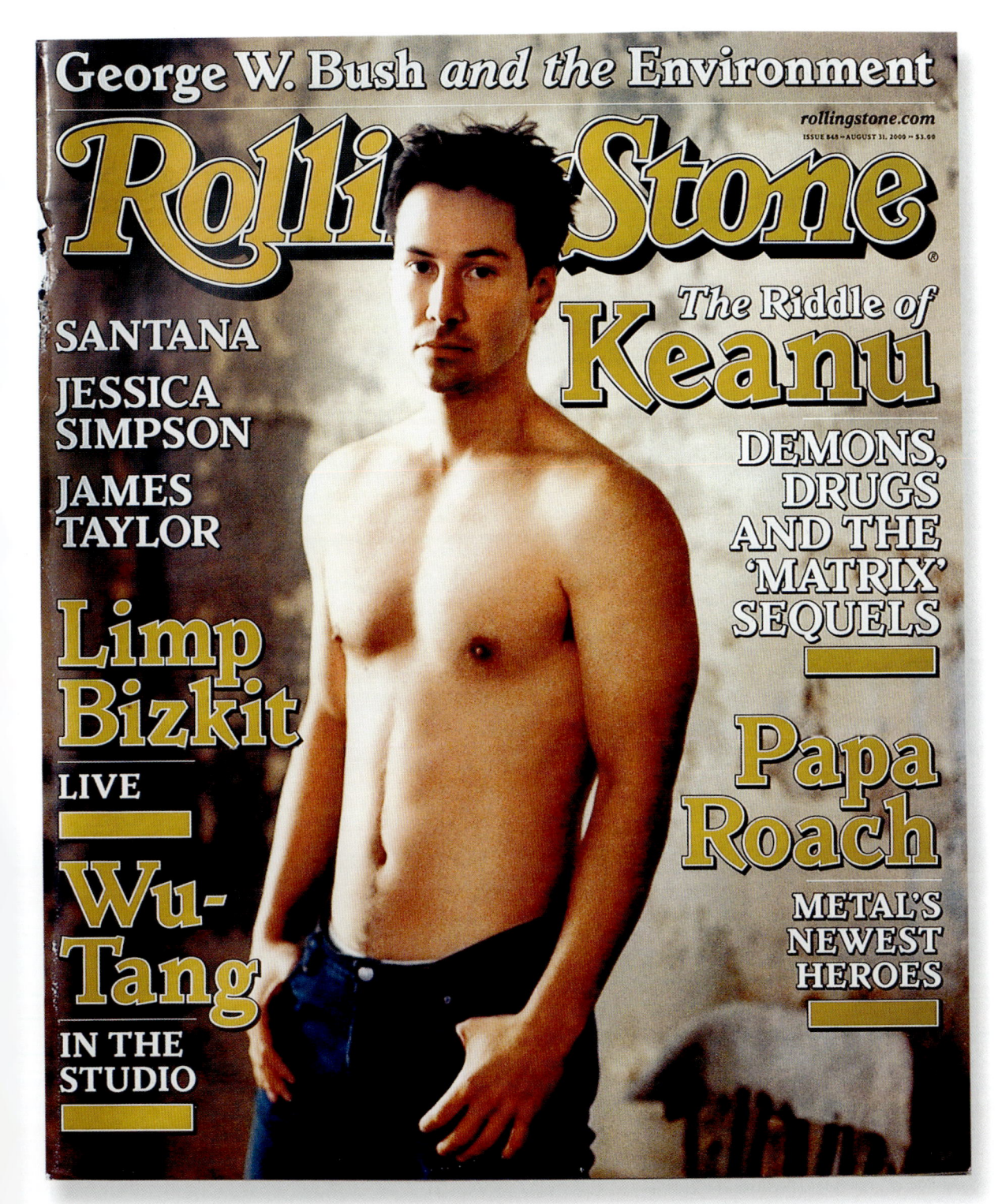

RS 848 | KEANU REEVES | August 31st, 2000 | Photograph by Mark Seliger

50 YEARS OF COVERS • 461

Rolling Stone

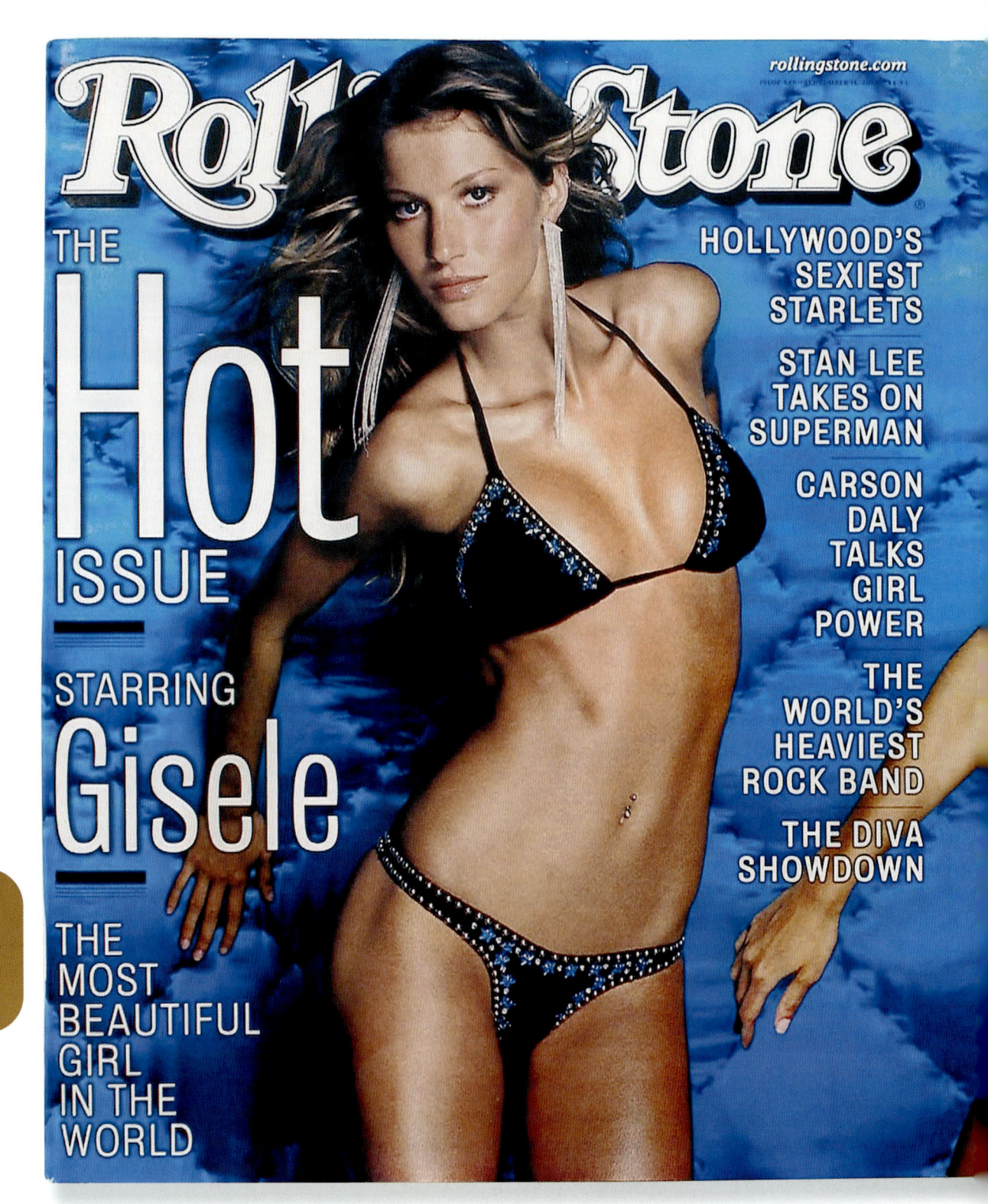

rollingstone.com

THE Hot ISSUE

STARRING Gisele

THE MOST BEAUTIFUL GIRL IN THE WORLD

HOLLYWOOD'S SEXIEST STARLETS

STAN LEE TAKES ON SUPERMAN

CARSON DALY TALKS GIRL POWER

THE WORLD'S HEAVIEST ROCK BAND

THE DIVA SHOWDOWN

2000s

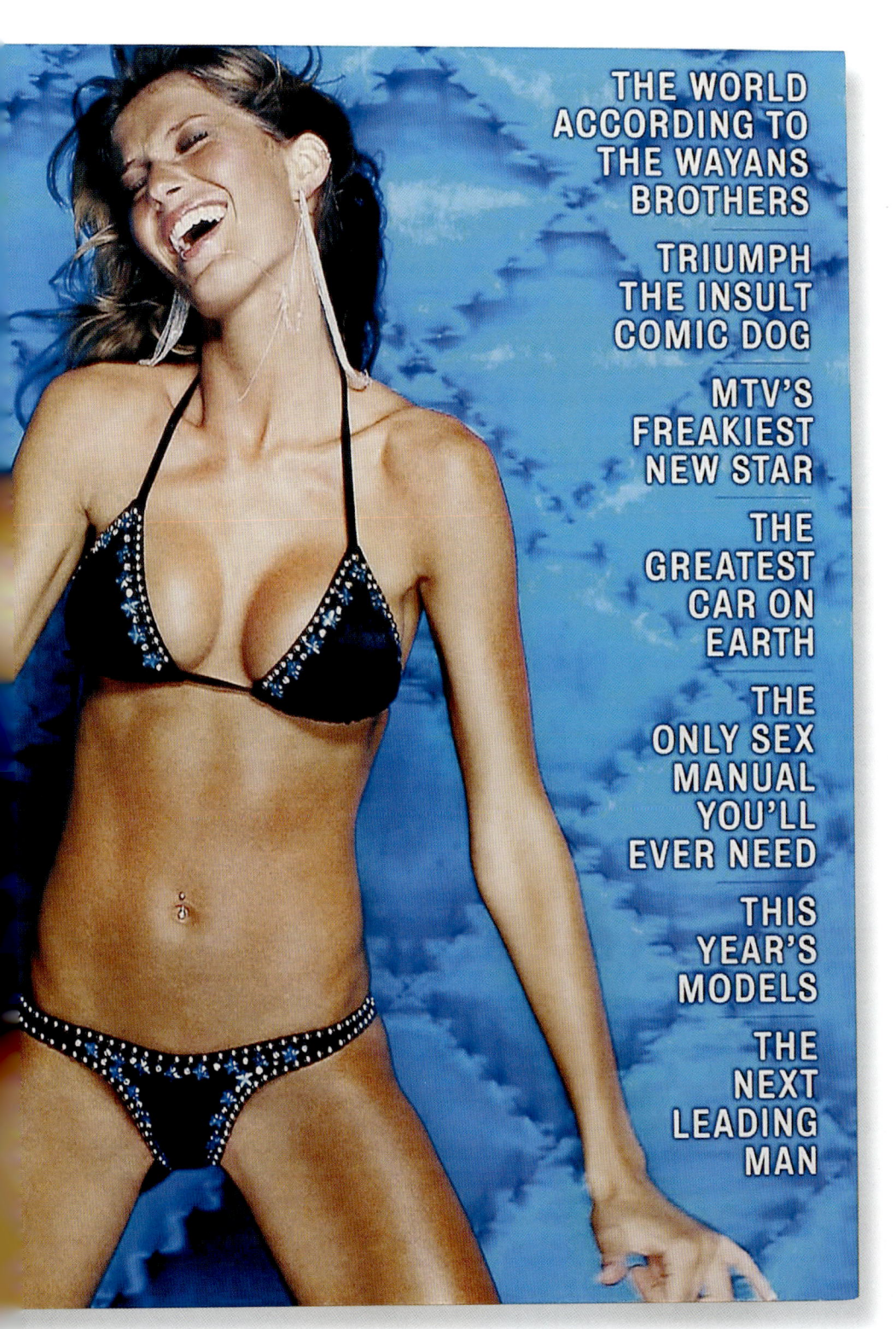

RS 849 | GISELE
September 14th, 2000
Photograph by
Mark Seliger

50 YEARS OF COVERS • 463

HISTORICAL RECONSTRUCTION, when done well, is like a game of charades with vivid hints. Some of the events in *Almost Famous* beg deciphering. Let's clarify a few things [with Cameron Crowe].

What about that scene where Russell, on a bad acid trip, climbs up on the roof of a fan's house and yells, "I am a golden god"?

Robert Plant – he was joking around and said it while looking over the Sunset Strip. He and Jimmy Page saw the movie, and when Billy Crudup's character is complaining about the story and says, "I didn't say, 'I am a golden god,'" Plant shouted, "Well, I did!"

Who is Russell Hammond, really?

I saw Glenn Frey at a dinner party recently, and I realized that so much of Russell is Glenn. He was the coolest guy I had ever met in 1972. I was backstage at a concert interviewing everybody – the Eagles, King Crimson, Ballin' Jack, Chaka Khan. In the Eagles' dressing room, everyone's talking about Glenn – the one guy who isn't there. He's out looking for babes. Everyone's like, "The thing about Glenn," "Oh, one time Glenn and I . . ." And then, like a one-act play, Glenn appears. He walks in a little buzzed, he's got a long-neck Bud, and he's like, "How ya doin'?" Just classic. That whole thing of "Tonight, friends – tomorrow, the interview" was him. And there's one line he really did say to me: "Look, just make us look cool."

[EXCERPT FROM RS 851 COVER STORY BY ANTHONY BOZZA]

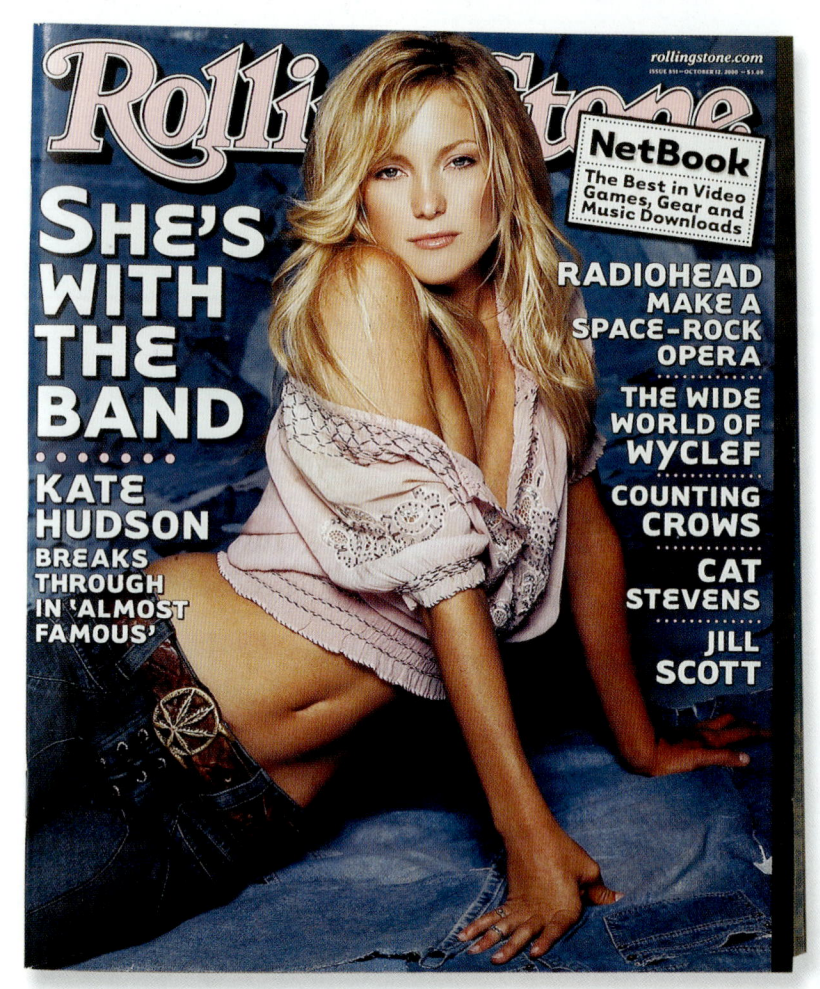

2000s

RS 851 | KATE HUDSON
October 12th, 2000
PHOTOGRAPH BY HERB RITTS

[**RS 851**] When Cameron Crowe started writing for ROLLING STONE in the 1970s, few could have guessed he would become one of Hollywood's most beloved directors, the man behind *Fast Times at Ridgemont High*, *Say Anything* and *Jerry Maguire*. But Crowe's own story was every bit as incredible as those he told on celluloid: When he joined the magazine's stable of writers, he was only fifteen. Crowe's misadventures on the road finally made it to the screen in *Almost Famous* – costarring RS 851 cover girl Kate Hudson – a movie that exponentially increased the number of unsolicited record reviews the magazine received from its eager young readers.

464 • ROLLING STONE

NELLY'S 'COUNTRY GRAMMAR' ROCKS THE NATION

Rolling Stone

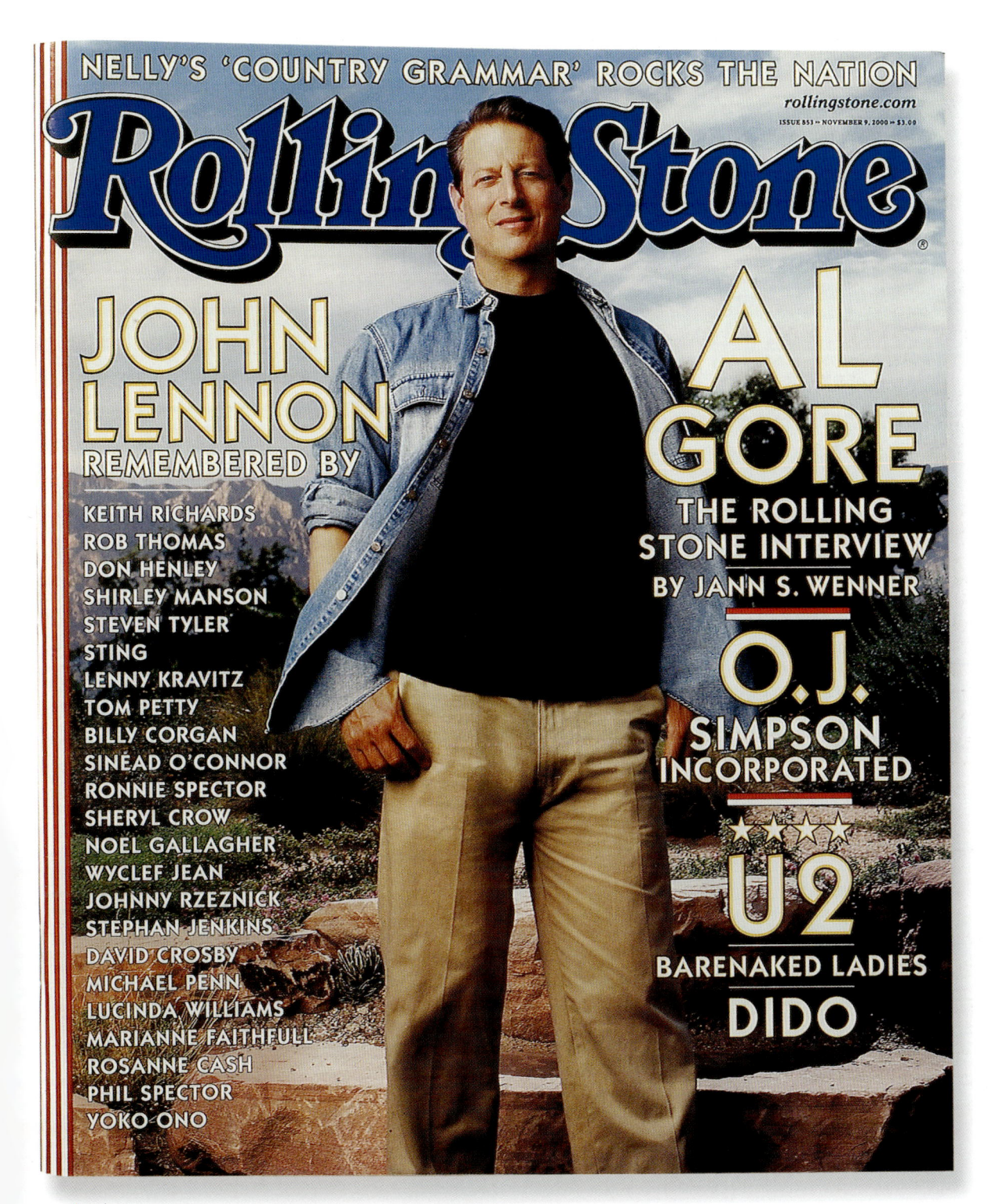

rollingstone.com
ISSUE 853 · NOVEMBER 9, 2000 · $3.00

JOHN LENNON
REMEMBERED BY

KEITH RICHARDS
ROB THOMAS
DON HENLEY
SHIRLEY MANSON
STEVEN TYLER
STING
LENNY KRAVITZ
TOM PETTY
BILLY CORGAN
SINÉAD O'CONNOR
RONNIE SPECTOR
SHERYL CROW
NOEL GALLAGHER
WYCLEF JEAN
JOHNNY RZEZNICK
STEPHAN JENKINS
DAVID CROSBY
MICHAEL PENN
LUCINDA WILLIAMS
MARIANNE FAITHFULL
ROSANNE CASH
PHIL SPECTOR
YOKO ONO

AL GORE
THE ROLLING STONE INTERVIEW
BY JANN S. WENNER

O.J. SIMPSON INCORPORATED

U2
BARENAKED LADIES
DIDO

RS 853 | AL GORE | November 9th, 2000 | Photograph by Mark Seliger

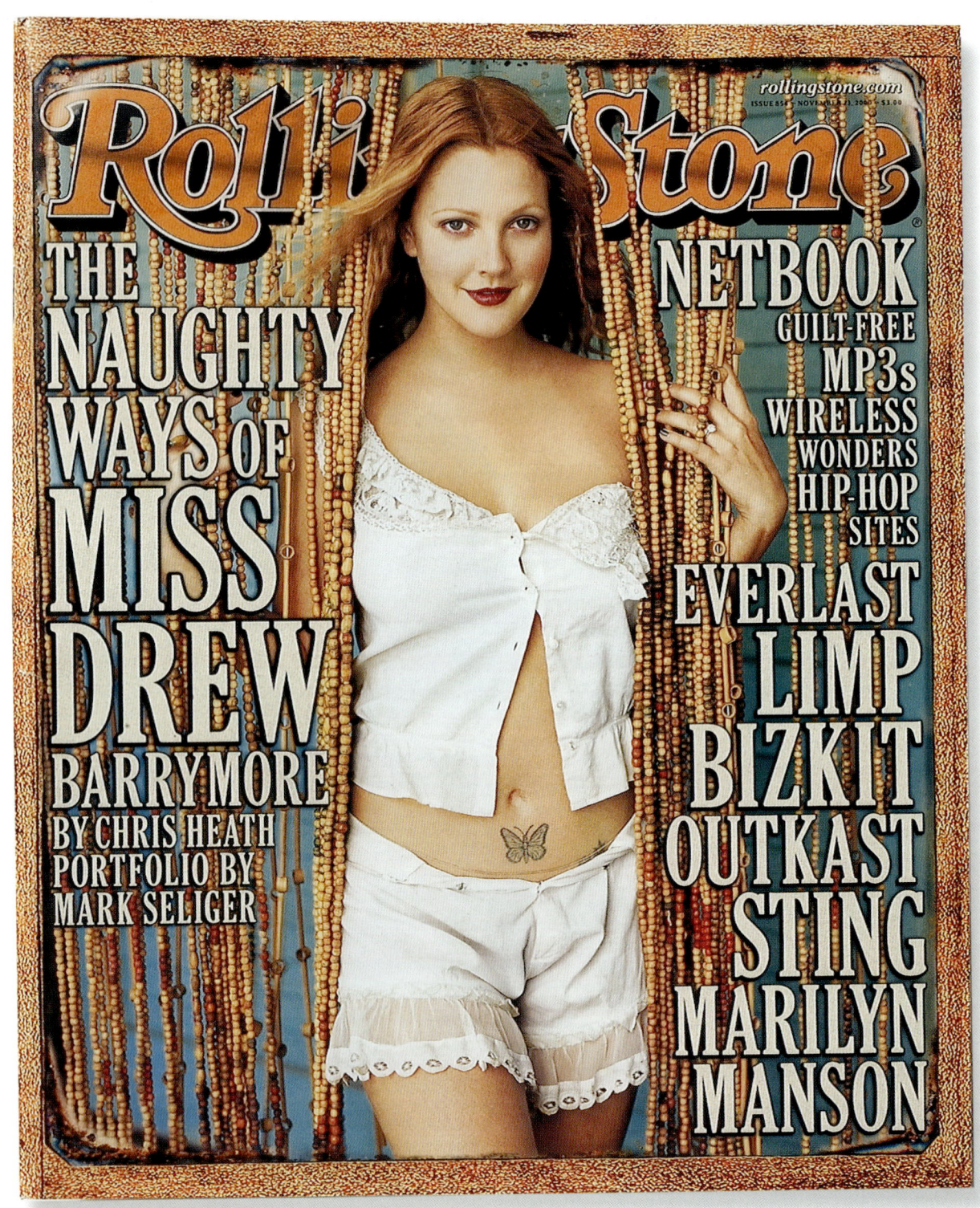

RS 854 | DREW BARRYMORE | November 23rd, 2000 | Photograph by Mark Seliger

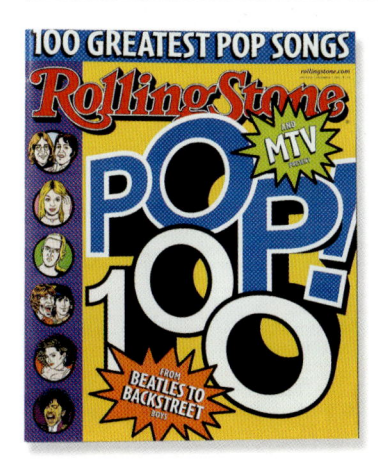

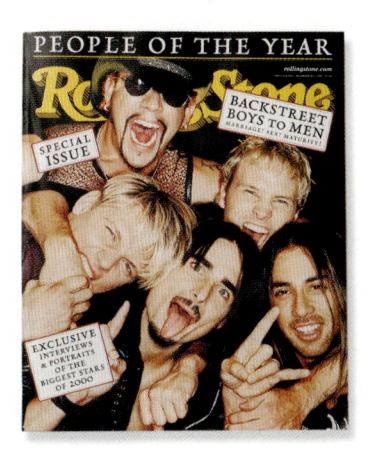

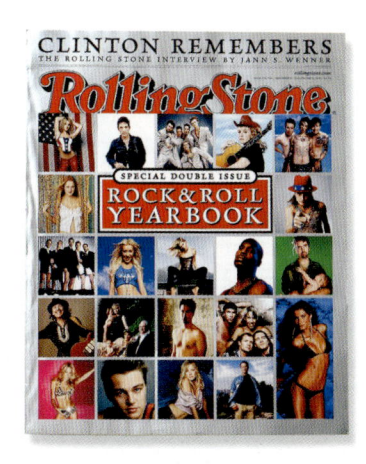

"*Drew is my quintessential* muse. She was responsible for elevating my work. She gave me the trust and time to let me create. Then she would embellish it and make it really powerful. . . . Usually when I talk to somebody beforehand, they're giving me their formula on what they want and what they won't do. She just let me go. That blew me away."

—Mark Seliger

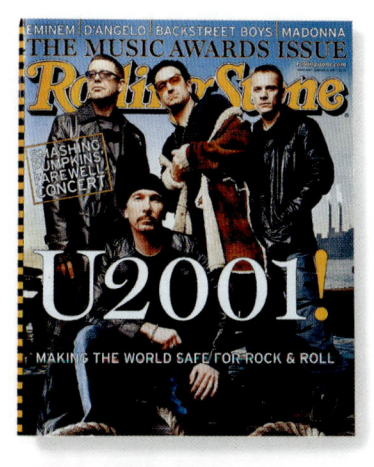

RS 855 | POP 100! THE 100 GREATEST POP SONGS
December 7th, 2000
ILLUSTRATION BY WARD SUTTON

RS 856/857 | BACKSTREET BOYS
December 14th – December 21st, 2000
PHOTOGRAPH BY DAVID LACHAPELLE

RS 858/859 | ROCK & ROLL YEARBOOK 2000
December 28th, 2000 – January 4th, 2001
VARIOUS PHOTOGRAPHERS

RS 860 | U2
January 18th, 2001
PHOTOGRAPH BY MARK SELIGER

50 YEARS OF COVERS • 467

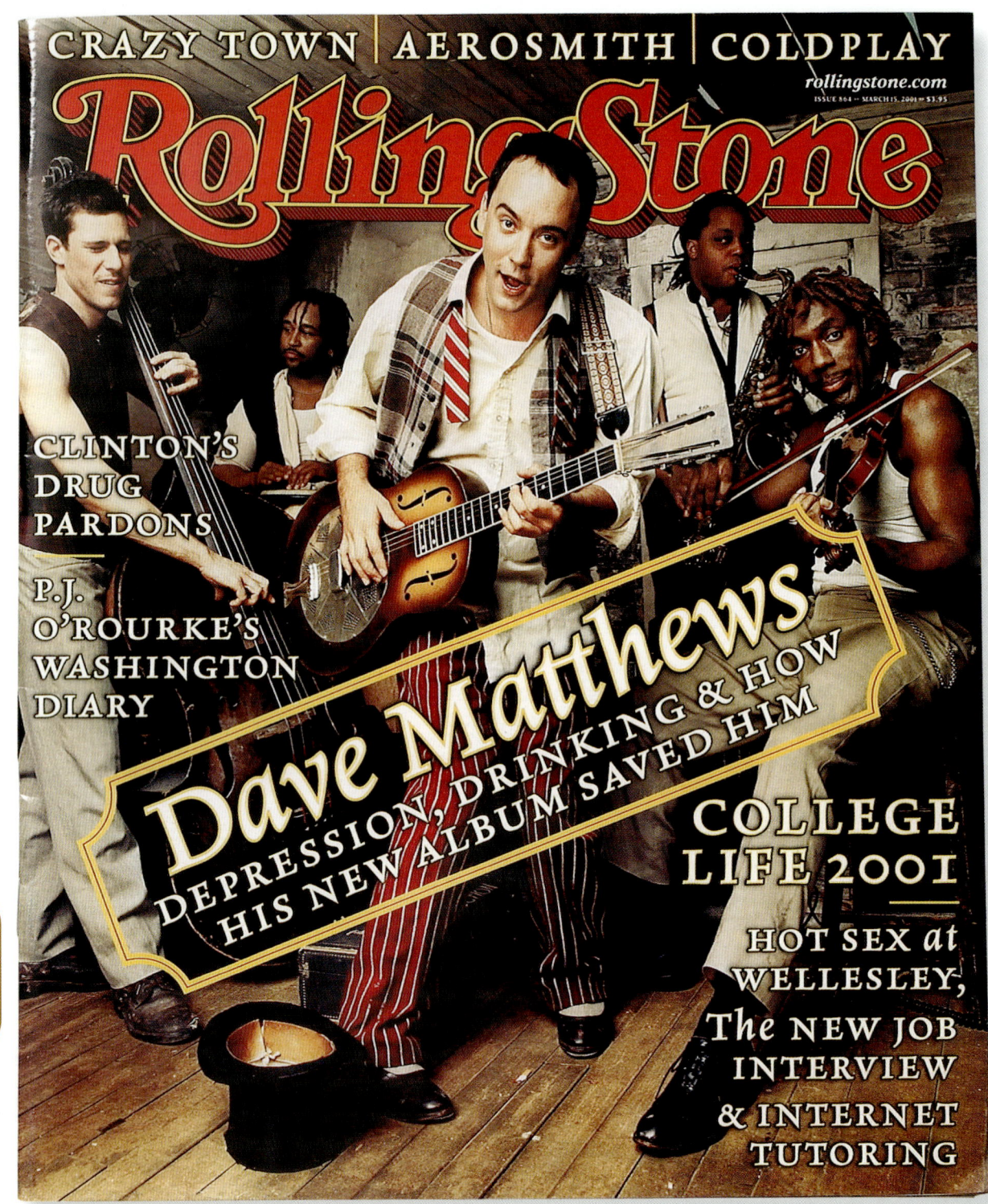

RS 864 | DAVE MATTHEWS BAND | March 15th, 2001 | Photograph by Mark Seliger

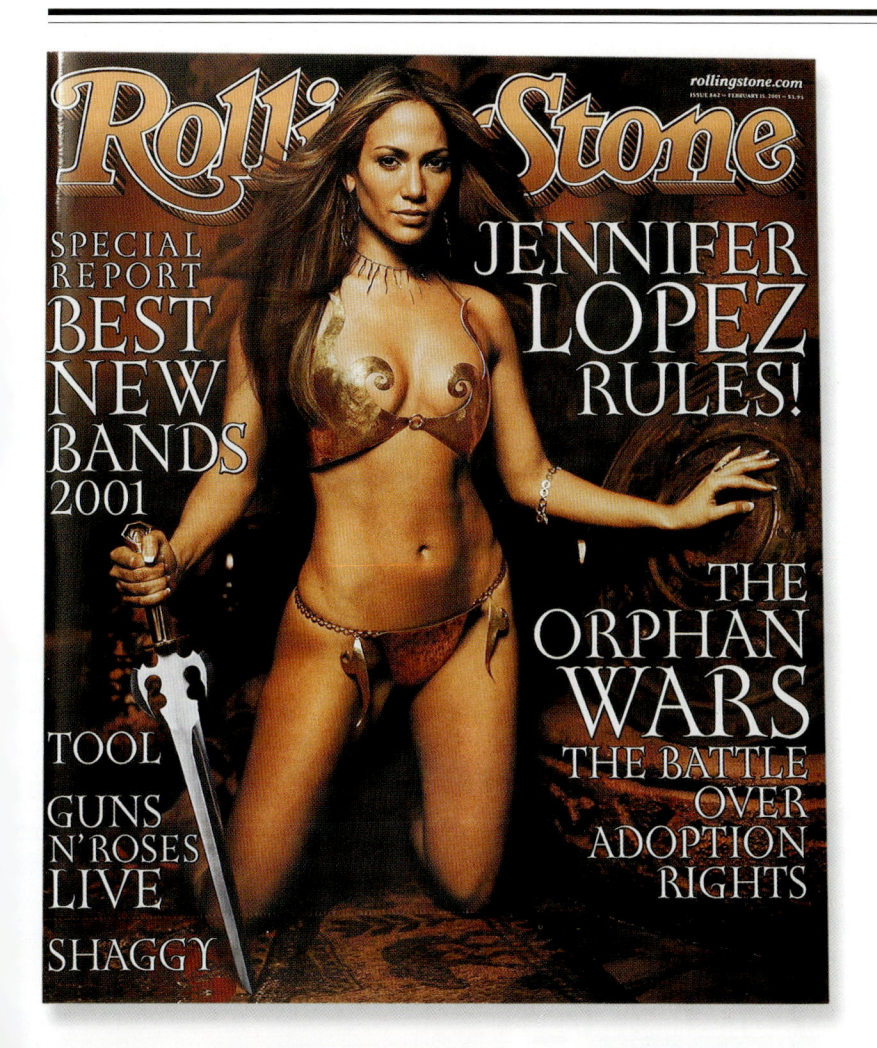

RS 862 | JENNIFER LOPEZ | February 15th, 2001 | Photograph by Mark Seliger

[RS 862] **The custom-made metal brassiere Jennifer Lopez wore for this cover now resides in the Rock and Roll Hall of Fame and Museum in Cleveland.**

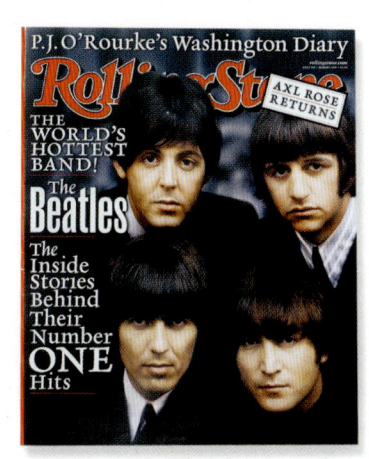

RS 863 | THE BEATLES
March 1st, 2001
Photograph by Robert Freeman

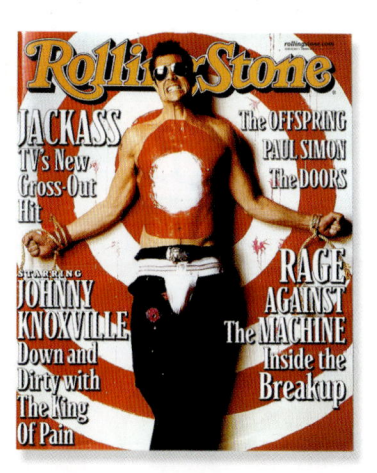

RS 861 | JOHNNY KNOXVILLE
February 1st, 2001
Photograph by Mark Seliger

50 YEARS OF COVERS • 469

Rolling Stone

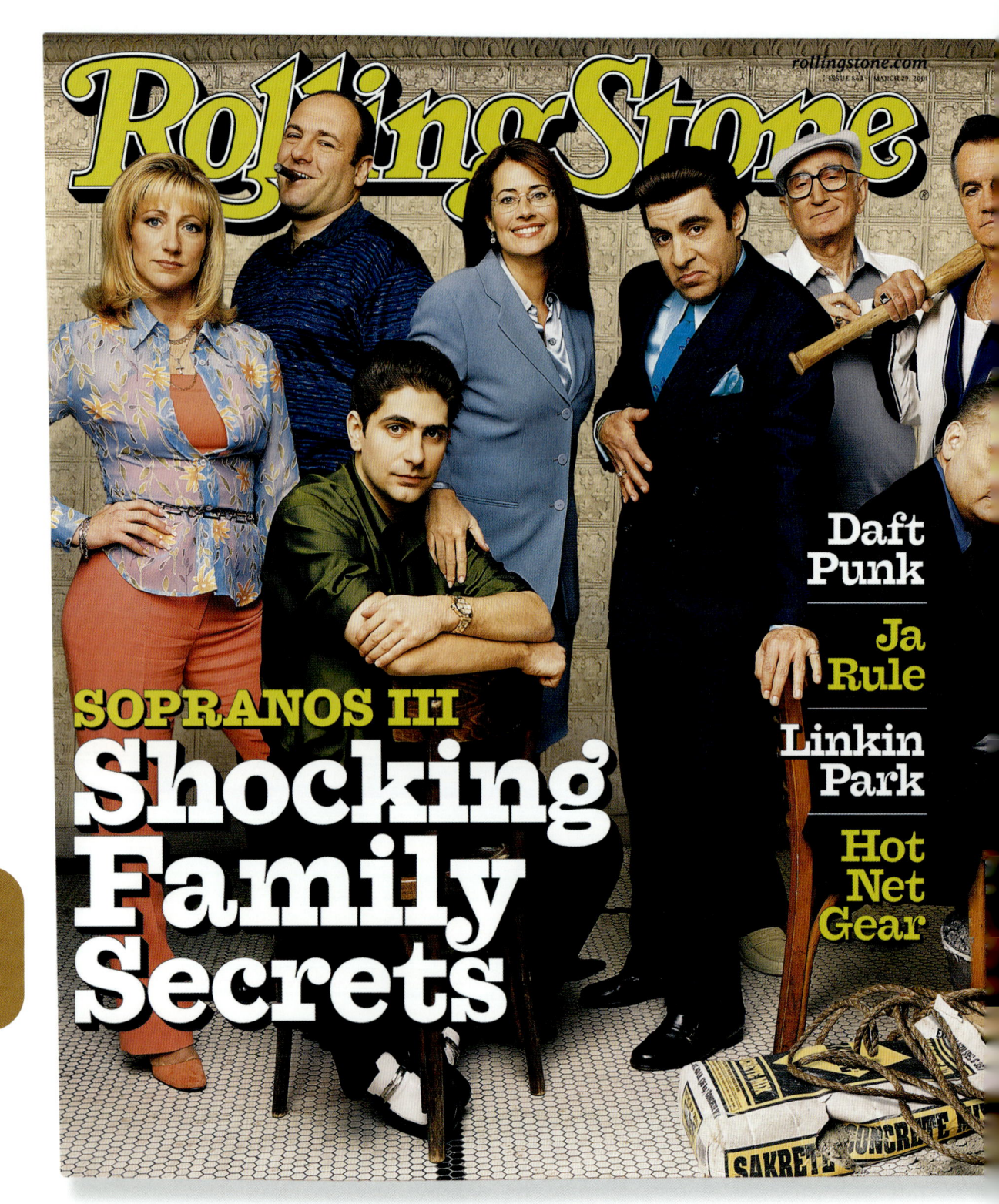

rollingstone.com

SOPRANOS III
Shocking Family Secrets

Daft Punk

Ja Rule

Linkin Park

Hot Net Gear

2000s

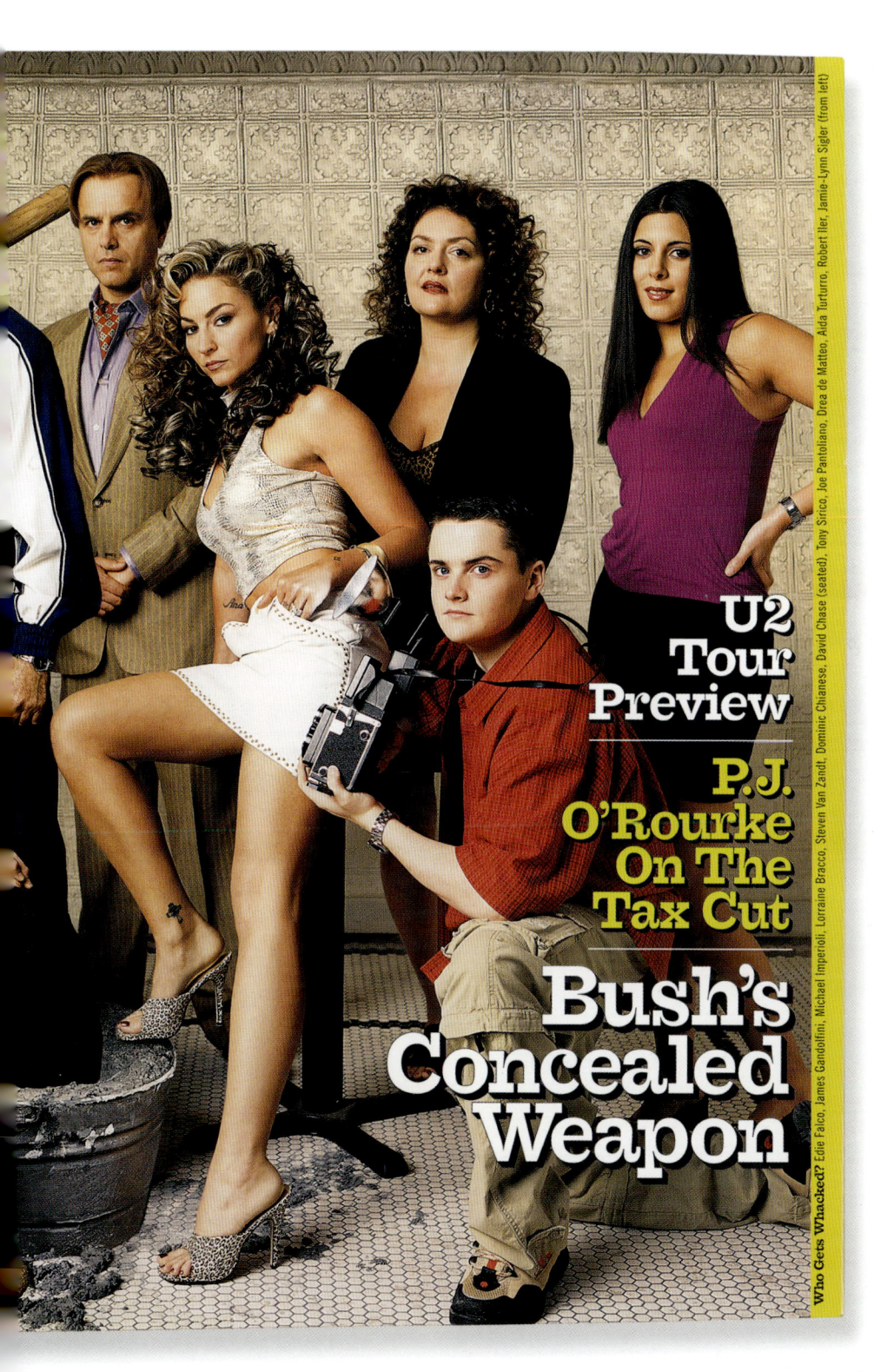

RS 865 | CAST OF 'THE SOPRANOS'
March 29th, 2001
PHOTOGRAPH BY MARK SELIGER

U2 Tour Preview

P.J. O'Rourke On The Tax Cut

Bush's Concealed Weapon

Who Gets Whacked? Edie Falco, James Gandolfini, Michael Imperioli, Lorraine Bracco, Steven Van Zandt, Dominic Chianese, David Chase (seated), Tony Sirico, Joe Pantoliano, Drea de Matteo, Aida Turturro, Robert Iler, Jamie-Lynn Sigler (from left)

50 YEARS OF COVERS • 471

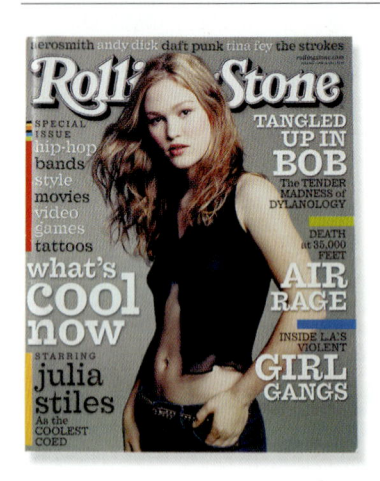

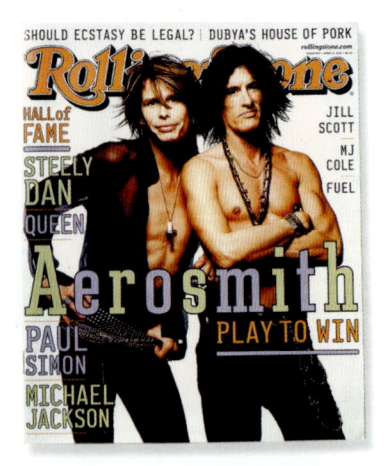

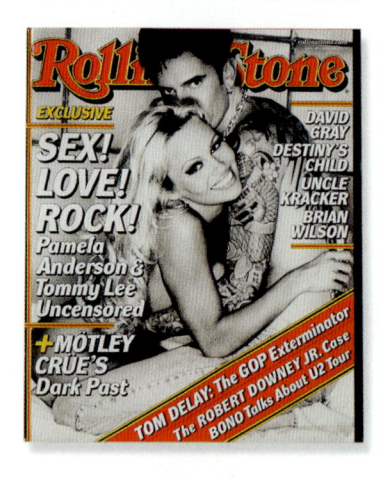

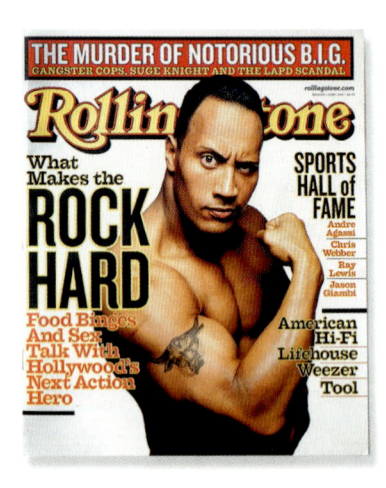

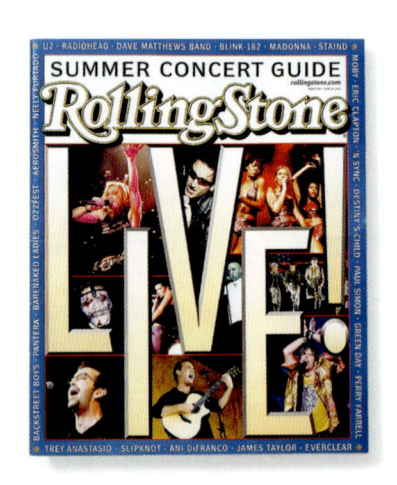

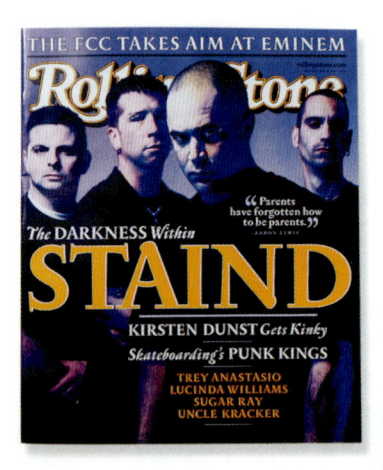

RS 866 | JULIA STILES
April 12th, 2001
Photograph by Patric Shaw

RS 870 | THE ROCK
June 7th, 2001
Photograph by Mark Seliger

RS 867 | STEVEN TYLER
& JOE PERRY
April 26th, 2001
Photograph by Mark Seliger

RS 871 | LIVE 2001
June 21st, 2001
Various photographers

RS 868 | PAMELA ANDERSON
& TOMMY LEE
May 10th, 2001
Photograph by Steve Wayda

RS 873 | STAIND
July 19th, 2001
Photograph by Mark Seliger

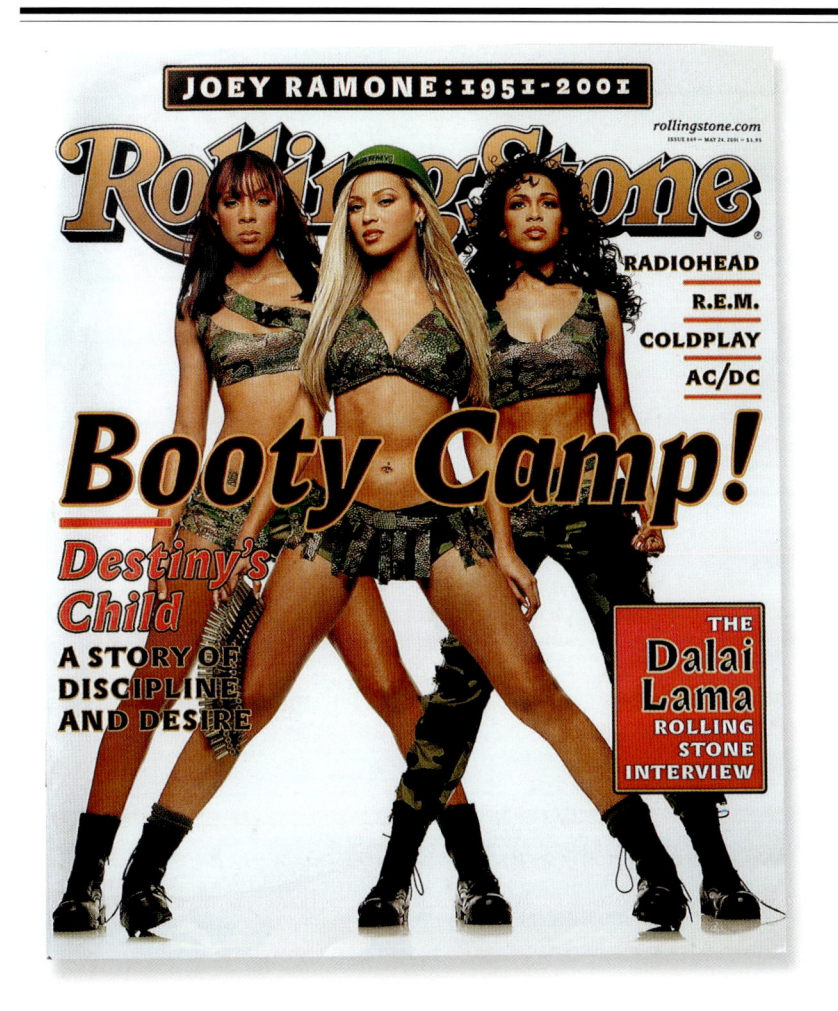

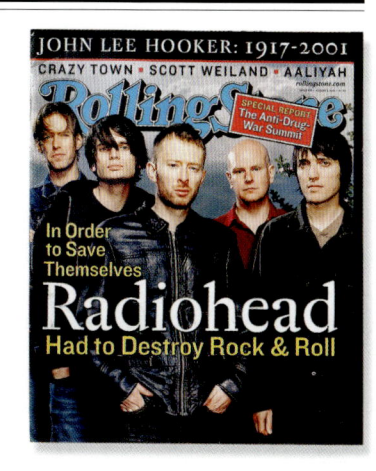

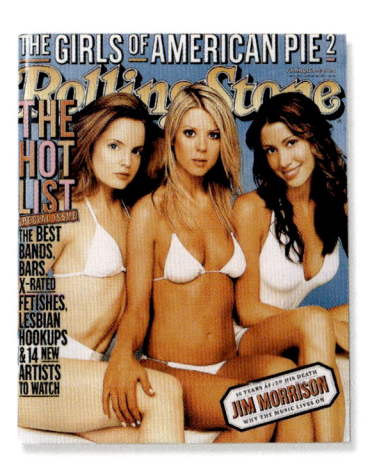

RS 869 | DESTINY'S CHILD
May 24th, 2001
PHOTOGRAPH BY ALBERT WATSON

RS 874 | RADIOHEAD
August 2nd, 2001
PHOTOGRAPH BY LEE JENKINS

RS 876 | THE GIRLS OF 'AMERICAN PIE 2'
August 30th, 2001
PHOTOGRAPH BY JIM WRIGHT

50 YEARS OF COVERS • 473

RS 875 | 'NSYNC: JC CHASEZ, LANCE BASS, CHRIS KIRKPATRICK, JUSTIN TIMBERLAKE & JOEY FATONE
August 16th, 2001
PHOTOGRAPHS BY MARK SELIGER

The editor's letter explains this multicover extravaganza: "For the first time in ROLLING STONE's history, we are publishing six separate, simultaneous covers. The five Brady-esque portraits of the members of 'NSync will travel to newsstands, supermarkets, bookstores and other destinations where single copies are sold; subscribers' copies feature a group shot." For the record, Chris Kirkpatrick was the only member to choose his own background hue: purple, his favorite color.

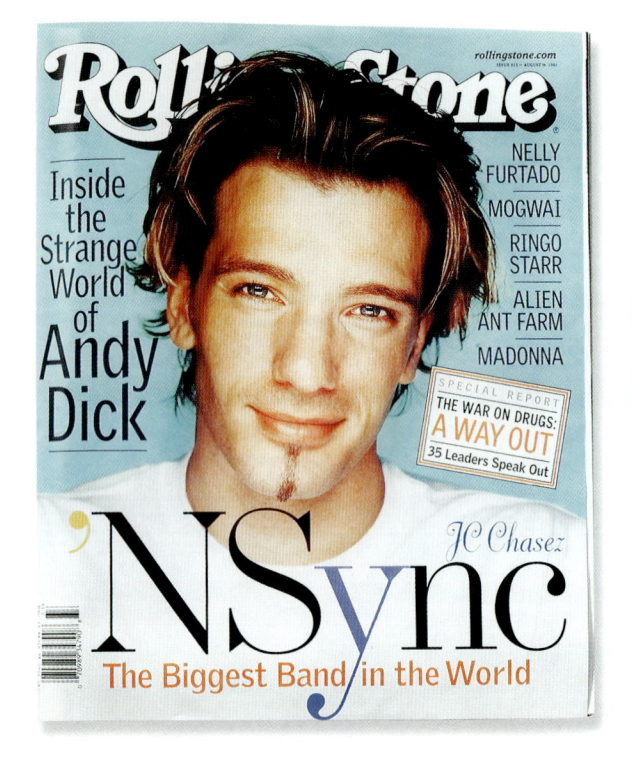

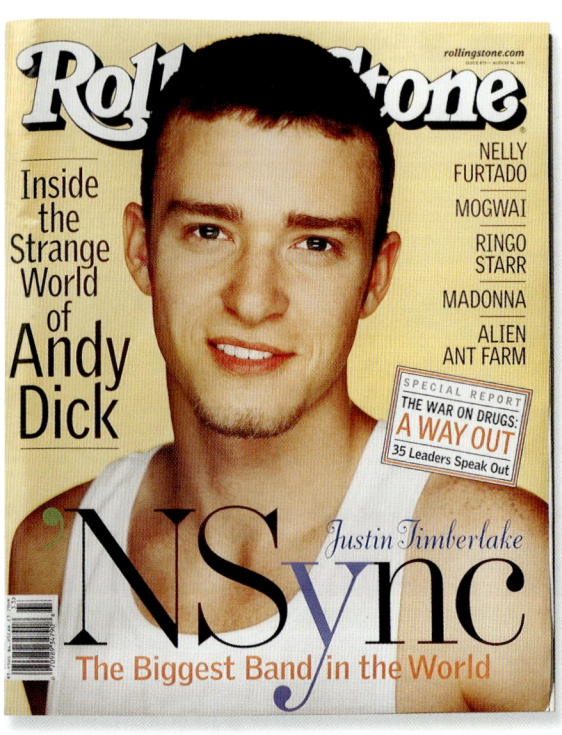

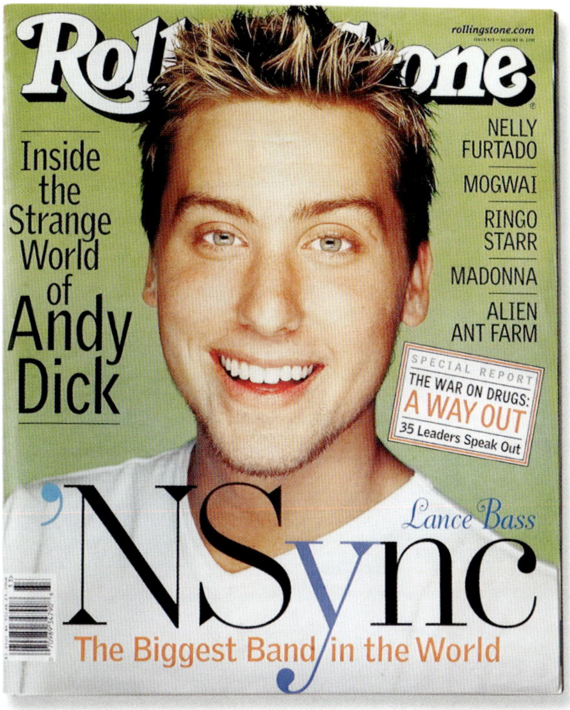
Rolling Stone
rollingstone.com
Inside the Strange World of Andy Dick
NELLY FURTADO
MOGWAI
RINGO STARR
MADONNA
ALIEN ANT FARM
SPECIAL REPORT
THE WAR ON DRUGS:
A WAY OUT
35 Leaders Speak Out
Lance Bass
'NSync
The Biggest Band in the World

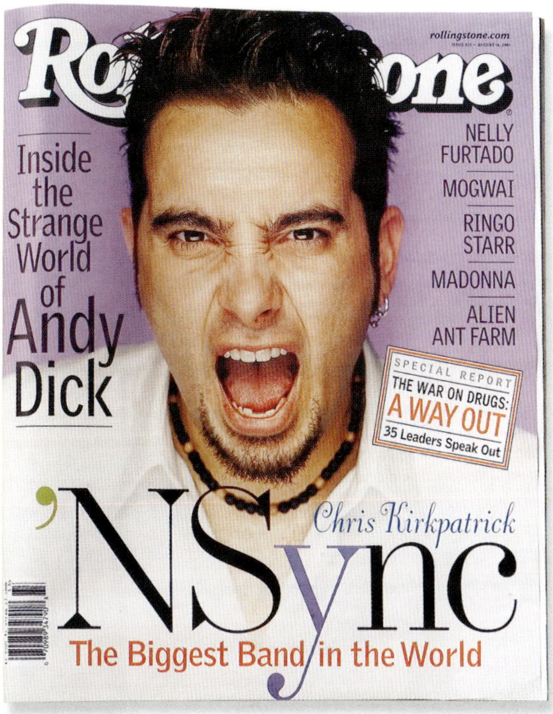
Rolling Stone
rollingstone.com
Inside the Strange World of Andy Dick
NELLY FURTADO
MOGWAI
RINGO STARR
MADONNA
ALIEN ANT FARM
SPECIAL REPORT
THE WAR ON DRUGS:
A WAY OUT
35 Leaders Speak Out
Chris Kirkpatrick
'NSync
The Biggest Band in the World

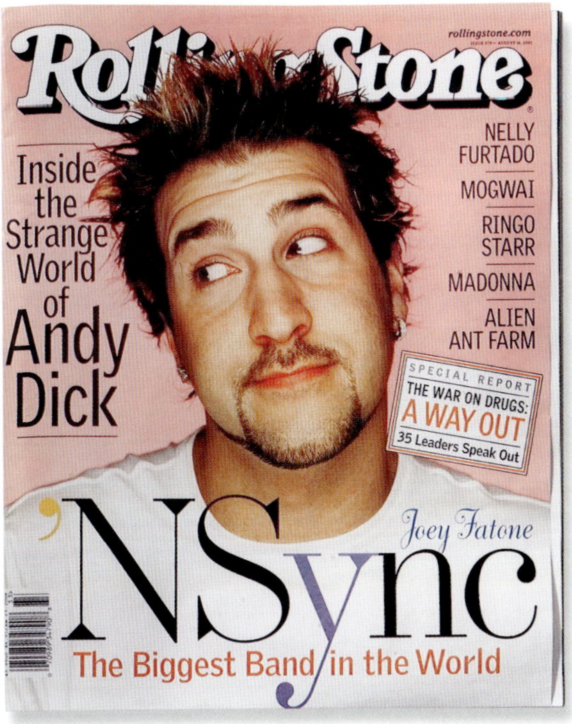
Rolling Stone
rollingstone.com
Inside the Strange World of Andy Dick
NELLY FURTADO
MOGWAI
RINGO STARR
MADONNA
ALIEN ANT FARM
SPECIAL REPORT
THE WAR ON DRUGS:
A WAY OUT
35 Leaders Speak Out
Joey Fatone
'NSync
The Biggest Band in the World

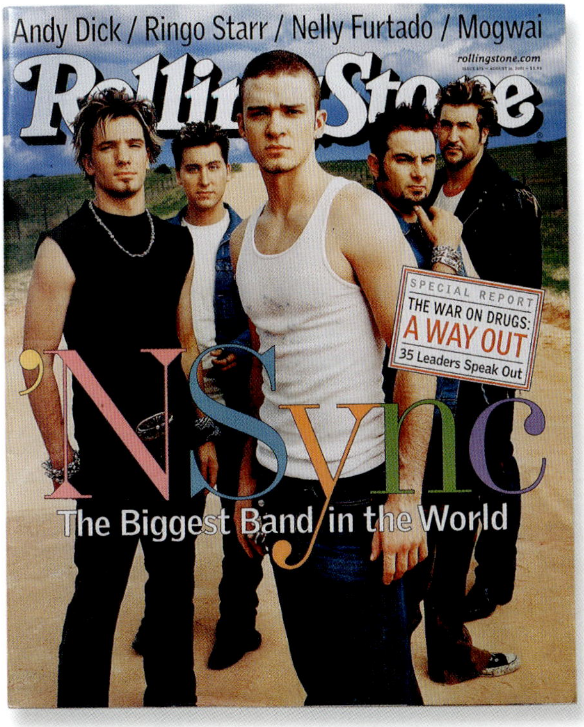
Andy Dick / Ringo Starr / Nelly Furtado / Mogwai
Rolling Stone
rollingstone.com
SPECIAL REPORT
THE WAR ON DRUGS:
A WAY OUT
35 Leaders Speak Out
'NSync
The Biggest Band in the World

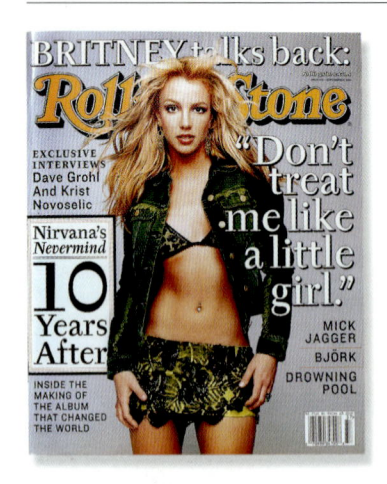

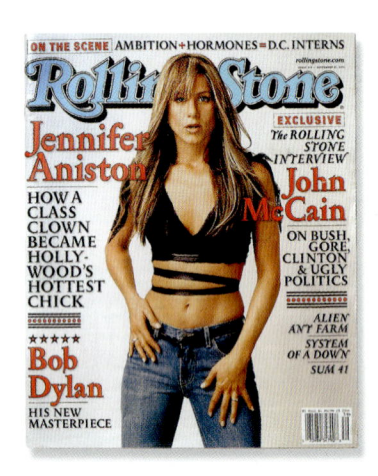

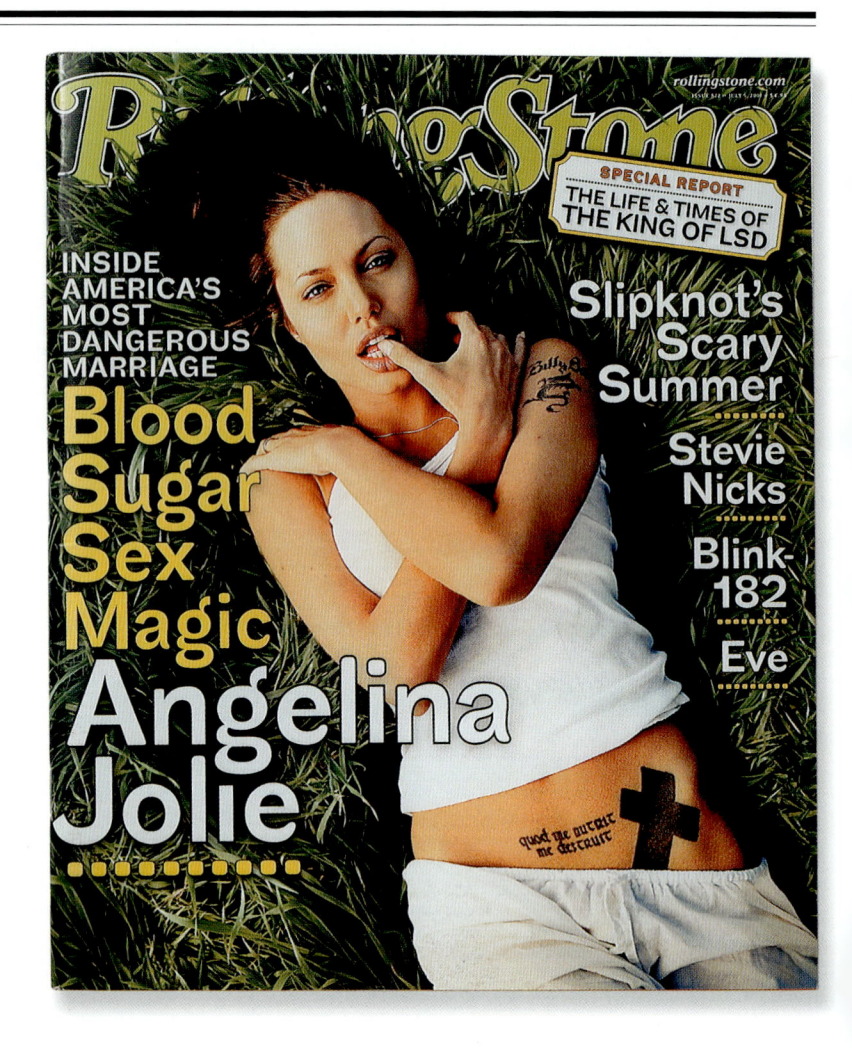

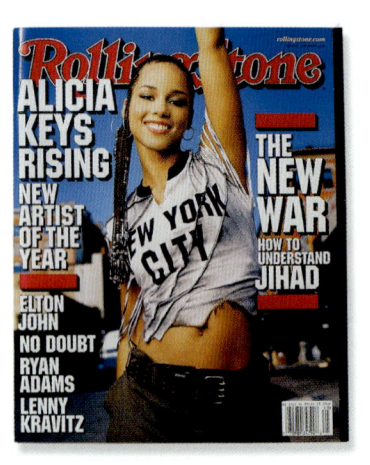

$\mathcal{RS}$ 872 | ANGELINA JOLIE
July 5th, 2001
Photograph by David LaChapelle

$\mathcal{RS}$ 877 | BRITNEY SPEARS
September 13th, 2001
Photograph by Patrick Demarchelier

$\mathcal{RS}$ 878 | JENNIFER ANISTON
September 27th, 2001
Photograph by Herb Ritts

$\mathcal{RS}$ 881 | ALICIA KEYS
November 8th, 2001
Photograph by Mark Seliger

2000s

476 • ROLLING STONE

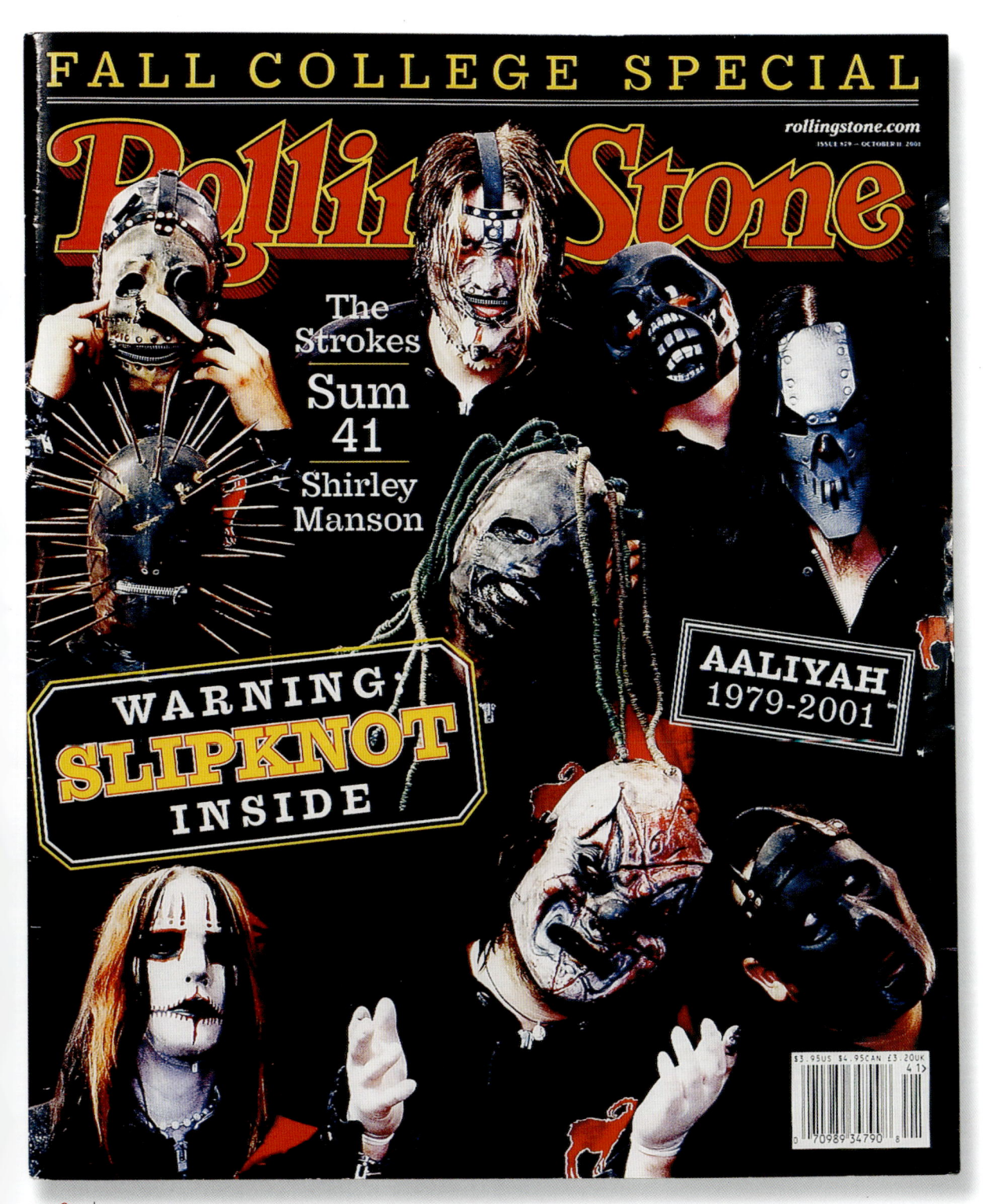

RS 879 | SLIPKNOT | October 11th, 2001 | Photograph by Martin Schoeller

A SPECIAL ISSUE | THE REALITIES OF GROUND ZERO...
HEROES OF NEW YORK... ELEGIES FOR AMERICA... MUSICIANS
UNITED... INSIDE THE HOLY WAR... MEMO TO THE PRESIDENT

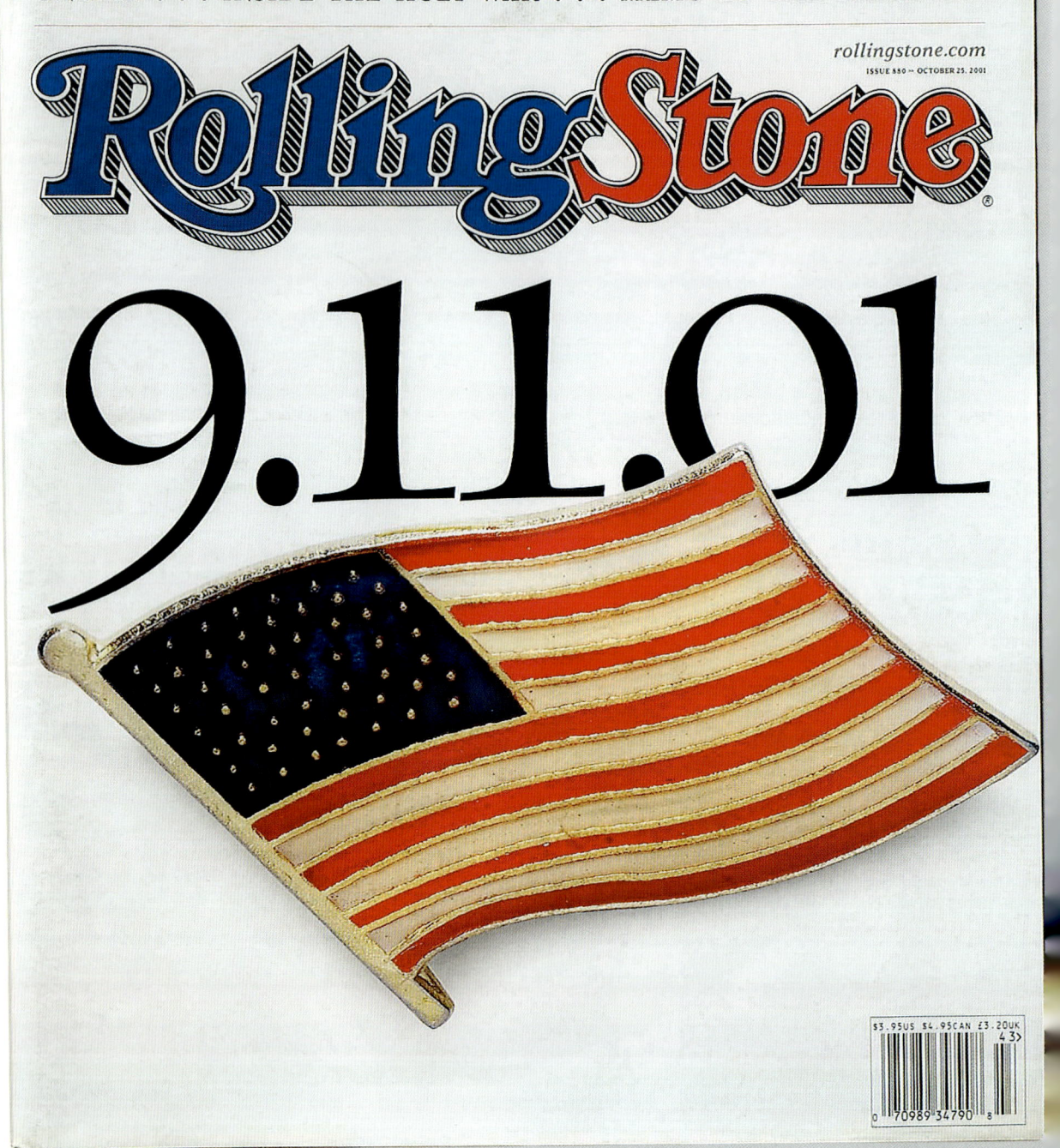

RollingStone

rollingstone.com
ISSUE 880 — OCTOBER 25, 2001

9.11.01

RS 880 | 9/11 – AMERICAN FLAG PIN | October 25th, 2001 | PHOTOGRAPH BY DAVIES & STARR

LETTER FROM THE EDITOR

New York City is our home.

It's been our home since 1977, when we moved the magazine here from San Francisco. The entire staff comes to work every day in an office tower next to Rockefeller Center that is four and a half miles north of where the World Trade Center stood. Most of us live in the city, some within a couple of blocks of the financial district, some close enough to it to have wondered why that airliner was flying so low on the beautiful new morning of September 11th.

On that Tuesday, the best of who we are was turned against us. Our open borders and immigration policies were exploited; our beneficent technology turned into tools of terror: the WTC towers, modern wonders of American engineering; four fully fueled Boeing jets, the most popular aircraft in the world and a testament to the superiority of American technology. The video images of the second jetliner knifing into the tower, the sharklike final turn, will be with us forever. The cold transaction of steel into steel, brought about by men armed with knives and razor blades.

There is cause to be worried about the future, about our economy, about our safety, about the men and women who are being called into service to protect us. September 11th is a pivot upon which we will view our future and our past.

—*Jann S. Wenner*

BUSH HAS JUST FINISHED HIS BIG talk to congress. The talk was planned to prepare us for war. It's going to get messy, everyone agrees. It's going to last for years and probably decades, everybody ruefully concedes. Nothing will ever be the same, everybody eventually declares.

Then why does it all sound so familiar? Because we are talking not just about war this time, but about the war above the war: the Real War. This war has already been waged, and it's not between the United States and the Taliban, but between the ancient, gut-wrenching, bone-breaking, flesh-slashing way things have always been and the timorous and fragile way things might begin to be. Could begin to be. Must begin to be, if our lives and our children's lives are ever to know honest peace. —*Ken Kesey*

"**WITH TERRORISM, WHETHER** you kill five people or five thousand, it is still a disregard for normal human values, what you expect in a civilized society. I never believed in violence as a way of achieving the political ends that we mentioned in songs like 'Street Fighting Man.' The people that believe in it – I have no time for them whatsoever.

"People are saying to me, and I felt the same way: 'I couldn't do anything for a week. My life, all my things, feel so trivial.' But to some extent, after the shock and mourning comes the adjustment to real life. During times of war, my parents tried to carry on as normally as much as you can, with adjustments. You can't let terrorists completely change your lifestyle. They would love that. That's a victory." —*Mick Jagger*

"I'm not leaving New York.

And neither is anyone else. We're here. We are quintessential Americans – we're not only American but New York–American."

—*Lou Reed*

I WAS ROCKETED OUT OF BED shortly before 9 A.M. by a bang that was shuddery even by New York's clamorous standards. Making our way down to the street, my girlfriend and I saw smoke filling the sky to the south, very nearby, and knots of puzzled people beginning to form on the corners below. Was it just a fire? A blown-out gas main? What? Then another explosion shook the scene, and suddenly an inconceivable word was in the air: terrorists.

Having raced back to the apartment to gather up our two dogs, I could hear the sounds of chaos and catastrophe mounting outside – sirens and screams and the horrendous, rumbling crunch of something unimaginably huge collapsing. Back down in the street, police and firefighters were everywhere. People were fleeing up Greenwich Street in unbridled panic. I braced myself against the wall of a building and stared up toward the twin towers of the World Trade Center, the neighborhood's most familiar and dominant sight. One of them – astonishingly, impossibly – gone. The other was hideously split and flaming.

—*Kurt Loder* [EXCERPTS FROM RS 880]

50 YEARS OF COVERS • 479

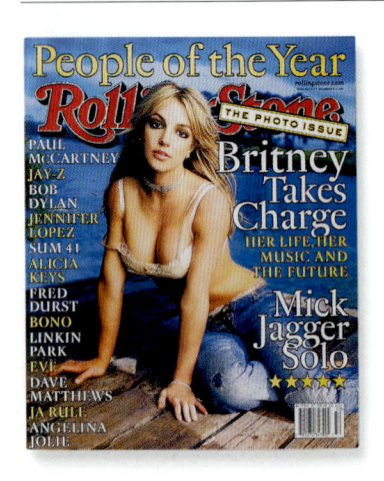

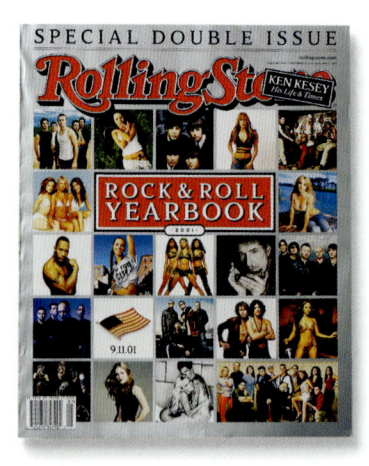

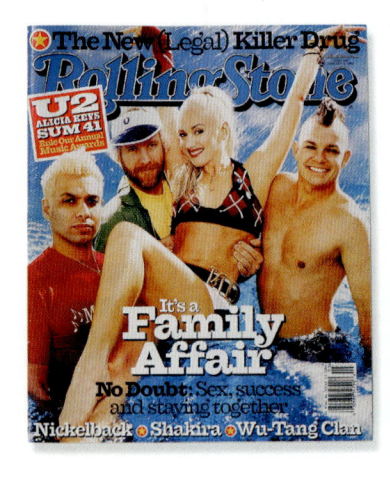

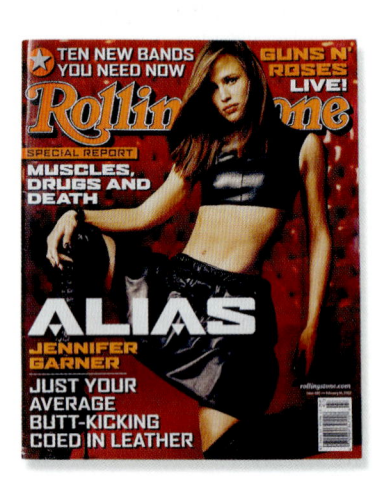

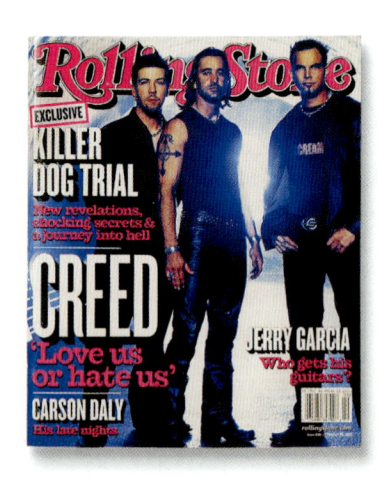

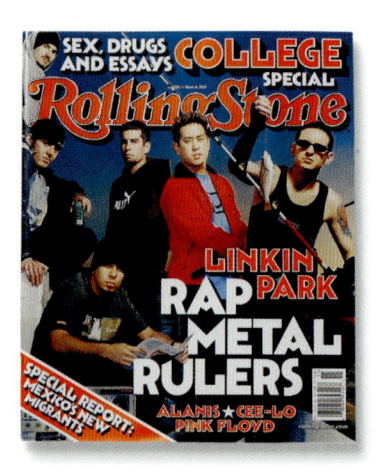

$\mathcal{RS}$ *883/884* | BRITNEY SPEARS
December 6th – December 13th, 2001
PHOTOGRAPH BY MARK SELIGER

$\mathcal{RS}$ *889* | JENNIFER GARNER
February 14th, 2002
PHOTOGRAPH BY ISABEL SNYDER

$\mathcal{RS}$ *885/886* | ROCK & ROLL
YEARBOOK 2001
December 20th, 2001 – January 3rd, 2002
VARIOUS PHOTOGRAPHERS

$\mathcal{RS}$ *890* | CREED
February 28th, 2002
PHOTOGRAPH BY LEN IRISH

$\mathcal{RS}$ *888* | NO DOUBT
January 31st, 2002
PHOTOGRAPH BY DAVID LACHAPELLE

$\mathcal{RS}$ *891* | LINKIN PARK
March 14th, 2002
PHOTOGRAPH BY MARTIN SCHOELLER

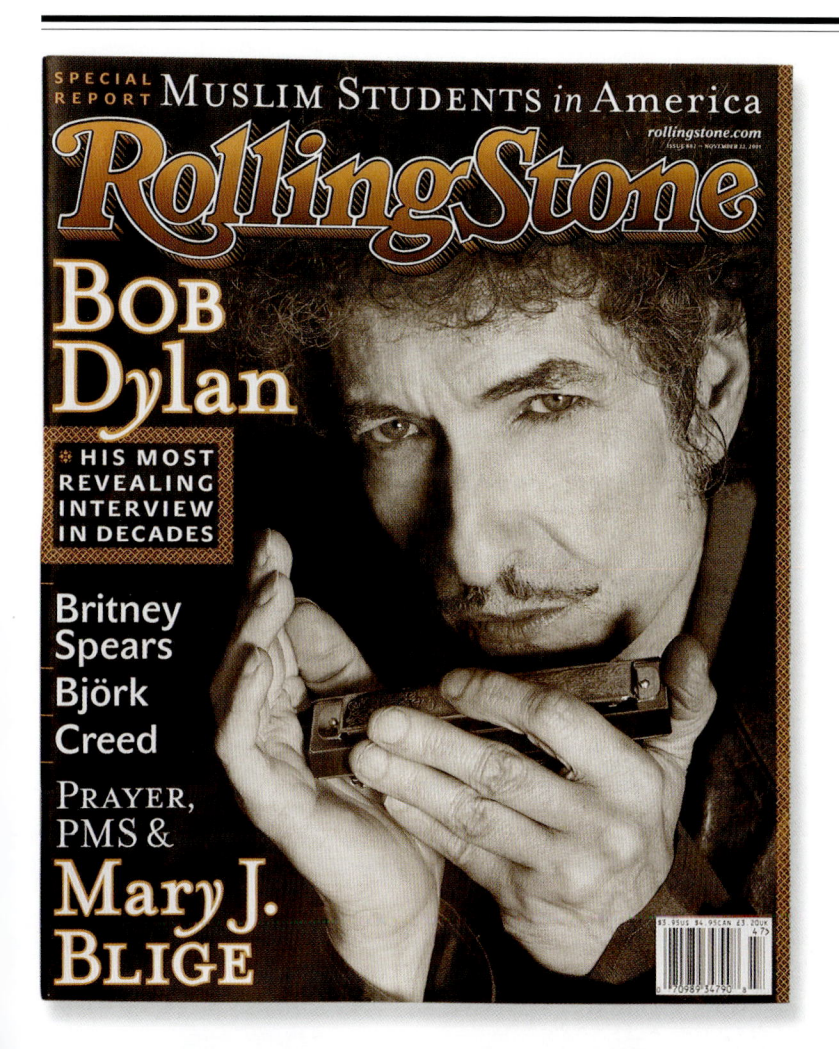

RS 882 | BOB DYLAN | November 22nd, 2001 | Photograph by Herb Ritts

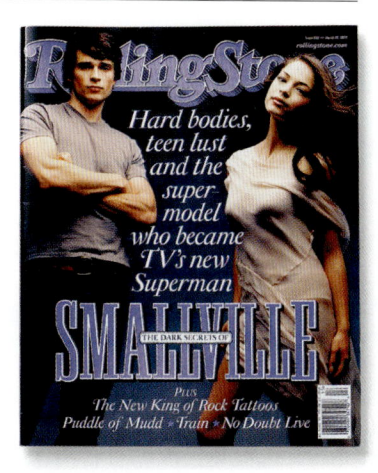

RS 892 | TOM WELLING AND KRISTIN KREUK OF 'SMALLVILLE'
March 28th, 2002
Photograph by Stewart Shining

"THERE ARE SO MANY WAYS to photograph something, so many interpretations. There's something about a photograph that can intrigue you. You can put it away and you want to see it again."

—Herb Ritts

Rolling Stone

rollingstone.com
ISSUE 887 · JANUARY 17, 2002

2000s

RS 887 | GEORGE HARRISON | January 17th, 2002 | Photograph provided by Michael Ochs Archives

HE LEFT THIS WORLD AS HE lived in it: conscious of God, fearless of death and at peace, surrounded by family and friends. He often said, "Everything else can wait, but the search for God cannot wait."

[FROM A STATEMENT BY OLIVIA AND DHANI HARRISON]

HE HAD BEGUN WORKING ON A NEW solo album when he was diagnosed with throat cancer in 1997. He later underwent surgery to have a nodule removed from his lung.... In May 2001, he again underwent surgery for lung cancer and, soon after, went to Switzerland for further treatment. The cancer, unfortunately, had spread to his brain. By the late fall, he was desperate to save his life, traveling first to Staten Island University Hospital in New York, and then to the UCLA Medical Center in Los Angeles. As all this was going on, in late November, keyboardist Jools Holland released a new album, with a track co-written by Harrison and Dhani, on which Harrison also plays guitar. It's called "Horse to the Water," and, in a perfect Harrison touch, the publishing credit reads RIP Music Ltd. 2001, a nod to the graveyard sendoff "rest in peace."

If anyone could view his own imminent death with a humorous detachment, Harrison could. This is a man, after all, who titled an album *All Things Must Pass* and wrote a song for it called "Art of Dying." Ever since he discovered Eastern religion in the mid-Sixties, he believed that this life was transient and that every human soul was on a journey to perfection. He moved in and out of the public eye, in and out of commercial favor, but his faith never wavered.

—*Anthony DeCurtis*

> "*He was a giant, a great,* great soul, with all the humanity, all the wit and humor, all the wisdom, the spirituality, the common sense of a man and compassion for people. He inspired love and had the strength of a hundred men.
>
> "He was like the sun, the flowers and the moon, and we will miss him enormously. The world is a profoundly emptier place without him."
>
> —*Bob Dylan*

> "**GEORGE WAS SO MANY THINGS** to the world: He was an innovative guitar player, a songwriter with words of wisdom and a man who introduced Eastern philosophy and music to the West. But in his private life, he was a man of wit and humor who made his friends laugh."
>
> —*Yoko Ono*

> "**GEORGE REALLY TREASURED HIS** friends. He once brought me four ukuleles in a week. I said, 'George, I don't think I need four ukuleles.' He said, 'Well, this one is better than the other ones. And it's just good to have them here – you never know when we're going to all be over and need them.' George's idea of a band was that everybody hung. From what he told me, the Beatles were that way. They were very, very tight. He really wanted the Traveling Wilburys to be like that. Like, 'If we're going to the party, we're all going.' I'm so glad I got to be in a band with him. He taught me so much."
>
> —*Tom Petty*

> "**GEORGE AND I KIND OF FORMED** – without talking too much about it, although we did have a laugh here and there – a bond, in that we felt we were fulfilling the same role within our respective bands. It was a nod and a wink to say, 'Well, they'd be nowhere without us.'
>
> He was a guy who only looked out for the best in people. I'm going to miss him. And if there is anything like heaven and shit like that, hopefully John and him are saying, 'How you doing, pal, want a drink?'"
>
> —*Keith Richards*

> "**WITHOUT GEORGE,** it all wouldn't have been possible. I'll miss him dearly and I'll always love him – he's my baby brother."
>
> —*Paul McCartney*

[EXCERPTS FROM GEORGE HARRISON TRIBUTE]

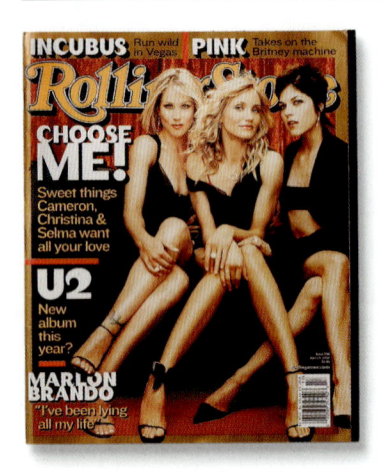

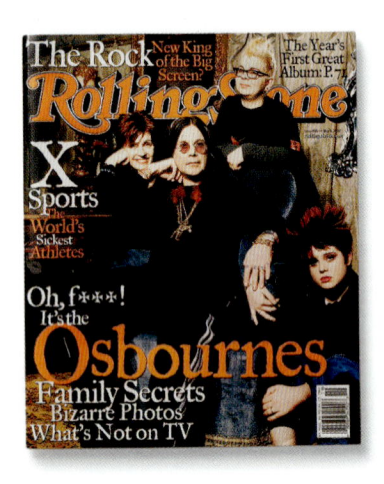

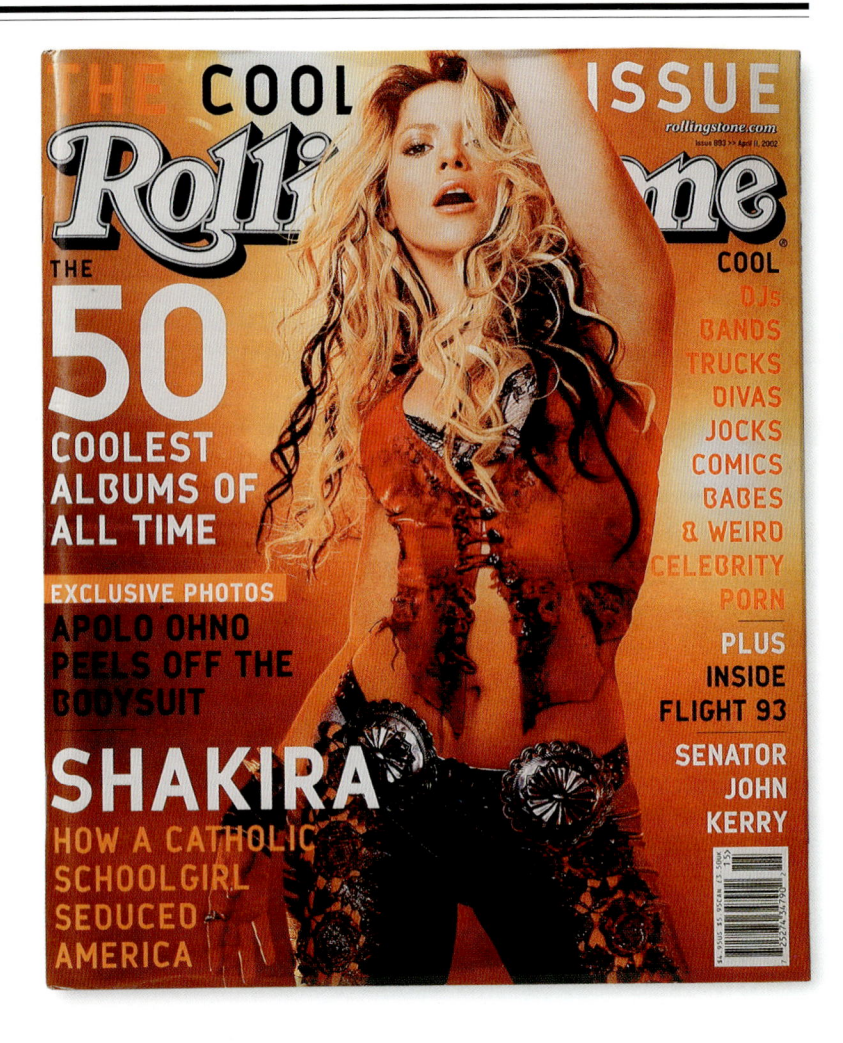

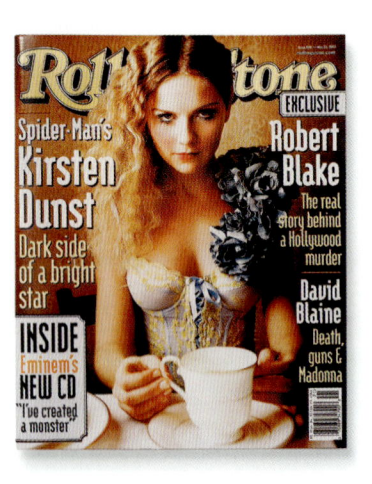

RS 893 | SHAKIRA
April 11th, 2002
PHOTOGRAPH BY MARTIN SCHOELLER

RS 894 | THE WOMEN OF 'THE SWEETEST THING'
April 25th, 2002
PHOTOGRAPH BY STEWART SHINING

RS 895 | THE OSBOURNES
May 9th, 2002
PHOTOGRAPH BY SOPHIE OLMSTED

RS 896 | KIRSTEN DUNST
May 23rd, 2002
PHOTOGRAPH BY DAVID LACHAPELLE

"*What is a* functional family? I know I'm dysfunctional by a long shot, but what guidelines do we all have to go by? The Waltons?"

—*Ozzy Osbourne*

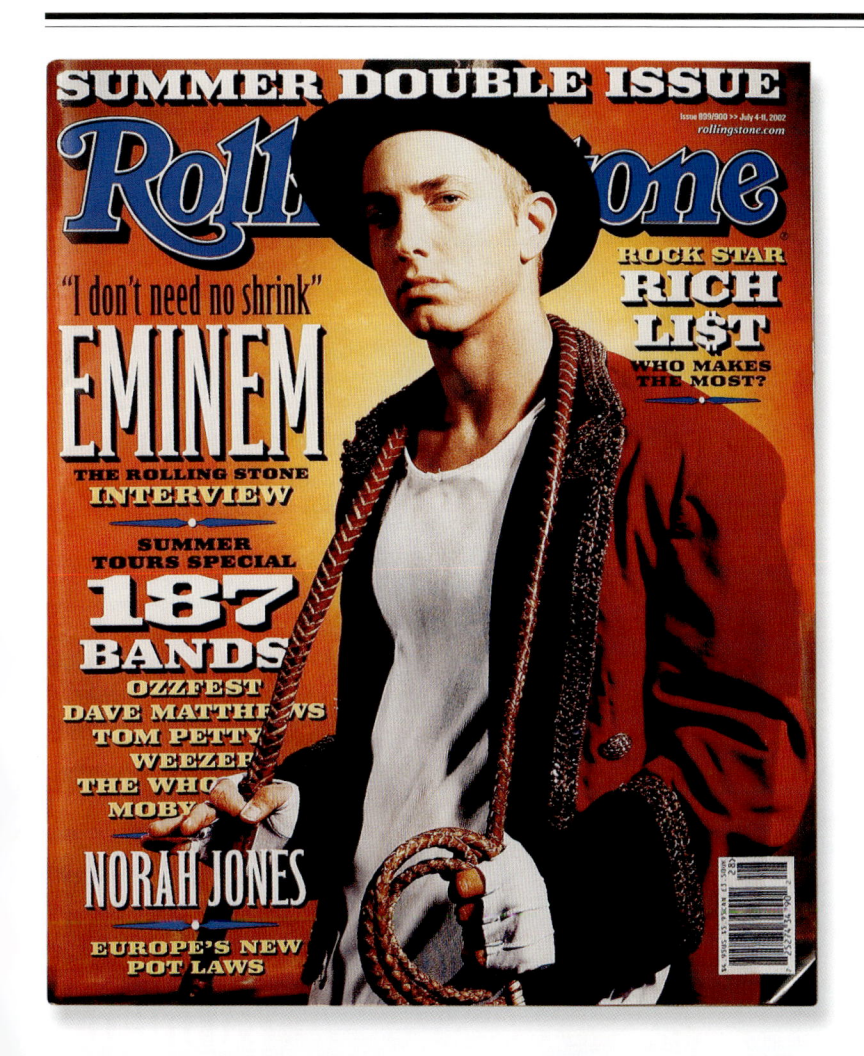

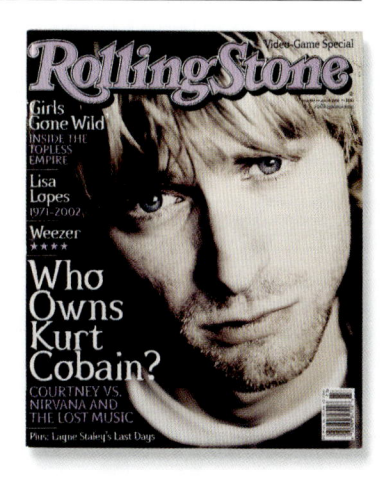

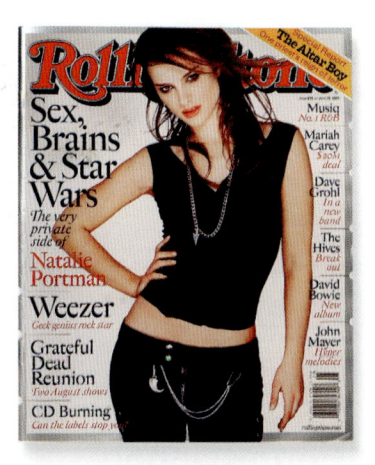

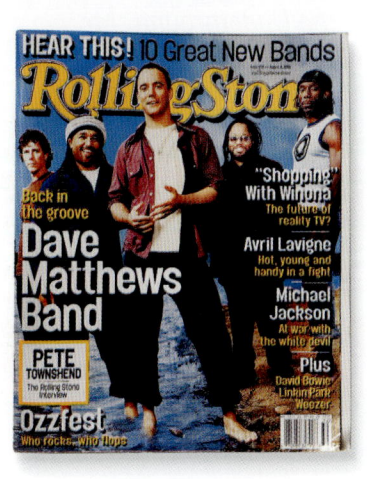

> "*It's obvious* to me that I sold double the records because I'm white. In my heart I truly believe I have a talent, but at the same time I'm not stupid."
>
> —*Eminem*

RS 899/900 | EMINEM
July 4th – July 11th, 2002
Photograph by Jeff Riedel

RS 897 | KURT COBAIN
June 6th, 2002
Photograph by Charles Hoselton

RS 898 | NATALIE PORTMAN
June 20th, 2002
Photograph by Albert Watson

RS 902 | DAVE MATTHEWS BAND
August 8th, 2002
Photograph by Martin Schoeller

SEX, DRUGS, DJs The World's Wildest Clubs

Rolling Stone

Issue 901 >> July 25, 2002
rollingstone.com

OZZY
The Rolling Stone Interview

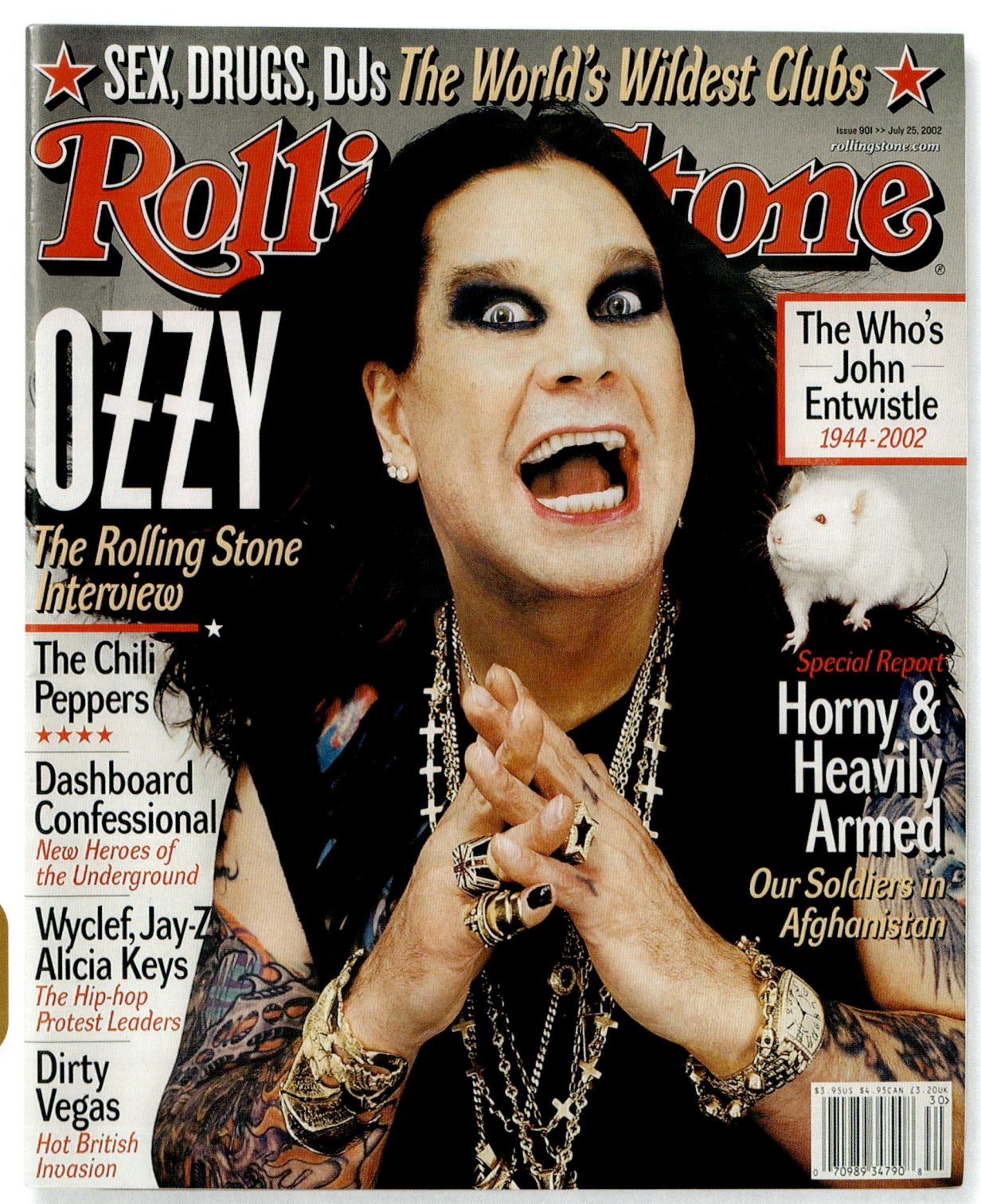

The Chili Peppers

Dashboard Confessional
New Heroes of the Underground

Wyclef, Jay-Z Alicia Keys
The Hip-hop Protest Leaders

Dirty Vegas
Hot British Invasion

The Who's John Entwistle
1944-2002

Special Report
Horny & Heavily Armed
Our Soldiers in Afghanistan

2000s

RS 901 | OZZY OSBOURNE | July 25th, 2002 | Photograph by Martin Schoeller

486 • ROLLING STONE

Issue 903 >> August 22, 2002
rollingstone.com

Rolling Stone

The White Stripes

THE NEW CARPENTERS?

Eminem
KILLS MOBY!

The Vines
ROCK & ROLL LUNACY

Stripper Sisters, Drugs & Murder

BUSINESS, ARIZONA-STYLE

Hip-hop's Wild Genius
IRV GOTTI UNCENSORED

The Gospel According to **BRUCE**

Plus: The Year's First ★★★★★ Album

RS 903 | BRUCE SPRINGSTEEN | August 22nd, 2002 | Photograph by Martin Schoeller

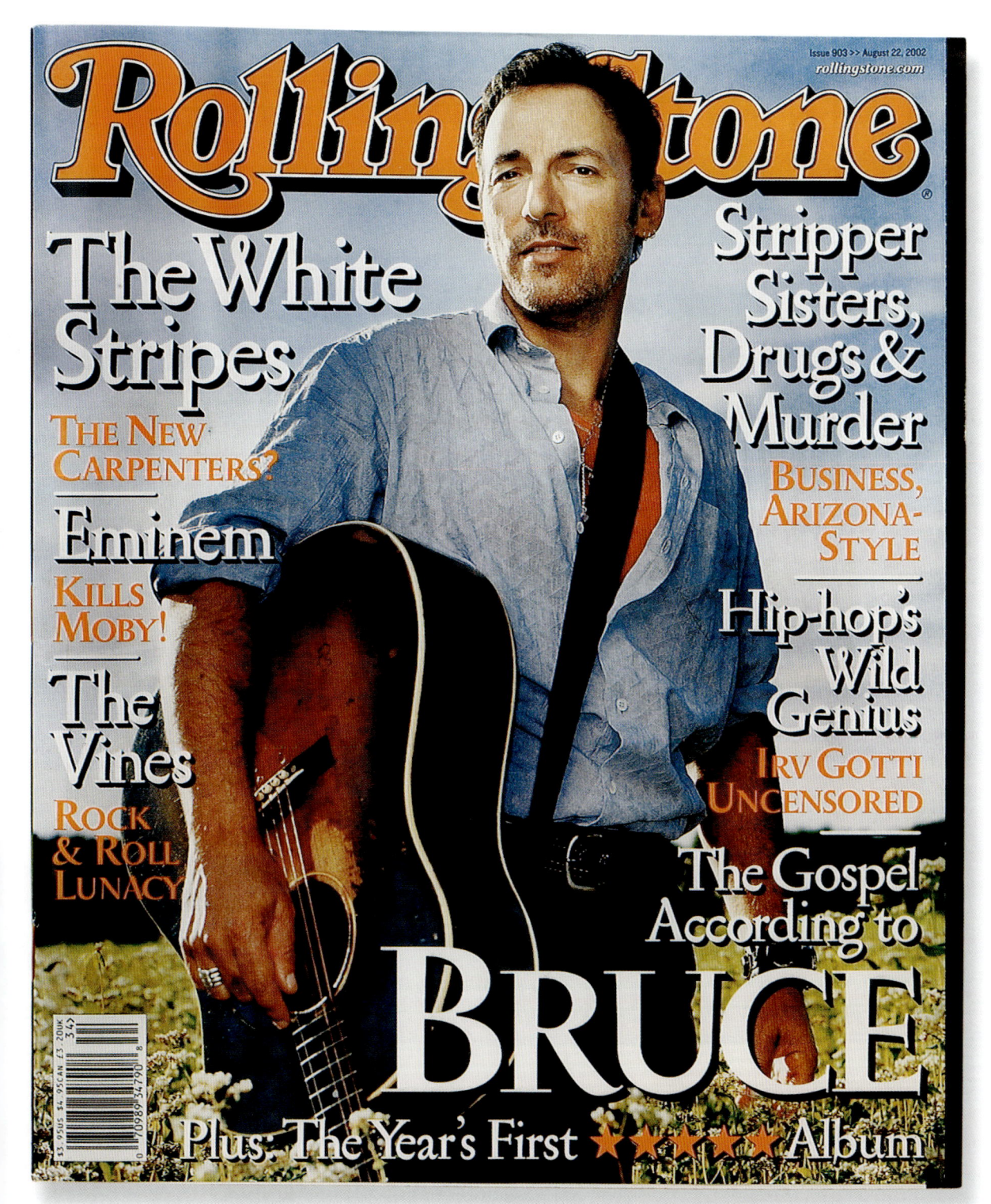

WOMEN IN ROCK SPECIAL ISSUE PLUS THE 50 B

Rolling Stone

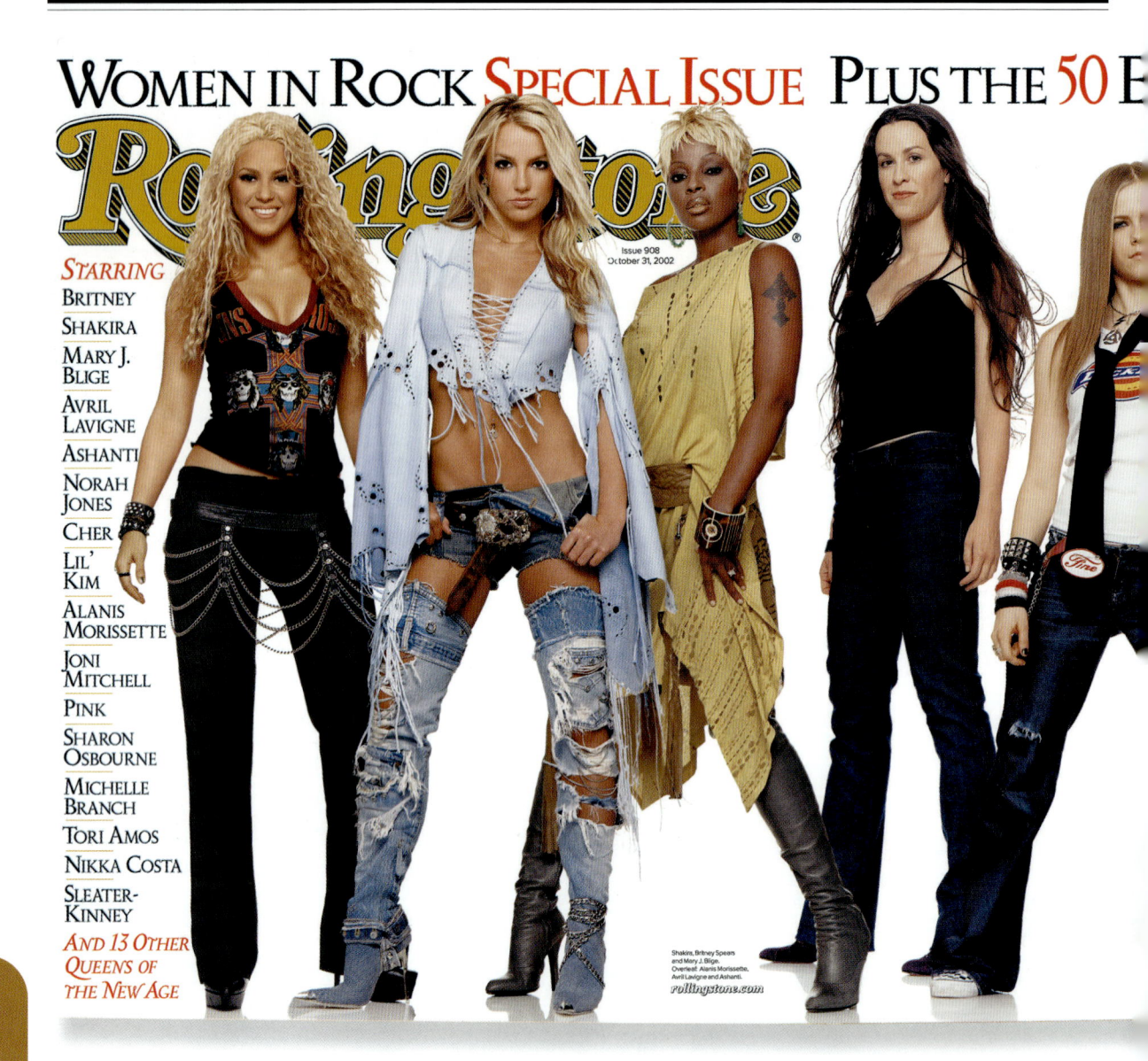

Issue 908
October 31, 2002

STARRING
BRITNEY
SHAKIRA
MARY J. BLIGE
AVRIL LAVIGNE
ASHANTI
NORAH JONES
CHER
LIL' KIM
ALANIS MORISSETTE
JONI MITCHELL
PINK
SHARON OSBOURNE
MICHELLE BRANCH
TORI AMOS
NIKKA COSTA
SLEATER-KINNEY

AND 13 OTHER QUEENS OF THE NEW AGE

Shakira, Britney Spears and Mary J. Blige. Overleaf: Alanis Morissette, Avril Lavigne and Ashanti.
rollingstone.com

2000s

RS 908 | WOMEN IN ROCK | October 31st, 2002 | PHOTOGRAPH BY ALBERT WATSON

488 • ROLLING STONE

ntial Albums

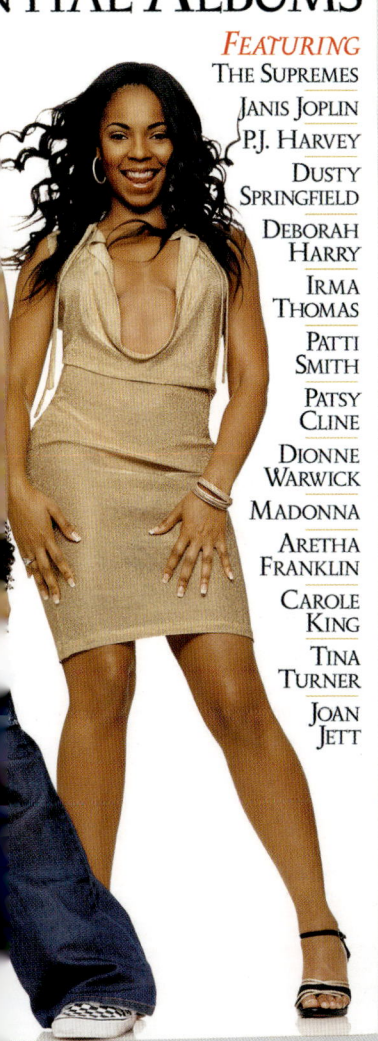

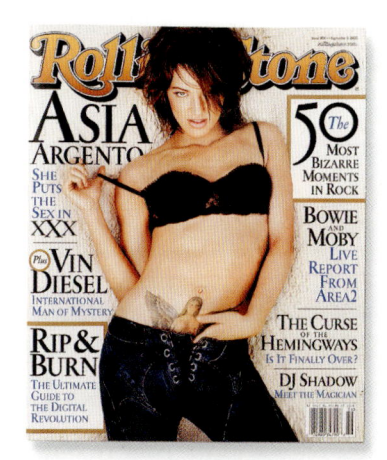

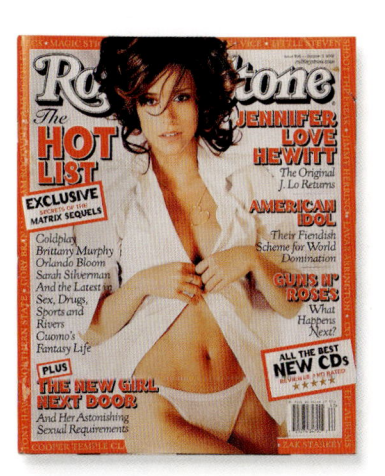

Featuring
THE SUPREMES
JANIS JOPLIN
P.J. HARVEY
DUSTY SPRINGFIELD
DEBORAH HARRY
IRMA THOMAS
PATTI SMITH
PATSY CLINE
DIONNE WARWICK
MADONNA
ARETHA FRANKLIN
CAROLE KING
TINA TURNER
JOAN JETT

RS 904 | ASIA ARGENTO
September 5th, 2002
PHOTOGRAPH BY TONY DURAN

RS 906 | JENNIFER LOVE HEWITT
October 3rd, 2002
PHOTOGRAPH BY MATTHEW ROLSTON

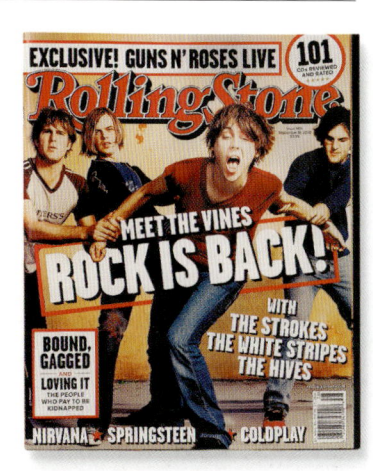

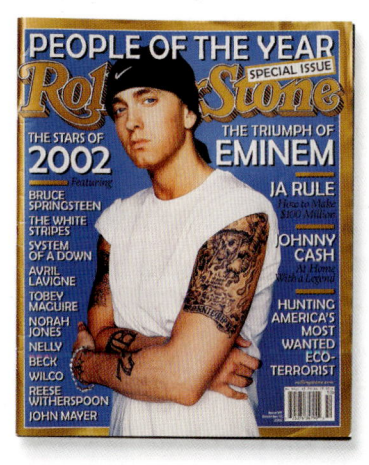

RS 905 | THE VINES
September 19th, 2002
PHOTOGRAPH BY MARTIN SCHOELLER

RS 911 | EMINEM
December 12th, 2002
PHOTOGRAPH BY MARY ELLEN MATTHEWS

50 YEARS OF COVERS • 489

RS 907 | KEITH RICHARDS | October 17th, 2002 | Photograph by Sante D'Orazio

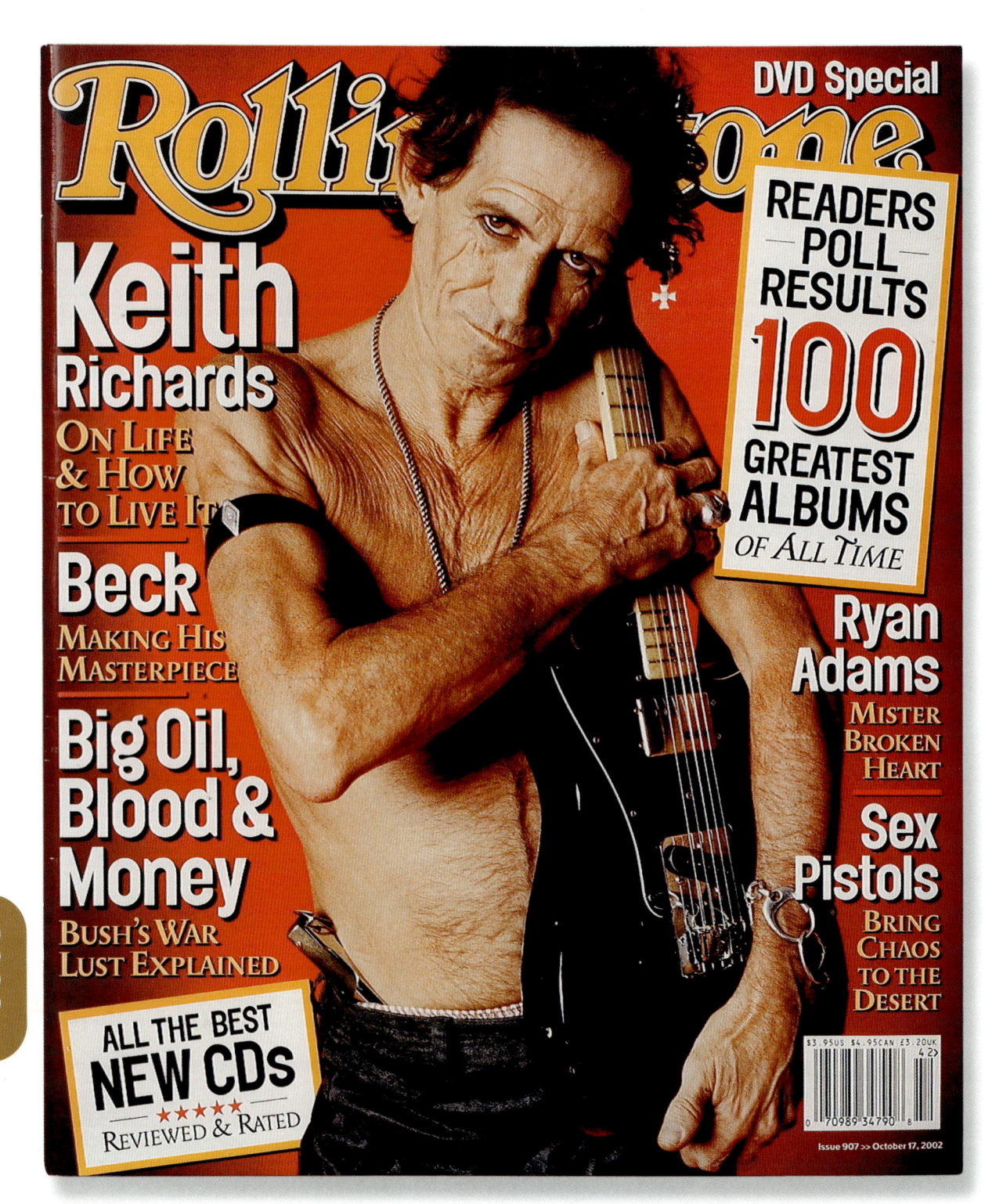

Rolling Stone

Issue 909 >> November 14, 2002
rollingstone.com

Ultra-Cool Cars
...and the Rock Stars Who Love Them

Plus
Bowie
Eminem
Nirvana
Tom Petty
The Hives
Bright Eyes
Foo Fighters

Are We Gun Crazy?
Michael Moore on America's Fatal Addiction

Christina Aguilera
Inside the Dirty Mind of a Pop Princess

RS 909 | CHRISTINA AGUILERA | November 14th, 2002 | PHOTOGRAPH BY ALBERT WATSON

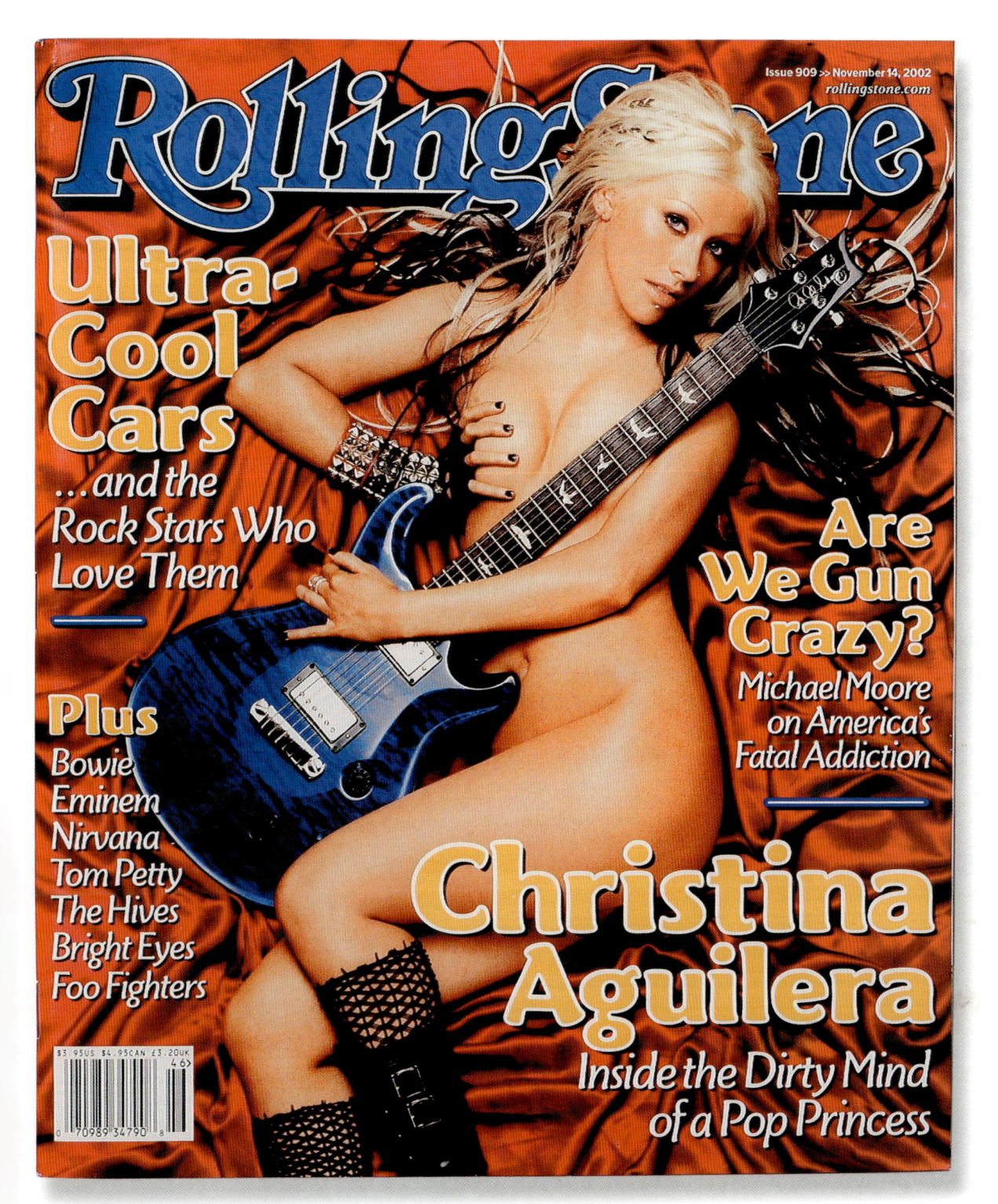

50 YEARS OF COVERS • 491

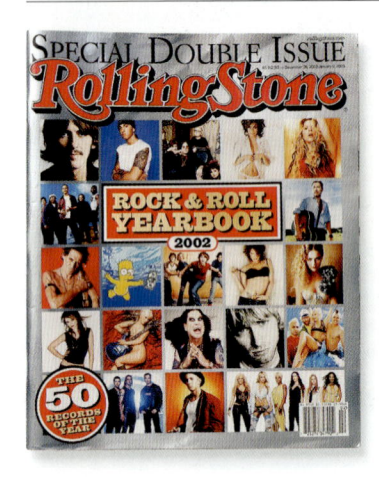

RS 912/913 | ROCK & ROLL YEARBOOK 2002
December 26th, 2002 – January 9th, 2003
VARIOUS PHOTOGRAPHERS

[RS 910] For our special Simpsons package, ROLLING STONE brainstormed with Matt Groening and the Simpsons art department to come up with the most iconic album covers to lampoon. Alas, we could only put three of them – Nirvana's *Nevermind*, Bruce Springsteen's *Born in the U.S.A.* and the Beatles' *Abbey Road* – on the front of our magazine. Herewith are some that didn't make the cut: Fleetwood Mac's *Rumours*, starring Homer and Marge as Mick Fleetwood and Stevie Nicks; Homer as both Michael Jackson on *Thriller* and David Bowie's *Aladdin Sane*; and Carl, Moe, Homer and Lenny, in front of a brick wall, spoofing the Ramones' self-titled debut. Of course in this instance, the word *Ramones* has been strategically vandalized to read RAMOES.

> "*I started out animating on* The Simpsons and now I'm the creative director over at Fox, so I do lots of magazine covers. I've done a lot of really cool ones, but those were by far the coolest covers I've ever done. I don't have any Simpsons work hanging up in my house, but I have the three covers framed. Matt Groening also sent me a letter thanking me, and he said that now he has something to show his mom."
>
> —Julius Preite

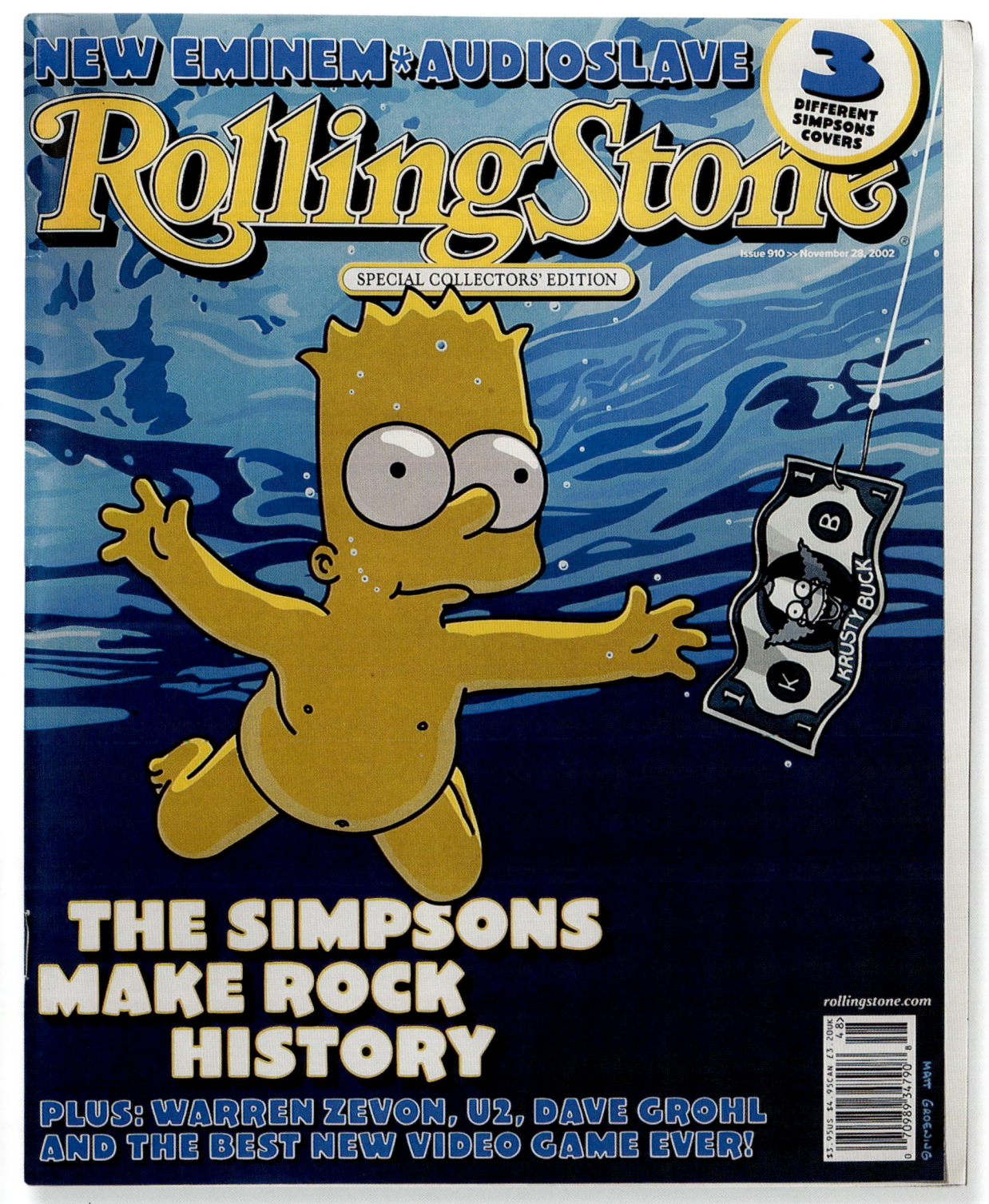

RS 910 | BART SIMPSON | November 28th, 2002 | Illustration by Julius Preite

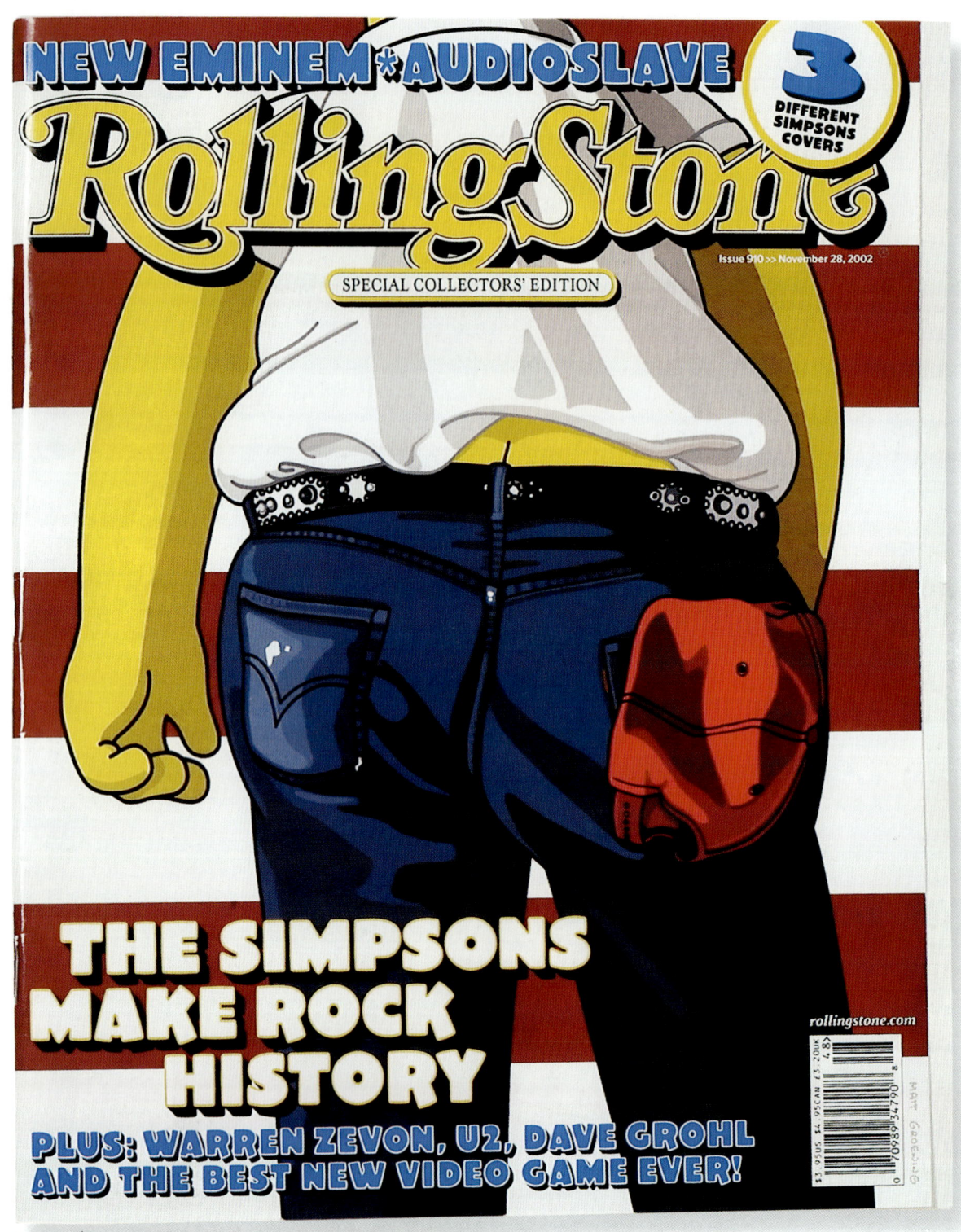

2000s

RS 910 | HOMER SIMPSON | November 28th, 2002 | ILLUSTRATION BY JULIUS PREITE

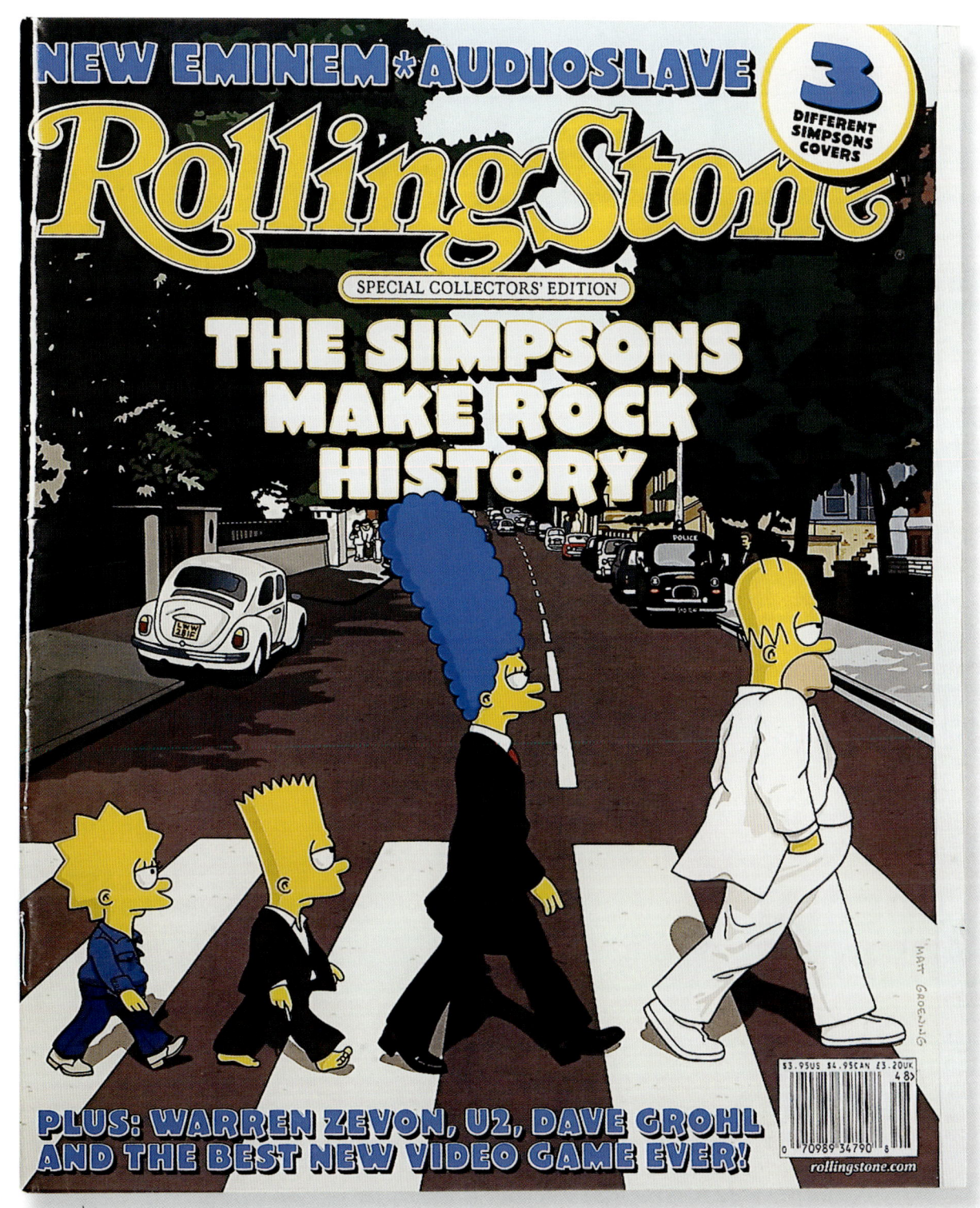

RS 910 | THE SIMPSONS | November 28th, 2002 | ILLUSTRATION BY JULIUS PREITE

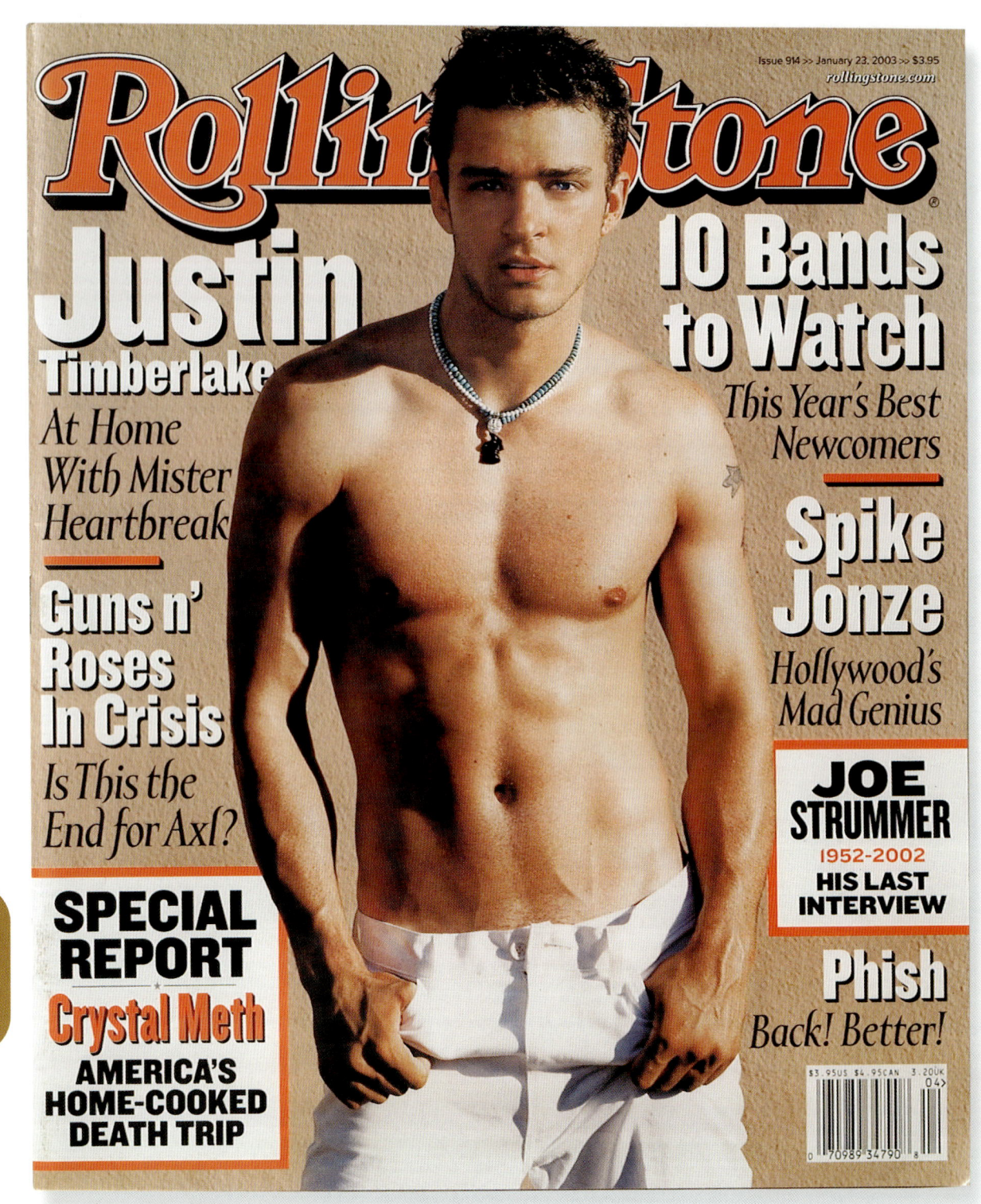

Rolling Stone

Issue 914 >> January 23, 2003 >> $3.95
rollingstone.com

Justin Timberlake
At Home With Mister Heartbreak

Guns n' Roses In Crisis
Is This the End for Axl?

10 Bands to Watch
This Year's Best Newcomers

Spike Jonze
Hollywood's Mad Genius

JOE STRUMMER
1952-2002
HIS LAST INTERVIEW

Phish
Back! Better!

SPECIAL REPORT
Crystal Meth
AMERICA'S HOME-COOKED DEATH TRIP

2000s

RS 914 | JUSTIN TIMBERLAKE | January 23rd, 2003 | Photograph by Herb Ritts

[RS 914] Justin Timberlake's first cover as a solo artist was also Herb Ritts's forty-sixth and final cover for ROLLING STONE. The photographer died of complications from pneumonia on December 26th, 2002.

"I'M A VERY LOVING, CARING

person," [Timberlake] was saying, "and if I start dating you – you know, as a girl – it may take me a long time to give myself away to you, but once I do, that's it. You can have whatever you want. But I've had my heart broken plenty of times."

He pressed his lips together and fluttered a sad noise.

"Three times, actually," he continued. "I was fifteen the first time. She cheated on me, and I broke up with her. That's reason enough, right? 'Oops, sorry, see you.' I'd been going with her for a year. The second one I saw for a year and a half. And the third one" – and here he paused, thinking of Spears – "was for three and a half years. It was the same with her as with the first girl who broke my heart and the second. They've all gone down the same way. All of them. Three strikes, I'm out. I mean, she has a beautiful heart, but if I've lost my trust in someone, I don't think it's right for me to be with them. I'm not going to let my baggage with somebody else become my baggage with a new person. But I'll tell you, man, I have little, little hope. Three strikes. Little hope."

So that's the way it is with him. The girls he loves apparently cheat on him. It's an embarrassing thing, especially for a star of Timberlake's magnitude; but worse, it's a terrible personal tragedy, excruciating to the heart and a burden on the soul.

[EXCERPT FROM RS 914 COVER STORY BY ERIK HEDEGAARD]

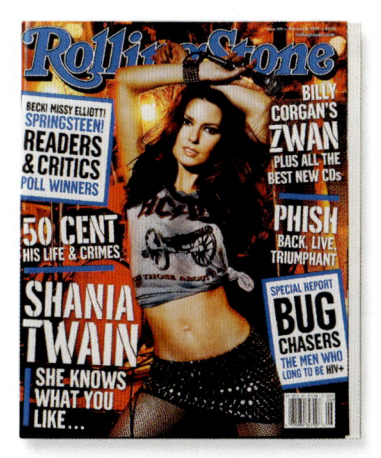

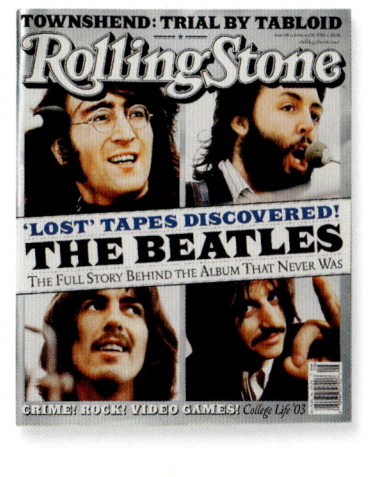

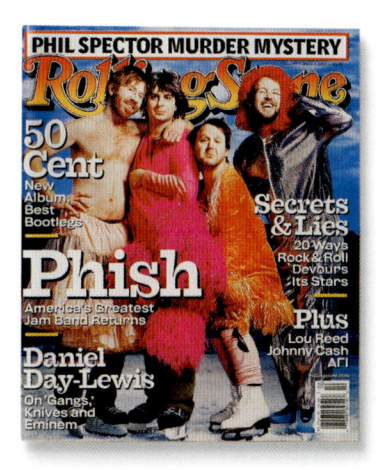

RS 915 | SHANIA TWAIN
February 6th, 2003
PHOTOGRAPH BY MICHAEL THOMPSON

RS 917 | PHISH
March 6th, 2003
PHOTOGRAPH BY MARTIN SCHOELLER

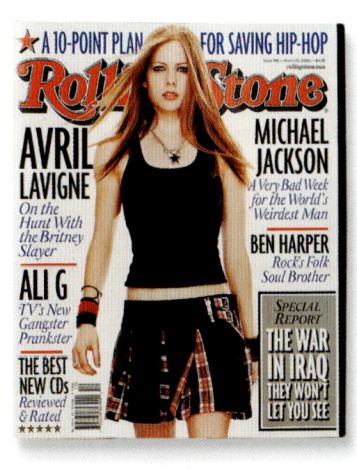

RS 916 | THE BEATLES
February 20th, 2003
VARIOUS PHOTOGRAPHERS

RS 918 | AVRIL LAVIGNE
March 20th, 2003
PHOTOGRAPH BY MARTIN SCHOELLER

VIOLENCE HAS BEEN A CONSTANT IN the life of twenty-six-year-old 50 Cent – government name Curtis Jackson, nickname Boo-Boo. His mother, a drug dealer, was killed when he was eight. At twelve, he became a dealer, and was nearly shot to death at twenty-four. His first hip-hop mentor, Jam Master Jay, was killed execution-style last year. Just four days before this very evening, an empty SUV owned by Busta Rhymes was hit with six bullets while parked in front of 50 Cent's manager's office. And right now, there are people who want 50 dead.

50 gets through his days in bulletproof trucks, walking with four to six bodyguards just inches away, ushering him briskly through streets and doors, but his body language and demeanor show him unmoved by the threats on his life. He never refuses to stop for an autograph or a photo request, even when it exposes him to danger. Is he worried about his grandparents, who still live in Queens, New York, in the house where he grew up? He says his reputation is enough to protect them. "They [his would-be killers] know how I am. Anything go on around there, they need to move everything they love. They mammy, they pappy, they kids, all that shit. That'd start some real nasty shit. And they don't wanna go through that." He seems confident he won't be killed, unperturbed by being hunted. "It don't matter to me," he says. "That shit is not important when you got finances. Do I look uneasy to you?"

[EXCERPT FROM RS 919 COVER STORY BY TOURÉ]

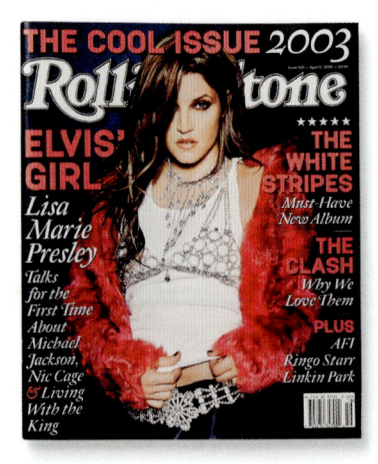

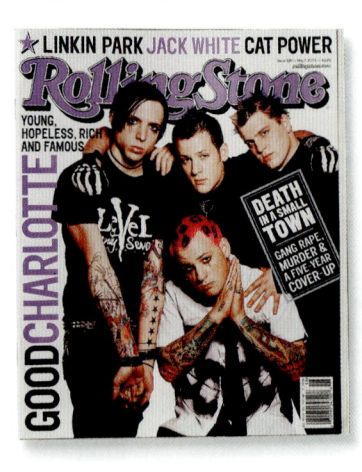

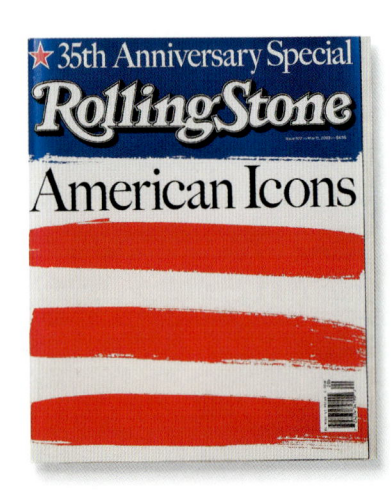

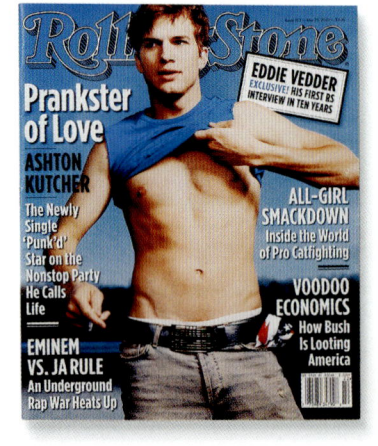

RS 920 | LISA MARIE PRESLEY
April 17th, 2003
PHOTOGRAPH BY MATTHEW ROLSTON

RS 922 | AMERICAN ICONS
May 15th, 2003
ILLUSTRATION BY ANDY COWLES

RS 921 | GOOD CHARLOTTE
May 1st, 2003
PHOTOGRAPH BY DAVID LACHAPELLE

RS 923 | ASHTON KUTCHER
May 29th, 2003
PHOTOGRAPH BY MARTIN SCHOELLER

[RS 922] Rather than assemble a retrospective on its history, ROLLING STONE chose to celebrate its thirty-fifth anniversary by documenting the people, inventions and images that define our times. Selected subjects included Elvis Presley, the Stratocaster, the iPod, the peace sign, Jack Daniels, the concept of the leading man—and, of course, the American flag that decorates the cover.

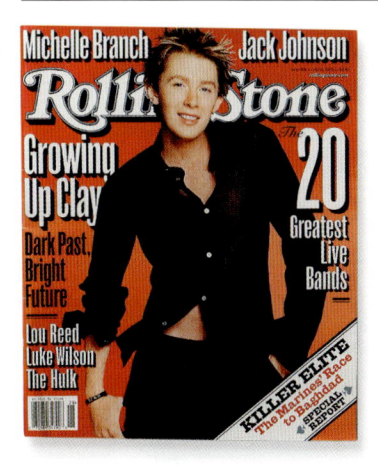

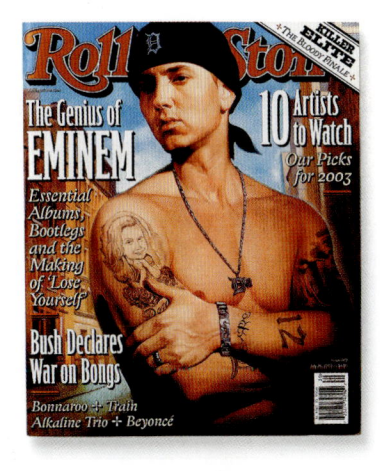

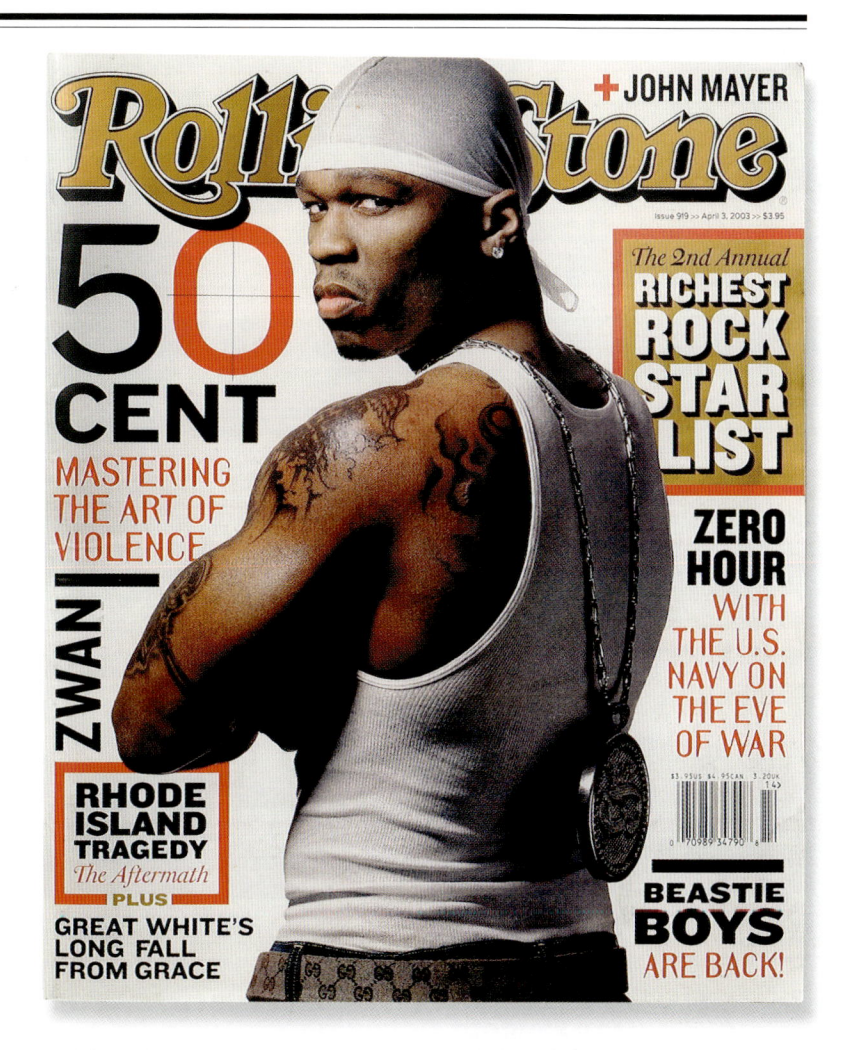

RS 926 | CLAY AIKEN
July 10th, 2003
Photograph by Matthew Rolston

RS 919 | 50 CENT
April 3rd, 2003
Photograph by Albert Watson

RS 927 | EMINEM
July 24th, 2003
Illustration by Roberto Parada

[RS 926] In summer 2003, Clay Aiken won the hearts and minds of the American public with his improbable run through *American Idol*. Despite his second-place finish, to Ruben Studdard, ROLLING STONE put Clay on the cover and was rewarded with one of its top-selling issues of 2003. Fans of Studdard weren't so happy and campaigned for their man to get a cover of his own. Three issues later, we caved in and were rewarded with one of our worst-sellers of the year.

50 YEARS OF COVERS • 499

ROLLING STONE

The Matrix › **Led Zeppelin** › **Sean Paul** › **12 Headbang**

Issue 924 >> June 12, 2003

SPECIAL ISSUE
MONSTERS OF SUMMER
ROCK HITS THE ROAD

12-Star Foldout Cover Including...
Dave Grohl › Lars Ulrich › Perry Farrell › Chester Bennington
Josh Homme › Brody Armstrong › Davey Havok › Dave Navarro ›››

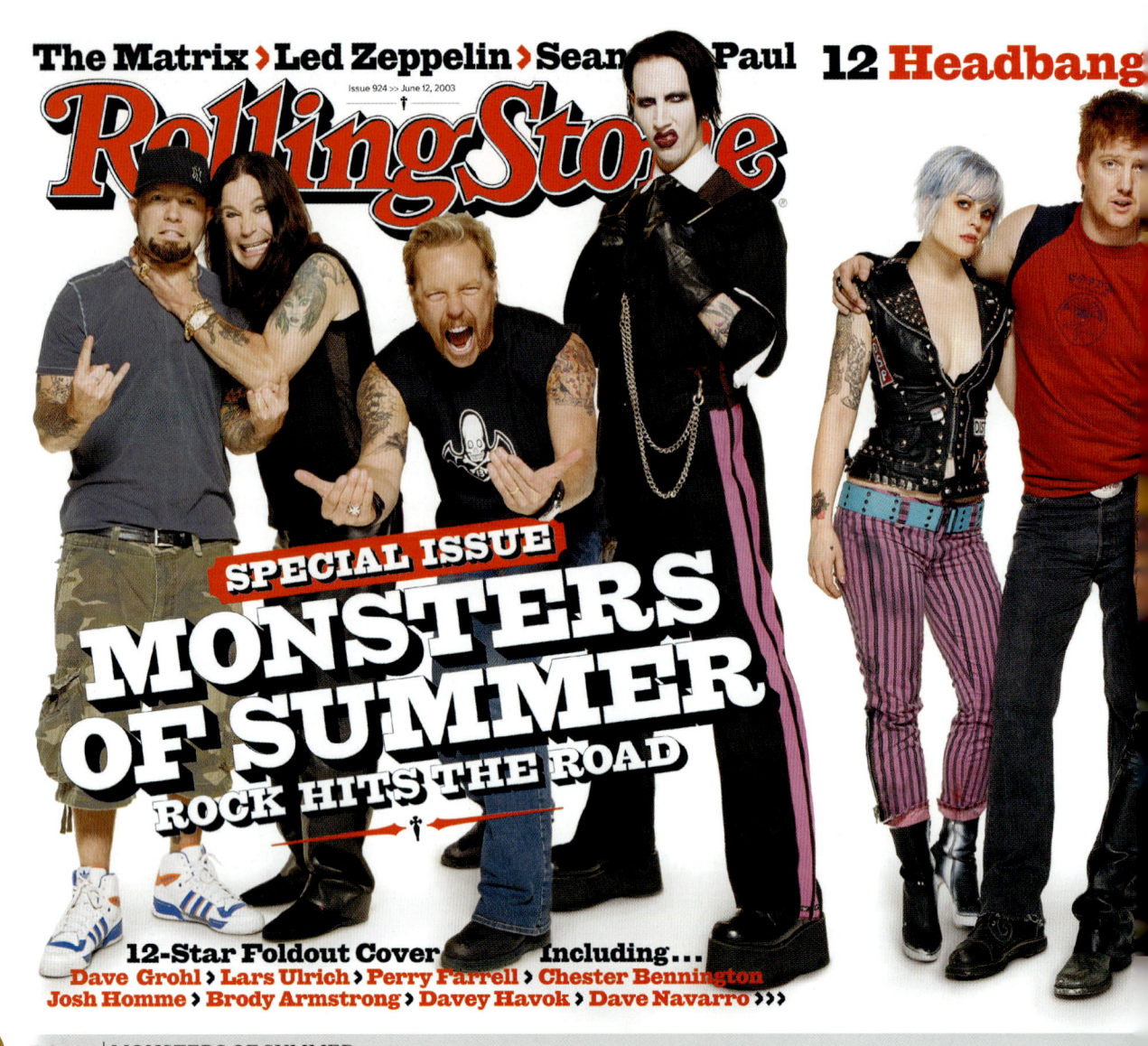

2000s

RS 924 | MONSTERS OF SUMMER | June 12th, 2003 | Photograph by Andrew MacPherson

[**RS 924**] It's never easy assembling this many egos, but for our Monsters of Summer issue, that turned out to be the least of our problems. The concept was that the cover would unfold to three times its regular size, thereby allowing us to cram twelve major players from the summer's biggest tours onto the front of our magazine. It was only after we designed the cover that we discovered our printing presses could handle just one foldout, not two. As a result, Linkin Park singer Chester Bennington, AFI vocalist Davey Havok, Metallica drummer Lars Ulrich and Perry Farrell were relegated to the flip side of the foldout. Thanks to the wonders of modern technology, they all appear here.

500 • ROLLING STONE

Interviews… With the Stars of Summer

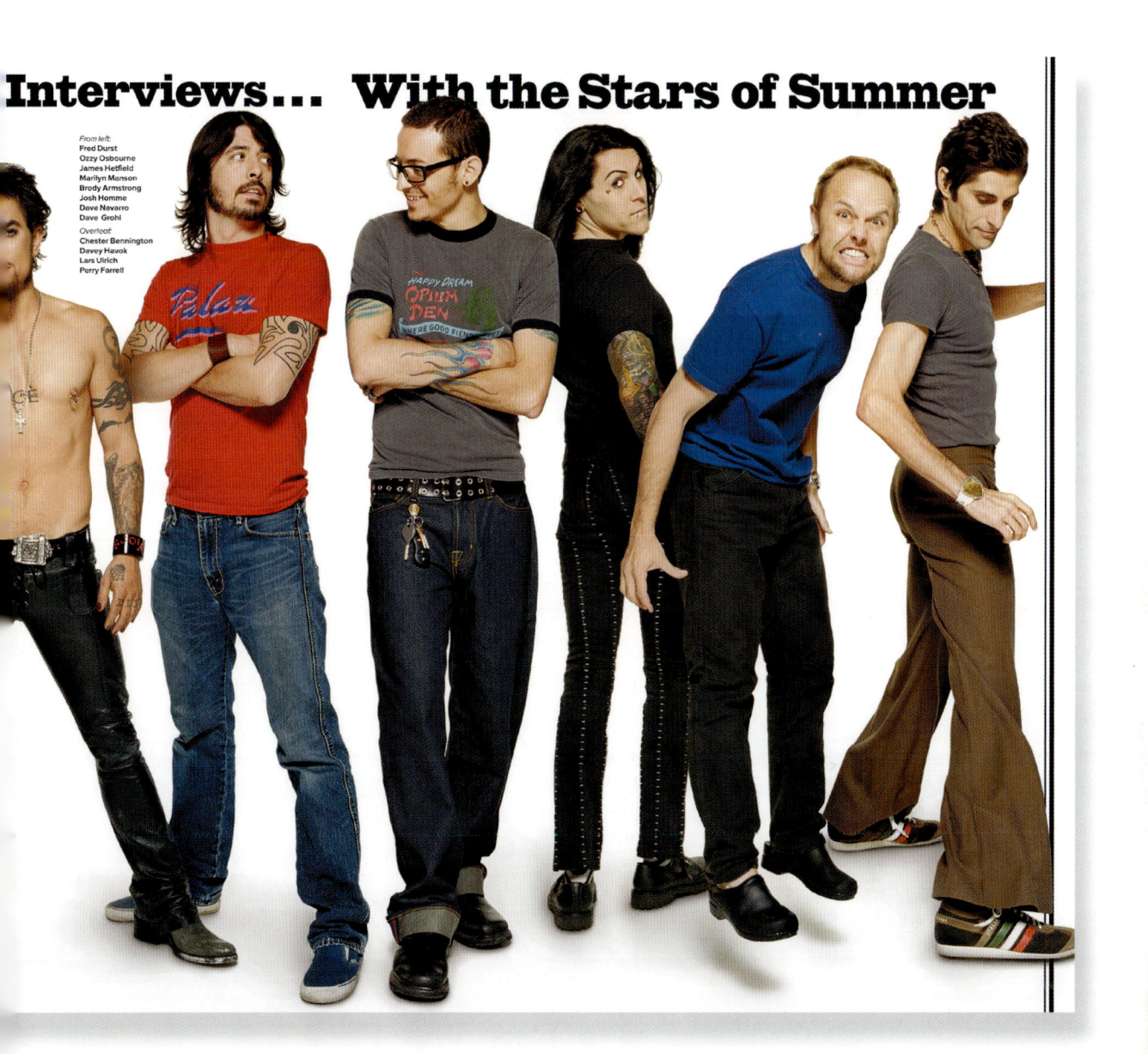

From left:
Fred Durst
Ozzy Osbourne
James Hetfield
Marilyn Manson
Brody Armstrong
Josh Homme
Dave Navarro
Dave Grohl

Overleaf:
Chester Bennington
Davey Havok
Lars Ulrich
Perry Farrell

50 YEARS OF COVERS • 501

Rolling Stone

rollingstone.com

KILLER ELITE
THE REAL STORY OF THE MARINES IN IRAQ

JON STEWART
THOM YORKE
EVANESCENCE
METALLICA

JUSTIN & CHRISTINA
DOUBLE TROUBLE
HOOKING UP FOR THE SEXIEST TOUR ON EARTH

2000s

Issue 925
June 26, 2003
$3.95

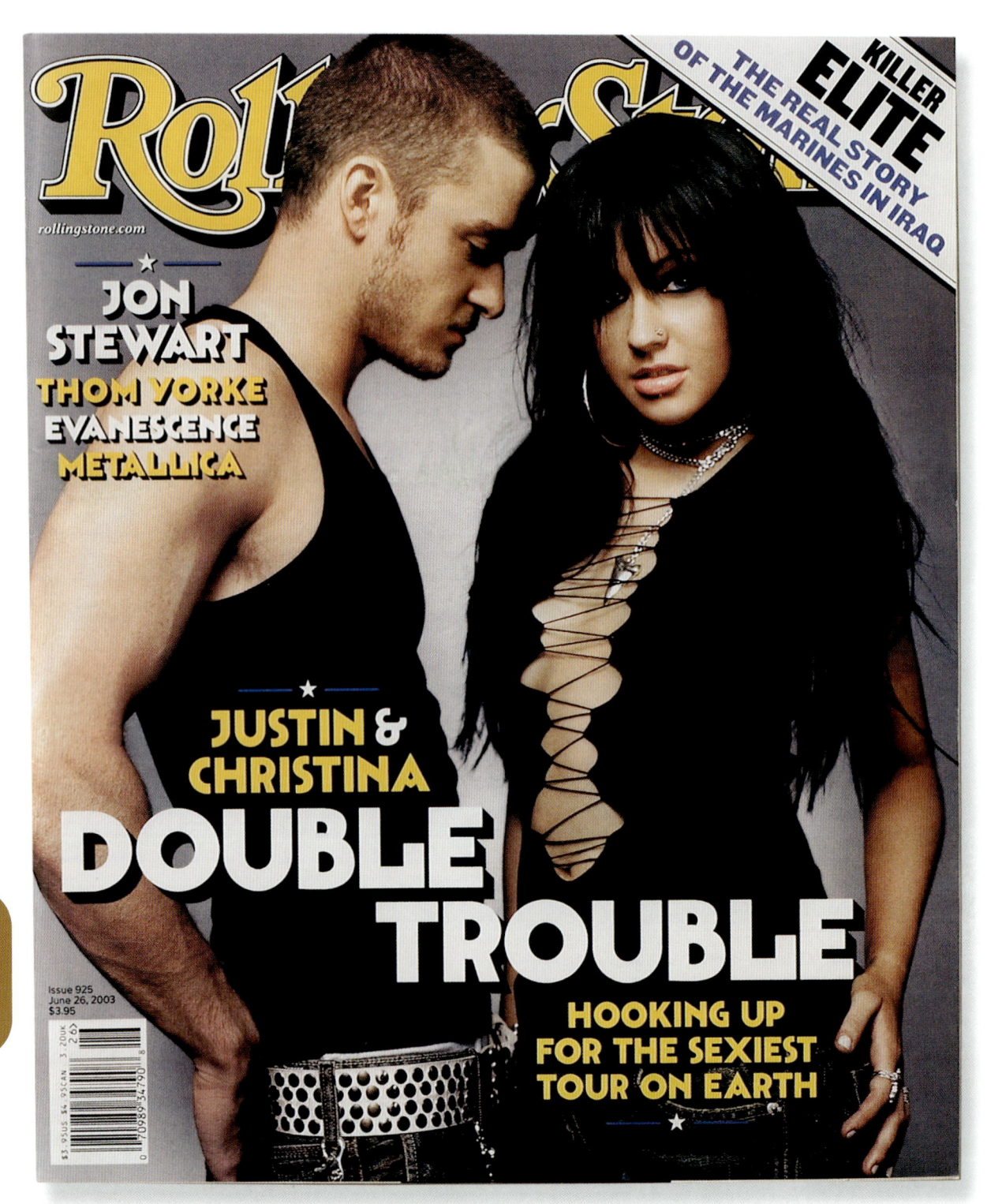

RS 925 | JUSTIN TIMBERLAKE & CHRISTINA AGUILERA | June 26th, 2003 | Photograph by Max Vadukul

Rolling Stone

Issue 928 >> August 7, 2003 >> $3.95
rollingstone.com

PHOTO SPECIAL

Hot & Single

ANGELINA JOLIE
On Sex, Her Dad & Leaving Billy Bob

Backstage and on the Road
With

RED HOT CHILI PEPPERS

FLAMING LIPS

LIL' KIM

JAMES TAYLOR

JOHN MAYER

Cannibalism & Chaos
Inside the World of Liberia's Child Soldiers

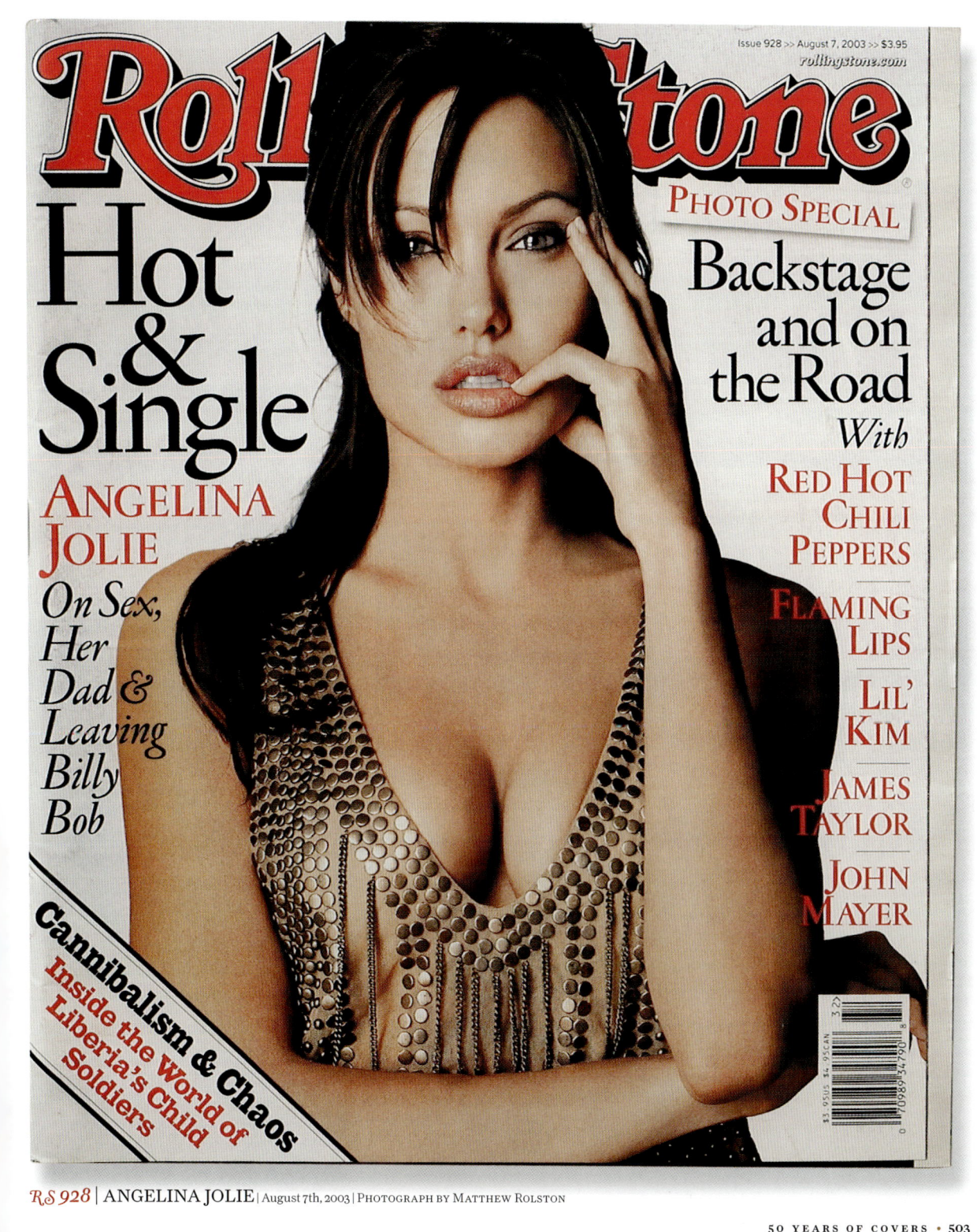

RS 928 | ANGELINA JOLIE | August 7th, 2003 | Photograph by Matthew Rolston

50 YEARS OF COVERS • 503

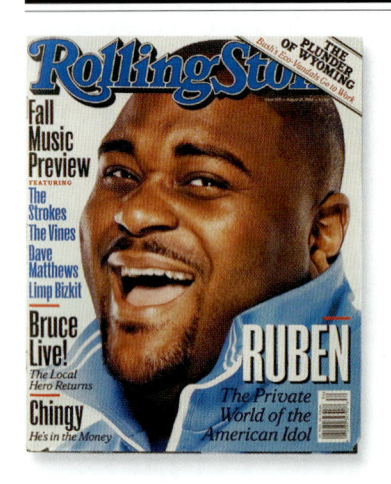

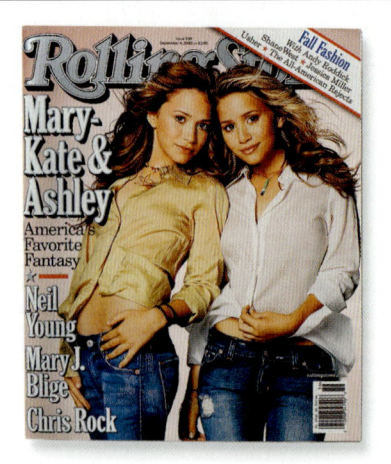

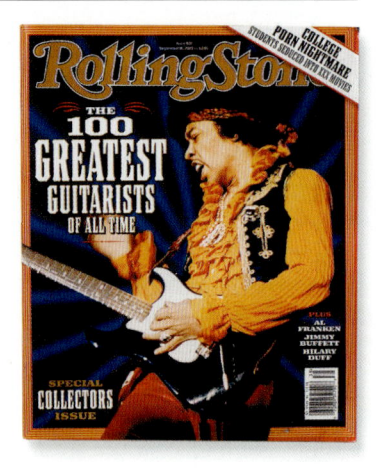

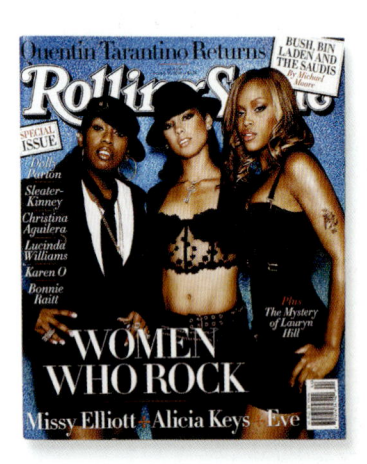

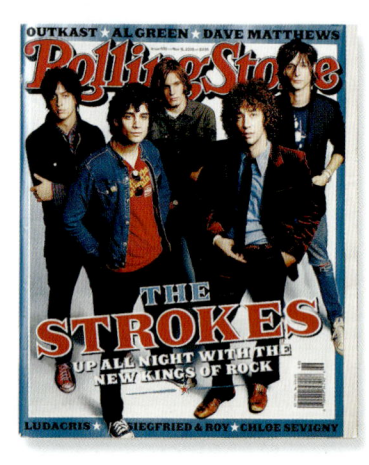

RS 929 | RUBEN STUDDARD
August 21st, 2003
Photograph by Andrew MacPherson

RS 934 | MISSY ELLIOTT, ALICIA KEYS & EVE
October 30th, 2003
Photograph by Max Vadukul

RS 930 | MARY-KATE AND ASHLEY OLSEN
September 4th, 2003
Photograph by Matthew Rolston

RS 935 | THE STROKES
November 13th, 2003
Photograph by Max Vadukul

RS 931 | THE 100 GREATEST GUITARISTS OF ALL TIME – JIMI HENDRIX
September 18th, 2003
Photograph by Jill Gibson

"*I think* every photo shoot I've done has been tasteful. I'll never be a vamp-vixen-sex-goddess."

—*Britney Spears*

2000s

504 • ROLLING STONE

Rolling Stone

Issue 932 >> October 2, 2003 >> $4.95
rollingstone.com

Britney
On Justin, That Kiss and Being Alone

David Bowie
John Mayer
Bill Murray

Martin Scorsese's History of the Blues

The 2003 Hot List

Viggo Mortensen
Scarlett Johansson
Ryan Adams
Brand New
Obie Trice
Aimee Mullins

Special Report
{ **AMERICA'S DIRTY WAR** }
The Deadly Cost of Radioactive Tank Busters

RS 932 | BRITNEY SPEARS | October 2nd, 2003 | Photograph by Matthew Rolston

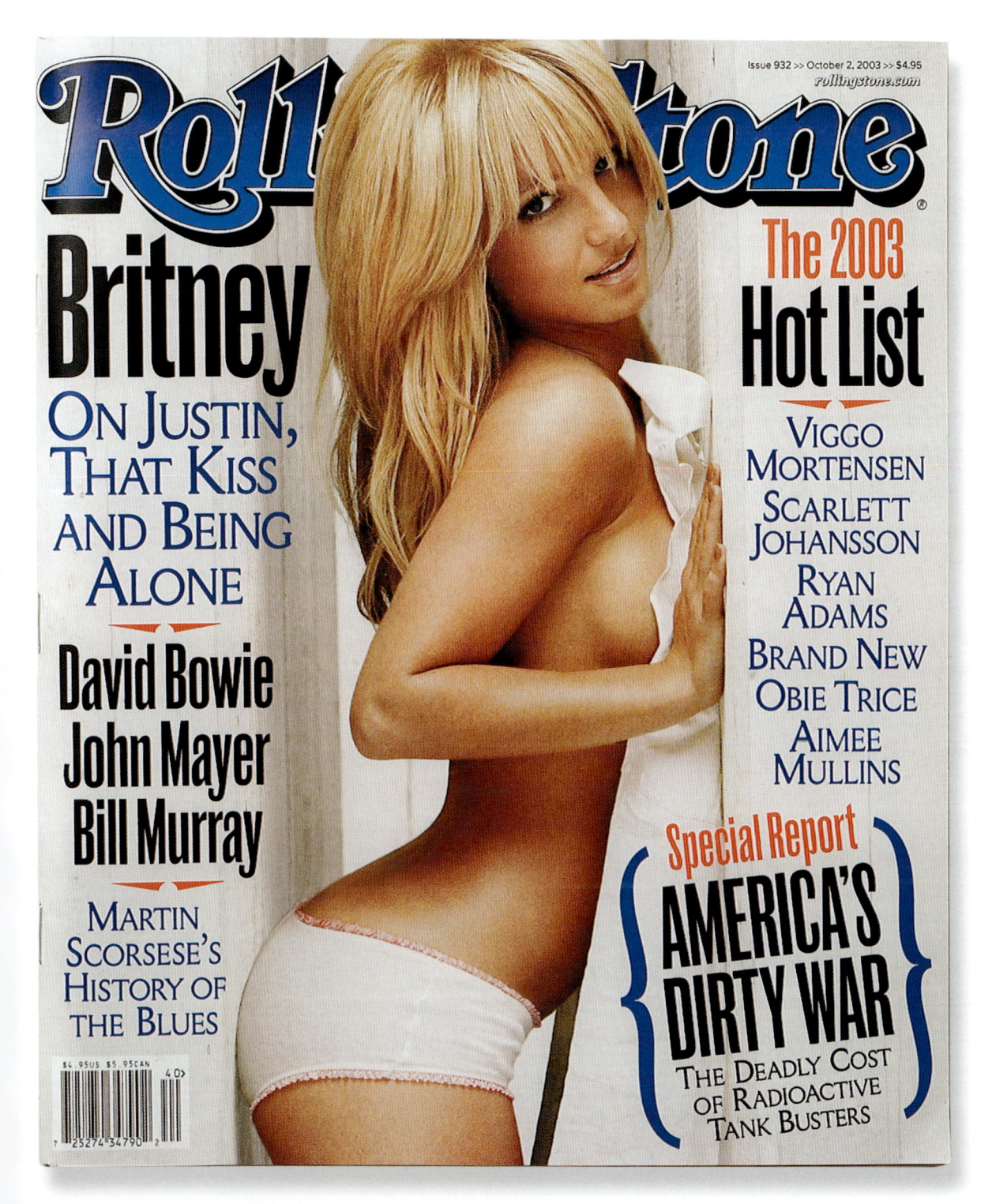

50 YEARS OF COVERS • 505

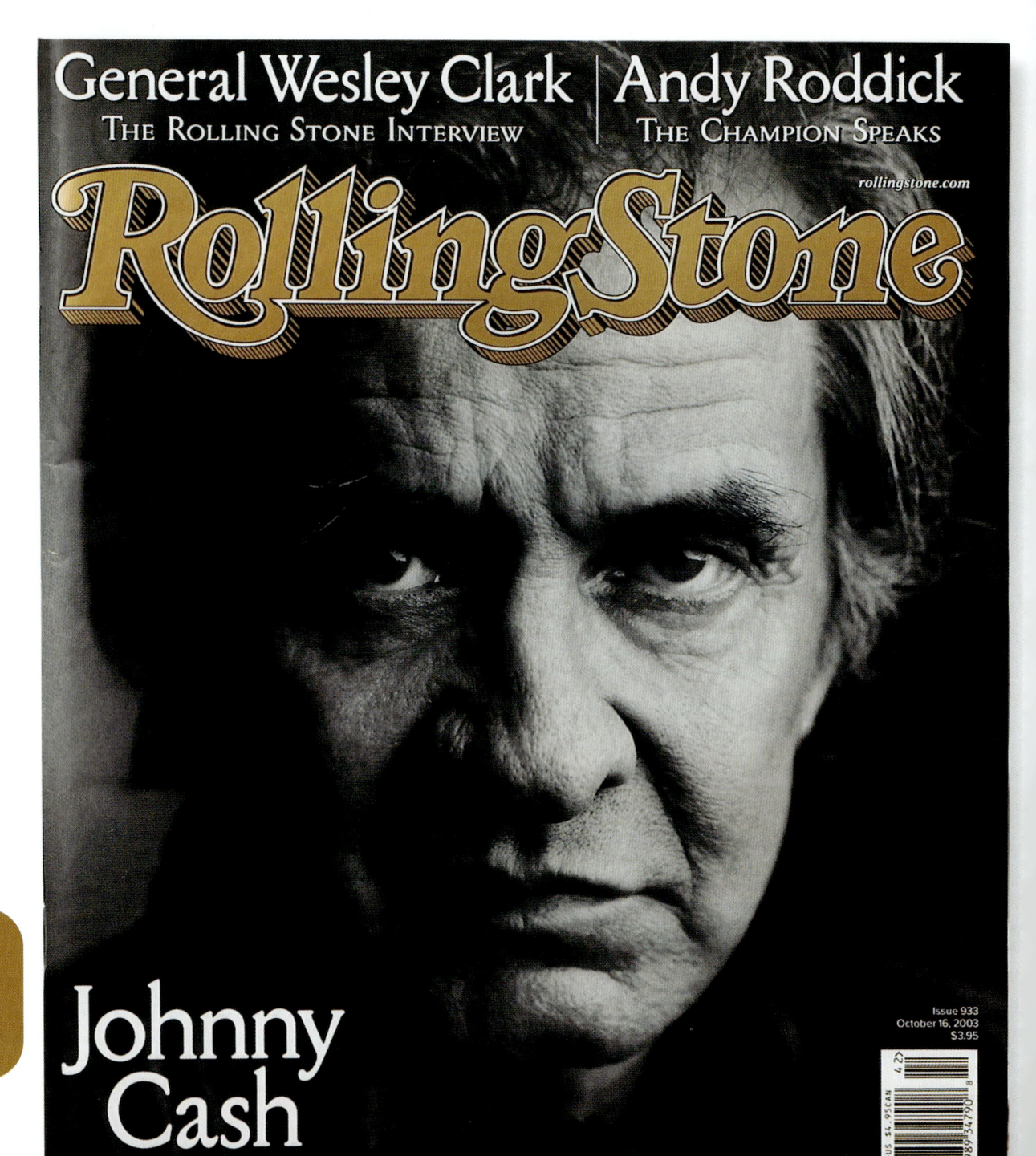

General Wesley Clark
THE ROLLING STONE INTERVIEW

Andy Roddick
THE CHAMPION SPEAKS

RollingStone

rollingstone.com

2000s

Johnny Cash
1932-2003

Issue 933
October 16, 2003
$3.95

RS 933 | JOHNNY CASH | October 16th, 2003 | Photograph by Mark Seliger

For so long it seemed that even death would have to back off from a final confrontation with the daunting eminence of Johnny Cash. Even after the singer was found to have an incurable, degenerative disease in 1997, he did not back down. Despite frequent hospitalizations, he recorded some of the best music of his career, made himself available for interviews, oversaw reissues of his extensive catalog of albums and made a heart-stopping video that racked up six nominations at this year's MTV Video Music Awards. On the night nearly six years ago when, from a concert stage in Michigan, he first publicly announced that he was ill, he said of his disease, "I refuse to give it some ground in my life." As always with Johnny Cash, his word proved rock-solid.

But when June Carter Cash, his wife of thirty-five years and the exquisite love of his life, died in May, it became anybody's guess how long Cash would be able to tolerate this world without her. This was the woman for whom he had written "Meet Me in Heaven": "At the end of the journey," he sang, "When our last song is sung/Will you meet me in heaven someday?" Perhaps Bono put it best when the subject of Cash's death came up. "Maybe it's not that sad," he said. "I mean, it's sad for us. But June went off to prepare the house. And he wasn't long behind her."

—*Anthony DeCurtis*

"EVERY MAN COULD RELATE TO HIM, but nobody could be him. To be that extraordinary and that ordinary was his real gift. That, and his humor and his bare-boned honesty. When I visited him at home one time, he said the most beautiful, poetic grace. He said, 'Shall we bow our heads?' We all bowed our heads. Then, when he was done, he looked at me and Adam Clayton and said, 'Sure miss the drugs, though.'"

—*Bono*

"IN PLAIN TERMS, JOHNNY was and is the North Star; you could guide your ship by him. The greatest of the greats then and now."

—*Bob Dylan*

"I HAD BEEN IN AWE OF HIM SINCE I saw him play in 1958, at San Quentin Prison, where I was an inmate. He'd lost his voice the night before over in Frisco and wasn't able to sing very good, but he won over the prisoners. He chewed gum, looked arrogant and flipped the bird to the guards – he did everything the prisoners wanted to do. He was a mean mother from the South who was there because he loved us. When he walked away, everyone in that place had become a Johnny Cash fan. There were five thousand inmates in San Quentin and about thirty guitar players; I was among the top five guitarists in there. The day after Johnny's show, man, every guitar player in San Quentin was after me to teach them how to play like him. It was like how, the day after a Muhammad Ali fight, everybody would be down in the yard shadowboxing; that day, everyone was trying to learn 'Folsom Prison Blues.'"

—*Merle Haggard*

[EXCERPTS FROM JOHNNY CASH TRIBUTE]

For RS 937, 'Rolling Stone' convened a panel of 273 musicians, producers, journalists and others to choose the 500 best albums ever made. These are the Top 25.

1.	SGT. PEPPER'S LONELY HEARTS CLUB BAND	THE BEATLES
2.	PET SOUNDS	THE BEACH BOYS
3.	REVOLVER	THE BEATLES
4.	HIGHWAY 61 REVISITED	BOB DYLAN
5.	RUBBER SOUL	THE BEATLES
6.	WHAT'S GOING ON	MARVIN GAYE
7.	EXILE ON MAIN STREET	THE ROLLING STONES
8.	LONDON CALLING	THE CLASH
9.	BLONDE ON BLONDE	BOB DYLAN
10.	THE BEATLES [THE WHITE ALBUM]	THE BEATLES
11.	THE SUN SESSIONS	ELVIS PRESLEY
12.	KIND OF BLUE	MILES DAVIS
13.	THE VELVET UNDERGROUND	THE VELVET UNDERGROUND & NICO
14.	ABBEY ROAD	THE BEATLES
15.	ARE YOU EXPERIENCED?	THE JIMI HENDRIX EXPERIENCE
16.	BLOOD ON THE TRACKS	BOB DYLAN
17.	NEVERMIND	NIRVANA
18.	BORN TO RUN	BRUCE SPRINGSTEEN
19.	ASTRAL WEEKS	VAN MORRISON
20.	THRILLER	MICHAEL JACKSON
21.	THE GREAT TWENTY-EIGHT	CHUCK BERRY
22.	PLASTIC ONO BAND	JOHN LENNON
23.	INNERVISIONS	STEVIE WONDER
24.	LIVE AT THE APOLLO	JAMES BROWN
25.	RUMOURS	FLEETWOOD MAC

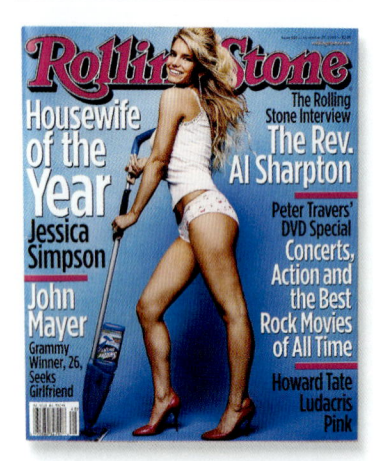

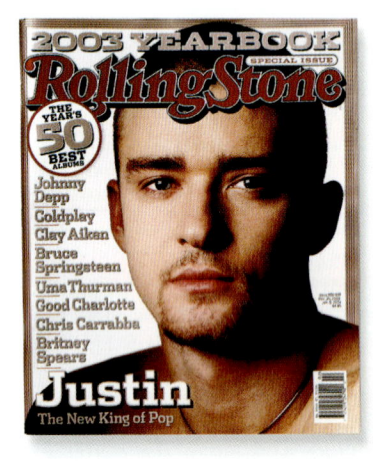

RS 936 | JESSICA SIMPSON
November 27th, 2003
PHOTOGRAPH BY MAX VADUKUL

2000s

RS 938/939 | JUSTIN TIMBERLAKE
December 25th, 2003 – January 8th, 2004
PHOTOGRAPH BY ALBERT WATSON

[RS 938/939] **The face of Justin Timberlake graced both our first and last issues in the year 2003. That feat, along with his appearance on RS 925 (with Christina Aguilera), makes Timberlake the first artist to notch three ROLLING STONE covers in a single calendar year.**

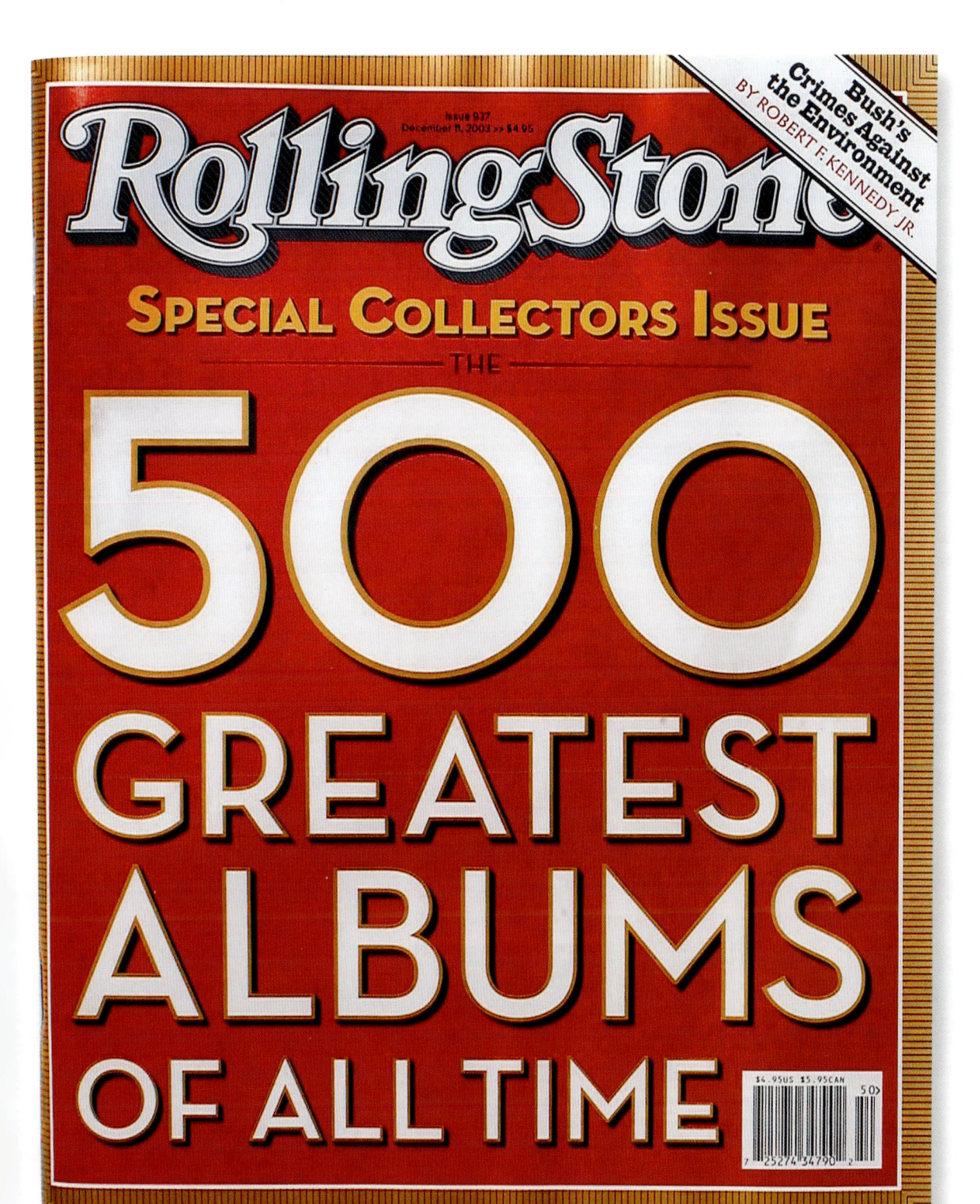

RS 937 | THE 500 GREATEST ALBUMS OF ALL TIME | December 11th, 2003 | Typography by Andy Cowles

Toby Keith, One Angry American

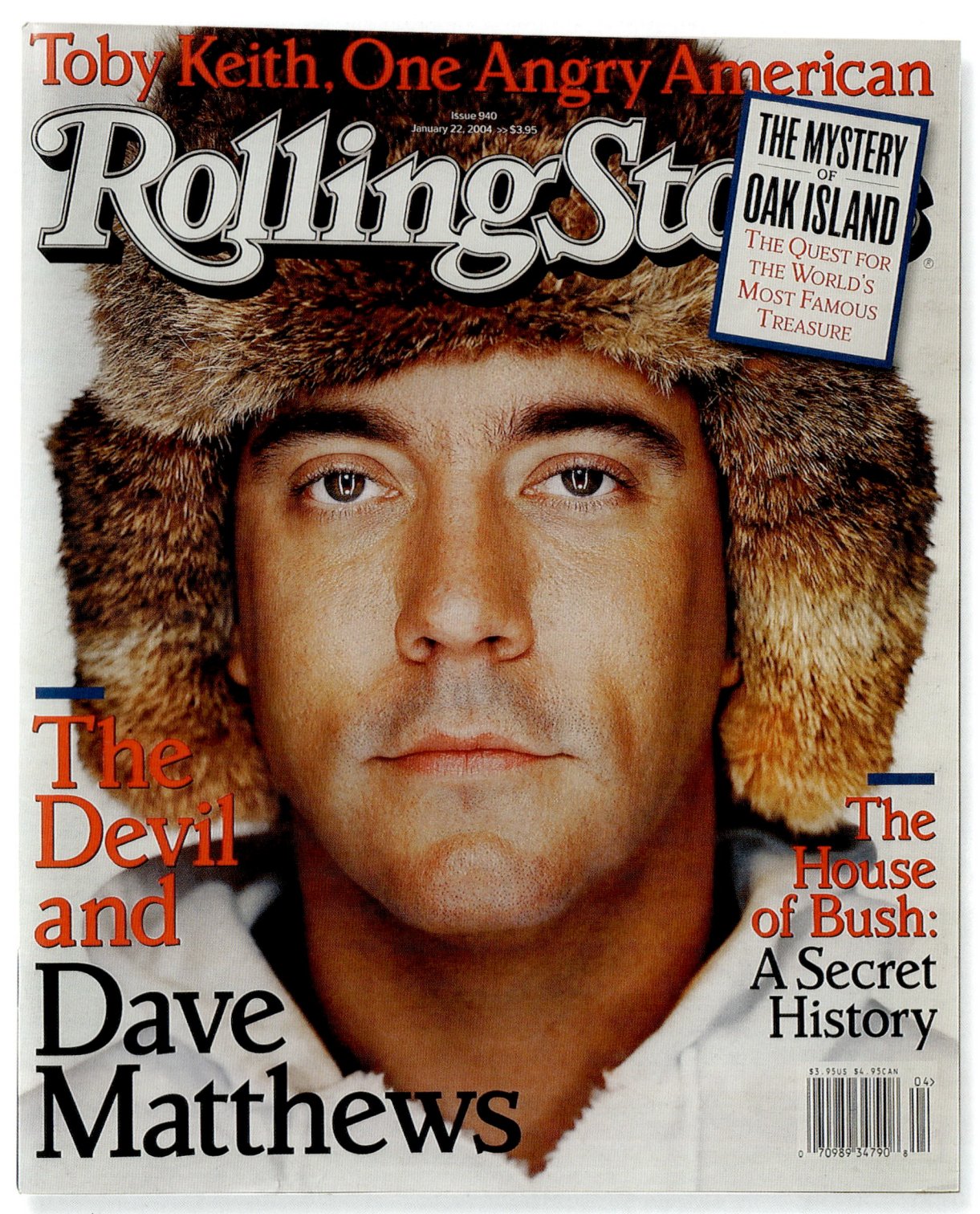

Rolling Stone

Issue 940
January 22, 2004 >> $3.95

THE MYSTERY OF OAK ISLAND
THE QUEST FOR THE WORLD'S MOST FAMOUS TREASURE

The Devil and Dave Matthews

The House of Bush: A Secret History

2000s

RS 940 | DAVE MATTHEWS | January 22nd, 2004 | Photograph by Martin Schoeller

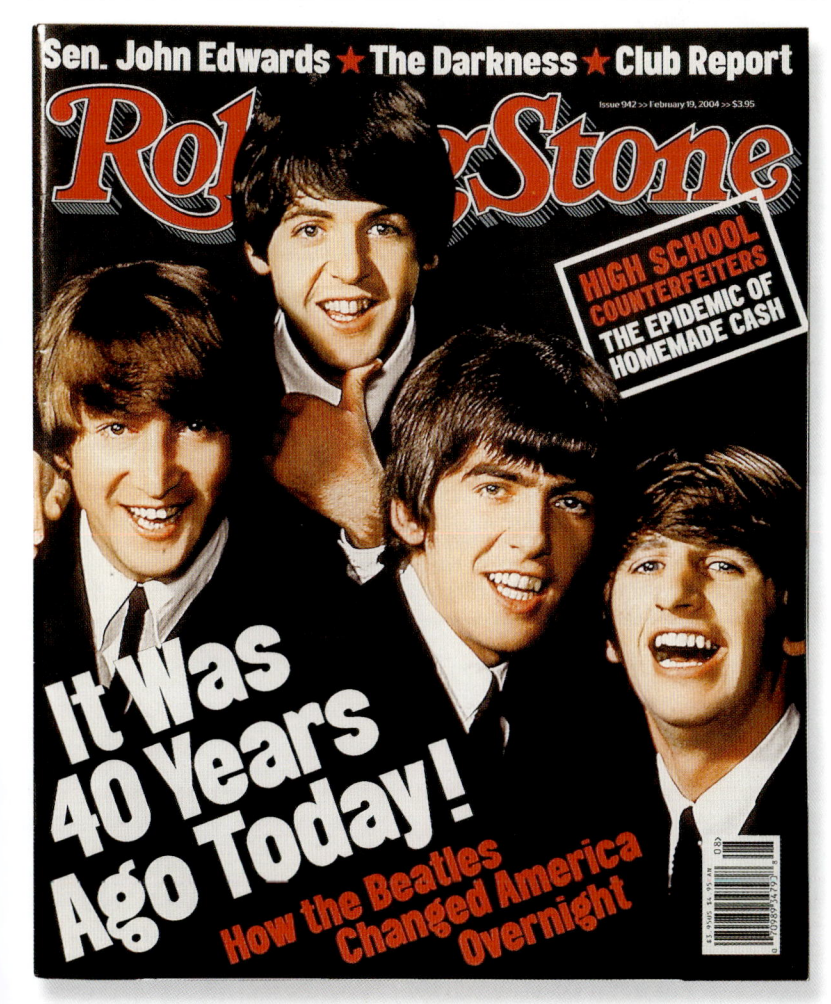

RS 942 | THE BEATLES | February 19th, 2004 | Photograph by John Dominis

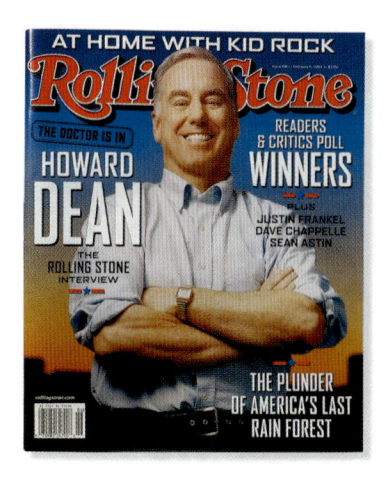

RS 941 | HOWARD DEAN
February 5th, 2004
Photograph by Stephen Danelian

[RS 941] When this issue hit newsstands on January 16th, 2004, Howard Dean was being touted as the savior of the Democratic Party. Three days later, following the Iowa Democratic Caucus, he suffered one of the most spectacular meltdowns in American political history with his notorious "Scream" speech. Sales suffered accordingly.

"When I put the fuzzy hat on, I laughed and said, 'This will be on the cover.' I thought it would be the shot that made me look the most stupid. Even though I've been teased about it at the coffee shop at home, I liked it."
—Dave Matthews

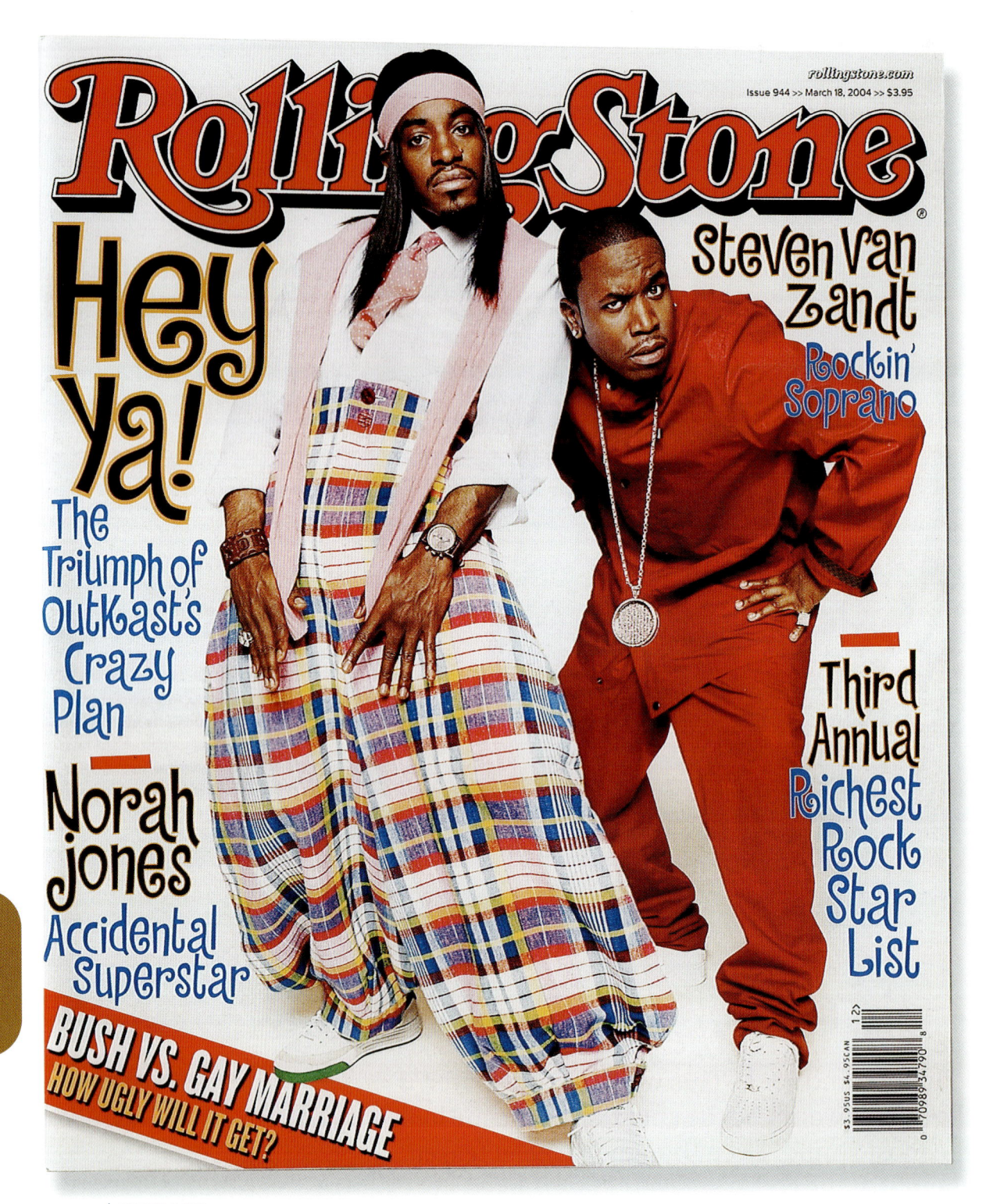

RS 944 | OUTKAST | March 18th, 2004 | Photograph by Andrew MacPherson

Rolling Stone

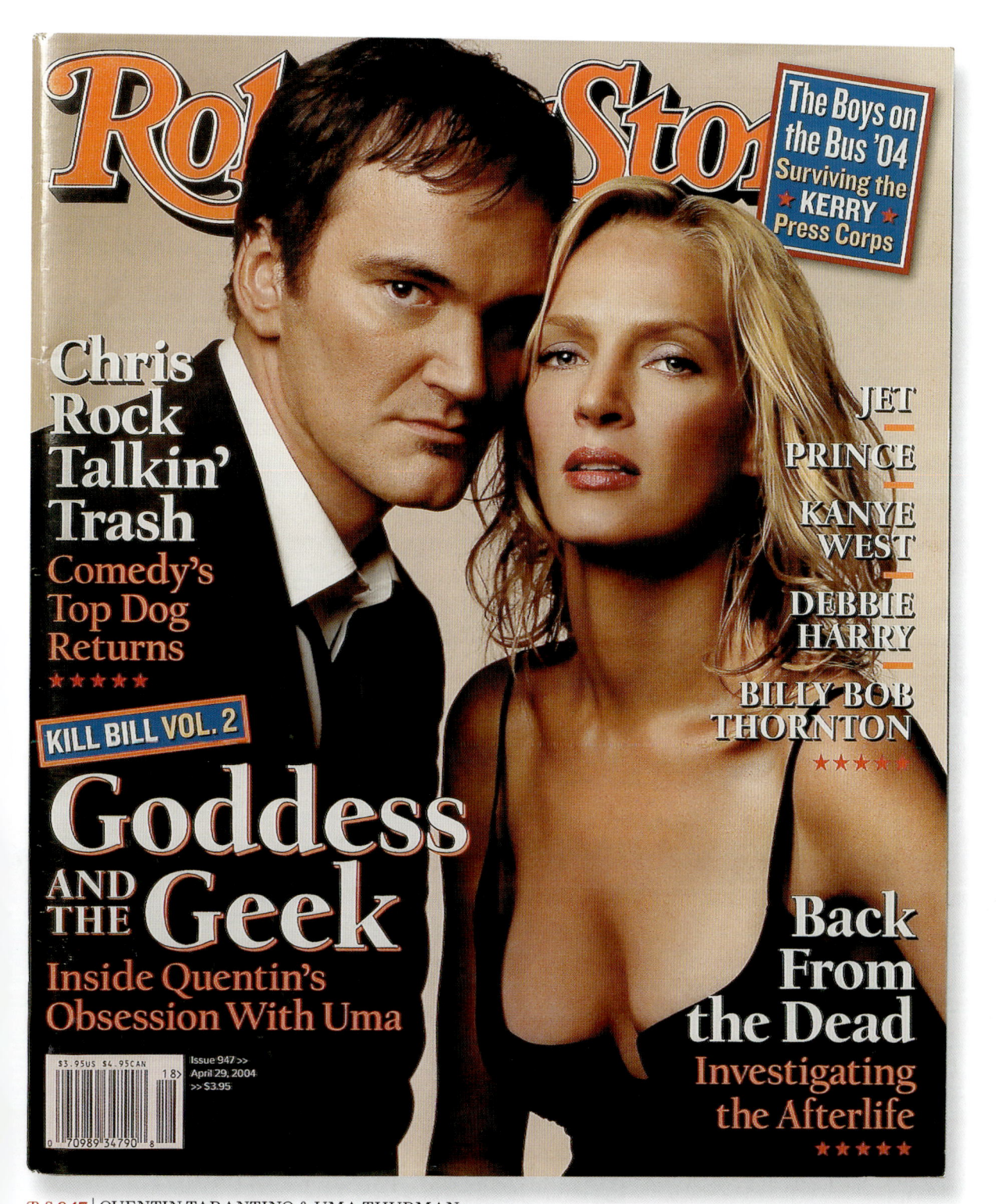

The Boys on the Bus '04 Surviving the ★ KERRY ★ Press Corps

Chris Rock Talkin' Trash
Comedy's Top Dog Returns
★★★★★

JET
PRINCE
KANYE WEST
DEBBIE HARRY
BILLY BOB THORNTON
★★★★★

KILL BILL VOL. 2

Goddess AND THE Geek
Inside Quentin's Obsession With Uma

Back From the Dead
Investigating the Afterlife
★★★★★

Issue 947 >>
April 29, 2004
>> $3.95

RS 947 | QUENTIN TARANTINO & UMA THURMAN | April 29th, 2004 | Photograph by Albert Watson

50 YEARS OF COVERS • 513

RS 943 | BEYONCÉ
March 4th, 2004
PHOTOGRAPH BY RUVEN AFANADOR

RS 945 | BEN AFFLECK
April 1st, 2004
PHOTOGRAPH BY DAVID LACHAPELLE

RS 948 | USHER
May 13th, 2004
PHOTOGRAPH BY MARTIN SCHOELLER

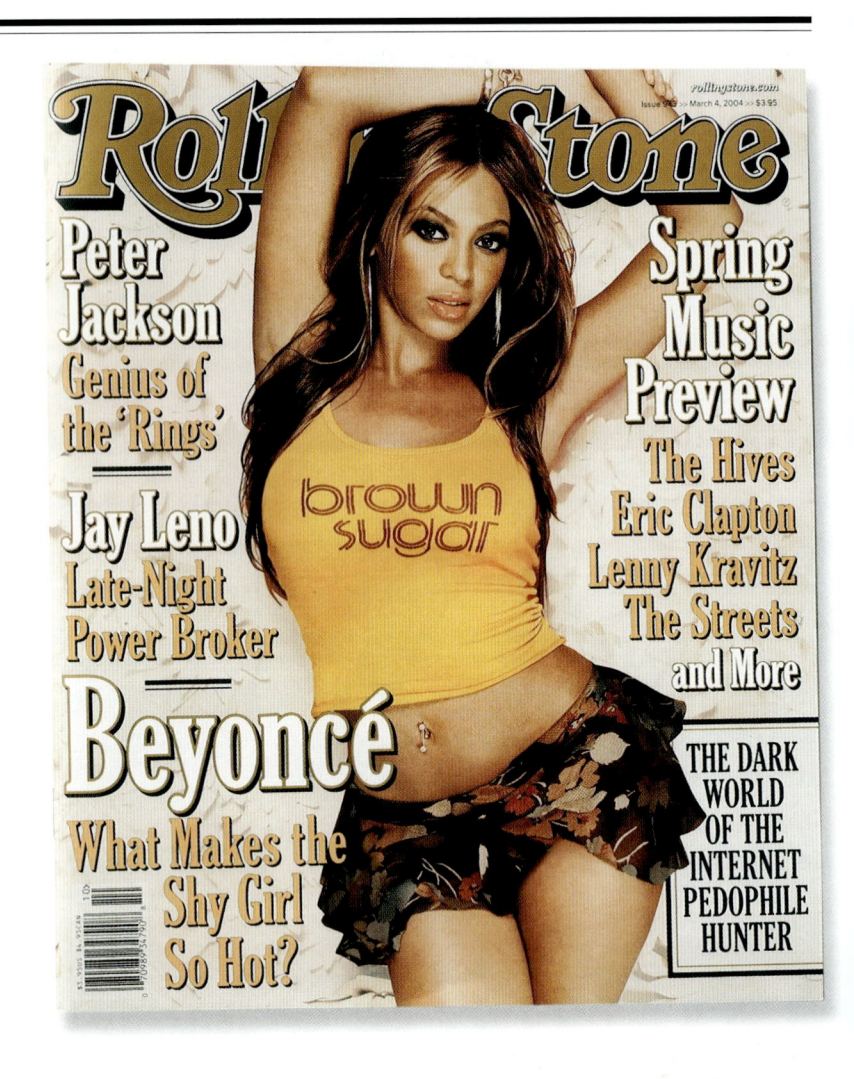

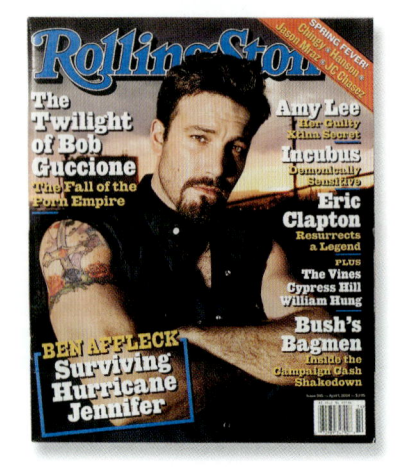

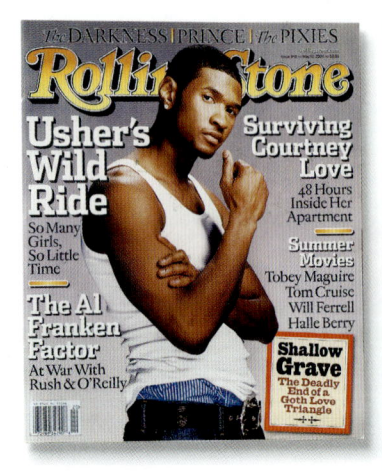

2000s

514 • ROLLING STONE

PATTI SMITH **HOWARD STERN** **D12**

rollingstone.com
Issue 949 >> May 27, 2004 >> $3.95

RollingStone

**FAITH!
FUNK! SEX!**

Prince
On Fire

**He's Still Got
That Red-Hot
Magic**

**Original
Jackass
In Pain With
Bam Margera**

**Honky-tonk
Woman**

**Loretta Lynn,
Amazing Again**

A SOLDIER'S STORY
★★★ **THE
AGONIZING
DEATH
OF PRIVATE
PIESTEWA**
The Unsung Heroine
of the Jessica Lynch
Ambush in Iraq

RS 949 | PRINCE | May 27th, 2004 | Photograph by Albert Watson

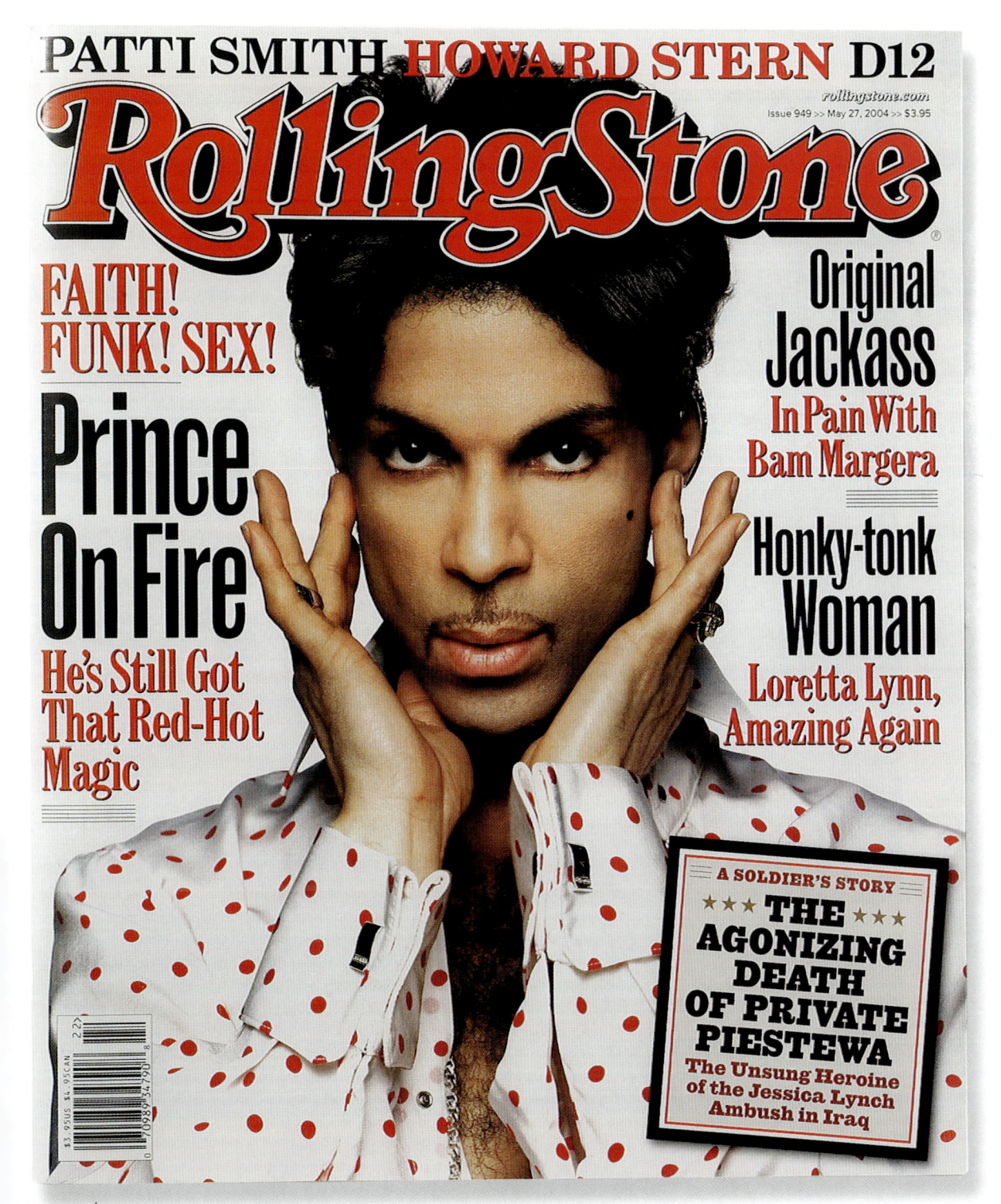

50 YEARS OF COVERS • 515

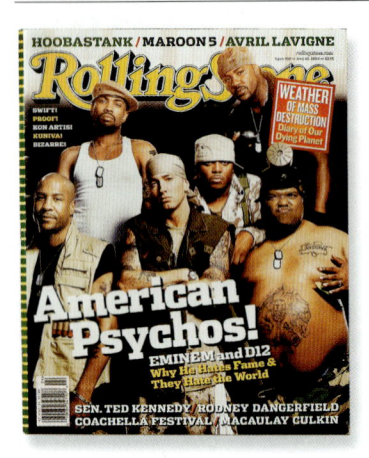

RS 950 | EMINEM & D12
June 10th, 2004
Photograph by Martin Schoeller

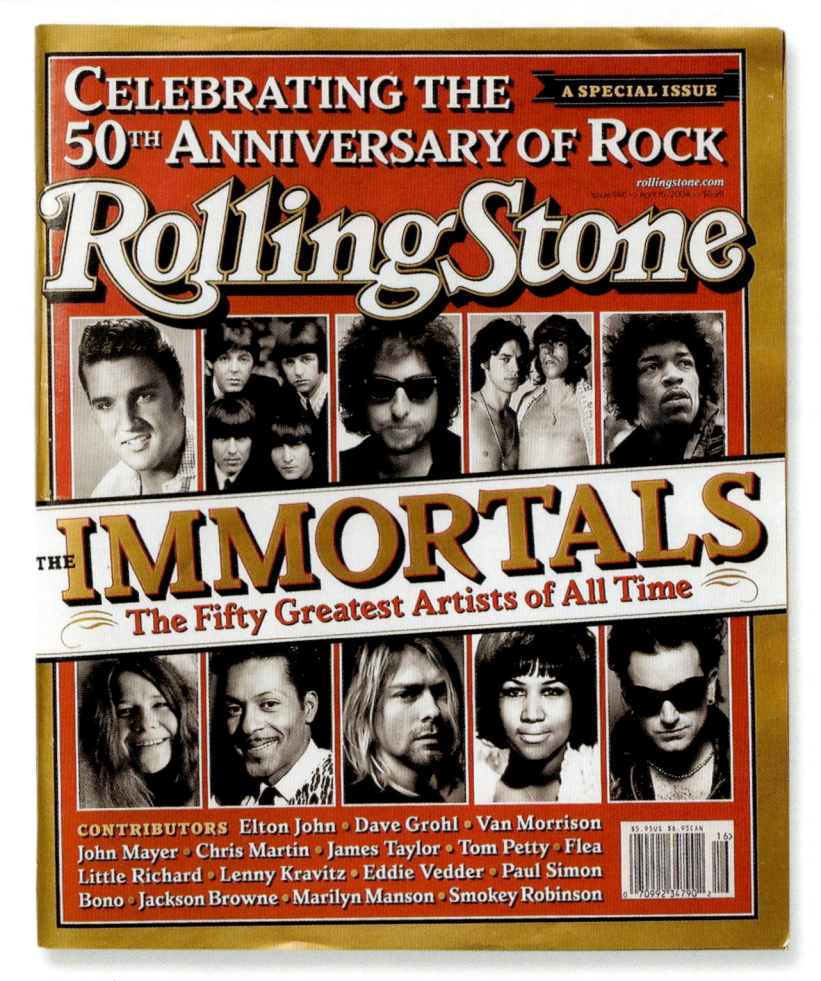

RS 946 | THE FIFTIETH ANNIVERSARY OF ROCK: THE IMMORTALS
April 15th, 2004 | Various photographers

THE IMMORTALS ARE THE GREATEST ROCK & ROLL ARTISTS OF ALL TIME. THEY ARE also more than that. The fifty men, women and bands celebrated in the following pages are the singers, songwriters, record makers and performers who are continually in the music – as pioneers, teachers and stars; touching our souls and pulling us to our feet, on a daily basis – even when they are no longer with us. And this is not just a list. It is a fundamental lesson in the history of rock & roll and its continuing power to inspire and transform. The Immortals is a tribute to those who created rock & roll, written by their peers and heirs, those who have learned from their innovations, struggles and legacies.

This year, rock & roll turns fifty, and this is the first of three special issues ROLLING STONE is publishing to mark the occasion. Scholars have debated the precise birth date for as long as the music has been around. We chose July 5th, 1954 – the day Elvis Presley recorded "That's All Right" at Sun Studio in Memphis. On that date, the nineteen-year-old truck driver not only made his first and most important single. He created a new world – initiating a way of life and expression – that, even at fifty, is still evolving. There is no better standard for rock & roll immortality.

[EXCERPT FROM RS 946]

2000s

516 • ROLLING STONE

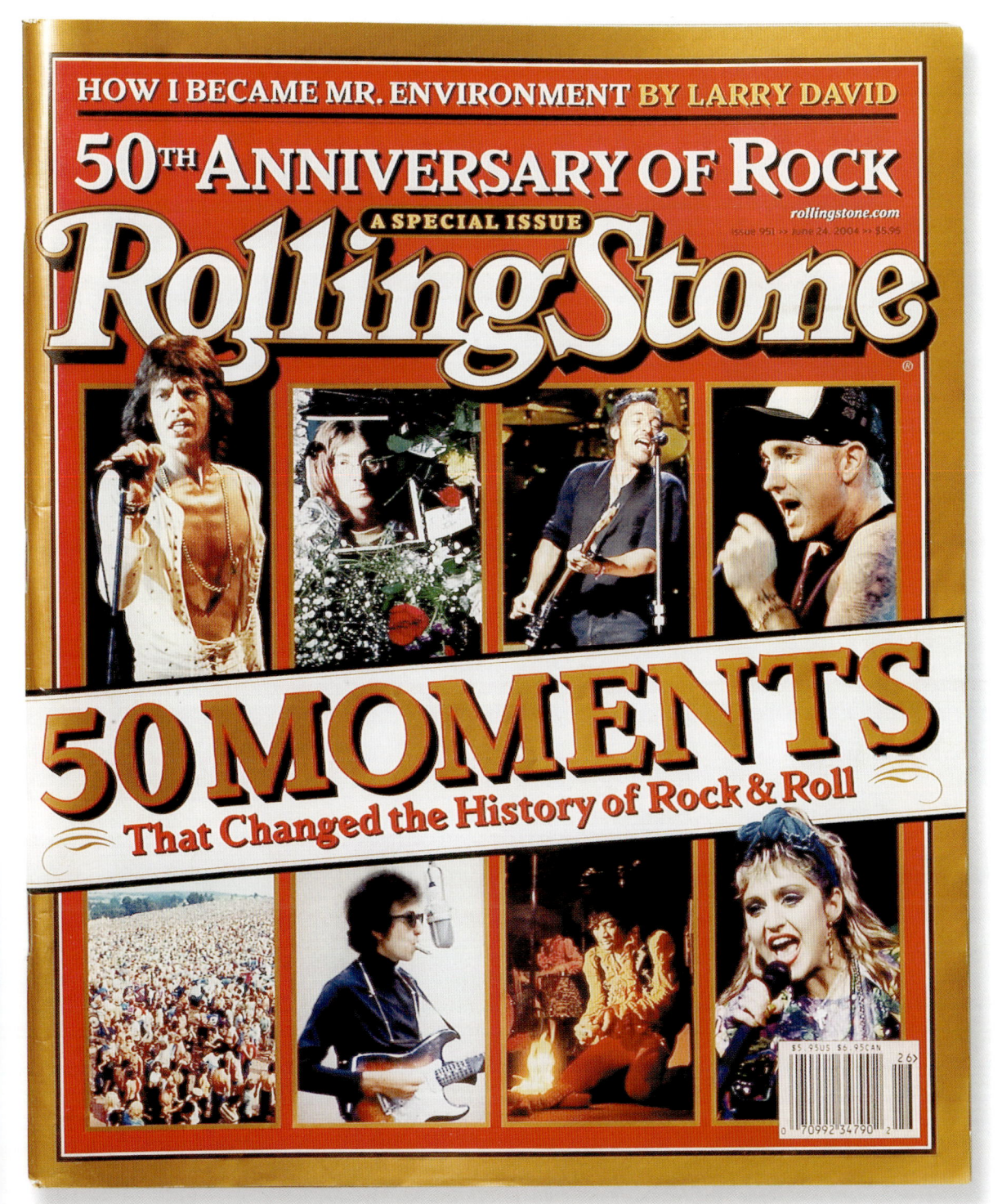

RS 951 | THE FIFTIETH ANNIVERSARY OF ROCK: FIFTY MOMENTS THAT CHANGED THE HISTORY OF ROCK & ROLL | June 24th, 2004 | VARIOUS PHOTOGRAPHERS

NEW REVELATIONS JIM MORRISON'S LAST DAYS

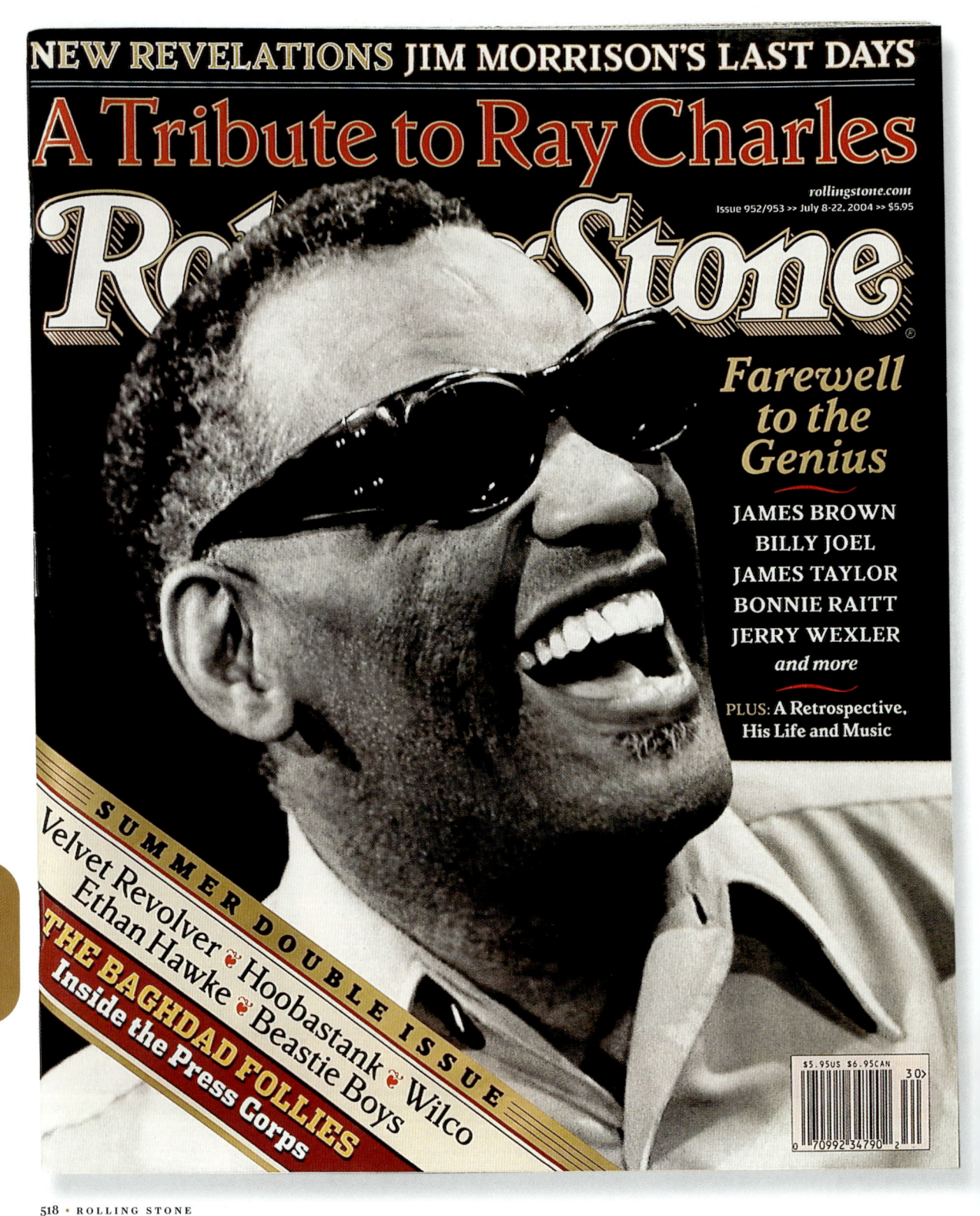

A Tribute to Ray Charles

Rolling Stone

rollingstone.com
Issue 952/953 >> July 8-22, 2004 >> $5.95

Farewell to the Genius

**JAMES BROWN
BILLY JOEL
JAMES TAYLOR
BONNIE RAITT
JERRY WEXLER**
and more

PLUS: A Retrospective, His Life and Music

SUMMER DOUBLE ISSUE

Velvet Revolver • Hoobastank • Wilco
Ethan Hawke • Beastie Boys

THE BAGHDAD FOLLIES
Inside the Press Corps

2000s

RS 952/953 | RAY CHARLES | July 8th – July 22nd, 2004 | Photograph courtesy of CBS/Everett Collection

"*Ray Charles' music got me* through high school. I loved him so much that back in 1963, after the Beach Boys got going, we used to do a live version of 'What'd I Say.' We did it because we wanted to turn people on to Ray Charles. It was always a real thrill for me to sing that song and think of Ray, so you can just imagine how I felt when, in 1986, Ray sang a version of our song 'Sail On Sailor.' Maybe most of all what I remember him for is his sensitive singing on cuts like 'I Can't Stop Loving You.' You can be sure the whole world will never stop loving you, Ray."

—*Brian Wilson*

"WHEN PEOPLE SAY, 'YOU AND Ahmet [Ertegun] produced Ray Charles,' put big quotation marks around produced. We were attendants at a happening. We learned from Ray Charles. My dear friend [writer] Stanley Booth once remarked, 'When Ahmet and Jerry got ready to record Ray Charles, they went to the studio and turned the lights on. Ray didn't need them.'"

—*Jerry Wexler*

"HE WAS THE FIRST TRUE CROSSOVER artist. I remember putting off a few of my so-called hipper friends when the *Jazz* album came out. They said, "Man, he's selling out." But Ray was rock & roll. He was rhythm & blues. He was jazz. He was country. He had such reach – and far-reaching effect."

—*Keith Richards*

"THIS MAY SOUND LIKE SACRILEGE, but I think Ray Charles was more important than Elvis Presley. I don't know if Ray was the architect of rock & roll, but he was certainly the first guy to do a lot of things. He was not a snob about style. Who the hell ever put so many styles together and made it work? He was a true American original."

—*Billy Joel*

"RAY WAS ALWAYS positive about what he was doing, and I admire him most for that. I tell you one thing: He could see a lot better than those with eyes."

—*James Brown*

"DEATH," RAY CHARLES TOLD ME when he first learned that cancer was devouring his body, "is the one motherfucker that ain't ever going away."

I met Ray Charles in 1975, when he agreed to let me ghostwrite his autobiography. He was vulgar, refined, funny, sexy, spontaneous, outlandish, brave, brutal, tender, blue, ecstatic. He would wrap his arms around his torso, hugging himself in a grand gesture of self-affirmation. In normal conversation, he preached and howled and fell to the floor laughing. He was, in his own words, "raw-ass country."

Because my job was to take the material of our dialogues and weave them into a first-person narrative, I had to make sure the dialogues were deep. I began tentatively by saying, "Now if this question is too tough . . ."

"How the fuck can a question be too tough? The truth is the truth."

The truth – at least Ray's truth – came pouring out: that his life had been rough; that his life had been blessed; that he had been a junkie; that he had given up junk only when faced with prison; that he still drank lots of gin and smoked lots of pot and worked just as tirelessly; that he had a huge appetite for women; that he wasn't even certain how many children he had fathered; that he was unrepentant about it all.

"When my mother died, I didn't understand death," he told me. "What do you mean, she's gone forever? I was fifteen, living at a school for the blind 160 miles away from home. She was all I had in the world. No, she couldn't be dead. Can't make it without her.

"That's when I saw what everyone sees: You can't make a deal with death. No, sir. And you can't make a deal with God. Death is coldblooded, and maybe God is, too."

—*David Ritz*

[EXCERPTS FROM RAY CHARLES TRIBUTE]

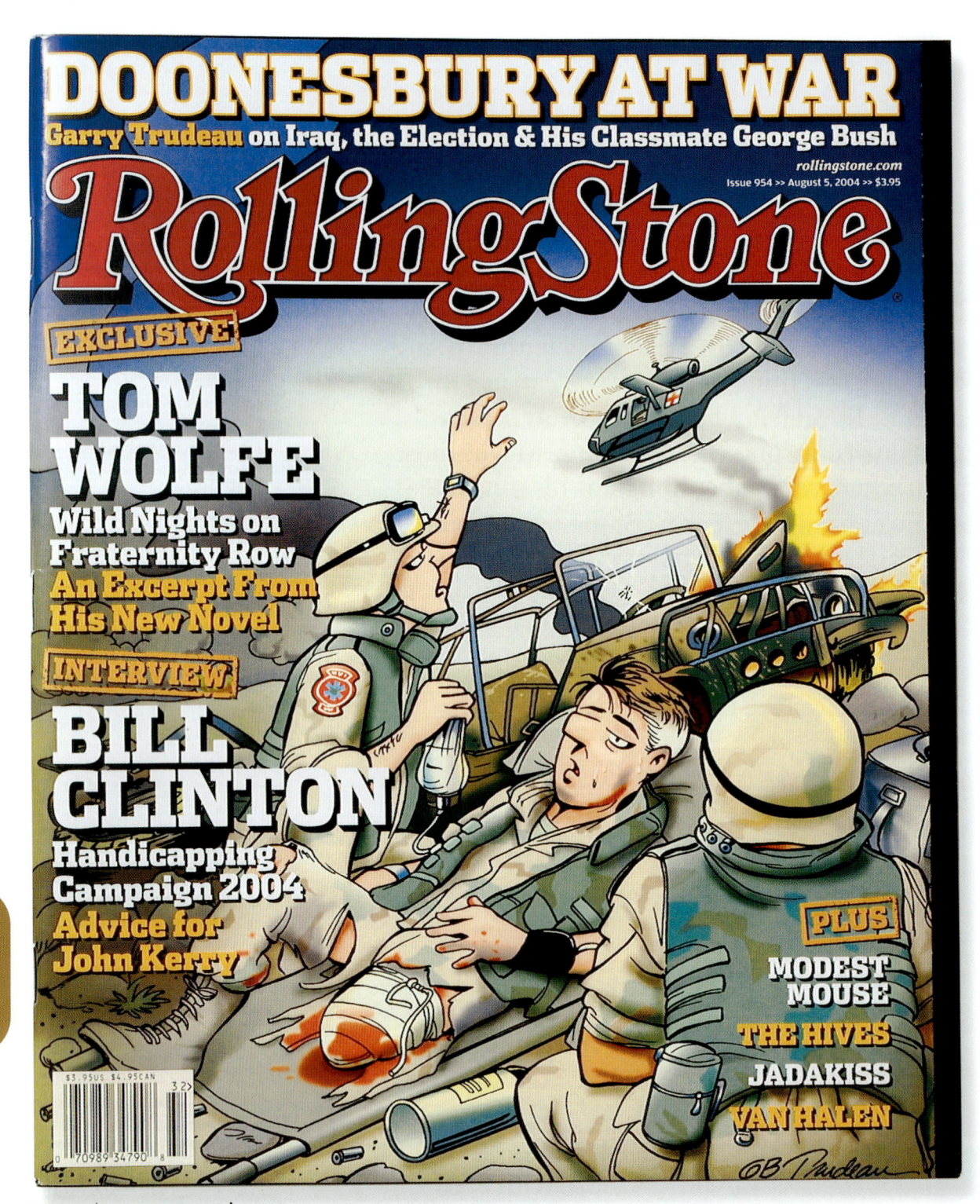

RS 954 | DOONESBURY'S B.D. | August 5th, 2004 | ILLUSTRATION BY GARRY TRUDEAU

NICHOLSON REMEMBERS BRANDO

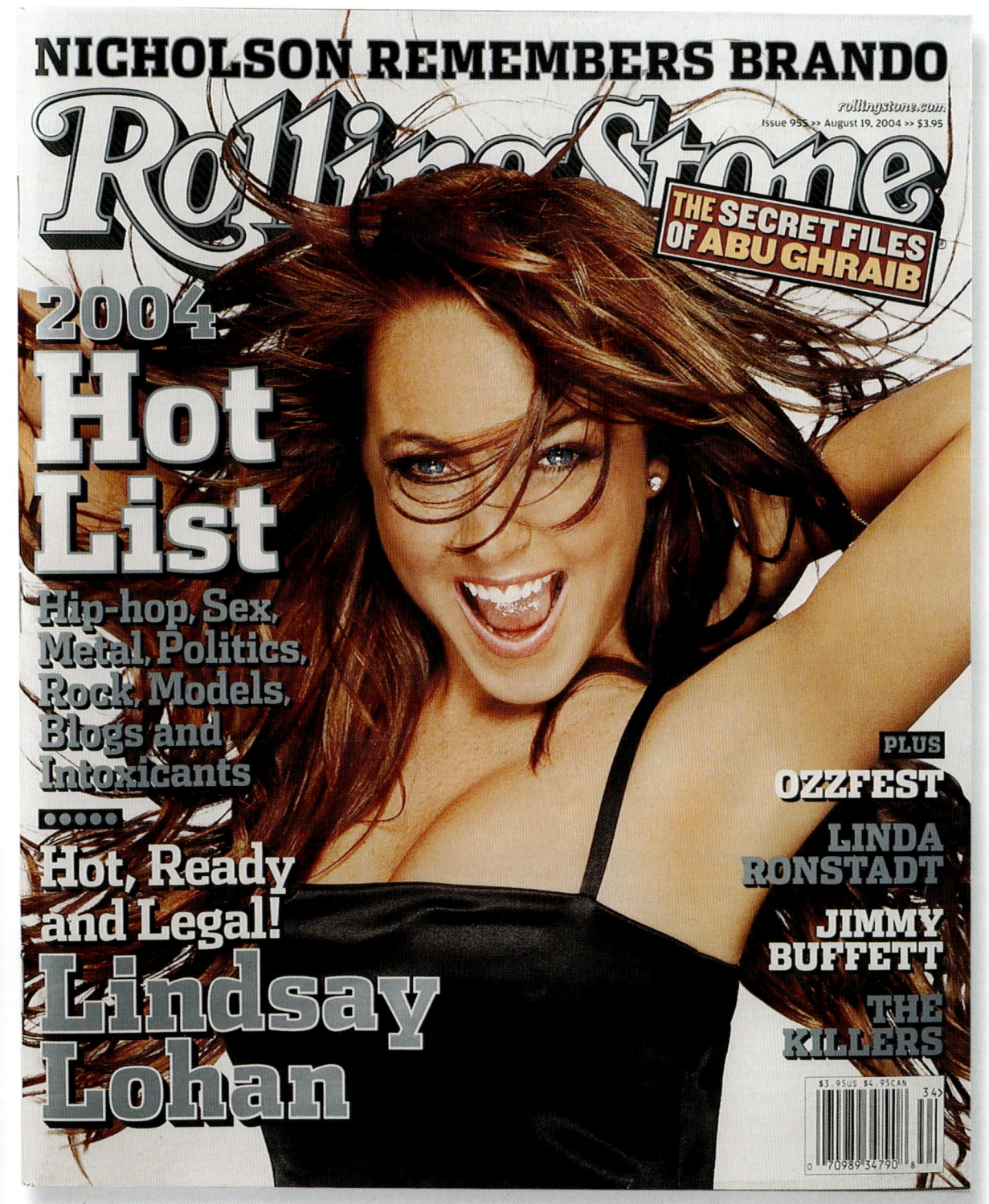

Rolling Stone

rollingstone.com
Issue 955 >> August 19, 2004 >> $3.95

THE SECRET FILES OF ABU GHRAIB

2004 Hot List

Hip-hop, Sex, Metal, Politics, Rock, Models, Blogs and Intoxicants

Hot, Ready and Legal! Lindsay Lohan

PLUS
OZZFEST
LINDA RONSTADT
JIMMY BUFFETT
THE KILLERS

RS 955 | LINSDAY LOHAN | August 19th, 2004 | Photograph by Matthew Rolston

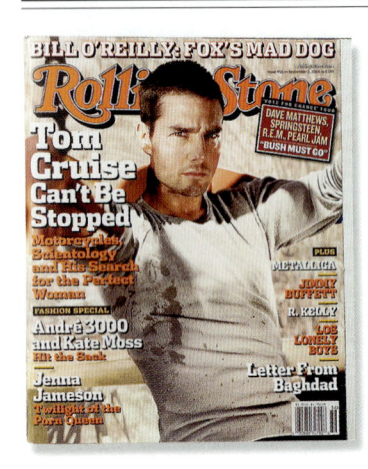

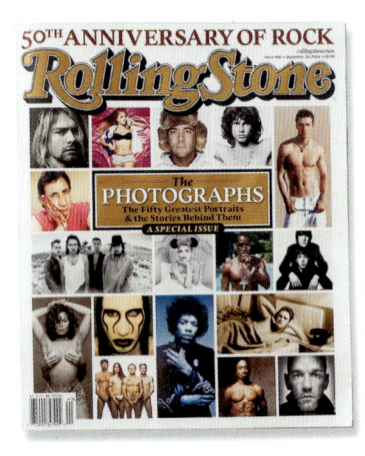

RS 956 | **TOM CRUISE**
September 2nd, 2004
Photograph by Tony Duran

RS 958 | **THE FIFTIETH ANNIVERSARY OF ROCK: THE FIFTY GREATEST PORTRAITS**
September 30th, 2004
Various photographers

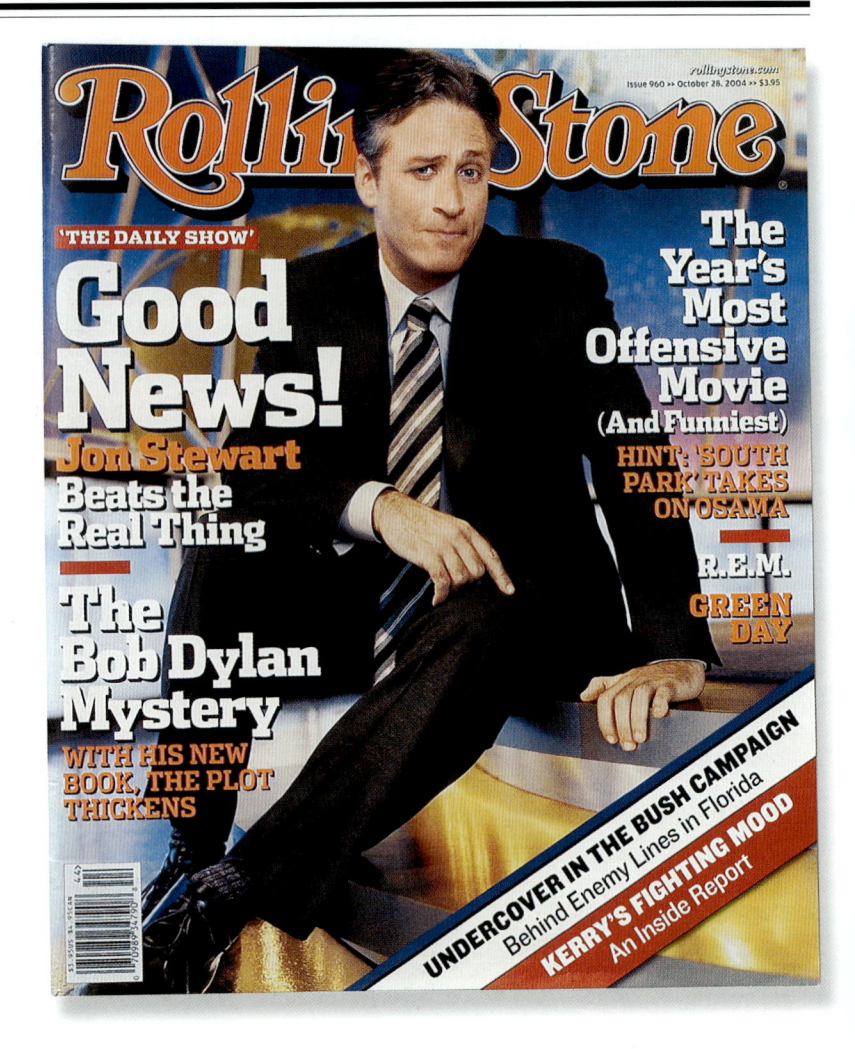

RS 960 | **JON STEWART** | October 28th, 2004 | Photograph by Michael O'Neill

"I THINK WE'VE CHANGED THE WORLD DRAMATICALLY. WHEN WE WERE picked up for broadcast by CNN International – I don't want to say a week later but maybe two weeks later – the border between Pakistan and India stood down. Direct correlation? I don't know what else you can point to."
—*Jon Stewart*

[*RS 957*] This cover, starring the incendiary documentary maker Michael Moore, followed a rather graphic depiction of the Iraq war by Doonesbury creator Garry Trudeau (RS 954) in a series of political covers that led up to Election Day 2004. After Moore came the Vote for Change Tour, a nine-day concert tour of the swing states organized to mobilize voters (RS 959); *Daily Show* host Jon Stewart (RS 960); and then–presidential nominee John Kerry (RS 961).

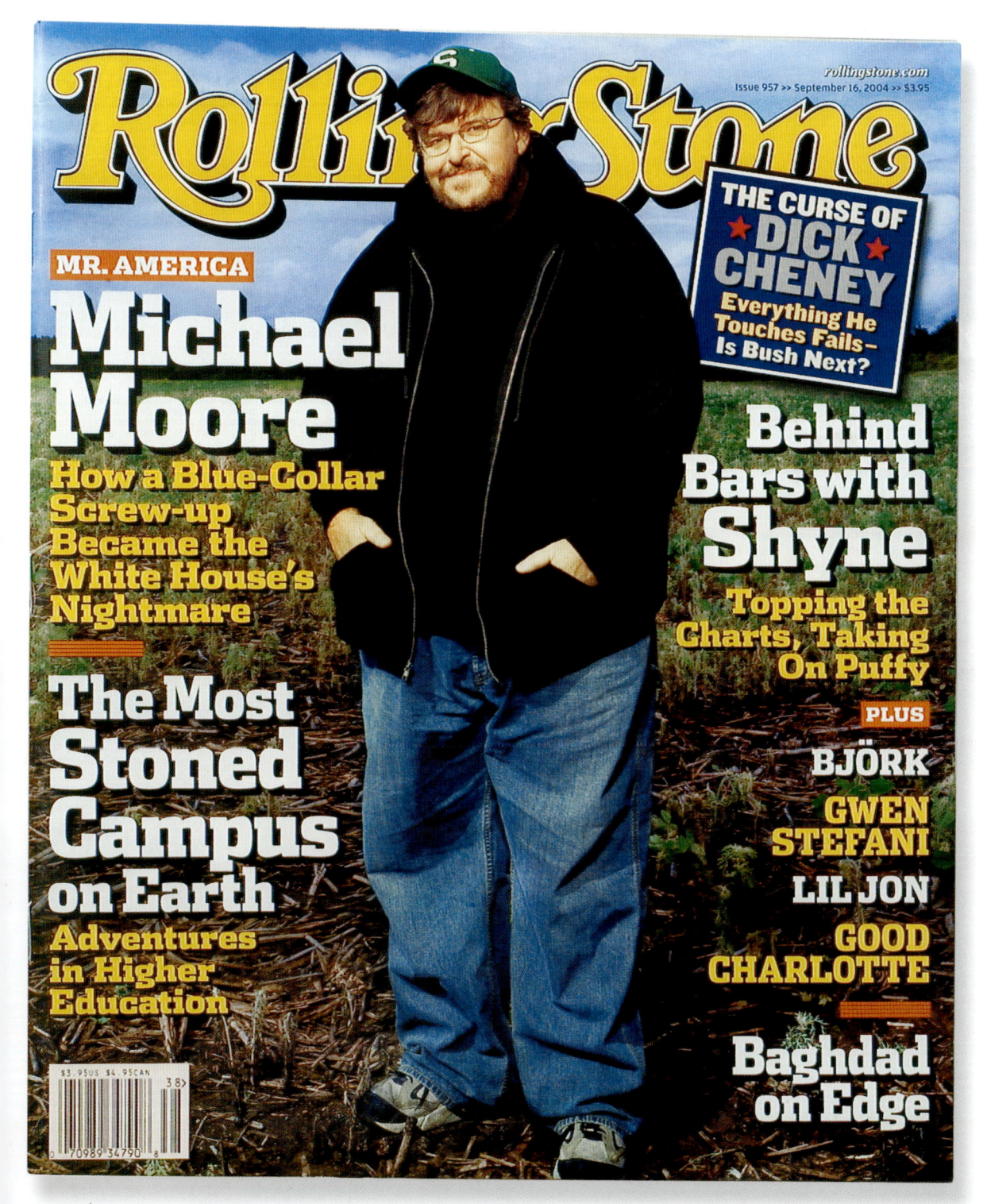

Rolling Stone

Issue 957 >> September 16, 2004 >> $3.95

THE CURSE OF DICK CHENEY
Everything He Touches Fails – Is Bush Next?

MR. AMERICA
Michael Moore
How a Blue-Collar Screw-up Became the White House's Nightmare

The Most Stoned Campus on Earth
Adventures in Higher Education

Behind Bars with Shyne
Topping the Charts, Taking On Puffy

PLUS
BJÖRK
GWEN STEFANI
LIL JON
GOOD CHARLOTTE

Baghdad on Edge

RS 957 | MICHAEL MOORE | September 16th, 2004 | Photograph by Albert Watson

50 YEARS OF COVERS • 523

THE LAST DAYS OF JOHNNY RAMONE

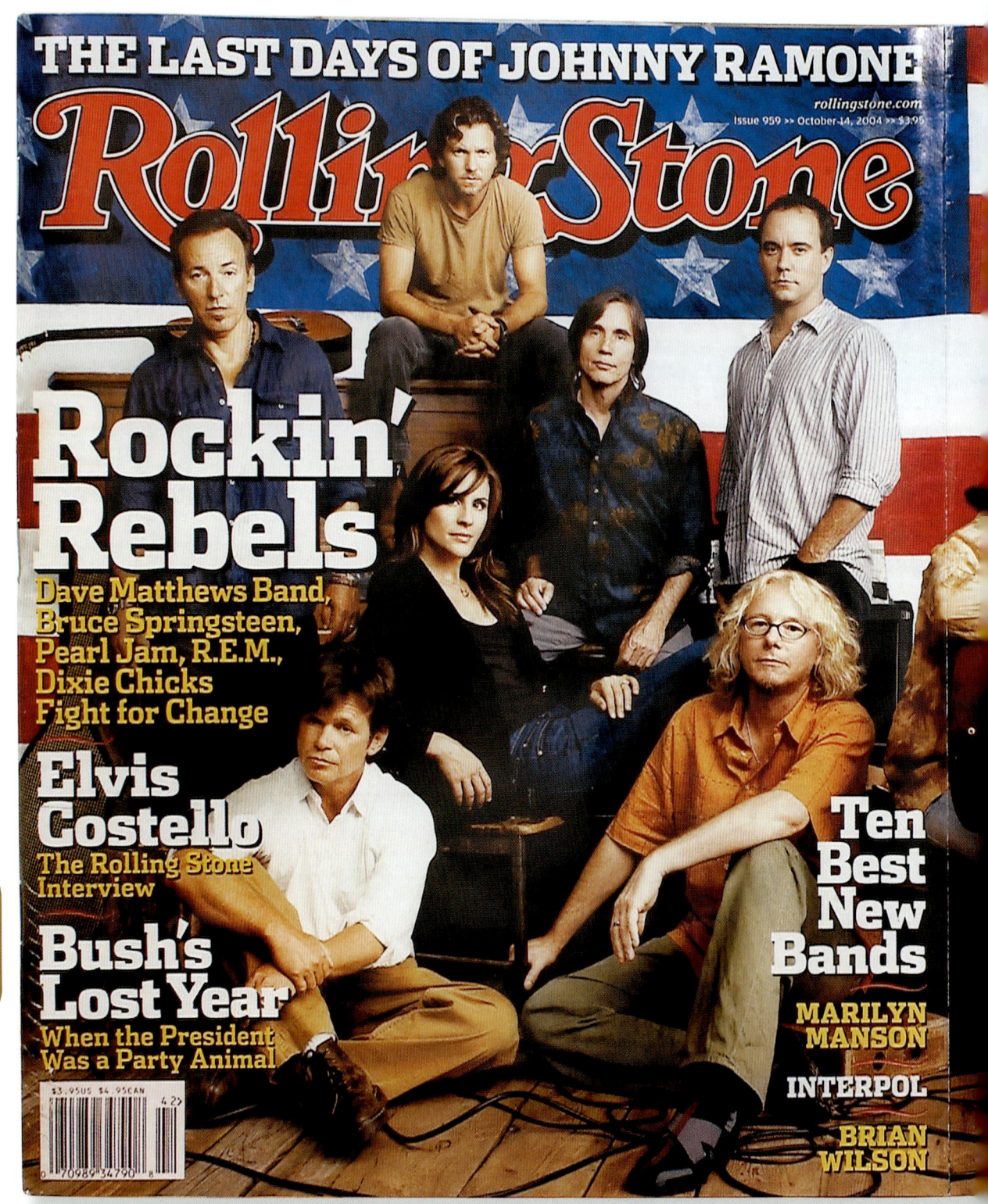

Rolling Stone

rollingstone.com
Issue 959 » October 14, 2004 » $3.95

Rockin' Rebels
Dave Matthews Band, Bruce Springsteen, Pearl Jam, R.E.M., Dixie Chicks Fight for Change

Elvis Costello
The Rolling Stone Interview

Bush's Lost Year
When the President Was a Party Animal

Ten Best New Bands
MARILYN MANSON
INTERPOL
BRIAN WILSON

2000s

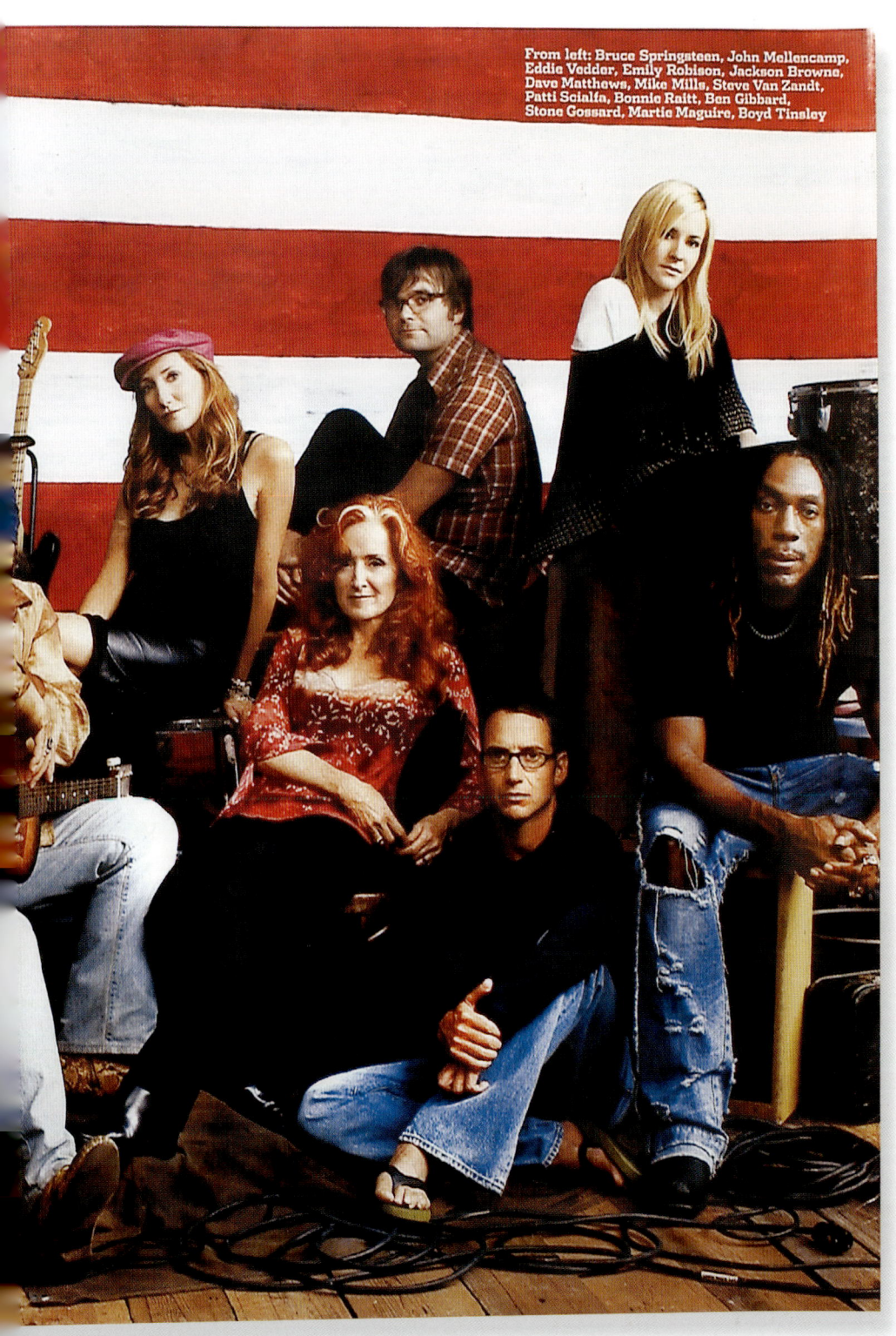

From left: Bruce Springsteen, John Mellencamp, Eddie Vedder, Emily Robison, Jackson Browne, Dave Matthews, Mike Mills, Steve Van Zandt, Patti Scialfa, Bonnie Raitt, Ben Gibbard, Stone Gossard, Martie Maguire, Boyd Tinsley

RS 959
MUSICIANS FROM THE VOTE FOR CHANGE TOUR
October 14th, 2004
PHOTOGRAPH BY NORMAN JEAN ROY

[RS 963] Finishing what it started with RS 937 (which compiled the 500 best albums ever recorded), ROLLING STONE pulled together an all-star panel of 172 voters to select the 500 greatest songs of all time. These are the Top 25.

1.	"LIKE A ROLLING STONE"	BOB DYLAN
2.	"(I CAN'T GET NO) SATISFACTION"	THE ROLLING STONES
3.	"IMAGINE"	JOHN LENNON
4.	"WHAT'S GOING ON"	MARVIN GAYE
5.	"RESPECT"	ARETHA FRANKLIN
6.	"GOOD VIBRATIONS"	THE BEACH BOYS
7.	"JOHNNY B. GOODE"	CHUCK BERRY
8.	"HEY JUDE"	THE BEATLES
9.	"SMELLS LIKE TEEN SPIRIT"	NIRVANA
10.	"WHAT'D I SAY"	RAY CHARLES
11.	"MY GENERATION"	THE WHO
12.	"A CHANGE IS GONNA COME"	SAM COOKE
13.	"YESTERDAY"	THE BEATLES
14.	"BLOWIN' IN THE WIND"	BOB DYLAN
15.	"LONDON CALLING"	THE CLASH
16.	"I WANT TO HOLD YOUR HAND"	THE BEATLES
17.	"PURPLE HAZE"	THE JIMI HENDRIX EXPERIENCE
18.	"MAYBELLINE"	CHUCK BERRY
19.	"HOUND DOG"	ELVIS PRESLEY
20.	"LET IT BE"	THE BEATLES
21.	"BORN TO RUN"	BRUCE SPRINGSTEEN
22.	"BE MY BABY"	THE RONETTES
23.	"IN MY LIFE"	THE BEATLES
24.	"PEOPLE GET READY"	THE IMPRESSIONS
25.	"GOD ONLY KNOWS"	THE BEACH BOYS

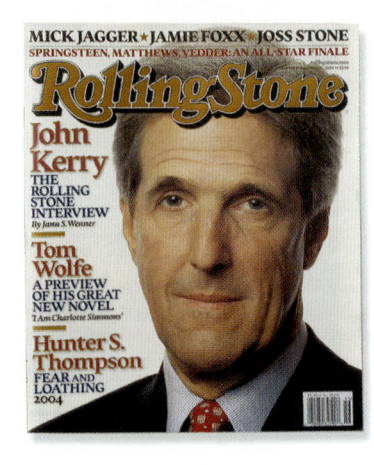

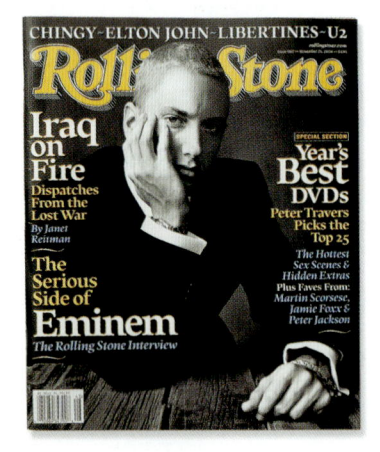

RS 961 | JOHN KERRY
November 11th, 2004
PHOTOGRAPH BY ALBERT WATSON

RS 962 | EMINEM
November 25th, 2004
PHOTOGRAPH BY NORMAN JEAN ROY

RS 963 | THE 500 GREATEST SONGS OF ALL TIME
December 12th, 2004
TYPOGRAPHY BY AMID CAPECI

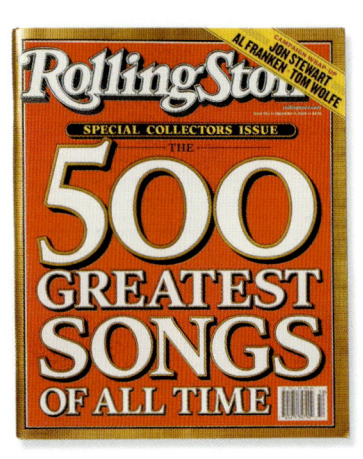

2000s

526 • ROLLING STONE

ANNUAL READERS & CRITICS' POLL

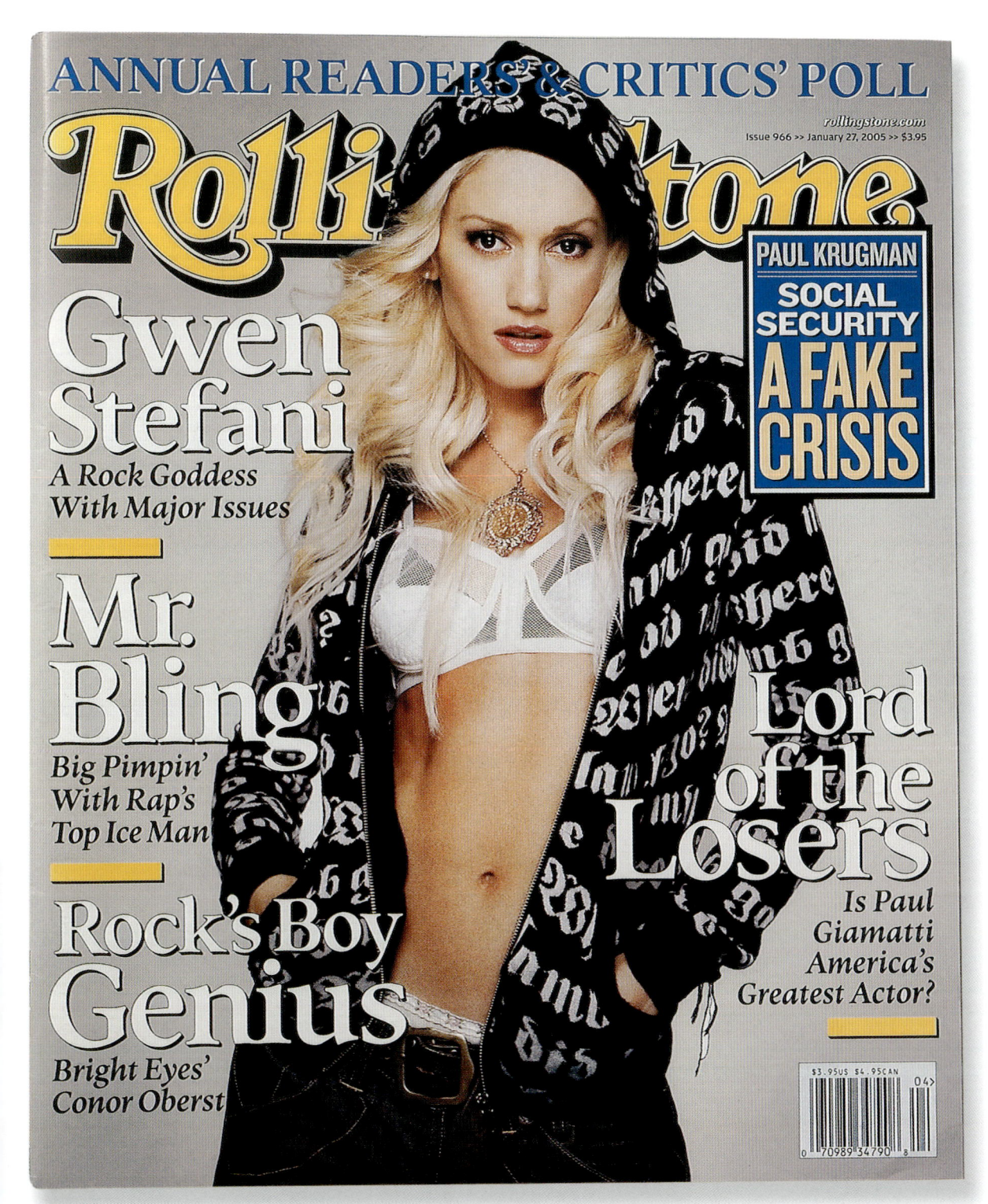

Rolling Stone

rollingstone.com
Issue 966 >> January 27, 2005 >> $3.95

Gwen Stefani
A Rock Goddess With Major Issues

Mr. Bling
Big Pimpin' With Rap's Top Ice Man

Rock's Boy Genius
Bright Eyes' Conor Oberst

PAUL KRUGMAN
SOCIAL SECURITY A FAKE CRISIS

Lord of the Losers
Is Paul Giamatti America's Greatest Actor?

RS 966 | GWEN STEFANI | January 27th, 2005 | Photograph by Max Vadukul

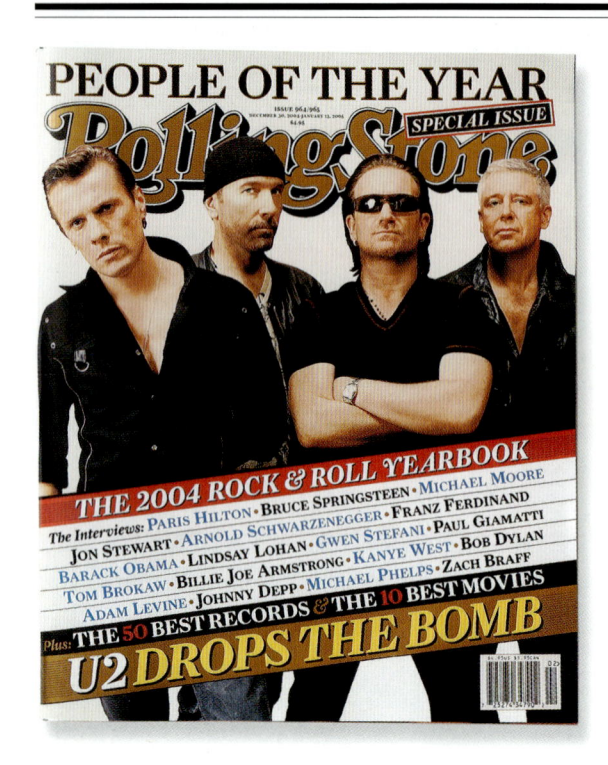

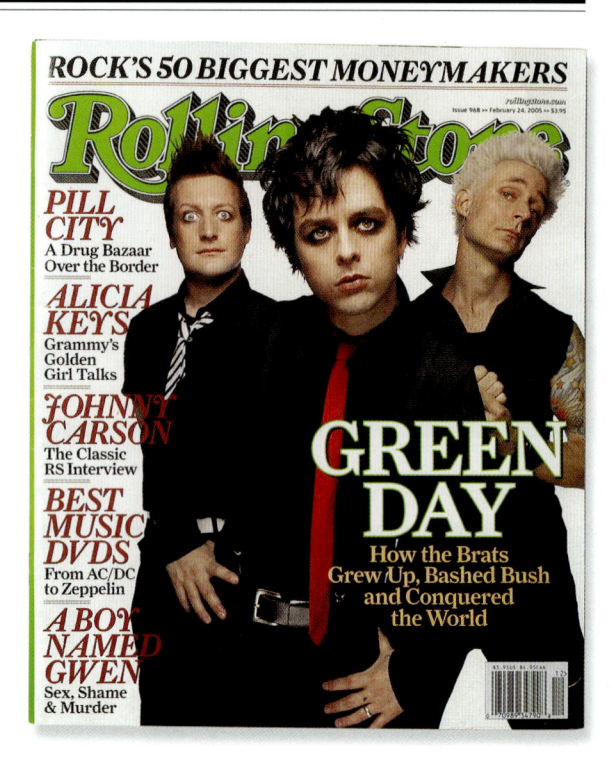

RS 964/965 | U2
December 30th, 2004 – January 13th, 2005
PHOTOGRAPH BY RUVEN AFANADOR

RS 968 | GREEN DAY
February 24th, 2005
PHOTOGRAPH BY JAMES DIMMOCK

RS 969 | BOB MARLEY
March 10th, 2005
PHOTOGRAPH BY ANNIE LEIBOVITZ

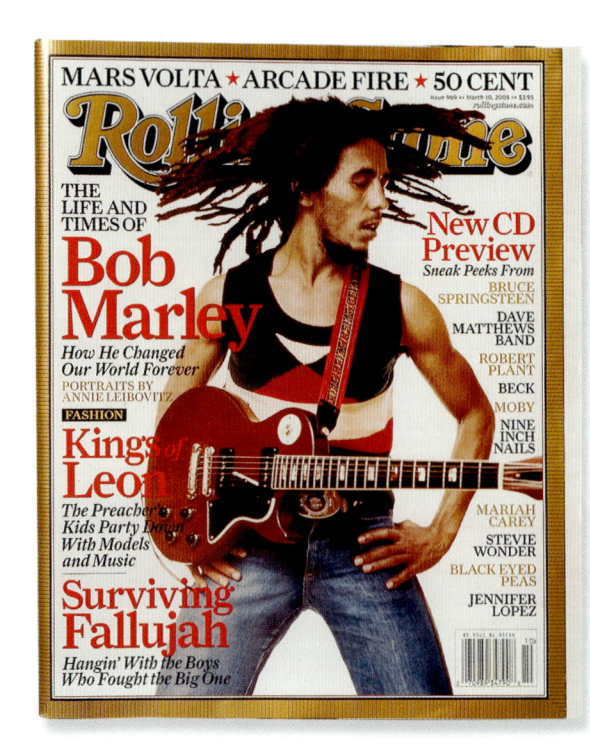

2000s

528 • ROLLING STONE

Rolling Stone

rollingstone.com
Issue 967 >> February 10, 2005 >> $3.95

Johnny Depp
Wild at Heart

King Rat
THE DARK WORLD OF THE DRUG WAR'S BIGGEST NARC

Michael Jackson On Trial
INSIDE HIS DEFENSE STRATEGY

The Game
DRE'S NEW HITMAN

Great Whales
PHOTOGRAPHS BY SEBASTIÃO SALGADO

RS 967 | JOHNNY DEPP | February 10th, 2005 | Photograph by Albert Watson

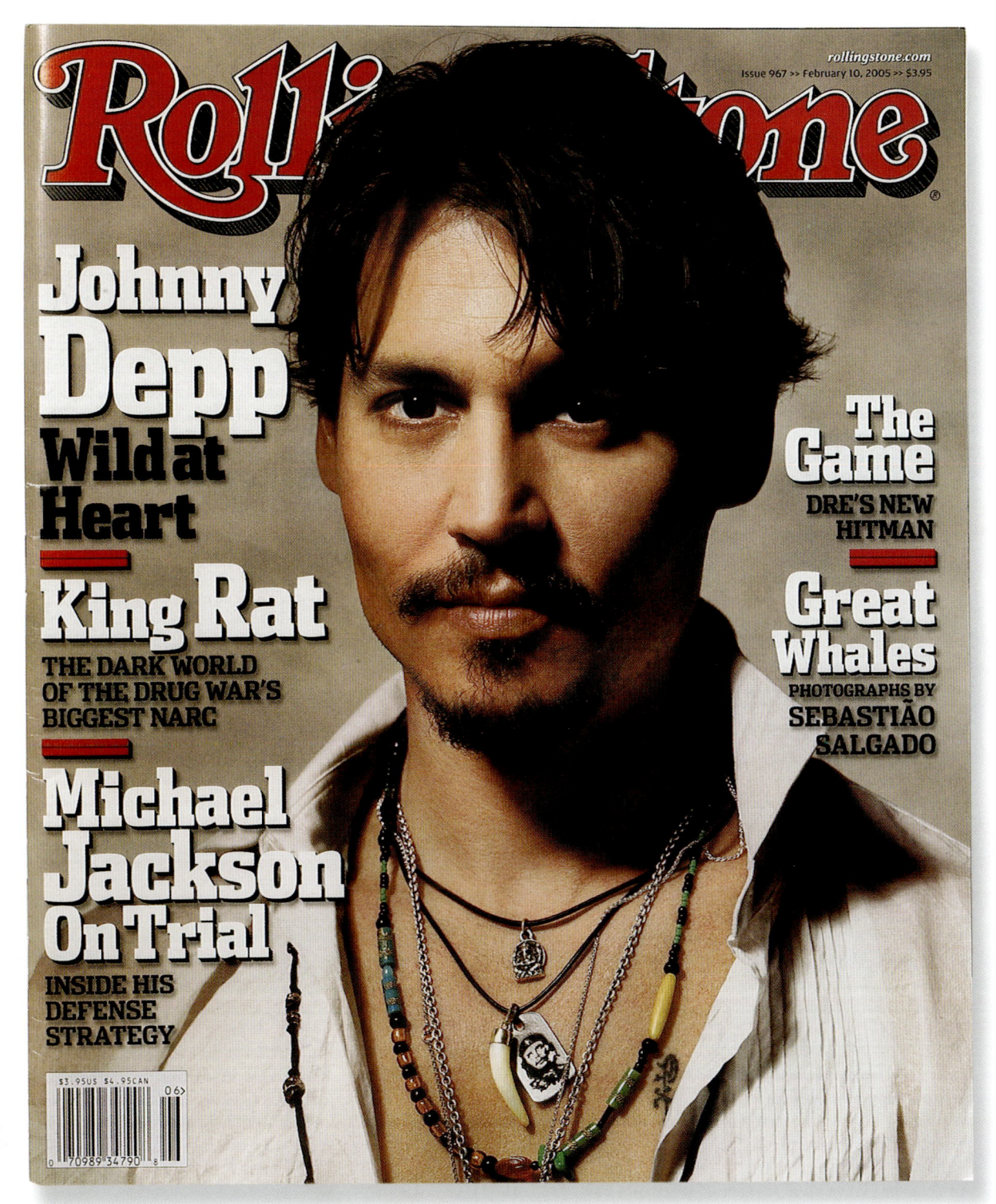

50 YEARS OF COVERS • 529

RS 970 | HUNTER S. THOMPSON | March 24th, 2005 | Photograph by David Hiser

These are sad days here at

Rolling Stone. This morning I cried as I struck "National Affairs Desk: Hunter S. Thompson" from the masthead – after thirty-five years. Hunter's name is now listed with Ralph Gleason's on what Hunter would have called "the honor roll." Hunter was part of the DNA of Rolling Stone, one of those twisting strands of chemicals around which a new life is formed. He was such a big part of my life, and I loved him deeply. He was a man of energy, physical presence, utter charm, genius talent and genius humor. It's very hard to have to give him up and to say goodbye...

Once I had Hunter all to myself, and now I don't have him at all. He was a careful, deliberate and calculating man, and his suicide was not careless, not an accident and not selfish. He was in a wheelchair toward the end of his life, and he decided he would not be able to live with extreme physical disability; it just wasn't him. He had already lived longer than he, or any of us, had expected. He had lived a great life, filled with friends, his genius talent and righteousness.

— *Jann S. Wenner*
[EXCERPT FROM HUNTER S. THOMPSON TRIBUTE]

"IT ALWAYS SEEMED TO ME THAT Hunter was a man fighting for the rights of American Independence. Inside he felt this deep outrage, because people were fucking with his beloved Constitution. In that way he was a real American, a pioneer, a frontiersman, with a huge and raging mind. He should be lying in state next to the Lincoln Memorial. That's how they should have done it. He was a genuine son of the Kentucky pioneers." —*Ralph Steadman*

"HE WAS INCISIVE. HE WAS DEEP. He played with facts, he slept with facts, he bathed with facts. They warmed him like a blanket. Facts were key, and they weren't arbitrary, they weren't ambiguous. They were precise. He was very, very precise.

"He was a great, great man. America has lost a great thinker."
—*Michael Stepanian*

"A FEW YEARS AGO HE SENT ME A wonderful photograph of himself leaping up on a golf course, like a gymnast, with both feet off the ground. He looks incredibly graceful. There's a wonderful passage from *The Great Gatsby*: 'Gatsby believed in the green light, the orgiastic future that year by year recedes before us. It eluded us then, but that's no matter – tomorrow we will run faster, stretch our arms out farther.' The picture of Hunter reminds me of that."
—*Lynn Nesbit*

"He makes us
laugh – we can't help it. When we're around or about [him], we all want to be brilliant."
—*Jack Nicholson*

"BUY THE TICKET, TAKE THE RIDE." These are the words that echo in my skull. The words that our Good Doctor lived by and, by God, died by. He dictated, created, commanded, demanded, manipulated, manhandled and snatched life up by the short hairs and only relinquished his powerful grasp when he was ready. We are here, without him. But in no way are we left with nothing. We have his words, his insights, his humor and his truth. For those of us lucky enough to have been close to him, which often meant rather lengthy and dangerous occasions that would invariably lead to uncontrollable fits of laughter, we have the memory of his Cheshire grin leading us wherever he felt we needed to go. Which was always the right direction, however insane it may have seemed. Yes, the doctor always knew best. I have, seared onto my brain, the millions of hideous little adventures that I was blessed enough to have lived through with him and, frankly, in certain instances, blessed to have lived through. He was/is a brother, a friend, a hero, a father, a son, a teacher, a partner in crime. Our crime: fun. Always, fun.
—*Johnny Depp*
[EXCERPT FROM HUNTER S. THOMPSON TRIBUTE]

"HE WAS A VERY MORAL MAN. To him, what's right was right. Anything else was wrong, and the bastards better pay for it.

"I'd get these faxes from him that would use up all of the paper in my machine: twenty pages of writing and drawings, in that jagged hand. They'd just keep on comin'. I'd think, 'Shit, I better put more paper in – Hunter's calling.'"
—*Keith Richards*

Tales From a Weird & Righteous American Saga

RollingStone

DR. HUNTER S. THOMPSON
1937-2005

GONZO

Issue 970
March 24, 2005
$3.95
rollingstone.com

2000s

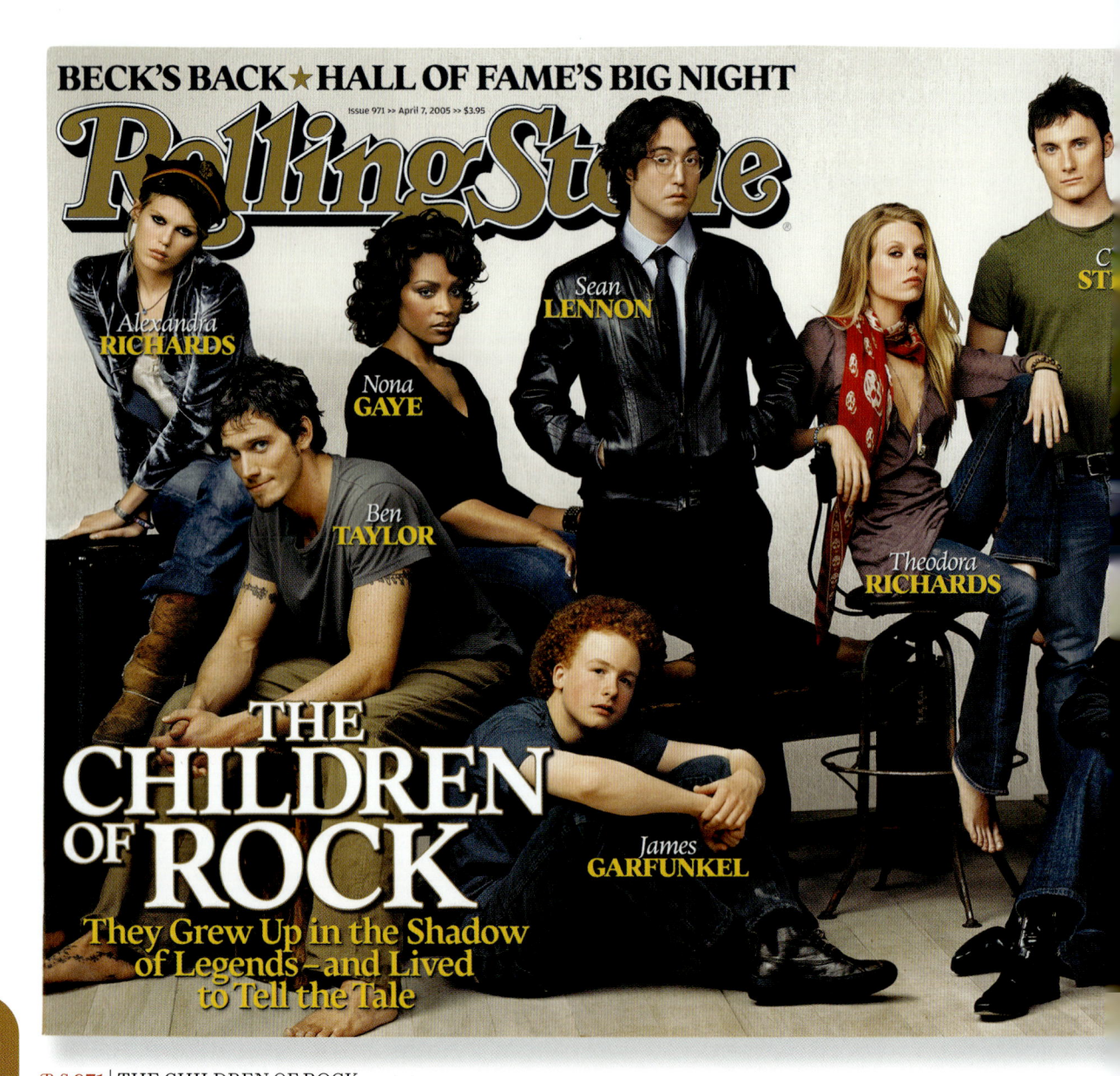

RS 971 | THE CHILDREN OF ROCK | April 7th, 2005 | Photograph by Norman Jean Roy

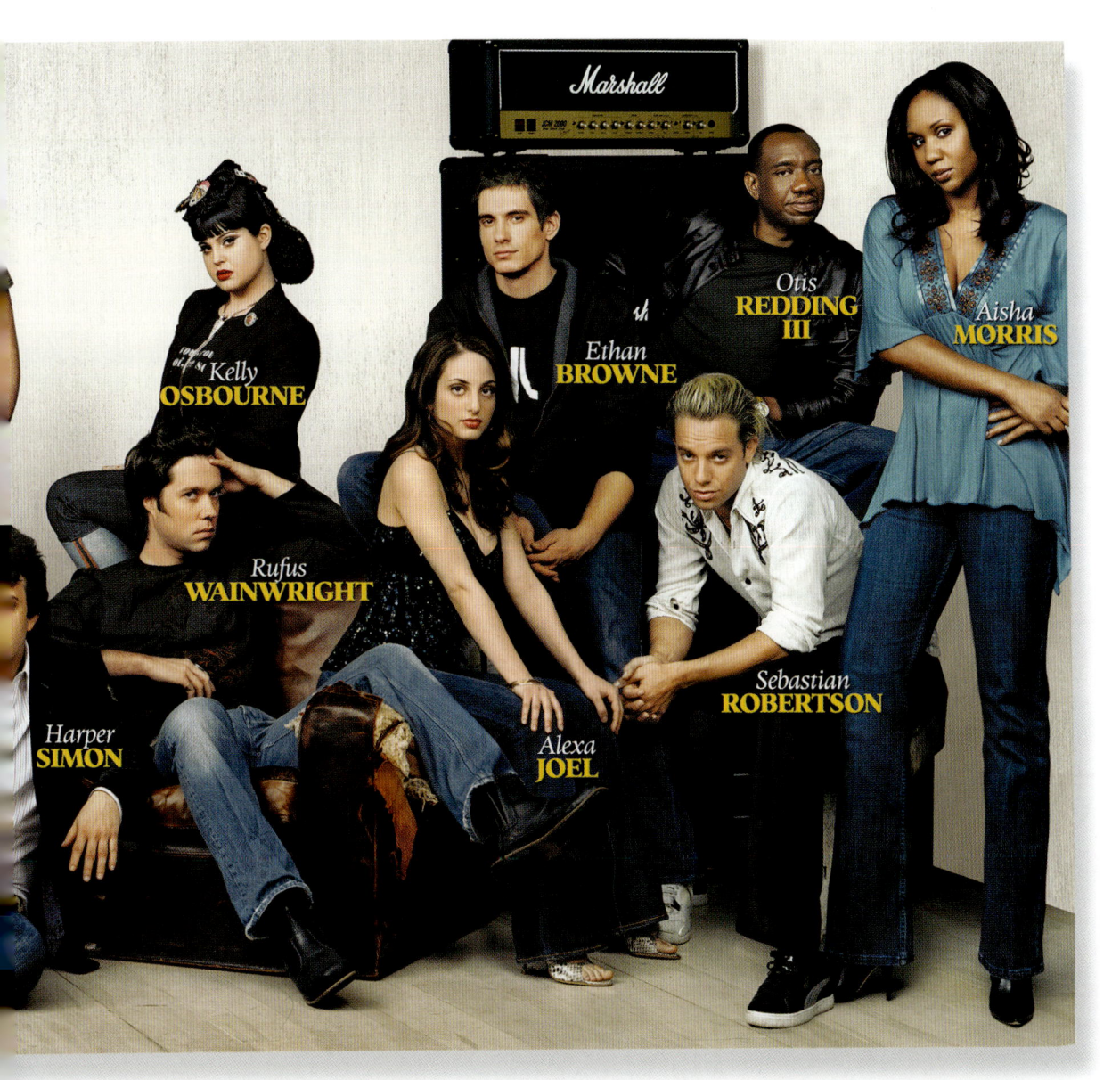

"**I think one of the reasons we all got along** [at the photo shoot] is because nobody was like, 'Oh, that's Stevie Wonder's daughter!' 'That's Marvin Gaye's daughter!' 'That's Paul Simon's son.' I mean, I can't tell you how many times I meet people and someone will say, 'This is Billy Joel's daughter!' I used to get mad and say, 'My name is Alexa!' Harper [Simon] and I were talking about how it was really nice, for once, to just discuss our own work and what we wanted to do with our own lives."

—*Alexa Joel*

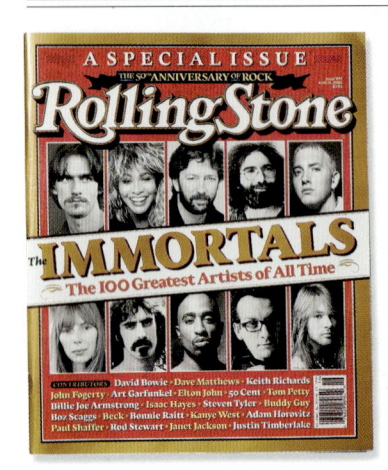

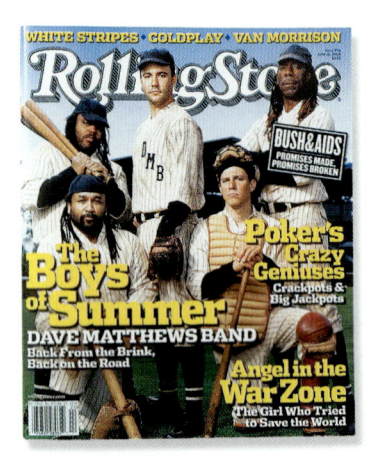

RS 972 | THE FIFTIETH ANNIVERSARY OF ROCK: THE IMMORTALS PART II
April 21st, 2005
VARIOUS PHOTOGRAPHERS

RS 976 | DAVE MATTHEWS BAND
June 16th, 2005
PHOTOGRAPH BY MARTIN SCHOELLER

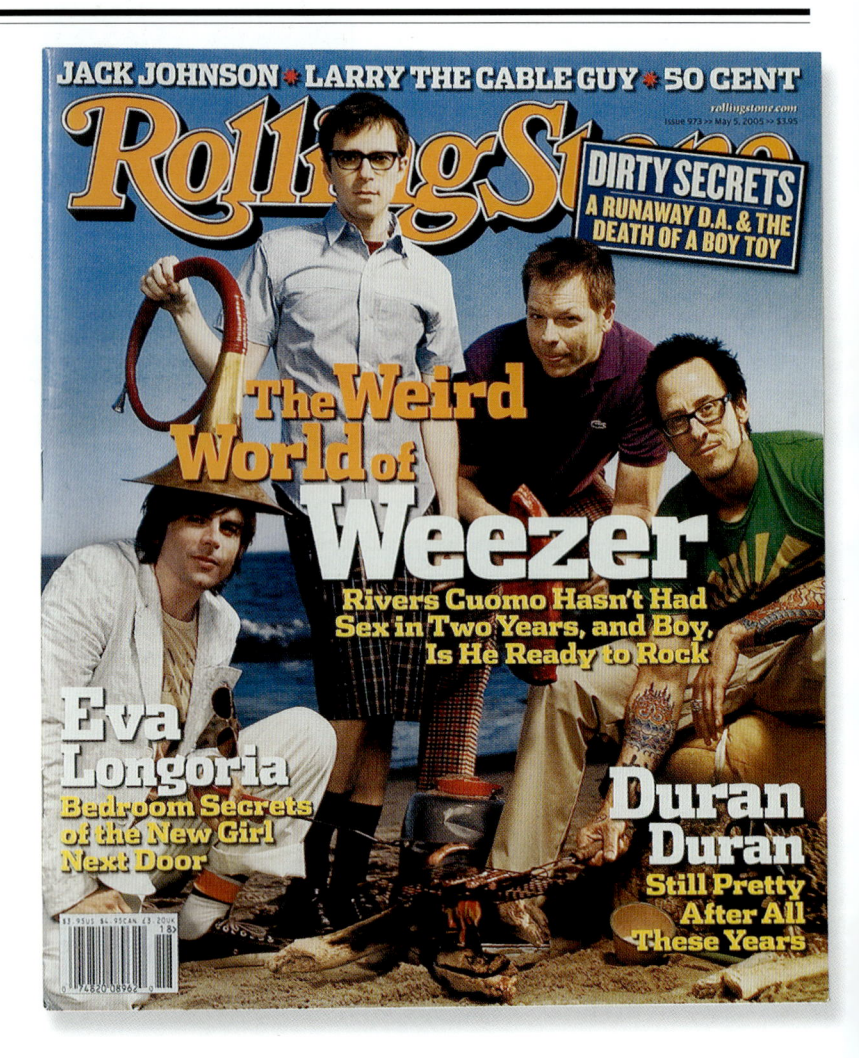

RS 973 | WEEZER
May 5th, 2005 | PHOTOGRAPH BY MARTIN SCHOELLER

BEFORE WE TURN IN FOR THE NIGHT, [ORLANDO] BLOOM TALKS ABOUT a phenomenon he experienced while filming *Kingdom of Heaven* in Spain. That phenomenon was himself. It was the first time he had to deal with mobs of screaming fans outside his hotel – so many that police barricades had to be erected. He eventually had to hire Brad Pitt's security guard. "I think I'm mentioning this because I feel slightly bad that I didn't cope with it better," he says. "I really feel like if I were ever back in Spain, I'd make an effort to spend time with those people. Because they were all so sweet. I felt like I froze."

Either Bloom is truly a good guy or he's a great actor. Perhaps even both.

[EXCERPT FROM RS 974 COVER STORY BY NEIL STRAUSS]

COLDPLAY'S PLAN FOR WORLD DOMINATION

Rolling Stone

rollingstone.com
Issue 974 >> May 19, 2005 >> $3.95

QUAGMIRE
A HARD LOOK AT THE IRAQ DISASTER

Sex on the Beach with Orlando Bloom

Hollywood's No. 1 Pretty Boy Finds His Inner Gladiator

Mötley Crüe Return

Sick Days, Twisted Nights, Lots of Naps

PLUS

CHRIS ROCK

ROBERT PLANT

WEEZER

DAVE MATTHEWS BAND

AUDIOSLAVE

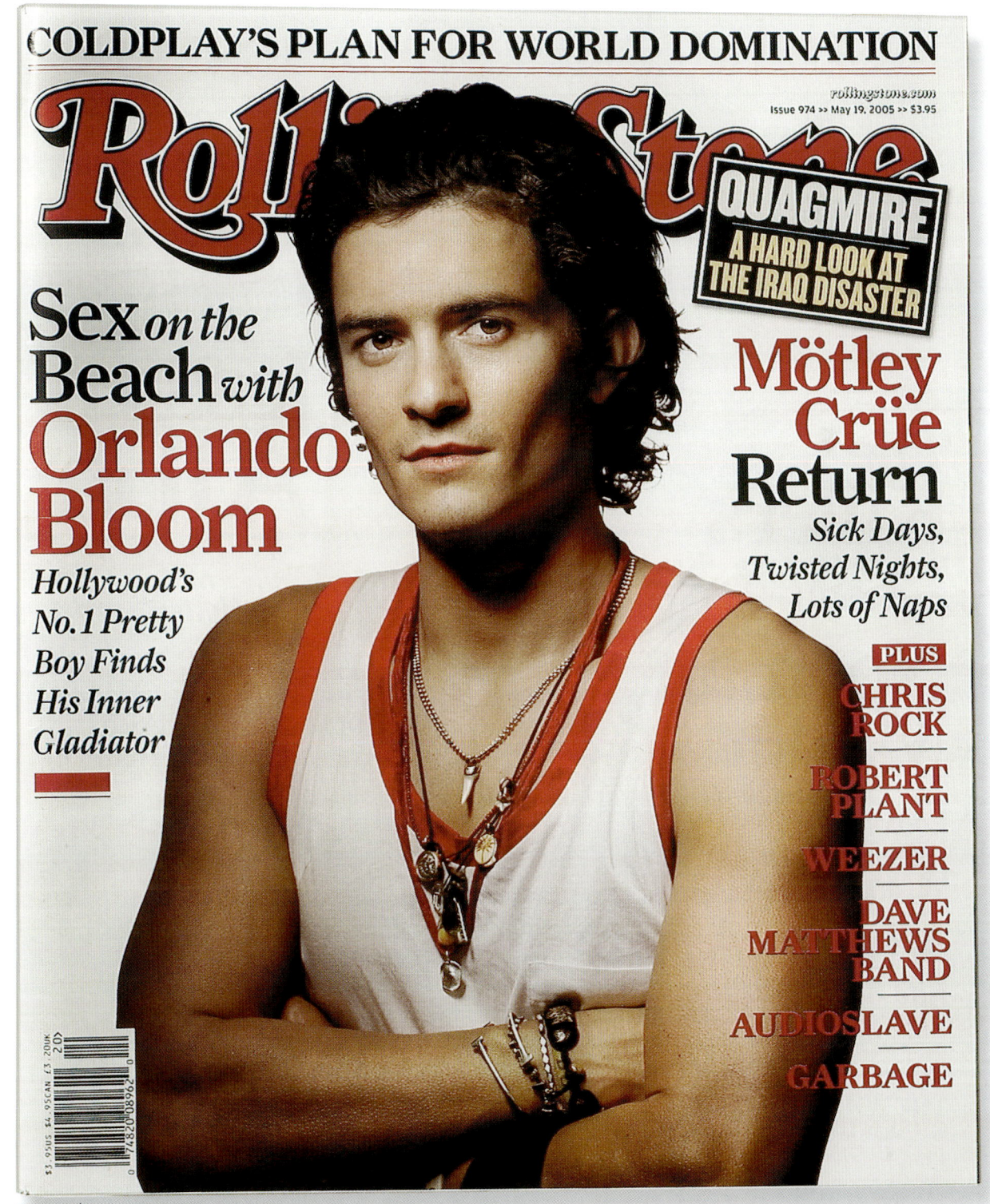

GARBAGE

RS 974 | ORLANDO BLOOM | May 19th, 2005 | Photograph by Albert Watson

50 YEARS OF COVERS • 535

SUMMER DOUBLE ISSUE

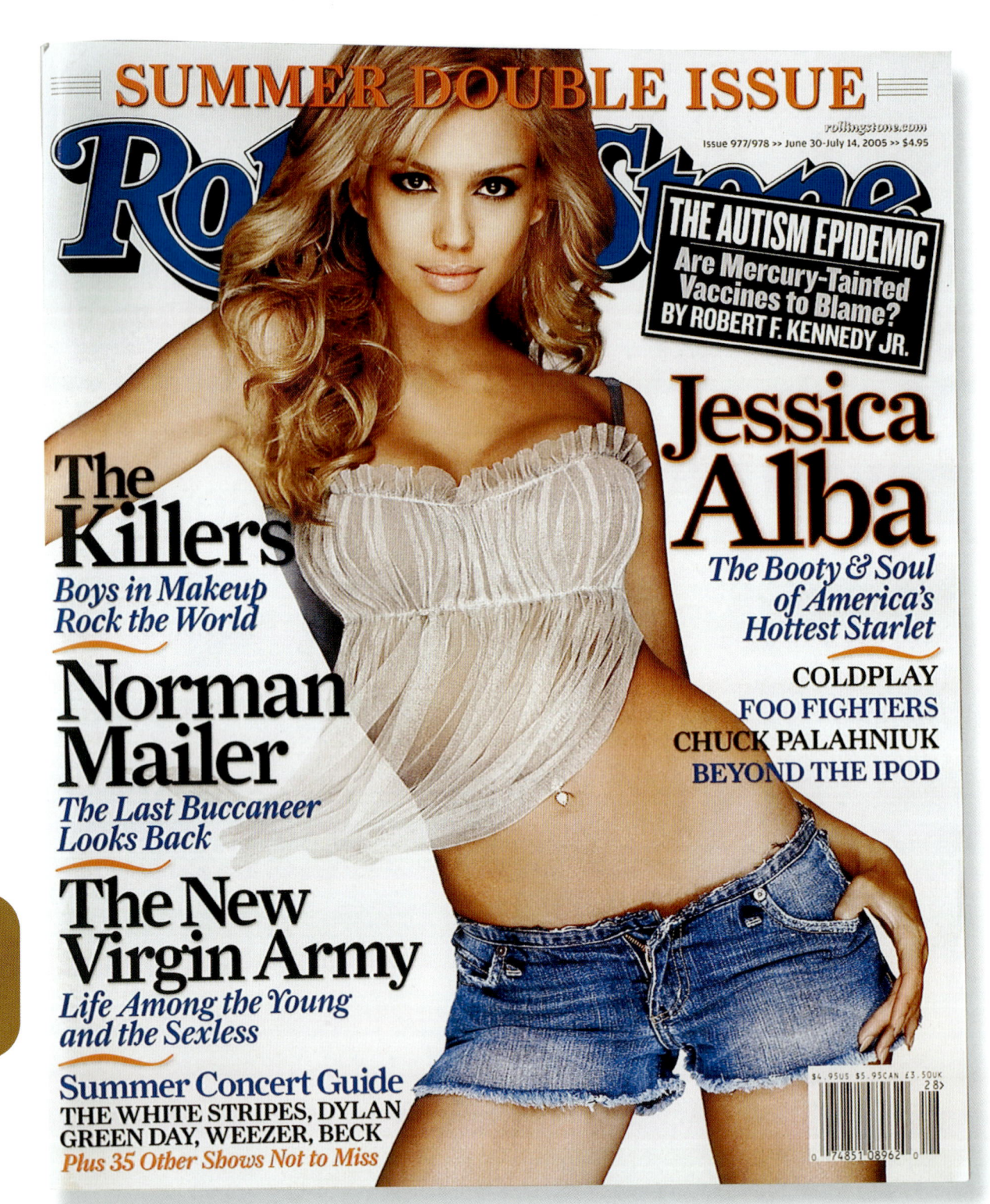

Rolling Stone

rollingstone.com
Issue 977/978 >> June 30-July 14, 2005 >> $4.95

THE AUTISM EPIDEMIC
Are Mercury-Tainted Vaccines to Blame?
BY ROBERT F. KENNEDY JR.

The Killers
Boys in Makeup Rock the World

Norman Mailer
The Last Buccaneer Looks Back

The New Virgin Army
Life Among the Young and the Sexless

Summer Concert Guide
THE WHITE STRIPES, DYLAN GREEN DAY, WEEZER, BECK
Plus 35 Other Shows Not to Miss

Jessica Alba
The Booty & Soul of America's Hottest Starlet

**COLDPLAY
FOO FIGHTERS
CHUCK PALAHNIUK
BEYOND THE IPOD**

2000s

RS 977/978 | JESSICA ALBA | June 30th – July 14th, 2005 | Photograph by Matthew Rolston

536 • ROLLING STONE

INSIDE LIVE 8 ★ COLDPLAY ★ BUSH vs. BIG BIRD

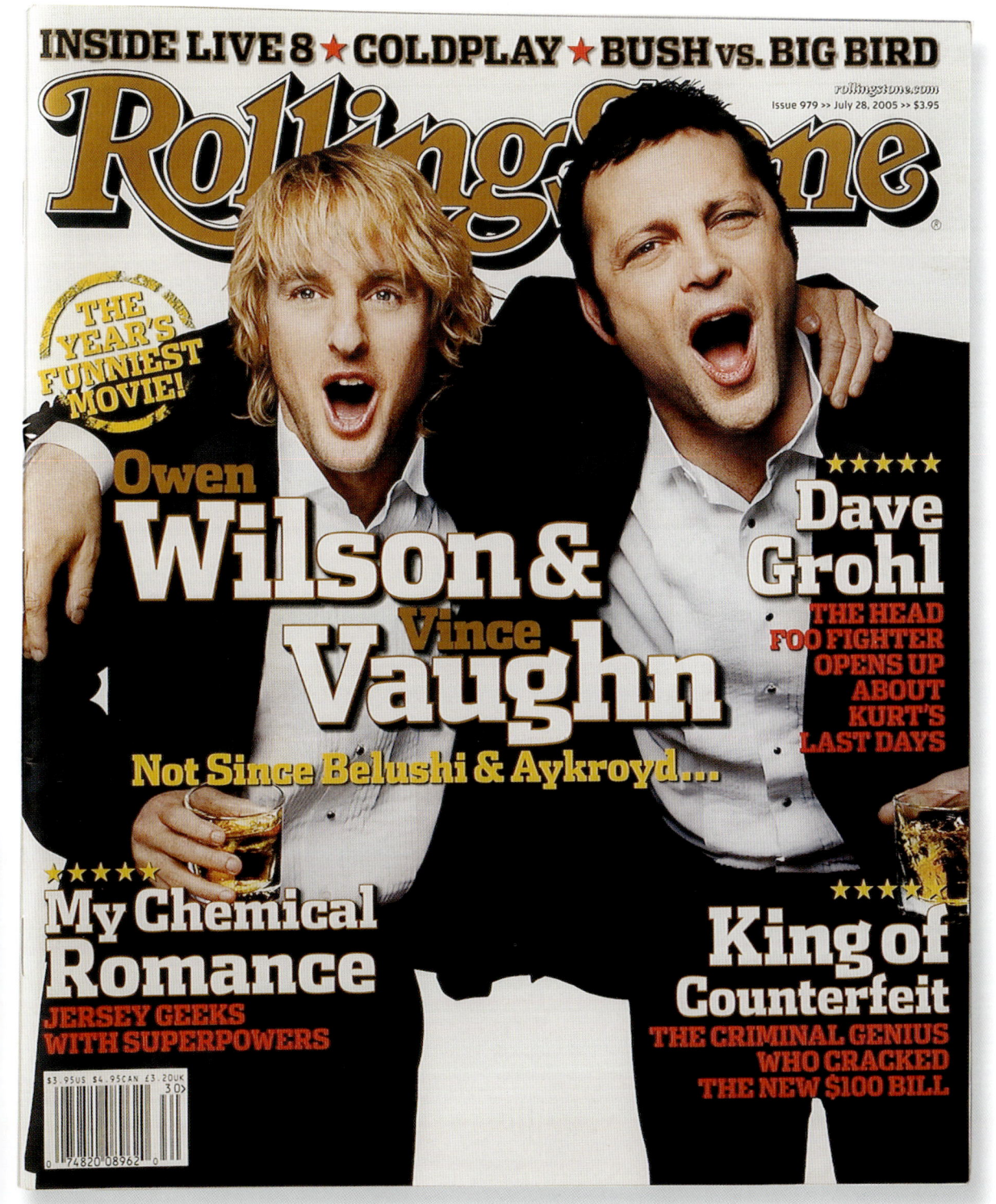

RollingStone

rollingstone.com
Issue 979 >> July 28, 2005 >> $3.95

THE YEAR'S FUNNIEST MOVIE!

Owen Wilson & Vince Vaughn

Not Since Belushi & Aykroyd...

Dave Grohl
THE HEAD FOO FIGHTER OPENS UP ABOUT KURT'S LAST DAYS

My Chemical Romance
JERSEY GEEKS WITH SUPERPOWERS

King of Counterfeit
THE CRIMINAL GENIUS WHO CRACKED THE NEW $100 BILL

RS 979 | OWEN WILSON & VINCE VAUGHN | July 28th, 2005 | Photograph by Max Vadukul

SYSTEM OF A DOWN: BIGGER & WEIRDER

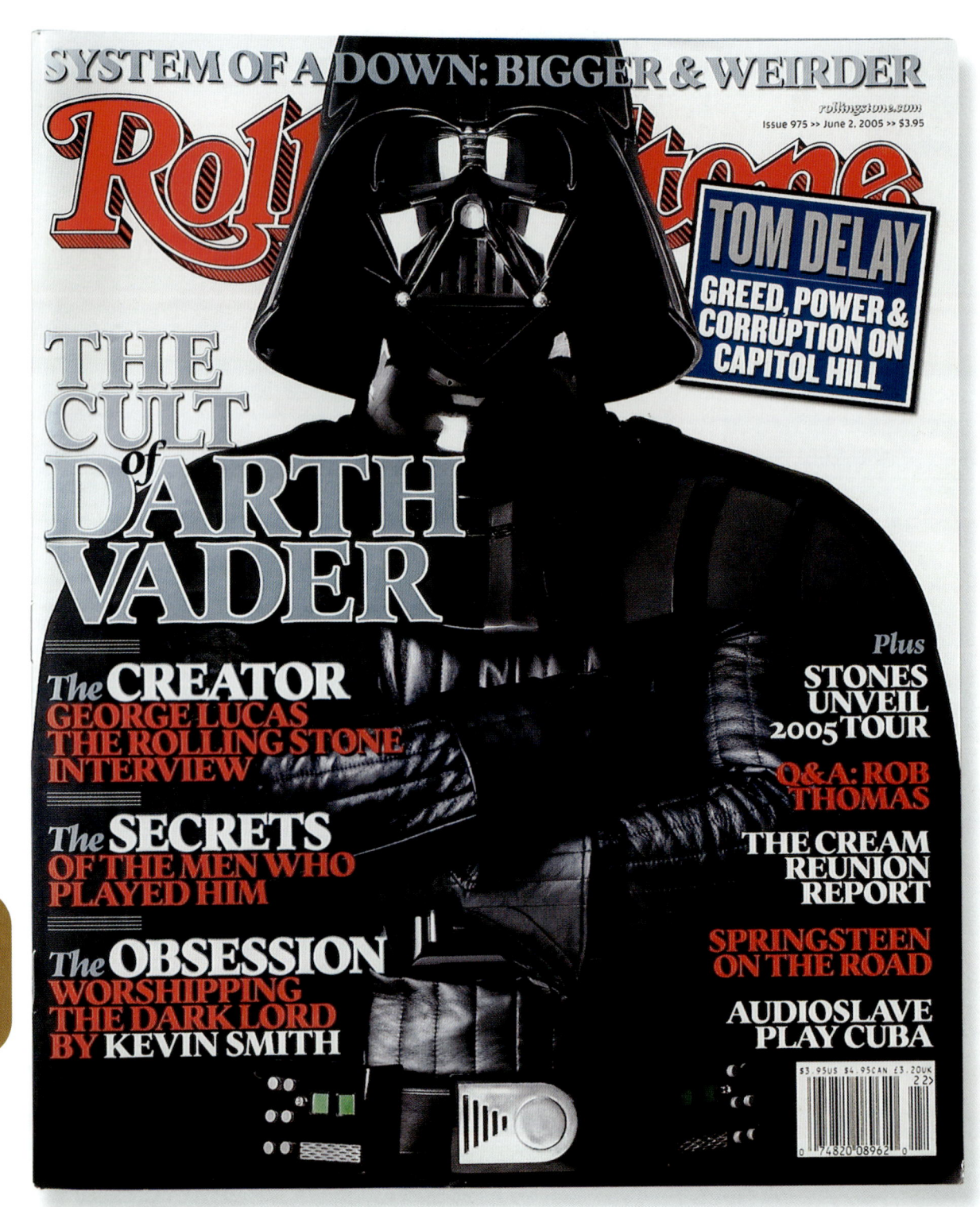

Rolling Stone

rollingstone.com
Issue 975 » June 2, 2005 » $3.95

TOM DELAY
GREED, POWER & CORRUPTION ON CAPITOL HILL

THE CULT of DARTH VADER

The CREATOR
GEORGE LUCAS
THE ROLLING STONE
INTERVIEW

The SECRETS
OF THE MEN WHO
PLAYED HIM

The OBSESSION
WORSHIPPING
THE DARK LORD
BY KEVIN SMITH

Plus
STONES
UNVEIL
2005 TOUR

Q&A: ROB THOMAS

THE CREAM
REUNION
REPORT

SPRINGSTEEN
ON THE ROAD

AUDIOSLAVE
PLAY CUBA

RS 975 | DARTH VADER | June 2nd, 2005 | Photograph by Albert Watson

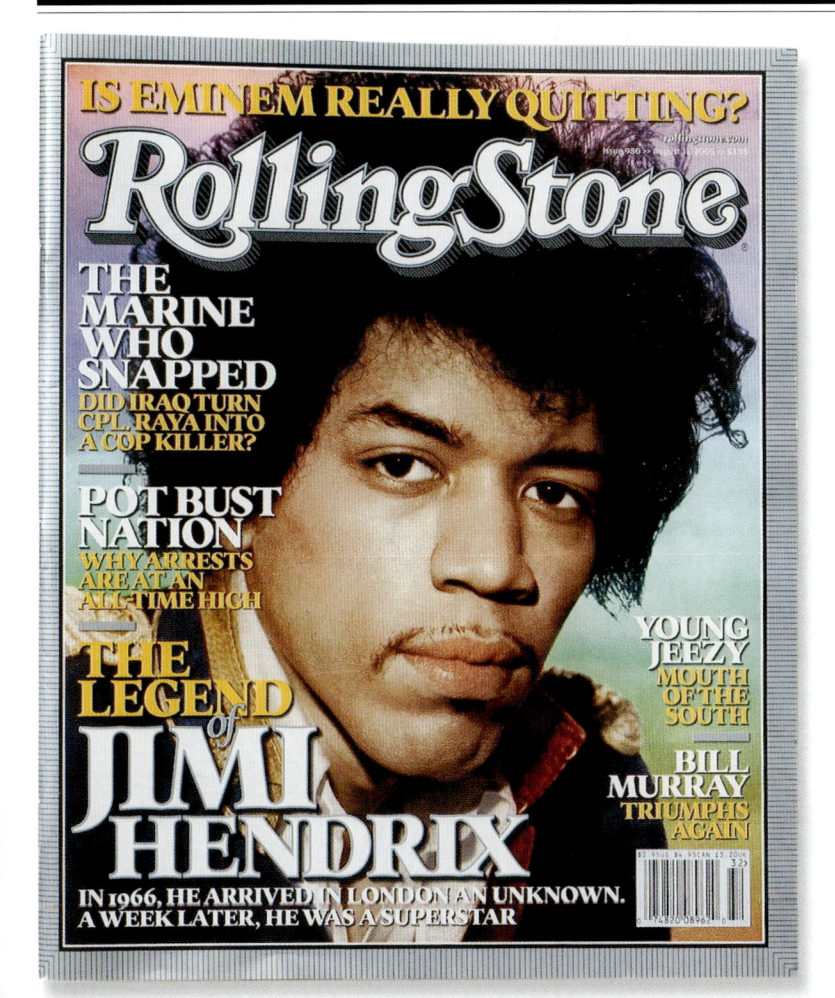

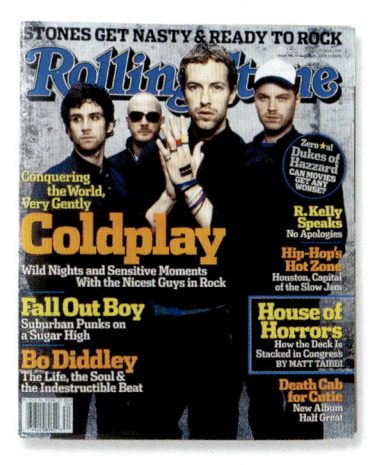

RS 980 | JIMI HENDRIX
August 11th, 2005
Photograph by Harry Goodwin,
Photo-illustration by Michael Elins

RS 981 | COLDPLAY
August 25th, 2005
Photograph by Anton Corbijn

"*It took about twenty minutes* to get suited up. There's no Darth Vader underwear; I wore my own. It starts off with the pants, followed by the boots and upper coverings, which come in a few layers. There's a leather jacket, then a fiberglass chest piece. Then there's a leather jock piece, which looks a little funny. Then it's the helmet and the cape. As each piece comes on, layer by layer, you feel the essence of Darth Vader overcoming you."

—Hayden Christensen

BUSH vs. THE ANTI-WAR MOTHER

Rolling Stone

Issue 982 >> September 8, 2005 >> $3.95

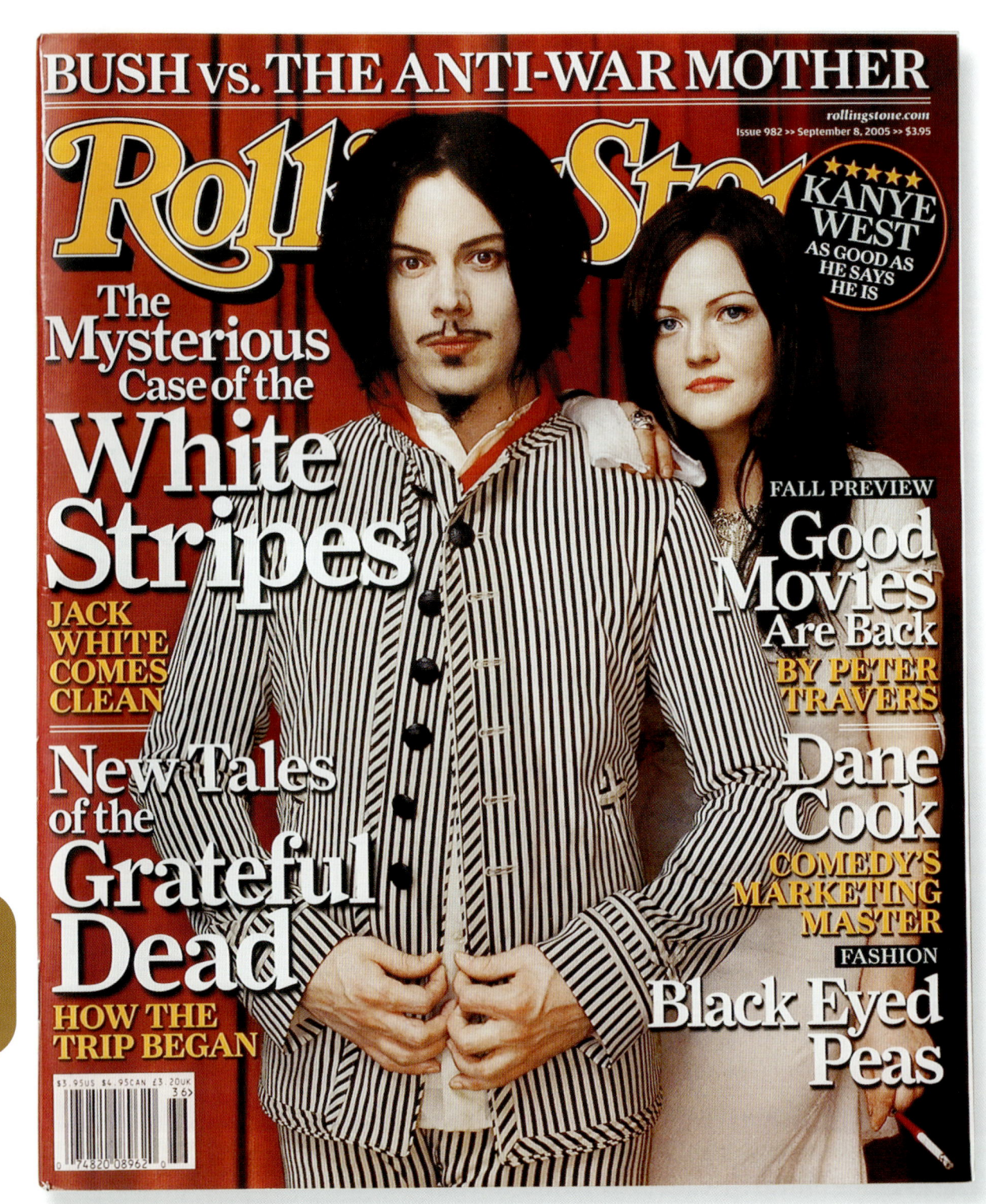

KANYE WEST AS GOOD AS HE SAYS HE IS

The Mysterious Case of the White Stripes

JACK WHITE COMES CLEAN

New Tales of the Grateful Dead

HOW THE TRIP BEGAN

FALL PREVIEW
Good Movies Are Back
BY PETER TRAVERS

Dane Cook
COMEDY'S MARKETING MASTER

FASHION
Black Eyed Peas

RS 982 | THE WHITE STRIPES | September 8th, 2005 | Photograph by Martin Schoeller

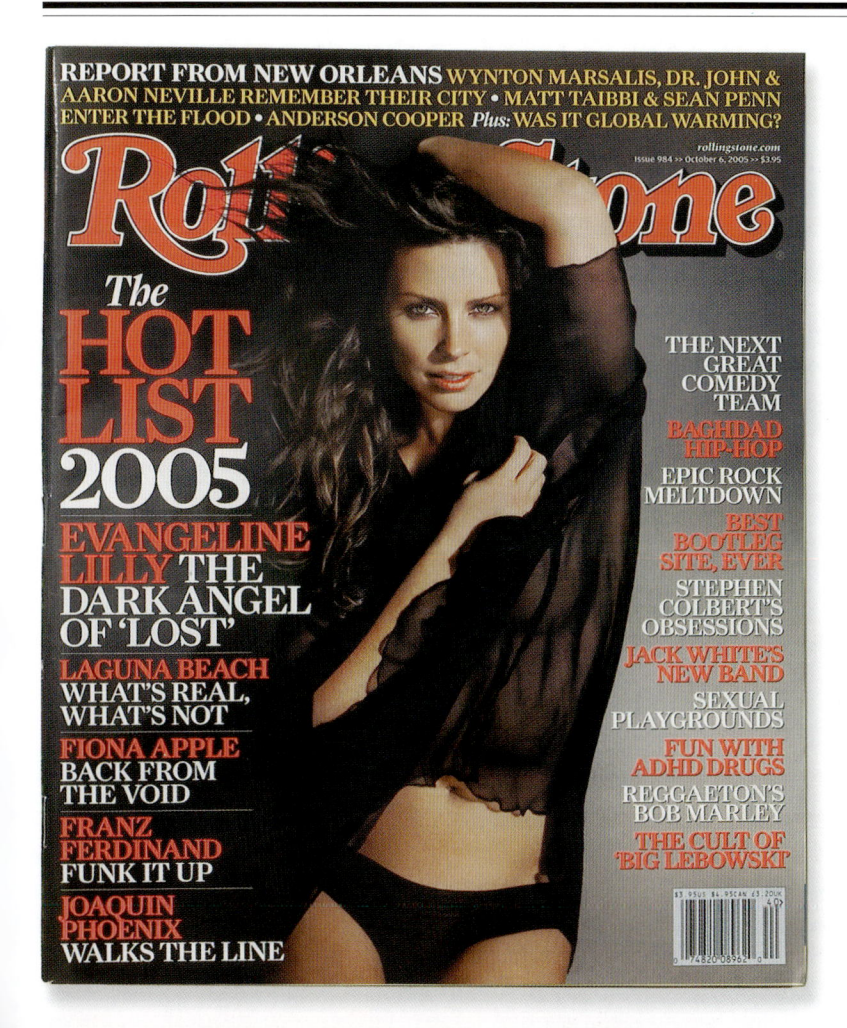

RS 984 | EVANGELINE LILLY
October 6th, 2005
PHOTOGRAPH BY TONY DURAN

[RS 984] When it came time to pick the face of our Hot List 2005, we wanted to go with Evangeline Lilly, the sexy star of TV's *Lost*. The business side of the magazine said no. Their reason? The show, in its first season, was not significant enough to warrant a cover girl. How did we get our way? It may have had something to do with the 2005 Emmy Awards, which were handed out during the making of the issue. Winner for best drama series? *Lost*.

"**The White Stripes' colors** were always red, white and black. It came from peppermint candy. I also think they are the most powerful color combination of all time, from a Coca-Cola can to a Nazi banner. Those colors strike chords with people. In Japan, they are honorable colors. When you see a bride in a white gown, you immediately see innocence in that. Red is anger and passion. It is also sexual. And black is the absence of all that." —*Jack White*

HUNTER S. THOMPSON'S WILD GOODBYE

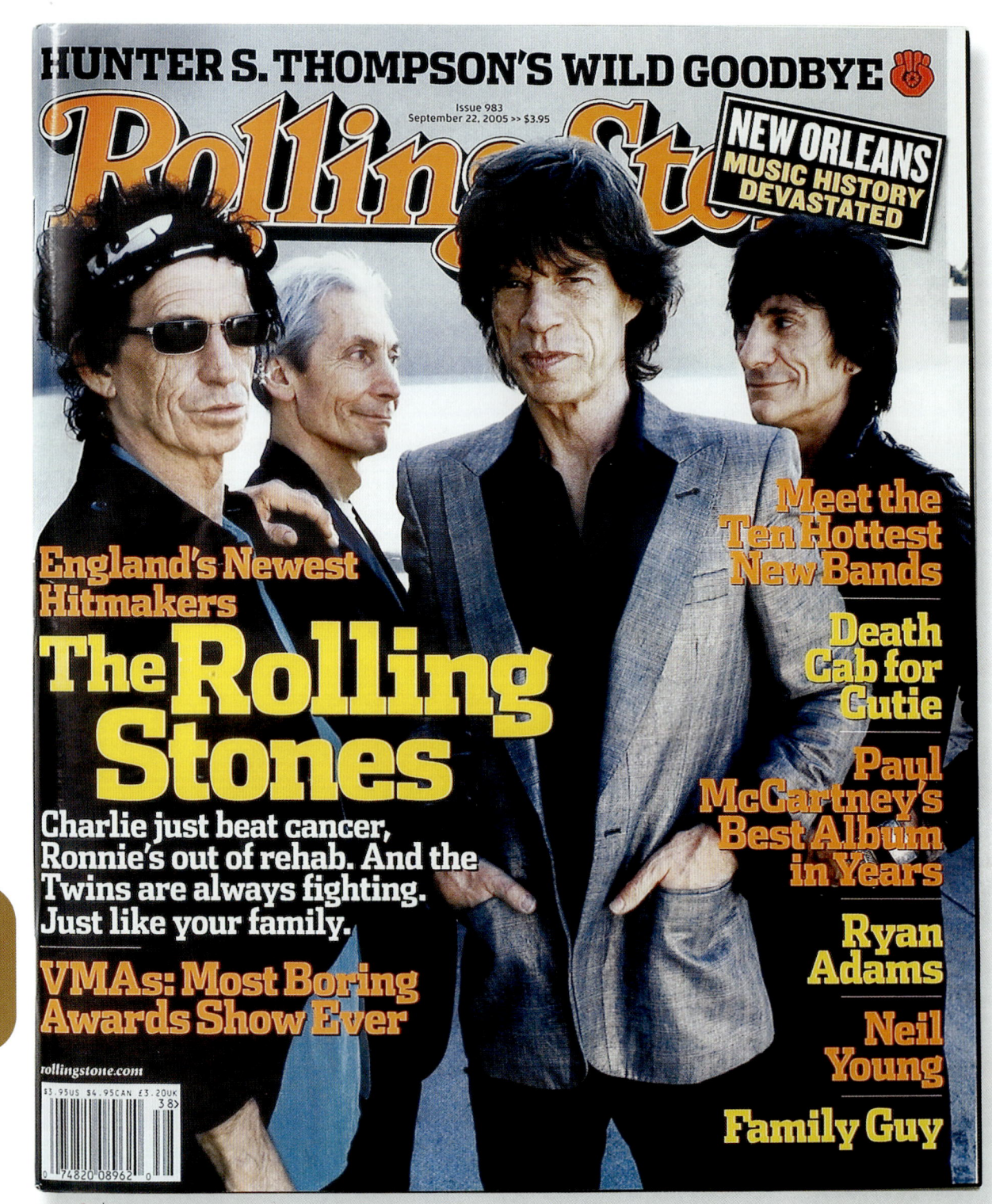

Rolling Stone

Issue 983
September 22, 2005 >> $3.95

NEW ORLEANS MUSIC HISTORY DEVASTATED

England's Newest Hitmakers

The Rolling Stones

Charlie just beat cancer, Ronnie's out of rehab. And the Twins are always fighting. Just like your family.

VMAs: Most Boring Awards Show Ever

Meet the Ten Hottest New Bands

Death Cab for Cutie

Paul McCartney's Best Album in Years

Ryan Adams

Neil Young

Family Guy

rollingstone.com

2000s

RS 983 | THE ROLLING STONES | September 22th, 2005 | Photograph by Anton Corbijn

542 • ROLLING STONE

THE WAR INSIDE THE PEACE MOVEMENT

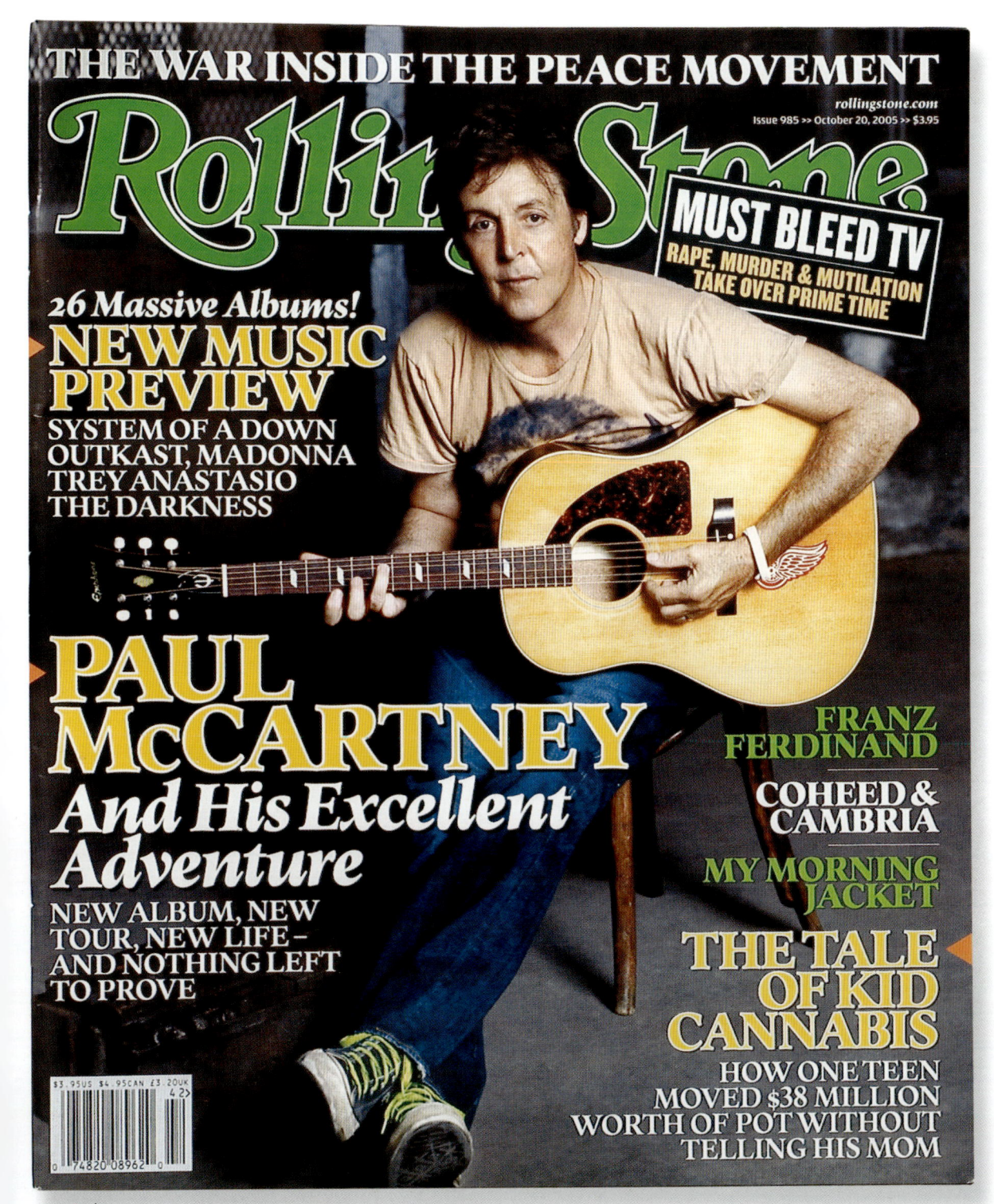

Rolling Stone

rollingstone.com
Issue 985 >> October 20, 2005 >> $3.95

MUST BLEED TV
RAPE, MURDER & MUTILATION TAKE OVER PRIME TIME

26 Massive Albums!
NEW MUSIC PREVIEW
SYSTEM OF A DOWN
OUTKAST, MADONNA
TREY ANASTASIO
THE DARKNESS

PAUL McCARTNEY
And His Excellent Adventure
NEW ALBUM, NEW TOUR, NEW LIFE – AND NOTHING LEFT TO PROVE

FRANZ FERDINAND

COHEED & CAMBRIA

MY MORNING JACKET

THE TALE OF KID CANNABIS
HOW ONE TEEN MOVED $38 MILLION WORTH OF POT WITHOUT TELLING HIS MOM

RS 985 | PAUL McCARTNEY | October 20th, 2005 | Photograph by Max Vadukul

SCIENCE vs. FAITH: EVOLUTION ON TRIAL

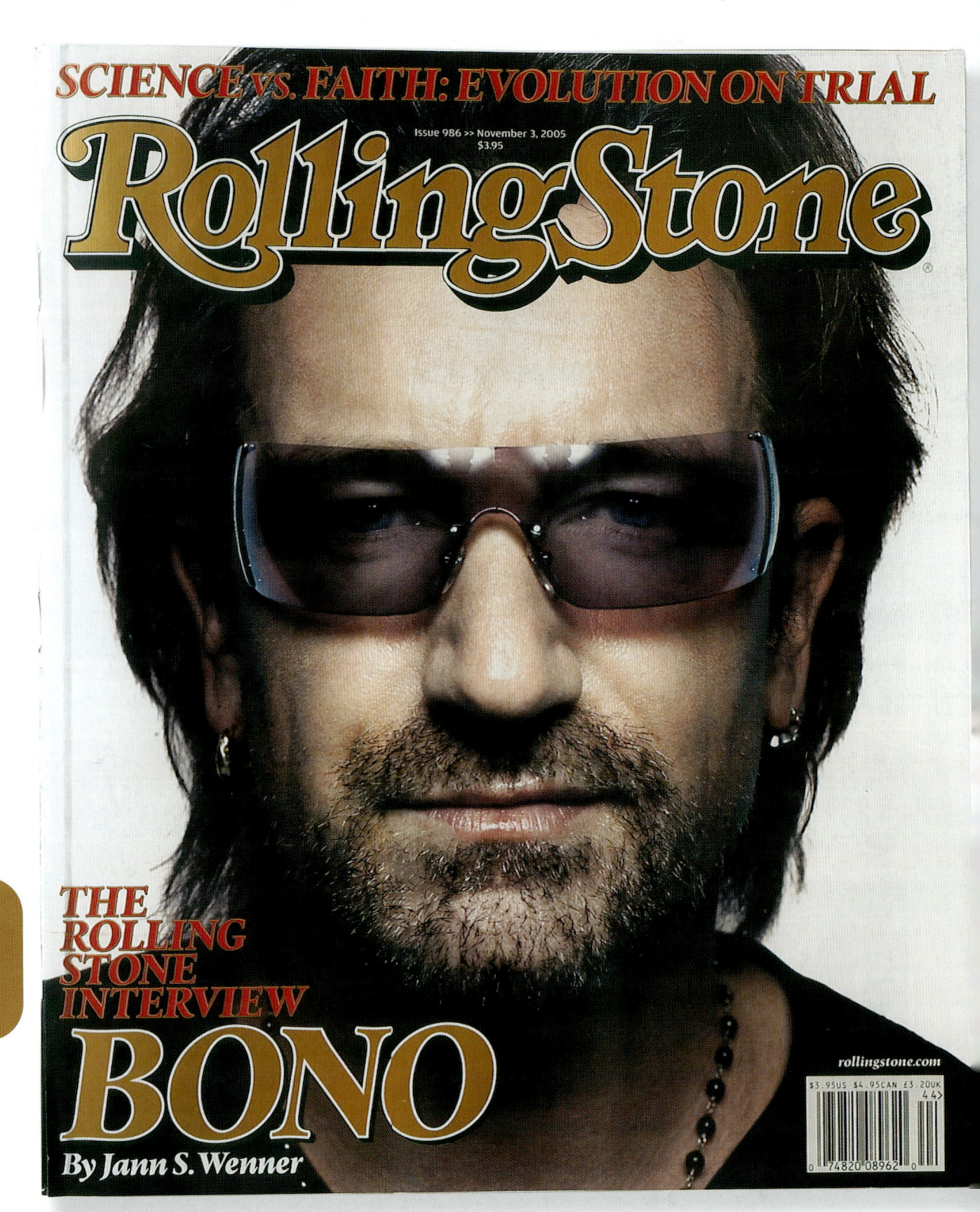

Issue 986 >> November 3, 2005
$3.95

Rolling Stone

2000s

THE ROLLING STONE INTERVIEW

BONO

By Jann S. Wenner

rollingstone.com

RS 986 | BONO
November 3rd, 2005
PHOTOGRAPH BY PLATON

WHAT ROLE DID RELIGION PLAY IN YOUR CHILDHOOD?

I knew that we were different on our street because my mother was Protestant. And that she'd married a Catholic. At a time of strong sectarian feeling in the country, I knew that was special. We didn't go to the neighborhood schools – we got on a bus. I picked up the courage they had to have had to follow through on their love.

Did you feel religious when you went to church?

Even then I prayed more outside of the church than inside. It gets back to the songs I was listening to; to me, they were prayers. "How many roads must a man walk down?" That wasn't a rhetorical question to me. It was addressed to God. It's a question I wanted to know the answer to, and I'm wondering, who do I ask that to? I'm not gonna ask a schoolteacher. When John Lennon sings, "Oh, my love/For the first time in my life/My eyes are wide open" – these songs have an intimacy for me that's not just between people, I realize now, not just sexual intimacy. A spiritual intimacy.

You never saw rock & roll – the so-called devil's music – as incompatible with religion?

Look at the people who have formed my imagination. Bob Dylan. Nineteen seventy-six – he's going through similar stuff. You buy Patti Smith: *Horses* – "Jesus died for somebody's sins/But not mine. . . ." And she turns Van Morrison's "Gloria" into liturgy. She's wrestling with these demons – Catholicism in her case. Right the way through to *Wave,* where she's talking to the pope.

The music that really turns me on is either running toward God or away from God. Both recognize the pivot, that God is at the center of the jaunt. So the blues, on one hand – running away; gospel, the Mighty Clouds of Joy – running towards.

And later you came to analyze it and figure it out.

The blues are like the Psalms of David. Here was this character, living in a cave, whose outbursts were as much criticism as praise. There's David singing, "Oh, God – where are you when I need you?/You call yourself God?" And you go, *this* is the blues.

Both deal with the relationship with God. That's really it. I've since realized that anger with God is very valid.

[EXCERPT FROM BONO INTERVIEW BY JANN S. WENNER]

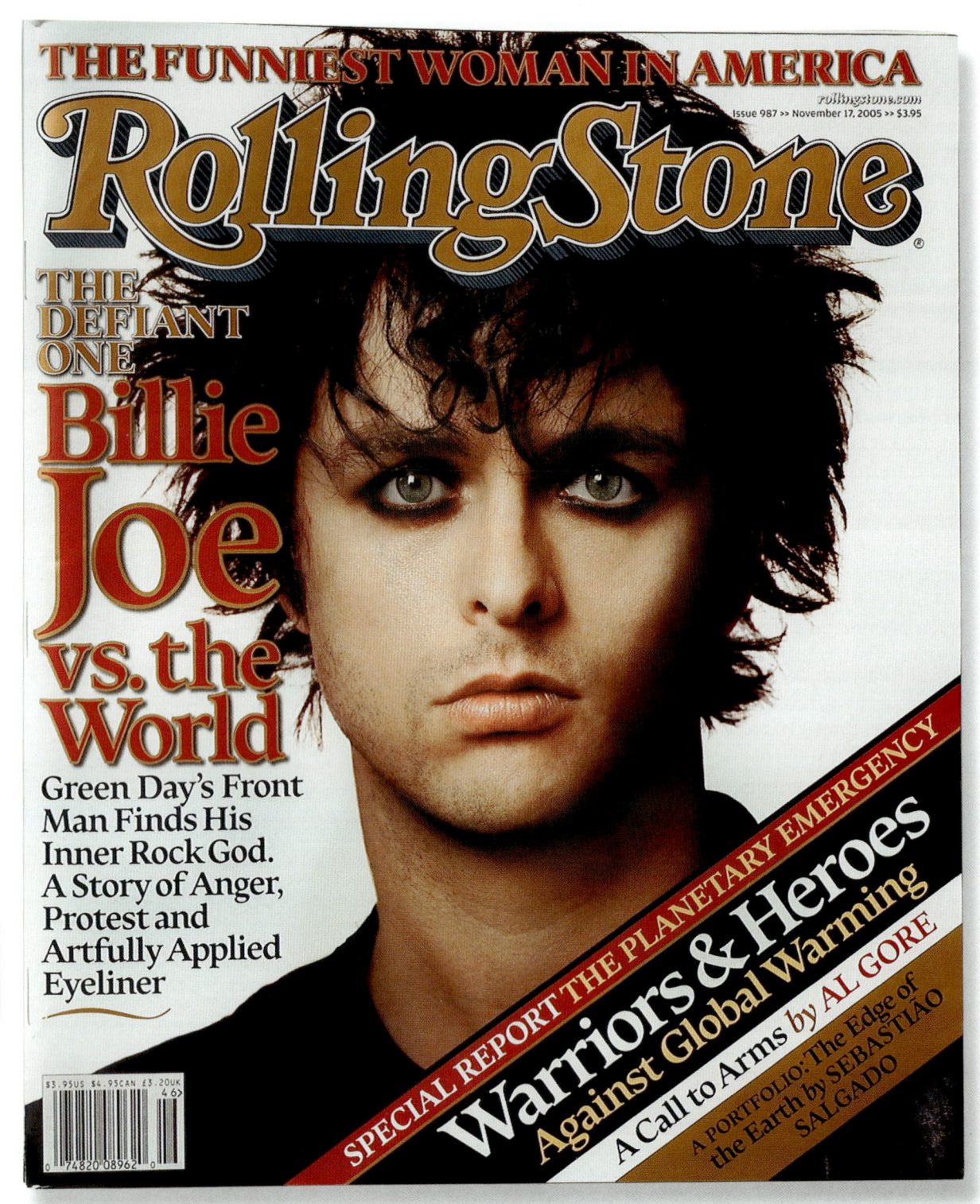

THE FUNNIEST WOMAN IN AMERICA

Rolling Stone

rollingstone.com
Issue 987 » November 17, 2005 » $3.95

THE DEFIANT ONE

Billie Joe vs. the World

Green Day's Front Man Finds His Inner Rock God. A Story of Anger, Protest and Artfully Applied Eyeliner

2000s

SPECIAL REPORT THE PLANETARY EMERGENCY
Warriors & Heroes Against Global Warming
A Call to Arms by AL GORE
A PORTFOLIO: The Edge of the Earth by SEBASTIÃO SALGADO

RS 987 | BILLIE JOE ARMSTRONG | November 17th, 2005 | Photograph by Albert Watson

JOHN LENNON: THE MAKING OF A GENIUS

SPECIAL ISSUE

Rolling Stone

rollingstone.com
Issue 989 >> December 15, 2005 >> $3.95

INSIDE JIHAD
AN INSURGENT TELLS ALL

Where It's At, Where It's Going

HIP HOP NOW

Rap's 25 Greatest Albums
By CHRIS ROCK

The Main Man Jay-Z

RS 989 | JAY-Z | December 15th, 2005 | Photograph by Albert Watson

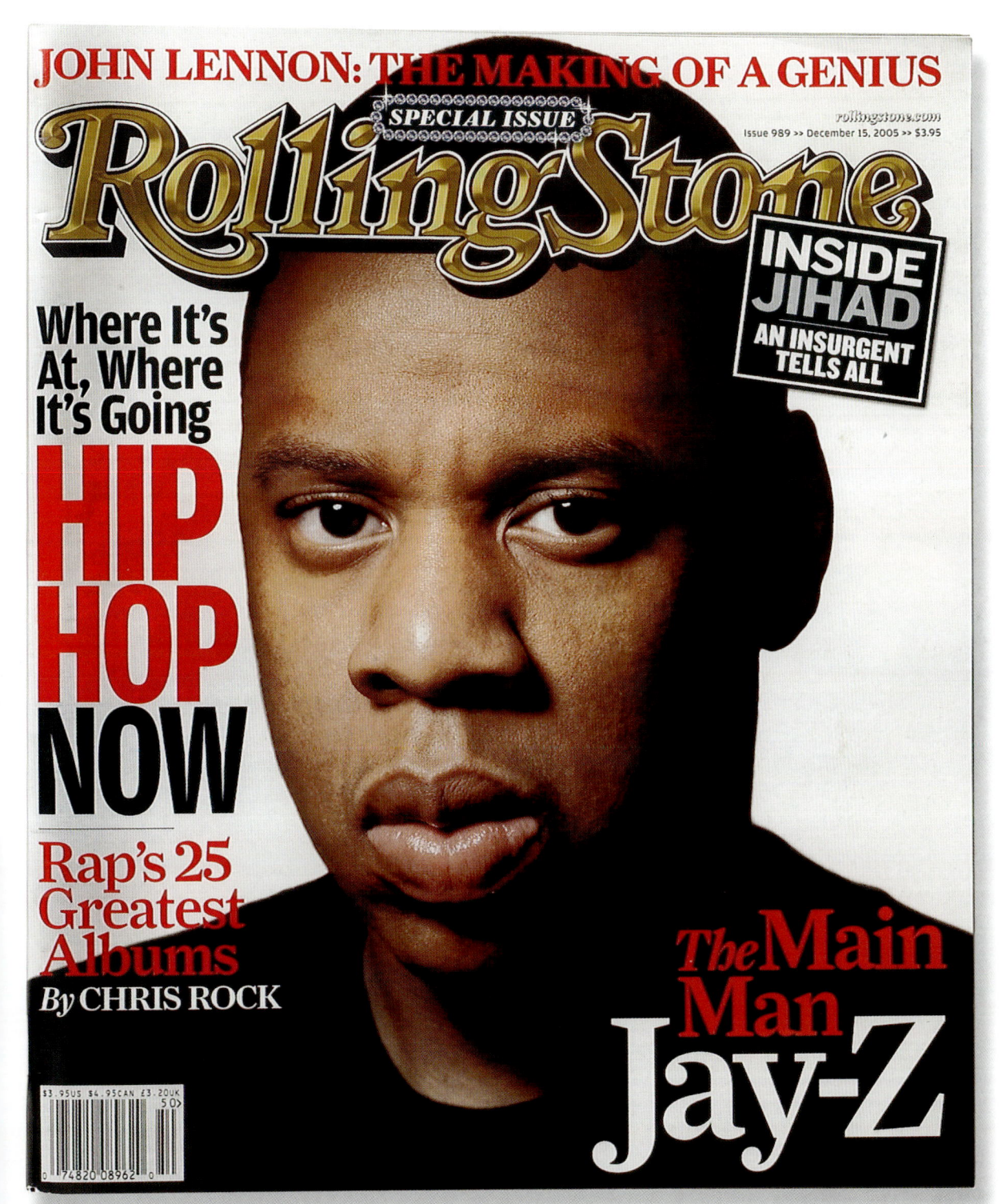

50 YEARS OF COVERS • 547

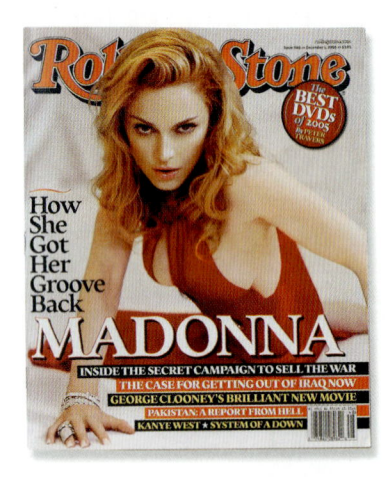

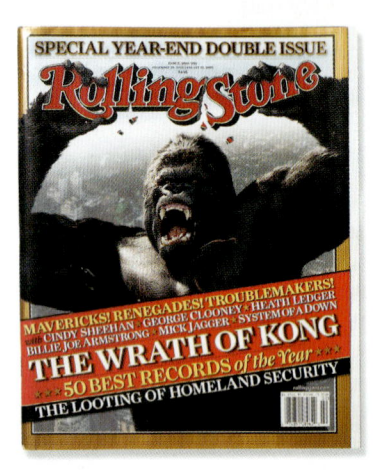

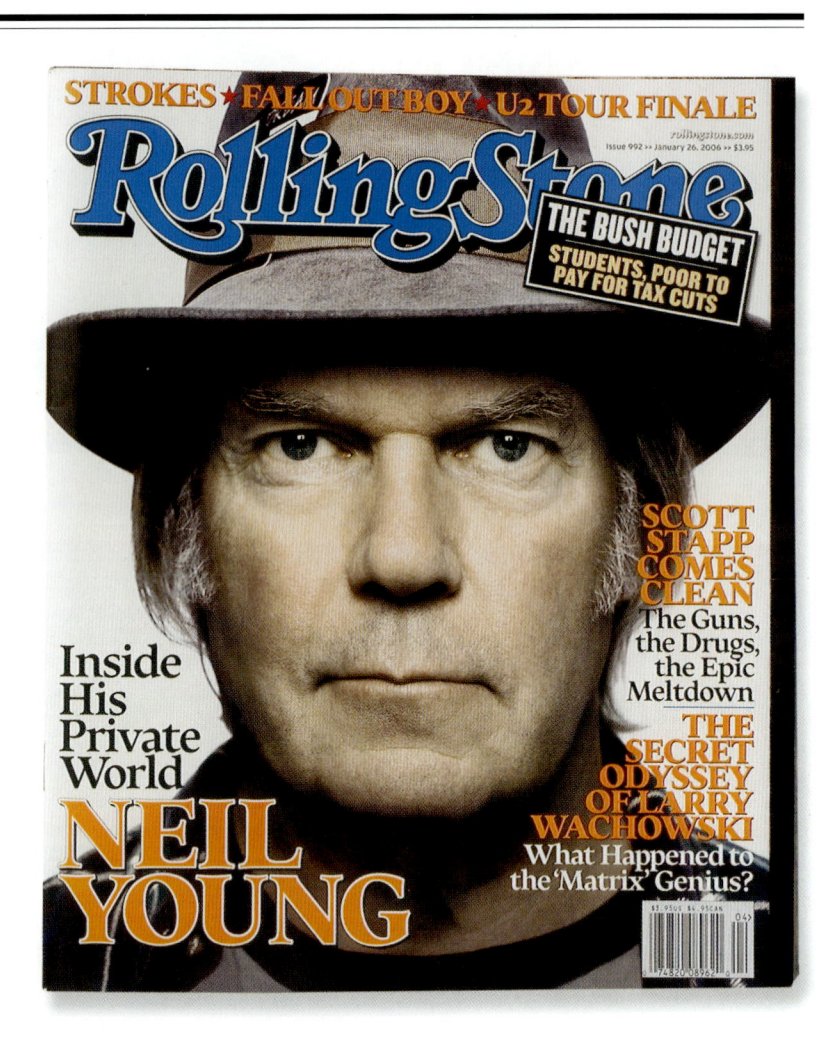

RS 988 | MADONNA
December 1st, 2005
PHOTOGRAPH BY STEVEN KLEIN

RS 992 | NEIL YOUNG
January 26th, 2006
PHOTOGRAPH BY PLATON

RS 990/991 | KING KONG
December 29th, 2005 – January 12th, 2006
PHOTOGRAPH BY WETA DIGITAL LTD

[RS 988] Madonna is the woman to appear most often beneath the ROLLING STONE logo: seventeen times, ranking her in a tie for fourth place along with Bono, Bob Dylan and Bruce Springsteen. This cover is her ninth solo showing; she has appeared eight times with others.

"In America, they want you to accomplish these great feats, to pull off these David Copperfield–type stunts. But let someone ask you about what you're doing, and if you turn around and say, 'It's great,' then people are like, 'What's wrong with you?' You want me to be great, but you don't ever want me to say I'm great?"

—*Kanye West*

548 • ROLLING STONE

CAT POWER + JAMES BLUNT + BILLY JOEL

Rolling Stone

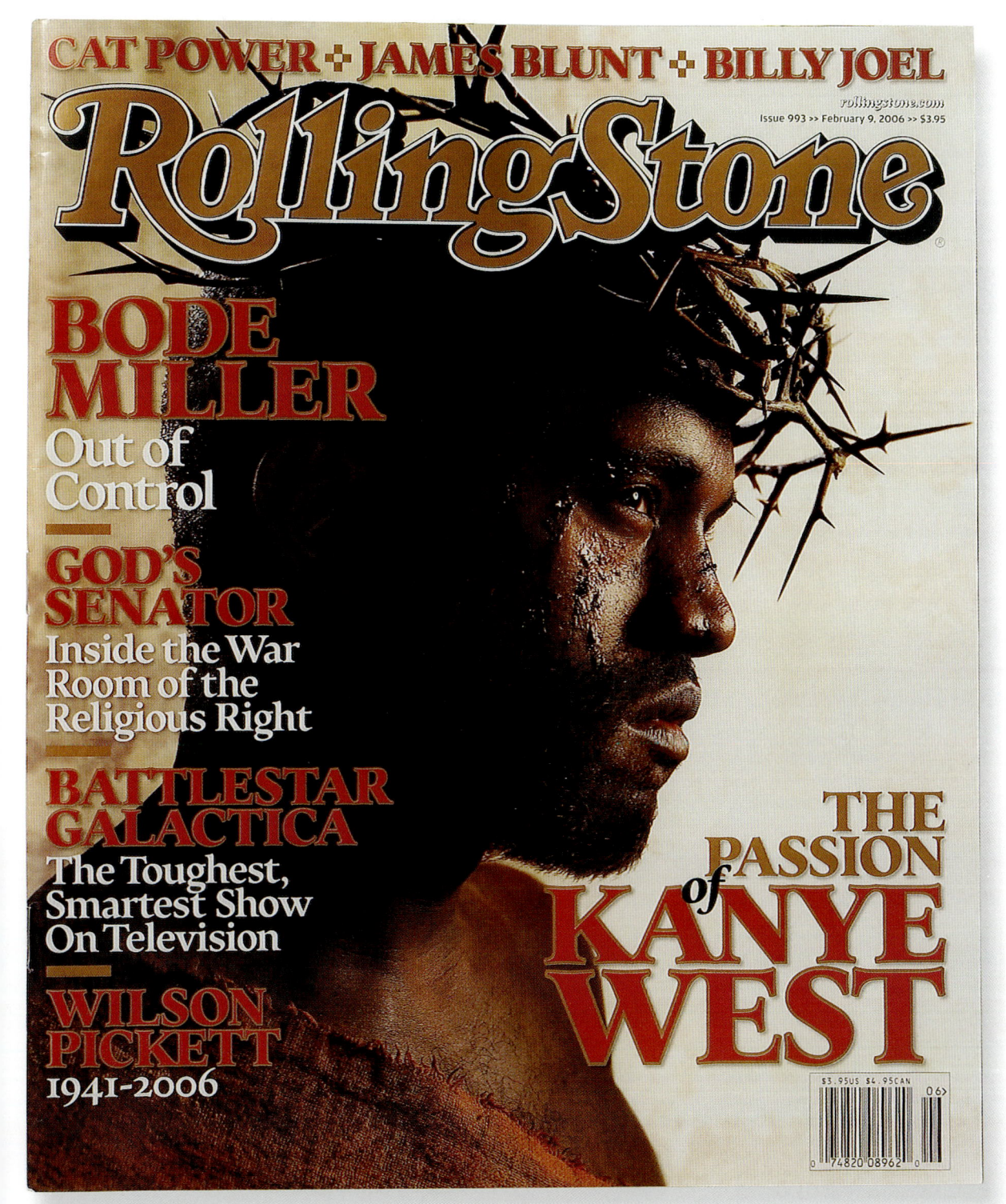

rollingstone.com
Issue 993 >> February 9, 2006 >> $3.95

BODE MILLER
Out of Control

GOD'S SENATOR
Inside the War Room of the Religious Right

BATTLESTAR GALACTICA
The Toughest, Smartest Show On Television

WILSON PICKETT
1941–2006

THE PASSION of KANYE WEST

RS 993 | KANYE WEST | February 9th, 2006 | PHOTOGRAPH BY DAVID LaCHAPELLE

50 YEARS OF COVERS • 549

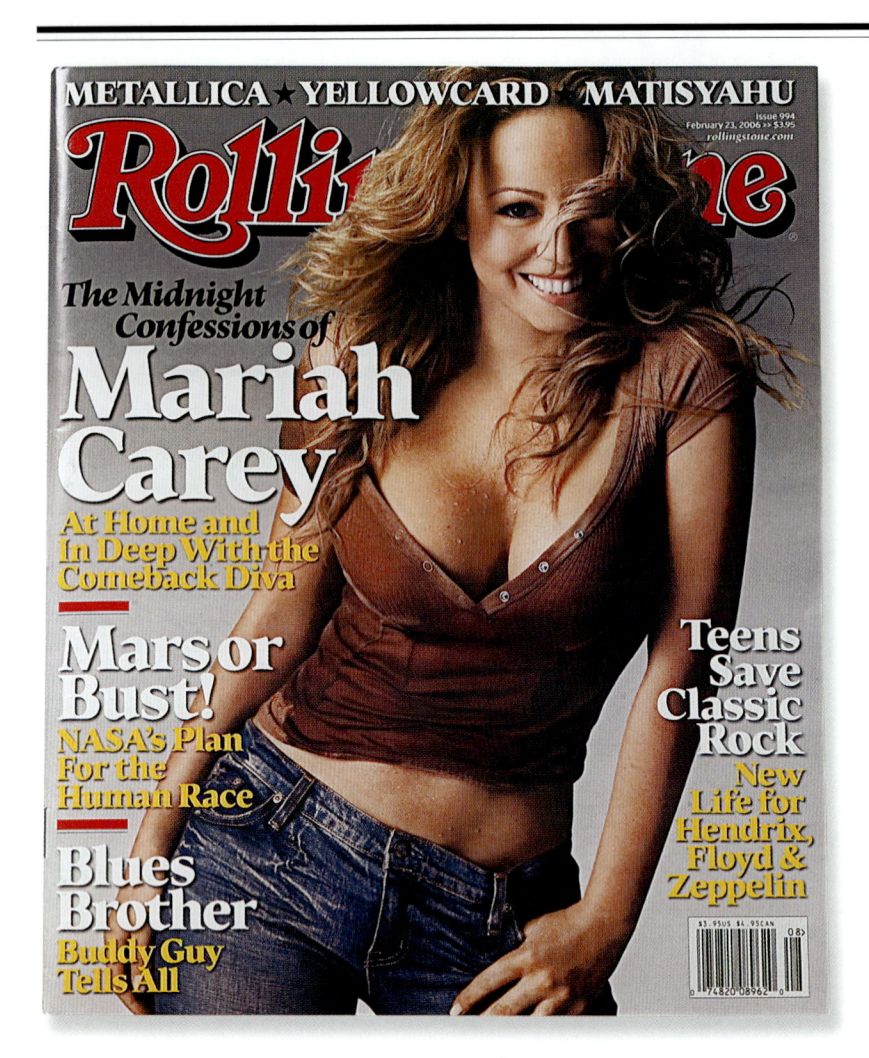

RS 994 | MARIAH CAREY | February 23rd, 2006 | Photograph by Brigitte Lacombe

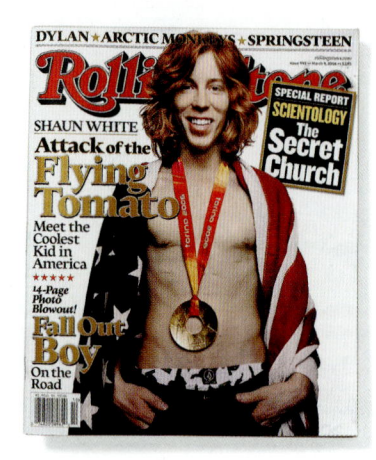

RS 995 | SHAUN WHITE
March 9th, 2006
Photograph by Platon

[RS 995] Shaun White is the third Olympic athlete to appear on the cover, along with swimmer Mark Spitz (RS 133) and Muhammad Ali (RS 78, RS 197 and RS 264). White had just won a gold medal for snowboarding when this issue came out. He was all of nineteen years old at the time.

2000s

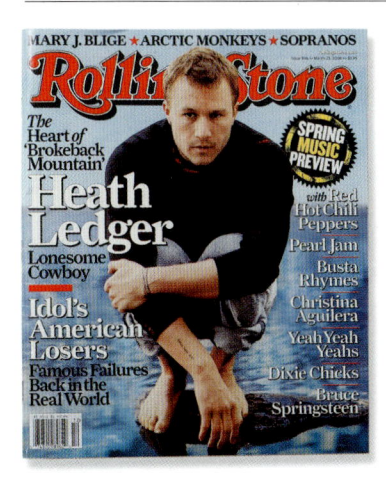

RS 996 | HEATH LEDGER
March 23rd, 2006
Photograph by Sam Jones

[RS 996] When Heath Ledger appeared on this cover, the actor had just emerged as a talent to be reckoned with, thanks to his star-making role as the gay cowboy Ennis Del Mar in Ang Lee's *Brokeback Mountain*. His performance earned the twenty-six-year-old his first Oscar nomination, for Best Actor.

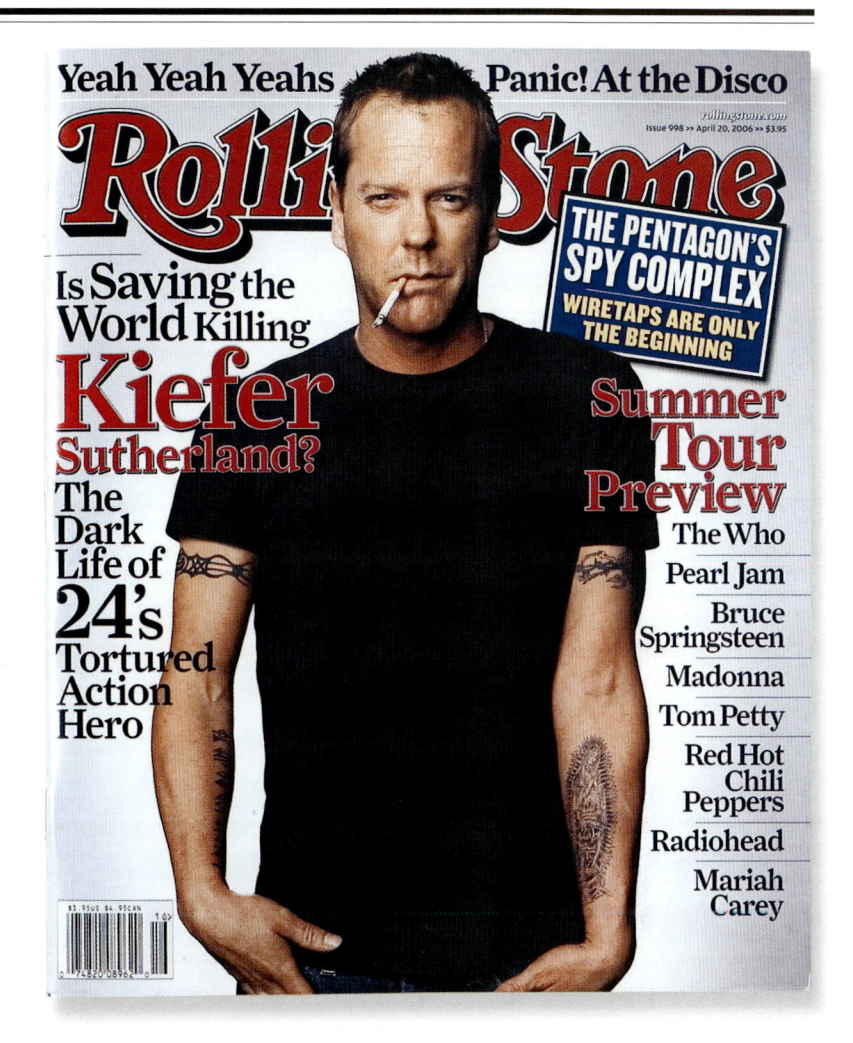

RS 998 | KIEFER SUTHERLAND | April 20th, 2006 | Photograph by Sam Jones

50 YEARS OF COVERS · 551

GEORGE W. BUSH'S PRESIDENCY appears headed for colossal historical disgrace. Barring a cataclysmic event on the order of the terrorist attacks of September 11th, after which the public might rally around the White House once again, there seems to be little the administration can do to avoid being ranked on the lowest tier of U.S. presidents. And that may be the best-case scenario. Many historians are now wondering whether Bush, in fact, will be remembered as the very worst president in all of American history....

The president came to office calling himself "a uniter, not a divider" and promising to soften the acrimonious tone in Washington. He has had two enormous opportunities to fulfill those pledges: first, in the noisy aftermath of his controversial election in 2000, and, even more, after the attacks of September 11th, when the nation pulled behind him as it has supported no other president in living memory. Yet under both sets of historically unprecedented circumstances, Bush has chosen to act in ways that have left the country less united and more divided, less conciliatory and more acrimonious.

There are too many imponderables still to come in the two and a half years left in Bush's presidency to know exactly how it will look in 2009, let alone in 2059. There have been presidents who have left office in seeming disgrace, only to rebound in the estimates of later scholars. But so far the facts are not shaping up propitiously for George W. Bush. He still does his best to deny it. Having waved away the lessons of history in the making of his decisions, the present-minded Bush doesn't seem to be concerned about his place in history. "History. We won't know," the told the journalist Bob Woodward in 2003. "We'll all be dead."

[EXCERPT FROM RS 999 COVER STORY BY SEAN WILENTZ]

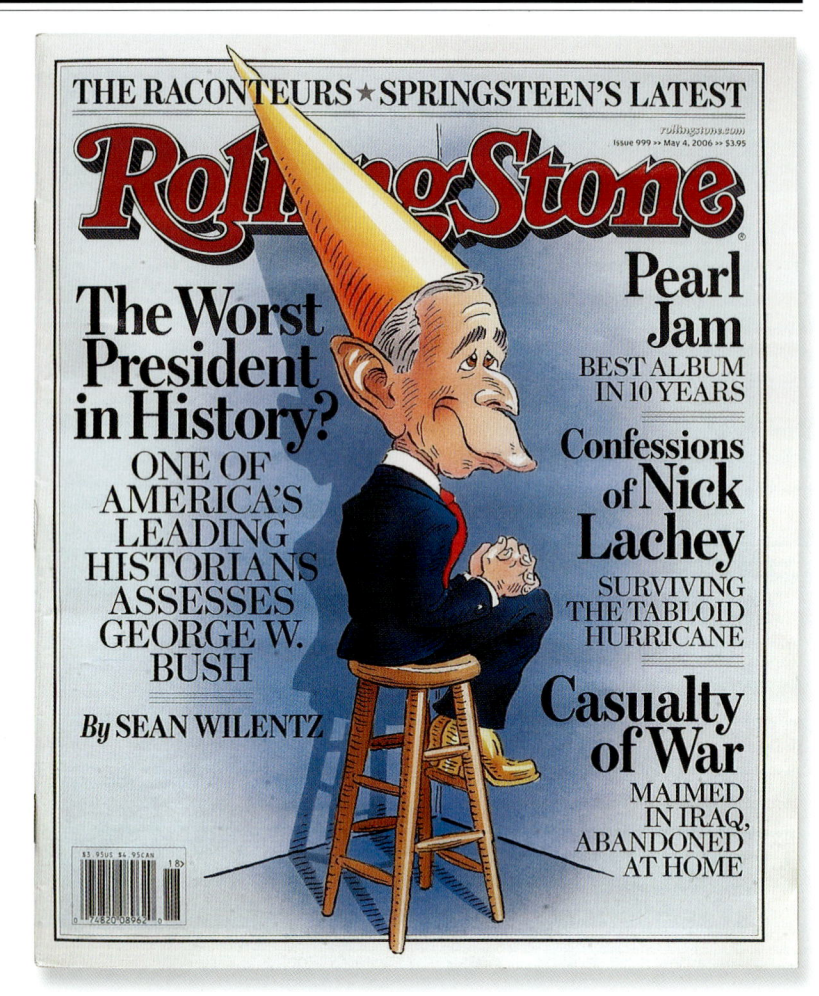

RS 999 | PRESIDENT GEORGE W. BUSH
May 4th, 2006 | ILLUSTRATION BY ROBERT GROSSMAN

[RS 997] In the original concept for this cover, *American Idol* judges Simon Cowell, Paula Abdul and Randy Jackson had an additional bedmate: the show's host, Ryan Seacrest. But after it was laid out, the slumber party looked too crowded, and it was decreed that someone had to go. Votes were cast, and Ryan was cut. A savvy editor, noticing the book in Randy's hands, then made this suggestion: If Ryan couldn't be on the magazine's cover, why not put him on the cover of Randy's book? A faux autobiography was mocked up, Photoshop was enlisted, and the show's crew of four was back together again. (For the record, the book actually held by Jackson was a pulp romance novel.)

OZZY, METALLICA, LYNYRD SKYNYRD, BLONDIE & SEX PISTOLS ROCK THE HALL OF FAME

rollingstone.com
Issue 997 >> April 6, 2006 >> $3.95

RollingStone

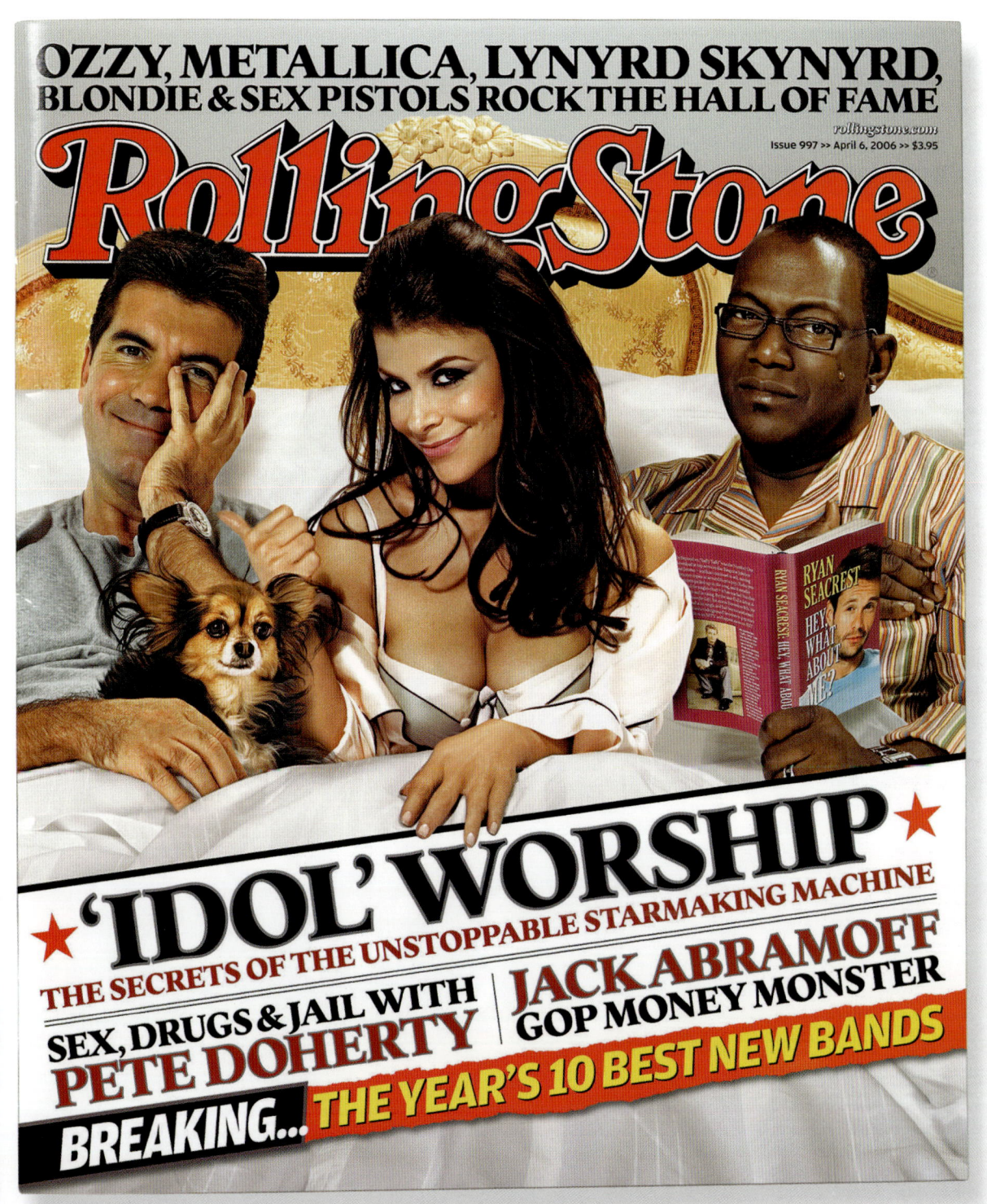

'IDOL' WORSHIP
THE SECRETS OF THE UNSTOPPABLE STARMAKING MACHINE

SEX, DRUGS & JAIL WITH PETE DOHERTY

JACK ABRAMOFF GOP MONEY MONSTER

BREAKING... THE YEAR'S 10 BEST NEW BANDS

RS 997 | SIMON COWELL, PAULA ABDUL & RANDY JACKSON OF 'AMERICAN IDOL'
April 6th, 2006 | Photograph by Michael Elins

2000s

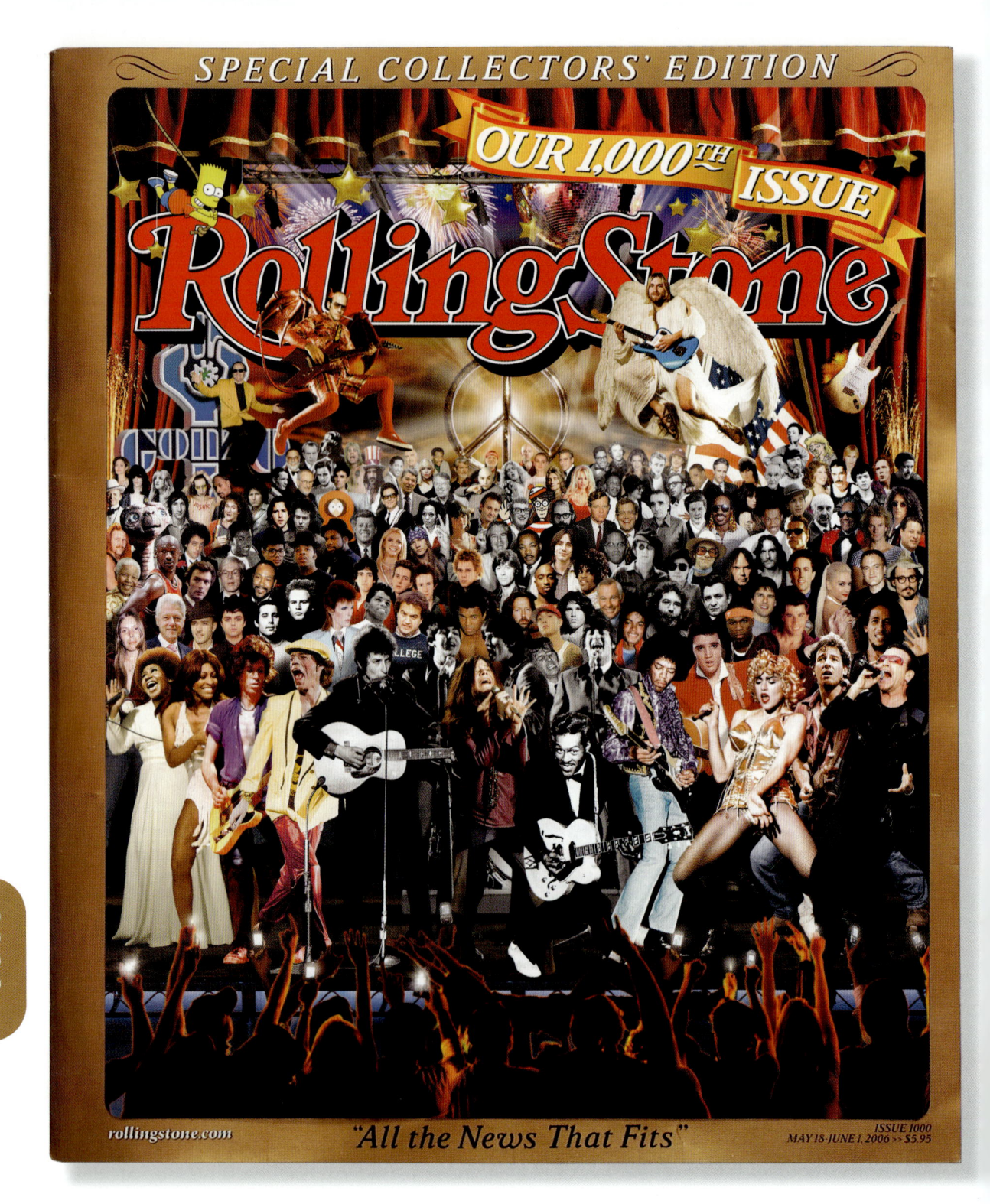

554 • ROLLING STONE

RS 1000 | THE THOUSANDTH ISSUE | May 18th, 2006 | Photo-Illustration by Michael Elins

This collectors' edition, in honor of ROLLING STONE's thousandth issue, celebrated the best covers the magazine ever produced. Capping off the issue was this splashy 3-D collage. Photo-illustrator Michael Elins began work on this landmark cover in the fall of 2005, an entire season before it was published. The editor's letter explained the process thus: "Elins meticulously built up the crowd, layer by layer, on his computer; in total, hundreds of layers create the 3-D effect. After the initial image was completed, Elins sent the enormous computer file to National Graphics, in Wisconsin, a printing company that patented lenticular technology, in which a thin, flexible plastic lens is adhered to the existing image. The project was so complex – Would the lens stick to the cover? Would the staples support the extra weight? – that the cover had to be finished in January" – three months before the the actual issue was completed.

The famous faces that appear on the cover were chosen by the magazine's editors. So that you can actually see who everyone is, the cover has been reproduced here in two dimensions rather than three.

"I WANTED IT TO BE LIKE A DREAM where you walk into the ultimate ROLLING STONE party."
—*Michael Elins*

To mark one thousand issues, we wanted to create a cover both extraordinary and celebratory. In searching for ideas, we discovered that technology for 3-D printing had come a long way and had never been used for a magazine cover as ambitious and mass-market as this one. It took two months to manufacture, and more than two million were made. *Sgt. Pepper's Lonely Hearts Club Band,* which came out in 1967, the same year as ROLLING STONE, was an album that changed our world forever. The 3-D idea, and a homage to the Beatles, seemed just right. . . .

For me, it's been a gas reading the stories behind the covers in this issue, shooting the breeze about all the fun we've had along the way. In many of the pieces, my name comes up, and I've gotten some pretty nice props here, but as many big decisions as I've made over the years as the editor of ROLLING STONE, the magazine stands, in all its glory, as a collaborative effort.

—*Jann S. Wenner*
[APRIL 23RD, 2006]

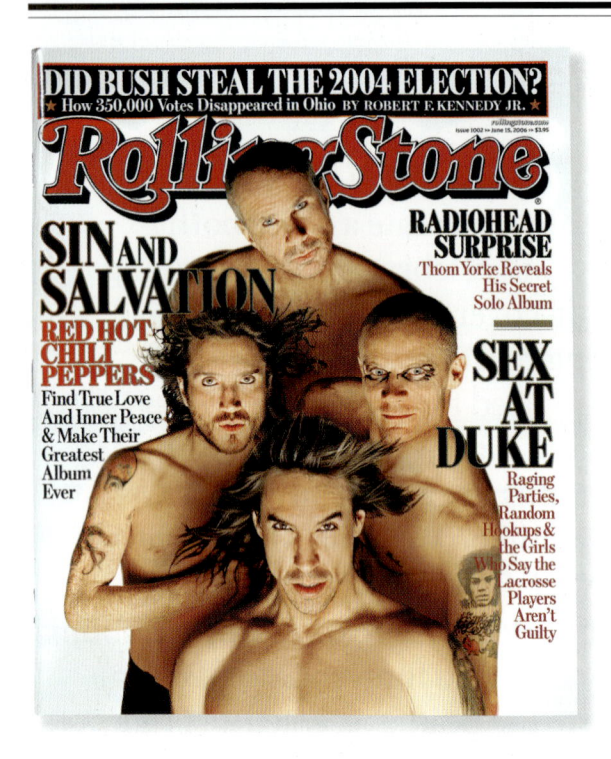

RS 1002 | RED HOT CHILI PEPPERS
June 15th, 2006
PHOTOGRAPH BY MATTHEW ROLSTON

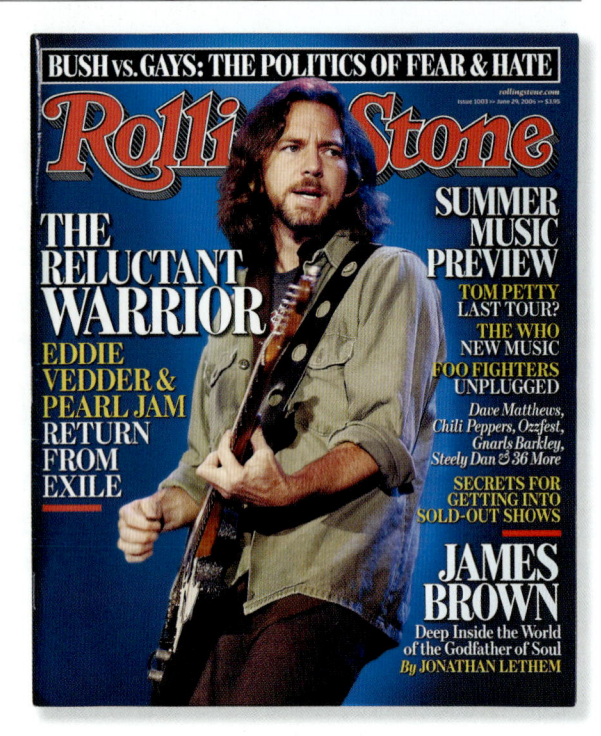

RS 1003 | EDDIE VEDDER
June 29th, 2006
PHOTOGRAPH BY NICK STEVENS/RETNA

[RS 1003] It doesn't happen often, but there are times when an artist isn't exactly thrilled with his or her cover. Case in point: fiercely independent grunge icons Pearl Jam. For Pearl Jam's sixth cover appearance, photographer Albert Watson shot the band backstage after a show in Chicago. Later, it was decided that the group photo worked better inside the magazine, and a solo shot of frontman Eddie Vedder was selected for the cover. Vedder wasn't happy about the decision. At a concert in Cincinnati later that year, he brought out a copy of the Pearl Jam issue and offered a colorful display of his displeasure. "I'm wiping my ass with ROLLING STONE magazine," Vedder told the crowd, literally rubbing the magazine on his butt. "Actually, I'm wiping myself off with…me."

Rolling Stone

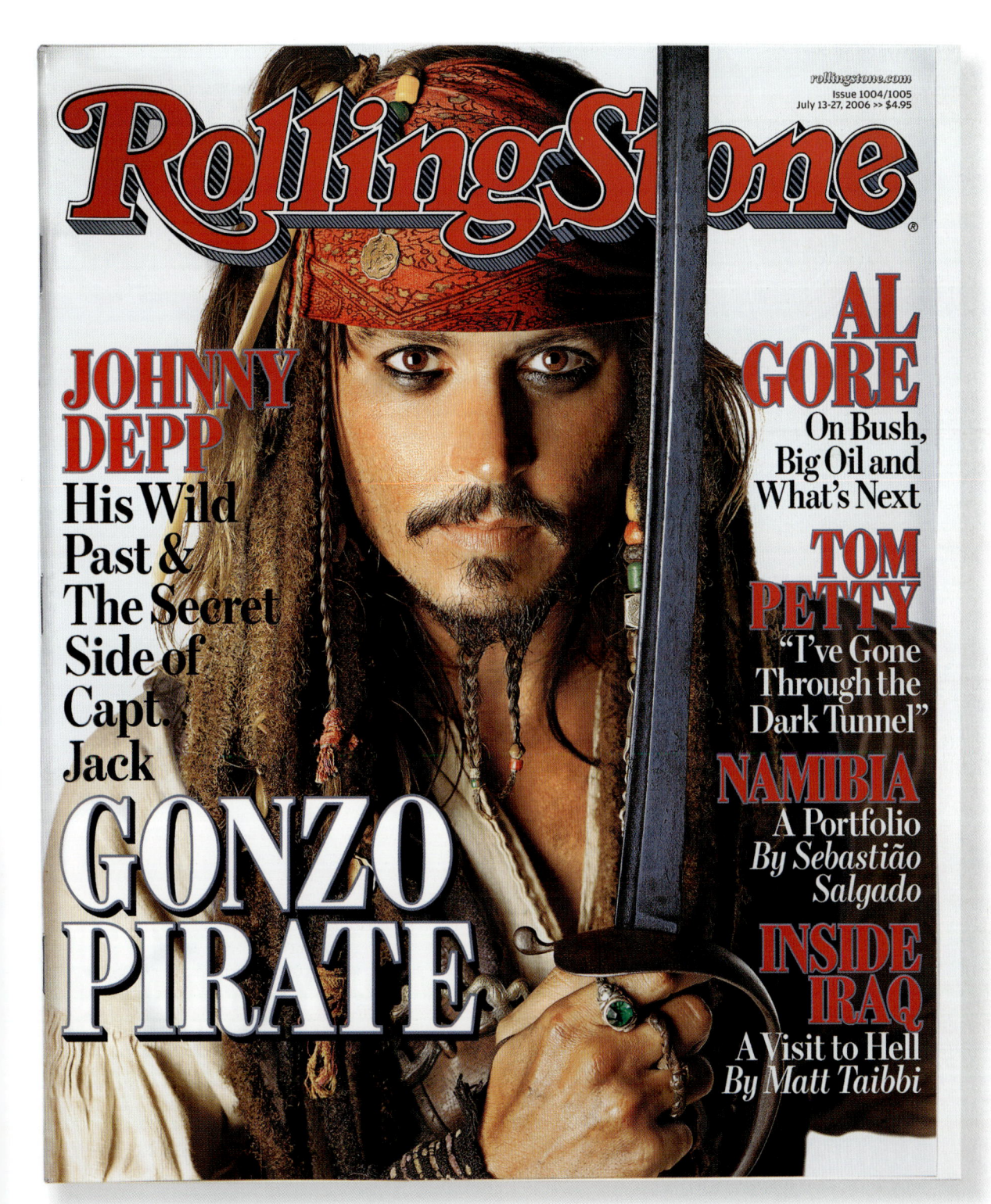

rollingstone.com
Issue 1004/1005
July 13-27, 2006 >> $4.95

JOHNNY DEPP
His Wild Past & The Secret Side of Capt. Jack

GONZO PIRATE

AL GORE
On Bush, Big Oil and What's Next

TOM PETTY
"I've Gone Through the Dark Tunnel"

NAMIBIA
A Portfolio By Sebastião Salgado

INSIDE IRAQ
A Visit to Hell By Matt Taibbi

RS 1004/1005 | JOHNNY DEPP | July 13th–27th, 2006 | Photograph by Matthew Rolston

50 YEARS OF COVERS • 557

THE 2006 FALL MUSIC PREVIEW

RollingStone

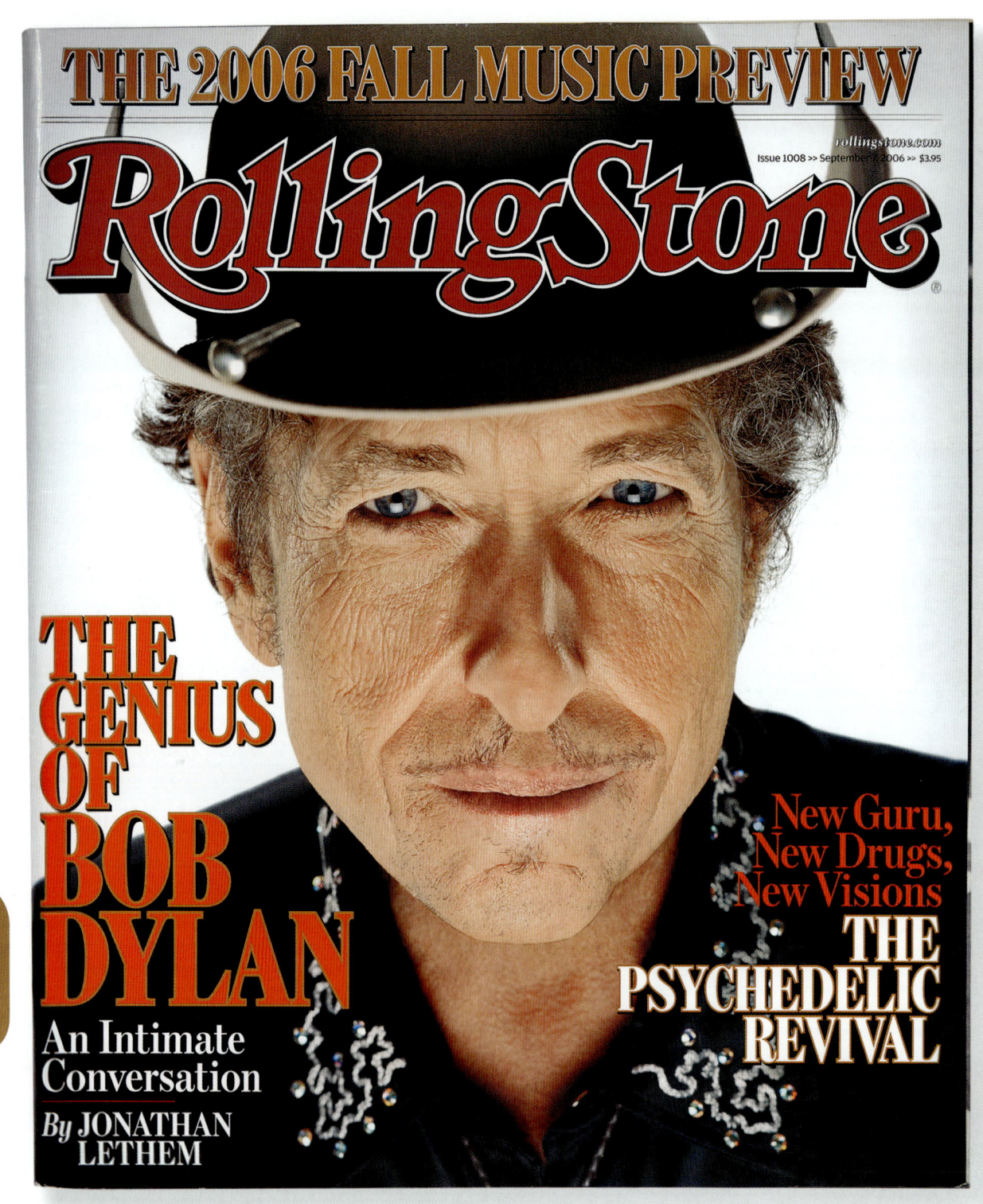

rollingstone.com
Issue 1008 >> September 7, 2006 >> $3.95

THE GENIUS OF BOB DYLAN

An Intimate Conversation

By JONATHAN LETHEM

New Guru, New Drugs, New Visions
THE PSYCHEDELIC REVIVAL

2000s

RS 1008 | BOB DYLAN | September 7th, 2006 | Photograph by Matthew Rolston

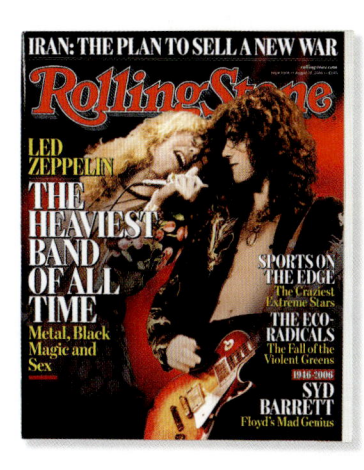

RS 1006 | LED ZEPPELIN
August 10th, 2006
Photograph by Adrian Boot,
Photo-Illustration by Michael Elins

"THIS COVER WAS REALLY ABOUT owning my body, embracing my power and fighting against stereotypes. I wanted it to be something that opened up conversations. It's still a work in progress, but it's beautiful to see women owning their own bodies of work and doing it for themselves."
—*Christina Aguilera*

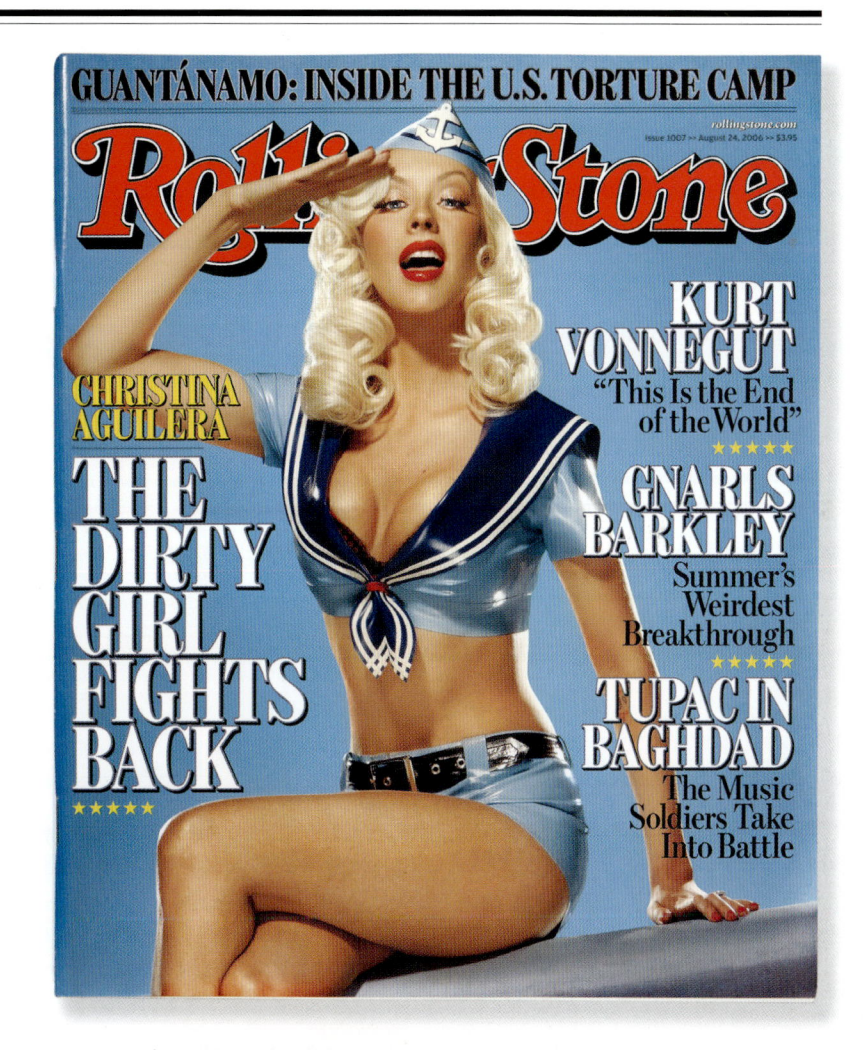

RS 1007 | CHRISTINA AGUILERA
August 24th, 2006
Photograph by Matthew Rolston

50 YEARS OF COVERS • 559

[**RS 1009**] "When I was a kid, I remember seeing Aerosmith on the cover of ROLLING STONE and thinking, 'Wow, they're rock stars,'" Justin Timberlake recalled in 2003. "And when 'NSync got our first ROLLING STONE cover, something didn't add up for me. We were definitely not rock stars." By 2006, Timberlake was definitely in rock-star territory, and ROLLING STONE celebrated that new status with a cover shot that was a homage to one of rock's greatest icons: Bruce Springsteen, specifically a 1988 ROLLING STONE cover photo of a sweat-soaked Bruce holding his guitar. The JT version had more of a wet-T-shirt beach feel, splitting the difference between pop idol and grown-up icon.

RS 1009 | JUSTIN TIMBERLAKE
September 21st, 2006
PHOTOGRAPH BY MAX VADUKUL

RS 1010 | JACK NICHOLSON
October 5th, 2006
PHOTOGRAPH BY MATTHEW ROLSTON

RS 1011 | FERGIE
October 19th, 2006
PHOTOGRAPH BY MAX VADUKUL

2000s

560 · ROLLING STONE

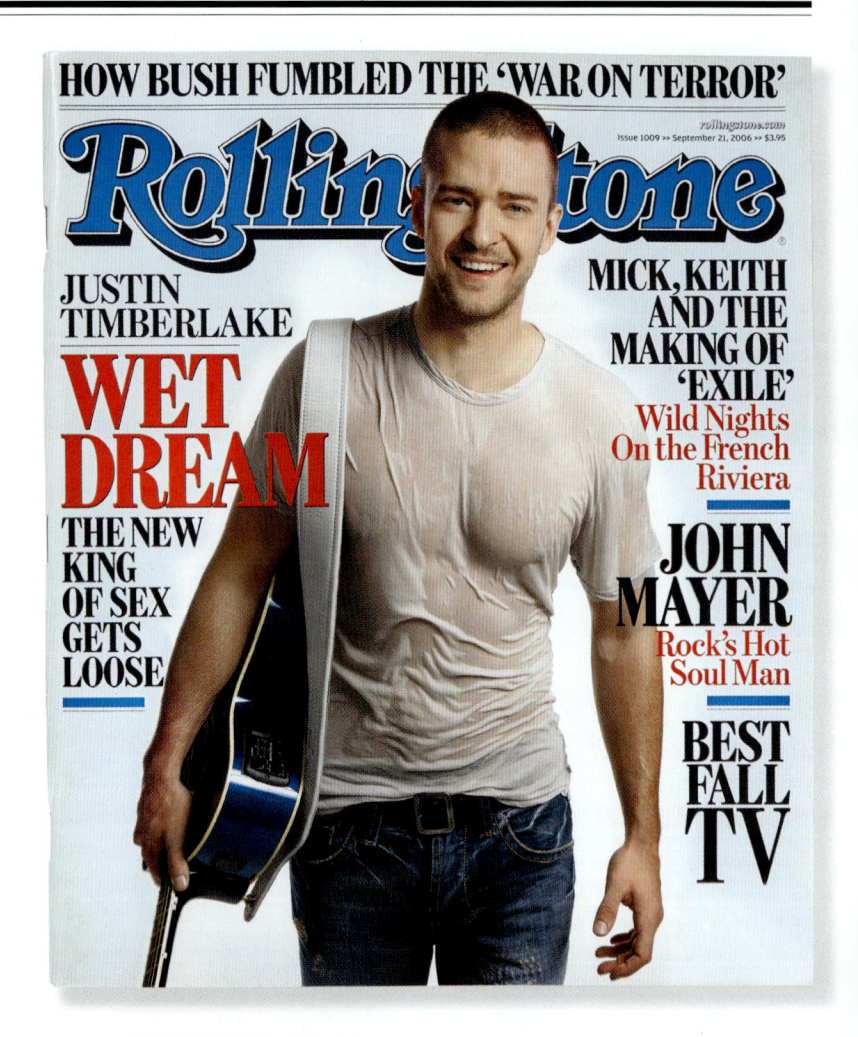

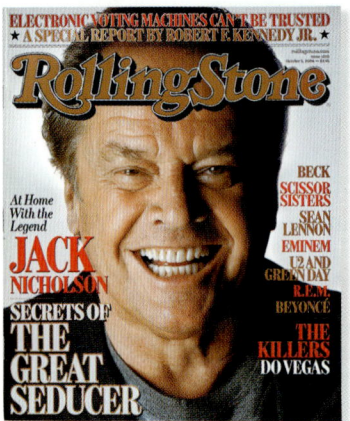

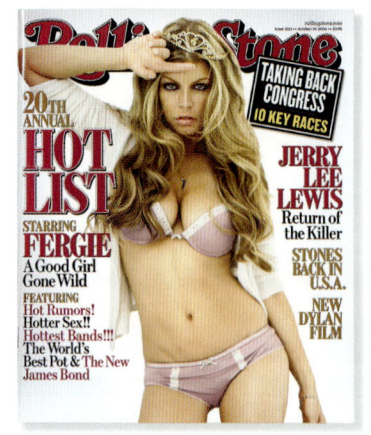

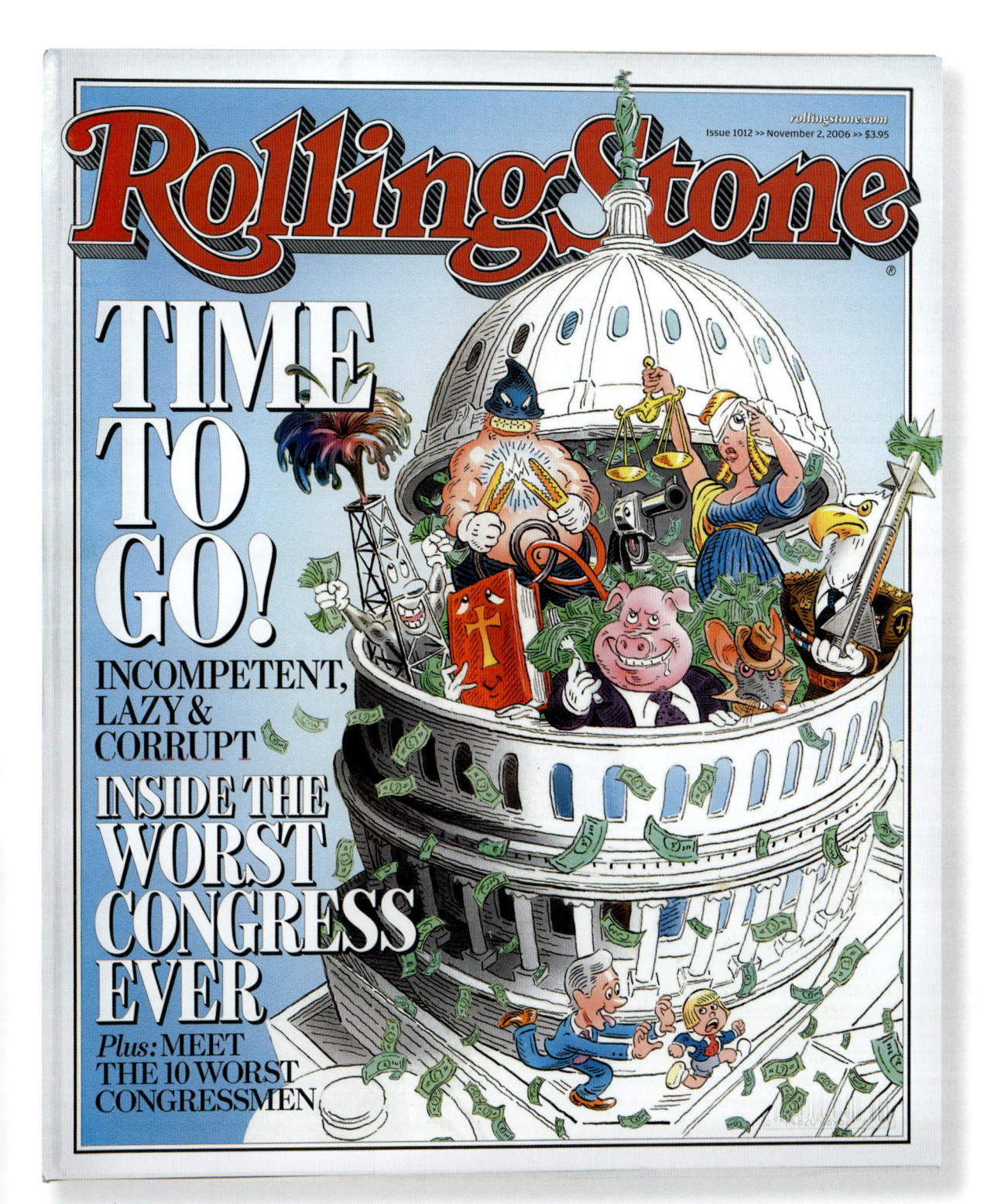

RS 1012 | WORST CONGRESS EVER | November 2nd, 2006 | ILLUSTRATION BY ROBERT GROSSMAN

50 YEARS OF COVERS • 561

IS THERE ANYTHING THAT'S considered going too far now? The other night you were joking that Bush could woo CNN White House correspondent Suzanne Malveaux with a down-home combination of "wildflowers and date rape." And within seconds you did an imitation of W. calling himself "a dick."

COLBERT: Jon has Tourette's. It mostly gets edited out.

STEWART: Here's the way I look at it. President Bush has uranium-tipped bunker busters, and I have puns. I think he'll be OK.

COLBERT: I don't know. The pen is mightier than the bunker buster.

STEWART: We rarely do ad hominem attacks. There's the occasional one – Cheney, I guess we do a little bit. But in general it's based in frustration over reality. We almost never do the, you know, Bush is dumb.

COLBERT: Ashcroft is a douchebag.

STEWART: I think Novak is a douchebag.

COLBERT: I'm sorry. I apologize. It's Robert Novak who's a douchebag. That's just fact. I think it's his confirmation name.

STEWART: When he joined Opus Dei...

COLBERT: "You shall be Saint Douchebag."

So it's impossible to go too far?

STEWART: I would hope that my sense of humanity prevents me from saying things that are so denigrating and derogatory as to be offensive. But I don't understand how anyone can consider jokes about this stuff worse than the reality of it.

[EXCERPT FROM RS 1013 COVER STORY BY MAUREEN DOWD]

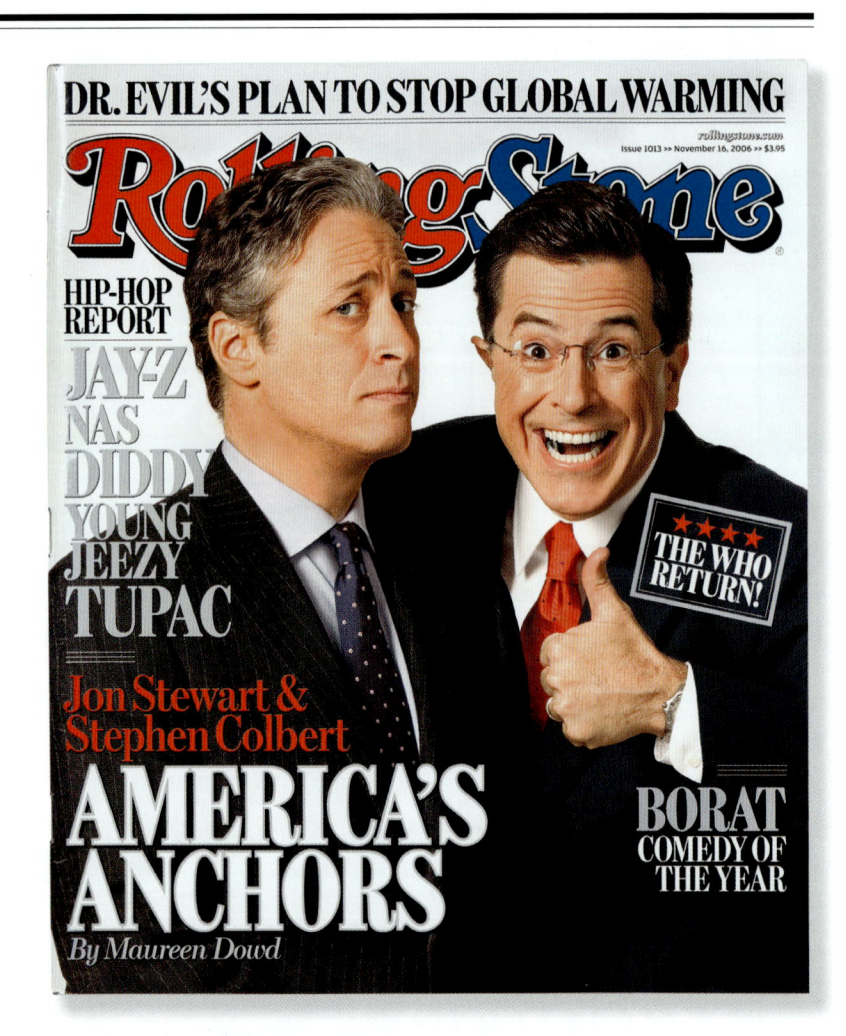

2000s

RS 1013 | JON STEWART AND STEPHEN COLBERT
November 16th, 2006
PHOTOGRAPH BY ROBERT TRACHTENBERG

562 • ROLLING STONE

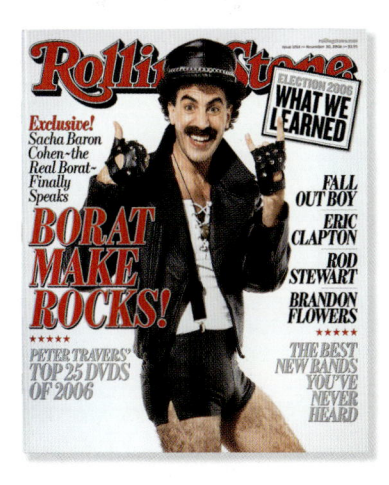

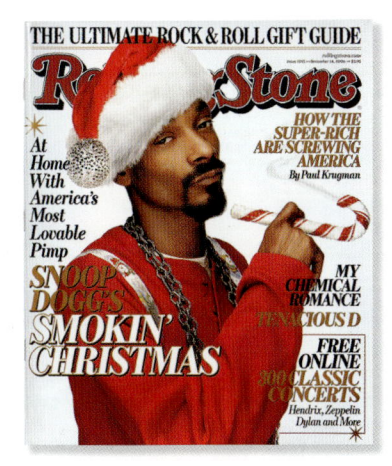

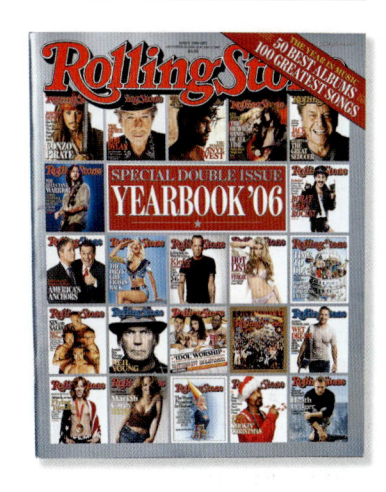

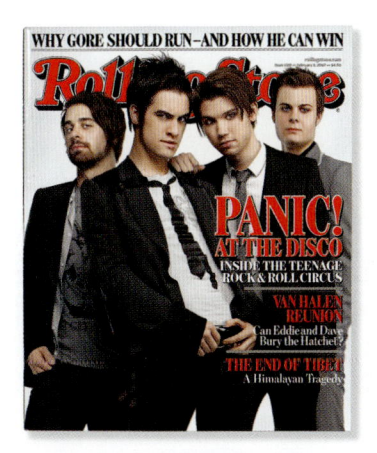

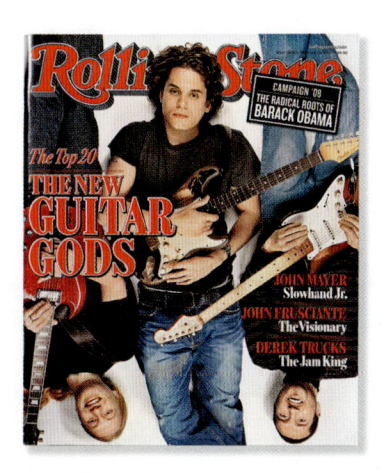

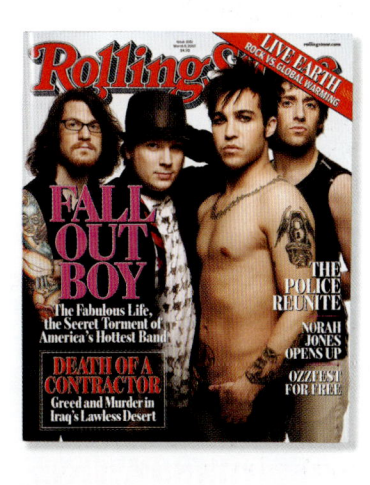

RS 1014 | SACHA BARON
COHEN AS BORAT
November 30th, 2006
PHOTOGRAPH BY ROBERT TRACHTENBERG

RS 1019 | PANIC! AT THE DISCO
February 8th, 2007
PHOTOGRAPH BY MAX VADUKUL

RS 1015 | SNOOP DOGG
December 14th, 2006
PHOTOGRAPH BY MATTHEW ROLSTON

RS 1020 | NEW GUITAR GODS
February 22nd, 2007
PHOTOGRAPH BY MATTHEW ROLSTON

RS 1016/1017 |
YEARBOOK 2006
December 28th, 2006–January 11th, 2007
VARIOUS PHOTOGRAPHERS

RS 1021 | FALL OUT BOY
March 8th, 2007
PHOTOGRAPH BY PETER YANG

Rolling Stone

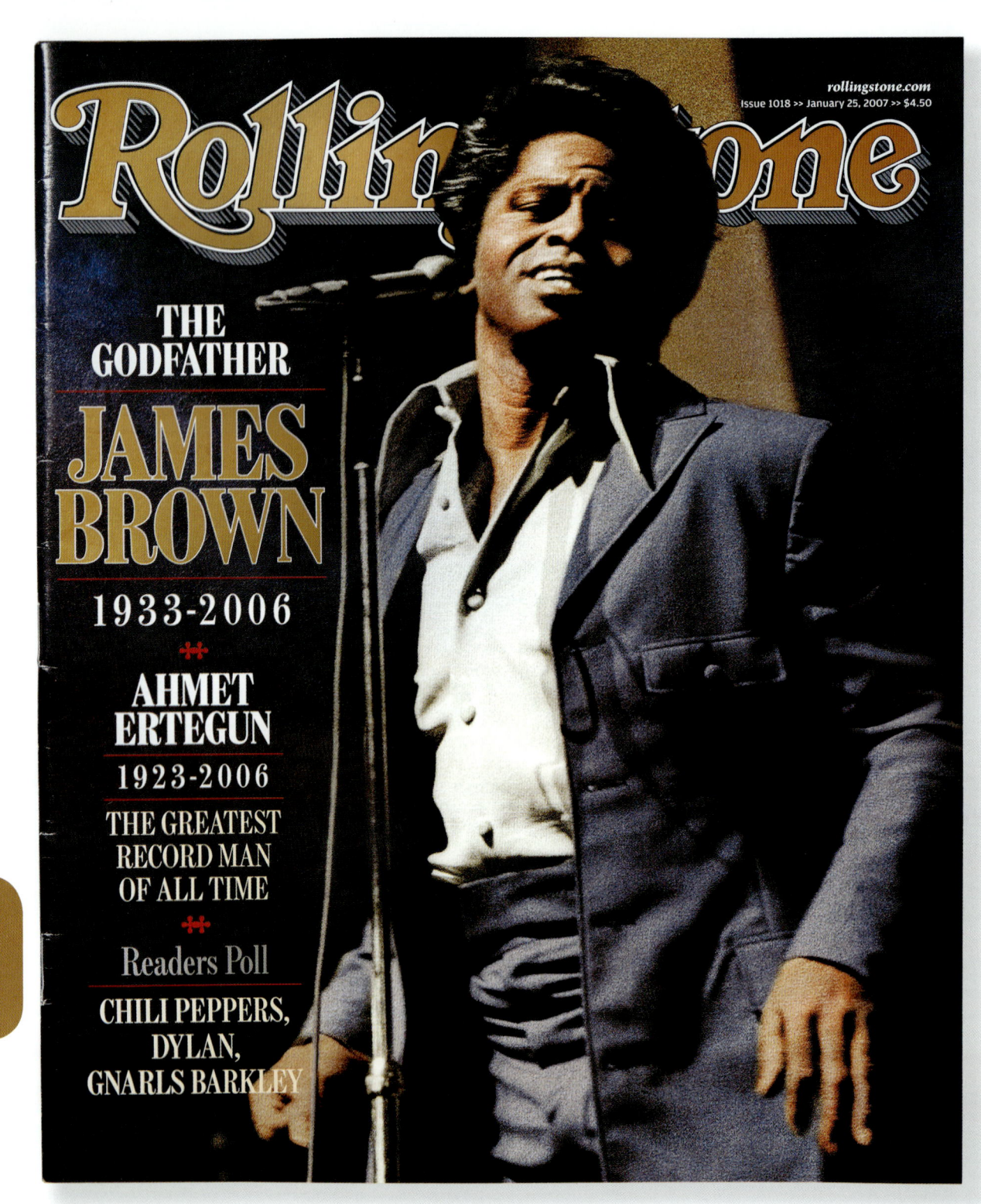

Issue 1018 >> January 25, 2007 >> $4.50
rollingstone.com

THE GODFATHER
JAMES BROWN
1933-2006

AHMET ERTEGUN
1923-2006
THE GREATEST RECORD MAN OF ALL TIME

Readers Poll
CHILI PEPPERS, DYLAN, GNARLS BARKLEY

2000s

RS 1018 | JAMES BROWN | January 25th, 2007 | Photograph by Gilles Caron/Contact Press Images, Photo Colorization by Michael Elins

On Christmas morning,

James Brown breathed his last in an Atlanta hospital. For a man whose trademark soul scream – black, American and proud – upended a half century of popular music, the end was uncharacteristically quiet. Congestive heart failure and pneumonia conspired to still the self-proclaimed (and undisputed) Hardest-Working Man in Show Business. A week earlier, he had been especially reflective when speaking to those close to him, almost as if he were taking stock. And when on December 24th, his worried dentist, suspecting pneumonia, sent him to Emory Crawford Long Hospital in Atlanta, JB – a man with incredible tolerance for pain and little patience for doctors – did not argue. At seventy-three, though he had gigs lined up through August 2007 on his Seven Decades of Funk Tour, it seems James Brown was ready.

His singular life, begun in unspeakable Jim Crow-era poverty, careened through phases of great fame, wealth, disgrace and redemption. He saw it this way: "My story is a Horatio Alger story. It's an American story, it's the kind that America can be proud of, but yet if you tell it in detail, if you tell all the things I fought to make it, it's like the Satchel Paige story."

[EXCERPT FROM RS 1018 COVER STORY BY GERRI HIRSHEY]

JAMES BROWN WAS THE Genius and Ray Charles the Godfather of Soul. Soul music was a pre-eminently vocal style, and while Brown was a magnificent singer, he was no Aretha Franklin or Ray Charles – as a lyrical interpreter, more in Wilson Pickett's class. Also, soul music had a forgiving softness to it. Brown strove to be hard, and before most white Americans knew what soul music was, he found his lifework with 1965's "Papa's Got a Brand New Bag." As he told Bruce Tucker in a terrific autobiography: "Aretha and Otis and Wilson Pickett were out there and getting big. I was still called a soul singer – I still call myself that – but musically I had already gone off in a different direction. I had discovered that my strength was not in the horns, it was in the rhythm." In other words, funk.

[EXCERPT FROM RS 1018 COVER STORY BY ROBERT CHRISTGAU]

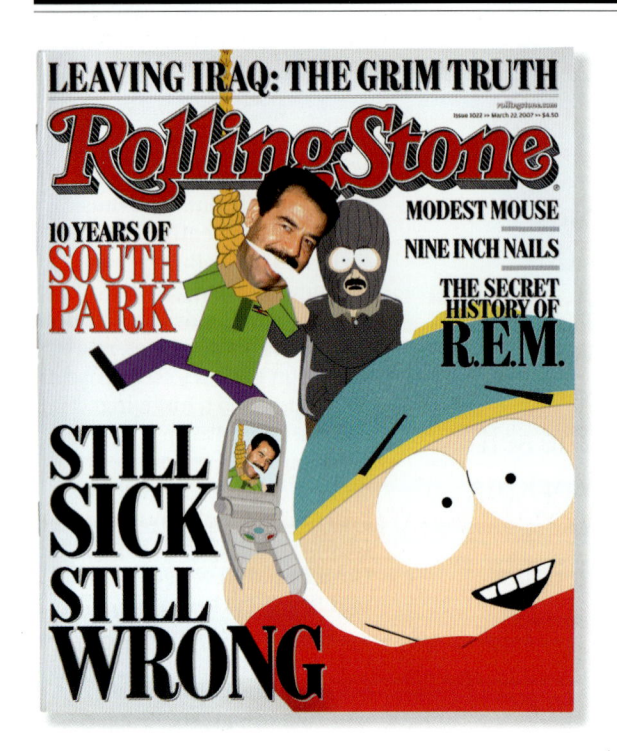

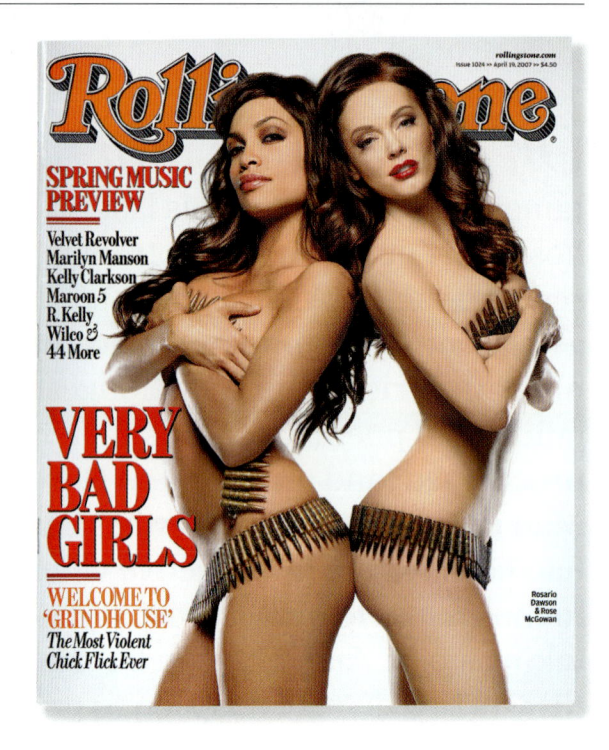

RS 1022 | 'SOUTH PARK'
March 22nd, 2007
ARTWORK BY SOUTH PARK STUDIOS

RS 1024 | ROSE McGOWAN
AND ROSARIO DAWSON
April 19th, 2007
PHOTOGRAPH BY MATTHEW ROLSTON

RS 1027 | KEITH RICHARDS
AND JOHNNY DEPP
May 31st, 2007
PHOTOGRAPH BY MATTHEW ROLSTON

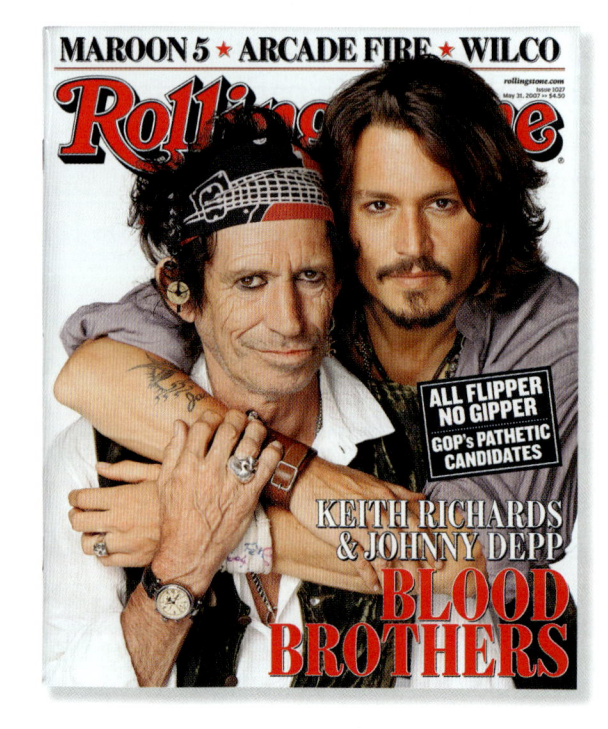

2000s

566 • ROLLING STONE

THE NEXT WAR ON DOWNLOADING

RollingStone

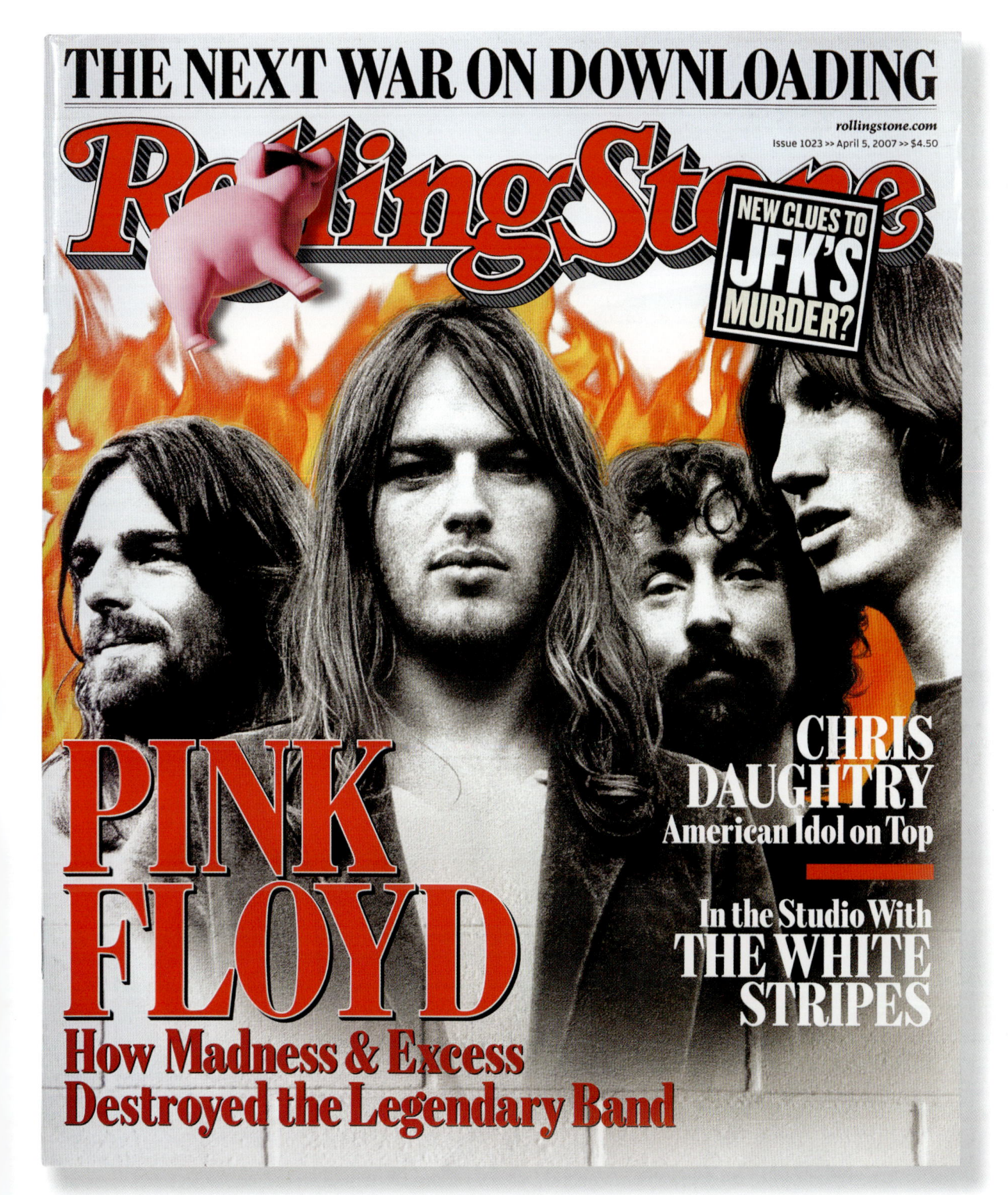

rollingstone.com
Issue 1023 >> April 5, 2007 >> $4.50

NEW CLUES TO JFK'S MURDER?

PINK FLOYD
How Madness & Excess Destroyed the Legendary Band

CHRIS DAUGHTRY
American Idol on Top

In the Studio With THE WHITE STRIPES

RS 1023 | PINK FLOYD | April 5th, 2007 | Photograph by Michael Ochs, Photo Colorization by Michael Elins

50 YEARS OF COVERS • 567

ROLLING STONE
THE FORTIETH ANNIVERSARY

2000s

RS 1025/1026 | FORTIETH ANNIVERSARY | May 3rd–17th, 2007 | GRAPHIC DESIGN BY CHIP KIDD

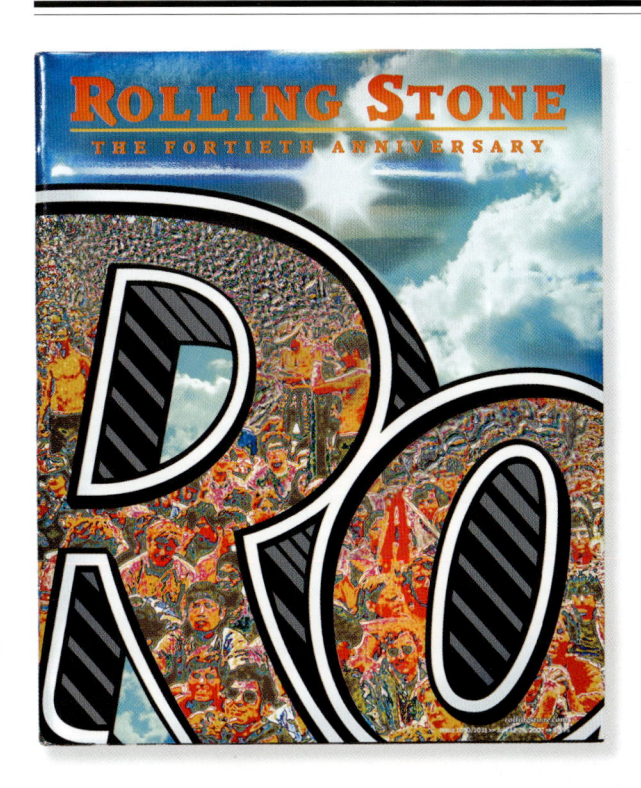

RS 1030/1031 | FORTIETH ANNIVERSARY
July 12th–26th, 2007
GRAPHIC DESIGN BY CHIP KIDD

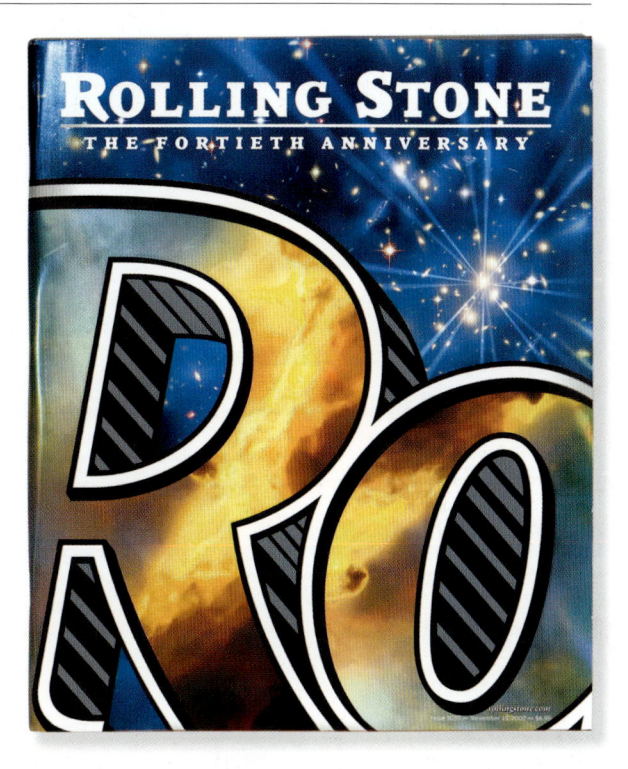

RS 1039 | FORTIETH ANNIVERSARY
November 15th, 2007
GRAPHIC DESIGN BY CHIP KIDD

"Age ain't nothing but a number." So began the Editor's Note to the first of three issues commemorating ROLLING STONE's 40th anniversary. "But 40 years is an impressive number indeed and one to be proud of." Preparing these three special collectors editions took more than a year. The finished products contained more than 100 interviews with musicians, filmmakers, actors, presidents, writers, scientists and other innovators who'd shaped the past four decades. The first issue focused on the baby-boom generation, from Bob Dylan to Steven Spielberg to Jimmy Carter. The second installment, which came out weeks later, was a tribute to 1967. The entire issue – from the Letters section to the news stories to the Charts – was dedicated to ROLLING STONE's founding year. The third anniversary edition looked ahead, with influential figures like Bill Gates, Jon Stewart, Bill Clinton and Bono assessing the future. "This is going to be an American century," Al Gore told us, striking an optimistic note amid the darkness of the Bush years. "We're going to come back strong."

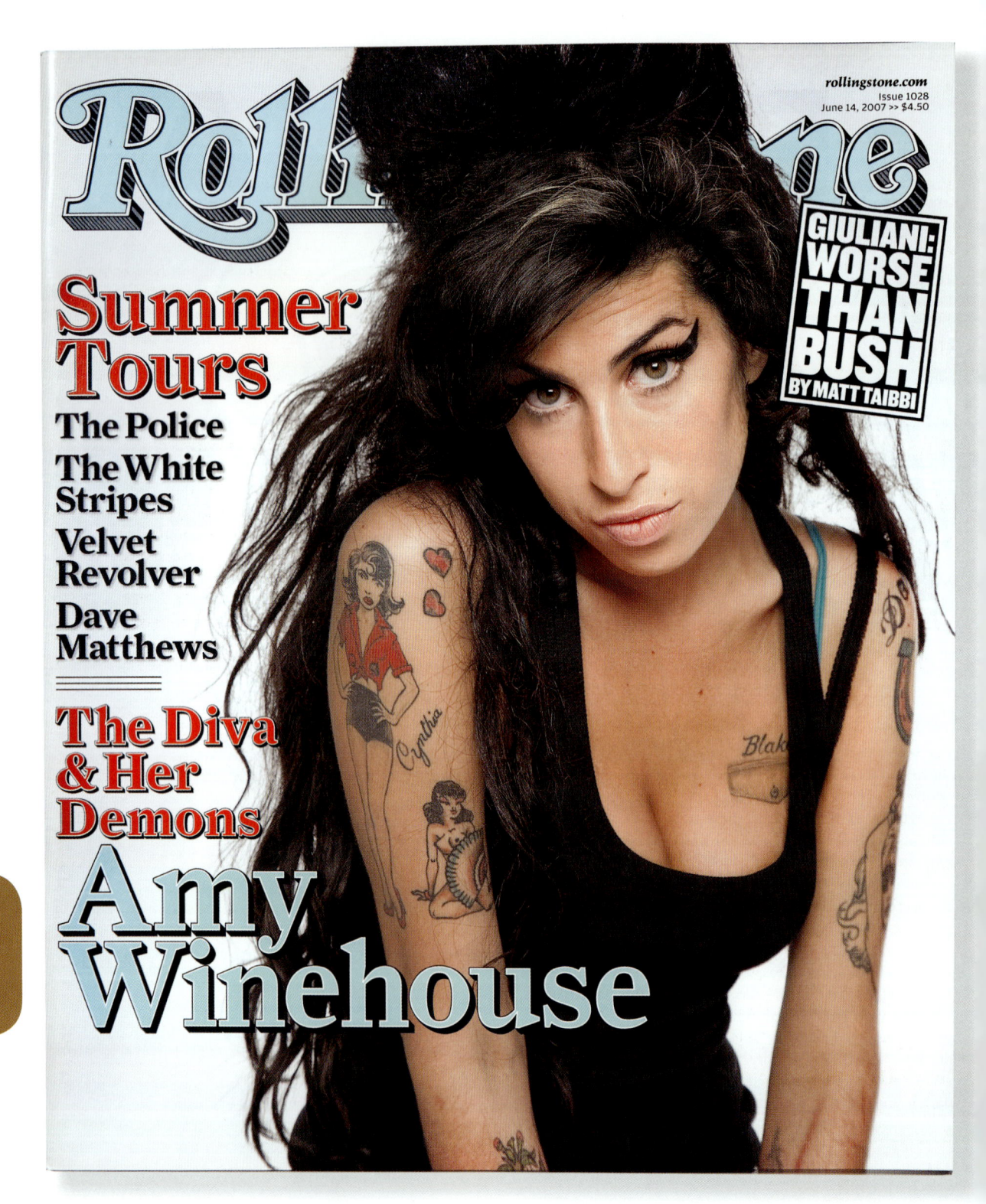

# Rolling Stone

rollingstone.com
Issue 1028
June 14, 2007 >> $4.50

GIULIANI: WORSE THAN BUSH
BY MATT TAIBBI

Summer Tours
The Police
The White Stripes
Velvet Revolver
Dave Matthews

The Diva & Her Demons
Amy Winehouse

2000s

570 • ROLLING STONE

RS 1028 | AMY WINEHOUSE | June 14th, 2007 | Photograph by Max Vadukul

In the universe of a twenty-three-year-old, "ages" is as relative as age is. Winehouse might say she's been singing for ages, though it's been less than a decade. Or that she's been in love with her Baby for ages, though it's been only a couple of years, with a span of months off in between. Or that the scars that cover her left forearm come from wounds she inflicted on herself ages ago, though they look considerably fresher than that. She might say any of those things, if she said much of anything at all.

Those who have only heard her voice express shock upon seeing the body that produces it: The sultry, crackly, world-weary howl that sounds like the ghost of Sarah Vaughan comes from a pint-size Jewish girl from North London, world-weary though she may be. Winehouse has also become notorious for allegedly drunken public appearances, including one time in January when she ran offstage during a performance to barf. At an awards show in the U.K. last fall, she heckled Bono during his acceptance speech with "Shut up! I don't give a fuck!" Then there are her album's frequent references to booze, weed and blow – most notably "Rehab," which narrates how her former management company tried to make her go to rehab, but, oh, you know what happened next.

[EXCERPT FROM RS 1028 COVER STORY BY JENNY ELISCU]

In many ways, the photo shoot for Amy Winehouse's lone ROLLING STONE cover was like a microcosm of her brief, tragic career. Photographer Max Vadukul traveled to Miami to shoot the singer, who was in such an upbeat mood that she volunteered to do a series of unplanned impromptu photos with her new husband, Blake Fielder-Civil, posing in their hotel room and on the beach. "They were so in love and so adorable," recalls ROLLING STONE creative director Jodi Peckman. But when it was time to take the photo that would actually appear on the cover, Winehouse's mood had darkened completely. Arriving at the studio five hours late in a sullen rage, she initially refused to have her picture taken at all. Eventually, Peckman and writer Jenny Eliscu talked her down, and Vadukul got the shot he needed. "She'd gone from bliss to agony," Peckman says. "You can see it in the photo."

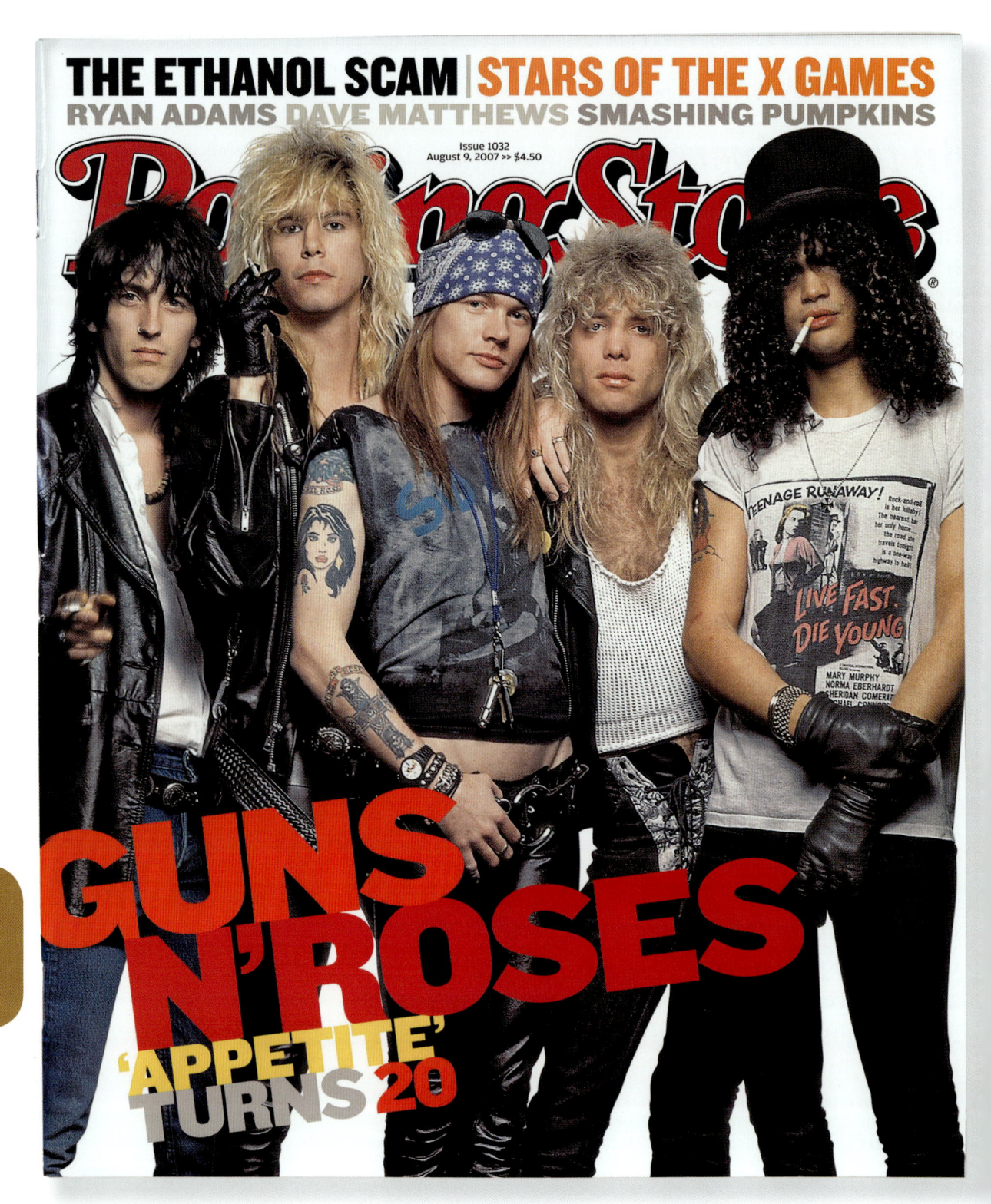

THE ETHANOL SCAM | **STARS OF THE X GAMES**
RYAN ADAMS DAVE MATTHEWS SMASHING PUMPKINS

Issue 1032
August 9, 2007 >> $4.50

GUNS N'ROSES
'APPETITE' TURNS 20

2000s

572 · ROLLING STONE

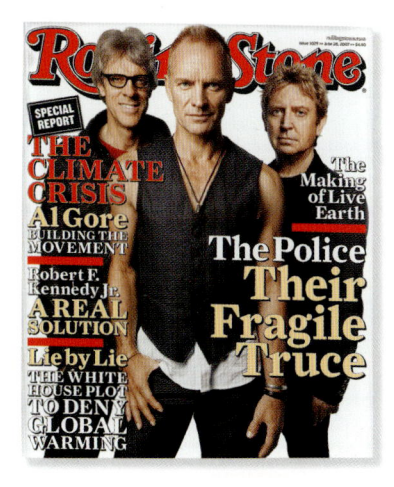

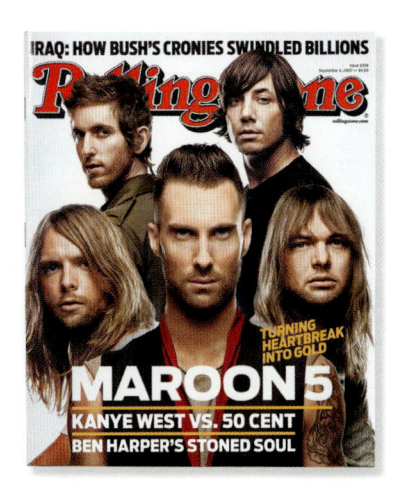

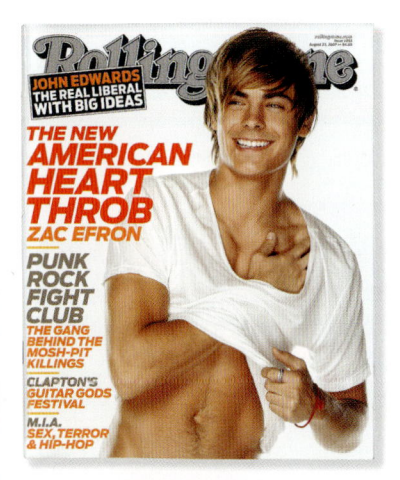

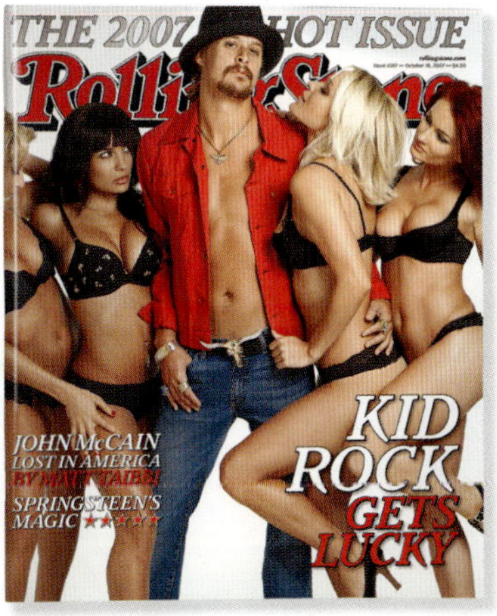

RS 1032 | GUNS N' ROSES
August 9th, 2007
PHOTOGRAPH BY NEIL ZLOZOWER

AXL ROSE WAS LYING NUDE inside a Manhattan recording studio's darkened vocal booth, working out some unorthodox last-minute overdubs. Tape was rolling, and he knew something wasn't right. Beneath him was a cute nineteen-year-old stripper named Adriana Smith, who happened to be his drummer's girlfriend. "Come on, Adriana, make it real," Rose barked, pausing mid-coitus. "Stop faking!" On that warm weekend evening in the spring of 1987, engineer Vic Deyglio had set up a top-of-the-line vocal microphone to capture the sounds of Rose and Smith having sex – and at one point, he had to dash into the booth to adjust the mike as they went at it. "It was like a Ron Jeremy set in there," Deyglio recalls. Smith wanted to get back at Guns n' Roses drummer Steven Adler for cheating on her – and had always liked the singer better anyway. "I would do anything Axl asked me to do," says Smith, now a forty-year-old mom. "He's fuckin' magical."

[EXCERPT FROM RS 1032 COVER STORY BY BRIAN HIATT]

RS 1029 | THE POLICE
June 28th, 2007
PHOTOGRAPH BY MAX VADUKUL

RS 1033 | ZAC EFRON
August 23th, 2007
PHOTOGRAPH BY MATTHEW ROLSTON

RS 1034 | MAROON 5
September 6th, 2007
PHOTOGRAPH BY MATTHEW ROLSTON

RS 1037 | KID ROCK
October 18th, 2007
PHOTOGRAPH BY MAX VADUKUL

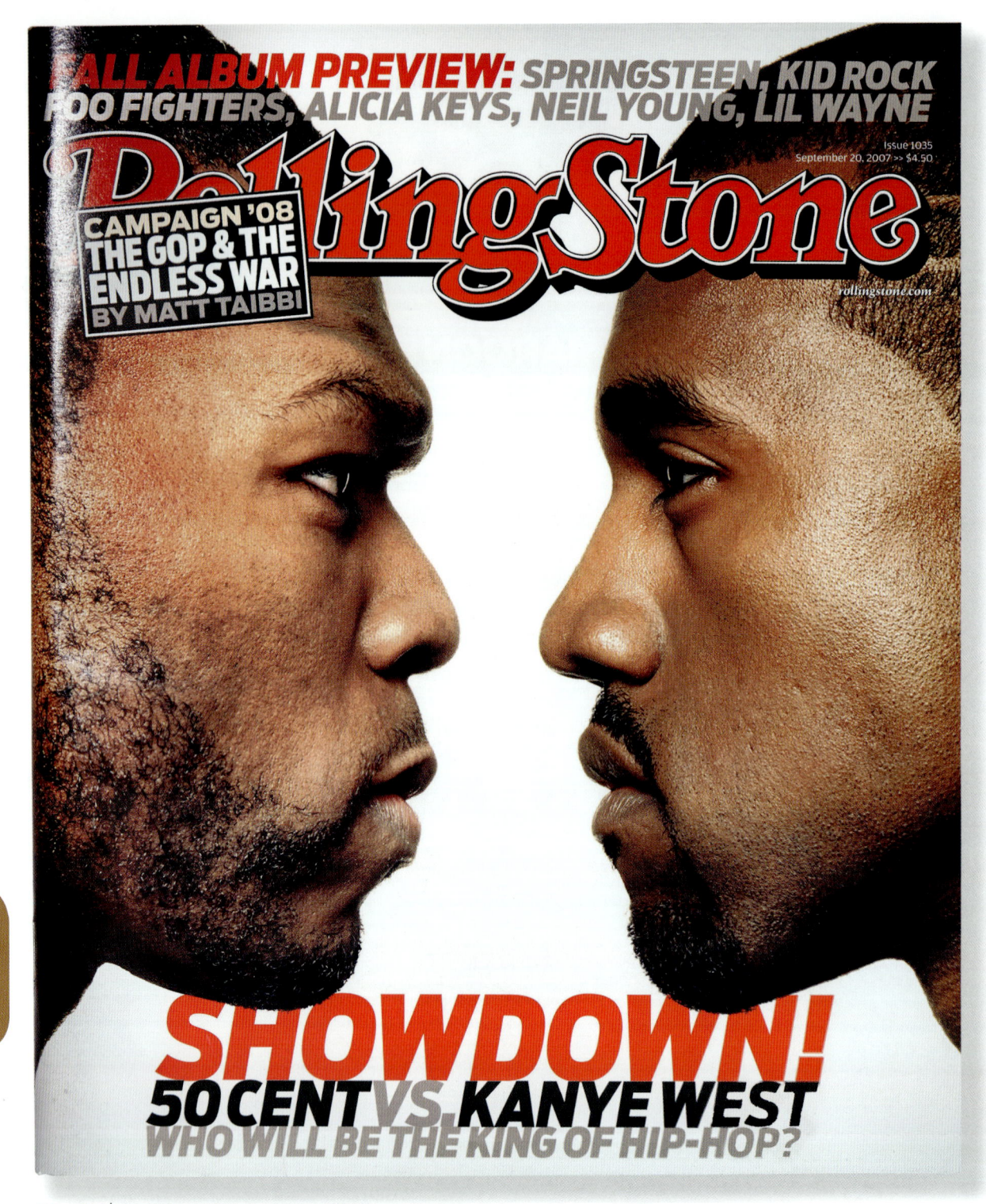

FALL ALBUM PREVIEW: SPRINGSTEEN, KID ROCK, FOO FIGHTERS, ALICIA KEYS, NEIL YOUNG, LIL WAYNE

Rolling Stone

Issue 1035
September 20, 2007 >> $4.50

**CAMPAIGN '08
THE GOP & THE ENDLESS WAR
BY MATT TAIBBI**

rollingstone.com

2000s

SHOWDOWN!
50 CENT VS. KANYE WEST
WHO WILL BE THE KING OF HIP-HOP?

RS 1035 | 50 CENT AND KANYE WEST | September 20th, 2007 | Photograph by Albert Watson

574 • ROLLING STONE

MICK JAGGER | JAMES BLUNT | SECRETS OF HALO 3

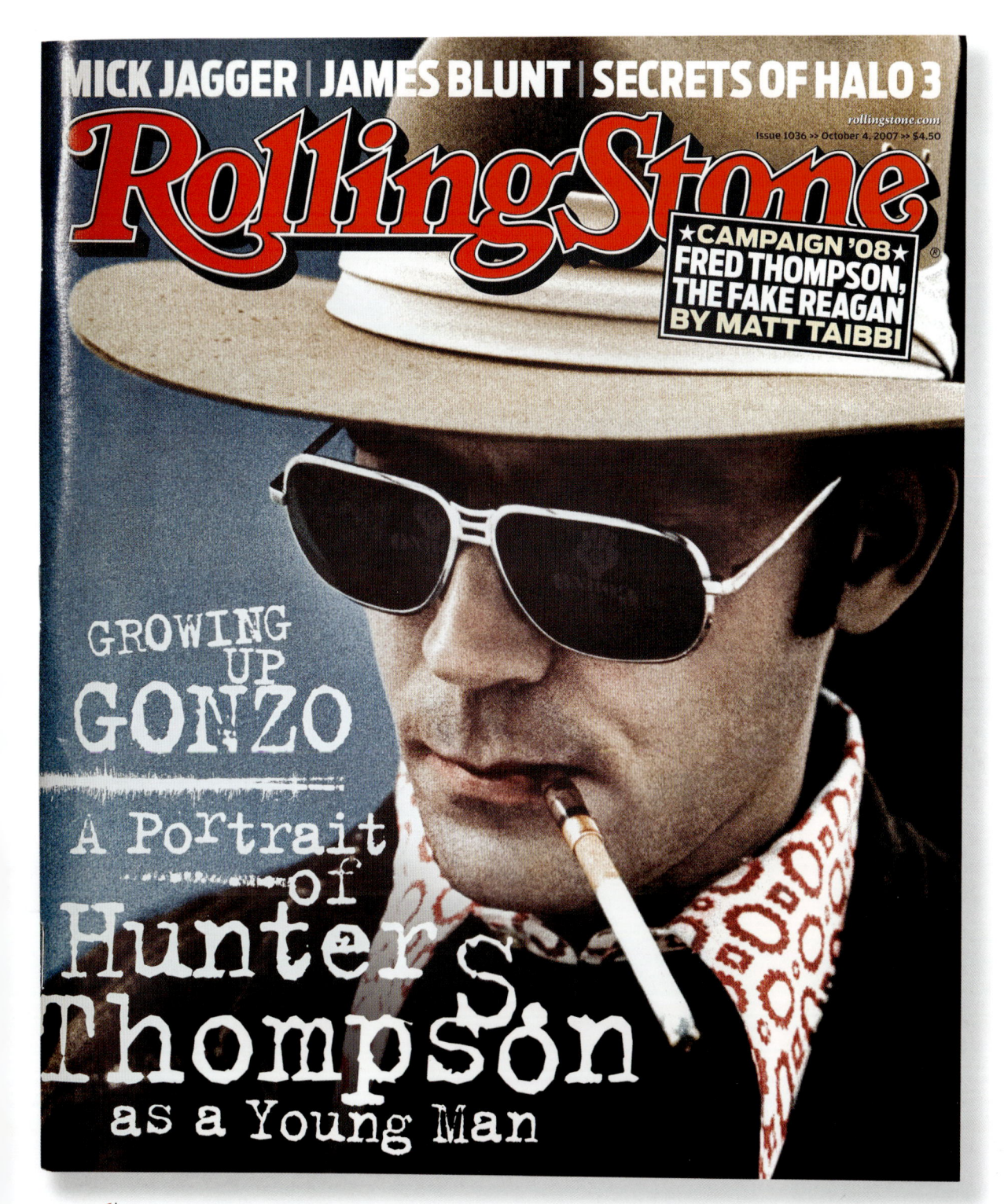

RollingStone

rollingstone.com
Issue 1036 >> October 4, 2007 >> $4.50

★ CAMPAIGN '08 ★
FRED THOMPSON,
THE FAKE REAGAN
BY MATT TAIBBI

GROWING UP GONZO

A Portrait of Hunter S Thompson as a Young Man

RS 1036 | DR. HUNTER S. THOMPSON | October 4th, 2007 | Photograph by Edmund Shea, Photo Colorization by Michael Elins

50 YEARS OF COVERS • 575

RADIOHEAD, EAGLES, JAY-Z, NEIL YOUNG

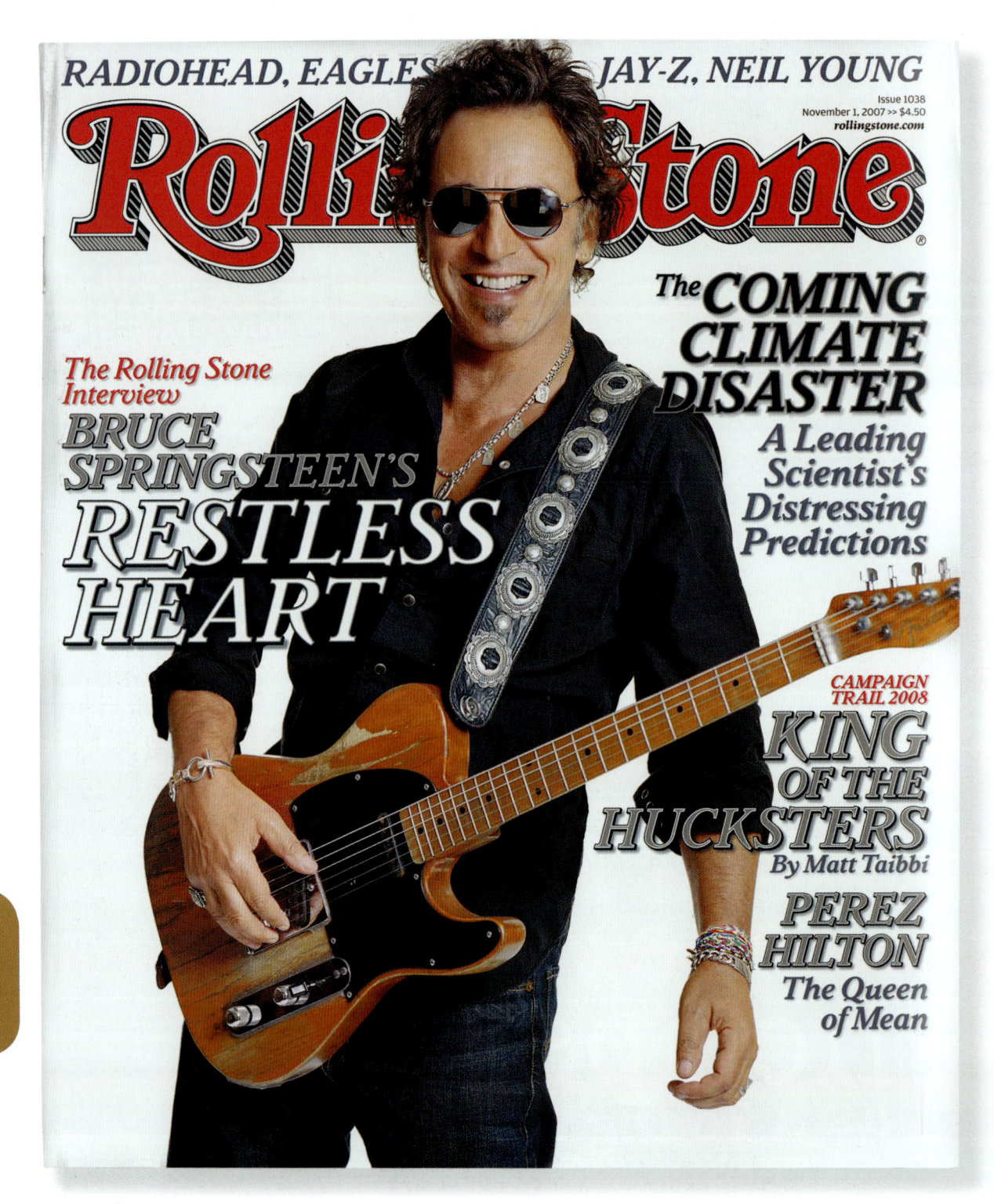

Rolling Stone

Issue 1038
November 1, 2007 >> $4.50
rollingstone.com

The Rolling Stone Interview
BRUCE SPRINGSTEEN'S RESTLESS HEART

The COMING CLIMATE DISASTER
A Leading Scientist's Distressing Predictions

CAMPAIGN TRAIL 2008
KING OF THE HUCKSTERS
By Matt Taibbi

PEREZ HILTON
The Queen of Mean

2000s

RS 1038 | BRUCE SPRINGSTEEN | November 1st, 2007 | Photograph by Max Vadukul

Rolling Stone

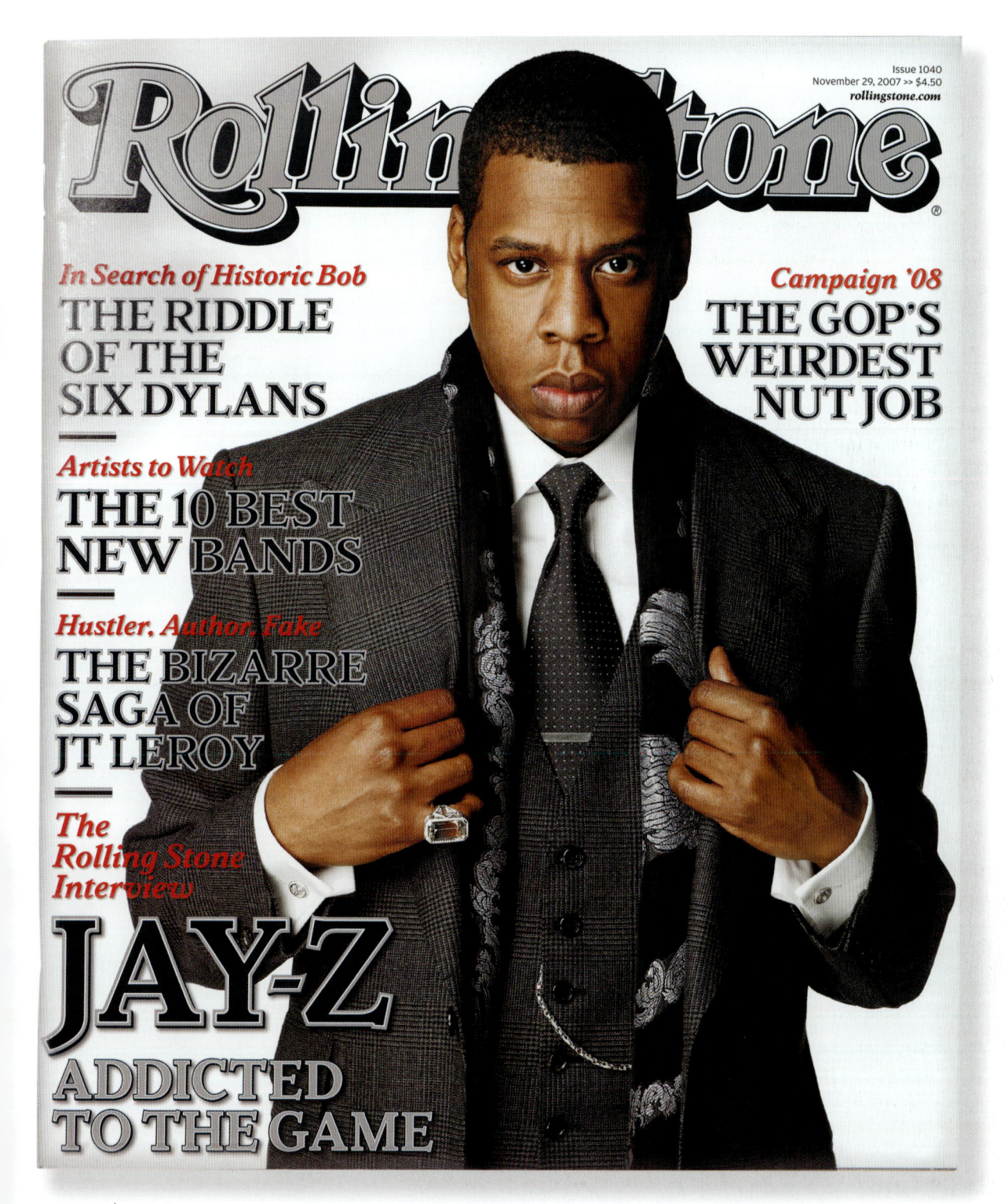

In Search of Historic Bob
THE RIDDLE OF THE SIX DYLANS

Artists to Watch
THE 10 BEST NEW BANDS

Hustler, Author, Fake
THE BIZARRE SAGA OF JT LEROY

The Rolling Stone Interview
JAY-Z
ADDICTED TO THE GAME

Campaign '08
THE GOP'S WEIRDEST NUT JOB

Issue 1040
November 29, 2007 >> $4.50
rollingstone.com

RS 1040 | JAY-Z | November 29th, 2007 | Photograph by Matthew Rolston

50 YEARS OF COVERS • 577

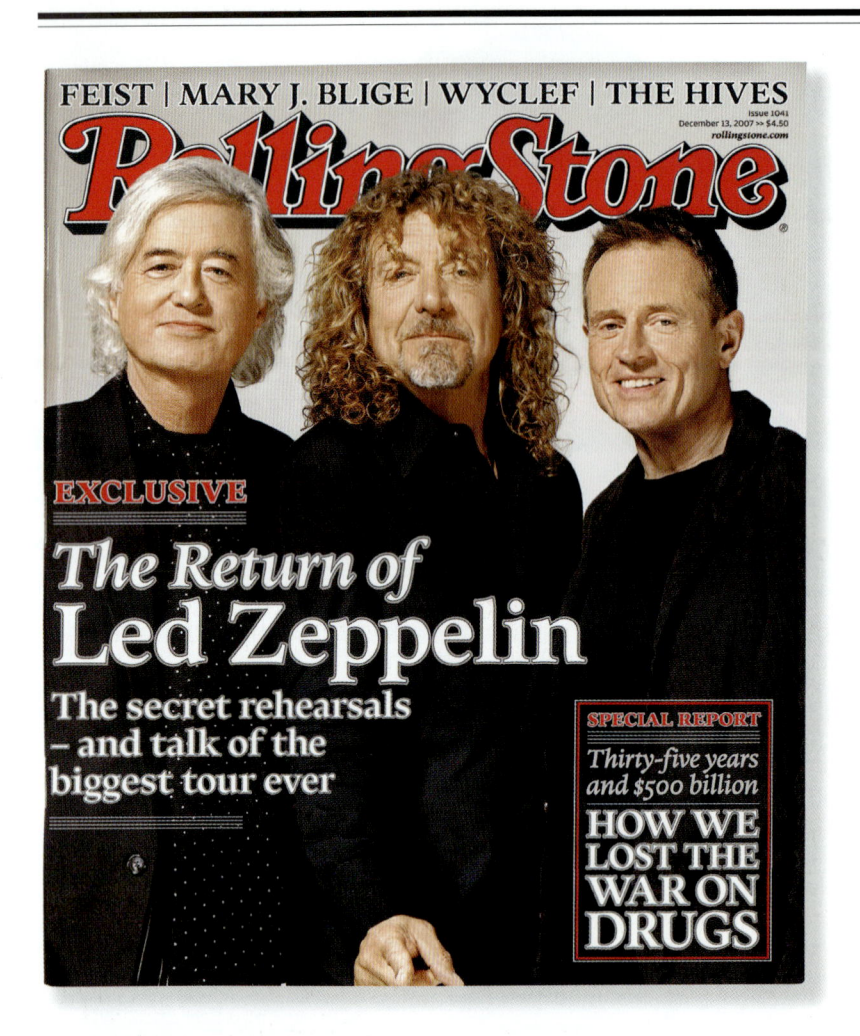

RS 1041 | LED ZEPPELIN
December 13th, 2007
Photograph by Perou

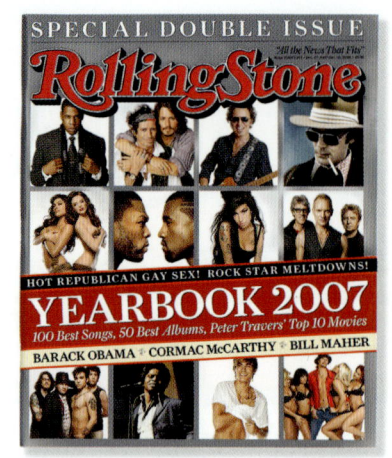

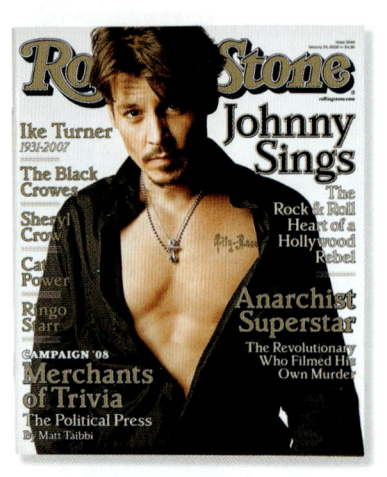

RS 1042/1043 | YEARBOOK 2007
December 27th, 2007–January 9th, 2008
Various Photographers

RS 1044 | JOHNNY DEPP
January 24th, 2008
Photograph by Matthew Rolston

2000s

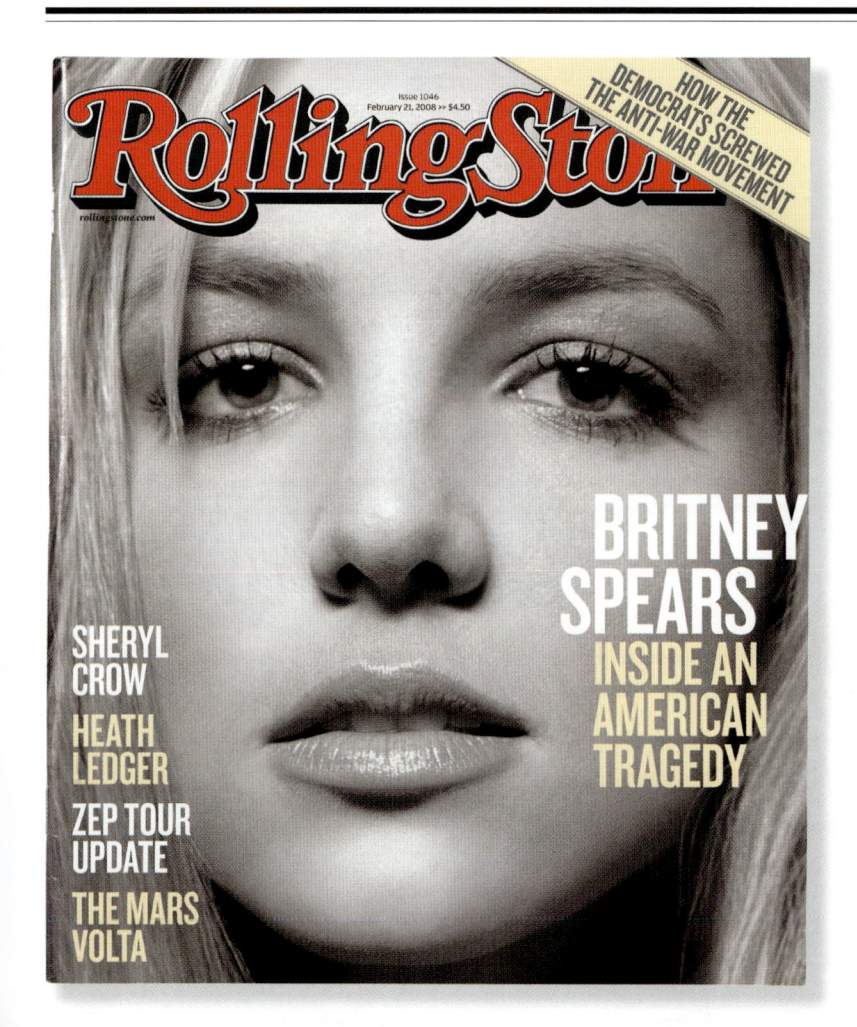

RS 1046 | BRITNEY SPEARS
February 21st, 2008
PHOTOGRAPH BY JAMES WHITE/CORBIS ONLINE

IF BRITNEY WAS really who we believed her to be – a puppet, a grinning blonde without a cool thought in her head, a teasing coquette clueless to her own sexual power – none of this would have happened. She is not book-smart, granted. But she is intelligent enough to understand what the world wanted of her: that she was created as a virgin to be deflowered before us, for our amusement and titillation. She is not ashamed of her new persona – she wants us to know what we did to her.

[EXCERPT FROM RS 1046 COVER STORY BY VANESSA GRIGORIADIS]

Rolling Stone

Issue 1045
February 7, 2008 >> $4.50

rollingstone.com

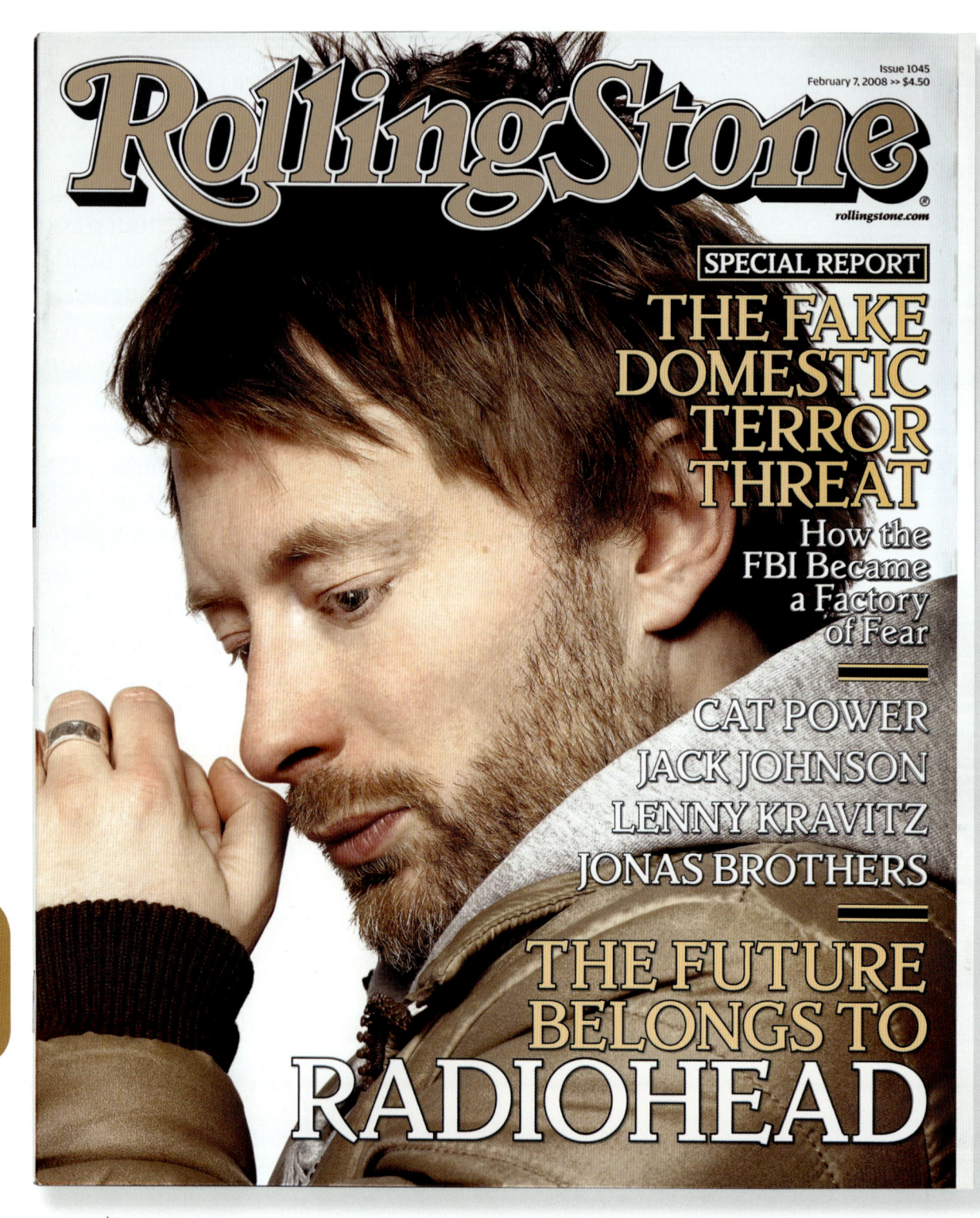

SPECIAL REPORT

THE FAKE DOMESTIC TERROR THREAT

How the FBI Became a Factory of Fear

CAT POWER
JACK JOHNSON
LENNY KRAVITZ
JONAS BROTHERS

THE FUTURE BELONGS TO RADIOHEAD

2000s

RS 1045 | THOM YORKE | February 7th, 2008 | Photograph by James Dimmock

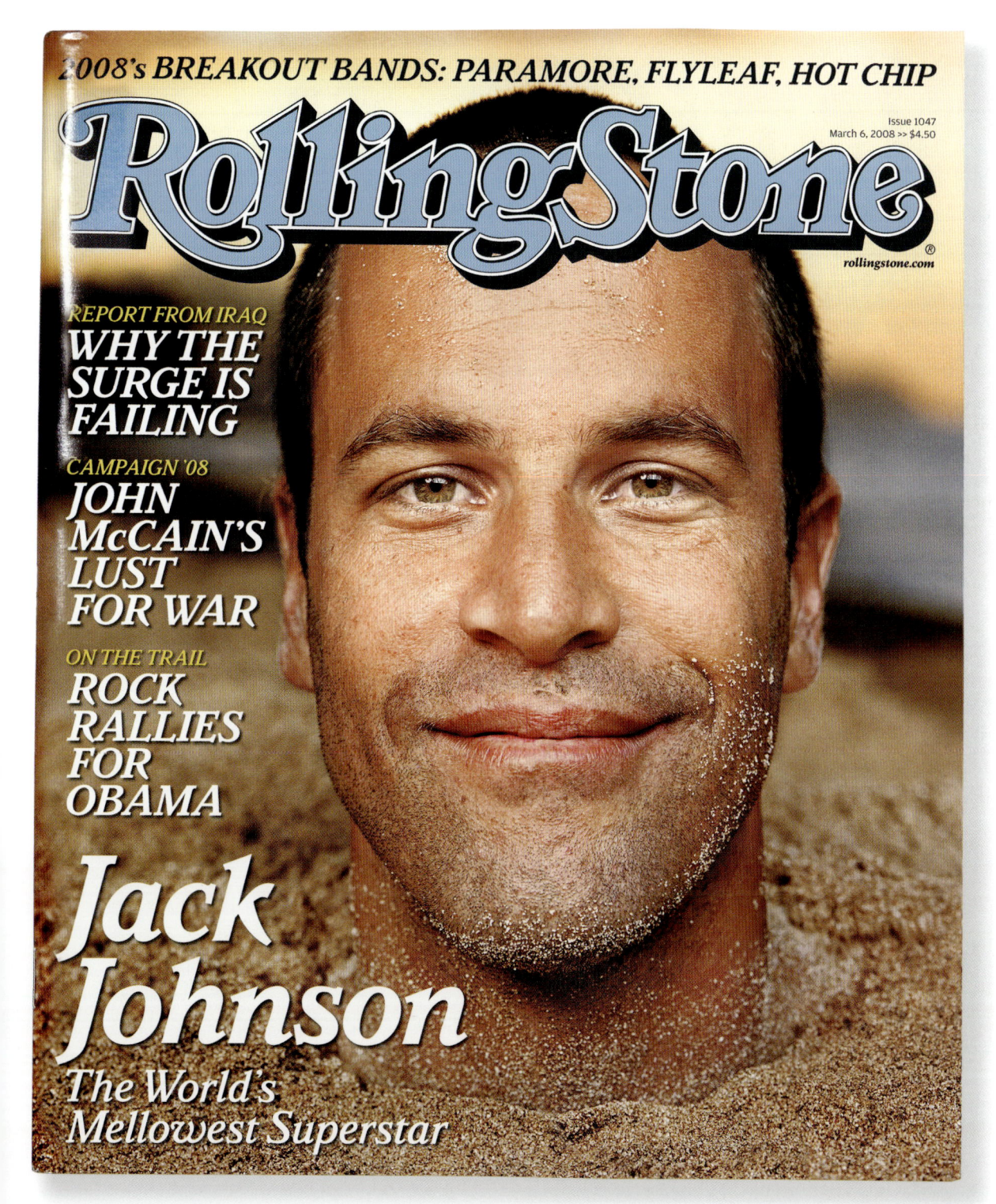

2008's BREAKOUT BANDS: PARAMORE, FLYLEAF, HOT CHIP

RollingStone

Issue 1047
March 6, 2008 >> $4.50

rollingstone.com

REPORT FROM IRAQ
WHY THE SURGE IS FAILING

CAMPAIGN '08
JOHN McCAIN'S LUST FOR WAR

ON THE TRAIL
ROCK RALLIES FOR OBAMA

Jack Johnson
The World's Mellowest Superstar

RS 1047 | JACK JOHNSON | March 6th, 2008 | Photograph by Martin Schoeller

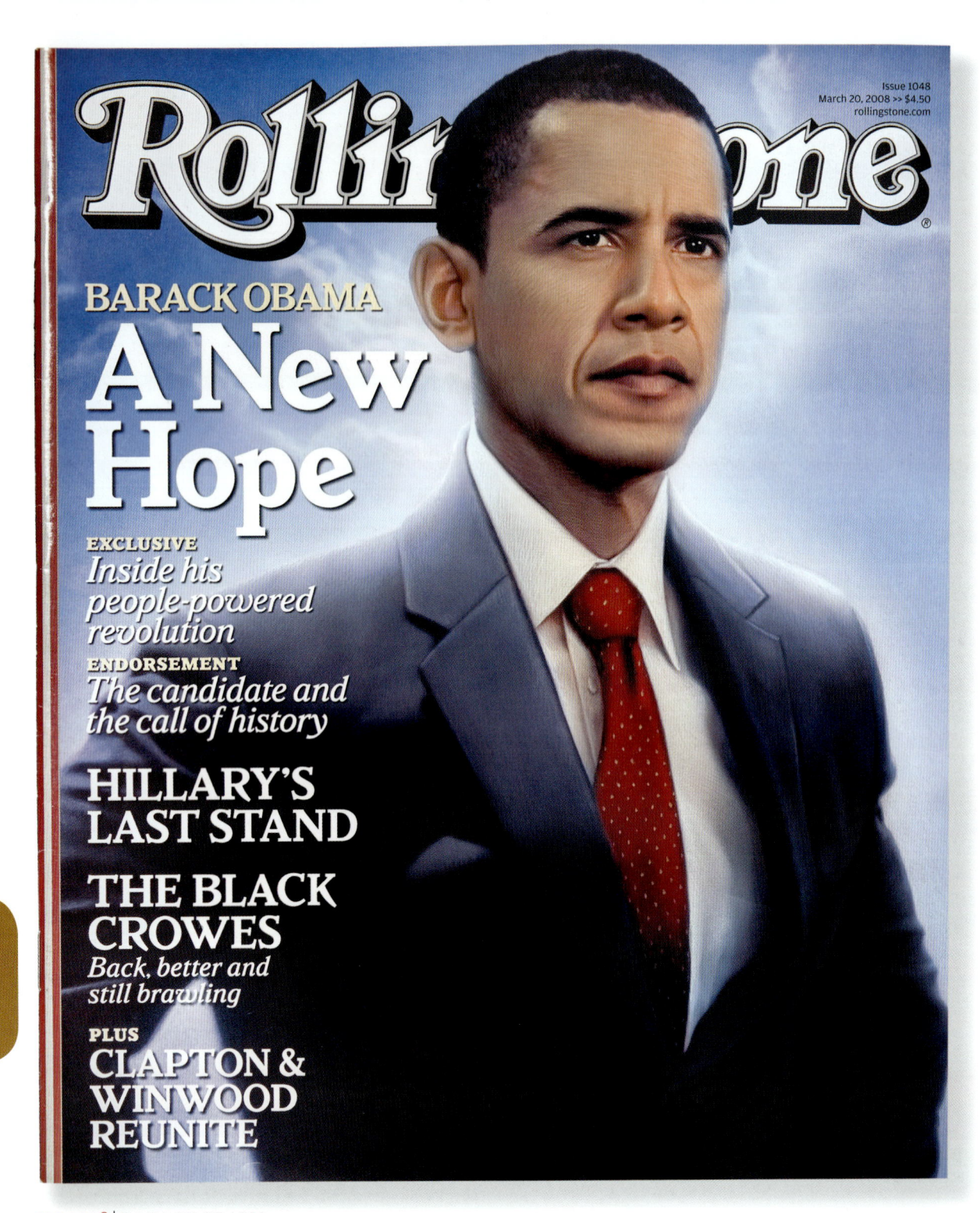

Rolling Stone

Issue 1048
March 20, 2008 >> $4.50
rollingstone.com

BARACK OBAMA
A New Hope

EXCLUSIVE
Inside his people-powered revolution

ENDORSEMENT
The candidate and the call of history

HILLARY'S LAST STAND

THE BLACK CROWES
Back, better and still brawling

PLUS
CLAPTON & WINWOOD REUNITE

2000s

RS 1048 | BARACK OBAMA | March 20th, 2008 | Illustration by Tim O'Brien

NINE INCH NAILS | COUNTING CROWS | VAN MORRISON

Rolling Stone

Issue 1049 >> April 3, 2008 >> $4.50
rollingstone.com

CHRIS ROCK
Hanging Out With the Funniest Motherf*#!er in the USA

HOME FROM WAR
Tragedy of the Marlboro Marine

CAMPAIGN '08
Hillary's Flimsy Case

★★★★
R.E.M.
Rock Again

RS 1049 | CHRIS ROCK | April 3rd, 2008 | Photograph by James Dimmock

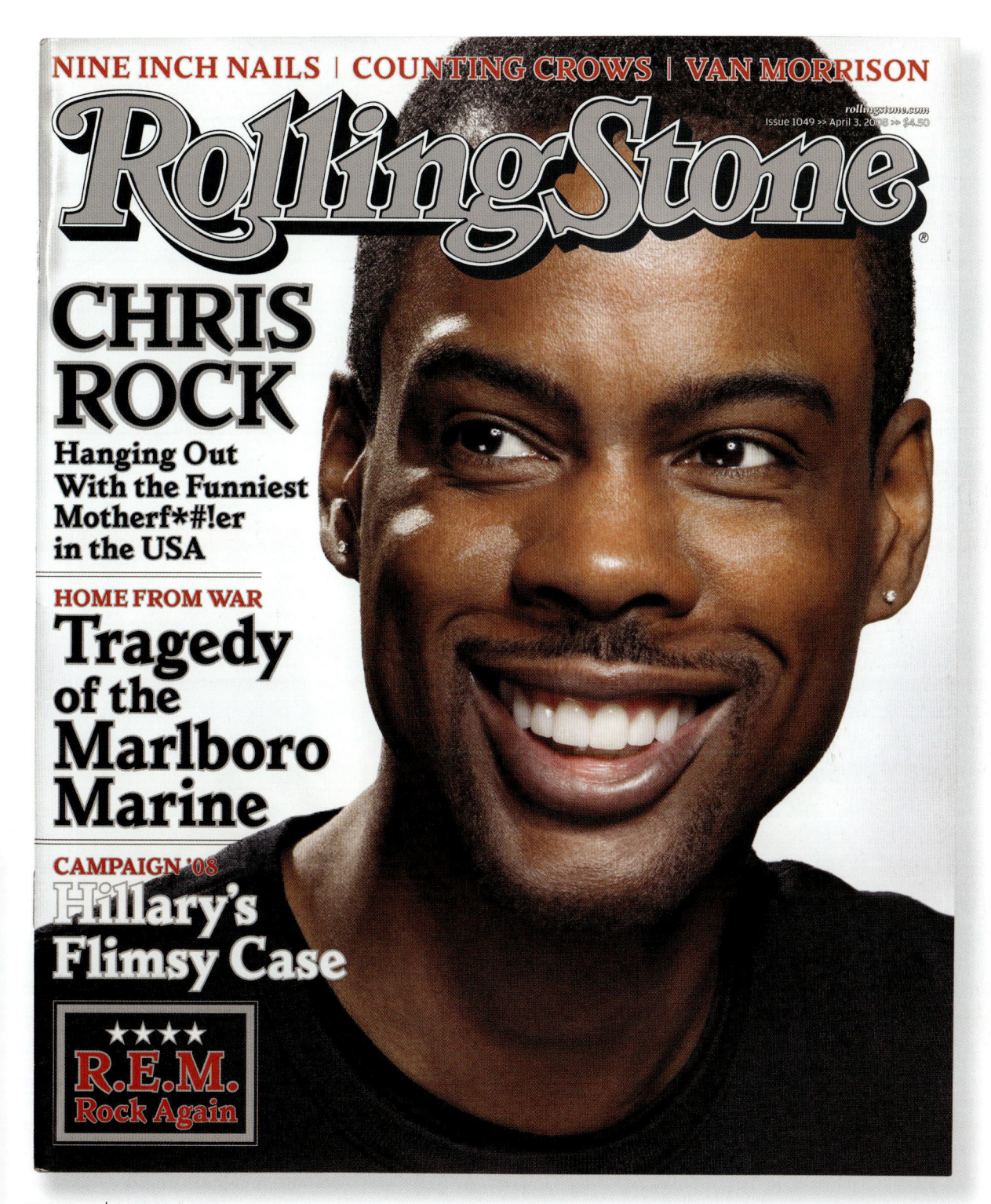

50 YEARS OF COVERS • 583

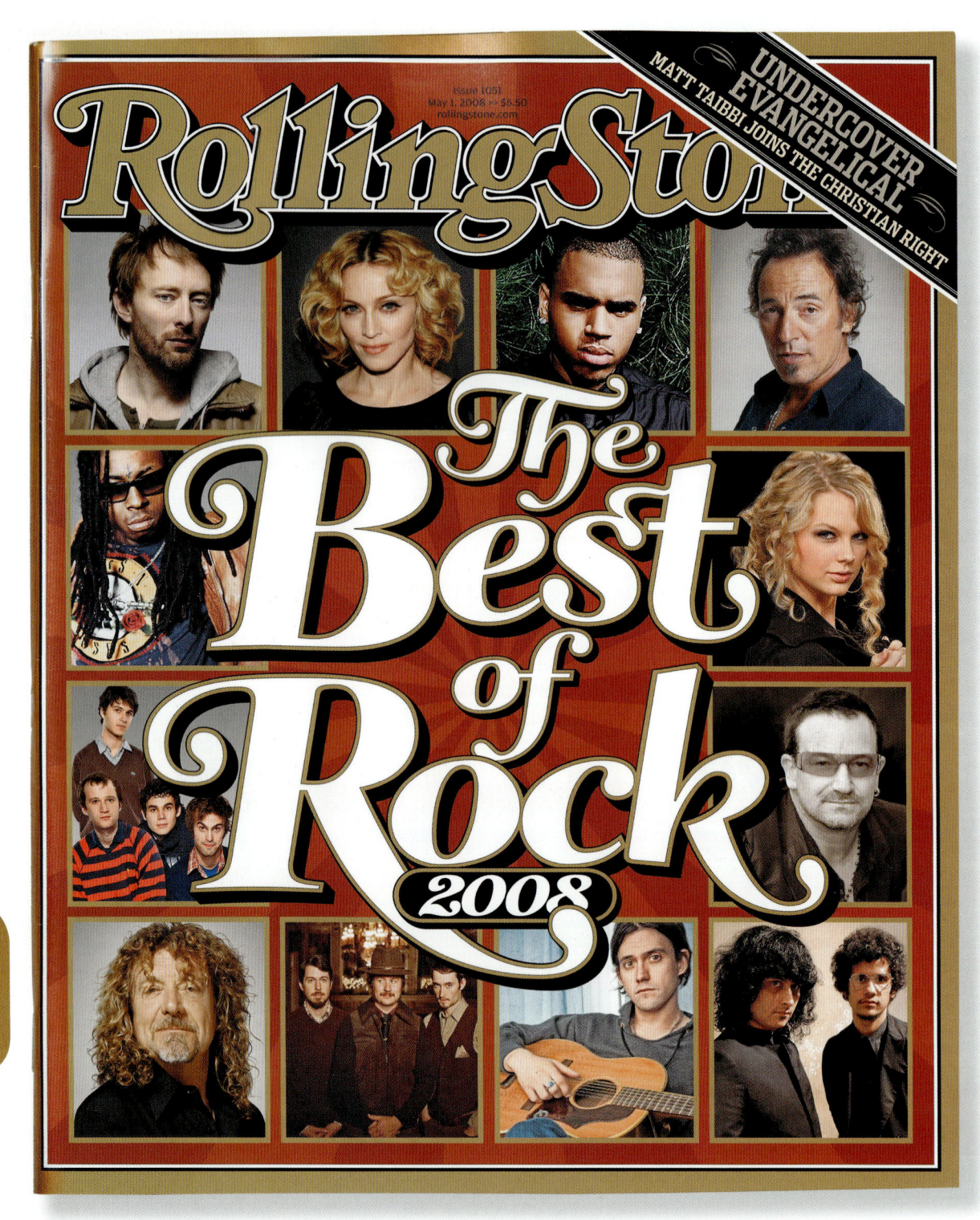

RS 1051 | THE BEST OF ROCK 2008 | May 1st, 2008 | Various Photographers

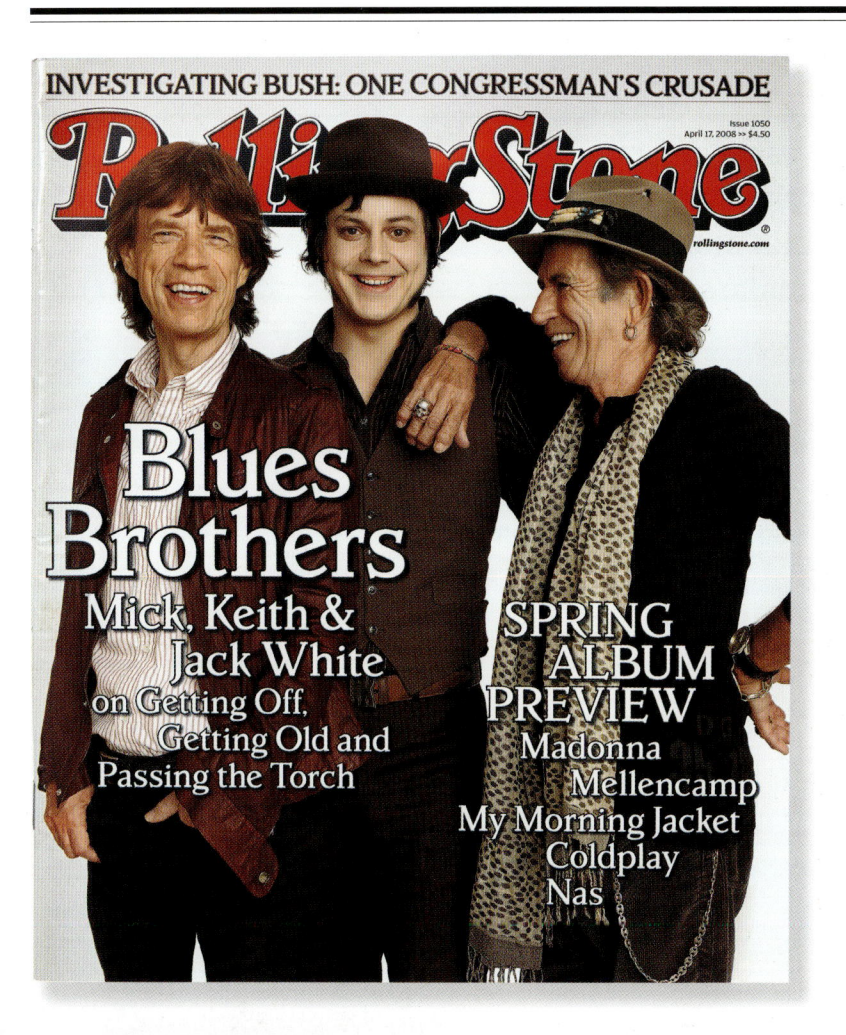

RS 1050 | MICK JAGGER, JACK WHITE AND KEITH RICHARDS
April 17th, 2008
Photograph by Max Vadukul

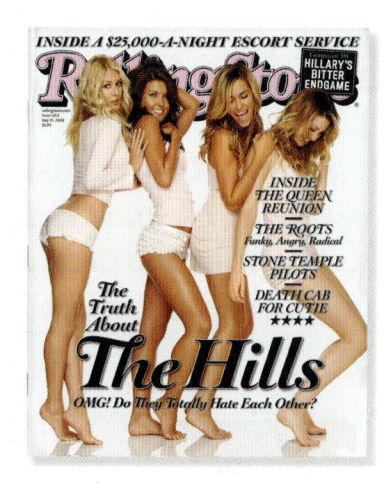

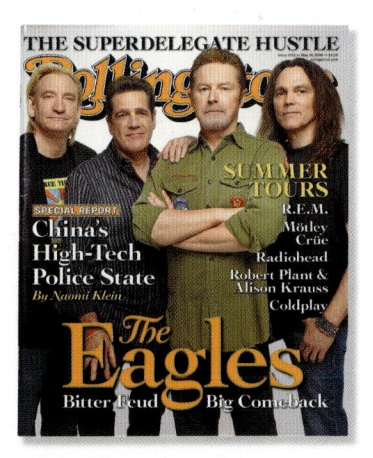

RS 1052 | CAST OF 'THE HILLS'
May 15th, 2008
Photograph by Matthew Rolston

RS 1053 | THE EAGLES
May 29th, 2008
Photograph by Max Vadukul

"**Well, guitar players** are a lot like the days of the Wild West. The one that played the fastest was the one that practiced the most. What I do mostly is try to play the note to make it make sense, not only to me but to you too." —B.B. King

[RS 1054] Any ROLLING STONE list is going to start debates and our guitar-related lists were no exception. "Look, how much room do you have?" asked senior writer David Fricke, whose encyclopedic knowledge of music history is indispensable in any list project. "For me, these songs are as natural as breathing."

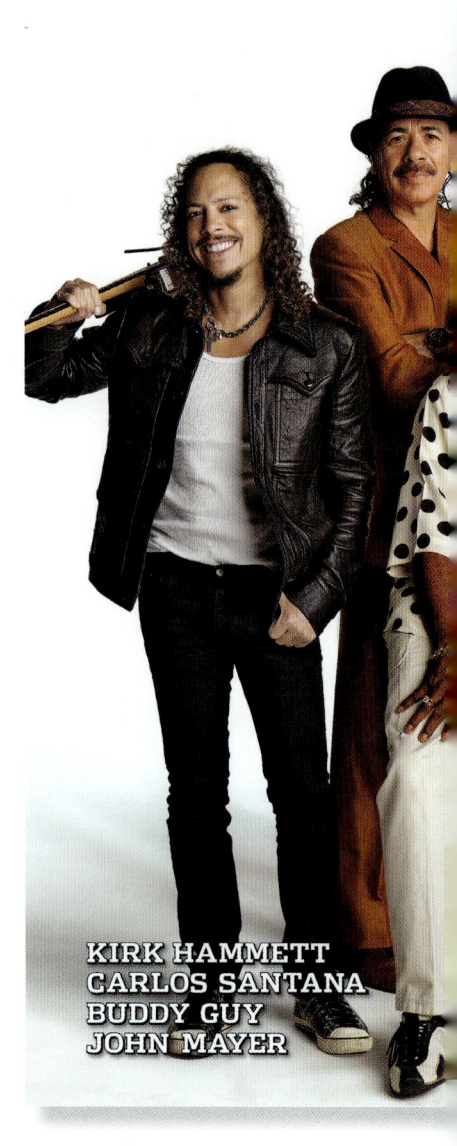

1.	"JOHNNY B. GOODE"	CHUCK BERRY
2.	"PURPLE HAZE"	JIMI HENDRIX
3.	"CROSSROADS"	CREAM
4.	"YOU REALLY GOT ME"	THE KINKS
5.	"BROWN SUGAR"	THE ROLLING STONES
6.	"ERUPTION"	VAN HALEN
7.	"WHILE MY GUITAR GENTLY WEEPS"	THE BEATLES
8.	"STAIRWAY TO HEAVEN"	LED ZEPPELIN
9.	"STATESBORO BLUES"	THE ALLMAN BROTHERS BAND
10.	"SMELLS LIKE TEEN SPIRIT"	NIRVANA
11.	"WHOLE LOTTA LOVE"	LED ZEPPELIN
12.	"VOODOO CHILD (SLIGHT RETURN)"	THE JIMI HENDRIX EXPERIENCE
13.	"LAYLA"	DEREK AND THE DOMINOS
14.	"BORN TO RUN"	BRUCE SPRINGSTEEN
15.	"MY GENERATION"	THE WHO

KIRK HAMMETT
CARLOS SANTANA
BUDDY GUY
JOHN MAYER

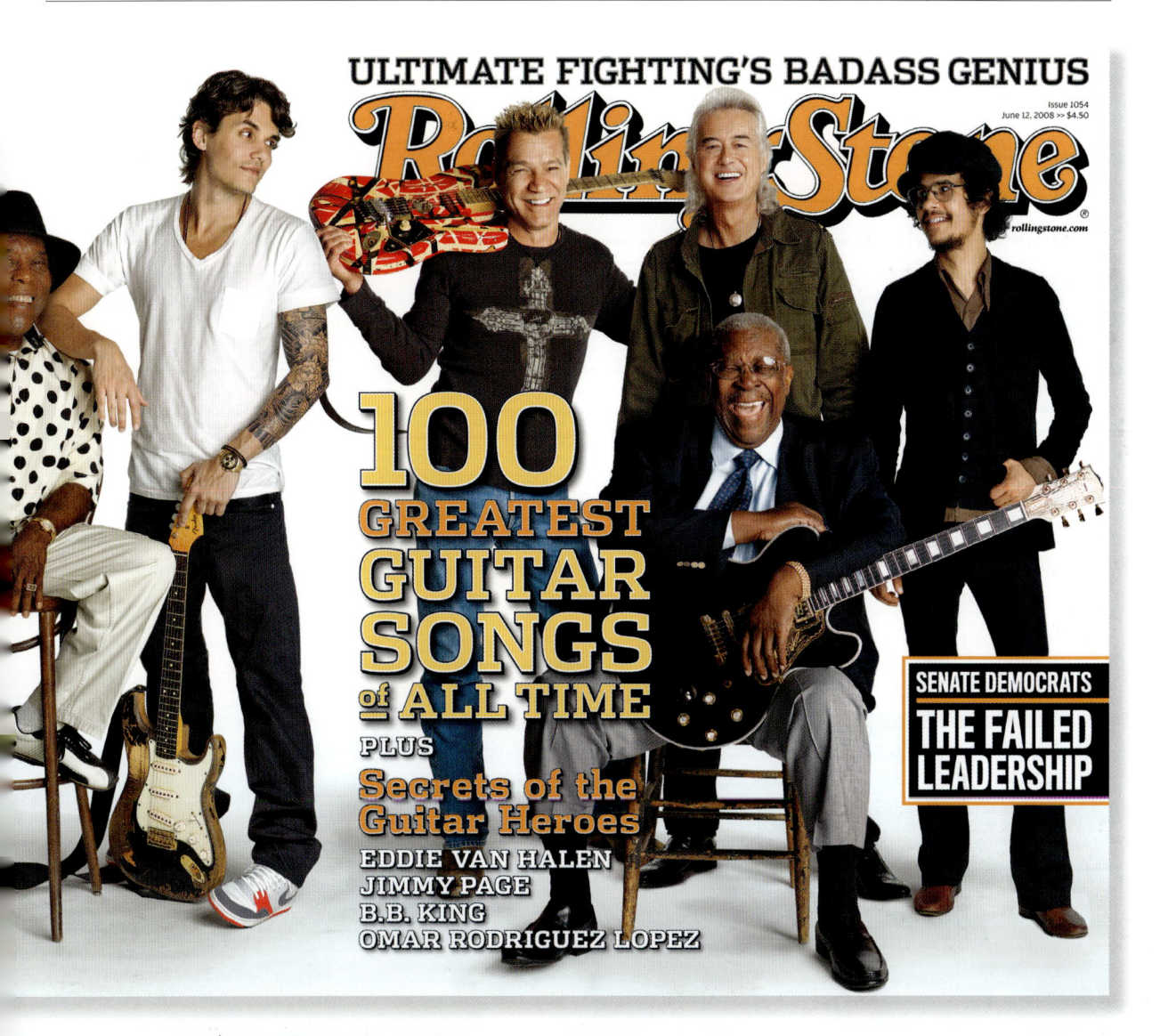

RS 1054 | 100 GREATEST GUITAR SONGS OF ALL TIME | June 12th, 2008 | Photograph by Max Vadukul and Ross Halfin

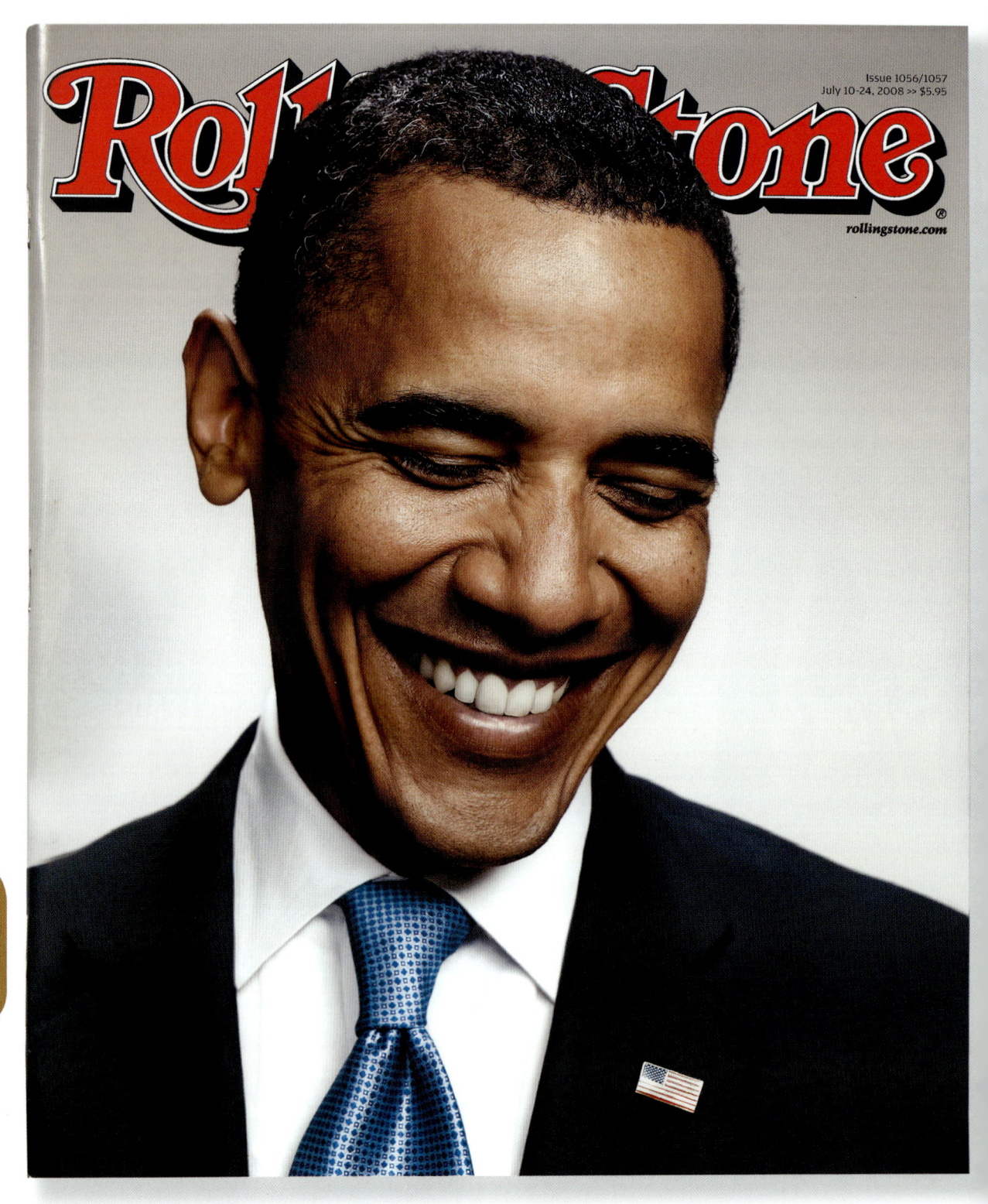

Rolling Stone

Issue 1056/1057
July 10-24, 2008 >> $5.95

rollingstone.com

2000s

RS 1056/1057 | BARACK OBAMA
July 10th–24th, 2008
Photograph by Peter Yang

WHAT HAVE YOU LEARNED IN THE CAMPAIGN ABOUT AMERICA THAT YOU MIGHT NOT HAVE KNOWN BEFORE?

I'm not sure if this is a new lesson, but it reinforced my belief that we're not as divided as our politics would indicate. You meet with the average person – I don't care whether they're Republican, Democrat, conservative, liberal – they don't think in labels. They're not particularly ideological. Everybody is sort of a mix of what you might consider some liberal ideas, what you might consider some conservative ideas. But there is a set of common values that everybody buys into: Everybody thinks you should have to work hard for what you get, everybody believes that things like equal opportunity should be real, not just a slogan.

Are you surprised by how optimistic everyone is in their hearts?

The American people are, I think, congenitally optimistic. Right now, they're not feeling particularly optimistic about Washington – they're genuinely concerned about the direction the country is moving in, they're anxious about globalization and whether we're going to be able to compete. But at bottom, they're not fatalists. They always feel like there's something we can do to make things better.

What have you learned about yourself during the campaign?

I've learned two things, and I think these two things are connected. One is that the older I get, the less important feeding my vanity becomes. I've discovered that I don't get a lot of satisfaction from being the center of attention, but I do get a lot of satisfaction about getting work done. And that, in turn, has led to a confirmation that I have a very steady temper. I don't get too high when things are high, I don't get too low when things are low, which has been very helpful during this campaign and is reflected in the people I hire and how we run our organization.

You've said you don't need to feed your vanity. How do you feed your sanity during the campaign?

Lately, because we've been campaigning in the Midwest, I get to go home each night. My nine-year-old is in the drama club, and last night they had a performance of *Odysseus*. It was outstanding. That's my unbiased review.

[EXCERPT FROM RS 1056/1057 COVER STORY BY JANN S. WENNER]

Rolling Stone

Issue 1055
June 26, 2008 >> $4.50
rollingstone.com

Coldplay's Chris Martin
Confessions of an Anxious Rock God

R.E.M.
METALLICA
DAVID COOK

Bo Diddley
1928-2008

CAMPAIGN '08
McCAIN'S WOUNDED PSYCHE

Stealing Facebook
Did a Dorm Room Theft Launch an Online Empire?

2000s

RS 1055 | CHRIS MARTIN | June 26th, 2008 | Photograph by Nadav Kander

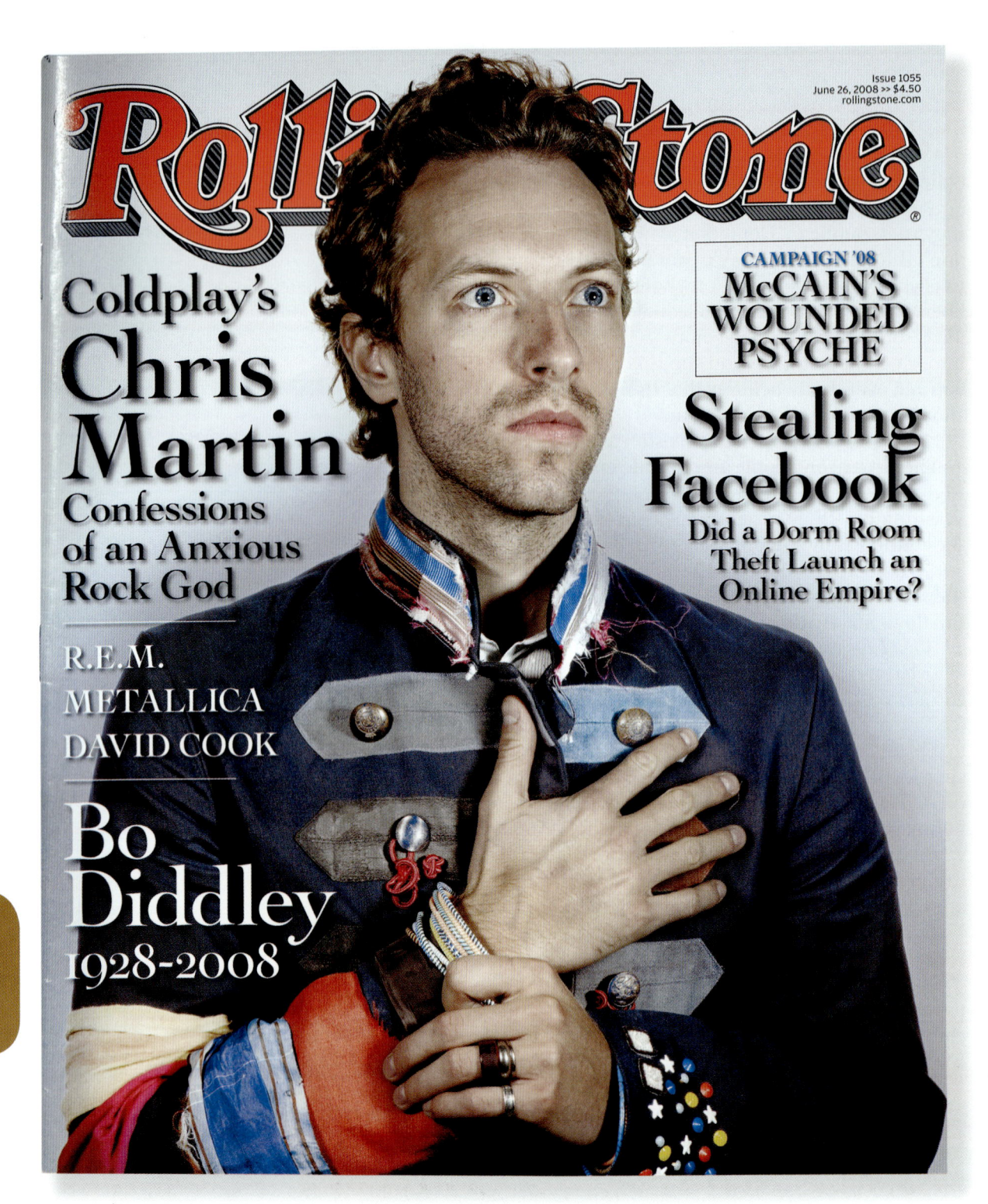

RollingStone

Issue 1059 >> August 21, 2008 >> $4.50
rollingstone.com

CAMPAIGN '08
MATT TAIBBI FOLLOWS THE MONEY

MICHAEL MOORE
How the Democrats Can Blow It

EIGHT DEAD at the MALL
A Tale of an Everyday Massacre

MELLENCAMP'S NEW BLUES

To Hell and Back With ROBERT DOWNEY Jr.

RS 1059 | ROBERT DOWNEY JR. | August 21st, 2008 | Photograph by Sam Jones

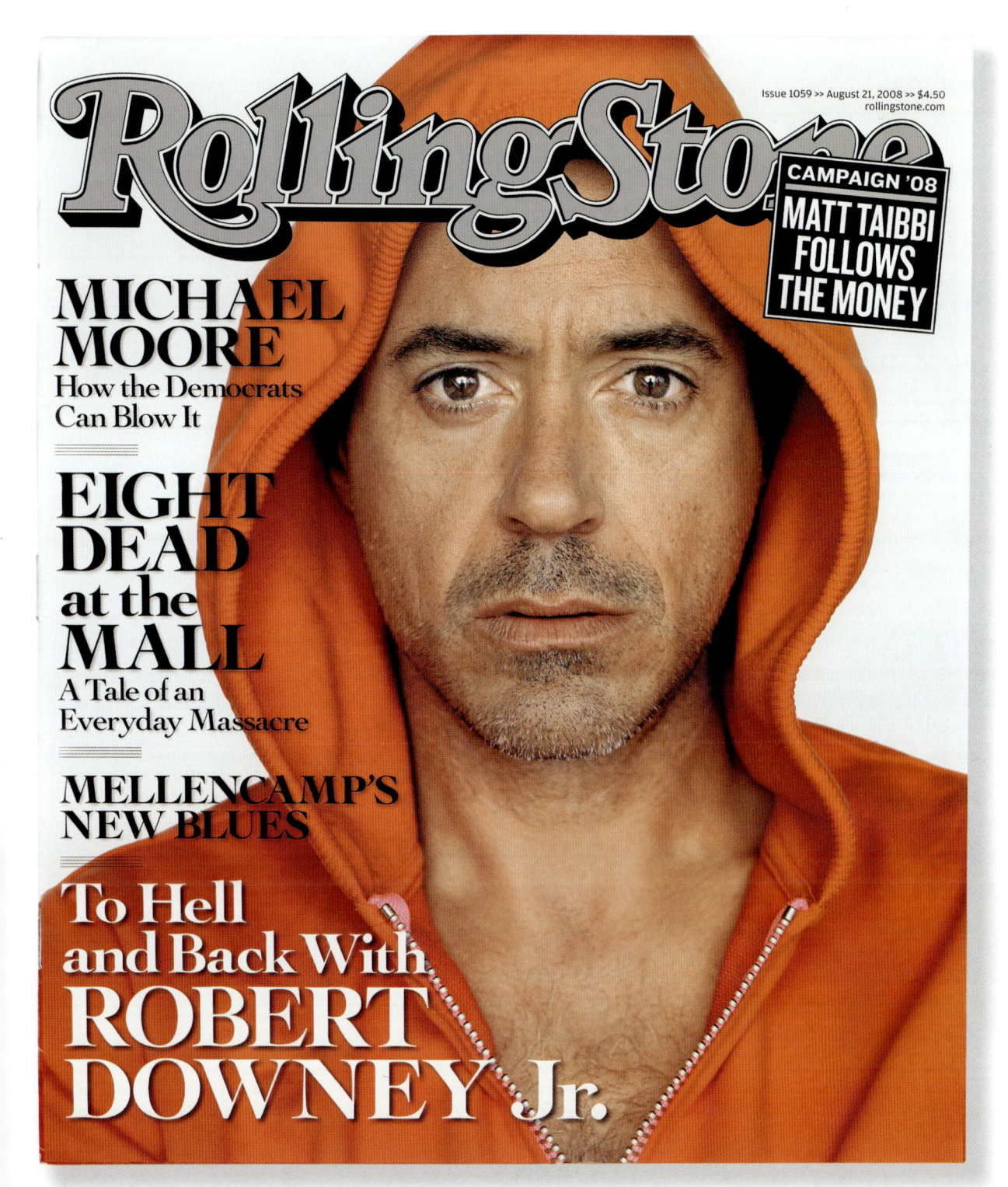

50 YEARS OF COVERS • 591

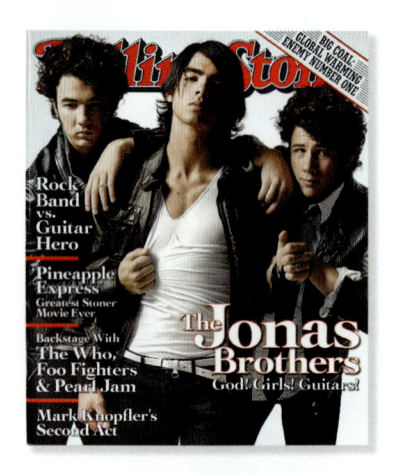

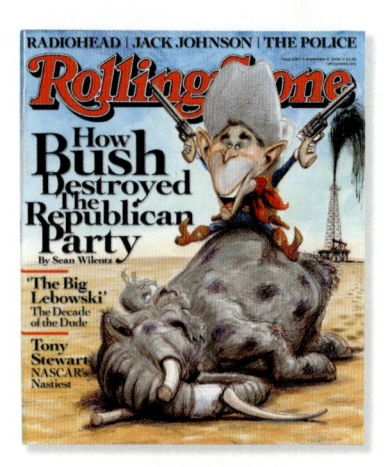

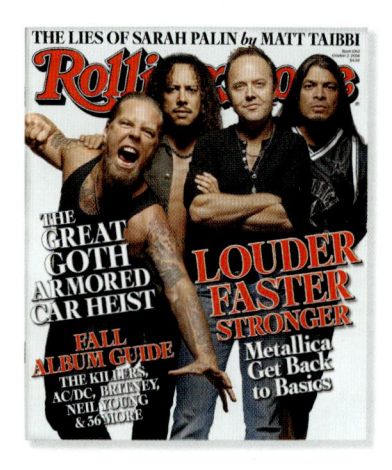

RS 1062 | METALLICA
October 2nd, 2008
PHOTOGRAPH BY JAMES DIMMOCK

[*RS 1064*] With RS 1064, the magazine made a radical change, going from the 10 × 12-inch format to the dimensions of a classic magazine, and trading staples for "perfect binding." The Editor's Note explained the decision thusly: "Like the man we are featuring on the cover for the third time in seven months – a record equaled only by John Lennon – we embrace the idea of change."

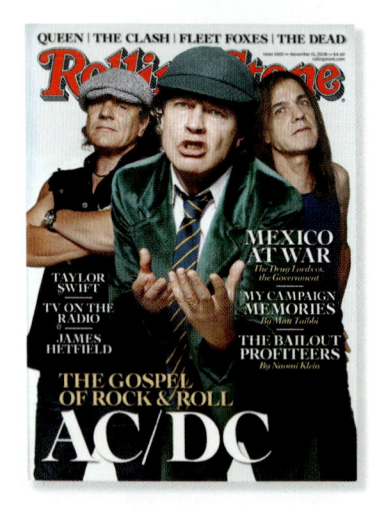

RS 1058 | THE JONAS BROTHERS
August 7th, 2008
PHOTOGRAPH BY MAX VADUKUL

RS 1065 | AC/DC
November 13th, 2008
PHOTOGRAPH BY JAMES DIMMOCK

RS 1060 | GEORGE W. BUSH
September 4th, 2008
ILLUSTRATION BY VICTOR JUHASZ

RS 1064 | BARACK OBAMA
October 30th, 2008
PHOTOGRAPH BY SAM JONES

2000s

592 • ROLLING STONE

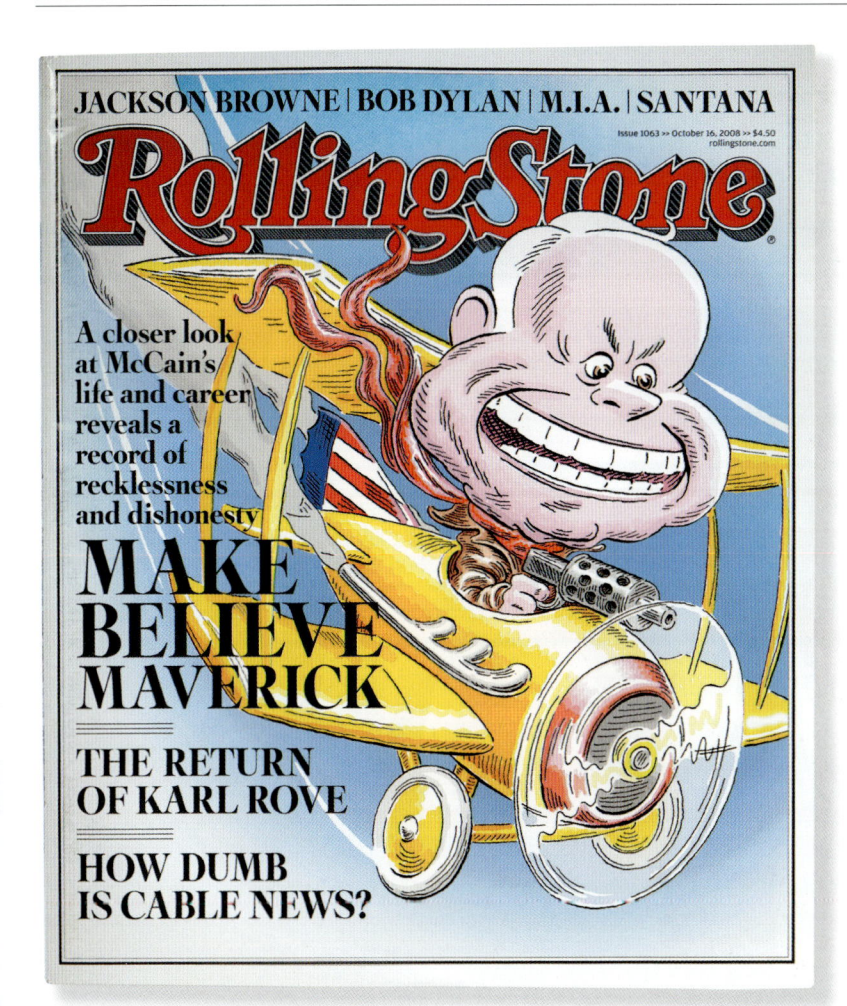

RS 1063 | JOHN MCCAIN
October 16th, 2008
ILLUSTRATION BY ROBERT GROSSMAN

"*The original* illustration I did for the McCain cover had Sarah Palin dancing on the wing of his plane. But they asked me to take that out. I think maybe I made her look too attractive."

—*Robert Grossman*

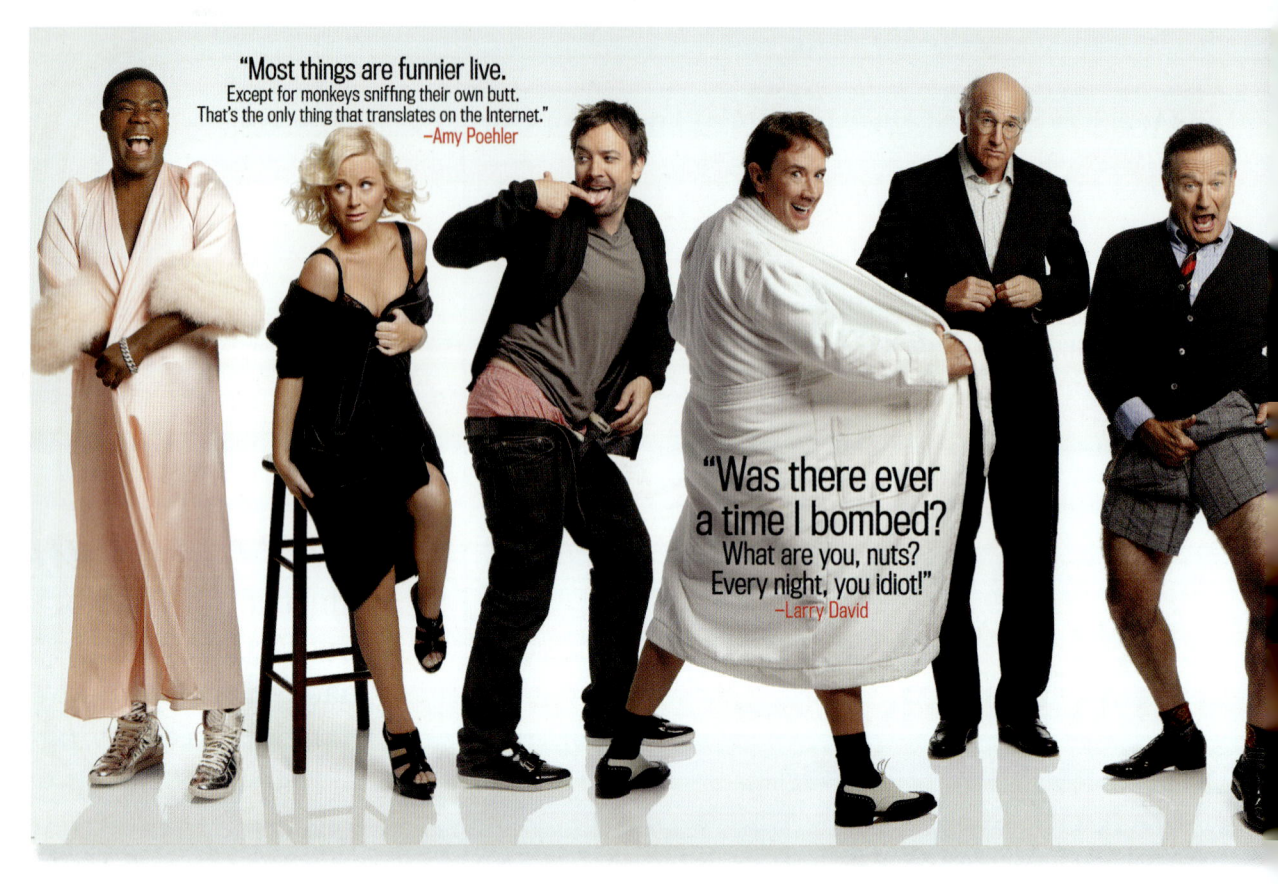

"Most things are funnier live. Except for monkeys sniffing their own butt. That's the only thing that translates on the Internet."
—Amy Poehler

"Was there ever a time I bombed? What are you, nuts? Every night, you idiot!"
—Larry David

RS 1061 | THE NEW GOLDEN AGE OF COMEDY | September 18th, 2008 | Photograph by Robert Trachtenberg

2000s

[RS 1061] Photographer Robert Trachtenberg had a unique challenge in getting 12 of the funniest people on the planet together for the gatefold cover of Rolling Stone's Comedy Issue. "The entire shoot revolved around this: [David] Letterman had not posed for a magazine cover in approximately 10 years. All these great comic minds couldn't just stand there, they had to be doing something. But what would Letterman actually be willing to do? Very little, it turned out. So I came up with the concept of having everyone either helping each other dress, and/or be in various states of undress – anything so they had an 'action.' Letterman (who could not have been nicer) was shot together with [Tina] Fey and [Chris] Rock. After that, it was just a question of 'building out' and assembling the photo in post production. Robin [Williams] was shot alone and, as usual, he delivered. Tracy Morgan said he was tired of being photographed nude or seminude, but within four minutes he was down to a negligee. [Don] Rickles was having back trouble so he had to sit, and Sarah Silverman could not have been sweeter or more touching. She adored him. [Jimmy] Fallon, [Amy] Poehler (pregnant, so a big coat) and Billy Crystal were each shot alone. Martin Short made Larry David laugh like I've never seen Larry David laugh. This is one of the few frames where he kept it together. Ultimately, eight different shoots that came together as one."

594 • ROLLING STONE

Rolling Stone

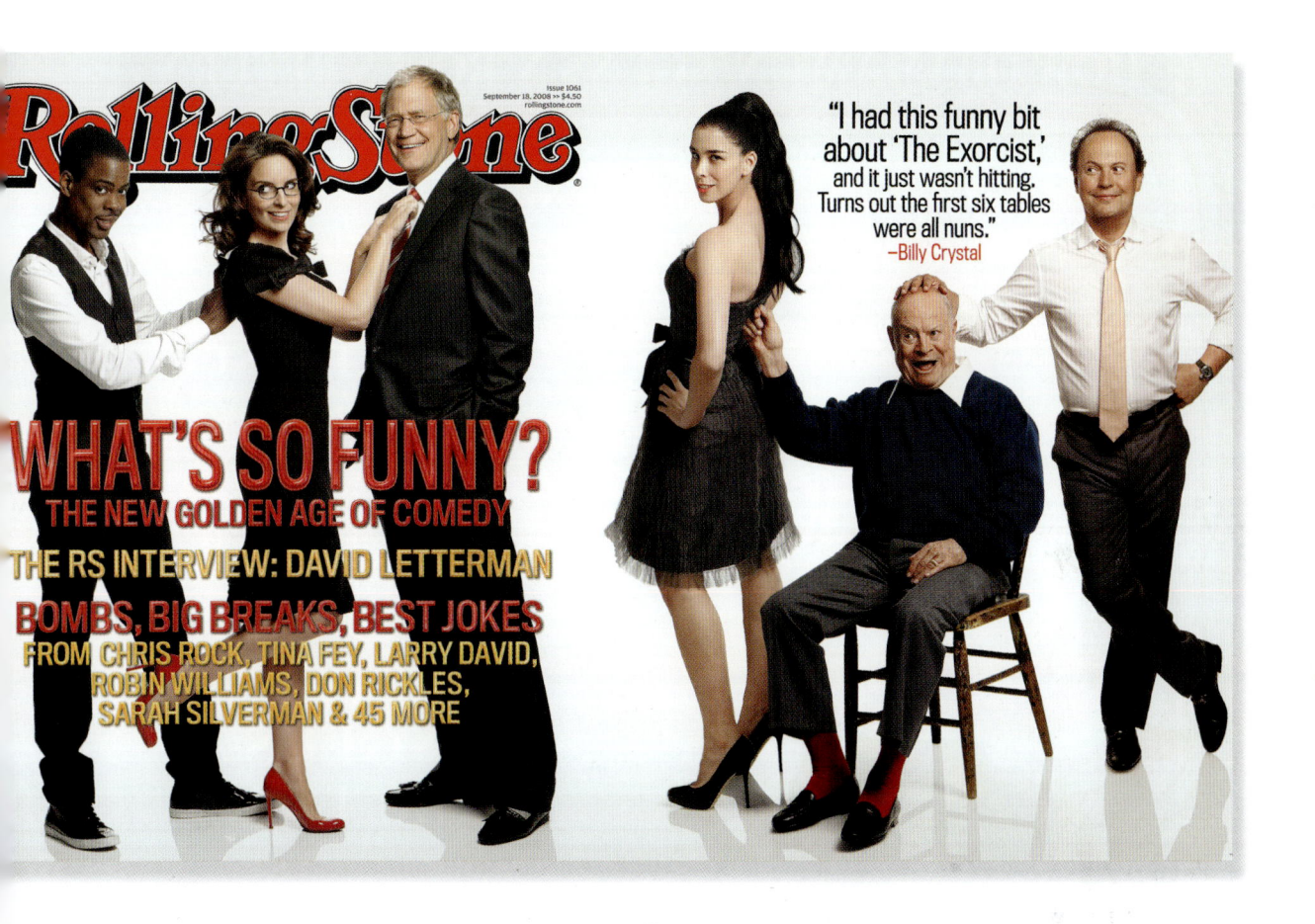

Issue 1061
September 18, 2008 • $4.50
rollingstone.com

"I had this funny bit about 'The Exorcist,' and it just wasn't hitting. Turns out the first six tables were all nuns."
—Billy Crystal

WHAT'S SO FUNNY?
THE NEW GOLDEN AGE OF COMEDY

THE RS INTERVIEW: DAVID LETTERMAN

BOMBS, BIG BREAKS, BEST JOKES
FROM CHRIS ROCK, TINA FEY, LARRY DAVID, ROBIN WILLIAMS, DON RICKLES, SARAH SILVERMAN & 45 MORE

50 YEARS OF COVERS • 595

HOW OBAMA WON ★ GUNS N' ROSES RETURN

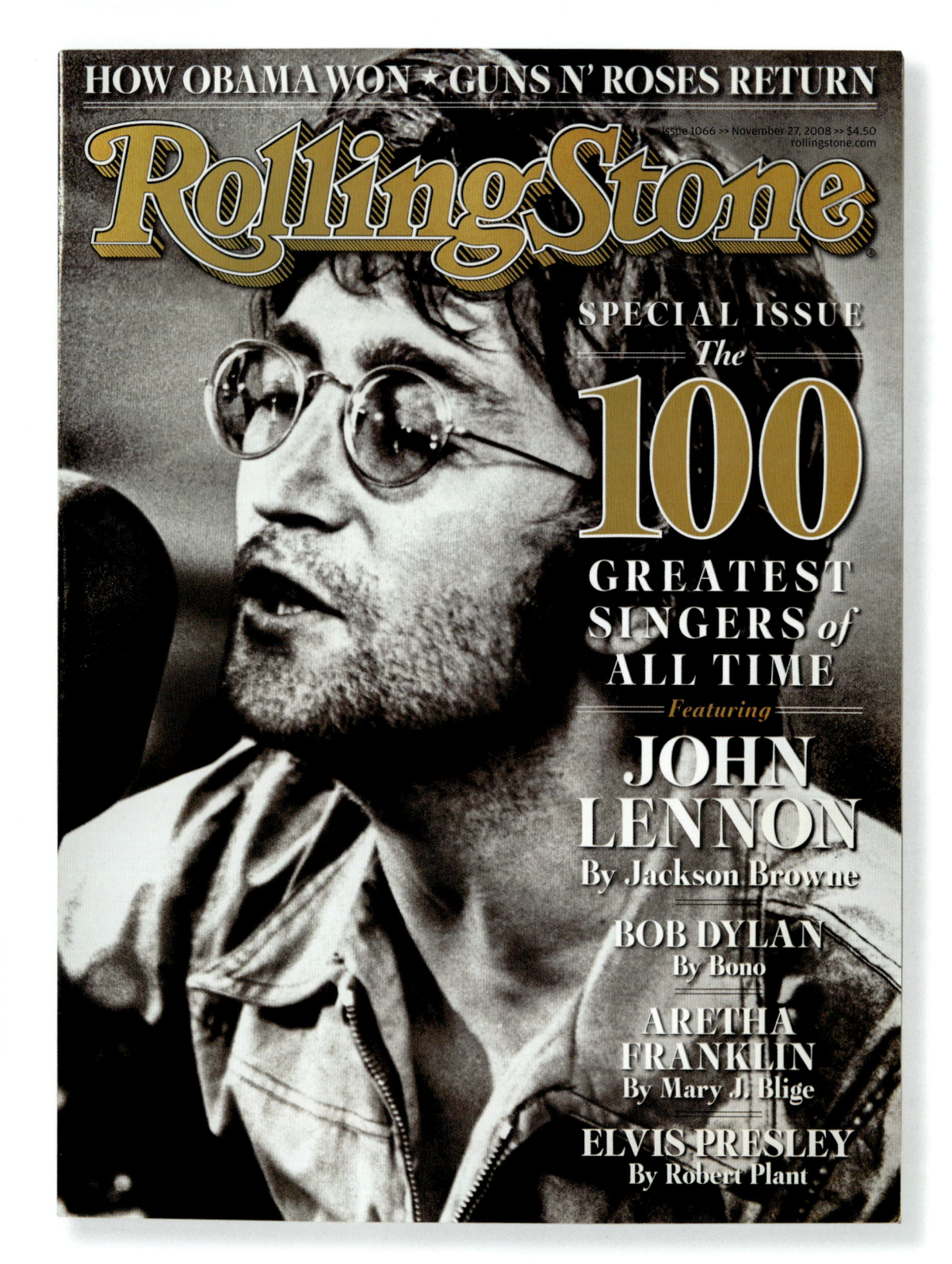

Rolling Stone

Issue 1066 >> November 27, 2008 >> $4.50
rollingstone.com

SPECIAL ISSUE
The
100
GREATEST SINGERS of ALL TIME

— *Featuring* —

JOHN LENNON
By Jackson Browne

BOB DYLAN
By Bono

ARETHA FRANKLIN
By Mary J. Blige

ELVIS PRESLEY
By Robert Plant

2000s

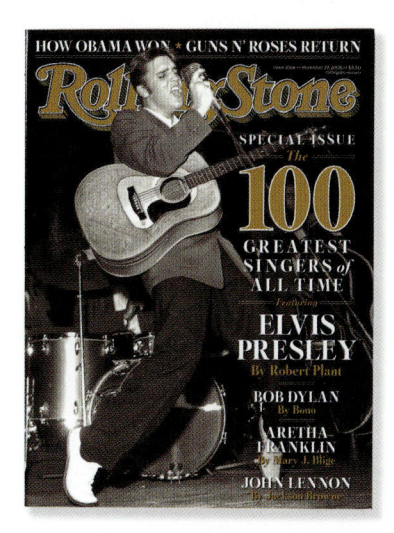

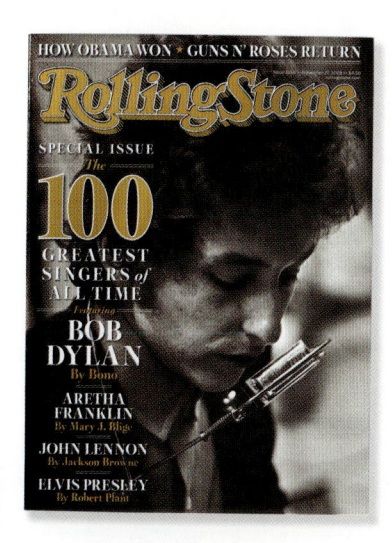

RS 1066 | 100 GREATEST SINGERS OF ALL TIME
November 27th, 2008
VARIOUS PHOTOGRAPHERS

We polled a wide range of rock and pop music luminaries for our ranking of the 100 Greatest Singers of All Time and divided the cover among four iconic voices: Bob Dylan, John Lennon, Elvis Presley and Aretha Franklin.

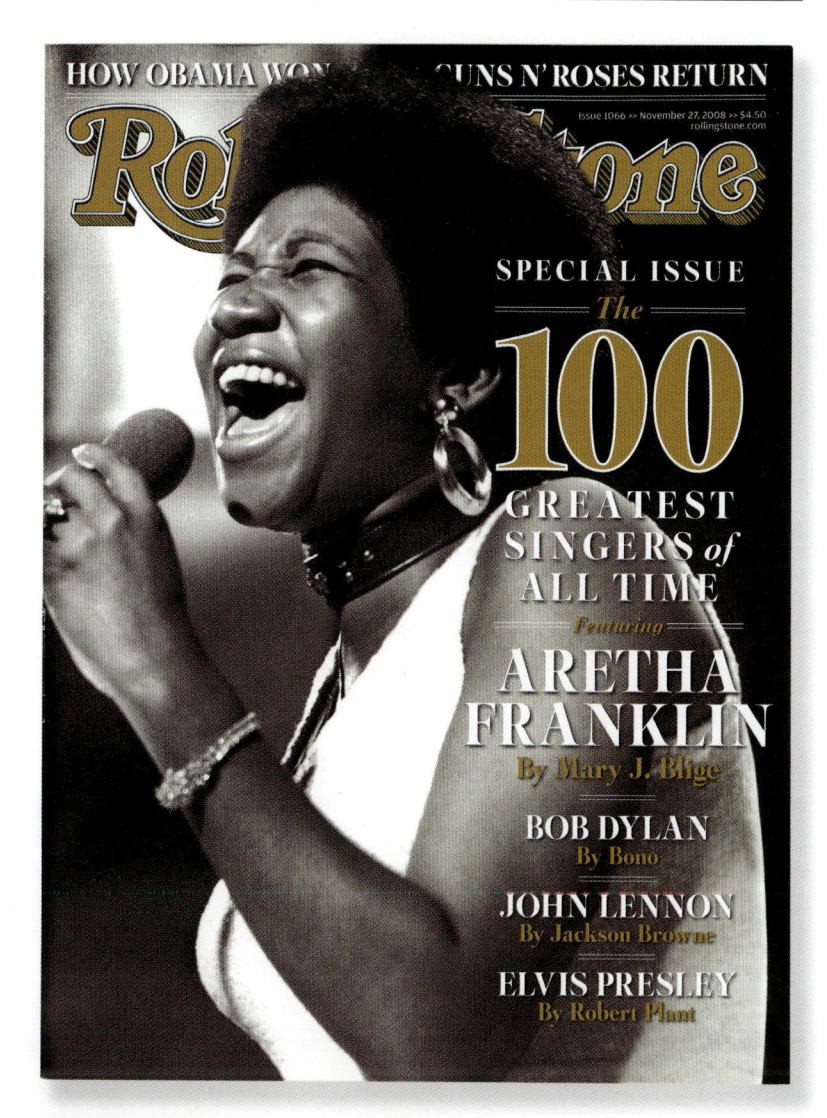

"*You know a force* from heaven. You know something that God made. And Aretha is a gift from God. When it comes to expressing yourself through song, there is no one who can touch her. She is the reason why women want to sing."

—*Mary J. Blige*

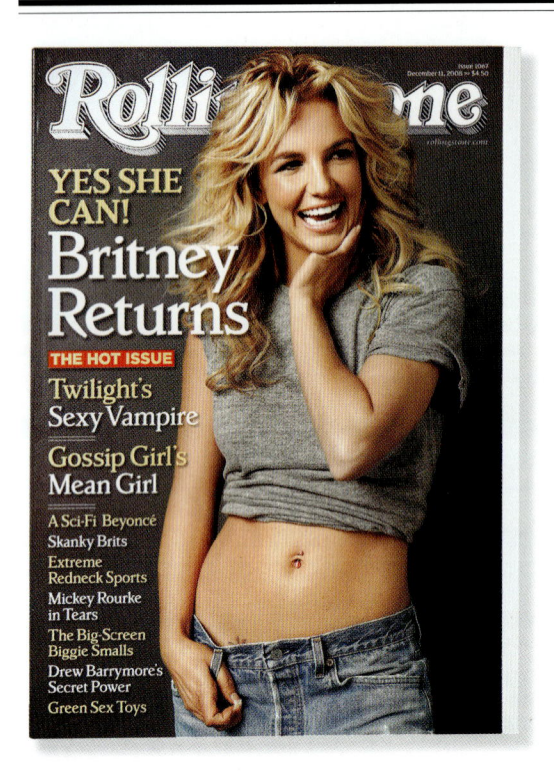

RS 1067 | BRITNEY SPEARS
December 11th, 2008
Photograph by Peggy Sirota

RS 1068/1069 | BRAD PITT
December 25th, 2008–January 8th, 2009
Photograph by Nadav Kander

RS 1070 | GEORGE W. BUSH
January 22nd, 2009
Illustration by Tim O'Brien, Based on a photograph by Shawn Thew

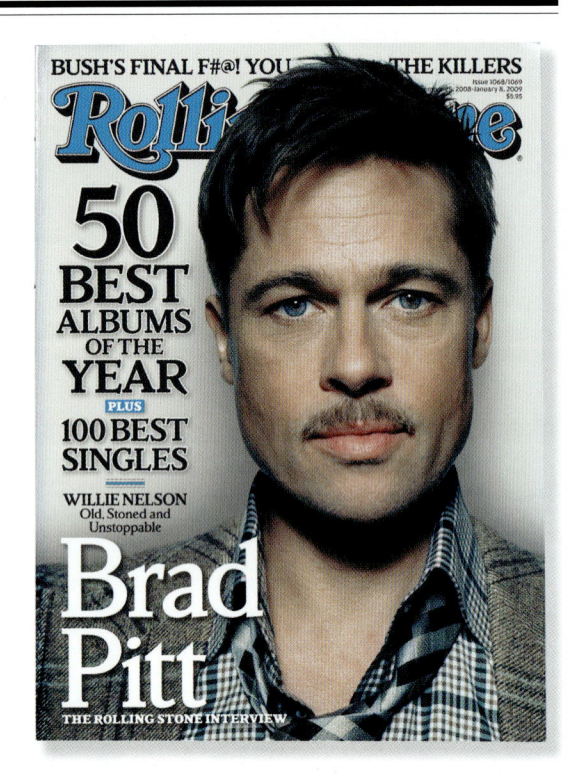

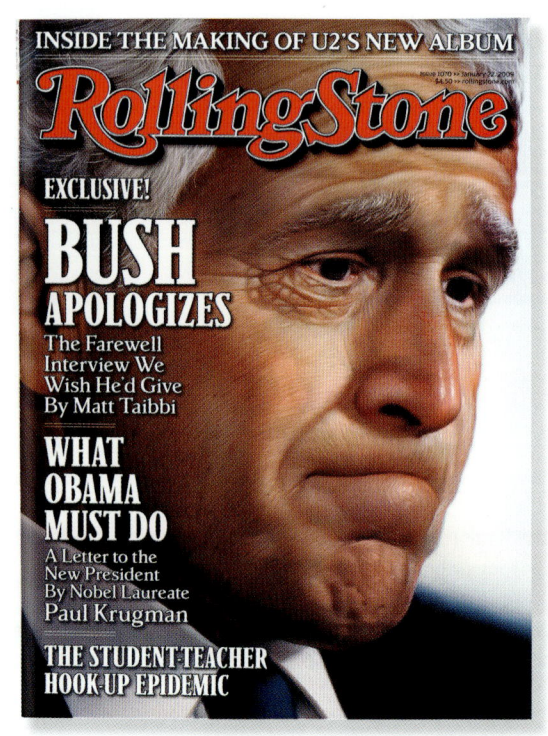

2000s

598 • ROLLING STONE

FRANZ FERDINAND | ANDY SAMBERG | ARTIE LANGE

RollingStone

Issue 1071
February 5, 2009
$4.50

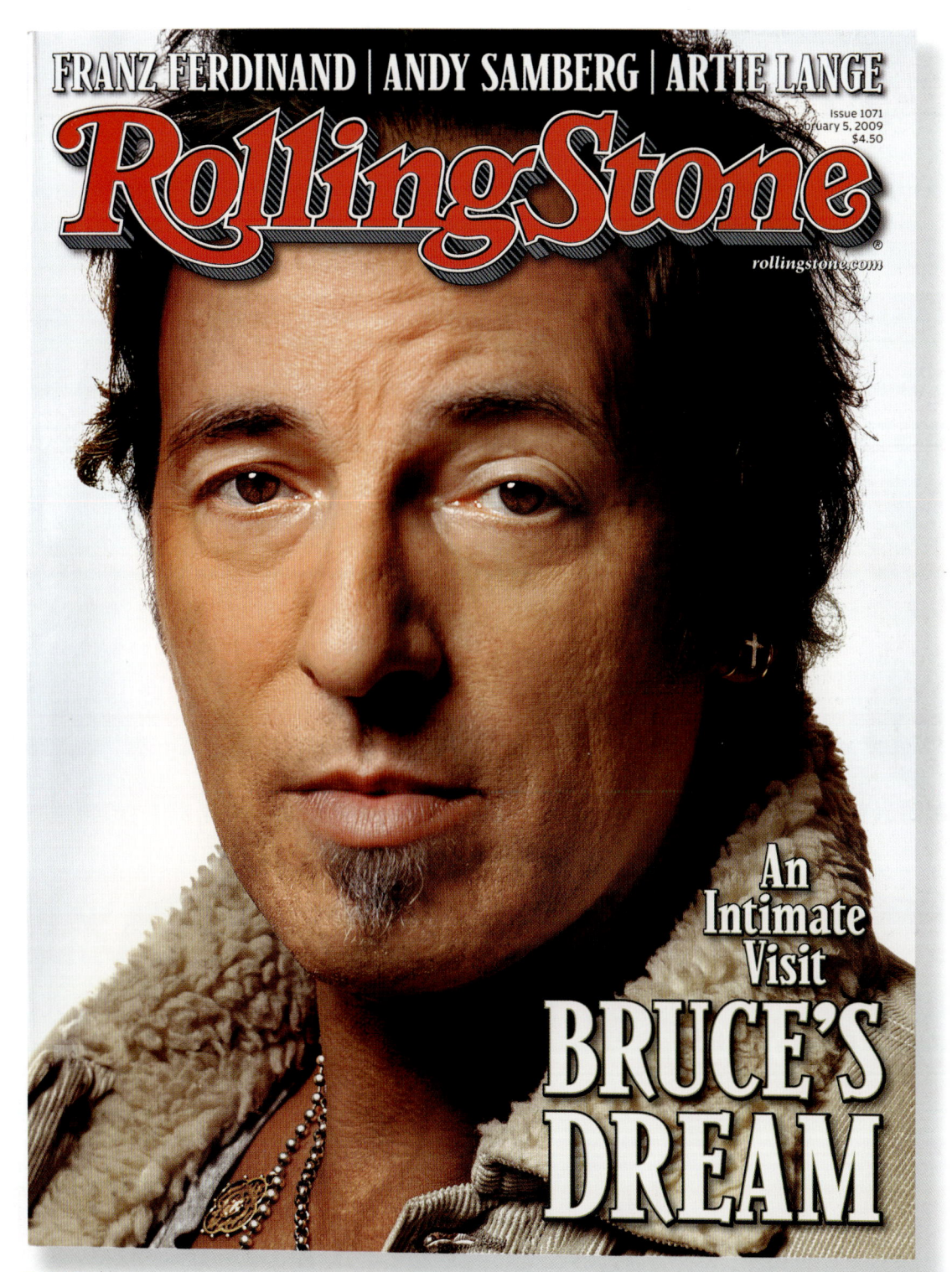

rollingstone.com

An Intimate Visit

BRUCE'S DREAM

RS 1071 | BRUCE SPRINGSTEEN | February 5th, 2009 | Photograph by Albert Watson

50 YEARS OF COVERS • 599

Issue 1073
March 5, 2009 >> $4.50
rollingstone.com

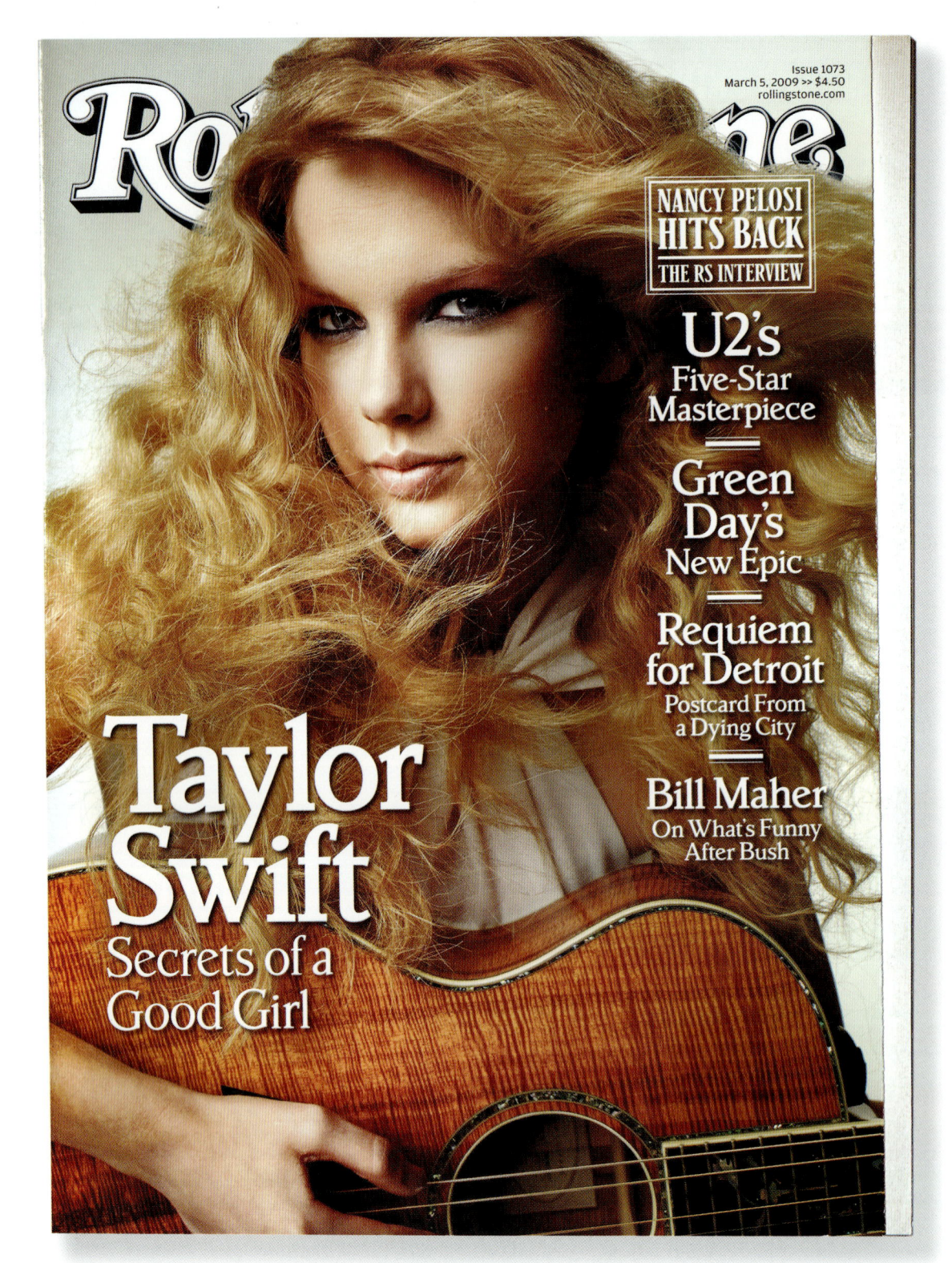

Rolling Stone

NANCY PELOSI HITS BACK
THE RS INTERVIEW

U2's Five-Star Masterpiece

Green Day's New Epic

Requiem for Detroit
Postcard From a Dying City

Bill Maher On What's Funny After Bush

Taylor Swift
Secrets of a Good Girl

RS 1073 | TAYLOR SWIFT | March 5th, 2009 | Photograph by Peggy Sirota

Swift wants to help adolescent girls everywhere feel better about themselves, and in the process heal her younger self. "In school, I loved reading *To Kill a Mockingbird*, and I'm very interested in any writing from a child's perspective," she says. At high school in Henderson, Tennessee, a suburb of Nashville – her parents agreed to move when she landed her RCA contract, at the beginning of her freshman year – Swift's interest in country music was obviously considered normal, but she still wasn't popular. She may be pretty now, and she eventually might have abused the power that comes with being a beautiful senior girl, but when she left high school, at 16, she was still a gangly sophomore. "There were queen bees and attendants, and I was maybe the friend of one of the attendants," she says. "I was the girl who didn't get invited to parties, but if I did happen to go, you know, no one would throw a bottle at my head."

In a way, Swift's emotional state seems to be stuck at the time when she left school. She says that she has only a half-dozen friends now – "and that's a lot for me" – and she talks constantly about her best friend, Abigail, a competitive swimmer and freshman at Kansas State, with a new nose ring and a new pet snake, doubtlessly having many experiences that Swift may not be ready for.

[EXCERPT FROM RS 1073 COVER STORY BY VANESSA GRIGORIADIS]

"THEY REALLY JUST CAPTURED where I was in that moment – as I've achieved more, I would set different goals. I'm totally freaking out because all these things are happening, like being on *SNL* and being on the cover of ROLLING STONE."

—*Taylor Swift*

Rolling Stone

RS 100 THE PEOPLE WHO ARE REINVENTING AMERICA

Issue 1075
April 2, 2009 >> $4.50
rollingstone.com

The NASTY THRILL of 'GOSSIP GIRL'

PHISH RETURN

THE TRUTH ABOUT THE BAILOUT
By Matt Taibbi

Blake Lively and Leighton Meester

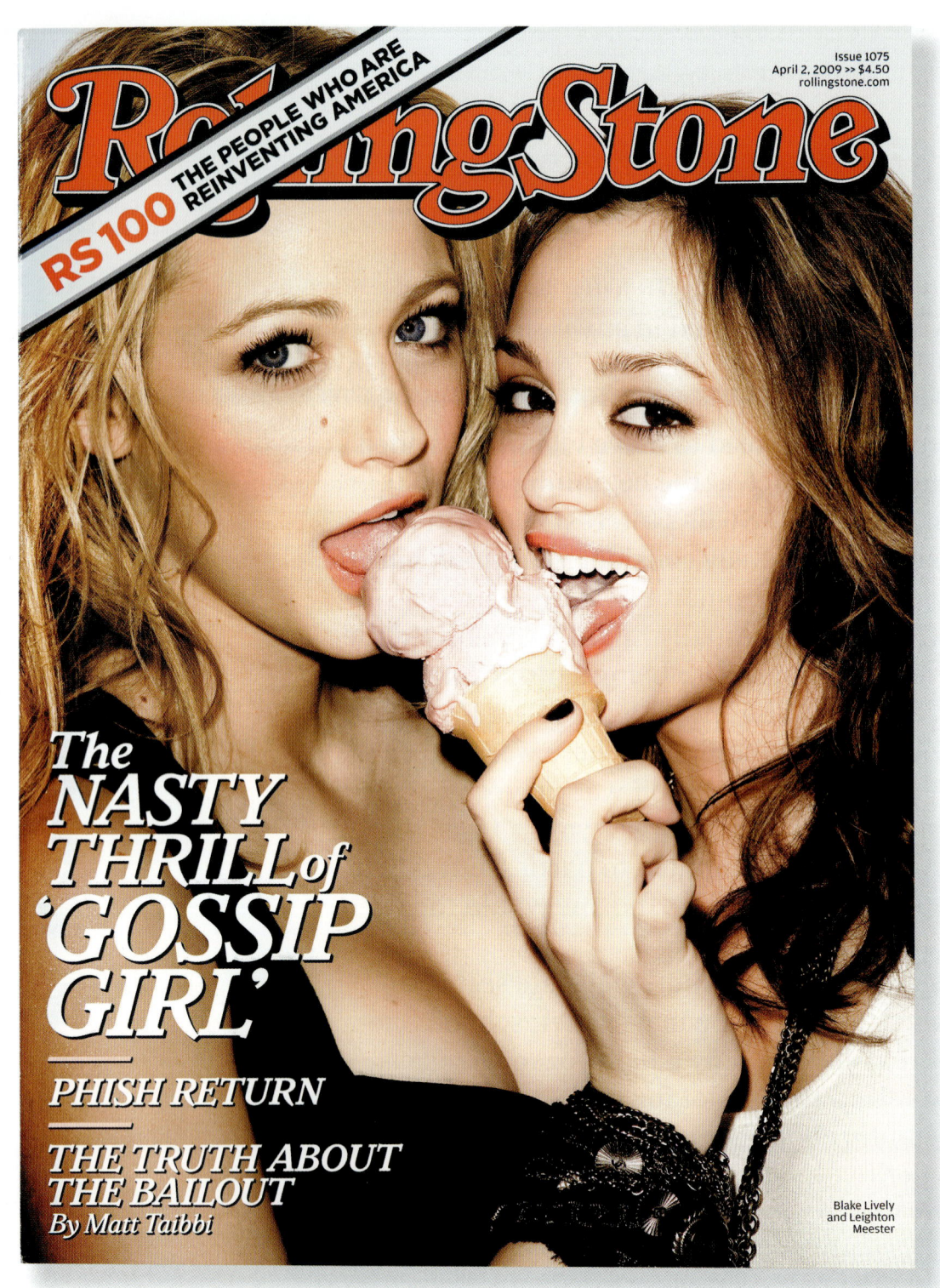

2000s

RS 1075 | BLAKE LIVELY AND LEIGHTON MEESTER | April 2nd, 2009 | Photograph by Terry Richardson

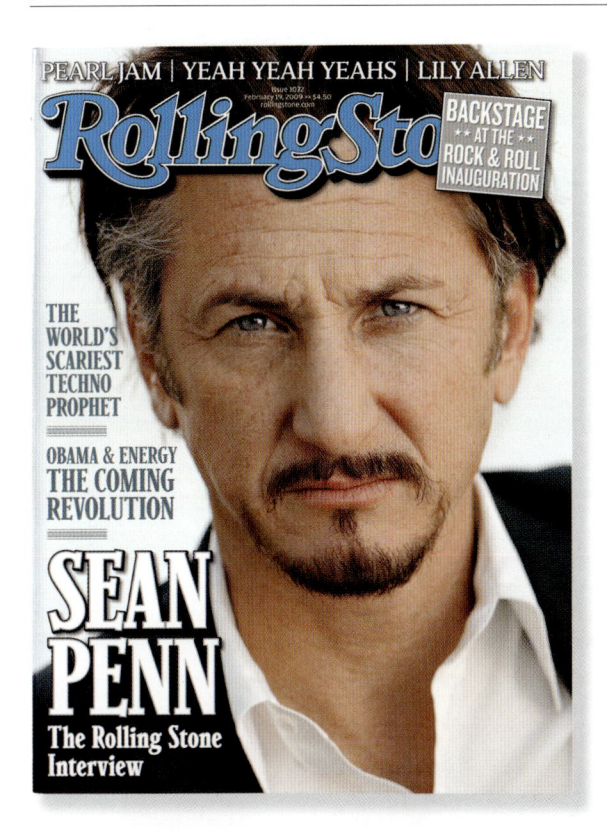

RS 1072 | SEAN PENN
February 19th, 2009
Photograph by Sam Jones

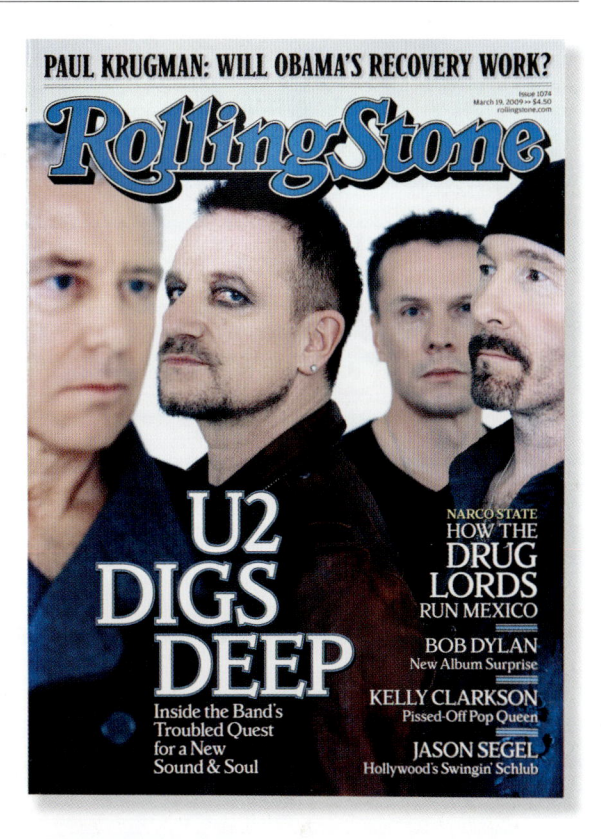

RS 1074 | U2
March 19th, 2009
Photograph by Anton Corbijn

[RS 1072] This was Penn's third appearance on the cover of ROLLING STONE. In his first, from 1983, the magazine declared him "the new James Dean." By 2009, he was a 49-year-old Oscar winner, but he hadn't mellowed much over the years. "We went to this takeout chicken place and just sat at a little table right in the parking lot, in this main street," recalls writer Mark Binelli. "I could see pretty much everybody recognized him. But not a single person approached him because of that reputation, because he looks kind of like a scary motherfucker."

Rolling Stone

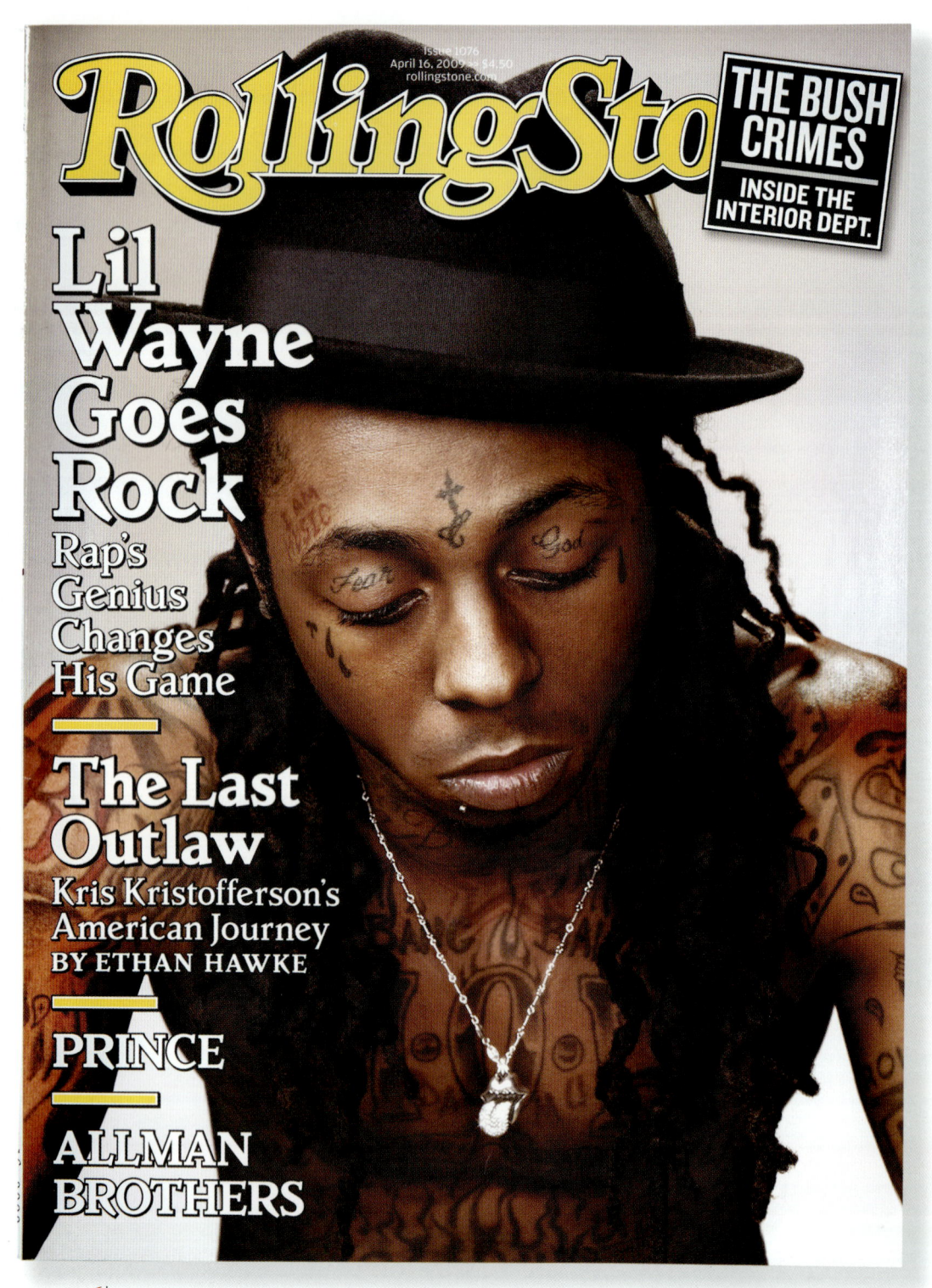

Issue 1076
April 16, 2009 • $4.50
rollingstone.com

THE BUSH CRIMES
INSIDE THE INTERIOR DEPT.

Lil Wayne Goes Rock
Rap's Genius Changes His Game

The Last Outlaw
Kris Kristofferson's American Journey
BY ETHAN HAWKE

PRINCE

ALLMAN BROTHERS

2000s

RS 1076 | LIL WAYNE | April 16th, 2009 | Photograph by Peter Yang

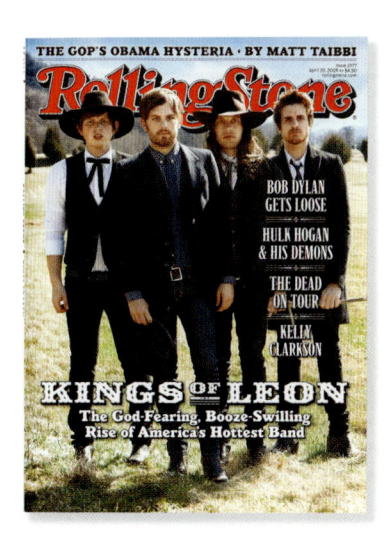

RS 1077 | KINGS OF LEON
April 30th, 2009
Photograph by Max Vadukul

"IT'S PECULIAR AND UNNERVING IN a way to see so many young people walking around with cellphones and iPods in their ears and so wrapped up in media and video games," he says. "It robs them of their self-identity. It's a shame to see them so tuned out to real life. Of course they are free to do that, as if that's got anything to do with freedom. The cost of liberty is high, and young people should understand that before they start spending their life with all those gadgets."

—*Bob Dylan*

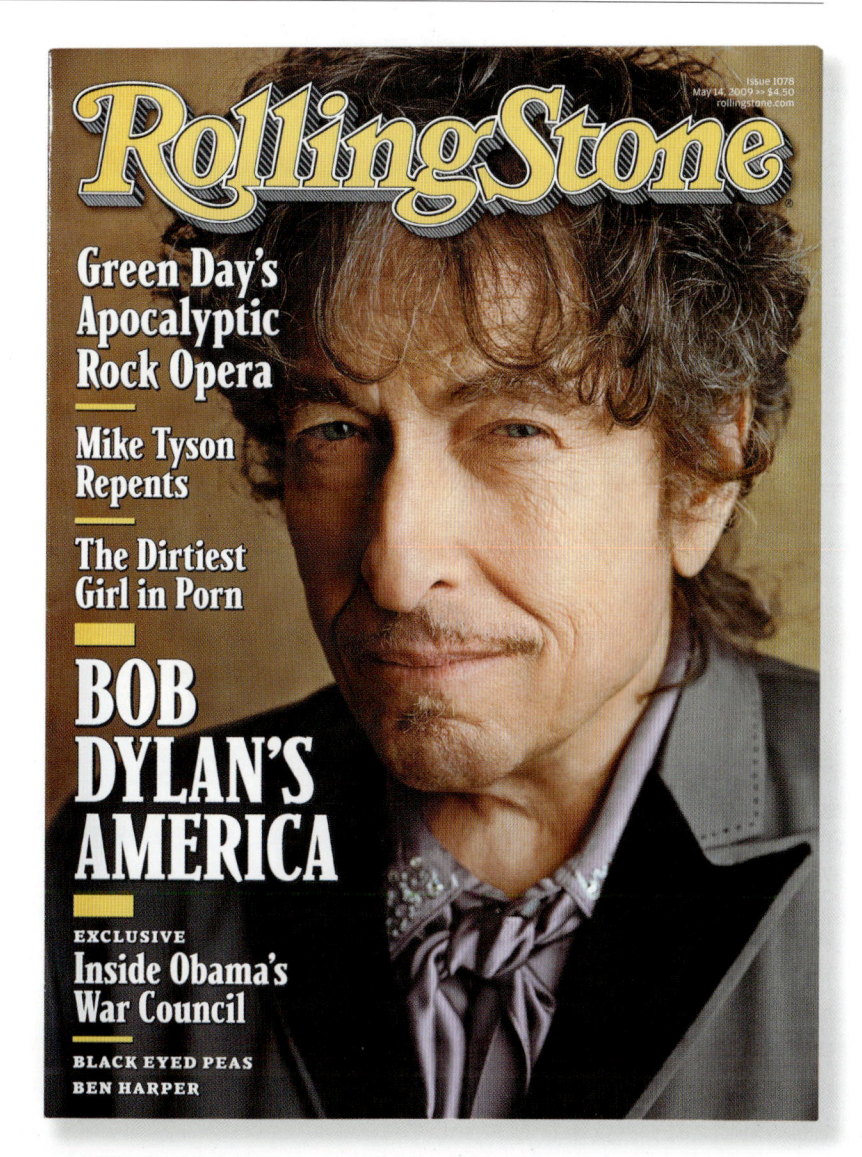

RS 1078 | BOB DYLAN
May 14th, 2009
Photograph by Sam Jones

50 YEARS OF COVERS • 605

RS 1079 | GREEN DAY
May 28th, 2009
Photograph by Sam Jones

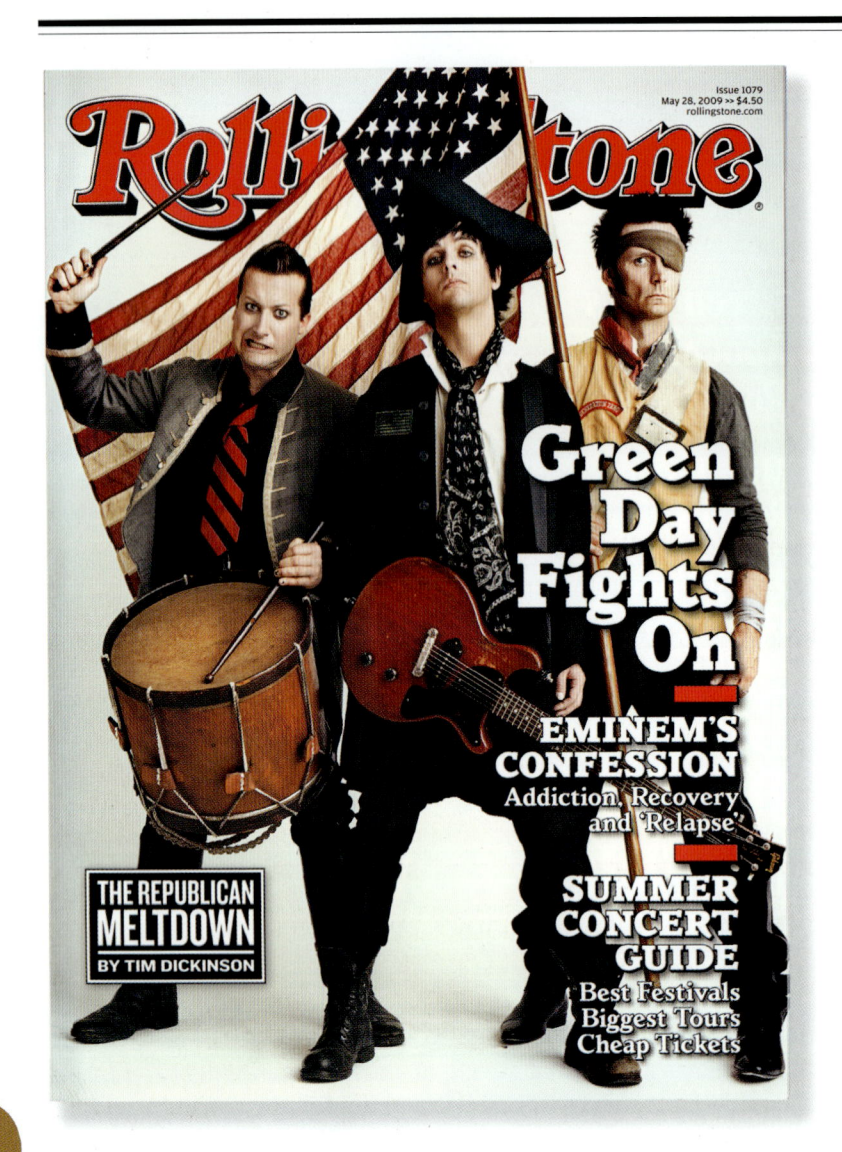

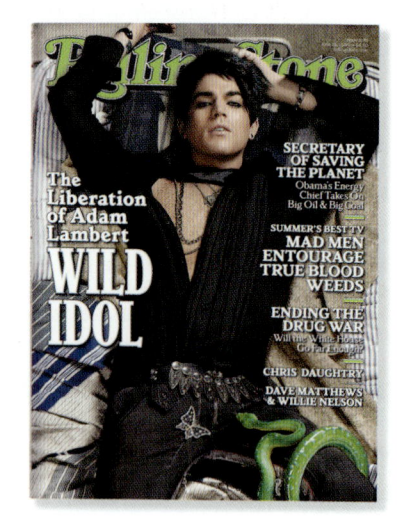

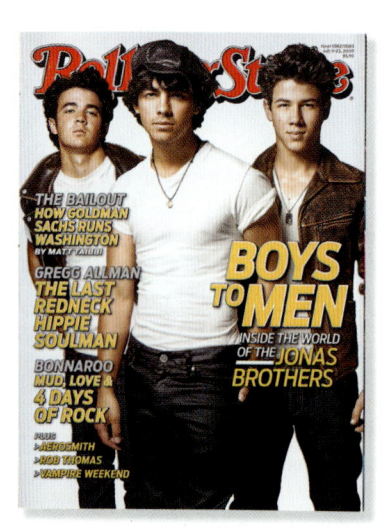

RS 1081 | ADAM LAMBERT
June 25th, 2009
Photograph by Matthew Rolston

RS 1082/1083 |
THE JONAS BROTHERS
July 9th–23rd, 2009
Photograph by Matthew Rolston

RS 1080 | LADY GAGA | June 11th, 2009 | Photograph by David LaChapelle

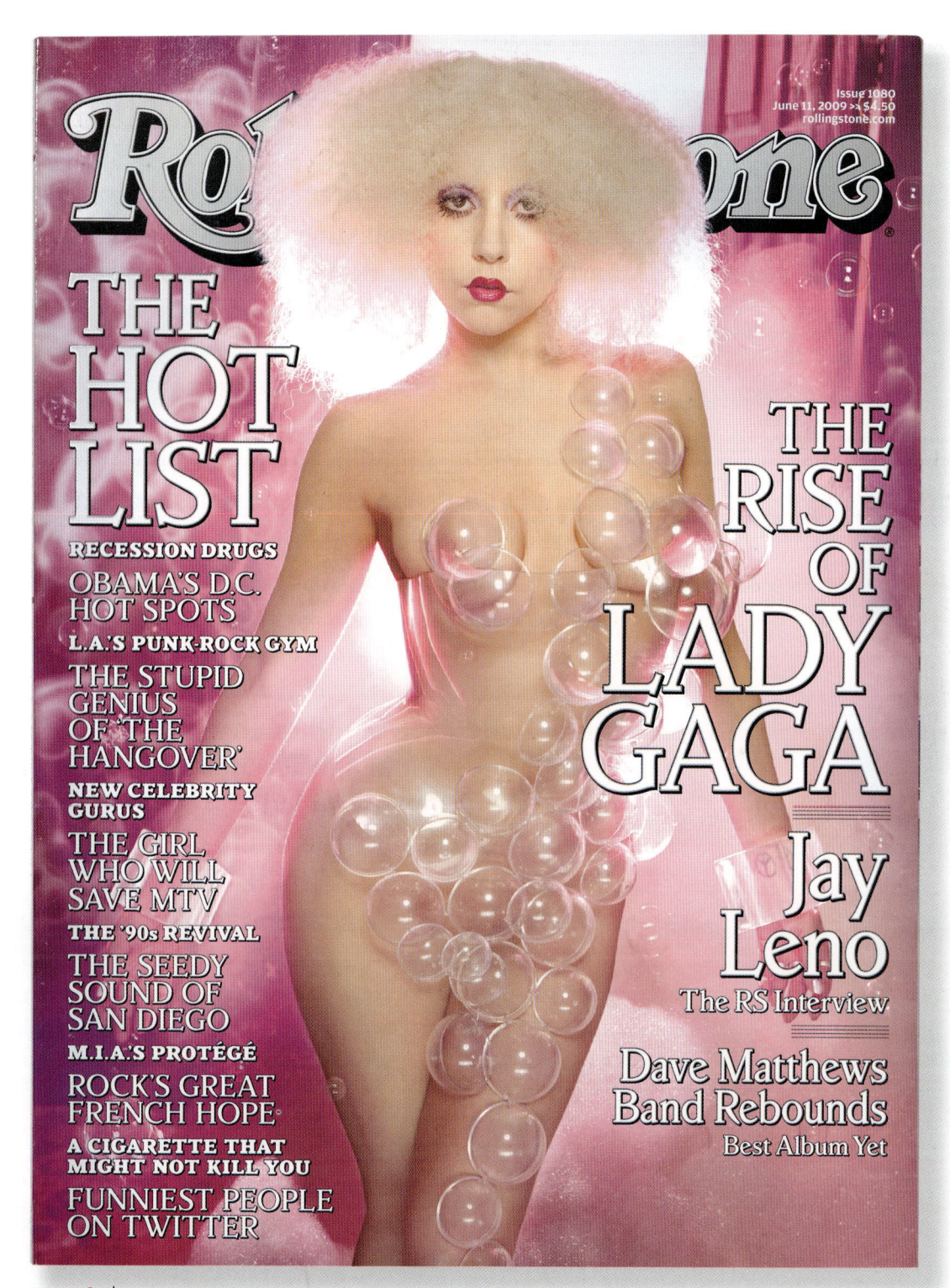

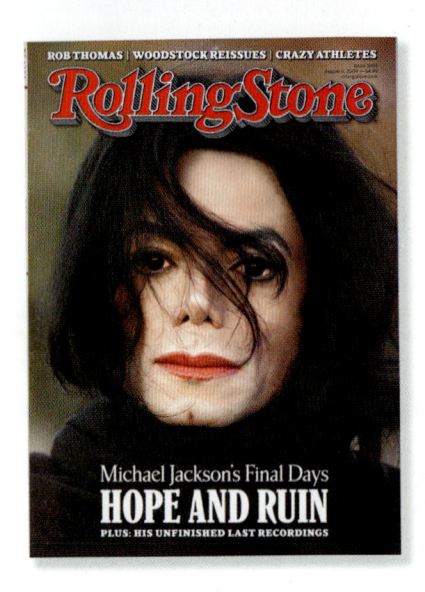

RS 1084 | MICHAEL JACKSON
August 6th, 2009
PHOTOGRAPH BY JONATHAN EXLEY,
CONTOUR BY GETTY IMAGES

Within hours of Michael's death, La Toya Jackson reportedly descended upon her brother's home, frantically searching for the bags of cash she knew he kept there, and in a matter of days, their mother raced to court to fight for control of Michael's estate and custody of his three children. The kids had followed Jackson to the hospital in a blue Escalade, and the job of telling them that their father was dead fell to Michael's manager, Frank DiLeo, who had nearly fainted when a nurse broke the news to him. This was the Michael Jackson that the world knew and mocked: the crazy family, the botched plastic surgeries, the two divorces, the charges of child molestation, the financial woes that had left him an estimated $500 million in debt.

But Michael had a different view. In his final days, he not only dreamed of a comeback, he worked as hard as he could to pull it off, maybe as hard as he ever had in his life. He wrote new songs, rehearsed hour after grueling hour to perfect the shows that would pay off his debts and mark his return to greatness, and planned every detail of his comeback tour – a massive spectacle that had already cost at least $25 million in preproduction alone. Jackson gave the tour its title, and the name said it all: This Is It. "This is real?" asked his friend Deepak Chopra. "You're coming back for real?" "For real," said Jackson, laughing.

[EXCERPT FROM RS 1084 COVER STORY BY CLAIRE HOFFMAN]

MATT TAIBBI: IS HEALTH CARE REFORM DOOMED?

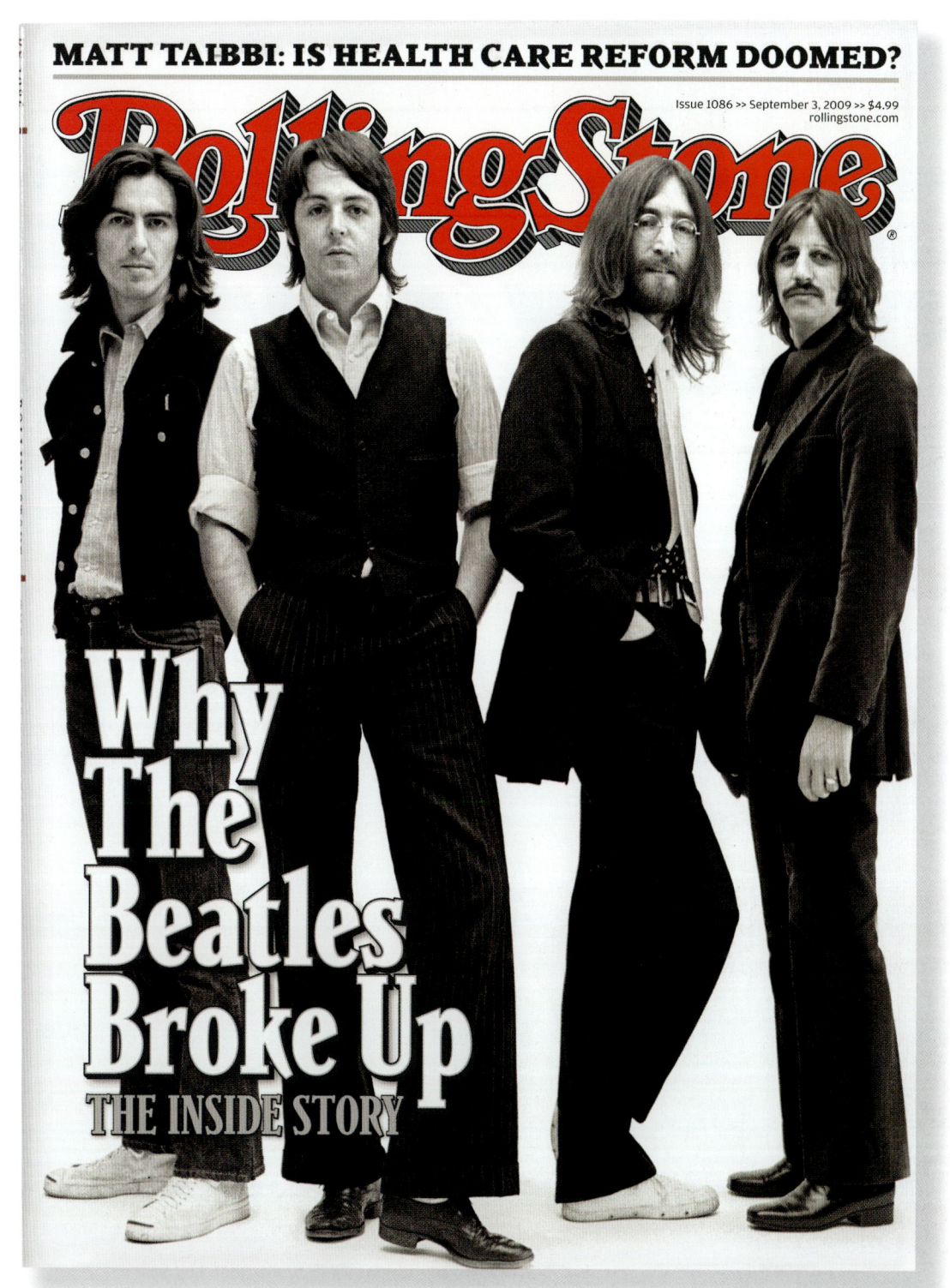

Rolling Stone

Issue 1086 >> September 3, 2009 >> $4.99
rollingstone.com

Why The Beatles Broke Up
THE INSIDE STORY

RS 1086 | THE BEATLES | September 3rd, 2009 | Photograph by Bruce McBroom/© Apple Corps Ltd. 2009

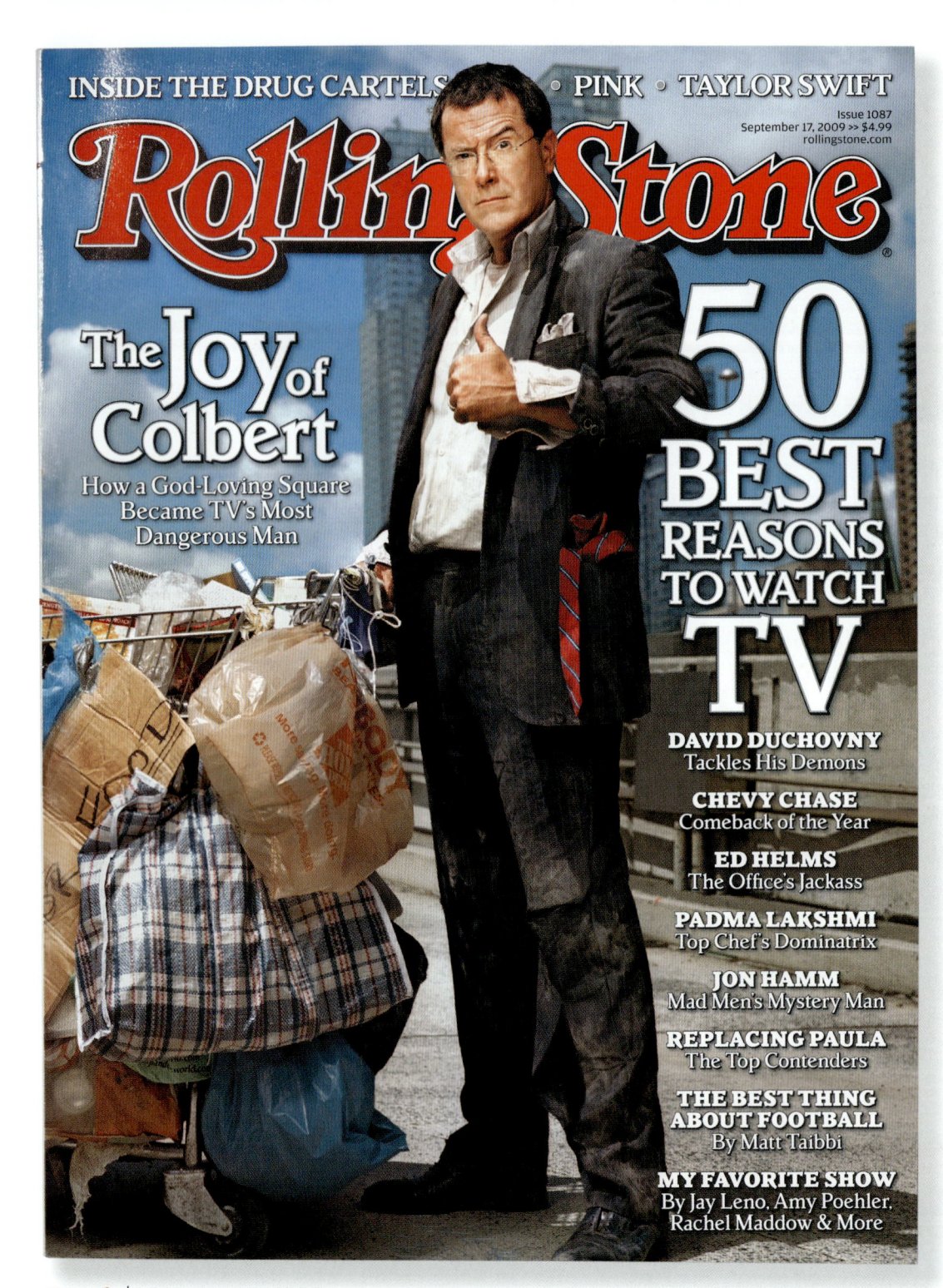

RS 1087 | STEPHEN COLBERT | September 17th, 2009 | Photograph by Martin Schoeller

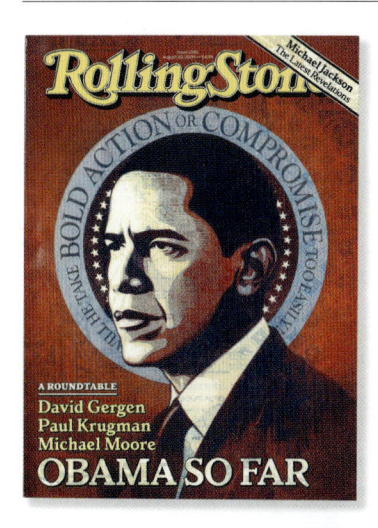

RS 1085 | BARACK OBAMA
August 20th, 2009
ILLUSTRATION BY SHEPARD FAIREY, BASED ON A
PHOTOGRAPH BY PABLO MARTINEZ MONSIVAIS

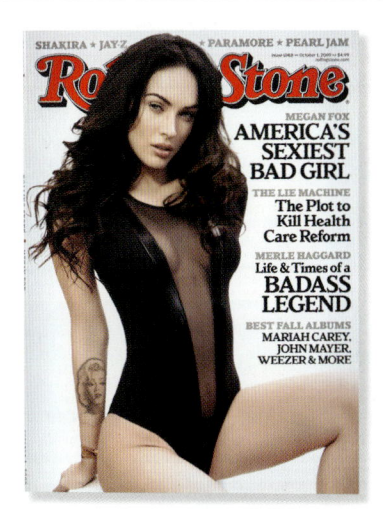

RS 1088 | MEGAN FOX
October 1st, 2009
PHOTOGRAPH BY MARK SELIGER

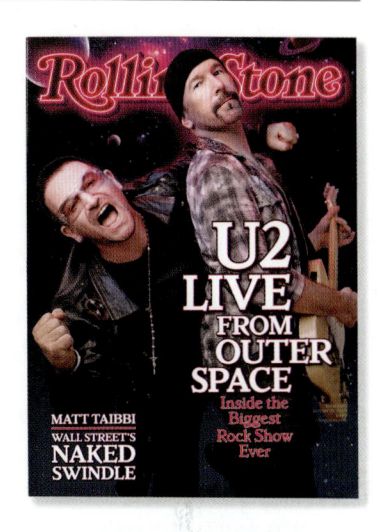

RS 1089 | U2
October 15th, 2009
PHOTOGRAPH BY SAM JONES WITH
BACKGROUND BY JOE ZEFF

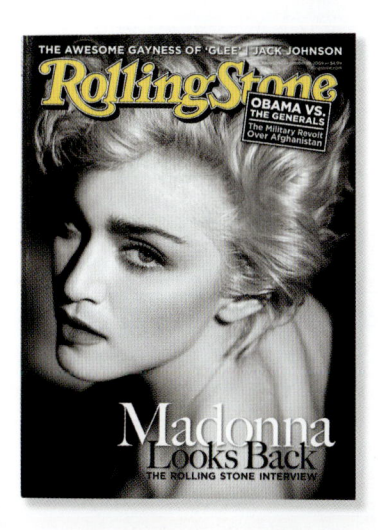

RS 1090 | MADONNA
October 29th, 2009
PHOTOGRAPH BY HERB RITTS

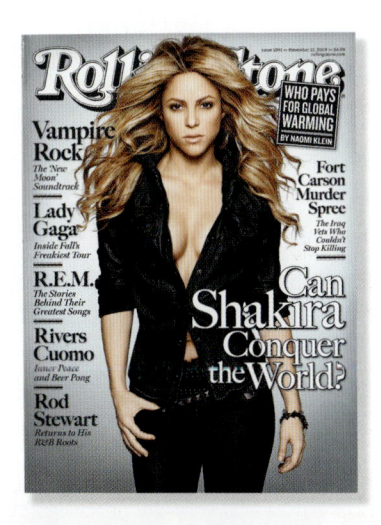

RS 1091 | SHAKIRA
November 12th, 2009
PHOTOGRAPH BY MAX VADUKUL

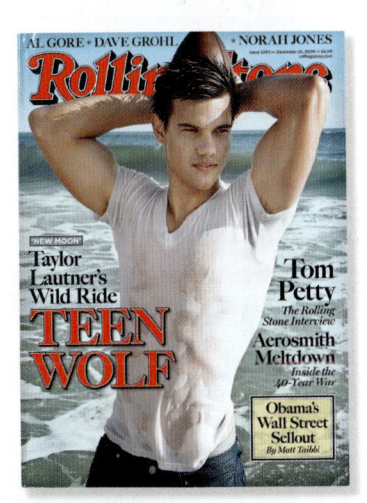

RS 1093 | TAYLOR LAUTNER
December 10th, 2009
PHOTOGRAPH BY MARK SELIGER

50 YEARS OF COVERS • 611

2000s

Rolling Stone

Issue 1092
November 26, 2009 >> $4.99

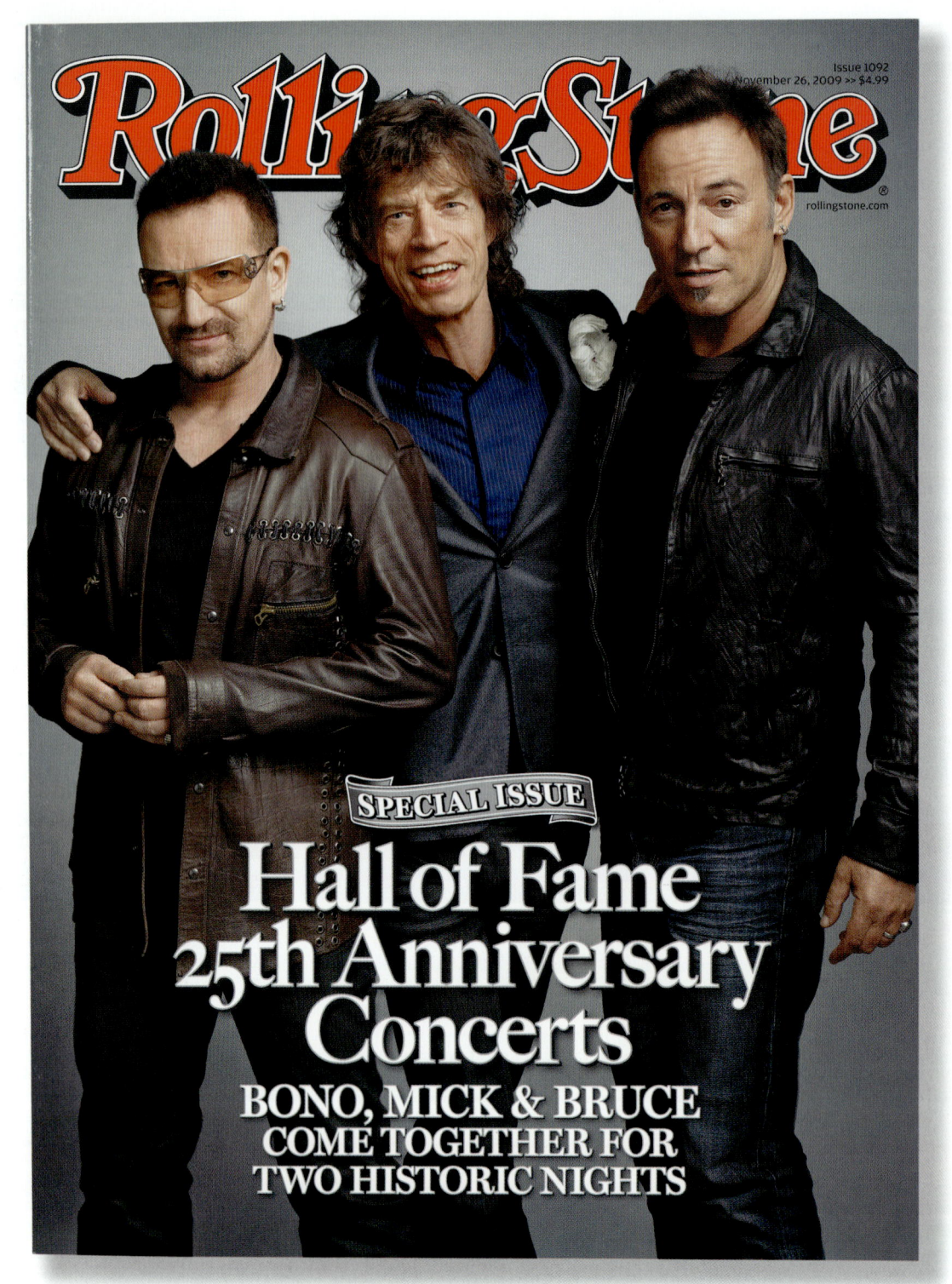

rollingstone.com

SPECIAL ISSUE

Hall of Fame 25th Anniversary Concerts

BONO, MICK & BRUCE COME TOGETHER FOR TWO HISTORIC NIGHTS

RS 1092 | BONO, MICK JAGGER AND BRUCE SPRINGSTEEN | November 26th, 2009 | Photograph by Mark Seliger

612 • ROLLING STONE

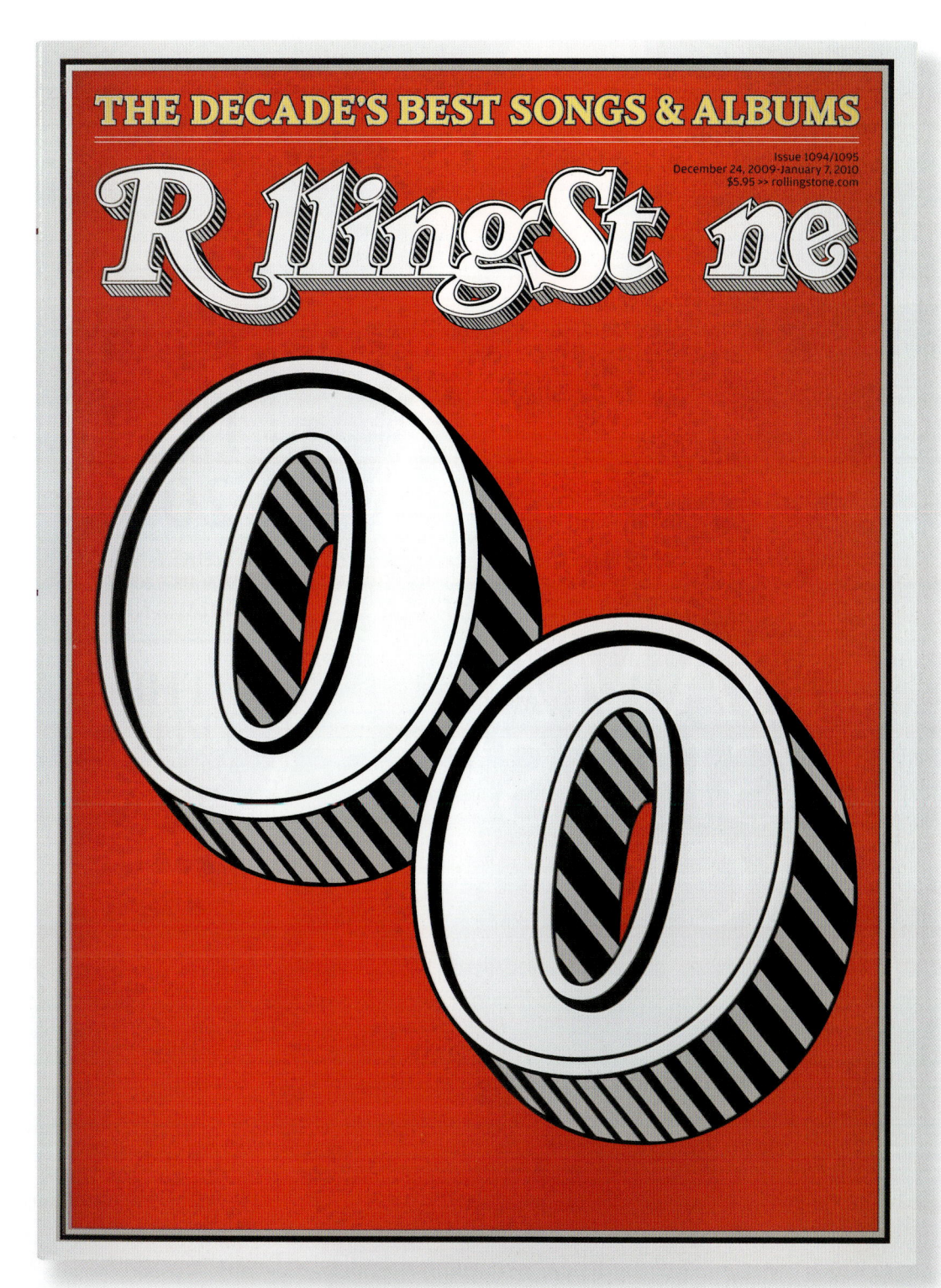

RS 1094/1095 | BEST OF THE DECADE | December 24th, 2009–January 7th, 2010
Concept by Chip Kidd, Logo Type by Jim Parkinson, Design by Joseph Hutchinson

Rolling Stone

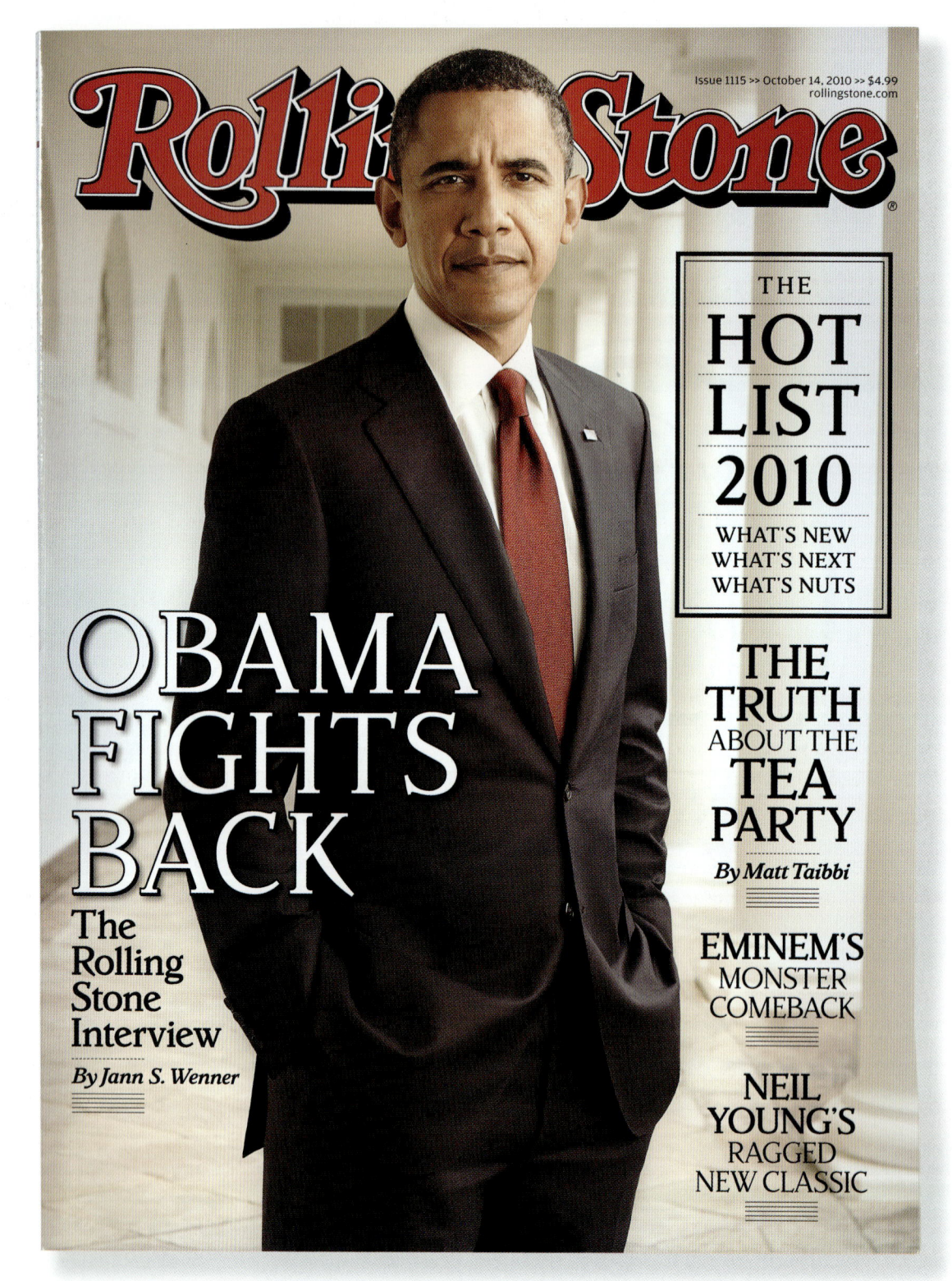

Issue 1115 >> October 14, 2010 >> $4.99
rollingstone.com

THE HOT LIST 2010
WHAT'S NEW
WHAT'S NEXT
WHAT'S NUTS

OBAMA FIGHTS BACK
The Rolling Stone Interview
By Jann S. Wenner

THE TRUTH ABOUT THE TEA PARTY
By Matt Taibbi

EMINEM'S MONSTER COMEBACK

NEIL YOUNG'S RAGGED NEW CLASSIC

2010s

614 • ROLLING STONE

RS 1096 – RS 1301

2010

The president brings the interview to a close

and leaves the Oval Office. A moment later, however, he returns to the office and says that he has one more thing to add. He speaks with intensity and passion, repeatedly stabbing the air with his finger. "One closing remark that I want to make: It is inexcusable for any Democrat or progressive right now to stand on the sidelines in this midterm election. There may be complaints about us not having gotten certain things done, not fast enough, making certain legislative compromises. But right now, we've got a choice between a Republican Party that has moved to the right of George Bush and is looking to lock in the same policies that got us into these disasters in the first place, versus an administration that, with some admitted warts, has been the most successful administration in a generation in moving progressive agendas forward. "The idea that we've got a lack of enthusiasm in the Democratic base, that people are sitting on their hands complaining, is just irresponsible.

"Everybody out there has to be thinking about what's at stake in this election and if they want to move forward over the next two years or six years or 10 years on key issues like climate change, key issues like how we restore a sense of equity and optimism to middle-class families who have seen their incomes decline by five percent over the last decade. If we want the kind of country that respects civil rights and civil liberties, we'd better fight in this election. And right now, we are getting outspent eight to one by these 527s that the Roberts court says can spend with impunity without disclosing where their money's coming from. In every single one of these congressional districts, you are seeing these independent organizations outspend political parties and the candidates by, as I said, factors of four to one, five to one, eight to one, ten to one.

"We have to get folks off the sidelines. People need to shake off this lethargy, people need to buck up. Bringing about change is hard – that's what I said during the campaign. It has been hard, and we've got some lumps to show for it. But if people now want to take their ball and go home, that tells me folks weren't serious in the first place." [EXCERPT FROM RS 1115 COVER STORY BY JANN S. WENNER]

RS 1115 | BARACK OBAMA | October 14th, 2010 | PHOTOGRAPH BY MARK SELIGER

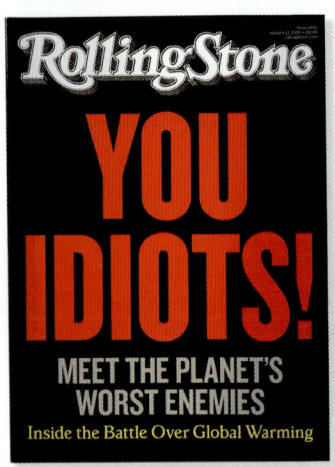

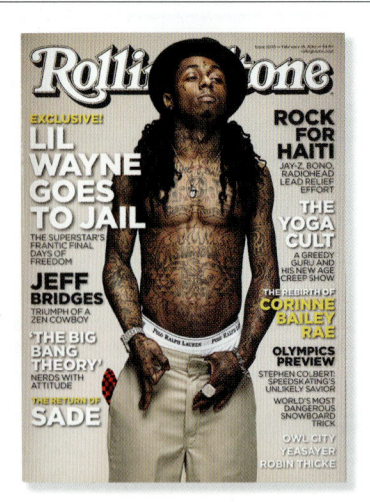

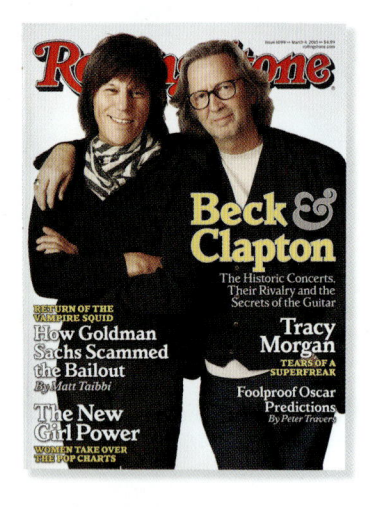

RS 1096 | YOU IDIOTS!
[GLOBAL WARMING]
January 21st, 2010
DESIGN BY JOSEPH HUTCHINSON

RS 1098 | LIL WAYNE
February 18th, 2010
PHOTOGRAPH BY PETER YANG

RS 1099 | JEFF BECK
AND ERIC CLAPTON
March 4th, 2010
PHOTOGRAPH BY SAM JONES

RS 1100 | SHAUN WHITE
March 18th, 2010
PHOTOGRAPH BY TERRY RICHARDSON

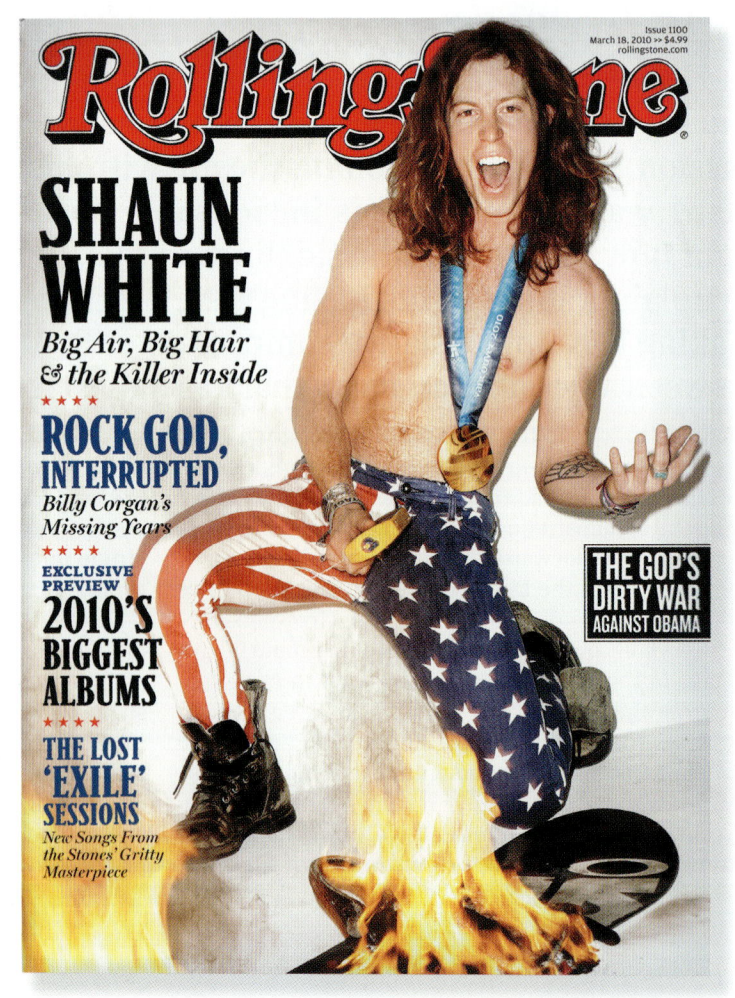

[RS 1096] RS 1096 was the rare instance in which our editors decided to go with a text-only cover. The first was the cover that featured Richard Avedon's iconic 1976 photo series "The Family" [RS 224]. In this case, the urgency of calling out the planet's worst climate villains demanded that kind of stark, eye-catching urgency. As the Editor's Note in the issue explained, "This is the biggest story of our time."

2010s

616 • ROLLING STONE

Rolling Stone

Issue 1097 >> February 4, 2010 >> $4.99
rollingstone.com

GETTING IT RIGHT
OBAMA'S TOP ECO-WARRIOR

VAMPIRE WEEKEND
SPOON
TAYLOR SWIFT
RINGO STARR

Son of Bin Laden
The Strange Journey of Osama's Heir Apparent

John Mayer
Dirty Mind, Lonely Heart

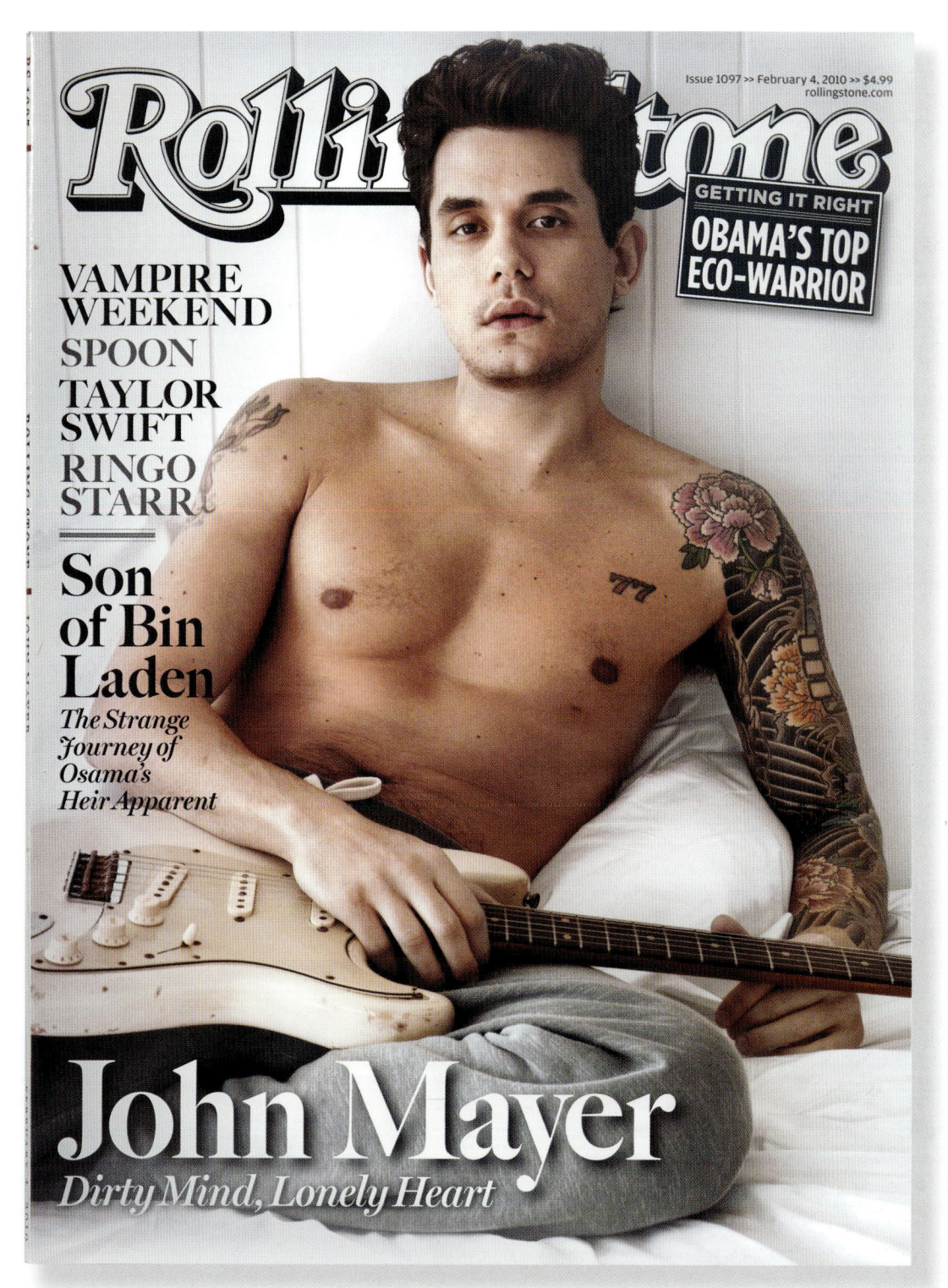

RS 1097 | JOHN MAYER | February 4th, 2010 | PHOTOGRAPH BY MARK SELIGER

50 YEARS OF COVERS • 617

MGMT • ERYKAH BADU • ALEX CHILTON • LADY GAGA

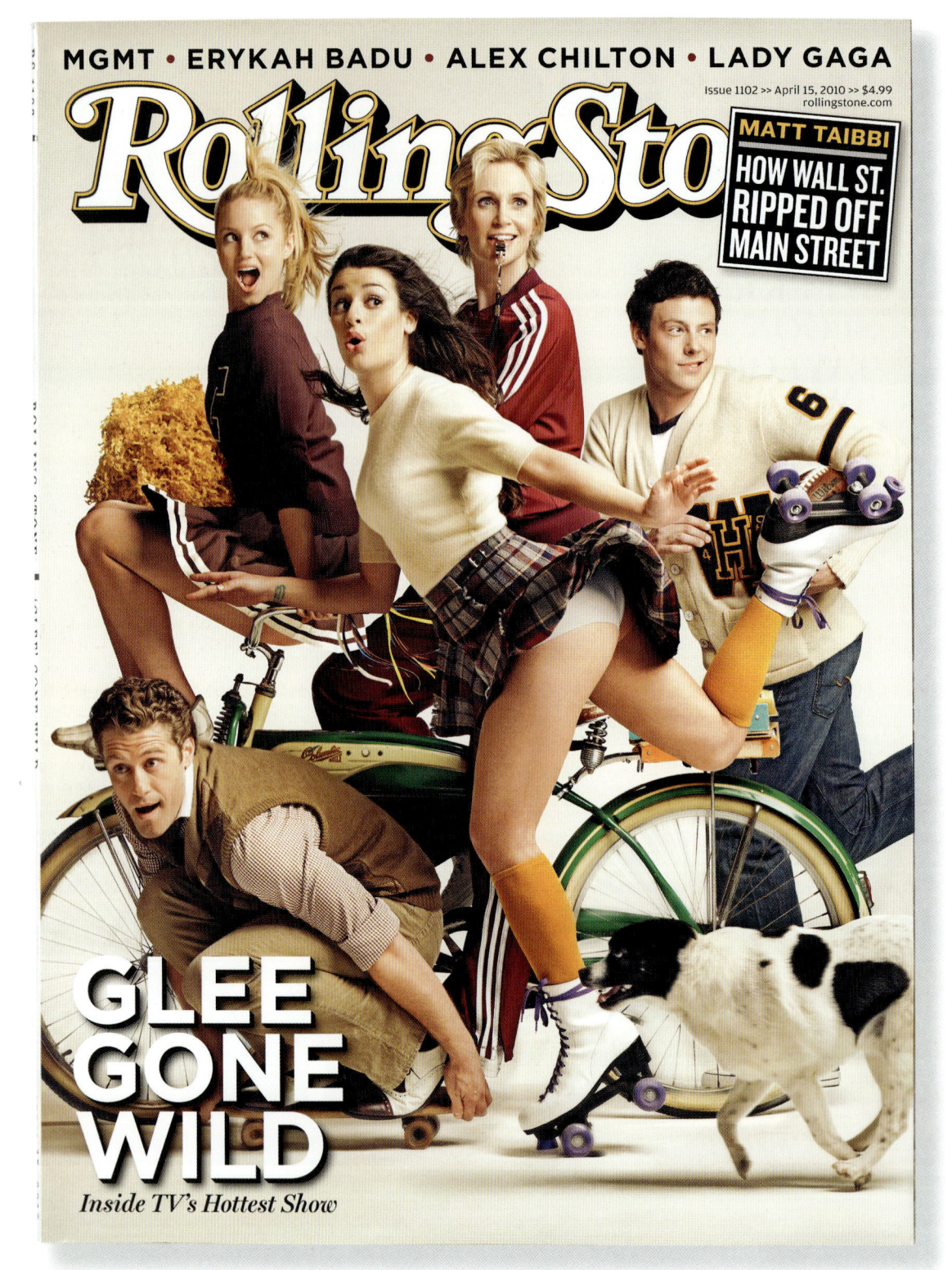

Rolling Stone

Issue 1102 >> April 15, 2010 >> $4.99
rollingstone.com

MATT TAIBBI
HOW WALL ST. RIPPED OFF MAIN STREET

GLEE GONE WILD
Inside TV's Hottest Show

2010s

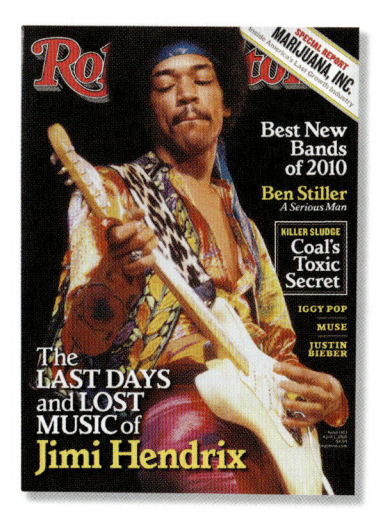

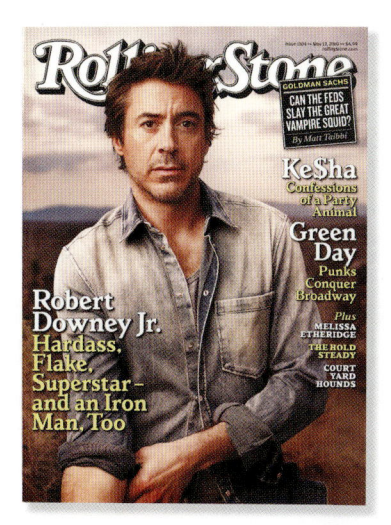

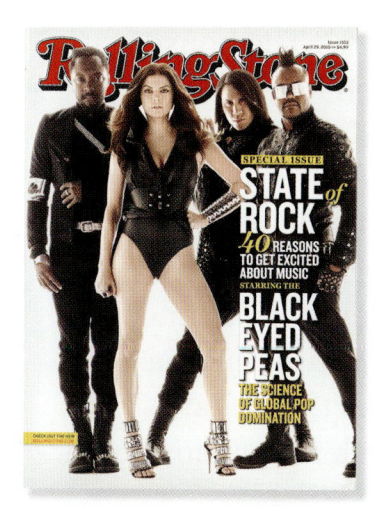

RS 1101 | JIMI HENDRIX
April 1st, 2010
Photograph by Gernot Plitz/Good Times/
Cache Agency

RS 1103 | BLACK EYED PEAS
April 29th, 2010
Photograph by Mark Seliger

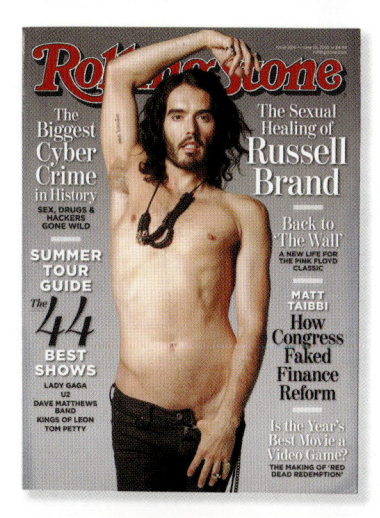

RS 1104 | ROBERT DOWNEY JR.
May 13th, 2010
Photograph by Mark Seliger

RS 1106 | RUSSELL BRAND
June 10th, 2010
Photograph by Theo Wenner

RS 1102 | CAST OF 'GLEE'
April 15th, 2010
Photograph by Mark Seliger

"I was a little strange myself in high school," says Chris Colfer, the 19-year-old gay kid who plays the gay kid Kurt. "I was in speech and debate and drama. I was president and the only member of the writers' club. At one point, I was 40 pounds overweight, with freckles, and I lost it because I thought I'd be more popular, but all I did was go from a fat loser to a skinny loser." He sighs. "My closest group of friends were the lunch ladies. I'm still very close with all of them." We go into Colfer's trailer and have a seat. He sits opposite us, a thin sapling of a boy with an agreeable semifeminine face and an impossibly high voice who when he hears himself on TV can only think, "'Do I really sound like that? What's wrong with me? I sound like a chipmunk! I don't want to be alive anymore.' Every year of adolescence, I'd ask my family doctor, 'Is my voice ever going to change?' 'Are you shaving?' 'Yes.' 'How long have you been shaving?' 'About a year.' 'Oh, you're screwed.' But all my disadvantages have become my advantages."

[EXCERPT FROM RS 1102 COVER STORY BY ERIK HEDEGAARD]

50 YEARS OF COVERS • 619

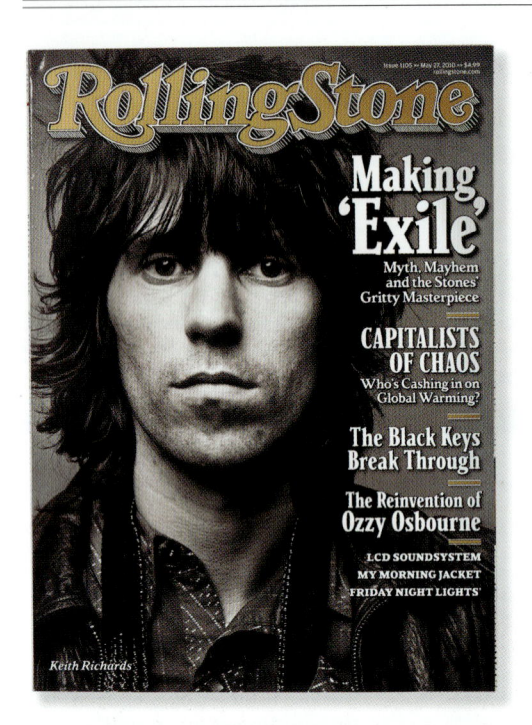

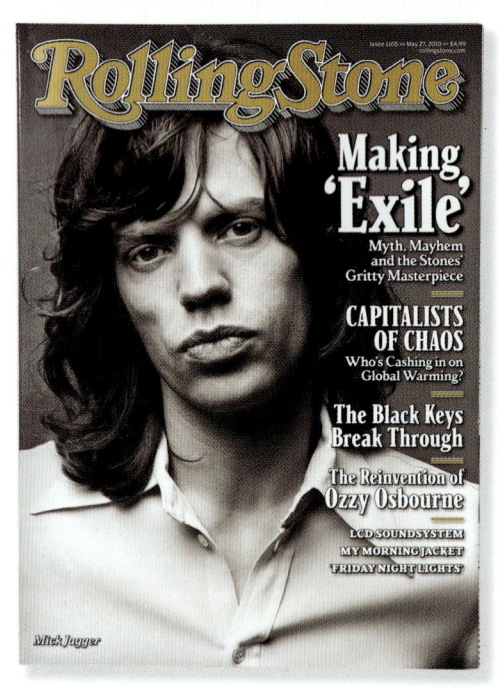

THE NELLCOTE MYTHOLOGY, THE often-told tales of decadent privilege, outlaw pleasures – one of which was Richards' heroin habit – and the house's supposedly sinister history, has inevitably colored the response to *Exile*. The room where Watts stayed, Johns recalls, "looked like a very expensive hooker's room. It had some sort of pink motif and a very large bed. In fact, I remember bonking some bird in there one night and getting discovered." The house was overrun with such louche visitors as Gram Parsons – who was so inelegantly wasted that he was asked to leave – and equally louche locals. At one point, work had to stop because somebody stole a bunch of guitars. "It's the South of France, what do you expect?" Richards says. "I mean, they stick up casinos down there, you know?

[EXCERPT FROM RS 1105 COVER STORY BY DAVID GATES]

[RS 1105] We celebrated the 40th anniversary of the Rolling Stones' 1972 landmark album, *Exile on Main Street*, with a deep dive into the making of the LP. The photos for the issue's split cover were taken that same year by Norman Seeff. "We were quite drunk and shot until the sun came up," he recalls. "I caught 12 shots and ended up turning them into tear-off postcards [inside] the album."

RS 1105 | MAKING 'EXILE'
May 27th, 2010
PHOTOGRAPHS BY NORMAN SEEFF

2010s

620 • ROLLING STONE

Rolling Stone

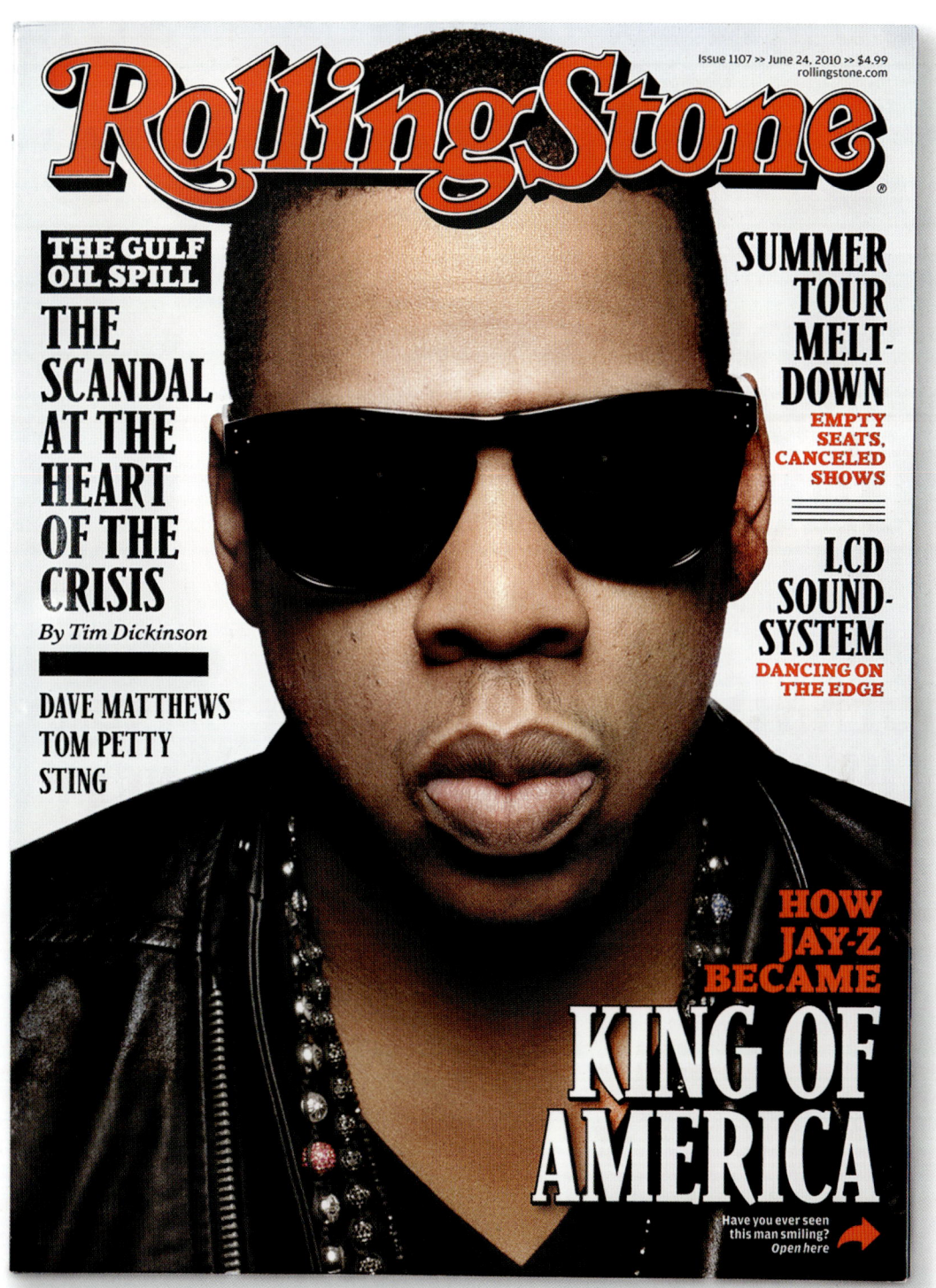

Issue 1107 >> June 24, 2010 >> $4.99
rollingstone.com

THE GULF OIL SPILL

THE SCANDAL AT THE HEART OF THE CRISIS

By Tim Dickinson

**DAVE MATTHEWS
TOM PETTY
STING**

SUMMER TOUR MELT-DOWN
EMPTY SEATS, CANCELED SHOWS

LCD SOUND-SYSTEM
DANCING ON THE EDGE

HOW JAY-Z BECAME KING OF AMERICA

Have you ever seen this man smiling? Open here ➡

RS 1107 | JAY-Z | June 24th, 2010 | Photograph by Mark Seliger

50 YEARS OF COVERS • 621

SUMMER DOUBLE ISSUE

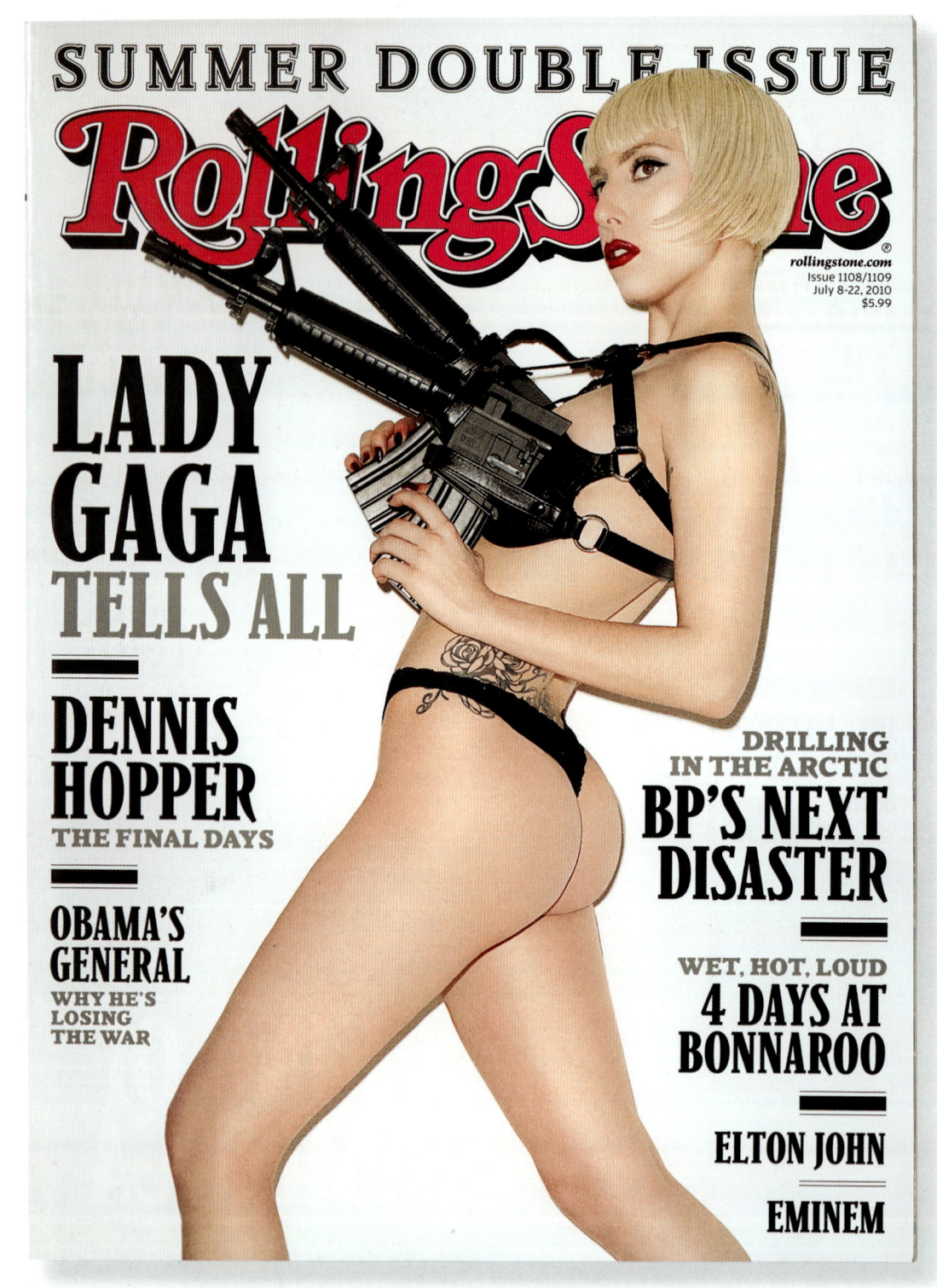

Rolling Stone

Issue 1108/1109
July 8-22, 2010
$5.99

LADY GAGA
TELLS ALL

DENNIS HOPPER
THE FINAL DAYS

OBAMA'S GENERAL
WHY HE'S LOSING THE WAR

DRILLING IN THE ARCTIC
BP'S NEXT DISASTER

WET, HOT, LOUD
4 DAYS AT BONNAROO

ELTON JOHN

EMINEM

RS 1108/1109 | LADY GAGA | July 8th–22nd, 2010 | Photograph by Terry Richardson

M.I.A. ★ SHERYL CROW ★ ARCADE FIRE ★ ROBERT PLANT

Issue 1110 >> August 5, 2010 >> $4.99
rollingstone.com

RollingStone

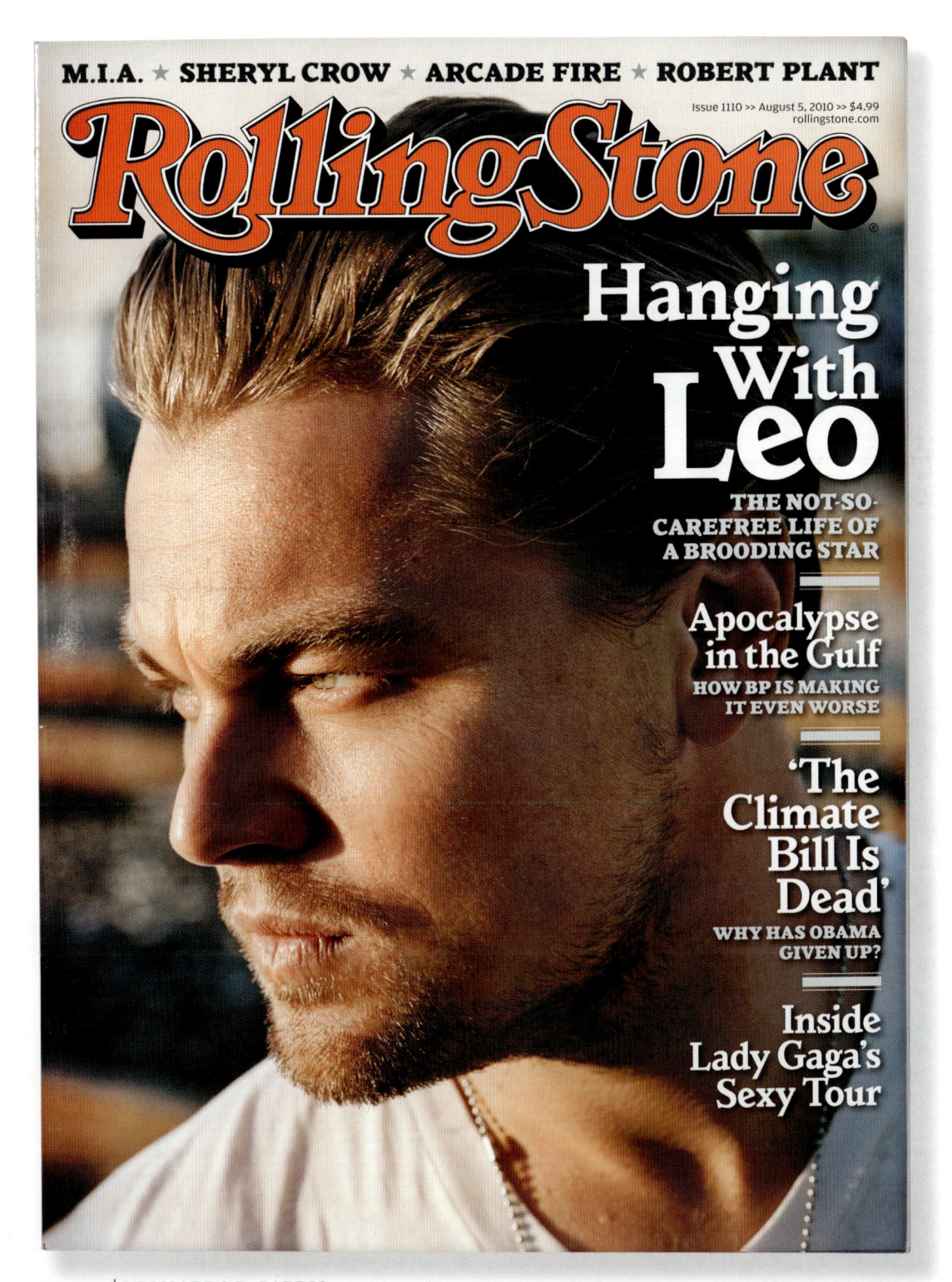

Hanging With Leo
THE NOT-SO-CAREFREE LIFE OF A BROODING STAR

Apocalypse in the Gulf
HOW BP IS MAKING IT EVEN WORSE

'The Climate Bill Is Dead'
WHY HAS OBAMA GIVEN UP?

Inside Lady Gaga's Sexy Tour

RS 1110 | LEONARDO DiCAPRIO | August 5th, 2010 | Photograph by Mark Seliger

50 YEARS OF COVERS • 623

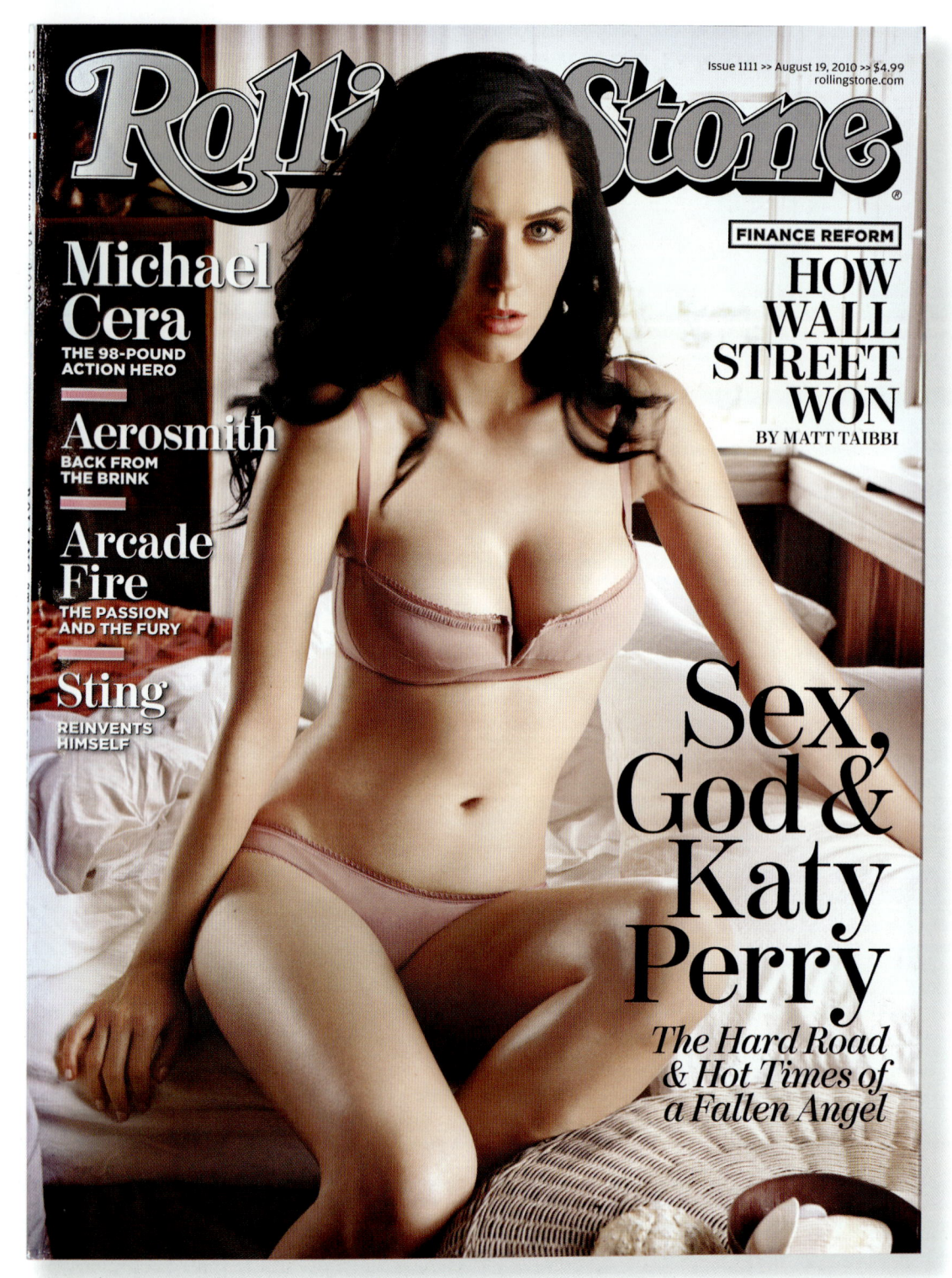

RS 1111 | KATY PERRY | August 19th, 2010 | Photograph by Mark Seliger

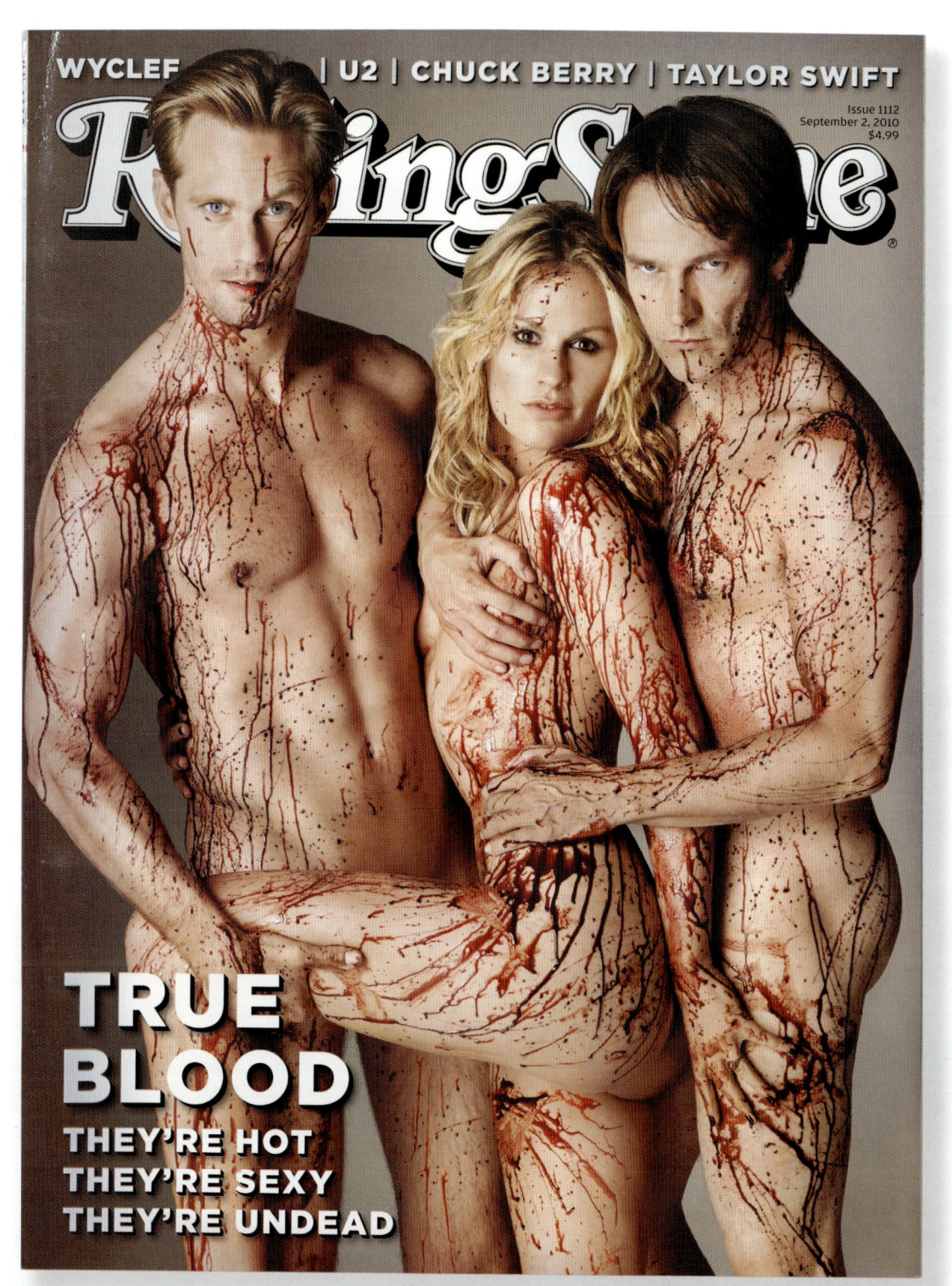

RS 1112 | CAST OF 'TRUE BLOOD' | September 2nd, 2010 | Photograph by Matthew Rolston

50 YEARS OF COVERS • 625

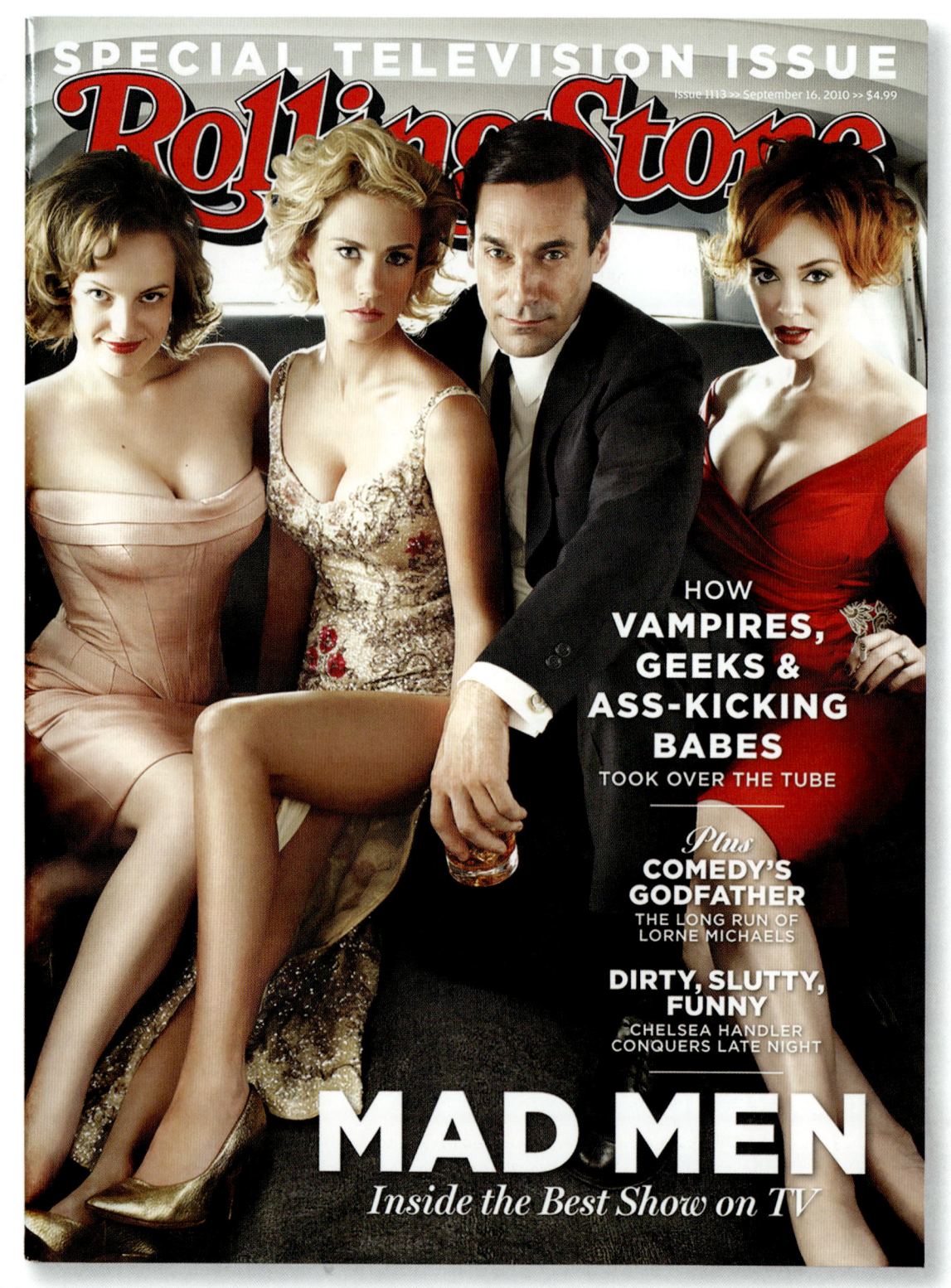

ROLLING STONE

SPECIAL TELEVISION ISSUE

Issue 1113 >> September 16, 2010 >> $4.99

HOW VAMPIRES, GEEKS & ASS-KICKING BABES TOOK OVER THE TUBE

Plus COMEDY'S GODFATHER
THE LONG RUN OF LORNE MICHAELS

DIRTY, SLUTTY, FUNNY
CHELSEA HANDLER CONQUERS LATE NIGHT

MAD MEN
Inside the Best Show on TV

2010s

RS 1113 | CAST OF 'MAD MEN' | September 16th, 2010 | Photograph by Robert Trachtenberg

WEINER WAS PICTURING LEADING MEN FROM THE SIXTIES WHEN HE created Don Draper. "James Garner played this kind of corrupt Boy Scout in a number of movies," Weiner says. "I saw black hair. I saw – if Gregory Peck and James Garner had had a baby, that guy."

The guy he got, Hamm, had been in Hollywood for a decade, with a list of credits split among forgettable TV shows (*The Division, Providence*), small-budget movies (*Kissing Jessica Stein*) and waiting tables at restaurants (at least one of which, Cafe Med, on Sunset Boulevard, wasn't bad). The year before he auditioned for *Mad Men*, he read for seven TV shows and completely struck out. "Seven tests, zero jobs," he says. "I was supernervous, nonpresent and terrified."

Hamm auditioned for *Mad Men* six times, but Weiner knew immediately that the actor had something in common with Draper. "That man was not raised by his parents," he famously told his casting director the moment Hamm left the first audition. The hunch was spot-on: Hamm's parents split up when he was two, and he was raised mostly by his grandmother. How could Weiner tell? "Without sounding too California, there's a kind of AM radio that goes on when we're casting that gives you an intuition about a human being," he says. "I got the feeling that Jon understood a kind of independence, and he had a wound."

This evening, drinking a gin and tonic at a rooftop bar high above Sunset Boulevard, Hamm comes across more like a handsome cop than a leading man: dark jeans, black sneakers, navy-blue windbreaker, aviator shades. He looks five years younger than Don Draper and moves with the easygoing, athletic boyishness of the high school jock he once was. "I play a character that's constantly dressed up," he says with a shrug. "I don't really have much in comparison to the way Don holds himself. I'm not that guy. I don't really look like that."

So do clothes make Don Draper? "Part of it is the suit, but another part is a choice," he says. "This is a person who takes himself very seriously at work, a guy who's going to walk in and command a room. I'm not that way in real life. I don't grab the mic." Still, he instantly identified with Draper's cutthroat nature. "My life at the time was trying to get a job," he says. "Talk about ruthless – being an actor in L.A. and not working is nothing but hustling. I just really responded to it on some visceral level, and that may have been what Matt picked up on. That may be why the character resonates coming from me." [EXCERPT FROM RS 1113 COVER STORY BY ERIC KONIGSBERG]

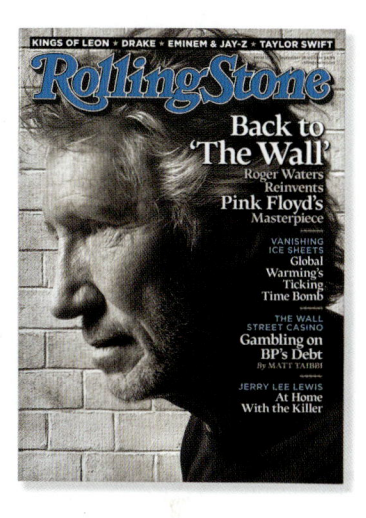

RS 1114 | ROGER WATERS
September 30th, 2010
Photograph by Albert Watson

[RS 1113] *Mad Men* was in the midst of its fourth season in 2010 when co-stars Elisabeth Moss, January Jones, Jon Hamm and Christina Hendricks appeared on the cover. When the actors arrived for the shoot, they didn't show up alone. *Mad Men* creator Matthew Weiner also brought along the show's hair, makeup and wardrobe team. "He wanted to make sure they looked authentic and in character," recalls photographer Robert Trachtenberg. "We punched the windshield out of a vintage Lincoln limo, and jammed the four of them in the backseat. I laid on my stomach across the hood and bruised my ribs getting the shot. Couldn't breathe right for a month."

LIL WAYNE ★ OZZY OSBOURNE ★ ARCADE FIRE

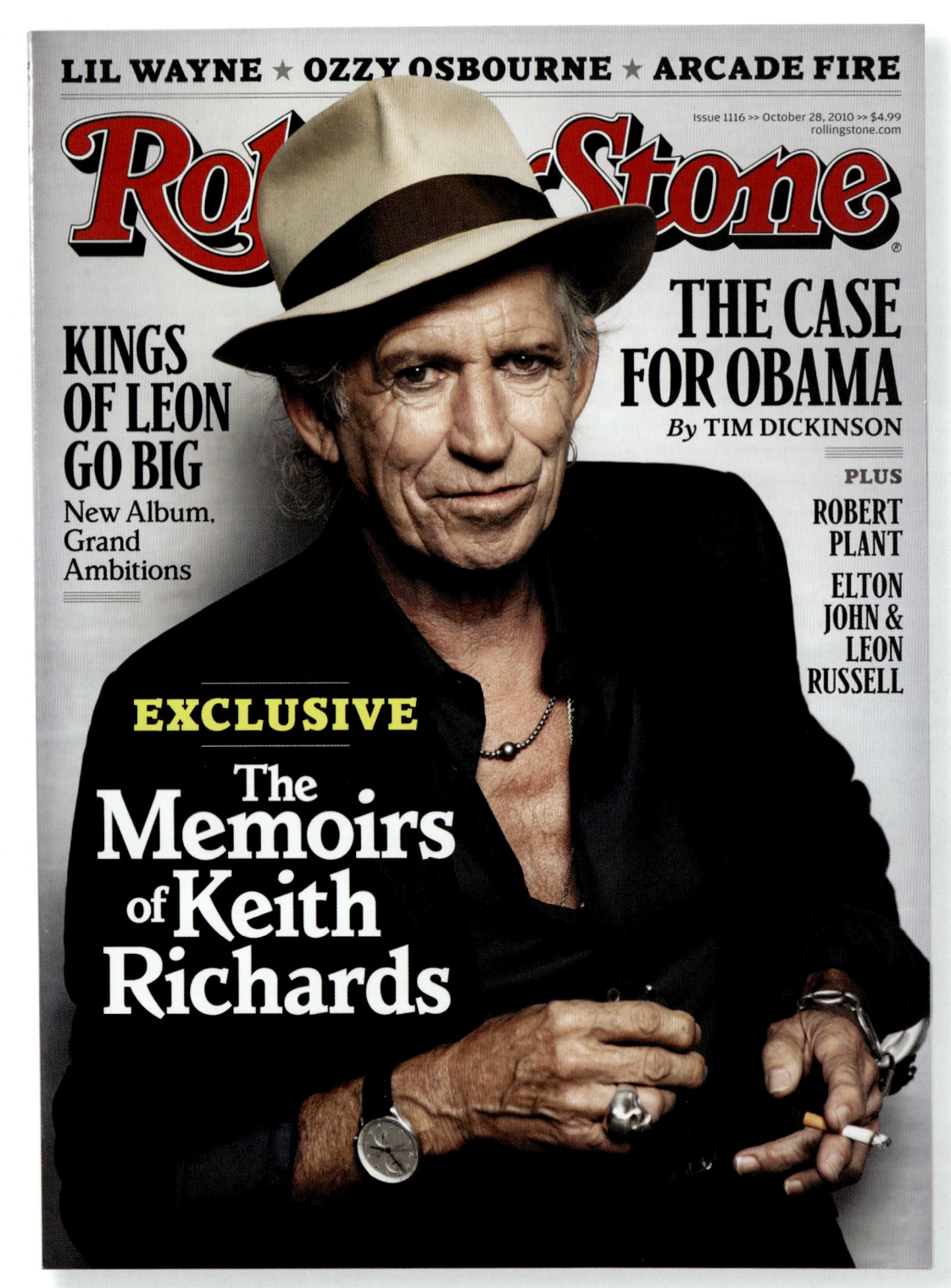

Rolling Stone

Issue 1116 >> October 28, 2010 >> $4.99
rollingstone.com

KINGS OF LEON GO BIG
New Album, Grand Ambitions

THE CASE FOR OBAMA
By TIM DICKINSON

PLUS
ROBERT PLANT
ELTON JOHN & LEON RUSSELL

EXCLUSIVE
The Memoirs of Keith Richards

2010s

RS 1116 | KEITH RICHARDS | October 28th, 2010 | Photograph by Peter Lindbergh

LIFE IS ULTIMATELY two stories: one of music, misbehavior and survival; the other a fond, perplexed, sometimes outraged telling of Richards' life with Jagger, including their battles over control and the destiny of their band. "I had a feeling Mick would have no problem with the truth," Richards claims. He goes quiet for a moment. "No doubt I was as infuriating to him as he can be to me."

Jagger read *Life*, Richards says, "and he was a bit peeved about this and that." But, the guitarist insists, "Mick and I are still great friends and still want to work together." Richards' proof: He and Jagger talked over the summer about new Stones action in 2011. There is another of those earthquake cackles. "Can you imagine if life went along smoothly and everybody agreed?" Richards asks. "Nothing would happen. There'd be no blues. There'd be no 'Happy,'" referring to his iconic blaze of joy on 1972's *Exile on Main Street*. There would certainly be no *Life*.

[EXCERPT FROM RS 1116 COVER STORY BY DAVID FRICKE]

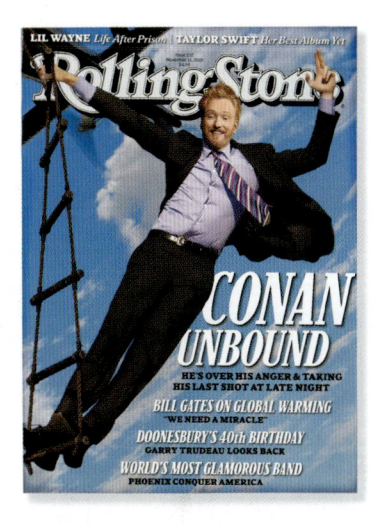

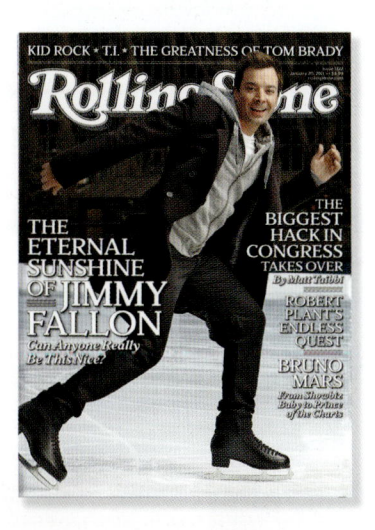

RS 1117 | CONAN O'BRIEN
November 11th, 2010
PHOTOGRAPH BY ROBERT TRACHTENBERG

RS 1122 | JIMMY FALLON
January 20th, 2011
PHOTOGRAPH BY ROBERT TRACHTENBERG

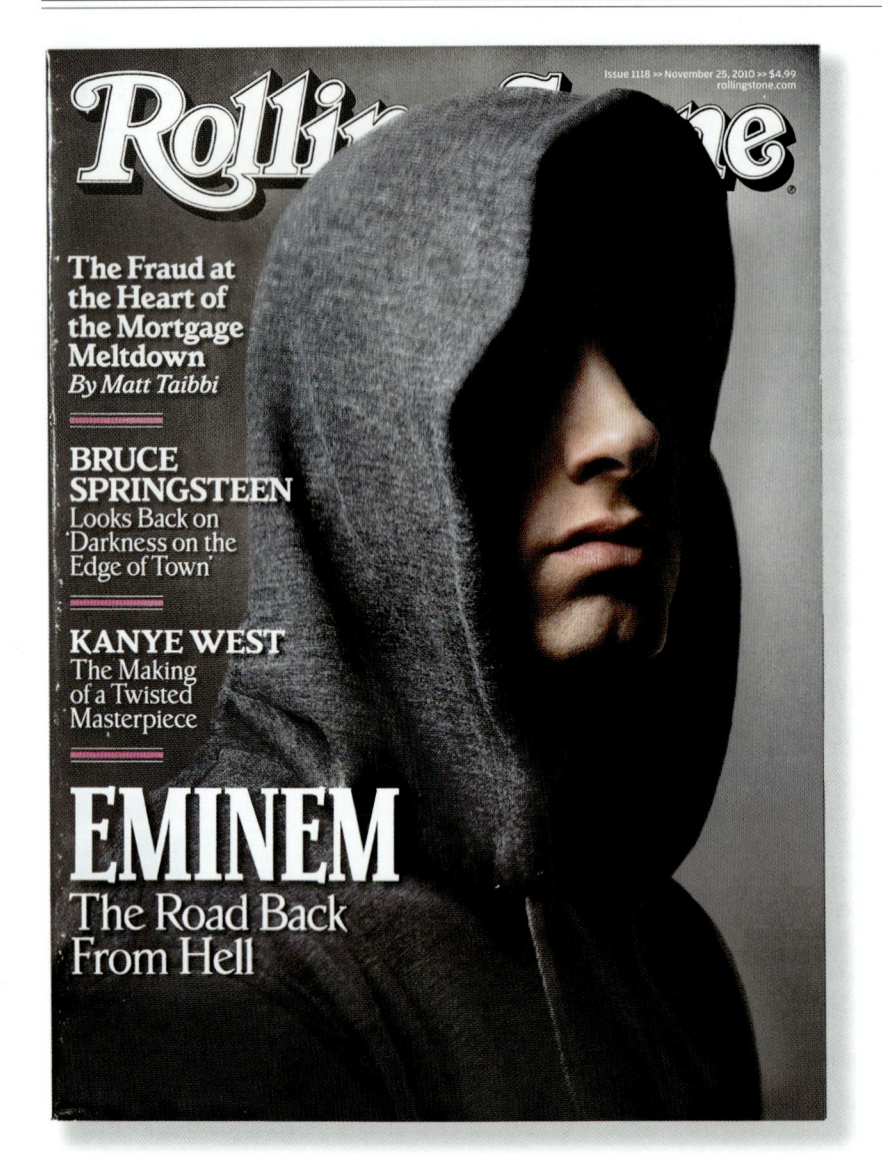

[RS 1119] The idea to do a Playlist Issue started with Roots drummer ?uestlove. We asked him to tell us his favorite songs, but he said he wanted to go deeper. "In my eyes, what defines a true artist is their filler," he said. "I happen to like the Stevie Wonder songs that aren't hits. I can say the same thing for Springsteen and Bob Dylan. Prince's hits are like a red carpet that he lays out to lead you to the good stuff."

RS 1118 | EMINEM
November 25th, 2010
PHOTOGRAPH BY MARK SELIGER

RS 1119 | THE PLAYLIST ISSUE
December 9th, 2010
PHOTOGRAPH BY CHARLES MASTERS

2010s

630 • ROLLING STONE

Yoko Ono loves the Beatles, but in choosing her late husband's favorite songs, she focused on the records Lennon made after the band's breakup. "He felt more free," says Ono. "He was getting down to what he was feeling. He was really speaking the truth."

1. "OH MY LOVE," 1971 In most love songs, you're making people feel hot or whatever about each other. But instead of that, he's saying, "I see it clearly for the first time." It's not so much about sexual interest or "I miss you" – it's more to do with true love.

2. "GIMME SOME TRUTH," 1971 "Gimme Some Truth" is so appropriate for now. He was before his time in a way. There's an edge to the music too – that kind of song didn't exist too much in those days.

3. "GIVE PEACE A CHANCE," 1969 You can't miss this one. It's proof that he could be very personal, but also he could cover the big picture and get people to think about that. And it worked. He really did affect the world a lot.

4. "GOD," 1970 A very powerful and daring song. The first time I heard it, when he sang "I don't believe in Beatles," I choked up. And so did many other people, for other reasons [*chuckles*]. It's very revolutionary, even more than the song "Revolution." It was breaking all the cobwebs and saying, "Here I am."

5. "GROW OLD WITH ME," 1984 He was saying it to me, but also to a whole generation: "Let's grow old together." After his passing, all I had was a cassette of it. I had it in my handbag. When I went to sleep, I had some bells on my door so if anyone came in, I'd hear it. I didn't want people to take it from me.

6. "IMAGINE," 1971 The chord structure and what it means are very direct and simple. And that was very important. He was good at anthems.

7. "SCARED," 1974 I thought this could be in the classical-music field. It's across the musical border.

8. "JEALOUS GUY," 1971 This was hard for him to get out – he was being very honest about being jealous. I don't think many songwriters owned up that way. They might tiptoe around that emotion.

9. "I DON'T WANNA BE A SOLDIER," 1971 A beautiful anti-establishment song, not just about a soldier but also a priest. He was just being himself. George's slide guitar is incredible. He was fantastic.

10. "MOTHER," 1970 John was coming out and saying, "Mother, I need you." He recognized the power and important position of women in society.

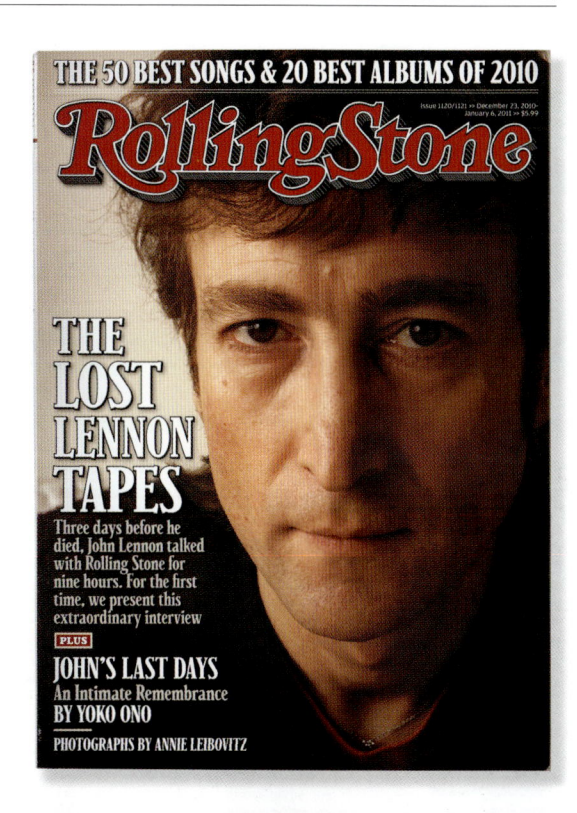

RS 1120/1121 | JOHN LENNON
December 23rd, 2010–January 6th, 2011
PHOTOGRAPH BY ANNIE LEIBOVITZ

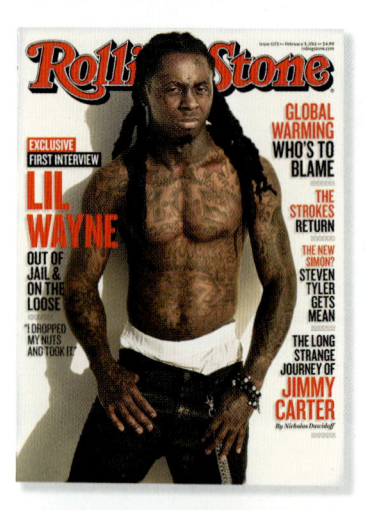

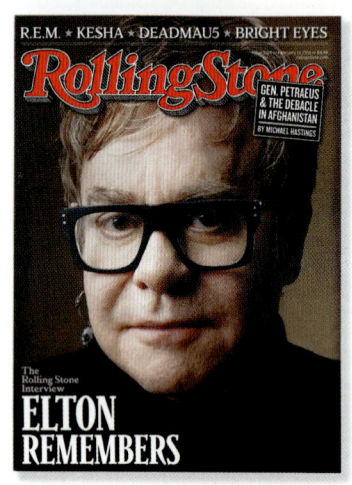

RS 1123 | LIL WAYNE
February 3rd, 2011
PHOTOGRAPH BY MARK SELIGER

RS 1124 | ELTON JOHN
February 17th, 2011
PHOTOGRAPH BY MARK SELIGER

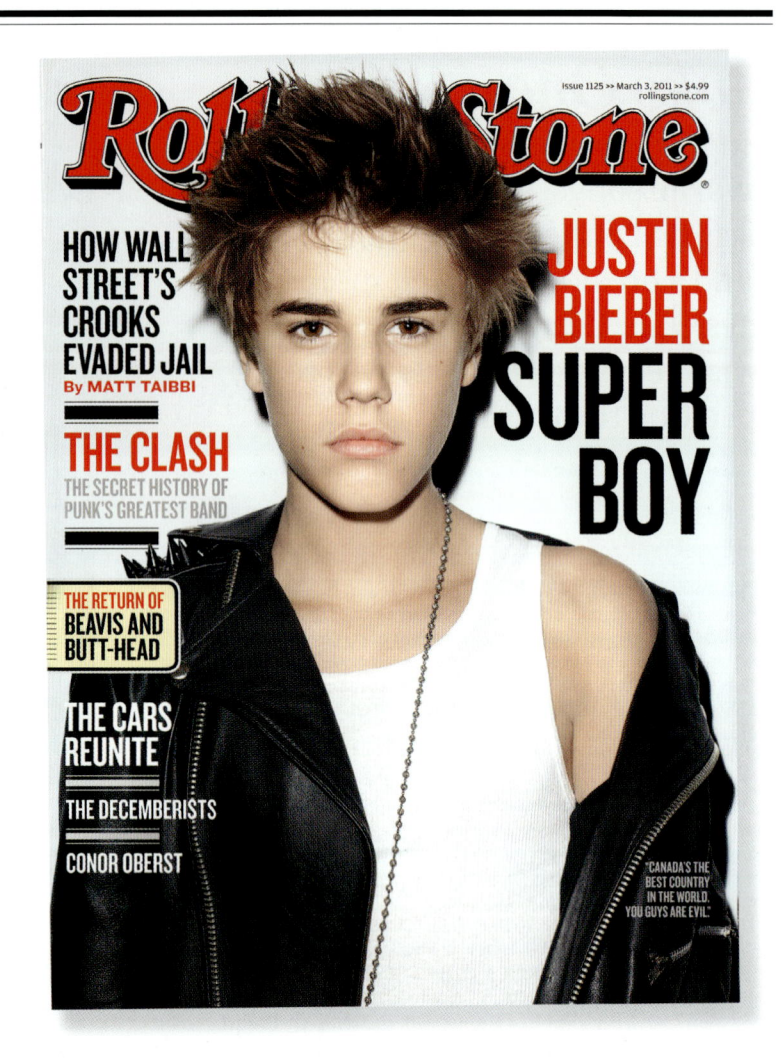

RS 1125 | JUSTIN BIEBER
March 3rd, 2011
PHOTOGRAPH BY TERRY RICHARDSON

[RS 1128] Stylist B. Akerlund had never worked with Rihanna before she got the assignment to choose her outfits for the singer's second ROLLING STONE cover – but she immediately had some ideas. "Her people told me the direction that we were going was if Kid Rock and Rihanna had a baby," she remembers. "So I tried to think of things she hadn't done. And everyone kept on saying, 'Supersexy, supersexy,' and I'm like, 'OK, I'll give you sexy.'" The result was a cover shot of Rihanna wearing a pair of barely-there, torn metallic shorts with a Levi's logo on the back, a midriff-baring white tank top and a red bandanna tied around her wrist. But it was the shorts that had everyone talking.

2010s

Rolling Stone

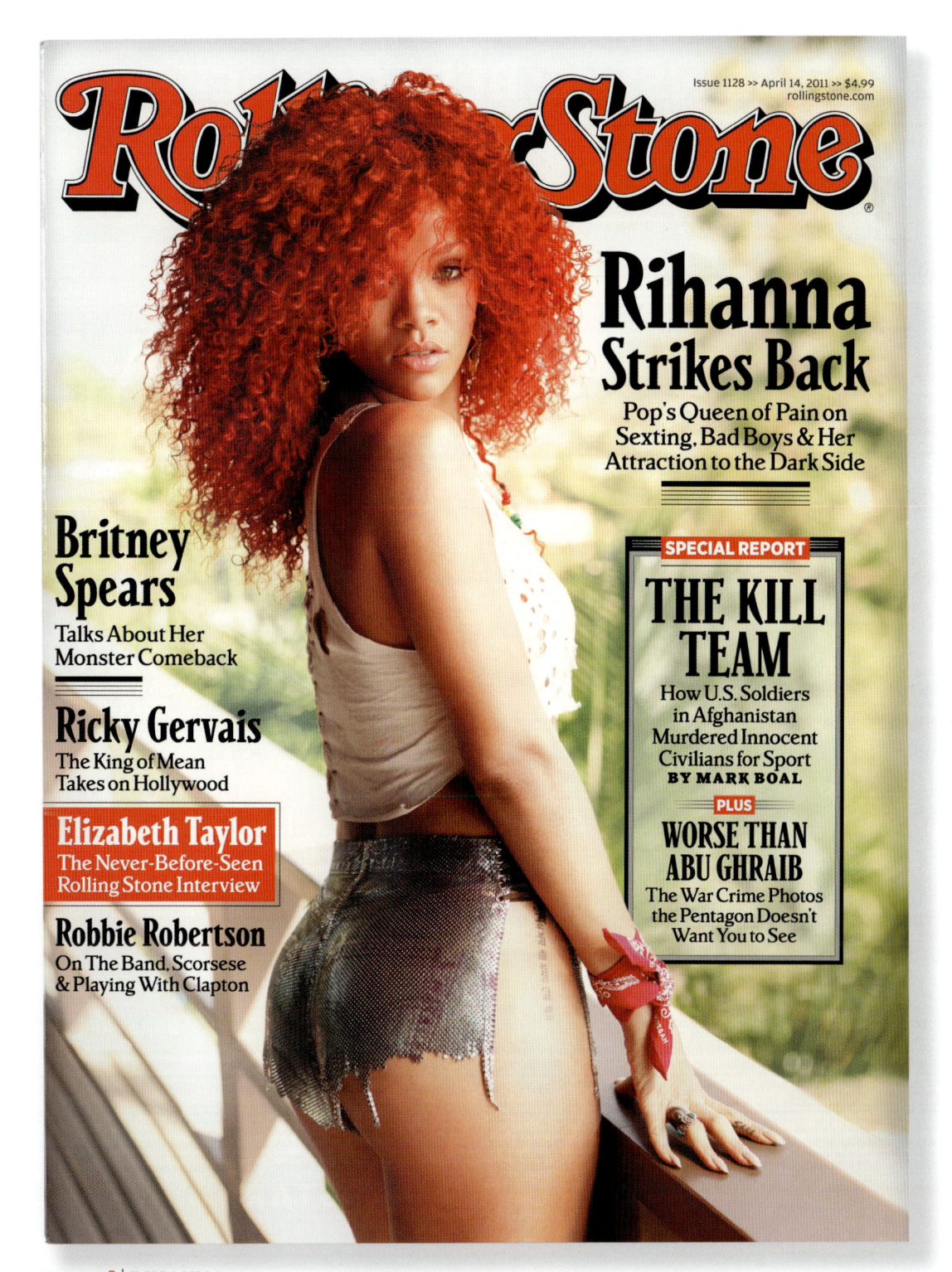

Issue 1128 >> April 14, 2011 >> $4.99
rollingstone.com

Rihanna Strikes Back
Pop's Queen of Pain on Sexting, Bad Boys & Her Attraction to the Dark Side

Britney Spears
Talks About Her Monster Comeback

Ricky Gervais
The King of Mean Takes on Hollywood

Elizabeth Taylor
The Never-Before-Seen Rolling Stone Interview

Robbie Robertson
On The Band, Scorsese & Playing With Clapton

SPECIAL REPORT
THE KILL TEAM
How U.S. Soldiers in Afghanistan Murdered Innocent Civilians for Sport
BY MARK BOAL

PLUS
WORSE THAN ABU GHRAIB
The War Crime Photos the Pentagon Doesn't Want You to See

RS 1128 | RIHANNA | April 14th, 2011 | PHOTOGRAPH BY MARK SELIGER

50 YEARS OF COVERS • 633

SPECIAL ISSUE: BEST OF ROCK 2011

RollingStone

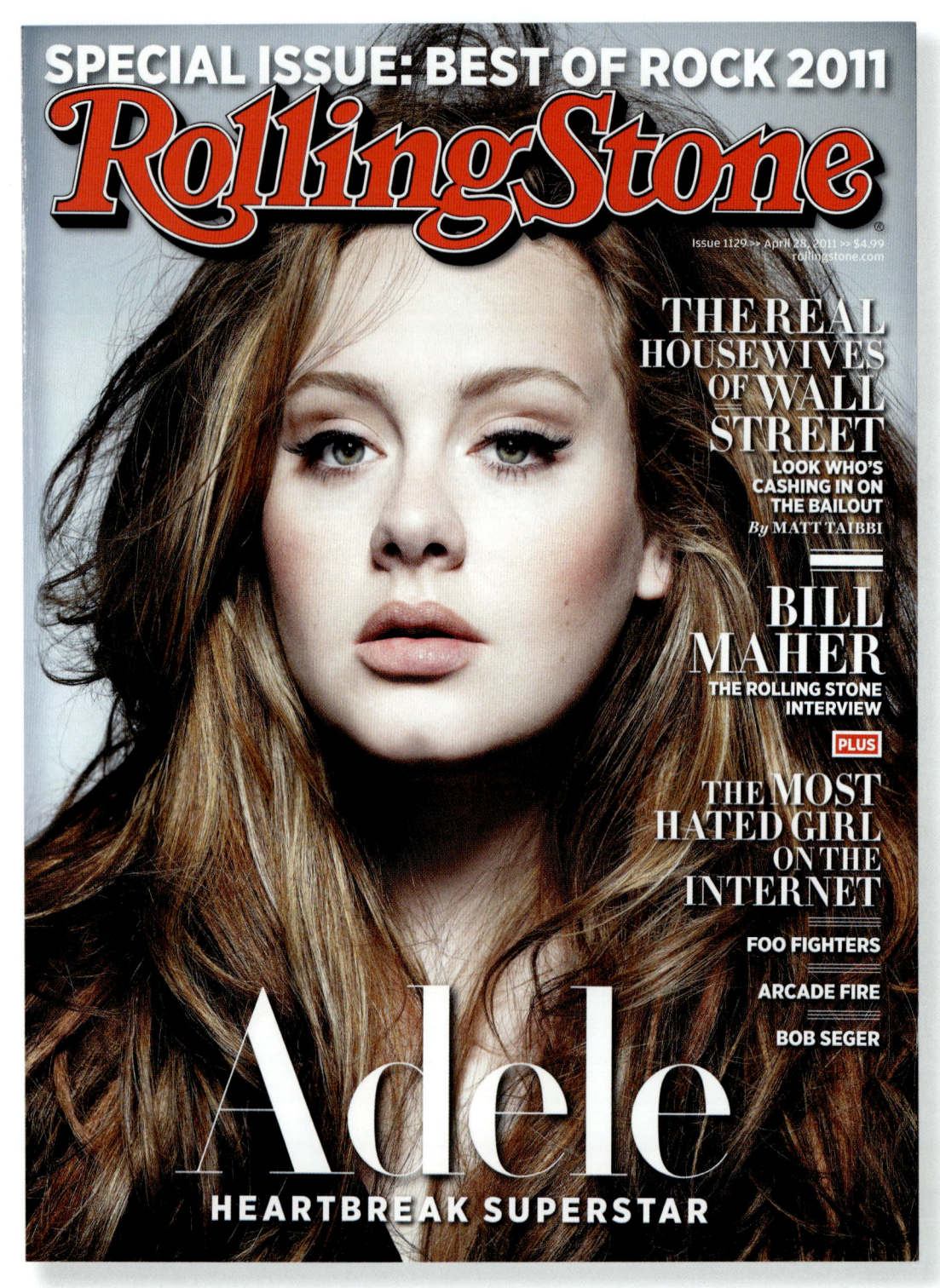

Issue 1129 >> April 28, 2011 >> $4.99
rollingstone.com

THE REAL HOUSEWIVES OF WALL STREET
LOOK WHO'S CASHING IN ON THE BAILOUT
By MATT TAIBBI

BILL MAHER
THE ROLLING STONE INTERVIEW

PLUS

THE MOST HATED GIRL ON THE INTERNET

FOO FIGHTERS
ARCADE FIRE
BOB SEGER

Adele
HEARTBREAK SUPERSTAR

2010s

RS 1129 | ADELE | April 28th, 2011 | Photograph by Simon Emmett

634 • ROLLING STONE

"*I have the shakes*," says Adele. It's 7:30 p.m. and she's in the basement dressing room of a 1,200-capacity club near Hamburg's red-light district, wearing the same black turtleneck sweater. She's been drinking coffee with Louis on her lap and smoking another cigarette. As always, she's got some stage fright. "I'm scared of audiences," she says. "I get shitty scared. One show in Amsterdam, I was so nervous I escaped out the fire exit. I've thrown up a couple of times. Once in Brussels, I projectile-vomited on someone. I just gotta bear it. But I don't like touring. I have anxiety attacks a lot."

How does she get herself onstage? "I just think that nothing's ever gone horrifically wrong," she says. "Also, when I get nervous, I try to bust jokes. It does work. I chat a lot of fucking shit, though." For most people who get stage fright, the nerves go away once the show starts, but for Adele, things get worse. "My nerves don't really settle until I'm offstage," she says. "I mean, the thought of someone spending $20 to come and see me and saying 'Oh, I prefer the record and she's completely shattered the illusion' really upsets me. It's such a big deal that people come give me their time."

[EXCERPT FROM RS 1129 COVER STORY BY TOURÉ]

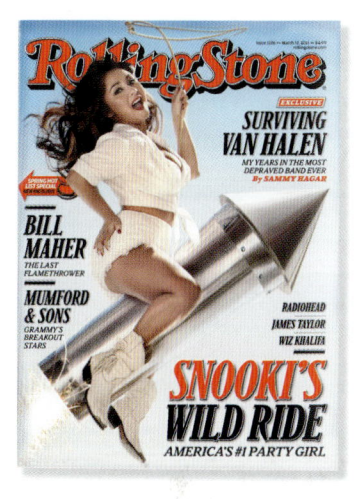

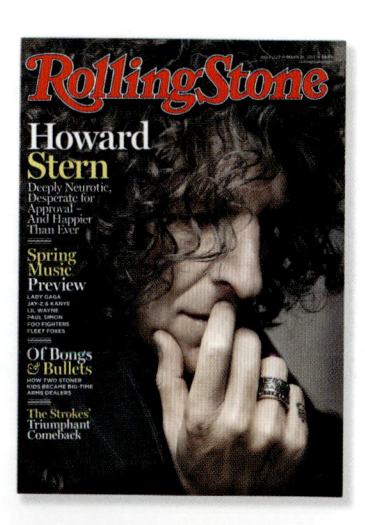

RS 1126 | NICOLE "SNOOKI" PIZZOLI
March 17th, 2011
Photograph by Mark Seliger

RS 1127 | HOWARD STERN
March 31st, 2011
Photograph by Mark Seliger

MUMFORD & SONS ★ WILCO ★ ANDY SAMBERG ★ METALLICA

Rolling Stone

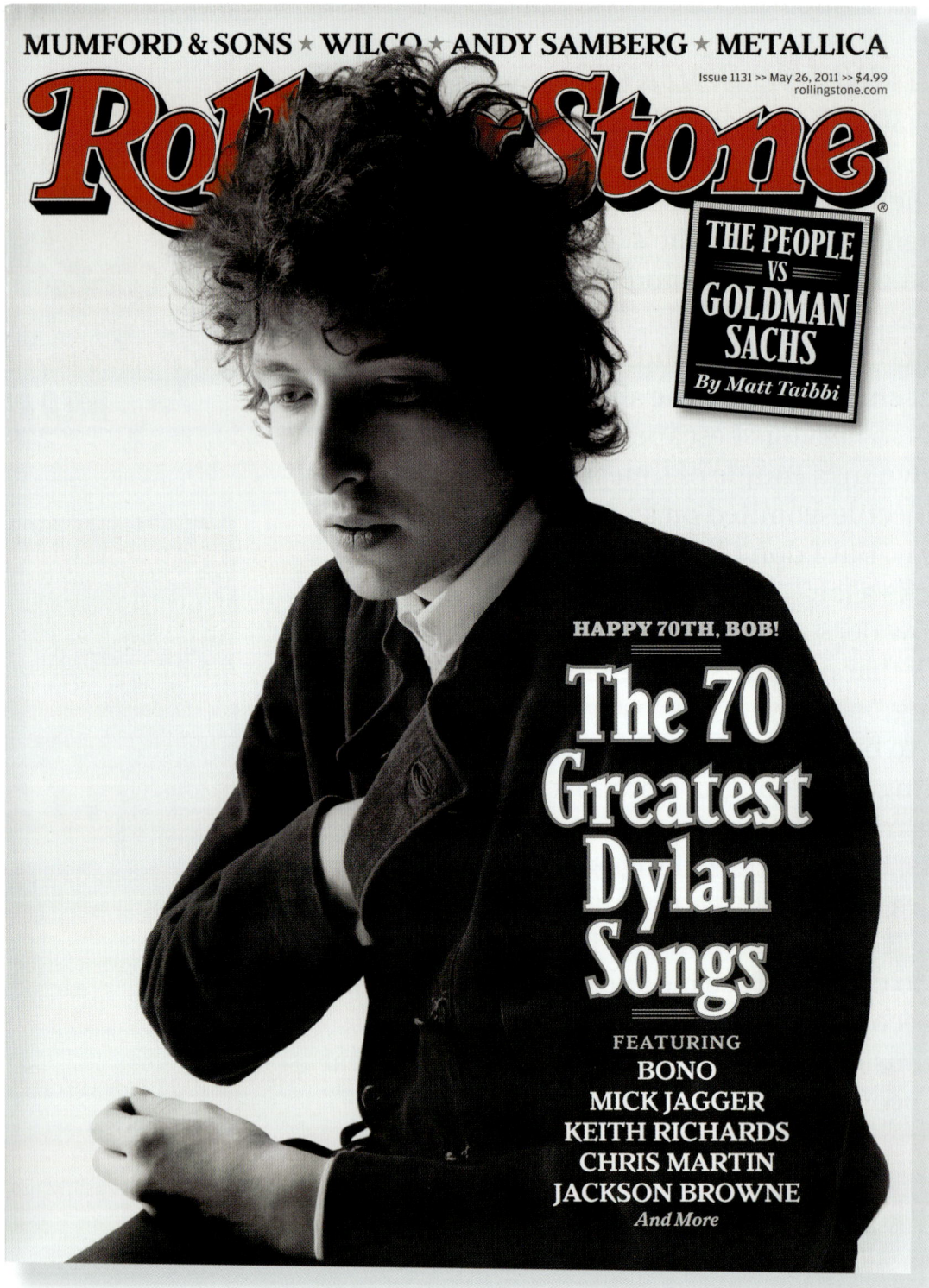

Issue 1131 >> May 26, 2011 >> $4.99
rollingstone.com

THE PEOPLE VS GOLDMAN SACHS
By Matt Taibbi

HAPPY 70TH, BOB!

The 70 Greatest Dylan Songs

FEATURING
BONO
MICK JAGGER
KEITH RICHARDS
CHRIS MARTIN
JACKSON BROWNE
And More

2010s

RS 1131 | BOB DYLAN | May 26th, 2011 | Photograph by JERRY SCHATZBERG/TRUNK ARCHIVE

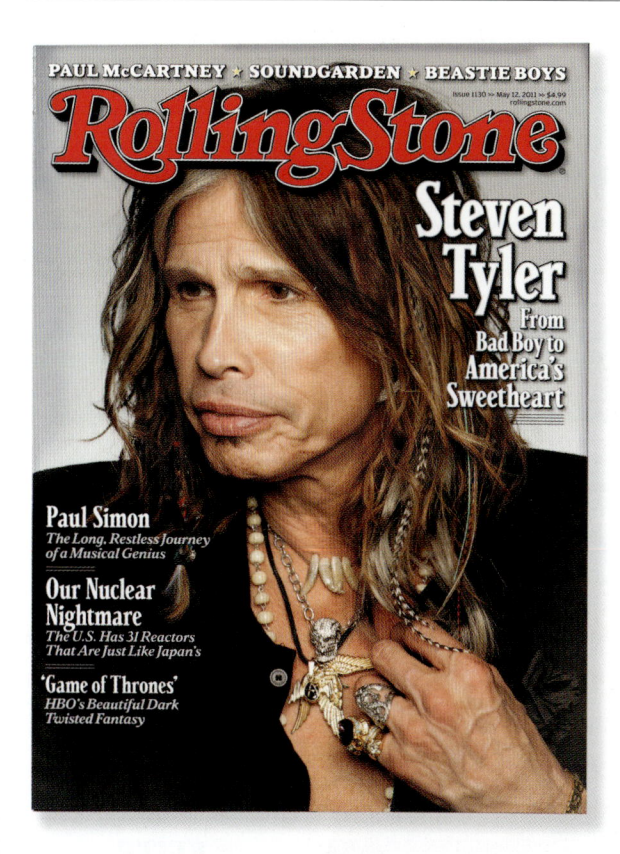

[RS 1131] For Bob Dylan's 70th birthday, we polled a group of experts and compiled a list of his 70 greatest songs. In an exclusive essay, Bono called "Like a Rolling Stone" the unsurprising list-topper, "a black eye of a pop song."

1.	LIKE A ROLLING STONE
2.	A HARD RAIN'S A-GONNA FALL
3.	TANGLED UP IN BLUE
4.	JUST LIKE A WOMAN
5.	ALL ALONG THE WATCHTOWER
6.	I SHALL BE RELEASED
7.	IT'S ALRIGHT MA (I'M ONLY BLEEDING)
8.	MR. TAMBOURINE MAN
9.	VISIONS OF JOHANNA
10.	EVERY GRAIN OF SAND
11.	IT'S ALL OVER NOW, BABY BLUE
12.	DESOLATION ROW
13.	SUBTERRANEAN HOMESICK BLUES
14.	HIGHWAY 61 REVISITED
15.	SIMPLE TWIST OF FATE

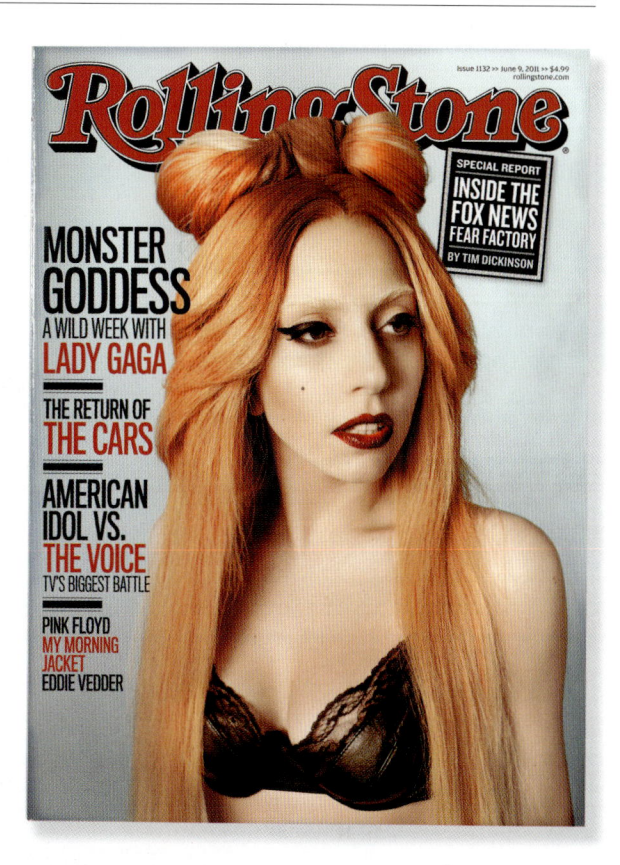

RS 1130 | STEVEN TYLER
May 12th, 2011
PHOTOGRAPH BY THEO WENNER

RS 1132 | LADY GAGA
June 9th, 2011
PHOTOGRAPH BY RYAN MCGINLEY

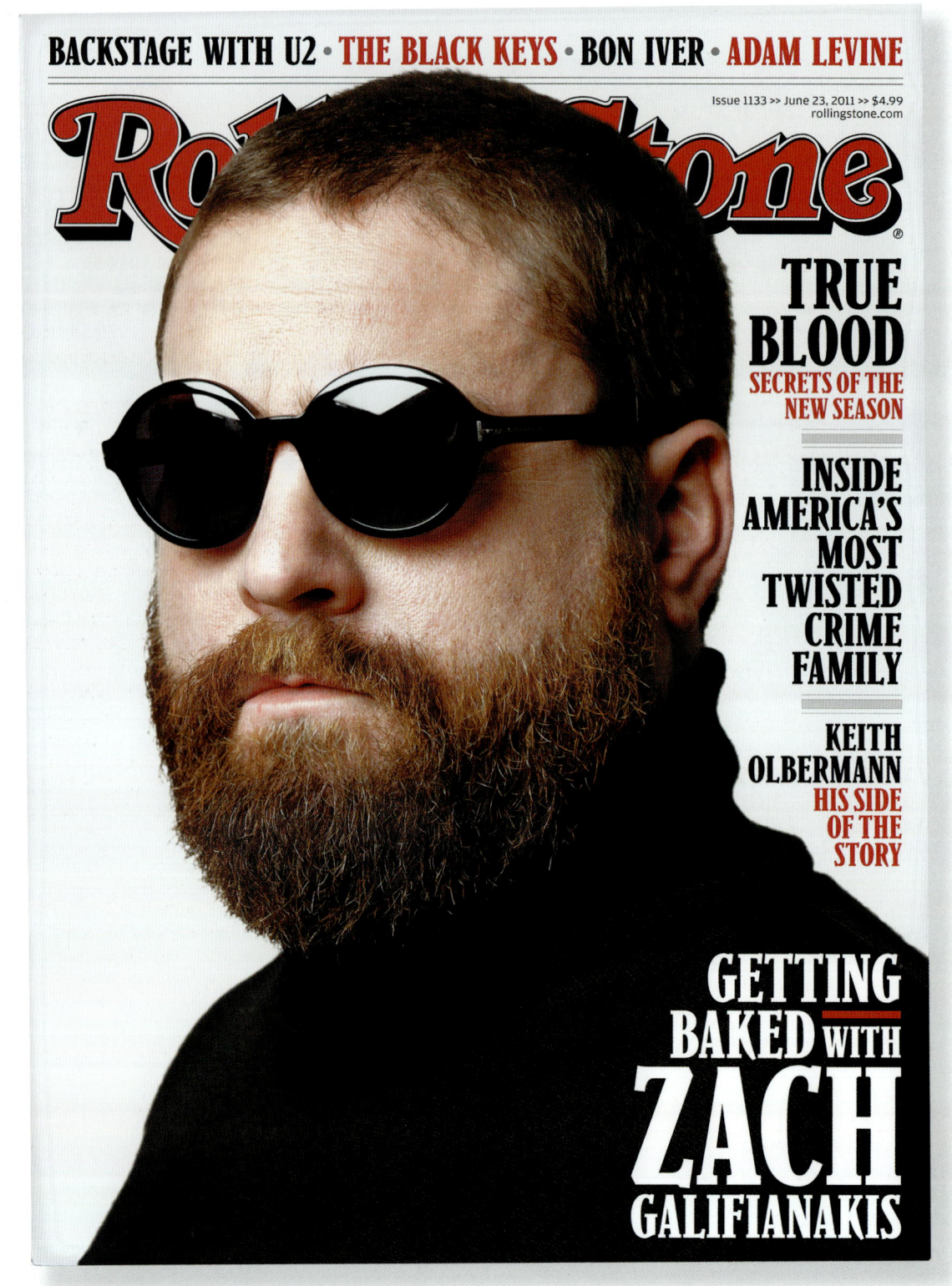

BACKSTAGE WITH U2 • THE BLACK KEYS • BON IVER • ADAM LEVINE

Rolling Stone

Issue 1133 >> June 23, 2011 >> $4.99
rollingstone.com

TRUE BLOOD
SECRETS OF THE NEW SEASON

INSIDE AMERICA'S MOST TWISTED CRIME FAMILY

KEITH OLBERMANN HIS SIDE OF THE STORY

GETTING BAKED WITH ZACH GALIFIANAKIS

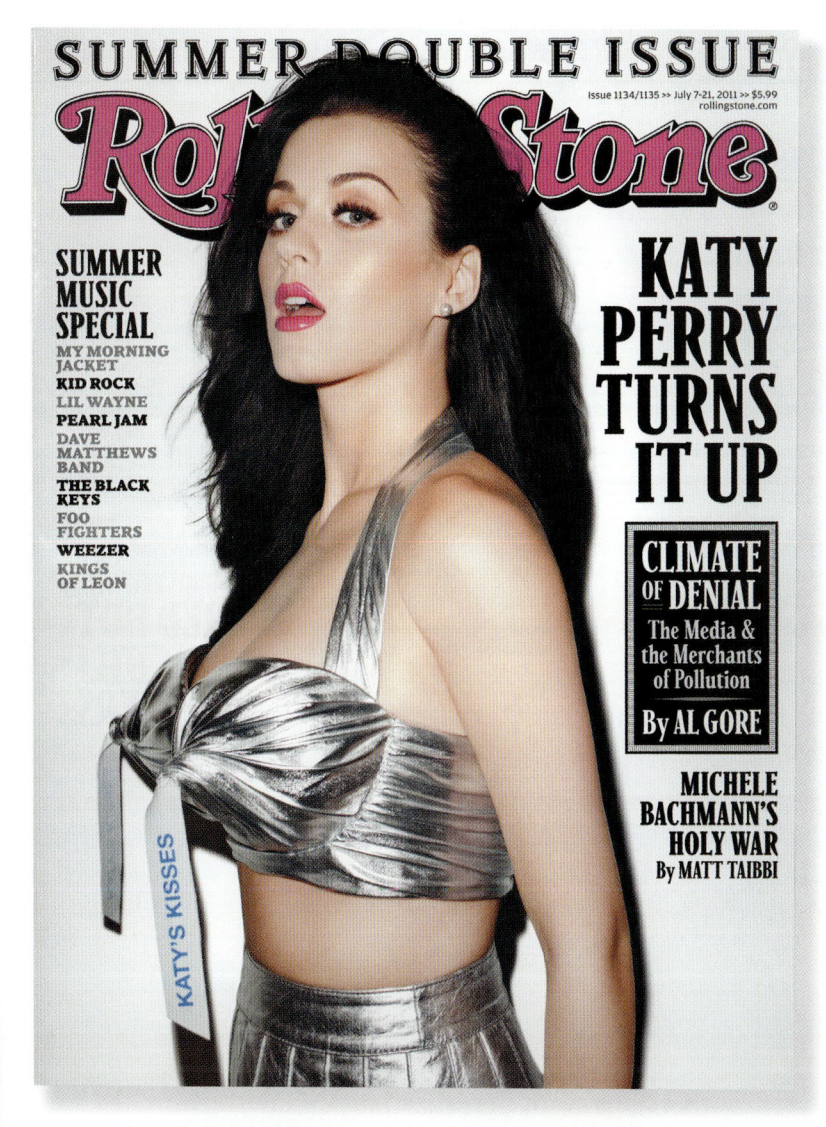

RS 1134/1135 | KATY PERRY
July 7th–21st, 2011 | Photograph by Terry Richardson

RS 1133 | ZACH GALIFIANAKIS
June 23rd, 2011
Photograph by Theo Wenner

THE PHONE BUZZES – IT'S a text from Galifianakis. "Running five minutes late. I got into a discussion with a pigeon. Lost track of time." He arrives at the East Village bar five minutes later, wearing a blue-and-green-striped polo and brownish pants. His hair is still short from when he shaved his head on *SNL* a few weeks ago (he walked out for the closing credits with a mohawk and announced, "Unfortunately, we didn't get to the Mr. T sketch"), and his celebrated beard does not disappoint. In his pocket is a rolled-up issue of *The New Yorker*, and around his neck, a pair of those black-foam headphones you get for free on a plane. "Hi," he says. "I'm Zatch Gassafanasky." He takes a seat at a sidewalk table and proceeds to remove his left shoe. He just walked here from his Brooklyn apartment, three miles across the bridge, and he thinks there might be something stuck inside. "I think it might be a dime. Do you know a good shoe detective?"

[EXCERPT FROM RS 1133 COVER STORY BY JOSH EELLS]

"I started praying for [breasts] when I was, like, 11. And God answered that prayer above and beyond, by, like, one hundred times, until I was like, 'Please, stop, God. I can't see my feet anymore. Please stop!'"
—*Katy Perry*

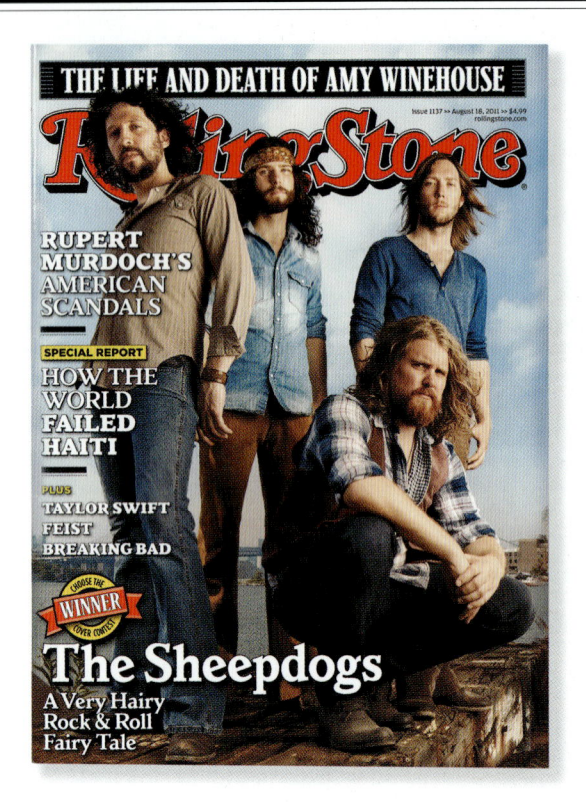

RS 1137 | THE SHEEPDOGS
August 18th, 2011
PHOTOGRAPH BY DANNY CLINCH

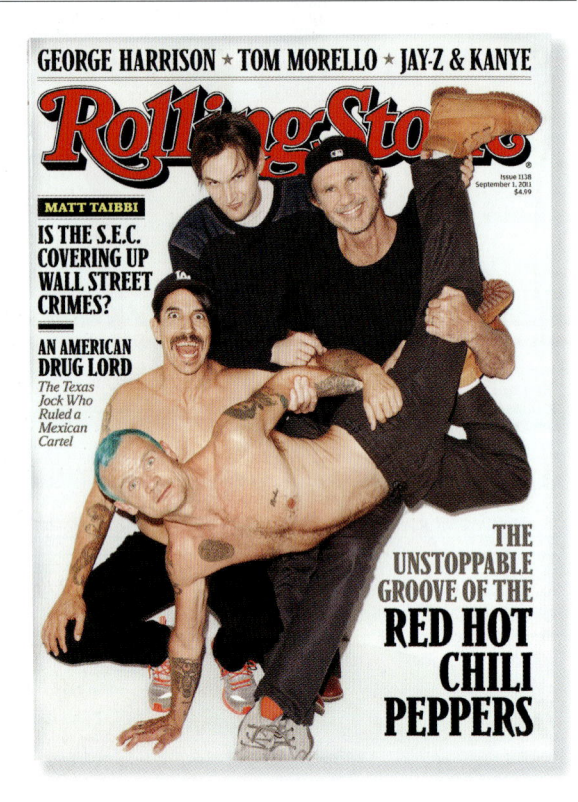

RS 1138 | RED HOT CHILI PEPPERS
September 1st, 2011
PHOTOGRAPH BY TERRY RICHARDSON

"I CAME UP WITH THE IDEA THAT LARRY SHOULD HAVE this cuddly little dog and show the gentler, kinder Larry David. Maybe there'd be a slight smile. Like, 'Oh, Larry David's finally had his cantankerous side softened by this little furry puppy.' But he said, 'No, no, no, I need to be annoyed with the dog.' So that was the joke. We had to get the dog trainer to put just a little peanut butter on his face. After having the peanut butter refreshed about 20 times, he was like, 'Alright, I'm done with this.'"

—*Mark Seliger*

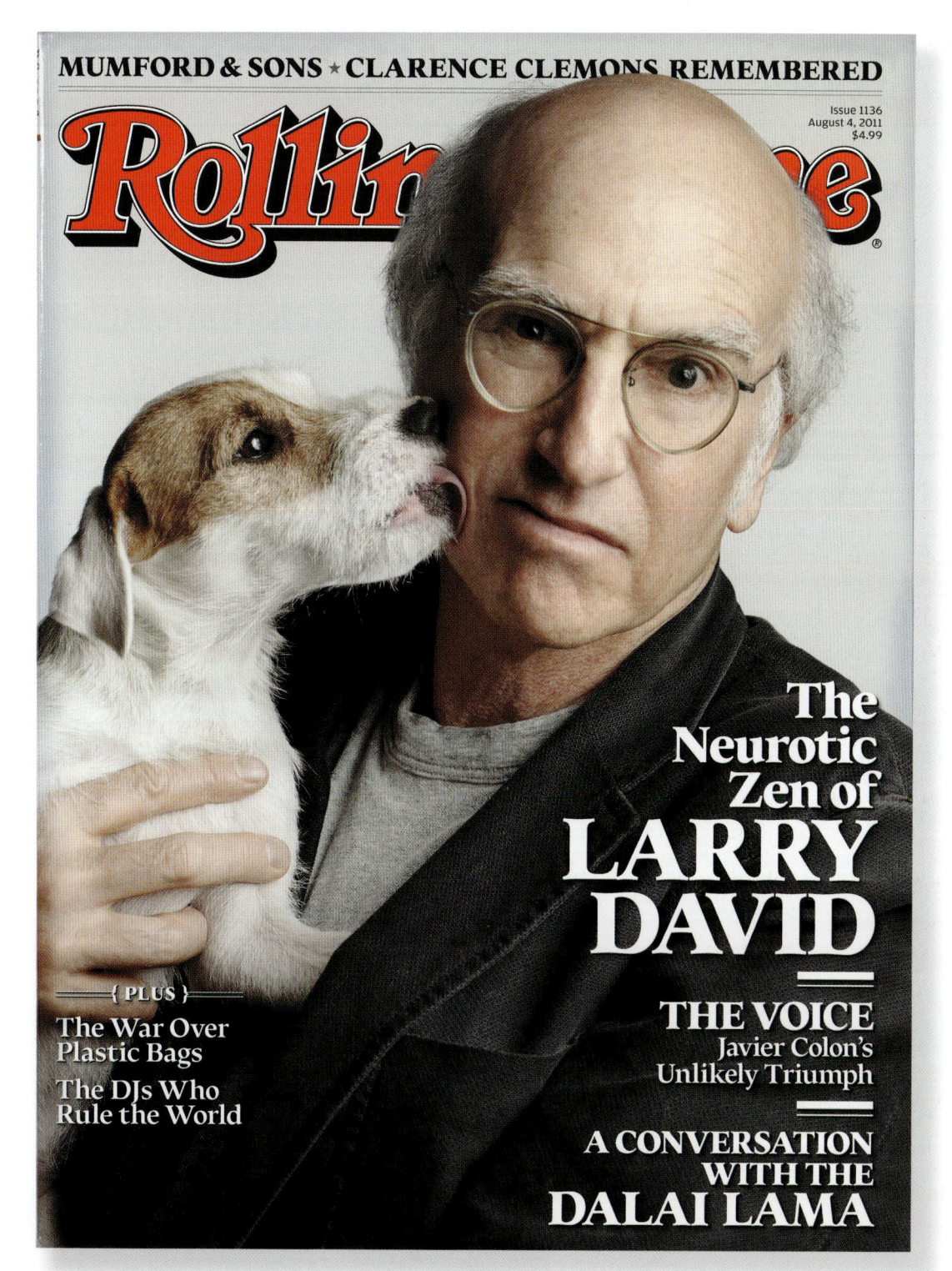

RS 1136 | LARRY DAVID | August 4th, 2011 | PHOTOGRAPH BY MARK SELIGER

THE CATHOLIC CHURCH'S SECRET SEX-CRIME FILES

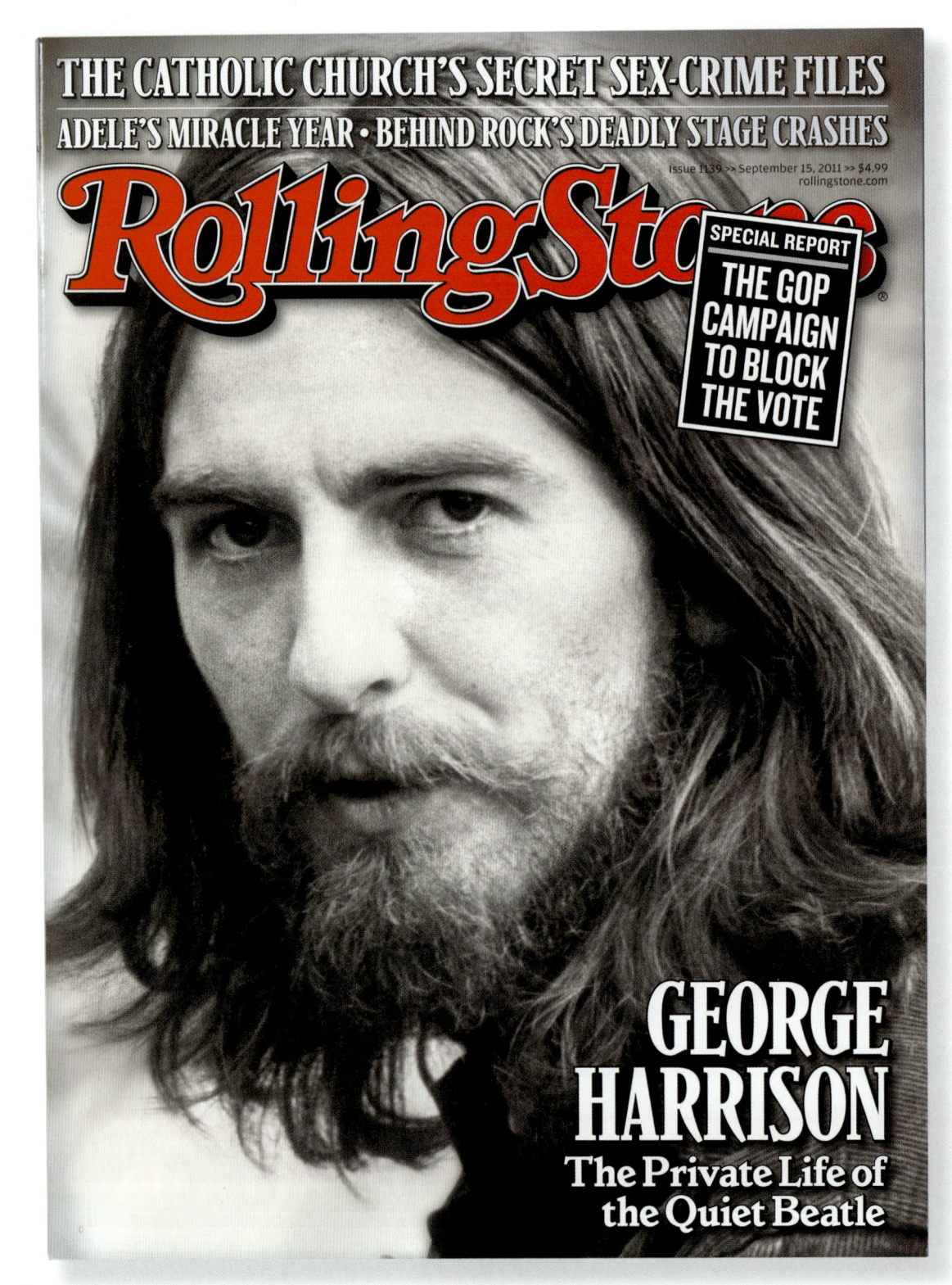

ADELE'S MIRACLE YEAR • BEHIND ROCK'S DEADLY STAGE CRASHES

Issue 1139 >> September 15, 2011 >> $4.99
rollingstone.com

RollingStone

SPECIAL REPORT
THE GOP CAMPAIGN TO BLOCK THE VOTE

GEORGE HARRISON
The Private Life of the Quiet Beatle

2010s

RS 1139 | GEORGE HARRISON
September 15th, 2011
Photograph by Arthur Steel/
Mirrorpix/Everett Collection

"*It's all well and good being* popular and being in demand, but, you know, it's ridiculous," Harrison told ROLLING STONE in 1987. "I realized this is serious stuff, this is my life being affected by all these people shouting." He felt physically unsafe. "With what was going on, with presidents getting assassinated, the whole magnitude of our fame made me nervous."
—*George Harrison*

"GEORGE DIDN'T SEE BLACK AND WHITE, up and down as different things. He didn't compartmentalize his moods or his life. People think, 'Oh, he was really this or that, or really extreme.' But those extremes are all within one circle. And he could be very, very quiet or he could be very, very loud. I mean, once he got going, that was it. He wasn't, you know, a wimp. I'll tell you that. He could outlast anyone."
—*Olivia Harrison*

"I KNOW THIS GUY," MCCARTNEY TOLD THE GROUP'S LEADER, JOHN Lennon. "He's a bit young, but he's good." Harrison passed his audition, playing the guitar instrumental "Raunchy" on the top half of a double-decker bus one night – and with that, he was a Beatle, or at least a Quarryman. But his bandmates never quite shook their idea of him as a junior partner – an "economy-class Beatle," in Harrison's sardonic formulation – and he soon began pushing for an upgrade. Harrison wasn't really the quiet Beatle: "He never shut up," said his friend Tom Petty. "He was the best hang you could imagine." He was the most stubborn Beatle, the least showbizzy, even less in thrall to the band's myth than Lennon. He was fond of repeating a phrase he attributed to Mahatma Gandhi – "Create and preserve the image of your choice" – which is odd, because his choice seemed to be no image at all. [EXCERPT FROM RS 1139 COVER STORY BY BRIAN HIATT]

MATT TAIBBI: THE WALL STREET PROTESTS

Issue 1142
October 27, 2011
$4.99

Rolling Stone

The Steve Jobs Nobody Knew

How an Insecure Hippie Kid Reinvented Himself – and Changed the World

INSIDE OBAMA'S WAR ROOM
By Michael Hastings

TOP 10s FROM

MICK JAGGER

BLACK KEYS

TOM PETTY

BON IVER

STEVEN TYLER

NORAH JONES

ADAM LEVINE

BEASTIE BOYS

KE$HA

LENNY KRAVITZ

DAVID GUETTA

The 2011 Playlist Special

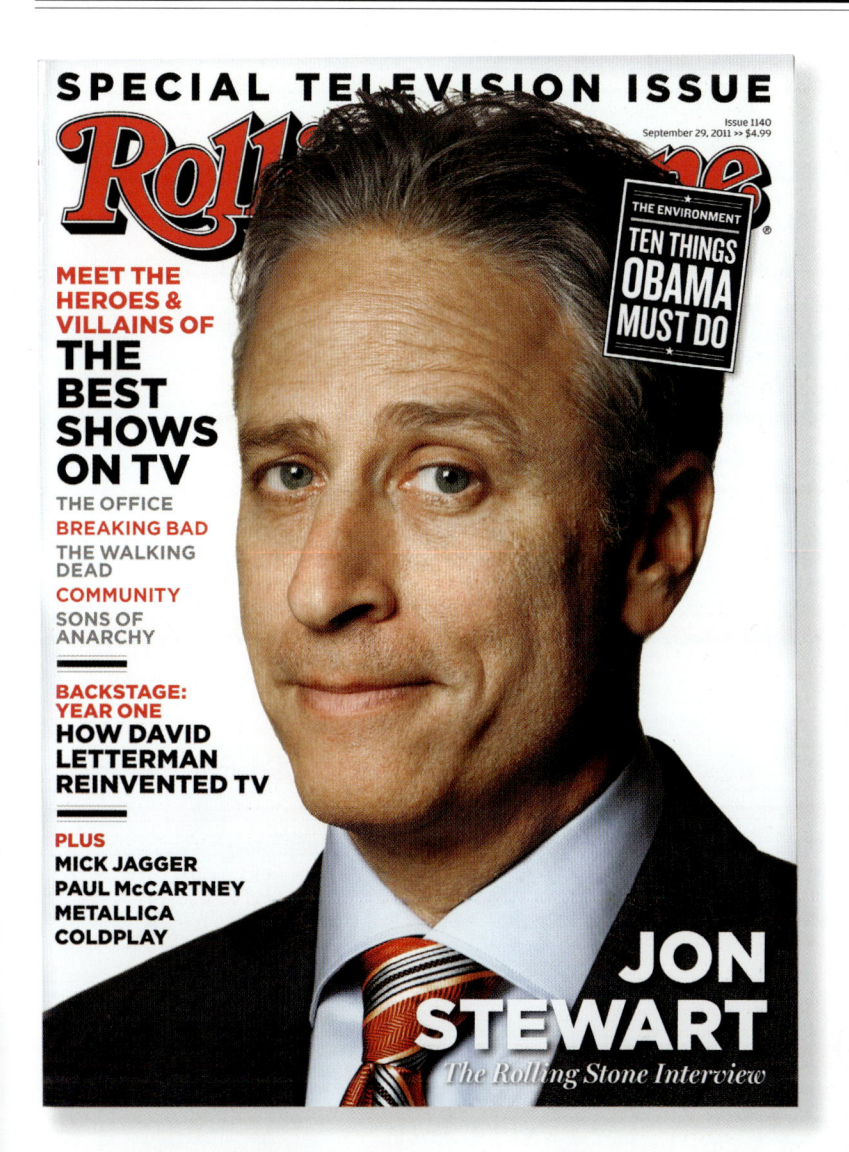

RS 1140 | JON STEWART
September 29th, 2011
PHOTOGRAPH BY ALBERT WATSON

RS 1142 | STEVE JOBS
October 27th, 2011
PHOTOGRAPH BY NORMAN SEEFF

"STEVE ALWAYS HAD THAT James Dean, live-fast, die-young thing," says Steve Capps, one of the key programmers on the first Apple Macintosh. As they worked late into the night to design and build the device that would revolutionize personal computing, Jobs would talk about death a lot. "It was a little morbid," Capps recalls. "He'd say, 'I don't want to be 50.'" Brennan recalls Jobs making similar comments when he was only 17. "Steve always believed he was going to die young," Brennan says. "I think that's part of what gave his life such urgency. He never expected to live past 45." In 2005, not long after he was diagnosed with the cancer that would eventually kill him, Jobs gave a now-famous commencement address at Stanford University, in which he hailed death as "very likely the single best invention of life," one that "clears out the old to make way for the new." Perhaps it was not unexpected that Jobs, the archetype of the modern inventor, would conceive of death in such terms – as if life itself were an idea that had been hacked together by a larger, more powerful version of himself in some big garage in the sky.

[EXCERPT FROM RS 1142 COVER STORY BY JEFF GOODELL]

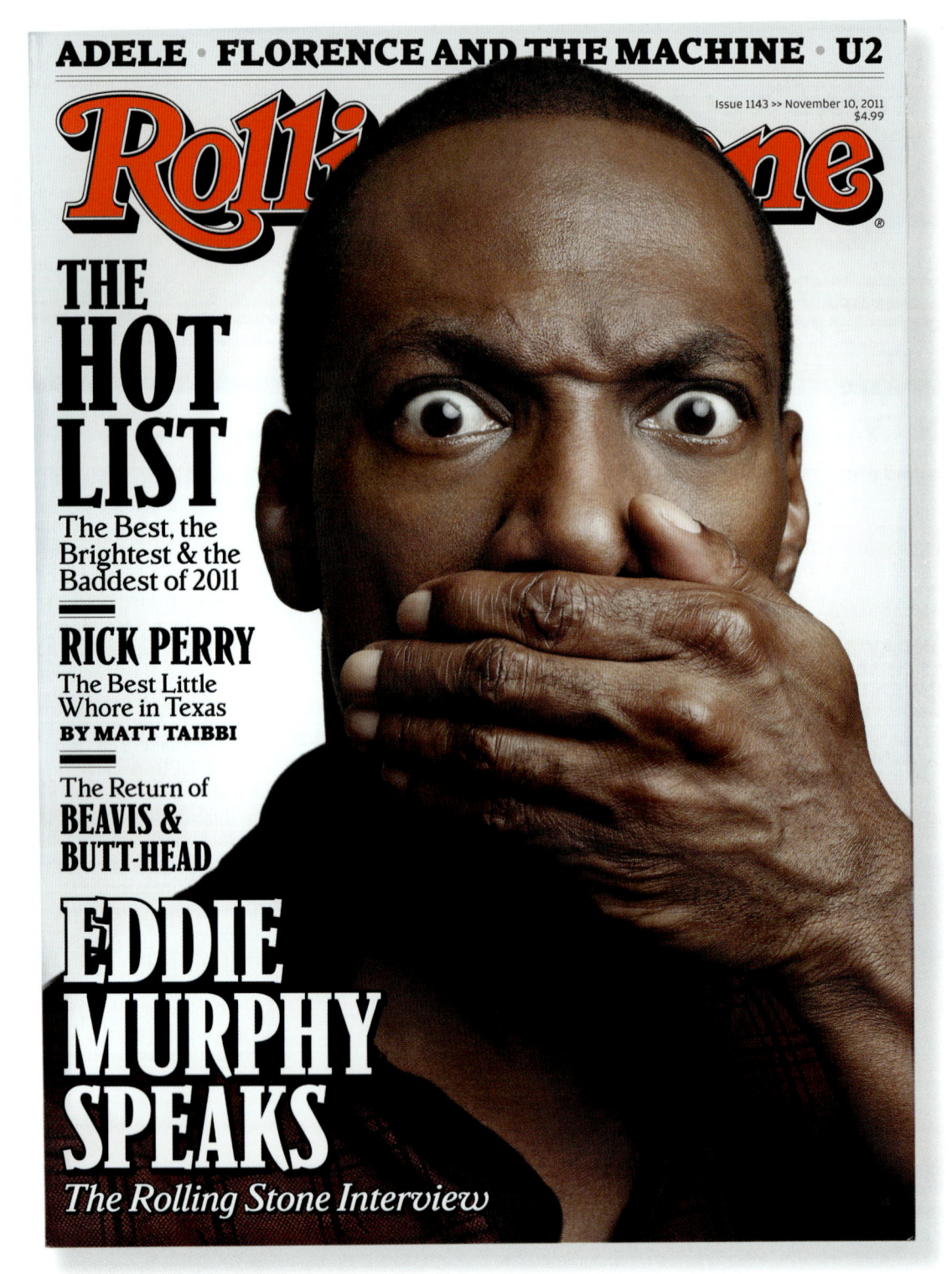

ADELE • FLORENCE AND THE MACHINE • U2

Rolling Stone

Issue 1143 >> November 10, 2011
$4.99

THE HOT LIST
The Best, the Brightest & the Baddest of 2011

RICK PERRY
The Best Little Whore in Texas
BY MATT TAIBBI

The Return of BEAVIS & BUTT-HEAD

EDDIE MURPHY SPEAKS
The Rolling Stone Interview

2010s

RS 1143 | EDDIE MURPHY | November 10th, 2011 | Photograph by Mark Seliger

646 • ROLLING STONE

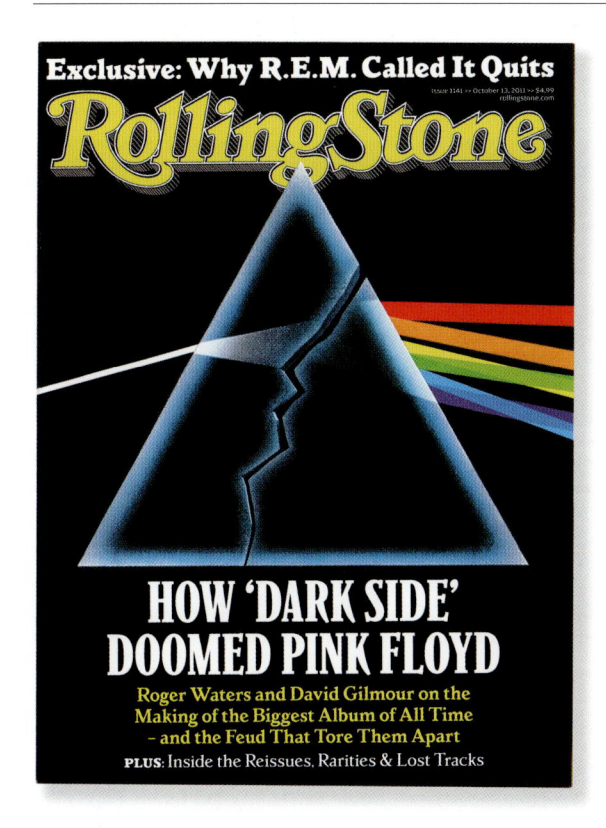

RS 1141 | PINK FLOYD 'DARK SIDE OF THE MOON'
October 13th, 2011
Design by Joe Zeff, Design based on Album Art (EMI Music)

RS 1144 | GEORGE CLOONEY
November 24th, 2011
Photograph by Mark Seliger

"YOU HAVE TO REMEMBER, THERE WAS NO HIP-HOP BACK then, or hip-hop was still novelty music, and for years I'm the whipping boy. Anybody that wanted to vent, I was the one. I got a lot of shit that wasn't fair. The root of it was racist. If I was rubbing you the wrong way, at the core of it was some racist shit: 'Look at this arrogant nigger, two thumbs waaaay down' [*laughs*]. Then, I wasn't helping, either. I wasn't giving no humble pie: 'Fuck y'all, suck my dick, motherfucker!'"
—*Eddie Murphy*

50 YEARS OF COVERS • 647

RS 1145 | 100 GREATEST GUITARISTS OF ALL TIME | December 8th, 2011 | Photographs by Various Photographers

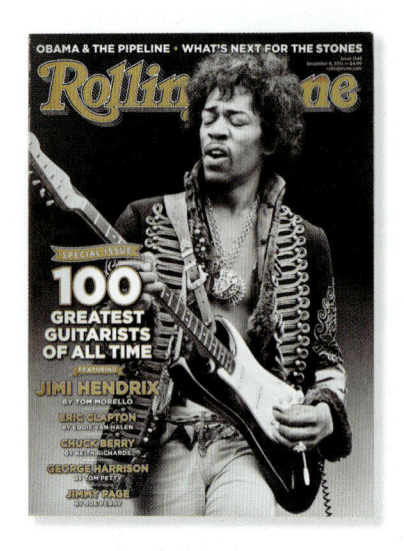

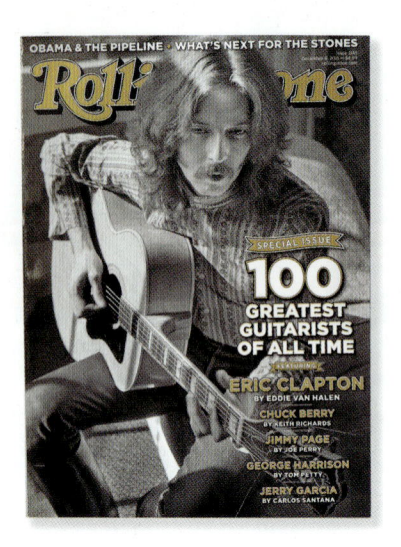

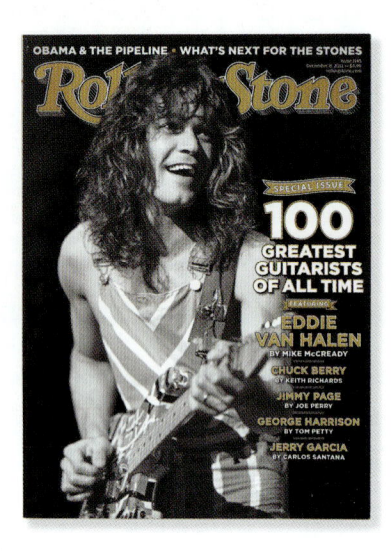

"His playing was effortless.

There's not one minute of his recorded career that feels like he's working hard at it – it feels like it's all flowing through him. The most beautiful song of the Jimi Hendrix canon is 'Little Wing.' It's just this gorgeous song that, as a guitar player, you can study your whole life and not get down, never get inside it the way that he does. He seamlessly weaves chords and single-note runs together and uses chord voicings that don't appear in any music book. His riffs were a pre-metal funk bulldozer, and his lead lines were an electric LSD trip down to the crossroads, where he pimp-slapped the devil." —*Tom Morello on Jimi Hendrix*

Our list of the 100 Greatest Guitarists of All Time came with four covers honoring Jimi Hendrix, Eric Clapton, Eddie Van Halen and Jimmy Page.

1.	JIMI HENDRIX
2.	ERIC CLAPTON
3.	JIMMY PAGE
4.	KEITH RICHARDS
5.	JEFF BECK
6.	B.B. KING
7.	CHUCK BERRY
8.	EDDIE VAN HALEN
9.	DUANE ALLMAN
10.	PETE TOWNSHEND
11.	GEORGE HARRISON
12.	STEVIE RAY VAUGHAN
13.	ALBERT KING
14.	DAVID GILMOUR
15.	FREDDY KING
16.	DEREK TRUCKS
17.	NEIL YOUNG
18.	LES PAUL
19.	JAMES BURTON
20.	CARLOS SANTANA

2010s

OBAMA & THE PIPELINE • WHAT'S NEXT FOR THE STONES

RollingStone

SPECIAL ISSUE

100 GREATEST GUITARISTS OF ALL TIME

FEATURING

JIMMY PAGE
BY JOE PERRY

ERIC CLAPTON
BY EDDIE VAN HALEN

CHUCK BERRY
BY KEITH RICHARDS

GEORGE HARRISON
BY TOM PETTY

JERRY GARCIA
BY CARLOS SANTANA

Issue 1145
December 8, 2011
$4.99
rollingstone.com

★ VAN HALEN'S FAST, FURIOUS COMEBACK ★

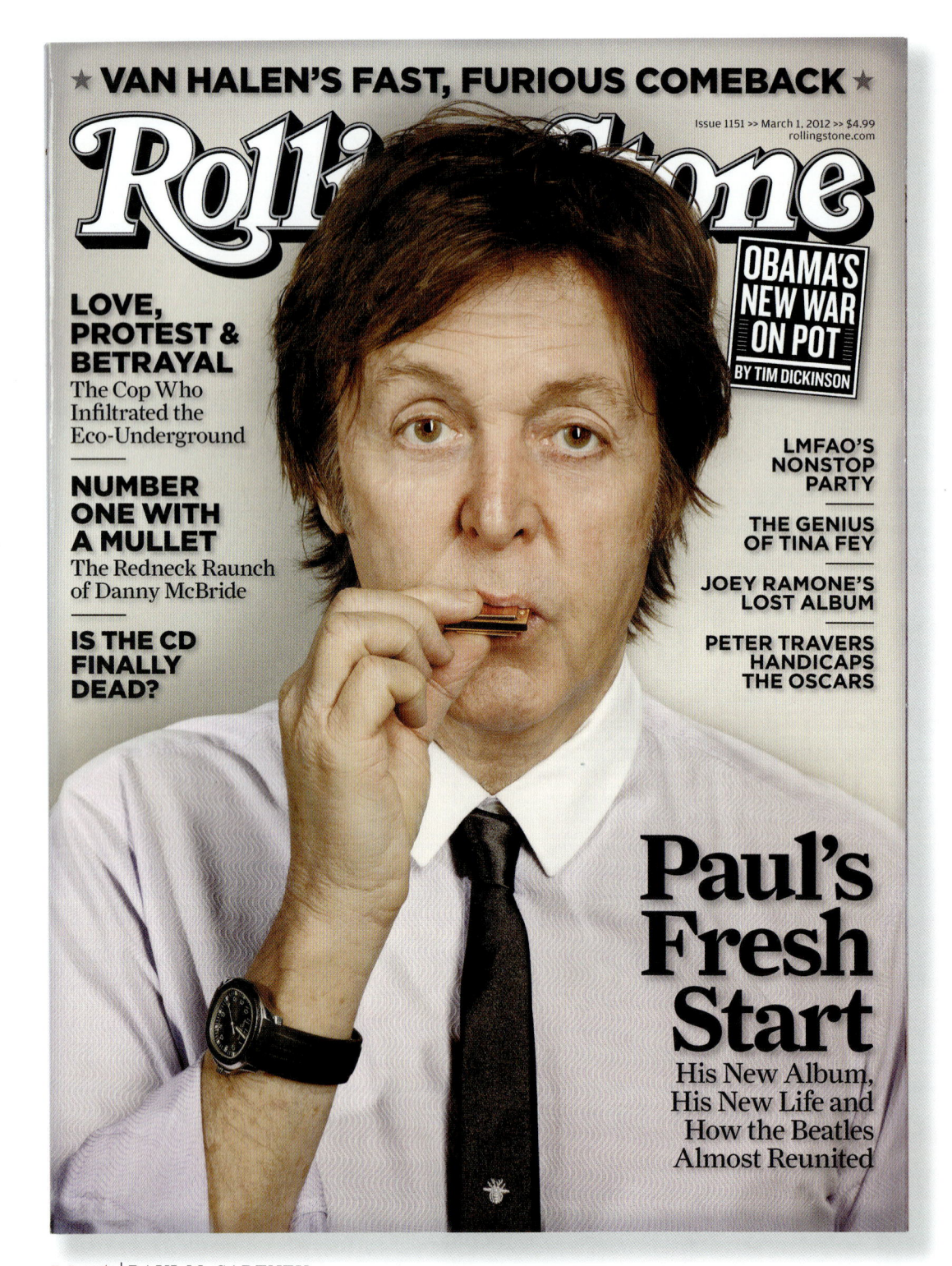

Rolling Stone

Issue 1151 >> March 1, 2012 >> $4.99
rollingstone.com

LOVE, PROTEST & BETRAYAL
The Cop Who Infiltrated the Eco-Underground

NUMBER ONE WITH A MULLET
The Redneck Raunch of Danny McBride

IS THE CD FINALLY DEAD?

OBAMA'S NEW WAR ON POT
BY TIM DICKINSON

LMFAO'S NONSTOP PARTY

THE GENIUS OF TINA FEY

JOEY RAMONE'S LOST ALBUM

PETER TRAVERS HANDICAPS THE OSCARS

Paul's Fresh Start
His New Album, His New Life and How the Beatles Almost Reunited

---

RS 1151 | PAUL McCARTNEY | March 1st, 2012 | Photograph by Nadav Kander

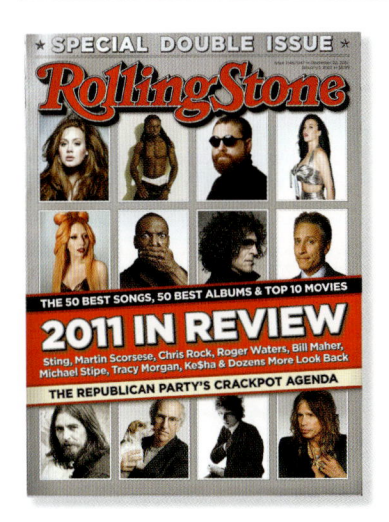

RS 1146/1147 | YEARBOOK 2011
December 22nd, 2011–January 5th, 2012
VARIOUS PHOTOGRAPHERS

"WHEN I WRITE A SONG, I HAVE MY other songs hanging over it. I suppose the minute you write a decent song, that's a curse. You're always like, 'Oh, shit, I've just written "Eleanor Rigby," how am I going to top that?' I think you go, 'I'm not.' You just realize you're not going to top it, but you write 'Blackbird.' You go in another direction or whatever if you're lucky. I've always been aware of that phenomenon, but I've never let it block me."
—Paul McCartney

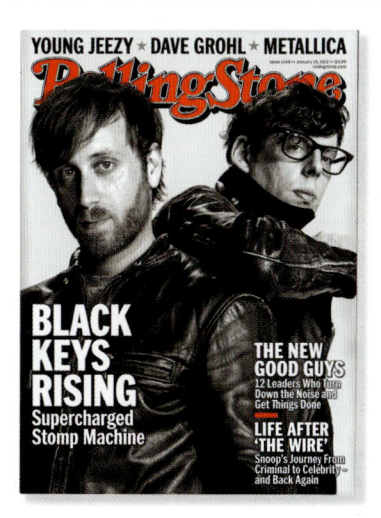

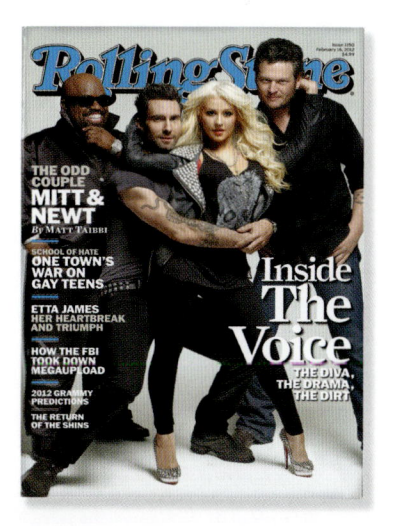

RS 1148 | THE BLACK KEYS
January 19th, 2012
PHOTOGRAPH BY THEO WENNER

RS 1150 | CAST OF 'THE VOICE'
February 16th, 2012
PHOTOGRAPH BY MARK SELIGER

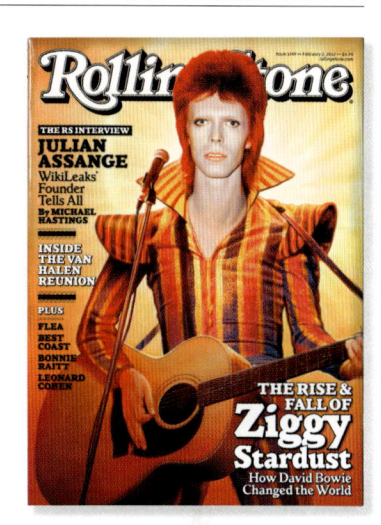

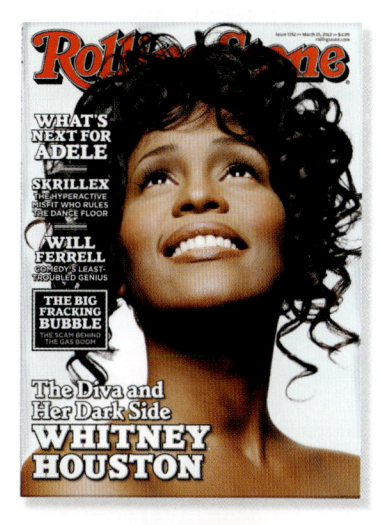

RS 1149 | DAVID BOWIE
February 2nd, 2012
ILLUSTRATION BY TIM O'BRIEN

RS 1152 | WHITNEY HOUSTON
March 15th, 2012
PHOTOGRAPH BY MICHAEL COMTE/
CORBIS OUTLINE

50 YEARS OF COVERS • 651

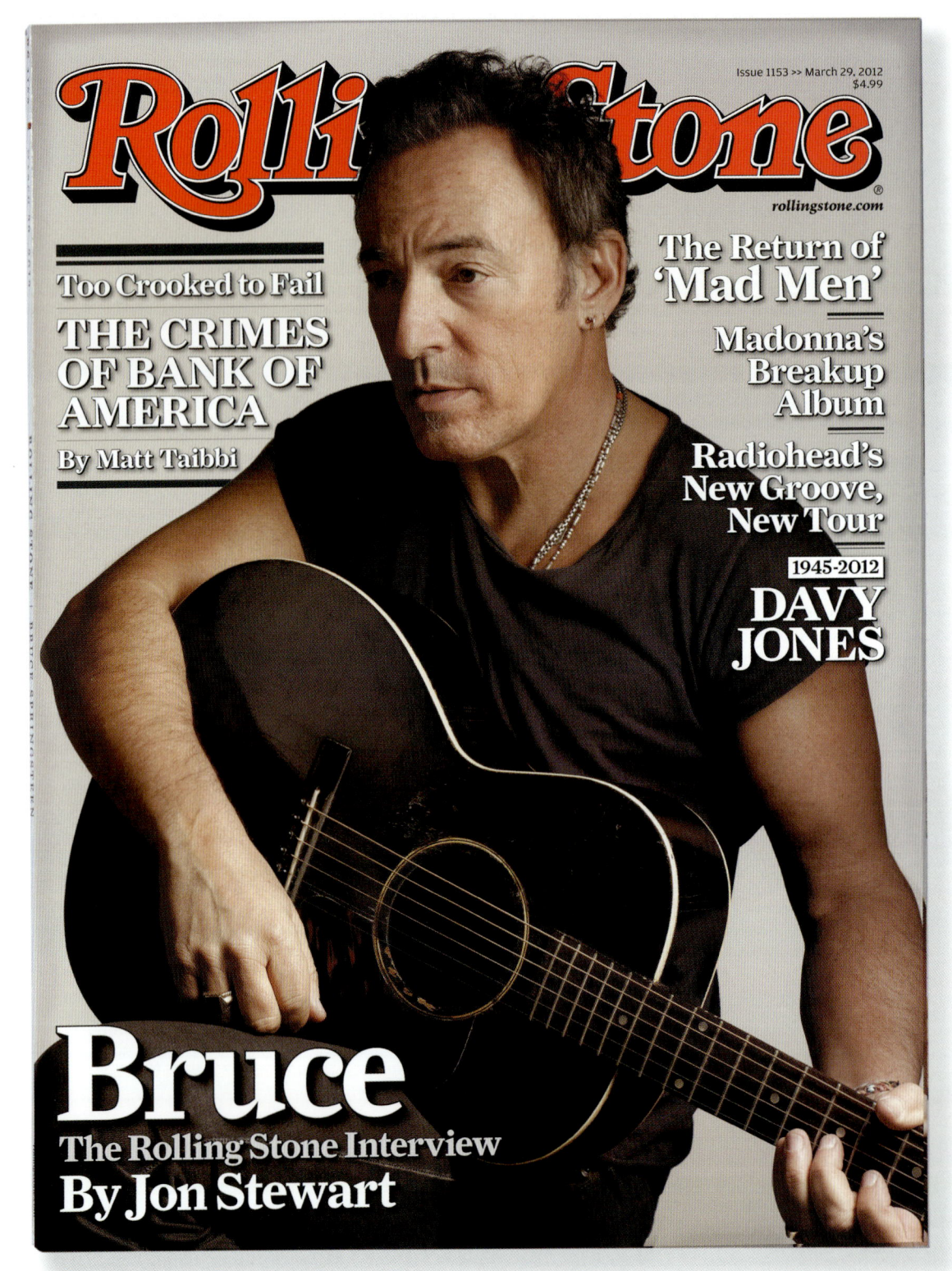

Rolling Stone

Issue 1153 >> March 29, 2012
$4.99

rollingstone.com

Too Crooked to Fail
THE CRIMES OF BANK OF AMERICA
By Matt Taibbi

The Return of 'Mad Men'

Madonna's Breakup Album

Radiohead's New Groove, New Tour

1945-2012
DAVY JONES

Bruce
The Rolling Stone Interview
By Jon Stewart

2010s

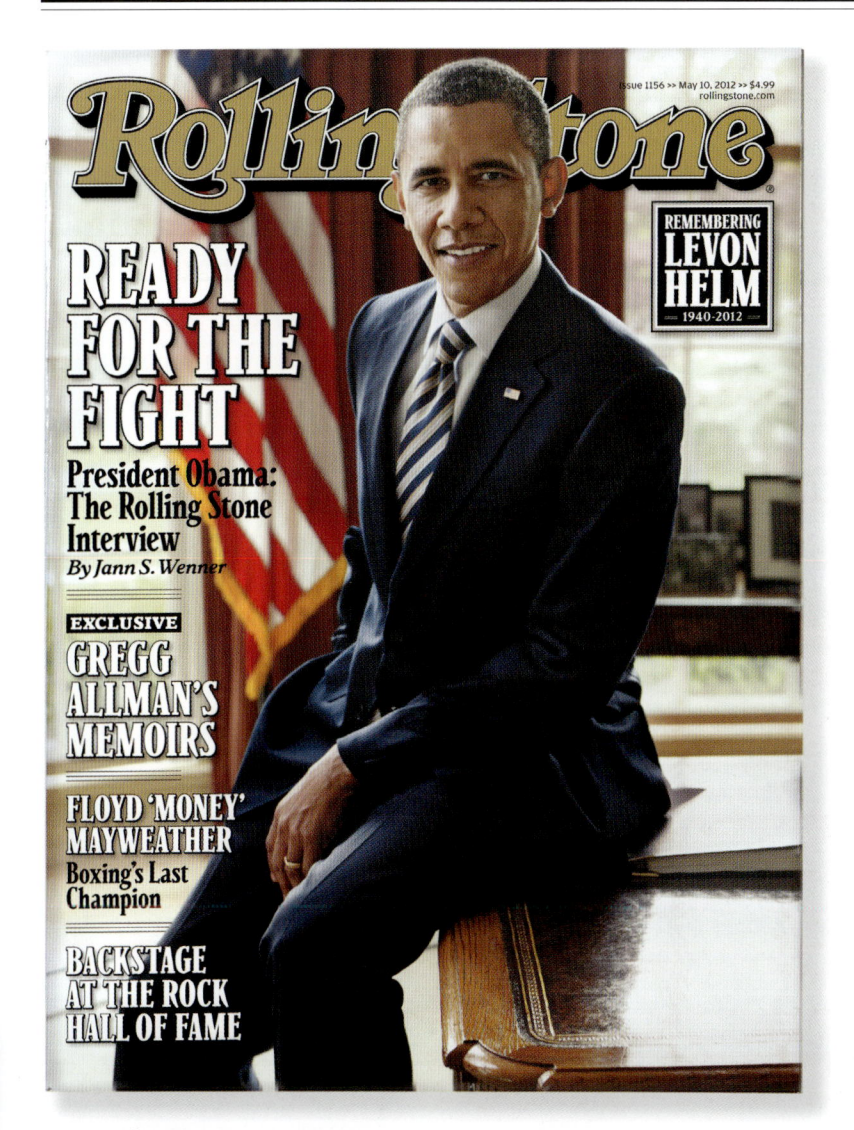

RS 1156 | BARACK OBAMA | May 10th, 2012 | Photograph by Mark Seliger

"MY VIEW ON RACE HAS ALWAYS BEEN THAT IT'S COMPLICATED. IT'S NOT JUST A MATTER of head – it's a matter of heart. It's about interactions. What happens in the workplace, in schools, on sports fields, and through music and culture shapes racial attitudes as much as any legislation that's passed. I do believe that we're making slow and steady progress. When I talk to Malia and Sasha, the world they're growing up with, with their friends, is just very different from the world that you and I grew up with." —*Barack Obama*

RS 1153 | BRUCE SPRINGSTEEN
March 29th, 2012
Photograph by Mark Seliger

JON STEWART: You've been writing about poor men wanting to be rich, rich men wanting to be king since the Seventies. That's what I like about what you were saying earlier – there's a certain universality to it that's ageless. The motivations don't seem to change.

BRUCE SPRINGSTEEN: For the majority of my lifetime, you saw an increase in inequality. It has only been in the news since Occupy Wall Street, but it was something that was a long, long time coming, and I think that, for better or for worse, I experienced the dynamic as a child, and it was something that I never forgot. I experienced what happens when, say, the male figure in your house struggles to work, can't find work, and the woman in the house becomes the primary breadwinner. That was my house. That's happening in homes all across America right now: guys that worked outside, guys that worked construction, guys that worked manufacturing, particularly those kinds of guys, suddenly those jobs disappeared. Their attitude, their education may not be suited immediately for the service economy – the economy now. It's been devastating on middle-class and blue-collar men, particularly. That was my story, that was the story I've written about.

[EXCERPT FROM RS 1153 COVER STORY]

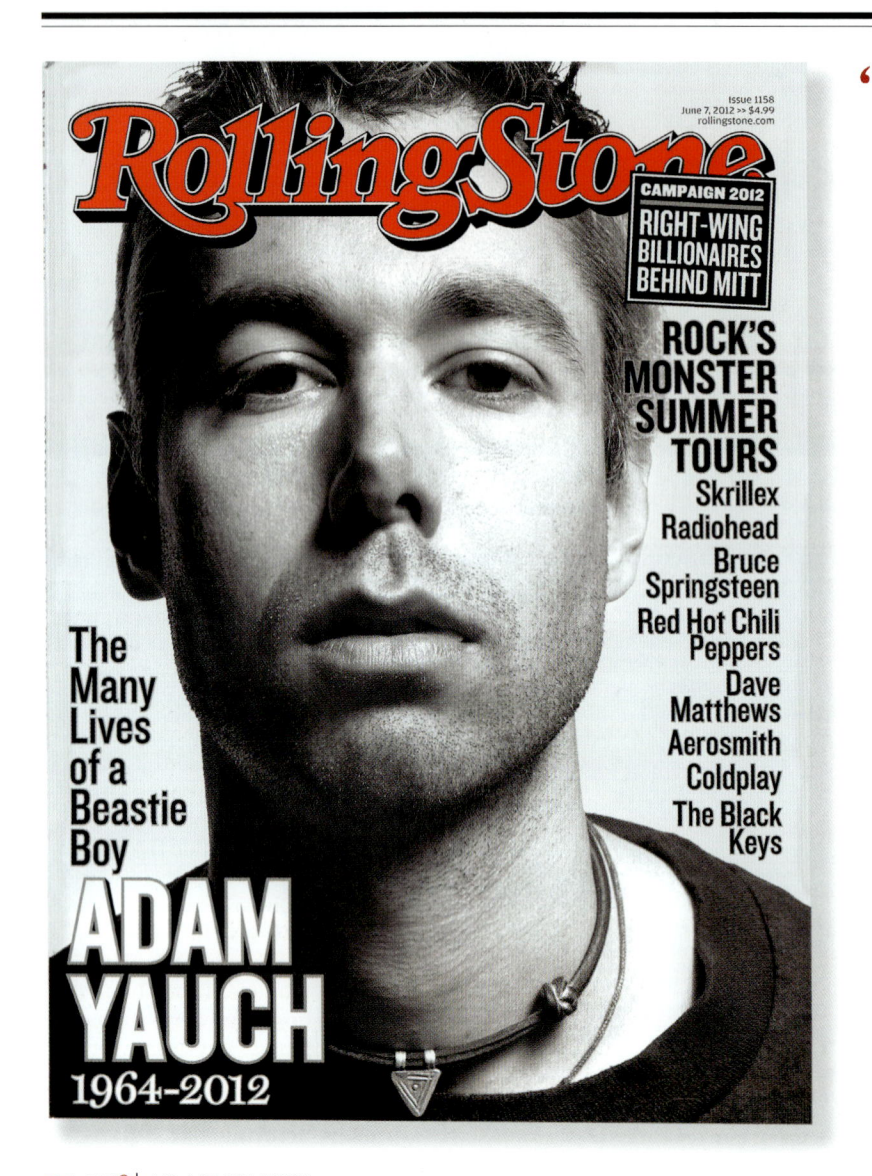

"**Western** society teaches us that if you get enough money, power and beautiful people to have sex with, that's going to bring you happiness. That's what every commercial, every magazine, music, movie teaches us. That's a fallacy. Maybe there was some realization of that during that *Licensed to Ill* period." —*Adam Yauch*

RS 1158 | ADAM YAUCH
June 7th, 2012
Photograph by Marina Chavez

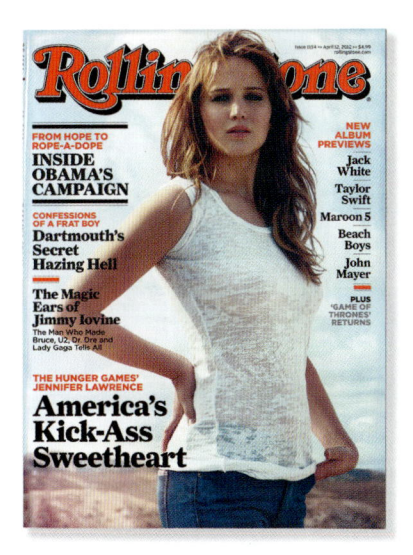

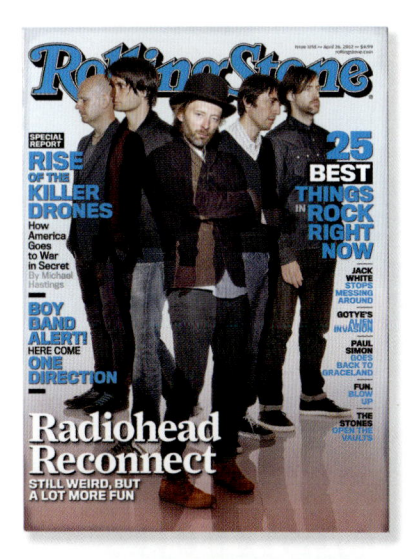

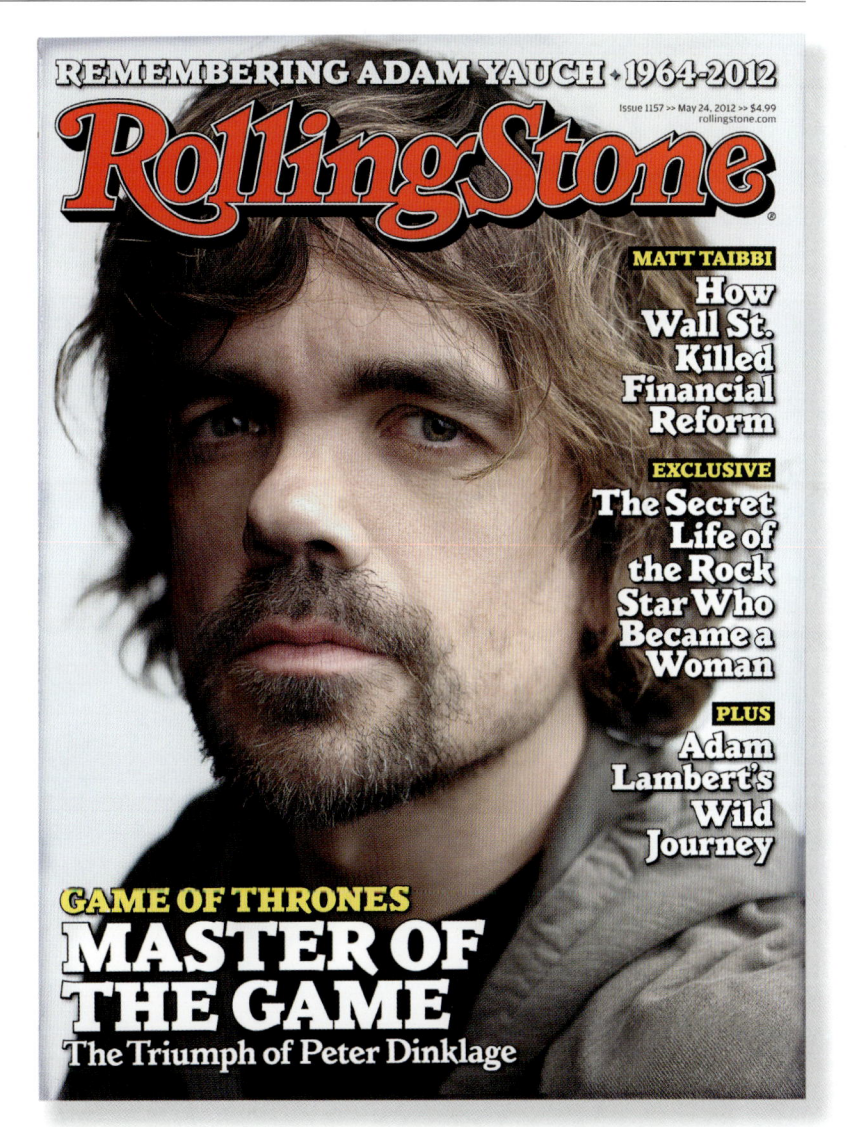

RS 1154 | JENNIFER LAWRENCE
April 12th, 2012
Photograph by Theo Wenner

RS 1155 | RADIOHEAD
April 26th, 2012
Photograph by Nadav Kander

RS 1157 | PETER DINKLAGE
May 24th, 2012
Photograph by Mark Seliger

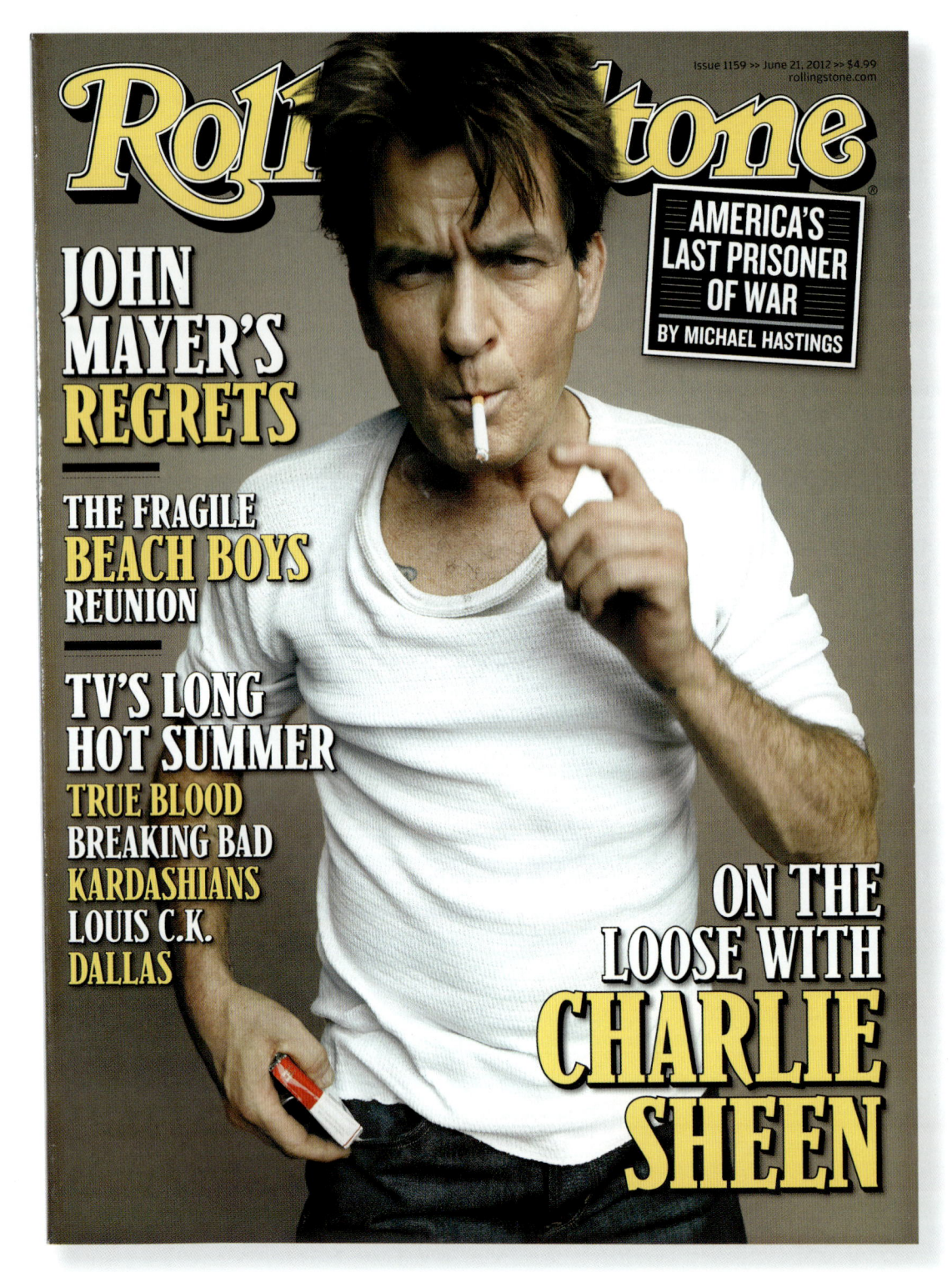

RS 1159 | CHARLIE SHEEN | June 21st, 2012 | Photograph by Peggy Sirota

TAIBBI: WALL STREET'S BID-RIGGING SCANDAL
RACHEL MADDOW'S QUIET WAR ON TELEVISION NEWS

Issue 1160/1161 >> July 5-19, 2012 >> $5.99
rollingstone.com

RollingStone

SUMMER SPECIAL

DANCE MADNESS!
THE CLUBS! THE FESTIVALS! THE DRUGS! AND THE DJS WHO RULE THE WORLD!
DEADMAU5
SKRILLEX
SWEDISH HOUSE MAFIA

RS 1160/1161 | DEADMAU5 | July 5th-19th, 2012 | Photograph by Albert Watson

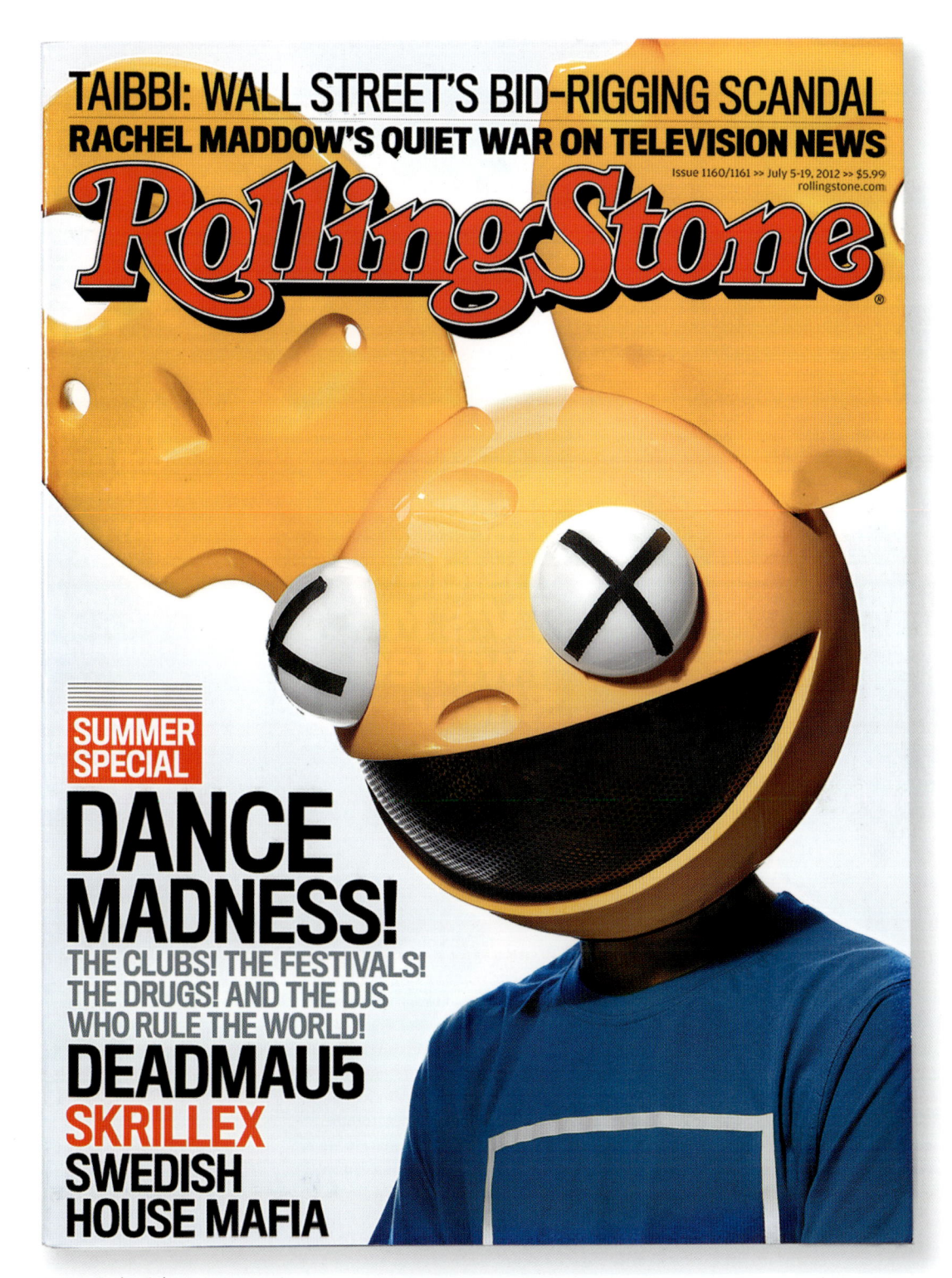

50 YEARS OF COVERS • 657

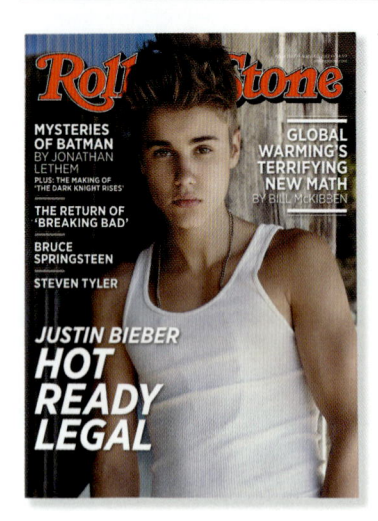

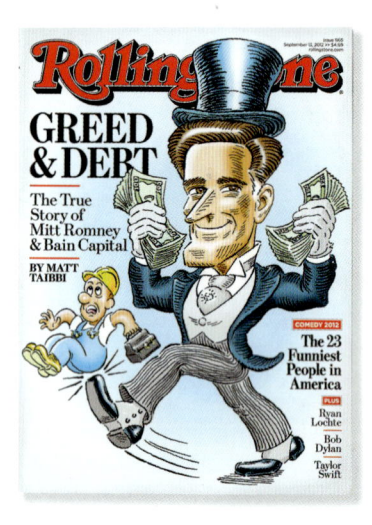

RS 1162 | JUSTIN BIEBER
August 2nd, 2012
PHOTOGRAPH BY MARK SELIGER

RS 1163 | BRYAN CRANSTON AND AARON PAUL OF 'BREAKING BAD'
August 16th, 2012
PHOTOGRAPH BY PETER YANG

RS 1165 | MITT ROMNEY
September 13th, 2012
ILLUSTRATION BY ROBERT GROSSMAN

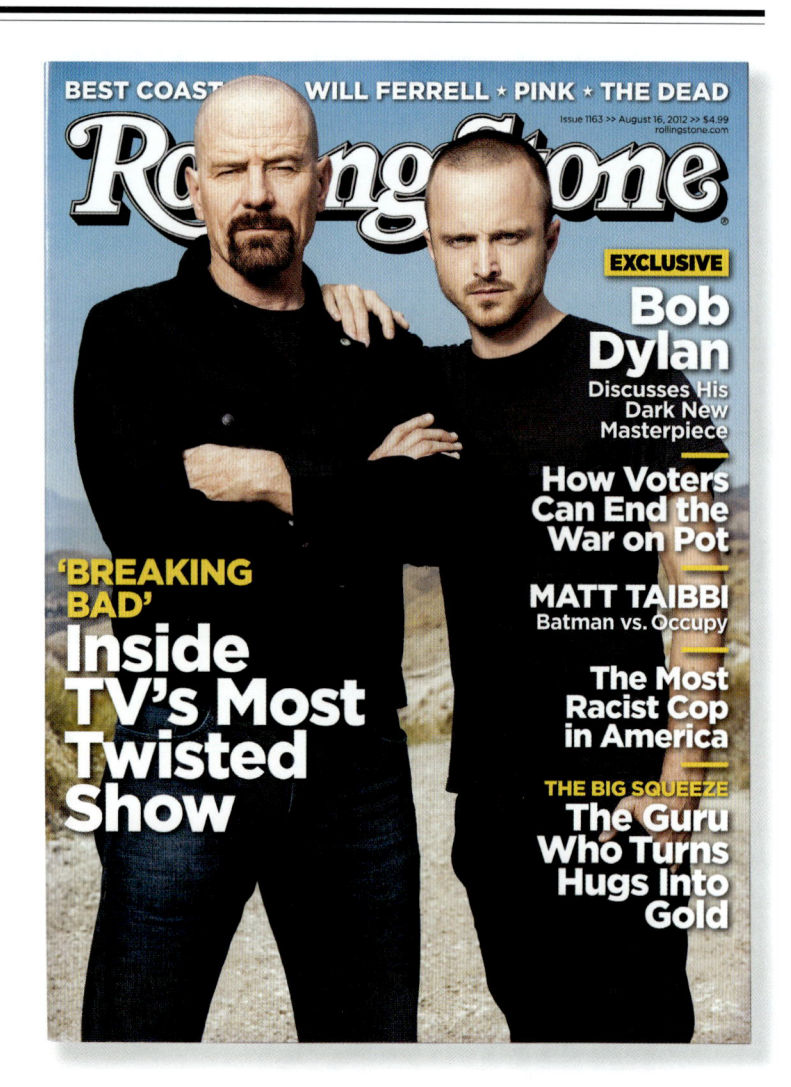

"YOU CAN HAVE A MAIN CHARACTER like Walter White or Tony Soprano or Don Draper, someone who does questionable things, but since they are the protagonist you can't help but see the world of the show more or less through their eyes. Sometimes I liken it almost to a Stockholm syndrome, where you as the viewer start to see things as they do, which is a danger when you're talking about a guy as warped as Walter White."

—*Vince Gilligan*

2010s

658 • ROLLING STONE

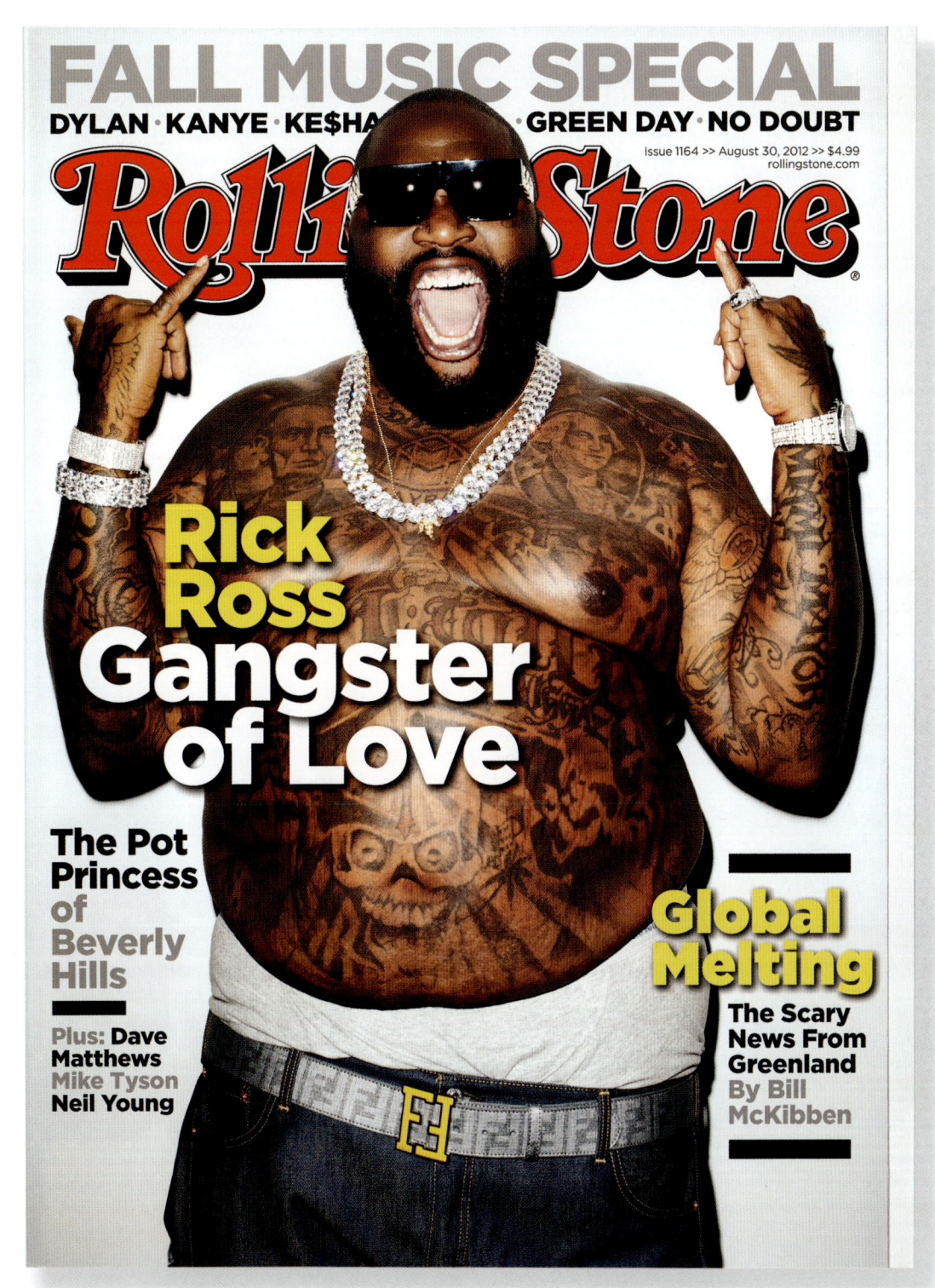

FALL MUSIC SPECIAL
DYLAN · KANYE · KE$HA · GREEN DAY · NO DOUBT

Issue 1164 >> August 30, 2012 >> $4.99
rollingstone.com

Rolling Stone

Rick Ross
Gangster of Love

The Pot Princess of Beverly Hills

Plus: Dave Matthews, Mike Tyson, Neil Young

Global Melting
The Scary News From Greenland By Bill McKibben

RS 1164 | RICK ROSS | August 30th, 2012 | Photograph by Terry Richardson

50 YEARS OF COVERS • 659

Rolling Stone

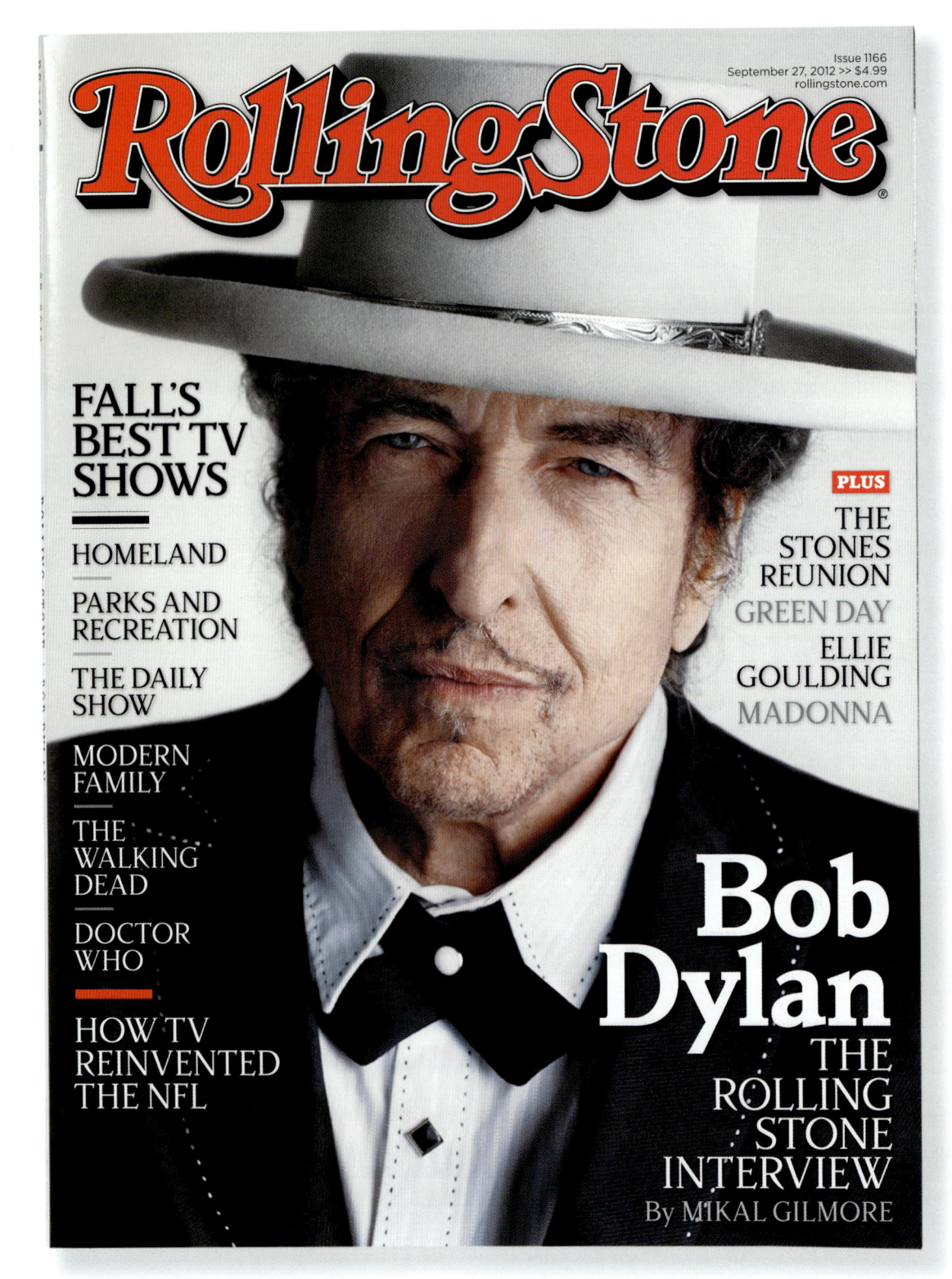

Issue 1166
September 27, 2012 >> $4.99
rollingstone.com

FALL'S BEST TV SHOWS

HOMELAND

PARKS AND RECREATION

THE DAILY SHOW

MODERN FAMILY

THE WALKING DEAD

DOCTOR WHO

HOW TV REINVENTED THE NFL

PLUS
THE STONES REUNION
GREEN DAY
ELLIE GOULDING
MADONNA

Bob Dylan
THE ROLLING STONE INTERVIEW
By Mikal Gilmore

2010s

DO YOU VOTE?

RS 1166 | BOB DYLAN
September 27th, 2012
PHOTOGRAPH BY SAM JONES

Uh...

Should we do that? Should we vote?

Yeah, why not vote? I respect the voting process. Everybody ought to have the right to vote. We live in a democracy. What do you want me to say? Voting is a good thing.

I was curious if you vote.

[*Smiling*] Huh?

What's your estimation of President Obama been when you've met him?

What do I think of him? I like him. But you're asking the wrong person. You know who you should be asking that to? You should be asking his wife what she thinks of him. She's the only one that matters. Look, I only met him a few times. I mean, what do you want me to say? He loves music. He's personable. He dresses good. What the fuck do you want me to say?

You live in these times, you have reactions to various national ups and downs. Are you, for example, disappointed by the resistance the president has met with? Would you like to see him re-elected?

I've lived through a lot of presidents! And you have too! Some are re-elected and some aren't. Being re-elected isn't the mark of a great president. Sometimes the guy you get rid of is the guy you wish you had back.

I've brought up the subject partly because of something you said the night he was elected: "It looks like things are gonna change now." Do you feel that the change you anticipated has been borne out?

You want to repeat that again? I have no idea what I said.

It was election night 2008. Onstage at the University of Minnesota, introducing your band's members, you said, "Tony Gamier, wearing the Obama button. Tony likes to think it's a brand-new time right now. An age of light. Me, I was born in 1941 – that's the year they bombed Pearl Harbor. Well, I been living in a world of darkness ever since. But it looks like things are gonna change now."

I don't know what I said or didn't say. As far as Tony goes, yeah, maybe he was wearing an Obama button and maybe I said some stuff because right there in the moment it all made sense. Maybe I said things looked like they could change. And maybe they did change. I don't think I could have predicted how they would change, but whatever was said, it was said for people in that hall for that night. You know what I'm saying? It wasn't said to be played on a record forever. Or did I go down to the middle of town and give a speech?

[EXCERPT FROM RS 1166 COVER STORY BY MIKAL GILMORE]

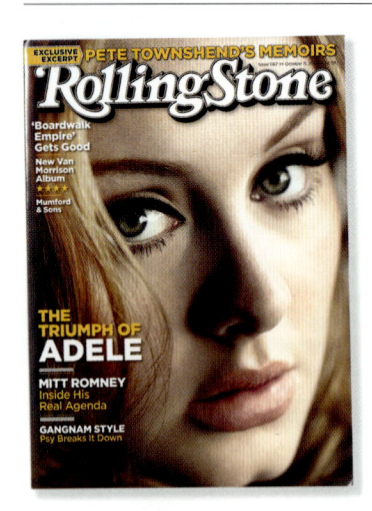

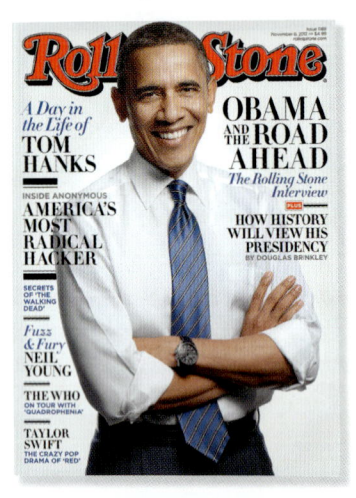

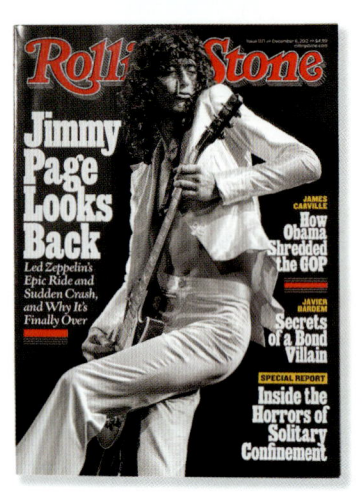

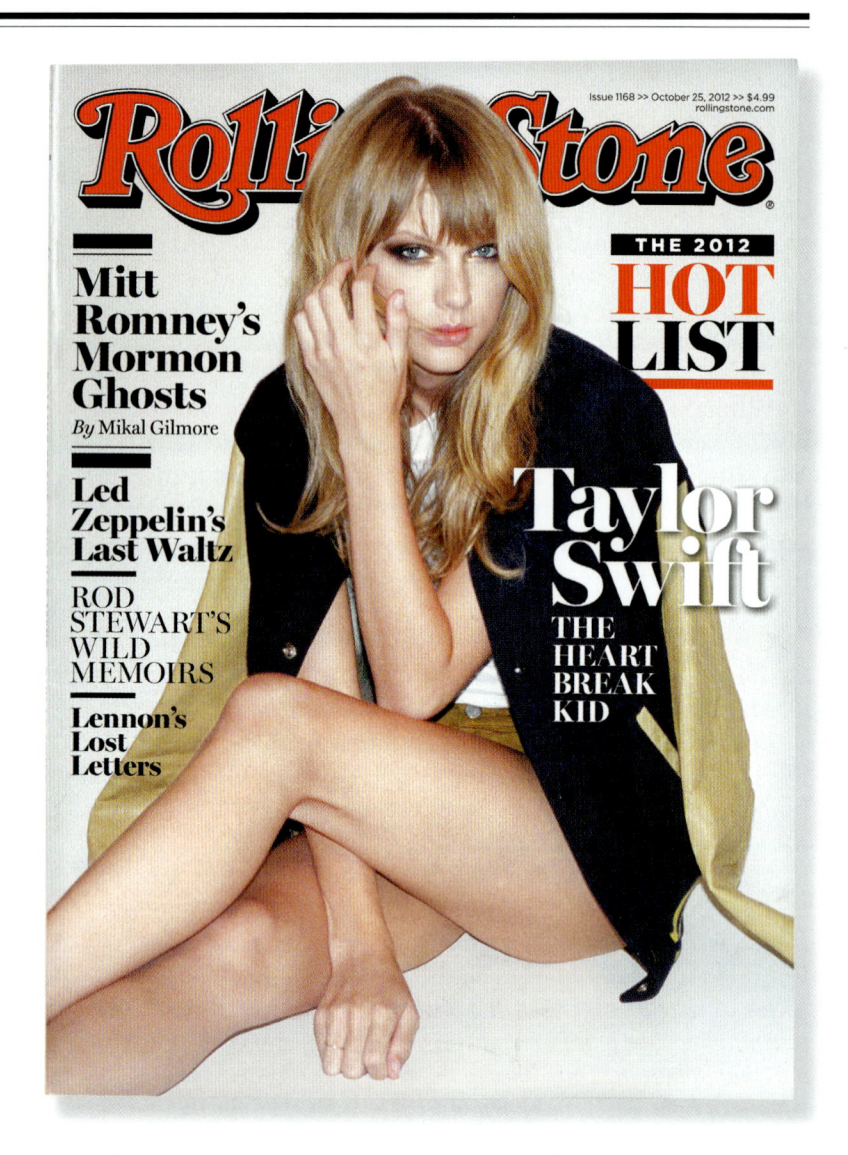

RS 1167 | ADELE
October 11th, 2012
Photograph by Simon Emmett

RS 1169 | BARACK OBAMA
November 8th, 2012
Photograph by Mark Seliger

RS 1171 | JIMMY PAGE
December 6th, 2012
Photograph by Neal Preston

RS 1168 | TAYLOR SWIFT
October 25th, 2012
Photograph by Theo Wenner

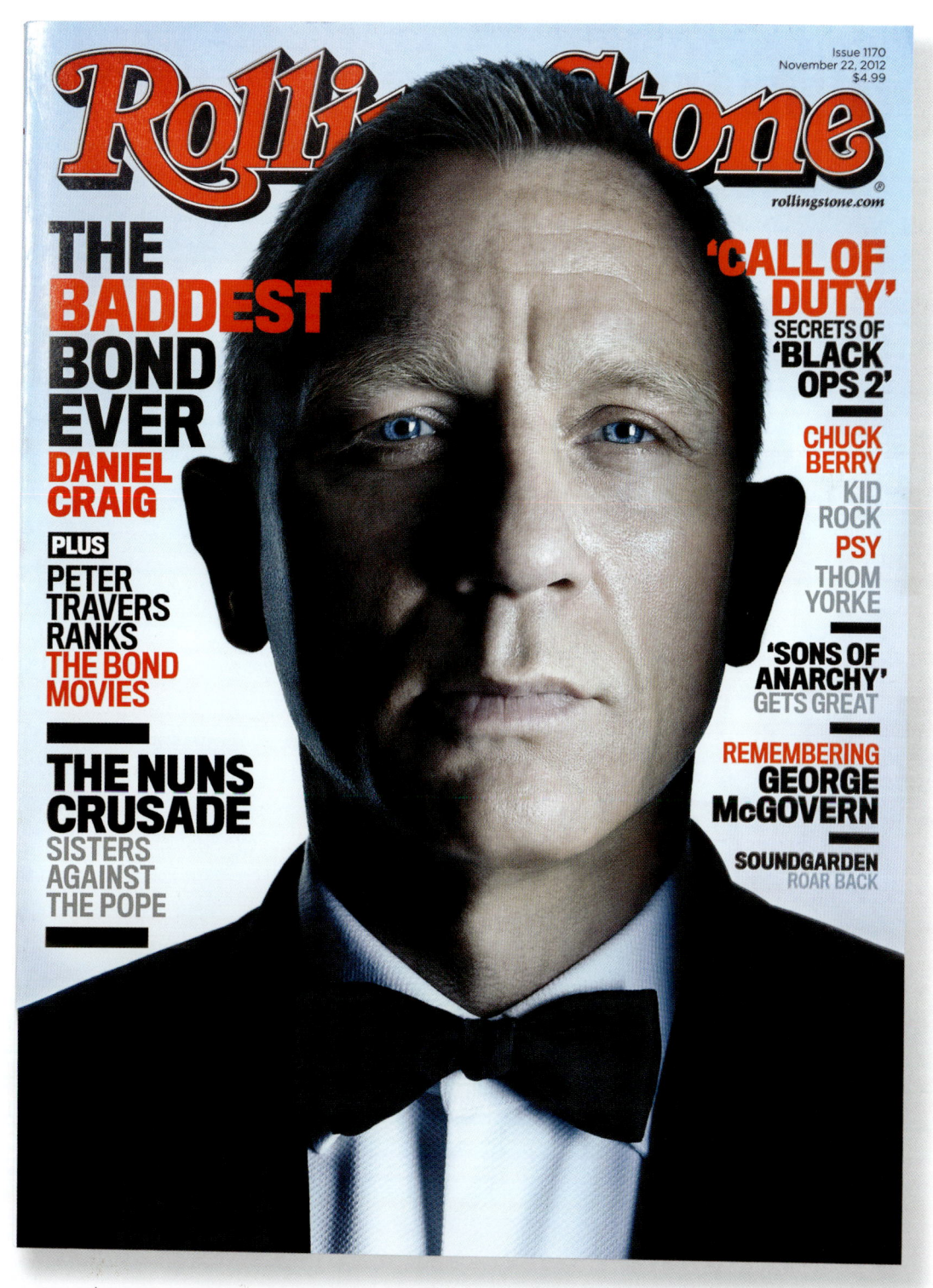

RS 1170 | DANIEL CRAIG AS JAMES BOND | November 22nd, 2012 | Photograph by Matthew Rolston

THE BEST ALBUMS & SONGS OF 2012

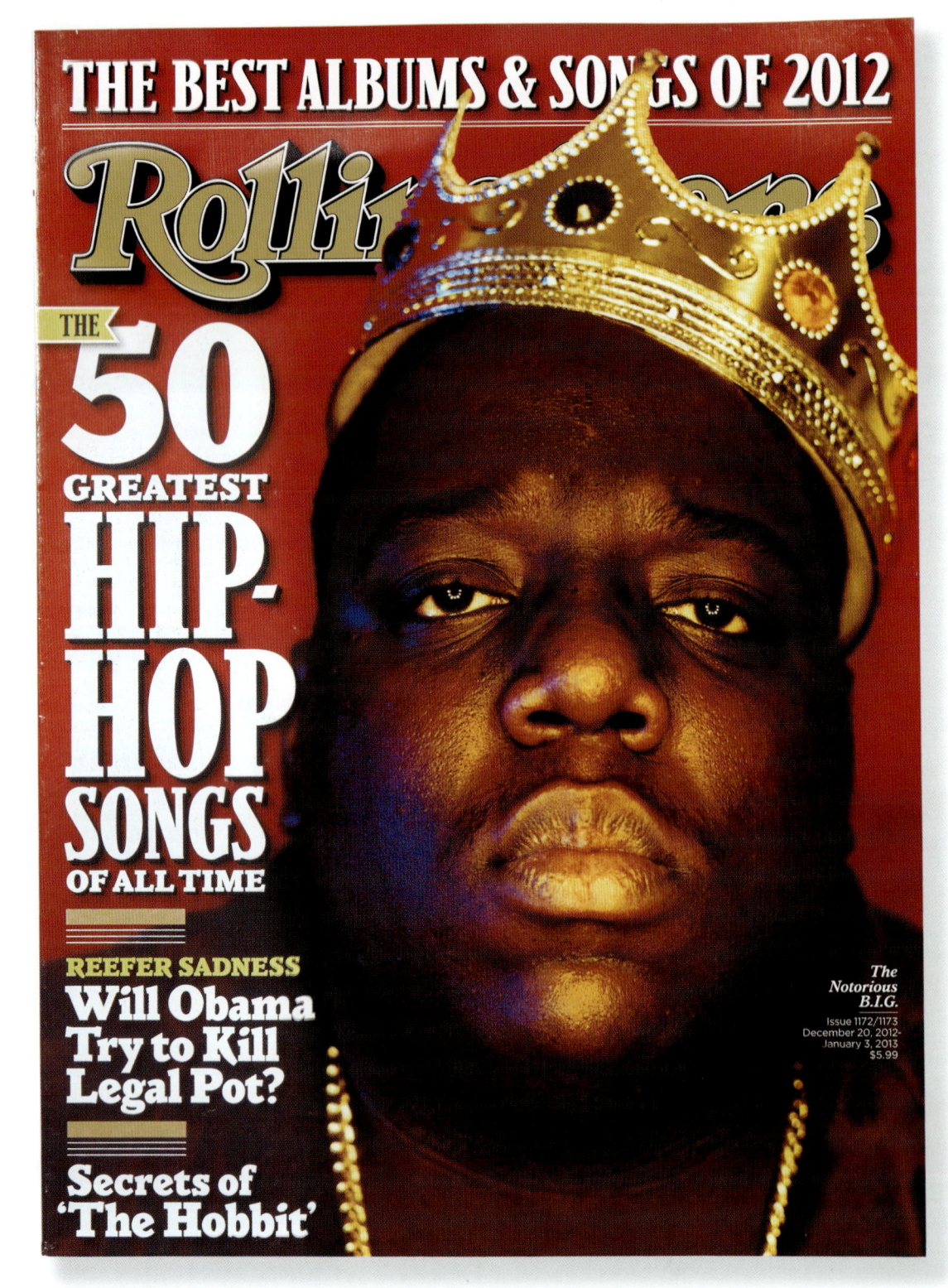

Rolling Stone

THE 50 GREATEST HIP-HOP SONGS OF ALL TIME

REEFER SADNESS
Will Obama Try to Kill Legal Pot?

Secrets of 'The Hobbit'

The Notorious B.I.G.
Issue 1172/1173
December 20, 2012–
January 3, 2013
$5.99

2010s

RS 1172/1173 | THE 50 GREATEST HIP-HOP SONGS OF ALL TIME | December 20th, 2012–January 3rd, 2013 | VARIOUS PHOTOGRAPHERS

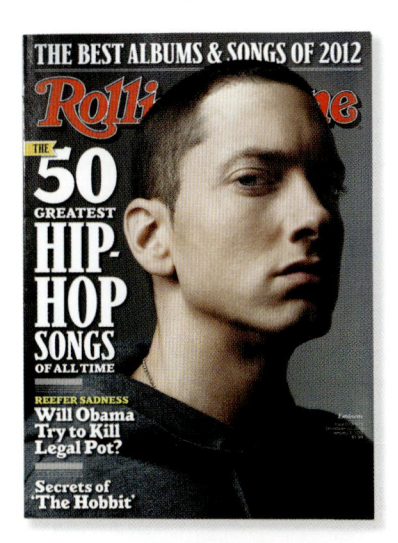

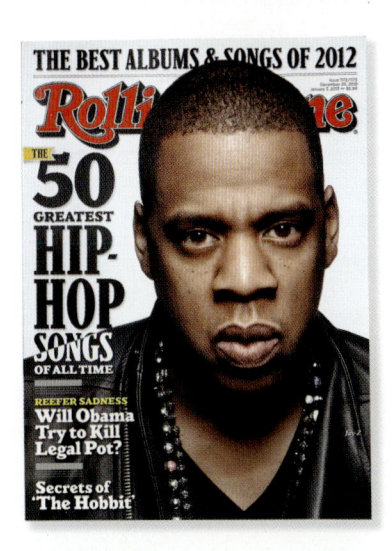

The photo of the Notorious B.I.G. was taken by Barron Claiborne just three days before the rapper's death, in March 1997. 2Pac was shot by Chi Modu in 1996. Mark Seliger's images of Eminem and Jay-Z are both from 2010. And the greatest hip-hop song of all time? "The Message," by Grandmaster Flash and the Furious Five.

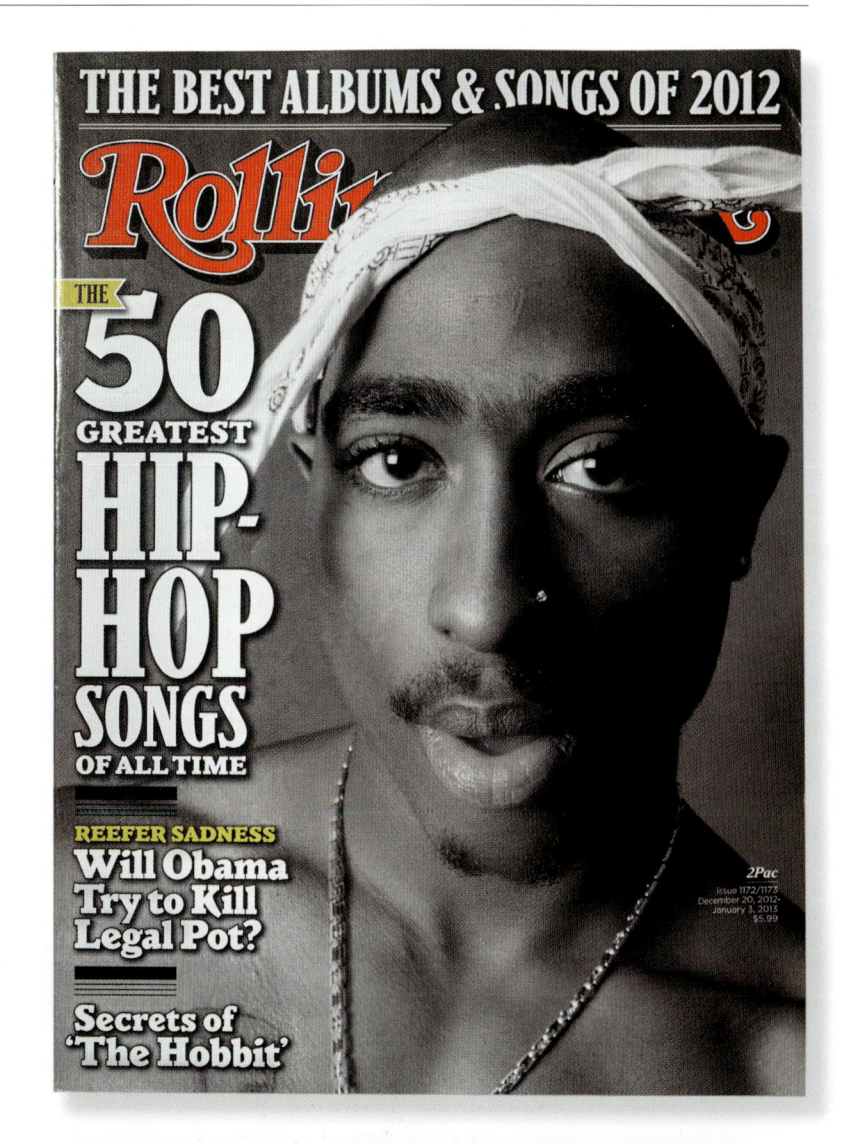

"*2Pac was able to go where* other MCs feared to tread: to address a song to his mother. He destroyed all other hardcore rappers by just saying 'Ya know, I'm gonna touch a soul.'"

—*Chuck D*

50 YEARS OF COVERS • 665

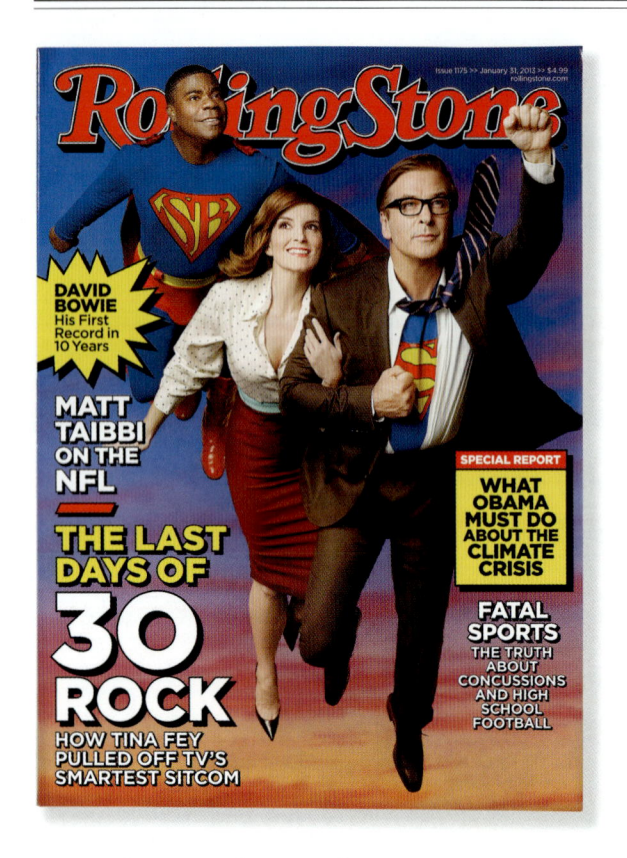

RS 1175 | CAST OF '30 ROCK'
January 31st, 2013
Photograph by Mark Seliger

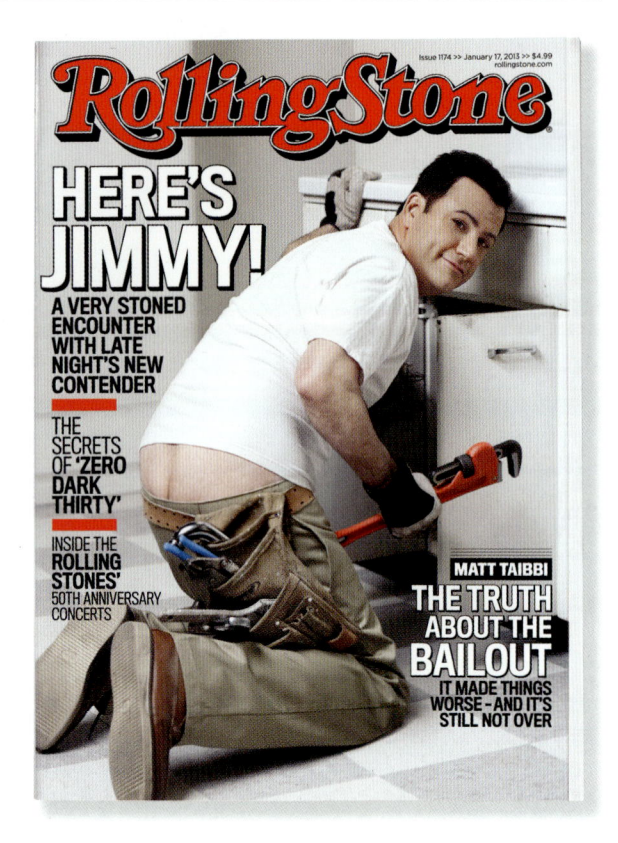

RS 1174 | JIMMY KIMMEL
January 17th, 2013
Photograph by Mark Seliger

"WHEN WE WERE GOING TO DO THE COVER, MY PUBLICIST Lewis was very much against showing my crack plumber-style, but I fought him on it. In retrospect, Lewis was correct."
—*Jimmy Kimmel*

2010s

666 · ROLLING STONE

Issue 1176 >> February 14, 2013 >> $4.99
rollingstone.com

Rolling Stone

BILLY JOEL
READY FOR A COMEBACK?

THE NRA VS. AMERICA
THE POWERS BEHIND THE MERCHANTS OF DEATH

RAPE & THE MILITARY
AN EPIDEMIC OF ASSAULT & COVER-UPS

MGMT
JIM JAMES

Rihanna
CRAZY IN LOVE

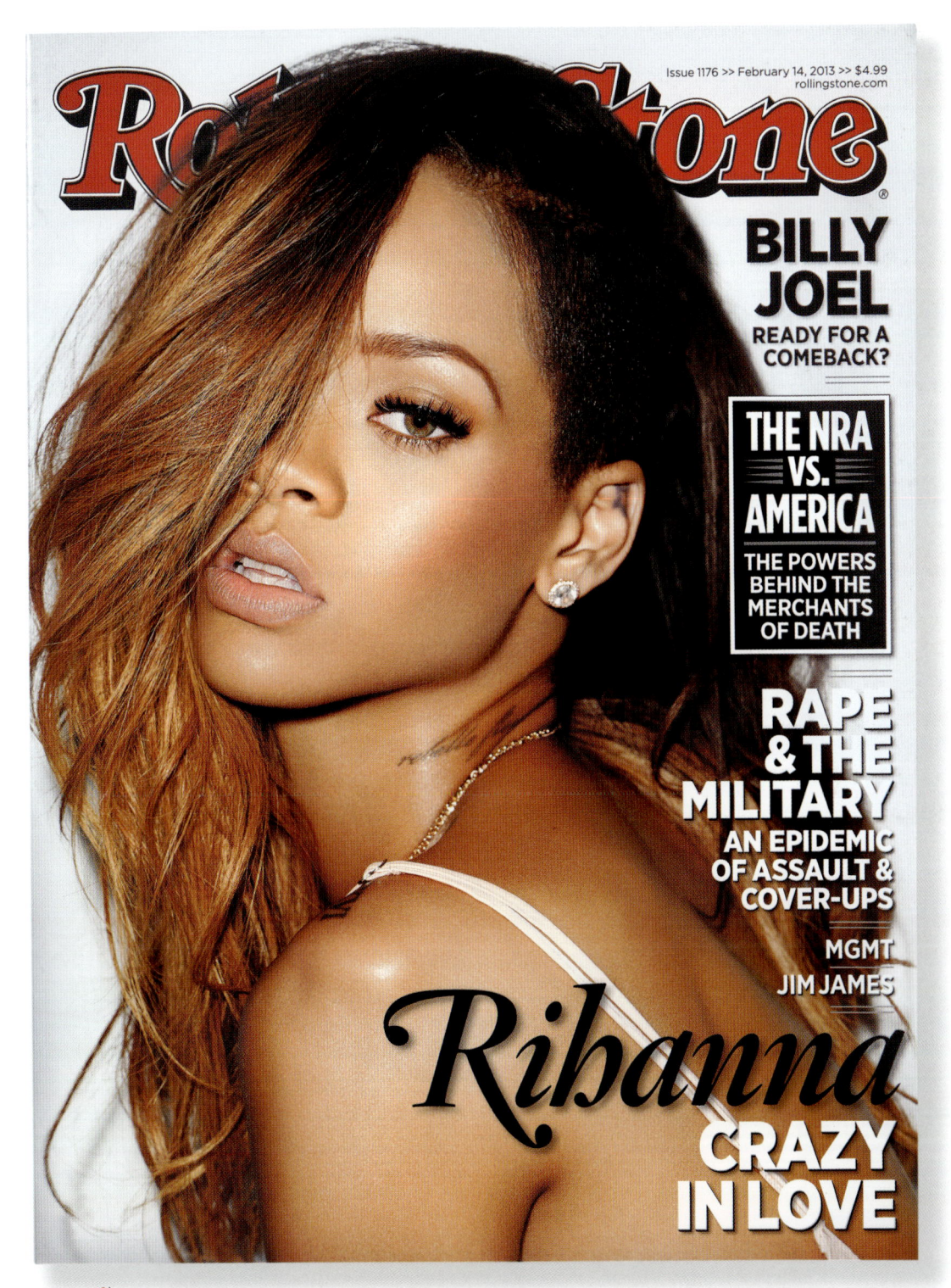

RS 1176 | RIHANNA | February 14th, 2013 | PHOTOGRAPH BY TERRY RICHARDSON

Rolling Stone

Issue 1177 >> February 28, 2013 >> $4.99
rollingstone.com

LENA DUNHAM
Anxiety, Bad Sex & the Best Show on TV

GANGSTER BANKERS
How HSBC Hooked Up With Drug Traffickers and Terrorists. And Got Away With It
BY MATT TAIBBI

BLACK SABBATH REUNITE

FUTURE SHOCK
AL GORE'S GRIM WARNING

ON THE ROAD WITH MUSE

PLUS
FALL OUT BOY
MACKLEMORE

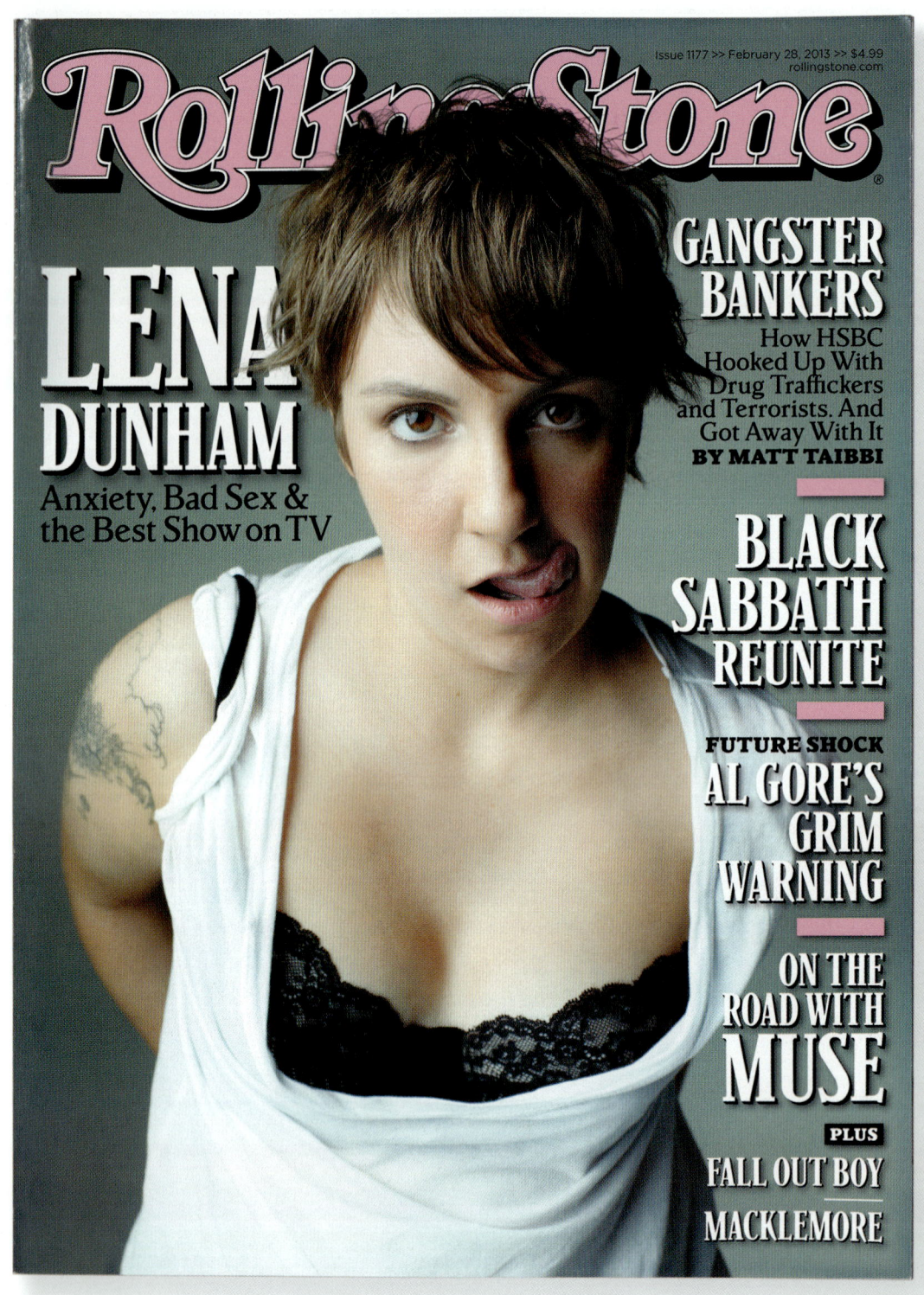

2010s

RS 1177 | LENA DUNHAM | February 28th, 2013 | Photograph by Peggy Sirota

DESCRIBE YOUR FIRST WEEK IN REHAB, AT HOME.

I was going through withdrawal. That was gruesome, laying on the bathroom floor and just feeling like... [*pauses*] I didn't realize how much that stuff affected me. And it's not the stuff that is immediately in your system. It goes back to how long you've been using. It was working its way out.

I was going through so much shit. Even into the second week, I was like, "I don't belong here. I'm not convinced." The sick part of it is I wanted to get all of the narcotics out of my system so I could start drinking. But that's the insanity of the whole thing. You make excuses. You rationalize. You can take a shit in a mailbox. That doesn't mean it's the right thing to do.

Did you speak with Mike or Tré while you were in rehab? Did you know what they were feeling?

There was semicontact. I think Tré was scared. Life got real serious there for a while. Mike was fucking pissed. Right when I got home, after [Las Vegas] happened, he said all this stuff. It was everything within three or four sentences: "You're scaring me. You're fucking up your life. You're fucking up everybody else's life. You need to get your shit together."

The great thing is we've known each other for so long that we can be like that without coming to blows. After about three and a half weeks [in rehab], I started going down to this doughnut shop to have coffee. And sure enough, one day, here comes Mike Dirnt, walking down the street. We sat down and had a great talk. Me and Mike have been friends since we were 10. Sometimes Green Day gets in the way of that, because we're around it so much.

[EXCERPT FROM RS 1178 COVER STORY BY DAVID FRICKE]

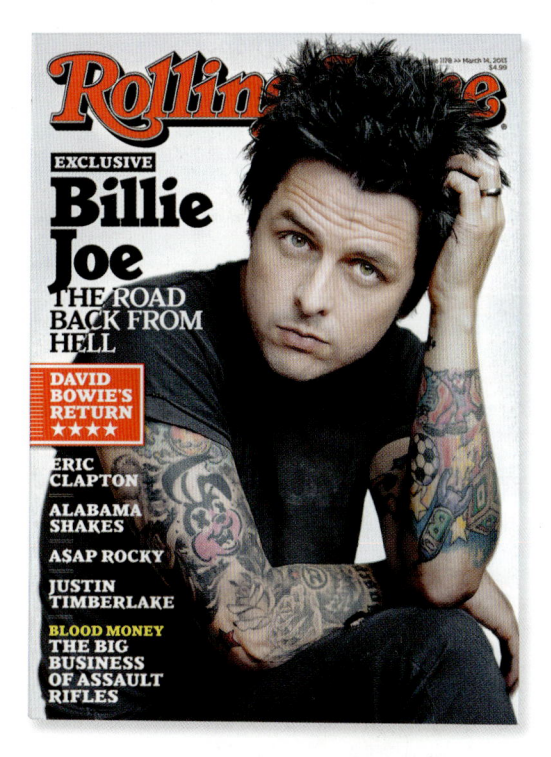

RS 1178 | BILLIE JOE ARMSTRONG
March 14th, 2013
Photograph by Danny Clinch

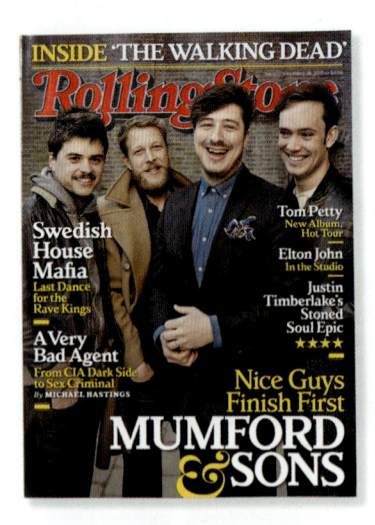

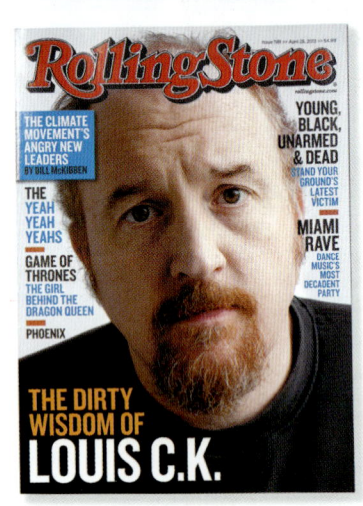

RS 1179 | MUMFORD & SONS
March 28th, 2013
Photograph by Sam Jones

RS 1181 | LOUIS C.K.
April 25th, 2013
Photograph by Terry Richardson

RS 1180 | JON HAMM
April 11th, 2013
Photograph by Mark Seliger

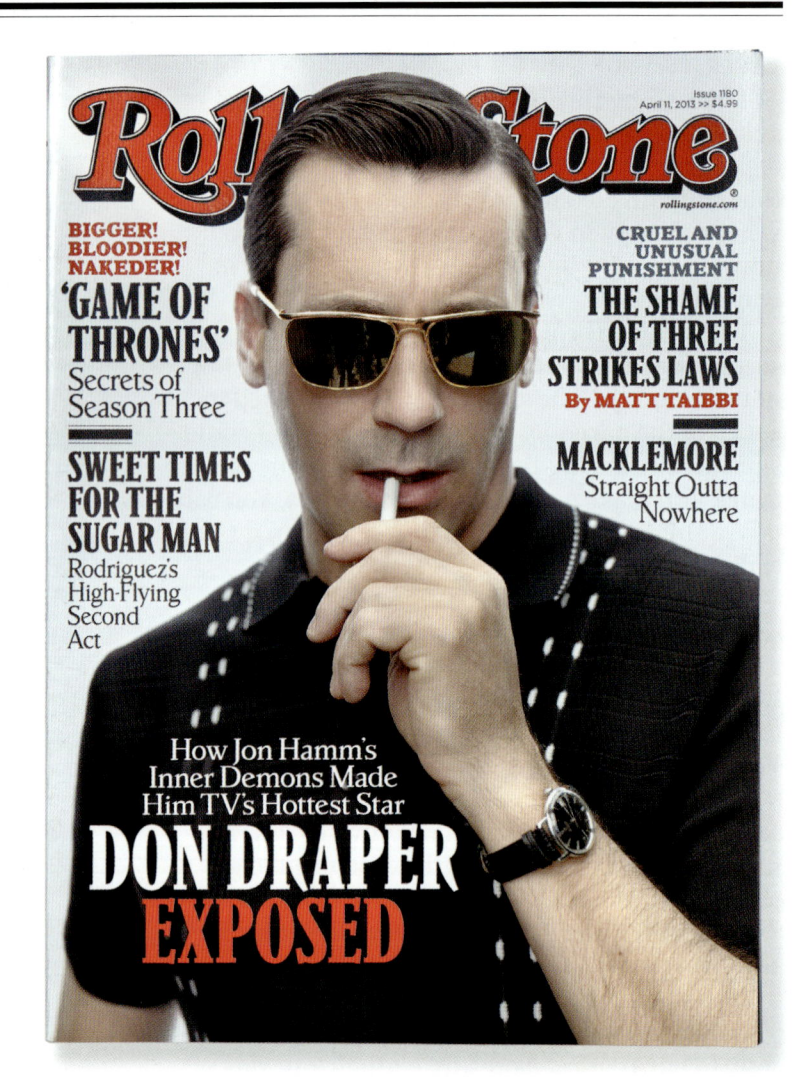

2010s

"*Don is a natural leader,* he's a natural salesman. He also has a tremendous creative streak. He'd probably publish Rolling Stone."

—*Jon Hamm*

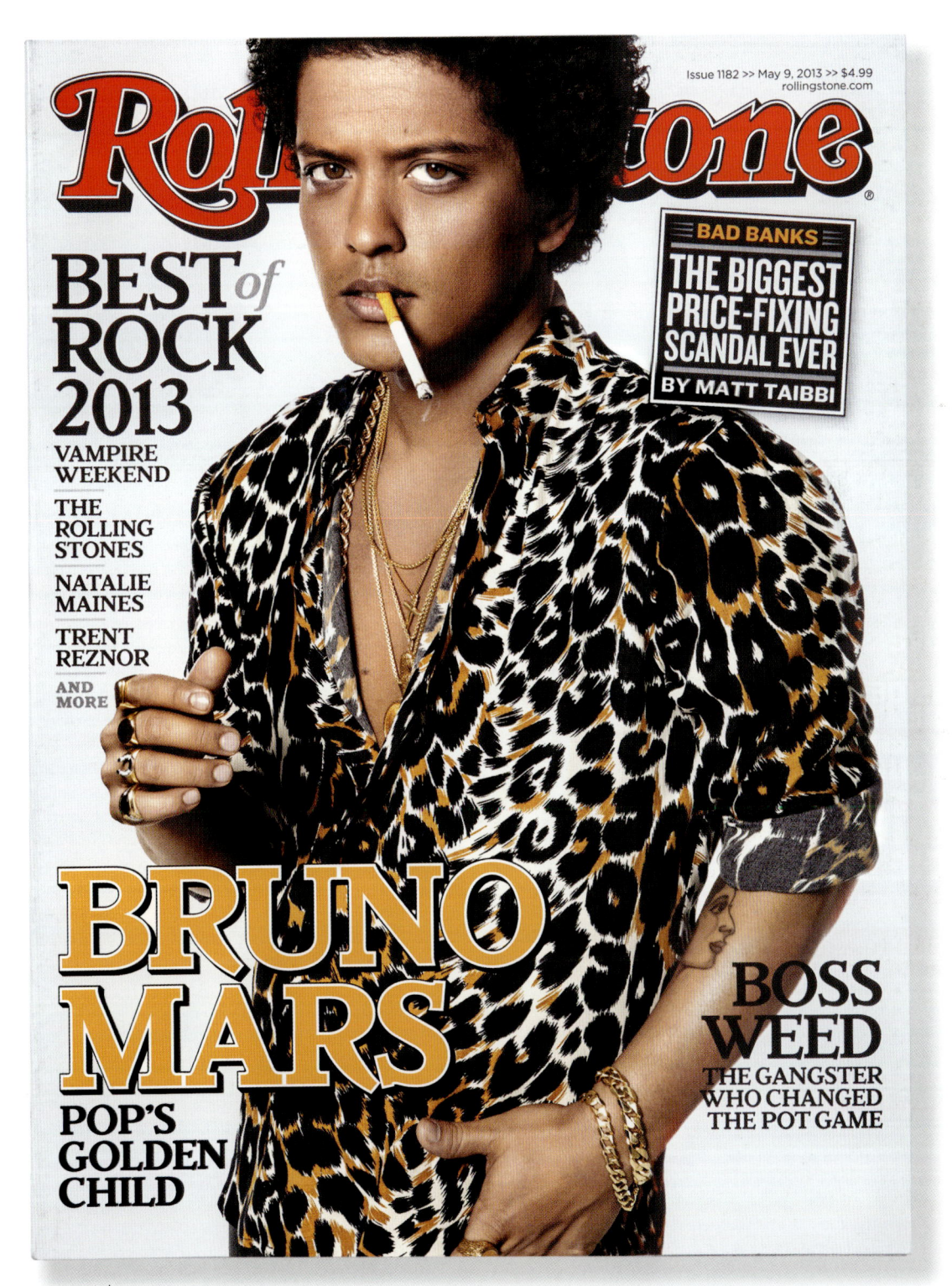

ROLLING STONE

Issue 1182 >> May 9, 2013 >> $4.99
rollingstone.com

BEST of ROCK 2013

VAMPIRE WEEKEND

THE ROLLING STONES

NATALIE MAINES

TRENT REZNOR

AND MORE

BAD BANKS
THE BIGGEST PRICE-FIXING SCANDAL EVER
BY MATT TAIBBI

BRUNO MARS
POP'S GOLDEN CHILD

BOSS WEED
THE GANGSTER WHO CHANGED THE POT GAME

RS 1182 | BRUNO MARS | May 9th, 2013 | Photograph by Theo Wenner

50 YEARS OF COVERS • 671

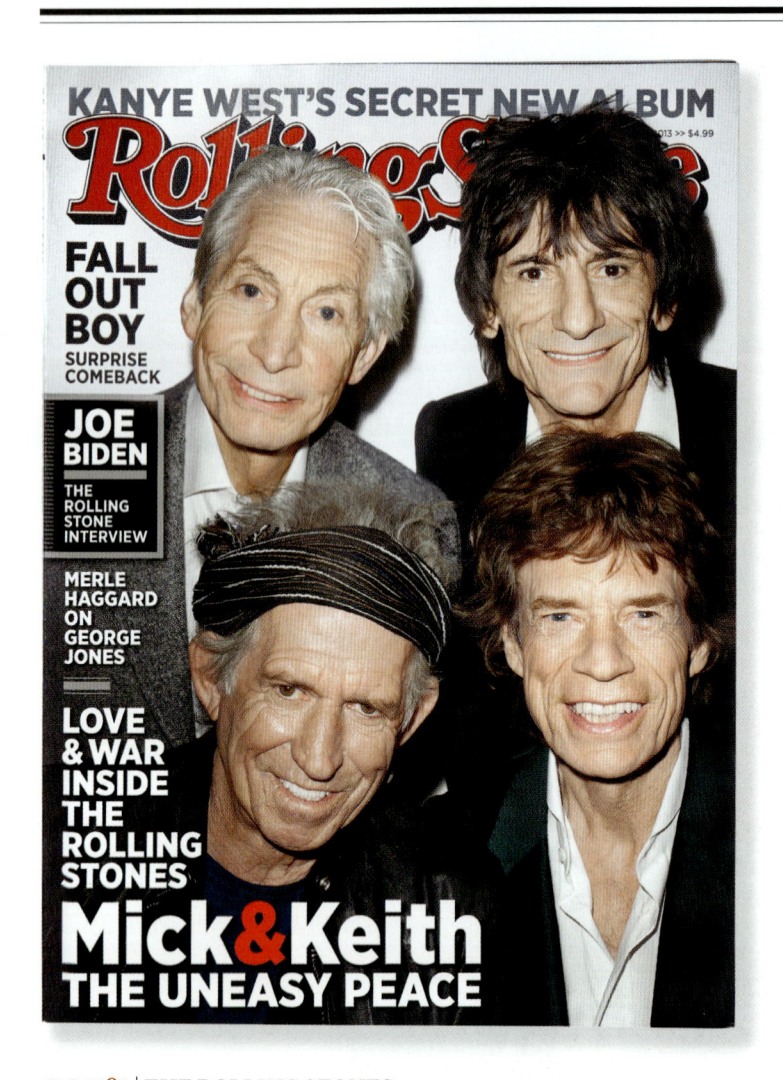

RS 1183 | **THE ROLLING STONES**
May 23rd, 2013
Photograph by Terry Richardson

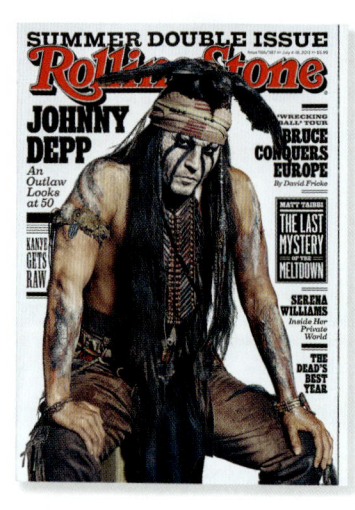

RS 1186/1187 | **JOHNNY DEPP AS TONTO**
July 4th–18th, 2013
Photograph by Theo Wenner

"**I don't have the physical need** for the drug alcohol. No, it's more my medication, my self-medication over the years just to calm the circus. Once the circus kicks in, the festivities in the brain, it can be ruthless. Maybe that's why Hunter [S. Thompson] and I got along so well. I'm able to continue for great periods of time, weirdly. For weeks. There's no great point to it, ultimately. You realize that you wouldn't treat your car that way."

—*Johnny Depp*

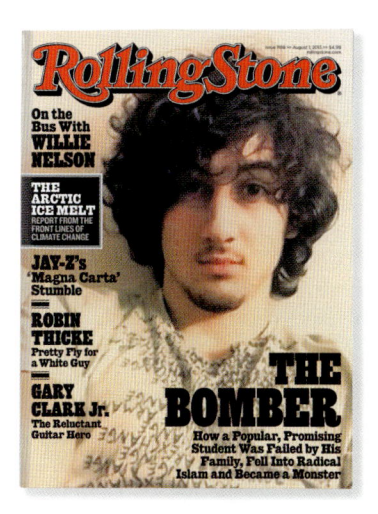

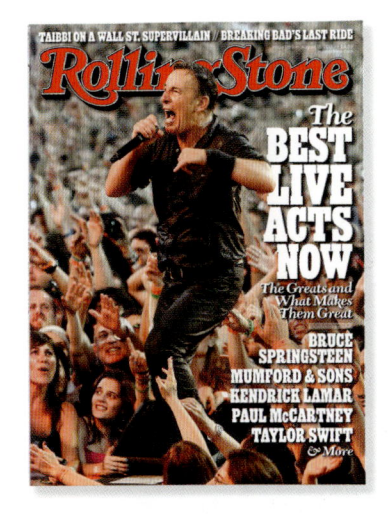

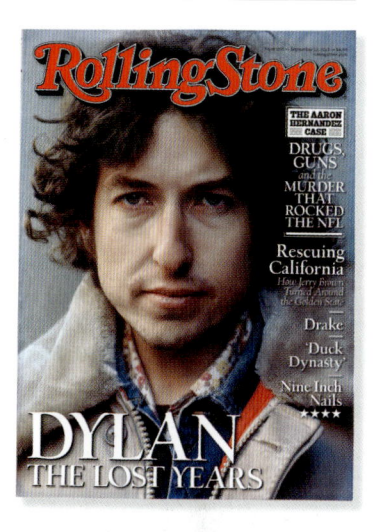

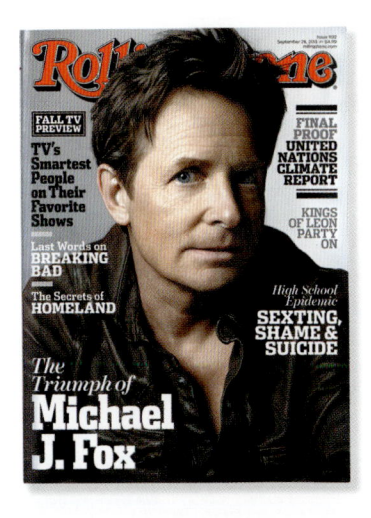

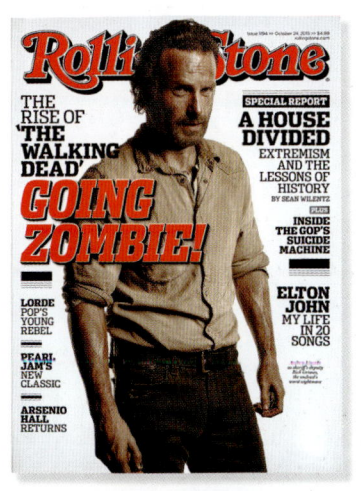

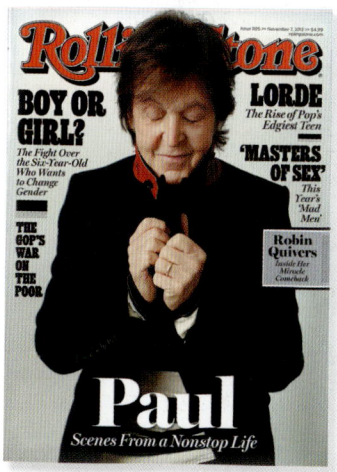

RS 1188 | DZHOKHAR
TSARNAEV
August 1st, 2013
Photo Illustration by Sean McCabe

RS 1192 | MICHAEL J. FOX
September 26th, 2013
Photograph by Mark Seliger

RS 1189 | BRUCE
SPRINGSTEEN
August 15th, 2013
Photograph by Jo Lopez

RS 1194 | ANDREW LINCOLN
OF 'THE WALKING DEAD'
October 24th, 2013
Photograph by Frank W. Ockenfels 3/AMC

RS 1191 | BOB DYLAN
September 12th, 2013
Photograph by David Gahr
(The Estate of 1971)

RS 1195 | PAUL McCARTNEY
November 7th, 2013
Photograph by Peggy Sirota

2000s

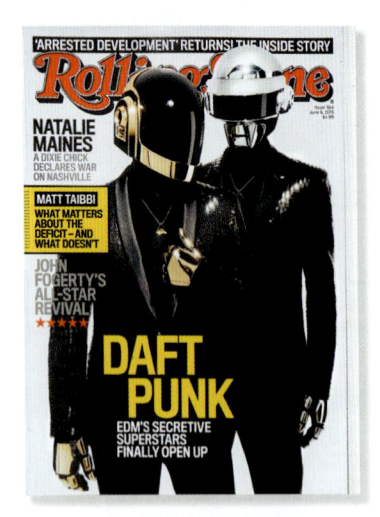

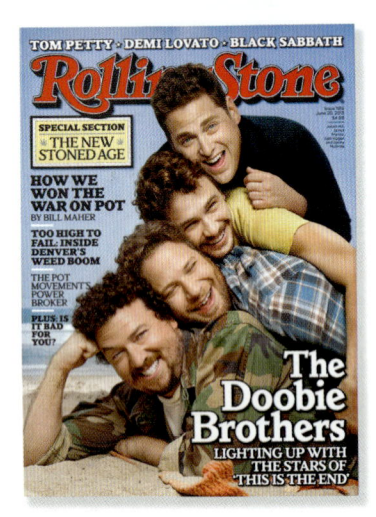

RS 1184 | DAFT PUNK
June 6th, 2013
PHOTOGRAPH BY PETER YANG

RS 1185 | CAST OF 'THIS IS THE END'
June 20th, 2013
PHOTOGRAPH BY MARTIN SCHOELLER

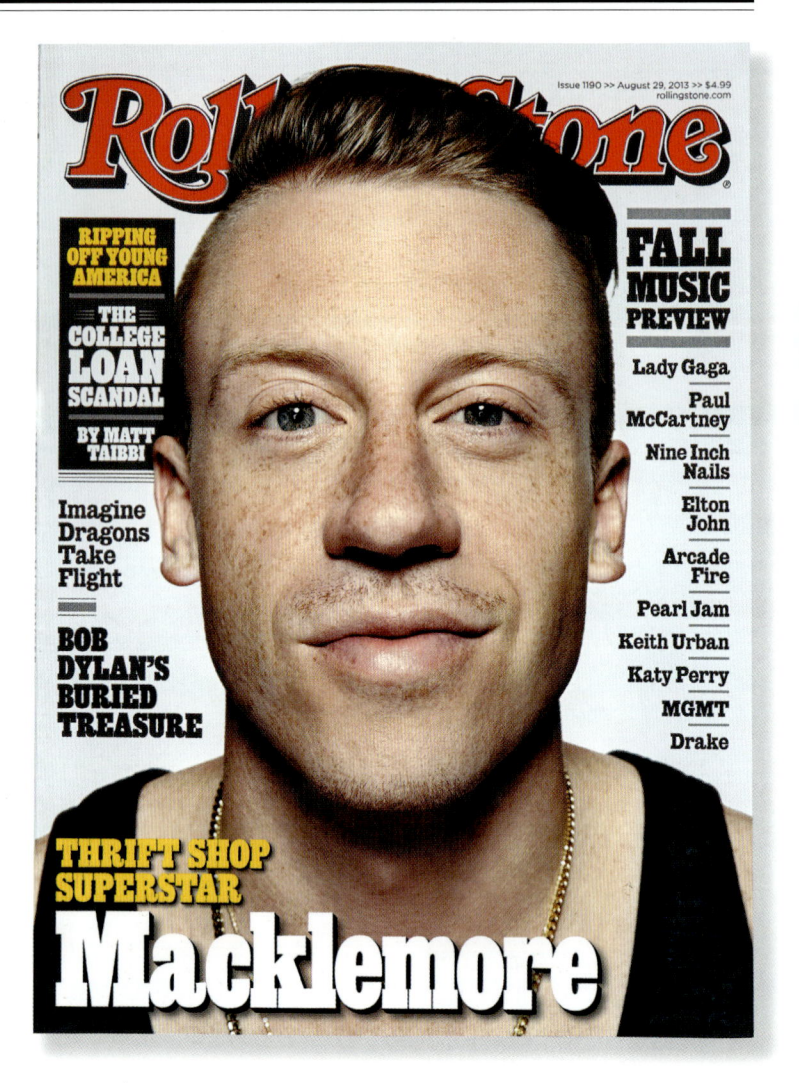

RS 1190 | MACKLEMORE
August 29th, 2013
PHOTOGRAPH BY PETER YANG

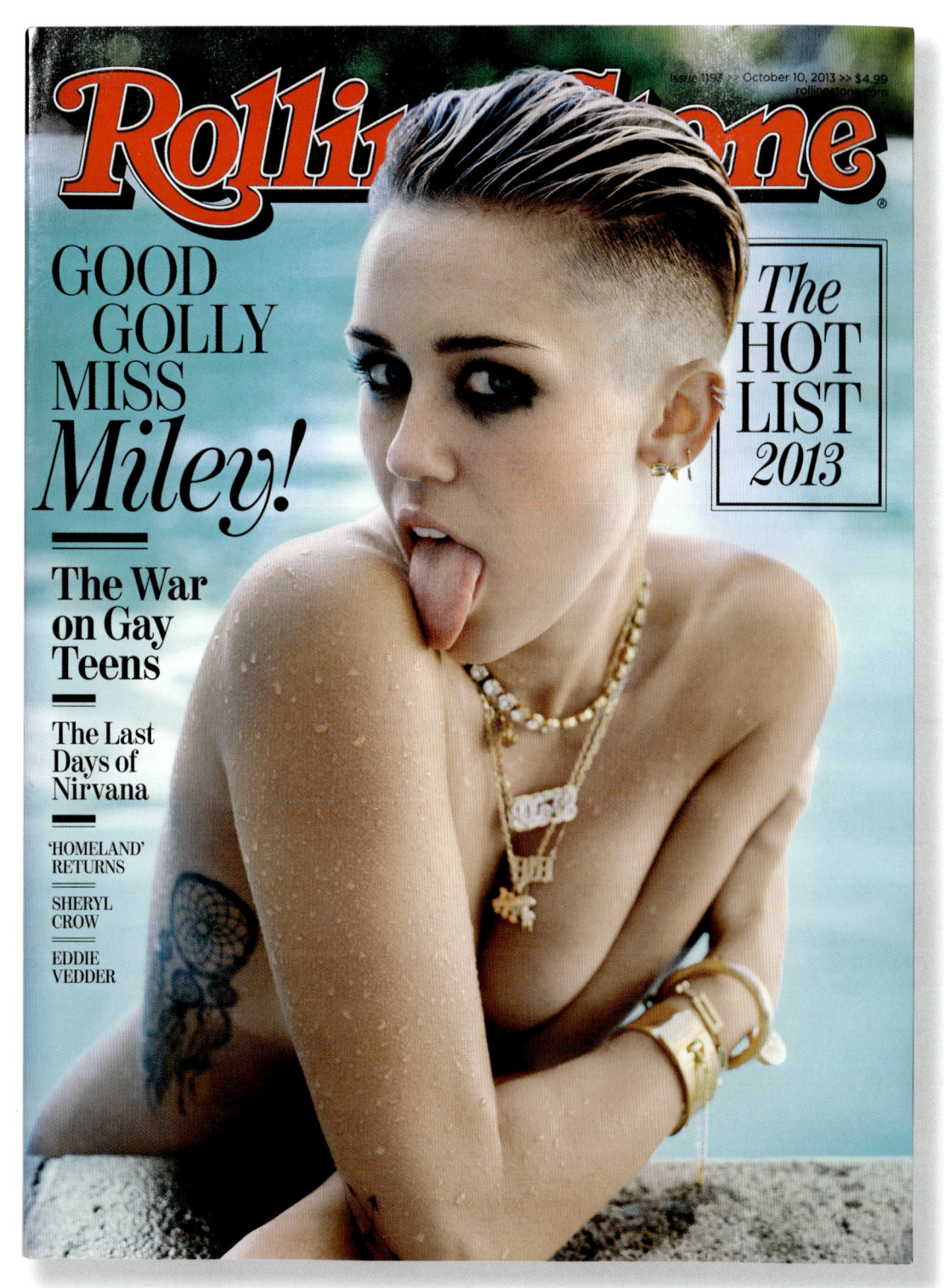

Rolling Stone

Issue 1193 | October 10, 2013 | $4.99
rollingstone.com

GOOD GOLLY MISS *Miley!*

The War on Gay Teens

The Last Days of Nirvana

'HOMELAND' RETURNS

SHERYL CROW

EDDIE VEDDER

The HOT LIST 2013

RS 1193 | MILEY CYRUS | October 10th, 2013 | Photograph by Theo Wenner

50 YEARS OF COVERS • 675

Rolling Stone

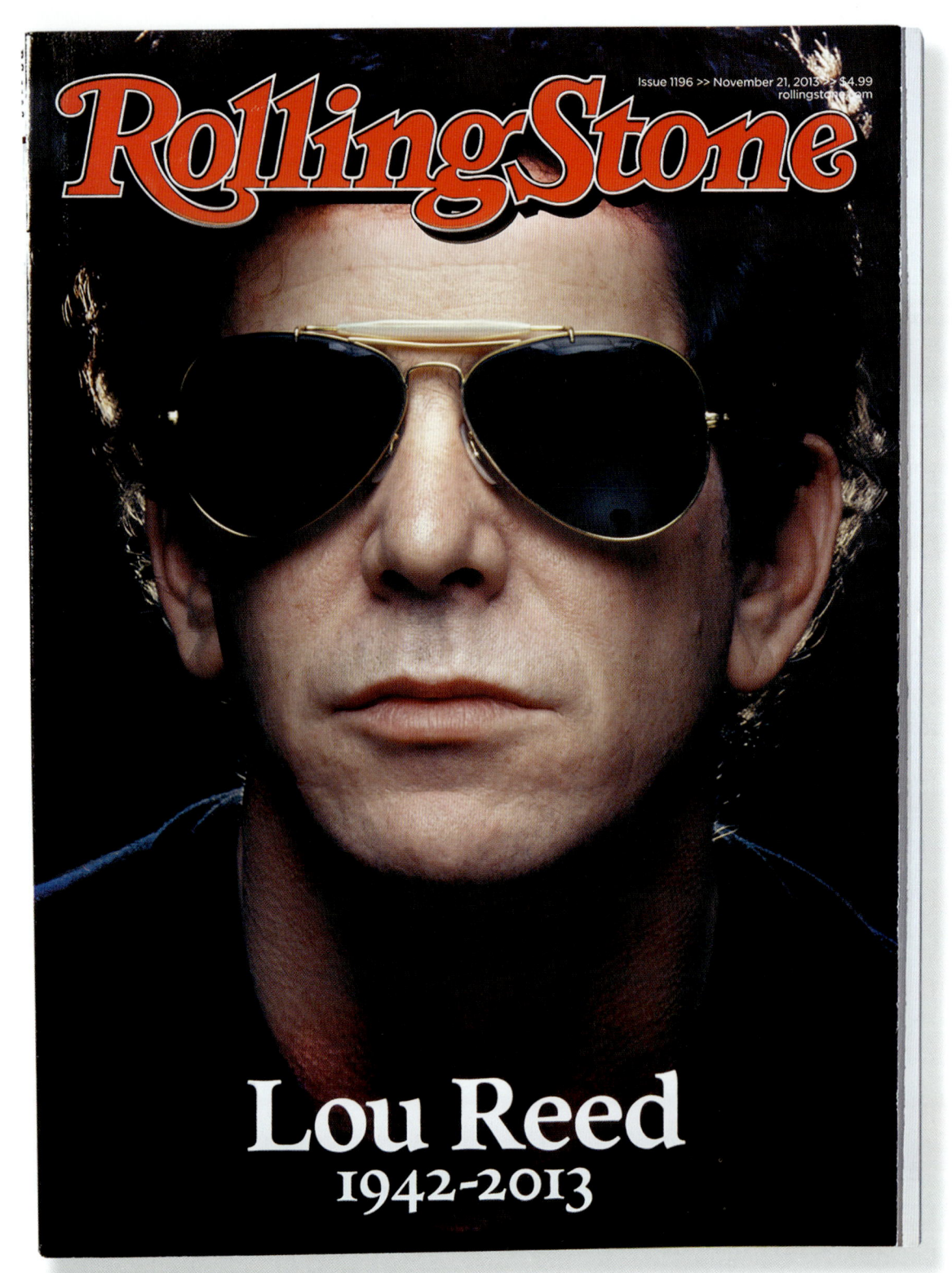

Issue 1196 >> November 21, 2013 >> $4.99
rollingstone.com

Lou Reed
1942-2013

| LOU REED | November 21st, 2013 | PHOTOGRAPH BY WARING ABBOTT/GETTY IMAGES

"*Lou and I played music* together, became best friends and then soulmates, traveled, listened to and criticized each other's work, studied things together (butterfly hunting, meditation, kayaking). We made up ridiculous jokes; stopped smoking 20 times; fought; learned to hold our breath underwater; went to Africa; sang opera in elevators; made friends with unlikely people; followed each other on tour when we could; got a sweet piano-playing dog; shared a house that was separate from our own places; protected and loved each other. We were always seeing a lot of art and music and plays and shows, and I watched as he loved and appreciated other artists and musicians. He was always so generous. He knew how hard it was to do. We loved our life in the West Village and our friends. And in all, we did the best we could do."

—*Laurie Anderson*

"**IF YOU THOUGHT OF [MY WORK] AS A BOOK,** then you have the Great American Novel, every record as a chapter. It tells you all about me, of growing up in the Sixties, Seventies and now the Eighties. That's what it was like for one person, trying to do the best he could, with all the problems that go along with everybody. Except mine took place in public. And I wrote about that too."

—*Lou Reed*

On October 27th, 2013, RollingStone.com broke the news that Lou Reed had died at 71. In the next few days, we prepared a cover package honoring the "godfather of punk," including a moving tribute from his wife, the artist Laurie Anderson, and an appreciation by senior writer David Fricke, who wrote that Reed "consistently challenged the rock & roll song's capacity for extremes."

"**AS A MAN HE WAS COMPLICATED.** I can remember us having... words with each other. But then I see pictures of us at CBGB. We're talking in such a caring manner. I step back and remember all the times he has been so warm and supportive – or sad. I've known other men like this. Their beauty or sorrow is so deep that they have to have a very strong mask."

—*Patti Smith*

"**NEW YORK CITY WAS TO LOU** Reed what Dublin was to James Joyce, the complete universe of his writing. He didn't need to stray out of it for material, there was more than enough there for his love and his hate songs. From *Metal Machine Music* to *Coney Island Baby,* from his work in the Velvet Underground to his work with Metallica, the city that he devoted his life to was his muse more than any other. Until Laurie Anderson came into his life 20 years ago, you could be forgiven for thinking that Lou had no other love than the noise of New York City. If he thought people could be stupid, he thought New Yorkers were the smartest of them."

—*Bono*

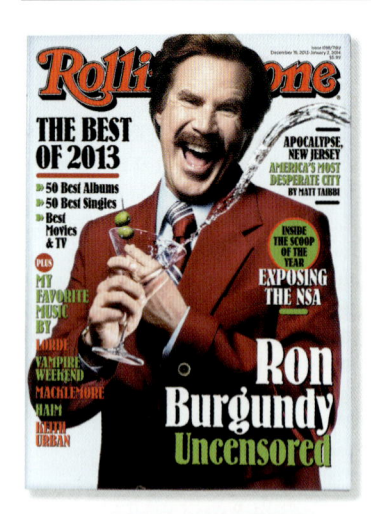

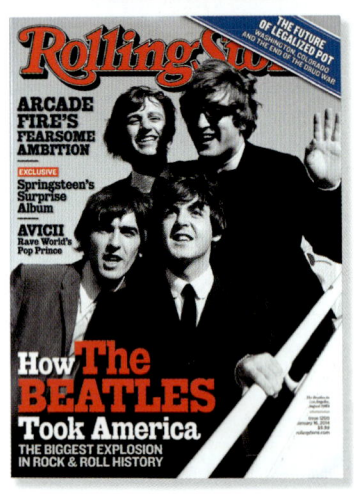

RS 1197 | EMINEM
December 5th, 2013
PHOTOGRAPH BY MARK SELIGER

RS 1198/1199 | WILL FERRELL AS RON BURGUNDY
December 19th, 2013–January 2nd, 2014
PHOTOGRAPH BY MARK SELIGER

RS 1200 | THE BEATLES
January 16th, 2014
PHOTOGRAPH BY BILL RAY/
TIME & LIFE PICTURES/GETTY IMAGES

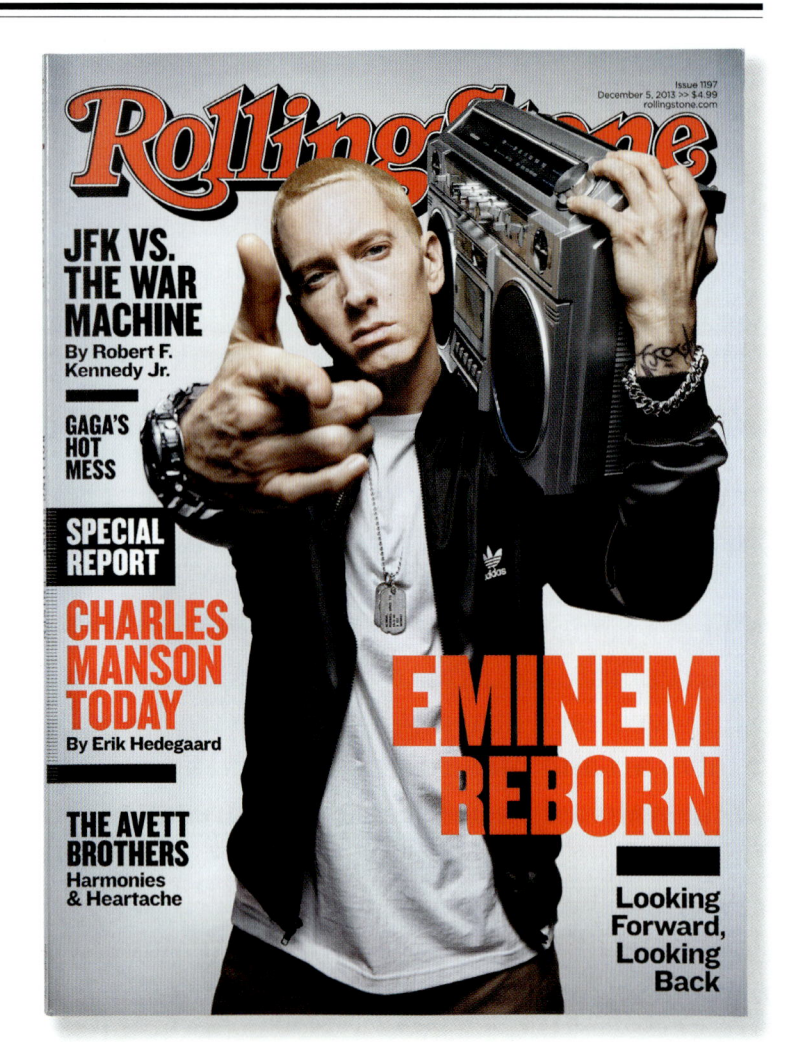

2010s

"*I get paralyzingly nervous* a lot of times, so I tried bravado. The way I dress and carry myself, a lot of people find it intimidating. I think my whole career can be boiled down to the one word I always say in meetings: strength."

—*Lorde*

Rolling Stone

Issue 1201 >> January 30, 2014 >> $4.99
rollingstone.com

Phil Everly
HARMONY & HEARTBREAK 1939-2014

BRUCE SPRINGSTEEN'S NEW CLASSIC

ROCK'S GREAT LOST GUITAR LEGEND

Adam Driver
GIRLS' MYSTERY HUNK

The Girl Who Broke the Rules

LORDE

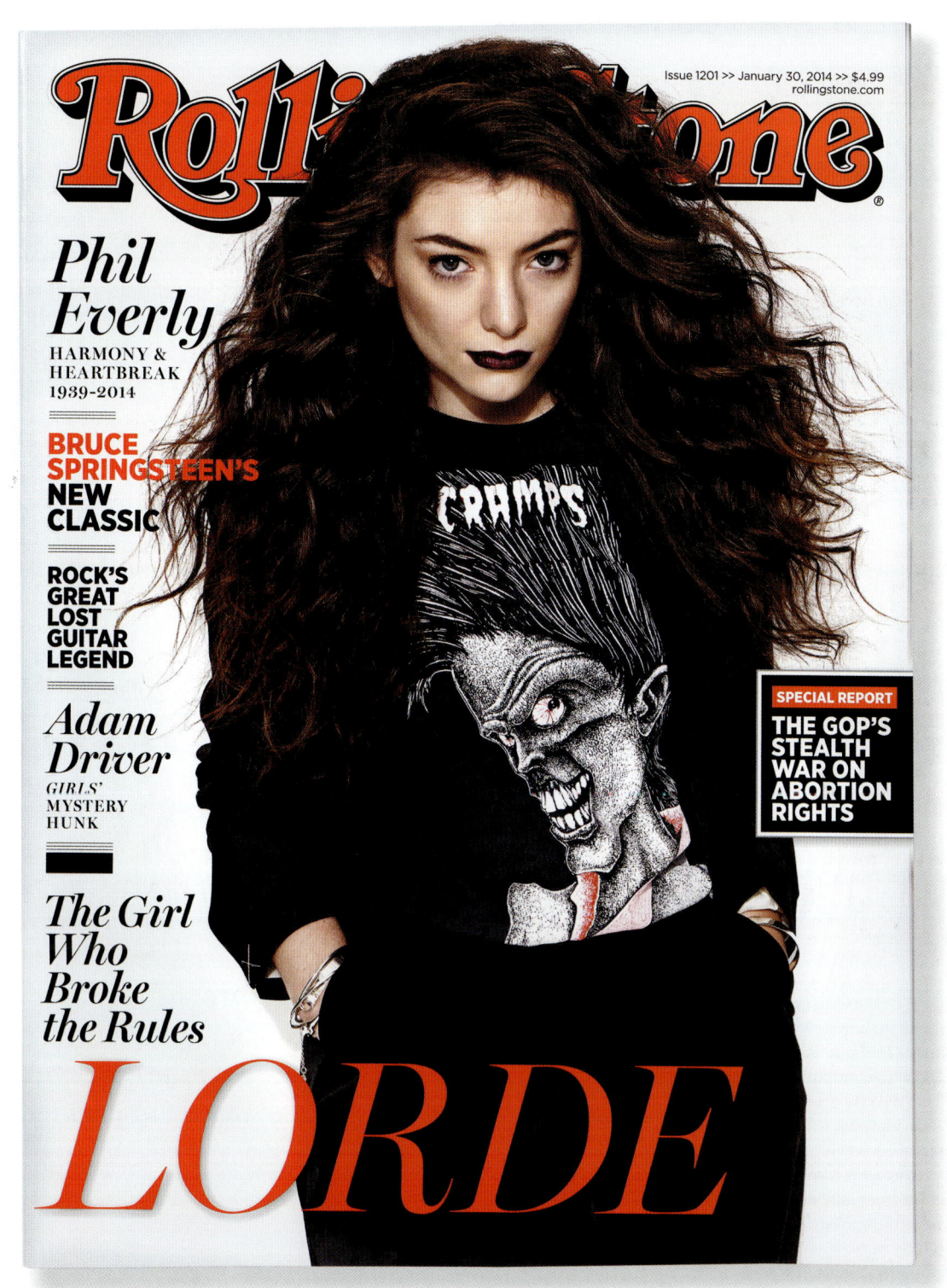

SPECIAL REPORT
THE GOP'S STEALTH WAR ON ABORTION RIGHTS

RS 1201 | LORDE | January 30th, 2014 | Photograph by Matthias Vriens-McGrath

50 YEARS OF COVERS • 679

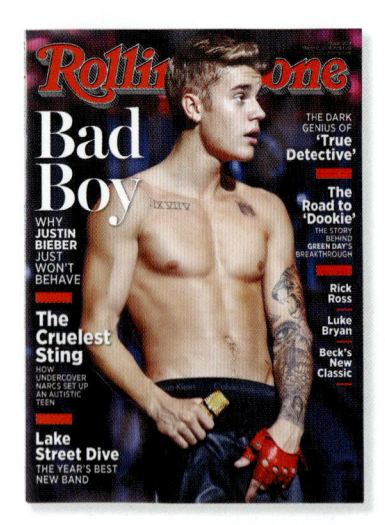

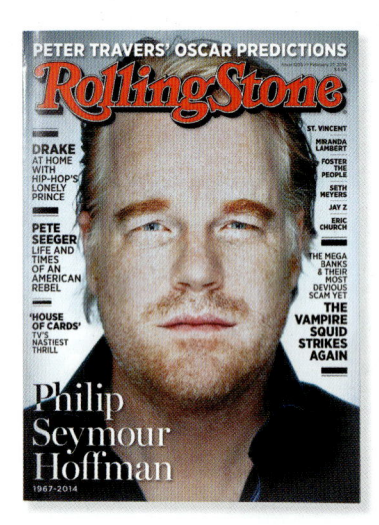

[RS 1203] Drake was supposed to appear on the cover of RS 1203. But just as the issue was going into production, actor Philip Seymour Hoffman died tragically. Drake lost his cover, and he wasn't happy about it. "The press is evil," he tweeted, and vowed to never do another interview again. He eventually cooled down and issued an apology, writing, "I completely support and agree with ROLLING STONE."

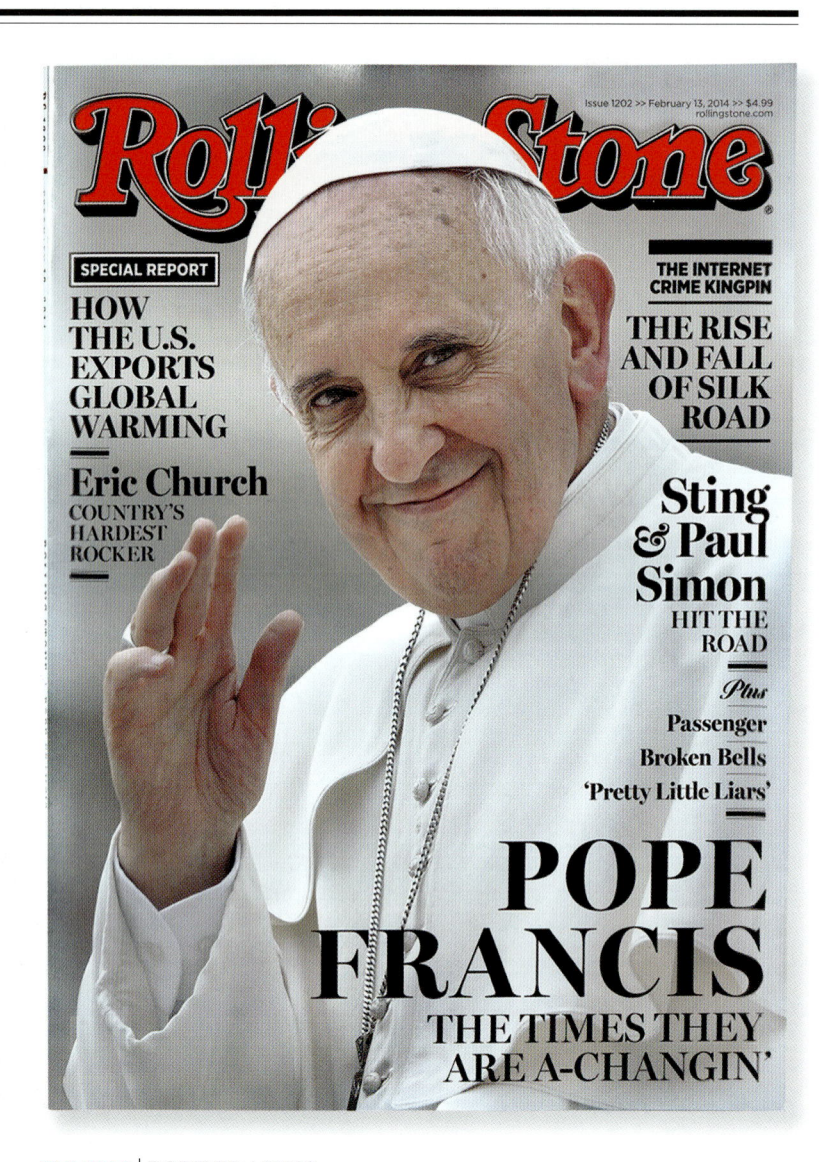

RS 1202 | POPE FRANCIS
February 13th, 2014
PHOTOGRAPH BY STEFANO SPAZIANI

RS 1203 | PHILIP SEYMOUR HOFFMAN
February 27th, 2014
PHOTOGRAPH BY MARTIN SCHOELLER/AUGUST

RS 1204 | JUSTIN BIEBER
March 13th, 2014
PHOTOGRAPH BY IMAGINECHINA/CORBIS

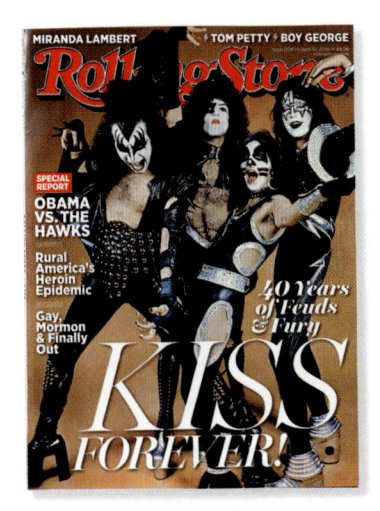

RS 1206 | KISS
April 10th, 2014
PHOTOGRAPH BY FIN COSTELLO

[RS 1206] When Kiss were (finally) inducted into the Rock and Roll Hall of Fame, we celebrated with the glam-rock icons' first cover appearance. The cover photo is a classic shot of the band from 1975. In 2014, co-founders Paul Stanley and Gene Simmons were still touring as Kiss, but original drummer Peter Criss and guitarist Ace Frehley had been out of the band for decades. "I keep thinking about Ace and Peter," Simmons told RS. " 'What are they doing now? How do you make any money? How do you pay your bills?' "

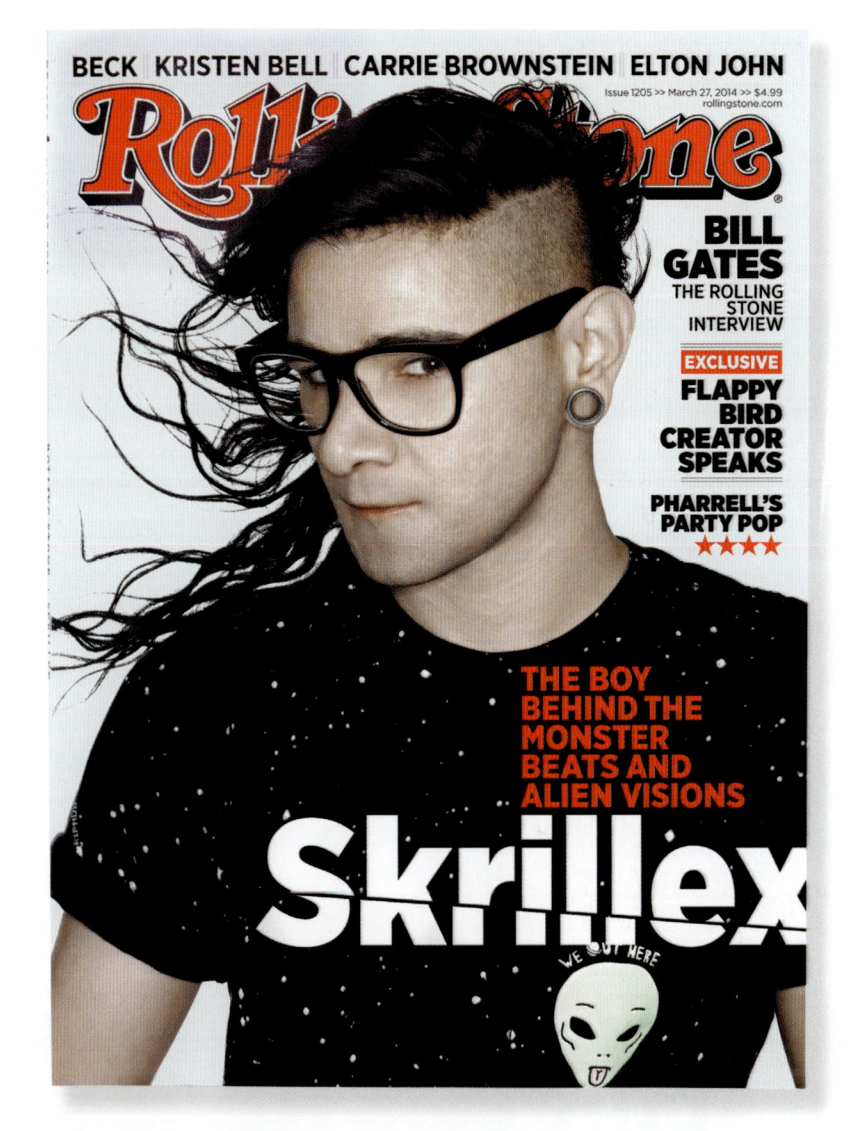

RS 1205 | SKRILLEX
March 27th, 2014
PHOTOGRAPH BY MARK SELIGER

Rolling Stone

Issue 1207 >> April 24, 2014 >> $4.99
rollingstone.com

FLEETWOOD MAC'S BIG REUNION

PHIL LESH Memories of the Dead

ED SHEERAN'S BITTER HEART

BLAKE GRIFFIN UNGUARDED

Julia Louis-Dreyfus Her Journey From 'Seinfeld' to 'Veep'

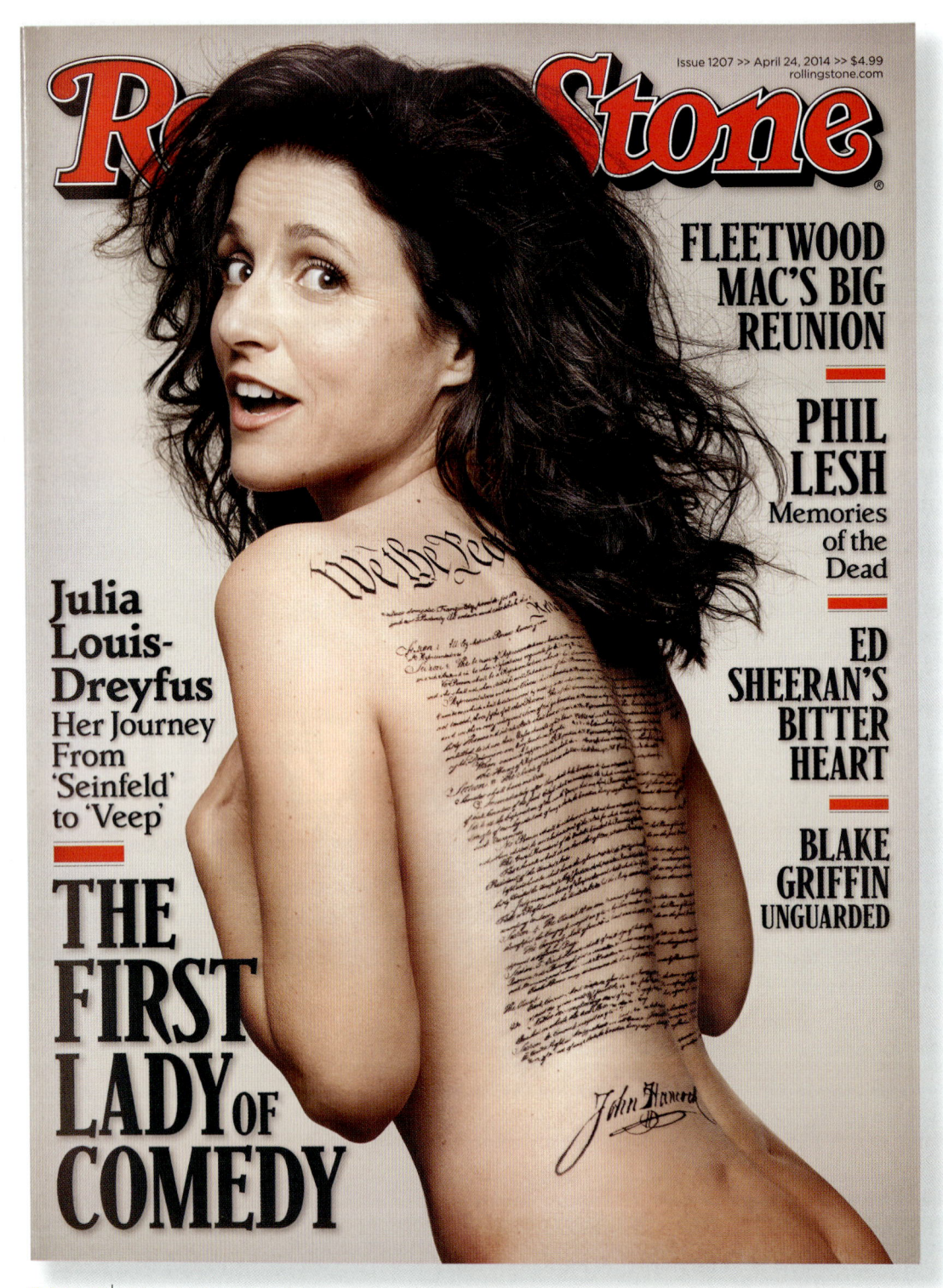

THE FIRST LADY OF COMEDY

RS 1207 | JULIA LOUIS-DREYFUS | April 24th, 2014 | Photograph by Mark Seliger

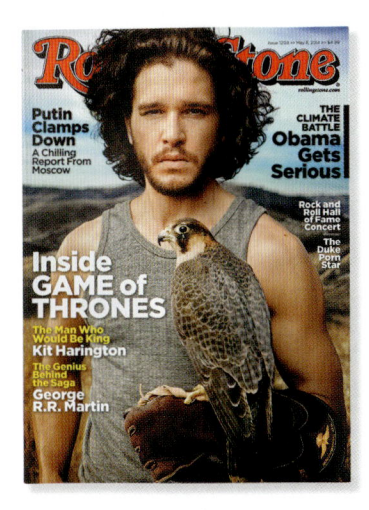

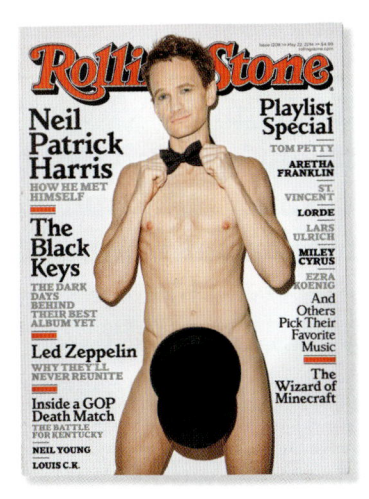

LOUIS-DREYFUS HAS BEEN AN ACTIVIST FOR ENVIRONMENTAL CAUSES for more than 20 years. Today, Louis-Dreyfus mostly works with the Natural Resources Defense Council and Heal the Bay, a Santa Monica-based charity that addresses water-quality issues in Southern California (she also worked on the successful campaign to ban plastic bags from Los Angeles), and is full of ideas about marketing environmentalism, like car manufacturers should have launched a hybrid vehicle after 9/11 called Patriot, and painted it red, white and blue, as she once suggested. "An actor is an actor, and you don't have to speak out because you're well-known – it's not your responsibility," she says. "I do it because I feel responsible. I am guilt-ridden, therefore I act."

Through her political work, as well as being a Hollywood star – or, perhaps, the irresistible combination of the two – Louis-Dreyfus has met several vice presidents, including Al Gore, "who did win, by the way," she says, raising a finger. Joe Biden even recently seated her next to him at a White House state dinner. "He loves to tell stories, and I'm a good listener," she says. "I loved that dinner. There was no cynicism, just a very earnest jubilation about being there. I got to meet Madame Christine Lagarde, Supreme Court Justice Kagan, Nancy Pelosi, Valerie Jarrett – you know, the list goes on." She smiles. "Dr. Jill Biden was also at my table, and she had this great idea. As soon as everyone sat down, she said, 'Let's each take the menu, get a pen, and we'll sign them.' So by the time we were done, everyone had a menu with everybody's name. Isn't that cool?" Her eyes sparkle. "Totally gonna sell that on eBay."

[EXCERPT FROM RS 1207 COVER STORY BY VANESSA GRIGORIADIS]

[RS 1207] Yep, we know. John Hancock signed the Declaration of Independence, not the Constitution. That historical error was an Easter egg for fans of HBO's political satire *Veep*, which starred Julia Louis-Dreyfus as craven, clueless Vice President Selina Meyer. When some readers missed the gag, Louis-Dreyfus spun the situation like a pro, joking that the tattoo was the fault of Meyer's incompetent communications director. "Yet another Mike screw-up," she wrote on Twitter. "Dummy."

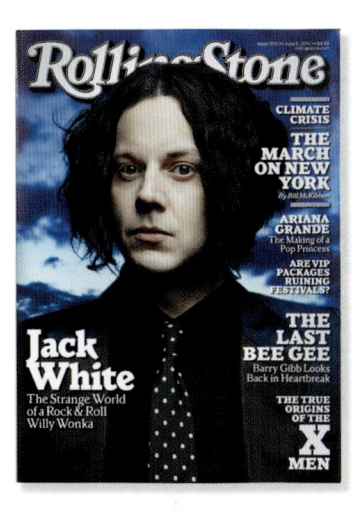

RS 1208 | KIT HARINGTON
May 8th, 2014
PHOTOGRAPH BY MARK SELIGER

RS 1209 | NEIL PATRICK HARRIS
May 22nd, 2014
PHOTOGRAPH BY TERRY RICHARDSON

RS 1210 | JACK WHITE
June 5th, 2014
PHOTOGRAPH BY MARK SELIGER

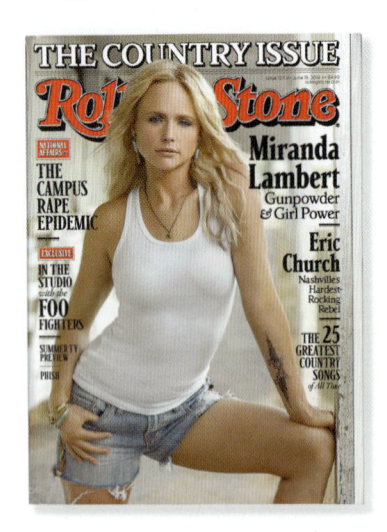

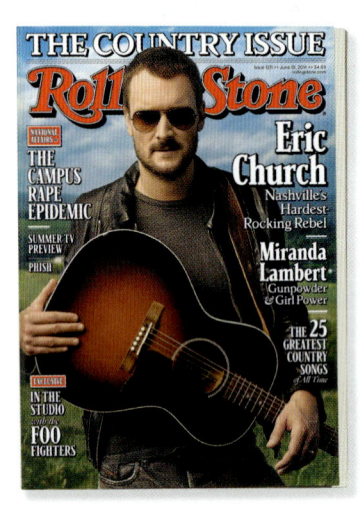

RS 1211 | RS COUNTRY
June 19th, 2014
PHOTOGRAPHS BY MARK SELIGER

In the summer of 2014, ROLLING STONE launched RS Country, a website based in Nashville and dedicated exclusively to country music. We celebrated by splitting the cover of RS 1211 between Grammy-winning singer Miranda Lambert and maverick artist Eric Church.

The town house Del Rey is staying in belongs to someone she calls "a friend": 31-year-old Francesco Carrozzini, a dashing Italian photographer who's shot her for various European magazines. He obviously does well for himself – "better than us," Del Rey jokes, as she shows me around. His four-story house is a seriously amazing bit of Manhattan real estate, a movie-star-worthy bachelor pad, its dark-wood walls covered with art photos and his shots of celebrities like Keith Richards. The house is on the same block where Bob Dylan moved with his family in 1969; Anna Wintour lives nearby, as does Baz Luhrmann.

On the second floor, on a coffee table, near a Serge Gainsbourg box set, there's a book called *The Boudoir Bible*. "No shame," Del Rey says with a grin. She's sitting on the brown couch, smoking Carrozzini's American Spirit cigarettes in her languid way, below a huge black-and-white photo of a bunch of slim, naked people, piled on top of one another. The midday sun is blazing through an open window, and her brown hair and fair skin are glowing in its haze – an Instagram filter or cinematographer couldn't do better. "I quit sometimes," she says, of the cigarettes. "And then stop quitting." She smokes onstage, too – it's pure craving, not an image thing. "I find, sometimes, halfway through the set, I definitely need to have a cigarette."

[EXCERPT FROM RS 1214 COVER STORY BY BRIAN HIATT]

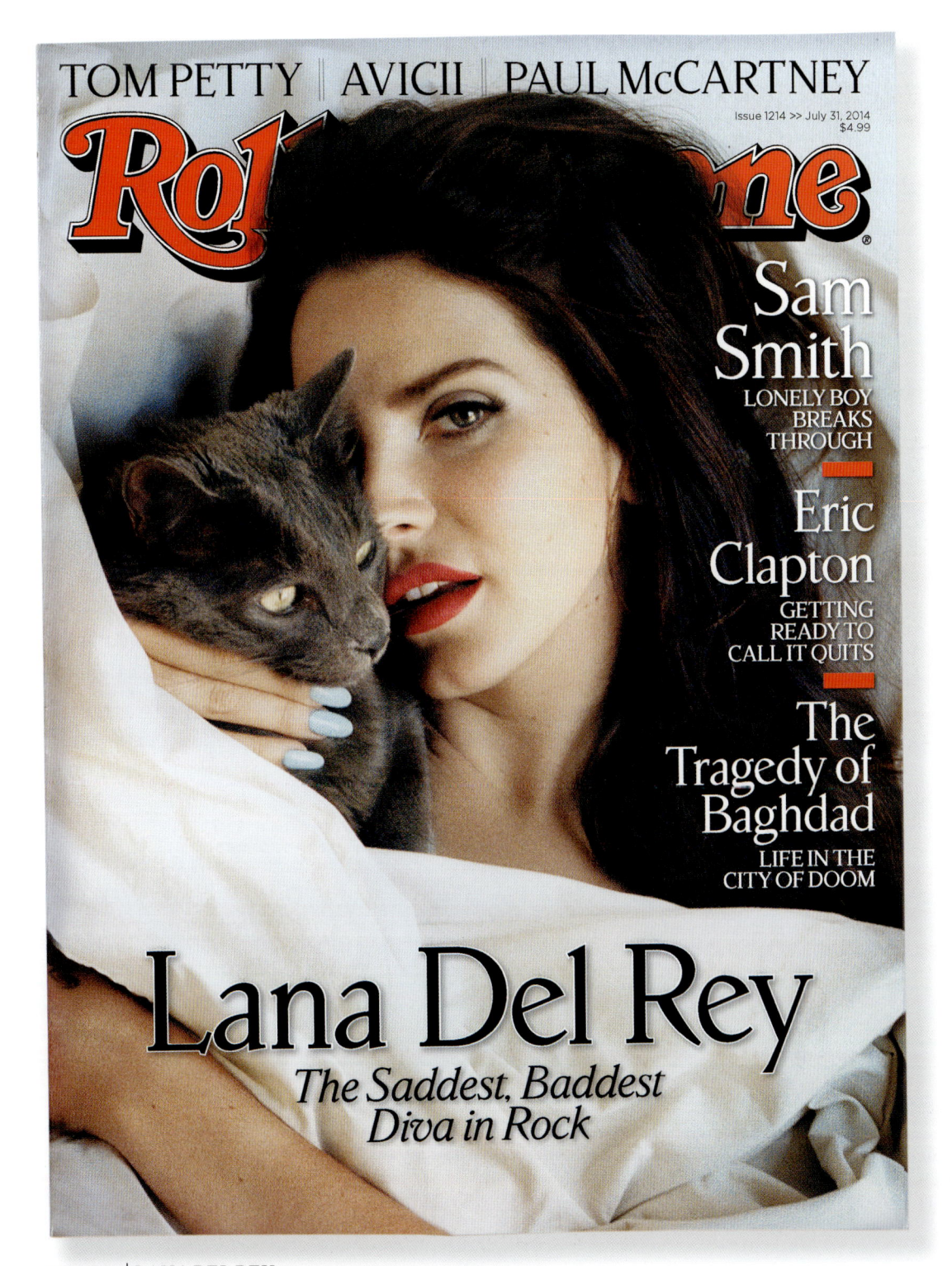

RS 1214 | LANA DEL REY | July 31st, 2014 | Photograph by Theo Wenner

50 YEARS OF COVERS • 685

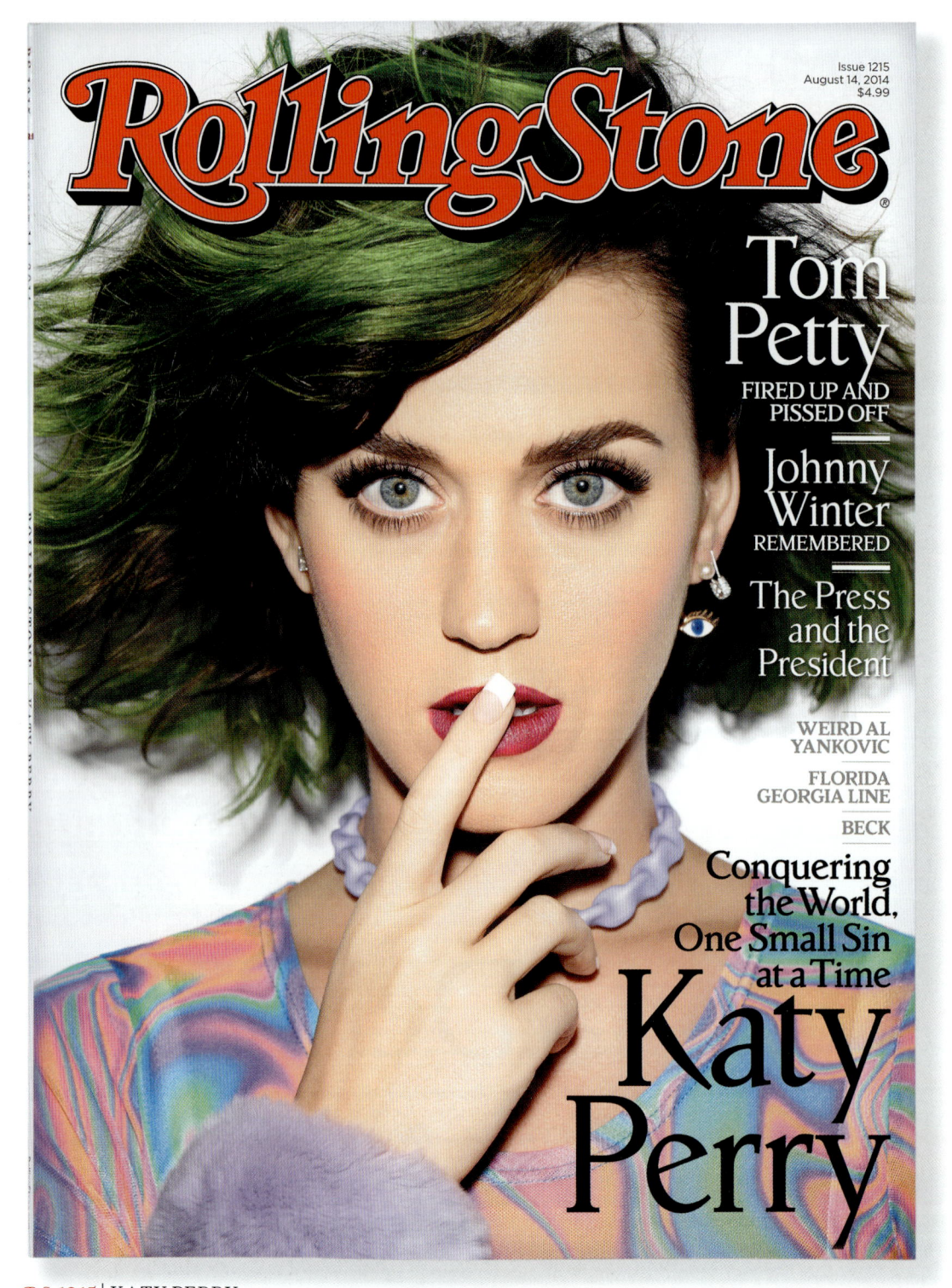

RS 1215 | KATY PERRY | August 14th, 2014 | Photograph by Peggy Sirota

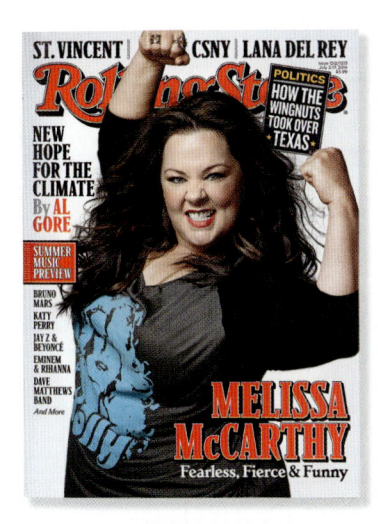

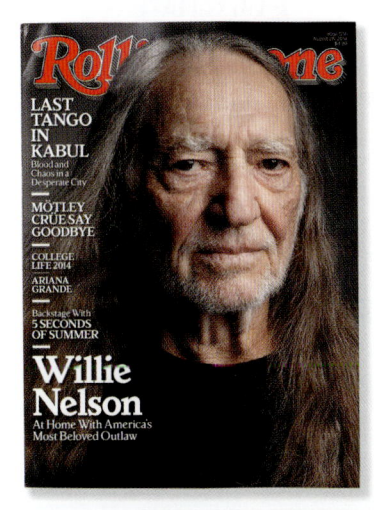

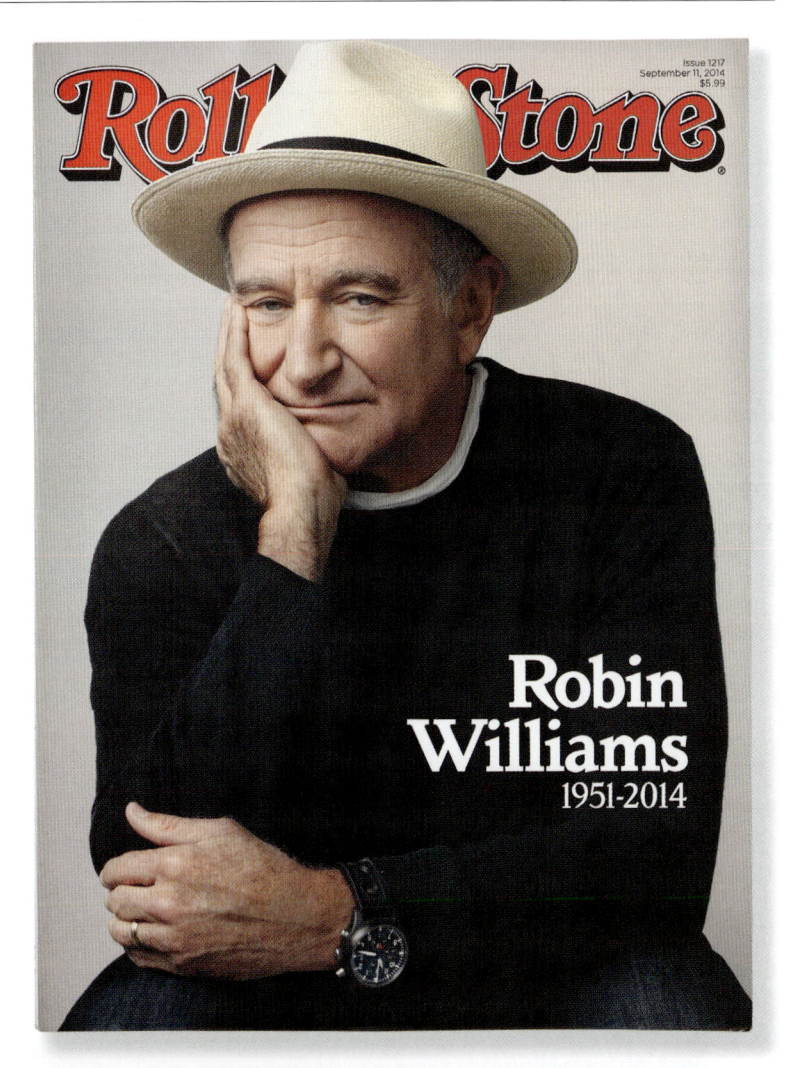

RS 1212/1213 |
MELISSA McCARTHY
July 3rd–17th, 2014
PHOTOGRAPH BY MARK SELIGER

RS 1216 | WILLIE NELSON
August 28th, 2014
PHOTOGRAPH BY MARK SELIGER

[RS 1216] Willie Nelson, who was 81 when this photo was taken, is the oldest person ever to appear on the cover of ROLLING STONE.

RS 1217 | ROBIN WILLIAMS
September 11th, 2014
PHOTOGRAPH BY PEGGY SIROTA/TRUNK ARCHIVE

"*He was doing something* so unique that no one could even attempt their version of it. He raised the bar for what it's possible to do, and made an enormous amount of us want to be comedians. He looked like he was having so much *fun*."

—*Judd Apatow, remembering Robin Williams*

50 YEARS OF COVERS • 687

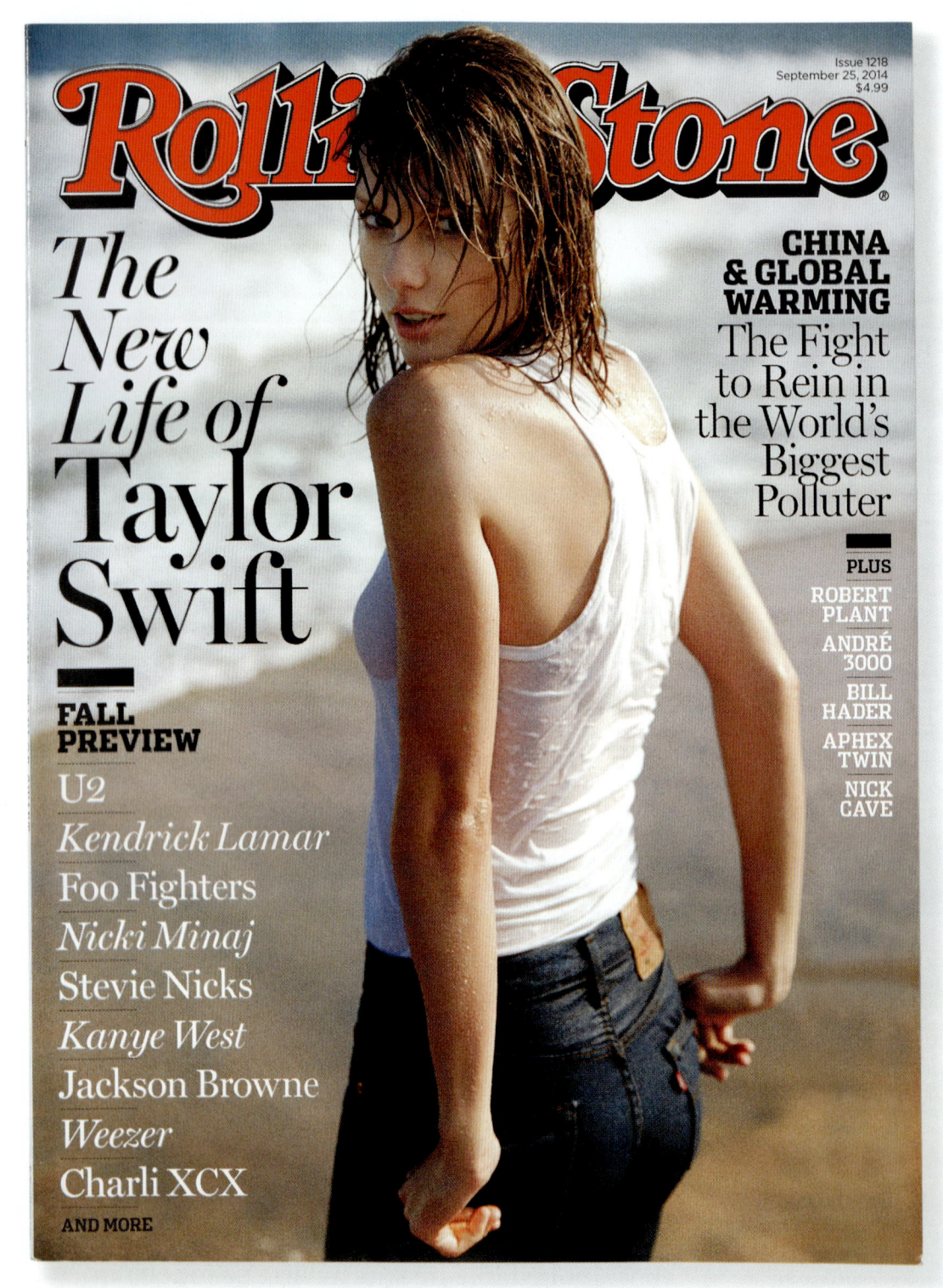

RS 1218 | TAYLOR SWIFT | September 25th, 2014 | Photograph by Theo Wenner

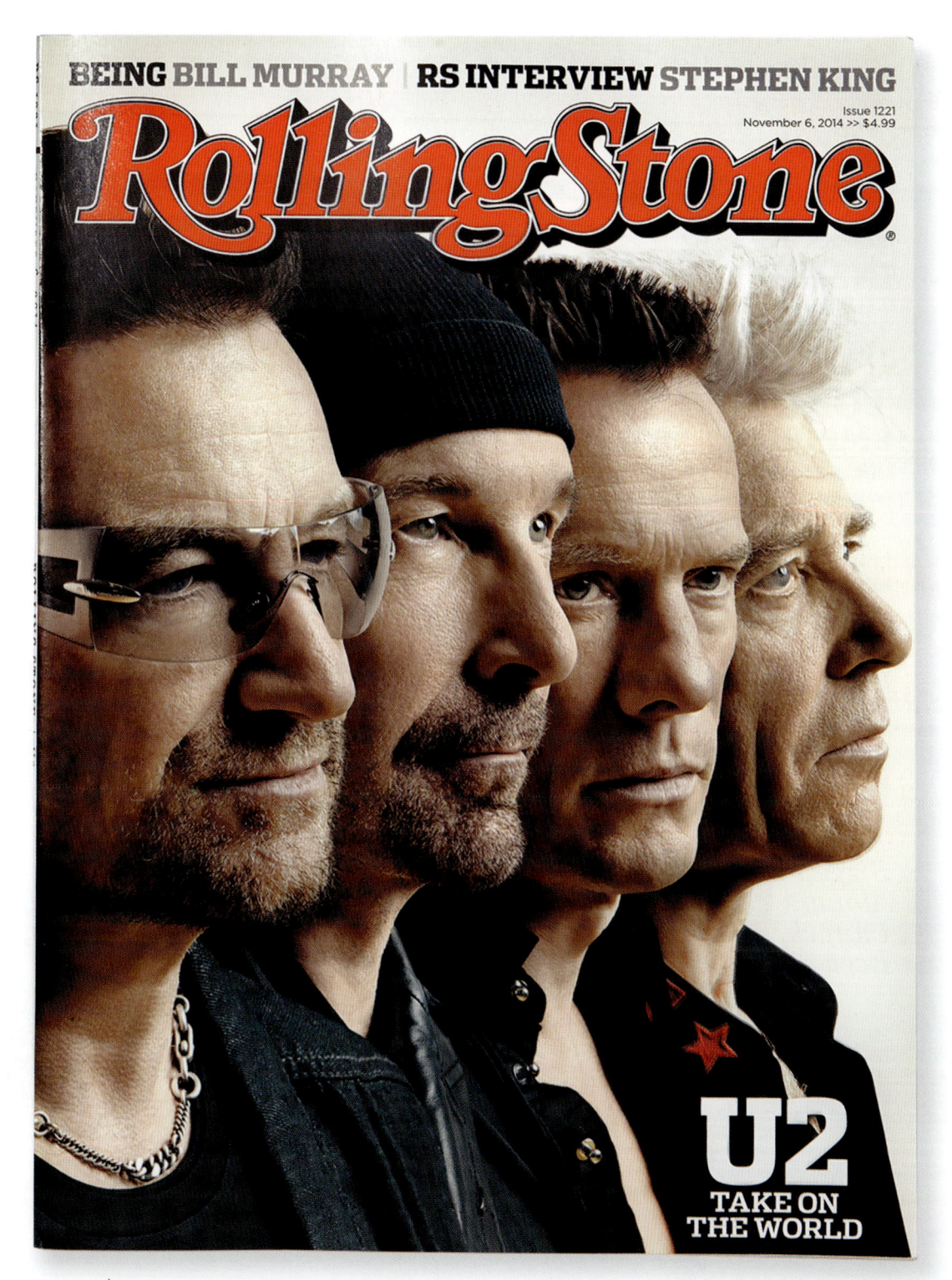

RS 1221 | U2 | November 6th, 2014 | Photograph by Mark Seliger

50 YEARS OF COVERS • 689

Rolling Stone

INSIDE THE KOCH BROTHERS' TOXIC EMPIRE

STEVIE NICKS

LENNY KRAVITZ

THE BLACK KEYS

LEONARD COHEN

U2
The Biggest Album Launch Ever

THE TV ISSUE

SONS OF ANARCHY

ADVENTURE TIME

BOARDWALK EMPIRE

FALL'S BEST (AND MOSTLY WORST) NEW SHOWS

PLUS THE GREATEST SHOWS THAT NEVER WERE

John Oliver
The Angriest Man in Fake News

Issue 1219
October 9, 2014
$4.99
RollingStone.com

RS 1219 | JOHN OLIVER | October 9th, 2014 | Photograph by Max Vadukul

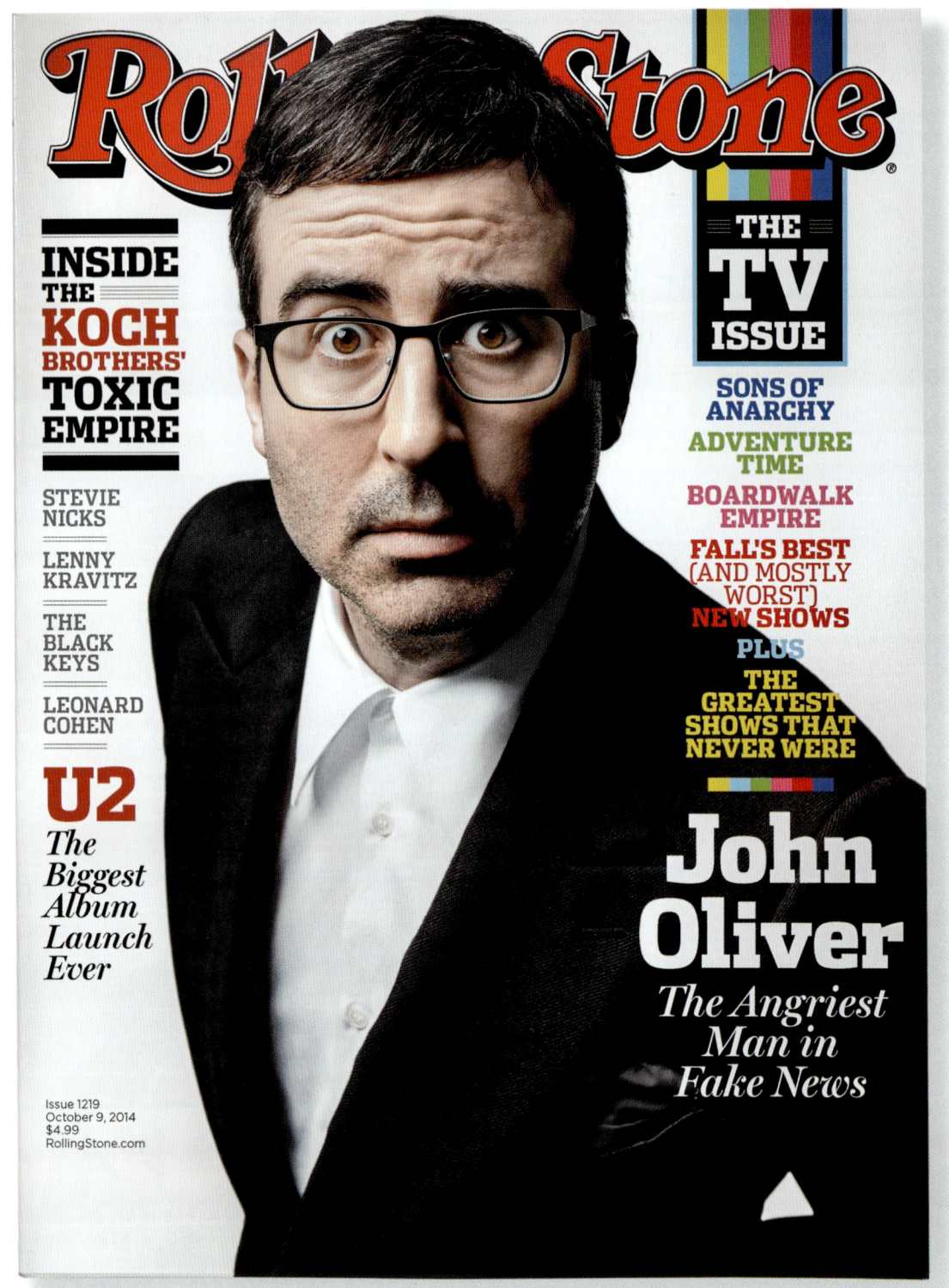

Digging into bleak corners of the American experience – payday loans, income inequality, the prison system – isn't exactly leavening Oliver's natural pessimism. "The more in-depth we go to things here, the darker you start to feel about it," he says. "When you start following the money in politics, that's where you start to think, 'Holy shit, is this thing broken beyond repair?' When we started looking at stories, even the Dr. Oz dietary-supplement stuff – you start to see how corrupted, at root, things have become. And the fact that there's this revolving door – that 50 percent of the people that leave the Senate go straight to lobbying positions, that one statistic alone is a dead canary in a coal mine. That is not good. There is something profoundly wrong at the heart of American politics."

And then there's the show's report on the United States' sloppy protection of nuclear-missile arsenals, which included an account of a drunk high-ranking general trying to get onstage with a Beatles cover band at a Mexican restaurant – in Russia. "Individually, the facts are horrendous," Oliver says. "But in their totality, you can get them to a point where you either have to laugh at them or you're about to walk into the river. You've got the choice."

[EXCERPT FROM RS 1219 COVER STORY BY BRIAN HIATT]

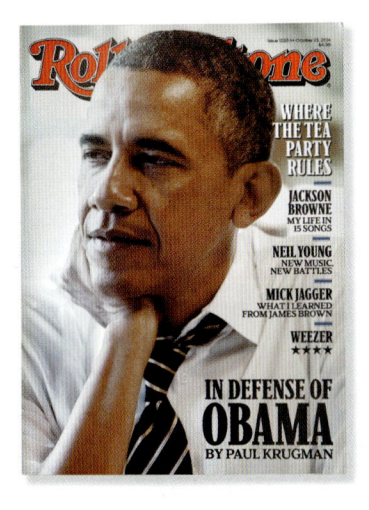

RS 1220 | BARACK OBAMA
October 23rd, 2014
PHOTOGRAPH BY OLIVER DOULIERY/ABACA USA

Rolling Stone

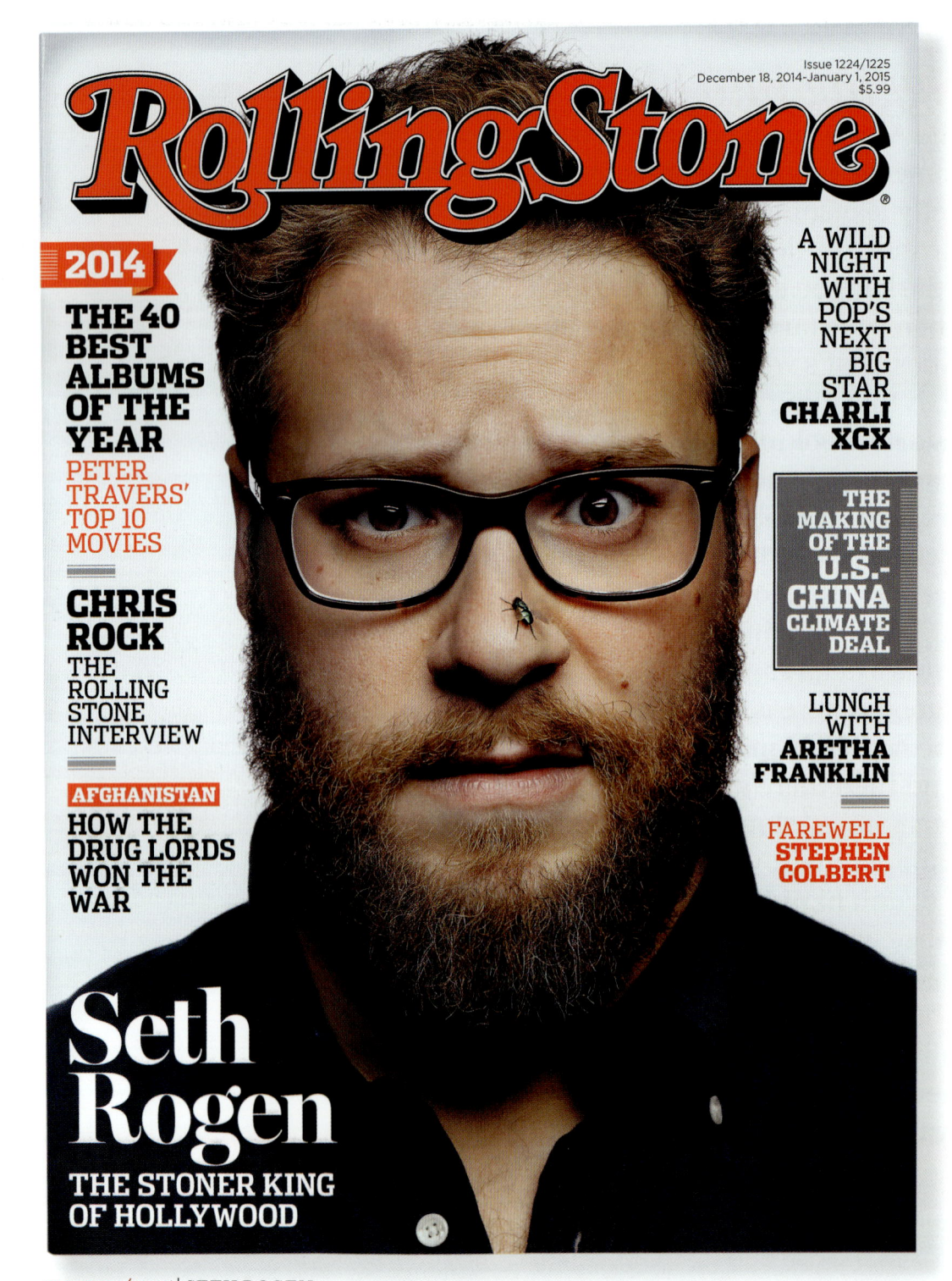

Issue 1224/1225
December 18, 2014 – January 1, 2015
$5.99

2014
THE 40 BEST ALBUMS OF THE YEAR

PETER TRAVERS' TOP 10 MOVIES

CHRIS ROCK
THE ROLLING STONE INTERVIEW

AFGHANISTAN
HOW THE DRUG LORDS WON THE WAR

A WILD NIGHT WITH POP'S NEXT BIG STAR **CHARLI XCX**

THE MAKING OF THE U.S.-CHINA CLIMATE DEAL

LUNCH WITH **ARETHA FRANKLIN**

FAREWELL **STEPHEN COLBERT**

Seth Rogen
THE STONER KING OF HOLLYWOOD

RS 1224/1225 | SETH ROGEN | December 18th, 2014 – January 1st, 2015 | Photograph by Mark Seliger

"*It's not until* you get your shit together that you can step back and say, 'I have a career; what am I going to do with it? Are you the kind of person that's happy just being a famous person, or are you the kind of person that thinks maybe I should try to contribute?' I think the answer for us right now is somewhere in the middle. We'll make a movie that maybe for two seconds will make some 18-year-old think about North Korea in a way he never would have otherwise." —*Seth Rogen*

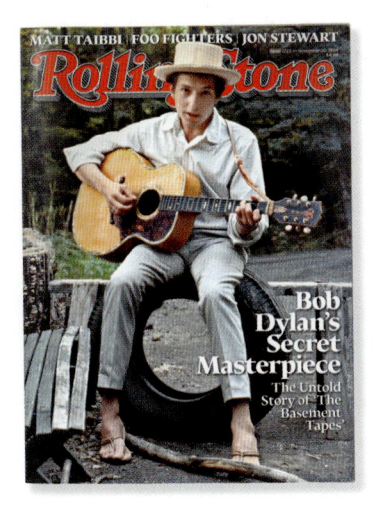

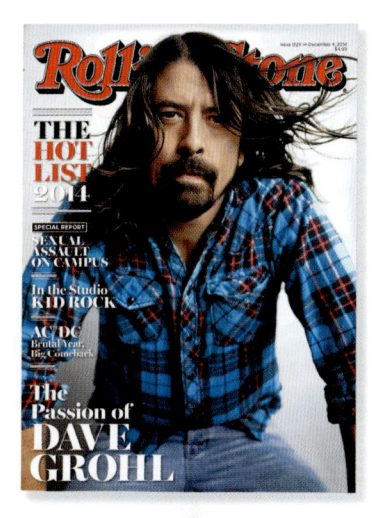

RS 1222 | BOB DYLAN
November 20th, 2014
PHOTOGRAPH BY ELLIOT LANDY ©

RS 1223 | DAVE GROHL
December 4th, 2014
PHOTOGRAPH BY PEGGY SIROTA

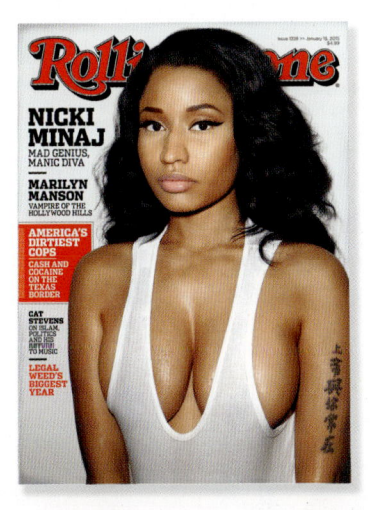

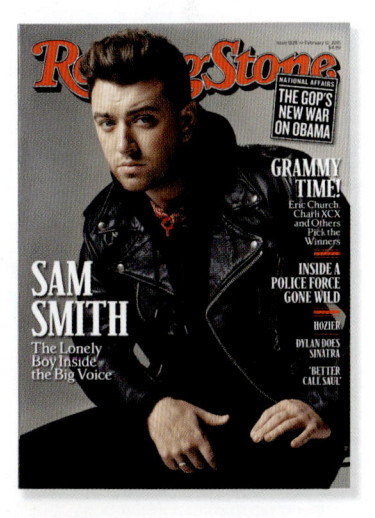

RS 1226 | NICKI MINAJ
January 15th, 2015
PHOTOGRAPH BY TERRY RICHARDSON

RS 1228 | SAM SMITH
February 12th, 2015
PHOTOGRAPH BY TERRY RICHARDSON

MADONNA | JOE COCKER | NICK JONAS

Issue 1227 >> January 29, 2015
$4.99

RollingStone

Stevie Nicks
A Rock Goddess Looks Back

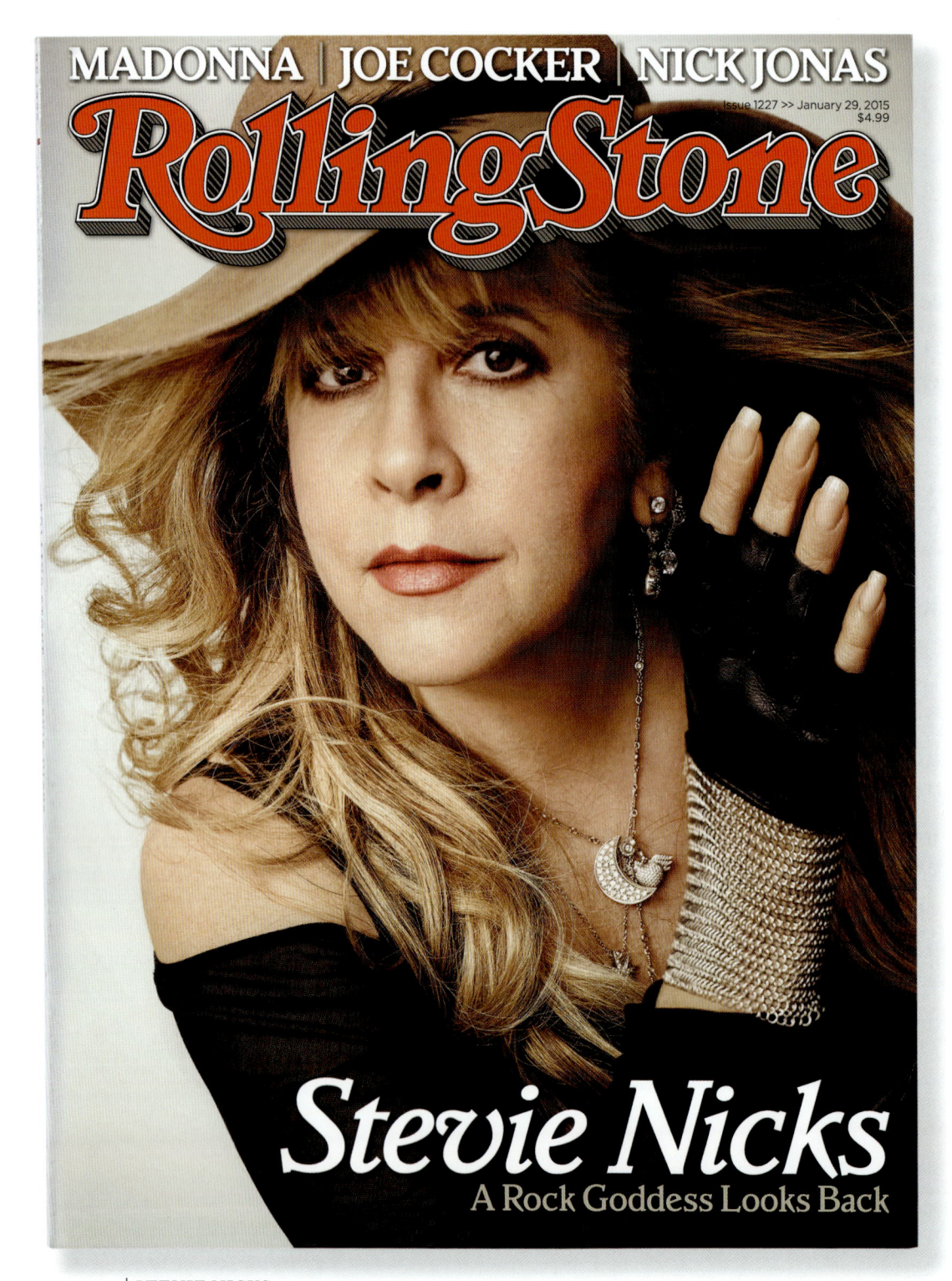

2010s

RS 1227 | STEVIE NICKS | January 29th, 2015 | Photograph by Peggy Sirota

RS 1229 | JOHN BELUSHI
February 26th, 2015
ILLUSTRATION BY ANITA KUNZ

[RS 1229] John Belushi wasn't just the obvious choice to top our definitive ranking of every *SNL* cast member, he made for a perfect cover too. "His characters were so memorable," says design director Joseph Hutchinson. "And visual." The cover illustration was done by Anita Kunz, who depicted Michael Jackson as Mickey Mouse in 1987, on the cover of RS 509.

1. JOHN BELUSHI
2. EDDIE MURPHY
3. TINA FEY
4. MIKE MYERS
5. DAN AYKROYD
6. BILL MURRAY
7. PHIL HARTMAN
8. AMY POEHLER
9. GILDA RADNER
10. CHEVY CHASE
11. DANA CARVEY
12. WILL FERRELL
13. BILL HADER
14. KRISTEN WIIG
15. CHRIS FARLEY
16. RACHEL DRATCH
17. ADAM SANDLER
18. MAYA RUDOLPH
19. JON LOVITZ
20. AL FRANKEN

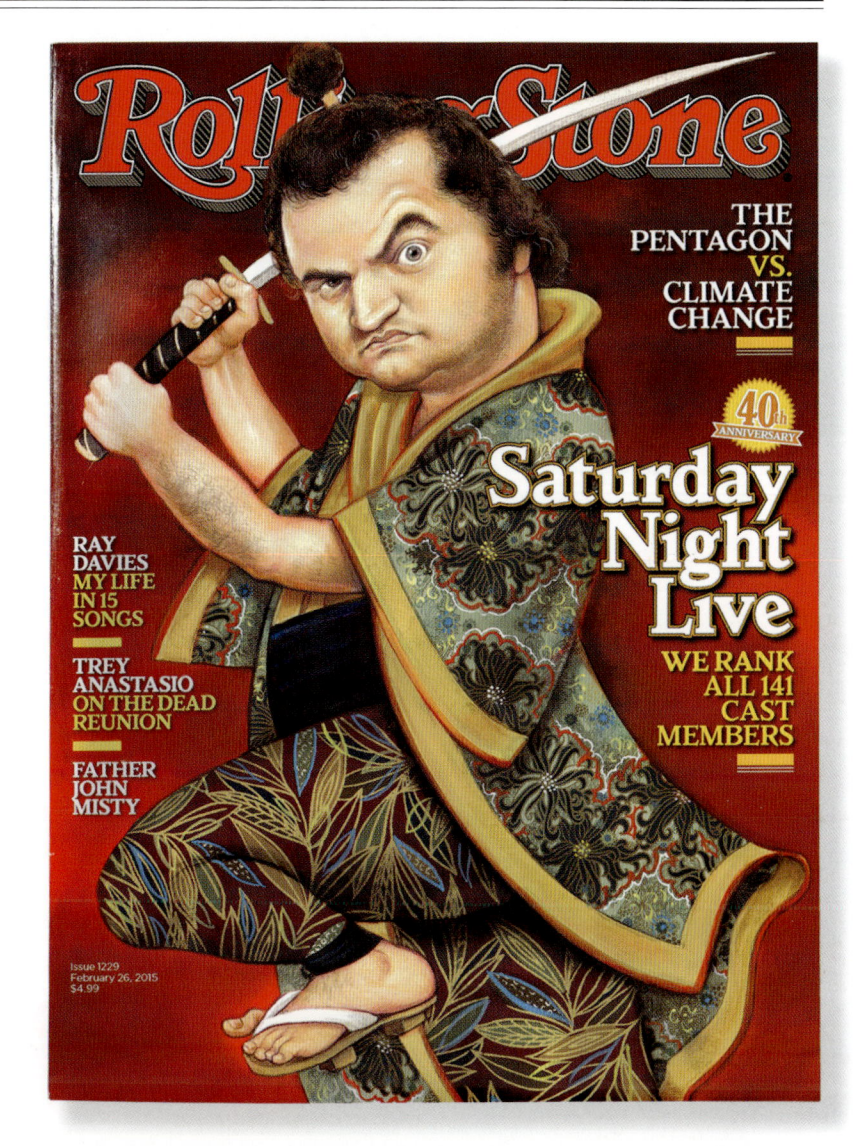

50 YEARS OF COVERS • 695

ROLLING STONE

MADONNA

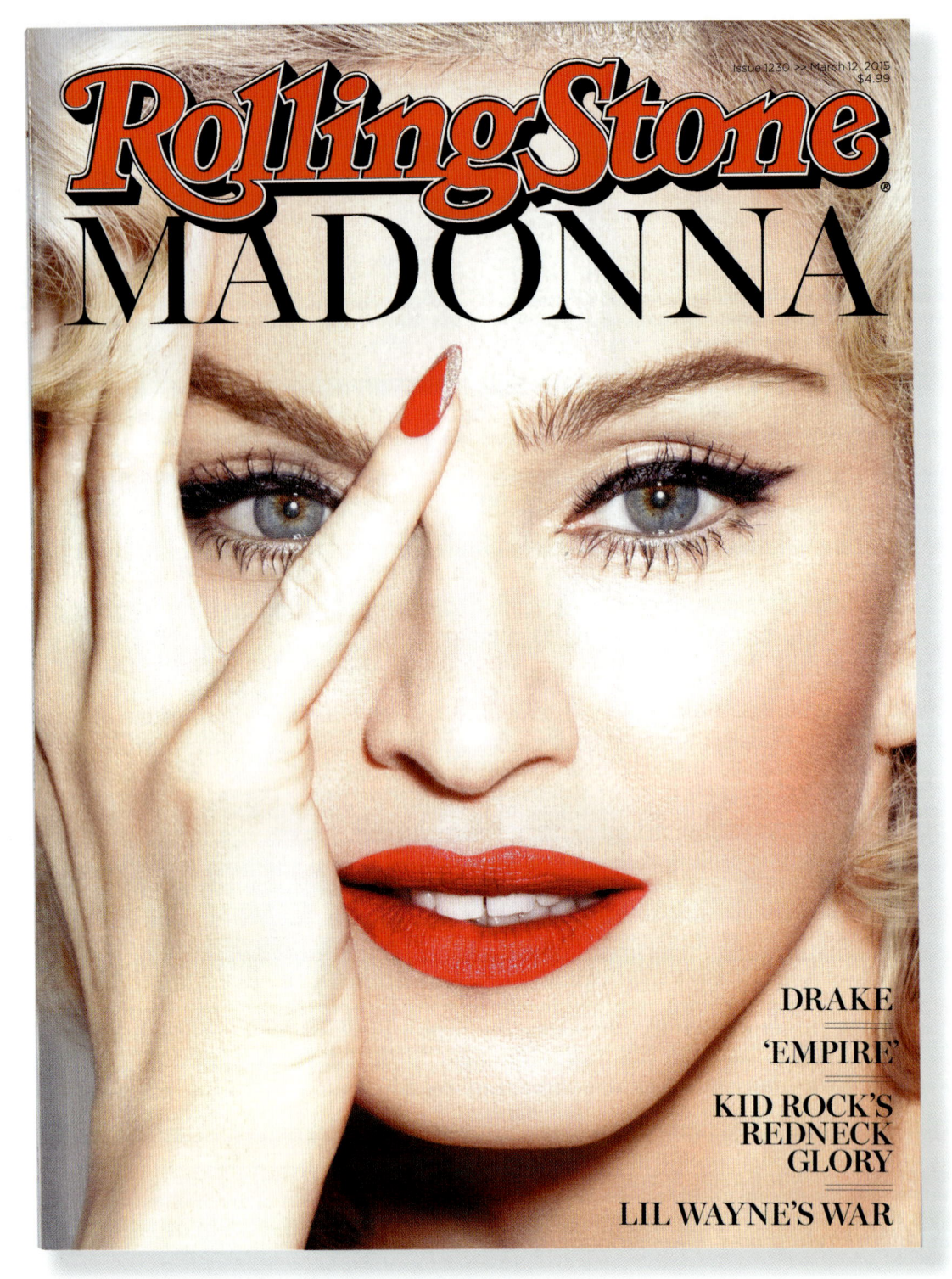

DRAKE

'EMPIRE'

KID ROCK'S REDNECK GLORY

LIL WAYNE'S WAR

Issue 1230 >> March 12, 2015
$4.99

2010s

RS 1230 | MADONNA | March 12th, 2015 | Photograph by Mert Alas and Marcus Piggott

696 • ROLLING STONE

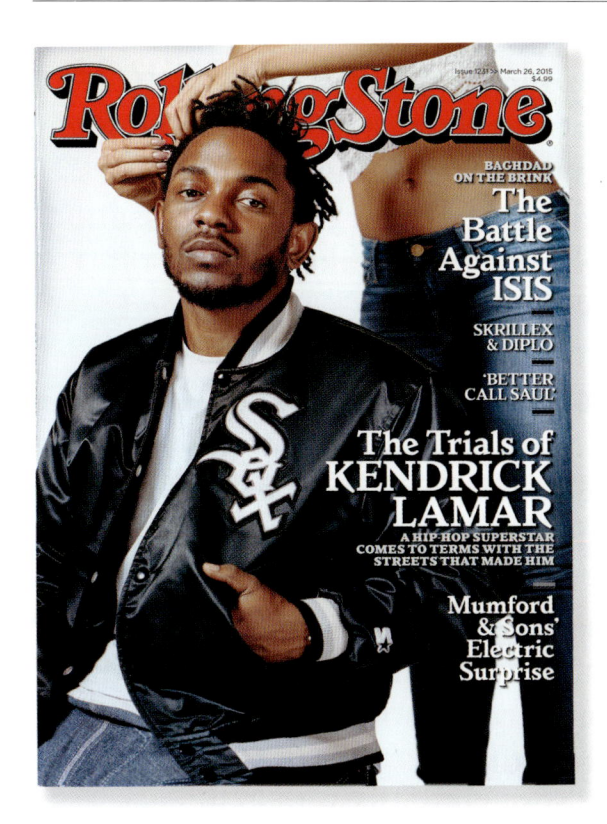

RS 1231 | KENDRICK LAMAR
March 26th, 2015
PHOTOGRAPH BY THEO WENNER

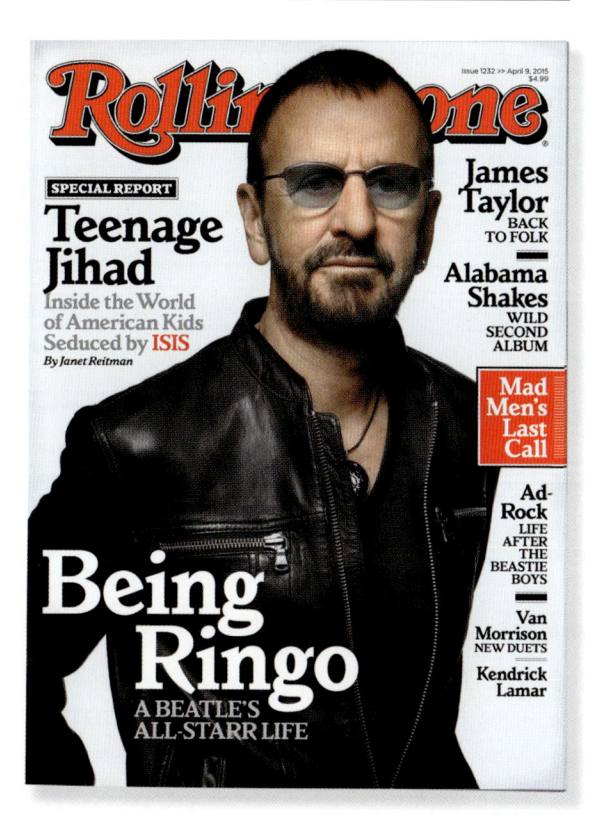

RS 1232 | RINGO STARR
April 9th, 2015
PHOTOGRAPH BY MARK SELIGER

[RS 1232] Along with being one of rock's greatest drummers, Ringo Starr is also a respected photographer. In 2015, the same year he appeared solo on the cover of RS for the first time since 1981, Starr released *Photograph*, a collection of his work. "Ringo's photography was exceptionally sophisticated for someone whose primary job was drumming in the world's most famous band," said Mark Seliger. "I don't separate Ringo the photographer from Ringo the drummer and songwriter. He is an artist through and through."

RS 1235 | DAVID LETTERMAN
May 21st, 2015
Photograph by Mark Seliger

A few days ago, Letterman celebrated his 68th birthday. He's an ongoing self-improvement project. Twenty-five years ago, a doctor suggested he try antidepressants, but he worried they might take the edge off his comedy. Then around 2003, he agreed to start a low dose of an SSRI, the class of serotonin-boosting drugs that includes Paxil and Lexapro. "I was suspicious, and skeptical, and nervous about it," he says. "But it changed my life. I used to have kind of a hair trigger; I used to put my fist through Sheetrock." Now he does transcendental meditation and no longer talks about "enduring" life beyond the show. He's also a regular in therapy – he calls it "an emotional tuneup." In fact, he's on his way to his therapist tonight, which in part explains the overalls. "I like them because they're comfortable and they're comforting," he explains.

Letterman once said there were two great motivators in his life: guilt and fear. Lately, he doesn't seem driven by either of them. He finds it hard to talk about his legacy: The closest he will come is an admission that he feels "wistful." Maybe it's because he's not ready to process it yet, or maybe it's too vast to reflect on with any perspective. "Ultimately, it's the body of work that speaks for itself," says Burnett. "It's 30 years. It's an ocean."

[EXCERPT FROM RS 1235 COVER STORY BY JOSH EELLS]

Rolling Stone

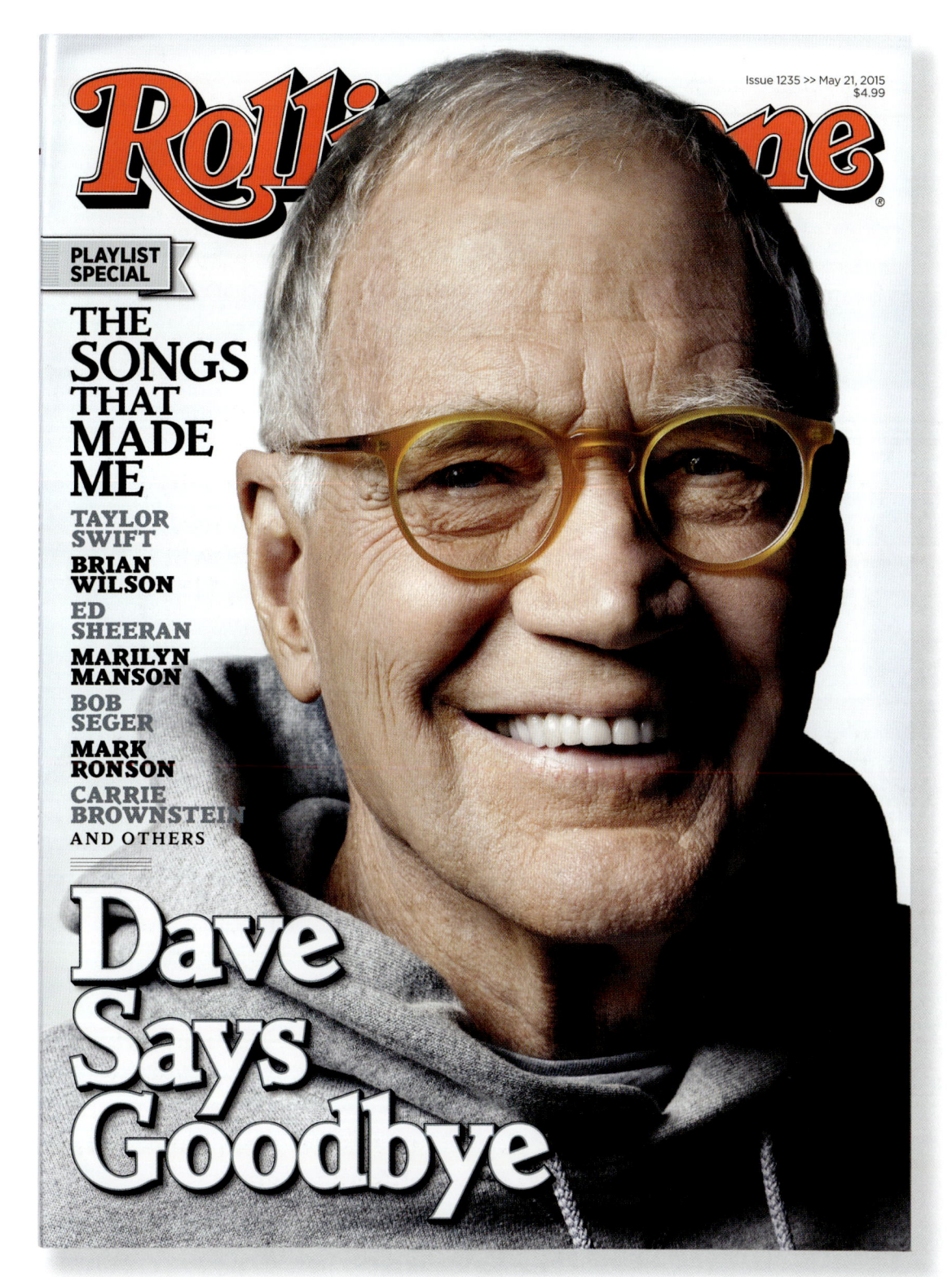

Issue 1235 >> May 21, 2015
$4.99

PLAYLIST SPECIAL

THE SONGS THAT MADE ME

TAYLOR SWIFT
BRIAN WILSON
ED SHEERAN
MARILYN MANSON
BOB SEGER
MARK RONSON
CARRIE BROWNSTEIN
AND OTHERS

Dave Says Goodbye

50 YEARS OF COVERS • 699

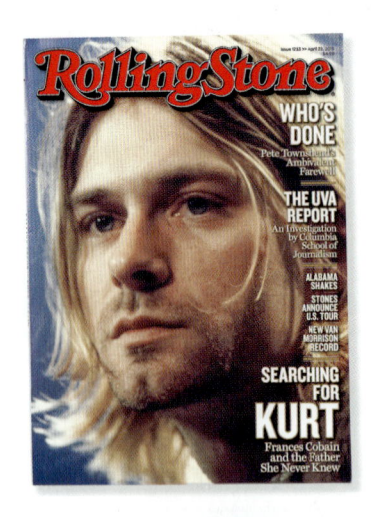

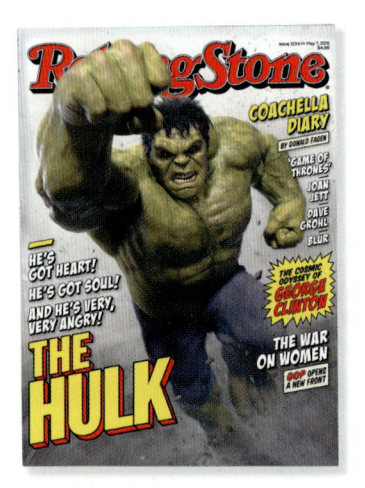

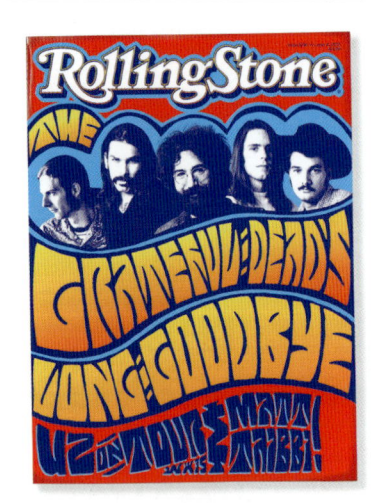

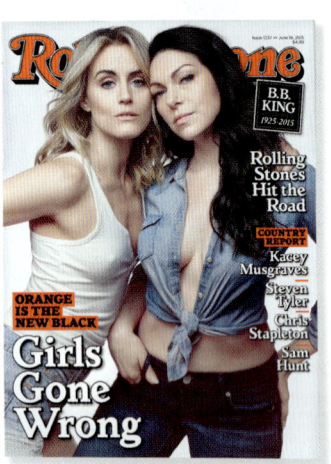

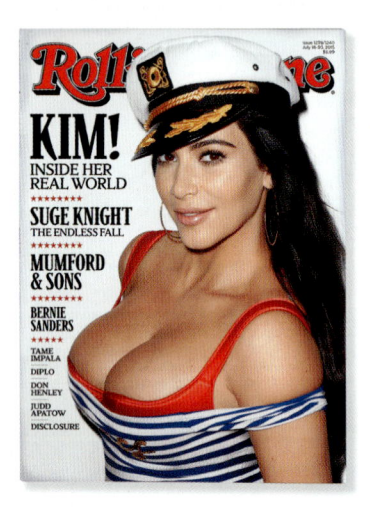

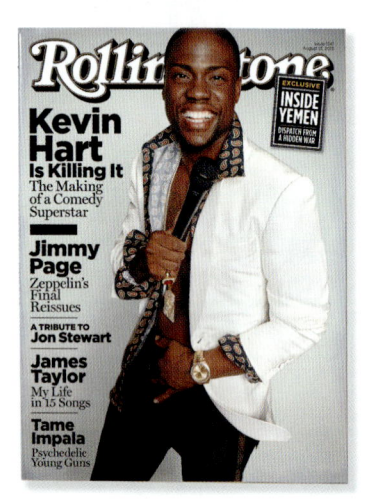

RS 1233 | KURT COBAIN
April 23rd, 2015
PHOTOGRAPH BY FRANK MICELOTTA/
GETTY IMAGES

RS 1234 | THE INCREDIBLE HULK
May 7th, 2015
ILLUSTRATION BY MARVEL 2015

RS 1236 | THE GRATEFUL DEAD
June 4th, 2015
VARIOUS PHOTOGRAPHERS; DESIGN AND LETTERING BY WES WILSON

RS 1237 | TAYLOR SCHILLING AND LAURA PREPON OF 'ORANGE IS THE NEW BLACK'
June 18th, 2015
PHOTOGRAPH BY MARK SELIGER

RS 1239/1240 | KIM KARDASHIAN
July 16th–30th, 2015
PHOTOGRAPH BY TERRY RICHARDSON

RS 1241 | KEVIN HART
August 13th, 2015
PHOTOGRAPH BY PEGGY SIROTA

2010s

700 • ROLLING STONE

RollingStone

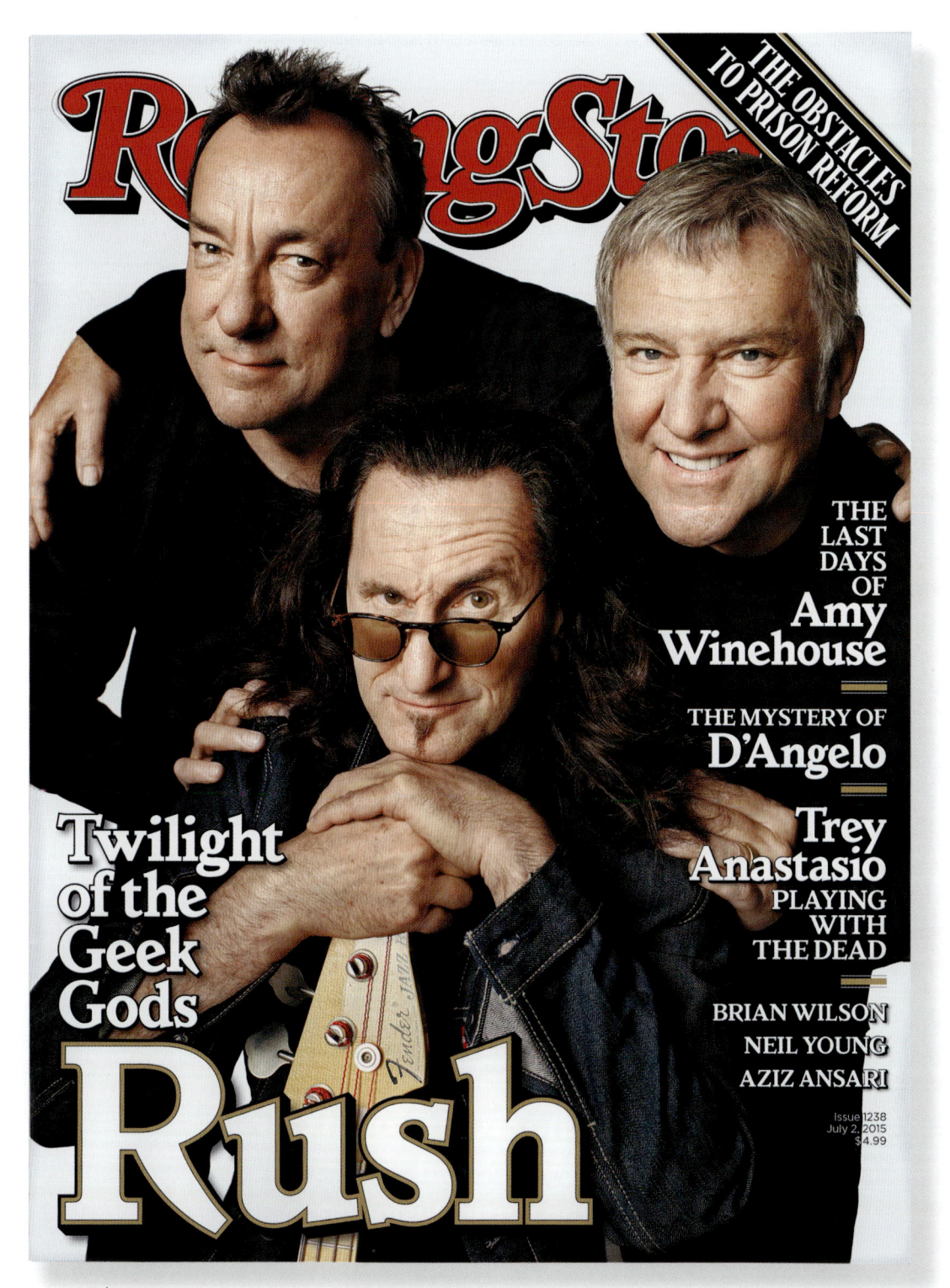

THE OBSTACLES TO PRISON REFORM

THE LAST DAYS OF **Amy Winehouse**

THE MYSTERY OF **D'Angelo**

Trey Anastasio PLAYING WITH THE DEAD

BRIAN WILSON
NEIL YOUNG
AZIZ ANSARI

Issue 1238
July 2, 2015
$4.99

Twilight of the Geek Gods
Rush

RS 1238 | RUSH | July 2nd, 2015 | Photograph by Peggy Sirota

50 YEARS OF COVERS • 701

RollingStone

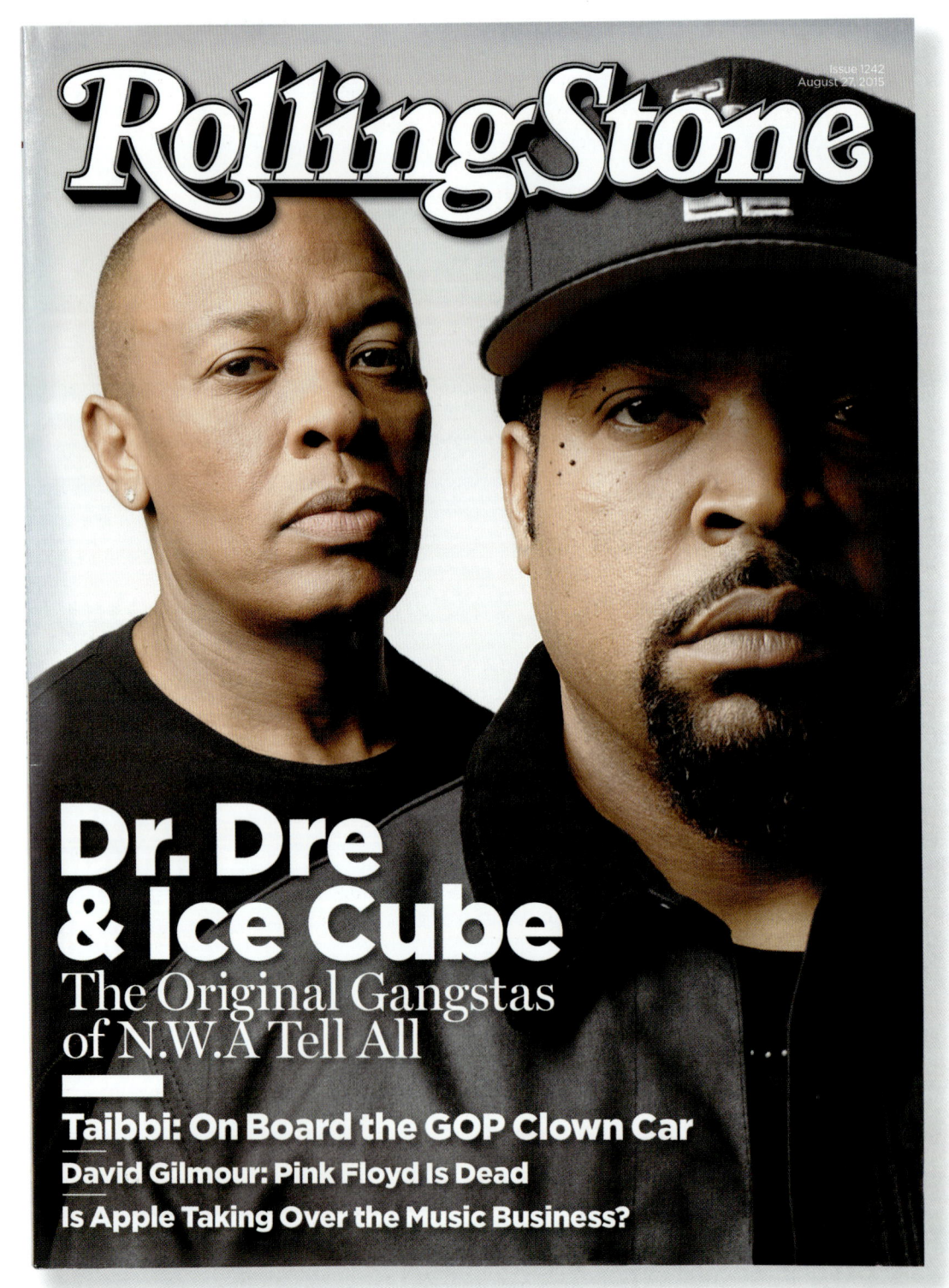

Issue 1242
August 27, 2015

Dr. Dre & Ice Cube
The Original Gangstas of N.W.A Tell All

Taibbi: On Board the GOP Clown Car
David Gilmour: Pink Floyd Is Dead
Is Apple Taking Over the Music Business?

RS 1242 | DR. DRE AND ICE CUBE | August 27th, 2015 | Photograph by Mark Seliger

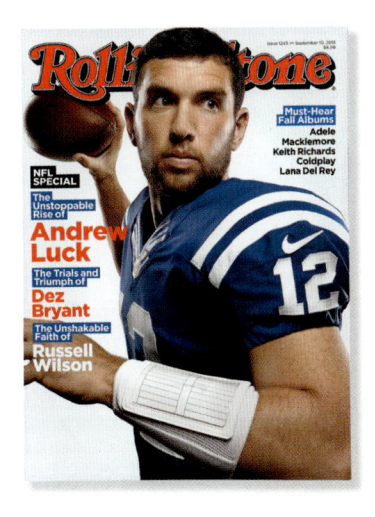

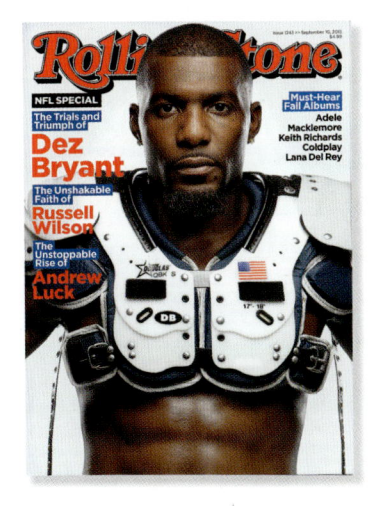

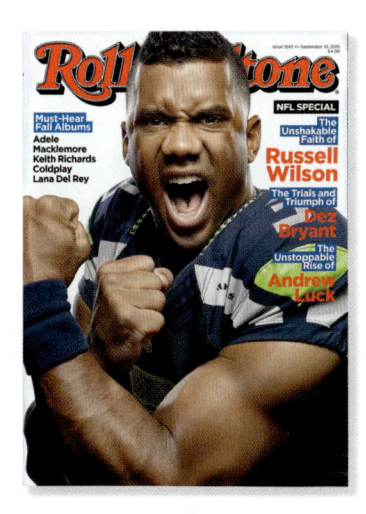

RS 1243 | ANDREW LUCK, DEZ
BRYANT & RUSSELL WILSON
September 10th, 2015
PHOTOGRAPH BY MARK SELIGER

DR. DRE PUTS ON A BLACK HOODED JACKET AND WALKS DOWN THE
hall to the complex's other studio. It's time to record the latest edition of his radio show, *The Pharmacy*, for Apple's Beats 1, with Cube and Compton director Gray as guests, along with regulars including Cube and Dre's old friend DJ Pooh, who co-wrote *Friday*. Cube is wearing a new-looking N.W.A T-shirt, sunglasses and a Dodgers cap.

Everyone is sitting around a circular table, wearing Beats by Dre headphones, surrounded by cameramen. "West Coast Mount Rushmore up in here," says Pooh. The only awkward moment comes when one of the DJs mentions that Dre and Cube used their own money to supplement the budget for a couple of scenes. Dre shakes his head. "Yeah, but we're not going to talk about that," he says.

Eventually, Gray thanks them. "Seriously, you guys, I'm honored you let me tell the story," he says. "It's a snapshot of American history."

They end the show by having Cube introduce the title track of *Straight Outta Compton*. "A-yo, wassup, it's your boy Ice Cube," he says, in full hype-man mode. "You know who I'm with? My homeboy Dr. Dre. We made history in 1989." He pauses. "Dre, let them know what they about to witness."

Dr. Dre smiles, and just as he did in a recording studio 30 miles, 26 years and many selves ago, he leans close to his microphone and intones 11 words — more reverently, this time, as if he's casting a spell: "You are now about to witness the *strength* of street knowledge."

[EXCERPT FROM RS 1242 COVER STORY BY BRIAN HIATT]

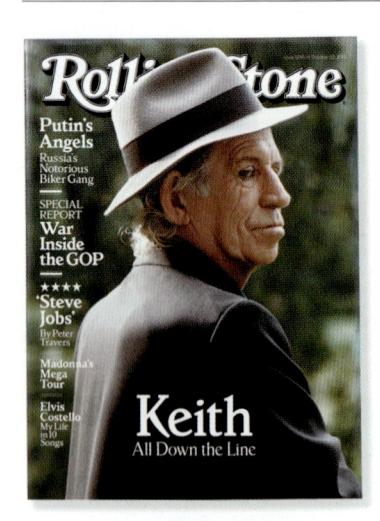

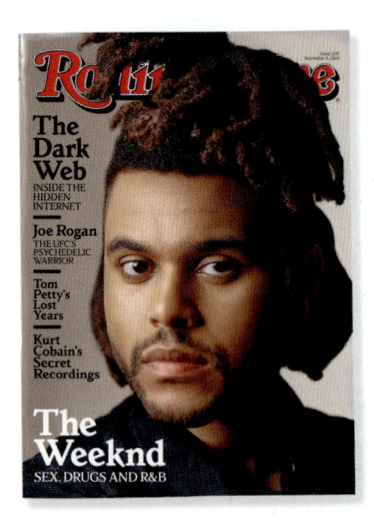

RS 1244 | DONALD TRUMP
September 24th, 2015
PHOTOGRAPH BY MARK SELIGER

RS 1246 | KEITH RICHARDS
October 22nd, 2015
PHOTOGRAPH BY THEO WENNER

RS 1247 | THE WEEKND
November 5th, 2015
PHOTOGRAPH BY MARK SELIGER

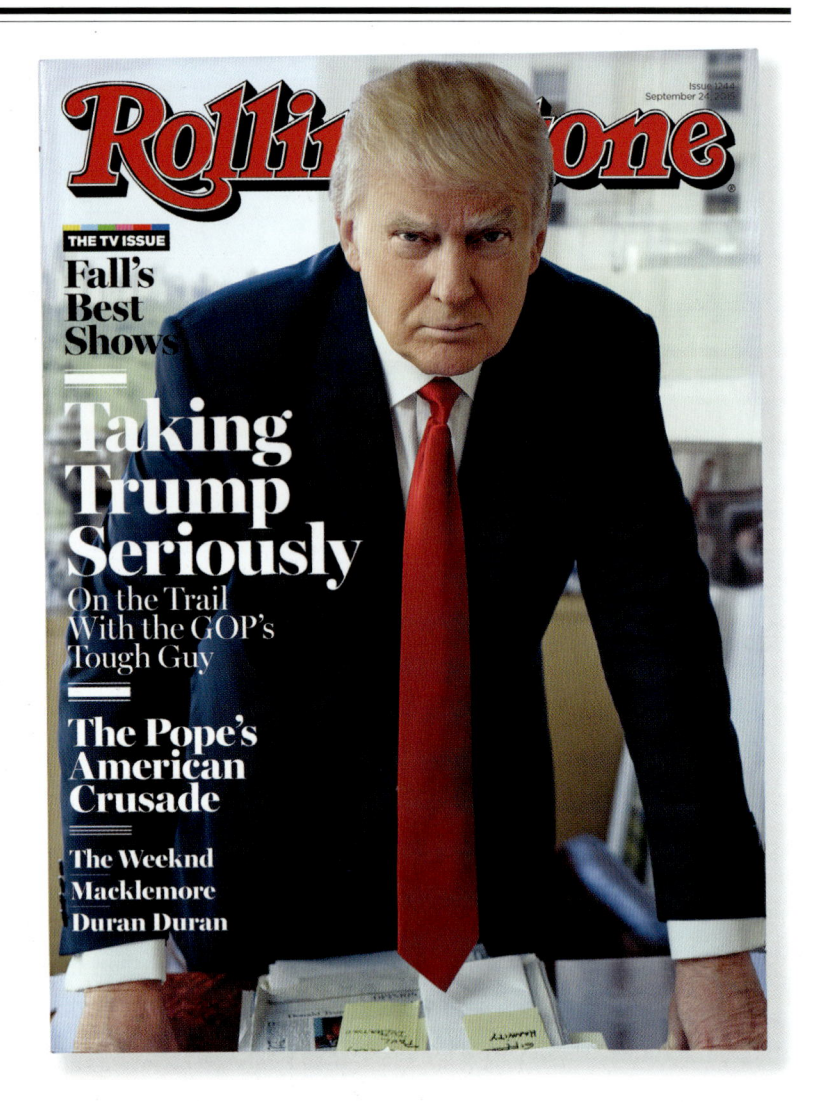

2010s

"*Typically, public figures* give you the expected situation. So the idea is to get the most unexpected moment. Usually, I just ask them to do things that we're told we can't actually ask them to do." —*Mark Seliger*

704 · ROLLING STONE

Rod Stewart's Comeback ★ Hip-Hop Smash 'Hamilton'

Rolling Stone

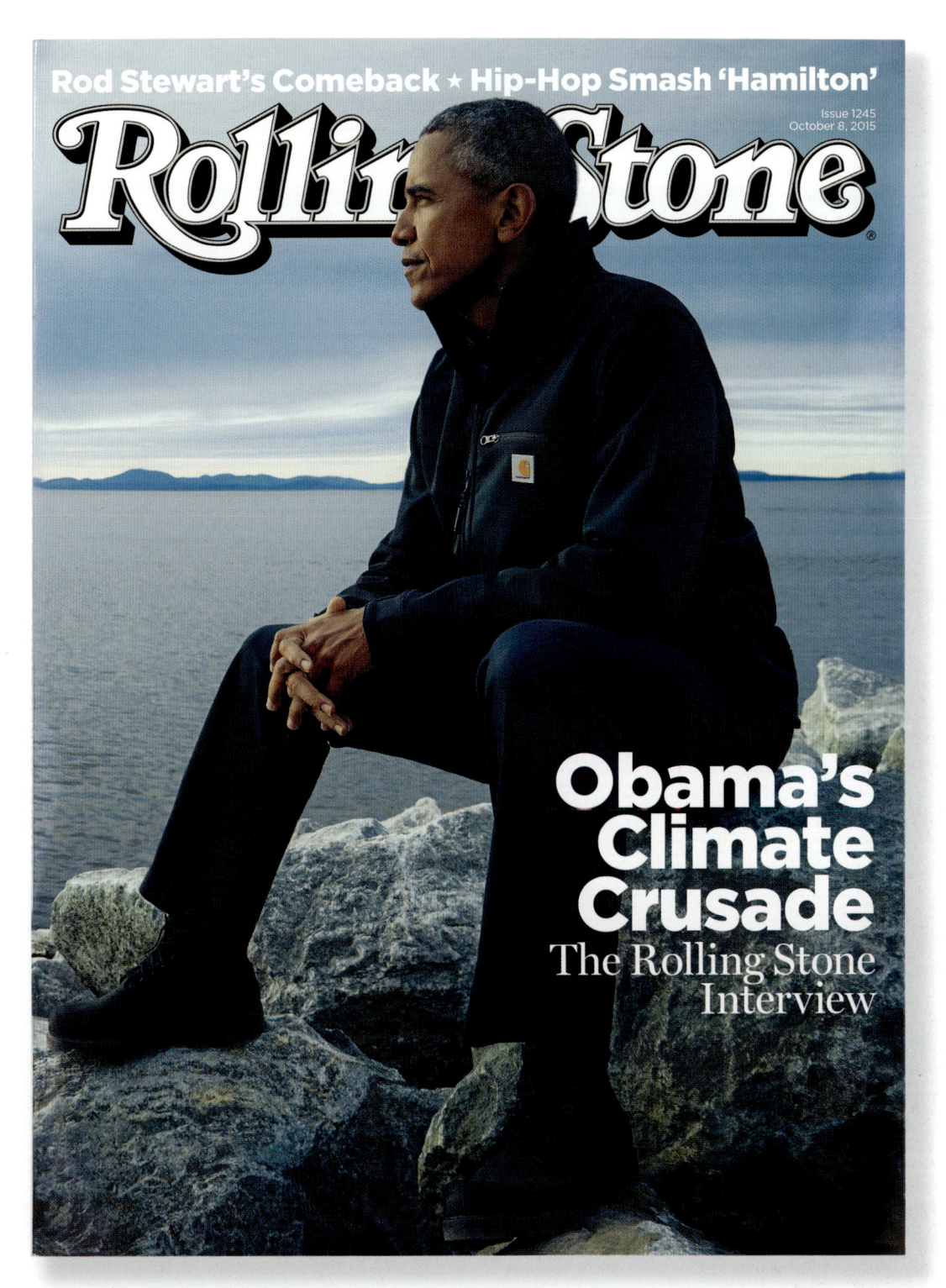

Issue 1245
October 8, 2015

Obama's Climate Crusade
The Rolling Stone Interview

RS 1245 | **BARACK OBAMA** | October 8th, 2015 | Photograph by Mark Seliger

RollingStone

Issue 1248 >> November 19, 2015

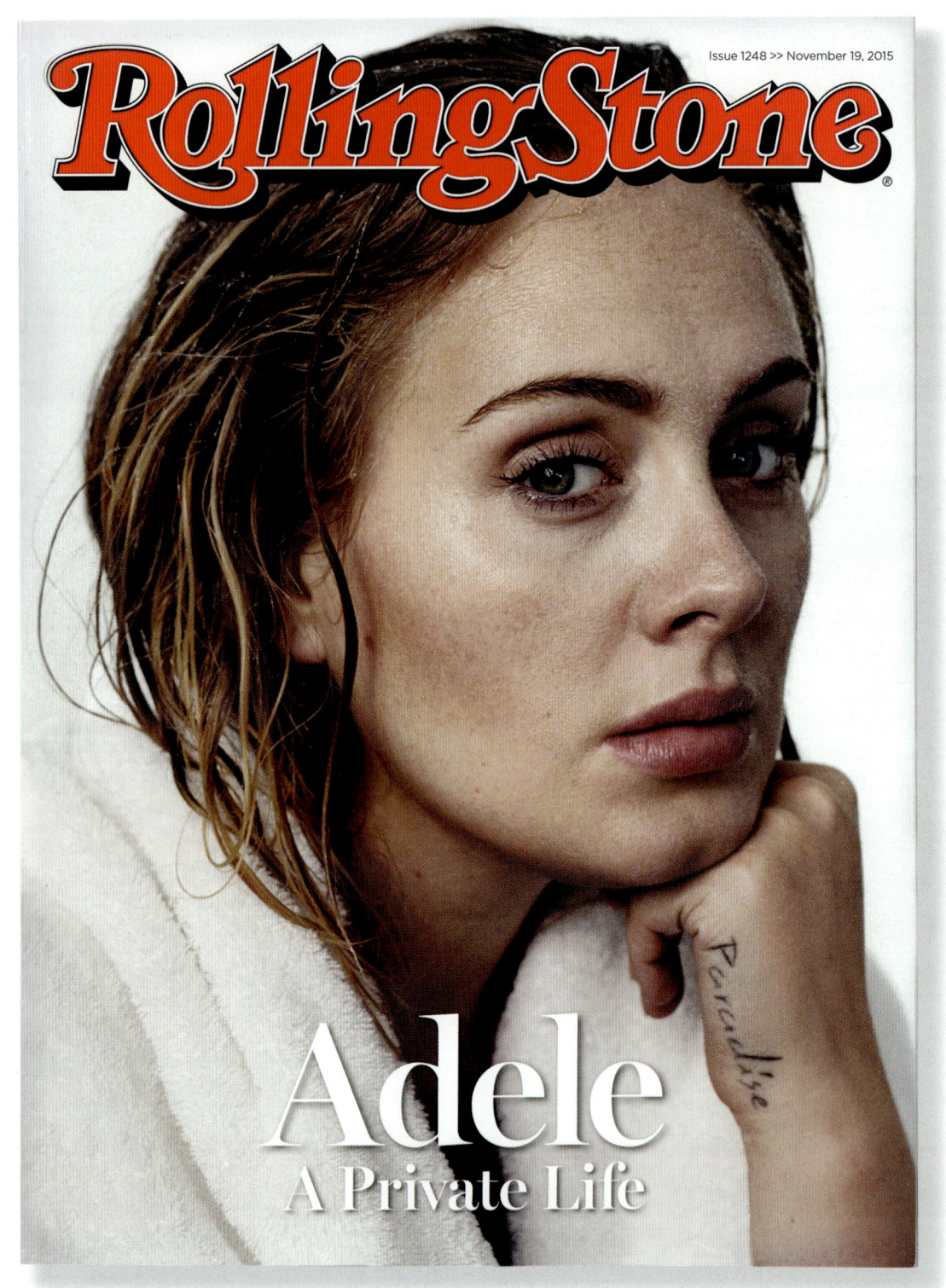

Adele
A Private Life

2010s

RS 1248 | ADELE | November 19th, 2015 | Photograph by Theo Wenner

"**I am a child** of the Sixties – I like the Motown sound and the Supremes and the Temptations. I am one of the few human beings – and this will not find favor with 'Rolling Stone' readers – but I like disco music. I like Abba. We played some Abba at my wedding. I like the Bee Gees. I am pretty across-the-board in my musical tastes. I like Celine Dion. I like country music."

—*Bernie Sanders*

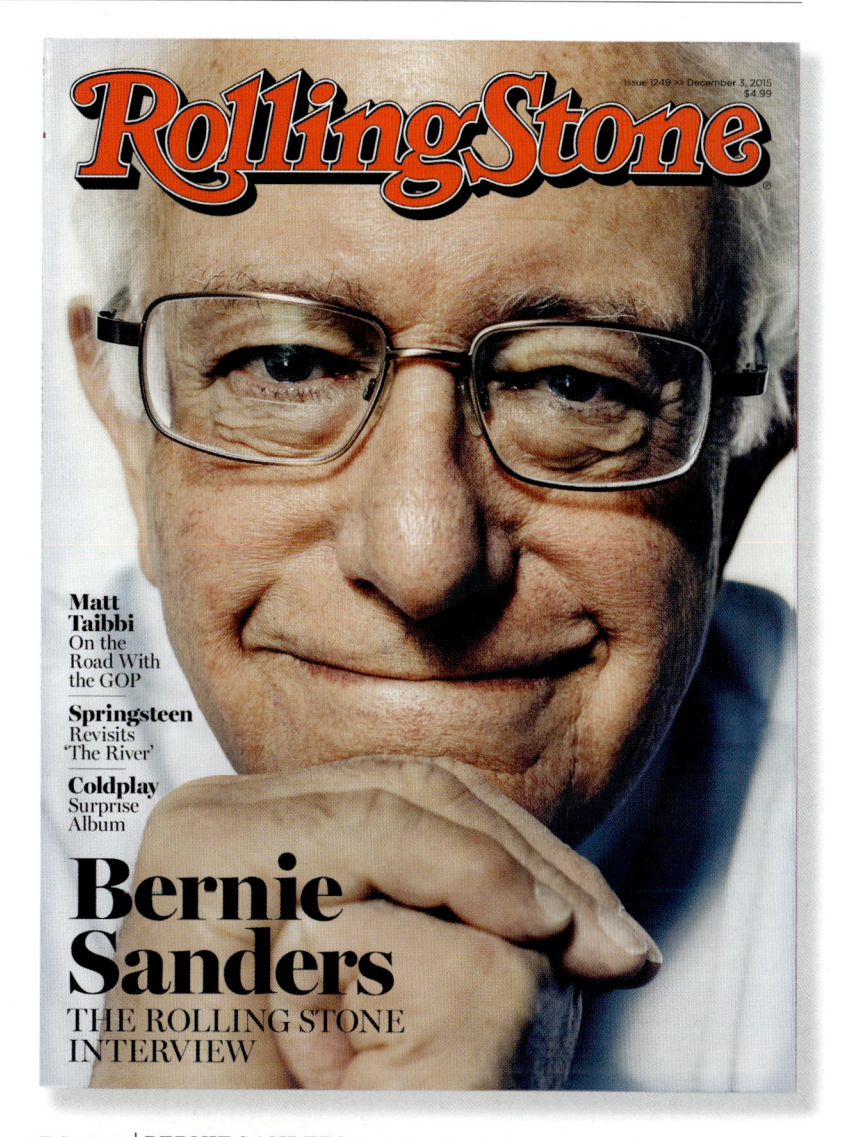

RS 1249 | BERNIE SANDERS | December 3rd, 2015 | Photograph by Christopher Anderson

[RS 1249] A true man of the people, Vermont senator and underdog Democratic presidential hopeful Bernie Sanders made things as easy as possible for the RS photo team by taking time out of his busy campaign schedule and dropping by our offices for an afternoon photo session. "I'm trying to create a movement," he told Tim Dickinson in his Rolling Stone interview. "That is what my campaign is about."

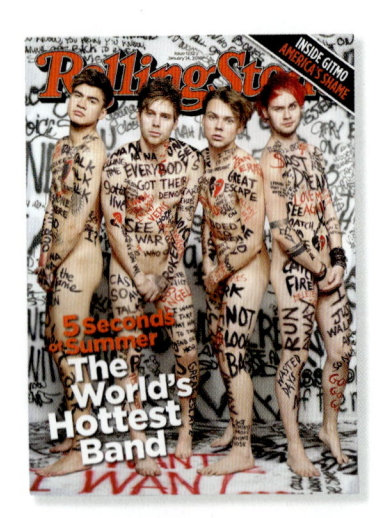

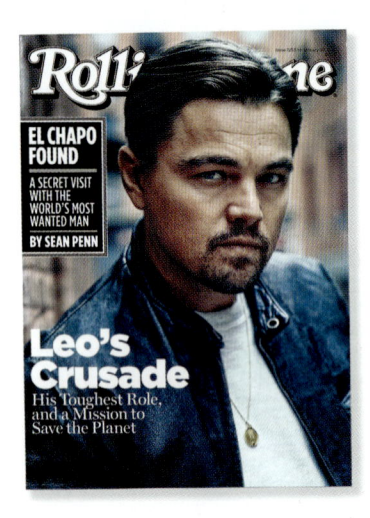

RS 1252 | 5 Seconds
of Summer
January 14th, 2016
Photograph by Martin Schoeller

RS 1253 | Leonardo
DiCaprio
January 28th, 2016
Photograph by Mark Seliger

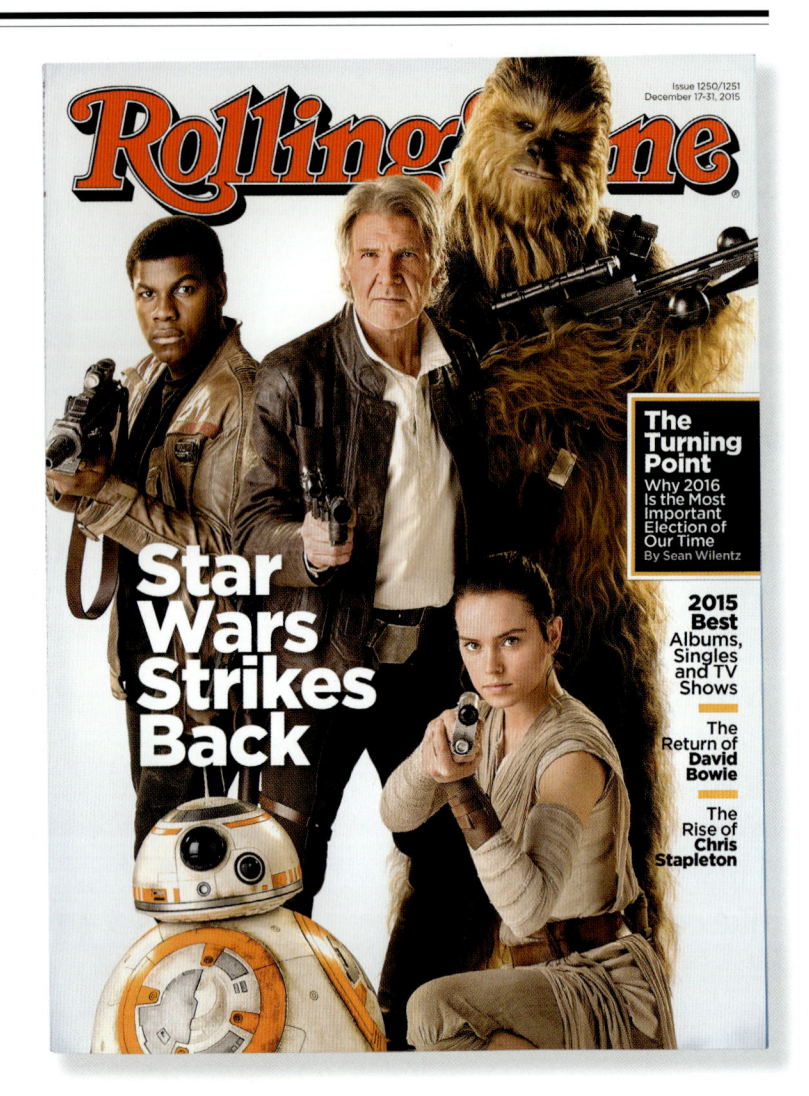

RS 1250/1251 | Cast
of 'Star Wars'
December 17th–31st, 2015
Photograph by Jules Heath/
© 2015 Lucasfilm Ltd.

Rolling Stone

Issue 1255
February 25, 2016

SPECIAL REPORT
The Koch Brothers Battle Solar Energy

The Revenant's Dark Genius

A Beach Boy Looks Back in Anger

Black Sabbath's Last Ride

Chris Martin
HEARTACHE & HEALING

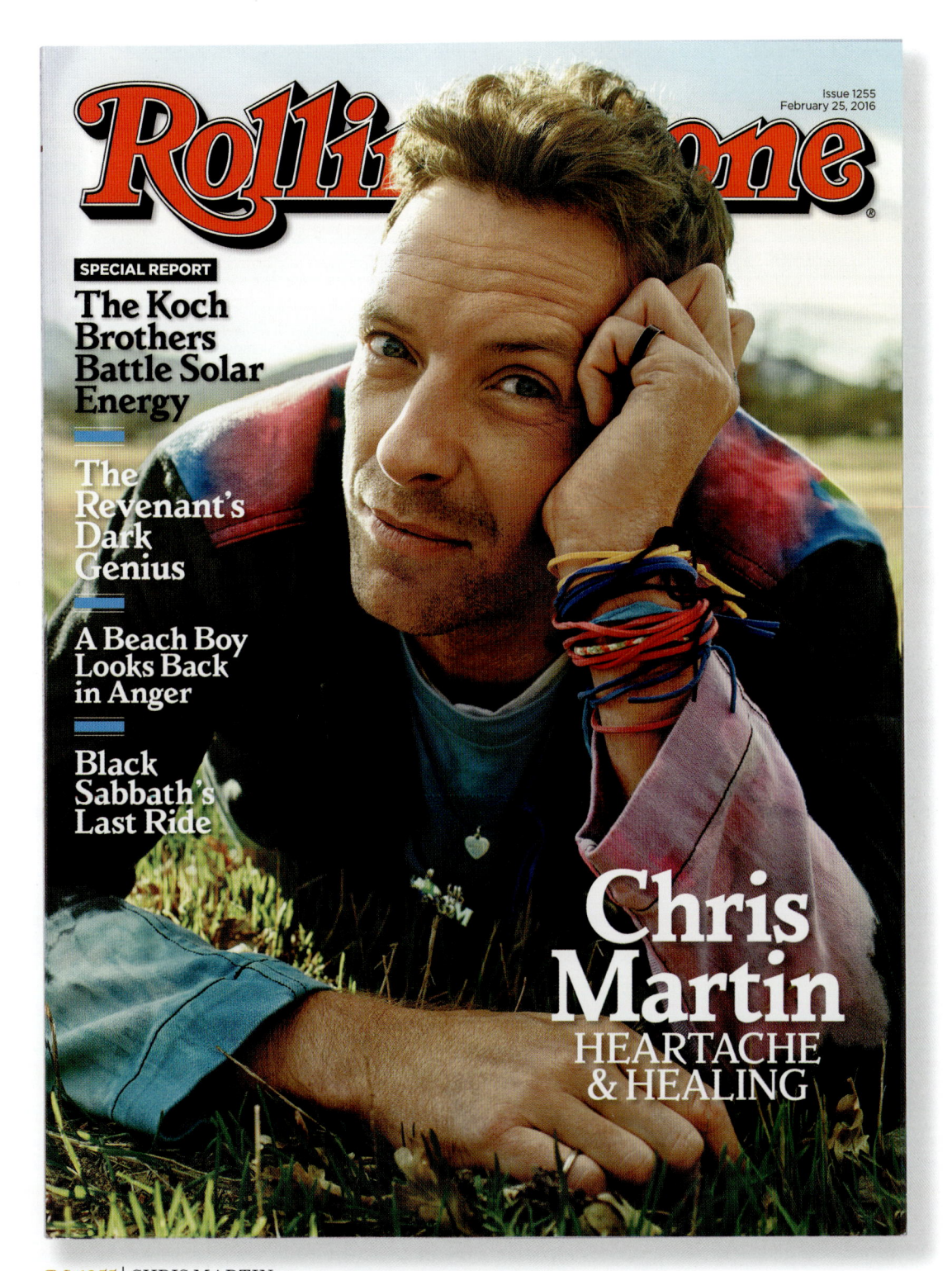

RS 1255 | CHRIS MARTIN | February 25th, 2016 | Photograph by Peggy Sirota

50 YEARS OF COVERS • 709

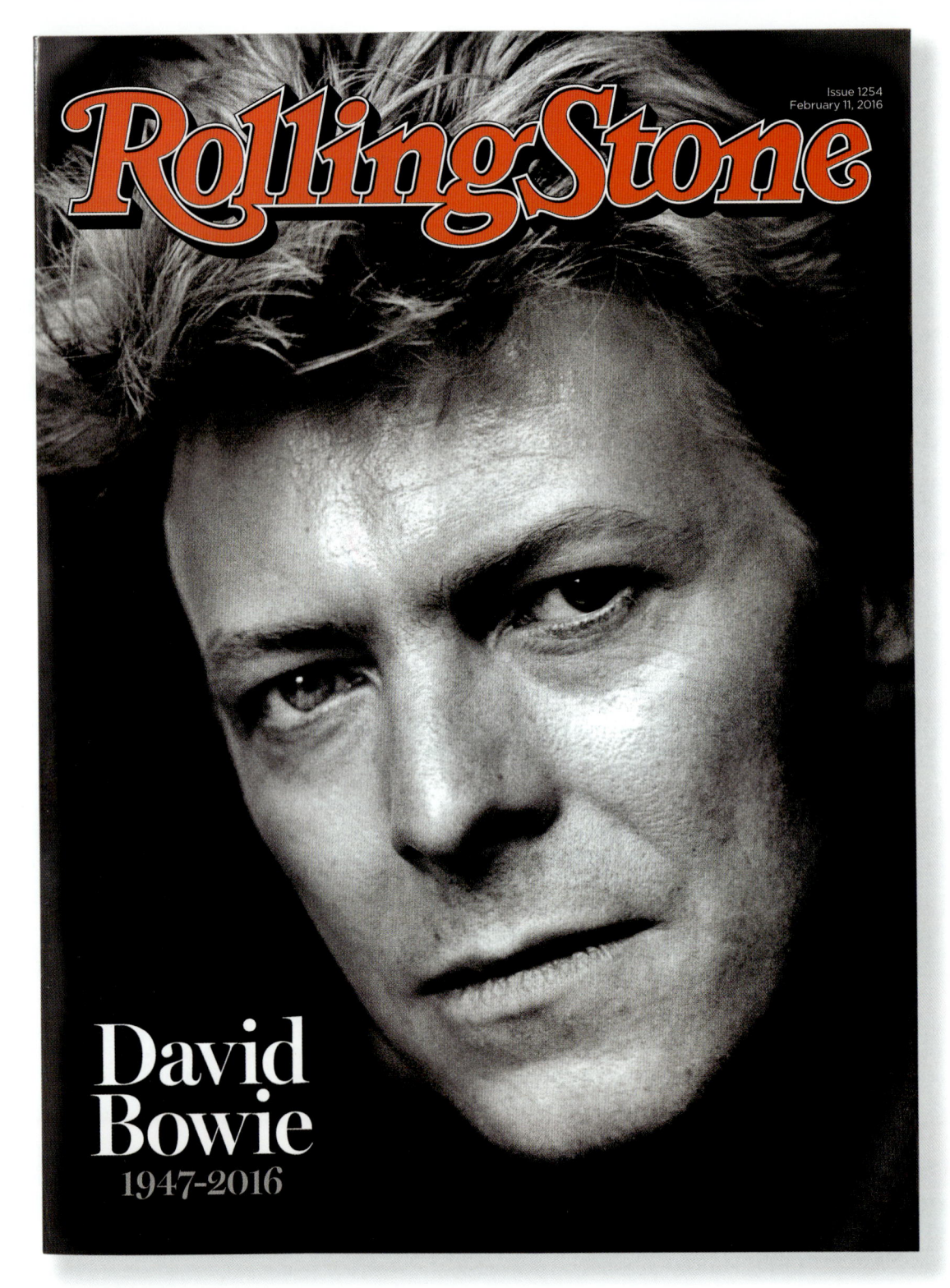

Rolling Stone

Issue 1254
February 11, 2016

David Bowie
1947–2016

RS 1254 | DAVID BOWIE | February 11th, 2016 | Photograph by Anton Corbijn

Death had been on David Bowie's mind in recent years. In "The Stars (Are Out Tonight)," from his surprise 2013 release, *The Next Day,* he could see it above and below: "Stars are never sleeping/Dead ones and the living/We live closer to the Earth/Never to the heavens." Most memorably, he spoke about it in lyrics from his new album, *Blackstar,* released just two days before his end. In the spellbinding "Lazarus," Bowie sang, "Look up here, I'm in heaven/I've got scars that can't be seen/I've got drama, can't be stolen/Everybody knows me now/Look up here, man, I'm in danger/I've got nothing left to lose." It was the least fanciful verse he'd ever written. For us, though, death didn't seem to become David Bowie. —*Mikal Gilmore*

"THE FIRST TIME I SAW HIM PERFORM WAS ON *Top of the Pops* in 1972, singing 'Starman.' He was so vivid. So luminous. So fluorescent. We had one of the first color TVs on our street, and David Bowie was the reason to have a color TV. I've said he was our Elvis Presley. There are so many similarities: the masculine-feminine duality, the physical mastery of being on a stage. They created original silhouettes, shapes now seen as obvious, that did not exist before." —*Bono*

"HE JUST CAME FRESH FROM A CHEMO session. And there was no way he could keep it a secret from the band. He told me privately, and I really got choked up when we sat face to face talking about it. He was so brave and courageous. And his energy was still incredible for a man who had cancer. He never showed any fear. He was just all business about making the album. I think he thought if he was going to die, this would be a great way to go. This would be a great statement to make." —*Tony Visconti*

"THERE WAS ALWAYS AN EXCHANGE of information within our friendship. And I suppose there was always an element of competition between us, but it never felt overwhelming. When he'd come over, we'd talk about our work – a new guitarist, a new way of writing, style and photographers. We had a lot in common in wanting to do big things onstage – using interesting designs, narratives, personalities. He'd always look at my clothes labels. When he would see me, he'd give me a hug, and I could feel him going up behind the collar of my shirt to see what I was wearing. He used to copy me sometimes, but he'd be very honest about it. If he took one of your moves, he'd say, 'That's one of yours – I just tried it.' I didn't mind sharing things with him, because he would share so much with me – it was a two-way street." —*Mick Jagger*

RollingStone

Issue 1260 >> May 5, 2016
$4.99

Merle Haggard
1937-2016
The Outlaw

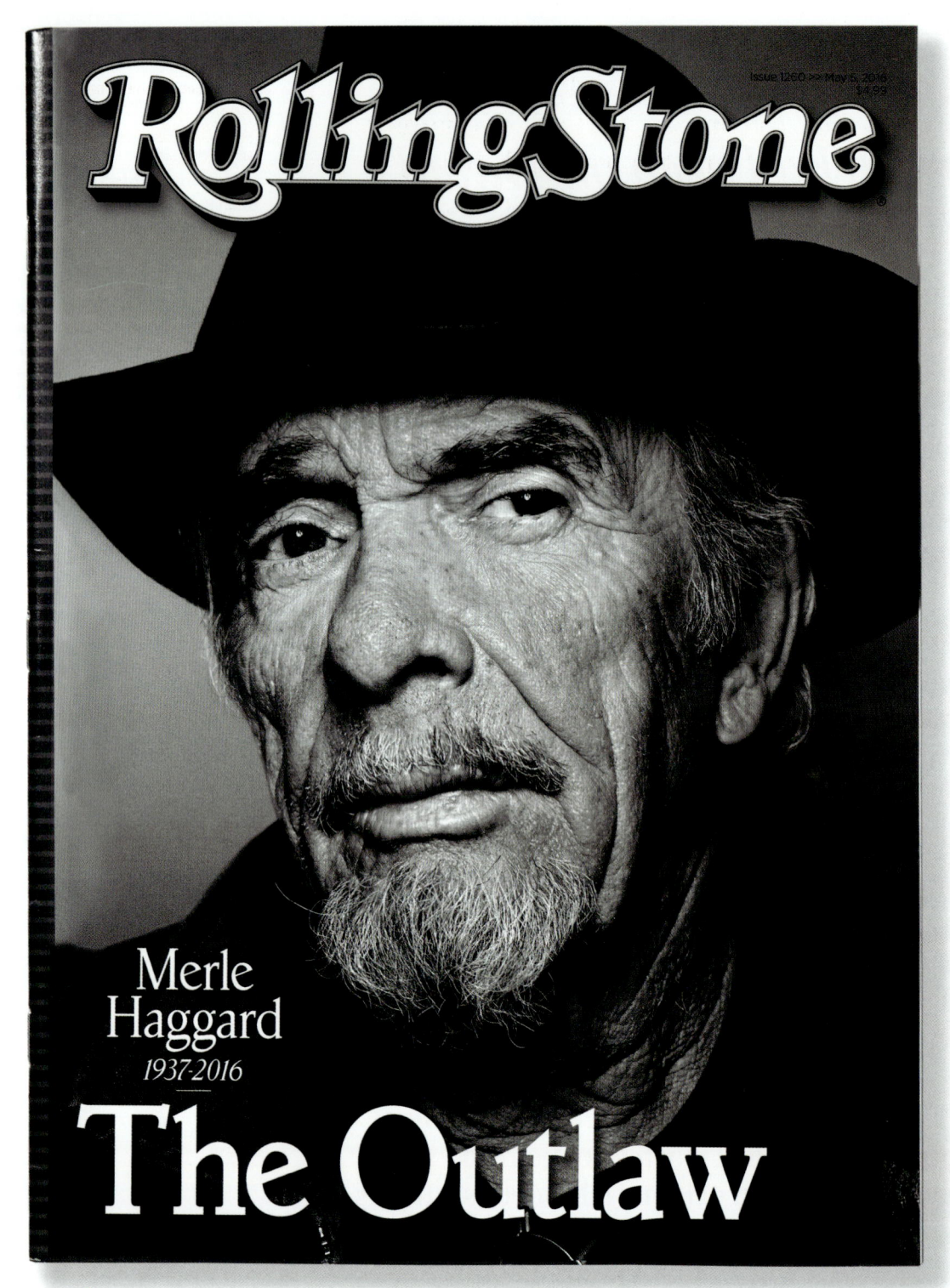

2010s

RS 1260 | MERLE HAGGARD | May 5th, 2016 | Photograph by Martin Schoeller/August

FROM THE START, he commanded attention with his voice. In contrast to Hank Williams' nervy drawl or Johnny Cash's rough-hewn, colloquial way of sharing predicaments, Haggard began with an impossibly beautiful voice. His brandy-toned, barroom plea could glide up a scale fluidly, without any discernible steps; it was a prodigy's feat, like Frank Sinatra's young mellifluence or Jim Reeves' plaintive Western croon. Haggard's voice yielded hard truths – songs about hearts lost in alcohol's shadow, men who couldn't find honest support and lived outside the law. Though his audience didn't know it for years, he was often singing about himself. Of all the country artists who bore or brandished an outlaw image, Haggard had come up against that life, and paid for it. That authenticity helped make him one of the most revered singers and songwriters that country music ever delivered. By the end of his life, 38 of his albums appeared on *Billboard*'s country-music Top 10 charts; more than a dozen made it to Number One. He also had 38 Number One singles. Hits like "Branded Man," "Sing Me Back Home," "Mama Tried" – about lives forfeited in punishment or desperation – found their way into Americans' conscience.

[EXCERPT FROM RS 1260 COVER STORY BY MIKAL GILMORE]

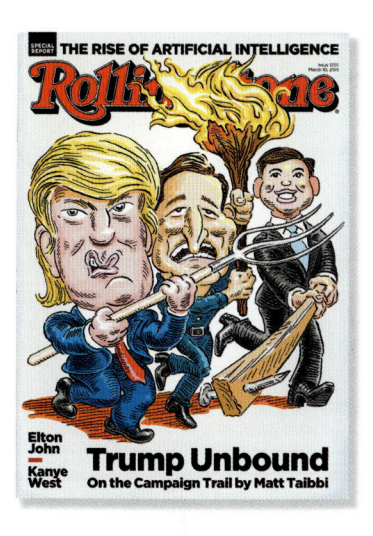

RS 1256 | DONALD TRUMP, TED CRUZ & MARCO RUBIO
March 10th, 2016
ILLUSTRATION BY ROBERT GROSSMAN

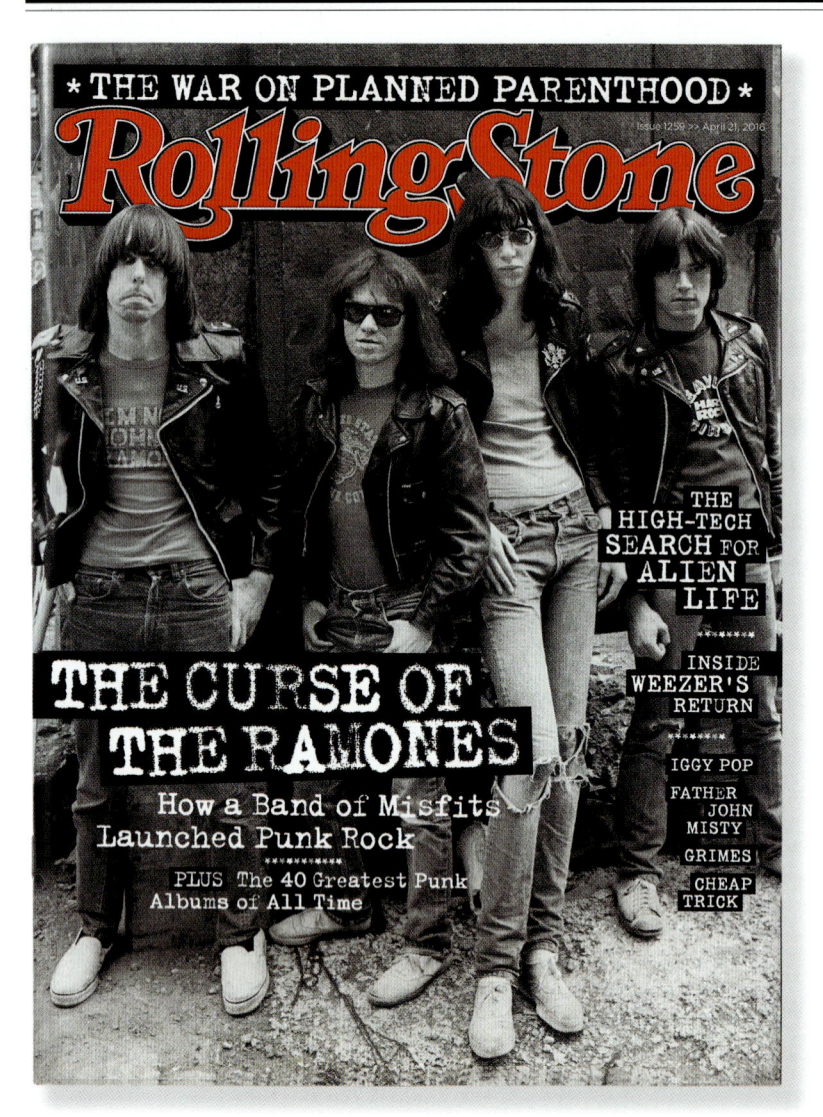

RS 1259 | THE RAMONES | April 21st, 2016 | Photograph by Ian Dickson/
© The Hell Gate/Corbis

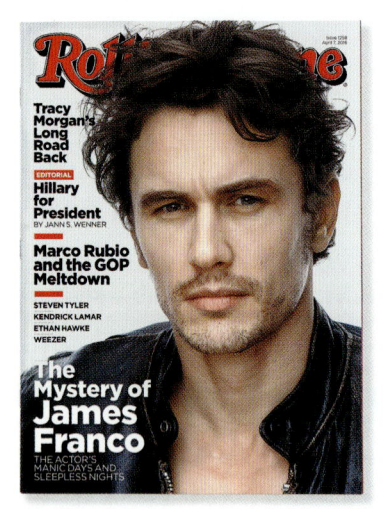

RS 1258 | JAMES FRANCO
April 7th, 2016
Photograph by Mark Seliger

[**RS 1259**] To celebrate the 40th anniversary of the Ramones' debut album, we ranked the "40 Greatest Punk Albums of All Time." Our master list of potential candidates had more than 200 LPs on it. Sadly, classics such as the Circle Jerks' *Wild in the Streets* and Halo of Flies' *Music for Insect Minds* didn't make the cut.

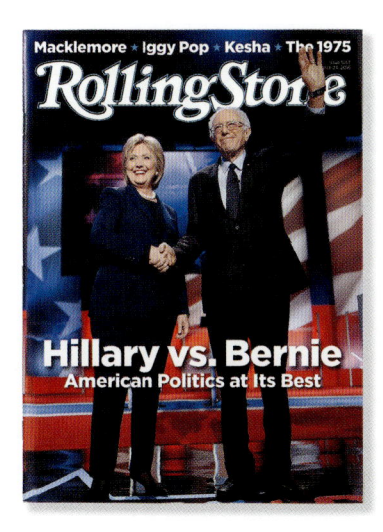

RS 1257 | HILLARY RODHAM CLINTON & BERNIE SANDERS
March 24th, 2016
PHOTOGRAPH BY JOE RAEDLE/GETTY IMAGES

"I KNOW IT SOMETIMES SEEMS A little odd for someone running for president, these days, in this time, to say we need more love and kindness in America. But I'm telling you, from the bottom of my heart, we do."
—*Hillary Rodham Clinton*

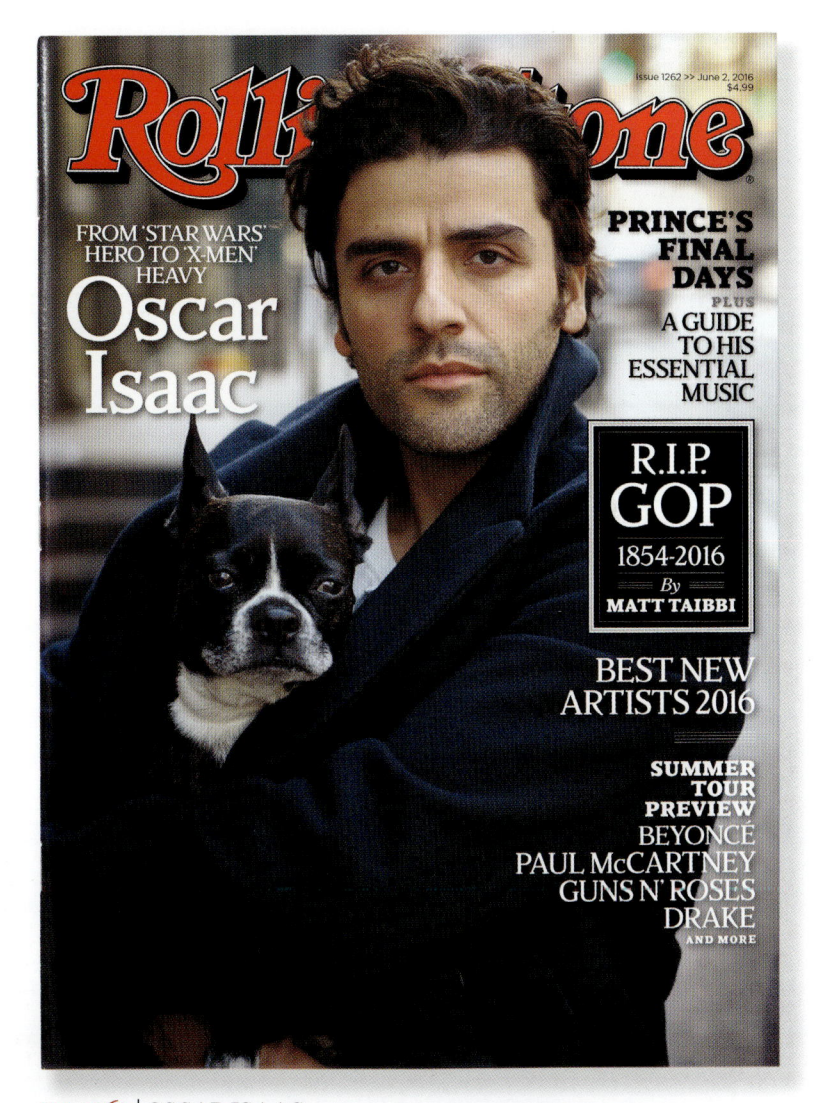

RS 1262 | OSCAR ISAAC | June 2nd, 2016 | PHOTOGRAPH BY MARK SELIGER

50 YEARS OF COVERS • 715

Issue 1261 >> May 19, 2016
$4.99

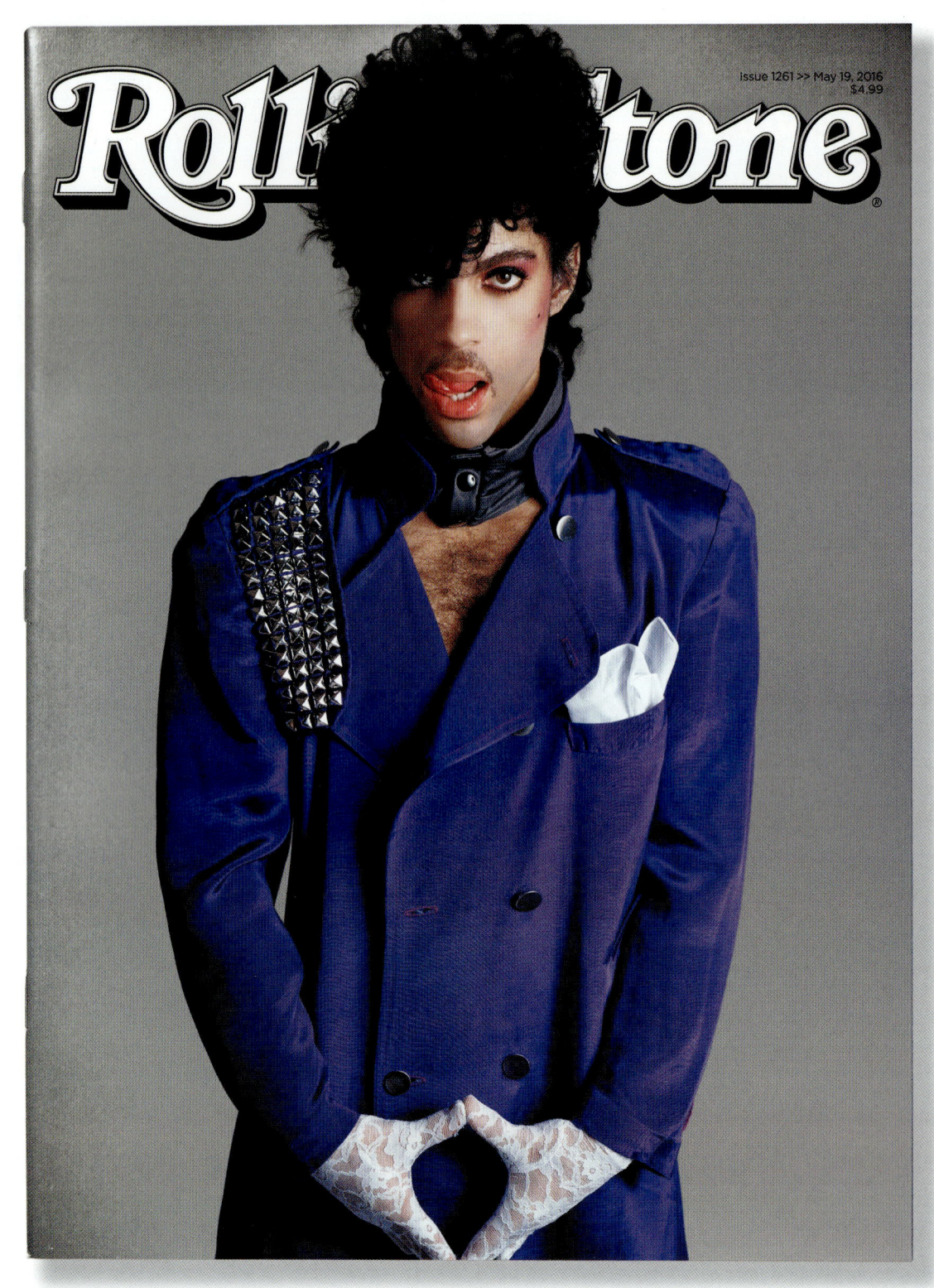

Rolling Stone

2010s

Thursday morning, April 21st, Prince was found in an elevator at Paisley Park. Sources say he had been living by himself in an apartment on the second floor in the back of the 65,000-square-foot complex. The last time he'd been seen alive was about 8 p.m. the previous night. A 911 call was placed at 9:43 a.m., but medics could not revive him and Prince was pronounced dead at 10:07 a.m. He was 57. In Minneapolis that night, the streets around First Avenue, the club where the performance scenes of the *Purple Rain* movie were filmed, were shut down, as thousands of people gathered to dance and sing along to Prince's music. They were not alone. They danced in Los Angeles and in Brooklyn.

They were gathered to enact the music, which has always been about community – the utopias of musical and sexual freedom he called Uptown, Paisley Park or Erotic City. He was rock's greatest trickster figure, the trick being that he could become whatever you imagined a rock star to be. "Am I black or white, am I straight or gay?" he asked in one song. The only answer was yes. He shifted his voice from male to female, and shrouded himself in mystery and impeccably tailored clothing (when he chose to wear clothing), selling fantasy in his music and image. Those fantasies were outrageously sexual and passionately religious, sometimes at the same moment.

[EXCERPT FROM RS 1261 COVER STORY BY JOE LEVY]

RS 1261 | PRINCE
May 19th, 2016
PHOTOGRAPH BY RICHARD AVEDON/
© THE RICHARD AVEDON FOUNDATION

Rolling Stone

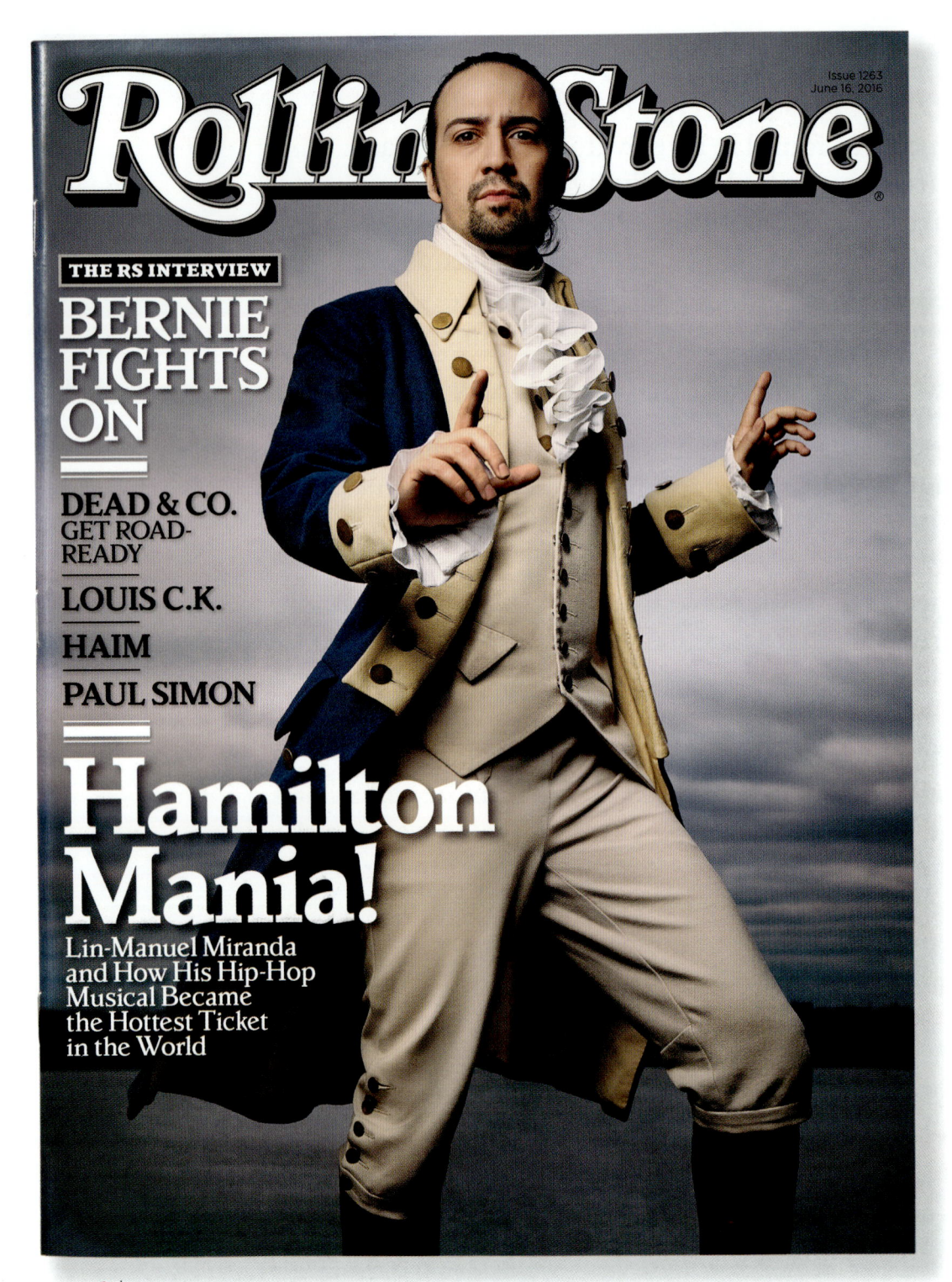

Issue 1263
June 16, 2016

THE RS INTERVIEW
BERNIE FIGHTS ON

DEAD & CO. GET ROAD-READY

LOUIS C.K.

HAIM

PAUL SIMON

Hamilton Mania!

Lin-Manuel Miranda and How His Hip-Hop Musical Became the Hottest Ticket in the World

RS 1263 | LIN-MANUEL MIRANDA | June 16th, 2016 | Photograph by Mark Seliger

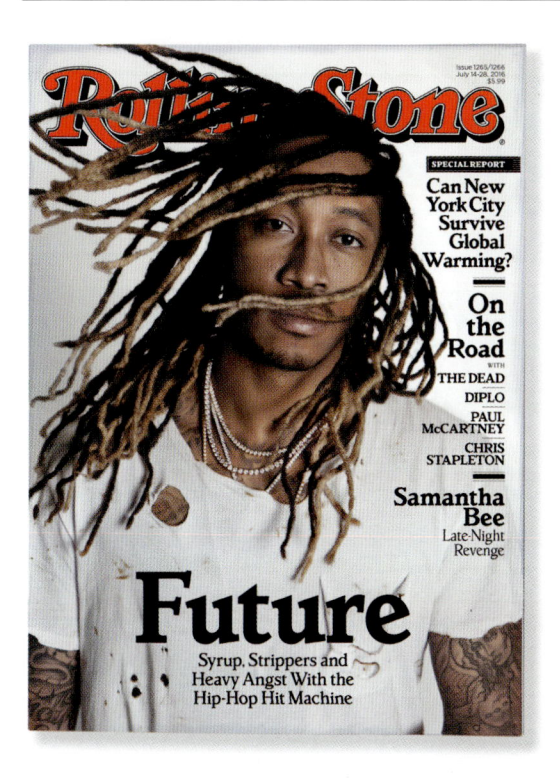

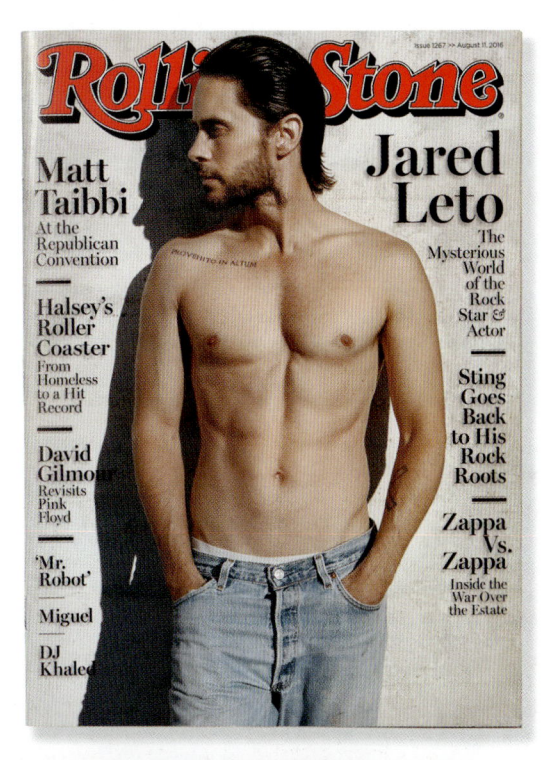

RS 1265/1266 | FUTURE
July 14th–28th, 2016
PHOTOGRAPH BY THEO WENNER

RS 1267 | JARED LETO
August 11th, 2016
PHOTOGRAPH BY THEO WENNER

RS 1268 | PAUL McCARTNEY
August 25th, 2016
PHOTOGRAPH BY MAX VADUKUL

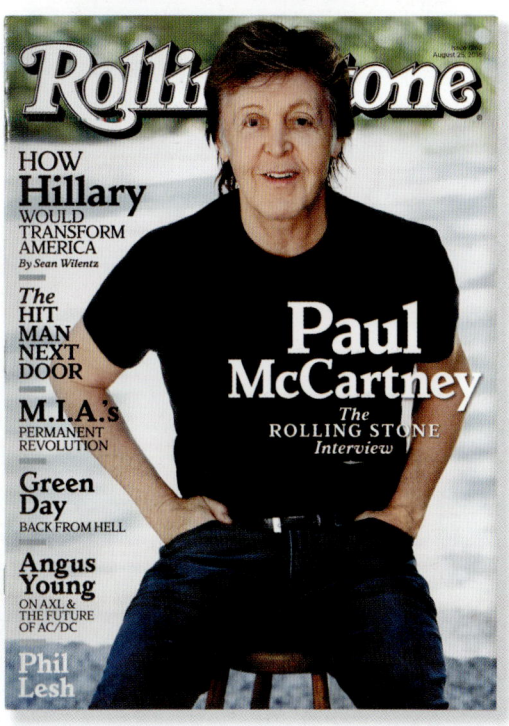

"*Lin came early,* and we built a platform on my roof. We had the perfect cloudy, overcast day. Then in post we took out New Jersey. It almost looks like one of those National Portrait Gallery paintings."

—*Mark Seliger*

50 YEARS OF COVERS • 719

Rolling Stone

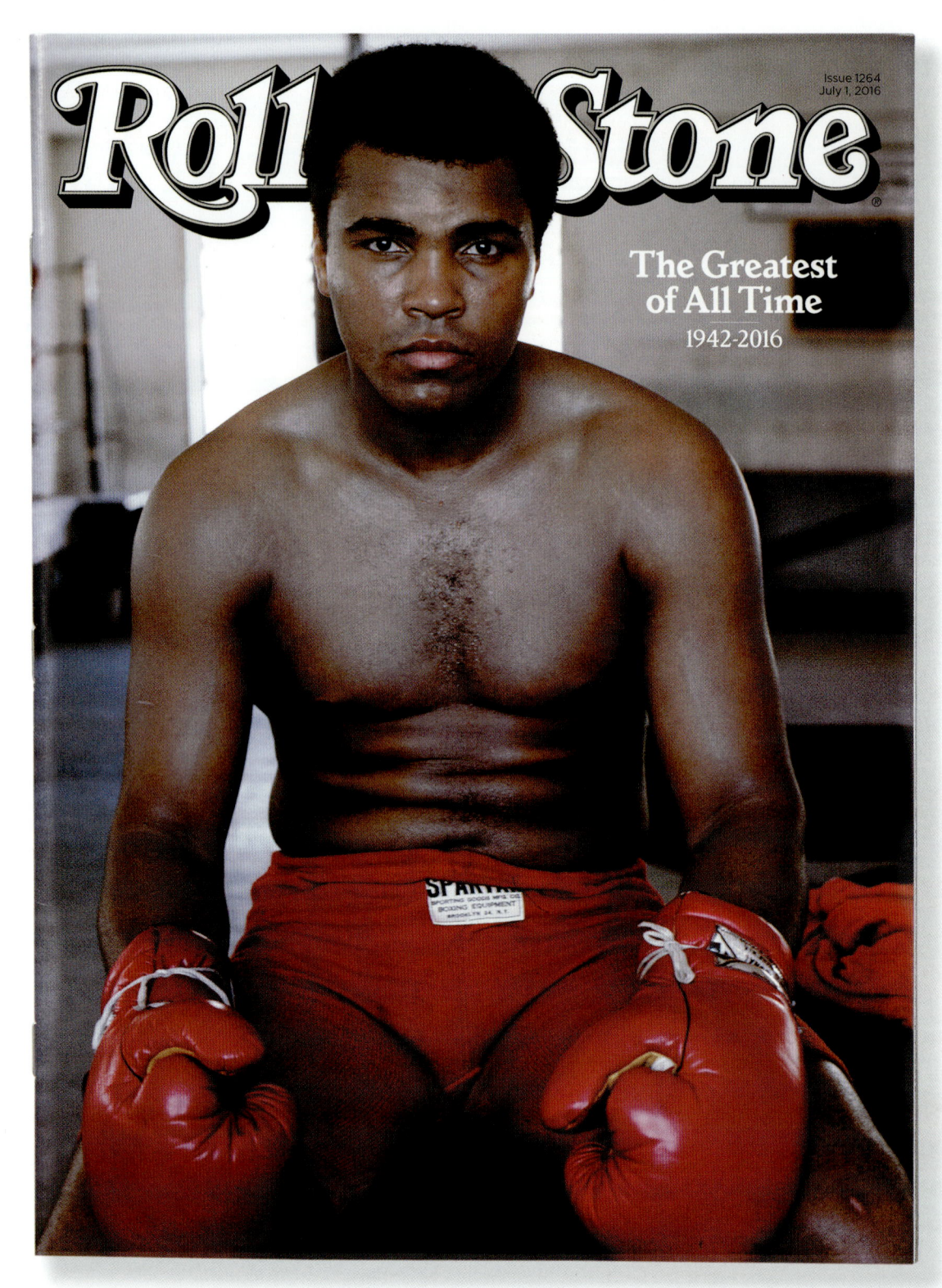

Issue 1264
July 1, 2016

The Greatest of All Time
1942-2016

2010s

RS 1264 | MUHAMMAD ALI
July 1st, 2016
Photograph by Gordon Parks/
© The Gordon Parks Foundation

Ali demanded respect and warranted it; he wouldn't be refused. In the process, he transformed the possibilities of pride, courage and recognition for many other black people – in athletics, certainly, but also beyond. "One of the reasons that the civil rights movement went forward," television journalist Bryant Gumbel said, "was that black people were able to overcome their fear. And I honestly believe that for many black Americans, that came from watching Muhammad Ali. He simply refused to be afraid."

That bravery went beyond both the remarkable feats and punishment he met within the ring. For half his life, he was stricken with Parkinson's; he could have been impatient, even bitter, about how his condition had undermined him for far longer than his prowess had served him. On occasion, when he felt uncomfortable with his slurred speech, he might cut short a conversation, either out of embarrassment or a desire not to be pitied, as he did during an interview with Ed Bradley on *60 Minutes*, in 1996. But Ali was nonetheless reflective about his disorder. "I know why this happened," Ali told David Remnick. "God's showing me that I'm just a man like everyone else. Showing you, too. You can learn from me that way." Nothing, though, would ever undermine all that he had done.

[EXCERPT FROM RS 1264 COVER STORY BY MIKAL GILMORE]

Rolling Stone

Issue 1269 >> September 8, 2016
$4.99

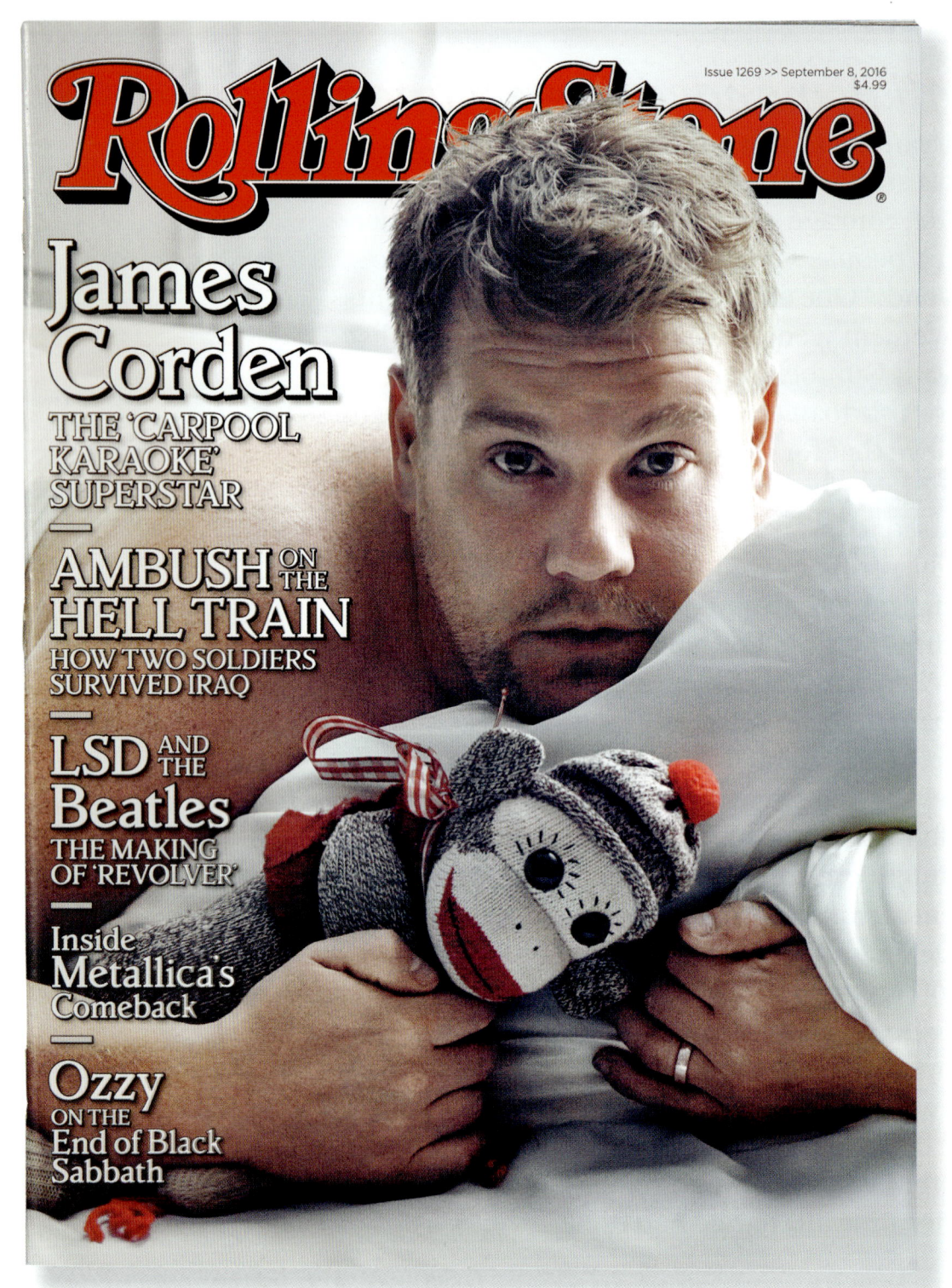

James Corden
THE 'CARPOOL KARAOKE' SUPERSTAR

AMBUSH ON THE HELL TRAIN
HOW TWO SOLDIERS SURVIVED IRAQ

LSD AND THE Beatles
THE MAKING OF 'REVOLVER'

Inside Metallica's Comeback

Ozzy ON THE End of Black Sabbath

2010s

RS 1269 | JAMES CORDEN | September 8th, 2016 | Photograph by Mark Seliger

Issue 1270
September 22, 2016

RollingStone

HOW TRUMP LOST HIS MOJO
By Matt Taibbi

LAURA JANE GRACE'S TRANSGENDER PUNK-ROCK BLUES

FRANK OCEAN

KANYE WEST

+

A GUIDE TO FALL'S BIGGEST ALBUMS

GREEN DAY
Louder, Faster, Angrier

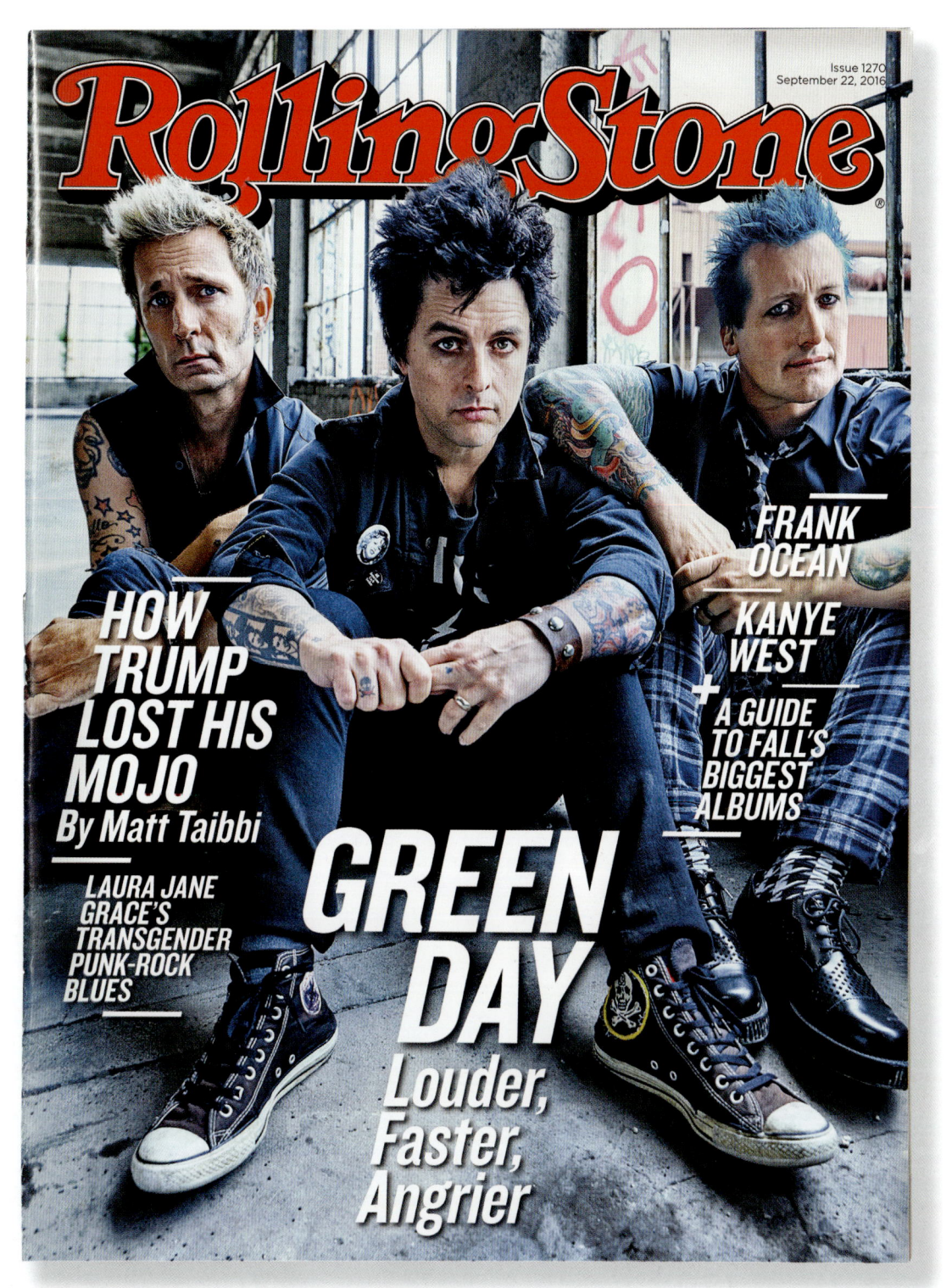

RS 1270 | GREEN DAY | September 22nd, 2016 | Photograph by Mark Seliger

Issue 1272 >> October 20, 2016
$6.99

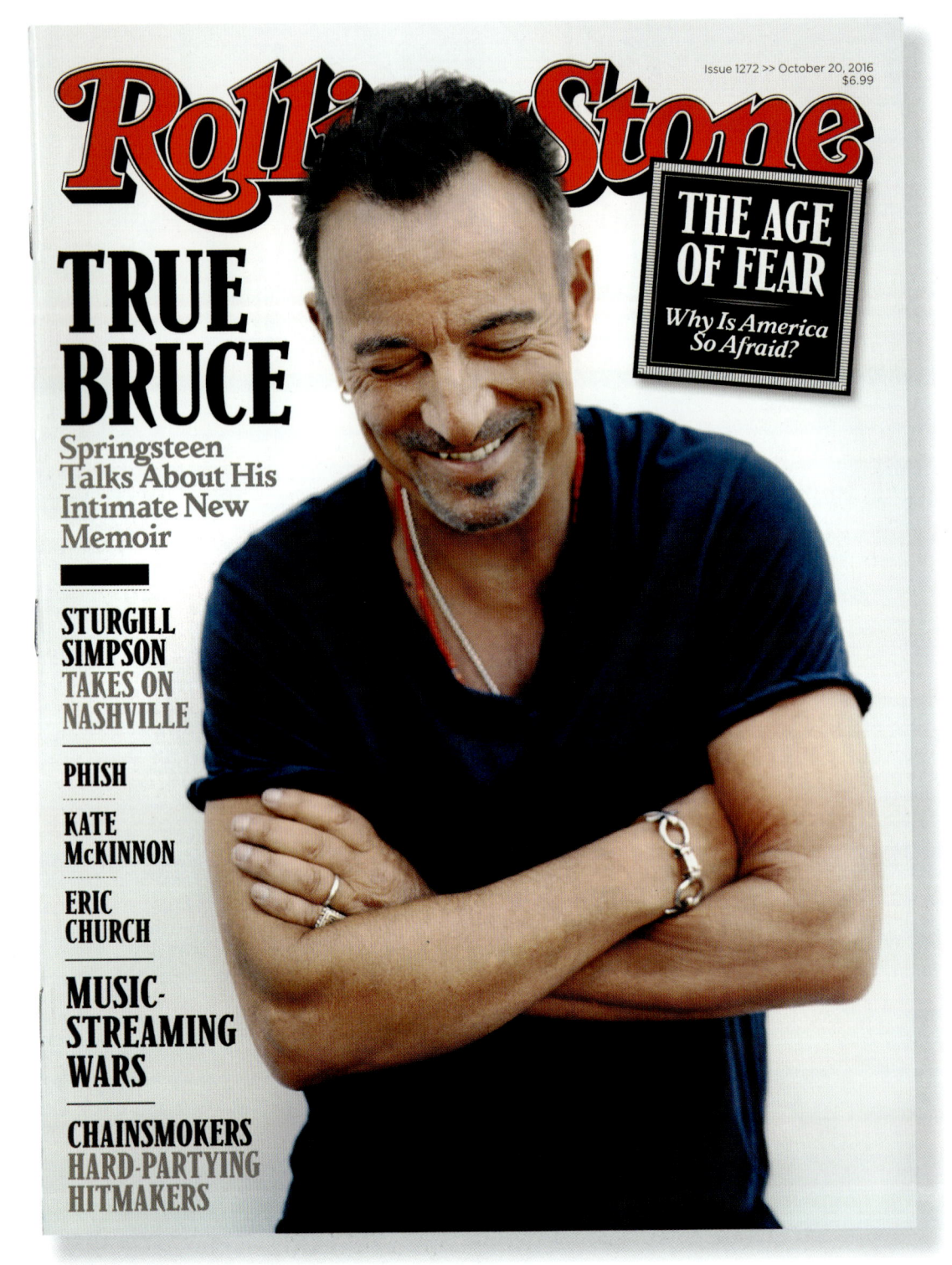

Rolling Stone

THE AGE OF FEAR
Why Is America So Afraid?

TRUE BRUCE
Springsteen Talks About His Intimate New Memoir

STURGILL SIMPSON TAKES ON NASHVILLE

PHISH

KATE McKINNON

ERIC CHURCH

MUSIC-STREAMING WARS

CHAINSMOKERS HARD-PARTYING HITMAKERS

2010s

RS 1272 | BRUCE SPRINGSTEEN | October 20th, 2016 | Photograph by Danny Clinch

RollingStone

Issue 1274 >> November 17, 2016

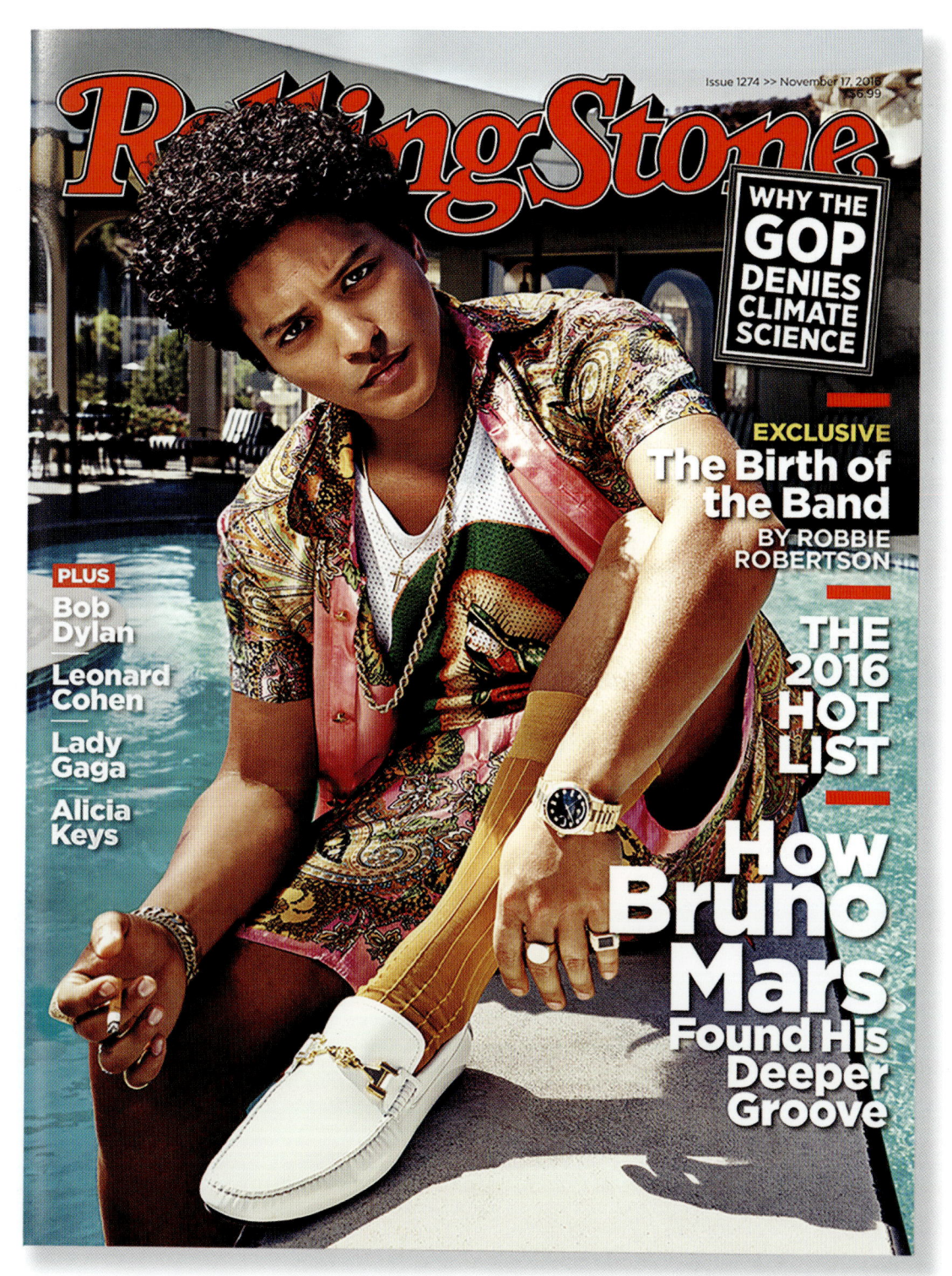

WHY THE GOP DENIES CLIMATE SCIENCE

PLUS
Bob Dylan
Leonard Cohen
Lady Gaga
Alicia Keys

EXCLUSIVE
The Birth of the Band
BY ROBBIE ROBERTSON

THE 2016 HOT LIST

HOW BRUNO MARS Found His Deeper Groove

RS 1274 | BRUNO MARS | November 17th, 2016 | Photograph by Mark Seliger

50 YEARS OF COVERS • 725

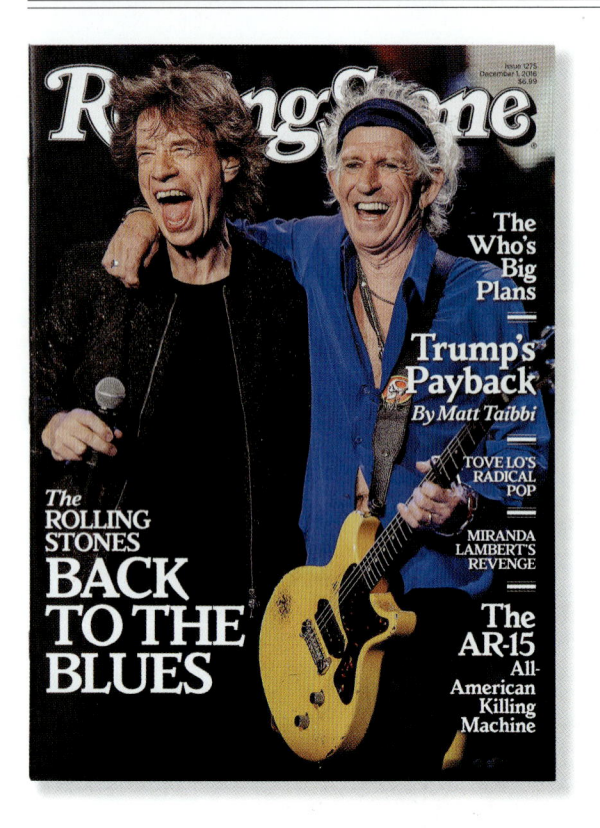

$\mathcal{RS}$ 1275 | MICK JAGGER AND KEITH RICHARDS
December 1st, 2016
Photograph by Carlos Muller

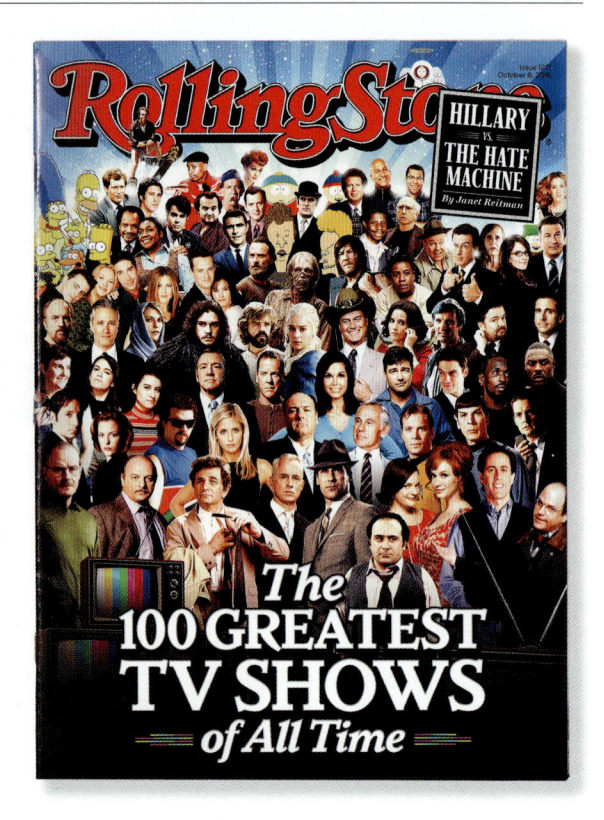

$\mathcal{RS}$ 1271 | THE 100 GREATEST TV SHOWS
October 6th, 2016
Photo Illustration by Sean McCabe

[RS 1271] **In compiling our list of the 100 greatest shows of all time, we polled actors, writers, producers and critics, including Judd Apatow, David Chase and Matt Groening.** "*Mad Men* was first on my ballot," says our TV critic Rob Sheffield. "Tragically, I was the only voter who stuck up for my beloved Seventies trash sitcom *Welcome Back, Kotter*."

1. THE SOPRANOS
2. THE WIRE
3. BREAKING BAD
4. MAD MEN
5. SEINFELD
6. THE SIMPSONS
7. THE TWILIGHT ZONE
8. SATURDAY NIGHT LIVE
9. ALL IN THE FAMILY
10. THE DAILY SHOW

Rolling Stone

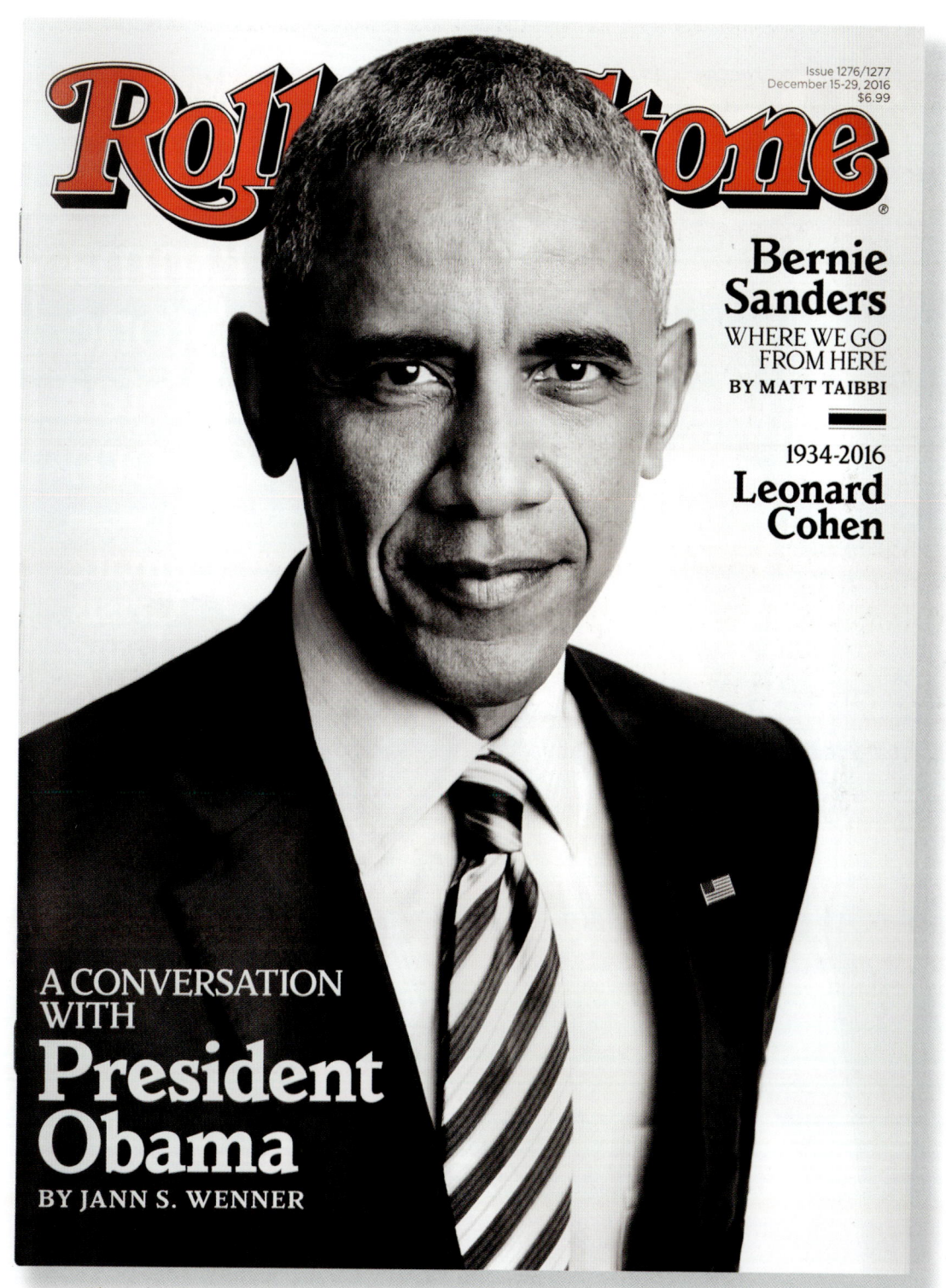

Issue 1276/1277
December 15-29, 2016
$6.99

Bernie Sanders
WHERE WE GO FROM HERE
BY MATT TAIBBI

1934-2016
Leonard Cohen

A CONVERSATION WITH
President Obama
BY JANN S. WENNER

RS 1276/1277 | BARACK OBAMA | December 15th–29th, 2016 | Photograph by Ruven Afanador

ROLLING Stone

50th ANNIVERSARY YEAR

Emma Stone A Star Is Born

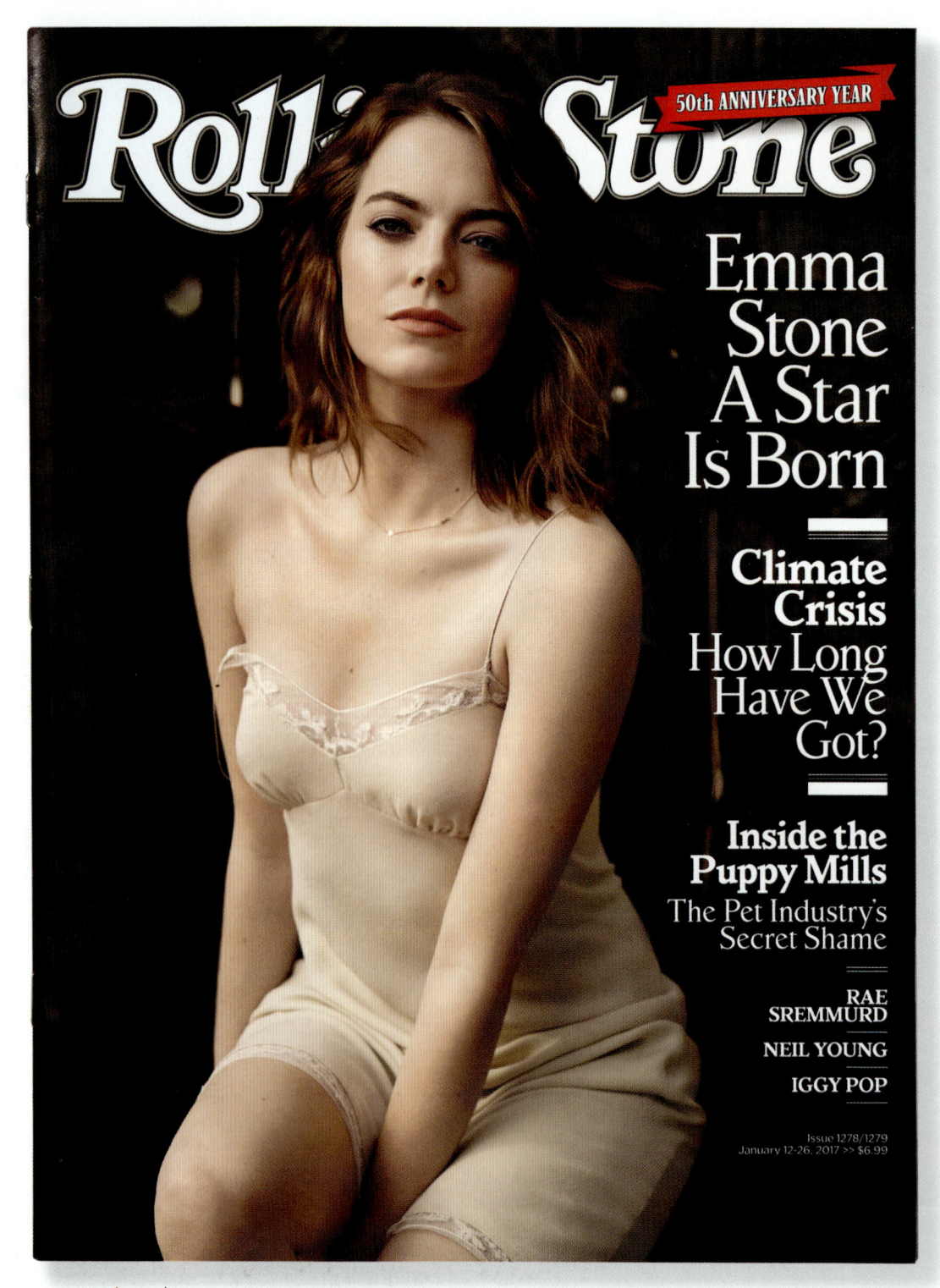

Climate Crisis
How Long Have We Got?

Inside the Puppy Mills
The Pet Industry's Secret Shame

RAE SREMMURD

NEIL YOUNG

IGGY POP

Issue 1278/1279
January 12-26, 2017 >> $6.99

RS 1278/1279 | EMMA STONE | January 12th–26th, 2017 | Photograph by Mark Seliger

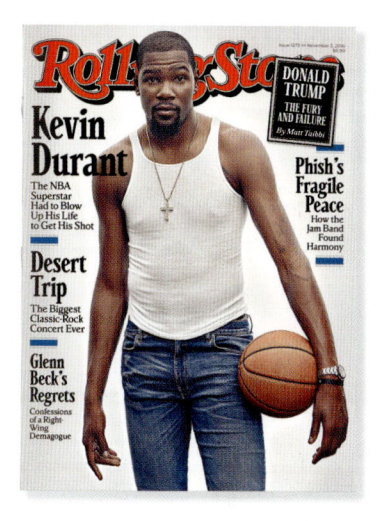

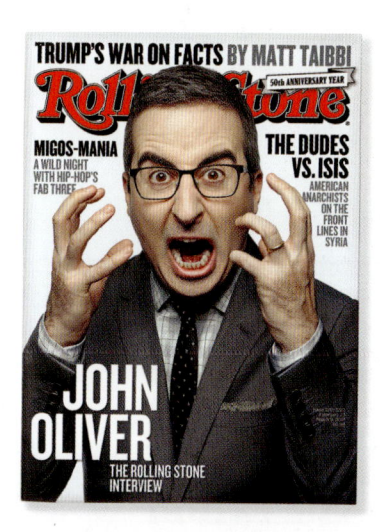

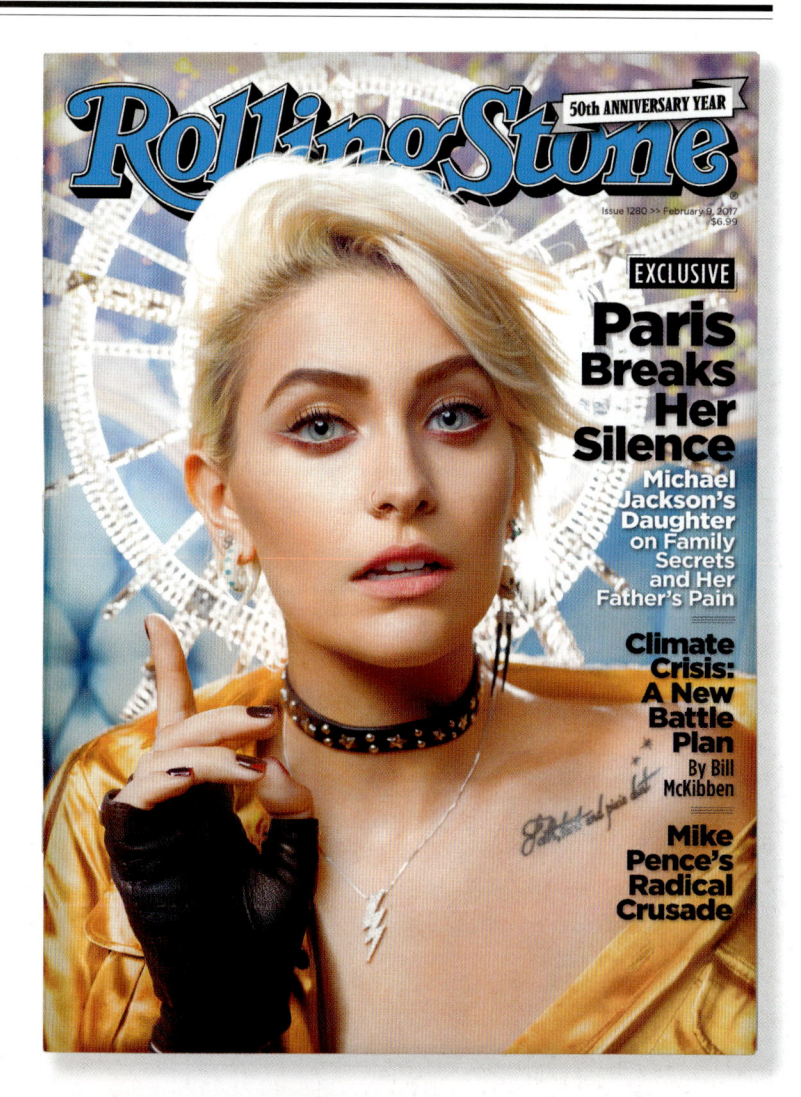

RS 1273 | KEVIN DURANT
November 3rd, 2016
PHOTOGRAPH BY MARK SELIGER

RS 1281/1282 | JOHN OLIVER
February 23th, 2017–March 9th, 2017
PHOTOGRAPH BY MARK SELIGER

"IN THE PAST, MAKING A MOVIE, I'VE been told that I'm hindering the process by bringing up an opinion or an idea. There have been times when I've improvised, they've laughed at my joke and then given it to my male co-star."
—*Emma Stone*

RS 1280 | PARIS JACKSON
February 9th, 2017
PHOTOGRAPH BY DAVID LACHAPELLE

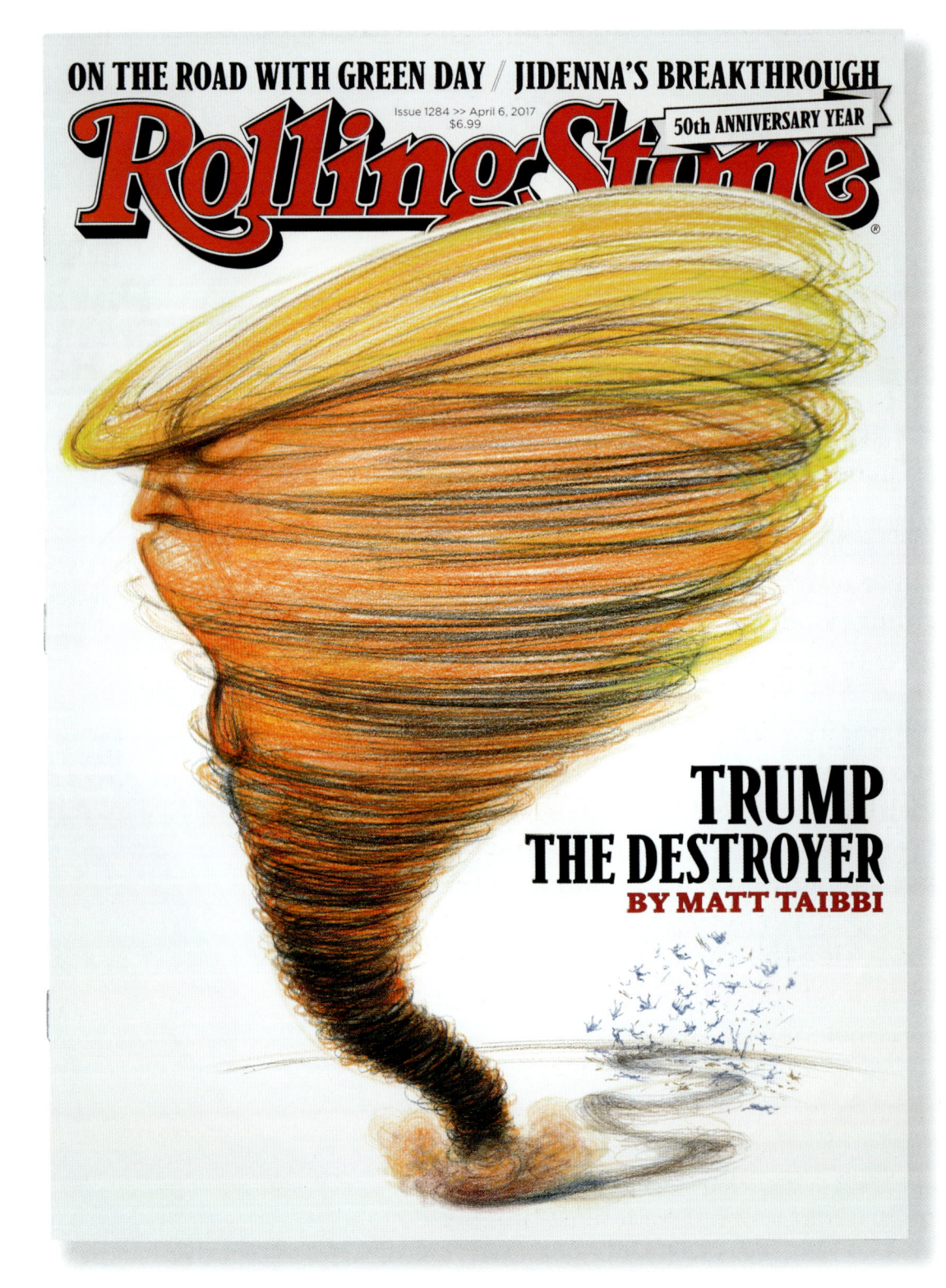

ON THE ROAD WITH GREEN DAY // JIDENNA'S BREAKTHROUGH

Rolling Stone

Issue 1284 >> April 6, 2017
$6.99

50th ANNIVERSARY YEAR

TRUMP THE DESTROYER
BY MATT TAIBBI

RS 1284 | DONALD TRUMP
April 6th, 2017
ILLUSTRATION BY VICTOR JUHASZ

Nearly two years into our relationship with Donald Trump, politician, his core schtick is no longer really a secret. The new president swings wildly between buffoon and strongman acts, creating confusion and disorder. While his enemies scramble to make sense of the outrages of a week before or yesterday or 10 minutes ago, and spend valuable energy wondering whether the man is crazy or stupid or cunning (or perhaps all three things at once), Trump continually presses forward. We always assumed there was a goal behind it all: cattle cars, race war, autocracy. But those were last century's versions of tyranny. It would make perfect sense if modern America's contribution to the genre were far dumber. Trump in the White House may just be a monkey clutching history's biggest hand grenade. Yes, he's always one step ahead of us, and more dangerous than any smart person, and we can never for a minute take our eyes off him. But while we keep looking for his hidden agenda, it's our growing addiction to the spectacle of his car-wreck presidency that is the real threat. He is already making idiots and accomplices of us all, bringing out the worst in each of us, making us dumber just by watching. Even if Trump never learns to govern, after four years of this we will forget what civilization ever looked like – and it will be programming, not policy, that will have changed the world.

[EXCERPT FROM RS 1284 COVER STORY BY MATT TAIBBI]

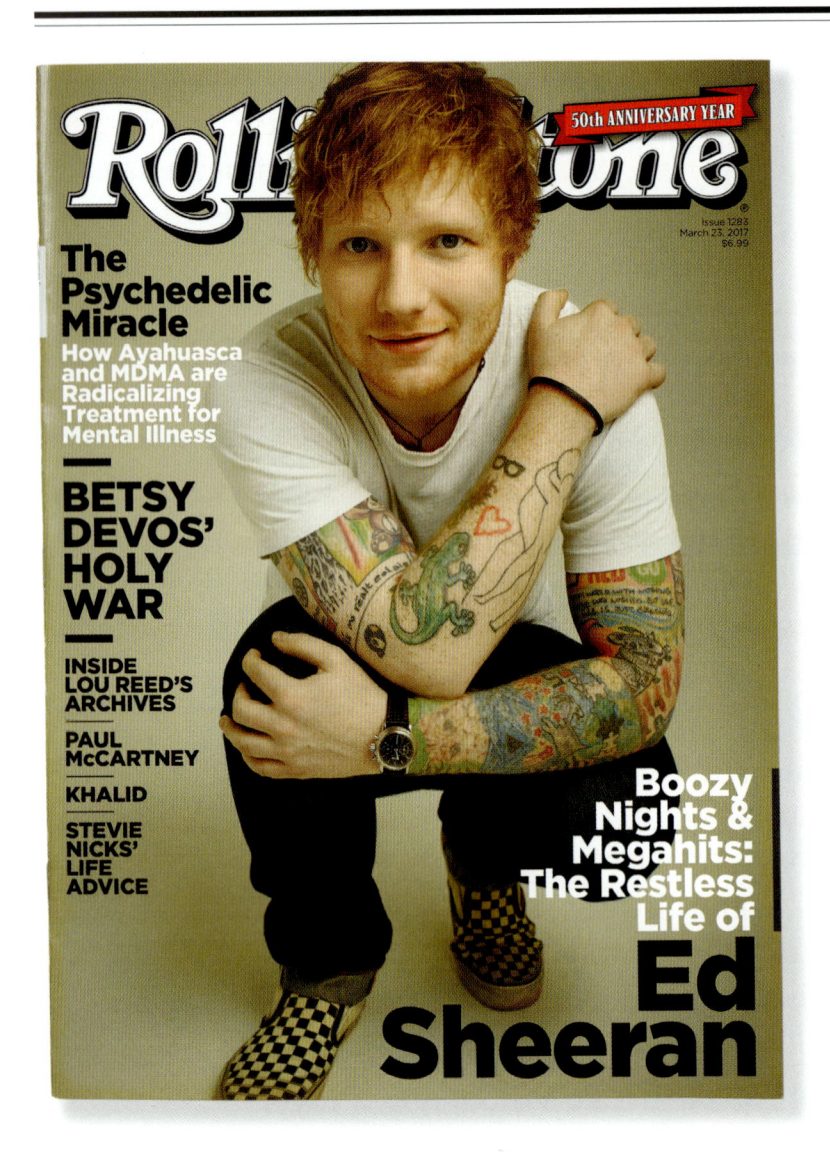

"COMING BACK INTO THIS ALBUM CAMPAIGN, THE ONLY THING I WANTED WAS a ROLLING STONE cover, and thankfully we did it. I'd never been on the cover of ROLLING STONE, and it was definitely something I had to tick off the list. I always feel really awkward at photo shoots. I'm not a massive fan of the way I look on camera. I walked in there and I was just like, 'Can we make this as quick and easy as possible?' There was a wardrobe. But it didn't really get used." —*Ed Sheeran*

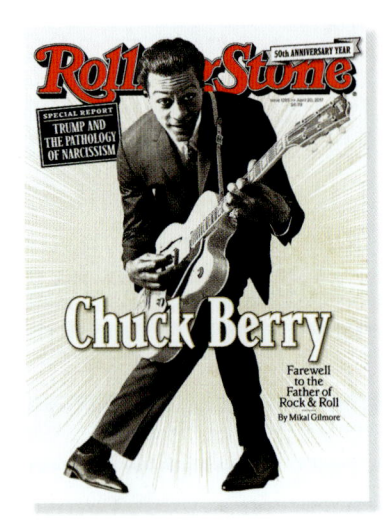

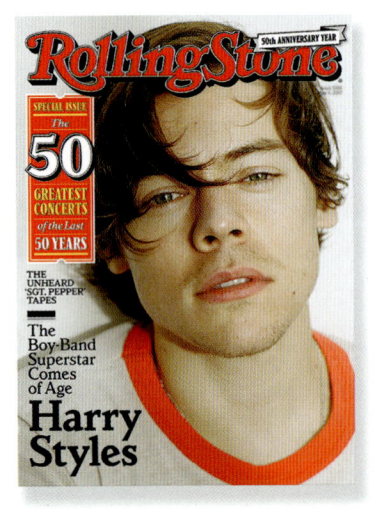

RS 1283 | ED SHEERAN
March 23rd, 2017
PHOTOGRAPH BY PEGGY SIROTA

RS 1285 | CHUCK BERRY
April 20th, 2017
PHOTOGRAPH BY MICHAEL OCHS

RS 1286 | HARRY STYLES
May 4th, 2017
PHOTOGRAPH BY THEO WENNER

2010s

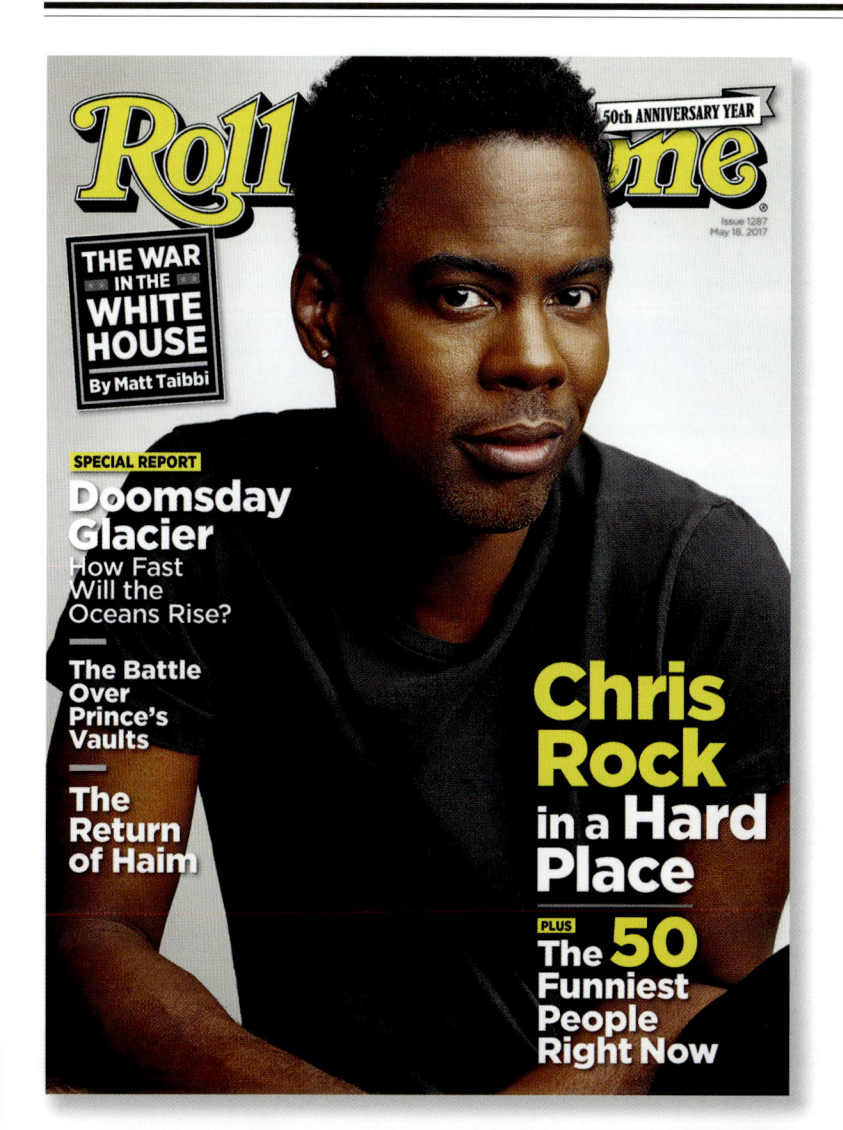

"**I LITERALLY GET** treated like a nigger a few times a day." He pauses. "I can't imagine what it is like for my brothers and what they go through every day." So Rock looks for some serenity in a familiar place. He talks in his set about finding God before God finds him. That is not persona Rock. "I wanna find some peace, 'cause people usually find that peace in a horrible time."

[EXCERPT FROM RS 1287 COVER STORY BY STEPHEN RODRICK]

RS 1287 | CHRIS ROCK
May 18th, 2017
Photograph by Mark Seliger

ROLLING STONE

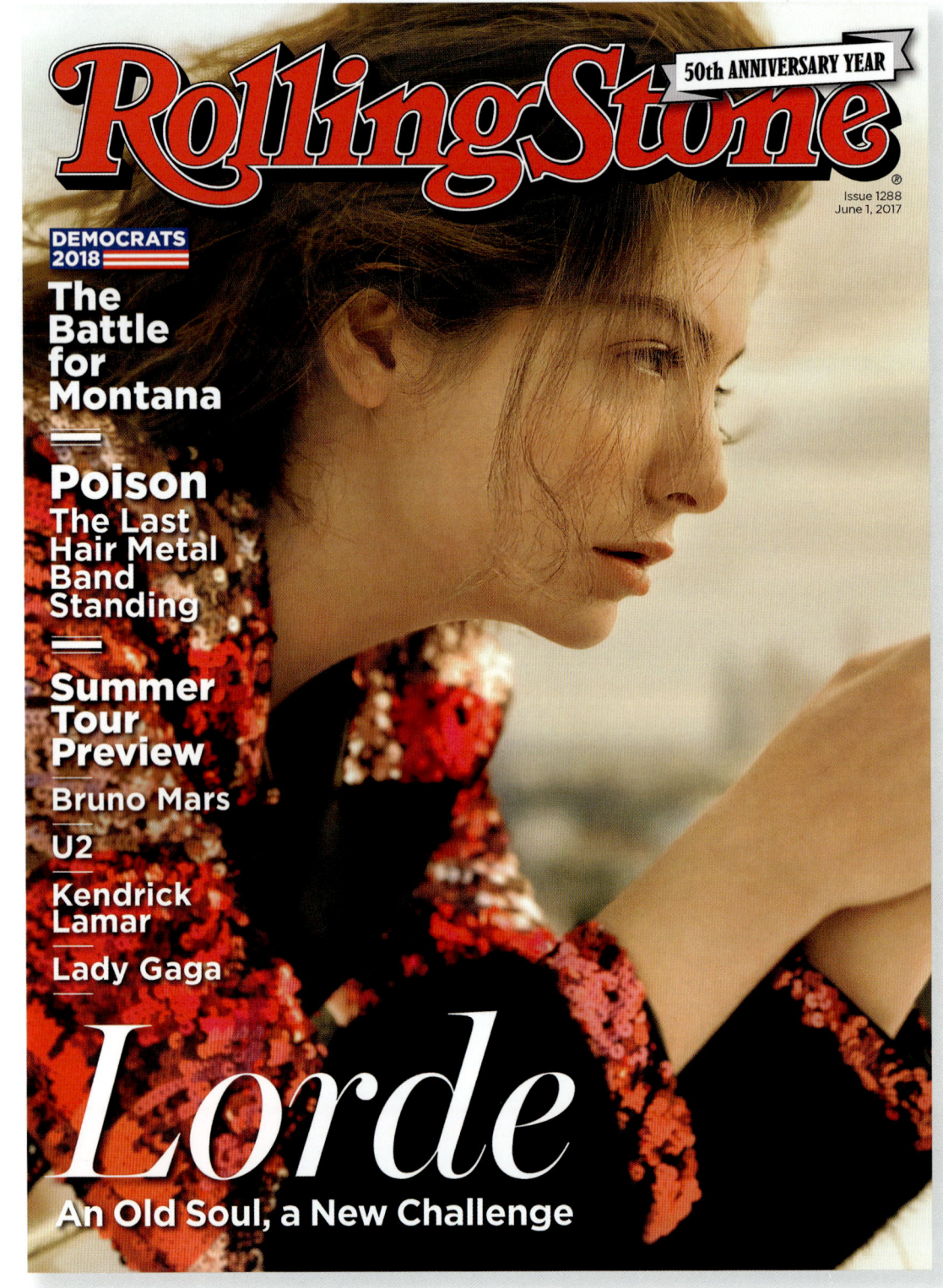

50th ANNIVERSARY YEAR

Issue 1288
June 1, 2017

DEMOCRATS 2018

The Battle for Montana

Poison
The Last Hair Metal Band Standing

Summer Tour Preview
Bruno Mars

U2

Kendrick Lamar

Lady Gaga

Lorde
An Old Soul, a New Challenge

2010s

734 • ROLLING STONE

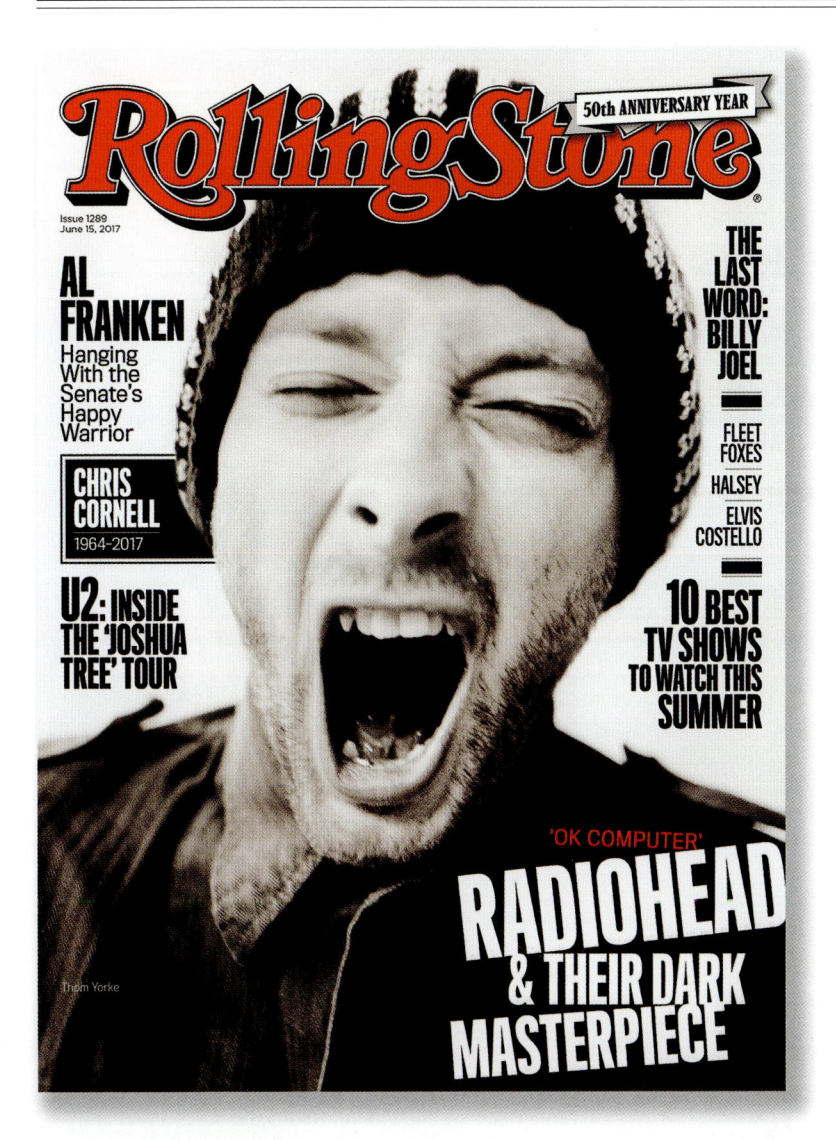

RS 1289 | THOM YORKE
June 15th, 2017
PHOTOGRAPH BY DANNY CLINCH

RS 1288 | LORDE
June 1st, 2017
PHOTOGRAPH BY PEGGY SIROTA

A COUPLE OF DAYS LATER, I meet Lorde in the outdoor dining area of the iconic L.A. hotel where she is staying despite its reputation as the sort of place someone like her might stay. She is there, she assures me, for the impressively deep pool. She wanted to do some "dives and shit," and to immerse herself fully in that silky, muffling blue. "It's a womb thing," she says. "Oh, it's so cozy." This is a particularly appealing sensation in the present moment. "I'm fucking nervous," she says, wearing the navy grunge dress she'd bought at Shareen. "I haven't performed in three years, and so it's like forced extroversion for a true introvert." In a rehearsal for the Coachella set a few nights before, it had been clear that much of the show was still coming together ("How do I not get electrocuted?" she'd asked of one stage stunt, to which a producer had replied, "And where does the water go without electrocuting everybody else?"). Now she all but holds her head in her hands. "I just got a prescription for some beta blockers. I was like, 'Let's do this. Give it to me, give it to me.'"

[EXCERPT FROM RS 1288 COVER STORY BY ALEX MORRIS]

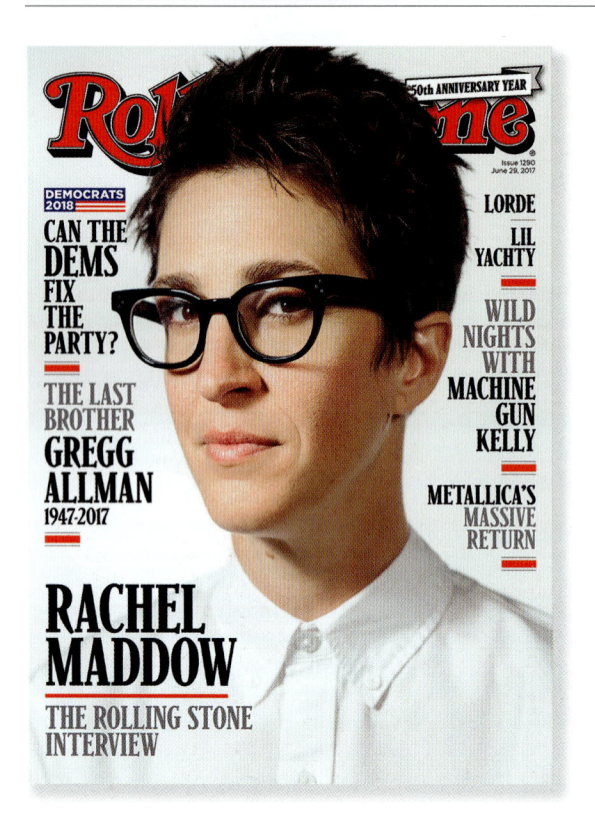

RS 1290 | RACHEL MADDOW
June 29th, 2017
Photograph by Mark Seliger

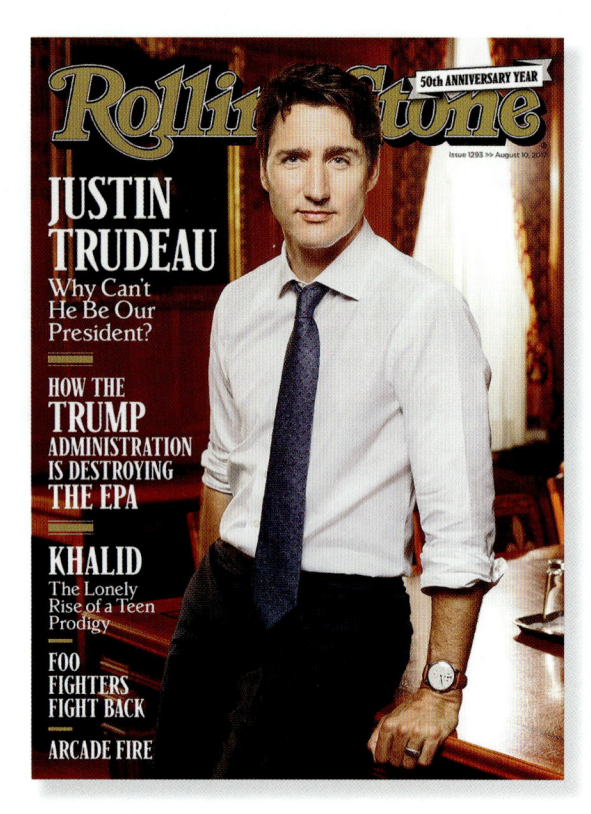

RS 1293 | JUSTIN TRUDEAU
August 10th, 2017
Photograph by Martin Schoeller

[RS 1293] Canadian Prime Minister Justin Trudeau is the first foreign leader to make the cover of ROLLING STONE. But this wasn't the first time a Trudeau has appeared in our pages. Justin's mother, Margaret, who was first lady of Canada during the Seventies and early Eighties, made a cameo hanging out with the Rolling Stones in a 1977 story chronicling Keith Richards' infamous Toronto drug bust.

Rolling Stone

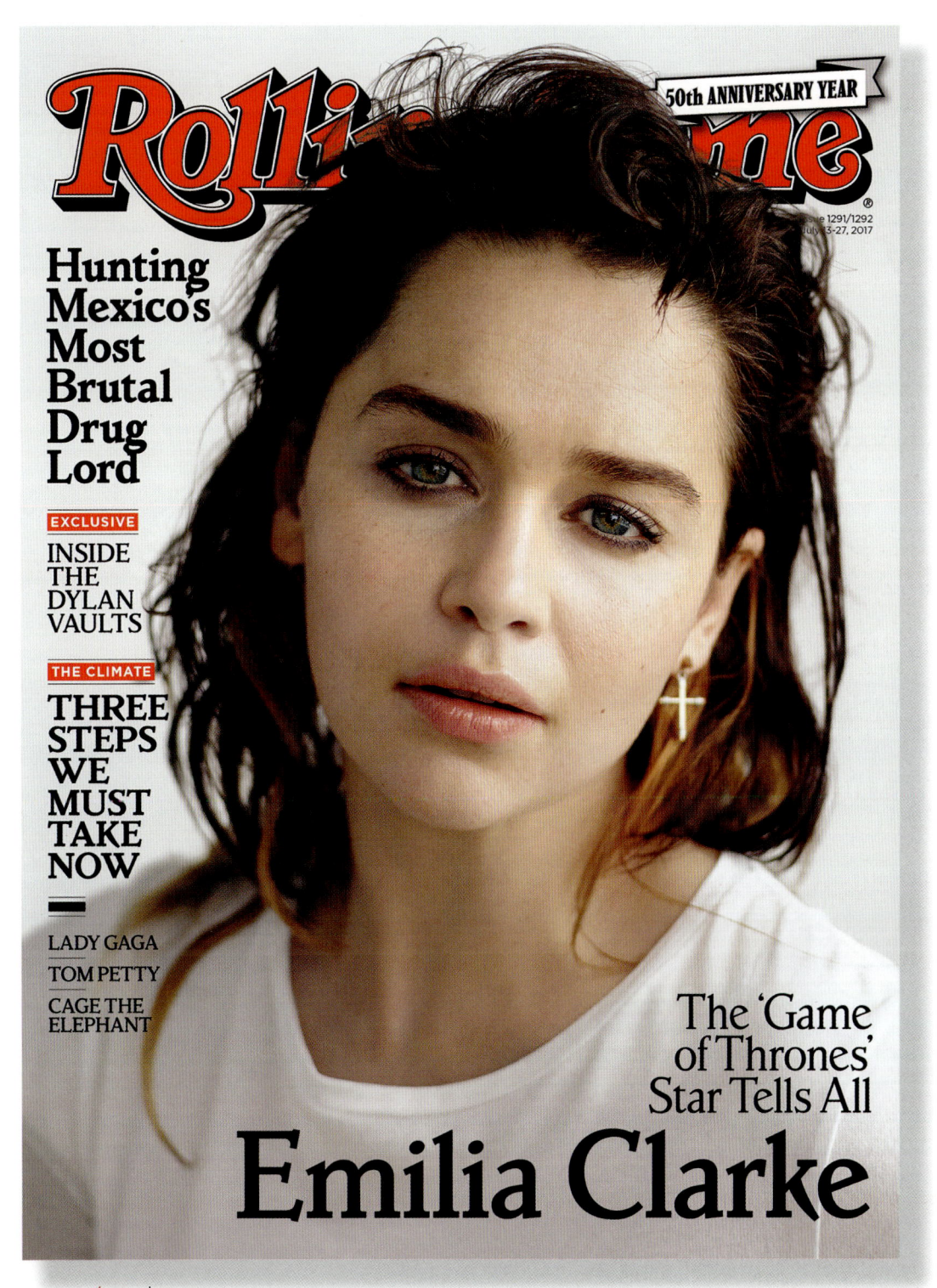

50th ANNIVERSARY YEAR

Issue 1291/1292
July 13-27, 2017

Hunting Mexico's Most Brutal Drug Lord

EXCLUSIVE
INSIDE THE DYLAN VAULTS

THE CLIMATE
THREE STEPS WE MUST TAKE NOW

LADY GAGA
TOM PETTY
CAGE THE ELEPHANT

The 'Game of Thrones' Star Tells All

Emilia Clarke

RS 1291/1292 | EMILIA CLARKE | July 13th–27th, 2017 | Photograph by Mark Seliger

ROLLING STONE

50th ANNIVERSARY YEAR

Issue 1294
August 24, 2017

Trump's Radical Attorney General

The Hunt for El Chapo

Chester Bennington's Last Days

THE ROLLING STONE INTERVIEW

Kendrick Lamar
The Greatest Rapper Alive

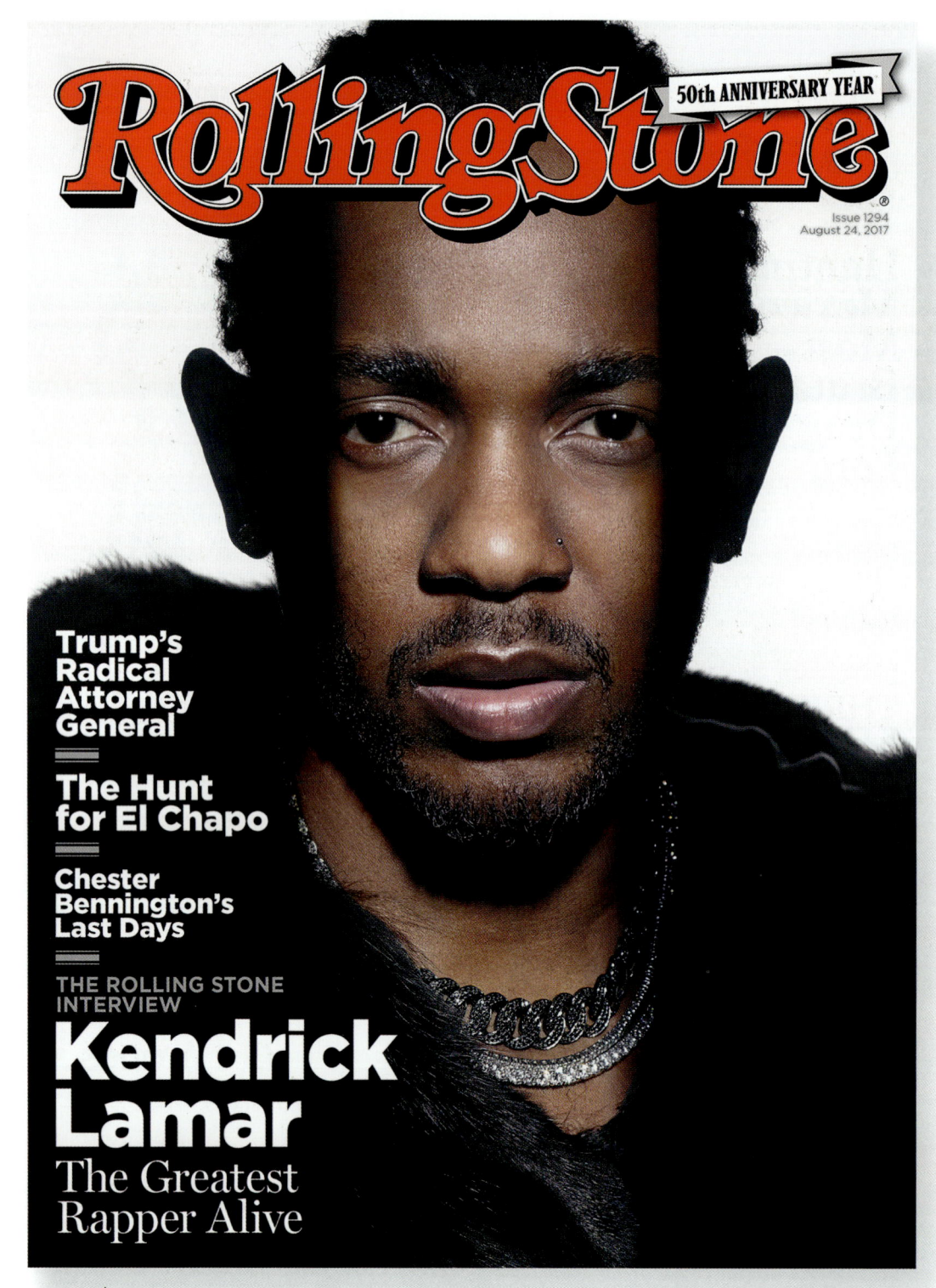

RS 1294 | KENDRICK LAMAR | August 24th, 2017 | Photograph by Mark Seliger

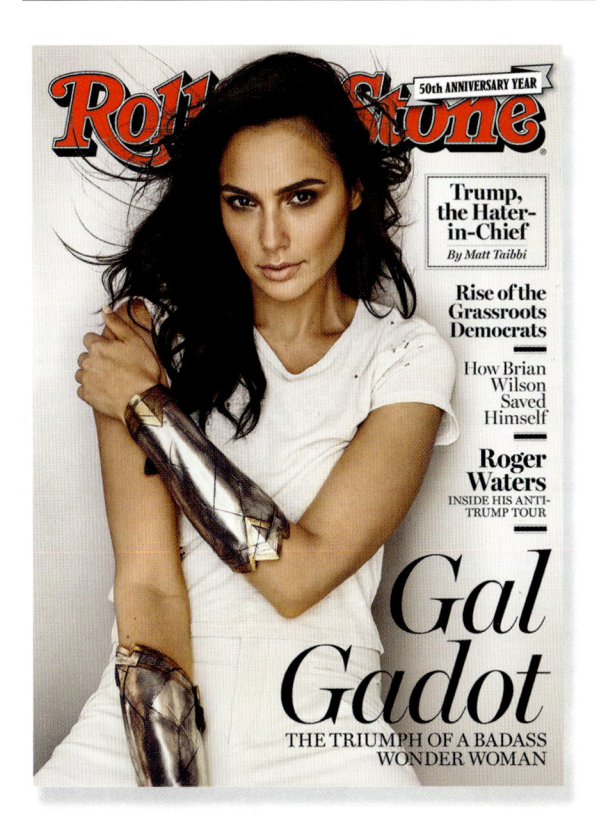

RS 1295 | GAL GADOT
September 7th, 2017
Photograph by Peggy Sirota

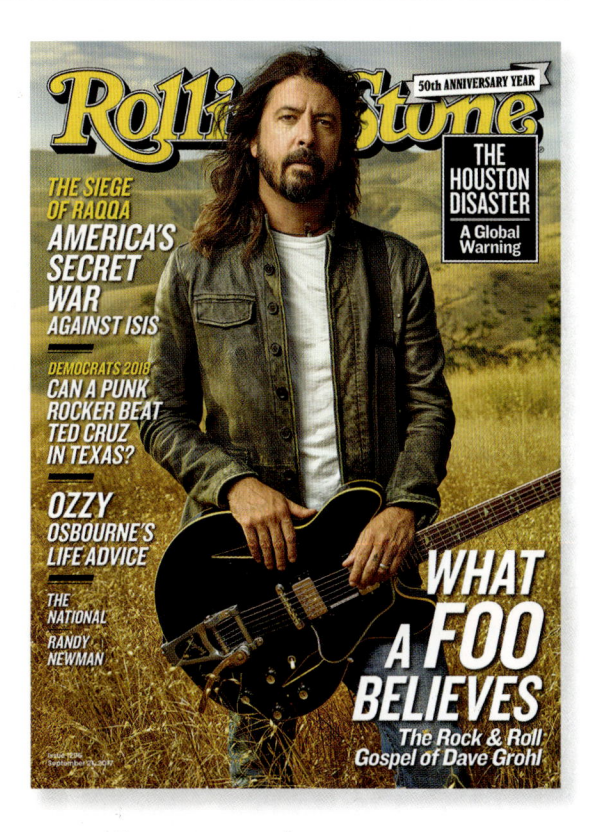

RS 1296 | DAVE GROHL
September 21st, 2017
Photograph by Mark Seliger

"*My biggest vice* is being addicted to the chase of what I'm doing. I shut off people that actually care for me. Being on that stage, knowing that you're changing people's lives, that's a high. Sometimes, when you're pressing so much to get something across to a stranger, you forget people that are closer to you."

—Kendrick Lamar

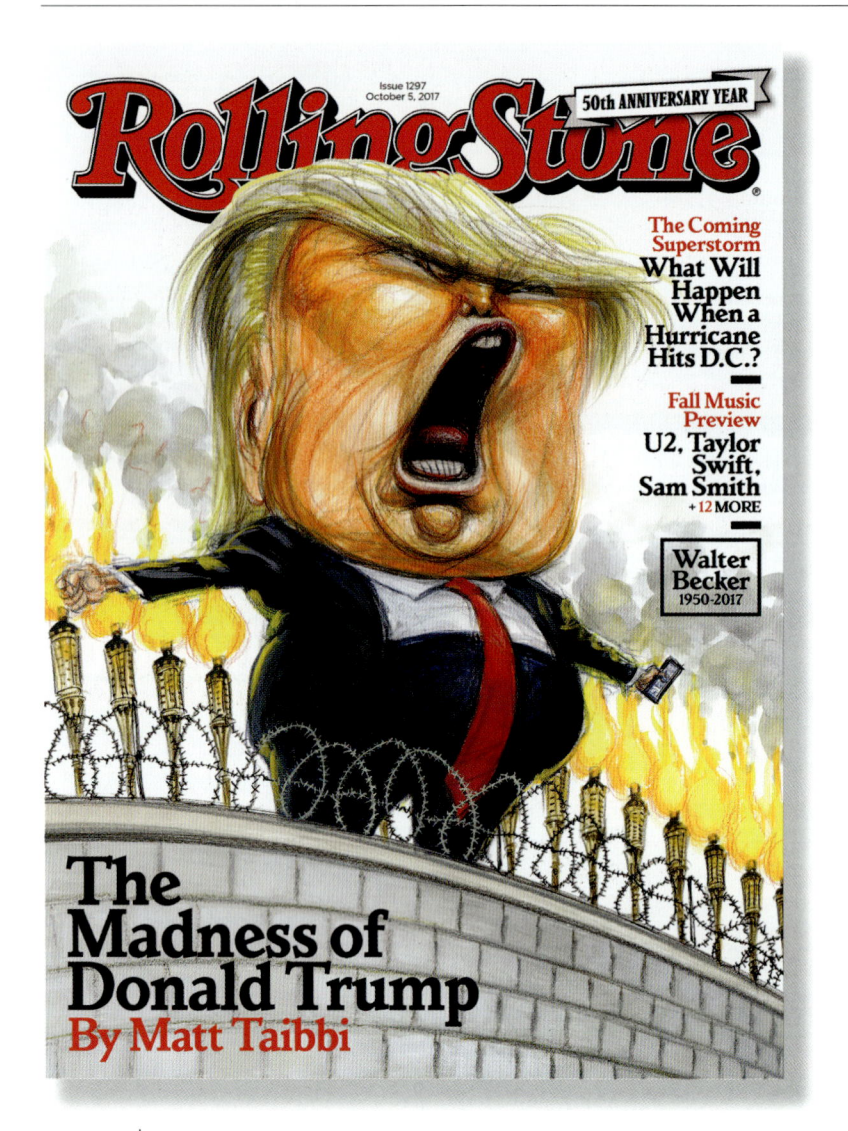

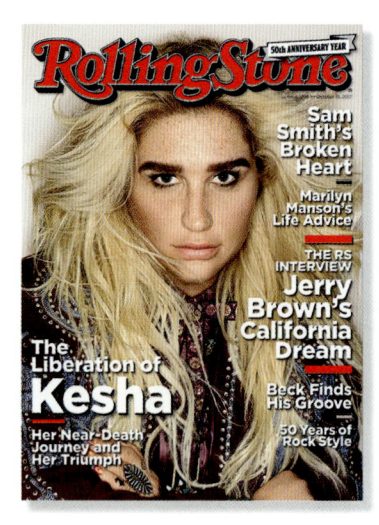

RS 1297 | DONALD TRUMP | October 5th, 2017 | Illustration by Victor Juhasz

RS 1298 | KESHA
October 19th, 2017
Photograph by Peggy Sirota

[RS 1297] **Both of our 2017 cover stories on the Trump presidency [RS 1284, "Trump the Destroyer," and RS 1297, "The Madness of Donald Trump"] came with cover illustrations by Victor Juhasz. "Illustrators are not great talkers, so this is how we get an idea across," says Juhasz. "I'm really happy with a piece if it feels like it's honest."**

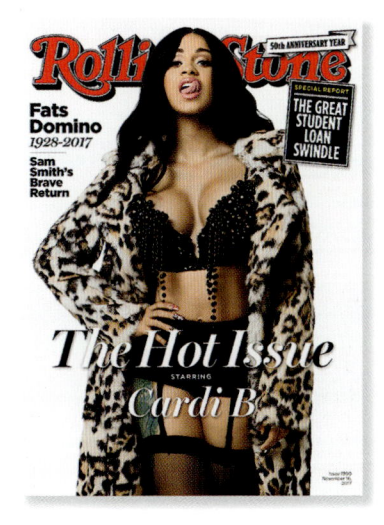

RS 1300 | CARDI B
November 16th, 2017
PHOTOGRAPH BY JUSTICE APPLE

"IT'S SAD THAT HE'S GONE, BUT IT WAS nice to be alive in his lifetime. Good songs stay written. Good records stay made. They are always filled with the promise and hope and life essence of their creator. Tom made a lot of great music, enough to carry people forward."
—*Bruce Springsteen*

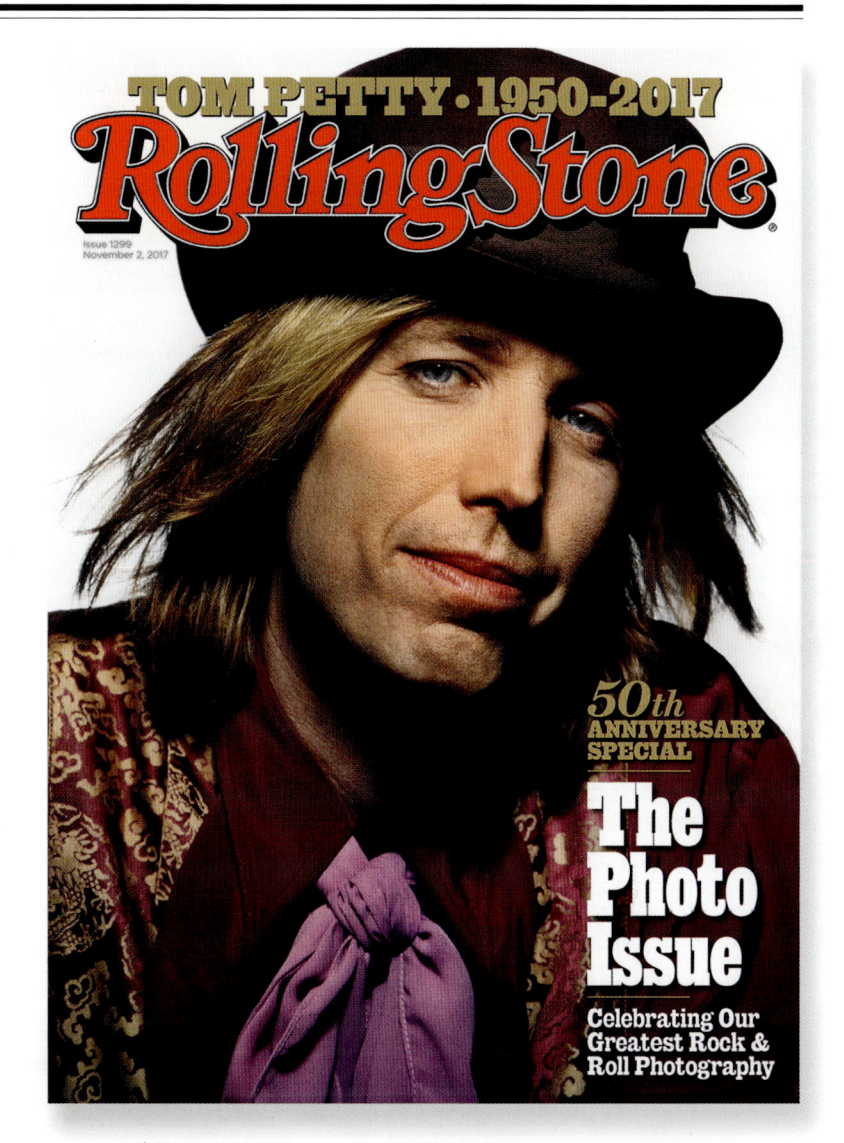

RS 1299 | TOM PETTY | November 2nd, 2017 | PHOTOGRAPH BY MARK SELIGER

50 YEARS OF COVERS • 741

Rolling Stone

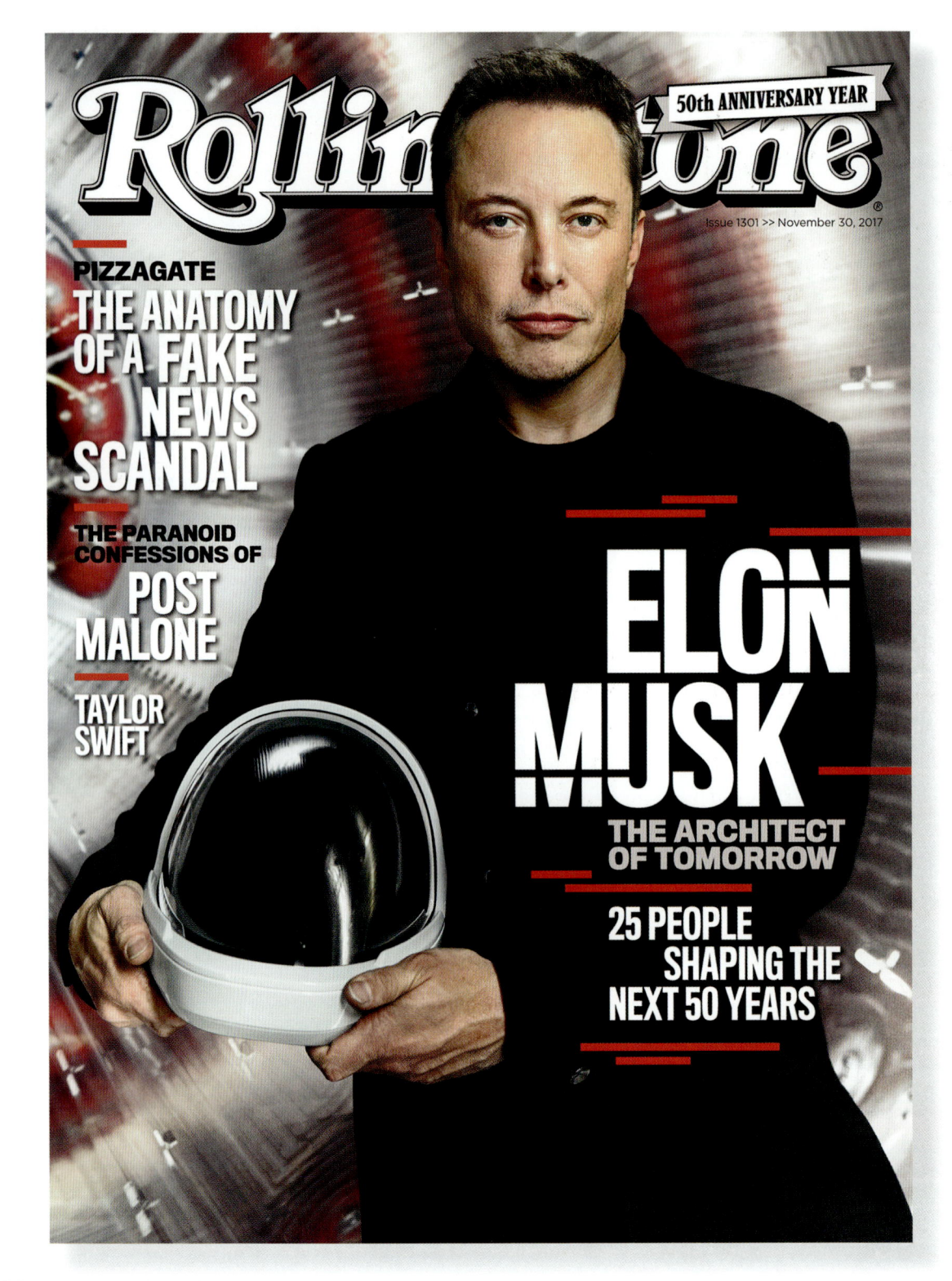

50th ANNIVERSARY YEAR

Issue 1301 >> November 30, 2017

PIZZAGATE
THE ANATOMY OF A FAKE NEWS SCANDAL

THE PARANOID CONFESSIONS OF POST MALONE

TAYLOR SWIFT

ELON MUSK
THE ARCHITECT OF TOMORROW

25 PEOPLE SHAPING THE NEXT 50 YEARS

2010s

RS 1301 | ELON MUSK | November 30th, 2017 | PHOTOGRAPH BY MARK SELIGER

Musk's career history decorates his desk. There's an item there from nearly all of his companies, even a mug for x.com, the early online bank he started, which became PayPal. The sale of Zip2 resulted in a $22 million check made out directly to Musk, which he used in part to start x.com. With the roughly $180 million post-tax amount he made from the sale of PayPal, he started SpaceX with $100 million, put $70 million into Tesla, $10 million into Solar City, and saved little for himself. One of the misunderstandings that rankles Musk most is being pigeonholed and narrowcast, whether as the real-life Tony Stark or the second coming of Steve Jobs. When, at a photo shoot, he was asked to wear a black turtleneck, the trademark garb of Jobs, he bristled. "If I was dying and I had a turtleneck on," he tells me, "with my last dying breath, I would take the turtleneck off and try to throw it as far away from my body as possible."

So what does tie Musk's companies together?

"I try to do useful things," he explains. "That's a nice aspiration. And useful means it is of value to the rest of society. Are they useful things that work and make people's lives better, make the future seem better, and actually are better, too? I think we should try to make the future better."

[EXCERPT FROM RS 1301 COVER STORY BY NEIL STRAUSS]

[RS 1301] Anchored by a cover story on visionary inventor and entrepreneur Elon Musk, RS 1301 featured profiles of "25 People Shaping the Next 50 Years." They included innovators like Chase Adam, head of a tech startup working to modernize the bureaucracy of health care; "all-natural architect" David Benjamin; and California Sen. Kamala Harris, "frontwoman for tomorrow's Democratic Party." Fifty years to the month after ROLLING STONE published its first issue, in November 1967, we were still looking ahead.

INDEX BY PHOTOGRAPHER & ILLUSTRATOR

CREDIT	ISSUE & COVER SUBJECT	PAGE	CREDIT	ISSUE & COVER SUBJECT	PAGE
ABBOTT, WARING	*RS* 1196 LOU REED	676	BLAKE, REBECCA	*RS* 443 U2	233
AFANADOR, RUVEN	*RS* 943 BEYONCE	514	BLANCH, ANDREA	*RS* 350 BILL MURRAY	180
	RS 964/965 U2	528	BOMAN, ERIC	*RS* 457 STING	240
	RS 1276/1277 BARACK OBAMA	727	BOOLE, TIM	*RS* 487 HUEY LEWIS	247
ALAS, MERT & PIGGOT, MARCUS	*RS* 1230 MADONNA	696	BOOT, TIM	*RS* 1006 LED ZEPPELIN	559
			BRAKHA, MOSHE	*RS* 459 STEVEN SPIELBERG	240
ALEXANDER, DAVID	*RS* 280 CHEECH & CHONG WITH KAREEM ABDUL-JABBAR	144		*RS* 488 RUN-D.M.C.	249
			BRANSON, BRADFORD	*RS* 445 DAVID LEE ROTH	234
	RS 290 RICHARD PRYOR	150	BROAD, JULIAN	*RS* 726 LIVE	390
ALLEN, JULIAN	*RS* 281/282 RICHARD DREYFUSS	144	BRODSKY, JOEL	*RS* 601 JIM MORRISON	314
	RS 284 NEIL YOUNG	145	BROWN, NACIO	*RS* 30 AMERICAN REVOLUTION IN 1969	18
	RS 295 PAUL McCARTNEY	152			
	RS 324 KEITH RICHARDS AND MICK JAGGER	169	BRUNO OF HOLLYWOOD	*RS* 205 PAT BOONE	95
			CALLIS, CHRIS	*RS* 474 MICHAEL J. FOX	244
	RS 340 ROMAN POLANSKI	175	CAMERON, NEVIS	*RS* 97 PETE TOWNSHEND	51
	RS 372 PETE TOWNSHEND	199	CAMP, E.J.	*RS* 397 CHRISTIE BRINKLEY AND MICHAEL IVES	210
ALLEN, TERRY	*RS* 565 THE 100 GREATEST ALBUMS OF THE EIGHTIES	289			
				RS 405 ANNIE LENNOX	212
	RS 576 THE FIFTIES	299		*RS* 420 DARYL HANNAH	219
ALTMAN, ROBERT	*RS* 44 DAVID CROSBY	22		*RS* 440 BILLY IDOL	230
	RS 45 TINA TURNER	22		*RS* 465 MICHAEL DOUGLAS	241
	RS 89 KEITH RICHARDS	48		*RS* 483 DON JOHNSON	247
ANDERSON, CHRISTOPHER	*RS* 1249 BERNIE SANDERS	707		*RS* 500 JON BON JOVI	254
ANDERSON, MICHAEL JR.	*RS* 56 DENNIS HOPPER	29		*RS* 506 MOTLEY CRUE	257
APPLE, JUSTICE	*RS* 1300 CARDI B	741		*RS* 577 BONNIE RAITT	298
AVEDON, RICHARD	*RS* 291 THE BEE GEES	151	CARAEFF, ED	*RS* 63 DAVID CROSBY	32
	RS 298 ROBIN WILLIAMS	154		*RS* 72 LEON RUSSEL	38
	RS 310 STEVIE NICKS AND MICK FLEETWOOD	162		*RS* 501 JIMI HENDRIX	255
			CARON, GILLES	*RS* 1018 JAMES BROWNE	564
	RS 313 BOB HOPE	162	CARROLL, PHIL	*RS* 180 THE ELECTRIC MUSE	81
	RS 332 DOLLY PARTON	171	CATES, GWENDOLEN	*RS* 592 KEVIN COSTNER	311
	RS 370 NASTASSIA KINSKI	198	CHAVEZ, MARINA	*RS* 1158 ADAM YAUCH	654
	RS 388 DUSTIN HOFFMAN	205	CHILDERS, MICHAEL	*RS* 342 RINGO STARR	176
	RS 390 THE STRAY CATS	208	CLINCH, DANNY	*RS* 746 TUPAC SHAKUR	400
	RS 394 PRINCE AND VANITY	209		*RS* 1137 THE SHEEPDOGS	640
	RS 399 EDDIE MURPHY	213		*RS* 1178 BILLIE JOE ARMSTRONG	669
	RS 402 JOHN TRAVOLTA	214		*RS* 1272 BRUCE SPRINGSTEEN	724
	RS 418 JACK NICHOLSON	218		*RS* 1289 THOM YORKE	735
	RS 419 EDDIE MURPHY	218	COMTE, MICHAEL	*RS* 1152 WHITNEY HOUSTON	651
	RS 422 CYNDI LAUPER	222	CORBIJN, ANTON	*RS* 499 U2	252
	RS 423 CULTURE CLUB	224		*RS* 547 BONO	281
	RS 429 PRINCE	225		*RS* 618 U2	324
	RS 449 JULIAN LENNON	238		*RS* 689 THE ROLLING STONES	368
	RS 585 JOHN LENNON	304		*RS* 702 ROBERT PLANT AND JIMMY PAGE	378
	RS 1261 PRINCE	716			
BAILEY, DAVID	*RS* 395 DAVID BOWIE	208		*RS* 719 RED HOT CHILI PEPPERS	388
	RS 416 THE POLICE	219		*RS* 737 METALLICA	395
	RS 533 ERIC CLAPTION	273		*RS* 745 R.E.M.	399
BECKMAN, JANETTE	*RS* 493 PEE-WEE HERMAN	250		*RS* 758 BECK	408
	RS 614 PEE-WEE HERMAN	321		*RS* 981 COLDPLAY	539

INDEX BY PHOTOGRAPHER & ILLUSTRATOR

CREDIT	ISSUE & COVER SUBJECT	PAGE	CREDIT	ISSUE & COVER SUBJECT	PAGE
CORBIJN, ANTON	RS 983 THE ROLLING STONES	542	EDELMANN, HEINZ	RS 9 JOHN LENNON AND PAUL MCCARTNEY	10
	RS 1074 U2	603	ELINS, MICHAEL	RS 980 JIMI HENDRIX	539
CORMAN, RICHARD	RS 1254 DAVID BOWIE	710		RS 997 'AMERICAN IDOL'	553
	RS 491 TALKING HEADS	248		RS 1000 THE THOUSANDTH ISSUE	554
	RS 409 MICK JAGGER	215	EMMETT, SIMON	RS 1129 ADELE	634
	RS 511 GEORGE HARRISON	262		RS 1167 ADELE	662
	RS 527 NEIL YOUNG	272	EPRIDGE, BILL	RS 209 LOUISE LASSER	95
COSTELLO, FIN	RS 566 JERRY GARCIA	291	EXLEY, JONATHAN	RS 1084 MICHAEL JACKSON	608
COUPON, WILLIAM	RS 1206 KISS	681	FAIREY, SHEPARD	RS 1085 BARACK OBAMA	611
	RS 409 MICK JAGGER	215	FEINGOLD, DEBORAH	RS 444 DON JOHNSON AND PHILLIP MICHAEL THOMAS	233
	RS 511 GEORGE HARRISON	262		RS 450 DAVID LETTERMAN	238
	RS 527 NEIL YOUNG	272		RS 461 MARK KNOPFLER	241
DALTON, DAVID	RS 566 JERRY GARCIA	291		RS 477 VAN HALEN	244
DAVIES & STARR	RS 32 STEVE WINWOOD	19		RS 495 MICHAEL J. FOX	251
	RS 462 BOB GELDOF	242		RS 502 ROBERT CRAY	257
	RS 556/557 THE WHO	285	FEINSTEIN, BARRY	RS 154 BOB DYLAN	69
DAVIS, PAUL	RS 880 9/11/01	478	FLESHER, VIVIENNE	RS 410 MICHAEL JACKSON AND PAUL MCCARTNEY	215
	RS 156 BOB DYLAN	70			
	RS 523 MARTIN LUTHER KING JR.	269	FOCUS, MARK	RS 176 GEORGE HARRISON	81
DAY, CORINNE	RS 740 JERRY GARCIA	397	FOOTHORAP, ROBERT	RS 106 THE ART OF SENSUAL MASSAGE	54
DEMARCHELIER, PATRICK	RS 704 DOLORES O'RIORDAN	379			
	RS 452/453 JOHN TRAVOLTA AND JAMIE LEE CURTIS	238	FREEMAN, ROBERT	RS 863 THE BEATLES	469
	RS 665 JANET JACKSON	351	GAHR, DAVID	RS 98 EVANGELIST MEL LYMAN	51
DANELIAN, STEPHEN	RS 877 BRITNEY SPEARS	476		RS 226 JANIS JOPLIN	108
DE RAEMY, LEONARD	RS 941 HOWARD DEAN	511		RS 1191 BOB DYLAN	673
DEZITTER, HARRY	RS 241 ROBERT DE NIRO	115	GATEWOOD, CHARLES	RS 137 ROD STEWART	63
DICKSON, IAN	RS 482 PAUL MCCARTNEY	247	GERSTEIN, GERRY	RS 131 DR. HOOK & THE MEDICINE SHOW	62
DILTZ, HENRY	RS 1260 THE RAMONES	714			
	RS 81 MICHAEL JACKSON	43	GIBSON, JILL	RS 931 JIMI HENDRIX	504
DIMMOCK, JAMES	RS 132 TRUMAN CAPOTE	61	GLASER, MILTON	RS 103 BOB DYLAN	53
	RS 968 GREEN DAY	528		RS 189 STEVIE WONDER	86
	RS 1045 THOM YORKE	580	GOLDBERG, NATHANIEL	RS 733 OASIS	395
	RS 1049 CHRIS ROCK	583	GOLDSMITH, LYNN	RS 272 BRUCE SPRINGSTEEN	141
	RS 1062 METALLICA	592		RS 273 MICK JAGGER AND KEITH RICHARDS	140
DOMINGO, RAY	RS 1065 AC/DC	592			
DOMINIS, JOHN	RS 173 EVEL KNIEVEL	80		RS 359/360 THE ROLLING STONES	192
DOONAN, JACK	RS 942 THE BEATLES	511		RS 403 STING	211
D'ORAZIO, SANTE	RS 269 WILLIE NELSON	137	GOMEZ, IGNACIO	RS 133 MARK SPITZ	63
DOULIERY, OLIVER	RS 907 KEITH RICHARDS	490	GOODHILL, DEAN	RS 15 MICK JAGGER	12
DURAN, TONY	RS 1220 BARACK OBAMA	691	GOODWIN, HARRY	RS 980 JIMI HENDRIX	539
	RS 904 ASIA ARGENTO	489	GORMAN, GREG	RS 384 BETTE MIDLER	204
	RS 956 TOM CRUISE	522		RS 433 DAVID BOWIE	228
EASTMAN, LINDA	RS 984 EVANGELINE LILLY	541	GOWLAND, PETER	RS 177 SUZI QUATRO	81
	RS 10 ERIC CLAPTON	9	GREENE, HERBIE	RS 120 JEFF BECK	57
ECCLES, ANDREW	RS 57 PAUL MCCARTNEY	28		RS 717 JERRY GARCIA	386
	RS 603 WILSON PHILLIPS	314	GRIFFIN, RICK	RS 17 ZAP COMIX	13
	RS 608/609 ROD STEWART AND RACHEL HUNTER	317	GRIMES, MELISSA	RS 513 PINK FLOYD	265
	RS 624 'BEVERLY HILLS, 90210'	328	GROENING, MATT	RS 581 BART SIMPSON	302

INDEX BY PHOTOGRAPHER & ILLUSTRATOR

CREDIT	ISSUE & COVER SUBJECT	PAGE	CREDIT	ISSUE & COVER SUBJECT	PAGE
GROSSMAN, ROBERT	RS 104 BOB DYLAN	53	JONES, SAM	RS 1079 GREEN DAY	606
	RS 148 JERRY GARCIA	67		RS 1089 U2	611
	RS 152 RICHARD NIXON	69		RS 1099 JEFF BECK AND ERIC CLAPTON	616
	RS 240 CROSBY, STILLS AND NASH	117			
	RS 275 THE WHO	142		RS 1166 BOB DYLAN	660
	RS 999 GEORGE W. BUSH	552		RS 1179 MUMFORD & SONS	670
	RS 1012 WORST CONGRESS EVER	561	JUDGE, MIKE	RS 663 BEAVIS & BUTT-HEAD	350
	RS 1063 JOHN MCCAIN	593		RS 678 BEAVIS & BUTT-HEAD	356
	RS 1165 MITT ROMNEY	658		RS 750/751 BEAVIS & BUTT-HEAD WITH PAMELA ANDERSON LEE	407
	RS 1256 DONALD TRUMP, TED CRUZ AND MARCO RUBIO	713			
GRUEN, BOB	RS 124 KEITH MOON	58	JUHASZ, VICTOR	RS 1060 GEORGE W. BUSH	592
	RS 250 JOHNNY ROTTEN	124		RS 1284 DONALD TRUMP	731
	RS 587 JIMMY PAGE AND ROBERT PLANT	306		RS DONALD TRUMP	740
			KANDER, NADAV	RS 1055 CHRIS MARTIN	590
HALFIN, ROSS	RS 748 EDDIE VEDDER	402		RS 1068/1069 BRAD PITT	598
	RS 1054 100 GREATEST GUITAR SONGS OF ALL TIME	586		RS 1155 RADIOHEAD	655
				RS 1151 PAUL McCARTNEY	650
HAMILL, BRIAN	RS 78 MUHAMMAD ALI	41	KATZ, JEFF	RS 472 PRINCE WITH WENDY & LISA	242
	RS 497 WOODY ALLEN	252		RS 589 PRINCE	308
HANAUER, MARK	RS 471 STEVIE WONDER	241	KIDD, CHIP	RS 1025/1026 FORTIETH ANNIVERSARY	568
HANSEN, CONSTANCE	RS 507 THE 100 BEST ALBUMS FROM 1967-1987	258			
				RS 1030/1031 FORTIETH ANNIVERSARY	569
HAYS, PHILIP	RS 128 BETTE MIDLER	60			
	RS 165 ERIC CLAPTON	74		RS 1039 FORTIETH ANNIVERSARY	569
HEATH, JULES	RS 1250/1251 STAR WARS	708	KING, BILL	RS 202 BONNIE RAITT	93
HELNWEIN, GOTTFRIED	RS 431 JOHN BELUSHI	228		RS 286 TED NUGENT	147
	RS 451 CLINT EASTWOOD	239		RS 289 THE VILLAGE PEOPLE	150
	RS 549 JAMES BROWN	282		RS 346 HARRISON FORD	181
HIRO	RS 190 LABELLE	84	KLEIN, STEVEN	RS 988 MADONNA	546
	RS 242 DIANE KEATON	118	KUNZ, ANITA	RS 509 MICHAEL JACKSON	260
	RS 266 CARLY SIMON	135		RS 1229 JOHN BELUSHI	695
	RS 271 JOHN BELUSHI	139	LACHAPELLE, DAVID	RS 789 TORI AMOS	424
	RS 524 DAVID BYRNE	270		RS 790/791 MADONNA	425
HISER, DAVID	RS 970 DR. HUNTER S. THOMPSON	531		ROS 802/803 JEWEL	433
HOSELTON, CHARLES	RS 897 KURT COBAIN	485		RS 810 BRITNEY SPEARS	435
HOUGHTON, JIM	RS 283 THE CARS	144		RS 811 EMINEM	438
HUTCHINSON, JOSEPH	RS 1096 YOU IDIOTS! [GLOBAL WARMING]	616		RS 818 RICKY MARTIN	442
				RS 830/831 THE PARTY 2000	448
IRISH, LEN	RS 890 CREED	480		RS 834 MARIAH CAREY	456
IMAGINECHINA/CORBIS	RS 1204 JUSTIN BIEBER	680		RS 856/857 BACKSTREET BOYS	467
JAFFE, STEVE	RS 139 TATUM O'NEAL	65		RS 872 ANGELINA JOLIE	476
JENKINS, LEE	RS 874 RADIOHEAD	473		RS 888 NO DOUBT	480
JOHN, ROBERT	RS 558 AXL ROSE	286		RS 896 KIRSTEN DUNST	484
JONES, SAM	RS 996 HEATH LEDGER	551		RS 921 GOOD CHARLOTTE	498
	RS 998 KIEFER SUTHERLAND	551		RS 945 BEN AFFLECK	514
	RS 1059 ROBERT DOWNEY JR.	591		RS 993 KANYE WEST	548
	RS 1064 BARACK OBAMA	592		RS 1080 LADY GAGA	607
	RS 1072 SEAN PENN	603		RS 1280 PARIS JACKSON	729
	RS 1078 BOB DYLAN	605	LACOMBE, BRIGITTE	RS 763 SANDRA BULLOCK	410

50 YEARS OF COVERS • 747

INDEX BY PHOTOGRAPHER & ILLUSTRATOR

CREDIT	ISSUE & COVER SUBJECT	PAGE	CREDIT	ISSUE & COVER SUBJECT	PAGE
LACOMBE, BRIGITTE	RS 994 MARIAH CAREY	549	**LEIBOVITZ, ANNIE**	RS 150 HUGH HEFNER	68
LAMANA, GEMMA	RS 274 GARY BUSEY	142		RS 158 MARVIN GAYE	71
LAMBRAY, MAUREEN	RS 262 BROOKE SHIELDS	133		RS 159 KRIS KRISTOFFERSON	71
LANDY, ELLIOTT	RS 16 THE BAND	12		RS 160 PAUL GETTY	72
	RS 1222 BOB DYLAN	693		RS 161 JACKSON AND ETHAN BROWNE	73
LANE, TONY	RS 64 JANIS JOPLIN	32			
	RS 187 CARLY SIMON	84		RS 164 KAREN AND RICHARD CARPENTER	72
	RS 200 PATTY HEARST (PT. 2)	93			
LASH, NAOKO	RS 28 JAPANESE ROCK	17		RS 166 MARIA MULDAUR	75
LAUNOIS, JOHN	RS 415 THE BEATLES	217		RS 169 RICHARD NIXON	76
LEATART, BRIAN	RS 261 DONNA SUMMER	132		RS 171 LILY TOMLIN AND RICHARD PRYOR	79
LEE, BUD	RS 192 RICHARD DREYFUSS	88			
	RS 211 PETER FRAMPTON	96		RS 174 ELTON JOHN	78
LEIBOVITZ, ANNIE	RS 60 ANTIWAR DEMONSTRATIONS	29		RS 181 KENNY LOGGINS AND JIM MESSINA	81
	RS 70 GRACE SLICK	38		RS 183 LINDA RONSTADT	83
	RS 73 ROD STEWART	38		RS 185 PETER FALK	83
	RS 74 JOHN LENNON	39		RS 188 PHOEBE SNOW	84
	RS 75 JOHN LENNON AND YOKO ONO	41		RS 191 MICK JAGGER AND KEITH RICHARDS	85
	RS 79 NICHOLAS JOHNSON	41		RS 195 MICK JAGGER	89
	RS 80 JOE DEALLESANDRA	42		RS 199 ROD STEWART AND BRITT EKLAND	90
	RS 82 PETER FONDA	42			
	RS 83 COUNTRY JOE MCDONALD AND ROBIN MENKEN	42		RS 208 DONNY OSMOND	95
				RS 212 CARLOS SANTANA	97
	RS 84 ELTON JOHN	44		RS 215 PAUL AND LINDA MCCARTNEY	101
	RS 87 IAN ANDERSON	46			
	RS 90 GEORGE HARRISON	47		RS 216 PAUL SIMON	102
	RS 92 JEFFERSON AIRPLANE	48		RS 218 JACK FORD	103
	RS 93 IKE AND TINA TURNER	48		RS 219 BOB MARLEY	104
	RS 94 THE BEACH BOYS	51		RS 220 STEVEN TYLER	105
	RS 99 CAT STEVENS	52		RS 222 NEIL DIAMOND	105
	RS 100 JERRY GARICA	52		RS 225 BRIAN WILSON	107
	RS 101 THE GRATEFUL DEAD	52		RS 227 LINDA RONSTADT	109
	RS 105 ALICE COOPER	54		RS 231 JEFF BRIDGES	112
	RS 107 VARIOUS	54		RS 232 PETER FRAMPTON	112
	RS 108 DAVID CASSIDY	55		RS 233 BOZ SCAGGS	113
	RS 109 JANE FONDA	55		RS 235 FLEETWOOD MAC	114
	RS 111 VAN MORRISON	56		RS 236 LILY TOMLIN	116
	RS 112 MICK JAGGER	56		RS 237 DARYL HALL AND JOHN OATES	115
	RS 114 HUEY NEWTON	56			
	RS 116 RANDY NEWMAN	56		RS 238 MARK FIDRYCH	115
	RS 117 THREE DOG NIGHT	57		RS 239 HAMILTON JORDAN AND JODY POWELL	115
	RS 122 PIMP JOE CONFORTE	57			
	RS 123 CARLOS SANTANA	58		RS 245 DIANA ROSS	119
	RS 127 DIANA ROSS	59		RS 247 O.J. SIMPSON	120
	RS 129 MICK JAGGER	61		RS 251 RON WOOD	126
	RS 134 ALICE COOPER	63		RS 253 STEVE MARTIN	126
	RS 140 PETER WOLF	65			
	RS 142 DAN HICKS	65			

748 • ROLLING STONE

INDEX BY PHOTOGRAPHER & ILLUSTRATOR

CREDIT	ISSUE & COVER SUBJECT	PAGE	CREDIT	ISSUE & COVER SUBJECT	PAGE
LEIBOVITZ, ANNIE	RS 255 JAMES TAYLOR, PETER ASHER AND LINDA RONSTADT	130	**LEIBOVITZ, ANNIE**	RS 330 MARY TYLER MOORE	170
				RS 331 JILL CLAYBURGH AND MICHAEL DOUGLAS	170
	RS 256 FLEETWOOD MAC	130		RS 335 JOHN LENNON AND YOKO ONO	172
	RS 257 BOB DYLAN	131			
	RS 260 JANE FONDA	132		RS 336 BRUCE SPRINGSTEEN	174
	RS 264 MUHAMMAD ALI	134		RS 339 WARREN ZEVON	176
	RS 265 JEFFERSON STARSHIP	135		RS 343 GUN CONTROL AND JOHN LENNON	178
	RS 267 JOHN TRAVOLTA	136			
	RS 268 MICK JAGGER	135		RS 349 RICKIE LEE JONES	180
	RS 270 PATTI SMITH	138		RS 351 STEVIE NICKS	182
	RS 279 LINDA RONSTADT, GILDA RADNER AND STEVE MARTIN	143		RS 353 YOKO ONO	184
				RS 354 MERYL STREEP	186
				RS 356 KEITH RICHARDS	188
	RS 285 THE BLUES BROTHERS, DAN AYKROYD AND JOHN BELUSHI	146		RS 357 WILLIAM HURT	187
				RS 361 JOHN BELUSHI	190
				RS 362 TIMOTHY HUTTON	191
	RS 287 JOHNNY CARSON	148		RS 363 STEVE MARTIN	193
	RS 288 MICHAEL AND CAMERON DOUGLAS	150		RS 364 PETER WOLF	192
				RS 356 ART GARFUNKEL AND PAUL SIMON	195
	RS 292 JOHN VOIGHT	150			
	RS 293 CHEAP TRICK	150		RS 367 MARIEL HEMINGWAY	194
	RS 294 BLONDIE	152		RS 368 JOHN BELUSHI	197
	RS 297 RICKIE LEE JONES	153		RS 369 SISSY SPACEK	199
	RS 299 JAMES TAYLOR	155		RS 373 SYLVESTER STALLONE	199
	RS 300 THE DOOBIE BROTHERS	156		RS 375 THE GO-GO'S	200
	RS 301 JIMMY BUFFET	156		RS 376 JEFF BRIDGES	199
	RS 302 SISSY SPACEK	157		RS 377 ELVIS COSTELLO	201
	RS 303 MARTIN SHEEN	158		RS 381 BILLY JOEL	202
	RS 304 MUSICIANS UNITED FOR SAFE ENERGY	156		RS 381 THE WHO	203
				RS 383 MATT DILLON	202
	RS 306 BETTE MIDLER	159		RS 591 BRUCE SPRINGSTEEN	310
	RS 311 TOM PETTY	160		RS 676 BOB MARLEY	356
	RS 314 LINDA RONSTADT	162		RS 969 BOB MARLEY	528
	RS 315 JOE STRUMMER AND MICK JONES	162		RS 1120/1121 JOHN LENNON	631
			LENNON, JOHN	RS 22 JOHN LENNON AND YOKO ONO	14
	RS 316 BOB SEGER	162			
	RS 317 ANN AND NANCY WILSON	164	**LINDBERGH, PETER**	RS 723 MICK JAGGER	391
	RS 318 THE PRETENDERS	164		RS 825 NICOLAS CAGE	446
	RS 319 EDWARD KENNEDY	164		RS 1116 KEITH RICHARDS	628
	RS 320 PETE TOWNSHEND	165	**LOPEZ, JO**	RS 1189 BRUCE SPRINGSTEEN	673
	RS 321 JOHN TRAVOLTA	166	**LUCHFORD, GLEN**	RS 680 SMASHING PUMPKINS	361
	RS 322 CAST OF 'THE EMPIRE STRIKES BACK'	167	**LUCKA, KLAUS**	RS 337 THE POLICE	175
			MACPHERSON, ANDREW	RS 562 ROLAND GIFT	287
	RS 323 JACKSON BROWNE	167		RS 580 SINEAD O'CONNOR	301
	RS 326 RODNEY DANGERFIELD	168		RS 651 BONO	345
	RS 327 ROBERT REDFORD	170		RS 657 STING	348
	RS 328 PAT BENATAR AND NEIL GERALDO	169		RS 667 THE EDGE	353
				RS 924 MONSTERS OF SUMMER	500
	RS 329 THE CARS	170		RS 929 RUBEN STUDDARD	504

INDEX BY PHOTOGRAPHER & ILLUSTRATOR

CREDIT	ISSUE & COVER SUBJECT	PAGE	CREDIT	ISSUE & COVER SUBJECT	PAGE
MACPHERSON, ANDREW	RS 944 OUTKAST	512	MULLER, CARLOS	RS 1275 MICK JAGGER AND KEITH RICHARDS	726
MAFFIA, DANIEL	RS 228 JACKSON BROWNE	110	MYERS, BILL	RS 55 ABBIE HOFFMAN	27
	RS 252 PETE TOWNSHEND	127	NESSIM, BARBARA	RS 537 JOHN LENNON	277
MAGGIA, MICHAEL	RS 50 ALTAMONT	24	NUTTER, DAVID	RS 223 ELTON JOHN	105
MAHURIN, MATT	RS 519 STING	264	O'BRIEN, TIM	RS 1048 BARACK OBAMA	582
	RS 690 TRENT REZNOR	369		RS 1070 GEORGE W. BUSH	598
	RS 711 SOUL ASYLUM	382		RS 1149 DAVID BOWIE	651
	RS 752 MARILYN MANSON	405	OCHS, MICHAEL	RS 1023 PINK FLOYD	567
	RS 798 MASTER P, WYCLEF JEAN AND JAY-Z	428		RS 1285 CHUCK BERRY	732
MAIER, FRANZ	RS 34 JIMI HENDRIX	19	OCKENFELS, FRANK W. 3	RS 586 M.C. HAMMER	305
MANKOWITZ, GERED	RS 623 JIMI HENDIRX	327		RS 607 R.E.M.	316
MAPPLETHORPE, ROBERT	RS 492 PETER GABRIEL	251		RS 692 LIZ PHAIR	372
MARK, MARY ELLEN	RS 213 MARLON BRANDO	98		RS 698/699 DAVID LETTERMAN	376
	RS 396 SEAN PENN	210		RS 720 ALANIS MORISSETTE	389
MARKUS, KURT	RS 653 GARTH BROOKS	348		RS 1194 ANDREW LINCOLN OF 'THE WALKING DEAD'	673
	RS 659 LAURA DERN	348	OLMSTED, SOPHIE	RS 895 THE OSBOURNES	484
MARSHALL, JIM	RS 39 BRIAN JONES	20	O'NEILL, MICHAEL	RS 504/505 THE GRATEFUL DEAD	257
	RS 66 THE GRATEFUL DEAD	33		RS 960 JON STEWART	522
	RS 68 JIMI HENDRIX	34	O'NEILL, TERRY	RS 246 CAST OF 'STAR WARS'	121
	RS 69 JANIS JOPLIN	36		RS 312 RICHARD GERE	163
	RS 145 ART GARFUNKEL	66	ORTIZ-LOPEZ, DENNIS	RS 576 THE FIFTIES	299
	RS 207 SAN FRANCISCO ROCKERS	95		RS 632 TWENTY-FIFTH ANNIVERSARY: THE GREAT STORIES	332
MASTERS, CHARLES	RS 1119 THE PLAYLIST ISSUE	630			
MATTHEWS, MARY ELLEN	RS 911 EMINEM	489	OVERACRE, GARY	RS 146 GENE AUTRY	66
MCBROOM, BRUCE	RS 1086 THE BEATLES	609	PALEY, STEPHEN	RS 54 SLY & THE FAMILY STONE	27
MCCABE, SEAN	RS 1271 THE 100 GREATEST TV SHOWS	726		RS 67 FELIX CAVALIERE AND THE RASCALS	33
MCGINLEY, RYAN	RS 1132 LADY GAGA	637	PALOMBI, PETER	RS 151 FUNKY CHIC	69
MCMULLAN, JAMES	RS 135 DIRK DICKENSON	63		RS 157 P.O.W. RICK SPRINGMAN	71
MEISEL, STEVEN	RS 432 TINA TURNER	227		RS 162 THE ECONOMY	72
	RS 435 MADONNA	229	PARADA, ROBERTO	RS 927 EMINEM	499
	RS 441 MICK JAGGER	231	PARKER, BEVERLY	RS 269 WILLIE NELSON	137
	RS 606 MADONNA	315	PARKER, TREY	RS 780 CAST OF 'SOUTH PARK'	419
MEOLA, ERIC	RS 244 ANN AND NANCY WILSON	118	PARKINSON, JIM	RS 254 RS 254 TENTH ANNIVERSARY	128
MERCER, LANCE	RS 822 EDDIE VEDDER	444			
METZLER, DOUG	RS 170 TANYA TUCKER	78		RS 512 TWENTIETH ANNIVERSARY	263
MICELOTTA, FRANK	RS 1233 KURT COBAIN	700	PARKINSON, NORMAN	RS 234 PRINCESS CAROLINE	112
MITCHELL, JACK	RS 366 WARREN BEATTY	195	PARKS, GORDON	RS 1264 MUHAMMED ALI	720
MONDINO, JEAN-BAPTISTE	RS 850 MADONNA	459	PAUL, ELIZABETH	RS 224 RICHARD AVEDON'S PORTFOLIO "THE FAMILY 1976"	106
MONTALBETTI/CAMPBELL	RS 734 DAVID DUCHOVNY AND GILLIAN ANDERSON	395			
MONTGOMERY, DAVID	RS 230 ROD STEWART	112	PAULINI, RUDOLF	RS 355 ELVIS PRESLEY	185
	RS 393 JOAN BAEZ	208	PEROU	RS 1041 LED ZEPPELIN	578
	RS 407 SEAN CONNERY	212	PETERSON, DON	RS 179 FREDDIE PRINZE	81
	RS 408 BOY GEORGE	215	PIEL, DENIS	RS 338 GOLDIE HAWN	175
	RS 414 DURAN DURAN	216		RS 347 MARGOT KIDDER	180
	RS 522 ROBERT PLANT	268			
MORRIS, DENNIS	RS 250 JOHNNY ROTTEN	124			

INDEX BY PHOTOGRAPHER & ILLUSTRATOR

CREDIT	ISSUE & COVER SUBJECT	PAGE	CREDIT	ISSUE & COVER SUBJECT	PAGE
PIETZSCH, STEVE	RS 534 THE 100 BEST SINGLES 1963-1988	274	**RICHARDSON, TERRY**	RS 1138 RED HOT CHILI PEPPERS	640
				RS 1164 RICK ROSS	659
PIGGOT, MARCUS & ALAS, MERT	RS 1230 MADONNA	696		RS 1176 RIHANNA	667
				RS 1181 LOUIS C.K.	670
PLATON	RS 986 BONO	5444		RS 1183 THE ROLLING STONES	672
	RS 992 NEIL YOUNG	547		RS 1209 NEIL PATRICK HARRIS	683
PLATON	RS 995 SHAUN WHITE	550		RS 1226 NICKI MINAJ	693
PLITZ, GERNOT	RS 1101 JIMI HENDRIX	619		RS 1239/1240 KIM KARDASHIAN	700
PREITE, JULIUS	RS 910 BART SIMPSON	493	**RIEDEL, JEFF**	RS 899/900 EMINEM	485
	RS 910 HOMER SIMPSON	494	**RITTS, HERB**	RS 371 DAVID LETTERMAN	199
	RS 910 THE SIMPSONS	495		RS 379 RICHARD GERE	202
PRESTON, NEAL	RS 182 JIMMY PAGE AND ROBERT PLANT	83		RS 448 RICHARD GERE	236
	RS 196 THE EAGLES	93		RS 447 MADONNA AND ROSANNA ARQUETTE	235
	RS 419 MARVIN GAYE	220		RS 455 MEL GIBSON AND TINA TURNER	238
	RS 442 BRUCE SPRINGSTEEN	231			
	RS 458 BRUCE SPRINGSTEEN	240		RS 460 DON JOHNSON	240
	RS 525 BRUCE SPRINGSTEEN	270		RS 466 JOHN COUGAR MELLENCAMP	241
	RS 573 KEITH RICHARDS AND MICK JAGGER	298		RS 476 TOM CRUISE	244
	RS 640 BONO	339		RS 480 JACK NICHOLSON	245
	RS 1171 JIMMY PAGE	662		RS 498 DAVID BOWIE	253
PUTNAM, JAMIE	RS 198 PATTY HEARST (PT. 1)	92		RS 508 MADONNA	259
RAEDLE, JOE	RS 1257 HILLARY RODHAM CLINTON AND BERNIE SANDERS	715		RS 529 TOM HANKS	274
				RS 532 TOM CRUISE	274
RAPOPORT, AARON	RS 345 JAMES TAYLOR	179		RS 535 TRACY CHAPMAN	275
	RS 348 TOM PETTY	180		RS 540 STEVE WINWOOD	277
	RS 374 E.T.	199		RS 543 MEL GIBSON	280
	RS 398 MEN AT WORK	212		RS 548 MADONNA	279
	RS 400/401 CAST OF 'RETURN OF THE JEDI'	210		RS 554 PAUL McCARTNEY	286
				RS 561 MADONNA	288
	RS 404 JACKSON BROWNE	212		RS 569 TOM CRUISE	294
	RS 420 THE PRETENDERS	219		RS 578 CLAUDIA SCHIFFER	300
	RS 430 HUEY LEWIS	226		RS 579 WARREN BEATTY	301
	RS 436 BRUCE SPRINGSTEEN	228		RS 582/583 TOM CRUISE	303
	RS 448 PHIL COLLINS	237		RS 584 JULIA ROBERTS	305
	RS 468 BRUCE SPRINGSTEEN	242		RS 595 JOHNNY DEPP	311
	RS 478/479 TOM PETTY AND BOB DYLAN	245		RS 597 STING	311
				RS 599 SINEAD O'CONNOR	313
RAY, BILL	RS 1200 THE BEATLES	678		RS 604 WINONA RYDER	314
REGAN, KEN	RS 204 JOAN BAEZ AND BOB DYLAN	93		RS 611 ARNOLD SCHWARZENEGGER	318
	RS 424 BOB DYLAN	223			
	RS 469 JIM McMAHON	242		RS 612 GUNS N' ROSES	319
RENARD, MORGAN	RS 278 BOB DYLAN	143		RS 621 MICHAEL JACKSON	325
RICHARDSON, TERRY	RS 1075 BLAKE LIVELY AND LEIGHTON MEESTER	602		RS 627 AXL ROSE	329
				RS 634/635 BATMAN'S SUIT	334
	RS 1100 SHAUN WHITE	616		RS 636 BRUCE SPRINGSTEEN	335
	RS 1108/1109 LADY GAGA	622		RS 638 MICHELLE PFEIFFER	337
	RS 1125 JUSTIN BIEBER	632		RS 672/673 CINDY CRAWFORD	355
	RS 1134/1135 KATY PERRY	639		RS 677 WINONA RYDER	357

INDEX BY PHOTOGRAPHER & ILLUSTRATOR

CREDIT	ISSUE & COVER SUBJECT	PAGE	CREDIT	ISSUE & COVER SUBJECT	PAGE
RITTS, HERB	RS 686/687 JULIA ROBERTS	366	ROLSTON, MATTHEW	RS 1010 JACK NICHOLSON	560
	RS 712/713 JIM CARREY	383		RS 1015 SNOOP DOGG	563
	RS 793 LAETITIA CASTA	427		RS 1020 NEW GUITAR GODS	563
	RS 800 ALANIS MORISSETTE	432		RS 1024 ROSE MCGOWAN AND ROSARIO DAWSON	566
	RS 816/817 NICOLE KIDMAN	441		RS 1027 KEITH RICHARDS AND JOHNNY DEPP	566
	RS 851 KATE HUDSON	464			
	RS 878 JENNIFER ANISTON	476		RS 1033 ZAC EFRON	573
	RS 882 BOB DYLAN	481		RS 1034 MAROON 5	573
	RS 914 JUSTIN TIMBERLAKE	496		RS 1040 JAY-Z	577
	RS 1090 MADONNA	611		RS 1044 JOHNNY DEPP	578
ROBATHAN, PETER	RS 767 THE PRODIGY'S KEITH FLINT	414		RS 1052 CAST OF 'THE HILLS'	585
				RS 1081 ADAM LAMBERT	606
ROCK, MICK	RS 121 DAVID BOWIE	57		RS 1082/1083 THE JONAS BROTHERS	606
ROLSTON, MATTHEW	RS 417 MICHAEL JACKSON	218		RS 1112 CAST OF 'TRUE BLOOD'	625
	RS 475 MADONNA	244		RS 1170 DANIEL CRAIG AS JAMES BOND	663
	RS 484 CYBILL SHEPHERD	247			
	RS 485 TINA TURNER	247	ROSE, TOM	RS 172 THE BEATLES	78
	RS 510 BONO	261	ROY, NORMAN JEAN	RS 959 VOICES FOR CHANGE	524
	RS 518 GEORGE MICHAEL	266		RS 962 EMINEM	526
	RS 521 U2	265		RS 971 THE CHILDREN OF ROCK	532
	RS 516 LISA BONET	271	RUSSELL, ETHAN	RS 19 MICK JAGGER	13
	RS 528 TERENCE TRENT D'ARBY	274	RYDEN, MARK	RS 809 JIMI HENDRIX	436
	RS 552 UMA THERMAN	284	SCAVULLO, FRANCESCO	RS 153 PAUL AND LINDA MCCARTNEY	69
	RS 563 ANDIE MACDOWELL	289			
	RS 572 JANET JACKSON	292		RS 186 JOHN DENVER	83
	RS 588 THE WOMEN OF 'TWIN PEAKS'	307		RS 211 PETER FRAMPTON	96
				RS 243 THE BEE GEES	118
	RS 500 JODIE FOSTER	311		RS 259 RITA COOLIDGE AND KRIS KRISTOFFERSON	132
	RS 679 ANTHONY KIEDIS	359			
	RS 688 BEASTIE BOYS	367		RS 276 LINDA RONSTADT	142
	RS 701 DEMI MOORE	377		RS 277 GILDA RADNER	143
	RS 722 LENNY KRAVITZ	390	SCHAPIRO, STEVE	RS 175 DUSTIN HOFFMAN	78
	RS 742 THE FUGEES	399		RS 206 DAVID BOWIE	94
	RS 754 GILLIAN ANDERSON	406	SCHATZBERG, JERRY	RS 1131 BOB DYLAN	636
	RS 760 JEWEL	408	SCHIFFMAN, BONNIE	RS 378 ROBIN WILLIAMS	202
	RS 766 PUFF DADDY	412		RS 389 MICHAEL JACKSON	207
	RS 769 NEVE CAMPBELL	414		RS 392 DUDLEY MOORE	208
	RS 906 JENNIFER LOVE HEWITT	489		RS 406 CHEVY CHASE	212
	RS 920 LISA MARIE PRESLEY	498		RS 413 ARMS CONCERT PARTICIPANTS	219
	RS 926 CLAY AIKEN	499			
	RS 928 ANGELINA JOLIE	503		RS 434 STEVE MARTIN	228
	RS 930 MARY-KATE AND ASHLEY OLSON	504		RS 470 BRUCE WILLIS	243
				RS 473 WHOOPI GOLDBERG	242
	RS 932 BRITNEY SPEARS	505		RS 496 THE BANGLES	252
	RS 955 LINDSAY LOHAN	521		RS 520 ROBIN WILLIAMS	267
	RS 977/978 JESSICA ALBA	536		RS 538 JOHNNY CARSON AND DAVID LETTERMAN	276
	RS 1002 RED HOT CHILI PEPPERS	556			
	RS 1004/1005 JOHNNY DEPP	557		RS 555 MICHAEL KEATON	290
	RS 1008 BOB DYLAN	558		RS 559 EDDIE MURPHY	286
	RS 1007 CHRISTINA AGUILERA	559			

752 • ROLLING STONE

INDEX BY PHOTOGRAPHER & ILLUSTRATOR

CREDIT	ISSUE & COVER SUBJECT	PAGE
SCHIFFMAN, BONNIE	RS 564 JAY LENO AND ARSENIO HALL	289
	RS 626 MIKE MYERS AND DANA CARVEY	327
SCHOELLER, MARTIN	RS 826 RAGE AGAINST THE MACHINE	446
	RS 839 RED HOT CHILI PEPPERS	454
	RS 879 SLIPKNOT	477
	RS 891 LINKIN PARK	480
	RS 893 SHAKIRA	484
	RS 901 OZZY OSBOURNE	486
	RS 902 DAVE MATTHEWS BAND	485
	RS 903 BRUCE SPRINGSTEEN	487
	RS 905 THE VINES	489
	RS 917 PHISH	497
	RS 918 AVRIL LAVIGNE	497
	RS 923 ASHTON KUTCHER	498
	RS 940 DAVE MATTHEWS	510
	RS 948 USHER	514
	RS 950 EMINEM AND D12	516
	RS 973 WEEZER	534
	RS 976 DAVE MATTEWS BAND	534
	RS 982 THE WHITE STRIPES	540
	RS 1047 JACK JOHNSON	581
	RS 1087 STEPHEN COLBERT	610
	RS 1185 CAST OF 'THIS IS THE END'	674
	RS 1203 PHILIP SEYMOUR HOFFMAN	680
	RS 1252 5 SECONDS OF SUMMER	708
	RS 1260 MERLE HAGGARD	713
	RS 1293 JUSTIN TRUDEAU	736
SCHOERNER, NORBERT	RS 759 NO DOUBT	408
SCOTT, GREG	RS 203 JEFFERSON STARSHIP	93
	RS 214 JIMMY CARTER	99
SEEFF, NORMAN	RS 296 JONI MITCHELL	150
	RS 305 THE EAGLES	156
	RS 1142 STEVE JOBS	644
	RS 1105 MICK JAGGER	620
	RS 1105 KEITH RICHARDS	620
SELIGER, MARK	RS 503 PAUL SIMON AND LADYSMITH BLACK MAMBAZO	256
	RS 546 SAM KINISON	280
	RS 551 LOU REED	283
	RS 574 THE B-52'S	297
	RS 575 AEROSMITH	298
	RS 590 LIVING COLOUR	309
	RS 596 SLASH	311
	RS 598 ROBIN WILLIAMS	312
	RS 605 THE BLACK CROWES	314

CREDIT	ISSUE & COVER SUBJECT	PAGE
SELIGER, MARK	RS 610 TOM PETTY	317
	RS 613 SEBASTIAN BACH	320
	RS 616 JERRY GARCIA	323
	RS 617 METALLICA	324
	RS 628 NIRVANA	330
	RS 629 DEF LEPPARD	328
	RS 633 RED HOT CHILI PEPPERS	333
	RS 637 ICE-T	336
	RS 639 BILL CLINTON	338
	RS 647 SPIN DOCTORS	342
	RS 648 NEIL YOUNG	343
	RS 650 DAVID LETTERMAN	344
	RS 654 JAMES HETFIELD	346
	RS 656 DANA CARVEY	347
	RS 660/661 CAST OF 'SEINFELD'	349
	RS 662 SOUL ASYLUM	352
	RS 664 JERRY GARCIA	352
	RS 666 DR. DRE AND SNOOP DOGGY DOGG	353
	RS 668 PEARL JAM	352
	RS 669 BLIND MELON	352
	RS 670 SHAQUILLE O'NEAL	353
	RS 671 BILL CLINTON	354
	RS 674 NIRVANA	356
	RS 675 HOWARD STERN	358
	RS 682 WOMEN OF 'MELROSE PLACE'	362
	RS 683 KURT COBAIN	365
	RS 684 SOUNDGARDEN	366
	RS 685 COUNTING CROWS	366
	RS 691 JERRY SEINFELD	370
	RS 693 R.E.M.	373
	RS 696 BRAD PITT	374
	RS 697 COURTNEY LOVE	375
	RS 703 ETHAN HAWKE	379
	RS 705 EDDIE VAN HALEN	379
	RS 706 BELLY	379
	RS 707 TOM PETTY	379
	RS 708 CAST OF 'FRIENDS'	380
	RS 710 DREW BARRYMORE	381
	RS 714 HOOTIE AND THE BLOWFISH	382
	RS 715 HOLE	384
	RS 721 SMASHING PUMPKINS	389
	RS 724/725 GREEN DAY	390
	RS 727 LAYNE STALEY	390
	RS 728 JOHN TRAVOLTA	390
	RS 729 JENNIFER ANISTON	392
	RS 730 JOAN OSBORNE	390
	RS 731 SEAN PENN	393

50 YEARS OF COVERS • 753

INDEX BY PHOTOGRAPHER & ILLUSTRATOR

CREDIT	ISSUE & COVER SUBJECT	PAGE	CREDIT	ISSUE & COVER SUBJECT	PAGE
SELIGER, MARK	RS 732 GAVIN ROSSDALE	394	**SELIGER, MARK**	RS 833 MELISSA ETHERIDGE, DAVID CROSBY AND FAMILIES	450
	RS 738/739 JENNY MCCARTHY	396			
	RS 741 CAMERON DIAZ	395			
	RS 743 CONAN O'BRIEN	398		RS 835 LEONARDO DICAPRIO	453
	RS 744 BROOKE SHIELDS	399		RS 836 CARLOS SANTANA	453
	RS 747 SHERYL CROW	402		RS 841 BRITNEY SPEARS	457
	RS 750/751 BEAVIS & BUTT-HEAD WITH PAMELA ANDERSON LEE	407		RS 842 TOM GREEN	454
				RS 843 KID ROCK	455
				RS 844/845 CHRISTINA AGUILERA	458
	RS 753 STONE TEMPLE PILOTS	407		RS 846 BLINK-182	460
	RS 756 HOWARD STERN	407		RS 848 KEANU REEVES	461
	RS 757 BRAD PITT	408		RS 849 GISELE	462
	RS 762 JAKOB DYLAN	409		RS 852 JAKOB DYLAN	454
	RS 764/765 SPICE GIRLS	411		RS 853 AL GORE	465
	RS 768 RZA AND ZACK DE LA ROCHA	414		RS 854 DREW BARRYMORE	466
				RS 860 U2	467
	RS 770 CHRIS ROCK	413		RS 861 JOHNNY KNOXVILLE	469
	RS 772 FLEETWOOD MAC	414		RS 862 JENNIFER LOPEZ	469
	RS 774 CAST OF 'SATURDAY NIGHT LIVE'	418		RS 864 DAVE MATTHEWS BAND	468
				RS 865 CAST OF 'THE SOPRANOS'	470
	RS 775 MICK JAGGER AND KEITH RICHARDS	416		RS 867 STEVEN TYLER AND JOE PERRY	472
	RS 776/777 TORI SPELLING	419		RS 870 THE ROCK	472
	RS 778 FIONA APPLE	419		RS 873 STAIND	472
	RS 783 SARAH MICHELLE GELLAR	420		RS 875 'NSYNC: JC CHASEZ, LANCE BASS, CHRIS KIRKPATRICK, JUSTIN TIMBERLAKE AND JOEY FATONE	474
	RS 784 RICHARD ASHCROFT	421			
	RS 786 JERRY SPRINGER	421			
	RS 787 CAST OF 'SEINFELD'	422			
	RS 792 BEASTIE BOYS	426			
	RS 794 SHANIA TWAIN	428		RS 881 ALICIA KEYS	476
	RS 795 KATIE HOLMES	428		RS 883/884 BRITNEY SPEARS	480
	RS 796 JANET JACKSON	428		RS 933 JOHNNY CASH	506
	RS 797 MARILYN MANSON	429		RS 1088 MEGAN FOX	611
	RS 799 BILL CLINTON	431		RS 1092 BONO, MICK JAGGER AND BRUCE SPRINGSTEEN	612
	RS 801 WILL SMITH	433			
	RS 804 BEASTIE BOYS	433		RS 1093 TAYLOR LAUTNER	611
	RS 805 ROB ZOMBIE	432		RS 1115 BARACK OBAMA	615
	RS 806 LAURYN HILL	432		RS 1097 JOHN MAYER	617
	RS 807 JENNIFER ANISTON	433		RS 1102 CAST OF 'GLEE'	618
	RS 808 MARK MCGRATH	434		RS 1103 BLACK EYED PEAS	619
	RS 812 KURT COBAIN	437		RS 1104 ROBERT DOWNEY JR.	619
	RS 813 BACKSTREET BOYS	439		RS 1107 JAY-Z	621
	RS 814 MIKE MYERS AS AUSTIN POWERS	440		RS 1110 LEONARDO DICAPRIO	623
				RS 1111 KATY PERRY	624
	RS 819 ANGELINA JOLIE	443		RS 1118 EMINEM	630
	RS 821 DAVID SPADE	444		RS 1123 LIL WAYNE	632
	RS 823 TRENT REZNOR	444		RS 1124 ELTON JOHN	632
	RS 824 BRAD PITT	445		RS 1128 RIHANNA	633
	RS 832 BACKSTREET BOYS	452		RS 1126 NICOLE "SNOOKI" PIZZOLI	635
				RS 1127 HOWARD STERN	635

INDEX BY PHOTOGRAPHER & ILLUSTRATOR

CREDIT	ISSUE & COVER SUBJECT	PAGE	CREDIT	ISSUE & COVER SUBJECT	PAGE
SELIGER, MARK	RS 1136 LARRY DAVID	641	**SELIGER, MARK**	RS 1294 KENDRICK LAMAR	738
	RS 1143 EDDIE MURPHY	646		RS 1296 DAVE GROHL	739
	RS 1144 GEORGE CLOONEY	647		RS 1299 TOM PETTY	741
	RS 1150 CAST OF 'THE VOICE'	651		RS 1301 ELON MUSK	742
	RS 1153 BRUCE SPRINGSTEEN	652	**SENDAK, MAURICE**	RS 229 WILD THINGS	111
	RS 1156 BARACK OBAMA	653	**SHAMES, STEVE**	RS 41 JOE COCKER	20
	RS 1157 PETER DINKLAGE	655		RS 43 THE UNDERGROUND PRESS	22
	RS 1162 JUSTIN BIEBER	658	**SHAW, PATRIC**	RS 866 JULIA STILES	472
	RS 1169 BARACK OBAMA	662	**SHEA, EDMUND**	RS 1036 DR. HUNTER S. THOMPSON	575
	RS 1175 CAST OF '30 ROCK'	666	**SHIELDS, CHARLES**	RS 143 SENATOR SAM ERVIN	65
	RS 1174 JIMMY KIMMEL	666	**SHINING, STEWART'**	RS 813 JENNIFER LOVE HEWITT	439
	RS 1180 JON HAMM	670		RS 837 NSYNC	453
	RS 1192 MICHAEL J. FOX	673		RS 840 SARAH MICHELLE GELLAR	454
	RS 1197 EMINEM	678		RS 892 TOM WELLING AND KRISTIN KREUK	481
	RS 1198/1199 WILL FERRELL AS RON BURGUNDY	678		RS 894 THE WOMEN OF 'THE SWEETEST THING'	484
	RS 1205 SKRILLEX	681	**SHUGRUE, STEPHEN**	RS 138 PAUL NEWMAN	63
	RS 1207 JULIA LOUIS-DREYFUS	682	**SIMON, PETER**	RS 113 PAUL SIMON	56
	RS 1208 KIT HARINGTON	683		RS 125 JAMES TAYLOR AND CARLY SIMON	58
	RS 1210 JACK WHITE	683			
	RS 1211 MIRANDA LAMBERT	684	**SIROTA, PEGGY**	RS 709 MELISSA ETHERIDGE	379
	RS 1211 ERIC CHURCH	684		RS 716 ALICIA SILVERSTONE	385
	RS 1212/1213 MELISSA MCCARTHY	687		RS 771 SALT-N-PEPA	414
	RS 1216 WILLIE NELSON	687		RS 773 THIRTIETH ANNIVERSARY: COURTNEY LOVE, TINA TURNER AND MADONNA	415
	RS 1221 U2	689			
	RS 1224/1225 SETH ROGEN	692			
	RS 1232 RINGO STARR	697		RS 781 KATE WINSLET	417
	RS 1235 DAVID LETTERMAN	699		RS 785 SARAH MCLACHLAN	421
	RS 1237 TAYLOR SCHILLING AND LAURA PREPON	700		RS 827 CHRISTINA RICCI	446
	RS 1242 DR. DRE AND ICE CUBE	702		RS 1067 BRITNEY SPEARS	598
	RS 1243 ANDREW LUCK	703		RS 1073 TAYLOR SWIFT	600
	RS 1243 DEZ BRYANT	703		RS 1159 CHARLIE SHEEN	656
	RS 1243 RUSSELL WILSON	703		RS 1177 LENA DUNHAM	668
	RS 1244 DONALD TRUMP	704		RS 1195 PAUL MCCARTNEY	673
	RS 1247 THE WEEKND	704		RS 1215 KATY PERRY	686
	RS 1245 BARACK OBAMA	705		RS 1217 ROBIN WILLIAMS	687
	RS 1253 LEONARDO DICAPRIO	708		RS 1223 DAVE GROHL	693
	RS 1258 JAMES FRANCO	714		RS 1227 STEVIE NICKS	694
	RS 1262 OSCAR ISAAC	715		RS 1241 KEVIN HART	700
	RS 1263 LIN-MANUEL MIRANDA	718		RS 1238 RUSH	701
	RS 1269 JAMES CORDEN	722		RS 1255 CHRIS MARTIN	709
	RS 1270 GREEN DAY	723		RS 1283 ED SHEERAN	732
	RS 1274 BRUNO MARS	725		RS 1288 LORDE	734
	RS 1278/1279 EMMA STONE	728		RS 1295 GAL GADOT	739
	RS 1273 KEVIN DURANT	729		RS 1298 KESHA	740
	RS 1281/1282 JOHN OLIVER	729	**SIRY, ERIC**	RS 695 GENERATION NEXT	372
	RS 1287 CHRIS ROCK	733	**SMALE, BRIAN**	RS 514 R.E.M.	265
	RS 1290 RACHEL MADDOW	736	**SNYDER, ISABEL**	RS 889 JENNIFER GARNER	480
	RS 1291/1292 EMILIA CLARKE	737	**SOREL, EDWARD**	RS 110 GEORGE MCGOVERN	55

INDEX BY PHOTOGRAPHER & ILLUSTRATOR

CREDIT	ISSUE & COVER SUBJECT	PAGE	CREDIT	ISSUE & COVER SUBJECT	PAGE
SOREL, EDWARD	*RS* 136 JESUS FREAKS	63	TURNER, PETE	*RS* 178 GREGG ALLMAN	81
SOUTH PARK STUDIOS	*RS* 1022 SOUTH PARK	566	VADUKUL, MAX	*RS* 925 JUSTIN TIMBERLAKE AND CHRISTINA AGUILERA	502
SPAZIANI, STEFANO	*RS* 1202 POPE FRANCIS	680			
STAVERS, GLORIA	*RS* 352 JIM MORRISON	183		*RS* 934 MISSY ELLIOTT, ALICIA KEYS AND EVE	504
STEADMAN, RALPH	*RS* 95 FEAR AND LOATHING IN LAS VEGAS (PT. 1)	50			
				RS 935 THE STROKES	504
	RS 96 FEAR AND LOATHING IN LAS VEGAS (PT. 2)	51		*RS* 936 JESSICA SIMPSON	508
				RS 966 GWEN STEFANI	527
	RS 115 1972 DEMOCRATIC CONVENTION	56		*RS* 979 OWEN WILSON AND VINCE VAUGHN	537
	RS 118 1972 REPUBLICAN CONVENTION	57		*RS* 985 PAUL McCARTNEY	543
				RS 1009 JUSTIN TIMBERLAKE	560
	RS 144 RICHARD NIXON	66		*RS* 1011 FERGIE	560
	RS 622 HUNTER S. THOMPSON	326		*RS* 1019 PANIC! AT THE DISCO	563
STEEL, ARTHUR	*RS* 1139 GEORGE HARRISON	642		*RS* 1028 AMY WINEHOUSE	570
STERMER, DUGALD	*RS* 126 APOLLO ASTRONAUT	58		*RS* 1029 THE POLICE	573
	RS 168 CROSBY, STILLS, NASH & YOUNG	75		*RS* 1037 KID ROCK	573
				RS 1038 BRUCE SPRINGSTEEN	576
STERN, BERT	*RS* 439 DARYL HALL AND JOHN OATES	231		*RS* 1050 MICK JAGGER, JACK WHITE AND KEITH RICHARDS	585
STEVENS, NICK	*RS* 1003 EDDIE VEDDER	556		*RS* 1053 THE EAGLES	585
STONE, GILBERT	*RS* 149 GREGG ALLMAN	68		*RS* 1054 100 GREATEST GUITAR SONGS OF ALL TIME	586
STONE, MATT	*RS* 780 CAST OF 'SOUTH PARK'	419			
SUMMA, ANN	*RS* 544 ROY ORBISON	280		*RS* 1058 THE JONAS BROTHERS	592
SUTTON, WARD	*RS* 855 POP 100!	467		*RS* 1077 KINGS OF LEON	605
TANNENBAUM, ALLAN	*RS* 380 JOHN LENNON AND YOKO ONO	202		*RS* 1091 SHAKIRA	611
				RS 1219 JOHN OLIVER	690
THOMPSON, MICHAEL	*RS* 915 SHANIA TWAIN	497		*RS* 1268 PAUL McCARTNEY	719
THURNER, JEFFREY	*RS* 652 NATALIE MERCHANT	348	VAN HAMERSVELD, JOHN	*RS* 163 JAMES DEAN	72
TRACHTENBERG, ROBERT	*RS* 1013 JON STEWART AND STEPHEN COLBERT	562	VARRIALE, JIM	*RS* 358 CARLY SIMON	189
				RS 387 PAUL NEWMAN	206
	RS 1014 SACHA BARON COHEN AS BORAT	563		*RS* 391 JESSICA LANGE	208
			VON UNWERTH, ELLEN	*RS* 649 NENEH CHERRY	342
	RS 1061 THE NEW GOLDEN AGE OF COMEDY	594	VRIENS-McGRATH, MATTHIAS	*RS* 1201 LORDE	679
	RS 1113 CAST OF 'MAD MEN'	626	WALZ, BARBARA	*RS* 428 BILL MURRAY	226
	RS 1117 CONAN O'BRIEN	629	WARHOL, ANDY	*RS* 249 BELLA ABZUG	125
	RS 1122 JIMMY FALLON	629	WATSON, ALBERT	*RS* 341 JACK NICHOLSON	177
TRAXEL, MEL	*RS* 119 SALLY STRUTHERS	57		*RS* 344 SUSAN SARANDON	179
TRETICK, STANLEY	*RS* 210 ROBERT REDFORD AND DUSTIN HOFFMAN	95		*RS* 425 THE GO-GO'S	226
				RS 486 BILLY JOEL	247
TRIMPE, HERB	*RS* 91 THE INCREDIBLE HULK	49		*RS* 494 BRUCE SPRINGSTEEN	251
TRUDEAU, GARRY	*RS* 194 DOONESBURY'S UNCLE DUKE	88		*RS* 517 MICHAEL DOUGLAS	265
				RS 536 KEITH RICHARDS	277
	RS 221 DOONESBURY'S GINNY SLADE AND JIMMY THUDPUCKER	105		*RS* 560 MICK JAGGER AND KEITH RICHARDS	287
				RS 615 ERIC CLAPTON	322
	RS 258 DOONESBURY'S JIMMY THUDPUCKER	132		*RS* 625 R.E.M.	328
				RS 630 SHARON STONE	331
	RS 954 DOONESBURY'S B.D.	520		*RS* 631 TOM CRUISE	331

INDEX BY PHOTOGRAPHER & ILLUSTRATOR

CREDIT	ISSUE & COVER SUBJECT	PAGE	CREDIT	ISSUE & COVER SUBJECT	PAGE
WATSON, ALBERT	RS 642 SINEAD O'CONNOR	340	**WENNER, THEO**	RS 1186/1187 JOHNNY DEPP AS TONTO	672
	RS 643 ELVIS' GOLD LAME NUDIE SUIT	341		RS 1193 MILEY CYRUS	675
	RS 644 DENZEL WASHINGTON	342		RS 1214 LANA DEL REY	685
	RS 655 ERIC CLAPTON	348		RS 1218 TAYLOR SWIFT	688
	RS 658 WHITNEY HOUSTON	348		RS 1228 SAM SMITH	693
	RS 694 LIV AND STEVEN TYLER	372		RS 1231 KENDRICK LAMAR	697
	RS 735 DAVID LETTERMAN	395		RS 1247 KEITH RICHARDS	704
	RS 749 DENNIS RODMAN	403		RS 1248 ADELE	706
	RS 761 U2	410		RS 1265/1266 FUTURE	719
	RS 779 MARIAH CAREY	419		RS 1267 JARED LETO	719
	RS 782 JACK NICHOLSON	419		RS 1286 HARRY STYLES	733
	RS 838 DMX	454	**WHITE, CHARLES E. III**	RS 130 ROBERT MITCHUM	61
	RS 869 DESTINY'S CHILD	473	**WHITE, TIMOTHY**	RS 530/531 VAN HALEN	275
	RS 898 NATALIE PORTMAN	485		RS 539 GUNS N' ROSES	278
	RS 908 WOMEN IN ROCK: SHAKIRA, BRITNEY SPEARS, MARY J. BLIGE, ALANIS MORISSETTE, AVRIL LAVIGNE, AND ASHANTI	488		RS 545 JON BON JOVI	280
				RS 550 R.E.M.	282
				RS 553 CAST OF 'GHOSTBUSTERS II'	286
				RS 570 BILLY JOEL	295
				RS 571 PAUL MCCARTNEY	296
				RS 1046 BRITNEY SPEARS	579
	RS 909 CHRISTINA AGUILERA	491	**WHITESIDES, KIM**	RS 141 ELTON JOHN	64
	RS 919 50 CENT	499		RS 193 NEIL YOUNG	87
	RS 938/939 JUSTIN TIMBERLAKE	508		RS 201 JACK NICHOLSON	91
	RS 947 QUENTIN TARANTINO AND UMA THURMAN	513		RS 325 BILLY JOEL	169
			WILLARDSON, DAVE	RS 147 DANIEL ELLSBURG	68
	RS 949 PRINCE	515		RS 167 STEELY DAN	75
	RS 957 MICHAEL MOORE	523	**WILLIAMS, JOHN**	RS 58 CAPTAIN BEEFHEART	29
	RS 961 JOHN KERRY	526	**WILSON, WES**	RS 1236 THE GRATEFUL DEAD	700
	RS 967 JOHNNY DEPP	529	**WINTERS, DAN**	RS 700 GREEN DAY	376
	RS 974 ORLANDO BLOOM	535		RS 718 FOO FIGHTERS	389
	RS 975 DARTH VADER	538		RS 755 TRENT REZNOR AND DAVID LYNCH	407
	RS 987 BILLIE JOE ARMSTRONG	545			
	RS 989 JAY-Z	546		RS 788 JOHNNY DEPP	423
	RS 1035 50 CENT AND KANYE WEST	574	**WOLFE, BRUCE**	RS 197 MUHAMMAD ALI	93
	RS 1071 BRUCE SPRINGSTEEN	599		RS 263 THE BEE GEES AND PETER FRAMPTON	132
	RS 1140 JON STEWART	645			
	RS 1114 ROGER WATERS	627	**WOLMAN, BARON**	RS 2 TINA TURNER	6
	RS 1160/1161 DEADMAU5	657		RS 5 JIM MORRISON	7
WATSON, NORMAN	RS 481 BOY GEORGE	246		RS 6 JANIS JOPLIN, GATHERINGS OF THE TRIBES BE-IN	7
WAYDA, STEVE	RS 868 PAMELA ANDERSON AND TOMMY LEE	472			
				RS 7 JIMI HENDRIX	8
WENNER, JANN	RS 18 PETE TOWNSHEND	13		RS 11 ROCK FASHION	10
WENNER, THEO	RS 1106 RUSSELL BRAND	619		RS 13 TINY TIM	11
	RS 1130 STEVEN TYLER	637		RS 14 FRANK ZAPPA	11
	RS 1133 ZACH GALIFIANAKIS	638		RS 23 DOUG AND SEAN SAHM	16
	RS 1148 THE BLACK KEYS	651		RS 26 JIMI HENDRIX	16
	RS 1154 JENNIFER LAWRENCE	655		RS 27 GROUPIES	17
	RS 1168 TAYLOR SWIFT	662		RS 31 SUN RA	19
	RS 1182 BRUNO MARS	671		RS 33 JONI MITCHELL	19

INDEX BY PHOTOGRAPHER & ILLUSTRATOR

CREDIT	ISSUE & COVER SUBJECT		PAGE
WOLMAN, BARON	RS 35	CHUCK BERRY	19
	RS 36	NUDIE COHN	19
	RS 40	JERRY GARCIA	21
	RS 42	WOODSTOCK	21
	RS 49	MICK JAGGER	22
	RS 52	CREEDENCE CLEARWATER REVIVAL	26
	RS 59	LITTLE RICHARD	30
	RS 76	JAMES TAYLOR	40
	RS 86	DOUG SAHM	44
WOODWARD, HANK	RS 155	FEAR AND LOATHING AT THE SUPERBOWL	69
WRIGHT, JIM	RS 876	THE GIRLS OF 'AMERICAN PIE 2'	473
YANG, PETER	RS 1021	FALL OUT BOY	563
	RS 1056/1057	BARACK OBAMA	588
	RS 1076	LIL WAYNE	604
	RS 1098	LIL WAYNE	616
	RS 1163	BRYAN CRANSTON AND AARON PAUL OF 'BREAKING BAD'	658
	RS 1184	DAFT PUNK	674
	RS 1190	MACKLEMORE	674
YORKE, ANNETTE	RS 51	JOHN LENNON AND YOKO ONO	26
ZEFF, JOE	RS 1141	PINK FLOYD 'DARK SIDE OF THE MOON'	647
ZIMMERMAN, JOHN	RS 217	THE BEATLES	100
ZLOZOWER, NEIL	RS 1032	GUNS N' ROSES	572

ADDITIONAL CREDITS

[RS 3] The Beatles and friends on location for *Magical Mystery Tour*: (from left, top row) Jeni Crowley, John Lennon, Spencer Davis, Jesse Robins, Paul McCartney, Maggie Right, Mel Evans, Alex Mardes, Bill Wall, Neil Aspinal, Shirley Evans, Ringo Starr; (from left, second row) Sylvia Nightingale, Pauline Davis & baby, Derek Royal, Mandy West, Linda Lawson, Amy Smedley, unknown couple; (from left, third row) Freda Kelley, Barbara Icing, Loz Harvey, George Claydon, Alf Mandos; (from left, front row) Michael Gladden, George Harrison, Nat Jackly, Leslie Cavendish, Ivor Cutler–*Photographer Unknown* [RS 4] Donovan–*Baron Wolman*; Jimi Hendrix, Otis Redding–*Photographer Unknown* [RS 8] Monterey Pop Festival Organizers John Phillips and Lou Adler–*Photographer Unknown* [RS 9] John Lennon and Paul McCartney in *Yellow Submarine*–*Photographer Unknown* [RS 11] Rock Fashion – Julianna Wolman–*Baron Wolman* [RS 20] Ringo Starr, Paul McCartney, John Lennon and George Harrsion–*Photographs from 16 magazine, Courtesy Gloria Stavers* [RS 28] Japanese Rock – Unidentified & Kenji "Julie" Sawada of Julie and the Tigers–*Naoko Lash* [RS 50] Altamont–*Michael Maggia/Photographies West* [RS 55] Abbie Hoffman–*Bill Myers/Praxis* [RS 107] Texas C&W Festival, Marvin Gaye, Hubert Humphrey–*Annie Leibovitz* [RS 115] George McGovern at the 1972 Democratic Convention–*Ralph Steadman* [RS 204] Joan Baez & Bob Dylan–*Ken Regan/Camera 5* [RS 207] Grace Slick, Jerry Garcia, Steve Miller, John Cipollina and Dan Hicks–*Jim Marshall* [RS 211] Peter Frampton–*Francesco Scavullo*; Peter Frampton–*Bud Lee*; Inset: SLA Hideout–*Alison Weir* [RS 230] Rod Stewart–*David Montgomery/Radio Times* [RS 234] Princess Caroline–*Norman Parkinson/Sygma* [RS 241] Robert De Niro–*Leonard De Raemy/Sygma* [RS 246] Mark Hamill, Carrie Fisher, Chewbacca and Harrison Ford–*Terry O'Neill* [RS 250] Johnny Rotten (left)–*Bob Gruen*; Johnny Rotten (right)–*Dennis Morris* [RS 262] Brooke Shields–*Maureen Lambray © 1977* [RS 304] Bonnie Raitt, Bruce Springsteen, Carly Simon, James Taylor, Jackson Browne, Graham Nash and John Hall–*Annie Leibovitz* [RS 309] Teva Ladd, Bryan Wagner, Connie Burns, James Warmoth, Karen Morrison, Peter Bowes, Jacqueline Eckerle, Phillip Snyder, David Heck, Stephan Preston, Walter Adams Jr.–*Photographers Unknown* [RS 322] Billy Dee Williams, Mark Hamill, Carrie Fisher and Harrison Ford–*Annie Leibovitz* [RS 342] Ringo Starr–*Michael Childers/Sygma* [RS 359/360] The Rolling Stones at Madison Square Garden–*Lynn Goldsmith* [RS 366] Warren Beatty–*Jack Mitchell/Outline* [RS 371] David Letterman–*Herb Ritts/Visages* [RS 400/401] Darth Vader, Ewok, Carrie Fisher and Gamurian Guard–*Aaron Rapoport* [RS 403] Sting–*Lynn Goldsmith/LGI* [RS 413] Eric Clapton, Jeff Beck, Jimmy Page, Joe Cocker, Charlie Watts, Bill Wyman, Kenney Jones, Paul Rodgers and Ronnie Lane–*Bonnie Schiffman* [RS 415] The Beatles–*John Launois/Black Star* [RS 421] Marvin Gaye–*Neal Preston/Camera 5* [RS 424] Bob Dylan–*Ken Regan/Camera 5* [RS 426] Tom Wolfe–*Annie Leibovitz/Contact Press Images*; Steven Spielberg–*Hiro*; Little Richard–*Ralph Morse/Life Magazine © Time Inc.* [RS 428] Bill Murray–*Barbara Walz/Outline* [RS 445] David Lee Roth–*Bradford Branson/Visages* [RS 454] Mick Jagger–*Albert Watson*; Bob Dylan, Madonna–*Ken Regan/Camera 5*; Paul McCartney–*Linda McCartney*; David Bowie–*Greg Gorman*; Chrissie Hynde, Phil Collins–*Aaron Rapoport*; Bono–*Photographer Unknown*; Bob Geldof–*Simon Fowler*; Ric Ocasek–*William Coupon*; Sting, John Taylor–*Eric Boman*; Robert Plant–*Ilpo Musto*; Eric Clapton–*David Montgomery*; Sade–*Brian Aris/Outline*; Pete Townshend–*Davies & Starr*; Bryan Ferry–*Lothar Schmid*; Tina Turner, Mark Knopfler, Bryan Adams; –*Deborah Feingold/Outline* [RS 456] Prince–*Raspberry Beret video still © 1985 PRN Productions* [RS 458] Bruce Springsteen–*Neal Preston/Camera 5* [RS 467] Elvis Presley–*Springer/Bettmann Film Archive*; Ray Charles, Buddy Holly–*James J. Kriegsmann*; Fats Domino, Jerry Lee Lewis, Chuck Berry, James Brown, Little Richard, the Everly Brothers, Sam Cooke–

ADDITIONAL CREDITS

Michael Ochs Archives [RS 469] Jim McMahon–*Ken Regan/Camera 5* [RS 497] Woody Allen–*Brian Hamill/Photoreporters* [RS 544] Roy Orbison–*Ann Summa/Onyx* [RS 553] Harold Ramis, Bill Murray, Sigourney Weaver, Ernie Hudson and Dan Aykroyd–*Timothy White* [RS 588] Lara Flynn Boyle, Sherilyn Fenn and Mädchen Amick–*Matthew Rolston* [RS 602] Chris Isaak–*Randee St. Nicholas/Visages*; Charlatans U.K., De la Soul, Nuno Bettencourt–*Mark Seliger* [RS 614] Pee-wee Herman–*Janette Beckman/Outline* [RS 624] Luke Perry, Shannen Doherty and Jason Priestly–*Andrew Eccles* [RS 660/661] Jason Alexander, Jerry Seinfeld, Julia Louis-Dreyfus and Michael Richards–*Mark Seliger* [RS 676] Bob Marley–*Annie Leibovitz/Contact Press Images* [RS 682] Laura Leighton, Josie Bissett, Heather Locklear, Daphne Zuniga and Courtney Thorne-Smith–*Mark Seliger* [RS 708] Jennifer Aniston, Matthew Perry, Lisa Kudrow, Courteney Cox, David Schwimmer and Matt LeBlanc–*Mark Seliger* [RS 724/725] Green Day, Jerry Garcia, Sheryl Crow, Billy Corgan, Courtney Love–*Mark Seliger*; John Travolta–*Richard Foreman*; Alanis Morissette–*Frank W. Ockenfels 3*; Coolio–*Albert Watson* [RS 734] David Duchovny and Gillian Anderson–*Montalbetti/Campbell for RS Australia* [RS 736] Perry Farrell, Billy Corgan–*Kevin Mazur*; "Independence Day"–*film still*; Alanis Morissette, Beck–*Frank W. Ockenfels 3*; Jimmy Buffett–*Randy Davey/LGI*; James Taylor–*Andrew Brucker*; Sandra Bullock–*Kate Garner/Visages*; Chris Cornell–*Mark Seliger*; John Popper–*Tom Wolff*; Kiss–*Costello/Retna* [RS 748] Eddie Vedder–*Ross Halfin/Photofeatures* [RS 761] U2–*Albert Watson*; Inset: Allen Ginsberg–*Fred W. McDarrah* [RS 767] Keith Flint–*Peter Robathan/Katz/Outline* [RS 774] Cheri Oteri, Will Ferrell, Molly Shannon and Chris Kattan–*Mark Seliger* [RS 787] Jason Alexander, Michael Richards, Julia Louis-Dreyfus and Jerry Seinfeld–*Mark Seliger* [RS 799] Bill Clinton–*Mark Seliger/Outline* [RS 812] Kurt Cobain–*Mark Seliger/Outline* [RS 815] Jar Jar Binks–*Image created exclusively for* ROLLING STONE *by Industrial Light & Magic, San Rafael, California, May 1999. Visual-effects supervision by Dennis Muren. SWI Image coordinator: Christine Owens. SWI image production assistant: Fay David. Animation director: Rob Coleman. Technical director: Damian Steel. CG animator: Kevin Martel. Photoshop artist: Claudine Gossett. © 1999 Lucasfilm Ltd. & TM. Digital work by ILM. All rights reserved. Used under authorization* [RS 820] Alanis Morissette, Wyclef Jean, DMX, Sheryl Crow, Jewel–*Tara Canova*; Jonathan Davis, Anthony Kiedis and Flea, Fred Durst, James Hetfield, Zack de la Rocha–*Kevin Mazur*; Kid Rock–*Len Irish*; Bruce Springsteen–*Mark Seliger*; Dave Matthews–*Rahav Segev*; Trey Anastasio–*Jay Blakesberg*; Tom Rowlands–*Rob Beccaris* [RS 828/829] Mick Jagger–*Jim Marshall*; John Lennon–*Annie Leibovitz*; David Bowie–*Mick Rock*; Britney Spears–*David LaChapelle*; Joni Mitchell–*Norman Seeff*; Lou Reed–*Andy Warhol*; Madonna–*Herb Ritts*; Bob Dylan–*M. Renard*; Jack Nicholson–*Albert Watson*; Kurt Cobain, Courtney Love and Frances Bean Cobain–*Kevin Mazur*; Aretha Franklin–*Linda McCartney*; Bruce Springsteen–*Lynn Goldsmith*; Bono–*Anton Corbijn*; Drew Barrymore–*Mark Seliger*; LL Cool J–*James Schnepf*; Keith Richards–*Peter Beard* [RS 830/831] The Party 2000–*David LaChapelle*; Historical photos *AP/Wide World Photo, Corbis, LGI/Corbis, Retuers/Corbis, UPI/Corbis, Michael Ochs Archives, Photofest* [RS 833] Jan Crosby, Bailey, Melissa Etheridge, Beckett, Julie Cypher and David Crosby–*Mark Seliger* [RS 847] Eminem, Dr. Dre–*Kevin Mazur*; Britney Spears–*J.K./All Action/Retna*; James Hetfield–*Kevin Winter/Image Direct*; Eddie Vedder, Kid Rock, Macy Gray–*Kelly A. Swift*; Bruce Springsteen–*Ethan Miller/Corbis*; Dave Matthews–*Rahav Segev*; Anthony Kiedis–*Yael/Retna*; Ozzy Osbourne–*Mark Seliger*; Mick Thompson–*Frank Forcino/London Features* [RS 855] John Lennon and Paul McCartney, Britney Spears, Eminem, Mick Jagger and Keith Richards, Madonna, Prince–*Ward Sutton* [RS 863] Paul McCartney, Ringo Starr, John Lennon and George Harrison–*Robert Freeman/© Apple Corps Ltd., circa 1965* [RS 865] Edie Falco, James Gandolfini, Michael Imperioli, Lorraine Braco, Steven Van Zandt, Dominic Chianese, David Chase, Tony Sirico, Joe Pantoliano, Drea de Matteo, Aida Turturro, Robert Iler and Jamie-Lynn Sigler–*Mark Seliger* [RS 868] Pamela Anderson and Tommy Lee–*Steve Wayda/Corbis/Outline* [RS 871] Madonna, Destiny's Child–*Kevin Mazur*; Bono–*Dave Hogan/ImageDirect*; Slipknot–*Martyn Goodacre/Retna UK*; Nelly Furtado–*David Atlas/Retna*; Moby–*Kevin Winter/ImageDirect*; 'NSync–*Framl Micelotta/ImageDirect*; Eric Clapton–*Steven Tackeff/ImageDirect*; Dave Matthews–*David Atlas/Retna*; Steven Tyler–*Scott Gries/ImageDirect* [RS 894] Cameron Diaz, Christina Applegate and Selma Blair–*Stewart Shining* [RS 895] Sharon, Ozzy, Jack and Kelly Osbourne–*Sophie Olmsted/Courtesy of* Revolver *magazine* [RS 897] Kurt Cobain–*Charles Hoselton/Retna* [RS 908] Shakira, Britney Spears, Mary J. Blige, Alanis Morissette, Avril Lavigne and Ashanti–*Albert Watson* [RS 910] Bart Simpson; Homer Simpson; Lisa, Bart, Marge and Homer Simpson–*Julius Preite. The Simpsons ™ and © 2002 Twentieth Century Fox Film Corp. All rights reserved* [RS 916] John Lennon, Paul McCartney, George Harrison, Ringo Starr–*Ethan Russell/Camera Press/RetnaEthan Russell © Apple Corps Ltd. AP* [RS 924] Fred Durst, Ozzy Osbourne, James Hetfield, Marilyn Manson, Brody Armstrong, Josh Homme, Dave Navarro, Dave Grohl, Chester Bennington, Davey Havok, Lars Ulrich and Perry Farrell–*Andrew MacPherson* [RS 931] The 100 Greatest Guitarists of All Time - Jimi Hendrix–*Jill Gibson ©/MichaelOchsArchives.com* [RS 933] Johnny Cash–*Mark Seliger/Outline* [RS 942] The Beatles–*John Dominis/Time Life Pictures/Getty Images* [RS 946] Elvis Presley–*Photographer Unknown*; The Beatles–*Robert Freeman/© Apple Corps Ltd./Everett Collection*; Bob Dylan, Mick Jagger and Keith Richards–© *Annie Leibovitz/Contact Press Images*; Jimi Hendrix, Janis Joplin–© *Jim Marshall*; Bono–© *Andrew MacPherson*; Aretha Franklin–*Everett Collection*; Kurt Cobain–*Mark Seliger/Corbis Outline*; Little Richard–*Michael Ochs Archives* [RS 951] Mick Jagger, Jimi Hendrix–© *Jim Marshall* ®; John Lennon memorial–*Lynn Goldsmith/Corbis*; Bruce Springsteen–*Hans Gutknecht/LADN/WireImage.com*; Eminem–*Peter Thompson/FilmMagic.com*; Madonna–*Neal Preston/Corbis*; Bob Dylan–*Rex USA*; crowd shot–*John Dominis/Time Life Pictures/Getty Images* [RS 952/953] Ray Charles–© *CBS/Courtesy Everett Collection* [RS 954] Doonesbury's B.D. –*G.B. Trudeau. Doonesbury* © 2004 *G.B. Trudeau, distributed by Universal Press Syndicate* [RS 958] Kurt Cobain, Red Hot Chili Peppers–*Mark Seliger*; Britney Spears–*David LaChapelle*; Dave Matthews–*Martin Schoeller*; Jim Morrison–*Joel Brodsky*; Justin Timberlake–*Herb Ritts*; Pete Townshend–*Annie Leibovitz/Contact Press Images*; U2–*Anton Corbijn*; Madonna–*Herb Ritts*; Sean Combs–*Michael Thompson*; John Lennon and Paul McCartney–*David Bailey*; Janet Jackson–*Patrick Demarchelier*; Marilyn Manson–*Matt Maburin*; Jimi Hendrix–*Gered Mankowitz*; Elvis Presley–*Jay Leviton*; Tupac Shakur–*Danny Clinch*; Michael Stipe–*Platon/CPI* [RS 959] Bruce Springsteen, John Mellencamp, Eddie Vedder, Emily Robison, Jackson Browne, Dave Matthews, Mike Mills, Steven Van Zandt, Patti Scialfa, Bonnie Raitt, Ben Gibbard, Stone Gossard, Martie Maguire and Boyd Tinsley–*Norman Jean Roy* [RS 971] Alexandra Richards, Ben Taylor, Nona Gaye, James Garfunkel, Sean Lennon, Theodora Richards, Chris Stills, Harper Simon, Rufus Wainwright, Kelly Osbourne, Alexa Joel, Ethan Browne, Sebastian Roberston, Otis Redding III and Aisha Morris–*Norman Jean Roy* [RS 972] James Taylor–*Baron Wolman/Retna*; Tina Turner–*MR Photo/Corbis*; Eric Clapton–*Terry O'Neill/Warner Bros. Records/Michael Ochs Archives*; Jerry Garcia–*Photofest*; Eminem–*Jack Chuck/Corbis Outline*; Joni Mitchell–*Henry Diltz*; Frank Zappa–*Michael Ochs Archives*; Tupac Shakur–© *Danny Clinch/Corbis Outline*; Elvis Costello–*Photofest*; Axl Rose–© *Herb Ritts Foundation/Visages* [RS 980] Jimi Hendrix–*Harry Goodwin/Michael Ochs Archives. Photo-Illustration by Michael Elins* [RS 990/991] King Kong–*Weta Digital LTD/Universal Studios*

ADDITIONAL CREDITS

[RS 1016/1017] Johnny Depp–*Matthew Ralston*; Bob Dylan–*Matthew Rolston*; Kanye West–*David LaChappelle*; Led Zeppelin–*Adrian Boot*; Jack Nicholson–*Matthew Rolston*; Eddie Vedder–*Nick Stevens*; Sacha Baron Cohen–*Robert Trachtenberg*; Jon Stewart & Stephen Colbert–*Robert Trachtenberg*; Christina Aguilera–*Matthew Ralston*; Kiefer Sutherland–*Sam Jones*; Fergie–*Max Vadukul*; Worst Congress Ever–*Robert Grossman*; Red Hot Chili Peppers–*Matthew Ralston*; Neil Young–*Platon*; American Idol–*Michael Elins*; The Thousandth Issue–*Michael Ellins*; Justin Timberlake–*Max Vadukul*; Shaun White–*Platon*; Mariah Carey–*Brigitte Lacombe*; President George W. Bush–*Robert Grossman*; Snoop Dogg–*Matthew Rolston*; Heath Ledger–*Sam Jones* [RS 1020]; John Mayer, Derek Trucks & John Frusciante–*Matthew Rolston* [RS 1042/1043]; Jay-Z–*Matthew Rolston*; Keith Richards & Johnny Depp–*Matthew Rolston*; Bruce Springsteen–*Max Vadukul*; Hunter S. Thompson–*Edmund Shea*; Rose McGowan & Rosario Dawson–*Matthew Rolston*; 50 Cent & Kanye West–*Albert Watson*; Amy Winehouse–*Max Vadukul*; The Police–*Max Vadukul*; Fall Out Boy–*Peter Yang*; James Brown–*Gilles Caron*; Zac Efron–*Matthew Rolston*; Kid Rock–*Max Vadukul* [RS 1051]; Thom Yorke–*James Dimmock*; Madonna–*Evan Agostini/AP Images*; Chris Brown–*Ture Lillegraven*; Bruce Springsteen–*Max Vadukul*; Taylor Swift–*Cliff Lipson/CBS/Landov*; Bono–*Mike Flokis/Headpress/Retna*; The Mars Volta–*Ross Halfin*; Conor Oberst–*Bill Sitzmann*; My Morning Jacket -*Autumn de Wilde*; Robert Plant–*Perou*; Vampire Weekend–*Mary Ellen Matthews/Corbis Outline*; Lil Wayne–*Jonathan Mannion* [RS 1052] Heidi Montag, Audrina Patridge, Lauren Conrad and Whitney Port–*Matthew Rolston* [RS 1054] B.B. King, Omar Rodriguez Lopez, Eddie Van Halen, John Mayer, Buddy Guy, Carlos Santana, and Kirk Hammett–*Max Vadukul*; Jimmy Page–*Ross Halfin* [RS 1061] Chris Rock, Tina Fey, David Letterman,Sarah Silverman, Don Rickles, Billy Crystal, Tracy Morgan, Amy Poehler, Jimmy Fallon, Martin Short, Larry David, Robin Williams–*Robert Trachtenberg* [RS 1066] Bob Dylan–*W. Eugene Smith/Black Star*; Elvis Presley–*Charles Trainor/Time & Life Pictures/Getty Images*; John Lennon–*Spud Murphy/© Yoko Ono*; Aretha Franklin–*Harry Goodwin/Rex USA* [RS 1102] Matthew Morrison, Dianna Agron, Lea Michele, Jane Lynch and Cory Montieth–*Mark Seliger* [RS 1112] Alexander Skaarsgard, Anna Paquin and Stephen Moyer–*Matthew Ralston* [RS 1113] Elisabeth Moss, January Jones, Jon Hamm and Christina Hendricks–*Robert Trachtenberg* [RS 1145] Jimi Hendrix–*Jim Marshall*; Eric Clapton–*Jim Marshall*; Jimmy Page–*Kevin Mazur/WireImage*; Eddie Van Halen–*Jon Sievert/Cache Agency* [RS 1146/1147] Adele–*Simon Emmett*; Lil Wayne–*Mark Seliger*; Zach Galifianakis–*Theo Wenner*; Katy Perry–*Terry Richardson*; Lady Gaga–*Ryan McGinley*; Eddie Murphy–*Mark Seliger*; Howard Stern–*Mark Seliger*; Jon Stewart–*Albert Watson*; George Harrison–*Arthur Steel/Mirrorpix/Everett Collection*; Larry David–*Mark Seliger*; Bob Dylan–*Jerry Schatzberg/Truck Archive*; Steven Tyler–*Theo Wenner* [RS 1150] Christina Aguilera, Blake Shelton, Cee-Lo Green and Adam Levine–*Mark Seliger* [RS 1172/1173] Tupac (2Pac) Shakur–*Chi Modu*; Jay-Z–*Mark Seliger*; The Notorious B.I.G.–*Barron Claiborne/Corbis Outline*; Eminem–*Mark Seliger* [RS 1175] Tracy Morgan, Tina Fey and Alec Baldwin–*Mark Seliger* [RS 1185] Danny McBride, Seth Rogen, James Franco and Jonah Hill–*Martin Schoeller* [RS 1236] Phil Lesh–*Herb Greene*; Mickey Hart, Jerry Garcia, Bob Weir, and Bill Kreutzmann–*©Baron Wolman/Iconic Images*. [RS 1250/1251] John Boyega, Harrison Ford, Peter Mayhew, Daisy Ridley and BB-8–*Jules Heath/© 2015 Lucasfilm Ltd.*